ENGLISH VERSE

BETWEEN

CHAUCER AND SURREY

English Verse
between Chaucer *and* Surrey

Being Examples of *Conventional Secular Poetry*,
exclusive of *Romance, Ballad, Lyric,* and
Drama, in the Period from Henry the
Fourth to Henry the Eighth

EDITED

WITH INTRODUCTIONS AND NOTES

BY

ELEANOR PRESCOTT HAMMOND

To know,
Rather consists in opening out a way,
Whence the imprisoned splendour may escape,
Than in effecting entry for a light
Supposed to be without.
—*Browning,* Paracelsus i: 733-37

1969

OCTAGON BOOKS

New York

Originally published 1927 by Duke University Press

Reprinted 1965
by special arrangement with Duke University Press

OCTAGON BOOKS
A DIVISION OF FARRAR, STRAUS & GIROUX, INC.
19 Union Square West
New York, N. Y. 10003

LIBRARY OF CONGRESS CATALOG CARD NUMBER: 65-25568

Printed in U.S.A. by
NOBLE OFFSET PRINTERS, INC.
NEW YORK 3, N. Y.

PREFACE

This volume is intended primarily for the advanced student of English literary history; and such intention has influenced both its plan and its mode of presentation. No single volume can fully represent the productivity of the century-and-a-half between the death of Chaucer and the birth of Spenser, and can also offer the necessary comment upon the published texts. For barren as is the period in one sense, it is nevertheless enormously prolific, and the aspects of its expression too varied for treatment in any compact anthology. The ballad and the religious drama, both of which lie partly within this tract of time, have been abundantly studied; investigation of non-dramatic religious poetry is well under way; the romances have their share of attention; but the field of what I may call for convenience "formal" verse, the mass of secular production partly narrative, partly didactic, partly satiric, partly amatory, partly descriptive, verse adhering anxiously to standardized forms and stylistic devices, is still nearly untouched. It is in this field that the soil of English literature most obviously becomes exhausted during the fifteenth century; and the study of these works may seem to the casual observer a thankless task. Yet without such a study the survey of English literary history is arbitrarily scanted; and every worker who views literature not as belles-lettres but as the expression of the national mind realizes that the functioning of that mind, like the movements of the racehorse or the boxer, is most clearly to be observed when the film is slowed. Elton has said that "the passage from older themes and styles into newer is best seen in the writers of middle rank and mixed performance"; and in this "Transition," of all periods in our literature, that possibility of analysis is present. The rockbottom qualities which affect the currents of literature are visible not at triumphant flood but at ebb-tide. The "Transition" has much to teach the student as to the working of psychic factors and the influence of the social environment on poetic expression; moreover, principles drawn thence are valid even among the greatest. After observing the excess of standardization in Lydgate or in Hawes, we regard the lessening in Spenser, the still more marked lessening in Shakespeare, not so much as a miracle but rather as a return to the balance long prevented by formalism.

Even with this limitation, it is impossible in a single volume to cover the field. In making a choice, the editor has endeavored to illustrate the different degrees of conservatism, the admixture now of satire, now of description, now of autobiography or of the personal, in the progress towards free treatment of the individual. A mass of verse at the close of the period is excluded because of its non-formal character. Copland's two poems, Cocke Lorel's Bote, Colyn Blowbole's Testament, etc., would greatly enlarge our picture of the national mind, but they are outside the scope of this volume. Much has also been omitted from considerations of expense; the Flower and the Leaf should be here, as representing a motif highly favored by the courtly poetry of the time, but it is accessible in a modern text, and has accordingly been withdrawn from this anthology. Gower is untouched here for the same reason. But a good deal of the contents of this volume is unobtainable by the student. Walton's Boethius, Lydgate's Dance Macabre, the translations of Orléans, Nevill, the Visions of Cavendish, and other poems, are accessible only in expensive editions if at all. And not only these poems, but most or all of those here printed are selected as illustrating dominant motifs of the time:—the anxious curiosity about death, the Fortune-formula, the laments over extravagance, the eagerness about trade and travel, the paraded encyclopedic knowledge, the bourgeois contempt for women and the cavalier deference for women, the rising interest in the scamp, the subservience to patrons, the lip-respect for Chaucer. In several poems either the influence of Chaucer is visible or a passage of Chaucer is illuminated, as in Bycorne and Chichevache, Canace's letter, Walton's Boethius, etc.

Wherever possible, the texts are printed as wholes or as portions complete in themselves. We might do as did Charles Lamb for the Elizabethan dramatists,—select passages showing the pictorial and emotional powers of their writers; but if in displaying the versifier's control over situation we conceal his ability, or inability, to get from situation to situation, we disguise facts necessary for the student, and cast a false light upon our period. It is incumbent upon the literary historian or editor to lay before workers proof how didactic was the fifteenth century at the emotional moment, how clumsy in managing transition, how crude in motiving action, how unable to release the subject in hand. Only from such a body of facts can we observe the irregular growth of English constructive power; and only long continuous excerpts, if not wholes, can provide a basis for observation. Even carelessly edited texts, like those put forth by Ritson and by Halliwell, retain their place with scholars just because they make wholes available for study.

But it has been impossible, however desirable, to place the whole of each of these texts before the student. Lydgate's Dance Macabre can be, and is, reproduced complete; the 36,000 lines of his Fall of Princes must necessarily be illustrated by extracts; nor can we refuse to make such excerpts, because a theme so important in West-European literature, a work so influential on the Continent and in England, cannot be omitted from our survey. The Garland of Laurell is printed entire; but portions only are possible of Hawes' Pastime, of Cavendish's Visions, of Barclay's Ship of Fools. Yet in all these cases the editor has endeavored to give chapters in full, to illustrate the mode of connecting chapters, to show the movement of the author's mind among his material.

The great amount of space given to Lydgate may provoke question; but since it is our problem to study the formal expression of the age, no apology is needed. For in this one man are represented so many of the aspects of such verse in the first half of the century that its standardized expression can almost be studied from him alone.

Criticism will also be aroused by my refusal to treat most of this verse as rhythmical composition. The work of Lydgate, for instance, has been taken very seriously by specialists; and only the inaccessibility of texts has prevented more of the verse of the period from receiving careful analysis on the model set up by German scholars. To such treatment I am for two reasons opposed. First, because the method is itself inadequate, a handling of verse line by line only and according to the number of syllables; secondly, because analysis is wasted upon a large portion of this verse, which is, e.g. in the Libel of English Policy, in Ripley's Compend, in Hawes' Pastime, sheer doggerel, guiltless of rhythm and conscious only of an approaching rime. This latter condition does not arise because of the badness of texts, for in the cases of both Hardyng and Cavendish we have the author's own manuscript, and yet the rhythm is as awkward as any of the period We can indeed study the attempts of Lydgate and Hoccleve to use Chaucer's pentameter line-flow, and we can recognize with pleasure the rhythmic command of the Orléans or of the Palladius-translator and of the writer of the Lover's Mass. But in most of this transitional work we have to note that a failure of sense-perception, a stale formality of simile and of phrase, accompanies this rhythmic poverty as its shadow,—or its substance. The cramping of the spirit by an environment which it cannot conquer through observation is at the basis of the Transition's failure to express, or indeed of a similar failure in any age. Given a partially-educated and insensitive group, obedient to external conditions, eager for moral and intellectual credit, and if it attempts expression, be it in the twentieth century or in the fifteenth, there will appear the same respect for the didactic, the same penchant for allegory, the same imitativeness and use of formulae, and the same failure to feel rhythm.

The textual presentation is academic. The original manuscript or printed copy is followed without deviation except in a few cases where the student might be led astray; in such cases the inserted or altered word is bracketed and the actual reading given at the foot of the page. All other changes, now suggested or made by previous editors, are relegated to the Notes. Modern punctuation has not been introduced; the markings of the original are scrupulously retained. For while the page may thus lose in clarity for the general reader, it gains greatly for the student, who is then given his proper share in the editorial problem of following the medieval mind. And when examining sentence-structure thus, the worker learns far more than when accepting uncritically the conclusions of an editor. Not only can an editor, even the best of editors, hypnotize his readers into false notions of the author's meaning, but the whole subject of Early English punctuation has been slighted and obscured because of such acceptance, continued century after century. We have made it impossible to obtain information on medieval theories of pointing by refusing to print texts with their pointing undisturbed; and the reasons for our refusal are the same as those once considered valid against the reproduction of the early spelling,—a matter long since settled. On all these accounts, the present editor has declined to impose modern punctuation here.

It will also be noted that the texts are not "critical". The establishment of a critical text, deduced from comparison of all existing copies of the work, suffers, and must always suffer, under two limitations. The surviving copies may be far indeed from the fittest; and in any case, the text constructed from them, though presumably antedating them, is not conclusively the original. It is "X"; but the identity of X with Chaucer or with Lydgate or with another cannot be asserted. Hence the labor of constructing such an hypothetical "Urtext", although an admirable exercise in acumen, arrives nowhither unless the number of copies be large and clearly grouped, unless moreover they be for the most part honestly executed. The present editor feels that the principle of critical text-construction is not something to be invoked "semper, ubique, et ab omnibus", but is to be applied according to mass and character of material. Some of the texts here assembled exist in but a single copy; of some we have a copy in the author's own hand; several are poorly preserved; and the few which survive in a number of copies, like Walton's Boethius, have received a treatment uniform with the others; that is, one text is printed verbatim et literatim, with mention of variants in the Notes.

In nearly every case the copies have been made by the editor. For the Palladius-text the photograph of the Wentworth Wodehouse MS was used by a Bodleian copyist; the Hoccleve texts have been revised by the Keeper of Manuscripts at the Henry E. Huntington Library, California, where the codices formerly Phillipps 8151 and Ashburnham Appendix cxxxiii now are. In this latter case errors in the Early English Text Society's edition have thus been removed.

The number of authors here represented has made it impossible to approach each text as would a specialist in that subject. No one of these introductions is, or attempts to be, exhaustive; no biography is fully given, no debatable point re-argued. The separate bibliographies are more complete, although the titles are condensed, and minor points left to the Dictionary of National Biography or to monumental editions like that of Skelton by Dyce. Similarly, in the glossary, it is assumed that the student has the New English Dictionary at hand, is familiar with Chaucer, and has a working knowledge of Early English otherwise. Etymologies are not given, nor dialectal peculiarities discussed.

I am indebted to the Press of Duke University, and especially to its editor-in-chief, Dr. Paull F. Baum, for the care and patience, the interested craftsmanship and scholarship, which they have devoted to this volume.

E. P. H.

TABLE OF CONTENTS

ENGLISH VERSE

BETWEEN

CHAUCER AND SURREY

GENERAL INTRODUCTION

The hundred and fifty years of the English "Transition" may fairly be treated in two periods, divided politically at the battle of Bosworth Field and intellectually at the establishment of printing. In the former of these periods, from 1400 to 1485, the Crown was long in dispute, the feudal nobility absorbed in foreign and in dynastic wars, the Church weakened by its dependence on the Crown, the commonalty engaged in using its first chance at accumulation of money. A shift of class-balance was in progress as result of the divisions and weakening of the landholders, of the economic power gained by the bourgeoisie; and English society was profoundly unsettled because of this readjustment. In the latter period, from 1485 on, the Tudor despotism established itself above a crippled aristocracy and Church, with the tacit consent of a commonalty not yet politically coherent and conscious. The education of the bourgeoisie proceeded slowly, taking at first a limited and pedagogic form, while courtly expression retained in large part the formulae of an earlier age.

Through the former period, ecclesiastical and chivalric standards of taste were still in force. Polite literature was formal, imitative, didactic; drama and the romance both submitted to pressure, and the traces of secular folk-expression outside the ballad are small. The numerous class of ecclesiastically-trained writers show the repressive, inhibiting power of the Church on letters; the Church contemned, as always, the human senses, contemned direct observation of any sort; it favored the symbol rather than the fact, and approved the didactic without any criticism of its quality. Its contribution to English literature was that of Christianity as a whole,—the idea of the struggle of vicious and virtuous impulses in the human heart,—an idea alien to the antique world. The Teutonic races obtained part of their intellectual discipline through the self-examination required by the Church; but the Church's opinion of the human senses acted as an inhibition to any real study of man by man; it created as sharp a cleavage in the possible whole of mental development as existed between the adoration of the Virgin Mother and the monastic horror of woman.

The medieval synthesis, both ecclesiastical and political, held firm while the Western world was still politically and linguistically a unit; it relaxed as the integration of separate nations and tongues progressed, a relaxation doubtless due in part to the difficulty of intercommunication over Western Europe. Upon this slow process another factor, the economic, acted as accelerant; with the use of coined money and the rise of an international banking system, democratic devices furthered by the aristocratic Crusades, the anti-synthetic particularistic tendency increased. As English commerce became more important, as the trading towns grew, as the dealers in wool accumulated wealth, the English bourgeoisie rose in power. Human ambition and human self-assertiveness, long denied expression to the "demos" by the rigid frame of feudalism, found opportunity; and during the Transition, especially during the second of its two periods, the bourgeoisie, vigorous, pushing, unscrupulous, with little education but with wide and widening human experience, comes more and more to the center of the stage. Like all natures of high animalism, no education, and unformulated ideas, the bourgeois was iconoclastic, insensitive, and greedy of emphasis; violent emotionalism, coarse jest, attack on all forms of the established order, appealed to him as they appeal to the new "proletariat" public today. Even at his worst, however, he was undulled by machine-service and by machine-made noise; his nature at its best is seen in the work of his hands and in his impulse to song.

As this confusion of tendencies, this strife between the overborne older order and the aggressive middle class, slowly worked to a height, it met incoming Humanism. A new cohesive force replaced the dissolving medieval theory. Every aspect of Humanism made for stability; a clarified expression, a standard of taste, a faith in man, were offered to a public sorely in need of them; and the concentration of interest upon the individual which characterized the Renaissance sweetened for the bourgeoisie the gift of Humanism which the Renaissance brought. It required time to train the new reading class; but as a small group of dramatic poets matured on the combined bourgeois and humanistic stimuli, the London public received the benefit in the theater, which taught through the emotions and the ear as well as the eye. To that conflict of good and evil in the human heart which was fundamental in Christian teaching, and to the human experience which the average man had acquired in the street and in the marketplace there was now added the Renaissance feeling for form, the Renaissance conception of the humane and the beautiful. Ideals are again revered; and men's imaginations, raised by such full faith in man as that of Spenser, are led to a newer and greater Romantic synthesis in Shakespeare, to a fusion not merely of human relations in a system, but of the seer with the thing seen. But in the years between Chaucer's death and the Elizabethan florescence, before the middle class had taken form or received education, English literature was in the hands of the conservatives.

Conservatism is as fundamental a force in literature and in character as is individualism, and as necessary. The greatest moments of artistic expression, whether in peoples or in the single workman, have been those of equipoise between these two forces. Such moments are brief and rare; there is usually a predominance of one element, a predominance determined often by conditions other than literary. The rigidity of the structure of feudalism, denying expression to all of lower rank, maintained the force of conservatism in literature for centuries. Had the English bourgeoisie obtained the upper hand in letters as well as in life, the chaos following on the shift might have been greater. But the incoming power of Humanism, almost coincident with the definite emergence of the bourgeoisie, equalized the thrust of individualism; and we have in the Elizabethan age one of the world's great moments of equipoise between the two contending forces. That it manifests itself in drama and in lyric is not surprising; for the agreement in spirit between the citizen community of Athens and the citizen community of Elizabethan London favored in both environments that drama which in each case had germinated within the limits of the established religion. In the outburst of individualism of our own day, accompanying the emergence of a new social class, we have an excess uncontrolled as yet by any conservative or humanistic force; and the unsettlement today of language and of morality, alongside the unsettlement and exaggeration of literary expression, are markedly parallel to the phenomena of the Transition.

Each of these social reconstructions, reconstructions which are but attempts to reach a balance, is confronted by the problem of educating a public new to power, untrained and indocile. And the psychology of human beings in the mass, of the "crowd-mind," is in each case an additional element in the struggle towards adjustment. The crowd-mind is self-assertive, but it is also self-protective, an impulse which is evident especially in the tendency to imitation, to the preservation of a standard once accepted. No matter how strong the individualistic assertion may be, it has no sooner obtained a hearing than it hardens into a creed. A process of stereotyping, insisted upon by the group, follows close upon revolt, close upon each attainment of balance; and how long its pattern endures will depend in great part upon external conditions. If an ecclesiastical and feudal framework is imposed upon society, as was the case all through the Middle Ages, literature will be standardized and held rigid by that framework. Should the inhibition be less heavy, as in fourteenth-century England, there may be here and there an attainment of balance, as in Chaucer, who represents in his isolated self the adjustment between group and individual, between book-education and human experience, between what George Eliot calls "separateness" and "communication." It is rare indeed to find a piece of literature which has not been influenced by social pressures and inhibitions, but the effect of this potent factor on the course of a nation's expression has not yet been studied. A view of English poetry which should regard it less as an evolution than as a constant struggle of the spirit against successive group-inhibitions would be of interest; nowhere would there be more material than in the period at which we are looking.

The society in which stereotypes prevail is one carefully and successfully guarded against change. It is not by chance that the two great modern social readjustments have each coincided with an expansion of the world in men's minds. The period of sailing out upon the oceans, in the late fifteenth century, is matched in the late nineteenth by immensely increased facilities for land travel, and by the conquest of undersea and upper air yet later. Such extensions of the ordinary man's horizon have incalculable consequences. They mean, of course, more human as well as more geographical knowledge; they mean increase of travel and commerce, exchange of ideas, enlargement of sympathies. But they bring difficulties as well as advantages. It is not that the laws of human nature, including the urge to imitate and to standardize, undergo any modification; but the speed and variability of their functioning increase enormously. In our own time the demolition of space-barriers which puts every variety of stimulus simultaneously before the people, and the articulate assertiveness of all classes in a democratic society, have tangled the threads of tendency to a degree hitherto unimagined. The necessity for swift and constantly repeated adaptation, in a society thus exposed to multifarious stimuli, is as disintegrating to personality as to literary standards. Beside the conditions of literature today, those of the fifteenth century are simplicity itself. In that last hour before the advent of printing and before the voyage of Columbus, the forces of established conservatism could offer to a new type, literary or religious, a resistance denser and more general than any novelty today will encounter. Looking over the history of our literature, we see that what we call periods were much longer before the invention of printing, that they shortened as commercial intercourse was facilitated, and that with cheap newspapers, steam, and the radio, the weakening of resistance to change has reached the danger point. The physical cause of this weakening is the immensely enhanced facility of human intercourse, which not only permits but compels a choice of stimuli at every moment, weakens the power of attention, and divides the individual against himself. The reduction in personality is as marked, in a hurried huddled age, as is the confusion of standards.

The Transition, defended yet awhile by the forces of feudalism against an uneducated, even if rising, middle class, is, as I have said, a simple problem compared to that of our own day. The two Transition publics and the two modes of expression, with the hybrids between them, can be traced with comparative ease. One body of production, the conservative and stereotyped, perpetuates earlier themes and forms; it draws its support from the privileged classes and accepts the dictation of a patronage which knows only traditional types of expression. As the years pass, the control of this patronage weakens, the force of imitation loses strength to resist increeping bourgeois qualities, and hybrids appear, as well as clumsy satire, jest, and description. This attempted description is for the most part of human or low-life figures, exaggerated often and often as overdone in another way as were the earlier stock-pattern figures. But poor and violent though the portraiture may be, it reaches out after real life; it attempts to use the senses, to redress the balance so long weighed towards the stereotype. And when this excess is in its turn reduced and steadied by Humanism, there is a brilliant though brief period of poise.

It is with the first of these three phases, the formal literature of the Transition, that we are concerned. The popular expression of the early sixteenth century is beyond our purview, as is the Renaissance. Yet though we emphasize the stereotyping society of the earlier Transition as principal cause of its failure in literary vitality, we have not thus given all the reasons for that failure. Even though we add the isolation of England during the Hundred Years' War, we have not fully explained her intellectual weakness then. The war indeed made itself felt on letters in the barrier which it set up between England and her nearest neighbors, in its denial of human intercommunication. If Mr. Belloc can say of Roman England that her separation from the Continent by barbarian Roman soldiers "lowered the general process of civilization in the eastern and starved into a still lower standard the isolated western part," this was equally true of the sundering force of the French war in the fifteenth century. But neither that war nor the contest of the Roses is the sole cause of English literary

conditions at the time. The tightening of inhibitions by the small arrogant litera-
ture-producing class has its effect in weakening English poetry; the break-down
of the aristocracy through war, the rise of the bourgeoisie through increase of
fluid wealth, account for the unsettlement of standards and the coarsening of
taste; the enforced separation from the Continent delays education. But none
of these, nor all taken together, tell the full story of the English Transition.

The "content" of any literary period varies in reality and power with the
weight of conviction and enthusiasm behind it. Carlyle, discussing the age of
Louis XV, remarked that "when the general life-element became so unspeakably
phantasmal, it was difficult for any man to be real." Morley says of Voltaire's
Henriade: "To form a long narrative of heroic adventure in animated, picturesque,
above all in sincere verse, is an achievement reserved for men with a steadier
glow, a firmer, simpler, more exuberant and more natural poetic feeling than
was possible in that time of mean shifts, purposeless public action, and pitiful
sacrifice of private self-respect." And Santayana may also be quoted: "When
chaos has penetrated into the moral being of nations, they can hardly be expected to produce great men." The new public of England was as uneducated
morally and ethically as it was mentally. It brought to secular literature no high
purpose, no faith in man, no sincerity; its narrow bourgeois greed, its measurement of life in terms of power and money, debarred it from giving out as a
people any real inspiration. And the men to whom England had to look as her
spokesmen were equally devoid of real inspiration; they were trained indeed to
some extent, but Church-trained, set firmly in the clerical mould, and as scanted
of liberal education as their public. Such writers had not either element of
literature; neither they nor their readers felt high purpose, and they themselves
possessed no craftsmanship. Milton's "various style" and "holy rapture" were
both lacking. There have been times in English literature when one of these
elements has alone sufficed to keep a body of poetry stable. In the spiritually meager age of Queen Anne, brilliancy of manipulation compensated in part for a
lack of sincerity, and Pope stamped an alloy of mean intrinsic value to pass
current for generations. But Lydgate, for example, had no such ability. And
though without the one basis, spiritual or intellectual, a body of literature may
stand, it cannot when devoid of both vital sincerity and technical excellence.
The weakness of the fifteenth century is no marvel; what were marvellous were
the growth of anything beautiful in verse under such conditions.

We do not endeavor, as appears from the foregoing, to explain the fifteenth
century as the outcome of the fourteenth. The doctrine of "continuous entity"
has value, but a mass of people moves not on the lines of the physical organ-
ism. The fifteenth century is not solely a degeneration nor an inheritance from
the years before it; it is not solely a period of gestation for a coming birth. The
Elizabethan Renaissance is less truly an upleap than an attainment of equilibrium after long effort at balance, an equilibrium at last made possible by the
break in social inhibitions, the advance in the new public's education, the enlarged
view of the world, and a more generous ideal of life. These are all conditions

external, in a sense, to literature; and it is now our problem to observe in more detail how such conditions formed in later medieval England.

During the ten centuries before the discovery of America the slowly integrating countries of Western Europe had developed on varying economic and political lines. The long sea-coasts of Italy and Britain, with their Oriental and Dutch frontages, had stimulated sea-borne trade. In Italy the growth of the textile industry was closely connected with the rise of that trade, and the two fostered each other. England did little weaving until the mid-fourteenth century; with her, minerals, and above all raw wool, were the export staples. This condition favored a large rural and a smaller trading class; and the habit of mind which is developed by artisan-skill was of late awakening in Britain. Her turn in the world's manufacturing economy came with the utilization of her iron and her coal, when Italy's primacy in textile work passed from her because of her lack of the minerals so abundant farther north.

The political development of the two countries was also very different. Italy's position on the Mediterranean Sea, the heart of ancient civilization, the seat of the Roman Empire and later of the Roman Church in her peninsula, the number and immediacy of her political contacts, the continuity of her intellectual life, made her widely different from insular, remote, untutored Britain. England's political and mental history hardly began until she was drawn, by the Norman Conquest, into the circle of the growing nations. There she found Italy, France, and the Low Countries her far more experienced and matured sisters. Her merchant trade built up slowly, and for generations her intellectual dependence was directly or indirectly on France, her conqueror and teacher.

It had been the great task of France to preserve the Latin tongue and to discipline the expression of Western Europe through her schools of philosophy and dialectic. Politically her position in the fourteenth century was midway between that of Italy and that of England. She was not split, as was Italy, into a half-hundred of jealous and contentious statelets, each torn also by local party strife; but her noble class was more numerous, compared with her bourgeoisie, than in England, owing to the social system which made every French younger son of aristocratic family also noble and privileged. The untaxed wealth of the Roman Church was much greater in France than in England; and after the division of territory among the sons of King John, the quarrels among the princes thus aggrandized and the Crown became violent. So far as letters and art were concerned, the rivalry between Burgundy, Anjou, Orléans, Berri, and the Ile de France stimulated the work of chroniclers, translators, painters, carvers, and scribes, even as was the case in the Italian peninsula among the rival despots. But the mass of the French people was heavily taxed, more so than in other countries, and lacked the political consciousness so swiftly developed in smaller and less agricultural states like Athens or Florence or Flanders. There was no check upon the dominant classes, and these continued in a round of imitation, so far as literature was concerned. Where the people could receive education, as in the handicrafts, art was vital; the architecture, the glass and metal work, the tapestry of the later Middle Ages, all bear witness to this. But the exclusively aristocratic literature of France suffered from the sterility of the aristocracy and the Church.

Communal development advanced faster in the small states north of France. The territory we now know as Holland and Belgium was in the fourteenth century divided into a group of thriving counties and duchies,—Brabant, Flanders, Hainault, Seeland, Holland, etc. The coast state of Flanders, in especial, was almost independent of the Empire, and her busy cities had grown rich by the manufacture of England's wool. During the latter fourteenth and early fifteenth centuries the French dukes of Burgundy came into possession, by marriage or by usurpation, of most of these little territories; and the marriage of Mary of Burgundy, sole heir of Charles the Bold, with Maximilian of Austria, carried the whole great Burgundian power to her grandson, the Emperor Charles the Fifth. The long years' struggle of the gallant little states of the North with Charles' son, Philip of Spain, is, however, no part of our history; at the period we are considering they were opulent manufacturing communities, famous for their glass, metal, and textile work, for their painters in oil, for their wealth, their growing political confidence and impatience of despotic control. Whatever their artificial dynastic bonds with France or with the Empire, the whole economic life of the Low Countries depended on England, from which they drew the wool for their weaving. And the connection of the two shores was other than commercial; the marriage of Edward III of England to Philippa of Hainault, and the constant intercourse between the English and the Burgundian courts in the next century, while Burgundy was supporting England against France, had almost as much influence on the arts and letters, the book-collecting and translating of England, as the similarity in trade-interests had on the bourgeoisie of the two countries. It was from the French-speaking court of the Burgundian dukes that much of England's fifteenth-century "culture" came; and it was from the court of a Burgundian duke and his English duchess that Caxton returned to London, carrying the Low-Country art of printing.

England's insular freedom from European political problems had left her, during the years since her royal house had become thoroughly English, in a position to grow more evenly and healthily than any Continental country. At the middle of the fourteenth century all signs were promising. In political, in literary, in social expression, she was full of vitality. The progress of Parliament towards control of government, the assertion of the nation against the Papacy in the statutes of Provisors and Premunire, the growing prosperity of English traders, the freer intercourse with the world, seemed to mean an awakened and intelligent group-consciousness. At that moment the Biblical drama, the ballads, the revival of the native verse, the rise of reforming feeling and of mystical thought, the technical power of Chaucer, all gave promise of a genuine literary florescence. Just then, it may be, if political class-agreements had continued the loosening of medieval inhibitions, if intercourse with the South of Europe had left the road open for intellectual growth, we might have had a noble national expression. Instead, everything conspired to check the development which seemed so certain, and to set the stage for a very different drama.

First in the sequence of untoward events was the Black Death. How large a proportion of England's population died in the series of epidemics which swept West Europe at intervals from 1348 on, we do not know; but it is clear that she lost so heavily from her working class that there was a sudden and a permanent shortage of labor, reflected by a rise in wages and in prices. The landowners, who largely constituted Parliament, refused to recognize the inevitable; and that energy which had been expended by them on control of king and nobles was diverted to a class-struggle with labor. Ten years before the first great wave of the plague, also, the disastrous Hundred Years' War with France had begun.

A strong and ambitious sovereign might have turned this rupture between landholders and commonalty to his own advantage. But the later years of Edward III were weak; the folly of Richard II brought him to ruin; and affairs weltered in chaos while peasants and Lollards were contending with landlords and Church. In the early fifteenth century we find England with her throne occupied by the keen and determined Lancastrians, her Church freed from Lollard criticism and sunk into apathy, her peasantry beaten into sullen dejection, the inhibiting feudal framework clamped again upon her literary expression, and all trace of her intellectual vigor gone with the barring of the Channel, the death of Chaucer, the death of religious freedom, the death of national unity. •

All unknown to king and noblesse, however, there was building up with their sanction a power which should undermine their rule more completely than the labor unrest. Where public and private obligations could be reckoned and collected in money, the country availing itself of that convenience was moving towards a time when political relations would cease to depend upon tenure of land; in other words, the feudal system was about to fall before the power of the bourgeoisie. There was no protest in this case from landholders or from Church, for that payment in coin which became the basis of trading prosperity was a convenience recognized alike by crusading nobles, absentee landholders, and the tax-collectors of the Roman Church.

On this new material foundation arose the bourgeoisie, in all its impulses antagonistic to the social order which had endeavored to hold it in check,—anti-feudal, anti-chivalric, anti-clerical, impatient, iconoclastic, ribald. Whatever the shortcomings of the falling order, it had nominally professed ideals,—loyalty to God, to the sovereign, to the beloved lady. But the rising bourgeoisie, during the long ensuing struggle with moribund feudalism, served no ideals; it had no apparent motive except self-aggrandizement. There was nothing in it of the respect for the past as a Golden Age, which chivalry had felt, nothing of the modern devotion to the future of the race, to the betterment of generations yet unborn. Its deficiency in enthusiasms, in convictions, in devotions, left it unendowed with literary force, as it was also undisciplined by training. The renewal of the Hundred Years' War under Henry V was no struggle against a Persian invader, a Spanish invader. Its motive was frankly lust of dominion. In speaking of the effect of the Persian war on Greece, Bury has said that in that war was illustrated "the operation of a general law which governs human societies. Pressure from without tends to produce unity within." Fifteenth-century England, however, was not rising to defend herself; she was not even venturing, as did Tudor England, into undiscovered countries and uncharted seas. She was seeking to aggrandize herself at the expense of an equal, a neighbor, a sister. Whatever Henry V's arguments of hereditary right, before his invasion of France in 1415, he appealed as much to the baser passions of the nation as did Bismarck. And the penalty which England paid was a spiritual one; she paid in the impoverishment of her literature, the deterioration of her Church, the delay of her emancipation and of her education. All that forming literary impulse which was just ready for the discipline of Humanism was stifled for many years. For not only did England's intellectual resources, still limited because of her belated admission to the European storehouse of thought, receive little or no food during most of the fifteenth century, but there was from decade to decade a steady loss in intellect and taste, caused by the ceaseless imitation, the starved inbreeding, of a race of ill-nurtured clerics. England in the fifteenth century, to quote Carlyle's phrase, saw life as "a thing whereby to do day-labor and earn wages"; she saw literature as a means of "eschewing idleness", in the current monkish phrase. And neither view ever inspired a soul to real utterance.

Both fundamental elements of a national literature were thus lacking in fifteenth-century England, the pressure of generous popular feeling and the presence of the technical artist. The previous century had felt the stirrings of high emotions, and had uttered them, often awkwardly enough, through the balladists, the mystics, Wyclif, Langland. One supreme artist, one man of both genius and technique, that century had possessed in Geoffrey Chaucer. Chaucer had certain essentials of artistic mastery as completely in his grasp as had the Greeks from whom he differed so widely. He knew the superiority of balance over symmetry; he understood and practiced restraint in expression; he studied contrast as no man but Shakespeare, in England, has studied it; he recognized the power of the selected detail; his senses were alert and keen. But neither these essentials nor his amazing technical mastery of his material could be communicated, and his touch was too light and shrewd to guide his followers.

In that technical mastery no comparison with his English predecessors is possible. His management of verse-flow, the vigor of his imagination, his perfect acquaintanceship with the creatures of his art and his power of bringing his readers into their presence, his understanding of his audience, have no prototype in England. We term such qualities "modern"; yet medieval Chaucer is as well. He used unhesitatingly and naturally many themes and forms which seem to us absurd; but by using this familiar material he kept himself understanded of the many, as Shakespeare did. In both of them was the "communication" with their fellows, and in both of them the "separateness" of genius.

And in yet another way Chaucer was a composite. He worked often with an eye on the aristocratic patron, used often aristocratic themes; but more and more, as he grows older, is the power released in him bourgeois. His kinship is with Boccaccio, with the French fabliau-makers, with Chrétien de Troyes or Jean de Meun. Like them his perceptions are quick, shrewd, amused; like them his study is by preference of human situation. Like them he excels in the smaller structural qualities; like them he makes little or no attempt to raise the pitch of life, as romance and allegory do, and as the bourgeois spirit never does. Yet simply and solely bourgeois, of the bourgeois ignorance of letters, the bourgeois-Philistine contempt for whatever it fails to understand, Chaucer was not. Always he is the composite, bourgeois enough to meet the bourgeoisie, courtly enough to meet the courtier, of genius sufficing to understand and to fuse both and to carry both into permanent literature. Bookman by taste and business man by profession; not deeply read but passionately addicted to reading; neither philosopher nor thinker, yet observer of everything human, interested in everything human, tolerant of everything human, without desire to teach or to preach; pliant to the literary customs of his time, yet understanding how to comply and to surpass with the same gesture,—Chaucer, like Shakespeare, struck a balance between individual assertion and conservative acceptance.

The century after his death saw the bourgeois and the aristocratic tendencies, which he had united, fall apart. Of the two publics into which England then split, publics more clearly defined after the establishment of printing, it was the aristocratic and formal which paid Chaucer deference and strove to imitate him. The group of his acknowledged followers had before them the same material, human and literary, which had lain before him; but their handling of books and of life is entirely different from his. No English "Chaucerian" looks at the written page as Chaucer had looked at it; there is only one man in the next age who is steeped in a book as was Chaucer,—Henryson in his Fables. Henryson, in his capacity of schoolmaster, must have taught and retaught Aesop until the Fox and the Wolf and the Cadger rose before him in their habit as they lived. But Lydgate, to take the most prolific of Chaucer's English admirers, has only a superficial contact with books, even with those he translates; he does not remember obvious facts about the Canterbury Tales, great as is the admiration he professes for it. His eye slides off the written page, slides off the human face; his senses are not alert, his interest not alive. No evidence is before us, and none may ever be obtainable, as to the actual condition of the human senses in any poetic period. But the appeal to them in "Romantic" periods is as marked as the lack of appeal to them when literature is held in stereotyped forms. It may be a fundamental fact in the Transition that its writers were so generally without visual and auditory sensitiveness. Description is abundant, but it moves in formulae; words are abundant, but the pregnant epithet, the revealing phrase, is not there. Chaucer was not one of the word-sensitive, as was Shakespeare or Keats; he cannot speak of "ardent marigolds" or of "warmèd jewels", but nevertheless his senses are not prisoners to formula. Whether it was Lydgate's ecclesiastical habit of mind, or the pressure on him of translation done to order, or his own temperamental sluggishness, which dulled him, we do not know; but his attention, his perception, his expression, are always blunted and diffused.

He had, however, more than many writers of his time, the access to books. The age was one of book-accumulation in England, as in Burgundy and in

France. Henry VI laid the foundations of the immense Royal collection of manuscripts now in the British Museum, and his uncle Humphrey of Gloucester presented his books to the University of Oxford. Balliol College, Oxford, received from her son William Grey, bishop of Ely, about two hundred volumes he had collected, three-quarters of which are still there. John Tiptoft Earl of Worcester, also a Balliol man, purchased so many books south of the Alps that he was said to have despoiled Italy in order to enrich England. He too gave books to Oxford. And at Oxford, until the dissolution of the monasteries, was the great library formed by Richard de Bury, bishop of Durham (died in 1345), an ardent amateur of books, as his friend Petrarch describes him, and ?author of the Philobiblon. Outside Oxford, too, was ample book-supply, especially in the Benedictine monasteries; and no one of these was better stocked than Lydgate's own house of Bury St. Edmunds.

Nor were royalty and the monastic houses the only book-lovers in England. We have still to decipher and arrange the evidence afforded by coats of arms painted in the books of their owners, which may reconstruct in part for us the collections of the Percies, the Stanleys, the Sinclairs, etc. And from the bequests in wills we can sometimes trace the passing of precious volumes from Sir John Morton to the Countess of Westmoreland, sometimes the bequest of the Canterbury Tales or of "Bochas" by one plain English citizen to another. The fifteenth century in England was not poor in the number of books from which sustenance could be drawn. The vibrating body and the transmitting medium were there, as they had been in the fourteenth century; the difference was in the receiving ear. To the very verge of the age of Elizabeth there were Englishmen full of enthusiasm for study, full of enthusiasm for travel, acquiring books, translating; but their efforts to express themselves can be classed as poetry only because of the accident of rime. Not all of Lord Morley's interest in Petrarch can make his translations endurable; the five years which Osbern Bokenam spent in Italy in no wise mitigated the clumsiness of his utterance; and neither Agincourt nor his Italian travels inspired John Hardyng to one rhythmical or readable line. What Cardinal Newman called "a haziness of intellectual vision" came, in the fifteenth century, from the same cause which Newman specified for his own time,—the lack of a really good education. It was the speaker's failure to see, to hear, to make fresh and independent comparisons, which deprived him of the power to understand or to express, which doomed his style to weakness and muddlement. Any form of education which quickened the perceptions of the English patron and the English clerk, or which could refine the taste of the bourgeois, would have served late medieval England, and did ultimately reach it in the form of drama; but from the inherited routine of study no stimulus came.

Higher education, in the fourteenth and fifteenth centuries, was obtainable in England at the monastic schools and universities and at the Inns of Court. Something more like a "finishing-school" training was to be found in great houses like that of John of Gaunt; a youth taken as page in such a household would become a complete courtier, able to speak and write French and a little Latin, to touch the lute, and to gather as much more knowledge as he could draw from the foreign-born physician or astrologer or Latin secretary who was so frequently to be found in the entourage of a great noble. The university man was definitely a logician or theologian, trained to the shaping of rhetorical periods or to scholastic argument in Latin; he often divided his later years between the penning of Latin letters for diplomats and a Church post given him as reward for secretarial duty. The lawyer received a more humane education, and may have lived a fuller life. Sir John Fortescue's classic account, although not particularized, tells us that in 1468-70, when he wrote, the training given by the Inns of Court included not only law and sacred and profane history, but singing, dancing, "and such other accomplishments as are usually practiced at Court." If Chaucer were a member of the Inner Temple, as now seems possible, his education was neither that of the desultory courtier nor of the secretarial monk; he must have learned how to mix with men as well as how to read many books. No match for him in personality came out of the Inns of Court in the fifteenth century; but whatever the determining power of Chaucer's own genius on his growth, some part of the difference between him and Lydgate, for example, may be due to the sharpening and clarifying of the one mind, the dulling and relaxing of the other, by the mental discipline received in young manhood.

The breaking-down of the difference between the two English publics, the beginnings of Humanism, are apparent first in the spread of secondary schools; and to this educational advance the new art of printing made early response. Caxton, with his strong personal interest in romantic narrative and his own activity as a translator, allied himself by preference with aristocratic patrons, with men of wealth. Only by such alliance, indeed, could he have published his ambitious folios. He tells us in one of his invaluable prefaces (to the Golden Legend) that the Earl of Arundel, when ordering the work, had promised him a buck and a doe each year, and to take a "reasonable number of copies." His issuance of Cicero's De Senectute was at Sir John Fastolfe's command; the Mirror of the World was printed for Hugh Brice, afterward Lord Mayor of London; and his earliest enterprise, the Recuyell of the Histories of Troy, undertaken while he was yet in Flanders, was at the command of Margaret duchess of Burgundy. The French versions used by Caxton for this last and for the Cicero had themselves been executed for ducal patrons; no man, indeed, could devote himself to such undertakings without assurance of support; and much of the formal large-scale literary production of the fifteenth century depended upon the taste of wealthy men. Caxton's successor, de Worde, was a more practical and less intellectual man than his master; under him and Richard Pynson the character of the London press changes, and reflects the state of the open market, the spread of education, the taste of the smaller customer. Gordon Duff states that of the ca.640 books printed by de Worde between 1500 and ?1535, over two hundred were school books. De Worde's hundred and fifty or so of poems and romances, beside this textbook production, shows how definitely a new sort of patron had appeared.

But whatever increase took place in the number of schools and of school-books, in the second half of our period, the mass of the English people was still little affected by education.   It was not by book-experience that they learned, but by life-experience, by enlarged discourse and enlarged intercourse among men. For this the growth of trade, of travel, and of the towns was responsible.   Not that there was any marked increase in the number of pilgrims to foreign shrines, or any clear effect on English culture caused by the travel of English gentlemen and scholars to Italy.   It was the many smaller and less obvious factors which counted; not the spectacular arrival of Erasmus in 1497, not the sojourn of Poggio, so much as e.g. the settlement near Winchester of Italian workers in metal and plaster.   It was not so much the presence in every great house of foreign secretaries, nor even the necessity for dealing with Flemish woolbuyers and Genoese moneylenders, as it was the extending of every citizen's horizon by enlarged buying power, repeated journeys near home, safer roads, wider acquaintance, aroused curiosity.   The freer circulation of money and the increase of trade as compared with agriculture pushed the key of bourgeois life nearer to that of the privileged classes, just as the Ford car and the highway system are pushing the change today.

That change proceeded very slowly.   Everything during the first half of our period combined to delay it; the distraction of England by class-quarrels, religious quarrels, dynastic quarrels, her cultural isolation by the French war, the lowering of her morale by that selfish and disastrous undertaking.   With the founding of the Tudor despotism and the establishment of printing, the confusion nominally ends; but it is long indeed before the bourgeoisie becomes able either to express itself or to make itself felt in national affairs.   And in the absence of any fresh creative impulse, the earlier formulae continue to endure.   Long after the introduction of printing, the expression of the people is still scarcely heard; the upperclass code, with its didactics, its allegories, its translations, its verbal stereotypes, persists.   However broken the aristocratic public politically, their taste regulates literary production.

Of this aristocratic literature, translation forms a large part.   At the opening of the century John Trevisa, the protégé of Lord Berkeley, made for his patron prose translations of Bartholomaeus De Proprietatibus Rerum, of Higden's Polychronicon, and of delle Colonne's De Regimine Principum.   The Polychronicon was printed by Caxton in 1482, emended by the editor-printer because of its "rude and old Englysshe, that is to wete certayn wordes which in these dayes be neither vsyd ne understanden."   The De Regimine was one of Hoccleve's sources for his verse Regement of Princes, dedicated to Henry V while Prince of Wales; and another of his sources, the Secreta Secretorum, so widely popular in the Middle Ages, was turned into English prose by James Young for the Earl of Ormonde about 1420, and into verse by Lydgate and a pupil a generation later. It was about 1410 that John Walton made his stanzaic translation of Boethius' De Consolatione at the command of Lord Berkeley's daughter.   Another didactic work, de Guilleville's three-part Pilgrimage, was turned into English several times before 1500, one verse-rendering of its second part being by Lydgate to the Earl of Salisbury's order. Much of Lydgate's activity, indeed, was as translator. He went over into the romantic-epic field at the bidding of Henry V, with his Troy Book; he may have pleasured himself with his Siege of Thebes, his Churl and Bird, his Dance Macabre; but his principal business was that of a large-scale didactic translator, from the saints' lives done for Henry V and for Henry VI, for the Countess of March, for the Abbot of St. Albans, to his heaviest undertaking, the 36,000 lines of the Fall of Princes, executed for Humphrey of Gloucester. Didactics mingled with narrative we find in the saints' legends of Bokenam, Bradshaw, Capgrave, in the Assembly of Gods, the Court of Sapience, the book of La Tour Landry printed by Caxton, and so on; and didactics were abundant unmixed, as in Cato, in Peter Idle's Instructions to his son, in Ashby's Activa Pollecia Principis, in Barclay's Mirror of Good Manners, in the whole group of Regements and Secrees on the one hand, of books of nurture on the other. The purpose of Hawes and of Barclay, later, is equally tutorial. Skelton translated Diodorus Siculus, Barclay translated Sallust; but into his freer work each of these men brought an air of contemporary life which we do not find in Hawes. Far more is this the case with Skelton; and beyond him, outside the limits of "formal" verse, there appears a mass of loudmouthed roughly written satire and foolery in which he too has a hand, though keeping his hold on standard subjects. Between the two extremes, hybrid forms exist; a poem like "How a Lover Praiseth his Lady" attempts to use stereotyped material, but constantly betrays a freer tone and spirit. Interest in everyday and low-class character shows itself, although the lists of beggars and knaves and drunkards are as definitely lists as was the Fall of Princes; and as far back as Hoccleve and Bokenam, in our period, the individual was talking about himself at the same time that he was writing correct and lifeless matter for publication. But all along with the increase of bourgeois feeling and with the hybrids ran the persistent stereotype. The Temple of Glass, the Black Knight, the Flower and Leaf, the Assembly of Ladies, the Court of Love, the Isle of Ladies, La Belle Dame, the Cuckoo and Nightingale,— all court poems of the Chaucerian school, are except the last, of the standard court-narrative model, conforming to French tradition. Most of the court-lyric, such as the translations of Charles d'Orléans and the anonymous love-poems of Fairfax 16, also follows copy. Features of interest, even of beauty, are presented by many of these poems; the grace of the Cuckoo and Nightingale or of the Lover's Mass, and the superiority of verse-flow in the Orléans translations as compared e.g. with Lydgate's work, are very marked. When the share of aristocratic writers in literary production increases, with the growing power of Humanism, the courtly lyric takes on new tones. But Wyatt and Surrey have already in their English blood a quality which they retain in the presence of the new material, and separate from it; they can most sweetly and clearly sing.

Neither in the narrative ballad nor in the form of pure song had lyric ever failed England. In the alehouse, the harvest field, the banqueting hall, the embrasure where ladies plied their needles, there had always been the group of singers or the solo lutist. During the fifteenth century we become aware that the individual aristocrat is writing and singing his own poems, a custom derived perhaps from Provence and France.   The Earl of Warwick, the Earl of Suffolk, later Sir Thomas Wyatt, the Earl of Surrey, Henry VIII himself, all try their hands at composition.   And we recognize also the power of Church music in England, not only what the Latin hymns must have meant for the writing of English religious verse, but what choral music meant for the carols, for the quality of pure song.   In the reigns of the Lancastrians the early music of England was in its bloom.   Little or nothing remains of the earliest English musical compositon; but the fifteenth century saw the development of what is known as "the second English school", of which the most eminent master was John of Dunstable.   It was the first great age of counterpoint; in solo singers and in composers England outdistanced France and Flanders.   Henry V, with his more military spirit, seems to have favored instrumental music; but Henry VI's taste was for vocal, especially for religious song.   His choir was famous, and compositions by the king himself are still extant.   Martin le Franc, writing his Champion de Dames in 1436-44, describes the envy of Continental musicians as they listened to the English at the Court of Burgundy and despaired of rivalling such melodies.   In 1442 the Privy Council[1] ordered Nicholas Sturgeon to "go and choose six singers of England such as the messenger that is come from the Emperor will desire for to go to the Emperor."   As far back as the beginning of the century, a Frenchman had celebrated the musicians of England,[2] and for generations she held her power.

But the beauty of song, whether on the lips of aristocrat, of cleric, or of the wandering harpist, is not paralleled in other fifteenth-century verse by a truly rhythmic sense.   Words which the medieval Englishman linked to tune often seem to have been born in a tune; but the words which he employed to carry lesson or story, which he intended to reach the intellect, have frequently no kinship with rhythm.

Of the many difficult problems in fifteenth-century verse criticism, the most persistent are the method of analysis to be adopted and the determination of a text to be analyzed.   The uncertainty which still surrounds the latter question renders inconclusive all the results which any method can at present yield.   No satisfactory argument can be based on a text such as Professor Skeat offers for Chaucer; and should we turn instead to the Canterbury Tales material offered by the Chaucer Society, we have but eight, of the many MSS, from which to generalize.   Of Chaucer's minor poems we have indeed all the texts, but no estimate has yet been formed of the different scribal personalities and their modes of interference with a copy.   For Lydgate and other fifteenth-century writers our position is far worse; we have in many cases only a single published text of each poem, giving us even less basis from which to argue.   Every statement here made is therefore only a suggestion.

Hitherto the method of analysis used on e.g. Lydgatian texts has been line-by-line.   This method has perhaps some basis in the classical and the early Teutonic line-conception of verse, a conception which the establishment of rime has

---

[1] Proceedings of the Privy Council, ed. Nicolas, v:218.
[2] Bibl. de l'Ecole des Chartes 62:716-19.

necessarily changed; but a stronger reason is the coercive power of the couplet-idea so marked in English. The writer who uses complex stanzas made up of unequal lines may earn from the critic a treatment stanza-by-stanza; but the man who writes in equal lines is assumed to have thought and worked line-by-line. One reason for the long popularity of the closed couplet was its adaptation to the metrical grasp of the average Englishman. He could see rime and rhythm in its small compactness, while its usual content of wit and wisdom was within his comprehension, and just enough above his power of expression to command his admiration. There was no uncomfortable tax on his knowledge, no "threat of loveliness" to chill him.

The line-by-line method will be used here only with limitations. Were it our sole mode of analysis, it would disguise the inadequacies of Chaucer's followers by fencing their work and his into small spaces where his power of phrase-manoeuvre cannot be seen. The way in which he surpassed the couplet-form his disciples did not recognize, nor do we if we treat him solely by line-types. The short phrase following the long breath-sweep of two lines and more, the line with less than five heavy syllables followed by the line of extra weight, the compounding of a twenty-line paragraph out of a half-dozen different sorts of line-movement adroitly interwoven, the running-over of one rime followed by pause and emphasis on the next, and the story proceeding all the while with perfect clarity and ease, its high points exactly met by the special stresses of the verse,—here is rooted the student's delight in Chaucer's line-management. Of course we seek in Chaucer nothing like the emotional contrasts of phrase-length as in Shelley. Shelley may write, in the Epipsychidion,—

> ———an antelope
> In the suspended impulse of its lightness   85
> Were less ethereally light; the brightness
> Of her divinest presence trembles through
> Her limbs, as underneath a cloud of dew
> Embodied in the windless heaven of June
> Amid the splendor-wingèd stars, the Moon
> Burns, inextinguishably beautiful.

But although there is here, as in Chaucer, the long breath-run followed by a short phrase, although there is a light swift line such as Chaucer could on occasion write, there are things impossible to Chaucer,—the iteration of long *i*-sounds standing out of narrow vowels in the opening sentence, and the slow close of the passage on lingering polysyllables, after the isolated emphatic word *Burns*. This management of vowel-color and of tempo, like the choice of simile and of epithet and the exalted passion of the poet, are too sophisticated, too subtle for Chaucer. We can find alliteration in Chaucer, but no such subtlety as Keats'

> The dreary melody of bedded reeds,   (Endymion I, 239)

with its long and short *e*'s and its half-submerged *d*'s. We can find skilful phrase-handling in Chaucer, but not such as Shelley's. Nor do we expect it. Chaucer is a master of the larger speech-unit which his narrative key requires, and no man working in his key has ever done better. Indeed, his immediate successors failed most conspicuously in that particular.

Lydgate is the striking example of this failure, just because Lydgate brought to a study of Chaucer the uneducated and timid mind moving line by line. He picked out from his master the kinds of line which might be written, and proceeded to use them without any of Chaucer's feeling for variety, for the pattern of the whole. He was by nature repetitive to excess, as his style shows, and the poverty of ideas which he joined to an unfortunate glibness resulted in an endless and ill-organized stream of words whenever he was commanded to speak. The verse in which he arranges those words has no structural quality outside the line; it escapes analysis as a long series of huts connected by passages escapes being called architecture. We may apply to him the five types used by Professor Schick for the classification of his verses; but it must be with the proviso that such a treatment accords only with the mind of Lydgate, and in no wise with the mind of Chaucer, that it has no validity for real poetry. One of the many likenesses between the fifteenth century and the eighteenth is the possibility of using on the verse of both periods the ruler five feet long. But for times of freer, larger feeling that ruler does not apply.

It has been said above that Chaucer understood the shift of weight from line to line,—a phrase which must be made clearer before we can proceed. English speech throws its major stresses upon the root-element of substantives, adjectives, and verbs; the iambic pentameter line has in theory five such stresses or heavy elements and five light or less important syllables, arranged alternately. In practice, an exact following of this pattern is not demanded; not only may the fall of verse-stress upon secondary syllables reduce the amount of grammatical stress in the line, and the appearance of important monosyllables in unaccented position change the balance of the line, but in all good verse this variation of the ripple, this shift of weight within the line, is sought by the artist. As Coventry Patmore says, the vital thing in English verse is "the perpetual conflict between the law of verse and the freedom of the language; each is incessantly though insignificantly violated for the purpose of giving effect to the other." Or, as Charlton M. Lewis has said, "the actual movement of the verse does not exactly correspond with the ideal rhythmical scheme deep down in our minds; it plays about—but never wholly forsakes it." An outward sign of a triumph of language over verse is the frequent appearance of a "trochee" among iambs, even of a spondee, or double heavy syllable, should the movement of thought require it; and this latter will make the line heavier just as the use of two syntactically unimportant words to make up a foot will reduce the total weight of the line. When Chaucer writes

> But trewely to tellen atte laste,

he has but three grammatically important syllables in a five-beat line; the verse is definitely underweighted; and this underweighting is well adapted to the merely connective function of the line.

Being a narrator by trade, Chaucer does not use the heavy line as often for a variant as he uses the light. The addition of stress to normal means, as we have noted, the presence in the text of pictorial or motor-words. The descriptive writer thus naturally makes more use of the full-weighted or the heavy line, while the forward-pressing narrator tends to reduce the stress-value of his total. Speaking a language in which the inflexional -*e* was still a separate element, Chaucer could conform his narrative to iambic rhythm more simply than can the modern poet; and in a full-stressed line he moves with a lighter tread. He has, normally, a high percentage of regular iambic lines, about fifty per cent of his work in each case; and heavy lines are not common. Underweighted lines which he introduces into his pentameter are not necessarily those carrying a notion of speed, such as "Or breke it at a renning with his heed," nor are they reduced in weight because of their small value in the narrative, like the line cited in our last paragraph above. They most often appear because there must be variety in any verse-flow, and because the lighter line is the natural variant for a story-teller. In this respect there is a noticeable difference between Chaucer and William Morris, for instance. Comparing two passages of similar function, the opening of the Squire's Tale and the opening of the tale of Cupid and Psyche, from the Earthly Paradise, we shall find that Chaucer has thirty normal iambic lines to Morris' eighteen, six heavy in one foot to Morris' fourteen; and that while Morris has a dozen or so of verses showing interior balance or compensation, i.e. a heavy and a light foot in the same line, Chaucer seeks this variant not at all. The Victorian's love of sense-appeal is reflected in his richer heavier rhythm. It may be objected that the two passages are not strictly parallel in content. But the characteristic difference between the two poets is that Chaucer opens a romantic tale and sets his stage with fewer properties; Morris produces at once his color, his draperies, and his emotions. It is the nature of the two poets which differentiates their modes of beginning, both in imagery and in rhythm.

Every poet of artistic sensibility steers a little east or west of regularity. A course in the direction of reduced line-weights gives a less obtrusive result; free use of the heavier line, or of the line with marked rhythmic divergence, challenges attention. If the words thus made conspicuous are important words, the variant is justified. When Chaucer puts into the four-beat movement of the Book of the Duchesse the line

> Blew, bright, clere was the air,

he writes a headless line, he places the adjective *bright* in unstressed position, and he uses two strong pauses to throw his descriptive epithets into prominence. Thus he heightens his effect both by rhythmic flow, by conflict of rhythm and language, and by marked catches in the breath-lengths. Nor does he dull the emphasis by using such an eccentric combination repeatedly or without purpose.

Eccentric lines may diverge from normal either in the grouping of their stressed syllables or in the total number of their syllables. The former variant is briefly mentioned above; as regards the latter, lines may vary by excess or by deficiency. If by excess, the line may have disyllabic or "feminine" rime, it may have an extra syllable at the opening (disyllabic upbeat), and it may have an extra syllable before the verse-pause, or "epic caesura." With these variants, the five-beat line may run to twelve syllables; the extra syllable elsewhere than at the line-opening (resolved arsis) is not proven for Chaucer. If the line varies not by excess but by deficiency of syllable, this happens either at the opening of the line or at the verse-pause, and results in either the "headless" or the "broken-backed" line. An unaccented syllable is lacking in such case. Students recognize the occurrence of the first of these line-forms in Chaucer, frequently in his four-beat work, less in his pentameter as time goes on. The headless line may occur in groups in the four-beat Hous of Fame, but the small number of such cases in the Canterbury Tales seem to serve a special purpose, to be used for cataloguing or for emphasis. As for the brokenbacked line, its sanction by Chaucer is still doubtful.

The four-beat work of Chaucer and that of his contemporary Gower differ markedly as regards these variants in syllable-count. Gower does not write head-less lines. The ten per cent of them in the Hous of Fame, book I, the approxi-mately fourteen per cent of them in book II, have no parallel in the Confessio Amantis. Gower also represses the natural lightenings and reversals of freely flowing speech; and the amount of rhythmic variety in his long poem is so rela-tively small that an effect of monotony results, an effect which closely cor-responds to the mental tone of the Confessio. But Lydgate shows in his work far more headless lines than Chaucer permitted in his pentameter; and he adds to his large number of lines short at their beginning an equal and some-times larger number of lines short an unaccented syllable at the verse-pause,—brokenbacked. For example:—

> And mony a tre mo then I can telle   Black Knight 81
> Theffect of which was as ye shal here   *ibid*. 217

As his basis of full pentameter lines is frequently below the fifty per cent usual in Chaucer, Lydgate has, instead of Gower's excess of normal over variant, an excess of variant over normal. And while Gower's substance and style are con-firmed by his rhythm, Lydgate's are in discord with it; they have none of the qualities which can justify such persistent emphasis. Now, if the thing said does not warrant the use of forceful variants, if the attention is summoned sharply to words not worth special emphasis, the effect on the listener is irritating. Lyd-gate's heavy demands on the rhythmic ear are not justified by his matter. These divergences, these headless and brokenbacked lines, also occur repeatedly and in close proximity, so that the reader has the threefold tax of an emphatic variant unsupported by a content deserving emphasis, and aggressively recurrent. The mechanical excess and the aesthetic or intellectual deficiency in Lydgate's verse so react upon one another that the result is more than doubly displeasing.

Beside Lydgate, Hoccleve leads the list of English Chaucerians. The person-ality of this partly pious, partly dissipated government clerk, who knew Chaucer and felt real affection for his master, this writer of begging-letters, railer at himself, translator, miracle-monger, wouldbe scamp, and wooden versifier, is far more interesting than that of Lydgate. The amount of Hoccleve's work is small as compared with that of Lydgate, and it includes no such proportion of com-missioned verse. Alongside the decorous hack-translation of the De Regimine

Principum done for Henry V, alongside a number of religious poems and a righteously indignant tongue-lashing of the heretic Oldcastle, are not a few compositions definitely autobiographical. Hoccleve's work is all stanzaic, in pentameter, and quite different as regards line-management from that of Lydgate. Here, as with Lydgate, there is uncertainty about the text; but so far as we can now see, Hoccleve writes very few of the lines scanted half a foot which are so common in Lydgate. His metrical characteristic is, that while holding steadily to the full ten syllables, he is not sensitive to the correspondence of syllables with verse-stress. He can write:—

And with him hir seruant to the ship wente,—

and many another such line syllable-filled and rhythm-empty. He and Lydgate had each a code; but while Lydgate erects Chaucer's variants into types and over-uses them, Hoccleve watches the number of his syllables and hears no rhythm. As Hoccleve's EETS editor points out, he "thwarts the run of his verse" at every turn by the prosaic arrangement of his syllables. Lydgate, on the other hand, is quite willing to write lines of less than ten syllables; but having adopted such variant-forms, his repetitive tendency overworks them to the injury of his whole.

The tendencies of later pentameter-writers in the century were determined neither by Hoccleve nor by Lydgate. Even men showing Lydgate's influence, like Metham, or Hawes or Cavendish in the sixteenth century, do not imitate his shortbreathed line-movement; and no one has a syllable-counting tendency. In most later cases there is no visible code on which verse is constructed. Perhaps because of the bewilderment caused by the loss of inflexional -e in pronunciation while it was still irregularly written, perhaps because of the cramping and inbreeding which weakened the intellectual fibre of the educated further with every decade, the rhythmic sense of most English writers slid to the level of doggerel. In the Libel of English Policy, an earnest plea to government for "high tariff," in the versified handbook of alchemy by George Ripley, in the romances of Lovelich, the awkward syllable-counting of Hoccleve and the awkward over-use of emphatic line-forms by Lydgate change to a reaching-after the rime-word without regard to the number or the placing of syllables in the line. This is doggerel; it becomes in the Libel a mere slither of words; and though there is less of a collapse of rhythm in Lovelich and in Hawes, their matter is so invertebrate that it disturbs the reader more than do the Libel's purposeful, if clumsy lines.

The codeless weakness of such degeneracy and the obstinately uncomprehending codes of Lydgate and Hoccleve are the more marked because of a few striking examples of rhythmic sensitiveness. Conspicuous among these is the translation of Palladius' De re rustica executed for Humphrey of Gloucester by an unnamed protégé at much the same time when Lydgate was beginning his Fall of Princes translation for the duke. I have elsewhere[1] commented on the remarkable smoothness and accuracy of the existing texts of this translation, and pointed out that in its first 1800 lines there are no cases of clipped lines, almost

[1] Modern Philology XXIII, 148.

no error in the scribe's treatment of inflexional -*e*, and every sign of a competent user of language and rhythm. The matter of the poem is unpoetical enough, with its instructions as to bee-keeping, poultry-management, the choice of soils, the times of planting, etc.; but there is no monotony and no clumsiness in the handling of the verse. The prologue and the connectives between books have much about Gloucester, and display adroit manipulation of rhetorical devices, as the passages included in this anthology will show. And there is clever workmanship in the stanza-variations of the Lover's Mass. When these pieces of work were done, and when the anonymous translations of Charles d'Orléans were executed, or earlier in the Boethius of Walton, some men were still sensitive to the relation between language and verse. But throughout the period, the incompetents are in the majority; and the further we go from Chaucer the feebler the general sense of rhythm. The incapacity of Hawes, the stiffness of Barclay, the mixture of lowclass slapstick and upperclass stereotype in Skelton, give place to the doggerel of Morley, the puerility of Nevill, and the curious double movement of Wyatt and of Surrey. Neither of these first masters of the sonnet walks very securely in the long line. Wyatt is much given to the wrenching of accent for rhythm's sake, a preciosity we can see in Walter's Guiscard and Sigismonda before him and in Swinburne or Rossetti after him; and Surrey's blank verse is tentative. But both they and Skelton can sing with perfect ease and sweetness. When they sing, they turn from older and from newer formal line-groupings and from pentameter, to shorter verses not equal in length; they find their full release by a variant other than the rhythmic, as the writer of the Lover's Mass had found it.

But generally throughout the Transition the stereotype of form is as heavy as is that of style and subject. It was *de rigueur* to write pentameter, and especially to write it in rime royal. The amount of seven-line stanza in the period is enormous, from Walton's translation of Boethius (part only) through Lydgate's Fall of Princes and Ripley's Compend of Alchemy to Hawes' Pastime of Pleasure and to Cavendish and Sackville. The romances had their own inherited strophes; but the religious, the didactic, and the occasional verse of the Transition preferred the seven-line stanza. The couplet, either four-beat or five-beat, was not apparently favored even by Chaucer's immediate followers to any such extent as was rime royal. How far this preference was the poets' own is uncertain. For although the great bulk of the Fall of Princes, the almost 6,000 lines of the Life of Our Lady, and the 3,700 lines of St. Edmund, raise the count of Lydgate's seven-line stanzas high over that of his eights, these are commissioned works, the Fall of Princes and the Palladius-translation both done to Gloucester's order at the same time in the same strophe-form. And Lydgate's eight-line stanza, constructed as a double quatrain, carries a large number of short poems, often religious, which may have been put into that form by his own choice. Hoccleve also uses the eight-line (and nine-line) stanza in his occasional poems, where he speaks more independently than in the Regement of Princes or in his narrative verse. But the later writers of the century preferred rime royal. Perhaps the taste of earlier patrons, imposed on the translations which they ordered, took effect on subsequent versifiers; certainly both Cavendish and Sackville had the Fall of Princes in mind when writing their seven-line stanzas.

Occasionally there is variation of form within the one work. Lydgate's Temple of Glass uses five-beat couplets and stanzas; Hawes changes from rime royal to couplet when he introduces the Godfrey Gobelive episodes into his Pastime; Barclay's insertion of a stanzaic Complaint into his pentameter-couplet Fourth Eclogue doubtless seemed to him very effective. But the narrow range of this variation, as compared with Chaucer in the Anelida, or with the Lover's Mass, or with Skelton in his Garland of Laurel, shows the timidity of the English Transition code. When the Humanistic change came it came at first in form more than in subject or in style; the sonnet and blank verse are more definitely novelties in form than was Barclay's introduction of the eclogue, and were addressed to a public more in need of new verse-moulds than was the public which enjoyed Skelton's tumbling verse. A road having been broken in one direction, the bourgeois subjects which were struggling into notice could push further forward. Sometimes they stumbled in the couplet, sometimes in the stanza, as either the political doggerel against Suffolk or the Hye Way to the Spyttelhous may show. And the disappearance of fourteenth-century stanzas derived from jongleur or from Latin hymns, of the complexities of strophe as in the Miracle Plays, is as marked as is the sixteenth-century appearance of humanistic forms and development of song.

Outside the stanza and couplet there is little verse-form in the Transition upon which to comment. Skeat assigns the partly terza rima Complaint to his Lady to Chaucer; the Anelida contains a rhetorical exercise in medial rime and in echo which we find again in the Lover's Mass and in Palladius; Skelton plays with short lines; and there are a few roundels in the period, from that at the close of the Parlement of Foules to those translated from Orléans. Some undated manuscripts contain free lyric verse which, if of the mid-sixteenth century, arrives when expected, and if of the fifteenth, is still more interesting. The Cambridge University codex Ff i, 6 is such a volume. But in general, there is less variety of verse-form, as of verse-tone, in the English post-Chaucerian period than in the Scottish.

The difference in social growth between England and Scotland in the fifteenth century may in part account for the fact that Chaucer's Scottish followers do not by any means suffer the rhythmic and intellectual disorder so marked in the Southern writers. English Chaucerians did over again, and botched, a work already done to admiration; but the master's influence was really felt by Scotsmen. When the spirit of Scottish nationality asserted itself, in the fourteenth century, the Bruce of John Barbour gave it enthusiastic expression, and the tide of national poetry began to rise. It continued throughout the fifteenth century, in the popular ballads and in the popular epic of Blind Harry's Wallace. Alongside this stream of genuine national expression, borne on the same tide of rising vitality, runs the more intellectual and formal poetry of King James the First, of Robert Henryson, of William Dunbar, and of Gavin Douglas, to all of whom, except perhaps to Dunbar, Chaucer is master and model. This more lettered aspect of the Scottish florescence shows itself first in King James (died 1437), and then in Henryson, the "Schoolmaster of Dunfermline," who died about 1506. In them and in Dunbar, who died in 1520, we find, looking at the technical side alone, a control of line and of stanza, a definiteness of purpose, and an assured ease of movement, which neither Lydgate nor Hoccleve ever attained. King James's one poem, the Kingis Quair, is somewhat hampered by its allegorical machinery, but James, like Henryson, has his verse under control. Henryson, though claiming for his Fables a "morale sweit sentence" which he considers it the duty of the poet to provide, keeps his moral from encroaching on his narrative,—a restraint impossible to Lydgate; and in his Testament of Cresseid he goes far from the shrewd and simple humor of the Fables to strike a note of passionate pity loftier than anything written by his more versatile and vigorous compatriot Dunbar, whom criticism generally terms the greatest of the group. Dunbar, rich in a begging friar's experience of life, is a professional poet of the stock of Skelton and the tribe of Rabelais. He tried his hand at many meters and managed all easily; he can praise the Virgin, abuse his fellowpoets, lash the vices of the time, and shudder at death, with equal fluency and force. And in quieter moods he can sound a note of solemn dignity in the Lament for the Makaris, and write the neat allegorical compliment of the Thrissill and the Rois. But his widemouthed boisterous vigor, the graceful sentiment of King James, and the quiet amused penetration of Henryson, all take something of their form and pressure from Chaucer; and all these poets are competent workmen.

Gavin Douglas, bishop of Dunkeld (died ca.1522), is a different personality. If Dunbar is akin to Skelton, Douglas is akin to Lydgate and to Hawes, though a much larger man than they. Certain of the conventions obeyed by them he has; his Palice of Honour is as heavily allegorical as the Court of Sapience or the Flower and Leaf; and in much of his work there is a straining for "aureat language" which, as in Hawes, speaks the rhetorician rather than the poet. This connects Douglas with such Frenchmen as St. Gelais and Molinet; indeed, his likeness to Octovien de St. Gelais, also bishop, rhetorician, and translator of Virgil, is marked. But wholly a pedant Douglas was not. The interesting escapes of personal expression and of nature-feeling in his prologues to the Aeneid, and his harsh but not systematically harsh treatment of the five-beat line, give him advantage over Lydgate, even over the nature-bits of the Troy Book. According to Professor Saintsbury, Douglas makes some use of the brokenbacked line; but until the relation of his verse to St. Gelais' Aeneid-translation, made in French pentameter couplet, can be worked out, there can be no full discussion of the technique of Douglas.

Verse-modeling and style develop parallel in all these writers. With the establishment of rime in late Latin and in the West European languages, the medieval system of "colores rhetorici" received additional floriations. To the accepted modes of literary amplification, to the "digressio," "descriptio," and "exclamatio" which we see used e.g. in Chaucer's more academic narratives, to the management of interpretation, of comparisons, and of word-play, there were added the effects obtainable by rime-combination. All varieties of stanza, all possibilities of medial rime, echo, interlace, etc., were worked by the French poet-rhetoricians, but were less favored in England. There the feeling for rime as a mode of stress might lead to its over-use by restless-minded men, but with the more sluggish-minded it led to the phrase-tag. The difference in its handling marks the difference between Skelton and Lydgate, just as its use now for emphasis, now in formula, now partially blurred by enjambement, marks the Chaucerian control of technique. A study of rime in Chaucer or in Lydgate is scarcely begun when its purity or impurity has been noted; the subjugation of rime to poetic purpose is the root of the matter, with its various aspects of phrase lengthened over the rime, phrase-formula used for rime's sake, shift of emphasis from rime-word to mid-line and back, etc. The second of these subjects, so far as Chaucer and Lygate are concerned, is discussed in the introductory essay on Lydgate here; but the two other aspects mentioned require far more comment than this book can give.

So with the question of vocabulary and word-usage in the Transition; the *rigor mortis* which held rhythm and held narrative-power pressed heavily on the treatment of the word   Something of this may be ascribed to the great amount of commanded translation in the period; but in passing the responsibility from poet to patron we do not remove it from the group. The late medieval versifier or reader had no notion of the metaphors latent but vital in words, of the power resident in the "fringe" of a verb or adjective and evocable by slightly shifting the angle of vision. There is a strong etymological interest in words, and there is abundance of abstract terminology new in English; but there is little or no development in meaning. Chaucer's "smoky rain," Lydgate's "restless stone" of Sisyphus, are rarities in Early English. Although Chaucer's senses were far more alert, his perceptual power far higher than those of his English followers, he is no specialist in word or phrase. The characteristic action which he sees so truly he presents in lines or in brief scenes. Concentration is not a quality of the Middle Ages. And as the Middle Ages yielded to the impact of Humanism, two general tendencies become marked in the use of words by English writers. There is the riotous extravagance of Skelton, in whose texts we find the inexplicable word as well as the inexplicable local allusion; such a word is obviously either a bit of showman's lingo or a boisterous coinage on Skelton's part. In Hawes and Nevill is the other tendency. Their pedantry strives for "aureat language"; Hawes loads his verse with terms like *depure, facundious, solacious, oblocucioun, pulchritude,* etc.; but both he and Nevill also use words, especially verbs, so vaguely and insecurely that we find no meaning in them.[1] We often do not know what Hawes intends to say by his use of *exemplify* or *inspect* or *ratify;* and his failure to pass on meaning is doubtless due to his own vagueness on the point. St. Gelais and the later rhétoriqueurs in France, Lyly or the seventeenth-century Latinists in England, show the same tendency, which is less a matter of chronology than of social and educational maladjustments. This attitude to language Hawes does not derive from his "master Lydgate"; Lydgate muddles his syntax badly, and employs the dead

[1] See note on the Pastime of Pleasure, line 78.

phrase for rime, but he rarely wanders from the essential meaning of a Latin word. His very large contribution to the English vocabulary[2] does not deepen or intensify language; it has no procreative power. He does not even carry it easily, as Hoccleve had carried his limited human common-sense vocabulary; but he does provide English with a mass of useful abstract terms which he manages with accuracy, but which the pedants of the later Transition blurred.

Chaucer attained his rhythmical and critical poise in an imperfectly developed and ill-adjusted age. He could not bequeath it. The power to control material can be received only by those mentally capable of receiving it; and the resettlement of the stereotype on English society just after his death, the increasing lack of educational opportunity of the early fifteenth century in England, smothered the growth of any such mentality. Pattern can be a relentless thing; if it encroaches on the imaginative field, the imagination either submits, or escapes only to extravagance and disordered unsymmetry. Not merely in Transitional rhythmic work and Transitional use of the formula or of the rhetorical code, does this appear, but in Transitional narrative.

At the opening of the fifteenth century the English narrator had before him as narrative-types the fabliau, the saint's legend, the allegory, and the romance. The first was frankly bourgeois, as the second was religious; both were small-scale. Allegory and romance are oftenest large-scale narratives, and the former has at its best a sense of causality working in human affairs which makes it an important factor in the development of structural feeling. Both it and the romance are also of moment in narrative-shaping because of their mass, because the mere handling of a great quantity of material urges a workman towards structure.

For several of these story-forms the work of Chaucer offered examples. He had brought the fabliau, especially, to a high state of finish as regards economy, dexterity, and single-figure portrayal; but in the eyes of his followers such tales were permissible only because their tellers were at the moment specially privileged; the presentation of such material would not only be impossible to the hand of Hoccleve or of Lydgate, but to their code. The "tragedy," as in the Monk's tale, or the saint's legend, as in those of Prioress and Second Nun, seemed, however, a very fit subject to the Transition workman, who probably saw no difference in the sincerity of Chaucer's attitude to the one and the other.

The saint's legend ran out, as a productive vein, by the close of the fifteenth century. It was hampered by its religious character. Its protagonist possessed no human failings, and the various antagonists no redeeming features; the two great opportunities of narrative, the dilemma and the error, were rarely permitted in the legend. Suspense, except in an elementary repetitive form, and complication, are absent. Visualization is infrequent; the stage is rarely set; and dialogue, used mainly for conversion or for miracle-working, shows no conflict of motive within the individual. Capgrave's St. Katherine endeavors to explain action and prepare for event; and in the lengthy discourses of the princess and her ministers regarding her marriage there is evident the author's sober legal

---

[2] See the Introd. to Lydgate, pp. 87 ff. below.

pleasure in weighing and stating a case. There is spirit in the speeches with which
the proposals of the steward are rejected, in Bradshaw's St. Werburge; but
generally the legends lack the mundane vigor of utterance which had been present in the miracle-plays, and are lacking also in the dignity and the pathos which
their circumstances permit. Nor does management of detail show a strong
hand. Capgrave sometimes notes facial expression, or uses a fortunate homely
simile; and in Bokenam there is another kind of leaning towards actuality in the
author's frank and even playful comment. But in the most prolific of all the
legend-writers of the period, John Lydgate, the personal or pictorial is at the
minimum, and the weak repetitive method is burdened by masses of didactic digression in which the narrative current almost disappears. Fifteenth-century
legend-writers brought narrative no nearer to the object of study. So far as
plot was concerned, the workmen striving after magnitude sought it on the
method of piling like details atop of one another; the notion of bringing the
figure closer to the eye, instead of increasing the size of the canvas, is outside
the comprehension of most medieval narrators. Was a narrative to be more impressive or more heroic, it had more tortures or more combats added to it. But
still more did the failure of the legend to quicken human feeling inhere in the
rigidity of its conception of human character. Its attempt to raise the pitch of
life was unsuccessful, while that of romance succeeded, because of its tenuous
contact with reality; its structure was often feebly repetitive; and the greatest
study in life, personality, could receive no furtherance from its refusal to see
aught but white and black.

The two great dangers of English literary expression, formlessness and
didacticism, were thus encouraged by legend-writing; and they were not combated by another medieval narrative type, the allegory. Allegory resembles the
legend, and differs from fabliau and romance, in the rigidity of its material and
in its attempt to instruct. There is little or nothing in allegory of the amused
bourgeois temper which appears in the fable or the fabliau, and rarely an interest
in humanity. Some advance there is over the saints' legends in the larger plan
and in the insistence upon causality; to this extent the hand of narrative is
strengthened, although clumsily and impersonally. The type is Eastern in its
origin and Christian in its development; in Christian literatures it is a hybrid
between the narrative and the homily. It became weak or restricted in the Transition; and we may query if this were not in a measure due to the new method
of treating the Biblical text, if the new exegesis did not affect the popularity of
the method. The necessity for an interpretation of Biblical language other than
the literal or surface had been maintained especially by the great Church father
Origen, followed by the greater St. Augustine in the fourth century. Such
Biblical exegesis, starting from belief in verbal inspiration and determined to
press the obstinate letter into harmony with Christian desire, dominated the
Middle Ages, and its method extended to creative narrative. It felt in the word
or in the narrative not those connotations for senses and for memory, not those
recognitions of human experience, which had been pagan and which were overborne by the Christian Church, but a set of moral and ethical precepts. The en-

cyclopedists, like Isidor or Fulgentius, give allegoric etymologies for terms and names; the treatment of pagan poets such as Virgil, Ovid, and Homer, is one of the curiosities of criticism; and the impulse goes over also into the creative field. Churchmen like Alanus de Insulis and Martianus Capella composed extensive allegorical narrative, peopled by personified abstractions; Dante himself lives in spite of, not because of, the method with which he is saturated; Petrarch, and even the bourgeois Boccaccio, viewed poetry, with Dante, as "concealing truth under the beauteous veil of the fable." Lydgate and Hawes accept this as the function of poetry; for them fable, or story, is a "covert" for truth, is a "cloaking colour."

Hawes, however, implies, and later writers confirm, a growing indifference to allegorical narrative on the part of the uncultivated public. He himself, in his Pastime of Pleasure, mixes his allegory with romantic combat and amour, with pseudo-learning, and with the farcical episode of Godfrey Gobelive,—perhaps to assure himself of a hearing with his royal patrons. In the bourgeois public, with its taste for the actual, loss of popularity for the allegory was bound to come; while from the best-educated, for another reason, there also came a limiting of the scope of allegory. The Augustinian doctrine of verbal inspiration, with its consequent desire to wrench and press the word, yielded, so far as the strongest minds were concerned, to the doctrine of historic interpretation held by St. Jerome, and championed in the early days of Humanism by Tyndale, by Colet, and by Erasmus.

Nevertheless, the tendency to personification, the interest in a double meaning or a concealment, were not eradicated by the Renaissance. Under disguise of chevalier or of censor the allegorical method persisted; Ariosto, Tasso, Spenser, use the one cloak, Skelton, Dryden, Swift, the other. Pure didactic allegory had its last great treatment in Bunyan and in Comus, but the method is not dead, nor will it die. As Lippmann has said, the will to find an implied meaning beneath an obvious is "the deepest of all stereotypes." Our classshift today has brought not only popular interest in riddle and puzzle, but in Shaw, in Barrie, in Capek. And although we have nominally accepted the "higher criticism," in thousands of pulpits the method of allegory lives on defiant.

Rigid itself, allegory links readily with those devices for expression which are rigid. The largest form in which it moves is the Pilgrimage or Quest; smaller and more static forms are the Procession or "Defile," and the Parliament. The Nuptials and Battles of the more pompous Latin were never popular in France or in England, although the "estrif," as a sort of midway-type between the contest and the Parliament, was favored in legally-minded France and Provence. The Pilgrimage-motive probably owed some of its popularity to its connection with reality, with that religious or chivalric taking of the road which meant so much to the medieval mind, and which, as a traveling toward the unknown, will always have fascination for humanity. These two could be forced into combination, as in the Anticlaudianus of Alanus, in Chaucer's Hous of Fame, in Christine de Pisan's Chemin de long Estude. And there was in them some chance for character-interplay, for episode, which the Procession had not. The mere line of figures "passing a given point," and all guided by a common feeling, as in Boccaccio's De Casibus or the Dance Macabre or the Ship of Fools, meets allegory only in so far as it uses personification, like Petrarch's Trionfi. It was such a list, when real persons were summoned, as by Cavendish or by Sackville, that contributed solid material to the Tudor drama; and from a list of actual people, be it of Chaucer's Prologue, or of the Ship of Fools, or of the seventeenth-century "characters," or of Henley's Hospital Sketches, or of the Spoon River Anthology, interest never dies out.

It was this intrusion of the real person, whether coming from past history or from contemporary life, into narrative, which most surely undermined the credit of Personification, as applied to abstractions or to qualities. After a long period of attempt to modify life, men began more correctly to report it; and any increase of human perception is in the line of human development. Conduct in narrative began to be determined not by precept but by human probability or by recorded fact; that is, it underwent just the same change that had been made in Biblical interpretation. The Tudor dramatic narrative, when tragic, insisted on that Causality which allegory had helped it to realize; and it attempted something which neither fabliau nor satire ever had, but which allegory and romance consciously sought,—a raising of the pitch of life.

Such a raising of life above the everyday was theoretically the business of romance as well as of allegory; but many romances, both English and French, are nearly as conventional in their central figures as if they were allegories. The hero is really Courage or Loyalty or Love, whatever his appellation. It is the event which is "romantic," the succession of ordeals to which the hero is subjected. In the degenerate romances the canvas is overloaded with such ordeals, with perils, deceptions, combats, even as the saint's legend was overloaded with tortures or miracles. In both, the repetitive method, the lack of purpose and of humanity, drive the type to exhaustion. But to this summary generalization there are three great West European exceptions,—Chrétien de Troyes in the twelfth century, Jean de Meun in the thirteenth, and Sir Thomas Malory in the late fifteenth century.

The work of de Meun, despite its allegorical disguise and romantic plan, belongs rather among satires than among romances; this was clearly perceived by Christine de Pisan and her group, and by an indignant Church. Chaucer recognized his intellectual kinsman, and was as well able as de Meun to use the double method, as well able as the Cock of his own Nun's Priest. But the fifteenth and early sixteenth centuries knew little or nothing of innuendo in satire; they used not the rapier but the bludgeon for criticism. The popularity of de Meun waned as the popularity of romantic allegory waned, not because of impatience with de Meun's real intention, but because men failed to see that intention through the outmoded stereotype.

Chrétien and Malory approach romantic material very differently from de Meun, and each possesses a characteristic not usually displayed in the romance-type. Malory has to a remarkable extent that sense of causality working in human experience which is to appear more powerfully in Shakespearian tragedy. And Chrétien, while handling romantic material, does it on occasion in a spirit as bourgeois as Chaucer's own, with as shrewdly amused a sense of human pretences and inconsistencies. Neither of these great qualities, the bourgeois understanding of average human nature or the tragic sense of the ills of life as self-caused, was possessed by the fifteenth century generally; but in Chaucer's age the former was there in full and the latter in an undeveloped form. Both, for instance, are in Boccaccio, in his Decameron and in his De Casibus.

Knowledge of Chrétien on Chaucer's part has not been demonstrated; but no student of literature can read the dialogues between Troilus and Pandarus without turning again to Chrétien's Yvain and pondering the conversations between the hesitating widow and her sprightly maid. Nor can a student refrain from drawing the spiritual comparison, whether contact between the two writers be proved or not. For if a nation's political and social conditions are of any effect upon her writers, then similarities in those respects between two Occidental countries may produce similar results without direct borrowing. Let a narrative outline come into the hands of two keen observers of human nature, each living in a period of strong political vitality, of rising bourgeois aspirations, and of a more clearly personal view of woman than heretofore, and those writers' handling of a human situation may well be similar. Chaucer may not have known the Decameron, he may not have read Chrétien; but he lived in a ferment of social conditions very like that around the Italian and the Frenchman, and towards that ferment his attitude was, as theirs, the ironic smile of the observer.

The mass of English romances is of the fourteenth century. Much of it came from France by translation, and to the student of narrative the handling of the French original by the English workman is especially interesting. The principal romances of the late Middle Ages which allow us to compare the existing French with the existing English are Partonopeus de Blois, William of Palerne, the Launfal stories, Li Biaus Desconus, and Chrétien de Troyes' Yvain,—in English as Ywain and Gawain. The treatment of these stories by English translators varies from William of Palerne, which is a free paraphrase, to a somewhat close rendering as in Partonope of Blois. Of course, any medieval adapter felt himself at liberty to expand or alter plot; it is the English treatment of character, of background, which particularly interests us.

It often happens, in the better romances, that real traits of character appear. The romance is not so rigid as the saint's legend; its protagonist may make mistakes, and may even be depicted in a ridiculous situation, as in Partonope of Blois and in Li Biaus Desconus. The background was often ample, and with many moving figures; though the effect might be that of the shallow crowding of tapestry, though "as in a faded tapestry, the brilliance of the dresses might outlast the flesh-color," yet the eye of the romancer could and did move from one focus to another.

The romance had a freer hand than the legend to develop not only character but structure; its manoeuvring-ground was larger than that of the fable or fabliau,

giving room not only for the delineation of character by dialogue but for anticipation, surprise, suspense, retard, for the management of transition. Chaucer's
strength had lain in the single scene, the Friar entering the cottage of the sick
churl, the conversation between the Cock and the Fox; and in some of the romances we can find larger-scale character-management. In Chrétien's Yvain, for
example, the hero is concealed by a pitying waiting-maid in the castle of a seigneur
whom he has pursued and slain on the castle's threshold, only to be trapped by the
fall of the portcullis behind him. From an upper window Yvain watches the
obsequies of the seigneur, and falls deeply in love with the widow. He must and
will wed her; and the waiting woman sets about the task of persuading her mistress.
The scenes in which this is accomplished, the picture of the widow's abating
anger and growing coquetry, and of the embarrassed first meeting of the two
lovers, are of extraordinary interest to students of narrative. This transfer of
interest from the physical combat or the intellectual disputation to the conflict of
human emotions is Chrétien's principal service to storytelling. He is not alone
in his occupation with it; many biblical narratives and much of Ovid before him,
Boccaccio's Filostrato and the sonnets of Petrarch after him, focussed attention
upon the ebb and flow of feeling. But where Chrétien, like Boccaccio, excelled,
was in his sense of time, his recognition of the need to make the change of emotional front gradual, of avoiding the leap from one narrative position to another.
Both he and Renaud, the author of Li Biaus Desconus, were aware of the effectiveness of hesitation. Renaud represents his hero as sitting on the side of his
bed and debating whether or not he shall go to his lady's room; he says:—

> Irai-je, ou ci remanrai?
> Ma dame le m'a desfendu,
> Et par sanblant ai je veu
> Ele veut bien que je i aille.

At last he ventures. But the lady is a fairy, and as he is about to cross her threshold, a spell falls on him; he finds himself hanging in the air over a raging torrent.
He shouts for help; but when the servants rush in with torches, the torrent disappears, and he seems the victim of a nightmare, to his great chagrin. Were this
magical episode presented without the hero's musing, we should treat it as mere
fantasy; but the stamp of reality is given it by the preceding very human hesitation
and by the comedy-discovery. One of the few noteworthy structural or psychological moments in Lydgate's mass of narrative, we may note, is the study, in
the Fall of Princes i: 4943 ff., of Althea's hesitation over the fatal brand. Here
the monk turns aside from his usual source, where the matter is dealt with in one
sentence, to follow Ovid's study of the mother's contending feelings; and inadequate though the English be, the choice of technique is a point in Lydgate's favor.

Another noteworthy feature of the better romances is the attention to ad-
ministrative (say) as well as to psychological transition. In the two French romances just mentioned there is obvious care in the fitting of joints. And in
Eger and Grine, an English story of which no French parallel is known, the
knight Grine passes a lady's castle on his way to avenge his comrade Eger; she
implores him to abandon the adventure, but he is obdurate and goes on. On his

return, successful, he knocks on the door of the room where the lady is sitting in anxiety for him; and her waitingwoman, opening it cries out, "O madam, now is come that knight That went hence when the day was bright." The inferior romances would have jumped this detail, would have seen the story intermittently, would have recorded merely that the knight returned and that the lady was rejoiced. It is in this spacing-out and continued visualization of story between major events that mastery of structure is most needed. A lyrical or emotional writer may depict situation with power, but the great narrative writer must possess also the ability to get from situation to situation without loss of power. Immature or degenerate narrative betrays its weakness in lack of transitional management quite as much as in failure at the emotional nodus. Even in a man so close to Shakespeare as was Marlowe the difficulty of making transitions is evident; the poet who wrote the death-scene of Edward II wrote also the clumsy shift of the king from one favorite to another, in the same play. This power is at bottom the power of continuing to visualize while the figures move.

With such visualizing power goes often a clear view of the background. In Li Biaus Desconus is a feeling for light and darkness comparable to that of Mrs. Radcliffe or of Coleridge, to scenes in Shakespeare's Julius Caesar. When the knight sits on his charger in the enchanted castle of the thousand windows and the thousand lights, with the thousand musicians clashing their instruments at him in one moment, and the whole brilliant scene plunged into utter darkness and silence at the next, the fantastic scene is made convincing to us by our own sense of the threat of darkness as a concealer. Renaud also understood, as Mrs. Radcliffe understood and as Hawthorne or Stevenson understood, the alarming and puzzling effect of sound without accompanying sight. The cries from the distance in the wood, which cause the Bel Inconnu to hurry to the rescue, throw his train into terror. Renaud never fails, either, to note the lighting of his scene; and this imparts reality even to the fantastic, as we have said. The coming-in of candles or torches is always mentioned by him, as it is in the Merchant of Venice; and moonlight is not omitted from his descriptions.

It is sensitiveness in the writer which brings the background into the story; it is sensitiveness which works against the earlier medieval "contempt of interval," to borrow a phrase from Leigh Hunt. And it is a failure of sensitiveness, an oppression by the stereotype, which deprives Transition narrators of the power to see and to develop motives, to see behind their characters, and even to see those characters distinctly, whether in life or in another man's pages. The Transition writer saw a list of personages, but saw not the method of portrayal; he saw a sumptuous array of trappings, for instance in the Knight's Tale, and believed, like the youthful Keats gazing into the clouds, that high romance was embodied in those symbols. Such poems as the Flower and the Leaf, the Assembly of Ladies, the Belle Dame sans Merci (translated), are episodes rather than narratives, and are handled like tapestry. The garden, the bridge, the pavilion, the mounted knight, the coiffed and jewelled ladies, the stiffly marshalled or conventionally dancing courtiers, are all seen in the same focus. But even when the foreground is more fully treated, as in the Churl and the Bird or the much longer

Troy Book, there is small gain in character-presentation. Nearest reality is the Medea of the Troy Book, a creature whom no ineptitude can wither or stale; but both there and in the Brunhilde of the Fall of Princes we must reckon with an earlier source. And we observe that when Lydgate goes outside courtly models for his material, as in the prologue to Thebes, in his Fables, in his Mumming at Hertford, we find no release of ability to draw character, not so much as in the clumsy prologue to the tale of Beryn. Nor do we find it in Hawes, when he shifts from his pedantic-romantic plot to introduce Godfrey Gobelive. And when the bourgeois spirit gets expression in character-portrayal, it has no better vision; it changes material but hardly method. Its list is of rapscallions instead of the illustrious unfortunate, the Hye Way to the Spyttelhous instead of the Fall of Princes; but the list remains, and the lack of vision remains. The latter comes, however, from a different source, from the insensitiveness of ignorance instead of from the insensitiveness caused by a paralyzing stereotype. When the ignorance is remedied, vision is attained; a sympathy for the human being, a consciousness of his surrounding life, are felt and expressed, and not till then. There is no more sense of snow and wind in the Hye Way to the Spyttelhous than there is of salt air in the Ship of Fools, and no more intention of recognizing it. Lydgate's rain-storms and sunrises in the Troy Book (for which we do not know his original) and Douglas' prefaces to the separate books of his Aeneid-translation are the best example in formal Transition verse of a natural background to narrative; but a mere touch during the course of the story, such as Nevill's unexpected picture of evening or Henryson's opening of the Testament of Cresseid, is of more value than set pieces.

But in the very midst of the Transition muddling of structure and blurring of vision, the Transition's blindness to the method of Chrétien or of Renaud or of Chaucer, a greater than Henryson, in England, laid his hand upon the already stiffened mass of romantic narrative, and raised the Arthurian story to permanent life. Malory's imagination was of far larger calibre than that possessed by Henryson; and to his sense-perception, his power of seeing, hearing, and feeling his personages, the way in which his eye holds the picture while his figures move, Malory adds a strong sense of structure. Perhaps the huge compilations of the latter Middle Ages brought gain to narrative in the sense of Causality which was pressed out of event by the sheer weight of material. Malory's greatest service to English narrative is here, a greater even than his character-portrayal, than his prose. He bound the Arthurian stories together by a sense for causality, for the unescapable consequences of human conduct; through the juxtaposed mass of separate narratives he drew the twisted thread of the three great Loyalties, to sovereign, to the beloved lady, to God; and by the shattering of the Round Table he showed that no man held those three in equal reverence, that no man served the Ideal, that punishment for such failure came here upon earth.

Malory works toward tragedy, as Henryson toward comedy. The actual drama of the period gains now an inch here, now an inch there, as it struggles with allegory, with biblical fact, with history. From each of its sources, except perhaps from the saint's legend, it received some advantage; allegory gave training in plot, the Bible-story stimulated to character-portrayal; and when the actual historical personage appeared among the abstractions of the Morality, the step to the chronicle-play was short. But in the earlier plays of the great period which succeeded, power over character and over scene is still much more evident than power over structure; even of Marlowe this is true. The lesson of structure was slowly learned by England; not until the long period of externalized morality was past, and the moral struggle restored to its natural arena, the human heart and our present life, could the growth of drama or of narrative proceed. All through the Transition, the courtly maker and the cleric were controlled by the stereotypes of their class.

That those stereotypes held so firm was due to the limitation of education and to the power of patronage. Their dominance in verse, especially, followed from the theory that the poet must write with a moral purpose, must use the cloak of fable in order to teach. The prose workman, not so restricted, might be supposed to move more freely; yet this freedom was not sought. From the argumentation of Wyclif and from the Boethius-translation of Chaucer down to Lord Berners' translation of Froissart, the major prose works are the encyclopedias of Trevisa, the travels of "Mandeville," the treatises of Pecock and of Fortescue, the translated romances and original prefaces of Caxton, and the Arthurian compilation of Malory. Briefer things, themselves longer than Caxton's prefaces, also exist, of which one of the most interesting is the Serpent of Division, presumably by Lydgate, with which may be compared the addition to the Brut, or prose chronicle of England, ascribed to him; or Bokenam's Mappula Anglie, the Paston correspondence, the Gesta Romanorum, the Master of Game, etc. The proportion of narrative is small, and of independently-handled narrative even smaller.

What strikes us in most of these men is the freer stronger use of language and the partial release both of the mind and of the senses, as compared with contemporary work in verse. Much less, too, is heard of a moral purpose,—a fact perhaps allied; and we constantly feel, even with the translator Trevisa at the opening of the century, that a personality is speaking. Already with him the English is vigorous and racy, despite some pedantries; and "Mandeville" surpasses him. In those fantastic Travels, moreover, there is narrative movement; the story marches as no tale by Lydgate knows how to step. Pecock's subject is of no such fascination as are the Oriental wanderings of Mandeville, and although his reasoning interests us, as showing both his mental quality and his command of English, neither he nor Fortescue exerted such influence as did the narrators, preëminent among whom are Caxton and Malory. Caxton is far the more medieval; he is constantly conventional in choice of subject, in sentence movement, and in phrase. Like Trevisa and like Lord Berners, he favors paired terms and rhetorical pleonasms, and labors with involved sentences. But either his subject or his fidelity to ornate correctness pleased his public; the more medieval his work, the more editions it apparently received. His Golden Legend was a better seller than his Malory.

Malory stands by himself in this list of prose writers, as he does among romancers. He and Mandeville are both, as narrators, concerned frankly with their story; but he alone creates an atmosphere. Mandeville can and does obtain credence as well as interest; he knows as well as Swift the value for the human mind of the trivial as proof of the tremendous. But we remain outside Mandeville's narrative, absorbed and delighted observers, but independent, detached. Malory removes our world and substitutes his. The integrity of his conviction, his feeling, his imagination, is such that we return from him with difficulty to that smaller and meaner life which we have called normal.

There is the same integrity in Malory's use of English; his speech, his phrasing, are as dignified as those of an epic, but entirely simple and sincere. He was not surpassed or equalled in English until, in 1549, the gravely simple diction and noble rhythms of the first Prayer Book were composed. Between him and it the tale of English writing, verse or prose, is a sorry one. There is no suavity, no simplicity, and no dignity in Hawes; he is hopelessly muscle-bound. There is no freedom in Barclay; although he has the wit to reach for novel forms, his touches of reality and independence are clamped down among didactic phrases. Skelton is but half free, medieval rather than humanistic, a lampooner and rebel more because he is unsuccessful than because he has ideas. George Cavendish too is but half free; with him, however, the division is between verse and prose, the former stiffly imitative, the latter honest, vigorous, alive—a real story told with a real voice. His life of his master Wolsey is almost the first of English biographies, antedated only by More's unfinished life of Richard III; and it has had few superiors in the four centuries since it was written. But while Cavendish was writing it, in the group of versifying courtiers around Henry the Eighth the "mode" was supreme, whether in song or in translation. Wyatt, Surrey, Nevill, Morley, obey it, each in his own way; and although the two last-named are more woodenly subservient to pattern, the two greater men are fortunate partly because their patterns are fortunately chosen. In pure song, indeed, they are truly English, and truly poets. But no man rises above an original, above a standardized pattern, as Malory had, until Cavendish creates biography, until the Prayer Book is written, and until with Spenser, Shakespeare, and the King James version of the Bible, the freedom of English utterance is attained.

Removal of the pressure of the stereotype does not restore at once the long-atrophied vision; from a hundred and fifty years' denial of perceptual power, from protracted over-assimilation of a few facts, from the exhausting effect of overworked motives and words, a national literature does not recover at a bound. With the appearance of a foreign-bred Humanism among English scholars and in a small class of aristocratic poets, the Renaissance gets under way in England. As society settles, as education spreads, as intercourse grows freer, the new modes of expression find more favor. But earlier themes and tendencies last over; and it takes a long time for Englishmen to obtain control of rhythm and of structure, two lessons which Humanism could not teach them. Yet, slow as was the process of social readjustment and education, slow as was the assimilative power of the new public, England's attainment of balance, in the

Elizabethan age, was on all the higher level because the sequence of events which brought her there had been just what it had been. The defeat of the Armada was a spectacular success indeed, a powerful stimulus to English patriotic pride and to the sense of national unity. But it came after a long series of lesser inconspicuous successes in the economic field, after a definite rise in the average of English comfort and security in private life, after the assertion of English religious self-control. The sense of unity and confidence derived from resistance to an invader had a more ample national basis on which to rest, because of previous partial adjustments. The Armada success did not, like Agincourt, engender forces hostile to regular growth; it was a definite and healthy phase in England's attainment of self-poise, partly because of the social and religious resettlement which preceded it.

And so with literature. The various elements of the English change passed slowly and firmly into relation with one another. That challenge of the moral basis of life which follows on a change in social structure, that challenge of the social basis of life which accompanies a new view of morality, took effect each upon the other, and were expressed in new moulds of form. The English Renaissance is far more socially penetrative, more deeply felt on literature, more earnest and ethical than that of the Continent, because in England a bourgeois self-assertion which might, with the break-up of feudal inhibitions, have assumed a more arrogant and illiterate form, was reined in by both Humanism and the Protestant Reformation. It persisted, but it was modified. A politically homogeneous and articulate people and a national sense of conduct were growing alongside that revival of perception, that increase of experiencing power, which permitted a revival of expression. It is not surprising that the dominant literary form of this fusion and interaction should be the drama; for no other utterance is so definitely social, and none admits of such a variety of tones. Every vulgarity, every pedantry, every vice, every upleap of vigor, every dignity of Englishmen is poured into the alembic of Shakespeare.

SELECT REFERENCE LIST I

The student will derive profit from Green's Short History of the English People and from G. M. Trevelyan's History of England, 1926; from H. W. C. Davis' edition, Oxford, 1924, of Medieval England; from G. C. Coulton's Chaucer's England, and from Trevelyan's England in the Age of Wycliffe; from H. S. Bennett's The Pastons and their England, Cambridge, 1922; from Eileen Power's Medieval English Nunneries; from E. Mâle's L'art réligieux de la fin du moyen-âge en France, Paris, 1908, and from Mâle's other work; from Ramsay's Lancaster and York, Wylie's Henry IV, and Cora L. Scofield's Edward IV; from Vickers' England in the Later Middle Ages, London, 1914; from Huizinga, Herbst des Mittelalters, Munich, 1924 (transl. London, 1924 as The Waning of the Middle Ages); from the Legacy of the Middle Ages, Oxford, 1926.

G. Le Bon, The Crowd, a Study of the Popular Mind, transl. London, 1896, from the
    French. Many reëditions.
Th. Veblen, Theory of the Leisure Class, N. Y., 1899.
G. Tarde, The Laws of Imitation, transl. N. Y., 1903, from second French ed.
G. Tarde, L'Opinion et la Foule, third ed., Paris, 1910.
W. Trotter, Instincts of the Herd in Peace and War, N. Y., 1916.
W. Lippmann, Public Opinion, N. Y., 1922.

The Complaint to his Lady is printed in Skeat's Oxford Chaucer, i :360.
The Black Knight, see ed. by Skeat in vol. vii of the Oxford Chaucer.
Walter's Guiscard and Sigismonde, see Zupitza in Vierteljahrschrift für Kultur u.
    Litteratur der Renaissance, i :63-102 (1886). See diss. by Clarence Sherwood,
    Berlin, 1892.
"How a Lover Praiseth his Lady," see ModPhil 21 :379-395.
The Flower and Leaf, the Assembly of Ladies, the Court of Love, La Belle Dame
    sans Merci, are included in Skeat vii as above.
The Isle of Ladies, see diss. by Jane Sherzer, Berlin 1905.
Hye Way to the Spyttelhous, by Robert Copland, is printed in Hazlitt's Early Popular
    Poetry, 1866, vol. iv.

Travel and Travellers of the Middle Ages, ed. A. P. Newton, N. Y., 1926.
Dawn of Modern Geography, C. R. Beazley, London, 3 vols., 1897, 1906.
Mandeville's Travels are ed. for EETS by Paul Hamelius, 2 vols., 1919, 1923. See
    also Sir George Warner's ed. for the Roxburghe Club, 1889.
Le Morte Darthur of Sir Thomas Malory, Vida D. Scudder, London and N. Y., 1917.
For Lydgate's addition to the Brut, see Robinson in Harvard Studies v.
Bokenam's Mappula Anglie is printed by Horstmann in EnglStud 10.
The Master of Game, by Edward duke of York, is ed. Baillie-Grohman, 1904 and 1909.
Standard but special reference-works, such as Thorndike's History of Magic or Kings-
    ford's studies in the English Chronicles, will be found in the separate refer-
    ence lists of this volume.

JOHN WALTON'S BOETHIUS-TRANSLATION

The poem here discussed is in most of the manuscripts marked as by "Johannes Capellanus," in one manuscript at least (the Phillipps) as by "Capellanus Johannes Tebaud alias Watyrbeche." In the early and carefully-written volume belonging to Balliol College (A), the author's name is given as "John Walton nuper canonicus de Oseneye"; and in the 1525 print of the poem an acrostic at the close not only names "Johannes Waltwnem" as author but states that his patroness was Elizabeth Berkeley. Nothing more is known of John Walton except that his work is definitely dated 1410 by a number of the MS-colophons; Elizabeth Berkeley was probably daughter to that Thomas lord Berkeley who employed Trevisa to translate various encyclopedic works, and wife to Richard earl of Warwick, himself the reputed author of a little courtly verse, and Lydgate's patron for the Pedigree of Henry the Sixth. In such case, it was their daughter the countess of Shrewsbury who commanded of Lydgate his Guy of Warwick; and the family, with its protégés Trevisa, Walton, and Lydgate, make one of the literary "groups" of the fifteenth century. Elizabeth countess of Warwick married before May, 1399, and died in 1423. See pp. 459-60 here.

Already Thomas Warton, in his History of English Poetry (see ed. by Hazlitt iii:39-40) had identified Walton as the translator of this work; but the vagueness of "Johannes Capellanus" led various students to attribute it to John Lydgate. Such is the statement of Casley's 1734 catalogue of the Royal MSS and of the 1838 catalogue of the Durham Cathedral MSS; also of Peiper in his 1871 ed. of Boethius' Consolation, and of Manitius in his 1911 history of medieval Latin literature included in the Handbuch der klassischen Altertums-kunde, ix, 2. The impossibility of Lydgate's authorship is clear, however, to any student of the matter; the direct definite advance of the translator's mind, the absence of digression and of rime tags, the comparative freedom of the verse from eccentric lines, are completely non-Lydgatian. Indeed, although Warton dismissed our versifier summarily as "contributing no degree of improvement to our poetry or our phraseology," this Boethius-translation deserves more attention and credit than it has received. It was of course a mistake on Walton's part, as ten Brink remarked, to force the whole work into verse,—a greater tactical error than Chaucer's reduction of the whole to prose. For thereby is lost the element of variety, the change of key from reflective to lyrical, so definitely sought by Boethius; and the use of verse for the whole imposes on the major portion of the work a key more appropriate to the minor portion. A somewhat similar ill-judgment may be seen in the French translation of Boccaccio's Fall of Princes, cf. p. 151 below.

The work which Walton here translates is one of the most potent of the Middle Ages. It exerted upon West-European letters an influence comparable only with that of the Roman de la Rose seven centuries later. Its author, Anicius Manlius Torquatus Severinus Boethius, was born about 480 A.D., and was executed by the emperor Theodoric in 525. Of good family, he was raised to the consular dignity in 510, and was holding important government office when his remonstrances against the imperial policy brought upon him the suspicion and wrath of Theodoric. He was thrown into prison, and there put to death. During a life of great political activity and responsibility, he had found time to translate several texts of Aristotle, with commentaries, which were the main source of later medieval knowledge of Aristotle; he also wrote on logic, and drew up manuals of arithmetic, music, geometry, etc., which were the standard for centuries. But the best-known and most influential of Boethius' writings was his last, the De Consolatione Philosophiae, written while he lay in prison, and in the knowledge of approaching death. It is an interview, in Latin prose interspersed with verse, between the prisoner and Philosophy, who appears to him as a marvellous female figure, and discusses with him the secrets of the universe.

The Consolatio not only made a profound impression on the medieval mind, but has remained interesting to modern students, as the many translations of it show. For the French versions, etc., see Stewart as below; English renditions are still more numerous. The earliest of these is by King Alfred, latest edition by Sedgefield, Oxford, 1899; to this is appended the alliterating Old Eng. version of the metres of Boethius. Chaucer's translation is entirely in prose, but there is a stanzaic rendering by him of one metre, the "Former Age." Of his first book there is a reshaping which exists in one MS (see note on A 26 of our text) and which may have been known to Walton when he speaks of "diverse men" who had preceded him. Later than Walton are:—George Colvile in 1556, ed. Bax, London, 1897; Queen Elizabeth in 1593, ed. EETS 1899, with appendix containing nine metres translated by Sir Thomas Challoner ?1563; transl. by John Bracegirdle, 1603-09, in hexameter etc., specimen printed by Flügel in Anglia, 14:499; by "I. T." in 1609, prose and verse, printed in the Loeb Library Boethius, 1918; the metres of books i and ii by Henry Vaughan in his *Olor Iscanus,* 1651; by "S. E. M.", London, 1654; by H. Conningesby, verse, 1695; by anon., prose and verse, Oxford, 1674; by Richard lord Preston, prose and verse, 1695; by William Causton, prose and verse, London 1730; by Philip Ridpath, prose and verse, London, 1785; by R. Duncan, Edinburgh, 1789; an anon. transl. of the metres, London, 1792; by H. R. James, prose and verse, London, 1897, 1906; by W. V. Cooper, prose, London, 1902.

Walton's notion of a translator's duty, as stated in his preface, is more than the usual patristic one of keeping the sense, whatever may happen to the word. He attempts to be true to the word also, so far as metrical exigencies permit; and although his "liftings" from Chaucer are frequent, he is often fortunate in his phrasing, and quite as likely to render the Latin correctly as was his great predecessor. His work, despite its borrowings, has vigor and honesty. And the handling of English rhythm by Walton is so much better than by either Hoccleve or Lydgate that he, with the translator of Palladius and the translator of Charles d'Orléans, deserves especial attention from students of the English metre written in this bewildered period. He is frequently driven by his verse-form to pad, but avoids the barren formulae to which Lydgate is so prone. He can be dignified without being floridly rhetorical; his most deliberate ornament is alliteration, which he employs e.g. in the first metre of the first book. The care and intelligence with which he worked can be well seen in the difficult discussion of "prescience" in book v, prose 4. Chaucer's cautious progress through this material was successful, but Walton's restatement of it in verse was a real task, even with the Chaucerian text before his eyes. The mentality which could accomplish this is of an order quite other than the mentality of Hoccleve or of Lydgate; and we may note the scanty use of Boethius by Lydgate (see p. 185 below). Whether or not Walton knew the versifying of Boethius in Troilus' soliloquy, Book iv of Chaucer's poem, is a point as yet uninvestigated.

Walton's translation runs to more than 7,500 lines, in eight-line stanzas to the close of book iii, and thereafter in sevens, with a special prologue of Walton's own composition marking the change. Four stanzas at the close return to the original construction.

Manuscripts containing the work are fairly numerous. Schümmer as below lists fourteen, viz.:—In the British Museum, Royal 18 A xiii, Harley 43, Harley 44, and Sloane 554; in the Bodleian, Rawlinson poetry 151 and Bodley e Museo 53; in Oxford colleges, Balliol 316 A and 316 B, New College 319, and Trinity College 21; in Cambridge, Gg iv, 18 of the University Library. Other MSS in Schümmer's list are Lincoln Cathedral A 4, 11, Durham Cathedral v ii, 15, and the MS formerly Phillipps 1099, now (1927) in the hands of Dr. Rosenbach, the New York collector and dealer. To this list Prof. Carleton Brown, in his Register of Middle English Religious Verse, adds five MSS:—the former Chetwode MS, now McClean 184 of the Fitzwilliam Museum at Cambridge; the Society of Antiquaries 134; Christ Church Oxford 151; Bodl. Douce 100; and St. John's College Cambridge 196. A Copenhagen MS is mentioned by J. H. Wylie in Athen. 1892, i: 600.

Walton's poem was printed in 1525 at Tavistock Monastery in Devonshire (where was situate the second press established in England) by Thomas Rychard, at the request of Master Robert Langdon; the book is exceedingly rare. Brief extracts from the translation are given by Todd in his Illustrations of Gower and Chaucer p. xxxii (2 stanzas only); by Blades in his Caxton, ii:68; by Wülker in his Altenglisches Lesebuch, ii:56-59; by Stewart as below; by Skeat in his Oxford Chaucer, ii:xvi-xviii; by Flügel, Neuengl. Lesebuch, p. 99. Cossack and Schümmer, as below, print much larger portions of the text. On Walton see Warton's HistEngPoetry, iii:39-40 of Hazlitt's edition.

For my text I have used the MS Royal 18 A xiii of the British Museum, a volume used also by Wülker, by Skeat, and by Schümmer; some variant readings are given as stated, usually from the MS Balliol College 316 A. The Royal volume is on vellum, of 114 leaves, 9¼ by 6¼ inches, in a very neat square conventional hand, with careful capitals to stanzas, and marginal markings of metres and proses, etc. There is no other work in the volume. The Balliol MS contains, besides Walton, two short hymns; it also is on vellum, of 108 folios, with a colophon giving Walton's name and ecclesiastical status,—whereas the Royal's colophon has the usual "per Capellanum Johannem." These and other MSS are described by Schümmer as below.

SELECT REFERENCE LIST II

Doyle, Official Baronage of England, 3 vols., London, 1886.
Warwick, Richard de Beauchamp earl of; for a virelay by him see PMLA 22:597.
Moore, Samuel, Patrons of Letters in Norfolk and Suffolk ca. 1450, *ibid.* 27:188-207, 28:79-105.

Stewart, H. F., Boethius, an Essay, London, 1871.

Cossack, H., Ueber die altenglische metrische Bearbeitung von Boethius, de Consolatione Philosophiae. Leipzig diss., 1889, pp. 69.

> Cossack uses the 1525 print for his analysis, which is of book i only; he
> proves the use of Chaucer by Walton.

Fehlauer, Fr., Die englischen Uebersetzungen von Boethius' de Consolatione Philosophiae, Berlin, 1909. Part pubd. as diss., Königsberg, 1908.

Schümmer, K., John Waltons metrische Uebersetzung der Consolatio Philosophiae. Untersuchung des handschriftlichen Verhältnisses und Probe eines kritischen Textes,
Bonner Studien 1914. Part pubd. as diss., 1912.

> Schümmer's "textproben" are book i entire, the first three sections of book
> iii and a selection from its latter half, the prologue to books iv and v,
> and part of book v. All in all, he gives over a third of the work.
> His apparatus of variants is printed below each stanza, and in his
> introd. he constructs a genealogical tree of MSS.

Hittmair, R., Das Zeitwort "do" in Chaucers Prosa, Leipzig, 1923, diss., has a comparison of the Boece with Alfred, Walton, Colville, and Queen Elizabeth.

The Bodleian MS Auct. F 3, 5, which contains a prose transl. of book i of the
Consolatio, is now marked Bodley 2684; see the Summary Catalogue i:492, and
Liddell in Academy 1896 i:199.

Recent studies on Chaucer's translation are by B. L. Jefferson, Princeton, diss., 1917,
and by Koch in Anglia, 46:1-51.

[A]

[PREFACE AND PROLOGUE: METRE 1, PROSE 1]

Insuffishaunce of cunnyng & of wyt
Defaut of langage & of eloquence
Þis work fro me schuld haue wiþholden
   ȝit
Bot þat yowre hest haþ done me violence
Þat nedis most I do my diligence   5
In thing þat passith myn abilite
Beseching to youre noble excellence
Þat be your help it may amended be

2

This subtile matire of boecius
Heere in this book of consolacion   10
So hye it is so hard and curius
fful (fer) abouen myn estimacion
Þat it be noght be my translacion
Defouled ne corrupt to god I praye
So help me wiþ his inspiracion   15
Þat is of wisdom bothe lok & keye

3

As fro þe text þat I ne vary noght
But kepe þe sentence in his trewe entent
And wordes eke als neigh as may be
   broght
Where lawe of metir is noght resistent 20
This mater whiche þat is so excellent

12. Royal reads *fair*; Balliol 316 A, *fer*.
24. Insertion from Balliol A.

And passeth both my cunnyng & my
   myght
So saue it lord in þi gouernement
Þat kannest reforme all þing (vn) to
   right

4

I haue herd spek & sumwhat haue y
   seyne   25
Of diuerse men þat woundir subtyllye
In metir sum & sum in prose pleyne
This book translated haue full suffishaunt-
   lye
In to englissh tonge word for word wel
   neye
Bot I most vse þe wittes þat I haue   30
Þogh y may noght do so yit noght for
   thye
With helpe of god þe sentence schale I
   saue

5

To chaucer þat is floure of rethoryk
In englisshe tong & excellent poete
This wot I wel no þing may I do lyk   35
Þogh so þat I of makynge entyrmete
And gower þat so craftily doþ trete

33. Balliol reads *was flour*, etc.

As in his book of moralite
Þogh I to þeym in makyng am vnmete
Ʒit most I schewe it forth þat is in me 40

6

Noght lyketh me to labour ne to muse
Vppon þese olde poysees derk
ffor crystes feith suche þing schuld refuse
Witnes vppon Ierom þe holy clerk
Hit schold not ben a cristenmannes
     werk   45
Tho fals goddes names to renewe
ffor he þat haþ reseyued cristes merk
If he do so to crist he is vntrewe

7

Of þo þat crist in heuene blis schall
Suche manere werkes schold ben set on
     side   50
ffor certaynly it nedeþ noght at all
To (whette) now þe dartes of cupide.
Ne for to bidde þat Venus be oure gide
So þat we may oure foule lustes wynne
On aunter lest þe same on vs betide
As dede þe same venus for hyre synne

8

And certayn I haue tasted wonder lyte
As of þe welles of calliope
No wonder þough I sympilly endite
Yet will I not vnto tessiphone   60
Ne to allecto ne to megare
Besechin after craft of eloquence
But pray þat god of his benignyte
My spirit enspire wiþ his influence

9

So þat in schenschip & confusion   65
Of all this foule worldly wrecchidnesse
He help me in this occupacion
In honour of þat suffrayn blisfulnesse
And eke in reuerence of youre worthi-
     nesse
This simple work as for an obseruance
I schall begynne after my sympelnesse
In wil to do your seruice & plesance
EXPLECIT PREFACIO TRANSLATORIS

INCIPIT PROLOGUS EIUSDEM SUPER
     LIBRUM BOECII

10

The while þat Rome was reignyng in hir
     floures
And of þe world held all þe monarchie
Sche was gouerned þenne be emper-
     oures   75

---

49. Balliol A, blisse.
52. Royal wete, Balliol whette.

And was renounned wondir nobelye
Til pride had set þaire hertes vppon hye
Þenne gan thei to vsen cruelte
And regne by rigour & by tyrannye
In sore oppressioun of þe commynalte

11

For right as pouert causeth sobirnesse
And febilnesse enforseth continence
Right so prosperite & sikernesse
Þe moder (is) of vice & necligence
And pouer also causeth insolence   85
And often honour changeþ goode þewes
Þere is none mo parelouse pestilence
Þan hyhe estates gyffen vnto schrewes

12

Of which was nero oon þe principall
Þat suche manere of tyrannye began   90
þough he bare dyademe imperiall
Yit was hym selfe a verry cursed man
So cruelly he began to reigne þan
He slowh his modir & his maistir both
And myche he dide þat tellen I ne can
Who so haþ hit rede he (knowyth) well
     þe sothe   96

13

The cheef of holychirche he slowh also
Seynt Paule & petir both vppon a day
And after þeym full many oþer mo
And of hym self it is I dar wel say   100
þat paule writeth þus it is no nay
And seith now is þe forme of wickednesse
And figure right of Antechristus lay
In whom schall been all manere cursed-
     nesse

14

For þei þat trwly techeth cristes lore 105
To maken men forletten of þeire vice
Antecrist will pursue þeym þerfore
And all þis prechyng setten at no prise
So was he gifen to lustes & delice
In what desire þat comen to his þoght
He wolde it done wiþ outen more avise
ffor no þing þereof spare wolde he noght

15

And he þat wolde agayn his vices speke
Conseilyng hym his lustes to refreyne
Wiþ outen more anon he wolde be
     wreke   115

---

78. Balliol for to vsen, etc.
     Beside stanza 11, in margin, is Nota per
     exemplum.
84. Royal omits is; inserted from Balliol A.
93. began; Balliol gan.
96. Balliol as here; Royal knowt.
110. Balliol þt what desire þt come unto, etc.

He wolde him put in torment & in peyne
And he þat wolde his lustes out wiþ
    seyne
He was but dede if þat he wolde appere
ffor suche a cause Boecius was slayn
Of whom this processe techeþ after
    heere   *120*

16

The yeere of crist fyue hondred & fiftene
Whan anastasius was Emperour
Boecius þe same of whom I mene
In Rome he was a noble senatour
Bot þo in manere of a conque(r)our *125*
Theodoricus regned in ytayle
And rome he held as heed & gouernour
He hadde it wonne by conquest & bataile

17

For anastasius was noght ilyke
Ne noght so strong of meyne atte lest
He was consentant þat theodorik
Scholde regne in Rome & holde it atte
    hest
And he wolde holde hym seluen in þe este
He seide it was accordant to his hele
And for his ese in sothe he chese it
    meste   *135*
ffor romayns ben ful perelus wt to dele

18

This kyng of rome þan theodorik
Was full of malice & of cursidnesse
And for causa he was an heretyk
Þe cristen peple gan he sore to
    oppresse   *140*
Boecius wiþ his besynesse
Wiþstode hym euere sparing none offence
And hym presente ful often tyme expresse
Reuersed (his) vnlawefull iuggementis

19

He spared noght þe helþe of his estate
But euer he spake ayayn his tyrannye
Wherfor þe kyng hym hadde sore in hate
And hym exciled in to Lumbardie
To prison in þe citee of Pavie
Where ynne he was for a recreacion *150*
Be twyne hym selphe & philosophie
He wrote þis book of consolacion

---

117 out; Balliol *ought.*
125. So Balliol; Royal *in a manere.*
132. Balliol *at his heste.*
141. MS Phillipps reads *with all his,* etc.
144. So Balliol; Royal *is.*
150. The MSS read *was* or *he was;* the print
    reads *as.*

20

In prose & metre enterchaungyngly
Wiþ wordes set in colour wonder wele
Of rethoryk endited craftily   *155*
And schewyng þat þis welþis temporele
As not to be desired noght a dele
Ne worldly meschief noþing for to drede
Enforsyng vs be resoun naturale
To vertu fully for to taken hede   *160*

21

When anastasius had made his fyne
As tyme of age in to his deth him drewe
Þan after hym was emperour Iustyne
A noble knyght a feithful & a trewe
ffor cristes lawes wonder wel he
    knewe   *165*
And keped hem as a verry crysten man
And heretikes faste he gan pursewe
Þat arrians were cleped than

22

His letters in to Rome þan he sent
fforto destroyen all þat heresye   *170*
And fully gaf hym in comaundement
Þat þei schulde putte hem out of com
    panye
Theodoricus took þis wonder hyhe
for he hym self was oonly oon of tho
This message he repelled vtterlye   *175*
And made a vow it schold not stande so

23

And swore but if þe arrians moste
Have fully pees & graunted hem ageyn
He nold not leuen oon in all þe coste
Of cristen feith þat he ne scholde be
    slayn   *180*
And þus he bade þe messangers sayn
Þat if he wold wt arrians stryve
Seie to þe Emperour in wordes playn
Of cristen wil I leue noon on lyue

24

To constantinopill he sent anone   *185*
Of senatoures whiche þat hym self leste
And so among(es) oþer pope Ione
And bad þaim laboren for þaire avne
    beste

---

157. Balliol *þeim ought to be,* etc.; Harley 44
    Areen, etc.
171. Balliol *yaf hem.*
174. Cambr. and New Coll. read *holly oon.*
175. One *l* of *repelled* is inserted with caret;
    Balliol *repeled.*
178. MS New Coll. *þes ygraunted.*
187. So Balliol; Royal *among.*
188. Balliol, *owne beste.*

And rufullyche þei maden þaire requeste
Þat Iustyne schold þis maundement
   relees   *190*
ffor cristen might noght be in reste
But if he graunted arrians pees

25

The emperour his malice vnderstode
Benyngly he graunted haþ hur bone
And wel he þoghte þat (þis) was as
   gode   *195*
Þat mater for to cessen til efte sone
And beter mighte it afterward be done
Be good avise of wyser ordinaunce
Þe arriens so he lete alone
To vsen forth þaire olde gouernaunce

26

These messagers to þe kynges pay
Retourned noght so hastely ageyn
As he desired at assigned day
Wherfor in hert he had gret dysdeyne
And Boece þat lay in prisoun & in
   peyne   *205*
Exiled in þe citee of Pavie
In myleyne þan he made him to be sleyne
In Pavie been his bones sikerlye

27

And whan these messagers at þe laste
Returned were in hert he gan to
   brenne   *210*
And pope Ioone in prison þan he caste
All fer in to þe citee of Ravenne
And made him closid in a narwe denne
Where he ne mighte torne him selfe ne
   wende   *214*
And sothe to seyn he went neuer þenne
Bot of his lyfe right þere he made an
   ende

28

Also þe worthi noble semachus
Þat was a man full grounded all in grace
Þat as in vertu was heroycus
Þere left not suche an oþer as he was *220*
Wiþ outen cause surfete or trespace
At Ravenne eke he slowe hym cruellye
And afterward in þat same place
Þe next yere he deyde sodeynlye

29

And as seynt Gregor doth hym self
   write   *225*
As his diologe makeþ mencioun
Þere was þat tyme an holy heremyte

191. Balliol, *þe cristene.*
195. Insertion from Balliol.
203. Royal *assigned a day;* cp. line 125.

As he was in his contemplacioun
He sawe theodorik in visioun
By twine Symachus an(d) pope Iohn
Right as a þeef to his dampnacioun
How he was led and after þt anon

30

In þe yle of vlcane was he casten þenne
Þat full is of a fury flaumbe of hell
Þer in alwey in peynes forto brenne *235*
And wt þe foule fendes forto dwell
ffor tyrantes þat so fers been & fell
Suche reward is arayed for þaire mede
I saye yow but as olde bookes tell
Nowe to my purpose tyme is þat I
   spede   *240*

31

And euery lord or lady what (ye) be
Or clerk þat likeþ for to rede þis
Beseching lowly wiþ humylite
Support where I haue seyde amys
Correcte only þere þat nedeful is   *245*
If worde & sentence be noght as hit
   scholde
My self I am vnsuffishaunt Iwys
ffor if I couthe haue beter done I wolde

EXPLICIT PROLOGUS

INCIPIT LIBER BOECII DE CONSOLACIONE
PHILOSOPHIE: METRUM PRIMUM

Carmina qui quondam studio florente
   peregi
Flebiles heu mestos . cogor inire modos

Allas I wrecche þat whilon was in welthe
And lusty songes vsid for to write   *250*
Nowe am y set (in) sorowes & vnselthe
Wt mornyng nowe my myrþe I most
   respite
Lo redyng muses techeþ me to endite (5)
Of wo wt wepyng weteþ þai my face
Thus hath disese distryed all my delite
And broght my blis & my bonechife all
   bace

33

And (þogh) þat I (with) myschef nowe
   be mete
Þat false fortune lourith þus on me (10)
No drede fro me ne myghte þese muses
   lete
Me for to sewe in myn aduersite   *260*
My ioyes þei were all in my iolite

241. Royal *he;* most MSS *ye.*
246. Balliol *or sentence.*
251. Balliol *in;* Royal omits.
253. *redyng;* see Notes.
257. Royal writes *þoght, witht.*

Of youthe that was so gladsom & so
grene
Nowe þai solacen my drery destine (15)
And in myn age my confort nowe þei
bene

34

Unwarly age cometh on me hast(e)ly
Hyeng on me for harme þat I haue had
And sorow his eld haþ hoten to be ney
Hore heris on myn hede to rathe ben
sprad   (20)
All toome of blode my body waxeþ bad
Myn ampty skyn begynneth to tremble &
quake   270
I knowe no cause wher of I scholde be
glade
But socourlese þus am I all forsake

35

A deth of men a blisful þing it were (25)
If he wolde spare þeym in þaire lusty-
nesse
And (com) to þem þat ben of heuy
chere   275
When þai him call to slaken þaire dis-
tresse
But out allas howe dull & deef is he
Wryeng awey fro wrecches when þei
clepe   (30)
And werneth þenne wt wonder cruelnesse
Þe eyen forto close þat waile & wepe

36

Bot while fortune vnfeithfull & vntrewe
Of lusty lyf was to me fauorabill   (34)
ffull sodainly myn hede down he drewe
Þe carefull oure of deth vnmerciabill
But nowe þat sche so chaunging &
vnstable   285
Hath turned vnto me hire cloudi face
This wrecchid lyf þat is vnconfortable
Wyll drawe along & tarieth nowe allas

37

Wher to (ye) frendes made ye your
awaunt   (41)
So often tymes of my felicite   290
This worldly welthe is noght perseueraunt
Ne neuere abidyng in stabilite
ffor he þat falliþ out of his degre
Ye knowen wel þat stable was he noght
Ne he stood neuer in full prosperite
Þat in to meschef is so lowe Ibroght

38

[Prose 1]

In mornyng þus I made my complaynt
And for to write my fyngres gan I folde
ffor drerynesse I wax all febill & feynt
Þat of my lyf almost noþing I tolde 300
But vpward atte laste I gan beholde
In sothe y seie so faier a creature
I couthe hire noght discriuen þogh I
wolde
So semely was hire schap & hir feture

39

Sche was so wonder reuerent of hiere
chere   305
Hire colour eke so lyuely and so bright
Hire eyen brend semyng as for clere (11)
Passing full fer abouen manis sight
As þogh sche were full fresshe & clene
of might
As sche had ben full yongly of corage
Yit semed (she) to euery worldly wyght
Þat she was ouerpassid manis age

40

Hire stature was of doutful Iugement
Somtyme þus of comune mannes meet
And somtyme was hire stature so
(extent)   315
Þat wt hire heed sche semed heuenes beet
And oþer while so hihe hire heed sche
geet   (21)
Sche persed heuene & might no more be
seyne
So þat we muste þe sight of hire forlete
And all oure lokyng after was in veyne

41

Hire clothis wroght were of þredes smale
But subtile craft of mater perdurable
And wiþ hire hondes by hire awne tale
Sche had hem wroght I trowe it be no
fable
Þe beaute of hem was full commend-
able   325
But dusk þei were forleten as for elde
As ymages þat in smook had stonden
stable   (31)
Þat ben not wasche ne wyped not but
selde

265, 275, 278. Royal writes *hastly, cometh, wryng.*
285. Royal *sche is so,* etc.
289. Royal and Balliol *þe.*

309. Balliol *And þauh,* etc.
311. Balliol *she,* Royal *he.*
314. Royal inserts *ly* after *comune,* with caret;
    the ink is different.
315. See Notes.
322. Several MSS read *By subtile,* etc.

42

And in (þe) hem byneþen made sche had
So as I couthe it knowe a grekysshe · P ·
And in þe bordure al abouen I rad   *331*
And þere also sche had made a ·T·
And so by twyne þe lettres might I see
Like a laddire what þat evire it mende
Wher on men myght all wey fro gre to
    gre   *335*
ffro þare byneþen vpward evire ascende

43

Neuerþeles sum men by violence   (41)
Had kyt þis cloth & pecis born awey
Suche as þei mighte wt outen reuerence
And dide þere wt as was vnto theier pay
This creature of whom I gan yov say *341*
In hire right hond smale bookes were
A septir also of full riche araye
In certeyn in hire oþer hand sche bere

44

And when (þis) womman sawe þese
    muses þere   *345*
Vnto my beddes side approchen neye (50)
Enditing wordes to my wepyng chere
She gan to loke vppon hem feruentlye
Who haþ sche seide let in þis companye
Þus wt hire song þis seek man to
    plese   *350*
Þat noþing helpeth hym of his maladie
But rather doth hym greuaunce & disese

45

Lo þese it been sche seide þat folkes
    feden
Wt swete venim of corrupcioun
And tendre hertes maken forto bleden
Wiþe thornes of þeire full affeccioun
Þei sleyn þe worþi fruytes of resoun (61)
And only bryngen siknesse in vsage
This is þe kynde of þeire condicioun
And not at all þe seknesse to aswage *360*

46

Yif ye sche seide wt youre daliaunce
Had fro me drawe sum foole vnprofitable

---

345. Balliol þis, Royal þese.

ffull lesse it wolde haue done me dis-
    plesaunce
I myght haue sustened þat as sufferable
ffor whi & suche a foole þat is vnable *365*
Mai not be harmed of my bysenesse (70)
Bot þeie þat euer in studie hath stonden
    stable
Schuld not be founden wiþ youre foly-
    nesse

47

Bot goo ye filthes out of my presence
Youre swetnesse wolde hym bryng at an
    ende   *370*
I schall him saue wt salue of my science
Þat schall be more confort to his kynde
And þus þis companye away gan wende
And bitterly abasched of þeire blame
Schewyng in sothe þe abyt of þeire
    mynde
Hangyng doon to grounde þaire heed for
    schame   *376*

48

I than þat neigh for teres sawh right
    noght   (81)
Merueiled myche what myght þis wom-
    man be
I wondred also gretely in my þoght
Þat so imperiall of a(u)ctorite   *380*
Sche made þat meigne smertly for to flee
I was abasched and heng myn hede to
    grounde
What sche wold done or after seie to me
Þan I abood & held me still a stound

49

Unto my bed þan gan sche me neighe
    nere   *385*
And on þe corner doun hire self sche
    sette   (90)
And sadly gan byholde vppon my chere
Þat so was wt teres al bywette
And right þus sche bygan wiþ oute lette
Compleynyng on my perturbacioun *390*
ffor cause of meschef wher wiþ I was
    mette
Of me sche made þis lamentacioun

---

385. Balliol has not *me.*

[B]

[BOOK II METRE 5: THE FORMER AGE]

Full wonder blisseful was þat raþer age
When mortal men couthe holde hymself
   payed
To fede þeym self wt oute suche outer-
   age
Wiþ mete þat trewe feeldes haue arrayed
Wiþ acorne þaire hunger was alayed   *5*
And so þei couthe sese þaire talent
Thei had yit no queynt craft assayed
As clarry for to make ne pyment

2

To deen purpure couthe þei noght
   beþynke
The white flees wyþ venym tyryen   *10*
Þe rennyng ryuer yaf hem lusty drynke
And holsom sleep þei took vpon þe grene
The pynes þat so full of braunches been
Þat was þaire hous to kepe vnder schade
The see to kerue no schippes were þere
   seen   *15*
Þer was no man þat marchaundise made

3

Thay liked not to sailen vp & doun
But kepe hem self where þei weren bred
Tho was ful huscht þe cruel clarioun
ffor eger hate þer was no blood Isched *20*
Ne þer wt was non armour yit bebled
ffor in þat tyme who durst haue be so
   wood
Suche bitter woundes þat he nold haue
   dred
Wiþ outen reward forto lese his blood

4

I wold oure tyme mygth lerne certanly *25*
And þise maneres alwey wt vs dwelle
But loue of hauyng brenneþ feruently
More fersere þan þe verray fuyre of helle
Allas who was þat man þat wold him
   melle
This gold & gemmes þat were keuered
   þus   *30*
Þat first began to myne I can not telle
Bot þat he fond a parelous precious

[C]

[BOOK II METRE 7]

Who þat supposen will vnwyttyly
In renoun soueren ioyes for to be
And late hym look vp in to þe heuene on
   hye
And so be holde vpon þat large cuntre
And after lat hym to þerþe see   *5*
So narwe it is þat soore it schal hym
   schame
Þat in so litell space of quantite
He may it not fulfille wt his fame

2

Allas what aylen fierce men & proute
To leften vp þaire nekkes so in vayn   *10*
This mortal yok whiche þat ye bere
   aboute
Schal payse it downe vnto þe grounde
   agayn
Thogh þat youre resoun passe many a
   playn
And so be spred aboute be many tung
Þat of your lynage hyhe & souereyn   *15*
In grete honour þe fame of yow be
   sprung

2. Balliol *hemselfe.*
25. Balliol *turne certeynly.*

3

Yit deth depayseth all youre hyhe renoun
Neiþer greet ne lytell wil he none knowe
Bot bothe in lyke he layth hire hedes
   doun
And euene he makyth þe hyhe wt þe
   lowe   *20*
Lo where ben nowe þe bones as we trowe
Of brutus & fabricious þe trewe
Of sterne Catoun þe fame is ouerblowe
And maked now in lettres bot·a fewe

4

And yit þo men we (knoweth) not at
   all   *25*
Thogh þat we knowe þeyre fayre names
   so
ffor þei be deth as euery oþer schall
Out of þe sight be passed & agoo
ffor wiþ þis lyf when þat ye passe fro
ffor to be knowen þen ye ben vnable   *30*
Youre worþi fame may no more doo
But fleyen aboute veyne & variable

25. Royal reads *knowt;* see ante, A 96.

5

And if ye wene to drawe *your* lyf on long
As be a lytell wynde of worldly fame
As fooles þen ye done yow seluen
    wrong   35

ffor when o cruell deth yow schall
    atame
Al your renou*n* schal tu*r*nen in to grame
Whiche þat ye han *pur*chased so wt pride
ffor after þat be styntyng of *your* fame
Ye must þen another deth abyde   40

[D]

[BOOK III METRE 12]

Full blisfull is þat man þt may behold
þe bright welle of verray blisiulnesse
And well is hym þt may hym self vnfolde
ffro bondes of þis worldly wrecchidnesse
The poet Orpheus wiþ heuynesse   5
His wyfes deth haþ (weiled) wepyngly
And wiþ his songes full of drerynesse
Made wodes for to renne wonderly

2

He made stremis stonden & abyde
Þe hynde fered not of hou*n*des fell   10
Sche lete þe lyon lien by here syde
The hare also ne dred noght a dell
To see þe hound hit lyked hym so well
To here þe songes þat so lusty were
And boldly thei dorste to gidres dwell
Þat nevire a best had of oþer feere

3

And when þe loue gan brenne*n* in his
    brest
Of erudice moste hote & feruently
His song þat had so many a wylde best
So meke made to lyuen comynly   20
They myghte hym not conforten vtterly
Of hyhe goddes gan he to compleyn
And seide þei deden wt hym cruelly
That þei sent hym noght his wyf ageyn

4

He went þan to houses infernall   25
And faste his strenges þere dressed he
And sowned out þe swete songes all
Þat he had tasted of þe welles thre
While þat his modres dere Calliope
Þat is goddesse & chief of eloquence   30
To wordes þat moste piteous myght be
As sorowe had taght hym be exp*er*ience

5

And loue also þat doubleth heuynesse
To helle began he his compleynt to make
Askyng mercy þere wiþ lawnesse   35

At þilke lordes of þe schades blake
And cerberus þat woned was to wake
Wiþ hedes thre & helle yates kepe
So hadden hym þese newe songes take
The swetnesse made hym forto falle on
    slepe   40

6

The fuyres þat ben vengoures of synne
And surfetoures smyteþ so wt feere
ffor heuynesse þt þis man was ynne
They gan to mourne & weped many a
    tere
Ne þo þe swift wheele had no powere   45
To torne about þe heed of (Yxion)
Ne tantalus for thrist all þogh he were
fforpyned longe watire wolde he none

7

The gryp þat ete þe mawe of tycius
And tyred on hit longe tyme he fore   50
This song to hym was so delicius
He left it of & tyred it no more
And when þat orpheus had mou*r*ned sore
Than seide þe Iuge of helle peynes strong
Pyte me haþ quyt I will restore   55
This man (his) wyf þus wonnen wt his
    song.

8

Bot with a lawe þis gift will I restreyne
Þat vnto he this bondes haue forsake
If he beholde vpon his wyf ageyne
His wyf fro hym eft sone will we take   60
Bot who to louers may a lawe make
ffor loue is rathir to hym self a lawe
When he was neygh out of þe bondes
    blake
He turned hym & erudice he sawe

9

Allas he lost & left his wif be hynde
This fable lo to yow p*er*teyneth right
ffor ye þat wolde lyften vp *your* mynde
In to þe hye blisfull soue*r*eyn light

6. Royal *veiled*, Balliol *wayled*.
9. Royal *strennis*.

41. *fuyres;* so Balliol. Read *furyes.*
46. Royal and Balliol, *yaon.*
56. Royal writes *is.*

If ye eftsone turne down youre sight
In to þis foule wrecchid erthly dell   70

Lo all þat evire your labour haþ you dight
Ye loose it when ye loken in to hell

EXPLICIT LIBER TERCIUS BOECII DE CONSOLACIONE PHILOSOPHIE

[E]

PREFACIO TRANSLATORIS IN LIBRUM QUARTUM & QUINTUM

[Walton here inserts a preface, nine stanzas of *seven* lines, lyrical]

O hye & riche tresour of science
And wisdom whiche in god eternally
Conteyned is so þat his iugement*es*
Ne mowe not be enserched certanly
Neither þe wey be knowen vtterly   5
Be whiche þis wonder worldes gouer-
    naunce
He kepith in suche a certayn ordy-
    naunce

2

Who wist his wit when he þis world
    began
Or who was he þt was his conseillour
When no thyng was who was þt gaf hym
    þan   10
To whom he is in daunger as dettour
Of hym is all for he is creatour
Be him it is þat all þing Is susteyned
In hym is all þing kyndly conteyned

3

Lo of so hye a matre for to trete   15
As after þis myn auctour doth pursue
This wote I well my wyttes ben vnmete
The sentence forto saue (in) metre trewe
And not forthi I may it not eschewe
Ye ben þe cause why I mote don þus   20
And schewe my seluen here presumptu-
    ous

4

Of hap of fortune & of destine
Þat marred haþ full many a mannes
    mynde
Supposyng þat oure kyndely liberte
Thus to & fro must all wey turne &
    wende   25
So þt oure werkes to a certan ende
Constreyned ben wher þt we will or noght
So þat none oþer wise þei may be wroght

5

To speken of divine purveaunce
Þt all þing knowith or it be bygonne   30
No worldly wight may haue þat suffi-
    saunce
With all þe wit & clergie þat þei konne

No more þan perce the myddes of þe
    sonne
As wiþ þe litell vigour of þaire sight 34
Wel myche more it passeth mannes myght

6

And þat (we) stonden in oure arbitrye
As fully set in verray liberte
So þat we mowe chesen wilfully
Bothe goode & euel bothe wel & wo to be
And yit þat god in his eternyte   40
So knoweth all þt evire schall betide
Who can þis two compownen & devide

7

It is not elles bot þat oure desire
Wolde kyndely þat conseyt comprehende
Right as we seen a litel flaumb of fuyre 45
How scharp it makeþ it seluen to ascende
And not forþi it failleþ of his ende
And is full fer from theder þat it scholde
So may we þenken or tell(en) what we
    wolde

8

Bot fuyre right of movynge of nature   50
Behold how scharp it makeþ it & light
And all so ferforth as it may endure
How it enforceth forto stye vp right
Bot we wolde haue not elles but a sight
And knowe þe height of goddes priuete
And will oure self all wey in erthe be

9

To þe þat art the welle of sapience
Almyghti lord this labour I commyt
Thogh I be fer fro craft of eloquence
Enforce þou my connyng & my wit   60
This mater forto treten so þat it
Be to þi honour & to þi plesaunce
So take it lord into thi gouernaunce

INCIPIT LIBER QUARTUS
[Prose 1]

And when (my) maistresse philosophie
Kepyng all wey hire sobirnesse & hire
    chere   65

18, 36. Balliol &c. have *in, we;* Royal omits.

64. Royal omits *my;* supplied from Balliol.

This song had songen wonder lustilye
So þat full sad all wey hire wordes were
I gan to speke & seide in þis manere
Noght all forgeten myn oppressioun
I made hire make an interrupcioun   70

O souereigne gidoresse of verrey light
Youre resouns ben so myghti & so fyne
Anon to þis & open to my sight
As in þaire (speculacioun) devine
Whiche as ye seide for angir & for
    pyne   75
fforgeten was (& falle) out of my þoght
Bot yit beforn (byknowen) were þei not

Bot þis is most my cause of heuynesse
So good a gouernour as hauen we
How þere may be so myche wikked-
    nesse   80
And suffred so vnponysched to be
How wonderful is þis now deme ye
And this wel more encreseþ my doloures
Þat wickednesse regneþ in his floures

And now not onely vertu wanteþ mede
Bot felons han defouled it & schent   86
And in þe stede of synne & coursidhede
Now vertu bereth peyne & (ponysche-
    ment)
Bot in þe rewme of god omnipotent
Þat seeth all þis & onely good he will
I may compleyne & wonder wel be skyll

Than seide sche þus a wonder þing it
    were
Abhomynable & verry menstruouse
If as þou feynest & supposest here
In a so well disposed lordes house   95
If vesselles þat ben riche & precious
Schuld so despised & defouled be
And foule vessell be made in preciouste

Bot sikerly sche seide it is noght so
ffor if tho thynges stondeth formely   100
That we before þis haue consented to
Now be þe help of souereyn god on hye
Of whom here he speketh (ententifly)
Thow schalt here after fully knowe &
    seen

Þat good folkes all wey myghti ben   105
And wicked folkes vnmyghti þere ageyne
Ne mede may fro vertu noght disseuere

74, 88, 103. Royal writes *spectaculacioun, poyn-
    yschement, entiflye.*
76. Royal writes *was for & all out,* etc.; 77, it
    writes *we knowen.* Readings from Balliol.

And þat þere is no vice wiþouten peyne
And good folke of welþe faillen nevire
And wicked folk ben infortunat euere
And myche þyng þat to þyn hertes ese
Availen schall and þi compleynt (appese)

Now here beforn I haue þe schewed
    expresse
As þou hast herd & seen it plenerly
Whiche is þe forme of verrey blisful-
    nesse   115
And where þou schalt it fynde verrayly
Lo all þis ouerpassen now will I
Whiche þat we moste over passe nede
And to my purpose faste I schall me
    spede

Unto thi home I schall þe schewe a
    wey   120
And pennes schall I pycche into þi mynde
Þat it arisen into height may
Al heuynesse left & put behynde
My path I will þe lede be þe hand
And cariage my self I schal þe fynde 125
Al hole & sound into þyn owne land

[iv, Metre 1]

Full swyft been my fetheres in þaire
    flight
Þat stieng into hyhe heuene ariseth
And when þei be into a mynde Ipight
Þe erthe þen it hateþ & despiseth   130
And setteþ all at (noght) as he deviseth
Þe speere of eyre he passeth all aboue
Behynde his bak he seeth þe cloudes houe

That mynde also þe spere of fuyre trans-
    cendeth
That is so hoot be movynge of þe
    heuene   135
And to þe sterred places he ascendeþ
Thurgh out þe speres of planetes seuene
And wt þe sonne his wey he ioyneþ
    euene
So at þe laste he meteþ wt þe old
Saturnus whos effectes ben so cold   140

So is þis sotill mynde made a knyght
Of god þat is þe souereyn sterre clere
And (so) þe cercle of þe sterres bright
Þe whiche ye may behold on nyghtes here
Wt his recours he passeth all in fere 145
And in theire speres be holden wele
Þe manere of þeire movynge euery dele

112, 131. Royal reads *aplese, not.*
143. Royal omits *so.*

And well he wot þat goddes ben þai not
Þe hyest heuen he leueth hym behynde
Till þat he haue araysed vp his þoght 150
Anone to hym þat auctour is of kynde
This worþi lyght he putteþ in his mynde
Þat of þis round world is lord & kyng
Þat kepeth & gouerneþ all þing

The swyft cours of sterres meveth he
Iuge of þinges bright & souereyn
Hym self stedfaste evire in oo degre
If þis wey may reduce þe ageyn
Vnto þi place þou schalt þi self seyn

Lo here it is þat I so longe haue soght 160
My cuntre & til now I knewe it noght

Fro hennes I come & in þis place right
I thynke to (abyden) & to dwell
And if þe list to cast a doun þi sight
Into þis foule derk erthly selle   165
Be holden myght þou þere tyrantes felle
Whiche þat of wrecches ben Idrede full
      wyde
Out of this lond exiled for þere pryde

163. Royal writes *byden*.
166. Royal *be halden*, etc.

THOMAS HOCCLEVE

Of the English followers of Chaucer, Thomas Hoccleve and John Lydgate are best known to modern students. Both were grown men at the time of Chaucer's death in 1400, and Hoccleve at least knew his master personally; but there is no evidence that they knew of each other's work or of each other's existence. Their lives ran in different grooves.

The country-born Lydgate entered a monastery while still a boy, and so far as we know spent his life thus. Hoccleve was a Londoner by adoption if not by birth, became a clerk in the Privy Seal office when he was about twenty, and there apparently remained. From his many autobiographical allusions it seems that he was a tavern-haunter and a waster of money, that after being disappointed of a clerical post in the Church he drifted into marriage, that he suffered under a long period of mental illness or madness, and that he turned, verses in hand, from one noble patron or government official to another in the hope of money-reward to eke out the irregular payments of the Crown. He was probably born about 1368; for he gives his age as fifty-three in a poem which terms Gloucester the Lieutenant of the realm; this was in 1421-22, while Henry V was still in France. He dates his translation of the De Regimine Principum, or Regement of Princes, made for Henry V, in 1411-12, and there says that he had been for twenty-four years at his Privy Seal desk; he must accordingly have entered the office when about twenty. An allusion to Prince Edward's tutor, in a poem addressed to Edward's father the Duke of York, may date that poem 1446-48, when the prince was four to six years old. Thereafter we know no more of Hoccleve, nor have we any record of pension-payments to him for many years preceding. An entry in the Close Rolls, pointed out by Professor Hulbert, shows that Richard II granted a corrody, or maintenance chargeable on a church, to Hoccleve in 1395; this the poet transferred in the first year of Henry the Fourth.

The earliest of his poems to which we can assign a date is the Letter of Cupid, translated from the French in 1402, as the writer tells us. In 1406, probably, he wrote La Mâle Règle, a series of self-reproaches for his irregular life, ending with a petition to the lord treasurer to pay him his overdue pension; this annuity had been granted him by Henry IV soon after accession. In 1411-12 Hoccleve compiled the Regement of Princes, from several sources; and in 1415 he wrote a severely pious reprimand to the heretic Oldcastle. Perhaps ten years later, in the Complaint and the Dialogue with a Friend, he talks of an intervening illness, says he is fifty-three years old, and mentions the return of Gloucester from France (1421). For the duke's pleasure Hoccleve then translates and appends to the Dialogue the Gesta Romanorum story of the Innocent Persecuted Wife,—Jereslaus' wife. His translation of the tractate Learn to Die, from Suso's Horologium Sapientiae, also (probably) planned for Gloucester, and a second Gesta-story similarly appended, are later work. Both pairs of poems, and the Complaint which serves as introduction to the earlier, were transcribed in a sequence and sent to the Countess of Westmoreland in a copy which still exists at Durham. If this Countess was the widowed daughter of John of Gaunt, then living at the same castle of Sheriff Hutton which was later the scene of Skelton's Garland of Laurel, she was the woman to whom Sir Thomas Morton in 1431 bequeathed a copy of Gower's English poem, and the same woman who after her nephew Henry V's death applied to the Council for the return of books she had lent him.

Other poems by Hoccleve are brief, and are either devotional,—including the Mother of God so long ascribed to Chaucer,—or occasional verse often of the begging-letter type. All in all, he has left about 13,000 lines of verse, written in stanzas of seven or eight and a few of nine lines, and including four roundels. Neither this amount of productivity nor Chaucer's 34,000 lines of verse (exclusive of the Romaunt-translation), looms very large beside Lydgate's ca.140,000 lines; but, it is needless to say, there are various factors to be considered in making a comparison.

Both Hoccleve's production and his range of production are very much smaller than those of Lydgate. There are in his work no long romantic-epic narratives, no lives of saints, no allegories, no tapestry or fresco-poems, no courtly love-addresses, no beast-fables, no mummings. The religious-didactic is Hoccleve's theme whenever he is not autobiographic; but his constant tendency to the autobiographical is the most interesting of his qualities. La Mâle Règle is a deliberate and frank self-confession, used as lengthy prelude to a begging-letter. The two long tasks undertaken for Henry V and for Gloucester are each preluded by a lively piece of dialogue in explanation of their origin. In the one case it is a friend, in the other a wise old beggar, who receives Hoccleve's laments over his muddled life and counsels him how to proceed. Where Lydgate would compose a prologue in imitation of Chaucer or in praise of the original he was translating, Hoccleve plunges awkwardly but vitally in another method. His dialogue is real dialogue, not alternating set speeches. He is limited enough in his handling; there is no setting for his two speakers, such as Chaucer or Henryson would have painted in; the voices, though lively in tone, are bodiless. And as soon as they cease, and the business of Jereslaus' Wife or the Regement of Princes begins, Hoccleve drops into the stereotype of his period. In the prolonged didactics of the Regement of Princes there are several moments, however, where the name of Chaucer breaks that spell of somnolence. Hoccleve goes out of his way to allude to his beloved master; and in one of these three short but deeply-feeling passages he says that he has had Chaucer's likeness inserted, in order that men may not lose remembrance of him. A portrait of Chaucer does indeed appear at that point in a few MSS of the Regement, and is, with the Host's teasing chaff in the headlink to Sir Thopas, our only real clue to Chaucer's personal appearance.

These mentions of Chaucer, the requests to a patron or superior for money, and the religious character of many of the shorter poems, are the lines on which Hoccleve and Lydgate can be compared as regards theme. And the student who puts Hoccleve's begging-letters beside Lydgate's pleas to Gloucester, Hoccleve's language about Chaucer beside Lydgate's far more numerous allusions, Hoccleve's autobiographical disclosures beside Lydgate's Testament, Hoccleve's religious lyric beside Lydgate's, will perceive two very different men. The trappings of convention lie much more heavily on Lydgate, who has no such restless urge to talk of himself, no such human directness of approach to other human beings, as Hoccleve had. Hoccleve is always livelier and simpler than Lydgate; and when he speaks of Chaucer it is with a true affection and regret that have sweetened his own memory for the after-world. He has lived more really than has

Lydgate, and the mixture in him of piety and cheap raffishness makes him a more genuine creature. Saintsbury calls him a "crimeless Villon"; and it might repay a student to follow out the likenesses and differences between the Englishman and the Frenchman. In their piety the difference is very marked; for Hoccleve is as sincerely pious as is the monk Lydgate. He cannot indeed rise to as true a passion of love for Christ crucified as Lydgate sometimes can; but on the other hand, there are in the small bulk of Hoccleve's verse no such depths of wordy inanity as too often occur in Lydgate's religious poetry. We may plead for Lydgate the compulsion under which he worked, a compulsion from which Hoccleve was free. But the vacuity remains.

On the technical side of the two men's work there is also a marked difference. Both men were followers of Chaucer; and Hoccleve, who knew his master personally, says that Chaucer "fayn wolde han me taght, But I was dul and lerned lite or naght." His verse shows, indeed, less of Chaucer metrically than does the verse of Lydgate. Hoccleve manages pentameter badly, and is insensitive to the weave of stressed and unstressed syllables, so long as their number is constant at ten. Very many lines run as do these:

Þat me yeuest any othir than thee	i:5/165
Of thy soule meekly to him confesse	i:11/94
We sholde no meryt of our feith haue	i:13/142
And as that the preest hir soules norice	i:15/212
To the taast of your detestable errour	i:17/293
Of the myghty Prince of famous honour	i:49/3
Ageyn thorsday next & it nat delaye	i:66/56
And shoop me him to offende no more	i:67/16
Yit thy deeth gat of the feend the maistrie	i:68/52
On the crois was thy skin in to blood died	i:69/68
Þat our soules þat the feend waytith ay	i:71/126

Lydgate, on the contrary, is aware of certain rhythmic variants in Chaucer, adopts them, and abuses them. The headless line and the line brokenbacked, or short an unaccented syllable at the verse-pause, are a staple with him. He could find the former at least in Chaucer, and may have built the latter by analogy; but their occurrence is infrequent in Hoccleve, so far as we can yet say. The repetition of a single line-type by Lydgate is as marked as is Hoccleve's unawareness of line-type. Neither man understood Chaucer's rhythm, but they misunderstand very differently.

They differ also in their management of the English language; and here the advantage is so much with Hoccleve that we can surmise why Chaucer should have attempted to teach him. Hoccleve has nothing of Lydgate's uncontrollable verbosity. He does not jumble finite verbs and participles; he does not overwork the ablative absolute; he does not leave long sequences of clauses wandering without a principal verb; he does not repeat himself; he uses the minimum of padding and of rime-formulae; he sees where he is going, in narrative, and goes there. His syntax-control and his feeling for dialogue show that he had some storytelling faculty; and probably Chaucer recognized it. Hoccleve can toss dialogue back and forth through a stanza in swift exchange, breaking the line or overrunning it as he chooses; he does not move in monotonous half-lines or dilute into entire stanzas as does Lydgate.

But with this advantage over Lydgate in the normal movement of speech, in the more competent use of English for expression, there goes, in Hoccleve, a lack of the "high spots" that we can find in Lydgate. Despite Lydgate's verbosity and tedium, there are more than a few strong lines in his work; see p. 81 here. But from Hoccleve it is not possible to glean such. He does say of his reckless habits that for many years "Excesse at borde hath leyd his knyf with me," and that "Ther never yet stood wys man on my feet." His lament for Chaucer is moving. But his sense-perceptions, his feeling for nature, his imagination, are not developed even as much as are those of Lydgate. The few striking bits that we can cite are autobiographical and personal.

Nor does Hoccleve echo Chaucerian phrase to anything like the extent seen in Lydgate. This is partly, of course, because of his relative lack of the narration and description so definitely the business of Chaucer and of Lydgate. He alludes to the Wife of Bath in his Dialogue, line 694; and in a few passages he may derive from Chaucer rather than from Chaucer's original; see the remark on a prudent workman's method in Dialogue 638 ff., and cf. Troilus i:1065 ff.; or see the dictum in Dialogue 764-5, or the phrasing of the Regement of Princes 629. But there is no such evidence of Chaucer's power over Hoccleve's memory as is clear for Lydgate, despite Hoccleve's strong personal feeling for his master. This may be in some measure due to the resistance of a lively egoist, which Hoccleve undoubtedly was; for his citations of any sort are a separate element in his work. He follows copy and cites copy, in his translations, but it is distinct from his own trend of thought; and although the religious emotion of many of his independent poems is deep, he turns more naturally toward himself than toward literature.

His choice of works to translate also shows a mind less literary than practical and moralistic; and he had no body of patrons whose larger curiosity about books sent him afield in letters. His connection with Humphrey of Gloucester was slighter than was that of Lydgate. That some of Hoccleve's work was popular we might argue from the number of copies of the Regement of Princes; but we must recollect that the subject was popular, by whomsoever treated, and that Hoccleve is not mentioned with Gower, Chaucer, and Lydgate, by following generations. William Browne, in the seventeenth century, did indeed say of him:—"There are few such swaines as he Now a dayes for harmony,"—but this critical judgment has not been endorsed by readers before or since. What recommends Hoccleve to us is his deep and genuine respect for Chaucer, the candid, even if contrite, relish with which he talks about himself, and his direct commonsense handling of his work. He has no "aureate language," no rhetorical colors; he is too honest to delay his advance about his business by playing with words, and too clearheaded not to see the way to state that business. If Chaucer tried to teach Hoccleve to write, it was because Chaucer saw in Hoccleve the possibilities which are still to be seen. In studying him we study some one who was very little of a writer, but a good deal of a man.

SELECT REFERENCE LIST AND BIBLIOGRAPHY III

Manuscripts

Of the Shorter Poems en masse:
  HM 111 of the Huntington Library, California, formerly Phillipps 8151.
      Described by L. Toulmin Smith in Anglia 5:20, and by G. Mason in his ed.
      of six poems from it in 1796. Contents printed EETS edition, vol. i, 1892.
  HM 744 of the same library, formerly Ashburnham Appendix cxxxiii. Contents,
      except Learn to Die, are printed EETS ed., ii, 1925. Its copy of the Legend
      of the Virgin was ed. for the Chaucer Soc. in 1902; see my Manual, p. 444.
  Durham Cathedral V iii, 9. Texts printed EETS ed., vol. i.
  Egerton 615 of the Brit. Mus. Texts printed EETS ed., iii, 1897.
Of Single Shorter Poems:
  The Letter of Cupid.
      Fairfax 16, Bodley 638, Tanner 346, Digby 181, Selden B 24, all of the
      Bodleian Library. In Univ. Libr. Cambr., Ff. i, 6. In Durham Cathedral
      V ii, 13, a Troilus MS; this text is unpubd., uncollated, and unmentioned
      either by Skeat, vii: 217, or in my Manual, p. 434. In HM 744. A late
      copy is in the Bannatyne MS. The poem was once in Longleat 258; see
      my Manual, p. 434, and p. 103 here.
  The Mother of God.
      Selden B 24 of the Bodleian; HM 111 as above; Advocates Libr., Edin-
      burgh, 18, 2, 8.
  To Henry V, for money.
      Fairfax 16. Text of Phillipps 8151 is printed EETS i: 62.
Of the "Series" of Linked Poems, i.e., Complaint, Dialogue, two Gesta Romanorum
    stories, Learn to Die.
      Bodley 221, of the Bodleian, has the Series, Lydgate's Dance Macabre, and the
          Regement of Princes. Laud 735, of the same library, has the same poems.
      Selden supra 53, same library, has the Regement (impf.), Series, and Dance
          Macabre.
      The lost Coventry School MS (see my Manual, p. 354) contained the Regement,
          the Series, the Dance Macabre, etc.
      Digby 185, of the Bodl. Libr. has the Regement and the two tales from the
          Series.
      Royal 17 D vi, Brit. Mus., has the Regement and part of the Series.
      Bodl. Eng. poet. d 4 has fragments of the two Tales of the Series.
      The MS formerly Phillipps 8267 (present owner unknown) has fragments of
          the Complaint.
Of the Regement of Princes (see also under "Series" above).
  Alone in the codex.
      Brit. Mus. Arundel 38, Harley 4866, Royal 17 C xiv, Royal 17 D xviii, Royal 17
          D xix, Sloane 1212, Sloane 1825.—Univ. Libr. Cambr. Gg vi, 17, Hh iv,
          11, Kk i, 3; Corp. Christi Coll. 496, Queen's Coll. 12, St. John's Coll. 223;
          McClean 185.—Bodl. Ashmole 40, Douce 158, Dugdale 45, Rawlinson poe-
          try 10; Rawl. poetry 168.—Advocates Libr., Edinb., 19, 1, 11, and Edinburgh
          Univ. D. b. vi. 7.—Lord Amherst's MS, now owned by Wilfrid Merton of
          London. The Ashburnham (paper) MS, now owned by Quaritch.

With various other works, not by Hoccleve.
> Brit. Mus. Adds, 18632, Arundel 59, Phillipps 1099 (in hands of Rosenbach),
> Phillipps 8980, Trin. Coll. Cambr. R 3, 22.

With various other works, not by Hoccleve.
> Brit. Mus. Harley 116, Harley 372, Harley 4826, Harley 7333 (dialogue only).
> Ellesmere 26 A 13, now Huntington (See JEGPh 9: 225 and MLNotes 25: 126).
> Soc. Antiquaries 134, McClean 182.

In the Harvard University Library, MS Eng. 532 F, is the transcript made from Harley
> 4866 (and Royal 17 D xix) by W. H. Black in 1843, in preparation for his
> projected Percy Society edition of the Regement, never carried out.

A page of Brit. Mus. Adds 18622 is reprod. in Garnett and Gosse's English Literature
> i, to face p. 190, and is wrongly marked as from the Siege of Thebes, in the
> same MS. It is from the Regement of Princes.

A page of HM 744 (then Ashburnham MS) is reprod. EETS ed. i, to face page xxviii

A page of Durham V iii, 9 is reprod. EETS ed. i, to face p. 242. *Ibid.*, p. xlix, Fur-
> nivall decides against either the Ashburnham, the Durham, or the Phillips as
> an Hoccleve autograph. See also Kern's Verslagen as below, p. 372.

A page of Durham V ii, 13 is reprod. by Root, The Manuscripts of Chaucer's Troilus
> Chaucer Soc. 1914, to face p. 12; description on p. 11. The Troilus is however in
> a hand different from that of the Hoccleve poem.

Brit. Mus. Adds. 24062, a collection of Privy Seal documents, is in Hoccleve's hand.

Editions

The standard edition of Hoccleve is pubd. by the EETS in 3 vols., i (1892), ii (1925),
> iii (1897). Vol. iii, ed. by Gollancz, is of 40 pages, and gives most of the con-
> tents of the then Ashburnham-Gollancz MS, now HM 744, including the 3
> roundels already printed by Gollancz in Academy 1892 i: 542; the third of these
> is also printed EETS ed. i, page xxxviii foot. This vol. excludes the "Ash-
> burnham" copy of Learn to Die, because "a good text" from the Durham MS
> is in ii:178.

George Mason pubd. in 1796 a volume entitled "Poems by Thomas Hoccleve, never
> before printed." These poems, six in number, were taken from the Askew-
> Phillipps MS, now Huntington 111, then in Mason's possession. Mason's texts
> were used by Morley and by Wülker as below.

The Letter of Cupid was printed with Chaucer's works from 1532 to 1721; see my
> Manual p. 434. Urry's 1721 text is repr. in Arber's Engl. Garner iv: 54, in re-
> ed., iv: 13-31. The Fairfax MS text of the poem is printed EETS i: 72 and
> Skeat vii: 217; the text of HM 744 is printed EETS ii: 20.

The Mother of God was printed with Chaucer's works from 1532 to 1866; see my
> Manual, p. 438. In EETS ed. it is printed i: 52, from the then Phillipps MS.

The poem To the King—and the Knights of the Garter was printed with Chaucer's
> works from 1532 to 1721; see my Manual, p. 459. It is printed EETS i: 41 and
> Skeat vii: 233 from HM 111, the former Phillipps MS.

The tale of Jonathas, forming part of the "Series", as above, was incorporated by
> William Browne into one of his Eclogues, and printed with his Shepheard's Pipe
> in 1614, repr. in Hazlitt's ed. of Browne, 1869. Browne in a note says that all
> Hoccleve's works are "perfect in my hands." He once owned MSS Durham

V ii, 15 and 16 (Lydgate), Durham V iii, 9 (Hoccleve), Ashmole 40 (the Regement of Princes), Ashmole 46 (Lydgate), Brit. Mus. Adds. 34360, Lansdowne 699, Stowe 952.

The Regement of Princes, or De Regimine Principum, was printed by Thomas Wright, London, 1860, from Brit. Mus. Royal 17 D vi. It is in the EETS ed., vol. iii, from Harley 4866. An extract from the Laud text of the poem, stanzas 58-73, is printed by Furnivall in Queen Elizabeth's Achademy, etc., EETS, pp. 105-8.

The poem to the heretic Oldcastle, copied by R. James from an earlier text, was ed. by Grosart with James' poems in 1880. It was printed from the then Phillips MS by L. Toulmin Smith in Anglia 5:9-43; Furnivall in EETS ed· i, page xliii, notes four errors in her text. The poem is in EETS i:8, from HM 111.

The story of the Virgin and her Sleeveless Garment was printed by the Chaucer Soc. 1902; see my Manual, p. 444. The poem is printed EETS ii:15, divided by the editor into two parts.

In JEGPh 8:260 MacCracken prints, from MS Univ. Libr. Cambr. Kk i, 6, a religious poem in ten eight-line stanzas for which he suggests Hoccleve's authorship.

Extracts from Hoccleve are in:—

Ward's English Poets, i:124-28.—Skeat's Specimens of English Lit. 1394-1579, pp. 13-22.—Wülker's Altengl. Lesbuch, ii: 47-56.—Morley's Shorter Engl. Poems, pp. 57-64.—Manly's Engl. Poetry 1170-1892, p. 47.—Neilson and Webster's Chief British Poets, 199-207.

Studies

Aster, Das verhältnis des altengl. gedichtes De Regimine Principum von Th. Hoccleve zu seinen Quellen. Leipzig diss., 1888.

Buchtenkirch, Der syntaktische gebrauch des infinitivs in Occleve's De Regimine Principum. Jena diss., 1889.

Vollmer, Sprache und Reime des Londoners Hoccleve, in Anglia 21: 201 (1898).

Bock, Studien zu Th. Hoccleve's Werken. Munich, diss., 1900, pp. 68.

Haecker, Stiluntersuchungen zu Th. Hoccleve's poetischen Werken. Marburg diss., 1914, pp. 104.

J. H. Kern, Een en ander over Th. Hoccleve en zijn werken, Amsterdam, 1915; pp. 365-390 of Verslagen en Mededelingen der Koninkl. Akad. v. Wetenschappen, reeks 5, vol. i.

——Zum texte einiger dichtungen Th. Hoccleve, in Anglia 39: 389-494 (1916).

——Hoccleve's Verszeile, in Anglia 40: 367-9.

——Date of Hoccleve's Dialog, ibid., 370-73.

——Der Schreiber Offorde, ibid., 374.

B. P. Kurtz, The Source of Hoccleve's Lerne to Dye, in ModLangNotes 38:337 (1923).

——The Prose of Hoccleve's Lerne to Dye, ibid., 39: 56.

——The Relation of Hoccleve's Lerne to Dye to its Source, in PMLA 40: 252-75.

Hoccleve is discussed:—Warton-Hazlitt, Hist. Eng. Poetry, iii: 42-7.—Morley's Engl. Writers, vi, chap. 5.—ten Brink's Hist. Eng. Lit., ii: 212-220.—Jusserand's Lit. Hist. Eng. People, i: 501-3.—Courthope's Hist. Eng. Poetry, i: 333-40.—Cambr. Hist. Eng. Lit., ii, chap. 8.—Garnett and Gosse's Engl. Lit., i:192-94.—Saintsbury's Eng. Prosody, i:231-4.

To the comment upon Hoccleve's verse in the EETS introd. add my paper in ModPhil 23:129 ff., on the Nine-Syllabled Pentameter Line in some Post-Chaucerian Manuscripts. Notes on Hoccleve's Reg. Princes text are in MLReview 4:235.

The MS Huntington 111, formerly Phillipps 8151, was described by Lucy Toulmin Smith, Anglia 5:20-21, as a small octavo of 8¼ by 6⅛ inches, containing 47 vellum leaves and bound in old dark leather stamped with the royal arms of England. It is said to have belonged to Prince Henry, son of James the First; since then, to Askew, G. Mason, Bishop Heber, and Sir Thomas Phillipps. It is a plain MS, with only two small colored initials, in a fifteenth-century hand but with headings in another and larger hand, probably contemporary. It contains 16 complete poems and a Complaint of the Virgin wrongly thrust in between two leaves of another poem; Tyrwhitt, whose letter to Mason is fastened inside the cover, suggests that this transfer was perhaps made to conceal the fact that the Complaint, once the first poem of the MS, is imperfect at beginning.

The codex is of careful and consistent orthography, and has some marks of punctuation which may be noted. These are of three sorts: the inverted semicolon, used apparently as a comma; the mark of interrogation, which is like ours but reversed; and a sign somewhat similar, but with a flattened curve and tipped very much down to the right. The first sign appears in Mâle Règle, end of line 17, in 319 after *why*; in 367 after *stele;* in To Carpenter, line 26, after *is,* and in To Bedford 14, 18, after *colours, mis.* The second sign is in Mâle Règle 37, in To Somer 22. The third is in Mâle Règle 265 after *A;* Mason here printed *Ah,* Furnivall *As.* It is also in To Carpenter, end of line 24.

For revision of the EETS texts of these poems with the MS I am indebted to the kindness of Capt. R. B. Haselden, Keeper of the Manuscripts in the Huntington Library, California.

HOCCLEVE'S MÂLE RÈGLE

[MS Huntington 111, fol. 16 verso]

CY ENSUYT LA MALE REGLE DE T. HOCCLEUE

1

O precious tresor inconparable
O ground & roote of prosperitee
O excellent richesse commendable
Abouen all / þt in eerthe be
Who may susteene thyn aduersitee   5
What wight may him avante of worldly
   welthe
But if he fully stande in grace of thee
Eerthely god / piler of lyf / thow helthe

2

Whil thy power / and excellent vigour
As was plesant vn to thy worthynesse
Regned in me / & was my gouernour
Than was I wel / tho felte I no duresse
Tho farsid was I with hertes gladnesse
And now my body empty is & bare

Of ioie / and ful of seekly heuynesse   15
Al poore of ese / & ryche of euel fare

3

If þt thy fauour twynne from a wight
Smal is his ese / & greet is his greuance
Thy loue / is lyf / thyn hate sleeth doun
   right
Who may compleyne thy disseuerance   20
Bettre than I þt of myn ignorance
Vn to seeknesse am knyt / thy mortel fo
Now can I knowe feeste fro penaunce
And whil I was wt thee / kowde I nat so

4

My grief and bisy smert cotidian   25
So me labouren & tormenten sore
Þt what thow art now / wel remembre I
   can

And what fruyt is in keepynge of thy lore
Had I thy power knowen or this yore
As now thy fo conpellith me to knowe *30*
Nat sholde his lym han cleued to my gore
For al his aart / ne han me broght thus
    lowe

5

But I haue herd men seye longe ago
Prosperitee is blynd / & see ne may
And verifie I can wel / it is so
For I my self put haue it in assay
Whan I was weel / kowde I considere
    it? nay
But what / me longed aftir nouelrie
As yeeres yonge yernen day by day
And now my smert accusith my folie *40*

6

Myn vnwar yowthe kneew nat what it
    wroghte
This woot I wel / whan fro thee twynned
    shee
But of hir ignorance hir self shee soghte
And kneew nat þt shee dwellyng was wt
    thee
For to a wight were it greet nycetee *45*
His lord or freend wityngly for toffende
Lest þt the weighte of his aduersitee
The fool oppresse / & make of him an
    ende

7

From hennes foorth wole I do reuerence
Vn to thy name / & holde of thee in
    cheef *50*
And werre make & sharp resistence
Ageyn thy fo & myn þt cruel theef
Þt vndir foote / me halt in mescheef
So thow me to thy grace reconcyle
O now thyn help / thy socour and
    releef *55*
And I for ay / mis reule wole exyle

8

But thy mercy excede myn offense
The keene assautes of thyn aduersarie
Me wole oppresse with hir violence
No wondir / thogh thow be to me con-
    trarie *60*
My lustes blynde han causid thee to varie
Fro me / thurgh my folie & inprudence
Wherfore / I wrecche / curse may &
    warie
The seed and fruyt of chyldly sapience

9

As for the more paart / youthe is rebel
Vn to reson / & hatith hir doctryne

Regnynge which /it may nat stande wel
With yowthe / as fer as wit can ymagyne
O yowthe / allas / why wilt thow nat
    enclyne
And vn to reuled resoun bowe thee *70*
Syn resoun is the verray streighte lyne
Þt ledith folk / vn to felicitee

10

Ful seelde is seen / þt yowthe takith
    heede
Of perils þt been likly for to fall
For haue he take a purpos / þt moot
    neede *75*
Been execut / no conseil wole he call
His owne wit he deemeth best of all
And foorth ther with / he renneth bry-
    dillees
As he þt nat betwixt hony and gall
Can iuge / ne the werre fro the pees *80*

11

All othir mennes wittes he despisith
They answeren no thyng to his entente
His rakil wit only to him souffysith
His hy presumpcioun nat list consente
To doon as þt Salomon wroot & mente *85*
Þt redde men by conseil for to werke
Now youthe now / thow sore shalt
    repente
Thy lightlees wittes dull of reson derke

12

My freendes seiden vn to me ful ofte
My mis reule me cause wolde a fit *90*
And redden me in esy wyse & softe
A lyte and lyte to withdrawen it
But þt nat mighte synke in to my wit
So was the lust y rootid in myn herte
And now I am so rype vn to my pit
Þt scarsely I may it nat asterte

13

Who so cleer yen hath & can nat see
Ful smal of ye auaillith the office /
¶ Right so / syn reson youen is to me
For to discerne a vertu from a vice *100*
If I nat can with resoun me cheuice
But wilfully fro reson me withdrawe
Thogh I of hire haue no benefice
No wondir / ne no fauour in hir lawe

14

Reson me bad / & redde as for the
    beste
To ete and drynke in tyme attemprely
But wilful youthe nat obeie leste
Vn to þt reed / ne sette nat ther by
I take haue of hem bothe outrageously

And out of tyme / nat two yeer or
three   110
But xxti wyntir past continuelly
Excesse at borde hath leyd his knyf wt
me

15

The custume of my repleet abstinence
My greedy mowth Receite of swich out-
rage
And hondes two / as woot my negli-
gence   115
Thus han me gyded / & broght in seruage
Of hire þt werreieth euery age
Seeknesse y meene riotoures whippe
Habundantly þt paieth me my wage
So þt me neithir daunce list ne skippe

16

The outward signe of Bachus & his lure
Þt at his dore hangith day by day /
Excitith folk / to taaste of his moisture
So often / þt man can nat wel seyn nay
For me I seye / I was enclyned ay   125
With outen daunger thidir for to hye me
But if swich charge / vp on my bak lay
That I moot it forbere / as for a tyme

17

Or but I were nakidly bystad
By force of the penylees maladie   130
For thanne in herte kowde I nat be glad
Ne lust had noon to Bachus hows to hie
Fy lak of coyn / departith conpaignie
And heuy purs with herte liberal
Quenchith the thristy hete of hertes
drie   135
Wher chynchy herte / hath ther of but
smal

18

I dar nat telle / how þt the fressh repeir
Of venus femel lusty children deere
Þt so goodly / so shaply were & feir
And so plesant of port & of maneere 140
And feede cowden al a world wt cheere
And of atyr passyngly wel byseye
At Poules heed me maden ofte appeere
To talke of mirthe / & to disporte &
pleye

19

Ther was sweet wyn ynow thurgh out the
hous   145
And wafres thikke / for this conpaignie
Þt I spak of / been sumwhat likerous
Where as they mowe a draght of wyn
espie

Sweete / and in wirkynge hoot for the
maistrie
To warme a stomak wt / ther of they
dranke   150
To suffre hem paie had been no courtesie
That charge I took / to wynne loue &
thanke

20

Of loues aart / yit touchid I no deel
I cowde nat / & eek it was no neede
Had I a kus / I was content ful weel
Bettre than I wolde han be wt the deede
Ther on can I but smal it is no dreede
Whan þt men speke of it in my presence
For shame I wexe as reed as is the gleede
Now wole I torne ageyn to my sen-
tence   160

21

Of him þt hauntith tauerne of custume
At shorte wordes / the profyt is this
In double wyse / his bagge it shal con-
sume
And make his tonge speke of folk amis
For in the cuppe / seelden fownden
is   165
Þt any wight his neigheburgh com-
mendith
Beholde & see / what auantage is his
Þt god / his freend / & eek him self
offendith

22

But oon auantage / in this cas I haue
I was so ferd / with any man to
fighte   170
Cloos kepte I me / no man durste I
depraue
But rownyngly / I spak no thyng on
highte
And yit my wil was good / if þt I
mighte
For lettynge of my manly cowardyse
Þt ay of strokes impressid the wighte 175
So þt I durste medlen in no wyse

23

Wher was a gretter maister eek than y
Or bet aqweyntid at Westmynstre yate
Among the taverneres namely
And Cookes / whan I cam / eerly or
late   180
I pynchid nat at hem in myn acate
But paied hem / as þt they axe wolde
Wherfore I was the welcomere algate
And for a verray gentil man y holde

24

And if it happid on the Someres day
Þt I thus at the tauerne hadde be
Whan I departe sholde / & go my way
Hoom to the priuee seel / so wowed me
Hete & vnlust and superfluitee
To walke vn to the brigge / & take a
   boot   *190*
Þt nat durste I contrarie hem all three
But dide as þt they stired me / god woot

25

And in the wyntir / for the way was
   deep
Vn to the brigge I dressid me also
And ther the bootmen took vp on me
   keep   *195*
For they my riot kneewen fern ago
Wt hem I was I tugged to and fro
So wel was him / þt I wt wolde fare
For riot paieth largely / eueremo
He styntith neuere / til his purs be
   bare   *200*

26

Othir than maistir / callid was I neuere
Among this meynee in myn audience
Me thoghte / I was y maad a man for
   euere
So tikelid me þt nyce reuerence
Þt it me made larger of despense   *205*
Than þt I thoghte han been / o flaterie
The guyse of thy traiterous diligence
Is folk to mescheef haasten / & to hie

27

Al be it þt my yeeres be but yonge /
Yit haue I seen in folk of hy degree
How þt the venym of faueles tonge
Hath mortified hir prosperitee
And broght hem in so sharp aduersitee
Þt it hir lyf hath also throwe a doun
And yit ther can no man in this con-
   tree   *215*
Vnnethe eschue this confusioun

28

Many a seruant / vn to his lord seith
Þt al the world spekith of him honour
Whan the contrarie of þt / is sooth in
   feith
And lightly leeued is this losengeour *220*
His hony wordes / wrappid in errour
Blyndly conceyued been / the more harm
   is
O thow fauele of lesynges Auctour
Causist al day / thy lord to fare amis

29

Tho combreworldes clept been enchan-
   tours   *225*
In bookes / as þt I haue or this red
That is to seye sotil deceyuou(r)s
By whom the peple is mis gyed & led
And with plesance so fostred and fed
Þt they forgete hem self & can nat
   feele   *230*
The soothe of the condicion in hem bred
No more / than hir wit were in hire
   heele

30

Who so þt list in the booke of nature
Of beestes rede / ther in he may see
If he take heede vn to the scripture
Where it spekth of meermaides in the See
How þt so inly mirie syngith shee
Þt the shipman ther with fallith a sleepe
And by hire aftir deuoured is he
From al swich song is good men hem to
   keepe   *240*

31

Right so the feyned wordes of plesance
Annoyen aftir / thogh they plese a tyme
To hem þt been vnwyse of gouernance
Lordes beeth waar / Let nat fauel yow
   lyme
If þt yee been enuolupid in cryme   *245*
Yee may nat deeme / men speke of yow
   weel
Thogh fauel peynte hir tale in prose or
   ryme
Ful holsum is it / truste hire nat a deel

32

Holcote seith vp on the booke also
Of sapience / as it can testifie   *250*
Whan þt Vlixes saillid to and fro
By meermaides / this was his policie
All eres of men of his compaignie
With wex he stoppe leet / for þt they
   noght
Hir song sholde heere / lest the armonye
Hem mighte vn to swich deedly sleep han
   broght

33

And bond him self / vn to the shippes
   mast
Lo thus hem all saued his prudence
The wys man is of peril sore agast
O flaterie o lurkyng pestilence   *260*
If sum man dide his cure & diligence
To stoppe his eres fro thy poesie

And nat wolde herkne a word of thy
    sentence
Vn to his greef it were a remedie

34

A nay / al thogh thy tonge were ago
Yit canst thow glose in contenance &
    cheere
Thow supportist with lookes eueremo
Thy lordes wordes in eche mateere
Al thogh þt they a myte be to deere
And thus thy gyse is priuee and ap-
    pert   270
With word and look / among our lordes
    heere
Preferred be / thogh ther be no dissert

35

But whan the sobre / treewe & weel
    auysid
Wt sad visage his lord enfourmeth
    pleyn
How þt his gouernance is despysid
Among the peple / & seith him as they
    seyn
As man treewe oghte vn to his souereyn
Conseillynge him amende his gouernance
The lordes herte swellith for desdeyn
And bit him voide blyue with mes-
    chaunce   280

36

Men setten nat by trouthe now adayes
Men loue it nat / men wole it nat cherice
And yit is trouthe best at all assayes
Whan þt fals fauel soustenour of vice
Nat wite shal how hire to cheuyce   285
Ful boldely shal trouthe hir heed vp bere
Lordes lest fauel / yow fro wele tryce
No lenger souffre hire nestlen in your ere

37

¶Be as be may / no more of this as now
But to my mis reule wole I refeere
Wher as I was at ese weel ynow
Or excesse vn to me leef was & deere
And or I kneew his ernestful maneere
My purs of coyn had resonable wone
But now ther in can ther but scant ap-
    peere   295
Excesse hath ny exyled hem echone

38

The feend and excesse been conuertible
As enditith to me my fantasie
This is my skile / if it be admittible
Excesse of mete & drynke is glotonye   300
Glotonye awakith malencolie

Malencolie engendrith werre & stryf
Stryf causith mortel hurt thurgh hir folie
Thus may excesse reue a soule hir lyf

39

¶No force of al this / go we now to
    wacche   305
By nightirtale / out of al mesure
For as in þt / fynde kowde I no macche
In al the priuee seel with me to endure
And to the cuppe ay took I heede & cure
For þt the drynke appall sholde noght
But whan the pot emptid was of moisture
To wake aftirward /cam nat in my thoght

40

But whan the cuppe had thus my neede
    sped
And sumdel more than necessitee
With repleet spirit wente I to my bed 315
And bathid ther in superfluitee
But on the morn / was wight of no
    degree
So looth as I / to twynne fro my cowche
By aght I woot / abyde / let me see
Of two / as looth / I am seur kowde I
    towche   320

41

I dar nat seyn Prentys and Arondel
Me countrefete & in swich wach go ny
    me
But often they hir bed louen so wel
Þt of the day / it drawith ny the pryme
Or they ryse vp / nat tell I can the
    tyme   325
Whan they to bedde goon / it is so late
O helthe lord / thow seest hem in þt
    cryme
And yit thee looth is / wt hem to debate

42

And why I not / it sit nat vn to me
Þt mirour am of riot & excesse   330
To knowen of a goddes pryuetee
But thus I imagyne / and thus I gesse
Thow meeued art of tendre gentillesse
Hem to forbere / and wilt hem nat chas-
    tyse
For they in mirthe and vertuous glad-
    nesse   335
Lordes reconforten in sundry wyse

43

But to my purpos / syn þt my seeknesse
As wel of purs as body hath refreyned
Me fro Tauerne / & othir wantonnesse

Among an heep / my name is now des-
teyned 340
My greuous hurt ful litil is conpleyned
But they the lak compleyne of my des-
pense
Allas þt euere knyt I was and cheyned
To excesse / or him dide obedience

44

Despenses large enhaunce a mannes
loos 345
Whil they endure / & whan'they be for-
bore
His name is deed / men keepe hir
mowthes cloos
As nat a peny had he spent tofore
My thank is qweynt / my purs his stuf
hath lore
And my Carkeis repleet with heuy-
nesse 350
Be waar Hoccleue / I rede thee therfore
And to a mene reule/thow thee dresse

45

Who so passynge mesure desyrith
As þt witnessen olde Clerkes wyse
Him self encombrith often sythe &
myrith 355
And for thy let the mene thee souffyse
If swich a conceit in thyn herte ryse
As thy profyt may hyndre or thy renoun
If it were execut in any wyse
With manly resoun thriste thow it doun

46

Thy rentes annuel / as thow wel woost
To scarse been greet costes to susteene
And in thy cofre pardee is cold roost
And of thy manuel labour as I weene
Thy lucre is swich / þt it vnnethe is
seene 365
Ne felt / of yiftes seye I eek the same
And stele for the guerdoun is so keene
Ne darst thow nat / ne begge also for
shame

47

Than wolde it seeme / þt thow borwid
haast
Mochil of þt þt thow haast thus de-
spent 370
In outrage & excesse and verray waast
Auyse thee / for what thyng þt is lent
Of verray right / moot hoom ageyn be
sent
Thow ther in haast no perpetuitee

Thy dettes paie / lest þt thow be
shent 375
And or þt thow ther to compellid be

48

Sum folk in this cas dreeden more offense
Of man / for wyly wrenches of the lawe
Than he dooth eithir god or conscience
For by hem two he settith nat (an)
hawe 380
If thy conceit be swich / thow it with-
drawe
I rede / and voide it clene out of thyn
herte
And first of god and syn of man haue
awe
Lest þt they bothe / make thee to smerte

49

Now lat this smert warnynge to thee
be 385
And if thow maist heere aftir be releeued
Of body and purs / so thow gye thee
By wit / þt thow / no more thus be
greeued
What riot is / thow taasted haast and
preeued
The fyr / men seyn / he dreedith þt is
brent 390
And if thow so do / thow art wel
ymeeued
Be now no lenger fool / by myn assent

50

Ey / what is me / þt to my self thus
longe
Clappid haue I / I trowe þt I raue
A / nay / my poore purs / and peynes
stronge 395
Han artid me speke as I spoken haue
Who so him shapith mercy for to craue
His lesson moot recorde in sundry wyse
And whil my breeth may in my body waue
To recorde it / vnnethe I may souffyse

51

¶O god o helthe vn to thyn ordenance
Weleful lord / meekly submitte I me
I am contryt / & of ful repentance
Þt euere I swymmed in swich nycetee
As was displesaunt to thy deitee 405
Now kythe on me thy mercy & thy grace
It sit a god been of his grace free
Foryeue / & neuere wole I eft trespace

52

My body and purs been at ones seeke
And for hem bothe / I to thyn hy
   noblesse
As humblely as þt I can byseeke
Wt herte vnfeyned / reewe on our dis-
   tresse
Pitee haue of myn harmful heuynesse
Releeue the repentant in disese
Despende on me a drope of thy
   largesse   415
Right in this wyse /if it thee lyke & plese

53

¶Lo lat my lord the Fourneval I preye
My noble lord / þt now is tresoreer
From thyn Hynesse haue a tokne or
   tweye
To paie me þt due is for this yeer   420
Of my yeerly .x.li. in theschequeer
Nat but for Michel terme þt was last
I dar nat speke a word of ferneyeer
So is my spirit symple and sore agast

54

I kepte nat to be seen inportune   425
In my pursuyte / I am ther to ful looth
And yit þt gyse / ryf is and commune

Among the peple now withouten ooth
As the shamelees crauour wole / it gooth
For estaat real / can nat al day werne
But poore shamefast man ofte is wroth
Wherfore for to craue moot I lerne

55

The prouerbe is / the doumb man no lond
   getith
Who so nat spekith / & with neede is bete
And thurgh arghnesse / his owne self
   forgetith   435
No wondir / thogh an othir him forgete
Neede hath no lawe / as þt the Clerkes
   trete
And thus to craue / artith me my neede
And right wole eek þt I me entremete
For þt I axe is due / as god me
   speede   440

56

And þt that due is / thy magnificence
Shameth to werne / as þt I byleeue
As I seide / reewe on myn impotence
Þt likly am to sterue yit or eeue
But if thow in this wyse me releeue 445
By coyn I gete may swich medecyne
As may myn hurtes all þt me greeue
Exyle cleene / & voide me of pyne

[TO SOMER]

[From the same MS, fol. 38 verso]

CESTES BALADE & CHANCEON ENSUYANTES FEURENT FAITES A MON MEISTRE .H.
SOMER QUANT IL ESTOIT SOUȜTRESORER

The Sonne wt his bemes of brightnesse
To man so kyndly is & norisshynge
Þt lakkyng it / day nere but dirknesse
To day he yeueth his enlumynynge
And causith al fruyt for to wexe &
   sprynge   5
Now syn þt sonne may so moche auaill
And moost with Somer is his soiournynge
That sesoun bou(n)teuous we wole assaill

2

Glad cheerid Somer / to your gouernaill
And grace / we submitte al our willynge
To whom yee freendly been / he may nat
   faill
But he shall haue his resonable axynge
Aftir your good lust be the sesonynge

Of our fruytes / this laste Mighelmesse
The tyme of yeer was of our seed
   ynnynge   15
The lak of which / is our greet heuynesse

3

We truste vp on your freendly gentillesse
Yee wole vs helpe / and been our sup-
   poaill
Now yeue vs cause ageyn this cristemesse
For to be glad / o lord / whethir our
   taill   20
Shal soone make vs with our shippes saill
To port salut? if yow list / we may synge
And elles moot vs bothe mourne & waill
Til your fauour vs sende releeuynge

4

We your seruantes Hoccleue & Baillay 25
Hethe & Offorde yow beseeche & preye

---

421. Marginal gloss: *annus ille fuit annus restrictionis annuitatum.*

Haasteth our heruest / as soone as yee
    may
For fere of stormes / our wit is aweye
Were our seed Inned / wel we mighten
    pleye
And vs desporte / & synge / & make
    game
And yit this rowndel shul we synge &
    seye
In trust of yow / & honour of your name

Somer þt rypest mannes sustenance

With holsum hete of the Sonnes warm-
    nesse
Al kynde of man thee holden is to blesse

Ay thankid be thy freendly gouernance
And thy fressh looke of mirthe &. of
    gladnesse
        Somer &c.
To heuy folke / of thee the remem-
    braunce
Is salue & oynement to hir seeknesse
For why we thus shul synge in Christe-
    messe
        Somer &c.

[TO CARPENTER]

[From the same MS, fol. 41]

See heer my maister Carpenter I yow
    preye
How many chalenges ageyn me be
And I may nat deliure hem by no weye
So me werreyeth coynes scarsetee
That ny Cousin is to necessitee   5
For why vn to yow seeke I for refut
Which þt of comfort am ny destitut

2

Tho men / whos names I aboue expresse
Fayn wolden þt they and I euene were
And so wolde I / god take I to wit-
    nesse   10
I woot wel I moot heere / or elles where
Rekne of my dettes / & of hem answere
Myn herte for the dreede of god & awe
Fayn wolde it qwyte / & for constreynt
    of lawe

Just above is, in margin, *A de B & C de D, &c.*
    See Notes.
6. Marginal gloss: *Ceste balade feust tendrement
    considere & bonement execute.*

3

But by my trouthe / nat wole it betyde *15*
And therfore as faire as I can & may
With aspen herte / I preye hem abyde
And me respyte / to sum lenger day
Some of hem grante / and some of hem
    seyn nay
And I so sore ay dreede an aftir clap *20*
That it me reueth many a sleep & nap

4

If þt it lykid / vn to your goodnesse
To be betwixt (hem) and me swich a
    mene
As þt I mighte kept be fro duresse
Myn heuy thoghtes wolde it voide
    clene   *25*
As your good plesance is this thyng
    demene
How wel þt yee doon / & how soone also
I suffre may in qwenchynge of my wo
        Cest tout

[THREE ROUNDELS]

[MS Huntington 744]

CY ENSUENT TROIS CHAUNCEONS / LUNE CONPLEYNANTE A LA DAME MONNOIE & LAUTRE
LA RESPONSE DELE A CELLUI QUI SE CONPLEYNT & LA TIERCE / LA
COMMENDACION DE MA DAME

I

[Compleynt]

Wel may I pleyne on yow lady moneye
Þt in the prison of your sharp scantnesse
Souffren me bathe in wo and heuynesse
And deynen nat of socour me purueye
Whan þt I baar of your prison the keye
Kepte I yow streite Nay God to witnesse
   Well may I
I leet yow out / O now of your noblesse
Seeth vn to me / in your deffaute I deye
   Well may I
Yee saillen al to fer retourne I preye
Conforteth me ageyn this Cristemesse
Elles I moot in right a feynt gladnesse
Synge of yow thus & yow accuse & seye
   Well may I

II

[La Response]

Hoccleue / I wole / it to thee knowen be
I lady moneie /of the world goddesse
Þt haue al thyng vndir my buxumnesse
Nat sette by thy pleynte risshes three

Myn hy might haddest thow in no cheertee
Whyle I was in thy slipir sikirnesse
   Hoccleue
At instance of thyn excessif largesse
Becam I of my body delauee
   Hoccleue
And syn þt lordis grete obeien me
Sholde I me dreede / of thy poor sym-
  plesse
My golden heed akith for thy lewdnesse
Go poore wrecche / who settith aght by
  thee
   Hoccleue
    Cest tout

III

[La Commendacion de ma Dame]

Of my lady wel me reioise I may
Hir golden forheed is ful narw & smal
Hir browes been lyk to dym reed coral
And as the Ieet / hir yen glistren ay

Hir bowgy cheekes been as softe as clay
Wth large Iowes and substancial
   Of my lady
Hir nose / a pentice is þt it ne shal
Reyne in her mowth / þogh shee vp
  rightes lay
   Of
Hir mowth is nothyng scant / wt lippes
  gray
Hir chin vnnethe / may be seen at al
Hir comly body / shape as a foot bal
And shee syngith / ful lyk a papelay
   Of

   Cest tout

HOCCLEVE'S DIALOGUE WITH A FRIEND

[EXTRACT]

The partially-linked set of poems and prose moralizations by Hoccleve, which I for convenience call a "Series," opens with a Complaint in soliloquy, of 413 lines rime royal; with it is connected a following Dialogue, of 826 lines in the same stanza, which introduces the tale of Jereslaus' Wife, from the Gesta Romanorum, of 952 lines similarly grouped. On this follow four stanzas of dialogue, and the prose moralization of the Tale which Hoccleve's friend therein demands. Earlier, in the Dialogue itself, the friend who is counseling Hoccleve learns from him that he is pledged to execute a piece of work for the duke of Gloucester, which is long overdue; the friend suggests something lighter than Hoccleve had had in mind, something to appease women, who have been angered by Hoccleve's translation of the Letter of Cupid. An "Innocent Persecuted Wife" story is accordingly told by the poet, a story closely allied to Chaucer's tale of Constance; but the rendition of "Learn to Die" which next follows (without connection) in the MSS of the "Series," may be the work originally planned for Gloucester. It, and a prose comment, are bound by another bit of dialogue with the same friend to a second narrative translated from the Gesta Romanorum, also with appended moralization; this closes the "Series."

Our extract is taken from the second link of the "Series," the Dialogue: it opens with Hoccleve's protest, in two stanzas, that he is quite capable of resuming composition after his long illness, and has no intention of overworking himself as his friend fears. The friend has the next three stanzas and two lines more; Hoccleve replies, and not only stanzas but lines are occasionally divided between the two in the animated dialogue which follows. A similar dialogue-method of introducing his work is employed by Hoccleve as preface to the Regement of Princes. The student will observe here the careful use of *Thomas* and of *freend* by the different speakers, for clearness.

The MS from which I print, Selden supra 53 of the Bodleian Library at Oxford, is described p. 124 here.

Freend I not medle of materis greete
Ther to not strecche may myn intellecte
I neuere yit was brent with studies
    hete   *500*
Let no man holde me therynne suspecte
If I not ligtly / may cacche the effecte
Of thing in wiche / laboure I me purpose
A deu my studie / anoon my book I close

By stirtis / whanne that a fresshe lust me
    taketh
Wole I me bisie now and now a lite
But whanne my lust dulleth & aslaketh
I stinte wole / and no lenger write
And parde frende / that may not hindre a
    mite
As that it semeth to my symple avis *510*
Iugeth youre silfe / ye bene prudent &
    wys

Siker Thomas / if thou do in suche wise
As thou seist / I am ful wel content
That thou vppon the take that emprise
Wiche that thou hast purposid and y ment
Un to that ende geue I myn assent
Goo thou ther to / in ihesu cristis name
And as thou hast me seide/do thou the
    same

I am sure that thi disposicioun
Is suche / that thou maist more take on
    honde   *520*
Than I first wende in myn opinioun
In many foold / thankid be goddis sonde
Do forth in goddis name / and not ne
    wonde
To make and write / what thing that
    thee list
That I not er knewe / is nowe to me wist

And of oo thing / nowe wel I me remem-
bre
Whi thou purposist in this book trauaile
I trowe that in the moneth of Septembre
Nowe last or not fer from it / it is no
faile
No force of the time / it shal not
auaile   530
To my matere / ne hindre or lette
Thou seidest / of a book thou were in
dette

Vn to my lorde / that nowe is lieutenant
Mi lorde of Gloucestre / was it not so
Yis sothly freend / and as by couenant
He shulde han had it many a day a go
But seeknesse and vnlust / and othir mo
Han bene the causis of impediment
Thomas / thanne this book hast thou to
him ment

Siker freend ye ful trewe is youre
demynge   540
ffor him it is / that I this book shal make
As blyue as that I herde of his comynge
ffro ffrance / I penne and ynke gan to
take
And my spirit I maade to a wake
That longe lurkid hath in ydelnesse
ffor any suche labour and besinesse

But of some othir thing / fain trete I
wolde
Mi noble lordis herte / ther with to
glade
And therto deepe I bounden am and
holde
On suche mater / by him that me
made   550
Wolde I bistowe many a balade
Wiste I what / good freend / telle on
what is best
Me for to make / and folowe am I prest

Next oure lege lorde oure kyng victorious
In al this wide worlde / lorde is ther
noone
Vn to me so good ne so gracious
And hath bene suche / yeeris ful manie
oone
God yelde it him / as sad as any stoone
His herte is sette / and not chaunge can
ffro me his humble seruant and his
man   560

For him I thougte han translatid
(Vegece)
Wiche tretith of the art of Chiualrie
But I see his Knygthod so encresce
That no thing my labour shulde edifie
ffor he that art / wel can for the maistrie
Bygonde he preued hath his worthinesse
And amonge other / Chirburgh to wit-
nesse

This worthi Prince laie bifore that holde
Wiche was ful stronge at sege many
aday
And thens for to departe hath he not
wolde   570
But knygtly there abood / vppon his pray
Til he by force it wan / it is no nay
Duke herry that so worthy was and good
ffolowith this Prince / as wel in dede as
blood

Or he to Chirborwe cam / in iourneiing
Of Costantin he wan the cloos and yle
ffor wich / laud and honour & bi preis-
ing
Rewarden him / and quiten him his wyle
Thoug he biforn that had a worthi stile
Yit of noble rennoun is that encrees   580
He is a famous Prince / and that is doute-
lees

For to reherce or telle in special
Euery act that his swerde / in steel wroot
there
And many a nother place / I woot not al
And thoug euery act come had to myn
eere   585
To expresse hem / my spirit wolde han
fere
Lest I his thanke par chaunce migt
abregge
Thorug vnkunnynge / if I hem shulde
alegge

But this I seie / he called is Humfrey
Conueniently as that it semeth me   590
ffor this conceit is in myn herte alweie
Batallous Mars / in his natiuite
Vn to that name / of verrey specialte
Titlid him / makinge him ther by prom-
esse
That strecche he shulde un to hie
prowesse

For humfrey / as vn to myn intellect
Man make I shal / in englissh is to seie
And that biheest / hath taken trewe effect
As the comune fame / can biwreie
Who so his worthi knygthod / can
    weie   600
Duely in hise conceitis balaunce
Ynowe hath / whereof his rennoun en-
    haunce

To cronicle hise actis / were a good dede
ffor thei ensaumple migt and encorage
fful many a man / for to taken hede
How for to gouerne hem in the vsage
Of armes / it is a greet auauntage
A man bifore him / to haue a mirrour
Therynne to see the path vn to honour

O lorde / whanne he cam to the seege of
    Roon   610
ffro Chirborwe / whether fere or coward-
    ise
So ny the wallis / made him for to goon
Of the town / as he dide I not suffice
To telle yow / in howe knygtly a wise
He loggid him there / and how worthily
He bar him / what / he is al knygt
    sothly

Nowe good frende / shoue at the cart I
    yow preie
What thing may I make vn to his
    plesaunce
With outen youre reede / noot I what to
    seie
O / no parde Thomas / o no ascaunce 620
No certein freend / as nowe no cheuis-
    aunce
Can I youre counseil is to me holsum
As I truste in yow ministrith me sum

Wel Thomas / trowest thou his hie
    noblesse
Not rekke / what mater that it be
That thou shalt make of no freend as I
    gesse
So that it be mater of honeste
Thomas and thanne I wole avise me
ffor who so reed and counseil geue shal
May not on heed / forthe renne ther with
    al   630

And that to so noble a Prince namely
So excellent / worthy and honourable
Shal haue / nedith good a vise sothly
That it may be plesaunt and agreable
To his noblesse / it is not couenable
To write to a prince so famous
But it be good mater and vertuous

Thow woost wel / who shal an hous
    edifie
Gooth not ther to with oute avisement
If he be wys for with his mental ye 640
ffirst is it seen / purposid / cast and
    ment
Howe it shal wrougt be / ellis al is shent
Certis for defaute of good forsigte
Mis tiden thingis / that wel bitiden migte

This may be vn to thee / in thi makinge
A good mirrour / thou wilt not haste I
    trowe
Vn to thy penne / and ther with wirche
    heedlinge
Or thou avised be wel / and wel knowe
What thow shalt write / o Thomas /
    manie a throwe
Smertith the fool / for lak of good a
    vis   650
But no wigt hath it smerted that is wys

For wel is he ware / or he write or
    speke
What is to do or leue / Who by prudence
Rule 'him shal / no thing shal oute from
    him breke
Hastily ne of rakel necligence   655
ffreend that is soth / o / nowe youre
    assistence
And helpe / what I shal make I yow
    biseche
In youre wys conceit / serche ye and
    seche

He a long while in a studie stood
And aftir warde thus he tolde his
    entente   660
Thomas saaf bettre avis I holde it good
Sithin howe the hooly sesoun is of lente
In wiche it sitt euery wigt him repente
Of his offence / and of his wickidnesse /
Be heuy of thi gilte / and thee confesse

And satisfaccioun do thou for it
Thou woost wel / on wymmen greet wite
    & lak
Ofte hast thou putt / bi war / lest thou
    be quit
Thy wordis fille wolde a quarter sak
That thou in white / depeintid hast with
    blak   670
In her repreef mochel thing hast thou
    wrete
Wiche thei not forgeue haue / ne forgete

Sumwhat nowe write in honour & preis-
    ing
Of hem / so maist thow do correccioun
Somdel of thin offence and mys heering
Thou art clene oute of hir affeccioun
Nowe sithen it is in thin eleccioun
Whether thee list / her loue a gein pur-
    chace
Or stonde as thou dost / oute of loue
    and grace

Be wys rede I / chese the bettir part 680
Triste wel this / wymen ben fel and wise
Hem for to plese / lith greet craft and
    art
Wher no fir made is / may no smoke
    arise
But thou hast ofte / if thou the wel avise
Made smoky brondis / and for al that
    gilt
Yit maist thou stonde in grace / if thou
    wilt

Bi buxum herte and bi submissioun
To her graces / yelding the coupable /
Thou pardoun maist haue and remiscioun
And do vn to hem plesaunce greable 690
To make partie / art thou no thing able
Humble thi goost / be not sturdy of herte
Bettir than thou art / han thei made to
    smerte

The wyf of Bathe take I for auctrice
That wymmen han no ioie ne deinte
That men shulde vppon hem putte any
    vice
I woot wel so / or like to that seith she
By wordis writen / Thomas yelde the
Euene as thou by scripture hast hem
    offendid
Rigt so / lat it be by writyng amendid 700

Freend / thoug I do so / what lust or
    pleisir
Shal my lorde therynne haue / noon /
    thinkith me
Yis Thomas yis / his lust and his desir
Is / as it wel sit / to his hie degre
ffor his disporte / and mirthe in honeste
With ladies / for to haue daliaunce
And this booke / wole he hem shewen
    par chaunce

And sithen he thi good lorde is / he be
    may
ffor thee suche a meene / that the ligtlyere
Shullen thei forgeue the / putte it in
    assay   710
My counseil / let see / not shal it thee
    dere
So wolde I do / if in thi plite I were
Leie hand on thi brest / if thou wilt so
    do
Or leue / I can no more seie ther to

But thoug to wymmen thou thin herte
    bowe
Axinge her graces / with greet repen-
    taunce
ffor thi giltees / thee wole I not alowe
To take on thee suche rule and gouer-
    naunce
As thei thee reede wolde / for greuaunce
So greet / ther folowe migt of it par
    cas   720
That thou repente it shuldist evere
    Thomas

Adam bigilid was thorug Eues reed
And siker so was she by the Serpent
To whom god seide / this womman thin
    heed
Breke shal / for thorug thin enticement
She hath y broke my comaundement
O sithen womman had on the fende suche
    migt
To breke a mannes heed / it semeth ligt

For why let noon housbonde / thinke it
    shame
Ne repreef vn to hym / ne vilenye 730
That his wijf dooth to him that selue same
Hir resoun axith haue of men the mais-
    trie
Thoug hooly writ witnesse it and testifie
Man shulde of hem hane dominacioun
It is the reuers in probacioun

Hange vp his hachet / and sette him
   adoun
ffor wom*m*en wole assente in no manere
Vn to that pointe / ne that conclusioun
Thomas / howe is it bitwixe the and thi
   fere
Wel wel quod I / what list you ther of
   to here   740
My wyf mygt hoker haue and greet dis-
   dein
If I shulde in suche caas / pleie a solein

Nowe Thomas / if thou list to lyue in
   ese
Prolle aftir wym*m*ens beneuolence
Thoug it be daungerous / good is hem
   plese
ffor harde is / to renne in her offence
What so thei seien / take al in pacience
Bettir art thou not / than thi fadris bifore
Han ben Thomas / be rigt wel ware
   therfore

Freende harde it is / wym*m*en to greue
   I graunte   750
But what haue I a gilte / for him that
   dide
Not haue I doon why / dar ye me auaunte
Oute of wym*m*ens gracis slippe or slide
Yis Thomas yis / in the epistle of Cupide
Thou hast of hem / so largely said
That thei ben blak wrooth / and ful yuel
   apaid

Freend / douteles sumwhat is ther in
That sowneth but rigt smal to her
   honour
But as to that / nowe for youre fadir
   kyn
Considre / I was thereof noon auc-
   tour   760
I nas in that caas / but a reportour
Of folkes tales / and that they seide /
   I wrote
I not affermed it on hem / god it woote

Who so that shal reherse a mannes sawe
As that he seith / moot he seie & not
   varie
ffor and he do / he dooth a gein the lawe
Of trouthe / he may tho wordis not
   contrarie
Who so that seith I am her Aduersarie
And dispreise her condiciou*n*s and port

ffor that I made of hem suche report /   770

He mis avisid is / and eke to blame
Wha*n*ne I it spak / I spake conpleiningly
I to hem thougte no repreef ne shame
What worlde is this / howe vndirstande
   am I
Loke in the same book / what stiketh by
Who so loketh aright / therynne may
   thei see
That they me ougte haue in greet chirtee

And ellis / woot I not what is what
The book concludith for hem / it is no
   nay
Vertuously / my good frende / dooth it
   nat   780
Thomas I not / for yit I neuere it say
No freend no Thomas / Wel trowe I in
   fay
ffor had ye red it fully to the ende
Ye wolde seie / it is not as ye wende

Thomas / howe so it be / do as I seide
Sithen it displesith hem / amendis make
If that some of hem thee ther of vpbreide
Thou shalt be besie y now I vndirtake
Thi kut to kepe / and nowe I thee bitake
To god / for I moot nedis fro the
   wende   790
The loue and thanke of wym*m*en / nowe
   god the sende

Amonge I thenke thee for to visite
Or that thi book fully finisshid be
ffor looth me were / thou shuldist ougt
   write
Wher thorug / thou migtest gete any
   mawgree
And for that cause / I wole it ouer see
And Thomas / nowe a dieu and fare
   weel
Thou finde me shalt / al so trewe as
   steel

Whane he was goon / I in myn herte
   dredde
To stonde oute of wym*m*ens beneuol-
   ence   800
And to fulfille that / that he me redde
I shope me to do my peine and diligence
To wynne hir loue by obedience
Thoug I my wordis can not wel por-
   treie /

Lo here the forme / howe I hem obeie

My ladies alle / as wisly god me blesse
Why that ye meued bene / can I not
   knowe
My gilte cam neuere yit to his ripenesse
Al thoug ye for youre foo / me deeme
   & trowe
But I youre frende be / bite me the
   crowe   810
I am al othir to yow / than ye wene
By my writing / hath it and shal be sene

But netheles / I lowly me submitte
To youre bountees / as fer as thei han
   place
In yow / vn to me wrecche it may wel
   sitte

To axe pardoun / thoug I not trespace
Leuer is me / with pitous chere and
   face
And meek spirit do so / than open werre
Ye make me / and me putte at the werre

A tale eke / wiche I in the Roman
   dedis   820
Nowe late sy / in honur & plesaunce
Of yow my ladies / as I moot nedis
Or take my way / for fere in to ffrance
Thoug I not shapen be / to prike and
   praunce
Wole I translate / and that my gilte I
   hope
Shal pourge / as clene / as keuer-
   chiefs dooth sope

[IN PRAISE OF CHAUCER]

[Stanzas from the Regement of Princes, from the copy executed for Henry Prince of
Wales, MS Arundel 38 of the British Museum. This volume has on fol. 37, at opening of the
poem after the introduction, a miniature of the poet presenting his work to Henry. The leaf
which probably carried the miniature of Chaucer, with lines 4990-5042, has been removed from
the manuscript.]

[MS Arundel 38, fol. 35b-36]
Wyth hert as tremblyng as the leef of asp
ffadir syn 3e me rede do so
Of my simple conceyt wol I the clasp
Vn do / And lat yt at his large go
But welaway / so ys myn hert wo
That the honour of englyssch tong is
   deed
Of which / I wont was han consail &
   reed   1960

O mayster dere and fadir reuerent
My mayster Chaucer flour of eloquence
Mirrour of fructuous endendement
O vniuersel fader in science
Allas that thou thyn excellent prudence
In thy bed mortel mightyst nort by
   quethe
What eiled deth Allas why wolde he
   slethe

O deth thou dedyst nou3t harm synguleer
In slaghtree of hym / but al þs land yt
   smertith
But natheles 3yt hastow no power   1970
He name sle / hys hye vertu astertyth
Vnslayn fro the / whych ay vs lyfly
   hertyth
Wyth bokes of hys ornat endityng
That ys to al thys land enlumynyng.

Hastow nou3t eeke my mayster Gower
   slayn
Whos vertu I am in sufficient
ffor to descryue. I woot wel in certayn
ffor to sleen al thys world thou hast I
   ment
But syn our lord cryst was obedient
To the in feyth. I can no ferther
   seye   1980
Hys creatures mosten the obeye

. . . . .

Symple as my goost and scars my let-
   terure   2073
Vn to 3our excellente for to write
Myn inward loue / and 3it aventure
Wil I me putte thogh I can but lyte
My dere mayster god ys soul quyte
And fadir Chaucer rayn wolde han me
   taght

Variants of Brit. Mus. Adds. 18632 (Ad) and
  Harley 4866 (H) are: 1954 *herte tremblyng*
  (Ad); 1955 *rede to do so* (HAd); 1957 *and
  at his large lat hit goo* (Ad); 1958 *herte* (HAd);
  1959 *tonge* (HAd); 1963 *entendement* (HAd);
  1964 *of science* (Ad); 1966 This MS errs: *not*
  (Ad), *naght* (H); 1967 *sle the* (HAd); 1971
  His name . . . astertith (HAd); 1978 *haast ment*
  (H); 1980 *no more seye* (Ad).
The MS formerly Phillipps 1099 reads in 1963
  endytement, in 1980 *no bettir seye*.

But I was dul . and lerned lyte or naght
Alas my worthy mayster honorable 2080
Thys landes verray tresour and rychesse
Deth by thy deth harme irriparable
Vn to vs don. her vengeable duresse
Despoyled hath this land of the swet-
nesse
Of rethorik / for vn to tullius
Was neuer man so lyk a monges vs

Also who was hier in philosophye
To aristotle / in our tonge but þu
The steppes of virgile in poesie
Thow filwedist eek wot wel I now 2090
That combre world þt þee my mayster
slow
Wolde I slayn were / deth was to hastyf
To renne on the and reue the þy (1)yf

Deth hath but smal consideracion
Vn to the vertuous I haue espyed /
No more as schewyth the probacion
Than to a vycyous mayster losel tried
A mong an heep / euery man ys mays-
tried
Wyth her as wel the poore as ys þe ryche
Leered and lewde eek standen al I
leche 2100

Sche my3tte han taried hir vengeance a
while

Variants of Adds. 18632 and Harley 4866 are:
2073 *Simple is* (HAd); 2074 *excellence* (HAd);
2075 *yit in auenture* (HAd); 2077 *soule* (HAd);
2082 *deth / hath harme* (HAd); 2088 *tonge þan
thow* (Ad)—note Ad's understanding of *hier*,
2087, as "higher", not as "heir"; 2090 *men wite
wel* (Ad); 2093 first letter of *lwf* is erased; 2104
MS reads *brange*; 2106 *for the beste* (Ad).
The scribe has made several corrections during
transcription.
The former Phillipps 1099 reads: 2073 *scars is
my;* 2079 *yong and lerne lyte;* 2096 *a scheweth
probacion;* 2099 *as the riche;* 2100 *eek ben vnto
hyre lyche;* 2104 *lyke brynge forth to the;* 2106
as for the beste.

Til that sum man had egal to þe be
Nay lat be þat / she knewe wel þt þys Ile
May neuere man forth bringe lyk to þe
And hyre office nedes do moot sche
God bad hire soo / I truste as for thi
beste
O maister maister / god þy soule reste

· · · · ·

[MS Brit. Mus. Adds. 18632, fol. 93b]
The firste foundere of oure faire langage 4978
haþ seid in caas.semblable.and oþer mo
so hily wel. that hit is my dotage
for to expresse . or touche ony of tho
allas my fader. is fro þe world go
my worþi maister Chaucer. him I mene
be þov aduoket for him . heuenes quene

As þov wel knowest . o . blessed virgine 4985
wt louinge herte . and hie deuociouny
in þin honour . he wrot ful many a lyne
o . nov þin help . and thin promociouny
to god þi sone . make a mociouny
hov he þi seruaunt was. maiden marie
and lat his loue . floure and fructifie

Al þouh his lyf be quent. þe resemblaunt
of him haþ in me .so fressh liflinesse
that to putte other men. in remembraunce
of his persone. I haue here his likinesse
do make to this ende. in sothfastnesse
that thei þt han of him lost þouht &
mynde 4997
bi þis peinture may. agein him fynde

Variant readings of Harley 4866 and of the remaining lines of Arundel 38 are: 4978 *finder, fyndere*
(AdH); 4982 *fro the world ys goo* (AdH);
4991 *queynt* (H); 4992 *resemblaunce* (H); 4995
lyknesse (H); 4997 *lest þought* (H).
The former MS Phillipps 1099 reads: 4978 *of
your faire;* 4985 *And thou;* 4991 *love;* 4997 *lost.*

[TO BEDFORD]

[MS Huntington 111, fol. 37]

CE FEUST MYS EN LE LIURE DE MONSR JOHAN LORS NOMEZ / ORE REGENT
DE FRANCE & DUC DE BEDFORD

Vn to the rial egles excellence
I humble Clerc with al hertes hum-
    blesse
This book presente / & of your reuerence
Byseeche I pardon and foryeuenesse
Þt of myn ignorance & lewdenesse   5
Nat haue I write it in so goodly wyse
As þt me oght vn to your worthynesse
Myn yen / hath custumed bysynesse
So daswed / þt I may no bet souffyse

2

I dreede lest þt my maister Massy   10
Þt is of fructuous intelligence
Whan he beholdith how vnconnyngly
My book is metrid / how raw my sent-
    ence
How feeble eek been my colours his
    prudence

Shal sore encombrid been of my folie 15
But yit truste I / þt his beneuolence
Compleyne wole myn insipience
Secreetly / & what is mis rectifie

3

Thow book / by licence of my lordes
    grace
To thee speke I / and this I to thee
    seye   20
I charge thee / to shewe thow thy face
Beforn my seid Maister / & to him preye
On my behalue / þt he peise and weye
What myn entente is þt I speke in thee
For rethorik hath hid fro me the keye 25
Of his tresor / nat deyneth hir nobleye
Dele with noon so ignorant as me

Cest tout

JOHN LYDGATE

John Lydgate, the "Monk of Bury," whose life was bounded by the years 1375 and 1448-9, is an apt example of that mutability of fortune which he and his contemporaries loved to dwell upon, of a reputation in his own day which has now faded as completely as has that of Cowley. He was born in the village of Lydgate, near the great Benedictine abbey of Bury St. Edmunds, Suffolk; he became as a lad a novice within its walls, and passed on through subdiaconate and diaconate to the priesthood in 1397. In 1421 he was made prior of Hatfield Broadoak, Essex, but after eleven years he relinquished that office and, so far as we know, returned to Bury. The last we hear of him through official documents is a receipt on his behalf for his semi-annual pension from the Crown, dated Sept. 1449; and in the 27th year of Henry VI, 1448-9, he is spoken of as dead by the versifier John Metham.

The tradition set on foot by Bale, that Lydgate studied at both Universities and traveled extensively abroad, has never received any corroborative proof. He seems to have been in France when the translation of the Dance Macabre was suggested to him; and headings by Shirley to some of the shorter poems state that they were composed in Oxford or in London; but there is no evidence that he did the bulk of his verse-production elsewhere than in his monastery. And if the most of his years were passed at Bury, it was in no secluded backwater of life that he dwelt. The seat of the Abbey was one of the larger towns of England. In Lydgate's lifetime and in that of Chaucer, London had between forty and fifty thousand inhabitants, while very few other towns numbered more than ten thousand; most of the English people dwelt in hamlets of three hundred or less. Bury, with its four thousand population, was an important place; and the frequent disputes of Town and Gown in the period show that it was by no means dominated by its great Benedictine House. Life there was not perhaps at the tension of life in London, but the town was no sleepy nook of silence; and literature also had its vicarious experience to offer to a monk of Bury. The Abbey Library was one of England's largest book-collections. John Boston of Bury, Lydgate's contemporary and fellow-monk, travelled all over England investigating and cataloguing monastic libraries; and none in his list was better stocked than that of Bury itself, with its two thousand or more volumes of both sacred and profane literature. Had Lydgate chosen, he could have studied there not only Cicero and Seneca, but Horace and Juvenal, Virgil, Statius, Plautus, and Terence.

Neither life nor letters, however, could yield to Lydgate quite the same opportunity as to Chaucer. The pressure of the monastic habit of thought, the monastic routine, lay heavy on a cloistered monk; and had Lydgate ever possessed the keen sensibilities with which Chaucer came to books, they must have been deadened by the amount of work which he did to order. He probably showed, in early manhood, a glibness with words and with rime which made him conspicuous in his monastery; one commission followed another, and his facile "eloquence" was soon in steady demand for any occasion requiring verses. A mumming by London merchants before the Lord Mayor, a "letter" to accompany Christmas gifts to the king, an explanation of the Mass for a pious Countess to keep in her chamber, a set of stanzas to serve up with the "subtlety" at a banquet, a complaint for a lovesick squire to offer his lady, the "histories" to accompany figures in a fresco or in tapestry, either for a graveyard or for a wealthy mercer's parlor, a colossal translation of Boccaccio's "tragedies" for the Duke of Gloucester,— are examples of the monk's varied commissions.

He has left a good many thousand lines of brief poems, religious and secular; but his larger pieces of work were the mainstay of his reputation for generations; and most of these were translations done to order. For Henry V, while still Prince of Wales, Lydgate translated the Troy Book, a rewriting, in 30,000 pentameter couplet lines, of the Trojan story, drawn apparently from Guido delle Colonne. This was begun in 1412 and finished in 1420, according to its own statements; and it was probably preceded by another work for the same prince, the Life of Our Lady, 6,000 lines long, in sevens. The Earl of Salisbury commissioned from Lydgate a translation of Deguilleville's Pèlerinage de la Vie Humaine, which Lydgate tells us was begun in 1426, and which runs to 25,000 lines, mainly short couplets. The poet's Guy of Warwick was done at the request of Margaret Lady Talbot, daughter of the Earl of Warwick; it is less ponderous,—of 592 lines only. Lady Talbot's father, Richard de Beauchamp Earl of Warwick, while Lieutenant-General of France after the death of Henry V, ordered of Lydgate, in 1426, a translation setting forth the hereditary right of Henry VI to the French crown,—329 lines in pentameter couplets. For presentation to the youthful king, and at the command of Curteys, abbot of Bury, Lydgate wrote, in 1433, the Lives of SS. Edmund and Fremund, 3,700 lines rime royal. Later, in 1439, the abbot of St. Albans requested of Lydgate a life of SS. Albon and Amphabell, which runs to 4,700 lines, in sevens. And the heaviest of Lydgate's undertakings, the 36,000 lines of the Fall of Princes, translated from Laurent de Premierfait's second prose version of Boccaccio's De Casibus Virorum Illustrium, was executed between 1431 and 1438 for Humphrey duke of Gloucester, brother of Henry V, first founder of the library of the University of Oxford, and Maecenas of his time.

Nor do these commissioned and datable poems exhaust the list of Lydgate's longer works. A translation from the French, entitled Reason and Sensuality, is dated conjecturally about 1408; it is of 7,000 lines in short couplets, unfinished. The Churl and the Bird, also from the French, may date even earlier. The Dance Macabre, another translation from the French, must postdate the execution of the wall-painting (1424) in Paris whence Lydgate says he took it; it is of almost 700 lines, in stanza. A tale supplementary to the Canterbury Tales, the Siege of Thebes, 4,700 lines in pentameter couplets, was perhaps written between 1420 and 1422. The poet's Testament, written presumably late in life, is of 900 lines in stanza; and according to a note in the manuscripts, his death occurred while he was engaged upon a version of the so-called advice of Aristotle, to Alexander, the Secreta Secretorum, of which Lydgate did about 1,500 lines in sevens, his follower Burgh(?) continuing the work.

To these ca.120,000 lines of well-authenticated verse we must add the mass of the shorter poems; and here we are on less certain ground. The list of Lydgate's works drawn up by Ritson (see below p. 99) has been denounced by Schick and dissected by MacCracken; but from its fault of method, its tendency to add to the Lydgatian canon any piece of fifteenth-century verse didactic in content, accurate in rime, and jerkily ambling in rhythm, we are not yet free. The collection of the monk's minor poems made by J. O. Halliwell in 1840 assigned to Lydgate work marked as his by any manuscript, or even appearing without author's name in a volume including some Lydgatian poems. No classification of MS-authorities according to their probable trustworthiness has yet been made, and no canon of Lydgate has been drawn up in which there is separation between the poems claimed by Lydgate in his text, the poems mentioned as his by contemporaries, the poems assigned to him by trustworthy scribes, and the poems without any external evidence as to authorship. The list of his writings in the Dictionary of National Biography is entirely uncritical, and the canon as endorsed by MacCracken, in his EETS edition of the Minor Poems, vol. i, is marred by the addition of a number of poems unmarked in any MS and accepted solely by Dr. MacCracken's personal judgment.

Relying first upon the few manuscripts written by Lydgate's contemporary, John Shirley, manuscripts very fully marked with authors' names—and upon one codex, Harley 2255 of the British Museum, which may have been compiled for Lydgate's own abbot, we can add to the canon of the monk's works some 15,000 lines of minor poems.[1] In few cases is it possible to date them. The Departing of Chaucer is probably of 1417; the epithalamium to the Duke of Gloucester is of 1422; the Coronation address to Henry VI must be of 1429; and the two mummings in honor of Estfeld's London mayoralty are of 1429 or 1437. But we can only conjecture as to the dates of the remaining mummings or of the tapestry poems, while for the prayers, the hymns, and the didactic verse we have no criterion other than internal, than the better or worse handling of rhythm and subject.

This standard is difficult of application to Lydgate. The student who had never read a line of his work might suspect, upon hearing of its enormous amount, that its quality was strained. It is indeed. And with Lydgate the period of life at which he writes has less to do with his power of expression than has his subject. The Testament may have been of his later years, but it contains fine stanzas of deep religious feeling, notably that praised by Churton Collins, in which Christ addresses the sinner thus:

[1] John Shirley, several of whose commonplace-books remain to us (see p. 192 here), not only transcribed a mass of poems by Chaucer and by Lydgate, but wrote for many of his copies full "gossippy" headings, from which we draw some curious particulars. A Shirley volume in the library of Trinity College, Cambridge (R, 3, 20), has 60 entries; nine of these are by Chaucer and one by Hoccleve, five mention no author (although another Shirley MS ascribes two of them to Lydgate), nine are in Latin or French, eight are mere bits, such as proverbs or recipes, and 28 are marked as by Lydgate. This collection includes his six mummings, which are preserved nowhere else, two tapestry poems, two personal poems addressed to Gloucester, and the Coronation Address to Henry VI; the rest are religious and didactic,— 4500 lines in all. A Shirley codex in the British Museum, Adds. 16165, has 23 entries, of which eight are there assigned to Lydgate, including the Temple of Glass, the Black Knight, the Departing of Chaucer, and a New Year's poem; the total is 2600 lines, or 3200 if we accept the complaint appended to the Temple of Glass, the genuineness of which is doubted by Prof. Schick, the EETS editor of the poem. Another Shirley volume, Bodl. Ashmole 59, besides reproducing ten of the entries made in the Cambridge and in the London codices, and copying as separate poems four extracts from longer works, adds to the above list 14 poems,— 1480 lines. Four of these latter are also contained in MS Harley 2255 of the British Museum. If the tiny coat of arms in its initial means that this codex was written for William Curteys, abbot of Bury during the last twenty years of Lydgate's life (on which point see Anglia 28:24), then the authority of its ascriptions is high. The number of its entries marked as by Lydgate is 24, four of which are already in our list; among the others are the Fabula Duorum Mercatorum, the Letter to Gloucester, the legend of St. Austin at Compton, and the Testament. Most of its contents are religious, and the number of lines assigned to Lydgate is 5800.

> Tarye no longer toward thyn herytage
> Hast on thy weye and be of ryght good chere
> Go eche day onward on thy pylgrymage
> Thynke howe short tyme thou shalt abyden here
> Thy place is byggyd aboue the sterres clere
> Noon erthly palys wrought in so statly wyse
> Kome on my frend my brother most entere
> For the I offred my blood in sacryfyce

Yet other late verse by Lydgate, such as the Secrees, has no value; and other religious verse by him, when done to order, as St. Albon was done to order, can drop to a very low level, not so low as Guy of Warwick, but weakly monotonous. In Lydgate's many and respectful allusions to Chaucer he pleases us; but when he attempts to imitate the Prologue he makes a lamentable failure. If the Flower of Courtesy be his (for which we have only the word of the editor of the 1561 Chaucer) he was capable of grace and sweetness of expression on a hackneyed subject; but his epithalamium to Gloucester is a wooden piece of work. His sunrises and spring settings were not unjustly praised by Warton; compare the picture of Spring in Reson and Sensuality 101 ff., and many passages in the Troy Book (e. g. i: 1197 ff., 1271 ff., 3094 ff., 3907 ff. etc.), pictures much better and more detailed than the monk permits himself in the Fall of Princes (cf. v: 1506-11 there). In this respect, as in others, the Troy Book is the most successful of Lydgate's longer works; in vivacity, in self-expression, in knowledge of life, it is much superior to the Siege of Thebes, although it be a commissioned task and a translation. If a religious emotion be absent, and if Lydgate lacks the restraint of a compact stanzaic original, such as he had for the Dance Macabre, he easily wanders; the slender substance of his meaning dries into the sands of his fluency, and he blunders among words, unable to advance to a goal which he does not clearly see. He spoils Canace's lament by a tasteless allusion to Cupid as causer of the tragedy; he cannot let Paris relate his dream, in Priam's family council, without a pedantic explanation of the attributes of Mercury. He can no more deny himself a digression, especially a didactic one, than could Browning; but it is not Browning's pressure of bounding vitality, like that of a dog quartering a new countryside, which drives Lydgate to utterance; it is a sort of "total recall," the inability to stop until a whole series of familiar and related phrases have been not only reeled off, but repeated. This verbosity, when joined to a lack of structural sense, is disastrous; and Lydgate had little or no structural sense. He had no notion of the value of brevity, of selection among details. Indeed, his proclaimed theory is to the contrary. He says, in the prologue to the Fall of Princes, lines 92, 93, that a story "constrained under wordes fewe" is no story; see page 158 here. But Chaucer's view is the more truly psychological; cf. the Squire's Tale lines 393 ff.:—

> The knotte, why that every tale is told,
> If it be taried til that lust be cold
> Of hem that han it after herkned yore,
> The savour passeth ever lenger the more,
> For fulsomenesse of his prolixitee.

The remark of Gosse, that Lydgate appears better in selections than in wholes, means of course that the monk's inability to conceive of structure, to treat any part of his work with reference to any other part, or to get from one episode or mood to another, is disguised by the process of selection. No writer is at once so slow and so breathless as Lydgate; his discourse advances at a crawl, with constant returns upon itself, but marks time with such volubility that the reader is bewildered.

It is indeed possible to collect some handfuls of good verses from the many thousand lines which Lydgate has left, mainly from the Troy Book and the Fall of Princes. For instance :—

And saue þe eye atwen was no message DuorMerc 54 is less striking.	Troy Book ii :3718
Solitarie in captiuite	Troy Book ii :3906
For many fader schal his sone se	
Hol in þe morwe þat schal be slawe or eve	Troy Book ii :4204-5
Lat vs with swerde & nat with wordis fight	Troy Book ii :4381
Þe swerde of rancour may nat alwey bite	Troy Book ii :7028
—þe fomy wawes wyde Þat to sight whelmen vp so grene	Troy Book ii :8036-7
And al þe eyr with schot of arowis kene Ischadwed was þat Phebus bemys bright Vp on þe soille was dirked of his light	Troy Book ii :8106-8
Aforn his swerd Grekis go to wrak Cf. ii :7272, iii :1470-71	Troy Book ii :8493
Of noyse of hors þe erþe gan to tremble	Troy Book iii :1562
Or þe heuene be clustred and depeynt With brighte sterris in þe Euenynge See Chaucer's Boece iv, metr. 1, 23-4.	Troy Book iii :2680-1
Liche as þe goddis wolde haue take wrak And had of newe assentid ben in oon Þe londe to drenche of Deucalyon From the Latin of Guido.	Troy Book iii :3294-6
With swiche colour as men go to her graue See Troilus iv :862-3.	Troy Book iii :4185
Furiously walkynge vp and doun	Troy Book iii :5143
And alweye fix on hir he hadde his loke See Knight's Tale 1949.	Troy Book iv :608
And verray wery of his owne lyf See FaPrinces i :3774, iii :2825, Thebes 2518.	Troy Book iv :2386
When þe hote mery somers day	
No dwery is but like a geant longe	Troy Book iv :3390-1
Nat Cleopatra goyng to her graue	Troy Book iv :3658
For euery wo by processe muste aswage See ii :458, 4086, etc.	Troy Book iv :3702
Liche þe sonne þat shyneþ in þe reyn	Troy Book iv :5224
Pes in þe face but in þe herte werre	Troy Book iv :6132
Ther was al merthe ther was al melodie	FaPrinces i : :593
Al worldli welthe shal fadyn as a rose	FaPrinces i :942
God hath a thousand handes to chastise (etc.) From Laurent's French.	FaPrinces i :1331 ff.

She may be troublid but ouercome neuere	FaPrinces i:1366
On to the deth he felte his herte colde	FaPrinces i:4480
Cf. Chaucer, MLTale 781, etc., Troy Book i:2050, iii:4546, v:3123, etc.	
Fame in her paleis hath trumpes mo than oon	FaPrinces i:5111
Oon bet the bussh another hath the sparwe	FaPrinces i:5127
The sterrid heuene is thi couerture	FaPrinces i:6161
Go foorth my soule peur & inmortal	FaPrinces ii:1310
From Coluccio's Latin, see ModPhil 25:56.	
Now heer now ther as botis hom to londe	FaPrinces iii:1321
Sum drope of pite lat in thyn herte fleete	FaPrinces iii:2040
For comparisouns doon ofte gret greuaunce	FaPrinces iii:2188
See HorseGooseSheep 526.	
The wise war the circumspect goddesse	FaPrinces iii:4237
Vnder that dirked and cloudi orizonte	FaPrinces iii:4345
Al for the werre & nothyng for the pees	FaPrinces iv:1817
See Troy Book ii:3319.	
Than gaff he sentence & theron he abood	FaPrinces v:455
Thi secre bosum is ful of stories	FaPrinces vi:309
In Laurent, "ton giron qui est tresgarny des hystoires."	
In Phebus presence sterris lese her liht	FaPrinces vi:2983
See note on FaPrinces G 36 here.	
The faire day men do praise at eue	FaPrinces ix:2024
See ModLangNotes 36:115-18.	

These are sufficiently striking. But it is to be remembered, first, that most rimesters can show a good line or two; John Hamilton Reynolds or Leigh Hunt has occasionally a verse or a bit of observation which reminds us that they were indeed contemporaries and friends of Keats. And secondly, these extracts or twice their number make hardly a ripple in the ocean of Lydgate's 140,000 and more lines, lines not only thin in substance but clogged with formulae. We dredge up such a bit as Achilles' plaint of his love for Polyxena, Troy Book iv: 707-8,—

> Or how shal I ben hardy to apere
> In the presence of hir eyen clere,—

and it is an excellence. In the text, however, it immediately follows,

> For how shuld I be bold to haue repaire
> Or dorn, allas, comen in hir sight.

That is, Lydgate's habit of repetition is constant, his power of expression easily overborne; and the linking of the happier couplet to the weaker injures the effect of the whole. The monk's habit of padding, too, is injurious. He has memory and appreciation enough to quote his great master; but when we find "For pitee renneth sone in gentil herte" appearing in the form

> For pite, who that kan aduerte,
> Renneth sone in gentyl herte,—   ResonandSens 6915-6

we recognize not only the merit of the attempt at citation, but the clumsiness of the formula which splits it.[1] And similarly with the monk's allusions to nature. They are often apparently fortunate; but we cannot with certainty praise, e.g., his feeling for the lark, and add to our list such a bit as

> ——til the larke song
> With notes newe hegh vp in þe ayr,   Thebes 2296-7

because in the Troy Book Lydgate so frequently uses the lark's song mechanically, to date the beginning of a battle. We cannot tell, in his work, when his imagination is perhaps for a moment free and when he is using a formula which by accident shapes into a "sport." And however interesting this list of detached lines, the sunrise and spring-descriptions of the Troy Book, the allusions to Chaucer, the feeling for little children, the monk's real lyrical adoration of his crucified Master, these passages are constantly damaged by his bad stylistic habits, and lost in the flood of his uncontrollable verbiage. Neither in structural power, descriptive power, emotional power, nor metrical power, is there any real parallel between Lydgate and his great exemplar Chaucer. His verbosity and his habit of repetition are superficial faults, but none the less displeasing; and deeper-seated than they are the monk's lack of feeling for structure and proportion, his dulness of perception. Lydgate's material overpowers him; he is the creature of routine phrase; and his deficiencies in sensitiveness, in control, in balance, are as evident in his versification as in his guidance of narrative. There also are the automatic repetition, the jerky hesitation, the failure to see the part in relation to the whole, which are stamped on his story-method.

But Lydgate's versification has been seriously and carefully discussed. Professor Schick, the first critical editor of a Lydgate-text, adopted for the pentameter line of the Temple of Glass (EETS 1891) five principal forms or types, which he differentiated according to the number of their syllables. His type 1 is regular, of five iambs; type 2 is like the preceding, but with an extra syllable at the verse-pause; type 3, the "Lydgate line," or brokenbacked line, lacks an unaccented syllable at the pause; type 4, the headless line, lacks the opening unaccented syllable; and type 5 has a trisyllabic first foot.

This classification takes account only of the syllabic compass of the single verse; it makes no mention of variety in rhythmic flow within the line, of the lengthening or shortening of the poetic phrase around the line-unit, of the line as part of the poetic paragraph, or of the relation between line-and-paragraph rhythm and poetic content. By discussing minutely the number of syllables, it creates the impression that Lydgate's versification has been analyzed; whereas everything important to rhythm has been passed over unnoticed. Professor Schick has no thought of rescuing Lydgate from censure by thus narrowing the scope of analysis; he speaks with emphasis of Lydgate's metrical shortcomings. But later students, still limiting themselves to the single line, have attempted to condone those shortcomings. In a monograph on the metric of the Chaucerian Tradition, published in 1910, Dr. Licklider treated the question more historically

---

[1] Chaucer often enough inserts a formula, for rime's sake, into a couplet; cf. for example BoDuchess 1065, 1119, the prol. LGW 454, and especially Troilus v: 1040-41. But nearly always in Chaucer the vigor, the moving force of his matter, carries us over such bare patches; while in Lydgate there is not sufficient impetus in the context to prevent the dead halt.

than did Professor Schick, with the aim of justifying, e.g., Lydgate's line-structure by that of modern poets.   Dr. Licklider assumes, to begin with, that the stresses of verse are fixed, that they invariably fall upon the syllables which schematically come under them, whether such syllables be verbs or indefinite articles.   Should a preposition thus appear under ictus, it is raised in value by "pitch-accent," and the effect of the line is heightened by this ennobling of its grammatically less dignified elements.   In such a verse, for example, as Milton's

Deep malice *to* conceal, couch *with* revenge,

the italicized words are raised to higher power by their position under stress; and any line in Lydgate, in the Transition, in later English poetry, which shows this "pitch accent on relational words" acquires value thereby.

This view of English pentameter line-structure is not here accepted.   It is obvious that the single line shows, in both modern and medieval English verse, a frequent coincidence of theoretic stress with unimportant syllable; but instead of explaining this coincidence, in any poet, as a heightening of word-value by the impact of immutable stress, I shall treat the line and the paragraph as plastic, subject at every moment to the shaping hand of the poet; I shall recognize, as already stated (p. 19), the "perpetual conflict" of the verse-norm and of language-freedom as the living foundation of English verse.   The line from Milton, above cited, I explain by the poet's shift of word-weight within the verse; a heavy first foot, a light second, a reversed fourth, challenge the reader's ear by their divergence from standard as regards the massing of stress, while the total weight of the line remains standard.   Chaucer, in his handling of rhythm, shows the same desire to vary it, now to reduce and now to increase line-weight, now to reduce and now to increase breath-length, to make up a paragraph out of slightly differing lines, that the greatest modern poets have shown.   He has not their subtleties of ear, their developed sense of balance within the single verse; such compensation, or poise of the heavy against the light foot, as that of Milton just noted, is not Chaucerian.   But the simpler variants of tetrameter and pentameter flow, underweighting and reversal, are very freely used by Chaucer, and with increasing skill as he grows older.   He also made, at first, extensive use of the line short a syllable at opening, a variant frequent in his Hous of Fame.   In that poem (using Skeat's text) we find not only very many single headless lines, but such lines grouped in pairs, occasionally in threes, and once in a sequence of four.   But in Chaucer's pentameter, so far as we can now judge, this lavishly-employed license of the short couplet becomes a minor variant; Skeat's text of the General Prologue has but nine acephalous lines, and the two pairs of such verses in the D-fragment, the two in the Knight's Tale, ser e for especial emphasis or for enumeration.

Chaucer's treatment of the line in this respect was not understood by Lydgate, who not only wrote the acephalous verse very freely in pentameter, but made as much or more use of another truncated line-form, that lacking an unaccented syllable just after the verse-pause.[1]   It looks as if the monk thought in half-lines, and, having accepted a line-form headless in the first half, saw no reason why the second half also should not be headless.   The existence of this

---

[1] How in manhod he was peréles   FaPrinces iii :3617 (headless)
Nor allë men may nat been iliche   FaPrinces i :5120 (brokenbacked)

brokenbacked line in Chaucer is still questionable; even the poorest Chaucer MSS show no drift to the type, and no evidence has yet been presented to prove that the dropping of inflexional -e would bring such a line into being oftener, e.g., than lines short in the fourth foot.   Moreover, the mind which would lay hold of lines accidentally shortened at the cesura by the scribe and erect them into a type is a mind already thinking, as I have said, in half-lines.   Lydgate's difference from other Transition versifiers in his use of these two truncated pentameter-forms is another reason for seeking their explanation in his individuality. The headless line was not written by Gower; it was not used by Hoccleve to any extent; it was not written by the scrupulous scribe of the Palladius; it is not common in later Transition verse.   We can find it in late sixteenth-century prints, for instance in The Flower and the Leaf; but there the textual conditions have become too complicated to serve as evidence.   So far as we yet see, the use of these two truncated line-forms centralizes in Lydgate, and in Chaucer there seems clear sanction for but one of them, the headless line.

An explanation of Lydgate's procedure has been variously but unsatisfactorily sought.   The fall of inflexional -e, as I have studied it in a small number of texts, produces lines clumsy in many ways, but not predominantly headless or brokenbacked; and there remain outside its influence a large number of truncated lines in Lydgate, and in Lydgate alone.   If the influence of the Old English alliterative verse, with its sharp medial break, was strong enough to develop the brokenbacked line in Lydgate, why not in other poets?   That Chaucer's truncated line-form should be taken up, and extended, by Lydgate and by Lydgate alone, of a group of versifiers using a common language and sharing a common history, argues some quality of difference in Lydgate himself.

That quality I see most clearly not in his adoption of the truncated line but in his excessive use of it and in his extension of truncation to the second half-line.   As regards the headless line which he could find in Chaucer, a man so prone to repetition as was Lydgate, so devoid of sensitiveness, of balance, and of feeling for variety as his narrative-wanderings and his continual formulae show him to have been, would not discriminate between Chaucer's use of a variant and his own mass-manufacture of a staple.   As regards the brokenbacked line, which is not Chaucer's, the student who works through a quantity of Lydgate's verse with an ear alert to its phrasing will recognize that the half-line is the favored breath-length, and that the great number of padding phrases filling just half a line either supports or helps cause this tendency.   If the monk felt his verse more in half-lines than in lines, the extent to which he uses the brokenbacked line may be due to that limitation in him rather than to his transference of it as a whole line from any source, Latin or English.

His excess of these truncated lines, his excess of padding phrases, find their explanation together in his lack of structural and aesthetic feeling.   Some part of them may be due to the rate at which he was compelled to produce; but that it was natural to him to repeat himself is as obvious as that he thereby gave no offence to the taste of his contemporaries.   Any man who carries repetition to the extent to which Lydgate carried it is a man in all respects insensitive, a man not quick nor clear of sight, not alive to the way character reveals itself in trivial action, dull of ear, deficient in taste, unaware of that "perpetual conflict" between language and rhythm which, though not formulated by Chaucer in theory, is revealed in his practice.   Such a man, because he lacks perceptual power, lacks therefore a plan; he repeats or dilutes himself because he is unclear about his next step; he knows that his story has an ending and has certain high points, but how to get from one to another, or how to make those points stand out, he knows not; yet he keeps talking. Lydgate's incompetences in rhythm, in style, in narrative-management, cannot be exemplified in a brief essay. The analysis of many passages parallel to Chaucer, will show us, so far as rhythm is concerned, that Lydgate habitually writes less than half his lines iambic-normal, Chaucer a full half or more; it will show Lydgate's constant use of the truncated line and Chaucer's decreasing use of it as time goes on; it will show that Lydgate treats Chaucer's rhythmic "easements" as if they were "staples," to borrow terms from Professor Saintsbury. The student of narrative can take the opening paragraph of the Siege of Thebes and compare it with Chaucer's mode of starting the Canterbury Tales; he can parallelize Chaucer's clear completion of his twice-repeated *Whan* by *Than,* his gradual narrowing of the reader's interest to focus on Canterbury, with Lydgate's helpless and verbless wanderings; he can examine the same Chaucerian passage beside Troy Book i:1197-1221 as regards the arrangement of line-types in a paragraph. And he will find the same man, whether rhythm, style, or narrative management be the angle of observation; a man floating in a tide of material which he cannot guide, check, or see. Lists of parallel passages, lists of line-types, do not show the differences between Lydgate and his master; they cannot make clear, for example, that a variant line may be pleasing or unpleasing according to its context and content; that the final thing in judging rhythm is not the rhythm itself but the union of rhythm and contained meaning.

Thus, in Chaucer's description of his Knight there occurs, lines 75-6, the following:

> Of fustian he wered a gipoun
> Al bismotered with his habergeoun.

Were this couplet analyzed rhythmically, the stressed *a* of the one line, the lack of upbeat to the other, would be rated as harsh, and the lines placed among aberrant types. But in the masterful flow of the Prologue they are carried with no sense of the disagreeable. For there we come upon them after the narrator has proved his power. We may have been but partially conscious of the strong sweep of the opening paragraph; we may not have noticed the effect of lengthened breath and of reversal in

> That fro the tyme that he first began
> To ryden out, he loved chyvalrye,
> Trouthe and honour, fredom and curteisye;

but we have been influenced by them, and by the roll of sounding place-names, names as proudly and deliberately trumpeted as Milton's or Moody's similar summons to the imagination. In such context, after such prelude, the single line of less rhythmical quality passes current. And as the context carries these, so does the content carry the third of the lines just quoted. There is an almost identical structure present in either of these verses:—

> ffourme and colour merite and beaute   Palladius iv:808
> Pees and quyete / concord and vnyte   Thebes 4703

But Palladius' enumeration of the points of a horse, Lydgate's generalized and overlapping terms, have none of Chaucer's stirring emphasis on the essential qualities of knighthood, an emphasis which for the moment raises the pitch of life.

Yet Lydgate has interest and value for the student. Historically, he sums up his age as definitely as did Pope or Dr. Johnson; technically his importance may be a negative one, but in his choice of verse-forms and subjects he is noteworthy; and his vocabulary is his most permanent and positive contribution to English. Among his verse-forms the pentameter seven-line stanza bulks largest, because of the Fall of Princes, the Life of Our Lady, and St. Edmund, which together run to over 45,000 of his ca.55,000 such lines. But the pentameter couplet, as in the Troy Book, Thebes, and three shorter poems, amounts to over 35,000 lines, the four-beat couplet to 32,000, for almost 25,000 of which the Pilgrimage accounts. The eight-line pentameter stanza is used for many of Lydgate's short religious poems; and as he may have had a freer hand there than in his long commissioned works, the stanza was perhaps more to his taste than it was to Chaucer's. Other verse-forms are few in the monk's work. One or two attempts at a roundel, a New Year's poem in threes, and an occasional shift of form within a poem, represent Lydgate's range. The Testament is in sevens and eights, the Temple of Glass in rime royal and couplet; the prologues to poems, as in St. Edmund, St. Albon, and the Pilgrimage, are sometimes in a form other than that of the poem itself. In all this we cannot trace any conscious adaptation of form to subject; the pentameter couplet is used for the Troy Book and also for the Mumming at Hertford, the seven-line stanza for both comedy and tragedy; the eight-line stanza, although apparently preferred for the shorter religious poems, is also used for the Letter to Gloucester and for Horns Away.

In choice of theme Lydgate has done some service to English. He introduced, it seems, the first bit of that Fool-literature which was carried so much further by Barclay under Brant's—or rather Locher's—influence; he brought in the Dance of Death motive; he wrote a few clumsy mummings which are apparently the first of their type in our literature; he set moving in English a pageant of "tragedies" which endured until the time of Shakespeare. None of his innovations had in it the germ of long life, but they count for something in our literary history.

It is Lydgate's services to the language which are both noteworthy and permanent. His is not the use of words at their full metaphorical power, which is one of the dangerous joys of the Romantic poet. No closepacked phrases, no epithets rich in imaginative thrill, have to be unfolded and tasted by the mind as we read him. His value is for the lexicographer. Although archaic and recondite terms do appear in his pages,—*amate, avale, blive, enose, fage, queme, suppowaile, ure,*—and although he unsuccessfully endeavors to obtain currency for *flaskisable* and *tarage*, a very large number of useful words make their first appearance in English under his auspices. For example:[1]—*abuse, adjacent, adolescence, aggregate*, arable*, attempt*, auburn, avaricious*, capacity*, circumspect, colic*, combine*, commodious, condign, confidence, conspirator, countermand, credulity*, criminal, debar, deception, delude*, depend*, detestable*, dial, disappear*, dislodge*, dismay*, duplicity, entitle*, equivalent*, excel, fallible, fraternal*, fraudulent, gallery*, gentlemanly, grandmother, humidity*, immutable, impregnable, incident, incredible, inexcusable*, infallible*, intermission*, interrupt, invincible, irrigate*, magnate, massive, musical, passionate*, paternal*, persuade*, pirate, powerless*, pretence*, provoke, rural, solicitude*, tedious*, ter-*

---

[1] Words marked with an asterisk are used by Lydgate earlier than the first case recorded in the New English Dictionary; and the list could be much extended.

rible*, timorous*, tolerance, transcend*, unoccupied*. Many of these are used repeatedly in the Troy Book and in the Fall of Princes, the *-ble* and *-ent* words often in rime. In a few cases we can see the word making the crossing from Laurent's French, e.g., *adolescence, magnate;* and the word *inexcusable,* standing at the head of the second chapter of Romans, may have caught Lydgate's eye there; for he, like Isidore and many another medieval rhetorician, was very much aware of language in the dictionary-sense. As one works with the New English Dictionary, it is noticeable how often the three principal fifteenth-century translators, Trevisa, Lydgate, and Caxton, are responsible for the introduction of abstract but useful terms, for the development of the power to express shades of thought.

Lydgate not only brings into English these convenient polysyllables, he makes a word familiar by repetition, often by repetition in rime or in formula. His padding-formulae are one of the most characteristic features of his style, and therefore especially revelatory of the man. Their abuse by him is precisely parallel to his abuse of the headless line; he found both in Chaucer, and employed neither in Chaucer's manner.

Chaucer used formulae all through his work, for the sake of rime; within about 400 lines of the Knight's Tale (264-676) we find *out of doute* 283, *I dar wel seyn* 293. *as olde bokes seyn* 340, 605, *sothly to telle* 341, 676, *pleynly for tendyte* 351; these are all handy tools for Lydgate. We find also the halfline *ther nis namor to seye* (264) a filler used by Lydgate a score of times in the Troy Book; we find in line 617 *as faste as euere he may*, which is worked by Lydgate, in the form *in al the haste he may*, another score of times in the same poem. All the lines and phrases of expedited narrative, so abundant in Lydgate, he could find in Chaucer; see this same KnTale passage, lines 330, 332, 343, 500, 522, 559. Chaucer uses as first half-line the phrase *This al and som,* cf. PoFoules 650, WBprol 91; Lydgate does the same thing ten or twelve times in the Troy Book.

But the medium in which Chaucer's padding formulae and expletives are carried is of so firm and flavored a quality that our attention is not diverted by them. They are not only less frequent than in Lydgate, but often seem formulae only when we have disengaged them from their context. Lydgate, however, does with these rime-tags as with his headless and brokenbacked lines; they are aggressive in number, aggressively defined against a slack and ineffective background, and emphatic of a half-line movement of thought. That the monk turned consciously and continually to line-tags is shown by his use of padding in the first half-line as well as in the second; e.g., *Withoute mor, Withoute abood,—* which occur some fifty times in the Troy Book. The pages of that poem are also sprinkled with colorless expletives such at *platly, pleynly, in soth, sothly,* used in mid-line; and the emptiness of these words and phrases to Lydgate's mind is shown by the way he redoubles them. He writes *in al the haste he may:—withoute mor delay,* as consecutive riming half-lines, Troy Book i:3993-4, ii:7917-18, 8329-30; he repeats his meaning as *shortly and make no delay* ii:1918-19 (see iv:1888); he more than doubles on himself in ii:8556, *Anon forthwith and make no delay*. With this last we may compare his frequent repetitions such as:—

> That he constreyned right of verray nede
> Compelled was iustly to procede
> To han redres only by rigour.   Troy Book ii:1773-5

See also the same poem i:3489-93, ii:2098-2100, 3761-3, iii:1231-36, 1541-3, 1677-78, 3538, iv:153-56, 258-59, 5051-55. Of the same character are his lengthened repetitions in the Fall of Princes, e.g., i:1898 ff. and 1905 ff., where Cadmus' prayer to Apollo is twice given in two consecutive stanzas.

Perhaps for this last Lydgate might see a precedent in passages like Chaucer's Clerk's Tale 410 ff. or Franklin's Tale 337-40. He might consider that his use of *pleynly eke withal,* Troy Book ii:949, or of *ouermore platly eke* (*ibid.* v:2475), was justified by Chaucer's *And eke also,* e.g., HoFame 178;[1] certainly the pupil uses the last-named reduplication often enough,—ten or fifteen times in the Troy Book alone. But whether he was following Chaucer or following a general rhetorical license, Lydgate was by nature prone to repetition and insensitive to its effect. No man with a feeling for style would have written the number of ill-fitting rime-tags which we find in the Troy Book; cf. prol. 101-2, i:95-6, 669-70, 3081-82 and iii:2757, ii:2155-56, 2785-86, 2789-90, 5179-80, 7809-10 and v:2101-2, etc. Probably neither Lydgate nor his readers saw any more incongruity in his Trojan heroes' bidding each other farewell "with St. John to borrow," Troy Book i:3082, iii:2757, than Lydgate saw in Chaucer's use of the phrase, Compleynt of Mars, line 9. But other formulae of this brief selection are more obviously inappropriate. The appearance of Achilles' name in rime, in line 96 of Troy Book i, calls out *platly this no les* as a balancing tag; the use of *wordes softe,* ii:2786, drives Lydgate to *lowe and nat alofte* to fill his couplet. The *eyen clere* or *eyen glade* of Trojan women are used more than once in padding phrases, for which Chaucer's Troilus iv:663 may have been authorization; and the formula *for sour or swete* appears three times in the poem, *for sote or sour* twice, *by south and not by east* once. This last, v:2102, is an exception to Lydgate's usual procedure in couplet, which is to put his clumsy padding in the earlier of the two lines. In his stanza-work, especially in the Fall of Princes, the padding phrase occurs anywhere and everywhere; some stanzas have as many as three half-line formulae, while tags filling an entire line I have not attempted to catalogue. Schick said of Lydgate that "his rime is in general pure, and skilfully handled." That the bulk of the monk's work is accurately rimed no student denies; but correctness is not skill, and such pairs as *multitude: platly to conclude, commendable: platly this no fable,* such formulae as are above exemplified, are too frequent in Lydgate for us to term him "skilful" in rime-management.

As all readers know, Chaucer made free use of rime-tags; and it is easy to believe that Lydgate imitated him in this respect as he did in the use of the acephalous line, exaggerating both, driven partly by the pressure of compulsory translation to abuse of both. But it is not clear that Lydgate found Chaucerian precedent for some of his licenses in rime, for his fairly frequent assonances and for his riming of *Troye:weye* (*woye*) fourteen times in the Troy Book. In that same poem alone there are fifteen cases of assonance, nearly all of them on *-ape:-ake.* The one definite case in Chaucer, Troilus ii:884-6, is on *-yke:-yte;* but this is surely insufficient to establish for Lydgate his right to a license which he uses from the Black Knight to the Secrees, all through his work.

The great number of "Chaucerian" formulae adopted by Lydgate would in itself lead a student to argue Chaucer's influence on the monk; but his imitations and borrowings of Chaucerian material and his frequent allusions to his "master"

---

[1] Or by "And ferther over now ayenward yit", Troilus iv: 1027, which represents Boethius' "atque e converso rursus."

are proof positive. The detailed story of Lydgate's dependence on Chaucer is still to be written; and in appraising the facts we have to bear in mind several aspects of medieval literature. The regulation tone of humility towards patron or master must be remembered; the tone of Lydgate towards Chaucer must be compared with that which he uses toward Guido or Boccaccio; the tone of Hoccleve, of the Palladius-translator, etc., must be paralleled with that of Lydgate. It is fairly easy to differentiate the three men's attitude to Humphrey of Gloucester, for instance. The slightness and formality of Hoccleve's connection with him, the conventional pomposity of most of Lydgate's allusions and the sudden warmth of his personal gratitude for money-gifts, the odd little glimpses of Humphrey in the Palladius-epilogues and the translator's sycophantic address of his patron (i:1194) as—

> But God me semeth best thou mayst resemble
> ffor verite Iustice and mansuetude,

are differences which mean degrees in the nearness of the three writers to the duke, and differences in their usage of stereotyped forms. In the attitude of Chaucer's two pupils toward him there is much more resemblance in tone, although Hoccleve's three allusions in the De Regimine—his only mentions of his master— have a warmth of personal affection and grief not to be found in Lydgate's many passages of praise. It is to be noted, as regards the amount of allusion by the two pupils, that most of Lydgate's are in long poems parallelizing work by Chaucer, such as the Siege of Thebes, the Troy Book, and the Fall of Princes; that Hoccleve's short religious and occasional compositions afforded no such opportunity for mention of the elder poet as did his one long poem, the De Regimine, in which the allusions appear. Also we remark that both this poem and Lydgate's Troy Book were executed for Henry the Fifth; since Hoccleve did not hesitate to insert a picture of Chaucer into his poem, is it not a fair surmise that Henry professed interest in Chaucer and favored allusion to him?

The Siege of Thebes, written as it was to supplement the Canterbury Tales, is naturally dependent on Chaucer. The prologue is an inept imitation of Chaucer's; the story narrates in detail the events which Chaucer had summarized in a few lines of the Knight's Tale. The poem entire is therefore a homage to the elder writer, and so far as we yet know a homage paid on the monk's own initiative. That it was written with the Knight's Tale near Lydgate's hand is evident from the crowding of Chaucer-phrases between Thebes 4480 and 4540; but that the Canterbury Tales-prologue was not so consulted for the Thebes-prologue is arguable from the lack of such direct liftings and from Lydgate's confusion of the Pardoner and the Summoner. With the Troy Book and the Fall of Princes, frequent as are allusions to Chaucer, we cannot be sure that Henry the Fifth and Gloucester, the monk's patrons, are not as much in his mind. The passages about women, in both poems, are as obviously attuned to the patron's ear as are the laudatory prologues and epilogues; the emphasis in the Troy Book on armor, on heraldic device, on methods of warfare and of encampment, is planned for the taste of King Henry just as the dissertations on literature in the Fall of Princes are adapted to Gloucester. For instance, in the latter work, Lydgate prefixes to its fourth book a long discourse in praise of writing and writers; he takes some of his generalities from John of Salisbury, but the particular cases, I would suggest, are derived from Gloucester's own library.[1] For in the catalogue of books given by Humphrey to Oxford a few years later are included not only John of Salisbury's Polycraticus and many of the Latin classics, but a Librum Dantes, a Commentaria Dantes, and many volumes of Petrarch; while in this prologue are discussed the Latin works of Petrarch and the writings of Virgil and of Cicero, with a meager but interesting allusion to Dante's Commedia.[2] I would think it possible that Lydgate was here aiming at his patron's taste, perhaps obeying that patron's command. In any case, the opinion of the patron has to be considered in estimating the allusions to Chaucer which are made by Hoccleve and by Lydgate.

Some of the briefer mentions of Chaucer in the Fall of Princes arise from the context. Among the unfortunates in Boccaccio's long procession are several included by Chaucer in the Legend of Good Women, the Monk's Tale, and the Doctor's Tale;—Lucretia, Philomena, Dido, Virginia, Cleopatra, Caesar, Nero, Zenobia, Ugolino. Lydgate's approach to these various tragedies differs. For Philomena (i:1786 ff.) and for Antony and Cleopatra (vi:3620 ff.) he declares that

> Thyng onys said be labour of Chauceer
> Wer presumpcioun me to make ageyn,

and sends his readers to the "legende of martirs off Cupide." For the story of Zenobia (viii:666 ff.) Lydgate says that because Chaucer has "compendiousli told al," he will pass it over; he devotes, however, some sixty lines to her. When he is dealing with Caesar's fall (vi:2815 ff.), with Nero (vii:600 ff.), with Dido (ii:1898 ff.), and with Virginia (ii:1345 ff.), we hear nothing of Chaucer. In his two introductions of Lucretia (ii:1002 ff., iii:960 ff.), the second only follows Laurent's French; the former, suggested by Laurent's mention of Junius Brutus, in a list of high-couraged men, as Lucretia's avenger on Tarquin, is accompanied by Lydgate's refusal to tell her story because Chaucer has already done so; but this refusal is set aside at Gloucester's command, and we have 43 stanzas of Lucrece's farewell speech, taken, as Lydgate states, from Collucius, i.e., from a "declamation" by Coluccio Salutati.[3] The scanty five lines given to Ugolino (ix:2049 ff.), not only make no mention of Chaucer but close with the remark "no mor of him I fynde"; and the elaborate treatment of the Canace-story condemned by Chaucer carries no explanation of Lydgate's reason for so doing.

This variation in Lydgate's treatment of Chaucer is paralleled by variation in the monk's method of quoting his "master." There are clumsinesses enough in

---

[1] This suggestion derives support from the allusion to Dante and to Petrarch found in book iii:3858-9, in a short begging-letter chapter not preserved by all MSS, and perhaps worked by scribes into the portion of the text with which it had been sent to Gloucester. Note also the two fragments of Greek, ii:1855 and iv:568, not in Laurent's French, with the copy of "Verba Graeca et interpretationes linguae Latinae" given to Oxford in 1443 by Humphrey with the Dante and the Petrarch books above mentioned. See Anstey's Munimenta Academica, pp. 768-772, and see note below on the Lucrece-tragedy.

[2] Writyng causeth the chaplet to be greene
Bothe of Esope and of Iuuenal
Dantis labour it doth also meynteene
By a report verray celestial
Sunge amonge Lombardis in especial
Whos thre bookis the grete wondres tell
Of heuene aboue of purgatorie & hell.   iv:134-140

[3] See my paper in Modern Philology 25:49-57.

Lydgate on occasion; it might be said that a man who renders line 80 of the Venus—

> Sith ryme in English hath swich scarsitee

in the two forms—

Syth þat in ryme ynglysch hath skarsete	Troy Book ii :168,
Seyn how that Ynglyssh in ryme hath skarsete	FaPrinces ix :3312,

is too careless and too obtuse to be considered a true admirer of Chaucer; it might be said that a man who (in Horns Away) confuses Alanus' description of Nature and Chaucer's description of Venus is no reader of the Parlement of Foules. Nevertheless, there are elsewhere in Lydgate, especially in the Black Knight, very faithful echoes of the Parlement; and at any moment in Lydgate there appear such phrases as "woful Myrrha," "vois memoriall," "hateful harm," "peple vnsad and euer vntrewe," "pres hath envie," "thoroughfare of woo,"— which must mean that reminiscences of his master's text came easily and naturally into Lydgate's memory. Considering this, and considering longer passages such as FaPrinces iv :2955-56 or St. Albon iii :457 ff., we can hardly assert that Lydgate's knowledge of Chaucer was superficial. We may find fault with Mr. Chesterton for talking of the "rescue of Miss Lammle," and point out that he has confused poor futile little Georgiana Podsnap with the designing Lammle-couple who tried to entrap her; but we should not be justified in saying that Mr. Chesterton has thus demonstrated his ignorance of Dickens. The present question resolves itself into a weighing of quantity against quality; and so far as I can now see, the amount of Lydgate's conscious and unconscious citation of Chaucer is great enough to prove his industrious reading of the elder poet.[1]

Classical authors have indeed exerted small influence on Lydgate's text, with the noteworthy exception of Ovid,—the more noteworthy because the Bury St. Edmunds library, although rich for its time in classics, contained apparently no Ovid. Their influence, or that of any writer on Lydgate, may be considered under one of four categories:—his translation of an entire work, his insertion of a long borrowed passage, his adoption of details from a classic into a work derived mainly from other sources, the recurrence all through his productivity of phrasal echoes. It is this last, as we have just seen, which clearly proves the power of Chaucer over Lydgate; taken in conjunction with the continual use of Chaucerian rime-tags and the steady abuse of a specifically Chaucerian line-type, it shows the pressure of Chaucer on a mind imitative, repetitive, careless, but none the less honestly admiring. No classical writer exerts any such influence on Lydgate.

There is only one classical writer, indeed, who can be said to exert any influence on Lydgate,—Ovid. Other writers of the ancient world are names or nearly names, especially the Greeks. Homer is for Lydgate, as for Chaucer, the honeymouthed father of song and the too-partial champion of Achilles; Plato holds the key "of dyvyn Ideie"; Euripides and Demosthenes are mentioned in dependence on Laurent's French; Aristotle, except in the pseudo-Aristotelian

---

[1] Lydgate's statement, FaPrinces, i :6452, that Samson's hair was cut by Dalila diverges from Judges xvi :17, where she "vocavit tonsorem," toward Chaucer's indefinite phrase in MoTale 77 that she "made to clippe" the sleeper's hair. Also note how the account of the Broche of Thebes, FaPrinces i :324-5, is influenced by Chaucer's Mars 245-50.

letter to Alexander, is as much a name as is Homer. Of the Latins, Virgil is less poet and more sorcerer to Lydgate than to Chaucer; Horace is unknown, as he was to Chaucer; Livy and Juvenal are names, as is Persius; Statius is nominal authority for the Theban story, but was probably no more used at first hand than was Boccaccio for the Fall of Princes. The subjects of several of Seneca's tragedies are known to Lydgate, and as moralist he is also often mentioned, but not so often as is Cicero ("Tullius"), from whom, however, but one (?) passage is quoted. Ovid only, of the classics, has to any degree passed into the fabric of Lydgate's work. He is frequently mentioned in the Fall of Princes, contrary to the practice of Lydgate's French source; and not only are Laurent's mythological narratives sometimes altered to follow the Metamorphoses, but Ovid's lines are on occasion translated and interwoven with the English.

It should be emphasized that all this happens in the Fall of Princes, and that the less conventional of Lydgate's classical allusions are nearly all to be found there. Not only is the list of Chaucer's work in that poem, but lists of the writings of Virgil, Cicero, Petrarch, etc., and whatever Lydgate knows about Dante. The prologues and epilogues to other poems, e.g., St. Edmund, and one of Lydgate's mummings, are liberally seasoned with a mixture of Helicon, Clio, Aurora, Polyphemus, Socrates, Tullius, Homer, and Atropos, but in an entirely lifeless and routine-fashion. The Fall of Princes allusions have some slender vitality in them, and for that vitality, I believe, Humphrey of Gloucester was largely responsible. The heavy task which he assigned to his protégé did indeed crush Lydgate's verse and style to worse than a dead level much of the time; but it was Gloucester who ordered Lydgate to read and use Coluccio Salutati, Gloucester who spurred Lydgate to talk about literature occasionally instead of about morality all the time, Gloucester for whom the attempts at humor were constructed, Gloucester whose library included both Petrarch and Dante. The interpolations from Salutati and from John of Salisbury in the Fall of Princes, the prologue to book iv with its catalogues, are of no literary value; but they are of a better substance than is the interpolation about false gods, in Troy Book ii, from Isidor. Lydgate's knowledge of Petrarch or of Dante was infinitesimal, but that a cloistered monk of his time should have that minute particle is of interest.

We cannot, it is true, understand why Lydgate should know so little of Dante and of Boethius, when he found their names so clearly-cut in Chaucer. Occasionally we think we hear a Dante-echo in him; the lines Troy Book iv:3014 ff. run much as does the "Taccia Lucan omai" of Inferno 25:94 ff.; but the contact is with Chaucer's MerchTale 488 ff. The most famous of all Dante-passages, paraphrased by Tennyson as "A sorrow's crown of sorrow is remembering happier things," comes to mind when we find in FaPrinces i:645-6,—

> For thilke sorwe surmountith euery sorwe
> Which next folwith afftir felicite,—

but Lydgate derives proximately from Chaucer's Troilus iii:1625-28, ultimately from the De Consolatione ii, prose 4. Of his several repetitions of the thought, FaPrinces i:3529-30, iii:722-24, iv:2308-10, only the second has the notion of remembrance as in Chaucer and in Dante; yet Lydgate's direct dependence upon Boethius is less likely than inexactness of Chaucer-memory on his part. For his knowledge of Boethius, except for one translated bit, is surprisingly small and colorless; see p. 185 here.

Other reading by Lydgate shows itself hardly more than in his following of a prescribed source, be it saint's life, Dance of Death, or Guido delle Colonne's Trojan story. There is one mention of Gower (FaPrinces ix:3410), but the allusion is only a citation from Chaucer; and although Macaulay has pointed out that the Glasgow MS of the Confessio Amantis is supposed to have come from the Bury library, the only hint of Lydgate's Gower-knowledge is his telling of the Canace-story. Hampole has just a mention. We do not here discuss Lydgate's Biblical knowledge, or his use of Josephus; but his reading of English writers outside Chaucer, or of any classical writer outside Ovid, is not proved. The extent of his acquaintance with such medieval writers as Fulgentius, John of Salisbury, or Isidor of Seville, is not yet investigated; his interpolation from Isidor into the Troy Book, and his other mentions of the Spanish encyclopedist, have especial interest when we recall the copy of Isidor's Synonyma in the Bodleian Library, MS Laud Misc. 233, on the last leaf of which is written "Sciant presentes ac futuri quod ego Iohannis Lydgate," and on the first leaf "Liber monachorum sancti Edmundi."

The use which Lydgate makes of his reading is mechanical, and he is always the ecclesiastic. He censures the vices of his time as a Churchman censures, not with desire to cleanse society for society's sake, but with desire that society shall submit to the Church. One thing of which he feels real personal horror is dissension within the State; to that subject he returns again and again, throughout all his work; and if the prose Serpent of Division be his, to that subject he has devoted a special tractate. The quarrels of kinsmen are so often lamented by Lydgate, the recoil of a bloody deed on its perpetrator so often emphasized, that it is impossible not to connect his strong feeling in these respects with the state of his times. Yet his direct allusions to contemporary history are not many; cf. for instance FaPrinces viii:2457. And although his general political ideas were doubtless ultra-conservative, he is too vague a thinker to grasp the full meaning of some passages which he quotes. Laurent, with similar insensitiveness, had translated for the duke of Berri, in his second book, all the vehement republicanism of Boccaccio against tyrants; and although Lydgate does indeed at this point substitute a long digression on "the body politic" from ?John of Salisbury, he later (FaPrinces ix:1443-46) says, quite in Boccaccio's key,

> Philisophres and poetis eek deuise
> In ther sawes prudent and notable
> Blood of tirauntis is noble sacrefise
> To God aboue whan thei be vengable.

There is enough of this language about tyrants in the churchman John of Salisbury[1] to give the fifteenth-century mind, either aristocratic or ecclesiastical, a view of the denunciation as a formula. It assuredly never occurred either to Laurent or to Lydgate that he could arouse any indignant feeling in his patron by copying the quotation. Lydgate's own idea of the poet's duty is independently expressed in the Fall of Princes iii:3830-36; he says—

> Ther cheeff labour is vicis to repreue
> With a maner couert similitude

---

[1] See Emerton, Humanism and Tyranny, Cambridge, 1925.

And non estat with ther language greeve
Bi no rebukyng of termys dul and rude
What euer thei write on vertu ay conclude
Appeire no man in no maner wise
This thoffice of poetis that be wise.

The same mixture of tone runs all through his work. He insists on the "poraile" as the support of monarchy more than once and more than twice, but his language about the instability of the commons is the same as that of Chaucer; and his horror of a churl in power is almost as great as his horror of civil dissension, although he praises natural "gentilesse" as Chaucer had praised it. Lydgate is, in fact, too little politician or satirist to have a consistent tone.

In minor or more personal aspects, Lydgate has been praised for his tenderness toward children, for his defence of women, for his strong nature-feeling; we are told that he can be both deeply pathetic and admirably humorous, and that on occasion he can show "a stiller kind of majesty." The first-named is indeed one of his most engaging qualities; he rarely mentions a child without dwelling on its smallness, its softness, its helplessness, even its smile. He may spoil his pictures by accompanying ineptitudes, as in the Canace-letter, but his feeling is real; and on such passages, or on, e.g., the (overlong) dying speech of Polyxena in Troy Book iv:6731 ff., rests much of his claim to command of pathos. His "humor" is almost entirely bound up with his language about women; and here the longer passages are a less trustworthy guide than the shorter. In the Troy Book he frequently bewails Guido's wicked anti-feminist tongue, and follows a lengthy attack on women, translated from the Latin, by a lengthier defense and a hearty rating of his author. But more than a few touches elsewhere in the work, touches of mock courtesy or of michievous comment, show that the poet's eye was on Henry the Fifth, and that he was alert to provide entertainment for his patron. Compare for instance the meeting of Jason and Medea or of Helen and Paris; and in the Fall of Princes the monkish jocularity over Orpheus' loss of his wife, i:5825-31, or the jest as to the fewness of good women, i:1805, 2849, etc., or the line closing the description of Candalus' queen, saying that Nature, busy in augmenting her beauty, "hadde forget for to make hir trewe." In these and other sex-gibes (cf. the Mumming at Hertford, also done as aristocratic amusement) is to be found the bulk of Lydgate's attempts at humor; and these are precisely in the medieval tradition, as is the contradiction between them and the lavish praise of woman, e.g., in the Flower of Courtesy. The ecclesiastic who both worshipped the Virgin Mother and shrank from every woman as the daughter of mischief-making Eve saw no incongruity in his pictures of woman.

Lydgate's nature-pictures are also of a mixed character. They often have a sort of freshness, especially the many of the Troy Book; but they are nearly always drawn with the help of mythology and of astronomy, servants who can easily overpower a master not possessed of word-magic. Chaucer had been successful as he opened the Canterbury Tales, but Lydgate is only at times partially successful. Here, as always in his work, the edge of sensation is not keen enough to bring the blood of real expression. Very rarely do we find a happy epithet, as in "smooth rain" or the "restless stone" of Sisyphus. There are two lines in the Troy Book, iii:2746-48, which remind us of Keats's "early sobbing of the morn," just as other passages seem to have given a hint to Shakespeare.[1] There is, very infrequently, a bit of real observation, such as the description of smoking lime, Troy Book iv:5927-28, or the several allusions to leaderless sheep; and the picture of convent-robbers in St. Edmund may owe its existence to actual experience. See also the (muddled) metaphor of harrowed soil in Fa- Princes ix:691-2, and best of all the line FaPrinces iii:252, where Lydgate says to the hated figure of Poverty, wandering from door to door, "And many a dogge hath on thi staff ignawe." Laurent spoke only of "barking dogs." Dulness of sense-perception on the one hand, the weight of stereotyped formula on the other, hold down Lydgate's feeling for nature just as they hold down his nar- rative progress.

Nearly all his work is lifeless. He did fairly well in beast-fables such as the Churl and the Bird, still better in the Horse, Goose, and Sheep, but failed completely in his Aesop stories. His religious narratives, except perhaps St. Margaret, are weakly done; St. Edmund is particularly wooden, although not so hopelessly bad as the Guy of Warwick. The longer romantic narratives, al- though unsteadily handled, and heavy with repetitions, have points of interest. In one channel only, the religious lyric, did the monk find occasionally free ut- terance; passages of the Testament, especially where Lydgate imagines his Savior as addressing him, have real sincerity and power.

But it was upon his two long narrative poems that the fame of Lydgate rested in the century after his death. The influence of the Troy Book is marked on Metham's Amoryus and Cleopes; Caxton not only professed himself un- worthy to bear Lydgate's inkhorn, when taking up the tale of Troy, but echoed the monk's phraseology in the proheme to his second edition of the Canterbury Tales and lavished praise on his "master" in his Book of Curtesye (see EETS ed., pp. 36-40). Lydgate was diligently read by Hawes, who is said to have known much of his verse by heart, and to have entertained Henry the Seventh therewith. The Fall of Princes was imitated by Cavendish, by the writers of A Mirror for Magistrates, and by Barclay; the reprint of it in 1554 and of the Troy Book in 1555 came close in time to the publication of Hardyng's Chronicle, to the third edition of Fabyan's Chronicle, and to the upgrowth of the English chronicle-play. In the seventeenth century Heywood rewrote the Troy Book as the Life and Death of Hector, and John Lane, the continuator of the Squire's Tale, published a supposed rewriting of Lydgate's Guy of Warwick, in which the monk appears as prologue and epilogue. Those functions, and that of Chorus, Lydgate had already filled in Tarlton's lost play of the Seven Deadly Sins. He appears, with Gower and Chaucer, in Ben Jonson's masque of the Golden Age Restored, and with them is cited by Jonson in his Grammar.

The association of Lydgate's name with Chaucer's, or with those of Gower and Chaucer, was long the rule. The fifteenth century apparently marked no difference between them. Hoccleve mentions Gower with Chaucer, terming him also "master," though with no such personal warmth as he gives to his language about Chaucer. Bokenam, in the prologue to his life of St. Agnes, makes

---

[1] With Troy Book ii:8197, where the bloody battleground is described as "That first was grene turned into red," or with the same phrasing i:4100-01, Thebes 2305-6, cp. Macbeth ii,2:64, "Making the green one red." With Troy Book iii:5662, "As he lyuede in his apparaile," cp. Hamlet iii,4:134, "in his habit as he lived."

Pallas say that her fresh flowers have all been gathered by Gower, Chaucer, and Lydgate, the third of whom yet lives. Burgh, although he begins his address of homage to Lydgate with a line which is ultimately Chaucer's, makes no mention of the elder poet in his list of famous rhetoricians, and terms Lydgate the flower and treasure of poetry. The unknown writer of the poem published p. 198 here calls Lydgate the fit successor of Chaucer; and the writer of How a Lover Praiseth His Lady, while commending Chaucer warmly, mentions Gower, Lydgate, Ovid, and Statius along with him. George Ashby wrote of "Maisters Gower, Chaucer and Lydgate, Primier poetes of this nacion"; and Forrest in the prologue to his Joseph names the three together. Hawes lavishes praise on Lydgate, and it is not until Skelton's Philip Sparrow that we find a discrimination among the three elder poets.

From the 1558 edition of the Fall of Princes through the seventeenth century there are no reprints of Lydgate except those of his poems which are carried along under Chaucer's name in the editions by Speght. But John Dart, modernizing the Black Knight in 1718, proclaimed Lydgate the greatest poet that England (or perhaps the world) had ever produced,—an opinion not shared by the candid Mrs. Cooper, editor of The Muses' Library, who in 1737 remarked that she had "waded through" a large volume of his work without finding any of the supposed equality with Chaucer. In 1802 Ritson called Lydgate "a voluminous, prosaic, and drivelling monk"; but Gray, in his essay on Lydgate, written much earlier but printed 1814, attributes the "long processes" of the monk's writing to the taste of his time, and praises him for his power of raising tender emotion and for a frequent "stiller kind of majesty" in expression. Lowell termed Lydgate's verse "a barbarous jangle"; and both Gosse and Saintsbury, in their histories of English literature, have spoken of his intolerable prolixity and his deficient metrical ear, although Gosse, as already noted, adds that a selection could probably be made which would do him greater credit than does the whole mass. Gosse also mentions appreciatively the gentleness and sympathy for which Gray had praised Lydgate; but Churton Collins, in our own day, has far outdone Gray in the warmth of his commendation. He declares that Lydgate was a poet of fine genius, that his descriptions of nature almost rival Chaucer's, that his powers of pathos are of a high order, that his style and verse are often of exquisite beauty, and that, at his best, he is one of the most musical of poets.

Of such an estimate of Lydgate it can only be said that the perspective of English poetry must have disappeared from before the eyes of a man who applies to Lydgate words better applicable to Keats.

If we turn from the opinions of single critics to the testimony of the press, we find that while about seventy MSS of the Canterbury Tales and sixteen of Troilus survive, there are forty of Hoccleve's De Regimine Principum and thirty of Lydgate's Fall of Princes, of Lydgate's Troy Book about a score, still extant. Caxton, who printed the Canterbury Tales twice and Troilus once, issued Lydgate's Horse, Goose, and Sheep thrice, the Churl and Bird twice, the Temple of Glass and the Life of Our Lady once each; also a few brief poems, perhaps as "fillers." Wynkyn de Worde published the Canterbury Tales twice and the Troilus once, the Temple of Glass three times and the Churl and Bird, the Horse, Goose, and Sheep, the Black Knight, the Siege of Thebes, and the Virtues of the Mass, once each; he also put out a set of extracts from the Fall of Princes, from Chaucer, etc., as "The prouerbes of Lydgate." It was Richard Pynson who undertook Lydgate's longer poems, printing both the Troy Book (1513) and two editions of the Fall of Princes, 1494 and 1527; he also reissued the Temple of Glass and the Churl and Bird, and printed the Testament. Minor printers issued, between 1515 and 1531, the Legend of St. Austin at Compton, the Life of St. Albon, and the Life of Our Lady. In the years between 1554 and 1558 there was a sudden "boom" in Lydgate's longer poems, the Fall of Princes appearing in 1554 and 1558, the Troy Book in 1555; but thereafter, for nearer three hundred than two hundred years, only a few of Lydgate's shorter poems and the Siege of Thebes remained in print, carried along with Chaucer in the editions of 1561 and following. In 1818, 1822, the Roxburghe Club reprinted, as literary rarities, Lydgate's Horse, Goose, and Sheep, his Churl and Bird, and his Black Knight; in 1827 Nicolas' Chronicle of London, in 1859 Wright's Political Poems, included several texts by Lydgate or ascribed to him; in 1840 the first collection of the monk's shorter poems was edited by J. O. Halliwell for the Percy Society,— a task most indifferently performed. Since 1864, when the Early English Text Society began publishing, texts of Lydgate have been steadily appearing; for them and for the poems edited by German doctorate-candidates, see the appended Select List of the monk's works. Various collections of Middle English verse have also included work by Lydgate, e.g., Skeat's Chaucerian and Other Pieces (vol. vii of the Oxford Chaucer), Horstmann's Altenglische Legenden, Neilson and Webster's Chief British Poets of the Fourteenth and Fifteenth Centuries.

Criticism of Lydgate:—

> Thomas Gray's essay, in Gosse's ed. of Gray's Works, vol. i.
> Warton's Hist. Eng. Poetry, in Warton-Hazlitt ed., iii:53 ff.
> Morley's English Writers, vol. vi.
> Ward's English Poets vol. i; ten Brink's Hist. Eng. Lit., vol. ii; Jusserand's Literary Hist. of the Eng. People, i:498-501; brief treatments by Gosse and by Saintsbury in their short hists. of English literature; Courthope in his Hist. Eng. Poetry, vol. i; Saintsbury in Cambridge Hist. Eng. Lit., vol. ii, chap. on The English Chaucerians. Sidney Lee's article in the DictNat-Biog. is compact, but needs revision, especially on the bibliographical side.
> The extravagant praise of Churton Collins in his Ephemera Critica, e.g., pp. 98, 115, 199, does not carry conviction to a careful student.
> Schick's introd. to his EETS ed. of the Temple of Glass is still the best guide to knowledge of Lydgate.
> Koeppel's monographs on the Fall of Princes (see p. 151 here, foot) and on the Siege of Thebes (p. 120) are of value; that by E. Gattinger on Die Lyrik Lydgates, Vienna, 1896, is unsound.

Essays on Special Points:—

> F. Reuss, Das Naturgefühl bei Lydgate, in Archiv 122:269-300.
> Moorman, Interpretation of Nature in Eng. Poetry, Quellen u. Forschungen, vol. 95 (1905). See chap. 9.
> G. Reismüller, Romanische Lehnwörter bei Lydgate, Munich, 1909.
> R. Hingst, Die Sprache Lydgates aus seinen Reimen, Greifswald, 1908.
> A. H. Licklider, Chapters on the Metric of the Chaucerian Tradition, Baltimore, 1910.
> H. Reger, Die epische Cäsur in der Chaucerschule, Bayreuth, 1910.

C. F. Babcock, The Metrical Use of Inflectional -e in Middle English, with particular reference to Chaucer and Lydgate, in PMLA 29:50 ff.

A. L. McCobb, The Loss of Unaccented -e in the Transition Period, in PMLA 29:39-41.

E. Hüttmann, Das partic. präsens bei Lydgate im Vergleich mit Chaucers Gebrauch, Kiel diss., 1914.

A. Courmont, Studies on Lydgate's Syntax in the Temple of Glass, Paris, 1912.

R. Hittmair, Das Zeitwort "do" in Chaucers Prosa, Leipzig, 1923. See pp. 85-91.

E. P. Hammond, The Nine-Syllabled Pentameter Line in some Post-Chaucerian MSS, in ModPhil 23:129-52.

THE CANON

The larger part of the work attributed to Lydgate may with tolerable certainty be treated as his; but a number of poems assigned to him, from the day of Hawes to our own, are doubtful or more than doubtful. Hawes, in his Pastime of Pleasure, stanzas 184-187, mentioned eight poems by the monk; for the passage see p. 281 here, and the Notes. More business-like bibliographies, so far as intention is considered, are to be found in:—

John Bale, Scriptorum illustrium Maioris Brytannie ——Catalogus, 1557. See pp. 586-7.

John Bale, Index Britanniae Scriptorum, ed. from the MS notebook of Bale by R. L. Poole and Mary Bateson, Oxford, 1902. See pp. 228-231.

John Stow's list of 112 works by Lydgate appended to the text of the Siege of Thebes in Speght's 1598 Chaucer. Stow cited usually from MSS, and is better worth heeding than is the flimsiness of Bale.

John Pits, Relationum Historicarum de Rebus Anglicis, tomus primus, Paris, 1619. See pp. 632-34. Based on Bale.

Thomas Tanner, Bibliotheca Britannico-Hibernica, ed. David Wilkins, 1748. See pp. 489-93 for long list of Eng. titles and MS-references.

For discussion of the above, see H. N. MacCracken's EETS ed. of the Minor Poems of Lydgate, vol. 1, 1911, xxxiv-xlii.

Joseph Ritson, in his Bibliographia Anglo-Poetica, 1802, printed a list of 251 "works" supposedly by Lydgate; this list Schick, in his EETS ed. of the Temple of Glass, 1891, pp. cxlviii-cliii, justly denounces as an "Augean stable of disorder, glaring mistakes, and inextricable confusion." Ritson was criticised and a new list prepared by MacCracken in an essay on the Lydgate Canon prefixed to his EETS volume above mentioned. This study I have elsewhere (Anglia Beiblatt 24:140-145) reviewed as not sufficiently judicial; a number of poems are added to the canon on Dr. MacCracken's opinion alone,—the subjective method for which we censure Stow's treatment of Chaucer.

The list of Lydgate's works in the DictNatBiog., s.v. Lydgate suffers from lack of method, and has frequent inaccuracies.

Notes contributory to the establishment of a Lydgate-canon will be found in Anglia 28:1-28 (1905), Anglia 30:320-48 (1907).

Life of Our Lady. No modern ed. yet available. To MacCracken's list of MSS add
Durham V, ii, 16, Hunterian U, 3, 5 at Glasgow, a portion in Huntington 144
(formerly Huth), etc.

London Lickpenny. Probably not by Lydgate. In this volume, p. 237, q. v.

Margaret, Life of St. In Horstmann, Altengl. Legenden, p. 446; in MacCracken,
i :173.

Margaret, see Queen Margaret.

Mass, The Lover's. Probably not by Lydgate. See p. 207 here.

Mass, Virtues of the. In Huth's Fugitive Tracts, 1875; in MacCracken, i :87.

Mumming at Hertford. In Anglia 22 :364, repr. Neilson and Webster p. 223. The other
mummings by Lydgate are in Brotanek's Englische Maskenspiele, 1902. These
clumsy but historically important poems were long supposed lost.

Nightingale Poems, Two, ed. Glauning, EETS, 1900. See Anglia Beiblatt 16 :360.

Order of Fools. In Halliwell, p. 164. In the EETS Booke of Precedence, p. 79.

Pilgrimage of the Life of Man, EETS, 1899-1904.

Prospect of Peace. In Wright, Polit. Poems, ii :209.

Queen Margaret's Entry into London. By Lydgate? Texts printed by Carleton Brown
in MLReview 7 :225, by Robt. Withington in ModPhil 13 :53.

Reason and Sensuality, ed. Sieper, EETS, 1901.

Secrees of Olde Philisoffres, ed. Steele, EETS, 1894. Corrections by Prosiegel, Book
of the Governance of Kings, Munich diss., 1903.

Stans Puer ad Mensam. In Reliquiae Antiquae, i :156; in EETS Babees Book, p. 26;
in EETS Booke of Precedence, p. 56.

Temple of Glass, ed. Schick, EETS, 1891. An extract from Schick is in Neilson and
Webster, p. 213. See MacCracken in PMLA 23 :129-40; see Courmont as
p. 99 ante.

Testament. In Halliwell, p. 232; in MacCracken, i :329.

Thebes, Siege of, or Story of, ed. Erdmann, EETS, 1911, text. Prologue in Wülker's
Altengl. Lesebuch, ii :105 (from Stow of 1561); in Anglia 36 :360; in Spurgeon's
Chaucer Allusion i :26-31; and p. 118 here. See my Chaucer Manual, p. 456.
A selection from part ii is in Skeat's Specimens Eng. Lit. 1394-1579.

Troy Book, ed. Bergen, EETS, 1906-08, text. A bit is repr. by Neilson and Webster, p. 216.

For Lydgate's prose work, see MacCracken's ed. of the Serpent of Division,
Oxford, 1911, and note by same in MLReview 8 :103. See, in the Harvard MS 530 F,
a continuation of the prose Brut, or chronicle of England, which the copyist John
Shirley in a long heading asserts to be the work of Lydgate. This heading is printed
Harvard Studies v :185.

Besides the Assembly of Gods, the Court of Sapience, the Lover's Mass, London
Lickpenny, etc., many other works have been falsely ascribed to Lydgate. Walton's
translation of Boethius was credited to Lydgate as noted on p. 39 here; Warton opined
that the Coventry Corpus Christi Play was "very probably" by Lydgate, and Wright
hinted his authorship of the Payne and Sorow of Euyll Maryage,—see p. 295 of Poems
of Walter Mapes, Camden Soc., 1841. The prose transl. of the Pilgrimage of the Soul
is frequently assigned to Lydgate, see Schick's ed. of the Temple of Glass, p. ci; and
this very dubious assignment is sanctioned by the New Eng. Dict. Other minor ascriptions are made by fifteenth-century scribes, and a major one by Henry Peachan, who
in 1622 announced that Lydgate "wrote that bitter Satyre of Peirs Plowman". Ritson's
pseudo-bibliography has been torn to pieces by Schick as cited, and the Canon-essay of
MacCracken does not classify Lydgate's works with regard to the quality of evidence
for the monk's authorship.

THE CHURL AND THE BIRD

The Churl and the Bird was one of the most popular of Lydgate's shorter poems, and is among the eight works attributed to him by Hawes in his Pastime of Pleasure; see p. 281 here. It was printed by Caxton twice, by de Worde, by Copland, and by Pynson. Its exact source has not been identified; the French "paunflete" which Lydgate mentions in line 35 would hardly have been the long narrative compilation of Petrus Alfonsus' Disciplina Clericalis in its French rendering Le Castoiement d'un Père à son Fils, but some perhaps separate version of the single tale which it contains on this subject. The Castoiement's recension of our story, which is nearer the English than is any other of the French versions, mentions a peasant as owner of the garden, describes the song of the bird, its capture, and the dialogue leading to its release; it presents the three "wisdoms" as: 1) que tu ne creies pas A toz les diz que tu orras, 2) que tu avras Ce que toen ert jà n'i faudras, 3) que ne deiz pas plorer Ne ne te deiz desconforter Se perdue as aucune rien.—The churl's despair is then described, the bird's reproof given, and the bird departs. See the poem (156 lines) as printed in Labouderie's ed. of the Disciplina, Paris, 1824, ii:130-36. This version, as appears, is close to the English.

Gaston Paris, in his Légendes du Moyen Age, essay on Le Lai d'Oiselet, prints and discusses a far fuller and more symmetrical French tale based on the same situation. In this version the garden depends for its existence upon the song of the bird, and although once the property of a chevalier, has now fallen into the hands of a "vilain". The bird still sang in the garden her wonderful song, which was of duty to God, and that God and love are one, and that love is supported by loyalty, courtesy, and honor. As the bird sings she sees the listening churl, who is evil-minded and covetous; and therefore she pours out praises of her former hearers, the noble knights and ladies. This incenses the churl, who snares the bird. The story then continues as here, with the added detail that the churl scorns the bird's three "wisdoms", and declares he is not so stupid as to need them. The rest of the narrative is as here, except that when the bird departs the beauty of the garden disappears, the streams and trees dry up, and the churl loses his all. This version may also be read in Barbazan and Méon's Fabliaux, iii:114; although such a developed tale bears no relation to Lydgate's source, it is interesting to note that when Elias Ashmole reprinted our poem in his Theatrum Chemicum Britannicum in 1652, he drew from it a "parabolicall and allusive interpretation"—although an alchemical one.

The date of the English rendering is uncertain. It has been suggested by Schick, page c of his edition of the Temple of Glass, that the translation was executed before the death of Chaucer, the allusion to "my maister" in line 380 being taken to mean Chaucer. But the argument is of doubtful validity. From the phrasing and movement of the poem we may, however, be inclined to place it early in Lydgate's career; for it is much fresher and lighter than is, e.g., the fable of the Cock and Precious Stone, where the narrative is very poorly managed. Both this poem and Bycorne and Chichevache seem to us early just because of this (comparative) freshness of handling; or it may be that the choice of models in them is fortunate, for Lydgate and for us, since their connection with the Manciple's tale or with the Clerk's envoy stimulates the modern reader's interest.

My text is in the main from MS Longleat 258, of the Marquess of Bath's library, for the use of which I am indebted to the present Lord Bath. Other copies are in Brit. Mus. Harley 116, Cotton Caligula A ii, Lansdowne 699; in Lansdowne's partial sister Leyden Vossianus 9; in Hh iv, 12 and Kk i, 6 of the University Library Cambridge; in Trin. Coll. Cambridge R 3, 19; in Balliol College Oxford, and a fragment in Christ Church College Oxford 152; in Lincoln Cathedral C 5,4; in a Gurney MS, in the Cardigan MS of the Canterbury Tales; and in a Huth MS, now No. 144 of the Huntington Library, California. Halliwell in his edition of the Minor Poems printed the Harley 116 text, reprinted in Neilson and Webster's Chief British Poets, p. 209. The second Caxton was reprinted for the Roxburghe Club in 1818, and the first Caxton (unique) was facsimiled in 1906 by the Cambridge University Press.

As the MS Longleat 258 is in private possession and difficult of access, I describe it in some detail. It is of 147 leaves 8⅝ by 5½ inches in size, mainly in eights, paper quires in vellum covers. It is written in one small legible current hand, evenly but not handsomely, three spaced stanzas to the page, without ornament. The titles of the poems are usually in colophons; a slovenly later hand has put in running titles. An inserted note by Henry Bradshaw discusses the loss of the fifth and sixth quires, with which went the whole of the Flower and Leaf and the first six stanzas of Chaucer's Mars. A contemporary table of contents on the last verso shows that the volume also once contained, at the beginning, the Letter of Cupid and "Vnum Carmen". This table is printed in Chaucer Soc. Odd Texts, p. 251, and also in ModLangNotes 20:77, where I described the MS. The contents are:—

1-32a, the Temple of Glass. Most of 32a was blank, and three stanzas were later written there, perhaps by Sir John Thynne, an early owner. These stanzas are printed, from MS B. M. Adds. 17942, by Flügel, Neuengl. Lesebuch 39. Fol. 32b is blank. See Schick's ed. of the Temple of Glass, EETS 1891.

(Two eights are missing)

49a-54b, Chaucer's Mars, impf. at beginning. Printed Chaucer Soc. SPT, p. 141.

55a-57b, Chaucer's Pity. Printed Chaucer Soc. Odd Texts, p. 251.

58a-75b, the Assembly of Ladies. This text not noted by Skeat, vii:380 ff.

76a-84a, Chaucer's Anelida. Printed Chaucer Soc. SPT 37. Fol. 84b is blank.

85a-101a, Chaucer's Parlement of Foules. Printed Chaucer Soc. SPT, p. 1. Fol. 101b is blank.

102a-119a, the Eye and the Heart. Printed Anglia 34:235-265. Most of 119a and all 119b are blank.

120a-136b, La Belle Dame sans Merci, by Ros. This text not noted by Skeat, vii:299. See my Manual, pp. 432-33.

137a-147a, the Churl and the Bird. Text here printed. Fol. 145b and all of 146 are blank; the last stanza of the poem, on 147a, is written by the usual scribe, but the three stanzas on 145a, i.e., 46, 47, and 48, are in the later hand of the codex, while the last gathering of the MS has nine paper leaves instead of the usual six. Two stanzas, 49 and 50, are lacking to the poem, as also in the Balliol copy. It seems probable that the scribe had an imperfect copy before him, recognized it as such, and enlarged his final quire to permit addition later, putting his last stanza after his estimated space to make it clear that more text was to come. Whatever copy the later scribe then found was short two stanzas, as is Balliol. Cf. p. 336 of my Manual for the procedure of the Fairfax and the Bodley MSS in the Book of the Duchesse under similar conditions.

Stanzas 49 and 50, missing from Longleat and from Balliol, are here supplied from MS Lincoln Cathedral C 5, 4. This MS, a damaged and somewhat mutilated volume of 86 paper leaves, contains but four entries, viz.: Lydgate's St. Albon and St. Amphabell, impf. at beginning and at close; the Churl and Bird, lacking 8 stanzas at beginning; Lydgate's St. Austin at Compton; and his Dance Macabre. These three latter poems appear in MS Lansdowne 699 in the same order and with the same headings; and the Dance Macabre text in both MSS is of the same recension, and closely similar. Could the codices be laid side by side, it might even appear that the writing was identical; so far as my visual memory served, the hands were not unlike.

In the Longleat MS a hand other than the scribe's has made some corrections; see lines 76, 225, 266, 280, 305, 306, in the footnotes. Special textual differences among the MSS are dealt with in the Notes; see lines 1, 51, 76, 115, 177, 210, 227, 352, 356-7.

Problemes of olde likenes and figures
Whiche proued ben ful fructuous of
    sentence
And han auctorite grounded on scriptures
By resemblaunce of notable Apparence
With moralite concluding on prudence 5
Like as the Bibyll rehersith by writyng
Howe trees sumtyme chose heim self a
    king

2
ffirst in thair chois they named the Olyve
To reigne amonge heim Judicum doth ex-
    presse
But he himself gan excusyn blyue   10
That he might not forsake his fatenesse
Ner the ffigge tre his amerous swetnesse
Ner the vyne his holsom fressh tarage
Whiche yevith comfort vnto almaner age

3
And sembla(b)ly Poetes Laureate   15
By derke parables ful convenyent
ffayn that birddes and bestes of estate
As Roial Egles and lyons of assent
Sent out writes to holde a perlament
And made decrees brevely for to saye
Summe to haue lordship and summe to
    obaye

4
Egles in the eyre highest take hir flight
Power of lyons on the grounde is sene
Cedre amonge trees highest is of sight
And the laurer of nature (is) ay grene 25
Of floures al flora goddes and quene
Thus (of) al thinges there ben diver-
    sites
Summe of estat and summe of low degres

5
Poites written wonderful liknesse
And vnder couert kepe heim self ful
    cloos   30
They take bestes and foules to witnesse
Of whois fe(y)nynges fables first aroos
And here I cast vnto my purpose
Oute of the frenssh a tale to translate
Whiche in a paunflete I red and saw but
    late   35

6
This tale whiche I make of mencion
In gros rehersith by writing thaire
Thre proverbes paied for the raunson
Of a faire brid that was take in a snare
Wondre desirous to scape oute of hir
    care   40
Of myn auctorite folowing the processe
So as it fil in ordre I shal expresse

2, 11. Only Longleat has *ful, that.*
4. Harl. and Kk have *nobill* inst. of *notable.*
17. Other MSS *ffeyne, ffeynyn.*

22. Other MSS *to take*: note the infinitives of 20, 21.
25, 27. Longleat omits *is, of.*
41. Other MSS *auctor* inst. of *auctorite.*

7

Whilom there was in a smal vilage
As myn auctour maketh rehersayl
A chorle whiche hade lust and gret
corage   45
Within him self by deligent trauayl
Taraye his gardyne with notable ap-
perayl
Of leng(t)h and brede elich square and
longe
Hegged and diched to make it sure and
stronge

8

Alle the aleys were made playne with
sonde   50
The benches couerd with new turvys
grene
Swete herbes with condites at honde
That welled vp ayenst the sonne shene
Like siluer stremes as any cristal clene
The burbly wawes (in ther) vp boyl-
ling   55
Rounde as birall thair stremes out shew-
ing

9

Amyd the gardyn stode a fressh laurere
Thereon a birde synging day and nyght
With sonnysh feders brighter then gold
were
Whiche with hir song made hevy hert*es*
light   60
That to be holde it was an heuenly sight
Howe towarde even and day dawynge
She dud hir payne moost amorously to
singe

10

Esperus enforced hir corage
Towarde even whan Phebus gan to
(w)est   65
Amonge the braunches to hir avauntage
To singe hir complaynt and than to go to
rest
And at the rising of the quene Alcest
To synge ayein as it was to hir dewe
Erly on morowe the day sterre to sa-
lewe   70

11

It was a verrey hevenly melodye
Evyn and morowe to here the bridd*es*
song

And the swete sugred Armonye
Of vncouth warbles and tewnes draw
along
That al the gardyn of the noys rong   75
(Tyl) on (a) morowe that Tytan shone
ful clere
The bride was trapped and taken in a
pantere

12

The chorle was glad that he this bride
had take
Mery of chere of loke and of visage
And in al hast he cast for to make   80
Within his hous a praty litel cage
And with hir song to reioyse his corage
Tyll at the last the cely bride abrayde
And sobirly thus to the chorle she saiede

13

I am now take and stand vnder daun-
gire   85
Holde straite that I may not flee
A dewe my songe wt al my notes clere
Nowe that I haue lost my liberte
Now am I thral and sum*m*e tyme•I was
free
And trust well while I stond in dis-
tresse   90
I can not syng ner make noo gladnesse

14

And though my cage forged were of gold
And the penacles of byral and cristal
I remembre a proverbe said of olde
Who lesith his fredome in faith he lesith
al   95
ffor I had leuer vpon a branche smal
Merely to singe amonge the wodes grene
Thenne in a cage of siluer bright and
shene

15

Songe and prison han noon accordaunce
Trowest thou I wol synge in prisou*n*
Songe procedith of Ioye and of pleas-
aunce
And prison causith deth and distruc-
ciou*n*
Rynging of fetters make noo mery sou*n*
Howe shuld he be glad or Iocunde
Ayeinst his wille that lithe in chaynes
bounde   *105*

---

55. Other MSS have *in ther* before *vp.* Harl. has
in.
62. Other MSS *and in the dawnynge.*
65. Longleat reads *gan to rest.*
67. Other MSS, except Hh, read *complyn* inst.
of *complaynt.*

---

76. Longleat has been corrected; see Note.
90. *while,* Harl, Trin.; *now,* Linc, Lansd. Kk.
104. Other MSS read *Or howe shuld,* etc.

16

What availith a lion to be kyng
Of bestes al shet in a Tour of stoon
Or an egle vnder streit kepyng
Called also kyng of foules echoon
ffye on lordship when liberte is goon *110*
Answere hereto and lete it not asterte
Who singith mery that singith not in
herte

17

But if thou wilt rejoys of my singyng
Lette me goo flee fre from al daunger
And euery day in the mornyng   *115*
I wil repair vnto thy laurer
And fresshely syng wt lusty notes cler
Vndre thy chambre and afore thy halle
Euery season whan thou list me calle

18

To be shitt vp and pynned vndre
dƒede   *120*
Noo thing accordith vnto my nature
Though I were fedde wt mylke & wastel
brede
And swete cruddes brought to my pasture
Yet had I leuer to doo my besy cure
Erly in the morowe to (shrape) in the
vale   *125*
To fynde my dyner amonge the wormes
smale

19

The labourer is gladder at the plough
Erly on the morowe to fede him on
bacou*n*
Than som man is that hath tresour
ynough
And of al deyntes plente and foyson *130*
And hath noo fredom with his posses-
sion
To goo at large but as a bere at the
stake
To passe his boundis but if he leve take

20

Take this answere ful for conclusion
To synge in prison thou shalt me not
constrayn   *135*
Tyll I haue liberte in wodd*es* vp and doon
To fleen at large on bowghes rough &
playn
And of reason thou shuldest not disdayn

Of my desires but laugh and haue good
game
But who is a chorle wold eche man were
þe same   *140*

21

Welle quod the chorle / sith it wol not be
That I desire / as by thyn talkynge
Maugre thyn hede / thou shalt chese oon
of thre
Within a cage merely to synge
Or to the kechyn I shal thy body
brynge   *145*
Pul thy feders that ben so bright and
clere
And after rost the / or bake the to my
dynere

22

Thenne quod the Bride to reason say not
nay
Toching my songe / a ful answere thou
hast
And when my feders pulled ben away *150*
If I be rosted other bake in past
Thou shalt haue of me a ful smal repast
But if thou wilt werke be my counsaille
Thou maist be me haue passing gret
availle

23

If thou wilt vnto my rede assent   *155*
And suffre me goo / frely from prison
Withoute raunsou*n* / or any other rent
I shal the yeve / a notable gwerdou*n*
Thre gret wisdomes according to reason
More of value take hede what I prof-
fre   *160*
Than al the gold / that shitt is in thy
cofre

24

Trust me wel / I shal the not disceyue
Welle quod the chorle telle on anoon lete
se
Nay quod the bride thou maist aforne
conceyue
Who that shal teche / of reason he must
goo fre   *165*
It sitt a maistre / to haue his liberte
And at large to teche his lessou*n*

109, 112. Other MSS read *euerichoon, of herte.*
115. See Note.
125. *sharpe* has been emended to *scrape;* other
MSS *shrape.*
134. Trin, Harl. *for ful;* Linc, Lansd, Hh, *for a
full.*

147. Trin, Hh omit first *the;* Linc, Lansd, omit
both. Harl reads—*the rooste and baake,*
etc.
148. Longleat inserts *I* before *say;* Lansd and
Calig insert *I* before *nay.*
152. Other MSS *of me haue.*
160. Other MSS *I do profre.*
164. Other MSS *thou must afore,* etc.

Haue me not suspecte I meane noo
   tresou*n*

25

Welle quod the chorle I holde me content
I trust thy promyse / which thou hast
   made to me *170*
The bride fligh forth the chorle was of
   assent
And toke hi(r) flight vp to the laurer tre
Then thought she thus / now that I
   stande fre
With snares panters I cast not al my
   lyve
Ner with noo lyme twigges any more to
   stryve *175*

26

He is a foole that scaped is daungere
Hath broken his (fetters) & fled is from
   prison
That wol resort for brent childe dredith
   fere
Eche man be ware of wisdome and rea-
   son
Of Sugre strawed that hidith fals poi-
   son *180*
There is noo more perlious venom of
   sharpnesse
Than when it hath of treacle a likenesse

27

Who dredith noo p*er*el in p*er*ell he shal
   falle
Smothe waters ben ofte sithes depe
The quayle pipe can moost falsly
   calle *185*
Tylle the quayle vndre the net doth
   creepe
A blere eyed fouler trust not though he
   wepe
Eschewe his thombe of weping take noon
   hede
That smale briddis can nype by the hede

28

And now that I suche daungier am as-
   kaped *190*
I wol be ware and afore prouide
That of noo fouler I wol no more be
   Iaped
ffrom thaire lyme twig*ges* I wol fle fer
   aside
Where perel is / (gret) perel is to abide

Come nere thou chorle take hede to my
   speche *195*
Of thre wisdomes that I wol the teche

29

Yeue thou not of wisdome to haste cre-
   dence
To euery tale ner to eche tything
But considre of reason and prudence
Amonge many tales / is many loude
   lesing *200*
Hasty credence causith gret hinderyng
Report of tales and tything*es* brought vp
   of new
Maketh many man to be holde vntrew

30

ffor oo party take this for my raunsou*n*
Lerne the secunde grounded on scrip-
   ture *205*
Desire thou not / by noo condiciou*n*
Thing that is impossible to recure
Worldly desire stondith al in aventure
And who desireth to clymbe to high on
   loft
By souden turne he falleth oft vnsoft

31

The threde is this / be warre both evyn
   & morowe
fforgete it not / but lerne this of me
ffor tresour lost / make neuer to gret
   sorowe
Whiche in noo wise / may recouerde be
ffor who taketh sorow / for losse in that
   degre *215*
Rekyn first his losse / and aft*er* rekyn
   his payne
Of oo sorowe he maketh sorowes twayne

32

After this lessou*n* / the bride began a
   song
Of hir eschape gretly reioysing *219*
And she remembring also of the wrong
Don by the chorle / first at hir taking
Of hir affray / and of hir prisonyng
Glad that she was at large and oute of
   drede
Saide vnto him howyng aboue his hede

33

Thou were quod (she) a verrey natural
   foole *225*

---

172. Longleat *his*, altered by corrector.
177. Longleat *feders;* see Note.
194, 197, 202. Longleat omits *gret*, inserts *thou*,
   inserts second *of*.

200. Other MSS *gret* inst. of *loude*.
201. Other MSS *hath causid* inst. of *causith*.
210, 227. See Notes.
221. Longleat reads *Down by*, etc.
225. The corrector of Longleat inserts *she*.

To suffre me depart / of thy lewdenesse
Thou augtest of right complayne & to
    make dole
And in thyn hert / haue gret heuynesse
That thou hast lost so passing gret
    rychesse
Whiche might haue sufficed by value of
    rekenyng   230
To pay the raunsoun of a mighty kyng

34

There is a stone whiche called is Iagounce
Of olde engendred within myn entrayle
Whiche of fyne gold peysith a gret vnce
Citheryn of colour like garnettes of
    entayle   235
Whiche maketh men victorious in batayle
And who so euer bere on him this stone
Is fully assured ayeinst his mortal foone

35

Who hath this stone / in possessioun
Shal suffre noo pouert / ner noon indi-
    gence   240
But of plente haue tresour and foysoun
And euery man shal doo him reuerence
And noon enemy shal doo him offence
But fro thyn handes now that I am goon
Playne if thou wilt (for) thy part is
    noon   245

36

It causith loue it maketh men gracious
And fauourable in euery man is sight
It makith accorde betwix folke envyous
Comfortith sorowful / and makith heuy
    hertes light
Like Topasion of coloure sonnysh
    bright   250
I am a fole to telle alle at ones
Or teche a chorle the prise of precious
    stones

37

Men shulde not put a precious Marga-
    rete
As Rubeis Sapheres / or other stones
    ynde
Emeraudes ner rounde perles white   255
To forne rude swyne / that loue draff
    of kinde
ffor a Sowe dili(ti)th as I fynde
More in foule draff / hir pigges for to
    glade

Then in al the perry / that cometh of
    garnade

38

Eche thing draweth to his semblable
ffisshe in the see / bestes on the stronde
The eyre for foules of nature is conven-
    able
To a plough man for to till the lande
And to a chorle a muke forke in his
    hande
I lese my tyme any more to tary   265
To telle a boyuer of a lapidary

39

That thou haddest / thou getest nomore
    agayne
Thy lyme twigges and panters I defye
To lete me goo thou were foule ouer-
    sayne
To lese thy richesse only of folye   270
I am now fre to sing / and for to flye
Where that me list / and he is a fole at al
That goth at large / and maketh him self
    thral

40

To here of wisdome thyn eres ben half
    defe
Like an Asse that listith on an harpe 275
Thou maist goo pipe in an hyvye lefe
Better is to me to sing / on thornes
    sharpe
Than in a Cage with a Carle to carpe
ffor it was saide of folkes yore agoon
A Chorles (thralle) is alwey woo begoon

41

The chorle felt his hert part on twayn
ffor verrey sorowe / and a sondre ryve
Alas quod he I may well wepe and playn
As a wreche neuer like to thryve
But forto endure in pouert al my lyve 285
ffor of foly / and of wilfulnesse
I haue now loste al holy my richesse

42

I was a lord I crye oute on fortune
Hade gret tresour late in my keping
Whiche might haue made me long to
    (contune)   290

---

245. Longleat omits *for.*
249. Harl, Hh, Calig, also have *and;* not in other
    texts.

259. Other MSS, except Lansd, have *oute of
    garnade.*
260. Harl, Linc, Lansd, Hh, *vnto.*
266. Lansd, Hh, Calig, read *chorl* inst. of *boveer.*
    and the corrector of Longleat has written
    chorl above *boyuer.*
280. The Lt. corrector writes *thralle* above *chorle.*
    Linc, Lansd, Harl, Trin, have *cherl,* Hh
    wyfe.
290. Lt. writes *contynue,* other MSS *contune.*

With thilke stone to haue lyued like a
    kyng
If that I hade sett it in a ryng
Borne it vpon me I had hade good ynough
I shulde no more haue goon vnto the
    plough

43

Whenne the Bride sawe the chorle thus
    morne   *295*
And how that he was heuy of his
    c(h)ere
She toke hir flight / and gan ayein
    retorne
Towarde him / and said as ye shal here
O dulle Chorle wisdomes for to lere
That I the taught al is left behinde   *300*
Raced awey / and clene oute of thy
    mynde

44

Taught I the not this wisdome in sen-
    tence
To euery tale brought vp to the of newe
Not to hastly to yeue therto credence
Vnto tyme thou knew that (it) were
    trewe   *305*
Alle is not gold that (sheweth) goldissh
    hewe
Ner stoones al by nature as I fynde
Be not Saphers / that shewen colour
    ynde

45

In this doctryne I lost al my laboure
To teche the suche *prouer*bes of sub-
    staunce   *310*
Now maist thou see thyn lewde blynde
    erroure
ffor al my body peysed in balaunce
Weyeth not an vnce rude is thy remem-
    braunce
I to haue more peyce in myn entrayle
Then al my body sett for countervayle

46

Alle my body wey(e)th not an vnce
Howe might then I haue in me a stone
That peyseth more than doith a gret
    Iagonce
Thy brayne is dulle / thy witte is almost
    goone
Of thre wisdomes thou hast forgoten
    oone   *320*

Thou shuldest not after my sentence
To euery tale yeue hasty credence

47

I bad also be warre (both) even and
    morowe
ffor thing lost / of sodeyne aventure
Thou shuldest neuer make to muche
    sorowe   *325*
When thou seist / thou maist not it recure
Here thou failist / whiche doth thy besy
    cure
In thy snare to cache me ayeine
Thou art a fole thy labour is in vayne

48

In the threde thou doost also rave   *330*
I bad thou shuldest in noo man*ere* wise
Coueyt thing / whiche thou maist not
    haue
In whiche thou hast forgote my enprise
That I may sey plainly to deuise
Thou hast of madenesse forgeten al
    thre   *335*
Notable wisdomes / that I taught the

49

It wer but foly / mor with the to carpe
Or to preche / of wisdamys more or lasse
I hold hym mad / that bryngeth forth
    his harpe
Ther on to teche / a rude fordullid
    Asse   *340*
And mad is he / that syngeth a fool a
    masse
And he most mad / that doth his besy-
    nesse
To teche a cherl / termys of gentilesse

50

And semblably / in Aprill & in May
When gentil briddis most make mello-
    dye   *345*
The cokkow syngen can but oo lay
In othir tunys / she hath no fantasye
Thus euery thyng / as clerkis specefye
ffrut on trees / & folk of eu*er*y age
ffro whens thei cam / thei take a
    tarage   *350*

51

The Vynteneer tretith / of his holsom
    vynes

---

296. Lt reads *clere* inst. of *chere*.
305. The corrector inserts *it*.
306. The corrector writes *sheweth* over *shyneth*.
309. No other MS has *al*.
315. Other MSS *countertayle*.

---

323. Longleat reads *but*, other MSS *both*.
    Stanzas 46, 47, 48, are in later hand; see
    introd. to this poem.
    Stanzas 49 and 50 are from the Lincoln
    Cathedral MS; see Introduction.
346. Harl and Trin read *can than but*, etc.

Off gentil frut / bostith eek the garden-
eer
The ffissher cast / his hookis & his lynes
To cachche ffissh / in euery fressh ryveer
Off tilthe of lond / tretith the boveer *355*
The gentylman talkythe of genterye
The cherl deliteth / to speke of ribaudye

52

All oon to the a facoun & a kite
As good an owle / as a Popyngay
A dongel doke / as deynte a's a snyte *360*
Who serueth a cherl / hath many a car-
ful day
Adieu sir cherl farweel I flye my way
I cast me nevir / hen(s)forth my
lyvyng
Afforn a cherl / any mor to synge

53
Verba auctoris

Ye folk that shal this fable seen &
reede   *365*
Newe forgid talis / I counsell you to
flee
ffor los of good / takith nat to gret heede

---

352. Other MSS, except Linc and Hh, have not
eek.
356-7. See Notes.
366. Harl and Hh as here; Linc, Lansd, have
conceileth inst. of *I counsell.*

Beeth nat to sorweful for noon aduersite
Coueiteth nat thyng that may nat be
And remembrith wher evir that ye
gon   *370*
A cherlis thrale / is alway woo begon

54

Vnto purpos / this proverbe is ful riff
Rad & reportid / bi old remembrance
A childis bird / & a knavis wiff
Haue ofte sith / gret sorwe & mys-
chance   *375*
Who hath freedam / hath al suffisance
Bett is freedam with litil in gladnesse
Than to be thral in all wordly richesse

55
Lenvoye

Goo litil quayeer & recomende me
Vnto my maistir / with humble affec-
cion   *380*
Beseche hym lowly / of mercy & pite
Off thi rude makyng / to haue compas-
sion
And as touchyng / thi translacion
Out of the frenssh / how euer the
ynglissh be
All thyng is seyd / vndir correccion *385*
With supportacion of your benygnyte
Explicit fabula de Aue & Rustico

HORNS AWAY

When Anne of Bohemia came to England in 1381 to marry Richard II, she
brought with her, says Miss Strickland in her Queens of England, three fashions
previously unfamiliar to Englishwomen. One was the use of pins, as we know
them; another was the sidesaddle; the third was the high forked headdress or
horned cap. "This cap," continues Miss Strickland, "was at least two feet in
height, and as many in width; its fabric was built of wire and pasteboard, like
a very widespreading mitre, and over these horns was extended glittering tissue
or gauze. Monstrous and outrageous were the horned caps that reared their
heads in England directly the royal bride appeared in one."

It was an age of extravagance in dress, not only in the use of costly ma-
terials, but in the cut and trimming of all garments. Richard II and his unworthy favorites excited the anger and contempt of the people by the fanciful
absurdity of their clothes. The anonymous play known as the Woodstock Play,[1]
which praises "plain Thomas" duke of Gloucester, in contrast to the foolish
prodigality of the king, has several scenes deriding the "wyld and antick habits"
of the courtiers. Among the fashions held up to laughter are the high pointed

---

[1] Printed in Jahrb. der deutschen Shakespeare-Gesellschaft 35:3-121 (1899).

shoes, connected with the hose by chains, or as the play has it, "a kynd coherence twixt the tooe and knee". There are also mentioned Italian cloaks and Spanish hats, their plumed tops "waving a cubit high above their wanton heads". See the "hygh cappis wytlesse" and "long peked schone" mentioned in a ballad printed by Wright, Political Poems, ii:251; and cf. notes here on Barclay's Ship of Fools, lines 456, 8479-85, where the English Acts of Apparel are cited. See also Hoccleve's Regement of Princes, 421-546, and the description of the Lombard kings in the Fall of Princes, ix:838 ff.

Women's headgear was as extravagant as men's. Chaucer's Wife of Bath wore to church kerchiefs weighing ten pounds; Piers Plowman's peasant is warned by Reason that he should not let his wife's head cost half a mark.[1] When the horned headdress was succeeded by the steepleshaped, expenditure was in nowise decreased, for jewels and long silk veils were added. See the headdresses reproduced in Shaw's Dresses and Decorations, ii, from MS Harley 6431, where Christine de Pisan presents a poem to Queen Isabella of France; and see *ibid.* from MS Royal 18 E ii (a Froissart MS) showing a masque before Charles VI of France; see also *ibid.*, the portrait of Constance, wife of John of Gaunt, wearing the horned headdress. Fairholt in his Costume in England has many small outline cuts taken from manuscript; this poem is cited p. 148 of his 1860 edition.

Horned headgear was also common, and derided, in France at an earlier date; see the Dit des Cornetes in Jubinal's Jongleurs et Trouvères, p. 87, reproduced by Fairholt in Satirical Songs, p. 29; see La Contenance des Femmes in Jubinal's Nouveau Recueil, pp. 174-5; see the Roman de la Rose 13500-03, ed. Méon, ii:338.

The fashion persisted long in England; see Elmham's Liber Metricus, where the author remarks of the crowds assembled to see Henry V pass,—

> Quaeque fenestra nitet
> Vultibus ornatis, utinam sine cornubus! illic
> Erexit cornu nobis Deus ipse salutis:
> Hinc confringantur cornua fulta malis.

Lydgate mentions the horned caps several times; in Reason and Sens 6565 he says that good women "dedely haten highe crestys And to be hornyd lych as bestys." In the Fall of Princes, ii:4231-2, he implies the same thing; in the golden world (*ibid.* iii:3158) "Women that age farsid were nor hornyd"; and again, vii:1206, "Of hornyd beestis no boost was then Iblowe."

This "high style" changed in Henry VII's time to a low flat cap, with the same suddenness and completeness as did the style of hair, of sleeves, and ot shoes.

Manuscripts of the poem are:—Bodl. Laud 683, printed Reliq. Antiq. i:79, pr. by Halliwell, p. 46, by Fairholt in his Satirical Songs, 1849, p. 51.—Univ. Libr. Cambridge Hh iv, 12, printed EETS PolitReligLovePoems, 1903, p. 45, collated with Harley 2255; this text is repr. by Neilson and Webster, Chief British Poets, p. 222, from the earlier EETS ed. of 1893.—Harley 2255, printed in Nicolas' Chronicle of London, 1827, p. 270, and here.—Jesus Coll. Cambr. 56.—Bodl. Rawl. C 86.—Trin.Coll.Cambr R 3, 19.—Bodl. Ashmole 59 is a corrupt and careless text.—Harley 2251 and Adds. 34360, sister texts, are of four stanzas only.—MacCracken's inclusion of Leyden Vossianus 9 in the list I do not find justified.

---

[1] B-text, passus v, line 31.

[MS Brit. Mus. Harley 2255, fol. 6]

Off god and kynde / procedith al bewte
Crafft may shewe / a foreyn apparence
But nature ay must haue þe souereynte
Thyng countirfet / hath noon existence
Twen gold and gossomer is gret differ-
    ence   5
Trewe metal / requerith noon allay
Vnto purpoos / by cleer experyence
Bewte wyl shewe / thouh hornes wer
    away

2

Riche attires / of gold and perre
Charbonclis rubies / of moost excel-
    lence   10
Shewe in dirknesse / liht wher so they be
By ther natural / heuenly influence
Doubletys of glas / yeve a gret evidence
Thyng countirfet / wil faylen at assay
On this mateer / concludyng in sen-
    tence   15
Bewte wyl shewe / thouh hornys wer
    away

3

Aleyn remembryth / his compleynt who
    lyst see
In his book / of famous eloquence
Clad al in floures / and blosmys of a
    tree
He sawh *nature* / in hir moost excel-
    lence   20
Vpon hir hed a keuerchef of Valence
Noon othir richesse / of countirfet array
Texemplefye / by kyndly providence
Bewte wil shewe / thouh hornys wer
    away

4

ffamous poetys of antiquyte   25
In *Grece* and *Troye* renoumyd of pru-
    dence
Wroot of queen Heleyne / and *Penelope*
Off *Polyceene* / with hir chaast Inno-
    cence
ffor wyves trewe / calle Lucrece to pre-
    sence
That they wer fayr / ther can no man
    sey nay   30
Kynde wrouht hem / with so gret dilli-
    gence

On the MS see p. **79** *ante* note. This poem
is a tour de force on three rimes; for Lydgate's
most' extensive case of this "rhetorical color" see
Rome Remember, p. 169 below.

Ther bewte couthe / hornys wer cast
    away

5

Clerkys recorde / by gret auctorite
Hornys wer yove / to beestys for dif-
    fence
A thyng contrary / to ffemynyte   35
To be maad sturdy / of resistence
But arche wyves egre in ther violence
ffers as *Tygre* for to make affray
They haue despyt / and ageyn con-
    science
Lyst nat of pryde / ther hornys cast
    away   40

6

Lenvoye

Noble pryncessys / this litel shoort ditee
Rewdly compiled / lat it be noon offence
To your womanly / merciful pitee
Thouh it be rad / in your audience
Peysed ech thyng / in your iust aduer-
    tence   45
So it be no displeasaunce to your ᵽay
Vndir support / of your pacience
Yeuyth example hornys to cast away

7

Grettest of vertues / is humylite
As *Salomon* seith / sone of *Sapience*
Moost was acceptyd / to the deite
Takith heed heer of / yevyth to this
    woord credence
How *Maria* / which hadde a premynence
Above alle women / in bedleem whan she
    lay
At cristes birthe / no cloth of gret dis-
    pence   55
She weryd a keverche / hornys wer cast
    away

8

Off birthe she was hihest of degre
To whom alle aungelis / did obedience
Of *Dauid*is lyne / which sprang out of
    iesse
In whom alle vertues / by iust conven-
    ience   60
Maad stable in god / by goostly confi-
    dence
This roose of *Jerycho* / ther greuh noon
    suych in May
Poor in spirit / parfight in pacience
In whoom alle hornys of pryde were put
    away

9

Mooder of Ihesu / myrour of chastite 65
In woord nor thouht / that nevir did
offence
Trewe examplaire / of Virginitie
Heedspryng and welle / of parfit conty-
nence

Was nevir clerk / by rethoryk nor science
Kowde all hir vertues / reherse to this
day   70
Noble Pryncessys / of meeke benyuo-
lence
Bexample of hir / your horns cast away
Explicit

BYCORNE AND CHICHEVACHE

The immediate original of this poem, although not yet identified, was in all probability French. Texts of French poems on Bigorne and on Chicheface are printed by Montaiglon in his Recueil as below, ii :187 and xi :277; both are in nine-line stanzas, alternate speeches by beast and by victim. Neither of these texts is earlier than the mid-sixteenth century, nor are the closely similar French versions printed by Bolte in Archiv 114 :80 ff. But Chicheface, the "beste maigre" who devours the meek-spirited, is alluded to in the French fifteenth-century Mys- tère de Ste. Geneviève, as if well-known; see Jubinal's edition as below, i :248. In a note *ibid.* i :390 Jubinal prints a poem of 68 lines, in couplets, on "Chinche- fache," from a French manuscript of the fourteenth century; and Chaucer, in the envoy to his Clerk's Tale, warns wives against patience, "Lest Chichevache yow swolwe in hir entraille." It was thus a current allusion before the fifteenth century.

The two names were originally Bigorne and Chi(n)chefache; and their coupling and contrast is a late medieval arrangement. The former word has not yet been explained etymologically, and is rare. Chicheface or Chinchefache is much the commoner of the two; the compound means "niggard-face", and *chinche* or *chynchy* appears in Middle English as well as in French to mean "stingy, tight"; see, e.g., Hoccleve's Mâle Règle, line 136. The French term is used to signify something like "scarecrow" in Martin Le Franc's Champion de Dames (ca. 1440), where the Adversary declares that woman, "celle Ciche- face", was made out of the leavings after man had been carefully created, just as a potter fashions a queer "marmouset" out of his clay remnants when the pot has been finished. A little earlier, in Baudet Herenc's Doctrinal de la séconde rhétorique of 1432, the "sotte amoureuse" is indignantly termed by the versifier "le laide cicheface"; and in the fourteenth-century Lamentations de Mathéolus, iii :3220 ff., the poet says he is "comme une chicheface, Maigre par dessoubs ma peaucelle."

These are all general terms. But in the fourteenth-century lines De la Chinchefache printed by Jubinal (as below), there is described a lean horrible monster, long-toothed and staring-eyed, whose function is to seize and devour such women as do not "talk back" to their lords. And in the Ste. Geneviève drama above mentioned, the angry bourgeois says to the saint, who is counselling patience, "Gardez vous de la chicheface; el vous mordra s'el vous encontre." Both these texts write the name with an *f*, and the former says nothing of any re- semblance between the monster and a cow; nor do most of the sixteenth-century pictures so represent Chichevache. That at the Château de Villeneuve has the body and head of a wolf, with horse's hoofs behind and claws in front; in her huge jaws she holds a struggling woman in bourgeois dress. Other cuts show the creature horned, however, and Lydgate (see stanza 12) is explicit. Doubtless as soon as the medial *f* was voiced enough to sound like *vache,* the legend responded.

For Bycorne or Bigorne there is much less to be said. Perhaps the change of *g* to *c,* giving the word the apparent meaning of "two-horned", followed the transmutation of Chichevache into a cow and the connection of the two beasts. There is a cow Bicorne in Nigel Wireker's Speculum Stultorum, a twelfth-century Anglo-Latin satire; but she merely cuts off her tail in despair when it is frozen into the ice, and has no function as a peripatetic censor. Lydgate mentions "Bycornys" in Troy Book ii :7702, with other woodland beings. The true French word *bigorne* meant either an iron-shod staff, or "argot", according to Godefroy; the transference to signify a beast of folk-lore is not yet explained. At the Château de Villeneuve the creature is represented as shortlegged, scaly-backed, and with a human head, in the huge jaws of which a man has disappeared all but the arms.

The use of verses to accompany tapestry or wall-paintings is an aspect of medieval art and letters not yet fully investigated. See Mâle's L'art réligieux de la fin du moyen-âge en France, Paris, 1908; see Jubinal, refs. of 1838 and 1840 in list below; see a few notes by me in Englische Studien 43 :10-26, prefacing prints of two tapestry-poems by Lydgate. See the text of "Dames illustres qui ont esté Roynes", stanzas written to accompany tapestries of eighteen queens, presented to Catherine de Médicis by their author, and at her bidding copied for Elizabeth of England. The transcript made for Elizabeth exists in Brit. Mus. Royal 20 A xx; see the 1921 catalogue of the Royal MSS. To some of its stanzas are prefixed directions for representing the figures; cf. Lydgate's procedure here. Stanzas painted, with their pictures, in the cloister of SS. Innocents at Paris served as Lydgate's original for the Dance Macabre; and he may have obtained the French of this poem in a similar way. There are some verbal resemblances between his lines and the surviving French poems on Bigorne and on Chinchefache; but structurally the English is quite different. In Lydgate the two monsters are represented, in the same poem, as husband and wife, and the text is arranged to suit a series of pictures.

The patient wife, and also the ungovernable wife, were stock subjects of medieval bourgeois narrative. Chaucer handled the former traditional theme, pitched in aristocratic key, in his Clerk's Tale of Griselda; but in the Clerk's envoy, so liberally used by Lydgate here, he adopted the bourgeois key. His Constance story, assigned to the Man of Law, is aristocratic in tone, with a few sly touches. Gower in his Constance-story, and Hoccleve in his tale of Jereslaus' Wife, are steadily aristocratic. Lydgate refers to Griselda here; and he refers to the Wife of Bath, Chaucer's full-length study of the ungovernable wife, both here and in his Mumming at Hertford. This latter, printed in Anglia 22 :364, and repr. by Neilson and Webster, p. 223, should be compared with this poem.

Three texts of this poem are known to me. The first, in Trinity College Cambridge R 3, 20, is here reproduced; it was written by John Shirley, the contemporary of Lydgate and admirer of Chaucer,—see p. 192 here. Another copy is in Brit. Mus. Harley 2251, a codex which in this part of its contents is copied from the Trinity College volume, and which has therefore no independent value at this point. A third copy is in Trin. Coll. Cambridge R 3, 19.

The poem was printed, from Harley 2251, in vol. xii of Dodsley's collection of old plays, eds. of 1780 and 1825-1827; and it was termed by Tyrwhitt, in his note on CantTales 9064, "a kind of pageant". But in the Gentleman's Magazine for 1834 ii:43, Thomas Wright published a notice of the R 3, 20 copy, and called attention to the detailed heading by Shirley describing the poem as intended for wall-hangings. The text was accordingly not reprinted by Hazlitt in his 1874 reëdition of Dodsley. It was again published from the Harley MS by Halliwell in his 1840 volume of Lydgate's minor poems, p. 129; and that text was reprinted by Montaiglon in his Recueil xi:280-83. Montaiglon also printed, *ibid.* ii:193-6, a translation of Lydgate into French prose. The poem, from MS Harley but with spelling somewhat modernized, was included by Henry Morley in his Shorter English Poems (1876), pp. 54-56. Halliwell's text was reprinted by Neilson and Webster, p. 220, with retention of Halliwell's errors; see the notes on our text.

SELECT REFERENCE LIST IV

Montaiglon, Recueil de poésies françoises des XVe et XVIe siècles, 13 vols., Paris, 1855-78.

Jubinal, Mystères inédits du XVe siècle, 2 vols., Paris, 1837.

Jubinal, Les anciennes tapisseries historiées, Paris, 1838.

Jubinal, Récherches sur l'usage et l'origine des tapisseries à personnages, Paris, 1840.

Le Franc, see dissertation by A. Piaget, Lausanne, 1888. Le Champion de Dames is discussed pp. 100-127; see pp. 111-12.

Wireker's Speculum Stultorum is ed. Th. Wright, Anglo-Latin Satirical Poets of the XII Century, Rolls Series, 1872, 2 vols.; see i:3 ff.

Les Lamentations de Mathéolus et la Livre de Léesce de Jehan le Fèvre, ed. with Latin original by A. G. van Hamel, 2 vols, Paris, 1892, 1905.

Langlois, ed. Recueil d'arts de séconde rhétorique, Paris, 1902, includes Baudet Herenc.

Neilson and Webster, Chief British Poets of the XIV and XV Centuries, Boston, 1916.

[MS Trinity College Cambridge R. 3, 20, p. 10]

LOO SIRS þE DEUISE OF A PEYNTED OR DESTEYNED CLOTHE FOR AN HALLE . A PARLOUR . OR
A CHAUMBRE DEUYSED BY JOHAN LIDEGATE AT þE REQUEST OF A WORþY
CITESEYN OF LONDOUN

ffirst þere shal
stonde an ymage in
poete wyse seying
þees thre balades

O prudent folkes takeþe heed
And remembreþe in youre lyves
Howe þis story / doþe proceed
Of þe housbandes / and of þeyre wyves
Of þeyre acorde / and of þeyre stryves   5
With lyf or deeþe / which to derrain
Is graunted / to þees beestis tweyn

2

Of *Chichevache* / and of *Bycorne*
Treteþe hooly / þis matere
Whos story haþe taught us here toforne   10
Howe þees beestis boþe in feere
Haue þeyre pasture / as yee shal here
Of men and wymmen / in se(n)tence
Thorugh soufferaunce or thoroughe inpacience

Shirley's running titles are: þe fourome of desguvsinges contreved by Daun Johan Lidegate.—þe maner of Straunge Desgysinges.—þe gyse of a right.
On the MS see p. 79 note.
Italicized words here represent underscorings by Shirley.

3

ffor þis *Bicorne* of his nature   *15*
Wil noon oþer maner foode
But pacient men in his pasture
And þene shalle And *Chichevache* . eteþe wymmen goode
þeer be portrayed And booþe þeos beestes by the Roode
twoo beestis oon Be fatte or leene / hit may not fayle   *20*
fatte anoþer leene Lyke lak or plente / of þeyre vitayle

4

þanne shall þer be Of Bycornoys / I am *Bycorne*
pourtrayhed a fatte fful fatte and rounde / here as I stonde
beest called By- And in maryage bonde and sworne
corne of the Cun- To *Chichevage* as hir husbande   *25*
trey of Bycornoys Whiche wil not ete on see nor lande
and seyne þees thre But pacyent wyves debonayre
balades filowing Which to hir husbandes. beon (not) contrayre

5

fful scarce god wot / is hir vitayle
Humble wyves she fyndeþe so fewe   *30*
ffor alweys. at þe countretayle
Þeyre tunge clappeþe and doþe hewe
Suche meke wyves / I beshrewe
Þat neyþer cane at bedde ne boord
Þeyre husbandes nought forbere on worde   *35*

6

But my foode and my cherisshing
To telle pleynly / and not tarye
Ys of suche folk / whiche þer living
Dar to þeyre wyves / be not contrarye
Ne frome þeyre lustis / dar not varye   *40*
Nor with hem holde / no chaumpartye
Alle suche my stomake . wol defye

7

þanne shal be pour- ffelawes takeþe heede and yee may see
trayed a companye Howe *Bicorne* . casteþe him to deuoure
of men comyng to- Alle humble men / boþe you and me   *45*
wardes þis beest Þer is no gayne vs may socour
Bicorne and sey Wo be þer fore in halle and bour
þees foure balades To alle þees husbandes . which þeyre lyves
Maken maystresses of þeyre wyves

8

Who þat so dooþe þis is þe lawe   *50*
Þat þis *Bycorne* wol him oppresse
And devowren in his mawe
Þat of his wyff makeþe his maystresse
Þis wol vs bring in gret distresse
ffor we for oure humylytee   *55*
Of Bycorne shal devowred be

9

We stonden pleynly in suche cas
Þat þey to vs maystresses be
We may wel sing and seyne allas

Þat we gaf hem þe souereynte 60
ffor we be thralle / and þey beo fre
Wher fore *Bycorne* þis cruell beste
Wol vs devowren at þe leest

10

But who þat cane be souereyne
And his wyf teeche and chastyse 65
Þat she dare nat a worde geyne seyne
Nor disobeye no maner wyse
Of suche a man I cane devyse
He stant vnder proteccioun
ffrome Bycornes . jurisdiccyoun 70

11

O noble wyves / beoþe wel ware
Takeþe ensaumple nowe by me
Or ellys afferme . weel I dare
Yee shall beo ded yee shal not flee
Beoþe crabbed . voydeþe humylitee
Or *Chychevache* / ne wol not fayle
You for to swolowe . in hir entrayle

*þanne shal þer be a
womman deuowred
yportrayhed in þe
mouþe of Chiche-
75 vache cryen to alle
wyves & sey þis
balade*

12

Chychevache . þis is my name
Hungry megre / sklendre and lene
To shewe my body I haue gret shame
ffor hunger / I feele so gret teene
On me no fattnesse wol beo seene
By cause þat pasture I fynde noon
Þer fore I am but skyn and boon

*þanne shal be þer
purtrayhed a longe
80 horned beest sklen-
dre and lene with
sharpe teethe and
on his body no
thinge saue skyn
and boone*

13

ffor my feding in existence 85
Is of wymmen þat beon meeke
And lyche *Gresylde* in pacyence
Or more þeyre bountee for to eeke
But I ful longe may goon and seeke
Or I cane fynde a gode repaaste 90
A morowe to breke with my faaste

14

I trowe þer beo a dere yeere
Of pacyent wymmen nowe þeos dayes
Who greueþe hem / with worde or chere
Let him be ware of suche assayes 95
ffor it is more þane thritty Mayes
Þat I haue sought frome lande to londe
But yit cane Gresylde neuer I fonde

15

I fonde but oone in al my lyve
And she was deed . sith go ful yore 100
ffor more pasture . I wil not stryve

Nor seeche for my foode no more
Ne for vitayle me to enstore
Wymmen beon wexen so prudent
Þey wol no more beo pacyent   *105*

16

þanne shal þere be My wyff allas devowred is
pourtrayhed affter Moost pacyente and mooste peysyble
Chichevache   an Sheo neuer sayde to me amysse
olde man with a Whome haþe nowe slayne þis beest horryble
bastoun   on   his And for it is an Impossyble   *110*
bakke manassing þe To fynde euer suche a wyff
beest for þe res- I wil lyve sool during my lyff
cowing of his wyff

17

ffor nowe of nuwe for þeyre prowe
Þe wyves of ful hyegh prudence
Haue of assent made þeyre avowe   *115*
ffor to exyle *pacience*
And cryed wolffes heed . *obedyence*
To make *Chichevache* fayle
Of hem to fynde more vitayle

18

Nowe *Chichevache* may fast longe   *120*
And dye for al hire cruweltee
Wymmen haue made hem self so stronge
ffor to outraye *humylyte*
O cely housbandes woo beon yee
Suche as cane haue no pacyence   *125*
Ageyns youre wyves vyolence

19

Yif þat yee suffre yee beo but deed
Þis *Bicorne* awayteþe yowe so soore
Eeke of youre wyves yee stonde in dreed
Yif yee geyne seye hem any more   *130*
And þus yee stonde / and haue doone yoore
Of lyff and deeth bytwix tweyne
Lynkeld in a double cheyne

PROLOGUE TO THE SIEGE OF THEBES

The Siege, or Story, of Thebes, 4716 lines in five-beat couplets, was written
by Lydgate as a supplementary Canterbury Tale. In his prologue he represents
himself as arriving at the Canterbury inn on the eve of the pilgrims' return to
London, as invited by the Host to join the party, and as beginning his tale at the
Host's command when the riders are outside town the next morning. The material of his narrative is part of that which Chaucer passed over as he opened
his Knight's Tale; Lydgate, however, did not use Chaucer's source, Boccaccio's
Teseide, nor the Latin of Statius, but, according to Koeppel, drew on some one
of the French prose romances connected with the rimed French Roman dé
Thèbes.

There is no evidence that the monk worked on commission, nor any external evidence as to the date of his translation. It appears possible not only that the Thebes was written soon after the Troy Book, as has been suggested, but also that it was written between the conclusion of the Troy Book (1420) and the composition of the Epithalamium for Gloucester, of latter 1421 or earlier 1422. The fact that Tydeus is brought in so unexpectedly and unusually as one of the great heroes with whom Gloucester is compared, and the fact that Calydon and Argos are mentioned in the Epithalamium to illustrate the union of countries by marriage, make it supposable that the Thebes-source, containing these details, had been already used by Lydgate. There are also stylistic points in which the Troy Book, the Thebes, and the Epithalamium show similarity. Aside from the romantic-epic tone of the two narratives, a tone faintly heard in the marriage-poem, note the management of the embassy-speech in Thebes 2016 ff. and compare Troy Book ii:1538; note the Shakespearean phrasing of Thebes 2305-6 and of Troy Book i:4100-01, ii:8197; note the leaning towards nature-pictures in Thebes, though to much less extent than in the Troy Book; cf. the formulae of Oedipus' wedding, Thebes 826 ff., with phrasings in the Epithalamium; cf. the detail of Thebes 1669 with Troy Book ii:3547, 4181. Other positive points might be adduced; and we may note the negative fact emphasized by Koeppel, that the death of Henry V (August 1422) is not mentioned in the Siege of Thebes,—also that Henry is still living when the Epithalamium is composed.

Failing any evidence of this poem's execution to order, it may be treated as a labor of love, an attempt on Lydgate's part to link his name with that of Chaucer and his effort with the Canterbury Tales. Yet it is not appended to many MSS of the Tales,—to but four so far as I have noted,—Adds. 5140 and Egerton 2864 of the British Museum, the privately owned Cardigan MS, and Christ Church College Oxford 152. Other copies of the poem are:—Brit. Mus. Arundel 119 (whence my text), Adds. 18632 (formerly the Denbigh MS), Adds. 29729, Cotton App. xxvii, and Royal 18 D ii; in the Bodleian Library are Bodley 776, Digby 230, Laud 416 and 557, and Rawlinson C 48; in the University Library Cambridge is Adds. 3137; in Trinity College Cambridge are O 5, 2 and R 4, 20; in the archiepiscopal library is Lambeth 742; in Durham Cathedral Library is Durham V ii, 14; in the library of Magdalen College Cambridge is Pepys 2011. Privately owned are a Gurney MS, Lord Bath's Longleat 257, Prince Frederick Dhuleep Singh's copy, formerly of the Tixall Library, and Lord Mostyn's MS containing the poem, bought in 1920 by Mr. Abbot.

To these twenty-four texts actually in existence we may add the copy in the lost Coventry School MS, for which see my Chaucer Manual, p. 354; and the copy bequeathed by John Baret of Bury in 1463 to his priestly cousin John Cleye. MacCracken's list erroneously includes Harley 262, which is a Turkish MS.

The poem was printed by de Worde ca.1500. In 1561 John Stow included it in his edition of Chaucer's Works, stating that it was by Lydgate; his own MS-copy exists in Brit. Mus. Adds. 29729. Subsequently collected eds. of Chaucer reprinted the poem, down to 1721, and it appears in Chalmers' English Poets, vol. i. It was edited for the EETS by Erdmann in 1911, vol. i, the text. Wülker, in his Altengl. Lesebuch, ii:105 (1879), reprinted the 1561 text of the Prologue, and was led by that into a few erroneous notes. The Arundel 119 text of the Prologue was printed by Miss Spurgeon in her EETS Chaucer Allusions i:26, and by me in Anglia 36:360, with notes.

The poem was modernized by Darton, London, 1904. Notes may be found in Gosse's ed. of Gray, i:387 ff., in Warton-Hazlitt's English Poetry, iii:74, and in ten Brink's English Literature, ii:225. See E. Koeppel, Lydgate's Story of Thebes, eine Quellenuntersuchung, Munich, 1884.

A work executed as appendage to Chaucer would naturally show the elder poet's influence. Ten Brink remarked that in this prologue Lydgate appeared almost as Chaucer's ape, a dictum warmly disputed by Churton Collins in his Ephemera Critica, p. 199. It is recommended to the student to trace these hundred and seventy-six lines, idea by idea and phrase by phrase, to their sources in the Canterbury Tales; to note the attempt at swinging sentence-management, at description of character, and at humor, and to establish thus an independent opinion of Lydgate's effort. There should also be read the prologue to Beryn, and perhaps Percy Mackaye's Canterbury Pilgrims.

Brit. Mus. Arundel 119, the manuscript here used, is dated by Ward, Catalogue of Romances, i:87, about 1430. The volume, which contains only this work, bears the arms of William de la Pole, earl of Suffolk, husband of Thomas Chaucer's daughter Alice; he died in 1450. As Lydgate's Virtues of the Mass was compiled for one of Suffolk's three wives, and as the monk's application, 1441, for renewed pension was supported by Suffolk, we recognize an associational value to this codex.

A few differences between the text of the prologue here printed and its EETS print have been verified by repeated collation. The Arundel MS has in the prologue one or two scribal slips; in 63 *take* is written for *tale,* in 110 *to* is omitted, and in 131 the *n* of *Canterbury* was not indicated by the customary horizontal line over the vowel.

[MS Brit. Mus. Arundel 119]

Phebus in Ariete	Whan briȝt Phebus / passed was þe ram
	Myd of Aprille / & in to bole cam
Saturnus in Virgine	And Satourn old / wt his frosty face
	In virgyne / taken had his place
	Malencolik / & slowgh of mocioun 5
	And was also / in thoposicioun
	Of lucina / the mone moyst and pale
	That many Shour / fro heuene made avale
	Whan Aurora / was in þe morowe red
Jubiter in capito cancri	And Iubiter / in the Crabbes Hed 10
	Hath take his paleys / and his mansioun
	The lusty tyme / and Ioly fressh Sesoun
	Whan that fflora / the noble myghty quene
	The soyl hath clad / in newe tendre grene
	With her floures / craftyly ymeynt 15
	Braunch & bough / wiþ red & white dopeynt
	ffletinge þe bawme / on hillis & on valys
	The tyme in soth / whan Canterbury talys
	Complet and told / at many sondry stage
	Of estatis // in the pilgrimage 20
	Euerich man / lik to his degre

Some of desport / somme of moralite
Some of knyghthode / loue and gentillesse
And some also of parfit holynesse
And somme also in soth / of ribaudye 25
To make laughter / in þe companye
Ech admitted / for non wold other greve
Lich as the Cook / þe millere and the Reve   *The cook the Mil-*
Aquytte hem silf / shortly to conclude   *lere and the reve*
Boystously in her teermes Rude 30
Whan þei hadde / wel dronken of the bolle
And ek also / with his pylled nolle
The pardowner beerdless al his Chyn   *Pardoner*
Glasy Eyed / and face of Cherubyn
Tellyng a tale / to angre with the frere 35
As opynly // the storie kan ȝow lere
Word for word / with euery circumstaunce
Echon ywrite / and put in remembraunce
By hym þat was / ȝif I shal not feyne   *Chaucer*
ffloure of Poetes / thorghout al breteyne 40
Which sothly hadde / most of excellènce
In rethorike / and in eloquence
Rede his making / who list the trouth fynde
Which neuer shal / appallen in my mynde
But alwey fressh / ben in my memoyre 45
To who be ȝoue / pris honure & gloyre
Of wel seyinge / first in oure language
Chief Registrer / of þis pilgrimage
Al þat was tolde / forȝeting noght at al
ffeyned talis / nor þing Historial 50
With many prouerbe / diuers & vnkouth
Be rehersaile / of his Sugrid mouth
Of eche thyng / keping in substaunce
The sentence hool / with oute variance
Voyding the Chaf / sothly for to seyn 55
Enlumynyng / þe trewe piked greyn
Be crafty writinge / of his sawes swete
ffro the tyme / that thei ded mete
ffirst the pylgrimes / sothly euerichon
At the Tabbard / assembled on be on 60   *At þe tabard in*
And fro Suthwerk / shortly forto seye   *Suthwerk*
To Canterbury / ridyng on her weie
Tellyng a ta(l)e / as I reherce can
Lich as the hoste / assigned euery man   *The hoste*
None so hardy / his biddying disobeye 65
And this whil / that the pilgrimes leye
At Canterbury / wel lo(g)ged on and all
I not in soth / what I may it call
Hap / or fortune / in Conclusioun
That me byfil / to entren into toun 70
The holy seynt / pleynly to visite
Aftere siknesse / my vowes to aquyte
In a Cope of blak / & not of grene   *Discryving of the*
On a palfrey / slender / long / & lene   *Monk*
Wiþ rusty brydel / mad nat for þe sale 75
My man to forn / with a voide male

Which of ffortune / took myn Inne anon
Wher þe pylgrymes / were logged euerichon
The same tyme / Her gouernour the host
Stonding in hall . ful of wynde & bost   80
Lich to a man / wonder sterne & fers
Which spak to me / and seide anon daun pers

The wordes of þe Daun Domynyk / Dan Godfrey / or Clement
host to the Monk 3e be welcom / newly into Kent
Thogh 3oure bridel / haue neiþer boos ne belle 85
Besechinge 3ou / þat 3e wil me telle
ffirst 3oure name / and of what contre
With oute mor . shortely that 3e be
That loke so pale / al deuoyde of blood
Vpon 3oure hede / a wonder thred bar hood   90
Wel araied / forto ride late

Lydgate I answerde / my name was Lydgate
Monk of Bery Monk of Bery / ny3 fyfty 3ere of age
Come to this toune / to do my pilgrimage
As I haue hight / I ha ther of no shame   95

The wordes of þe Dan Iohn quod he / wel broke 3e 3oure name
host Thogh 3e be soul / beth right glad & light
Preiyng 3ou / soupe with vs to nyght
And 3e shal han / mad at 3oure devis
A gret puddyng / or a rounde hagys   100
A ffranchmole / a tansey / or a froyse
To ben a Monk / Sclender is 3oure koyse
3e han be seke / I dar myn hede assure
Or late fed/ in a feynt pasture
Lift vp 3oure hed / be glad take no sorowe   105
And 3e shal hom ride with vs to morowe
I seye whan 3e rested han 3our fille
Aftere soper / Slepe wol do non ille
Wrappe wel 3oure hede / clothes rounde aboute
Strong notty ale / wol mak 3ou (to) route   110
Tak a pylow / þat 3e lye not lowe
3if nede be / Spar not to blowe
To holde wynde / be myn opynyoun
Wil engendre / collis passioun
And make men to greuen / on her roppys   115
Whan þei han filled / her mawes & her croppys
But toward nyght / ete some fenel Rede
Annys / Comyn / or coriandre sede
And lik as I / pouer haue & myght
I Charge 3ow / rise not at Mydnyght   120
Thogh it so be / the moone shyne cler
I wol my silf / be 3oure Orloger
To morow erly / whan I se my tyme
ffor we wol forþ / parcel afore Pryme
A company / parde / Shal do 3ou good   125
What look vp Monk / for by kokkis blood
Thow shalt be mery / who so þat sey nay
ffor to morowe anoon / as it is day
And that it gynne / in þe Est to dawe
Thow shalt be bound / to a newe lawe   130
Att goyng oute of Ca(n)terbury toune

And leyn aside / thy professioun
Thow shalt not chese / nor þi silf withdrawe
ȝif eny myrth / be founden in thy mawe
Lyk the custom / of this Compenye   *135*
ffor non so proude / that dar me denye
Knyght nor knaue / Chanon / prest / ne nonne
To telle a tale / pleynly as thei konne
Whan I assigne / and se tyme opportune
And for that we / our purpoos will contune   *140*
We wil homward / the same custome vse
And thow shalt not / platly the excuse
Be now wel war / Stody wel to nyght
But for al this / be of herte liȝt
Thy wit shall be / þe Sharper & the bet   *145*
And we anon / were to Soper set
And serued wel / vnto oure plesaunce
And sone after / be good gouernaunce
Vnto bed goth euery maner wight
And touarde morowe / anon as it was light   *150*
Euery Pilgryme / both bet & wors
As bad oure hoste / toke anon his hors
Whan the sonne / roos in the est ful clyere
ffully in purpoos / to come to dynere
Vnto Osspryng / and breke þer oure faste   *155*
And whan we weren / from Canterbury paste
Noght the space / of a bowe draught
Our hoost in hast / haþ my bridel raught
And to me seide / as it were in game
Come forth dan Iohn / be ȝour Cristene name *160*
And lat vs make / some manere myrth or play
Shet ȝoure portoos / a twenty deuelway
Is no disport / so to patere & seie
It wol make ȝoure lippes / wonder dreye
Tel some tale / and make ther of (a) Iape   *165*
ffor be my Rouncy / thow shalt not eskape
But prech not / of non holynesse
Gynne some tale / of myrth or of gladnesse
And nodde not / with thyn heuy bekke
Tell vs somme thyng / that draweþ to effekke *170*
Only of Ioye / make no lenger lette
And whan I saugh / it wolde be no bette
I obeyde / vnto his biddynge
So as the lawe / me bonde in al thinge
And as I coude / with a pale cheere   *175*
My tale I gan / anon / as ȝe shal here

         Explicit prologus

THE DANCE MACABRE

There exist in English two somewhat different recensions of a poem known as the Dance Macabre,[1] Dance of Death, or Dance of Paul's, a poem translated by John Lydgate from the French at the end of the first quarter of the fifteenth century. In this "dance" or procession, Death addresses in turn all classes of men, from Pope and Emperor to Laborer and Hermit, bidding them follow him; for each character who appears there is a stanza of summons by Death and a stanza of lamenting reply by the personage called. One of these two recensions, here termed A, is distinguished by five introductory stanzas in which Lydgate tells us that he had seen the French verses "depict upon a wall" at SS. Innocents' church in Paris, by an envoy of two stanzas in which he makes the conventional apology for his "rude language" and gives his name, and by several characters added to the French, notably the "tregetour" or juggler of Henry the Fifth. There are 36 personages in this version; it runs quite close to a French text (here printed), of which it frequently retains the rime-words.

. The other recension (B), is without the introduction and envoy; it omits a half-score of characters present in A, notably the Usurer, Tregetour, and Parson; and it adds a half-dozen to the earlier version. As it often gives its personages[2] a name not coincident with that given in A, and as it several times rewrites the stanzas, we cannot always determine whether B is rewriting A or substituting a different character. But that B is based upon A rather than upon the French is evident, e.g., from its retaining three of the five characters added by Lydgate to the French; see also the notes on lines 64, 137, 297. Only a complete parallel-text edition can show the many differences and resemblances of the two recensions, and the divergences of B-MSS from each other as compared to the general agreement of A-texts. The texts of B however resemble one another in a colorlessness, a tendency to empty generalities, wherever the A-type is abandoned.

A text of the earlier recension, that bearing Lydgate's name, is here printed, from the manuscript Selden supra 53 of the Bodleian Library at Oxford.[3] So

---

[1] The word *Macabre* should be pronounced trisyllabic and with last syllable stressed,— Mac-a-bray. For its meaning see note on line 24.

[2] Of the characters which the two recensions have in common, the arrangement is a little different. The order Pope-Emperor-Cardinal is the same in both, but in the sequence of the next nine characters B makes an interesting alteration. Lydgate had followed the French in putting King next to Cardinal, with Patriarch, Duke, Archbishop, Baron, Bishop, Squire, Abbot, in the order named. The B-reviser transposed the pairs King-Patriarch, Duke-Archbishop, etc., so as to give precedence to the spiritual dignitary in each case. The juxtaposition of two ecclesiastical lords, Cardinal and Patriarch, was avoided in B by the insertion of the Empress after the Cardinal. Similarly, the Emperor is not in B termed "hiest of noblesse", but is "surmountyng of noblesse"; and yet while A, in line 60, gives the Pope sovereignty over "the chirche and states temporal", the B-version alters to "the chirche most in especial".

[3] Bodl. Selden supra 53 is on vellum, in eights, of 159 leaves 10¼ by 7½ inches, and is impf. at beginning. It is well written in one strong square neat professional hand, with numerous marginal rubrics and small red and blue capitals to stanzas. It contains:—Hoccleve's Regement of Princes, impf. at beginning, ending 76 a.—Hoccleve's Complaint, Dialogue, etc., i.e. the group of his poems termed "the Series" p. 57 here.—The Dance Macabre, foll. 148 a– 158 b. No heading; in the margin, red, "Verba translatoris". Colophon in red, leaf rubbed, —"Here e............ the Daunce of De........" Below, on 158 b, a different hand has written the two Empress-stanzas; cf. the B-recension. Leaf 159, a guard-leaf, darkened, carries a copy of "Earth upon earth".

far as I know, five other texts of that type exist, in Brit. Mus. Harley 116, in Bodley 221 and Laud 735 of the Bodleian, in Trinity College Cambridge R 3,21, and in a codex formerly belonging to the Earl of Ellesmere, now in the Huntington Library, California.[1] The lost manuscript of Coventry School, described by Bernard in his 1697 Catalogus as containing this poem, agreed in contents with Laud and Bodley.

The B-recension appears in five manuscripts:—Bodley 686 of the Bodleian Library, Corpus Christi College Oxford 237, Lansdowne 699 of the Brit. Mus., and its partial sister Leyden Vossianus 9 of Leyden, Holland; this last I have not seen. It is also in the MS Lincoln Cathedral C 5,4; and a fragment exists in Brit. Mus. Cotton Vespasian A xxv. The miscellaneous Lydgate-codices Lansdowne (and Leyden?) show very free handling in all their texts, so free that in this poem they do not fairly represent the B-type.

The A-version of the Dance Macabre was printed by Tottel with the 1554 Fall of Princes; this was reprinted by Dugdale in his History of St. Paul's Cathedral, 1658, and in his Monasticon Anglicanum, 1673, vol. iii; the text may also be found in Francis Douce's monograph on Holbein's Dance of Death, London, 1790, and in Montaiglon's edition of Holbein's Alphabet of Death, Paris, 1846. With his edition of Lydgate's Fall of Princes, 1923, vol. iii, Dr. Henry Bergen printed the Tottel text of the Dance, collated with Harley 116 and "in part with Lansdowne 699".

As Lydgate says in his stanzas of introduction and envoy, he found the original of his poem at Paris, "depict vppon a walle" at the Church of the Innocents; and being urged by French clerks, he undertook a translation and sent it home to England. That the monk was in Paris about 1426 is probable from his Pedigree of Henry VI, done in that year from the French at the request of the Earl of Warwick, who was then in France; it is further probable from the fact that the Dance-fresco had since 1424 been upon the walls of SS. Innocents, and had made a strong impression upon beholders.

A similar use was made of Lydgate's translation, or some modified form of it, in London. Stow in his Survey of London (ed. Kingsford, i: 327) says that about the cloister of St. Paul's was "artificially and richly painted the dance of Machabray, or dance of death, commonly called the dance of Pauls: the like whereof was painted about S. Innocents cloyster at Paris in France: the meters or poesie of this dance were translated out of French into English by Iohn Lidgate Monke of Bury, the picture of death leading all estates, at the dispense of Ienken Carpenter, in the raigne of Henry the sixt." As Kingsford points out, this painting was known to Sir Thomas More, who alludes to it as the Daunce of Death. The cloister was pulled down in 1549.

No trace now remains of the few fifteenth or sixteenth-century English representations of the Dance Macabre. There was a tapestry of "Makaborne" in the collection of Henry VIII; there was a fresco in the archiepiscopal palace at Croydon, one in Salisbury Cathedral, and one in Wortley Hall, Gloucestershire. Whether these, or any of these, were of the same processional character as the pictures of St. Paul's, we do not know; nor do we know whether or not they had accompanying texts, except that the late and poor Cotton MS text of our Dance is said to be that of Wortley Hall. The verses of Lydgate were

---

[1] Collations of the MS El 26 A 13 I owe to the kindness of Capt. R. B. Haselden, Keeper of MSS in the Huntington Library.

separately preserved, and there are a number of English poems on death which allude to the Dance of Paul's or to some similar picture; for example, a clumsy poem transcribed in MS Brit. Mus. Adds. 37049, in which the tenth stanza begins,—"Man remembyr of þe dawnce of makabre"; or in two poems printed with Lydgate's by Halliwell, pp. 34, 77.

Both as picture and as text, the Dance of Death, or Triumph of Death, is a West-European phenomenon. Sometimes restricted to the limits of an illumination in a missal, sometimes extended all along the arcades of a cloister or a bridge, or carved in the tympanum of a cathedral porch, the idea was widespread and powerfully effective. In Italy we have such graveyard monuments as the great fresco of the Campo Santo at Pisa, with a row of corpses stretched before the feet of an unwary party of gay riders; or the picture in the Church of the Disciplini at Clusone, depicting three huge skeletons standing upon an open tomb surrounded by imploring popes, kings, and ecclesiastics, while below passes the procession of humanity, each figure escorted by a skeleton. In France there were the pictures and texts of Paris and of Kermaria in Britanny, the pictures of La Chaise-Dieu in Auvergne, and the tapestries of Amiens Cathedral. In Germany and in Switzerland traces are numerous, although the texts once in Basel, Berlin, and Lübeck are now largely illegible, and the later work of Holbein and the well-known pictures of the Mühlenbrücke at Lucerne are more famous than their prototypes. The "Death-motif" which inspires the Dance also inspired the representations of the Three Living and Three Dead (another branch of this subject) and inspired the many Triumphs of Death, of which latter Petrarch's poem and its woodcut-illustrations are the most striking examples.

In the pictures and texts of Northern Europe there is a tone quite different from the more formal Triumph as seen in Italy, a tone belonging to the later medieval, bourgeois society out of which these Northern dances grew. The Dance of Death has a number of elements. There is the figure of a guide or leader to the after-life, a motive of great antiquity; there is the processional motive, also very old; there is the dialogue-form; and there are two ideas of quite different date,—the feeling of Death's malignant satisfaction in his work, and the insistence on a social classification of his victims. While the former of these ideas is by no means foreign to the Etruscan grave-frescoes, executed before the Christian era, the emphatic combination of the two, as in the Dance here discussed, may indicate the condition of a society in which the Black Death was rampant and in which the feudal system was breaking up.

The appearance of those summoned by Death in an ordered class-list is not so very late in the medieval period. A Latin poem of perhaps the twelfth century, the "Vado Mori", introduces twelve figures, from Pope to pauper, each speaking two lines of farewell to life; and in a probably later development of this theme, the dialogue-structure appears, some interlocutor (not Death) speaking a companion couplet beginning "Vive Deo" each time. So far as I know, these are the earliest texts to make the classed arrangement; for although the Etruscan frescoes were so interpreted at first, recent investigation has rejected the possibility of any "class-idea" in the procession depicted, for instance, in the Grotto del Cardinale at Corneto.

I subjoin a text of the Vado Mori, from MS Brit.Mus.Lansdowne 397.

Dum mortem meditor crescit michi causa
  doloris
Nam cuntis horis mors venit ecce citor
Pauperis et regis communis lex moriendi
Dat causam flendi si bene scripta legis
Gustato pomo nullus transit sine morte
Heu (misera) sorte labitur omnis homo

Vado mori papa qui iussu regna subegi
Mors michi regna tulit eccine vado mori

Vado mori rex sum quid honor quid
  gloria regum
Est via mors hominis regia vado mori

Vado mori presul cleri populique lucerna
Qui fueram validus langueo vado mori

Vado mori miles victor certamine belli
Mortem non didici vincere vado mori

Vado mori monachus mundi moriturus
  amori
Vt moriatur amor hic michi vado mori

Vado mori legista fui defensor egenis
Causidicus causas (desero) vado mori

Vado mori logicus aliis concludere noui
Conclusit breuiter mors michi vado mori

Vado mori medicus medicamine non
  redimendus
Quicquid agat medici pocio vado mori

Vado mori sapiens michi nil sapiencia
  prodest
Me reddit fatuum / mors fera vado mori

Vado mori diues (ad) quid michi copia
  rerum
Dum mortem nequeat pellere vado mori

Vado mori cultor collegi farris aceruos
Quos ego pro vili computo vado mori

Vado mori pauper quem (semper) Chris-
  tus amauit
Hunc sequar euitans omnia vado mori

Bracketed words above are from the MS Brit. Mus. Adds. 38131. Similar texts are found in Brit. Mus. Adds. 24660 and Royal 5 E xxi, in a MS at Erfurt printed by Fehse in Zeitschr. f. deut. Philol. 42:277, and in two MSS mentioned by Storck *ibid*. 42:422. Versions expanded by additional characters are mentioned by Storck, and are in Brit. Mus. Adds. 18347 and Royal 7 E vii. For the expanded or dialogue-version, see my article in Modern Philology, vol. 8.

This "Vado Mori" idea and phrasing were popular as all Death-poetry was and is popular. Citations, or English versions of bits, appear in many MSS; thus, in Brit. Mus. Cotton Faustina B vi, and in Stowe 39, are rimed alliterative versions of a few stanzas, introducing the king, the knight, and a cleric,—e.g., "I wende to dede knight stithe in stoure Thurghe fyght in felde I wane þe flour Na fightes me taght þe dede to quell I weend to dede soth I yow tell." And detached stanzas of the Latin are at the top of some pages of the 1490 French Danse des Hommes in Guyot Marchand's edition.

It seems obvious that these stanzas were intended to accompany either paintings or a mimetic presentation. Whether the repetition of *Vado Mori* at the end of each distich were an exit-phrase for the moving figure, or merely a rhetorical device, is uncertain; and in the expanded form of the text it is also uncertain who is the speaker of the "Vive Deo" distich. It may well have been not Death, but a homilist into whose sermon this pageant was inserted, and who from his pulpit commented on each passing figure. Such indeed is the view of Mâle, in his admirable work on late medieval religious art, p. 392, who suggests that the origin of the Death-dances is to be sought in the "illustrated" medieval sermon. While the preacher warned and exhorted, the costumed figures of king, soldier, laborer, etc., passed below his pulpit; and impressive as might be the oratorical warning each time repeated, the effect of the shrouded seizing Death-figure, later perhaps of the speaking Death-figure, must have been powerful indeed. On such a theory, the Dance Macabre, in its rudimentary or its developed form, would have its fountain-head even where the medieval drama rose. Such a presentation, after it began to use the visible figure of Death which at first did not appear, could manage with one Death, who met and seized each personage as he entered from the "wings" and convoyed him across in front of the congregation. But the treatment of the theme in a series of wall-paintings, broken into arcades as were the cloisters of SS. Innocents at Paris, compelled the painter to repeat each time the figure of Death, a device accepted by the onlookers with no more imaginative difficulty than Romans felt in viewing the column of Trajan with its ninety-times-repeated figure of the Emperor. The endeavor of some scholars to explain the numerous skeletons of the Dance Macabre paintings as the Dead escorting their living brethren, rather than as Death, is based upon a reading of modern ideas into medieval artistic conditions. The repetition of the skeleton puzzled no medieval understanding.

The immense attraction of the theme for all humanity needs no comment. But the many visitations of the plague to West Europe between 1348 and 1450 must have especially affected the imagination and the art-expression of those years. When we consider that in the first month alone of the World War there were some 1500 cartoons of Death on the battle-field, it is easy to believe that the swiftness, the deadliness, and the impartiality of the Black Death assisted in raising the tide of Death-literature and Death-painting that flowed over Europe in the fifteenth century. Every third spade-thrust into manuscript-mould of that period brings up a farewell or an epitaph or a dialogue of Soul and Body or a lyric on this haunting theme, with occasionally a direct allusion to "stroke of pestilence", such as Lydgate here makes. Some share the Black Death must have had in giving this mass of grave-literature its frequent hard fierceness of tone.

But not all the popularity of the motive in the fifteenth century is due to the especial sense then prevalent of the uncertain tenure of life. Elsewhere in this volume are pointed out similarities between the fifteenth and the eighteenth century; and this is another. An age lacking in enthusiasms and convictions, an age of dull sense-perceptions and low creative power, that is, an age of strong inhibitions, tends to the acceptance of authority, to formulae, and to the expression of those didactic and melancholic feelings which the torpid or the conventionalized mind considers "decorous". The wide popularity of the "grave-yard school" of the eighteenth century, the mass of imitations of Gray's Elegy, the welcome extended by Germany and by France to Young's Night Thoughts (1742-44) and to Blair's Grave (1743), the tomb-sculptures and the engravings of the period, all indicate, not the insecurity and terror of plague or war, but the reduction of creative power. The eighteenth-century pre-occupation with death is less harshly conspicuous than that of the fifteenth century because, in the three hundred and fifty years which had elapsed since Chaucer, England had laid down what we may call, in the combined phrase of Carlyle. Sainte-Beuve, and Fitzgerald, a "substratum of intellectual peat", a soil which by 1750 had become so deep that no temporary drought could deprive it of its living forests. No poetic luxuriance obliterates the tendency to the didactic and the melancholic, which is especially marked in the Northern races; even in the greatest there is the horrified cry of Claudio, the musing of Jaques and the gloom of Hamlet, the farewell of Prospero. But with Shakespeare the figure of Death remains well beyond the crowded doorway of life. Not only the imminence of terror, but the absence of vigor, the dulling of perception, can make his figure assume disproportionate magnitude. And in the fifteenth century both elements, the physical fear and the lowered intellectual vitality, combined to spread the Death-fascination.

So far as the Dance Macabre is concerned, England took her text from France, through Lydgate. The French text is definitely literary as compared with the single existing Spanish Dance of Death and with a German text (Lübeck) which resembles the Spanish in addressing the eighth and last line of each Death-speech to the next victim. Such a peculiarity is neither pictorial nor literary; it implies representation by living beings. And however the patriotic dispute as to priority of Dance-text may be waged, the student perceives that one class of texts is of the dramatic-sermon type and another of the wall-fresco type. To the latter category belonged the poem translated by Lydgate. The pictures which accompanied his text, and its original, both perished in the sixteenth century by the destruction of St. Paul's cloisters and of the Church of SS. Innocents in Paris; but both the French and English poems survive in transcripts,[1] and a French wall-picture at Kermaria, Brittany, is copied, in figures and in text, from the Paris Dance. (See Soleil as below.)

The length of stanza in French and in English was no obstacle to the use of these poems in fresco or in tapestry. Stained-glass windows no larger than those of the little church of Our Lady at Grand Andelys, Normandy, carry four-line stanzas descriptive of the Clovis and Clotilde pictures they present; Lydgate in his Bycorne and Chichevache, or Sir Thomas More in his poems written for tapestries in his father's house,[2] used the seven-line stanza; the tapestry-verses written in French for Catherine de Médicis[3] ran in some cases to twenty lines for the "Dames illustres" there represented; and much earlier, in the third century, Prudentius drew up a Diptychon or Dittochaeon of 49 hexametric four-line stanzas to serve as legends for sacred pictures.

Lydgate's translation of the French is, he says, "not word by word but following the substance"; it adheres much more closely to its original, however, than is usual with him. The structure of the poem compelled him to fidelity and restrained his verbosity. The desire to retain the proverbial line with which each stanza of the French closes,—a literary device which appealed strongly to his taste,—also led him to take over much of the French rime-scheme. The proverbial line and its mate gave him but two of his eight lines and one of his three rimes; two more rime-sounds had to be found, one of which must serve for four lines; and his resort for this latter to words of Romance endings should be compared with the French. Occasionally, as in stanzas 21 and 48, none of the French rime-sounds is preserved; and in the stanzas added by Lydgate to the French he has a closing proverb only in the case of the Abbess. As the French line is of four beats and the Lydgatian of five, there is a small amount

---

[1] The French text preserved in a MS of the Bibliothèque Communale at Lille, which is very close to Lydgate's version, is printed in the Notes below. Whether this MS still exists or not, after the fire during the German occupation of Lille, I cannot say; I have no reply to inquiries.

[2] These stanzas are reprinted by Flügel, Neuengl. Lesebuch, pp. 40-42.

[3] See the British Museum Catal. of Western MSS in the Old Royal and Kings' Collections, 1921, under Royal 20 A xx.

of padding in the English, increased somewhat by the exigencies of rime and by Lydgate's natural tendency to set phrases such as:—as I reherce can, whoso takith hede, who prudently can se, if I shall nat tarie; etc.

Such merit as the poem possesses is, of course, due to its French original; but even in the somewhat wooden translation of Lydgate the subject arouses interest. A study of Death, be it a wall-fresco of the fifteenth century or a sculpture such as the Paris *Aux Morts* of the twentieth, reaches the imagination of the man in the street. And the fifteenth-century Dance derived additional power from its satiric character. In it the rich, the mighty, the gifted, are as helpless as the laborer; all the artificial and ephemeral distinctions of life disappear. The bourgeois spectator of the Dance shared the harsh satisfaction of Death himself in levelling social differences. In such and similar insistences on the fragility of human prosperity the spirit of the time revelled; as Gaston Paris has said:—"Deux thèmes revenaient sans cesse dans cette littérature; des considérations sur la puissance et les vicissitudes de la fortune et des réflexions sur l'inéluctabilité de la mort."

SELECT REFERENCE LIST V

Douce, The Dance of Death . . . . . ascribed to Macaber and Hans Holbein, London, 1794?, 1833, etc.

Langlois, Pottier, Baudry, Essai historique, philosophique, et pittoresque sur les dances des morts, 2 vols., Rouen, 1852.

Soleil, Les heures gothiques et la littérature pieuse au xve et xvie siècles, Paris, 1882

Seelmann, Die Totentänze des Mittelalters, Leipzig, 1893.

Vigo, Le danze macabre in Italia, Bergamo, 2d ed., 1901.

Fehse, Der Ursprung der Totentänze, Halle, 1907.

Dimier, Les dances macabres et l'idée de la Mort dans l'art chrétien, Paris, 1908.

Mâle, L'art religieux de la fin du moyen-âge en France, Paris, 1908.
    See also his art. in Revue de deux mondes 32:647-679 (1906).

Künstle, Die Legende der drei Lebenden und der drei Toten und der Totentanz, Freiburg, 1908. See chap. v for survey and criticism of previous work.

Fehse, Das Totentanzproblem, in Ztschr. f. deut. Philol. 42:261-286 (1910). Combating Künstle's theory of the derivation of the Dance from the Legend.

Storck, Die Legende von den drei Lebenden u. von den drei Toten, Tübingen diss., 1910.

Storck, Das "Vado Mori", in Ztschr. f. deut. Philol. 42:422-28 (1910).

Hammond, Latin Texts of the Dance of Death, in ModPhil 8:399-410 (Jan. 1911).

Durwächter, Die Totentanzforschung, in Festschrift f. G. von Hertling, i:390 ff., 1913.

Glixelli, Les cinq poèmes des Trois Morts et des Trois Vifs, Paris, 1914.

Huet, Notes d'histoire littéraire: iii, La Danse Macabre, Paris, 1918. (On the word *macabre*.)

Martha, J., L'art étrusque, Paris, 1889. See p. 393.

Weege, F., Etruskische Malerei, Halle, 1921. See p. 77 for the Tomba del Cardinale.

Poulsen, F., transl. Andersen, Etruscan Tomb Painting, Oxford, 1922. See p. 58, and plate to face, for the Tomba del Cardinale.

[MS Bodleian Selden supra 53, fol. 148a]

Verba translatoris

O ȝee folkes / harde hertid as a stone ·
Wich to þe worlde / haue al ȝour aduer-
tence
Liche as it shulde / laste euere in oone ·
Where is ȝour witt / wher is ȝour pru-
dence
To se aforn / the sodeine violence ·   5
Of cruel dethe / þat be so wis and sage ·
Wiche sleeth allas / by stroke of pesti-
lence ·
Boþe ȝong and olde / of lowe & hy
parage ·

2

Deeth sparith not / lowe ne hy degre ·
Popes kynges ne worthy Emperours ·   10
Whan þei shyne / most in felicite ·
He can abate / þe fresshnes of her
flours ·
The briȝt sonne / clipsen with his shours ·
Make hem plunge / from her sees lowe ·
Magre þe myȝt / of alle these conquer-
ours ·   15
ffortune hath hem / from her whele
ythrowe ·

3

Considerith þis / ȝe folkes that be wys ·
And it enprentith / in ȝoure memorial ·
Like þensaumple / wiche þat at Parys ·
I fonde depict / oones in a wal ·   20
fful notably / as I reherce shal ·
Ther of frensshe clerkis / takyng aquein-
taunce ·
I toke on me / to translatyn al ·
Oute of þe frensshe / machabres daunce ·

4

By whos avys / and counceil atte þe
leste ·   25
Thoruȝ her steryng / · and her mocioun ·
I obeide / vn to her requeste ·
Ther of to make / a playn translacioun ·
In englissh tonge / of entencioun ·
That proude folkes / wiche þat be stout
& bold ·   30
As in a mirrour / to for in her resoun ·
Her ougly fine / may cleerly ther bihold ·

5

By exaumple / þat þei in her ententis ·
Amende her lif / in euery manere age ·

The wiche daunce / at seint Innocen-
tis ·   35
Portreied is / with al þe surpluage ·
To shewe þis worlde / is but a pilgrimage ·
ȝove vn to vs / our lyves to correcte ·
And to declare / the fyne of oure passage ·
Riȝt anoon / my stile I wole directe · 40

6

Verba auctoris

O creatures / ȝe that be reasonable ·
The lyf · desiring / wiche is eternal ·
ȝe may se here · doctrine ful notable ·
ȝoure lif to lede / wiche þat is mortal ·
Ther by to lerne / in especial ·   45
Howe ȝe shul trace / þe daunce of
Machabre ·
To man & womman / yliche natural ·
ffor deth ne spareth / hy ne lowe degre ·

7

In þis mirrour / euery wiȝt may finde ·
That him bihoveth / to goo vpon þis
daunce ·   50
Who goth to forn / or who shal goo be
hinde ·
Al dependith / in goddis ordinaunce ·
Wherfore eche man / lowly take his
chaunce ·
Deeth spareth not / pore ne blood royal ·
Eche man þerfore / haue in remem-
braunce ·   55
Of o mater / god hath forged al ·

8

Deeth to the Pope[1]

O ȝee þat be set / most hie in dignite
Of alle estatis / in erthe spiritual
And like as Petir had þe souereinte
Overe þe chirche / and statis temporal 60
Vpon þis daunce / ȝe firste begyn shal
As moste worthy lorde / and gouernour
ffor al þe worship / of ȝoure astate papal
And of lordship / to god is the honour

9

The Pope aunswerith

First me bihoueth / þis daunce for to
lede ·   65
Wich sat in erþe / hiest in my see ·

[1]This and other stanza-headings are in the margin
of the MS.

The state ful perillous / ho so takith
   hede ·
To occupie / Petris dignite ·
But al for that / deth I may not fle ·
On his daunce / with other for to trace ·
ffor wich / al honour / who prudently
   can se ·
Is litel worth / that doþe so sone pace ·

10

Deeth to the Emperour

Sir Emperour / lorde of al the ground ·
Souerein prince / and hiest of noblesse ·
Ȝe must forsake / of golde ȝour appil
   round ·   75
Septre and swerd / and al ȝoure hy
   prowesse ·
Behinde leve / ȝour tresour and ricch-
   esse ·
And with othir / to my daunce obeie ·
Aȝein my myȝt / is worth noon hardi-
   nesse ·
Adamis children / alle þei moste deie ·

11

The Emperour answerith

I note to whom / þat I may (me) apele ·
Touching deth / wiche doth me so con-
   streine ·
There is no gein / to helpe my querele ·
But spade / and pikois / my graue to
   ateyne ·
A simple shete / ther is no more to
   seyne ·   85
To wrappe in my body / and visage ·
Ther vpon sore / I may compleine ·
That lordis grete / haue litel avauntage ·

12

Deeth to þe cardinal

Ȝe be abaisshid / it semeth and in drede ·
Sir cardinal / it shewith by ȝoure chere ·
But ȝit for thy / ȝe folowe shulle in
   dede ·
With oþir folke / my daunce for to lere ·
Ȝoure grete aray / al shal bileven here ·
Ȝoure hatte of reed / ȝoure vesture of
   grete cost ·
Alle these þingis / rekenyd wele y
   fere ·   95
In greet honour / good avis is lost ·

---

81. Bracketed word from Harley 116.

13

The cardinal answerith ·

I haue grete cause / certis this is no
   faille ·
To bene abaisshid / and greetly drede
   me ·
Seth deeth is come / me sodeinly to as-
   saille ·
That I shal neuere / her aftir clothed
   be ·   100
In grys ne ermyn / like to my degre ·
My hatte of reed / leue eke in distresse
By wiche I haue / lyved wel and see ·
Howe þat al Ioie / endith in heuynesse ·

14

Deeth to the kyng ·

O noble kyng / moste worþi of renoun ·
Come forþe anone / for al ȝoure worþi-
   nesse ·
That somtyme had / aboute ȝow envir-
   oun ·
Greet rialte / and passing hy noblesse ·
But riȝt anoone / (for) al ȝoure grete
   hynes ·
Sool fro ȝoure men / in hast ȝe shul it
   lete ·   110
Who moste aboundiþ / here in greet
   ricches ·
Shal bere with hym / but a sengle shete ·

15

The kyng answeriþ ·

I haue not lernyd / here a forn to
   daunce ·
No daunce in sooth / of footyng so
   sauage ·
Wherfore I see / by clere demon-
   straunce ·   115
What pride is worth / force or hy lyn-
   age ·
Deeth al fordoþe / this is his vsage ·
Greet and smale / þat in þis worlde
   soiourne ·
Ho is most meke / I hold he is most
   sage ·
ffor he shal al to dede asshes tourne · 120

16

Deeth to þe Patriarke ·

Sir Patriarke / alle ȝoure humble chere ·
Ne quite ȝow not / ne ȝoure humilite ·
Ȝoure double crosse / of gold and stones
   clere ·
Ȝoure power hoole / and al ȝoure dignite ·

Some othir shal / of verrey equite · *125*
Possede anoone / as I reherce can ·
Trustiþ neuere / that ȝe shulle pope be ·
ffor foly hope / deceiveth many a man ·

17

The Patriarke aunsweriþ ·

Worldly honour / greet tresour & rich-
esse ·
Han me deceivid / sothfastly in dede · *130*
Myn olde Ioies / be turned to tristesse ·
What vailith it / suche tresour to pos-
sede ·
Hy clymbyng vp / a falle hath for his
mede ·
Grete estates / folke wasten oute of
noumbre ·
Who mountith hy / it is sure and no
drede   *135*
Greet berthen / doþe hym ofte encom-
bre ·

18

Deeth to þe constable ·

It is my riȝt / to reste and ȝow constreine ·
With vs to daunce / my maister sir
Constable ·
ffor more strong / þan euere was Char-
lemayne ·
Deeth hath aforced / and more wor-
shipable ·   *140*
ffor hardines / ne knyȝthood / þis is no
fable ·
Ne stronge armvre / of plates ne of
mayle ·
What geyneth armes / of folkes moste
notable ·
Whan cruel deeth / lest hem to assaille ·

19

The constable answeriþ ·

My purpos was / and hool enten-
cioun ·   *145*
To assaille castelles / and miȝty forteresses ·
And bringe folke / vn to subieccioun ·
To seke honour & fame / and grete
richesses ·
But I se wel / þat al worldly prowesses
Deeth can abate / wich is a grete dis-
pite ·   *150*
To him al oone / sorwe and eke swet-
nesses ·
ffor aȝein deeth / is founden no respite ·

20

Deeth to þe Archebisshop ·

Sir Archebisshoppe / whi do ȝe ȝow
withdrawe ·
So frowardly / as it were by disdeyn ·
Ȝe muste aproche / to my mortel lawe ·
It to contrarie / it nere not but in veyn ·
ffor day by day / þere is noon othir geyn ·
Deeth at þe hande / pursueth euery
coost ·
Prest and dette / mote be ȝolde aȝein ·
And at o day / men counten wiþ her
oost ·   *160*

21

The Archebisshoppe · answerith ·

Allas I woote not / what partie for to
flee ·
ffor drede of dethe / I haue so grete
distresse ·
To ascape his myȝt / I can no refute se ·
That who so knewe / his constreint and
duresse ·
He wolde take resoun to maistresse · *165*
A dewe my tresour / my pompe and pride
also ·
My peintid chaumbres / my port & my
fresshnesse ·
ffor thing that bihoveth / nedes must
be do ·

22

Deth to þe Baroun ·

Ȝe þat amonge lordis / and barouns ·
Han had so longe / worship and re-
noun ·   *170*
fforȝete ȝoure trumpetis / and ȝoure
clariouns ·
This is no dreme / ne simulacioun ·
Somtime ȝoure custome / and entencioun ·
Was with ladies / to daunce in þe shade ·
But ofte it happith / in conclusioun · *175*
That o man brekith / þat a noþir made ·

23

The Baroun or the knyȝt answerith ·

Ful ofte siþe / I haue bene auctorised ·
To hie emprises / and þinges of greet
fame ·
Of hie and lowe / my thanke also
deuised ·
Cherisshed wiþ ladies / and wymmen hie
of name ·   *180*
Ne neuere on me / was put no defame ·
In lordis court / wiche þat was notable ·

But deeþis strook / hath made me so
lame ·
Vndre heuene / in erþe / is no thing
stable ·

24

Deeth to þe lady of grete astate ·
Come forþe anone / my lady and Princesse ·   *185*
3e muste also / goo vp on this daunce ·
Not may availle / 3oure grete straunge-
nesse ·
Nouþer 3oure beute / ne 3oure greet
plesaunce ·
3oure riche aray / ne 3oure daliaunce ·
That svmtyme / cowde so many holde an
honde ·   *190*
In loue for al / 3oure double variaunce ·
Ye mote as nowe / þis footing vndirstonde ·

25

The lady answerith ·
Allas I see / ther is none othir boote ·
Deeth hath in erthe / no lady ne maistresse ·
And on his daunce / 3it muste (I) nedis
foote ·   *195*
ffor þere nys qwene contesse ne duchesse ·
fflouringe in bounte / ne in fairnesse ·
That she of deeth / mote deþes trace
sewe ·
ffor to (oure) bewte / and countirfeet
fresshnesse ·
(Oure) rympled age / seith fare wele
a dewe ·   *200*

26

Deeth to þe Bisshoppe ·
My lorde sir Bisshoppe / with 3oure
mytre & croos
ffor al 3oure ricchesse / sothly I ensure ·
ffor al 3oure tresour / so longe kept in
cloos ·
3oure worldly goodes / and goodes of
nature ·
And of 3oure sheep / þe dredly goostly
cure ·   *205*
With charge committid / to 3oure pre-
lacie ·
ffor to acounte / 3e shulle be brou3te to
lure ·
No wi3t is sure / þat clymbeth ouere hie ·

27

The Bisshoppe answeriþ ·
My herte truly / is nouþer glad ne myrie

Of sodein tidinges / wiche þat 3e
bring   *210*
My fest is turned / in to a simple ferye ·
That for discomfort / me list no þing
syng ·
The worlde contrarie nowe / vn to me
in workyng ·
That alle folkes / can so disherite ·
He þat al withhalt / allas at oure part-
ing ·   *215*
And al shal passe / saue only oure
merite ·

28

Deeth to þe Squier ·
Come forth sir Squier / ri3t fresshe of
3oure aray ·
That can of daunces / al þe newe gise ·
Thou3 3e bare armes / fressh horsed
3isterday ·
With spere and shelde / at 3oure vnkouþe
deuise ·   *220*
And toke on 3ow / so many hy emprise
Daunceth with vs / it wil no bettir be ·
Ther is no socour / in no manere wise ·
ffor no man may / fro deþes stroke fle

29

The Squier aunswerith ·
Siþen þat deþe / me holdith in his
lace ·   *225*
3et shal y speke / o worde or y pase ·
A dieu al myrþe / a dieu nowe al solace ·
A dieu my ladies / somtime so fressh of
face ·
A dieu beute / plesaunce and solace ·
Of deþes chaunge / euery day is
prime ·   *230*
Thinkeþ on 3oure soules / or þat deth
manace ·
ffor al shal rote / and no man wote what
tyme ·

30

Deeth to þe Abbot ·
Come forth sir Abbot / wiþ 3oure brood
hatte ·
Beeth not abaisshed / þou3 3e haue ri3t ·
Greet is 3our hood / 3our bely large &
fatte ·   *235*
3e mote come daunce / þou3 3e be no
þing li3t ·
Leve vp 3oure abbey / to some othir
wi3t ·
3oure eir is of age / 3oure state to
occupie ·

Who þat is fattest / I haue hym behiȝt ·
In his graue / shal sonnest putrefie · 240

31
The Abbot answeriþ ·
Of thi þretis / haue I noon envie ·
That I shal nowe / leve al gouernaunce ·
But þat I shal / as a cloistrer dye ·
This doth to me / passinge grete grev-
aunce · 244
Mi liberte / nor my greet habondaunce ·
What may availe / in any manere wise ·
Ȝit axe I mercy / with hertly repen-
taunce ·
Thouȝ in diynge / to late men hem
avise ·

32
Deeth to the Abbesse ·
And ȝe my lady / gentil dame Abbesse ·
Wiþ ȝoure mantels / furred large and
wide · 250
Ȝoure veile ȝoure wymple / passinge of
greet richesse ·
And beddis softe / ȝe mote nowe leie a
side ·
ffor to þis daunce / I shal be ȝoure
guyde ·
Thouȝ ȝe be tendre / and born of gentil
blood ·
While þat ȝe lyve / for ȝoure silfe
prouide · 255
ffor aftir deeth / no man hath no good ·

33
The Abbesse · answerith ·
Allas that deeth / hath þus for me or-
deined ·
That in no wise / I may it not declyne
Thouȝ it so be / ful ofte I haue con-
streyned ·
Brest and throte / my notes out to
twyne · 260
My chekes round / vernysshed for to
shyne ·
Vngirt ful ofte (to walke at þe large ·
Thus cruell deth doth all estates fyne
Who hath no chippe muste rowe in bote
or barge)

34
Deeth to þe Bally ·
Come forþe sir bailly / that knowen al
þe gise · 265
By ȝoure office / of trouþe and riȝtwis-
nes ·
Ȝe must come / to a newe assise ·
Extorciouns / and wronges to redres ·
Ȝe be somonyd / as lawe bit expres ·
To ȝelde acountes / þe Iuge wole ȝow
charge · 270
Wiche hath ordeyned / to exclude al
falsnes ·
That euery man / shal bere his owne
charge ·

35
The Bayly · answerith ·
O þou lorde god / this is an hard
iourne ·
To suche a fourme / I tooke but litel
hede ·
Mi chaunge is turned / and þat for-
thinkiþ me · 275
Sumtyme wiþ Iuges / what me list to
spede ·
Lay in my myȝt / by fauour or for mede ·
But sithen þere is / no rescws by
bataille ·
I holde hym wys / þat cowde see in
dede ·
Aȝein deeth / þat none apele may
vaille · 280

36
Deeth to þe Astronomere ·
Come forþe maister / þat loken vp so
ferre ·
With Instrumentis / of Astronomy ·
To take þe grees / and heiȝte of euery
sterre ·
What may availe / al ȝoure astrologie ·
Sethen Adam and / alle the Genola-
gie · 285
Made ferst of god / to walke vppon þe
grounde ·
Deeth dooth areste / þus seith The(o)lo-
gie ·
And al shal die / for an appil round ·

---

244. The second half-line reads in the B-recension *somwhat the lesse grevaunce.*
262-4. Inserted from Harley 116; Selden is
blank after *ofte*, and Bodley 221, Laud,
lack line 7 of the stanza. Trinity and
Ellesmere agree with Harley, reading *shyp,
ship* in line 264.

274. Harley reads, "To the which aforne," etc.
275. Trinity, Harley, read *chaunce;* Ellesmere as
Selden.
285. Harley and the B-recension read: "Sith of
Adam all þe Genelogie".

37

The Astronomere answerith

For al my craft / kunnynge or science ·
I can not finde / no prouisioun ·　　　*290*
Ne in the sterris / serche oute no de-
fence ·
By domefiynge / ne calculacioun ·
Safe finally / in conclusioun ·
ffor to discrive / oure kunnynge euery-
dele ·
Ther is no more / by sentence of re-
'soun ·　　　　　　　　　*295*
Who lyueth ariȝt / mote nedis dye wele

38

Deeth to þe Burgeys ·

Sir burgeis / what do ȝe lenger tarie ·
ffor al ȝoure aver / and ȝoure greet
ricchesse ·
Thouȝ ȝe be straunge / deynous & contrarie ·
To this daunce / ȝe mote ȝow nedis
dresse ·　　　　　　　*300*
ffor ȝoure tresour / plente and largesse ·
ffrom oþere it cam / and shal vnto
straungers ·
He is a fool / that in suche bysynes ·
Woot not for whom / he stuffith his
garners ·

39

The Burgeis · aunswerith ·

Certis to me / it is greet displesaunce · *305*
To leve al this / and may it not assure ·
Houses rentes / tresour and substaunce ·
Deeth al fordoþe / suche is his nature ·
Therfore / wys is no creature ·
That set his herte / on good þat moot
disseuere ·　　　　　　*310*
The worlde it lente / and he mot it
(recure) ·
And who most hath / loþest dieth euere ·

40

Deeth to þe Chanoun ·

And ȝe sir Chanoun / with many grete
prebende ·
Ȝe may no lenger / haue distribucioun ·
Of golde and siluer / largely to dis-
pende ·　　　　　　*315*
ffor þere is nowe / no consolacioun ·

---

311. Selden, Laud, Bodley 221, read *recouere;*
　　　Harley, Trinity, Ellesmere, read *recure.*

But daunce with vs / for al ȝoure hie
renoun ·
ffor ȝe of deeth / stonde vppon þe brink ·
Ȝe may ther of / haue no dilacioun ·
Deeth comyth ay / whan men lest on
him þink ·　　　　　　*320*

41

The Chanoun answeriþ ·

My benefices / with many personage ·
God wote ful lite / may me nowe com-
forte ·
Deeth hath of me / so grete avauntage ·
Al my ricches / may me not disporte ·
Amys of grys / þei wole aȝein re-
sorte ·　　　　　　*325*
Vn to þe worlde /surplys and prebende ·
Al is veinglorie / truly to reporte ·
To die wel / eche man shulde entende ·

42

Deeth to þe Marchaunt ·

Ȝe riche Marchaunt / ȝe mote loke hider-
warde ·
That passid haue / many diuers
londe ·　　　　　　*330*
On hors on foot / hauynge moste reward ·
To lucre and wynnyng / as I vndirstond
But nowe to daunce / ȝe mote ȝeue me
ȝoure honde ·
ffor al ȝoure labour / ful litel availeth
ȝow ·
A dieu veinglorie / boþe of free and
bonde ·　　　　　　*335*
No more coueite þan þei þat haue ynow ·

43

The Marchaunt answeriþ ·

By manie an hil / and many a straunge
vale ·
I haue traueilid / with my marchandise ·
Ouere þe see / do carie many a bale ·
To sundry Iles / mo þan I can
deuise ·　　　　　　*340*
My herte Inwarde / ay fret with couet-
ise ·
But al for nouȝt / nowe deeth doiþ me
constreine ·
By wiche I seie / by recorde of the wise ·
Who al embraceth / litel shal restreine ·

44

Deeth to þe Chartereux ·

Ȝeue me ȝoure hond / wiþ chekis dede
& pale ·　　　　　　*345*

Causid of wacche / and longe abstinence ·
Sir chartereux / and ȝoure silfe avale ·
Vn to this daunce / with humble pa-
cience ·
To stryve aȝein / may be no resistence ·
Lenger to lyve / set not ȝoure mem-
orie ·   *350*
Thouȝ I be lothsom / as in apparence ·
Aboue alle men / deth hath þe victorie ·

45
The Chartereux aunswerith
Unto þe worlde / I was dede longe
agone ·
By my ordre / and my professioun ·
Thouȝ euery man / be he neuere so
stronge ·   *355*
Dredith to die / by kindly mocioun ·
Aftir his flesshly Inclinacioun ·
But plese it to god / my soule for to
borowe ·
ffrom fendis myȝt / and from dampna-
cioun ·
Some bene to day / þat shulle not be to
morwe ·   *360*

46
Deeth to þe Seriaunt
Come forþe sir Sergant / with ȝoure
statly mace ·
Make no defence / ne no rebellioun ·
Not may availe / to grucche in þis cace ·
Thouȝ ȝe be deynous / of condicioun ·
ffor nouther pele / ne proteccioun · *365*
May ȝow fraunchise / to do nature
wrong
ffor þere is noone / so sturdy champioun ·
Thouȝ he be myȝty / anoþer is as
stronge ·

47
The Sergant answerith
Howe dare þis deþe / sette on me
areste ·
That am þe kinges chosen officere · *370*
Wiche ȝisterday / boþe west and este ·
Min office dide / ful surquidous of chere ·
But nowe þis day / I am arestid here ·
And may not flee / þouȝ I hadde it
sworn ·
Eche man is lothe / to die ferre and
nere ·   *375*
That hath not lerned / for to die aforn

---
353. The rime is imperfect in the A-recension; the
B-recension reads —*dede ago ful longe.*

48
Deeth to þe Monke
Sir monke also / with ȝoure blak habite ·
Ȝe may no lenger / holde here soiour ·
Ther is no þing / þat may ȝow here
respite ·
Aȝein my myȝt / ȝow for to socour · *380*
Ȝe mote acounte / touching ȝoure labour
Howe ȝe haue spent it / in dede worde
& þouȝt ·
To erþe and asshes / turneth euery flour ·
The life of man / is but a þing of
nouȝt ·

49
The monke answerith
I hadde leuere / in þe cloistre be · *385*
At my book / and studie my seruice ·
Wiche is a place / contemplatif to se ·
But I haue spent / my life in many vice ·
Liche as a fool / dissolut and nyce ·
God of his mercy / graunt me repent-
aunce ·   *390*
By chere outwarde / harde (is) to
deuise ·
Alle be not mery / wich þat men se
daunce ·

50
Deeth to þe vsurere ·
Thou vsurer / loke vp and biholde ·
Vn to wynnygne / þou settist al þi peine ·
Whos couetise / wexiþ neuere colde · *395*
Thy gredy þrust / so sore þe doth con-
streine ·
But þou shalt neuere / þi desire ateyne ·
Such an etik / thin herte frete shal ·
That but of pite / god his hande re-
freine ·
O perillous strook / shal make þe lese
al ·   *400*

51
The vsurere answerith
Nowe me bihoueth / sodeinly to dey ·
Wiche is to me / grete peine & greet
grevaunce ·
Socour to finde / I see no maner wey ·
Of golde ne siluer / by no chevesaunce ·
Deeth þoruȝ his haste / abit no pur-
veaunce ·   *405*
Of folkes blinde / þat can not look wel ·

---
391. I insert *is* from Bodley 221 and Laud; not in
Selden, Harley, or Trinity.
402. Ellesmere is with Selden; Bodley 221, Harley, and Trinity read *and grevaunce.*

 fful ofte happith / by kinde or fatal
chaunce ·
Some haue faire ey3en / þat see neuere
a dele ·

52
The pore man to þe vsurere
Vsure to god / is ful grete offence ·
And in his si3t / a grete abusioun · 410
The pore borwith / par cas for indi-
gence ·
The riche lent / by fals collucioun ·
Only for lucre in his entencioun ·
Deeth shal hem boþe / to acountes fette ·
To make rekenynge by computacioun ·
No man is quit / þat is bihinde of dette

53
Deeth to þe ffisician
Maister of phisik / wiche on 3oure vryne
So loke and gase / and stare a3ein þe
sonne
ffor al 3oure craft / and studie of medicine
Al þe practyk / and sience þat 3e
konne   420
3our lyves cours / so ferforþe is Ironne
A3ein my my3t / 3oure craft may not
endure
ffor al þe golde / þat 3e ther by haue
wonne
Good leche is he / þat can him silfe recure

54
The ffisician answerith
fful longe a goo / that I vn to phisik · 425
Sette my witt / and my dilligence ·
In speculatif / and also in practik ·
To gete a name / þoru3 myn excellence ·
To finde oute / a3ens pestilence ·
Preseruatiues / to staunche it and to
fine ·   430
But I dar seie / shortly in sentence ·
A3ens deeth / is worth no medicine ·

55
Deeth to þe Amerous Squier
3e þat be gentil / so fresshe and amerous ·
Of 3eres 3onge / flouringe in 3oure grene
age ·
Lusty free / of herte eke desirous · 435
fful of devises / and chaunge in 3oure
corage ·

Plesaunt of port / of look and of visage ·
But al shal turne / in to asshes dede ·
ffor al bewte / is but a feint ymage ·
Wiche steliþ a weye / or folkes can take
hede ·   440

56
The Squier answeriþ
Allas · allas / I can nowe no socour ·
A3ens dethe / for my silfe provide ·
A dieu of 3ouþe / þe lusty fresshe flour
A dieu veinglorie / of bewte and of
pride ·
A dieu al seruice / of þe god Cupide · 445
A dieu my ladies / so fressh so wel be
sein ·
ffor a3ein dethe / no þing may abide ·
And windes grete / goo doun with litil
reyn ·

57
Deeth to þe gentil womman amerous
Come forþe maistresse / of 3eris 3onge
and grene ·
Wiche holde 3oure silfe / of bewte
souereyne   450
As faire as 3ee / was somtyme Polycene ·
Penolope / and the quene Eleyne ·
3it on þis daunce / þei wente boþe
tweine ·
And so shulle 3e / for al 3oure straunge-
nesse ·
Thou3 daunger longe / in loue haþ lad
3oure reine ·   455
Arestid is / 3oure chaunge of doubil·
nesse ·

58
The gentil womman answerith
O cruel deeth / þat sparest none estate
To old and 3onge / þou art indifferent ·
To my bewte / þou hast yseide chek-
mate ·
So hasty is / thi mortal Iugement 460
ffor in my 3ouþe / this was myn entent ·
To my seruice / many a man to haue
lured ·
But she is a fool / shortly in sentement ·
That in hir bewte / is to moche assurid ·

59
Deeth to the man of lawe
Sir aduocate / short processe for to
make ·   465
3e mote come plete / afore þe hi3e Iuge ·
Many a quarel / 3e haue vndirtake

And for lucre / to do folke refuge ·
But my fraunchise / is so large & huge ·
That Counceile none / availe may but
trouþe ·   470
He skapiþ wisely / of deeth þe greet
deluge ·
To fore þe doom / who is not teint wiþ
slouþe ·

60
The man of lawe answerith
Of riȝt and resoun / by naturis lawe ·
I can not putte / aȝein deeth no defence ·
Ne by no sleiȝte / me kepe ne wiþ-
drawe ·   475
ffor al my wit / and my greet prudence ·
To make apele / from this dredful sent-
ence ·
No þing in erthe / may a man preserve ·
Aȝeins his myȝt / to make resistence ·
God quite al men / like as þei de-
serve ·   480

61
Deeth to þe Iourrour
Maister Iurrour / wiche þat at assise
And atte Shires / questes doste embrace ·
Departist londe / like to þi deuise ·
And who most ȝaf / moste stode in þi
grace ·
The pore man / lost londe and place · 485
ffor golde þou cowdest / folkes dis-
herite ·
But nowe lete se / with þi teint face ·
To fore þe Iuge / howe þou canst þe
quite ·

62
The Iourour answerith
Somtyme I was clepid / in my cuntre ·
The belle wedir / and þat was nat a
lite ·   490
Nouȝt loued / but drad / of lowe and
hie degre ·
ffor whom me list / by craft I coude
endite ·
And hange the trewe / and þe theef
respite ·
Al þe cuntre / by my worde was lad ·
But I dar sey / shortly for to write · 495
Of my dethe / many a man is glad ·

63
Deeth to þe Minstral
O thou mynstral / þat canst so note and
pipe ·

Vnto folkes / for to do plesaunce ·
By þe riȝt honde / I shal anoone þe
gripe ·
With these other / to goo vp on my
daunce ·   500
There is no scape / neiþer avoidaunce ·
On no side / to contrarie my sentence ·
ffor in Musik / by craft and acordaunce ·
Who maister is / shewe his (science) ·

64
The minstral answeriþ
This newe daunce / is to me so
straunge ·   505
Wondir diuerse / and passingly contra-
rie ·
The dredful fotyng / doth so ofte
chaunge ·
And þe mesures / so ofte sithes varie ·
Wiche nowe to me / is no þing neces-
sarie ·
If it were so / þat I myȝt asterte · 510
But many a man / if I shal not tarie ·
Ofte daunceth / but no thing of herte ·

65
Deeth to þe Tregetour
Maistir Iohn Rikele / some tyme Tregetour ·
Of noble Harry / kyng of Engelond ·
And of ffraunce / þe miȝty conquer-
our ·   515
ffor alle þe sleiȝtes / and turnyng of þin
hond ·
Thou must come ner / this daunce to
vndirstond ·
Nouȝt may auaile / al thi conclusions ·
ffor deeth shortly / nouþer on see ne
lond ·
Is nouȝt deceivid / by none illusions 520

66
The Tregetour answerith
What may availe / magik natural ·
Or any craft / shewid by apparence ·
Or cours of sterres / aboue celestial ·
Or of þe heuene / al the influence ·
Aȝeins deeth / to stonde at defence · 525
Legerdemeyn / nowe helpiþ me riȝt
nouȝt ·

504. Selden, *shewe his sentence;* Ellesmere,
Laud, Bodley 221, *shew his science;* Trinity,
sheweþ his science; Harley, *shall schew his
science.*

ffarewel my craft / and al suche sapience ·
ffor deth moo maistris / ʒit þan I hath
wrouʒt ·

67
Deeth to / þe Persoun
O sir curat / þat bene nowe here pre-
sent ·
That had ʒoure worldly Inclinacioun · 530
ʒoure herte entire / ʒoure studie and en-
tent
Moste on ʒoure tithes / and oblacioun ·
Wiche shulde haue bene / of conuersa-
cioun ·
Mirrour vn to othir / liʒt and exaum-
plarie ·
Like ʒoure desert / shal be ʒoure guer-
doun · 535
And to eche labour / dewe is þe salarie ·

68
The Persoun answerith
Maugre my wille / I must condiscende ·
ffor deth assailiþ / euery lifly thing ·
Here in þis worlde / who can compre-
hende ·
His sodein stroke / and his vnware com-
yng · 540
ffarewele tithis / and farewel myn off-
ryng ·
I mote goo counte / in ordre by and by ·
And for my shepe / make a iust rek-
enyng ·
Whom he aquyteth / I holde he is happy ·

69
Deeth to þe laborer ·
Thou laborer / wiche in sorwe and
peine ·
Hast lad þi life / in ful greet trauaile ·
Thou moste eke daunce / and þerfore not
disdeyne ·
ffor if þou do / it may þee not auaile ·
And cause why / þat I þee assaile ·
Is oonly þis / from þee to disseuere · 550
The fals worlde / þat can so folke faile ·
He is a fool / þat weneth to lyne euere ·

70
The laborer answerith
I haue wisshed / aftir deeth ful ofte ·
Al be þat I wolde haue fled hym now · ⁻
I had leuere / to haue leyn vnsofte · 555
In winde and reyn / & haue gone at
plow ·

With spade & pikoys / and labourid for
my prow ·
Dolve and diched / and at þe carte
goone ·
ffor I may seie / and telle pleinly howe ·
In þis worlde here / ther is reste
none · 560

71
Deeth to þe frere menour
Sir cordeler / to ʒow myn hand is
rauʒt ·
To þis daunce / ʒow to conveie and lede ·
Wiche in ʒoure preching / haue ful ofte
Itauʒt ·
Howe þat I am / moste gastful for to
drede ·
Al be þat folke / take þerof noon hede ·
ʒit is þer noon / so stronge ne so hardy ·
But deth dare reste / and let for no
mede · 567
ffor deeth eche hour / is present and
redy ·

72
The frere answeriþ
What may þis be / þat in þis world no
man ·
Here to abide / may haue no surete · 570
Strengþe ricchesse / ne what so þat he
can ·
Worldly wisdom / al is but vanite ·
In grete astate / ne in pouerte
Is no þing found / þat may fro deþe
defende ·
ffor wiche I seie / to hie and lowe
degre · 575
Wys is þat synner / þat dooth his life
amende ·

73
Deeth to the childe
Litel enfante / þat were but late yborn
Shape in þis worlde / to haue no ples
aunce ·
Thou must with other / þat goone here
to forn ·
Be lad in haste / by fatal ordinaunce ·
Lerne of newe / to goo on my daunce ·
Ther may noon age / escape in soth
þerfroo · 582
Lete euery wiʒt / haue þis in remem-
braunce
Who lengest lyveth / moost shal suffre
woo ·

74
The childe answeriþ

A · A · A · o worde I can not speke · 585
I am so ȝonge / I was bore ȝisterday ·
Deeth is so hasty / on me to be wreke ·
And list no lenger / to make no delay ·
I cam but nowe / and nowe I goo my
    way ·
Of me no more / no tale shal be told · 590
The wil of god / no man with stonde
    may ·
As sone dieth / a ȝonge man as an old ·

75
Deeth to the Clerke

O ȝe sir clerke / suppose ȝe to be free ·
ffro my daunce / or ȝoure selfe defende ·
That wende haue rysen / vn to hie degre ·
Of benefices / or some greet prebende ·
Who clymbeth hiest / some tyme shal
    dissende ·   597
Lat no man grucche / aȝens his fortune ·
But take in gree / what euere god hym
    sende ·
Wiche ponissheth al / whan tyme is
    oportune ·   600

76
The clerke aunswerith ·

Shal I þat am / so ȝonge a clerke nowe
    deye ·
ffro my seruice / and haue no bettir
    guerdoun ·
Is ther no geyn / ne no bettir weye ·
No sure fraunchise / ne proteccioun ·
Deeth makith alweie / a short conclu-
    sioun ·   605
To late ware / whan men bene on þe
    brinke ·
The worlde shal faile / and al posses-
    sioun ·
ffor moche faileth / of þing þat foles
    thinke ·

77
Deeth to þe Hermyte

Ȝe þat haue lived / longe in wildernesse ·
And þere contynued longe in abstinence ·
At þe laste / ȝet ȝe mote ȝow dresse · 611
Of my daunce / to haue experience ·
ffor þere aȝein / is no recistence
Take nowe leue / of þin Ermytage ·
Wherfore eche man / aduerte this sent-
    ence ·   615
That þis life here / is no sure heritage ·

78
The Hermite answeriþ

Life in desert / callid solitarie ·
May aȝein deþe / haue no respite ne
    space ·
At vnset our / his comyng doth not
    tarie ·
And for my part / welcome be goddes
    grace ·   620
Thonkyng hym / with humble chere and
    face ·
Of al his ȝiftes / and greet habondaunce ·
ffynally / affermynge in this place ·
No man is riche / þat lackith suffisaunce ·

79
Deeth aȝein to þe Hermite

That is wel seide / and þus shulde euery
    wiȝt ·   625
Thanke his god / and alle his wittis
    dresse ·
To loue and drede hym / with al his
    herte & myȝt ·
Seth deeth to ascape / may be no siker-
    nesse ·
As men deserue / god quit of riȝtwis-
    nesse ·
To riche and pore / vppon euery side · 630
A bettir lessoun / þer can no clerke ex-
    presse ·
Than til to morwe / is no man sure to
    abide ·

80
*The kyng ligging dede and eten of
wormes*

Ȝe folke þat lokyn / vpon this portrature ·
Biholdyng here / alle the states daunce ·
Seeth what ȝe bene / and what is ȝoure
    nature ·   635
Mete vn to wormes / not ellis in sub-
    staunce ·
And haue þis mirrour euere in remem-
    braunce ·
Howe (I) lie here / somtyme crownyd
    kyng ·
To alle estates a trewe resemblaunce ·
That wormes food / is fyne of oure
    lyuyng ·   640

81
Machabre þe doctour

Man is not ellis / platly for to thinke ·
But as a winde / wiche is transitorie ·
Passinge ay forþe / wheþer he wake or
    winke ·

Towarde þis daunce / haue þis in memorie ·
Remembringe ay / þer is no bet vic-
torie ·   *645*
In þis life here / þan fle synne at þe
leste ·
Than shul ȝe regne / in paradys with
glorie ·
Happy is he / þat maketh in heuene his
feste ·

82

Ȝit ther be folke / mo þan six or sevene
Reckles of lyf / in many maner wise *650*
Like as þer were / helle none nor heuene
Suche false errour / lete euery man dis-
pice
ffor hooly seintis / and oolde clerkis wise
Writen contrarie / her falsnes to deface
To lyue wel / take this for best em-
price   *655*
Is moche worth / whan men shul hens
pace

83
Lenvoye de Translatour
O ȝe my lordis / and maistres alle in fere

Of auenture / þat shal þis daunce rede
Lowly I preie / with al myn herte entere
To correcte / where as ȝe see nede *660*
ffor nouȝt ellis / I axe for my mede
But goodly support / of this transla-
cioun
And with fauour / to sowponaile drede
Benignely / in ȝoure correccioun

84

Out of þe frensshe / I drewe it of en-
tente   *665*
Not worde by worde / but folwynge þe
substaunce
And fro Paris / to Engelonde it sente
Oonly of purpos / ȝow to do plesaunce
Rude of langage / I was not born in
fraunce
Haue me excusid / my name is Iohn
Lidgate   *670*
Of her tunge / I haue no suffisaunce
Her corious metris / in englisshe to
translate

Here endith the daunce of Deeth

EPITHALAMIUM FOR GLOUCESTER

Humphrey duke of Gloucester, youngest of Henry the Fourth's four sons,
was born about 1390, some years before his father's seizure of the English crown.
He took no conspicuous part in English politics until the renewal of the French
war by Henry the Fifth, and the absence of all his brothers in France, devolved
on him the governance of England. Either his own temperament, or a shrewd
perception of the future of the English middle class, then led him to championship
of the bourgeoisie. He became in consequence the idol of the people, and also
in consequence, a man suspect by his own class. With the death of Henry the
Fifth (1422) and of Thomas duke of Clarence (1421) in France, the administration of the Anglo-French dominions was divided between John duke of Bedford, who remained abroad to prosecute the war, and Humphrey duke of Gloucester, who was entrusted with the protectorate of England. In this duty, and
in the guardianship of the infant Henry VI, there were associated with Gloucester the Lords of Council, among whom the most powerful was Beaufort bishop
of Winchester, illegitimate half-brother of Henry the Fourth, a man of great
wealth and great ability, and strongly inimical to Gloucester. The remainder of
Humphrey's life, until his death under suspicion of poison in 1447, is, politically,
a struggle between his party and that of Beaufort and Suffolk.
    Were this political fencing the whole of Gloucester's activity, we should
have to term him a factious schemer, and little more. But his life has other as-

pects. Interesting, at least, are his relations with Jacqueline of Hainault, who became his wife in spite of political prudence; interesting also, in their own way, are his desertion of Jacqueline for Eleanor Cobham, the protest of English women to Parliament against his conduct, the later trial of Eleanor for sorcery, and that taper-bearing public penitence of the duchess through London streets, "hoodless save a kerchef", which is so astonishing a fact in Humphrey's life.

There is much that is violent and ignoble in all this; Gloucester's private life, indeed, was one of excess; but we can turn from such facts to a far finer side of Humphrey, his love of books and his patronage of men of letters. The man who first founded the library of the University of Oxford, the man who corresponded with Italian scholars and rewarded English writers, has a claim on the gratitude of students which outweighs many political errors. Humphrey after his elevation to power was reckless, selfish, unstable; he carried the soldier's temperament into affairs where caution and diplomacy were needed. But the afterworld has forgotten the politician, and forgiven the patron of letters.

Our admiration of his patronage of literature has, however, to be qualified by the sort of literature which he patronized. Humphrey had no Virgil to encourage and reward, not even the Tasso of a Renaissance despot. Like an Este or a Medici, though, he dispensed his favors. There is, as Tout has said, "something almost Italian about Gloucester, both in his literary and his political career." His personal vices, his restless instability, his condottiere swagger, his real love of learning and generosity to learning, are those of Ferrara or Florence. It is, however, too much to say, as Vickers says (*op. cit.* below, p. 348), that "what Petrarch did for the world, Humphrey did for England." The interest which Humphrey showed in the classics was indeed greater than that evinced by his royal brother; and Aeneas Sylvius commended the better Latin style which Gloucester's zeal for polite learning had introduced into England. But the blend of classicism, medievalism, and the new lyric self-expression which is in Petrarch is very differently proportioned in Humphrey, with far more of the medieval, as his literary patronage shows. Among the works dedicated to him or executed for him are Capgrave's commentary on Genesis, Gilbert Kymer's Dietarium, Nicholas Upton's De officio militari, Whethamstede's Granarium, the anonymous translation of Palladius De re rustica, Lydgate's translation of the De Casibus of Boccaccio, and Hoccleve's rendition of a story from the Gesta Romanorum. Another of Boccaccio's works, the Italian poem Il Corbaccio,—an attack upon women,—has recently come to light, says Vickers, pp. 377-79, in an English version by one of Gloucester's Latin secretaries. The duke's "poet and orator" Titus Livius wrote at his bidding a Latin biography of Henry the Fifth; Livius, and other of Humphrey's secretaries, were Italians, and Gloucester was in correspondence with Italian scholars. Aretino translated the Politics of Aristotle for him; Pier Candido Decembrio dedicated to him the Latin version of Plato's Republic. Gloucester's intellectual curiosity was keen, and he read both French and Latin. But his princely gift of manuscripts to the University of Oxford is the most truly humanistic act of his life.

His taste, as revealed in his choice of books for translation into English, does not appear to us humanistic. His election of the Fall of Princes for Englishing, was, however, quite in keeping with the preference of his age for large-scale didactics; and as a landholder he may have been interested in the translation of Palladius, which he seems to have supervised himself. Both from that work and from Lydgate's translation we get a few glimpses of Gloucester personally, though for the most part beclouded with extravagant conventional laudation. But other occasional poems by Lydgate,—the Epithalamium and the appeal for money printed below, especially the curious composition bewailing Humphrey's desertion of Jacqueline and endeavoring to explain it by witchcraft,—throw a little more light on the man. That Gloucester was reckless at Rouen we can read in the lines of John Page and of Hoccleve; that he was piously cruel to heretics we can read in the commendations of Lydgate and of the Palladius-translator; that London citizens, despite their indignation at his treatment of Jacqueline, agreed with him against Beaufort in his narrowly militaristic policy, his opposition to the liberation of the duke of Orléans, we can find from the chronicles. He was faithless to his unfortunate foreign wife; he was injudicious and selfish in matters political. But his generosity to scholars, his manner to the common citizen, have kept his memory green as "the good Duke Humphrey".

Jacqueline of Hainault, the princess to whom this poem is addressed, was the last of the Holland-Wittelsbach line to hold the throne of Holland and Seeland. She was only sixteen on accession, and but a part of her father's dominions recognized her, Holland going over to her uncle, John the Pitiless. She determined to marry her cousin, John of Brabant, hoping thus to strengthen herself against her uncle; but when this hope failed, and her husband became personally odious to her, she fled to England in 1421 for protection and for support in her plea to the Pope for a divorce. Undoubtedly her dominions were a pawn in the political game, but Henry the Fifth moved cautiously, unwilling to antagonize the duke of Burgundy, who also had his eye on Jacqueline's territories, and whose support was earnestly desired by England against France. Gloucester, however, was influenced by no motives of international diplomacy. He and Jacqueline fell in love with each other; and as Henry the Fifth's death soon left Gloucester unchecked, he married the now divorced Jacqueline, and in 1424 entered Holland with an English force to support her claims. Suddenly thereafter, perhaps because of Burgundy's suggestion of a personal duel to decide matters, perhaps for private reasons, Humphrey dropped the campaign and returned to England; the duke of Burgundy seized the deserted and helpless Jacqueline, who vainly implored her husband's aid; and she survived her fall but a few years, recognizing her marriage to Humphrey as void in 1428. Gloucester then married Eleanor Cobham, a former lady-in-waiting of Jacqueline, whom he had brought back from Holland with him, and for whom his passion had aroused general indignation and disgust. His popularity with Londoners was seriously shaken by his conduct to his deserted wife; in 1428 a group of women entered Parliament and formally protested against his neglect of Jacqueline and connection with Eleanor. Also, there exists in contemporary manuscript a poem, marked as Lydgate's, expressing strong sympathy for Jacqueline; in this it is interesting to observe the suggestion of sorcery as explanation of Gloucester's errors, inasmuch as it was for witchcraft that Eleanor of Gloucester later suffered punishment. Its anxious attempt to excuse Humphrey is notable in view of the praise which Hoccleve and Lydgate lavish on him for his "stableness",—a quality entirely foreign to Humphrey.

The poem below is far more conventional, and its complacent ignorance of the actual political situation, of the danger to the Burgundian alliance and to the French war which Humphrey was courting, is truly monastic. Lydgate realized only that a compliment to his patron's beloved would please his patron; and this huddle of extravagant encomiums and conventional formulae must have been presented to Jacqueline not only before her marriage to Humphrey in the autumn of 1422, but before the death of Henry V in August of that year, since he is spoken of as living, in line 48 here. As Jacqueline was in England by June 1421, the limits for composition of this poem are fairly narrow.

It survives in three copies, Shirley's MS now Trin. Coll. Cambridge R 3,20 (whence my text), and two transcripts from Shirley in Brit. Mus. Harley 2251 and Adds. 29729; the latter is in the hand of John Stow the antiquary, who died in 1605. For notes on Stow and on Shirley see pp. 191-94 below; and on the MS here used see p. 79 n., above.

SELECT REFERENCE LIST VI

Vickers, K. H., Humphrey Duke of Gloucester, London, 1907. With extensive bibliography.

Anstey, Munimenta Academica, 1868. See pp. 758-772 for lists of books given by Humphrey to Oxford.

Tout, T. F., art. on Gloucester in the DNB.

Palladius, De re rustica, transl. See p. 202 here.

Gloucester's desertion of Jacqueline, poem by Lydgate?, printed by me in Anglia 27:381.

The Siege of Rouen, by John Page; see Gairdner's Hist. Collections, Camden Society, 1876.

The relief of Calais by a force under Gloucester is described in a Ballad against the Flemings, printed by MacCracken in Anglia 33:283 as Lydgate's.

For Humphrey's protest against the liberation of Orléans see Speed's Hist. of Great Britain (1611), p. 660; see Vickers, pp. 264-5.

For the King's reply see Stevenson, Letters and Papers, ii:451-460, Rolls Series, 1861-4.

For the London women's protest against Gloucester's treatment of his wife see the Chronicon rerum gestarum in monasterio S. Albani, prefixed to the Rolls Series ed. of the Annales Sancti Albani, i:20.

For the public penance of Eleanor Cobham, duchess of Gloucester, see the "Lament of the Duchess of Gloucester", pr. by Hardwick in the Cambridge Antiq. Soc. Communications, i:177 (1855), and from a shorter text by Wright, Polit. Poems, ii:205, by Flügel in Anglia 26:177, by Dyboski, EETS vol. of Songs and Carols, 1908, p. 95.

Gloucester and his duchess Eleanor both appear in A Mirror for Magistrates; see Haslewood's 1815 ed., pp. 112, 128 of vol. ii.

[MS Trinity College Cambridge R 3, 20, foll. 158-64]

AND NOWE HERE BEGYNNEþE A COMENDABLE BALADE BY LYDEGATE DAUN JOHAN AT þE
REUERENCE OF MY LADY OF HOLAND · AND OF MY LORD OF GLOUCESTRE TO FORE
þE DAY OF þEYRE MARYAGE IN þE DESYROUS TYME OF þEYRE TRUWE LOVYNG

Thorugh gladde aspectis / of þe god *Cupyde*
And ful acorde of his moder deere
fful offt syþes / list aforne provyde
By cours eterne / of þe sterres cleere

Hertis in loue / for to Joyne in feere 5
Thoroughe bonde of feyth *per*petuelly tendure
By influence of god / and of nature

2

Italicized words are underscored by Shirley in the MS.

þe heven aboue / disposeþe many thinges
Which witt of man can not comprehende

Þe faatal ordre / of lordes and of
    kynges   10
To make som*m*e / in honnour hye as-
    cende
And som*m*e al so ful lowe to descende /
And in loue eeke / to lacen and con-
    streyne
Hertes tenbrace / in *Jubiters* cheyne

3

Þus cam in first / þe knotte of aſly-
    aunce   15
Betweene provynces / and worþy regy-
    ouns
ffolkes to sette in pees / and acordaunce
To beon alloone / in þeyre affeccouns
And to exclude / alle devysyouns
Of contekk stryff of batayle and of
    werres   20
Þe first cause pourtreyed in þe sterres

4

ffor noman may þordeynaunce eschuwe
Thinges disposed / by cours celestyal
Ner destenye / to voyde nor remuwe
But oonly god / þat lordshipeþe al 25
ffor thorughe his might moost Imperyal
Þeternal lord / moost discrete and saage
He brought in first / þordre of maryage

5

Ensaumple in bookes / þer beon moo
    þane oon
Þinward pithth / whoo so list to
    charge   30
Executid is / of so yoore agoon
Recorde I take / of *Calydoyne* and *Arge*
Howe þoo landes / so broode / so wyde
    / so large
Were maked oon / þe story list not feyne
By maryage / wheeche a fore were
    tweyne   35

6

And in cronycles autentyk and olde
Many a story / of Antiquytee
Vn to þis pourpoos / rehersed is and
    tolde
Howe maryages / haue grounde and
    cause be
Betwene landes / of pees and vnytee 40
And here to forne / as made is remem-
    braunce
Þe werre stynt of England and of
    ffraunce

7

And as I hope of hert and menyng truwe
Þe mortal werre / ceesse shal and fyne
Betwene þoo booþe / and pees ageyne
    renuwe   45
To make loue / with cleer beemys shyne
By þe meene of hir / þat heeght Kath-
    eryne
Ioyned til oon / his deedis can you telle
Henry þe fyffte / of knighthoode sours
    and welle

8

And firþerdovne / for to specefye 50
Þe dewe of grace / distille shal and reyne
Pees and acorde / for to multeplye
In þe boundes here of oure brettaygne
To fynde a wey / wherby we may at-
    teyne
Þat Duchye of holand / by hool af-
    feccoun   55
May beo allyed / with Brutus Albyoun

9

Þat þey may beo / oon body and oon
    hert
Rooted on feyth / devoyde of double-
    nesse
And eeke to seen cleerly / and aduerte
A nuwe sonne / to shynen of glad-
    nesse   60
In booþe londes / texcluden al derk-
    nesse
Of oolde hatred and of al rancour
Brought in by meene / of oon þat is
    þe floure

10

Thoroughe oute þe worlde / called of
    wommanheed
Truwe ensaumple and welle of al goode-
    nesse   65
Benyngne of poorte / roote of goodely-
    heed
Sooþefast myrrour of beaute and fayr-
    nesse
I mene of holand / þe goodely fresshe
    duchesse
Called *Jaques* / whas birth for to termyne
Is by descent / Imperyal of lyne 70

11

As *Hester* meeke / and as *Judith* saage
fflouring in youþe / lyke to *Polixseene*
Secree feythful / as *Dydo* of *Cartage*
Constant of hert / lyche *Ecuba* þe
    qweene

And as *Lucresse* / in loue truwe and
cleene 75
Of bountee fredame / and of gentylesse
She may be called / wel lady and maystresse

12

Ffeyre was *Heleyne* / liche as bookes
telleþe
And renommed as of seemlynesse
But sheo in goodnesse / fer aboue ex-
celleþe 80
To rekken hir trouthe and hir stedfast-
nesse
Hir gouuernaunce / and hir hye noblesse
Þat if she shal shortly (beo) compre-
hendid
In hir is no thing þat might beon amend-
ed

13

Þer to she is descreete / and wonder
sadde 85
In hir appoorte / who so list taake heede
Right avysee / and wommanly eeke
gladde
And dame *prudencc* / dooþe ay hir brydel
leede
Ffortune and *Grace* and *Raysoun* eeke in
deede
In alle hir werkis / with hir beon allyed 90
Þat thoroughe þe worlde / hir naame is
magnefyed

14

To þe poore she is / also ful mercyable
Ffful of pytee / and of compassyoun
And of nature / list not to beo vengeable
Þoughe hit so beo / sheo haue occasy-
oun 95
Þat I suppose nowe in no regyoun
Was neuer a better / at alle assayes
founden
So miche vertu / dooþe in hir habounden

15

A heven it is / to beon in hir presence
Who list consydre / hir governaunce
at al 100
Whas goodely looke / in verray ex-
istence
So aungellyk / and so celestyal
So femynyne / and in especial
Hir eyeghen sayne / who so looke weel
fforyoven is oure wraththe euery deel 105

16

And hir colours / beon black whyte and
rede
Þe reed in trouthe / tookeneþe stabul-
nesse
And þe black / whoo so takeþe heede
Signefyeth / parfyt soburnesse
Þe whyte also / is tooken of clen-
nesse 110
And eeke hir word / is in verray sooþe
Ce bien raysoun / al þat euer she dooþe

17

And sith she is / by discent of blood
Þe grettest borne / oone of hem on lyve
And þer with al / moost vertuous and
goode 115
Þe trouthe pleynly / yif I shal des-
cryve
Suche grace I hope / of nuwe shal ar-
ryue
With hir komyng / thoroughe al þis
lande
Þat þer shal beo a perpetuelle bande

18

Parfourmyng vp / by knott of mary-
age 120
With helpe of god / betweene þis lady
bright
And oon þat is sooþely of his aage
Thoroughe al þis worlde / oon þe best
knyght
And best pourveyed / of manhood and
of might
In pees and werre / thoroughe his ex-
cellence 125
And is also / of wisdam and prudence

19

Moost renommed / for to rekken al
Ffrome Eest to west / as of heghe prow-
esse
In daring doo / and deedes marcyal
He passeþ alle / thorughe his worþy-
nesse 130
Þat yif I shall / þe trouthe cleer ex-
presse
He haþe deserved / thoroughe his
knyghtly name
To beo regystred / in þe hous of ffaame

20

Egally ye with þe worþy nyen
Ffor with *Parys* he haþe comlynesse 135

In trouth of loue / with *Troyllus* he
dooþe shyne
And with *Hectour* / he haþe eeke hardy-
nesse
With *Tedeus* he haþe fredam and gentylnesse
Wal of Bretayne / by manly vyolence
Ageyne hir foomen / to standen at defence   *140*

21

Slouth eschuwing / he dooþe his witt
applye
To reede in bookis /wheeche þat beon
moral
In hooly writt with þe Allegorye
He him delyteþe / to looke in specyal
In vnderstonding / is noone to him
egal   *145*
Of his estate expert in poetrye
With parfounde feeling of Phylosofye

22

With *Salamoun* haþe he sapyence
ffaame of knighthoode / with *Cesar
Julius*
Of rethoryk and / eeke of eloquence *150*
Equypollent with *Marcus Tulius*
With *Hamibal* he is victorious
Lyche vn to *Pompey* / for his hyeghe
renoun
And to gouuerne / egale with *Cypyoun*

23

Þis Martys sone / and sooþefastly his
heyre   *155*
So wolde god of his eternal might
He Ioyned were with hir þat is so feyre
Þe fresshe duchesse / of whome I speek
now right
Sith he in hert is hir truwe knyght .
ffor whome he wryteþe / *in goode aven-
ture*   *160*
Sanz plus vous belle perpetuelly tendure

24

Þane were þis lande in ful sikurnesse
Ageyns þassaute / of alle oure mortell
foone
ffarewell þanne / al trouble and hevynesse   *165*
Yif so were þees landes / were alle oon

And god I prey / it may beo doone
anoon
Of his might / so gracyously ordeyne
Þat pees fynal / were sette betweene hem
tweyne

25

And I dare weel afferme fynally
Thorughe oute þis lande / of hye and
lowe degree   *170*
Þat alle folkes / preyen ful specyally
Þis thing in haast may executed be
And þou þat art oon and twoo and thre
Þis gracious werk dispoose for þe best
ffor to conclude þe fyne of þeyre re-
quest   *175*

26

And *ymeneus* / þow fortune þis matere
Thoroughe helpe of *Iuvo* / nexst of þyne
allye
Maake a knotte feythful and entiere
As whylome was betweene *Phylogenye*
And *Mercurye* eeke / so hyegh a bove
þe skye   *180*
Wher þat *Clyo* / and eeke *Calyope*
Sange with hir sustren / in noumbre
thryes three

27

And alle yee goddes beoþe of oon acorde
Þat haue youre dwelling / aboue þe
firmament
And yee goddesses / devoyde of al des-
corde   *185*
Beoþe weel willy / and also dilygent
And þowe fortune / bee also of assent
Þis neodful thing / texecut yerne
Thorugh youre power / which þt is
eterne

Lenvoye

Pryncesse of bountee / of fredam Em-
paresse   *190*
Þe verray loodsterre / of al goodelyhede
Lowly I prey / vn to youre hyeghe
noblesse
Of my Rudenesse / not to taken heed
And wher so it be / þis bille þat yee
reed
Haþe mercy ay / on myn Ignoraunce
Sith I it made / bitwix hope and dreed
Of hoole entent / yowe for tyl do ple-
saunce

LETTER TO GLOUCESTER

These stanzas exist in four manuscripts, so far as I know. The soundest and probably the oldest text is that here printed from Brit. Mus. Harley 2255, in which the poem is without heading. In Brit. Mus. Lansdowne 699 it is headed "Litera missura domini Joh*ann*is Lidgate ad ducem Glouc*ester*"; and in the sister-volumes Brit. Mus. Harley 2251 and Adds. 34360 there is a colophon which adds to the description as in Lansdowne the words "in tempore translacionis libri Bochasii *pro* Oportunitate pecunie." These two MSS are in this part of their contents derived from a lost volume in the hand of Lydgate's contemporary Shirley, which gives their account of the poem some validity; more is derived from comparing this poem with the prologue to the Fall of Princes (*liber Bochasius*), book iii, in which Humphrey's generosity is rapturously acknowledged, and in which there are some similarities of phrasing to the text below. We may conjecture that between the thanks of that prologue and this begging-letter there intervened a money-gift to Lydgate from his patron.

Lydgate, like Hoccleve in his numerous pleas for money, is aware that he must catch and hold his superior's attention. Gloucester's tastes were doubtless known to his protégé, and the metaphors here worked so elaborately,—medical, nautical, monetary,—are well adapted to please Humphrey. The proverbs are popular literary stuff, as is the refrain; and the employment of a stanza-form slightly different from that of the Fall of Princes may be noted. The occurrence of another begging-letter in the Fall of Princes, book iii, lines 3837-3871, is a somewhat curious fact as coming so soon, in space at least, after acknowledgment of a gift in the prologue to that same book. For this begging-letter see Anglia 38:133-34.

The poem was printed from this MS by Nicolas in his Chronicle of London (1827), p. 268; it was printed from Harley 2251 by Halliwell in his MinPo, p. 49, with the colophon as heading; it was printed from this MS by me in Anglia 38:125-26. On our MS see p. 79 n., above; on Harley 2251, see Anglia 28:24.

[Brit. Mus. Harley 2255, fol. 45b]

Riht myhty prynce / and it be your wille
Condescende / leiser for to take
To seen the content / of this litil bille
Which whan I wrot / myn hand I felte
    quake
Tokne of mornyng / weryd clothis
    blake   5
Cause my purs / was falle in gret rerage
Lynyng outward / his guttys wer out
    shake
Oonly for lak / of plate / and of coign-
    age

2

I souhte leechys / for a restoratiff
In whom I fond / no consolacioun   *10*
Appotecaryes / for a confortatiff
Dragge nor dya / was noon in Bury
    toun

Botme of his stomak / was tournyd vp
    so doun
A laxatif / did hym so gret outrage
Made him slendre / by a consump-
    cioun   15
Oonly for lak / of plate / and of coign-
    age

3

Ship was ther noon / nor seilis reed of
    hewe
The wynd froward / to make hem ther
    to londe
The flood was passyd / and sodeynly of
    newe
A lowh ground ebbe / was faste by the
    stronde   20
No maryneer durste / take on honde
To caste an ankir / for streihtnesse of
    passage

The custom skars / as folk may vndirstonde
Oonly for lak of plate / and of coignage

4

Ther was no tokne / sent doun from the
Tour   25
As any gossomer / the countirpeys was
liht
A ffretyng Etyk / causyd his langour
By a cotidian / which heeld hym day &
nyht
Sol and Luna / wer clypsyd of ther liht
Ther was no cros / nor preent of no
visage   30
His lynyng dirk / ther wer no platys
briht
Oonly for lak / and scarsete of coign-
age

5

Harde to likke hony / out of a marbil
stoon
ffor ther is nouthir / licour nor moisture
An ernest grote / whan it is dronke and
goon   35
Bargeyn of marchauntys / stant in aventure
My purs and I / be callyd to the lure
Off indigence / our stuff / leyd in morgage
But ye my lord / may al our soor recure
With a receyt / of plate and of coignage   40

6

Nat sugre plate / maad by thappotecarye
Plate of briht metal / yevith a mery soun

In boklers bury / is noon such letuary
Gold is a cordial / gladdest confeccioun
Ageyn Etiques / of oold consump-
cioun   45
Aurum potabile / for folk ferre ronne in
age
In quynt essence / best restauracioun
With siluer plate / enprentyd with coign-
age

7

O seely bille / whi art thu nat ashamyd
So malapertly / to shewe out thy con-
streynt   50
But pouert hath / so nyh thy tonne at-
tamyd
That nichil habet / is cause of thy com-
pleynt
A drye tisyk / makith oold men ful
feynt
Reediest weye / to renewe ther corage
Is a fressh dragge / of no spycis
meynt   55
But of a briht plate / enpreented with
coignage

8

Thu mayst afferme / as for thyn excus
Thy bareyn soyl / is sool and solitarye
Of cros nor pyl / ther is no reclus
Preent nor Impressioun / in al thy seyn-
tuarye   60
To conclude breefly / and nat tarye
Ther is no noyse herd / in thyn hermyt-
age
God sende soone / a gladdere letuarye
With a cleer soun / of plate / and of
coignage

Ext qd Lydgate

THE FALL OF PRINCES

(Extracts)

Lydgate's longest poem, the Fall of Princes, extending to more than 36,000
lines in rime royal,[1] was not translated direct from the Latin prose of Boccaccio's De Casibus Virorum Illustrium which is its ultimate original, but is a free
paraphrase, with many changes and additions, of a French prose version of Boc-

---

[1] Stanzas of eight lines occasionally appear in envoys; see iv:3445 ff., v:1590 ff. and 1846 ff.,
ix:2017 ff.; also ix:3239 ff., 3541 to close.

caccio made by Laurent de Premierfait in 1409.[1] Boccaccio is best known to the
modern world by his Decameron, and he made his strongest impression on his
contemporary Chaucer by the poems which Chaucer worked over into the Knight's
Tale and Troilus and Criseyde; but England and France generally, in the period
before the full Renaissance, took more interest in Boccaccio's Latin encyclopedic works, written during the latter half of his life,—the De Casibus, the De
Claris Mulieribus, the De Genealogia Deorum. In France, at the book-loving
court of Charles V, where the king and the royal dukes of Anjou, Berri, and
Bourbon encouraged translators and paid liberally to scribes and poets, as also
at the brilliant rival court of the dukes of Burgundy, there flourished the earliest
modern school of professional littérateurs. Possibly the most famous member
of the group was Christine de Pisan, one of the first women to earn her living by
her pen; but Laurent de Premierfait, translator and scribe, was not the least of
the circle. He translated Cicero for the duke of Bourbon, Boccaccio for the
duke of Berri; but though he laboriously manufactured a translation of the
Decameron[2] through the intervention of a Latin prose rendering done by an
Italian monk, it is his version of the De Casibus which has kept his name alive
with modern students.

The plan of the De Casibus is simple. A long procession of unfortunates,
from Adam and Eve to King John of France taken prisoner at Poitiers in 1356,
passes lamenting before Boccaccio as he sits in his study recording the "tragedy"
of each. The series of mournful narratives, for which Biblical and classical
history are both drawn upon, is varied in several ways: by disputes between Fortune and Poverty, between Boccaccio and Brunhilda, Atreus and Thyestes, etc.;
or by digressions of author's comment on the vices which cause these "tragedies";
or by brief group-chapters headed "Conventus Dolentium", "Miseri Quidam",
"Pauci Flentes", and so on, in which several or many persons are dismissed with
a mere mention. The whole work is in the Latin divided into nine books, of
nine to twenty-seven chapters each, usually of about twenty; and the first four
books have brief prologues.

Laurent twice translated the De Casibus; his first and more literal rendering
was made in 1400; the second, much amplified, was apparently the only French
version known to Lydgate. The general plan of the second recension follows
that of Boccaccio; thus, in the first book the division into nineteen chapters is
preserved and the same figures appear. But all the personages who in Boccaccio
pass rapidly as members of a group are by Laurent treated in detail, the "Conventus" chapters thus becoming among the longest of the work, and the scheme
losing the effect of alternate expansion and contraction given it on Boccaccio's
plan. Laurent also diverges and amplifies wherever excuse for divergence offers;
the mention by Boccaccio of a place, a custom, a person, sends Laurent off on a

---

[1] For Boccaccio's Latin and the French see:—Hortis, Sulle opere latine del Boccaccio,
Trieste, 1879; E. Koeppel, Laurents de Premierfait u. John Lydgates Bearbeitungen von
Boccaccios De Casibus Virorum Illustrium, Munich, 1885; see Hauvette, De Laurentio Pri-
mofato, Paris, 1903, also his paper in "Entre Camarades," Paris, 1901, pp. 279-297. Liberal
excerpts from the Latin and the French texts will be found in vol. iv of Bergen's ed. of the
Fall of Princes, 1927.

[2] A copy of this rendering, and of Premierfait's transl., are in Brit. Mus. Royal 19 E i.
The French transl. is also in Brit. Mus. Adds. 34322-3; and Humphrey of Gloucester's copy
is in Paris, Bibl. nat. fonds français 12421.

detour. Brief though many of these additions are, they are so numerous and their
character is often so much that of footnotes that the narrative is clogged while
it is extended.

Laurent's prose was rendered into English stanzaic verse by Lydgate at
the command of Humphrey duke of Gloucester, brother of Henry the Fifth, an
Englishman as royal in his patronage of letters and as turbulent in his meddling
with politics as were his French compeers. The date at which the work was
undertaken may be deduced from the opening prologue, in which Lydgate speaks
of Gloucester as Lieutenant of England during Henry VI's absence in France
(1430-Jan. 1432) and commends the duke for dealings with heretics which probably refer to the Lollard executions of 1431. For the ending of the work we
have only Lydgate's remark, in the prologue to book viii, that he is over sixty
years of age. As he had in the prologue to Thebes spoken of himself as nearly
fifty, students are inclined to place Thebes and the Fall of Princes in the intervening years, and to assign to the longer work four-fifths of the time.

In Lydgate's hands the De Casibus was again expanded.[1] He adds, of
course, at will to the narratives, drawing both from classical writers like Ovid
and from medieval encyclopedists and commentators; he sometimes cuts the
stories, as with Theseus and with Agamemnon, and may send the reader either to
Chaucer or to his own work; he alters and develops, as in the Orpheus and the
Althaea narratives of book i; and he everywhere diverges into moralization. He
has too much fact-material ready to his hand in Laurent to wander into a didactic
morass as he does in his version of Aesop, where the slender narrative is engulfed in
moral comment. And for a part of his moralizings here Lydgate has excuse;
Gloucester commanded him to follow up each tragedy by "a Lenvoy conveyed
by reason", which should point the lesson (see ii:145 ff.). These envoys con-

---

[1] The usual recension of the Fall of Princes, from which so far as I know only Harley
1766 differs, runs as follows:—
Book i:—Prologue, 67 stanzas. 23 chapters, Adam to Canace. Includes Nimrod, Saturn and
    the Golden Age, Cadmus, Jason, Oedipus, Atreus and Thyestes, Theseus, Althaea,
    Hercules, Orpheus, Priam, Samson, and a defence of women.
Book ii:—Prologue, 23 stanzas. 31 chapters, Saul to Hostilius, with an envoy "Rome, Re-
    member." Includes The Human Body and the Body Politic, Mucius Scaevola, Lucrece,
    Virginia, Jeroboam, Ahab, Dido (with a satirical envoy to widows), Cyrus, Midas,
    Belshazzar, Croesus, Romulus.
Book iii:—Prologue, 23 stanzas. 27 chapters, opened by a dialogue between Fortune and Pov-
    erty and closing with Artaxerxes and Darius. Lucrece again, Coriolanus, the Golden
    Age, Alcibiades, Haman, Esther.
Book iv:—Prologue on Poets and Writing, 30 stanzas. 26 chapters, Marcus Manlius to Arsinoë.
    Includes a discussion of Roman triumphs and crowns, Dionysius of Syracuse, Alexander,
    Agathocles the "crowned ass", Brennus.
Book v:—No prologue. 33 chapters, from a discourse against pride in beauty to Jugurtha.
    Includes Regulus, Scipio, Hannibal, the Gracchi.
Book vi:—No prologue. 16 chapters, opening with a dialogue between Fortune and Boccaccio,
    and closing with Antony and Cleopatra. Includes Caius Marius, Julius Caesar, Cicero,
    a chapter against those who defame rhetoric, Pompey.
Book vii:—No prologue. 9 chapters, from Antony the younger to the fall of Jerusalem.
    Includes Herod, Nero, and the dispute between Messalina, Caligula, and Tiberius. The
    Golden World is described,—see Book i also.
Book viii:—Prologue, 29 stanzas. 27 chapters, from Domitian to Rosamond. Includes many
    emperors, Constantine, Julian, Arthur, Boethius.
Book ix:—No prologue. 38 chapters, from Mauritius to John of France. Includes Brunhilde,
    Mohammed, Lombard emperors, Pope Boniface, Ugolino of Pisa.
Envoy to Gloucester.

stitute a structural change as compared with Laurent's work; and in some small measure they restore the narrative rhythm of Boccaccio's group-chapters set among the detail-chapters. But for a good deal of the difference in size between the French and the English we may look to Lydgate's rambling and verbose method of narration. When Laurent says that Nimrod "fut maistre des veneurs et eut entre eulx seigneurie", this becomes in Lydgate—

> He was callid cheeff prynce of venerie
> Desirous euer for to han victorie
> Off beestis wilde to be put in memorie
> And haue a pris amongis these champiouns
> Tigres to daunte bores and leouns.

> Ther was no beeste in wodes so sauage
> That durste ageyn hym make resistence
> His furious ire so mortal was and rage
> The erthe quook for feer off his presence.   i :1060 ff.

Again, in the inquiry of Cadmus at the oracle of Apollo, i:1898 ff., we find :—

> To what parti that he myhte drawe
> He praied the god to wissyn him & reede
> Sum tokne shewe or sum maner lawe
> Onto what ile that he myhte hym speede
> Or that he wolde graciously hym leede
> Where as he myhte bilden a cite
> That were accordyng for hym & his meyne

> And to Apollo he dede sacrefise
> And maad to hym his oblacioun
> The god requeryng goodli to deuise
> To what lond or to what regeoun
> For his duellyng and habitacioun
> He sholde drawe withoute mor obstacle
> For hym and hise to make his habitacle.

And yet a third stanza is required by Lydgate before he can relinquish the fact of Cadmus' question to Apollo, and proceed to the answer.

Not all of his expansions of Laurent are as unsuccessful as these. There is perhaps some narrative method, some attempt at dramatic delay, in the Althaea tragedy. Laurent says of Meleager's slaying of his uncles that Althaea, hearing the news, fell senseless, "et apres pour la vengeance du delict que feist Meleager elle bouta au feu le tison que elle auoit garde iusques lors." Lydgate makes eight stanzas out of the queen's hesitation between filial love and the desire for revenge, but sorely muddles his effect by allusions to the Fates and to Fortune. See i : 4943 ff.

The repetitive tendency, whether of a narrative point, a moral lesson, a stylistic formula, or a line-mould, is, as already said, Lydgate's most marked characteristic and his greatest failing. He can escape from it for an instant at a time, in a line or a pair of lines; see the examples above cited p. 81. Given a religious emotion and a good model, he can keep clear of his besetting sin for several verses, as here in i:1331-4. Laurent wrote:—"Dieu a mil mains / dieu a mil iauelots / dieu a mil arcs et manieres de pugnir les peches et les pecheurs." This becomes in the English :—

> God hath a thousand handis to chastise
> A thousand dartis off punycioun
> A thousand bowes maad in vnkouth wise
> A thousand arblastic bent in his dongoun　. . .

It is of such passages as this, or of the prayer of Theodosius, that Gray thought when he praised Lydgate for a "stiller kind of majesty."

But the felicity of a small number of lines, the dignity of a smaller number of passages, in the Fall of Princes, is overborne by the narrative failure of the whole, by its unvarying drone of misery, and in Lydgate's hands by its aggressive sermonizing and its faults of style. One may insist on the antiquarian value of his prologues, on the interest of his attempts at humor (usually against women), and plead the crushing size of his commanded task; but the fact remains that he did not do his work as well as did Boccaccio or Laurent. The monotony which always threatens stories in a framework, a monotony so evident in Gower and in the Monk's Tale, is here doubled by weakness and monotony of style.

The Monk's Tale and the Legend of Good Women were, however, constantly in Lydgate's mind as he worked at the Fall of Princes. It never occurred to him that Chaucer's voice in the former was as deliberately affected as was the falsetto of Sir Thopas, or that each piece of work betrays the author's weariness of his subject. In Lydgate's eyes Chaucer, like Seneca and Boccaccio and Petrarch, was a zealous writer of "tragedies". There is much about Chaucer in the Fall of Princes; but, as already said (p. 91 here), Lydgate's procedure regarding his master varies; he praises him lavishly, he often fears to "auaunce the penne" in rivalry, but again he leaves him unmentioned where we expect a reference, as in the Virginia or the Ugolino story, and he tells the Canace-story condemned by Chaucer. Of phrase-echo of the elder writer there is little here, as compared with the Troy Book or the Siege of Thebes.

Naturally the bulk of Lydgate's material comes from his French original; and there is no clear trace of his use of Boccaccio's Latin. His phrasing, however, would make it seem that he had recourse directly to Boccaccio; for after the formal introduction of Laurent in the opening prologue, Lydgate constantly speaks of his authority as "Bochas" or "John Bochas", i.e. Boccaccio. Laurent had not done this, but had spoken in Boccaccio's person, using the pronoun of the first person singular.

The general plan of Boccaccio's work remains clear through the changes and additions made by his translators; it was a plan and theme congenial to the age in which he lived. Though lacking utterly in the qualities which make Dante's Inferno immortal, the De Casibus yet gropes among material not unlike that which Dante transformed. The half-scholarly, half-monkish figure of Boccaccio seated in his study and visited by the shades of fallen greatness bewailing their lot; the monstrous figure of Fortune dominating the scene; the varying of the "tragedies" by denunciations of women, praise of poverty and of "rhetoric", by occasional dialogue-episodes,—these gathered together into this one book many of the philosophico-literary elements dear to the medieval mind. The connection of the always interesting theme of the mutability of Fortune with a list of imposing historical personages set a poetic fashion which persisted long.   Chaucer dallied with it; the Burgundian Chastellain imitated it in his prose Temple de Bocace; Laurent and Lydgate translated it; it was followed later by Lodowick Lloyd's Pilgrimage of Princes, by Cavendish's Visions, and by A Mirror for Magistrates; Barclay, in his Ship of Fools, refers to Lydgate's work and shows acquaintance with it; and it ultimately exerted its influence upon the historical plays of the Tudor age.   That age, however, discovered that for purposes of art, the part is greater than the whole, and that tragedy isolated is far more impressive than tragedy massed; it discovered also that tragic effect was enhanced by the interpolation of a lighter or a varied element.   This latter truth may have hovered before Boccaccio when he interspersed dialogue and group-scene among his single-figure studies; and when we look at the composition of the B^2 fragment of the Canterbury Tales or at the variety of its framework as a whole, we feel strongly that it was the craving for structural variety which led Chaucer, the potential dramatist, to hold up his earlier-written Monk's Tale to scorn, and to abandon the Legend of Good Women.

Lydgate's work was popular in its time.   Thirty or more MSS remain, and selections from it appear in many fifteenth-century commonplace-books.   It was twice printed by Pynson, in 1494 and 1527, by Tottel in 1554, and by Wayland in 1558.   Much of the opening prologue was printed by Miss Spurgeon in her EETS Chaucer Allusions i :37-40, from MS Harley 1766; and for Dr. Bergen's edition see below.

Manuscripts of the Fall of Princes at present (1927) known to me are:—
At Oxford:—
  In the Bodleian Library—
    Bodley 263: used as basis of the edition by Bergen as below.
    Bodley e Musaeo 1 (formerly 215).
    Hatton 2 (formerly 105).
    Rawlinson C 448.
    Corpus Christi College 242.
In London:—
    British Museum Harley 1245, 1766, 3486, 4197, 4203.   Fragment in Harley 2202.
    Brit. Mus. Royal 18 B xxxi, Royal 18 D iv, Royal 18 D v.
    Brit. Mus. Sloane 4031.   Eight leaves in Sloane 2452.
    Brit. Mus. Adds. 21410, impf.
    Brit. Mus. Adds. 39659, given by Baroness Zouche.
    Lambeth Palace Library 256.   ˙
In Other Public Libraries.
    Rylands Eng. 2, formerly owned by the Earl of Jersey at Osterley Park.
    Hunterian S i. 5 at Glasgow University.
In Private Possession.
    Rutland, or Belvoir Castle, owned by the Duke of Rutland.
    Longleat, owned by the Marquess of Bath.
    Mostyn, sold to Francis Edwards, 1920; now in the hands of Rosenbach, New
      York City.
    Wollaton Hall, Lord Middleton's MS, sold in 1925 to Quaritch.
    Plimpton, owned by George A. Plimpton, New York City, formerly by F. W.
      Bourdillon.
    Phillipps 4254, in the hands of Rosenbach, New York City.

Phillipps 4255, in the hands of Quaritch.

Phillipps 8117, owned by Robert Garrett of Baltimore; bought 1905.

Phillipps 8118, owned by John Gribbel of Philadelphia.

Morgan 124, formerly owned by the Lee family, and by Henry White, now in the Morgan Collection, New York.

Huntington 268, the Ecton Hall copy, in the Huntington Library, California. Impf. Bought in 1924.

Extracts from the poem are common in late fifteenth-century MSS. The longest collection of such extracts known to me is in Harley 2251 of the Brit. Mus.; see also Trin. Coll. Cambridge R 3, 19 and R 3, 20, Ashmole 59, McClean 182, etc., and the "Proverbs of Lydgate" printed by de Worde.

Two MSS mentioned in the Bernard Catalogus of 1697, owned by Abram Seller and by the Earl of Peterborough, I have not identified. (The former was destroyed by fire in 1700; see Dr. Bergen's Bibliographical Introduction, p. 3.)

The MS Royal 18 D iv bears at the foot of its first written page the arms of Tiptoft Earl of Worcester, died 1470; as the complicated marshaling shows the arms of Beauchamp duke of Warwick, it was probably executed for Tiptoft after his marriage, in 1446, with Cecily, daughter to the Earl of Salisbury and widow of Warwick.

The MS Royal 18 D v bears at close, set into the text, the arms of Percy Earl of Northumberland, gartered. This and several other MSS are occasionally mutilated or confused in sewing; the Corpus MS is both, its twelve opening leaves belonging between books v and vi. But the agreement in contents among most MSS is so close as to make the case of Harley 1766 the more conspicuous. This volume, which is ornamented with clumsy and garish pictures, looking as if wafered on to the margins and coarsely executed, has been extensively cut and rearranged as regards text. Most of books iii, iv, v, and vi, classical material, is not present, and the grouping of the chapters into books is not the usual one. The opening prologue and the final epilogue to Gloucester are there, but not the prologue to book iii with the thanks to him for his munificence. The codex also lacks the five stanzas of appeal to Gloucester for money which follow chapter 18, book iii, as lines 3837-3871; but this trait it shares with other texts, e.g. Rawlinson C 448, Bodley e Musaeo, Royal 18 D iv and v, Phillipps 4254. The lines appear, so far as I have noted, in Bodley 263, Harley 4197 and 4203, Hatton, Royal 18 B xxxi, and Morgan 124. In Anglia 36:121-36 I suggested that this envoy was a letter, appended by Lydgate to sheets which he submitted for Gloucester's inspection, and which in some copies became incorporated with the text. The duke's habit of examining the work of his translators while it was in progress may be inferred from the words of the Palladius-translator here cited, p. 206.

Full descriptions of all MSS and prints of the Fall of Princes will be found in vol. iv of Dr. Henry Bergen's edition of the poem for the Carnegie Institution, 1927; text in vols. i-iii, 1923. I am indebted to Dr. Bergen for much friendly help as to the MSS.

A

THE GENERAL PROLOGUE

[MS Brit. Mus. Royal 18 D iv.]

He that whilom dede his diligence
The book of bochas in frensch to trans-
    late
Out of latyn / he callid was laurence
The tyme trewli remembrid and the date
Theere whan kynge iohn / thoruh his
    mortail fate   5
Was prisoner brouht / to this regiown
Whan he first gan on this tra(n)slacioun

2

In his prologe affermynge off reson
Artificeres / hauyng exercise
Mai chaunge and turne bi good discre-
    cioun   10
Shappis formys and newli hem deuyse
Make and vnmake in many sondri wise
As potteris which to that craft entende
Breke and renewe ther vesselis to amende

3

Thus men of craft may of due riht   15
That ben inventiff and han experience
ffantasien in ther inwarde siht
Deuises newe thoruh ther excellence
Expert maisters han ther to licence
ffro good to beter for to chaunge a
    thinge   20
And semblabli thes clerkis in writynge

4

Thynge that was maid of auctours hem
    beforn
Thei may off newe finde and fantasie
Oute of olde chaff trie out ful clene corn
Mak it more fressh and lusti to the eie 25
Ther subtil wit and ther labour applie
With ther colours agreable off hewe
Make olde thinges for to seeme newe

5

Afforn prouidyd that no presumpcion
In ther chaungynge haue noon aucto-
    rite   30
And that meeknesse haue domynacion
ffals envie that she not present be
But that ther grounde with parfit charite
Conueied be to ther avauntage
Treuly rootid amyd off ther corage   35

6

Thus laurence fro hym envie excludid
Thouh toforn hym translatid was this
    book
Withynne hym silff he fulli hath con-
    cludid
Vpon that labour / whan he caste his
    look
He wolde ame(n)de it but first he for-
    sook   40
Presumpcion / and took to hym meeknes
In his prologe / as he doth expresse

7

In which processe lik as I am lerid
He in his tyme off connyng dede excelle
In ther langage therfore he was re-
    querid   45
Off estatis which can hym eek compelle
Among hem holde of rethorik the welle
To vnderfonge this labour thei hym
    preie
And he ther request lowli dede obeie

8

fful wel he felte the labour was not-
    able   50
The fall of nobles with euery circum-
    staunce
ffrom ther lordshippis dreedful & vn-
    stable
How that thei fill to putte in remem-
    braunce
Therin to shewe fortunes variaunce
That other myhte as in a myrovr see 55
In worldli worshipe may be no surete

9

Bi exaumple as ther is no rose
Spryngyng in gardyns but ther be sum
    thorn
Nor fairer blossum than nature list dis-
    pose
Than may ther beute as men ha seyn to
    forn   60
With bittir wyndis be fro ther braunchis
    born
Nor noon so hih in his estat contune
ffre fro thawaityng and daunger of for-
    tune

10

Wherfore bochas for a memoriall
Considryng the grete dignytees   65
Off ·worldli pryncis in ther power royall
Grete emperours estatis and degrees
How fortune hath cast them fro ther
    sees
Nameli such as kowde hem silff not
    knowe
fful sodeynli to make hem lyn ful lowe 70

11

This seide auctour avise and riht sad
Hath gadred out / with rethoriques
    sueete
In diuerse bookes / which that he hath
    rad
Off philisophers / & many an old poete
Besied hym / bothe in cold & heete   75
Out to compile / and writen as he fonde
The fall of nobles in many dyuerse londe

12

Upon whos book in his translacion
This seid laurence rehersyth in certeyn
And holdith this in his opynyon   80
Such language as opyn is & pleyn
Is more acceptid as it is offte seyn
Than strange termys which be not vnder-
    stande
Namli to folkes / that duellen vp on
    lande

13

As he seith eek that his entencion   85
Is to amenden / correcten and declare
Nat to condempne of no presumpcion
But to supporte / pleynli and to spare
Thyng touched shortli off the stori bare
Undir a stile breeff & compendious   90
Hem to prolonge / whan thei ben ver-
    tuous

14

ffor a stori / which is nat pleynli told
But constreyned / vndir wordes fewe
ffor lak off trouth / wher thei be newe or
    old
Men be report / kan nat the mater
    shewe   95
Thes ookes grete be nat doune jhewe
ffirst at a strok / but bi longe processe
Nor longe stories a woord may nat ex-
    presse

85. *As he seith*, etc. MS Bodley reads *And he*,
    etc.

15

ffor which pleynli this noble translatour
Cast off purpos / thes stories for to
    write   100
And for to doon / his diligent labour
As thei fill / in ordre to endite
That men aftir / myht hem silff delite
Auentures so as thei fill in dede
Off sondri pryncis / to beholde &
    reede   105

16

And haue a maner contemplacion
That thynges alle / where fortune may
    atteyne
Be transitori off condicion
ffor she off kynde / is hasti & sodeyne
Contrarious hir cours for to re-
    st(r)eyne   110
Off wilfulnesse she is so variable
When men most trust / than is she most
    chaungeable

17

And for hir chaunge / & for hir doubil-
    nesse
This bochas but that men sholde encline
Sette ther hertis / void off vnstabil-
    nesse   115
Upon thynges which that ben deuyne
Wher as joie perpetueli doth shyne
Withoute eclipsyng in that heuenli see
Void off alle cloudis of mutabilite

18

Among this bochas / writith off swet-
    nesse   120
And off maters / that lusti ben & glade
And sumwhile he writt / off wrechid-
    nesse
And how fortune / kan floure & after
    fade
Joie vnder cloude / prosperite in the
    shade
Enterchaungyng / off euery manere
    thyng   125
Which that men feele / here in this
    world lyuyng

19

And in his processe / who so list be-
    holde
Off alle estatis of hih and louh degre
And off pryncis / bothe ȝong and old

114. *but.* So MS. Read *bit*, i.e. biddeth.

ffro the begynnyng / which in this world
  ha be   *130*
Lyuynge in joie / or in aduersite
ffro the first / he descendith doun
Of ther fortune / bi pleyne descripciovn

20

Off the most noble he spareth noon
But settith hem in ordre ceriousli   *135*
Gynnyth at adam / & endith at kyng
  John
Ther auentures / rehersyng bi and bi
Off this kyng iohn / concludyng finali
How that he was for (al) his gret puis-
  saunce
Off prince edward take prisoner in
  ffraunce   *140*

21

This seid bochas auctour of this book
Which off stories had gret inteligence
Summe he leffte summe also he took
Such as he leffte was off no necligence
Supposyng & demynge off credence   *145*
Alle the stories which that comoun be
Other knew hem also wel as he

22

And that folk wold haue had disdeyn
Thynges comoun / to put in memoire
Therfore bochas / thouhte it was but
  veyne   *150*
To his name / noon encres off gloire
To remembre no cronycle nor histoire
But tho that wern / for ther merit not-
  able
Auctorised famous and comendable

23

In his labour / hauyng a delite   *155*
That the mater gretly myhte auayle
Do plesaunce to the comon profit
Off noble stories / to make rehersaile
Shewynge a merour / how all the world
  shal faile
And how fortune / for al ther hih re-
  novn   *160*
Hath upon princis iurediccion

24

The which thyng / in ful sobre wise
He considred / in his inwarde entente
In his resun gan to aduertise

134. Bodley 263 . . . *he ne spareth* . . .
139. Our MS reads *as;* bracketed word from MS
    Bodley. See 160, 181.
148. Bodley 263 reads *And lest that folk,* etc.

Seyng off princis / the blynd entende-
  ment   *165*
With worldi worshep how that thei be
  blent
As thei sholde euer / her estatis keepe
And as fortune were J . leid to sleepe

25

As thei hade of fortune the maistrie
Her enchanted / with ther pociouns   *170*
Bi sum crafte / off newe sorcerie
Or bi power off incantaciouns
To make stable / ther domynaciouns
With iren cheynys / for to laste longe
Lokkid to rokkis off adimantis stronge

26

Supposyng in ther surquedie   *176*
Ther estatis / sholde be durable
But fortune kan frowardli denye
Pleynli proue / that thei be chaungable
And to pryncis / for thei be nat
  stable   *180*
ffortune ful oft / for al ther gret estat
Unwarli chaungeth / & seith to hem
  chekmat

27

ffor lordis summe / in ther magnificence
Off roiall power / sette of god riht nouht
Thei nat consider / his longe pa-
  cience   *185*
Nor auertise / his power in ther thouht
But in ther hertis / ʒiff it were wel
  souht
How he is meke / & pacient to abide
Thei wolde of reson / ther pompe leyn a
  side

28

But for ther taryeng / & ther necly-
  gence   *190*
That thei to hym wil nat resorte a geyn
ʒit of his mercy / & benyuolence
With oute vengaunce / rigour or dis-
  deyn
As a meke fader / in alle his werkis
  pleyn
Assaieth his ʒerde of castigacion   *195*
So for to bringe hem / to correccion

29

Summe he kan ful fadyrly chastise
Where he loueth by punshyng of siknesse
And of his mercy in many a nothir wise
Bi aduersite of sum worldli distresse *200*
And he nat asketh / for (his) kyndenesse

201. Bracketed word from MS Bodley 263.

Off hih nor low / who so kan aduerte
Noon othir tresor / but a mannys herte

30

And as myn auctour / list to compre-
hende
This john bochas / bi gret auctorite 205
It is almesse to correcten and amende
The vicious folk / off euery comounte
And bi exaumplis / which that notable be
Off pryncis olde / that whilom dede fall
The lowere poeple / from ther erroure
call   210

31

Bi smale whelpis / as summe clerkys
write
Chastised is the myhti fers leon
And whan the swerd off vengeaunce eek
doth bite
Upon pryncis / for ther transgression
The comon poepil / in ther opynyoun 215
ffor werrai dreed tremble doun and quake
And bi such mene / ther vices thei for-
sake

32

And such also / as ha be defoulid
In ther vices / bi long contynuance
Or in ther synnys rustid & jmowled 220
Bi good exaumple may come to repent-
aunce
Who hym repentith the lord will hym
auaunce
And hym accepte in hih and louh estate
The meek preserue punyssch the obsty-
nat

33

This said mater / touchyng such
thynges   225
Myn auctour bochas / heeraffter shal de-
clare
Be exeaumple of princis / & of myhti
kynges
What was ther fyne / & nat the trouth
spare
And theih my stile nakid be & bare
In rethorik myn auctour for to sue   230
3it fro the trouthe / shal I nat remue

34

But on the substaunce / bi good leiser
abyd
Affter myn auctour / lik as I may atteyne

And for my part / sette eloquence aside
And in this book / biwepen & com-
pleyne   235
Thassaut off fortune froward & sodeyne
How sche on pryncis / hath kid here
variaunce
And of her malice the dedli mortal
chaunce

35

But o allas / who schal be my mvse
Or vnto whom shal j for helpe calle 240
Calliope my callyng will refuse
And on pernaso / here worthi sustren
alle
Thei will there sugre tempre with no
galle
ffor ther suetnesse / and lusti fressh
syngyng
fful ferre discordith / fro materis com-
pley(ny)ng   245

36

Mi maistir chauncer / with his freissh
comedies
Is deed alas / cheeffe poete of briteyne
That whilom made / ful pitous tragedies
The falle of pryncis / he dede also compleyne
As he that was / of makyng souer-
eyne   250
Whom al this land / shold of riht
preferre
Sith of oure language / he was the lode-
sterre

37

Senek in Rome / thoruh his hih prudence
Wrot tragedies of gret moralite
And tullius / cheeff welle of elo-
quence   255
Maade in his tyme / many fressh dite
Franceis petrak / of florence the cite
Maade a book / as I can reherce
Of too fortunys / welful & peruerse

38

And ageyn bothe / wrot the remedies 260
In bookis tweyne / made a deuysion
Amonge rehersyng many freissh stories
The first book / is thus conueied doun
A dialoge twen gladnesse & resoun
The secunde / can bere me weel wit-
nesse   265
Maad atwen resoun / & worldli heuy-
nesse

39

The matir / is wondirful delectable
Thouh wo with joie / haue int(e)resse
And john bochas / wrot mateers lament-
able
The fall off pryncis / where he doth ex-
presse   270
How fro ther joie / thei fill in gret dis-
tresse
And alle thes writers / thoruh ther fam-
ous renoun
Gret worshipe dede vnto ther nacion

40

And semblabli as I ha told toforn
Mi maistir chauncer / dede his besy-
nesse   275
And in his daies / hath so wel hym born
Out off oure tunge / tawoiden al reud-
nesse
And to refourme it / with colours of
suetnes
Wherfore lat vs yiue hym laude & glory
And put his name / with poetis in mem-
ory   280

41

Off whos labour / to make mencion
Wherthoruh of riht / he sholde com-
mendid be
In ȝouthe he made a translacion
Off a book which is callid trophe
In lumbard tunge / as men may reede
& see   285
And in oure vulgar / longe or than he
deide
Gaff it the name / of troilus & cresseide

42

Which for to reede / louers hem delite
Thei ha therin / so gret deuocion
And this poete / hymsilff also to
quyte   290
Off boeces book / the consolacion
Maad in his tyme / (an) hool transla-
cion
And to his sone / that callid was lowis
He made a tretys / ful noble & of gret
prisse

43

Upon thastlabre / in ful notable
fourme   295
Sett hem in ordre / with ther dyuysions
Mennys wittis / tapplien and confourme

268. Bodley 263 reads *have an interesse.*

To vndirstonde / bi ful experte resons
Bi domefieng of sundri mansions
The roote oute souht / at the ascen-
dent   300
Toforn or he gaff / any iugement

44

He wrot also / ful many day agone
Dante in inglissh / hym silff so doth ex-
presse
The pitous story / of ciex and alcione
And the deth eek / of blaunche the
duchesse   305
And notabli / dede his besynesse
Bi gret auys / his wittis to dispose
To translate / the romaunce of the rose

45

Thus in vertu / he sette all his entent
Ydilnesse and vices for to flee   310
Off foulis also / he wrot the parlament
Theryn remembryng / of roial eglis thre
How in ther chois / thei felte aduersite
Tofore nature / profred the batayle
Ech for his parti / ȝif it wolde availe 315

46

He dede also his diligence and peyne
In oure vulgar / to translate & endite
Origen vpon the maudeleyn
And of the leoun / a book he dede write
Off anneleida / & off falls arcite   320
He made a compleynt / doolful & pitous
And of the broche / which that Vulcanus

47

At thebes wrouhte / ful dyuerse of na-
ture
Ouyde writeth / who ther off hade a siht
ffor hih desir / he shold not endure 325
But he hit hadde / neuer be glad nor liht
And ȝif he hadde it / onys in his myht
Lich as my maistir / seith & wrott in
dede
It to conserue / he sholde ay liue in
dreede

48

This poete wrot at requeste of the
quene   330
A legende / of parfyt hoolines
Off good wommen / to fynde out nyn-
teen
That dede excelle in bounte & fairnesse
And for his laboure / and bisines

Was inportable / his wittis to en-
combre   *335*
In al this world / to fynde so gret a
nombre

49

He made the book off cantirbury talis
Whan the pilgrimes rood on pilgrymage
Thoruhout Kent by hillis & bi valis
And alle the stories / told in ther pas-
sage   *340*
Enditid hem ful wel in oure language
Summe of knyhthod & summe off gentil-
esse
And summe off loue & summe of parfit-
nesse

50

And summe also / off gret moralite
Summe of disport encludyng gret sent-
ence   *345*
In prose he wrot / the tale off Melibe
And off his wiff / that callid was pru-
dence
And off Grisildis parfit pacience
And how the monk / of stories newe &
olde
Pitous tragedies / bi the weie tolde   *350*

51

This said poete / my maister in his daies
Maad & compiled ful many a fressh dite
Compleyntis / baladis / roundelis / virrelaies
fful delectable / to heeryn and to see
ffor which men sholde off riht &
equyte   *355*
Sith he of inglissh / in makyng was the
beste
Praie vnto god / to ʒiue his soule reste

52

And thes poetis / J make off mencioun
Were bi old tyme / had in gret deynte
With kynges pryncis / in euery re-
gioun   *360*
Gretli preferred / after ther degre
ffor lordis hadde / plesance for to see
To studie among / & to caste ther lookis
At good leiser / vpon wise bookis

53

ffor in the tyme / off cesar Julius   *365*
Whan the triumphe / he wan in rome
toune
He entre wolde / the scoole off tullius
And here his lecture / off gret affeccioun

And not withstondyng / his conquest &
renoun
Vn to bookis / he gaff gret atten-
daunce   *370*
And hadde in stories / yoie and gret
plesaunce

54

Eek in this lond / I dar afferme a thyng
Ther is a prince / fful myhty of puys-
saunce
A kynges sone / vncle to the kynge
Henry the sexte / which is now in
fraunce   *375*
And is lieftenant / & hath the gouern-
aunce
Off our breteyne thoruh whos discrecion
He hath conserued / in this regioun

55

Duryng his tyme off ful hih prudence
Pes and quiete / and sustened riht   *380*
ʒit natwithstandyng / his noble prouy-
dence
He is in deede / prouyd a good knyht
Eied as argus / with reson and forsiht
Off hih lectrure / I dar eek off hym
telle   *384*
And treuli deeme / that he doth excelle

56

In vndirstondyng / all othir of his age
And hath gret joie / with clerkis to
commune
And no man is / mor expert off language
Stable in studie alwei he doth contune
Settyng a side / alle chaunges of fortune
And wher he loueth / ʒiff I schal nat
tarie   *391*
Withoute cause / ful loth he is to varie

57

Duc off Gloucestre / men this prince
calle
And natwithstandyng / his staat & dig-
nyte
His corage neuer / doth appalle   *395*
To studie in bookis / off antiquite
Therin he hath so gret felicite
Vertuousli / hym silff to ocupie
Off vicious slouth / to haue the maistrie

58

And with his prudence & wit(h) his
manheed   *400*

Trouthe to susteyne / he fauour set aside
And hooli chirche meyntenyng in dede
That in this land / no lollard dar abide
As verrai support / vpholdere & eek
   guyde
Spareth non / but maketh hym silff
   strong   *405*
To punysshe alle tho / that do the chirch
   wrong

59

Thus is he both manly & eek wise
Chose of god to be his owne knyht
And off o thynge he hath a synglar price
That heretik dar non comen in his siht
In cristes feith / he stant so hool vpriht
Off hooli chirche / defence and cham-
   pion   *412*
To chastise alle / that do therto treson

60

And to do plesance to our lord Ihesu
He studieth euere / to haue intelligence
Reedinge off bookis / bring(e)th in
   vertu   *416*
Vices excludyng / slouthe & necligence
Maketh a prince / to haue experience
To knowe hym silff / in many sundry
   wise
Wher he trespaseth his errour to chastise

61

And among bookis / pleynli this is the
   cas   *421*
This said prynce / considred of resoun
The noble book off this John bochas
Was accordyng in his opynyoun
Off gret nobles & reputacioun   *425*
And vnto pryncis gretli necessarie
To ʒiue exaumple / how this world doth
   varie

62

And for this cause as in his entent
To shewe thuntrust / of al worldli thyng
He gaffe to me / in comaundement *430*
As hym sempte / it was riht wel sityng
That I sholde / after my cunynge
This book translate / hym to do ples·
   aunce
To shewe the chaunge / of worldli vari-
   aunce

63

And with support of his magnificence *435*
Vnder the weengis of his correccion
Thouh that I haue / lak of eloquence
I schal procede / in this translacioun
ffro me avoidyng / all presumpcioun
Lowli submyttyng / eueri hour & space
Mi rude language / to my lordis grace

64

And as I haue o thyng wel in mynde
He bad me I scholde / in aspeciall
ffolowyng myn auctour / write as I fynde
And for no fauoure / be nat parciall *445*
Thus I mene to speke in generall
And noon estat / sengulerli depraue
But the sentence / of myn auctour saue

65

Al this conseyued I gan my stile dresse
Thouht I wolde / in my mater pro-
   ceede   *450*
And for the mater abraide on heuynesse
Off freissh colours I took no manere
   heede
But my processe / pleynly for to leede
As me sempte it was to me most mette
To sett a parte alle rethoriques sueete *455*

66

Dites of murnyng & of compleynynge
Nat appertene vnto Calliope
Nor to the muses that on pernaso synge
Which be remembrid in noumbre thries
   thre
And vnto maters off aduersite   *460*
With ther sugred aureat licour
Thei be nat willi for to don fauour

67

But off disdeyne / me settyng ferre abak
To hynder me off that I wolde endite
Hauyng no colours / but onli white &
   blak   *465*
To the tragedies / which that I shal
   write
And for I can my sylff no bet acquyte
Vndir support / of alle that shal it reede
Upon bochas / riht thus I will proceede

B

THE LETTER OF CANACE TO MACAREUS
Fall of Princes i : 6882-7049

At the end of the first book of the De Casibus, after the tragedy of Samson and a chapter "In Mulieres" apparently suggested by the perfidy of Delilah, Boccaccio inserts one of his group-chapters, entitled "Miseri Quidam". In it he says that he had not yet written sufficient of the wickedness of women when he heard a clamour of lamentation headed by Pyrrhus, him who was slain by Orestes in the temple of Apollo with the fraudulent connivance of the priest Macareus. Boccaccio gives no further detail regarding Macareus; he says "sic et plurimi succedebant", and concludes Book I.

Apparently Laurent, the French translator of Boccaccio, seeing the word Macareus, thought of the story of Canace and her brother Macareus, to which he had already alluded in his twelfth chapter without any suggestion from Boccaccio. He therefore added at this point a dozen lines telling briefly the tragedy of the wretched children of Aeolus, in which he says that historians are silent as to Canace's fate, although Macareus escaped and became priest of Apollo at Delphos. Lydgate, in his turn, saw the allusion to Canace; but instead of adhering to the short inconclusive tale told by Laurent, he launched into a full portrayal of Canace's anguish and death, giving at length her farewell letter to Macareus.

His distribution of emphasis among the various parts of the story is quite different from that of Ovid or of Gower. Ovid dwells upon the physical details, and makes one or two tasteless word-plays; Canace says, according to him, that her father Aeolus has the savage temper of the winds which are his subjects, that she herself in the pangs of childbirth was a "soldier new" to such service, and that she will not long be called "or mother or bereaved". In the Latin the narrative of preceding events and the lyric lament are both incorporated in the letter. Gower separates these elements in his treatment of the story, Confessio Amantis iii :143 ff. He disposes of all in less than 200 lines, eliminating most of Ovid's physical detail, and compressing the letter into 28 lines, as follows:—(MS Bodl. Fairfax 3)

O þou my sorwe and my gladnesse		Let him be beried in my graue	
O þou myn hele and my siknesse	280	Beside me so schalt þou haue	
O my wanhope and al my trust		Vpon ous boþe remembrance	
O my desese and al my lust		ffor þus it stant of my greuance	
O þou my wele o þou my wo		Now at þis time as þou schalt wite	
O þou my frend o þou my fo		Wiþ teres and wiþ enke write	
O þou my loue o þou myn hate		This lettre I haue in cares colde	
ffor þee mot I be ded algate		In my riht hond my Penne I holde	300
Thilke ende may I noght asterte		And in my left þe swerd I kepe	
And ʒit wiþ al myn hole herte		And in my barm þer liþ to wepe	
Whil þat me lasteþ eny breþ		Thi child and myn which sobbeþ faste	
I wol þe loue into my deþ	290	Now am I come vnto my laste	
Bot of o þing I schal þee preie		ffare wel for I schal sone deie	
If þat my litel Sone deie		And þenk how I þi loue abeie	

The word-plays of Ovid are not here, but there is an attempt at "rhetorical color" in the use of lines beginning alike and in the balancing of "opposites". Little material is actually retained from the Latin, and that little does not come from the last part of the Epistle, the lines 111-120 which Ovid's editor Palmer calls "the greatest achievement of the *Heroides*". What Gower transfers is Canace's request that she and her child be buried in one grave, and the picture of her with which the Epistle opens, a pen in her right hand, the sword in her left. To this Gower adds the child in its mother's lap, falling from it as she stabs herself, and rolling in the blood; but according to Ovid the infant had already been carried away, to be abandoned in some solitary place.

The Ovidian portrait of Canace, with pen and sword, was retained by Petrarch in his Trionfo d'Amore, IIa, 181-3; he there says, without using Canace's name :—

> E quella che la penna da man destra,
> Come dogliosa e disperata scriva,
> E 'l ferro ignudo tien dalla sinestra.

Lydgate also is struck by the picture of Canace, which he presents in Gower's, not in Ovid's form, with the child in her lap. He dissolves Gower's balanced "opposites", lines 279 ff., into his lines 4-18, and makes in 33-35 Canace's request for the burial of her child with her, found in both Ovid and Gower. He greatly expands the mother's wail of anguished tenderness over her child, evincing a feeling deeper than Ovid's and much deeper than that of Gower. The twenty-three stanzas of this letter do not, however, get their length from the added pathos; there is a deviation into ill-placed classicism in lines 99-126, and there is recurring blame of King Aeolus. Gower, indeed, uses the whole story as an example not so much of criminal love as of "malencolie" or unbridled anger; in the Confessio it is the king-father who is the awful example rather than the unhappy victims of the God of Love. Gower speaks, in line 172, of "lawe positif", the *lex positiva* of the Church, which had made incestuous unions wrong. He discusses the subject fully at the opening of Book viii of the Confessio, where he points out that in the early world marriages between brother and sister were usual, but that the Pope (line 144) had imposed restrictions. His tone on the matter is so calmly legal that there may be some relation between it and the condemnation which Chaucer strongly expresses in the Man of Law's headlink, choosing this very story for especial censure and declaring it unfit material for narrative. Alanus de Insulis, in his Anticlaudianus I, 5:11-12, had already said, in general, that "Nec nitor argenti nec fulgure gratius aurum   Excusare potest picturae crimen adultum." Although Ovid had protested his horror, he had recounted at length the stories of Byblis and of Myrrha; and the Christian Boccaccio, in his Amorosa Visione xxv, gives fully the prayer of Byblis to her brother, in which she rejects "il superflue nomen di fratello"; just preceding, there is brief mention of "Canace e Macareo dolenti". Later writers, in fifteenth- and sixteenth-century England, include Byblis, Canace, Pasiphae, among the great tragic lovers of the world. So in Feylde's Controversy between a Lover and a Jay; but as he there applies the epithet "so hynde" to Queen Tomyris, we may regard him with a little suspicion. And Skelton, making extraordinary comparisons between the Countess of Surrey's gentlewomen and some classical heroines,—see Garland of Laurel 910 and note,— is doubtfully sincere.

Lydgate does not seem to have given the matter much moral consideration; his remarks on incest, in the next book of the Fall of Princes (4068-71), are very brief. He either forgot or disregarded Chaucer's censure of the Canace story as unfit for narrative; and once launched on it, he let his sympathy run away with

him. That sympathy is not all, however, for the unhappy lovers, it is for the
child, a feeling so strong, in this cloistered and pedantic monk, that it occasionally
breaks the crust of the inhibiting formula and leaps out in a flash of sincerity.
All who have read the Fall of Princes have caught and welcomed this gleam; the
passage was selected by Gray, and by Campbell for his 1819 Specimens of the
British Poets; and part of it was included by Gilfillan (1860) in his Specimens
of the Less-Known British Poets, i : 46-48. The letter is too long, just as the dying
speech of Polyxena, Troy Book iv:6731 ff., is too long; but both passages have
points of reality.

It should be noted that Lydgate scans *Canace* as of three syllables; Gower
treated it as a dissyllable.

[MS Brit. Mus. Harley 1766]

Out of hire swowh whan she did abrayde
Knowyng no meene but deth in hire
   dystresse   (6883)
To hire brothir / ful pitously she sayde
Cause of my sorwe / roote of myn hevy-
   nesse
That whylom were / cheeff sours of my
   gladnesse   5
Whan bothe our Ioyes / be wel so dys-
   posyd
Vndir o keye / our hertys to be enclosyd

2

Whylom thou were / suppoort and syker-
   nesse
Cheeff reioysshing of my worldly
   plesaunce   (6890)
But now thow art / the ground of my
   syknesse   10
Welle of wanhope of my dedly penaunce
Which haue of sorwe / grettest habun-
   daunce
That euere yit hadde / ony creature
Which mvt for love / the deth allas
   endure

3

Thow were whylom / my blysse and al
   my trust   15
Sovereyn counfort / my sorwes to apese
Spryng and welle / of al myn hertys lust
And now allas / cheef roote of my
   dysese
But yiff my deth / myght do the ony
   ese   (6900)
O brothir myn / in remembraunce of
   tweyne   20
Deth shal to me / be plesaunce and no
   peyne

4

My cruel ffadir / moost vnmercyable
Ordeyned hath / it nedys mvt be so
In his rygour he is so vntretable
Al mercylees / he wyl that it be doo   25
That we algate / shal deye bothe twoo
But I am glad / sith it may be noon
   othir
Thow art escapyd / m(y) best belouyd
   brothir

5

This is myn ende I may it nat
   asterte   (6910)
O brothir myn / ther is no more to
   seye   30
Lowly besechyng with al myn hool herte
ffor to remembre / specially I preye
Yiff it be falle / my litel sone deye
That thow mayst afftir / som mynde
   vpon vs have
Suffre vs bothe / to be buryed in o
   grave   35

6

I holde hym streyghtly atwen myn armys
   tweyne
Thow and nature / leyd on me this
   charge
He gyltles / with me mvt suffre peyne
And sith thow art at ffredom and at
   large   (6920)
Lat kyndenesse / our love not so dys-
   charge   40
But haue a mynde / wher euere that
   thow be
Oonys a day / vpon my chyld and me

7

On the and me dependith the trespace
Towchyng our gylt / and our greet
   offence

But weylleway / moost au*n*gelyk of
  fface   45
Our yonge chyld / in his pure inno-
  cence
Shal ageyn ryght / suffre dethys violence
Tendre of lymes / god wot ful gyltles
The goodly ffayre / which lith here
  spechelees   (6930)

8

A mouth he hath / but wordys hath he
  noone   50
Can nat compleyne / allas for noon outrage
Nor gruccheth nat / but lyth here al
  aloone
Stylle as a lamb / moost meke of his
  visage
What herte of steel / cowde doon to
  hym damage
Or suffre hym deye / beholdyng the
  man*ere*   55
And look benygne / of his tweyne eyen
  clere

9

O thow my ffadir / to cruel is the wreche
Hardere of herte / than tygre or lyon
To slen a chyld / that lyth withoute
  speche   (6940)
Voyd of al mercy / and remyssyon   60
And on his modir / hast no compassyon
His youthe considred / with lyppes soffte
  as sylk
Which at my breest / lyth stylle and
  soukith mylk

10

Is ony sorw remembryd be wrytyng
Vn to my sorweful / syhes co*m*parable 65
Or was ther eu*ere* / creature levyng
That felt of dool / a thyng more lament-
  able
ffor cou*n*fortlees / and vnrecuperable
Ar thylke heepyd sorwes ful of
  rage   (6950)
Which han with woo / oppressyd my
  corage   70

11

Rekne al meschevys / in especial
And on my myscheef / remembre and
  ha good mynde
My lord my ffadir / is myn enmy mortal
Exp*er*ience Inough / thereof I ffynde
ffor in his pursewt / he hath lefft be
  hynde   75

In destruccyon of the my Chyld / and
  me
Routhe and al mercy / and ffadirly pite

12

And the my brothir avoyded from his
  syght
Which in no wyse / his grace mayst
  attayne   (6960)
Allas that rygour / vengau*n*ce and cruel
  ryght   80
Shulde above mercy / be lady sou*e*reyne
But cruelte doth at me so dysdeyne
That though my brothir / my chyld /
  and also I
Shal deye exylled / allas from al mercy

13

My ffadir whylom / by many sundry
  signe   85
Was my socour / my supportacion
To the and me / moost gracious and
  benygne
Our worldly gladnesse / our consolacyon
But love and fortune / ha turnyd vp so
  don   (6970)
Our *grace* allas / our welffare and ou*r*
  ffame   90
Hard / to recure / so sclau*n*dryd is our
  name

14

Spot of dyffamyng / is hard to wasshe
  away
Whan noyse and rumour / abrood do
  ffolk manace
To hyndre a man / ther may be no delay
ffor hatful ffame / fleth fferre in ful
  short space   95
But of vs tweyne / ther is noon othir
  grace
Save oonly deth / and afftir deth allas
Eternal sclaundre / of vs thus stant the
  caas

15

Whom shal we blame / or whom shal
  we atwyte   (6980)
Our grete offence / sith we may it nat
  hyde   *100*
ffor oure exskus reportys to respyte
Meene is ther noon / except the god
  Cupyde
And though that he / wolde for vs provyde

---

57. *the wreche.* Read *thi wreche,* as in Bergen's
  edition.

83. *though.* So MS. Read *thou,* as in Bergen's
  edition.

In this matere / to been our cheef
reffuge
Poetys seyn / he is blynd to been a
Juge   *105*

16

He is depeynt / lych a blynd archere
To marke aryght / fayllyng dyscrecyon
Holdyng no mesour / nouthir ferre nor
neer
But lyk ffortunys / dysposicion   (6990)
Al vpon hap / voyde of al reson   *110*
As a blynd Archeer / with arwes sharpe
grounde
Off aventure / yiveth many a mortal
wounde

17

At the and me / he wrongly did marke
ffelly to hyndre / our ffatal aventures
As ferre as Phebus / shyneth in his
arke   *115*
To make vs reffuce / to alle creatures
Callyd / vs tweyne / vn to the wooful
lures
Off dyffame / which wyl departe neu*er*e
Be new repoort / the noyse encresyng
eu*er*e   (7000)

18

Odyous ffame / with swyfft wynges
ffleth   *120*
But al good ffame / envye doth re-
streyne
Ech man of othir / the dyffautys seth
Yit on his owne / no man wyl compleyne
But al the world / out cryeth on vs
tweyne
Whoos hatful yre / by vs may not be
quemyd   *125*
ffor I mvt deye / my ffadir hath so
demyd

19

Now farewel brothir / to me it doth
suffyse
To deye allone / for our bothes sake
And in my moost / feythful humble
wyse   (7010)
Vn to my deth ward / though I tremble
and quake   *130*
Off the for eu*er*e / now my leve I take
And oonys a yeer / forget nat but take
hede
My ffatal day / this lettre for to rede

20

So shalt thow han / on me som remem-
brau*n*ce

My name enprentyd / in thy calen-
deer   *135*
Be rehersaylle / of my dedly greva*un*ce
Were blak that day / and make a doolful cheer
And whan thow comyst / and shalt
aproche neer
My sepulture / I pray the nat dys-
deyne   (7020)
Vpon my grave / som teerys for to
reyne   *140*

21

Wrytyng hire lettre / awhappyd and in
drede
In hire ryght hand / hire penne gan to
quake
And a sharp swerd / to make hire herte
blede
In hire lefft hand / hir ffadir hath hire
take
And moost hire sorwe / was for hire
chyldes sake   *145*
Vpon whoos fface / in hire barm slep-
yng
fful many a teer / she wepte in compleynyng

22

Afftir al this / so as she stood and
quook
Hire chyld beholdyng / myd of hire
peynes smerte   (7030)
Withoute abood / the sharpe swerd she
took   *150*
And rooff hire sylff / evene to the herte
Hire chyld / ffyl don / which myght
nat asterte
Havyng noon helpe / to socoure hym nor
save
But in hire blood the sylff / be gan to
bathe

23

And thanne hire ffadir / moost cruel of
entent   *155*
Bad that the chyld / shulde anoon be
take
Off cruel houndys / in haste for to be
rent
And be devouryd / for his moder sake
Off this tragedye / thus an ende I
make   (7040)
Processe of which / as men may rede
and se   *160*
Concludeth on myscheef / and ffuryous
cruelte

C

ROME, REMEMBER

Fall of Princes, ii : 4460 ff.

In this envoy, which closes the second book of the Fall of Princes, Lydgate carries his usual procedure a step further. His envoys, added at Gloucester's bidding as he says ii :145, have of course no parallel in the prose of Laurent, and are regularly constructed on three rimes for the whole, with a refrain-phrase or line; they are for the most part of three to five stanzas. Chaucer, in the envoy to the Clerk's Tale, had also used three rimes, but he there composed no more than thirty-six lines; Lydgate, like many another insensitive imitator, seems to have felt that emphasis and amplification of a device increase its effectiveness, and he here extends his scheme through 126 lines, on the three rimes *-oun, -ing,* and *-ine.* Similarly, in his poem with the refrain "So as the crabbe goth forward", copied by Shirley in the MS R 3, 20 of Trinity College Cambridge, there are fifty-six lines on three rimes, while the original French, also transcribed by Shirley with a request to readers to make comparison, is of twenty-five lines. Compare Lydgate's poem to St. Denis, printed by MacCracken i :127-9, and running through nine octave stanzas on three rimes, with refrain; cf. also his Fall of Princes ix: 2371 ff., and the poem Horns Away, p. 110 *ante.*

There is in the Fall of Princes, book viii, lines 2528 ff., another lament over Rome's wretchedness and vices, but this is far more interesting because of its use of the "Ubi Sunt" motive, a theme so popular in the Middle Ages that examples of it might be multiplied indefinitely. Its most famous expression is in Villon's *Ballade des dames du temps jadis,* with the refrain "Mais où sont les neiges d'antan?" which Rossetti rendered "But where are the snows of yesteryear?" Villon, however, had many predecessors. The direct line of connection, in which the "Ubi Sunt" motive is combined with a list of personages, runs back of Villon and Regnier to the Latin hymns of the eleventh-thirteenth centuries; one of these, ascribed to Jacopone da Todi, begins:

> Dic, ubi Salomon, olim tam nobilis,
> Vel ubi Sampson est, dux invincibilis?
> Vel pulcher Absalon, vultu mirabilis,
> Vel dulcis Jonathas, multum amabilis?
> Quo Caesar abiit, celsus imperio?
> Vel Xerxes splendidus, totus in prandio?
> Dic ubi Tullius, clarus eloquio?
> Vel Aristoteles, summus ingenio?

Another hymn, *Audi tellus,* contains the passage:

> Transierunt rerum materies,
> Ut a sole liquescit glacies.
> Ubi Plato, ubi Porphyrius,
> Ubi Tullius aut Virgilius;
> Ubi Thales, ubi Empedocles,
> Aut egregius Aristoteles;
> Alexander ubi rex maximus;

Ubi Hector Troiae fortissimus;
Ubi David rex doctissimus;
Ubi Salamon prudentissimus;
Ubi Helena Parisque roseus—
Ceciderunt in profundum ut lapides;
Quis scit, an detur requies?

The English Franciscan, Thomas de Sales, in his *Luve Ron,* of the thirteenth century, has:

Hwer is Paris and heleyne
Þat weren so bryht and feyre on bleo
Amadas tristram and dideyne
Yseude and alle þeo
Ector wiþ his scharpe meyne
And cesar riche of wordes feo
Heo beoþ iglyden ut of þe reyne
So þe scheft is of þe cleo.

Boccaccio's third Canzone, see ed. Moutier xvi:115 ff., is a lament over Rome and her fallen great; it contains a long passage beginning:

Ove li duo gentil Scipioni,
Ov' è il tuo grande Cesare possente?
Ove Bruto valente?

One of the chants-royaux of Deschamps (see his works iii:182), of fifty-six lines with the refrain "Tuit y mourront, et li fol et li saige," has in its third stanza:

Ou est Artus, Godefroy de Buillon,
Judith, Hester, Penelope, Arrien
Semiramis, le poissant roy Charlon,
George, Denys, Christofle, Julien,
Pierres et Pols, maint autre cretien,
Et les martires? La mort a tous s'applique.

A long passage of Olivier de la Marche's Triumphe des Dames, stanzas 165-178 of the ed. by Kalbfleisch, 1901, opens each stanza with the words "Qui est devenu—" and bewails the power of Death on a long catalogue of noble dames. The monk Ryman, a contemporary of Lydgate (see Zupitza in Archiv 89:167 ff., esp. 256) wrote:

Where is become king Salamon
And Sampson of myght strong
King Charles also and king Arthure
With alle the worthies nyne
Diues also with his richesse
Contynued not longe

Jehan Regnier's Balade Morale que le Prisonnier fit (see ed. Lacroix 1867), has a stanza beginning:

Ou est Artus, ou est Hector de Troye?

In the anonymous poem of MS Brit. Mus. Adds. 37049, cited p. 126 here as alluding to the Dance Macabre, there is a passage of the same nature as Ryman's, beginning "Wher is now Salamon with all his prudence" etc. Nevill in his Castell of Pleasure has the "Ubi Sunt" motive with list, see p. 293 here. The Lament for Edward IV, ascribed to Skelton, has an allusion to the motive, see Dyce i :4. Barclay in his Ship of Fools uses it; see Jamieson's ed. i :268-70. Sir Thomas More, in his Book of Fortune (see Anglia 26 :142) introduces Fortune as saying:

> Ou est Dauid et Salamon
> Mathusale Josue Machabee
> Olofernes Alexandre et Sampson
> Julles Cesar Hector ausy Pompee
> Ou est Vlyxes et sa grant renommee
> Artur le roy Godefroy Charlemaine
> Daires le grant Hercules Tholomee
> Ilz sont tous mors ce monde est chose vaine.

Feylde's Controversy between a Lover and a Jay has a passage beginning:

> What is become
> Of Phylys and Demophon
> Alcumena and Alphytyon

and continuing: "Where is Semele and Jocasta Cleopatre and Ixionya Semyrramys and Syluya So fayre of fauoure." And at the end of The Disobedient Child, written about the middle of the sixteenth century, Thomas Ingelond added a song with the lines:

> Where is now Salamon, in wisdom so excellent?
> Where is now Samson, in battle so strong?
> Where is now Absolon, in beauty resplendent?
> Where is now good Jonathas, hid so long?
> Where is now Caesar, in victory triumphing?
> Where is now Dives, in dishes so dainty?

Discourses on death or on the mutability of Fortune naturally developed such passages whenever the medieval writer's taste turned to the use of the favorite medieval list. A more general treatment, with very brief list or none, bewailing either the transitoriness of human fame or the frailty of earthly joys, is found in all periods of literature. In Cicero, in Ovid (see Metam. xv :429-30), in Boethius' De Consol. Philos. ii, metre vii, in the Old Eng. Wanderer, in a line of Petrarch's Triumphus Mortis, in Henryson's Cresseid, in Arnold's Thyrsis, in James Flecker's Donde Estan,—to take widely remote examples,— the theme appears. See J. L. Lowes' Convention and Revolt in Poetry, chap. iii.

This passage has been copied, as a separate extract, in the MSS Ashmole 59 and Harley 4011; it is transcribed, with many others from the Fall, in Harley 2251.

[MS Bodleian Rawlinson C 448]

Rome remembre / of thi funda-
cion   (4460)
And of what peeple / þu tok þi gynyng
Thi beldyng / gan off fals discencioun
Off slauhtre / moordre / & outrarious
robbyng
Yevyng to us / a maner knowlechyng 5
A fals begynnyng / autours determyne
Shal bi processe / come on to ruyne

2

Wher be thyn Emporours / most sover-
eyn off renoun
Kingis exilid / ffor outrarious levyng
(Thi) senatours / with worthi Scip-
ioun   10
Poetis olde / þi triumphes reher-
syng   (4470)
Thi laureat knyhtis / most staatly þer
rydyng
Thyne aureat gloire / þi noblesse ten-
lumyne
Is bi longe processe / brouht on to ruyne

3

Wher is now Cesar / þat took posses-
sioun   15
ffirst of þempire / þe triumphe usurpyng
Or wher is Lucan / þat makith mencioun
Off al his conquest / bi serious writyng
Octavyan most solempnest regnyng
Wher is be come / þer lordschippe or
þer lyne   20
Processe off yeris / haþe brouht it to
ruyne   (4480)

4

Wher is Tullius / cheef lanterne off þi
toun
In retorik / all oþre surmountyng
Morall Senek / (or) prudent sad Ca-
toun   (4490)
Thi comoun profite / allewei proferryng
Or rihtfull Traian / most (iust) in his
deemyng   26
Which on no party / list nat to declyne
Bot longe processe / haþ brouht al to
ruyne

5

Wher is the temple / off þi proteccioun
Made bi Virgile / moost corious off
beeldyng   30

10, 24, 26. The MS reads thei, off, iustli.

Ymagis errect / for euery regioun
Whan any land / was founde rebellyng
Toward þat parte / a smal belle herde
ryngynge
To that prouynce / thymage dede en-
clyne   (4500)
Which bi longe processe / was brouht
on to ruyne   35

6

Wher is also / the greet extorcioun
Off counseilleris / & prefectis oppres-
syng
Off dictatours / the fals collucioun
Off Decemvir / the ffroward deceyuyng
And off Trybunys / þe fraudelent werk-
yng   40
Off all ecchoun / the odious rauyne
Hath bi processe / the brouht on to
ruyne

7

Wher is be come / thi domynacioun
Thi gret tributis / thi tresours (en-
richyng)   •(4510)
The world all hool / in thi subieccioun 45
Thi swerd off vengaunce / al peeplis
manacyng
Euer gredi / tencrese in thi getyng
Nothyng / bi grace / which þat is
devyne
Which hath þe / brouht / bi processe tc
ruyne

8

In thi most hihest / exaltacioun   50
Thi proude tirauntis / prouyncis con-
queryng
To god contraire / bi longe rebellioun
Goddis Goddessis / falsly obeieng
Aboue the sterris / bi surquedous
clymbyng   (4520)
Till vengaunce thi noblesse / dede
ontwyne   55
With newe compleyntis / to shewe þi
ruyne

9

Ley doun thi pride / and thi presumpcioun
Thi pompous boost / thi lordschippis
encresyng
Confesse þine outrage / & lei thi boost
adoun
Alle false goddis pleynly diffieing   60
Left vp þine herte / on to þat hevenli
kyng

Which with his blood thi sorowis for to
fyne
Hath maad thi raunsoun to saue þe ffrom
ruyne

10

ffrom olde Satourne drauh þine affec-
cioun   (4530)
His goldene world / ffulli disprisyng 65
And ffro Jubiter / make a digressioun
His seluerene tyme / hertli dispreisyng
Resorte a geyne / with will and hool
menyng
To him þat is lord / off thordris nyne
Which meekli deide to saue þe fro
ruyne   70

11

Thouh Mars be myhti in his assencioun
Bi Influence victories disposyng
And briht Phebus / yeueth consolacioun
To wordli pryncis / þer noblesse
auaunsyng   (4540)
ffor sake þer rihtis / & thi fals offryng 75
And to þat lord / bowe doun þi chyne
Which shadde his blood / to saue þe
fro ruyne

12

Wynged Mercurie / cheeff lord and
patroun
Off eloquence / and off fair spekyng
fforsak his seruise / in thyn opynyoun 80
And serue the lord / that gouerneth all
thyng
The sterrid heuene / the speeris eek
meuyng
Which for thi sake / was crownyd with
a spyne
His herte eek perced / to saue the fro
ruyne   (4550)

13

Cast vp off Venus / the fals derisioun 85
Hir firi brond / hir flatereris remevyng
Off Diana / the transmutacioun
Now briht now pale / now cleer now
dreepyng
Off blynde Cupide / þe ffraudelent
mokkyng
Off Juno Bachus / Proserpyna Lucyne 90
ffor noon but crist / may saue þe fro
ruyne

14

Voide off Circes the bestial poisoun

Rawl. C 448 omits stanza 12, which I supply from
    Bodley 263.

Off Cirenes / the furious chauntyng
Lat nat Medusa / do þe no tresoun
And ffro Gorgones / turne þi lokyng 95
And lat Synderesis ha þe in kepyng
That crist Jesu may be þi medicyne
Geyn such raskaill / to saue þe fro
ruyne   (4564)

15

Off false Idolis / mak abiuracioun
To symulacres do no worshippyng   100
Make thi resorte to cristis passioun
Which may bi mercy / redresse þin
erryng
And bi his grace / repare thi fallyng
So thou obeie / his vertuous discyplyne
Truste þat he shal / restore thi ruyne

16

His mercy is surmountyng / off foi-
soun   (4573)
Euer encresyth / withoute amenusyng
Ay atte the fulle / ecche tyme & ecche
sesoun
And neuyr wanyth / bi noon eclipsyng
Whan men list make / deuoutli ther
rekenyng   110
To leue þer synne / & come to his doc-
tryne
He redi is / to keepe hem fro ruyne

17

O Rome Rome / al olde abusyoun
Off cerimonyes / falsli disusyng   (4580)
Lei hem a side / and in a conclusioun
Cry god mercy / thi trespacis repentyng
Truste he wil nat / refuse þine axyng
The to resseyue / to laboure in his vyne
Eternaly / to saue þe ffro ruyne

18

O noble pryncis / off hih discrecioun 120
Seeth in this worlde / þer is noon abid-
yng
Peisith consiens / attwen will & resoun
While ye haue leicer / of herte Imagyn-
yng
Ye ber nat hens / but your deseruyng
Lat this conseit / ay in your þouhtis
myne   (4591)
Bexample off Rome / how al goþe to
ruyne   126

D

THANKS TO GLOUCESTER

Fall of Princes, Prologue to Book iii

As in the prologue to book i above, so here Lydgate follows more than one thread. In the earlier and general introduction he had given Laurent's explanation of the purpose of his work; he had praised in detail his master Chaucer; and he had eulogized his patron Gloucester. Here again he uses Laurent's material, but he incorporates also in his translation a song of praise to Humphrey for his gracious reward of the effort thus far expended by the poet.

There exist in several MSS copies of a letter addressed by Lydgate to the duke, asking for money, a letter which according to one pair of texts was composed "in tempore translacionis libri Bochasii". This letter (here printed p. 149) shows enough similarity in phrasing to suggest that it was sent at this point in the work, after the completion of books i and ii. If such be the case, we have here an outburst of gratitude from Lydgate for Humphrey's gift of money, made in reply to a supplication still existing. There are many begging-letters yet preserved in the manuscripts of this period, and many adulatory poems; but it would be hard to match this case of plea and thanks both remaining to us.

The prologue divides into:—a stanza of simile, the poet comparing himself to a tired thirsty pilgrim; an explanation, in two more stanzas, of the simile; a disquisition on the pressure of age, incapacity, and poverty upon the poet; a paean of gratitude to "my lord" for relieving that poverty; a return to the pilgrim-simile of the first stanza, this time followed, according to the French text, through stanzas 14-18; an introduction of Boccaccio's name, and the arrival at Book iii.

Of all this, only the pilgrim-simile comes from Laurent; the rest is either "original" with Lydgate or from John of Salisbury, some of whose phrases are borrowed.

Stanzas 1-13 were printed by me, from this MS, in Anglia 38:129-132.

[Brit. Mus. Royal 18 D v, fol. 70b]

Like a pilgrime which that gooth on
  foote
And hath none hors to Releue his trau-
  aile ·
Hoote drie werie and finde mai no boote ·
Of welle colde whan thrust him doth as-
  saile ·
Wyne nor licoure that mai to him availe ·
Riht so fare I which in my besinesse · 6
No socoure finde my reudenesse to re-
  dresse ·

2

I meene as thus I haue no fressh licoure
Out of the conductis of Calliope
Nor throuh Clio · in Rethorik no floure
In my laboure · for to refressh me · 11
Nor of the sustren · in noumbre thries
  thre ·
Which with Cithera on Pernaso dwell

Thei neuer me gaff drink oonis of ther
  well

3

Nor of ther springis cleere and cristal-
  line   15
That sprang bi touching of the Pegase ·
Ther fauour lakkith my making to enlumine
I finde ther bawme of so grete scarsete ·
To tame ther tunnys with som drope of
  plente ·
ffor poliphemus throuh his grete blynde-
  nesse ·   20
Hath in me dirkid of Argus the brihtnesse ·

4

Our life here short of witte the grete
  dulnesse ·

The heui soule troublid with trauail
And of memoire the glacing brotilnesse ·
Dreede and vnkonning hath made a
    strong batail ·   25
With werinesse my spirit to assail
And with ther subtil creping in most
    queinte ·
Hath made my spirit in making for to
    feinte

5

And ouermore the fereful frowardnesse ·
Of mi stepmodir callid obliuioun   30
Hath made a bastile of foryetilnesse
To stoppe the passage and shadwe mi
    resoun
That I myht haue no clere direccioun
In translating of newe to quik me
Stories to write of oolde antiquite ·   35

6

Thus was I sette and stood in double
    were ·
At the meting of fereful weies twein
The tone was this who euer list to lere ·
Where as god wil gan me constrein
Bochas to accomplish for to do mi pein
Cam ignoraunce with a maas of dreede ·
Mi penne to arest I durst nat proceede ·

7

Thus bi my silff remembring on this
    booke ·
It to translate how I had vndirtake ·
fful pale of cheere astonid in my looke ·
Myne hand gan tremble my penne I felt
    quake ·   46
That disespeirid I had almost forsake ·
So grete a laboure dreedful & import-
    able ·
It to parfourme I fond mi silff so on able

8

Twene the residewe of this grete iornee
And litil part there of that was begunne
I stood chek maate for feere whan I gan
    see ·   52
In mi weie how litil I had runne ·
Lik to a man that failid dai & sunne ·
And had no liht to accomplissh his viage ·
So ferre I stood a bak in my passage · 56

9

The nyht cam on dirkid with ignoraunce
Mi witte was dulle be cleernesse to dis-
    cern ·
In Rethorik for lak of suffisaunce ·

The torchis out & queint was the lantern ·
And in this case my stile to gouern   61
Me to forthre I fond non othir muse
But hard as stone Pierides & Meduse

10

Supporte was none my dulnesse for to
    guie ·
Pouert approchid in stal crokid age ·   65
Mercuri absent and Phil(ol)ogie
Mi purs ai liht and void of al coignage
Bachus ferre of to glade mi corage ·
An ebbe of plente scarcete atte full
Which of an olde man makith the spirit
    dull   70

11

But hope and trust to put awei dispaire
In to my mynde of new gan hem dresse
And cheef of all to make the wethir
    faire
Mi lordis freedam and bounteuous lar-
    gesse
In to mi hert brouht in such gladnesse 75
That throuh releuing of his beningne
    grace ·
ffals indigence list me no more manace ·

12

A how it is an ertheli reioishing
To serue a prince that list to aduertise ·
Of ther seruauntis the feithful iust meen-
    ing   80
And list considre to guerdone ther seruise
And at a neede list (hem nat despise) ·
But from al daungere that shold hem noie
    to greue ·
Been euer redie to helpe hem and releue ·

13

And thus releuid bi the goodliheede · 85
And throuh the noblesse of this moost
    knihtli man
Al mistis clerid of dispeir and dreede ·
Trust hope and feith in to my hert Ran ·
And on my labour anon forth with I gan ·
ffor bi clere support of mi lordis grace ·
All forein letting fro me I did enchace ·

14

ffolkis that use to make grete viagis
Which vndirfong long trauaile and
    laboure
Whan thei haue don grete part of ther
    passagis
Of werinesse to asswagin the Rigoure 95

Agein feyntice to finde som fauour*e*
Loke oft agein parcel to be releuid
To seen hou moch ther*e* iourne is acheuid

15

Cause whi thei so ofte loke agein
Bakward turne look & eeke visage ·   *100*
Is oonli this that it mai be sein
To them hou moch is don of ther*e* viage ·
Eke weri folk that gon on pilgrimage
Rest hem som while a ful large space ·
Laborious soote to wipin from ther*e*
    face   *105*

16

Ther*e* heui ffardell among thei cast doun
At certein boundis to do ther*e* bakkis
    ese
At wellis coolde eke of entenciou*n*
Drink fressh watris ther*e* greuous thurst
    to apese ·
Or holsom winis ther appetite to plese *110*
Rekning the milis bi computaciou*n*s
Which the(i) haue passid of castillis &
    tovnis

17

It doth hem ese the noumbre for to know ·
Sith thei began of mani grete iornees ·

Of hih mounteinis and of valis low · *115*
And straunge sihtis passing bi contrees ·
The vncouth bilding of borowis & Citees ·
Counting the distaunce fro tovnis & the
    spacis
This ther talking at ther resting placis ·

18

The residew and the surplusage ·   *120*
Thei rekne also of ther labour coming
Think it is a man*er* vauntage ·
To haue and seen a cleere knowleching
Of thingis passid & thingis eke folowing
ffor to ther*e* hertis it doth ful grete
    plesaunce ·   *125*
Whan all such thing is put in remem-
    braunce ·

19

And semblabli Iohn Boch*as* as I fynde
Gan turne his bak look and contenauns ·
And to remembre a poy(n)ting in his
    mynde ·
To the stories rehersid in substauns *130*
In his two bookis of sorow and dis-
    plesauns ·
Him silf astonid merueling a grete dele
The falle of princis fro fortunis whele

[Four more stanzas complete the prologue
to Book iii]

E

THE TRAGEDY OF CAESAR

Fall of Princes vi : 2920 ff.

In Boccaccio's De Casibus Caesar appears only in the chapter devoted to
Pompey and in the group-chapter between that and the story of Cicero, in which
latter Caesar's murder is again briefly mentioned. Laurent expands this treatment
in the eleventh chapter of his sixth book, which is parallel to Boccaccio's group-
chapter; but he mentions the murder of Caesar only to emphasize the ingratitude
of Brutus and Cassius. This he expressly states; he says that if any one wonders
at his including the noble and victorious Caesar in this crowd of unfortunates, he
replies that all he has said of great Caesar is by way of describing the wretched
fate of Brutus and Cassius; Caesar is not to be classed with those miserable ones
whose own crimes flung them down from prosperity,— it was disloyal conspiracy
which caused his fall.

Lydgate makes no allusion to this explanation by Laurent. In his work the
struggle of the tyrannicides against Octavian is not included: the remainder of
Laurent's chapter is not used, and the envoy, on the fate of Caesar, brings the
story of Caesar into equal prominence with that of Pompey. Brutus and Cassius
occupy a very minor position in the English treatment.

One of Lydgate's dominant notions about Caesar, taken from Lucan, is that he asked and was refused a triumph, before he seized power at Rome. In the fifteenth-century prose Serpent of Division, ascribed by one MS to Lydgate, and employing a vocabulary markedly Lydgatian, this refusal is very amply treated, and the struggle between Caesar and Pompey is made an "exemplum" of the evils of civil discord. The editor of the only modern text of the Serpent, Dr. MacCracken, conjecturally dates the work in 1422, when England was threatened with disorder by the sudden death of Henry V; and he suggests Gloucester as the patron of the translation,—the exact source of which is not yet determined.

Were these suggested circumstances, i.e. authorship, date, and patron, all proved fact, we might expect some allusion to the earlier work in Lydgate's return here to the subject of Caesar and Pompey, even as he refers back to his Troy Book from i: 5946 of the Fall of Princes. No such mention is made, yet it appears to me very probable that the Serpent of Division is from Lydgate's hand. True, that work and the Fall, or this part of the Fall, are shaped to teach different lessons, the one urging the horrors of civil dissension, the other emphasizing the vanity and instability of earthly success. And there is in the Serpent a mass of material not used in the Fall at this point. But the agreements in vocabulary and in movement, still more the absence of differences on those points between the two works, are greater than between any two Middle English productions by different authors known to me. Whoever wrote the Serpent not only admired and quoted—or rather misquoted—his master Chaucer, but uses easily a number of words frequent in Lydgate; for instance, *ambiguity, contagious, disappear, contune, entrike, ratify, supprised, make mention*, the metaphor of the ebbtide, the phrase "whirlid up" for the chariot of the Sun, etc. There is the same sort of agreement in vocabulary between the Serpent and the Fall that exists between the Fall and the Troy Book; and the absence of padding phrase is to be expected when the constraint of rime is absent. Furthermore, there are one or two points of agreement between the Serpent and this part of Laurent's version of Boccaccio; for instance, the list of portents before civil war in Rome, and the ingenuous comment by Laurent on Caesar's refusal to read the letter of warning. It may be added that both the Serpent and the Fall give the bearer of this letter the name Tongilius (not in Laurent), and that they use an identical phrase in introducing him (see line 43 and note).

But that the Serpent was translated in 1422, or antedated the Fall, is not proved by resemblances in vocabulary and phrasing. We do not assert that the writer of the Serpent used Laurent's book, or that Lydgate knew nothing of Laurent until Gloucester entrusted him the volume for translation; but the date of the Serpent is not clearly of Henry VI's accession, nor is Gloucester obviously its inspirer. A tolerably plausible argument could be constructed, indeed, for one of Gloucester's opponents as the patron of the prose work, or for a date much nearer the Wars of the Roses; but the entire question is unsolved. The only point on which we may build is the probable identical authorship of the Fall and the prose treatise.

As Dr. MacCracken says, the Serpent of Division is the earliest separate treatment in English of the life of Caesar; its existence, alongside the encyclopedia of tragedies, is a phenomenon worth noting.

[MS Brit. Mus. Harley 1245]

Thus bi processe all holly þe kynrede
Of Pompeyus for shorte conclusioun
Bi Cesar wern & be his men in deede
Wtout mercy brouht to destruccioun
Thus gan encres þe fame & þe renoun
Of Julyus conquest on se & eke on
    londe   (2820)
Whos mortall swerde ther myht noon
    wtstonde

2

ffirst in Libye Spayn & eke Itaile
Thexperience of his Roiall puyssaunce
In Germany by many stronge bataile   10
His power previd in Germanye & in
    ffraunce
Brouht all thes kyngdamys vndir tho-
    beisaunce
Of þe Romayns peisid (al) this thyng &
    seyn
Touchyng his guerdoun his labour was
    in veyn

3

Towarde Rome makyng his repaire
Bi hym appesid Civile Dissenciouns
Of throne Imperiall clymbyng on þe
    stayre
for þe conquest of xiiine regiouns
Of þe triumphe requerid þe guerdouns
Which to (recure) his force he hath
    applied   20
Albe þe senate his conquest hath denyed

4

And his name more to magnyfye
To shew þe glory of his hih noblesse
To þe Capitoile fast he gan hym hye
As Emperour his Doomys ther to dresse
Þat day began wt joy & gret glad-
    nesse   (2840)
Þe eve no thyng accordyng wt þt
    morowe
Þe entre glad þe eende trouble & sorowe

5

Calapurnya which þt was his wiff
Had a dreme þe same nyht toforn   30
Toknes shewid of þe ffunerall striff
How þt hir lorde was likly to be lorn
By conspiracye compassid & sworn
If he þt day wtout avisement
In þe Capitoile satt in Jugeme(n)t   35

6

She drempt allas as she lay & slept (2850)
Þt hir lorde thoruhgirt wt many a
    wounde
Lay in hir lapp & she þe body kept
Of womanheede like as she was bounde
But oo Allas to soth hir Dreme was
    founde   40
Þe next morow no lengir made Delaye
Of his Parody was þe fatall Daye

7

A poor man callid Tongilyus
Which secretly þe tresoun did espye
Lete write a lettre toke it Julyus   45
Þe caas declaryng of þe conspiracye
Which to rede Cesar list nat applye
But oo Allas ambicious necligence
Causid his moordre by unware violence

8

Cesar sittyng myd þe consistorye   50
In his astate most Imperiall
Afftir many conquest & victorye
ffortune awaityng to yeve hym a fall
Wt bodkyns percyng as an all
He moordrid was wt many a mortall
    wounde   55
Lo how fals trust in worldely pompe is
    founde   (2870)

Lenuoye
9

Thoruh all this booke radde ech tragedye
Afforn rehercid & put in remembraunce
Is noon more woofull to my fantasye
Þan is þe fall of Cesar in substaunce 60
Which in his hihest Imperiall puyssaunce
Was while he wende ha be most glorious
Moordrid at Rome of Brutus Cassyus

10

This marciall Prince ridyng thoruh Lom-
    bardye
Ech Contre yolde & brouht to obey-
    saunce   65
Passyng thallpies roode thoruh Ger-
    manye   (2880)
To subieccioun brouht þe Rewme of
    ffraunce
Gat Brutus Albioun bi long contynuaunce
To lustris passid this manly Julyus
Moordrid at Rome by Brutus Cassyus

11

Among þe Senate was þe conspiracye
All of assent & of oon accordaunce
Whos Tryumphe thai proudly gan denye
But maugre them was kept þe obseru-
    aunce
His chaier of golde wt stedis of ples-
    aunce   75
Conveied thoruh Rome this prince most
    pompous
Þe moordre folwyng by Brutus Cas-
    syus   (2891)

12

Rekune his conquest rekune vp his
    chyualrye
Wt a cowntirpeise of worldely vari-
    aunce
ffortunys chaungis for his purpartye   80
Wey all togidre cast hem in ballaunce
Sett to of Cesar þe myschevous chaunce
Wt his parody soden & envyous
Moordrid at Rome bi Brutus Cassyus

13

Bookis all & cronyclis specifye   85
Bi Influence of hevenly purveiaunce
Mars & Jubiter þe(r)favour did applye

Wt glad aspectis his noblesse to en-
    haunce
Mars gaff hym knyhthoode Jubiter gov-
    ernaunce
Amongis princis holde oon þe most fam-
    ous   90
Moordrid at Rome bi Brutus Cassyus

14

Biholde of Alisaundre þe gret monarchye
Which al þe worlde hadd vndir obeisaunce
Prowesse of Ector medlid wt gentrye
Of Achilles malencolik vengeaunce   95
Rekune of echon þe queveryng assur-
    aunce   (2910)
Among remembryng þe fyne of Julyus
Moordrid at Rome bi Brutus Cassyus

15

Pryncis considrith in marciall policye
Is nouthir trust feith nor affiaunce   100
All stant in chaunge wt twynkelyng of
    an eye
Vp towarde heven sett your attendaunce
Þe worlde vnsure & all worldely ples-
    aunce
Lordshipp abitt nat Recorde on Julyus
Moordrid at Rome bi Brutus Cassyus 105

F

OCTAVIAN'S REVENGE

Fall of Princes vi : 2920 ff.

[MS Brit. Mus. Royal 18 D v]

Affter the moordre of this manli
    man   (2920)
This noble prince this famous emperour
His worthi Nevewe callid Octouian
To regne in Roome was next his succes-
    sour
Which did his deueere bi dilligent
    labour   5
To punsshe al tho of nature as he ouhte
Bi rihtful dome that the moordre wrouhte

2

Cheeff conspiratour was Brutus Cassius
Which of this moordre made al the orde-
    naunce

Anothir Brute surnamid Decius   10
Was oone also conspiring the veni-
    aunce   (2930)
Wrouht on Cesare he affter slain in
    ffraunce
Here men mai seene what costis þt men
    wende
How moordre al wai requerith an evil
    eende

3

With in the space almoost of thre yere 15
Destroied wern al the conspiratours
Bi sodein dethe and som stoode in
    daungere
To be bansshid or exilid as tretours

And as it is croniclid bi auctours
Space of thre yere reknid oone bi oone 20
Deied at myscheeff the moordereris
    euerychone
                    4
To moordre a prince it is a pitous
    thing   (2941)
God of his riht wil take ther of veniaunce

Nameli an emperour so famous in eche
    thing
Which al the worlde had in gouern-
    aunce   25
Rekne his conquest digne of Remem-
    braunce
Al peisid in oone bochas berith witnesse
In hih estate is litil sikirnesse

G

THE TRAGEDY OF CICERO

Fall of Princes vi : 2948-3276

In this chapter Lydgate in general follows Laurent, although he adds the
list of Cicero's works, lines 215-227, from Vincent of Beauvais, and takes details
of the dream and of Cicero's death from Valerius Maximus.

Cicero occupied in the imagination of medieval clerks a place with Homer
and Aristotle, and was much better known than they. Allusions to him, citations
from him, practices supported by his authority, are scattered all over medieval
literature. Lydgate could find his name, and a citation, at every turn in grammarians such as Priscian or Nonius Marcellus; he could read excerpts in John
of Salisbury ("prudent Carnotence" to Lydgate) and in Isidor; he could find
anecdotes of Cicero in Aulus Gellius, in the Polychronicon, and sheaves of selections in Vincent of Beauvais. Isidor and Valerius Maximus were, we know, in
the great library of Lydgate's own monastery; and the way in which he quotes
Aulus Gellius ("Agellius") and Vincent shows that he had access to the texts,
both of which were in the possession of Humphrey of Gloucester, as was an "Ex-
positio super Valerium Maximum." But citations from Cicero, or "Tullius", as
Lydgate always calls him, are not numerous in the monk's work, and are of a
sort that could derive from an Ars dictandi or a Florilegium. There is no proof
of any such intimacy as was John of Salisbury's, for instance.

[MS Brit. Mus. Royal 18 D v]

Myne auctour here writ no long processe
Of Julius dethe compleining but a while
To write of Tullie in haste he gan him
    dresse   (2950)
Compendiousli his liff for to compile
Compleining first seith his barein stile 5
Is insufficient to write as men mai seen
Of so notable a Rethoricien

                    2
Laumpe and lanterne of Romaine ora-
    tours
Amonge hem callid prince of Eloquence
On Pernaso he gadrid up the flours   10
This Rethoricien most of excellence
Whos meritis treuli to recompence

The musis nyne me thouht as I toke
    heede   (2960)
A croune of laurer set uppon his hede

                    3
Bochas astonid gan of him silff con-
    clude   15
His looke abasshid dulle of his corage
Thouht his termis & resouns were to rude
That he lakkid konning & language
Where bi he sholde to his auauntage
Thouh he laborid writing al his lyue 20
Of Tullius the meritis to descryue

                    4
Wher of supprisid he kauht a fantasie
With in hym silff remembring anone
    riht   (2970)

Thouh it so falle som tyme a cloudie skie
Be chaacid with wynde affore the sonne
   briht   25
Yit in effecte it lassith nat his liht
So bochas dempte that his dulle writing
Eclipsid nat of Tullius the shining

5

With rude language a man mai wele
   reporte
The laude of triumphees and conquestis
   meruelous   30
Which thing remembring greteli gan comforte
The herte of bochas & to him silff spak
   thus
Too colours sein that be contrari-
   ous   (2980)
As white and blak it mai be none othir
Eche in his kinde shewith more for
   othir   35

6

In phebus presence sterris lese there liht
Clere at myddaie apperith nat lucine
The fame of Tullie whilom shone so
   briht
Prince of fair speche fadir of that doc-
   trine
Whos briht beemys in to this houre do
   shine   40
Sotheli quod bochas of wham whan I
   endite
Myne hand I fele quaking while I write

7

But for to yeue folk occasioun   (2990)
Which in Rethorik haue more experiens
Than haue I and more inspeccioun   45
In the colours and crafft of eloquens
Them to excite to do there dilligens
Vnto my writing whan thei mai attende
Of compassioun my rudenesse to amende

8

Vnto him silff hauing this language   50
Bochas to write gan his penne dresse
Vndir support afforcid his corage
To remembre the excellent noblesse
Of this Oratour which with the suetnesse
Of his ditees abroode as thei haue
   shined   55
Hath al this world most clereli enlumined

9

This Tullius this singulere famous man
ffrist to remembre of his natiuite
Born at Arpinas a Cite of Tuskan

Of bloode Roial descendid who list se 60
Grekissh bookis of olde antiquite
Made of Rethorik and in there vulgare
   songe
He translatid in to latine tonge   (3010)

10

In tendir youthe his contree he forsoke
And fro Tuskan his passage he gan
   dresse   65
Toward Rome the riht weie he toke
Entring the Citee the renommed noblesse
Hid in his persone shewid the brihtnesse
Of diuers vertuis tyme while he abood
That lik a sonne his fame sprad abrood 70

11

ffor his vertuis made a Citesein
The good reporte of him shone so cleere
Lik as he had be born a Romain   (3020)
In there fauoure his name was so enteere
Among hem chose for a consuleere   75
Agein the Cite tyme of his consulat
Whan Cataline was with hem at debat

12

Bi the prudence of this Tullius
And his manhood reknid bothe Ifeere
Catalina most cruel & irous   80
ffroward of porte & froward of his cheere
Besy euer to fynde out the manere
How he myht bi any tokne or signe
Agein the Cite couertli maligne   (3031)

13

Sixe hundrid yere foure score told and
   nyne   85
Reknid of rome fro the fundacioun
This cruel tiraunt this proud Catalyne
Made with othre a coniuracioun
Agein ffraunchises and ffredam of the
   toun
ffirst discurid as bookis tel can   90
In the parties and boundis of Tuskan

14

The purpos holie of this Catalyne
Ymaginid on fals couetice   (3040)
Was to bring Rome on to Ruine
And there uppon in many sondri wise 95
ffond out meenys weies gan devise
To his entent bi dilligent laboure
In the Citiee gan gete him grete fauoure

15

But finalli his coniuracioun
Discurid was bi oone Quincius   100

Which was afforne fals on to the toun
Tolde al the caas vn to Tullius
Bi whose prudence and werking meruel-
ous   (3050)
Bi helpe of Antoyne that was his fellawe
The coniuracioun was broken & with
drawe   105

16

Bi witte of Tullie al the coniuratours
Espied werne and brouht on to mys-
chaunce
There namys rad to fore the Senatours
Of there falsheede tolde al the gouer-
nauns
Manli ordeinid throuh his purueauns 110
With al his peeple as made is mencioun
Catalyna departid from the toun

17

With Antoyne the said Catalyne   (3060)
Beside Pistoye had a grete batail
Slayne in the ffeelde he myht nat de-
clyne   115
ffor he aboode whan the feelde gan fail
Powere of oone litil mai auail
Nameli whan falsheed of malice and of
pride
Ageins trouth dare the bronte abide

18

Ther was anothir callid lentulus   120
Of his fellawis that namid was ffabyne
The thridde of hem eeke callid Ceregus
All assentid and sworne to Catalyne
Stranglid in prisoune at myscheeff did
fyne   (3071)
Cause Tullius did execucioun   125
Tulliane was callid the prisoun

19

Thus koude he punsshe tretours of the
toun
Outraie there enemies of manhod &
prudence
Callid of there Cite gouernour & patroun
Sent from aboue to be there diffence 130
There champioun most digne of reuer-
ence
Chose of there goddis there Cite for to
guy   (3079)
Bi too prerogatiuis knyhthod & clergy

20

Lik a sonne he did hem enlumine
Bi hih prowesse of knihtli excellens 135
And throuh the world his bemys did shine

Of his Rethorik and his eloquens
In which he had so grete experiens
Bi circumstauncis that nothing did lakke
He transcendid Policius & Gracce   140

21

Of Oratours it is put in memorie
This Tullius throuh his hih renoun
Of al echone the honour and the
glorie   (3090)
Was youe to him as made is mencioun
Surmountid alle and in conclucioun 145
The golden trumpe of the hous of fame
Throuh al the world bleuh abrode his
name

22

He kneuh secretis of philosophie
Cam tathenis to scole for doctrine
Where he profitid so greteli in clergi 150
In al sciencis heuenli & divine   (3098)
That he was callid as auctours determine
Amonge Romains of verrai dewe riht
Of eloquence the lanterne & the liht

23

It is remembrid among Oratours   155
How Tullius pletid causis tweyn
In the Romain courte affore the Sena-
tours
The cause diffending bi language sou-
ereyn
Of too accusid gein hem þt did plein
On there diffautis them sauing fro mis-
cheeff   160
The court escaping fro daunger & mys-
cheeff

24

Thes causis twein he pletid in latyn
With so excellent flouring fair lan-
guage   (3110)
With such resouns concludid atte fyn
That he be wisdam kauht the auaun-
tage   165
In his mateeris with al the surplusage
That myht auaile vnto his partie
What he said there coude no man denie

25

Among Greekis at Athenis the Citee
He was so grete of reputacioun   170
So famous holde of auctorite
To be comparid bi there oppinioun
To the philosophre that callid was pla-
ton   (3120)
To whos cradille bees did abraid
And hony soote thei on his lippis laid 175

26

A pronostik lik as bookis telle
Plato shold bi famous excellens
Of Rethorik be verrai sours & welle
ffor his language meroure of eloquens
Yit the Greekis recordin in sentens   *180*
How Tullius in partie and in all
Was vnto Plato in Rethorik egall

27

Throuh his language this said Tul-
    lius   (3130)
Reconsilid bi his soote Orisouns
To the lordshippe and grace of Julius *185*
Princis kingis of diuers Regiouns
That suspecte stood bi accusaciouns
Be cause thei did Julius disobeie
Were enclyned with Romains to Pompeie

28

He koude appese bi his prudent lan-
    guage   *190*
ffolkis that stood at discencioun
Bi crafft he had a special auauntage
ffauour singulere in pronunciacioun
In his demening grete prudence and
    resoun   (3141)
ffor the pronouncing of mateeris in sub-
    staunce   *195*
His thank receivith bi cheere & contin-
    aunce

29

To a glad mateere longith a glad cheere
Men trete of wisdam with woordis of
    sadnesse
Pleyntis requeere affter the mateere
Greuous or mortal a cheere of heui-
    nesse   *200*
Lik as the cause outhir the processe
Yevith occasioun to hynderen or to
    speed
The doctrine in Tullius men mai
    reed   (3150)

30

The name of Tullie was kouthe in mani
    place
His elloquence in euery lond was riff
His language made hym stonde in grace
And be preferrid during al his liff
Maried he was and had a riht fair wiff
Childre many seruauntis yonge & oolde
And as I fynde he heelde a good hous-
    oolde   *210*

31

De officijs he wrote bokis thre
De amicicia I fynde how he wrote oone

(continued)

Of age anothir notable for to se   (3160)
Of moral vertu thei tretid euerychone
And as Vincent wrote ful yore agone *215*
In his meroure callid historiall
Noumbre of his bookis be there remem-
    brid all

32

He wrote also the dreme of Scipioun
Of Rethorikes compilid bookis tweine
And tweine he wrote of diuinacioun *220*
Of cithe lond to write he did his peine
A large booke of glorie that is veine
De Repuplica and as he seyth him
    selue   (3170)
Of his Orisouns he wrote bookis twelue

33

And of his dictes that callid be morall *225*
Is remembrid notabli in deede
In the said meroure historiall
And yit this said Tullius as I reede
Mid his worshippis stoode all wai in
    dreede
Of ffortune for in conclucioun   *230*
He by envie was bansshid Rome toun

34

Beyng in exile this famous Tullius
In campania at Ative the Cite   (3180)
Receivid he was of oone Plancius
A man þt tyme of grete auctorite   *235*
And while that he aboode in that contre
Sleping a nyht the booke makith men-
    cioun
How that he had a wondir visioun

35

He thouht thus as he laie sleping
In a deserte and a grete wildirnesse   *240*
ffynding no pathe but to & fro erring
How he mette clad in grete richesse
Gayus Marrius a prince of grete no-
    blesse   (3190)
Axing Tullie with sad contenaunce
What was cheeff ground & cause of his
    greuaunce   *245*

36

Whan Tullius had him the cause toolde
Of his desese and his mortal woo
Marrius with his hand set on him hoolde
To a seriaunt assignid him riht thoo
And in all haste bad he shold goo   *250*
To conveie him doon his besi cure
In al haste possible to his sepulture

37

Wher he shold haue tidingis of ples-
  aun̄ce   (3200)
Of his repair into Rome toun̄
Been allegid of his olde greuaun̄ce   255
This was the eende of his avisioun̄
The next morowe as made is mencioun̄
Ther̄e was hold to Tullius grete avail
To fore Jubiter in Rome a grete counsail

38

Within the temple bilt bi marrius   260
The Senatours accordid were certein
To reconcile this prudent Tullius
Out of his exile to calle him home
  agein   (3210)
Afft̄er receivid as lord and souer̄ein
Of elloquence be assent of the Senat
ffulli restorid vn to his frist estat

39

This thing was done whan þt in Rome
  toun̄
The striiff was grettist twene Cesare and
  Pompeie
And for Tullius drouh him to Catoun̄
With Pompeius Cesare to werreie   270
And of Iulius the partie disobeie
Out of Rome Tullius did him hih
ffled with Pompeie in to Thessalie (3220)

40

Cesare afft̄er of his free mocioun̄
Whan that he stood hihest in his glori 275
Hym reconciled agein to Rome toun̄
Vppon Pompeie accomplisshid the vic-
  tori
But Julius slain in the consistori
Be sixti Senatours beyng of assent
Tullius agein was into exile sent   280

41

And in a cite callid ffaryman
Tullius his exile did endure   (3229)
ffor Antonyus was to him enmy than
Be cause that he par cas of auenture
Compiled had an Inuentiff scripture 285
Agein Antony rehersing al the caas
Of his diffautis & of Cleopatraas

42

Thus of envie and of mortal hattereed
His dethe compassid by Antonyus
And afft̄erward execut in deed   290
Bi procuring of oone Pompilius
Gat a commissioun̄ the storie telleth thus
Of fals malice and foorthe anone went
  he   (3240)

In to Gayete of Compaigne a cite

43

And bi the vertu of his commissioun̄ 295
Taking of Antoyne licence and liberte
Cheeff Rethorician that euer̄ was in the
  toun̄
Among Romains to worship the cite
Was slain allas of hate and enmyte
Bi Pompilius roote of al falsheed   300
Profring him silff to smyten of his heed

44

Tullius afforn had ben his diffence
ffro the Galwes and his dethe eke
  let   (3250)
Which had disseruid for his grete offence
To haue ben hangid vppon an hih
  Gibet   305
Who saueth a theeff whan the Rope is
  knet
About his neck as olde clerkis write
With som fals turne the bribour̄ wil him
  quite

45

Lo here the vice of ingratitude
Be exper̄ience brouht fulli to a preeff 310
Who in his hert tresoun̄ doth include
Cast for good wille to doon a man repreeff
What is the guerdoun̄ for to saue a
  theeff   (3260)
Whan he is scapid looke ye shal fynde
Of his nature euer̄e to be vnkynde   315

46

This Pompilius tretour most odible
To shewe him silff fals (cruel & venge-
  able)
Toward Tullie did a thing horrible
Whan he was deede this bribour most
  coupable
Smet of his riht hand to heere abhomin-
  able   320
With which honde he leuln̄g on him toke
To write of vertuis mani a famous boke

47

The hand the heede of noble Tul-
  lius   (3270)
Which euer̄i man auhte of riht com-
  pleine
Were take and brouht bi Popilius   325
Vppon a stake set up bothe tweine
There to abide where it did shine or reine
With wynde and wedir til thei were
  diffied
In tokne al fauour was to him denied

H

THE TRAGEDY OF BOETHIUS
Fall of Princes viii:2626-2660

Laurent de Premierfait's eighteenth chapter, which represents one of Boccaccio's group-chapters and very much expands it, mentions among other ill-fated sovereigns the Eastern Roman emperor Leo, the emperor Zeno who dethroned and succeeded Leo, the anxiety of Zeno at Odoacer's seizure of Italy, the campaign of Theodoric, Zeno's Ostrogothic general, against Odoacer, Theodoric's assumption of the crown after Odoacer's defeat, and the subsequent abuse of Theodoric's power by unworthy ministers, against whom Boethius protested. The French writer warmly praises Boethius, going much more into detail than did Boccaccio, who gave but a very brief account, with no mention of the cause of Boethius' imprisonment, which Laurent discusses quite fully; Laurent says that among the accusations against Boethius was that "de auoir familiarite auec les mauuais esperitz", because he, "comme vray philosophe", had avoided the multitude and preferred solitude. He calls Boethius not only "noble docteur de philosophie" but "homme catholicque", and denounces the cruelty of Theodoric, who even threw down the images on Boethius' tomb after his death. His emphasis on Boethius' wisdom and on the permanence of his influence is repeated several times.

But nothing of Laurent's sympathy appears in Lydgate, whose account is cool and brief. The facts are from Laurent, but Laurent's tone is not there, nor Chaucer's respect, nor Walton's knowledge and admiration. There are in Lydgate four other references at least to Boethius; he is mentioned in the list of Chaucer's works, Fall of Princes i: 291-2 (see p. 161 here), and in Troy Book iv: 3008-11 his warning against trusting Fortune is cited. The same warning appears in the poem Thoroughfare of Woe, printed by Halliwell, p. 122; and in the Entry of Henry VI, *ibid*. p. 11, Boethius represents the art of music.

Were these all the traces of Boethius in Lydgate, the monk's neglect of a writer so beloved of Chaucer would seem marked indeed; but in the Fabula Duorum Mercatorum 743-46 I find a close and spirited translation of a bit from the opening metre of the Consolatio, a translation entirely independent of Chaucer. It runs:

> O deth, desyred in aduersite,
> Whan thu are callyd, why nylt thu wrecchys heere
> And art so redy in felicite
> To come to them that the nothyng desire.

[MS Bodl. Rawl. C 448]

Afftir thes mischeeuys / Symak ga*n* hi*m*
   drawe ·
Toward bochas / with a ful pitous face ·
Boys cam with hi*m* / þt was his sone
   i*n* lawe ·
Which amonge Romayns / gretly stood
   i*n* grace ·
But i*n* this mateer / breeffly forth to
   pace ·   5

The said Boys / oonly for his trouthe ·
Exilid was / allas it was gret
   routhe ·   (3632)
        2
ffor comon profite / he was vnto the
   tou*n* ·
In mateers / that grou*n*did were on riht ·
Verray protectour / & stedfast cham-
   piou*n* ·   *10*

A geyn to tyrauntis / which off force &
  miht ·
Hadde in the poraill / oppressid many a
  wiht ·
Bi exacciouns & pillagis gonne off newe ·
Vppon the comons / ful fals & riht
  vntrewe ·

3

Whan Theodorik / off Gothes lord &
  kyng ·   15
Took vppon him / bi fals Intrusioun ·
To regne in Rome / the peeple oppres-
  syng ·   (2642)
Bi his too prouostis / as maad is men-
  cioun ·
Dide in the Citee / gret oppressioun ·
Confederat / as brothir vnto brothir ·   20
Coningaste & Trigwille was the tothir ·

4

Compendiously this mateer to declare ·

To saue his comon / Boys stood in diffence ·
ffor liff nor dethe / he list nat for to
  spare ·
To withstonde / off tyrauntis / the sentence ·   25
Kyng Theodorik / off cruel vio-
  lence ·   (2652)
Banschid him / bi hateful tyrannye ·
He & his fadre / tabide in Pauye ·

5

Afftirward / Theodorik / off hatreede ·
Lik a fals Tyraunt / off malis & envie · 30
Yaff Jugement / that bothe too were
  dede ·
But touchyng / Boys / as bookis specefie ·
Wrotte dyuers bookis / off philosophie ·
Off the Trynyte / maters / þat were
  dyuyne ·
Martryd for crist / and callid Seueryne ·

K

FROM THE EPILOGUE TO THE FALL OF PRINCES
Book ix: 3387-3442

The portion of the Fall of Princes epilogue here cited is preceded by twelve
stanzas addressed directly to Gloucester, describing the fears with which Lydgate
undertook the assigned task, and his own shortcomings; Lydgate prays his lord
to have compassion on his ignorant efforts. In the thirteenth stanza, at which
point our extract begins, the monk turns to the general public; and the fourteen
stanzas beyond line 3442 discuss the De Casibus as a book, and the mutability of
Fortune. Another six stanzas, with separate heading, are directed to Gloucester,
and a final five dismiss the book to the world. It is the general apology to the
public which we have here, an apology with more literary flavor than other parts
of the Epilogue.

In it Lydgate protests his ignorance of Homer, of Seneca, of Virgil, of Ovid,
of Dares Phrygius, of Chaucer; he mentions Gower, Strode, and the Hermit of
Hampole as judges of these matters, and Chaucer as the peerless narrator. Chaucer wrote tragedies, as did Petrarch and Boccaccio; but he, Lydgate, has ventured
into that field only "by constreynt." His inadequacy is hopeless; he was never
favored of the Muses, and can only say that he has done his poor best.

[MS Brit. Mus. Royal 18 B xxxi]

And semblably thouh I goo nat vpriht
But stoupe & halt / for lake of ello-
  quence
Thouh Omerus heeld nat the torch liht

To forthre my penne wt colours of
  cadence   (3990)
Nor moral Senec most sad of his sen-
  tence   5

Gaf me no part / of his moralites
Therfor I say / thus knelyng on my knes

To al tho that shal þis booke beholde
I them beseeke to haue compassion
& therwtal / I pray hem that þei wolde *10*
ffavoure the metre & do correccion
Of gold nor assur / I had no foison
Nor othir colours / þis processe ten-
    lumyne
Sauf whit & blake & þei but dully
    shyne   (3400)

I nevir was acqueyntid wt Virgile   *15*
Nor wt þe sugrid ditees of Omer
Nor Dares frigius / wt his golden stile
Nor wt Ouyd / in poetre most enteer
Nor wt þe sovereyn balladis of Chauncer
Which among al þat euer wer rad or
    song   *20*
Excellid al othir / in our ynglish tong

I can nat been a Iuge in this mateer
As I conceive folwyng in fantasy
In moral mateer / ful notable was
    Gower   (3410)
And so was Stroode / in his Philosophy
In parfit lyvyng / which passith poysy
Richard Hermyte / contemplatif of sen-
    tence
Drouh in ynglissh / the prike of con-
    science

As þe gold tressid / briht somer sonne
Passith othir sterris wt his bemys cleer *30*
And as Lucyna cacheth skyes donne

The frosty nyhtis whan Espirus doth
    apper
Riht so my maister had neuer peer
I meene Chauncer / in stories þat he
    tolde   (3420)
And he also wrot / tragedies olde   *35*

The fal of princis / gan pitously com-
    pleyn
As Petrake did / and also Iohn Bochas
Laureat Franceis Poetis both tweyn
Tolde howe princes / for ther gret tres-
    pace
Wer ove(r)throwe / rehersyng al þe
    cas   *40*
As Chaucer did in þe monkis tale
But I that stonde / low doun in the vale

So gret a booke in ynglyssh to trans-
    late
Did it by constreynt & no presump-
    cion   (3430)
Born in a village / which called is
    Lidgate   *45*
In olde tym / a famous castel toun
In Danys tyme / it was bett doun
Tyme whan seynt Edmond martir maid
    & Kyng
Was slayn at Oxne / record of writyng

I me excus / now this booke is do   *50*
How I was neuer / yit at Citharon
Nor on þe monteyn callid Pernaso
Wher nyne musis / ha ther mansion
But to conclude / myn entencion   (3440)
I wil proceed / forth wt whit & blake *55*
And wher I faile / late Lidgate bere þe
    lake

BENEDICT BURGH'S LETTER TO JOHN LYDGATE

Very little is known of Benedict or "Benet" Burgh, an ecclesiastic of some standing in the latter fifteenth century. He was born ca.1413, received an University training and a Master's degree at Oxford (1433), and died in 1483 as Archdeacon of Colchester and Canon of St. Stephen's Westminster. His prosperous although inconspicuous career in the Church seems to have been bound up with the patronage of the influential Bourchier family, but on one occasion at least a rich prebend was given him by the hand of Edward the Fourth direct. In the few bits of literary work which Burgh has left there is little or nothing of the personal such as we find abundantly in Hoccleve, more than a little in Bokenam, occasionally in the Palladius-translator. This address to Lydgate is the least didactic and most living of his productions. He is credited with: 1, a paraphrase of the Disticha Catonis so exceedingly popular in the late Middle Ages; 2, a Christmas Game or poem on the Apostles, twelve stanzas, preserved in only one MS of the latter fifteenth century; 3, the continuation of Lydgate's Secreta Secretorum after his master's death; 4, the brief poem below printed, preserved only by John Stow in a copy of 1558; 5, a five-stanza "Lesson to keep well the tongue", similarly preserved; 6, the "ABC of Aristotle", now known to be not Burgh's, but by Benet of Norwich. For this last fact see Foerster, in Archiv 117:371-5; and for prints of the poems numbered 2, 4, and 5 see Foerster, Archiv 101:29-64, where the data on Burgh's life are brought together.

There is no certain date for this brief production, but Foerster, in his careful article on Burgh, Archiv 101, suggests the years 1433-40, while Burgh was, it is supposed, Vicar of Maldon in Essex. This is supported by the author's dating of his letter from Bylegh Abbey, at Little Maldon; a detail unmentioned by Foerster is that not many miles separated the Abbey from Hatfield Broadoak, Essex, where Lydgate was Prior from 1423 to 1434. It is not impossible, although entirely conjectural, that Burgh at the opening of his Maldon life wrote (and sent?) this verse-tribute to the older man for whom he professes so ardent an admiration, and whose neighbor he had just become.

In the poem Burgh discourses enthusiastically on Lydgate's scholarship, and enumerates the classics known to Lydgate's "innate sapience",— Virgil, Homer, Boethius, Ovid, Terence, Persius, Lucan, Martianus Capella, Horace, Statius, Juvenal, and Boccaccio. Two of this list, Terence and Horace, are so far as I know unmentioned and unquoted by Lydgate; Lucan and Statius are named twice or thrice each, but there is no evidence that either the Pharsalia or the Thebais was used by Lydgate. To Virgil and to Homer his allusions, though fairly frequent, are mere formulae. Persius is once mentioned (FaPrinces iv:61), in a prologue on "letters" which, as I have suggested, was composed not only in deference to Gloucester's taste, but in dependence on his books, or at least on their titles. Juvenal is named in the same prologue, along with Aesop, and in the Fall of Princes Lydgate twice cites the bit about the poor man singing before the thief, without Juvenal's name; but he could get this, and the author's name, from the Wife of Bath's Tale of Chaucer. Nor, in his three allusions which I have noted to Martianus Capella and the De Nuptiis, is there anything which could not come from Chaucer's remark in the Merchant's Tale or from the mere heading of the work. The monk's very slight knowledge of Boethius, despite the interest felt by Chaucer, is discussed p. 185 here; Boccaccio's De Casibus, in a French prose version, was perhaps at this very time in Lydgate's hands, and he seems to have used the De Genealogia direct in other poems. But the only author of this list whom Lydgate not only mentions but has read sufficiently to quote of his own volition is Ovid; and this happens mainly in the Fall of Princes, on which the monk was engaged from ?1431 to 1438.

Burgh's compliment could hardly have less real foundation.

Other prints of Burgh's work have been:—

Steele, ed. of the Secreta Secretorum for the EETS, 1894.

Foerster, ed. of the Cato, Archiv 115:298-323 and 116:25 ff., from 24 MSS. Cp. Goldberg, Der englische Cato, Leipzig diss., 1883.

The Christmas Game, ed. by Thomas Wright in his volume of Carols, 1841, pp. 28-31; by Furnivall in Notes and Queries for May 16, 1868; by Flügel, Anglia 14:463-66. Foerster, Archiv 101:52, gives a list of Flügel's errors.

This poem to Lydgate is printed by Steele as above, p. xxxi-xxxii. Foerster in Archiv 101:47-48 gives a list of Steele's errors.

On the manuscript see p. 194 below.

[John Stow's MS, Brit. Mus. Adds. 29729, fol. 6]

Nat dremyd I in ye mownt of pernaso
ne dranke I nevar at pegases welle
the pale pirus saw I never also
ne wist I never where ye muses dwelle
ne of goldyn Tagus can I no thynge
    telle   5
And to wete my lippis I cowde not
    atteyne
In citero or elicon sustres tweyne /

2

The crafte of speche that some tyme
    founde was
of the famous philosophers moste perfite
Aristotell gorge and ormogenes   10
nat have I . so I have lerid but a lite
As for my party thowgh I repent I may
    go qwite
of tullius frauncis and quintilian
fayne wolde I lere . but I not conceyve
    can /

3

The noble poete virgil the mantuan   15
Omere the greke and torqwat sovereyne
Naso also that sith this worlde firste be
    gan
the marvelist transformynge all best can
    devyne
Terence ye mery and plesant theatryne

———
Stow's heading is nearly all trimmed away, but his copy is from some one's "booke dwelyng at wyndsor."

porcyus lucan marcyan and orace   20
stace Iuvenall and the lauriate bocase /

4

All thes hathe seyne . youre Innate sapience
ye have gadred flowris in this motli mede
to yow is yeven the ver(r)ay price of
    excellence
thowghe they be go yet the wordis be
    not dede   25
thenlumynyd boke where in a man shall
    rede
thes and mo be in this londe legeble
ye be the same ye be the goldyn bible /

5

O yet I truste to be holde and see
this blisfull booke wt ye goldyn claspes
    seven   30
ther I wyll begyne and lerne myne a.b.c.
that wer my paradyse, that wer my heven
gretar filicitie can no man neven
so god my sowle save, a benedicite
Maister lidgate, what man be ye /   35

6

Now god my maister, preserve yow longe
    on lyve
that yet I may be yowr prentice or I dye
then sholde myne herte at ye porte of
    blise aryve

ye be the flowre, and tresure of poise
the garland of Ive, and lawre of vic-
    torye   40
by my trowghte & I myght ben a em-
    perowr
for yowr konynge I shulde yowr heres
    honor /

7

writen at thabbey of bylegh chebri place
with frosti fingers, and nothynge pliaunt
when from the high hille I men yᵉ mownt
    canace   45
was sent in to briton the stormy per-
    saunt
that made me loke as lede & chaunge
    semblant
and eke yᵉ sturdi wynde of yperborye
made me of chere vnlusti sadde & sory /

8

The laste moneth that men clepe de-
    cembre   50
when Phebus chare was dryven a bowte
    yᵉ heven
yf we reken a ryght & well remembre
fowre tymes onys and aftar ward seven
that is to sey passid ther war days a
    leven
of the moneth when this vnadvisid
    lettar   55
writ was, but wt yowr helpe here aftar
    bettar /

explicit
*per magistrum burgh ad Ioannem
lidgate /*

JOHN SHIRLEY: TWO VERSIFIED TABLES OF CONTENTS

John Shirley, a warm admirer and zealous copyist of Chaucer and of Lydgate, was for the latter part at least of his ninety-years' life a resident of London, where he died in 1456. Stow in his Survey mentions the monument to him and his wife in the church of St. Bartholomew the Less; see Kingsford's edition of the Survey, ii : 23-4, for the verse-epitaph on that monument. The Dict. Nat. Biog. describes Shirley as "translator and transcriber"; and from an entry in the records of St. Bartholomew's Hospital it appears that in 1456 John Shirley was renter of a large tenement with four shops, belonging to the Society.[1] Considering the character of Shirley's existing manuscripts and the number of volumes partly copied from his work, it becomes a question if Shirley were not one of England's earliest publishers. These two tables of contents, and his verse "bookplate", show him as the proprietor and manufacturer of a lending library; and in his long "gossiping" headings to separate poems,—as Bradshaw termed them,—Shirley addresses "my lords and ladies" much in the tone of a modern publisher's jacket, explaining the work to follow and commending it to his readers with friendly respect. This also befits the lending library; but Shirley was a translator as well. Most of his existing work of that sort is in the MS Brit. Mus. Adds. 5467, a volume not written in his hand but probably copied from him, as it retains his headings and his tricks of spelling. This volume has been discussed by Gaertner in his dissertation on Shirley, Halle, 1904, and by Brusendorff, pp. 213-15.

There are two facts which contribute to the supposition that Shirley may have managed more than a lending library, that his London shops were used on a larger scale than one man's activity would need. First, a number of existing MSS which do not show his script show the influence of his text. For instance, two codices of the British Museum, Harley 2251 and Adds. 34360, written in one and the same hand, reproduce texts with Shirley's headings, derived probably from his volume now Trin. Coll. Cambr. R 3,20; this is especially true of the Harley manuscript. Also, the copy of the Canterbury Tales in Brit. Mus. Harley 7333, although not in Shirley's hand, preserves his marginalia, his "Nota per Shirley" against passages that interested him. And a single isolated text may in similar way show a Shirleyan archetype; cf. the poem printed by MacCracken on p. 260 of his EETS edition of Lydgate's Minor Poems, from MS Brit. Mus. Cotton Titus A xxvi. When we observe that the same man who wrote the Harley and Additionals volumes above mentioned also wrote the copy of the Canterbury Tales surviving in the College of Physicians' library, and wrote part of that in the MS Brit. Mus. Royal 17 D xv, etc.; when we see another man working with him on this latter volume; when we recognize the possibility that both men were writing in a place where a Shirley volume (? R 3, 20) and other manuscripts were at hand,—we conjecture again as to the business conducted in those four shops in Shirley's later years.

The extent of Shirley's influence on English "publishing conditions" has yet to be estimated; his importance as a preserver of Chaucerian and Lydgatian texts

---

[1] See Sir Norman Moore, History of St. Bartholomew's Hospital, London, 1918, 2 vols., ii :30.

is already recognized, reduced although it be by his failings. For Chaucer's work, he is our sole or main authority for including in the canon Anelida, Mars, Venus, Pity, Stedfastnesse, Truth, and the Words to Adam; of the last he has preserved the only copy. For Lydgate, also, Shirley did yeoman service; in the Trinity College MS above mentioned exists the only known set of Lydgate's clumsy but important Mummings, long supposed lost; and various traces of Lydgate's personal connection with Humphrey of Gloucester are preserved by Shirley, or his copyists, alone. His tone when speaking of the monk is friendly, even familiar; and he evidently had especial opportunities of obtaining Lydgate's work. For a piece of prose-translation which Shirley asserts to be Lydgate's, see p. 101 here.

The codices written by Shirley himself are nearly all commonplace-books, or collections of shorter works and scraps; they are now Brit. Mus. Adds. 16165, Bodl. Ashmole 59, and Trinity College Cambridge R 3,20; also an imperfect volume at Sion College, London, part of the volume Harvard University 530 F, and a few leaves each of Brit. Mus. Harley 78 and of the Earl of Ellesmere's MS 26 A 13, now in the Huntington Library, California. The first-named has been described by me in MLNotes 19:35-38 and in Mod. Phil. 1:331; the Ashmole has been described by me in Anglia 30:320-48; the Trinity College MS by me in Anglia 22:364-374; the Harvard volume by F. N. Robinson in Harvard Studies, vol. v. For the Sion College MS see my Chaucer Manual, p. 333; and on the general subject of the Shirley volumes see Brusendorff, pp. 207-236. In MLNotes 36:184 I queried if the imperfect Sion College MS could be the missing part of the Trinity College volume.

Codices derived in part at least from Shirley are Brit. Mus. Adds. 5467, Harley 2251, Adds. 34360, and Harley 7333; also John Stow's MS Brit. Mus. Adds. 29729, in which he transcribes a mass of material from the Trinity College volume, at that time his property. The first-named MS has been discussed by Gaertner as above, the next two by me in Anglia 28:1-28, Harley 7333 briefly by Gaertner op. cit. p. 19, more at length in my Chaucer Manual, pp. 176-77. The originals of Adds. 5467 and Harley 7333 are unknown to us, but a number of the poems in Harley 2251 and Adds. 34360 are in the Trinity College MS, with identical headings. There has as yet been no investigation to determine how far the copyists of Shirley are influenced by his shortcomings. Invaluable although Shirley's work is historically and archaeologically, it is textually most disappointing. The disorganization and corruption which he inflicts upon a text of Chaucer are often painful to witness. He had no feeling for rhythm, and either because of the fall of inflexional -e or because of his own insensitiveness, he did not perceive the speech-flow of Chaucer. The muddled conditions and omitted passages of Ashmole 59 may be due in part to Shirley's great age when that volume was compiled; but everywhere in his work the lines are jarring in ways which we may partly explain, but cannot reform. All the volumes in his own hand are characterized by this text-maltreatment, by his script, by his "gossiping" headings, by his orthography, and often by his device.

On the title-pages of Ashmole 59 and on a leaf of the former Ellesmere MS 26 A 13 is a device, resembling a composite letter, surmounted by a crown and flanked on the one side by the words "ma ioye", on the other side by the word "Shirley." This appears also on two MSS owned but not written by Shirley, both in French; one is a copy of Vegetius on the art of chivalry, in de Meun's translation, and is in the British Museum as Royal 20 B xv; the other is a French poem on Edward the Black Prince, formerly in Lord Mostyn's collection and after his sale presented (1921) to the present Prince of Wales. This latter volume is described by Sir Israel Gollancz in a small privately printed brochure, to which is prefixed a full-size photograph of Shirley's device. A very small drawing of the device is in the British Museum catalogue of the Royal MSS, with the description of the codex above mentioned; the device is there termed a "sort of monogram", but Gollancz affirms positively that it is an *A*. The letter of the Royal MS is identical with that of the former Ellesmere MS, I am informed by the Keeper of MSS in the Huntington Library; and it is identical with that of the Ashmole. The first leaves of the Trinity College MS are missing, possibly with the device; and the MS Adds. 16165 carries a simplified mark, the word *Shirley* with *ma ioye* above it, and between them a smallish ordinary *a* as in his usual script, uncrowned. I have previously suggested that this "device" may be a composite letter, representing perhaps MARIA or AMOR, and in the nature of an invocation or formula at beginning, like, e.g., the rubric "Assit principio sancta maria meo" on many MSS, such as Bodl. Laud 683 or those of the Bury Library as described by Dr. James. Shirley does indeed occasionally use this composite letter where an *A* is to be expected; but the difference between his device in Adds. 16165 and in the French MSS above mentioned or in Ashmole 59 may be one of date. The devices of the early printers may be compared.

Shirley's script is reproduced in the Chaucer Society Autotypes from the Adds. MS and from the Sion College MS; in Harvard Studies v from the MS Harvard 530 F; in Brusendorff to face p. 280, from MS Brit. Mus. Adds. 16165.

Besides Shirley's translations and copies there remain some bits of original verse by him:—a rimed table of contents in his autograph, here printed; a similar table existing only in Stow's copy of it, also here printed; a single stanza used as a sort of bookplate in MS Ashmole 59, and printed thence in Reliq. Antiq. ii :163, in Anglia 30: 329, in Gaertner's diss. as cited, p. 23 footnote, and by Brusendorff, p. 460; the same stanza is in the Trinity College MS, and is printed thence in James' catalogue of the MSS, ii: 81. Shirley perhaps also composed a sort of epitome of Chaucer's Legend of Good Women, in nine eight-line stanzas, which is printed by the Chaucer Society, Odd Texts, appendix, p. vi, and by Gaertner, *op. cit.*, p. 66, from the Ashmole volume. The two versified Tables of Contents here given are printed by Brusendorff, pp. 453-460; that in MS Adds. 16165 is printed by Gaertner, pp. 63-66. None of these bits has any literary value, and I include these Tables here mainly as illustration of the "publishing conditions" of the period and as parallel to the dialogue between Robert Copland and young Nevill, printed below pp. 287 ff. On Shirley see Brusendorff, pp. 453 ff.

More than a hundred years later than Shirley, the London tailor and antiquary John Stow, who died in 1605, owned and annotated a number of Shirley, Shirleyan, and other MSS. No list of Stow's known library has yet been compiled, but we find his memoranda, e.g., in Bodl. Fairfax 16, in Shirley's MS Trin. Coll. R 3,20 and in the MS preserved *ibid.* as R 3,21, in Brit. Mus. Adds. 34360, and in a former Huth MS now Huntington 144, not to mention transcripts in Stow's own hand in Stowe 952, ?Adds. 29729, Harley 542, etc., etc. In Stow's Survey as ed. by Kingsford, ii: 24, he says of Shirley,—"This Gentleman, a great traueller in diuers countries, amongst other his labours, painefully collected the workes of Geffrey Chaucer, Iohn Lidgate, and other learned writers, which workes hee wrote in sundry volumes to remayne for posterity. I haue seene them, and partly do possesse them."

It is possible that between 1598, when Stow wrote this, and 1558 when he compiled his MS Adds. 29729, he had come into possession of the Trinity MS R 3, 20, the Shirley volume from which he probably copied at the earlier date. His book 29729 is, he says, made up not only from "the boke of John Sherley", but from "master Blomfields boke", "master Hanlays booke", "master Philyppes boke", and "master Stantons boke". . (See description of the MS by Sieper in his EETS edition of Lydgate's Reson and Sensuality, introduction). At the end of his set of Shirley extracts Stow copies the second of the versified Tables of Contents here printed, a table no longer in the Trinity MS because of its loss of quires at the beginning; and he follows it with "Here endeth ye werkes of John lidgat which John Stow hath caused to be coppyed out of an owld booke som tyme wrytten by John Sherleye as is aboue made mencyon / John Sherley wrat in ye tyme of John lydgate in his lyffe tyme".

Stow was an author as well as a collector. The two most notable works of his busy life are the Chaucer edition of 1561 and the topographical Survey of London published in 1598. He also drew up a list of Lydgate's works for the Speght Chaucer of 1598. The first-named piece of work has made Stow suspect with modern students so far as matters literary are concerned; for it foisted upon Chaucer many poems which are obviously not his, and which it has cost a long struggle to remove from the Chaucer-canon. See Skeat, Oxford Chaucer i:31 ff. Stow's list of Lydgate's works is discussed by MacCracken in his EETS ed. of Lydgate's Minor Poems, with the conclusion that there, as in his Chaucer-ascriptions, Stow "has no great claim to credit". But Stow's evidence as an antiquary is another matter; and however we may censure and doubt his testimony or Shirley's on textual points, we owe deeply to both for their interested zeal as transcribers.

Stow's script may be seen in photographs of nine pages of Brit. Mus. Adds. 29729, preserved in the library of Harvard University, with other photographs, as "Poems and Ballads: photographs of selected folios of Lydgate's MSS in the British Museum."

[MS Brit. Mus. Adds. 16165, fol. 2a]

þE PROLOGE OF þE KALUNDARE OF þIS LITTLE BOOKE

Boicius in prose
Of Nichodeme
þe maistre of þe game
þe dreme for lovers
þe Ruyle of preestis
þe compleynt of a lover
þe compleynt of anelida
Item xii oþer litel balades
  complaintes & roundelles

¶ If þat you list / for to entende /
Of þis booke / to here legende /
Suche as is / right vertuous /
Of maner of mirthe nought vicious /
As wryten haue / þees olde clerkes /
Þat beon appreued / in aile hir werkis /
By oure eldres / here to fore
Remembraunce / ellys were forlore /
¶ Wher fore / dere sirs / I you beseche
Þat ye disdeyne not / with my speche /   *10*
ffor affter þe symplesse / of my witt /
So as feblesse / wolde suffice hit /
Þis litell booke / with myn hande /
wryten I haue / ye shul vnderstande /
And sought þe copie / in many a place /
To haue þe more thank / of youre grace /

¶ And doon hit bynde / In þis volume /
Þat boþe þe gret / and þe comune /
May þer on looke / and eke hit reede
Þeyres beo þe thanke / and þe meede   20
Þat first hit studyed / and owt founde
Nowe beon þey dolven / deep in þe grounde /
Beseche I god / he gyf hem grace /
In hevens blisse / to haue a place /
¶ And for to put hit / in youre mynde /
ffirst þus by ordre / shul ye fynde /
Of Boece / þe hole translacyoun /
And Phylosofyes / consolacyoun /
Laboured by *Geffrey Chaucier*
Whiche in oure wolgare / hade neuer his
    pere /   30
Of eloquencyale retorryke /
In Englisshe / was neuer noon him lyke /
Gyff him þe prys and seyþe þer hoo /
For neuer knewe ye / suche na moo /
¶ Þe passyoun þanne / of Nichodeme /
fful wel translated shul ye seen /
Þe whiche of Berkeley / lord Thomas
Whome god assoyle / for his grace /
Lete oute of latyn / hit translate /
By *Johan Trevysa* / þat hit made   40
A maystre in Theologye /
Appreued clerk / for þe maystrye /
Thankeþe þe lord / and þe Clerk /
Þat caused first / þat holy werk /
¶ Þanne filoweþe nexst / as in wryting /
Þe notablest story of huntyng
Þat euer was made / to fore þis day
Redeþe and proue hit by assaye
Maystre of þe game / men hit calle
I prey to god feyre mot him falle   50
Duk of york / þe last *Edwarde*
Þat dyed in þe vauntwarde
Of þe bataylle In Picardye /
At Agincourt / þis is no lye /
ffor as of huntyng / here to fore
Was neuer taught so truwe lore
To alle þat beon gentyl of kynde /
Beon bounde / to haue his soule in mynde
And namelych / of þis oure regyoun
Whiche was cleped Albyoun /   60
Þat nowe is called Engeland /
¶ Þanne shul ye wit / and vnderstand /
Of an Abstract made in latyne /
Al in proose / eke lyne by lyne /
Grounded vpon holy writte /
Regula sacerdotalis / men clepen hit /
God helpe so / as þat I not /
Who first hit made / ne hit wrot /
Þer fore noon Auctour / I allegge /

Drynkeþe to my lady / and I hir plegge /   70
Lest some folk wolde / me mysse construwe /
Þanne and ye wol þe wryting suwe /
¶ Shul ye fynde wryten / of a knyght
Þat serued his soueraine / lady bright /
As done þees louers amerous /
Whos lyff / is offt seen parillous /
Askeþe of hem / þat haue hit vsed
A dieux Joenesse I am refused
Whos complaynt is al in balade
Þat daun *Johan* of Bury made /   80
Lydegate þe Munk cloþed in blacke
In his makyng / þer is no lacke /
And thankeþe / daun Johan for his peyne /
Þat to plese gentyles / is right feyne /
Boþe with his laboure / and his goode /
God wolde of nobles / he hade ful his hoode /
¶ And oþer balades moo þer beon /
Right godely / looke and ye may seen
And whane ye haue þis booke ouerlooked /
Þe right lynes / with þe crooked /   90
And þe sentence / vnderstonden /
With Inne youre mynde hit fast ebounden
Thankeþe þauctoures þat þeos storyes
¶ Renoueld haue / to youre memoryes /
And þe wryter / for his distresse
Whiche besechiþe / youre gentylnesse
Þat ye sende þis booke ageyne
Hoome to *Shirley* / þat is right feyne
If hit haþe beon / to yowe plesaunce /
¶ As in þe reedyng / of þe romaunce /   100
And alle þat beon / in þis companye
God sende hem Joye / of hir ladye
And euery womman of hir loue
Prey I to god þat sitteþe aboue /
                    Explicit

II

[Brit. Mus. Adds. 29729, fol. 177 b]
[John Stow's MS]

KALUNDARE OF JOHN SHIRLEY WHICH HE SET IN Yᴱ BEGINNINGE OF HIS BOOKE

O ye my lordes whan ye be holde
this boke or list it to vnfould
or ye yᵉ leues turne to rede
looke this calender and then proced
for ther is titled compendyously   5
all yᵉ storyes hole by and by
eche after other in ther chapytles
as yᵗ sheweth pleyne / by ther tytles
and for I haue but shorte space
i must yᵉ lyttler ouer pase   10

besechynge / you be not to wroth
ffor as I could / wt outen coth
and as my febles would suffyse
in my rude vplandishe wise
thus haue I them in ordre sete   15
yᵗ fere were eft / now here ben mette
I meane yᵉ copyes / ne douteth noughte
In sondry place / haue I them soughte
on this hallfe / and beyonde yᵉ see
as fortune hathe them brought to me   20
ffirst yᵉ humayne / pilgrymage

In margin by II:10 is: *i. John Shirley.*

sayd all by proose in fayre langage
and many a roundell and balade
whiche ye munke of bury hath made
and sayd them wt hys sugred mouthe   25
in straunge metres so vnkouthe
of morall mater / and holynesse
of salmes / and of ympnes expresse
of loue and lawe / and of pleyinges
of lordes of ladyes of qwenes of
    kynges   30
his rymyng / is so moralysed
that hym aught well / be solempnysed
of all oure engelishe / nacion
for his famus / translacyon
Of this booke and of other mo   35
suche as he is haue we no mo
yet for all his much konnynge
which were gret / tresore to a kynge
I meane this lidgate / munke dame John
his nobles bene spent / I leue ychon 40
and eke his shylinges nyghe by
his thred bare coule / woll not ly
ellas ye lordis / why nill ye se
and reward his pouerte
ye liff also of sainte margarete   45
y^t holy virgine so fayre and swete
dame John hath it to translate
at ye request now but late
of my lady of huntyngeton
which here fast by / nere to london   50
lythe entered at sainte Kateryn
ye contesse of ye marche in hur tyme
almightye god so graunte hur grace
In heuen blysse to haue a place
ther bene also deuocyons   55
and dyuers medytacions
sayde bothe by lordes and by clerkes
which bene accostomed / to suche werkes
In french in engelishe and latine
y^t I haue wryt in this margyn   60
rede and persayue it by assaye
beseche I god þt to your paye

In margin by lines 24, 36, are: i. dame John
    lidgate, i. dame John.

and to your plesaunce it mought be
whan y^t ye rede ther on or se
ffor than my trauayle is welle sett   65
I aske of you no other dett
bot wher defaute is or ye blame
y^t it nenpayr ye auctors name
as for fayllinge of ye scripture
of ye meter / or ortografyure   70
wouch saue it to correcte
elles of ye defaute am I suspecte
y^t thorugh your supportacion
yow list to make correccion
sith to such craffte I am not vsed   75
of your grac hath me excused
So whan ye had thos storyes rede
be ye fastyng or be ye fede
as y^t I dare I you beseche
y^t ye disdayne not wt my speche   80
but sendeth this boke to me agayne
shirley I meane which is right fayne
if ye ther of haue had plesaunce
as in ye weddinge of ye romance
than am I glad by god onlyue   85
as I were lord of tounes fyue
and so at your commaundement
It shall bene eft when you list send
wt all ye saruice y^t I can
as he y^t is your oune man   90
and all y^t in this company
ben knight squyer or lady
or other estat what euer they be
ye god of loue / wher so y^t he ....e
be in heauen or here in yearth   95
he brynge them to the heuen forthe
if they in loue be founden true
wt stedfast hert and nought renew
nether in ernest nor in game
but kepe ther worshipe and ther name 100
he send them lord such guerdonynge
as they deserue in ther menynge
be hit female be it male
now seche and rede some other talle
                Explicit

A REPROOF TO LYDGATE

This poem exists, so far as is yet known, only in the volume from which it is here printed. In that manuscript it appears as one of a group of short courtly love-poems, separately headed in some cases as Balade, Compleynt, etc. Without title itself, this poem is immediately preceded by a "Compleynt" of the unpitied but loyal lover, and immediately followed by a sixteen-stanza "Parlement" of Cupid which is the last poem of the group. There is no mark of authorship to these poems in the manuscript; but H. N. MacCracken, publishing them as below, suggested the Earl of Suffolk (died 1450), and also suggested Suffolk as translator of the French poems by Charles d' Orléans, a number of which are printed in this volume (pp. 214 ff.).

That Suffolk dabbled in authorship we know from short French poems of his, preserved by John Shirley and also published by MacCracken, *ibid*. The two main reasons for binding his name upon this English collection appear to be, first, his relations with Orléans, whose gaoler he was for a part of the duke's captivity in England, and whom he afterward visited in France; and, secondly, the fact that one of the poems of this Fairfax series exists in the most important of the French volumes of Orléans' verse, a manuscript argued to be of his own compilation and partly in his own hand. MacCracken would regard the presence of a ?Suffolk-poem in such an album, along with poems by the duke's French circle, as a natural outcome of the close connection between Suffolk and Orléans; he therefore suggests that this English poem just mentioned (printed p. 222 here) is by Suffolk, and deduces thence Suffolk's authorship of the rest of the group as copied in Fairfax, including of course this present text.

The theory is interesting but inconclusive. The French savant Champion's suggestion of Alice countess of Suffolk as the "inamorata" and English instructor of the captive Orléans was interesting and not improbable; but the discovery of Anne Molins' name, inserted acrostic-wise, in one of Orléans' attempts at an English poem (see p. 222 here) puts a new face on the matter. And other facts may appear which will throw light on this group of courtly verses, especially on the tone here assumed toward Lydgate, who is both invoked as aid and censured for his language about women. The particular Lydgate-passages in the author's mind may be those of the Fall of Princes; for in the commonplace-book Harley 2251, where are copied a mass of "tragedies" from the Fall, the scribe has written indignant marginal comments on the aspersions against women contained in the tragedies of Hercules and of Samson. These notes, foll. 127-43 of the codex, are: "Ye be shent. Ye leese your thank. So shul ye be pese. Holdith your pees. Ye haue no cause to say so. Ye wil be shent. Be pees I bidde you. Ye haue no cause to say so. Late hem compleyne that neode have. I pray yow to be pees.——— Be my trowth ye wilbe shent. Be pees or I wil rende this leef out of your booke. There is no good womman that wilbe wroth ne take no quarell agenst this booke as I suppose."—etc. See Brusendorff, pp. 461-465.

This last comment is perhaps suggested by Lydgate's own text, Fall of Princes i: 6702-4; and when we note the characteristic Shirley-spelling of *neode* in these marginalia, we may wonder if they and their text were not copied from one of Shirley's volumes, as is much of this particular Harley-manuscript. It may be a corroboration to note that in Shirley's own copy of Lydgate's mummings (printed as below) there is found a jesting query by him against one of Lydgate's sly digs at women in the text. Lydgate says:—"I mene it þus, þat worde and werke were oon; It is no wonder, for wymmen soo beon echoon." And Shirley exclaims, in the margin: "A daun Iohan, est y vray?"

It is, however, not certain that the Fall of Princes passages are meant; and regarding authorship there is only conjecture as yet. That the poem must date before Lydgate's death in 1448-9 is clear.

Although the larger half is devoted to Lydgate, the opening stanzas allude, apparently, to "a strife of the Flower and the Leaf" in which our writer has chosen the Flower. This "sentimental strife" of two Orders is mentioned in Chaucer's prologue to the Legend of Good Women, in various short poems by Chaucer's French contemporary Eustache Deschamps, perhaps in Gower's Confessio Amantis viii: 2462 ff., and clearly in Charles d'Orléans' verse a generation later. Students have generally referred this "strife" to the age of Chaucer and Deschamps; but its fullest literary statement is in the anonymous "Flower and Leaf", a poem probably of the latter fifteenth century. Were we to take these fictions at their face value, we should infer that there existed, in France at least, two courtly "Orders", one vowing allegiance to the beauty of the Flower, the other making the Leaf the symbol of constancy and service. Such an inference passes well with what we know of the "Cour Amoureuse" of Charles the Sixth, the association of French chivalry and French letters in protest against the encroachment of the bourgeois spirit. That association, broken by the fall of so many of its members at Agincourt and by the long following war with England, was short-lived; but its code, or the code of a "sentimental strife", lingers in a few pieces of Transition verse.

SELECT REFERENCE LIST VII

MacCracken, "An English Friend of Charles of Orléans," PMLA 26:142 ff. See p. 218 here for comment on this paper.

Shirley, see p. 191 here.

Champion, "A propos de Charles d'Orléans," Romania 49:580-4.

Hammond, E. P., "Charles of Orléans and Anne Molyneux," ModPhil 22:215-16.

Lydgate's mummings are printed, all but the Mumming at Hertford, by Brotanek as appendix to his Englische Maskenspiele, 1902. The Hertford mumming is printed by me, Anglia 22:364; repr. Neilson and Webster, p. 223.

On Harley 2251 see my Chaucer Manual, p. 329; earlier and fuller material in Anglia 28:1 ff.

The Flower and the Leaf is ed. Skeat in Chaucerian and Other Pieces. See my Chaucer-Manual, p. 423. See G. L. Marsh, Sources and Analogues of the Flower and the Leaf, Chicago diss., 1906 and ModPhil iv.

On the Cour Amoureuse see Alma, LeDuc in Romanic Review 8:145,290, and Piaget in Romania 31:597.

[MS Bodl. Fairfax 16, foll. 325-327]

Myn hert ys set and all myn hole entent
To serue this flour in my most humble
　　wyse
As faythfully as can be thought or ment
Wyth out feynyng or slouthe in my
　　seruyse
ffor wytt the wele yt ys a paradyse
To se this flour when yt bygyn to sprede
Wyth colours fressh ennewyd white and
　　rede

2

And for the fayth I owe vn to thys
　　flour
I must of reson do my obseruaunce
To flours all bothe now and euery our　10
Syth fortune lyst that yt shuld be my
　　chaunce
If that I couthe do seruyse or plesaunce
Thus am I set and shall be tyll I sterue
And for o flour all othyr for (to) serue

3

So wolde god that my symple connyng
Ware sufficiaunt this goodly flour to
　　prayse
ffor as to me ys non so ryche a thyng
That able were this flour to countirpayse
O noble chaucer passyd ben thy dayse
Off poetrye ynamyd worthyest　　　　20
And of makyng in alle othir days the
　　best

4

Now thou art go / thyn helpe I may not
　　haue
Wherfor to god I pray ryght specially
Syth thou art dede and buryde in thy
　　graue
That on thy sowle hym lyste to haue
　　mercy
And to the monke of bury now speke I
ffor thy connyng ys syche and eke thy
　　grace
After chaucer to occupye his place

5

Besechyng the my penne enlumyne
This flour to prayse as I before haue
　　ment　　　　　　　　　　　　　30

And of these lettyrs let thy colours shyne
This byll to forthir after myn entent
ffor glad am I that fortune lyst assent
So to ordeyn that yt shuld be myn vre
The flours to chese as by myn aventure

6

Wher as ye say that loue ys but dotage
Of verey reson that may not be trew
ffor euery man that hath a good corage
Must louer be thys wold I that ye knew
Who louyth wele all vertu will hym
　　sew　　　　　　　　　　　　　40
Wherfor I rede and counsail yow ex-
　　presse
As for thys mater take non heuynesse

7

These clerkys wyse ye say were brought
　　full lowe
And mad full tame for alle thair sotelte
Now am I glad yt shall ryght wele be
　　know
That loue ys of so grete autoryte
Wherfor I lat yow wyt as semeth me
It is your part in euery maner wyse
Of trew louers to forther the seruyse

8

And of women ye say ryght as ye
　　lyst　　　　　　　　　　　　　50
That trouth in hem may but awhile en-
　　dure
And counsail eke that men shuld hem not
　　tryst
And how they be vnstedfast of nature
What causeth this for euery creature
That ys gylty and knowyth thaym self
　　coulpable
Demyth alle othir thair case semblable

9

And be your bokys I put case that ye
　　knewe
Mych of this mater which that ye haue
　　meuyd
Yit god defende that euery thing were
　　trew
That clerkes wryte for then myght thys
　　be preuyd　　　　　　　　　　60
That ye haue sayd which wyll not be
　　byleuyd
I late yow wyt for trysteth verely
In your conseyt yt is an eresy

There is no heading to the poem in the MS; it is
　　separated from that preceding by a space
　　of three lines and a horizontal bar. In the
　　perhaps contemporary table of contents at
　　the front of the Fairfax MS, this poem
　　is described as "How þe louer ys sett to
　　serue the floure." The MS is described
　　in my Chaucer Manual, pp. 333 ff.; see
　　also Notes below, p. 461.

10

A fye for schame O thou envyous man
Thynk whens thou came and whider to
   repayr
Hastow not sayd eke that these women
   can
Laugh and loue nat parde yt is not fair
Thy corupt speche enfectyth alle the air
Knoke on thy brest repent now and euer
Ayen therwyth and say thou saydyst yt
   neuer   70

11

Thynk fully this and hold yt for no fable
That fayth in women hath his dwellyng
   place
ffor out of her cam nought that was
   vnable

Saf man that can not well say in no place
O thou vnhappy man go hyde thy face
The court ys set thy falshed is tryed
Wythdraw I rede for now thou art as-
   pyed

12

If thou be wyse yit do this after me
Be not to hasty com not in presence
Lat thyn attournay sew and speke for
   the   80
Loke yf he can escuse thy necglygence
And forther more yit must thou recom-
   pence
ffor alle that euer thou hast sayde byfore
Haue mynde of this for now I wryte no
   more

PALLADIUS ON HUSBANDRY

The Prologue and Some Linking Stanzas

This straightforward translation of an unliterary Latin treatise, De re rustica, written in the fourth century by Palladius Rutilius Taurus Aemilianus, in prose, has great interest for students of fifteenth-century English verse. Its translator is unnamed and unknown; in his prologue he tells us that he is at the time of writing under the protection of Humphrey duke of Gloucester, after being in some way misused by an enemy. He seems to have been set to work by Humphrey at this task, and he declares that the duke has taught him "metring", and is the watchful critic of the text as he produces it. The metrical management here is noticeably competent and assured, at the very time when Lydgate, for instance, was producing his mechanical and monotonous translation of the Fall of Princes, also done for Gloucester. There is here a clarity of intention, a sureness of phrasing, a manipulation of rhythm, and a variety in breath-length, which Lydgate has not. This unknown workman has also animation in his personal touches, and interests us by his attempts at complex medial rime in his prologues; but the general rhythmical handling is especially important for students of the Transition. Sharp twists of syntax and somewhat strained uses of words occur in the prologue because of the elaborate "rhetorical color", the use of medial rime and of stanza-linking by echo. Such devices had been employed by Chaucer in parts of his Anelida; and see pp. 208, 211 here for their appearance in the Lover's Mass. This man moves less gracefully, but he controls his material.

Two manuscripts of the poem have been edited. In 1873 and 1879 the Colchester Castle MS, now Add. A 369 of the Bodleian at Oxford, was printed for the Early English Text Society by Barton Lodge. He wrongly assigned the codex to ca.1420; its text is imperfect at beginning and close, and less valuable than that of the MS owned by Earl Fitzwilliam and preserved at Wentworth Wodehouse. This latter was edited by Mark H. Liddell, Berlin, 1896, vol. i, text; notes, and discussion of the relation of the English to the Latin, have not appeared. The Fitzwilliam MS was apparently transcribed from the duke's own copy, as it bears his arms in the capital letter of book i; its text is complete and very carefully written, with the interesting prologue lacking in the Colchester-Bodley copy. A photographic reproduction of it exists in the Bodleian Library, marked Eng. poet. d. 27, and from this my extracts are made. According to Vickers' life of Gloucester, pp. 434-5, the Fitzwilliam MS is not now known to exist at Wentworth Wodehouse. There is another MS, Hunterian T, 5,6, at Glasgow, according to Archiv 100:156; it is imperfect, but it is textually close to the Fitzwilliam.

The work may be dated with some exactitude from allusions in the prologue. Gloucester's gifts of books to the University of Oxford, so enthusiastically lauded here, were in 1439 and 1443; in the second list[1] we find a copy of the Latin of Palladius, possibly the very book used by this translator. The prologue also speaks, stanza 8, of Gloucester's "annoying" Orléans; and this must refer to the sharp

---

[1] See Anstey, Munimenta Academica, 1868. See pp. 758-772 for list of books given by Gloucester to Oxford.

controversy between the Beaufort party and Gloucester regarding the liberation of Charles duke of Orléans, a controversy terminated, over Gloucester's protest, by the departure of the duke in November, 1440. The donation to Oxford here mentioned must accordingly be that of November, 1439, and the translation must belong in 1440.

It might be argued, from the tone of this work, of Lydgate's Fall of Princes, and of Hoccleve in his Dialogue, toward Gloucester, that the Palladius-translator was closely associated with the duke, that Lydgate saw him occasionally, and that Hoccleve saw him scarcely at all. The difference is more than one of tone; the emphasis of this man and of Lydgate (stanzas 58, 59 of the Fall of Princes prol.) on Gloucester's activity against heretics may indeed be due to the two writers' connection with the Church, but as years had elapsed since the executions of Sharp and of Wawe (line 51 below) it is also possible that the duke wished his piety commemorated, and that Hoccleve did not know of this wish. Our translator is, moreover, at this time residing, it would seem, in one of Gloucester's manors, perhaps that of "Plesaunce" at Greenwich, the duke's most famous abode; and in stanza 13 he mentions members of the household. Perhaps it was this very nearness to the powerful patron which urged him to a fulsomeness of praise greater even than Lydgate's, and much in excess of Hoccleve's. Lydgate is lavish, but with conventional formulae and comparisons; this man, although he has more of actual fact than Lydgate gives us, runs occasionally into hyperbole—see note on line 29 below—of which Lydgate would not be capable. But here again, as remarked in the note on line 51, the fact of Gloucester's waning political power may have urged his supporters to greater emphasis on his ability.

The work runs to nearly 6700 lines, mainly in rime royal, although the prologue and the connective-stanzas between books are of eight lines. The author thus uses a slightly different form when speaking in his own person; compare the use of refrain, occasionally of eight-line stanzas, in the envoys added by Lydgate, at Gloucester's command, to the Fall of Princes translation. The elaborate rime-echo of the prologue has some small reflection in the body of the work, where each book opens with the closing phrase of the book preceding, or rather of the inserted connective. Of these books the Palladius has thirteen, one for each month of the year and one introductory.

SELECT REFERENCE LIST VIII

Struever, C., Die mittelenglische Uebersetzung des Palladius: ihr Verhältnis zur Quelle und ihre Sprache. Göttingen diss., pubd. Halle, 1887, pp. 82. (This is based on the EETS edition, the inadequacies of which Liddell has shown; the MS used for that ed. also lacks the prologue.)

Liddell's collations of the EETS text with the Colchester-Bodley MS, correcting its many errors, are pubd. EETS 1896, and in his own ed. as above.

See: "The Nine-Syllabled Pentameter Line in Some Post-Chaucerian Manuscripts," by Eleanor P. Hammond, ModPhilol. 23:129-152, sect. IV of paper.

[Bodl. Eng. poet. d. 27, photogr. from MS Fitzwilliam]

Agriculture as in nature and art
Tendure of creature AlCreatour

List to prouide and duc H(umfrid)e his part

Verse 1 is written with 8-line gilt capital A, to the right of which appears, in a narrow vertical column, the remainder of the first line cut up into two- and three-letter pieces, viz.:—

GRI CUL TU RE AS IN NA TU RE AND ART. These smaller capitals are white or yellow on lake or blue ground.
Lines 3, 4, 8, 27 are blotted where brackets appear in text above.

Diuide of either side a(dd)ynge honour
So high that we of *princis* se the flour 5
Hym be So sende he me sense and science
Of my balade away to rade errour
Pallade and do t(o gl)ade his excellence

2

His excellence O trine and oon eterne
Almyghty lord Alsapyent al good 10
Thy *Prouidence* as sterismon and sterne
Emforth this word now refluent now
flood
Now in concord now violent and wood
By lif present so list extende in grace
That of his woord his werk entent or
mood 15
Noon inuident may *reprehende* an ace

3

An ace apoynt y vndirstonde is werk
Disioynt mys take on honde of his sup-
port
Wroght *euer* kynge or *prince* or knyght
or clerk
A thynge other then right by his con-
fort 20
Though opon fame ha maad thus pleyn
report
Yit lame is she tatteyn onto the dede
Of myghtiest to hym is glad resort
Of meest and leest is had his loue and
drede

4

His loue and drede in brestis sprede his
wit 25
And *grace* in sondri place is so fecounde
That sapienc(e in) his prudence is knyt
As seyn in trewthis pleyn that list
abounde
In myn entent the Sapient secounde .
Is fonde into euery londe whos fame is
born 30
And worthy straunge her londis chaunge
& founde
Exp*resse* of his prowess at eye aforn

5

At eye aforn is hym right here in sight
To here and noon was lorn of their
labour
Whos *vertu* seyn and doon disport
aright 35
Resort han su*mm*e ayeyn wt gret honour
And yiftis grete and su*mm*e vnder this
flour

Are heer and thyngis trete of high emprise
ffor lif p*resent* for lif future vche hour
His cure and iust entent who kan com-
prise 40

6

Who kan comp*rise* in werkis wise in
right
In sadde avise as forto wise a londe
The duc p*eriure* who made assure in
flight
Calise endure who made and sure in
honde
The kyngis right who made vpright to
stonde 45
Who hath insight to stynte vnright
adu*erse*
Who hath be p*rest* the chirche in rest to
londe
As trewthe is best let feithfullest reherce

7

Let feithfullest reherce y treste hym
beste
Yf heretike ought kouthe pike him fro 50
Yf Sharp or Wawe hadde of the lawe
a feste
Yf right was fond in al this londe vnto
Hit to gou*erne* he doon the sterne vnto
Of eu*ery* poynt a kyng ennoynt of bothe
Englond and ffraunce hath conysaunce
also 55
Nis ther noo lord that nil record hem
sothe

8

Record hem sothe hit self the dede ap-
perith
Wul he for bothe alyue and dede es-
ploye
To saue vs here and hem in ffraunce hit
cherith
His wit to here and Orliaunce ennoye 60
Wel myght a kynge of suche a flour
enioye
To seen hit sprynge in fyn odour & huys
Strenght & sauour hym ou*eral* to ioy
In whos fauour science and al v*ertu* is

9

Uertu is fonde if goldon Sapience 65
Haue intellect and consel ffortitude
If pite stonde enaured wt science
That hem connect the Lordis drede en-
clude
Man thus confect is voide of dedis rude

This kyngis dere vncul & sone and
  brother   70
Hath god prouect His werkis to conclude
His werkis here or where is suche another

10

Another felyng so the philosophre
In bokis natural as is phisic
Metaphisic also thus prompt to profre 75
Vche art quadriuial and hath practic
With theoric moral as is Ethic
Politic monastic yconomye
In gramer ground of al growyng logic
ffor fruyt and rethoric to florifie   80

11

To florifie in artificial
Science and al thorgh se philosophie
Beth thyngis hie And yiftis natural
Hit is not smal to haue as memorie
What thynge engyne vpfynde or reson
  trie   85
And iustifie in tresor to reclyne
Is not indigne if good phisionomye
Vche organ eye and al figure & lyne

12

At Oxenford thys lord his bookis fele
Hath euery clerk at werk They of hem
  gete   90
Methaphisic phisic these other feele
They natural moral they rather trete
Theologie here bye is with to mete
Hem liketh loke in boke historial
In deskis xij hym selue as half a strete 95
Hath boked thair librair vniuersal

13

For clergie or knyghthod or husbondrie
That oratour poete or philosophre
Hath tretid told or taught in memorie
Vche lef and lyne hath he as shette in
  cofre   100
Oon nouelte vnnethe is hym to profre

Yit Whethamstede and also Pers de
  Mounte
Titus and Antony and y laste ofre
And leest Our newe is old in hym ta-
  counte

14

But that his vertu list vs exercise   105
And moo as fele as kan in vertu do
He sapient is diligent to wise
Alle ignoraunt and y am oon of tho
He taught me metur make and y soso
Hym counturfete and hope aftir my
  sorow   110
In god and hym to glade and aftir woo
To ioy and aftir nyght to sey good morow

15

And hym that held as doubil mortal foo
Ten yeer my self and myne in wrong
  oppresse
And yit my chirche and al my good me
  fro   115
Hath in effect yit treste y god redresse
But this matere as here is not texpresse
As y seid erst in hope y thynke abide
And to that princis werk my wit com-
  presse
My wronge my woo my care y sette
  aside   120

16

And hym that lord that wt his woundis
  wide
ffrom deth vs bought and hath our lif in
  cure
Thorgh al this werk so derk he be my
  gide
My wight he right my number and mesure
That first for hym and thenne his creature   125
His princis flour good fruyt & fressh
  plesaunce
Vpgrowe on hit in his Agriculture
Maad at his hest and his Consideraunce
  Explicit Prohemium

[EPILOGUE-STANZAS FROM THE PALLADIUS TRANSLATION]

(A)

(The final stanza of Book II, January)

A now my lord biholdith on his book
ffor sothe al nought he gynnyth crossis
    make
With a plummet and y noot whow his
    look
His cheer is straunge eschaunge Almeest
    y quake
ffor ferd y shrynke away no leue y take
ffarwel my lord do forth for y am heer
And metur muse out of this prosis blake
And heer y wul sette on At ffeueryeer

(B)

(The final stanza of Book III, February)

Good hope is reste and al yit shal amende
Theron y treste And al this longe yeer
Of husbondrie in hast y thynke anende
The forme book is doon and Ianyueer
And lo my lord in honde hath ffeueryeer
Wul he correcte by what have y to done
He wul doon as a lord Thenne aftir heer
Asfaste y thynke on sette At Marchis
    mone

(C)

(The final stanza of Book V, April)

And heer an ende er then y wende y
    fynde
Eek done is in this mone art taught
    aforn
O Saluatour o iesse flour so kynde
Of oon for euerychoon that list be born
And for vs hynge a crowne vsynge of
    thorn
Honour be to The flour of flouris ay
Thy princis werk away fro derk vpborn
So make as heer y take ayeyn at May

(D)

(The final stanza of Book VI, May)

Lo May is ronne away in litil space
The tonge is short and longe is his
    sentence
fforride y se my gide and hym y trace
As he as swyft to be yit y dispence
O sone o god allone o Sapience
O hope of synys drope or fraude immuyn
Louynge y to the synge as my science
Kan do and forth y go to werk at Iuyn

THE LOVER'S MASS

The only copy of this poem known to the present editor bears, in the manuscript Fairfax 16 of the Bodleian Library at Oxford, no title; in the (perhaps contemporary) table of contents prefixed to the volume it is described as "The observaunce of Venus goddes of love". In structure the work is plainly an imitation of the Mass, and a title recognizing this has been given the poem on each of its appearances in print. It was published by the Rev. T. F. Simmons in the appendix to his Lay Folks' Mass-Book, EETS 1879, as Venus' Mass, and by me in the JourEngGerPhilol for 1908 (vii : 95-104) as The Lover's Mass. I adopted this wording to bring the poem into line with other medieval "parodies" such as the Missa Potatorum, Messe des Oisiaux, etc.

Although "parody" of the Mass is not here carried through, breaking off after the Epistle, and although the headings do not exactly represent the parts of the Mass so far as the work goes, the trend is yet closely parallel. The eucharistic ritual opens with the Introibo ad Altare, continues with a Confiteor to which "Misereatur" is the response, and then, after versicles and a silent prayer by the priest, proceeds to the Kyrie, the Gloria, the Collects for the day, the Epistle, and so on. Here the headings are Introibo, Confiteor, Misereatur, Officium, Kyrie, Gloria, Orison, and Epistle.

In discussion of this exceedingly interesting and graceful piece of writing, there are two main lines to be followed: its place among the mass of religious "parodies" of the late Middle Ages, and its varied verse-structure. Among definite parodies the poem hardly belongs; and indeed, many medieval writings so classified have but small parodic intent. Such compositions, when based on the Church service, may be divided into those which incorporate phrases from the ritual into a lay text, and those which follow the structure of the whole service, while presenting material of quite different character. The phrase-borrowing poems are the most numerous; they may employ the phrases as a sort of tail-rime, or incorporate the words firmly into a macaronic poem of love or politics, or scatter them through what is in reality a character-study, as are the striking French Patenostre de l'Usurier and Credo au Ribaut. In the former of these two poems, the contrast between the routine lip-service of phrase and the busy suspicious usurer-mind at work behind the automatic lips is drawn with an attempt at "psychology". And neither this poem nor many another of the large class to which it belongs is true parody; the writer's intent is elsewhere.

In the larger-scale type of poem various subdivisions may be made. The service may be gone through by headings only, to bring forward an array of speakers united by a common feeling, as in the clumsy English poem on the death of the duke of Suffolk, or as in the various bird-Masses of France and of England. There may be actual parody of the Mass both in structure and in language, in which case it is Latin prose, and runs beyond the bounds of piety and of taste, as in the Missa Potatorum or the Officium Lusorum. There may be a definite religious attempt at putting the Mass into current language, as in the Lay Folks' Mass-Book. And the religious headings of the service may be used to introduce a series of lay compositions having little or no trace of ritualistic language or purpose. Of this last-mentioned sort is the poem here printed, the only parallel to which, so far as I know, is the Spanish Misa de Amores.

The accessible text bearing that title is by Suero de Ribera, who is said by Amador de los Rios, the historian of Spanish literature, to have imitated the Misa de Amores of Juan de Dueñas. Both men were of the reign of John II of Castile, 1406-1454. The poem of de Dueñas is still unpublished, but that of de Ribera has been twice printed, as noted below. Between it and our English text there is no comparison in metrical variety; the Spanish work is a sequence of short love-lyrics arranged under the headings of the Mass and continued through it, the separate parts being often of no more than one stanza, the stanzas varying from six to twelve lines, and these lines being of uniform length.

Whether the English writer obtained his suggestion of a Lover's Mass from Spain or not, his work is far more striking, even in its incompleteness, than that of de Ribera, because of its change of metrical flow to support every change of tone. Shifts of form to suit an altered key can be adduced from earlier literatures, but few are noteworthy. The first which I have observed is the Ephemeris of Ausonius; in this poem, which narrates the events of a day, the vehicle changes from Sapphic to iambic as the poet passes from the awakening of the sleeper to the preparations for rising; the long Oratio is in hexameter, the ten-line Egressio in tetrameter, the giving of invitations to friends in hexameter again, and so on. Less rapid variations are easier to find. The most usual is that from verse to prose and back, two very conspicuous examples of which are the Consolatio of Boethius and the De Planctu Naturae of Alanus; as a later, French, case, we may note Froissart's Méliador. Still simpler, and still more frequent, is the shift from couplet to stanza, as in Lydgate's Temple of Glass or Hawes' Pastime of Pleasure; also the change from one stanza of equal lines to another, as may be seen in the envoys and prologues of works in rime royal. Later French poets and rhétori-queurs, such as Octovien de St. Gelais, freely used change of stanza to represent change of mood; and something of this is found in Machaut, in Chaucer's time. But the only compact yet elaborate instance of such work in early English is Chaucer's Anelida, which its copyist John Shirley declared was written in "þe mooste unkouþe metre coloures and Rymes þat euer was sayde tofore þis day." Shirley does not use any such language of the Chaucerian Complaint to his Lady, printed by Skeat i : 360; but this also has a variety of stanza.

From all these our poem differs in the intensive management it makes of strophic variation. Its author is not merely dexterous and graceful in the complex-ities of the Kyrie, and aware of the clear singing quality of the Gloria-stanza, but he is sufficiently sensitive to make the change to the deeper slower seriousness of the Orison. It is this quick and complete yielding to the shift of mood which makes it impossible to believe that Lydgate was the author of the Lover's Mass.

Yet Simmons, in his edition as above, ascribed the poem to Lydgate; and he was followed by W. A. Neilson in his monograph, The Origins and Sources of the Court of Love (see p. 233 there). Also the New English Dictionary, s. v. assuage, entitle, adopts the assignment. Lydgate can indeed reach a fairly high lyric-re-ligious note; parts of his Testament show this. But this variety, this swift clean release of each tone, are not his. He is able in a small way to change his key, but not with this firm quickness, this control of material, this absence of repetition and padding. There are, it is true, certain contacts between the Mass and the work of Lydgate; but even when these contacts are recognized, the primary facts of speed and suppleness remain to dispute the monk's authorship.

One such contact is between the pilgrim-simile used in the Epistle here and the pilgrim-simile of Boccaccio's De Casibus, bk. iii, developed thence by Laurent in his French prose, developed still more by Lydgate in the prologue to bk. iii of the Fall of Princes. The Latin and the French may be read in the note on the Fall of Princes C 92, here; and a comparison of them with the Epistle will show that Laurent's French was probably known to the writer of the Mass. He is occasionally close to Laurent's phrasing, he keeps at least one bit not retained by Lydgate, and he has a possible mistranslation not made by Lydgate. But did we take this agreement in source as evidence for Lydgate's authorship of the Mass, we should have to assert that no English writer but Lydgate was in this period acquainted with Laurent's translation of Boccaccio.

Another and more important "contact" between the Mass and Lydgate is in the movement and phrasing of the prose Epistle here as compared with those of the prose passage, lines 16275 ff., of Lydgate's Pilgrimage of the Life of Man. But the whole subject of prose in this period has still to be examined, and we do not as yet know, e.g., how far doublets may have been a conventional stylistic feature. It is therefore impossible to weigh such similarities of phrasing judicially.

But a third "contact", that of vocabulary, we can appraise. Suggestive although it may be, at first glance, to see the word *contune* used in the Mass, we must note that it appears in Bokenam as well as in Lydgate; that, also, words like *allege, assuage,* though common indeed in Lydgate, are not his sole property. An argument from vocabulary is too often the argument of the excluded middle; we cannot assert that no other writer used the term. Nor can we assert that the reminiscences of Chaucer's Anelida, or the false scansion of *Citheron* (line 5), or the padding phrase in line 34, mean Lydgate's authorship; for all these are features common to the age. Lydgate's composition of the poem seems very improbable, in the present state of our critical knowledge, because of traits in it larger than these; but any positive theory of authorship we cannot offer.

Nor can a definite theory as to the source be presented at this time. Very little is as yet known of the relation between English and Spanish letters in the fifteenth century. The alliances of Henry VIII with Katharine of Arragon and of Mary Tudor with Philip of Spain are so conspicuous in English history that we forget the earlier connections of England with Spain through John of Gaunt. His marriage with Constance of Castile in 1371 and his subsequent placing of his two daughters upon the thrones of Castile and of Portugal set a far earlier possible date for the transference of court-poetry from peninsula to island; and the bonds of commerce, the importation of Spanish secretaries, Spanish physicians, Spanish traders, into England before Tudor times, may have played some part in spreading West-European themes like the Dance Macabre or the confessions of a lover. Boccaccio's De Casibus was translated into Castilian quite as soon as into French, and had a greater success in Spain than in France, to judge from the number of imitations. In fact, the identity of courtly taste between Castile, France, Burgundy, and England in this changing age is so marked that no study of the formal poetry of the period can be complete without an evaluation of Spain's part,—for which, unfortunately, much of the source-material is still unpublished.

An editor of the Lover's Mass is therefore compelled to leave one possible line of the poem's origin with the barest comment; and as regards authorship even

less is to be said.   It could only be a cause of trouble for future students, to bind
any name conjecturally upon this fresh and gracious fragment, which Chaucer
need not have been ashamed to sign.

SELECT REFERENCE LIST IX

On parody and on religious parody see:—

Paul Lehmann, Die Parodie im Mittelalter, Munich, 1922.

Paul Lehmann, Parodistische Texte, Munich, 1923.

Eero Ilvonen, Parodies de thèmes pieux dans la poésie française du moyen âge,
    Paris, 1914.

Adolph Franz, Die Messe im deutschen Mittelalter, Freiburg, 1902.

Francesco Novati, La Parodia sacra nelle letterature moderne, in Studi Critici, Turin,
    1889.

Missa Potatorum, in Lehmann, p. 59; in Franz, p. 754; in Novati, p. 289, in Reliquiae
    Antiquae (1843), ii:208.

Messe des Oisiaus, by Jean de Condé, in vol. iii of A. Scheler's ed., Brussels, 1866-67.

Patenostre a l'Userier, in Ilvonen, pp. 44, 66; in Barbazan et Méon, Fabliaux, iv:99.

Credo au Ribaut, in Ilvonen, p. 123; in Barbazan et Méon, op. cit., iv:445.

Officium Lusorum, in Lehmann, p. 68; in Carmina Burana, ed. Schmeller (1883), p.
    248; in Franz, p. 754.

The Laborintus, by Evrard l'Allemand, is printed in Leyser's Hist. Poetarum, p. 796 ff.;
    in Faral, p. 336 ff.

Poem on the Earl of Suffolk's death; see Wright's Polit. Poems, Rolls Series, ii:232;
    see PolitReligandLove Poems, EETS 1903, pp. 6-11.

Lay Folks' Mass Book, EETS 1879.

Misa de Amores of Suero de Ribera; see E. de Ochoa's ed. of 'Rimas Ineditas' by the
    Marquess de Santillana and others, Paris, 1844, 1851, appendix.   See also the
    Cancionero Castellano del Siglo XIV, vol. ii, Madrid, 1915.

Octovien de St. Gelais, see monograph by H. J. Molinier, Paris, 1910, especially chap.
    on 'Le Séjour d'Honneur.'

For English and Spanish letters in the xv century see:—

Note sulla fortuna del Boccaccio in Ispagna nell' Età Media, by A. Farinelli, in
    Archiv 114:397-429 (De Casibus); ibid. 115:368-388 (De Claris Mulieribus);
    ibid. 116:67-96 (De Genealogia Deorum, etc.); ibid. 117:114-141 (Teseide,
    Filostrato, etc., Decamerone).

[MS Bodl. Fairfax 16, fol. 314]

¶ Introïbo
Wyth all myn hool herte enter
To fore the famous Riche Auter
Of the myghty god of Love
Whiche that stondeth high above
In the Chapel / of Cytheron   5
I will wyth gret devocion
Go knele / and make sacrifyse
Lyke as the custom doth devyse
Afor that God / preye and wake

Of entent I may be take   10
To hys seruyse / and ther assure
As longe / as my lyf may dure
To contune / as I best kan
Whil I lyve / to ben hys man

¶ Confiteor
I am aknowe / and wot ryght well   15
I speke pleynly as I fel
Touchynge / the grete tendyrnesse
Of my youthe / and my symplesse
Of myn vnkonying / and grene age

On the MS see note bottom p. 200.

Wil lete me han noon avantage   20
To serue loue I kan so lyte
And yet myn hert / doth delyte
Of hys seruauntys / for to here
By exaumple of hem / I myghte lere
To folowe the wey / of ther seruyse   25
Yif I hadde konnyng to devyse
That I myght a seruant be
Amongys other in my degre
Havynge ful gret repentaunce
That I non erste me gan avaunce   30
In loue court / my selfe to offre
And my seruyse / for to profre
ffor ffer of my tender youthe
Nouther be Est / nouther be Southe
Lyst Daunger / putte me a bake   35
And dysdeyn / to make wrake
Wolde hyndre me / in myn entente
Of al this thyng / I me repente
As my conscience / kan recorde
I sey lowly Myserycorde   40

¶ Misereatur

By god of louys Ordynaunce
ffolkys / that haue repentaunce
Sorowful in herte / and no thyng lyght
Whiche ha nat spent hys tyme aryght
But wastyd yt in ydelnesse   45
Only for lake of lustynesse
In slep / slogardye / and slouthe
Of whom / ys pyte / and gret routhe
But when they repente hem ageyn
Of al ther tyme / spent in veyn   50
The god of love / thorgh hys myght
Syth that Mercy passeth ryght
The mot acceptyd be to grace
And pute daunger out of place
This the wyl of Dame *Venus*   55
And of hyr Bisshop *Genivs*

¶ Officium

In honour of the god Cupide
ffirst that he may be my guyde
In worshepe eke of the pryncesse
Whyche is lady / and Maystresse   60
By grace they may / for me provyde
Humble of herte / devoyde of pryde
Envye and rancour set asyde
With oute change / or doubilnesse
    In honour of the   65
    ffirst that he
Joye and welfare in euery tyde
Be yove to hem / wherso they byde
And yive to hem grace / on my dystresse
To have / pyte / of ther hyghnesse   70

ffor in what place / I go or ryde
    In honour
    ffirst that

¶ Kyrie

Mercy : Mercy : contynuely : I crye
In gret disioynt : vpon the poynt : to
    deye   75
ffor that pyte : ys vnto me : contrayre
Daunger my ffo : dysdeyn also : whylk
    tweye
Causen myn herte : of mortal smert :
    dyspeyre
ffor she that ys : fayrest ywys : of
    ffayre
Hath gladnesse : of my syknesse / to
    pleye   80
Thus my trouble / double and double /
    doth repayre

¶ Christe

Repeyreth ay : which nyght nor day //
    ne cesseth nought   •
Now hope / now dred / now pensyff-
    hede / now thought
Al thyse yfere / palen myn chere / and
    hewe
Yet to hyr grace ech hour / and space /
    I ha besought   85
Hyr lyst nat here / ffor hyr daunger /
    doth ay renewe
Towardys me / for certys she / lyst
    nat rewe
Vp on my peyne / and thus my cheyne /
    ys wrought
Which hath me bounde / neuer to be
    founde / vntrewe

¶ Kyrie

Vntrewe nay : to se that day : god for-
    bede   90
Voyde slouthe / kepe my trouthe / in
    dede
Eve and morowe / ffor Joye or sorowe /
    I have behyght
Til I sterve : euere to serve / hir
    womanhede
In erthe lyvynge / ther is no thyng /
    maketh me so lyght
ffor I shal dye : ne but wer hir Mercye /
    mor than ryght   95
Off no decertys / but Mercy certys /
    my Journe spede
Adieu al play : thus may I say / I
    woful wyght

¶ Gloria in excelsis

Worsshyppe / to that lord above
That callyd ys / the god of love
Pes / to hys seruantes euerychon   100
Trewe of herte / stable as ston
    That feythful be
To hertys trewe of ther corage
That lyst chaunge / for no rage
But kep hem / in ther hestys stylle   105
In all maner wedris ylle
    Pes concord and vnyte
God send hem / sone ther desyrs
And reles / of ther hoote ffyrs
That brenneth at her herte sore   110
And encresseth / more and more
    This my prayere
And after wynter / wyth hys shourys
God send hem counfort / of May
    flourys
Affter gret wynd / and stormys kene 115
The glade sonne / with bemys shene
    May appere
To yive hem lyght affter dyrknesse
Joye eke after hevynesse
And after dool / and ther wepynge   120
To here / the somer foullys synge
    God yive grace

ffor ofte sythe men ha seyn
A ful bryght day / after gret reyn
And tyl the storme / be leyd asyde   125
The herdys vnder bussh abyde
    And taketh place

After also the dirke nyght
Voyde off the Mone / and sterre lyght
And after nyghtys / dool and sorowe 130
ffolweth ofte a ful glade morowe
    Of Auenture

Now lorde that knowest hertys alle
Off louers / that for helpe calle
On her trouthe / of mercy rewe   135
Namly on swyche as be trewe
    Helpe to recure
    Amen

¶ The Oryson

Most myghty / and most dredful lord
That knowest / hertys fals and trewe
As wel ther thynkyng as ther word   140
Bothe of lovers / old and newe
Off pyte / and of mercy rewe
On thy seruauntes / that be stable
And make ther Joye / to renewe
Swich as wyl neuer be chaungable   145

¶ The Epystel in prose

ffrom the party of the por plentyff in love wyth many yers of probacon professyd to be
trewe / To all the holy ffraternite and Confrary: of the same bretherhede / And to
alle hospytlerys and Relygious / nat spottyd / nor mad foul wyth no cryme of Apos-
tasye / nouthyr notyd nor atteynt wt no double fface / of symulacon nor constreyned
countenaunce of ypocrysye // To alle swiche chose chyldre of stabylnesse wyth [150
oute variaunce of corage / or of herte Joye / Elthe /: and long prosperyte / wyth
perfeccon of perseueraunce / in ther trouthe perpetually / tabyde // Experyence
techeth / that pilgrymes / and folkes custoumable to vyage // Whan they vnderfange /
any long / weye wiche that ys laboryous // Somwhile off consuetude / and custoum /
they vse a maner to reste on ther wey // Off entent to wype / and wasshe [155
away / the soot of ther vysages // And sum also vsen to ley adoun the hevy ffardellys
of ther bake // ffor to alleggen ther wery lemys / of her grete berthene / And
somme outher vsen to gadryn wyne / And somme to drynken outher water or wyn //
of ther botell or Goordys to asswage / the grete dryhnesse of ther gredy thruste //
And somme of hem somwhile / rekne and accounten / how myche they ha [160
passyd / off ther Journe / And sodeynly tourne ageyn ther bakkys towardys / som
notable seteys Which they of newe / be partyd fro / And therwyth al Recorden /
and remembren hem / of Cytes / Castelles / and touns which they ha passyd by /
and nat forgete / hylles ne valeys / dygne / to be put in remembraunce of hyt / for a
Memoryal / Somme entytlen hem / in smale bookes of Report / or in tablys / to [165
callen hem to mynde / whan they sene her tyme / And som ought callen to mynde gret
Ryuers and smale / And pereylles of the see that they ha passyd by / And whan they
han alle accountyd / and ageyn Relatyd the partyes passyd off her Journe / Off

newe they take to hem force / vigour / and strengthe / myghtyly Wyth oute feyntyse /
to performe / and manly to acomplysshe / the Resydue and the remnaunt of her [170
labour // And thus .I. in semblable wyse / al the tyme of my lyff / ffrom my grene
tendre youthe / And tyme that I hadde / yerys of dyscrecon beynge / and contynuynge
/ as an Errynge pylgrym / in the seruyse of the myghty and dredful god of loue
/ how many perylous / passages / and wayes / that I ha passyd by / How ofte in
compleynynge I have setyn don // to wypen away the soot of myn inportable labour [175
And dronken euer among of my botell and Goordes / the bytter drynkes / of drerynesse / And offte sythes assayed / to casten adoun the inportable fardel / of myn
heuy thoughtys / And amongys al this thyngys // lookyd bakward to consydren /
and sen the fyn and the ende of my worthy bretheren / and predecessours in love //
that ha passyd the same pilgrymage toforn // And ther I ha founden / and seyn [180
the grete trouthe of Troylus / perseuerant to hys lyves ende // The trewe stable
menyng of penalope / The clennesse of polycene // The kyndenesse off Dydo / quen
of cartage / And rad also ful often in my contemplatyff medytacons The holy legende
of Martyrs / of Cupydo / The secre trouthe of Trystram and ysoude And the smale
Gerdouns of woful Palamydes / All thyse / and anhondryd Thousand mo callyd [185
to mynde / me semeth / amonges all I am on of the most forsake / And ferthest
set behynde of grace / And moste hyndred to þe mercy of my lady dere / Nat wyth-
stondynge the grete party of my pilgrymage / that I ha don But that I shal euere /
for lyfe or deth / contynue / and perseuere trewe to my lyves Ende // Besechynge
ful lowly / to alle yow my brethere / vn to whom thys lytel Epystel ys dyrect // [190
That yt lyke yow / of pyte / amonge your / devout obseruaunces to han me Recom-
endyd / wt som Especial Memorye / in your prayers / That yet or I dye / I
may sum mercy fynde / Or that the god of love / Enspyre my ladyes herte of hys
grace what I endure for hyr sake /—/

CHARLES D'ORLÉANS

Charles duke of Orléans, of the blood royal of France, was nephew to Charle VI, and son to that Louis d'Orléans who was murdered in 1407 by members o the household of the duke of Burgundy. He was born in 1391, and his mothe was Valentine Visconti, of the great Milanese house of despots. Charles was bu sixteen when he succeeded to his father's position as one of the four greatest feu dal nobles of France; he had been married a year earlier to Isabella, widow o Richard II of England, who died in 1409; the young duke married a second tim in the following year, and in 1415 he was taken prisoner at Agincourt and carrie to England. There he remained for twenty-five years, his ransom constantly dis cussed and as constantly deferred by disputes over the attendant conditions; an there a large amount of his French poetry was written. During his captivity hi second wife, Bonne d'Armagnac, died; and immediately upon his liberation, in 1440 Charles married a niece of the duke of Burgundy, the principal agent in his release He died in 1455, having spent much of his time since his return to France at hi own court of Blois.

Charles left behind him a large mass of lyrical poetry, cast in the forms o ballade, chanson, and rondeau, and purporting to be autobiographical. The theme are courtly:—reproach of the loved one's coldness, praise of her excellences, com plaints against separation. One body of the poems, written in England, has muc of exile and love-longing; many of the poems written after Charles' return to France are more of the poetic-exercise type. His work was exceedingly popula in aristocratic circles of his own and the next age; for instance, in the long post humous Chasse et Départ d'Amours of Octovien de St. Gelais a great numbe of Charles' poems were incorporated, and the plan of his Poème de la Prison adopted. (See Molinier's monograph on Octovien.) Also, several poems by Charle are included in the Jardin de Plaisance, printed by Vérard about 1501; see th facs. reproduction by the Soc. des anciens textes français, and Piaget in Romani 21:581 ff. (Piaget on St. Gelais should be checked by Molinier as above.) An the translation of so much of Charles' verse into English is a notable phenomenon

It is with these translations that we are especially concerned. They wer termed "rubbish" by Hilaire Belloc, writing in the Athenaeum for 1904, ii:146 but few students of medieval verse will agree with this verdict. There is ver little English verse in the fifteenth century worthy of comparison with thes faithful, vigorous, and often graceful translations. Their editor has not yet arisen although Sauerstein's article below mentioned is an excellent preliminary study of the question; but when he arrives, he will discuss various points indicating an other than Charles as the author of the English versions. He will note, of course the easy command of English in them, as compared with the stiff insecurity of the English bits preserved in French volumes; and he will have to consider the possi bility either that lapse of years brought Charles to mastery of his gaolers' language or that in the French MSS the French scribe has garbled a fairly good English text. He will have to reckon with the fact that the personality behind the English recension is a more forceful and buoyant one than is the personality of the mass of the French poems; and he will have to note the presence in the translations of an occasional Chaucerian trace not in Charles' French.

These Chaucerian tinges may have filtered to our author through a second
dilution, as in the phrase "morow gray", or the car of Phoebus "whirlid up so
high" (see poem xix of this group). But the reproach to Death has verbal echoes
of the Book of the Duchesse, and line 877 of that poem is reflected in the line
"Me thynkith youre eyen mercy seith." Also, evening "revith day his light", and
birds sing "Right as the wood therewith should forshyuere" (see Charles' poem
xiv here). A very marked allusion to Chaucer is in the poem beginning, "When
y am leyd to slepe as for a stound"; the lover cannot rest,

> For all the night myn hert aredith round
> As in the romaunce of plesaunt chaucer.

Here the French has,—"Rommant de Plaisant Penser." Further, both Troilus
and Anelida have given our writer such clues as "Thus ay diyng y lyue and neuyr
dede" (Trolius iv: 280), "How love for love is skilful gerdonyng" (Troilus
ii: 392), and "So thrillith me in my remembraunce" (Anelida 211).

The translator has a good ear for rhythm, something noteworthy in fifteenth-
century England. He inserts ejaculations such as *Mafay, Lo,* especially the
latter, to fill out his metre, and places those ejaculations carefully. See poems xiii,
xvi, xviii, here; note also the use of the dissyllabic *apast* in xvi and the insertion
of *even* in xvi's refrain-line. The change from French to English is not accomplished without frequent padding; but the way this is handled, and the way the
French rime-sounds are now retained and now discarded is worth study. The rime
-ft: -ght is fairly frequent; the verb *square* and the metaphor of a shirt recur. The
translator more than once refers to his "derked eyen". Whoever that translator was,
he was both bilingual and a good metrist. He twists his syntax with a strong hand,
using sometimes difficult inversions. He wastes no words; he is not clumsy, and
he does not blur the light tenderness of the French, though he does occasionally
add firmness and freshness. Whether he be the duke of Suffolk, as Dr. Mac-
Cracken suggests (see below p. 218), or an unknown clerk, he is not writing "rubbish". There are degrees of ease and of excellence among these translations, of
course, but whoever wrote—

> When I am hushed it marvel is to me
> To hear my heart how that he talketh soft,

was not writing rubbish. Whoever wrote the dialogue between the lover and his
heart,—

> Seest thou not well that fortune doth us fail?
> Hast thou good lust to live in sorrow?—Nay,
> Iwis,—he said—I trust more to attain;
> I had a pretty look yet yesterday,
> As me reported have mine eyen twain,—

was not writing rubbish. The spell of allegory and of the courtly love-code was
heavy on Charles and on his translator, but both walk well despite their burden.

BIBLIOGRAPHY

In the year 1734 the abbé Sallier read to his fellow-members of the French
Institut Royal a paper on a "recueil manuscrit de poésies de Charles d'Orleans",
the MS in question being the "Colbert", now in the Bibliothèque Nationale as

fonds français 1104,—according to Champion. This paper was published in 1740, in the Memoires de littérature tirez des registres de l'Academie royale des Inscriptions et belles Lettres, xiii:580-592. The abbé's purpose was the demonstration of Charles' priority over Villon in the rebirth of French poetry. He cited portions of Charles' French verse.

Sallier was cited by the abbé Goujet in his Bibliothèque françoise, ou Histoire de la littérature françoise, 18 vols., Paris, 1741-46; the discussion of Charles is in vol. ix: 230-287, and citations are more liberal than with Sallier. On p. 265 Goujet remarks that Charles has among his poems "plusieurs en anglois"; no examples of these are adduced. Goujet notes the fact that the Jardin de Plaisance borrowed from Charles.

According to d'Héricault's ed. of Charles' poems, ii: 281, the Annales poétiques ou Almanach des Muses has in its vol. i, Paris, 1778, a "Choix de Poésies de Charles d'Orléans". (This I have not seen.) The Marquis de Paulmy, in his Mélanges tirés d'une grande Bibliothèque, 68 vols. and index 69, Paris, 1779-88, treats of Charles, with extracts (French only), in vol. iv: 239-267.

The first citation of Charles' English verse seems to have been made by Mlle. de Keralio, in vol. iii of her Collection des meilleurs ouvrages françois, Paris, 1786-88. This collection, issued by subscription, was run to about 36 vols., of which 14 appeared. The editor devotes pp. 140-167 to Charles, citing at length from Sallier, and supporting his point as to Charles' superiority over Villon by printing Villon's Ballade des dames du temps jadis and the Ballade addressed to the women of Paris. Villon, she says, obviously studied and imitated Charles, but "n'obtint jamais la gloire de l'égaler", as these poems, beside the duke's, clearly prove. She speaks as if she used the MS known to Sallier, but when printing two English poems by Charles she states: "Je n'ai trouvé que deux essais de cette nature dans le manuscrit." Goujet, however, used the words "plusieurs en Anglois", and the MS fonds français 1104 has, according to Guichard, nine English poems. The texts printed by Mlle. de Keralio are those here numbered I and II. She appends to each a French prose paraphrase, and adds: "Ceux qui connaissent la langue Angloise jugeront que ces vers sont assez bien tournés pour le temps, à l'exception de quelques mots qui ont vielli, et d'une ortographe assez mauvaise."

Horace Walpole, in his Catalogue of the Royal and Noble Authors of England, reprinted Mlle. de Keralio's two texts, and sneered at her high valuation of Charles, not as in comparison with Villon, but as a French poet. For "such is the poverty and want of harmony of the French tongue that one knows how very meagre thousands of couplets are which pass for poetry in France."

The existence of a mass of translations from Charles' French into English, in the MS Brit. Mus. Harley 682, was apparently first noticed by Joseph Ritson; he gave a specimen of what he assumed to be Charles' English work in the dissertation prefixed to his Ancient Songs and Ballads, London, 1790.

George Ellis, in his Specimens of the Early English Poets, first ed. 1790, fifth ed. 1845, printed i: 253-4 (1845 ed.) three English poems by Charles, which are found with a large quantity of his French work in MS Brit. Mus. Royal 16 F ii. The texts form part of Ellis' footnote on King James of Scotland; in this volume they are nos. IVb, X, and XI. See remark on the London Magazine below.

Charles' French poems were first edited in 1803, and three times since; of his editors only one has included the English texts found among his French verse. See below, following notes on the MSS.

In Park's 1806 edition of Walpole's work, Charles is treated i:174-186. Park adds bits from the MS Brit. Mus. Harley 682, and expresses surprise at Walpole's ignoring of the London codices of Charles' poems.

Manuscripts

The MS Bibliothèque nationale, fonds français 25458, is fully described by Champion in Le manuscrit autographe des poésies de Charles d'Orléans, Paris, 1907. Champion considers the codex as the verse-album of the court of Blois, after Charles' return from captivity, and as partly in the script of Charles himself. He explains the composite appearance of the volume by supposing this sequence of facts:—1, That a professional scribe copied Charles' work, that done while in England as prisoner, in the first part of the volume, and that Charles made corrections upon this with his own hand. 2, That in the following pages later poems, mainly by Charles himself, but also by others, were copied by various scribes, Charles being one. 3, That while the book as originally planned contained many chansons written in the lower parts of pages with the upper halves left blank for the music, a change of plan or need of space led to the use of those upper half-pages for poems subsequently entered.

This MS contains, among the French, nine English poems, here printed. The similar texts found in the Grenoble MS, which is less complete than this "autograph" MS, were printed by Champollion-Figeac in his ed. of Charles, and reprinted from him by Bullrich (three texts), by Sauerstein (two texts), and by MacCracken (eight texts).

The MS Bodl. Fairfax 16, described in my Chaucer Manual, pp. 333 ff., contains one of the nine English poems found in the "autograph" MS, transcribed into Fairfax with a body of courtly verse of similar nature. See the suggestion by MacCracken as to authorship, below.

The MS Brit. Mus. Royal 16 F ii is a very large and handsome vellum volume, written, as Sir George Warner has suggested, for Arthur prince of Wales, son of Henry VIII, ca.1500. It is in a big deeply black professional hand, the enormous illuminated capitals and the line-capitals stiff with gilt; it contains several fine fullpage illuminations, one of which, representing the Tower of London and Charles seated at a window, has been several times reproduced. See Edgar Taylor's Minnesingers, London, 1825, to face p. 286; see Warner's Illuminated MSS of the British Museum, 1893; see the illustrated ed. of Green's Short History of the English People, ii:640; see frontispiece to Benham's Tower of London, 1906; see Champion's Vie de Charles d'Orléans, Paris, 1911, frontispiece. On the MS see Warner as cited, Sauerstein as below, and the Catalogue of Western MSS in the Old Royal and Kings' Collections, London, 1921.

This MS contains among the French three English poems, one of which is also in the "autograph" manuscript. The three are printed by Ellis as above; two are printed by Costello and by Champollion-Figeac, three by Sauerstein and by Mac-Cracken.

The MS Brit. Mus. Harley 682, which consists of a great number of English translations of Charles' French verse, is a moderate-sized vellum volume of 148 leaves, written in one smallish neat unprofessional hand, apparently of the fifteenth century. In transcription, spaces were left for capitals, which were never supplied. It has been freely corrected by the same or a similar hand in a manner which often suggests translator's rather than scribe's revision; but this and all

questions connected with the codex are too closely bound up with the problem
of authorship to enter upon here. The book contains, according to Sauerstein, 222
poems; for discussion of it see Sauerstein as below.

This codex, unmentioned by Walpole or by Ellis, was noted by Ritson as
above; he printed one text from it in 1790; and Walpole's editor, Park, in 1806,
added several others. In 1838 the savant Francisque Michel, sent by his government to investigate French MSS in English libraries, reported fully on this volume;
see his Rapports à M. le ministre (etc.), 1838. Previous to Michel's investigation,
in 1827, there had been issued for the Roxburghe Club a print of the entire contents of Harley 682, edited by George Watson Taylor, who assumed that the translations were the work of Charles himself. His edition, which is defaced by very
many textual errors and prefaced by a scanty and valueless introduction, was
published in but 44 copies. His assertion as to Charles' authorship was doubted
by a writer in the Retrospective Review for 1827, p. 147; but Sir Frederick Madden, in his book on Illuminated Ornament, London, 1833, took the authenticity
of the translations as proved, and it was nearly seventy years before the papers
of Bullrich and of Sauerstein (see below) dealt more exactly with the question.
Bullrich opined that the Harley 682 poems show an easy flowing style, the English
poems included in French MSS a stiff and shambling movement. He concluded
that the Harley 682 translations were the work of an Englishman. Sauerstein,
going more fully into the subject, arrives at the same conclusion; and Saintsbury,
in his Encycl. Brit. article on Charles, thinks the attribution to Charles "without
certainty".

An interesting suggestion as to the translator's identity was made by H. N.
MacCracken in PMLA 26:142 ff. (1911), viz., that the author of the group of
English love-poems preserved in MS Bodl. Fairfax 16 and the author of these
translations is one and the same person,—the earl of Suffolk, William de la Pole,
made duke of Suffolk in 1449, the year before his death. Suffolk was for several
years Charles' English custodian, and the two men became friends, Suffolk visiting Charles at Blois in 1444, after the French duke's liberation. A few French
poems by Suffolk still exist, in MS Trinity College Cambridge R 3,20, and one
of the English poems of Fairfax 16 appears also in Charles' "autograph" MS,
whence it is here printed, p. 222 below. Dr. MacCracken thinks that this English
poem, like the rest of the Fairfax group, was by Suffolk, and was translated into
the "Blois album" in the same way that various other poems by Charles' friends
were there included. Both the Fairfax group of love-poems and the Harley 682
translations show metrical command and show the influence of Chaucer; but the
attributions of the two sets of texts to one person and the identification of that
person as Suffolk are as yet matter of conjecture.

Since Taylor's print, no complete edition of the Harley 682 poems has appeared. In Wülker's Altengl. Lesebuch, Halle, 1874-80, ii:122-4, are printed three
English texts from Harley, headed as by Charles. Twelve texts from it are printed
in this volume; but a fac-simile of Harley 682, with full discussion of the authorship problem, is a desideratum.

Four English poems translated from Charles and apparently part of a collection similar to that in Harley 682, are in a MS-fragment owned by the antiquary
Thomas Hearne; they are reprinted from Hearne's Diaries by Hausknecht in
Anglia 17:445-7, and may be seen also in Bliss' Reliquiae Hearnianae, London,
1869, i:265-67.

Manuscripts of Charles' French poems, other than the "autograph MS", are not here discussed; see the French editors and biographers of Charles as below.

Editions of Charles' French Poems.

The earliest of these was by P. V. Chalvet, librarian of the Grenoble collection, pubd. Grenoble 1803, repr. 1809. The texts are from the less complete Grenoble MS of Charles' work, and the editing is severely censured by Champollion-Figeac. I have not seen the book.

Poésies de Charles d'Orléans,—d'après les manuscrits des bibl. du Roi et de l'Arsénal, J. M. Guichard, Paris, 1842.

Les poésies du duc Charles d'Orléans, publiées sur le manuscrit de la bibl. de Grenoble conferé avec ceux de Paris et de Londres, etc., A. Champollion-Figeac, Paris, 1842.

> Guichard's text appeared eight days previous to that of Champollion-Figeac, apparently in deliberate rivalry; and each editor followed up his text by an introduction or appendix censuring the procedure of the other. Guichard's preference for the La Vallière MS, now known as the "autograph", will be endorsed by modern students; his omission of the nine English poems from his print, an omission censured by his rival, will not be endorsed. The English poems are printed by Champollion-Figeac from the Grenoble MS, and reprinted from him by MacCracken as above, with some conjectural emendations.

Poésies complètes de Charles d'Orléans, revues sur les manuscrits,—etc., C. d'Hèricault, Paris, 1874, 2 vols. Again 1896. The English poems are not printed. Text based on the "autograph" MS.

There are French poems, marked as by Charles, in various English MSS. See the texts of Trinity College Cambridge R 3, 20 as above mentioned; also four quatrains in Brit. Mus. Harley 7333, printed thence by MacCracken in PMLA 26:145 note.

Translations from Charles' French, other than those in Harley 682

In the London Magazine for Sept. 1823, pp. 301-6, is an unsigned article on Charles, with the text of five French poems from the ed. of 1809 and an English verse-translation of each. These are followed by the statement that the writer has found three English poems by Charles in a MS of the British Museum; the subjoined texts are those in Royal 16 F ii, nos. IVb, X, XI as here printed. The emendations of Ellis are repeated or adopted; is the translator George Ellis? See above, p. 216.

In Edgar Taylor's Lays of the Minnesingers, London, 1825, pp. 286-93, is a discussion of Charles, with verse-translations of five poems. One of these coincides with one of the London Magazine set, and comparison is interesting.

Verse-translations of nineteen poems by Charles, and a print of two of his English poems from the Royal MS (IVb, X as here), are included in Louisa S. Costello's Specimens of the Early Poetry of France, London, 1835.

Prose ascribed to Charles

One French prose work, a debate between the heralds of England and of France, was ascribed to Charles by Henry Pyne, in his England and France in the Fifteenth Century, London, 1870. The attribution was successfully disputed by P. Meyer in:—

> Le débat des hérauts d'armes de France et d'Angleterre, suivi de "The debate between the heralds of England and France by John Coke." Paris, 1871, SATF.

Studies on Charles' Life and Work.

L. Champollion-Figeac, Louis et Charles d'Orléans, leur influence sur les arts, la littérature, et l'esprit de leur siècle, d'après des documents inédits, Paris, 1844.

C. Beaufils, Etude sur la vie et les poésies de Charles d'Orléans, Coutances, 1861.

F. Kuhl, Die Allegorie bei Charles d'Orléans, Marburg diss., 1886.

G. Bullrich, Ueber Charles d'Orléans u. die ihm zugeschriebene englische Uebersetzung seiner Gedichte, progr. Berlin, 1893.

K. Münster, Die Lautverhältnisse in der neuengl. Uebersetzung der Gedichte des Herzogs von Orléans, progr. Berlin, 1894.

P. Sauerstein, Charles d'Orléans u. die englische Uebersetzung seiner Dichtungen, Halle, 1899.

P. Champion, Le manuscrit autographe des poésies de Charles d'Orléans, Paris, 1907.

—————, La librairie de Charles d'Orléans, avec un album de facsimiles, Paris 1910.

—————, Vie de Charles d'Orléans, Paris, 1911.

H. N. MacCracken, An English Friend of Charles of Orleans, in PMLA 26:142 ff.

P. Champion, A propos de Charles d'Orléans, in Romania 49:580-4 (1923).

This article consists of two notes: 1, La dame anglaise de Charles d'Orléans, and 2, Recueils imprimés contenant des poésies de Charles d'Orléans. With the first cf. my note as below, in Mod. Phil.; with the second cf. Piaget in Romania 21:581, "Une edition gothique de Charles d'Orléans"; and see Molinier Essai . . . sur Octovien de St. Gelais, chap. iv (1910).

E. P. Hammond, Charles of Orleans and Anne Molyneux, ModPhil 22:215-6 (1924).

The verse-work of Charles may be classed in four groups. 1, His French poems, preserved in a dozen or more MSS in England and France. 2, A small body of rondeaux written in English, preserved among these French poems. 3, A considerable body of English translations from his existing French verse, probably not by Charles himself, and remaining in but one MS, Harley 682 of the British Museum. 4, About 77 English poems, mainly in stanza, intermingled with the poems of 3, in the same MS, but having so far as yet known no French original. This last subdivision I do not here consider, and I make it merely for the convenience of future investigators. With the first subdivision I am now concerned only in so far as the French poems are the sources of work in our third or English group; to this third, and the second, we limit ourselves. There are here printed the entire body of Charles' recognized English verse, and twelve selections from the English translations of his verse. Regarding this last, one word further.

Charles was twenty-five years a prisoner in England, and the honorable confinement in which he was held did not preclude his meeting with the households of his various gaolers, perhaps with their English friends. M. Pierre Champion's article in Romania 49 as above calls attention to a passage in King René of Anjou's Livre du Cuer d'Amours Espris; René, who knew Charles well, there says that "——prins fuz des Anglois et mené en servaige, Et tant y demouray qu'en aprins la langaige, Par laquel fus acoint de dame belle et saige, Et d'elle si espris qu'a Amours fis hommaige, Dont maints beaux ditz dictié bien prisez davantaige", etc. In the MS the blank here left at the beginning of the extract is filled by the name of "Charles quint de France, roy vertueux et saige"; this, M. Champion says, must be a scribal alteration, as the facts fit only Charles of Orleans. Should the substitution of Orleans' name be justified, we have René's support not only for the fact of Charles' learning English, but for his becoming enamoured of his instructress. Champion suggests the countess of Suffolk, Alice Chaucer, as the tutor and beloved lady, and seems to feel that the Harley 682 poems may be the amorous verse to which René refers. But the existence of the name *Anne Molins* in one of Charles' original English rondeaux (see no. VI here) inclines to the belief that a lady of that name was more probably the admired of Charles, and that the poems addressed to her may be no more than the half-score composed in English by him.

These English poems written by Charles have been often printed, viz.: Two by Mlle. de Keralio, nos. I, II here, from a Bibl. nat. MS; these were reprinted by Walpole. Three by Ellis from the Royal MS,—nos. IVb, X, XI here. Two by Costello from the Royal MS,—nos. IVb, X here. The entire group by Champollion-Figeac from the Grenoble and the Royal MSS, in his edition of Charles. Three by Bullrich from that edition,—nos. II, X, XI here. Four by Sauerstein from that edition and from the Royal MS,—nos. IVb, X, XI, I here. Two were printed from the Royal MS (X, XI), one from the Fairfax MS, and eight from Champollion-Figeac, by MacCracken as above. The three printed by Ellis are also in the London Magazine for 1823, pp.301-6, as ante.

A

POEMS WRITTEN IN ENGLISH

I
[Bibl. Nat. fonds franç. 25458, p. 346]

Myn hert hath send glad hope in hys
    message
Vnto comfort plesans Ioye and sped
I pray to god that grace may hym leed
Wythout lettyng or daunger of passage
In tryst to fynd profit and auauntage   5
Wyth yn short tym to the help of hys ned
    (M)yn hert &c.
    (V)nto comfort &c.
Till þat he come myn hert yn ermytage
Of thoght shall dwel alone god gyve hym
    med   10
And of wysshynge of tymys shal hym fed
Glad hope folyw & sped wel thys viage
    (M)yn hert &c.

II
[*ibid.*]

Whan shal thow come glad hope fro þi
    vyage
Thow hast taryd to long many a day
ffor all comford is put fro my away
Tyll that I here tythynge of þy message
(W)hat that had be lettyng of thy
    passage   5
Or tariyng alas I can not say
    (W)hen shal &c.
    (T)how hast &c.

Thow knows ful wel þat I have gret
    damage
In abydynge of the that is no nay   10
And thof y synge & dauns or lagh and
    play
In blake mournyng is clothyd my corage
    (W)han shal &c.

III
[Bibl. Nat. fonds franç. 25458, p. 310]

A ȝens the comyng of may
That is ful of lustynes
Let vs leue al heuynes
As fer as we can or may

Now is tym of myrth and play   5
Wynter weth hys ydylnes
Is dyscomfet as y ges
And redy to fle away
    Aȝens &c.

Wherfore ladys. I ȝow pray
That ȝe take in ȝow gladnes   10
And do al ȝour besynes
To be mery nyght and day
    Aȝens &c.

IV A
[Bibl. Nat. fonds franç. 25458, p. 310]

Go forth my hert wt my lady

Loke that ye spar no bysynes
To serue hyr wyth seche lowlynes
That ʒe get hyr grace and mercy

Pray hyr of tymes pryuely   5
That sche guippe trewly hyr promes
    Go forth &c.
I most as a hertles body
Abyde alone in heuynes
And ʒe schal do wel wyth your mais-
   tres   10
In plesans glad and mery
    Go forth &c.

IV B

[Brit. Mus. Royal 16 F ii, fol. 69a]
Go forth my hert wt my lady
Loke that ye spare no bysynes
That ye gette her oftyme pryuely
That she kepe truly her promes   5
    Go forth &c.
Iniust as a helis body
Abyde alone in heuynes
And ye shal dwell with your mastres
In plaisauns glad and mery
    Go forth &c.

V

[Bibl. Nat. fonds franç. 25458, p. 311]
for the reward of half a ʒere
Tow trewe louys upon the brest
hyt ys y now to brynge yn rest
A hert that loue hold yn dangere
Whenne he hath be sume wat stran-
   gere   5
To hym ys holyday and fest
    For the &c.
Thousch hyt be a Juel ful dere
And a charme for the tempest
Yet y conseille hym to be prest   10
And fore aʒens the warderere
    For the &c.

VI

[ibid.]

A las mercy wher shal myn hert yow fynd
Neuer had he wyth yow ful aqwaintans
Now com to hym and put of hys greuans
Ellys ye be vnto yowr frend vnkynd

Mercy he hath euer yow in hys mynd   5
Ons let hym haue sum conforth of plesans
    Alas mercy &c.

Let hym not dey but mak at ons a uende
In al hys woo an right heuy penans
Noght is the help that whyl not hym
   avans   10
Slauth hys to me and euer com be hynde
    Alas mercy &c.

VII

[ibid., p. 312]

Ye shul be payd after your whylfulnes
And blame nothyng but your mysgouern-
   ans
For when good loue wold fayn had yow
   auans
Then went ye bak wyth wyly frawhyed-
   nes

I know anon your sotyl wyleness   5
And your danger that was mad for ascans
    Ye schal be &c.
Ye might haue been my lady and maistres
For euer mor with outhyn varians
But now my hert yn yngland or in
   france   10
Ys go to seke other nyw besynes
    Ye schal be &c.

VIII

[ibid., p. 312]

So fayre so freshe so goodely on to se
So welle dymeynet in al your gouernans
That to my hert it is a grete plesans
Of your godenes when y remembre me
And trustyth fully wher that euer y be   5
I wylle abyde vndyr your obeyssance
    So fayre &c.

For in my thought ther is nomo but ye
Whom y haue seruid wythout repentance
Wherfore y pray yow sethe to my greu-
   ance   10
And put o syde all myn aduersite
    So fayre &c.

IX

[ibid., p. 318]

O thou fortune which hast the gouernance
Of all thynges kyndely meuyng to se fro
Thaym to demene after thyn ordonnance
Right as thou lyst to grante hem wele
   or wo
Syth that thou lyst that I be on of tho   5
That must be rewlyd be thyn auisines
Why whylt thou not wythstand myn
   heuynes

2

Me thyng thou art vnkynde as in thys
    case
To suffre me so long a whylle endure
So grete a peyn . wehout mercy and
    grase   10
Which greuyth me right sore I the ensure
And syth thou knawst / I am that crea-
    ture
That wolde be fauourd be thy gentilles
Why whylt thou not wythstand myn
    heuynes

3

What causyth the to be myn aduersarie 15
I haue not done which that schuld the dis-
    plese
And yit thou art to myn entent contrarie
Which makyth alwey my sorous to en-
    crese
And syth thou wotst myn hert ys not in
    ese
But euer in trouble wythout sykyrnenes 20
Why wylt thou not wythstand myn heuy-
    nes

4

To the allonly thys compleynt I make
For thou art cause of myn aduersite
And yit I wote welle thou mayst vnder-
    take
For myn welfare if that thou lyst agre 25

I haue no cause to blame no wyght but
    the
For thys thou doste of verrey wylfulnes
Why wylt thou not wythstand myn
    heuynes

X

[Brit. Mus. Royal 16 F ii, fol. 118a]

My hertly loue is in your governauns
And euer shal whill þat I lyue may
I pray to god I may see that day
That we be knyt with trouthfull alyans
Ye shal not fynd feynyng or variauns 5
As in my part that wyl I trewly say
    My hertly &c.

XI

[ibid., fol. 131a]

Ne were my trewe innocent hert
How ye hold with her alïauns
That somtym wt word of plesauns
Desceyued you vnder couert
Thynke how the stroke of loue com
    smert   5
Without warnyng or deffiauns
    Ne were my &c.
And ye shall pryuely or appert
See her by me in loues dauns
Wyth her faire femynyn contenauns 10
Ye shall neuer fro her astert
    Ne were my &c.

B

TRANSLATIONS FROM CHARLES' FRENCH

XII

Lue soit cellui qui trouua
Premier le maniere descripre
En ce grant confort ordonna
Pour amans qui sont en martire
Car quant ne peuent aler dire   5
A leurs dames leur grief tourment
Ce leur est moult dallegement
Quant par escript peuent mander
Les maulx quilz portent humblement
Pour bien et loyaument amer   10

Honure and prays as mot to him ha-
    bound
That first did fynde the wayes of writyng
ffor comfort gret ordeynyd he that
    stounde
To suche as haue of louys payne felyng
ffor when to speke they naue tyme nor
    metyng   5
To say ther ladies of ther aduersite
Yet doth it them a gret tranquyllite
ffor to endite and sende as in writyng
What grevous lyf they lede as semeth me
Only for loue and feithful trewe serv-
    yng   10

Quant vng amoureux escripra
Son dueil qui trop tient de rire

Who so that write how he is wrappid &
    wounde

Au plustost quenuoye laura
A celle qui est son seul mire
Si lui plaist a la lettre lire   *15*
Elle puet veoir clerement
Son douloureux gouuernement
Et lors pitie lui scet monstrer
Qui dessert bon guerdonnement
Pour bien et loyaulment amer   *20*

In suche greef as kan kepe him from
    laughyng
And so may sende it to his lady round
Which is the leche to all his soore felyng
If then to rede hit be to her plesyng   *15*
She may right wele therin perceyue and
    se
What woofull gouernaunce endewrith he
Of whiche pite may geue hir hit mevyng
That his desert is reward of mercy
Only for loue and feithfull trewe serv-
    yng   *20*

Par mon cuer ie congnois pieca
Ce mestier car quant il soupire
Iamais rapaisie ne sera
Tant quil ait enuoye detire
Uers la belle que tant desire   *25*
Et puis sil puet aucunement
Oyr nouuelles seullement
De sa doulce beaulte sans per
Il oublie lennuy quil sent
Pour bien et loyaulment amer   *30*

That hit is thus in myn hert haue y
    found
And knowe the craft for when he tath
    sekyng
No thyng kan him appese vpon the ground
To he haue send or made sum endityng
On the fayre which is his most likyng   *25*
Of which if so that his fortune be
To haue a response of hir gret bounte
He tath therin so huge a reioysyng
That forget is he had on his party
Only for loue and feithfull trewe serv-
    yng   *30*

Lenuoy

Madame dieu doint que briefment
Uous puisse de bouche conter
Ce que iay souffert longuement
Pour bien et loyaulment amer

But what madame crist ewre me so that
    ye
May vndirstonde as bi my mouth telyng
What y haue dewrid in tymys quantite
Only for loue and feithfull trewe servyng

From MS Brit. Mus. Royal 16 F ii, foll. 31 b-32 a.

From MS Brit. Mus. Harley 682, fol. 16.

XIII

Fortune vueillez moy laissier
En paix vne fois ie vous prie
Trop longuement a vray conter
Auez eu sur moy seigneurie
Tousiours faictes la rencherie   *5*
Uers moy et ne voulez oyr
Les maulx que mauez fait souffrir
Il a ia plusieurs ans passez
Dois ie tousiours ainsi languir
Helas et nest ce pas assez   *10*

O ffortune dost thou my deth conspyre
Onys let me pese y pray thee hertily
ffor all to longe y fynde withouten wyre
That thou hast had vpon me the maystry
Whi dost thou straunge when y thi mercy
    cry   *5*
Hast thou disdayne me caytiff forto here
That thus wt payne hast brought vnto þe
    bere
That how y ben so longe y mervell how
With greef y haue endewrid many yere
Alas alas and is this not ynough   *10*

Plus ne puis en ce point durer
A a . mercy . mercy ie crie
Souspirs mempeschent le parler
Uoir le pouez sans mocquerie
Il ne fault ia que ie le die   *15*

Longe in this lyf may y not dewren here
A a fortune mercy y cry mercy
Of my compleynt harke þe carfull matere
And not arett my rewdisshe speche mok-
    kery

Pource vous vueil ie requerir
Quil vous plaise de me tolir
Les maulx que mauez amassez
Qui mont uns iusques au mourir
Helas et nest ce pas assez   20

Tous maulx suis content de porter
Fors vng seul qui trop fort mennuye
Cest qui me fault loing demourer
De celle que tiens pour amye
Car pieca en sa compaignie   25
Laissay mon cuer et mon desir
Uers moy ne veulent reuenir
Delle ne sont iamais lassez
Ainsi suis seul sans nul plaisir
Helas et nest ce pas assez   30

Lenuoy
De balader Jay beau loisir
Autres deduitz me sont cassez
Prisonnier suis damour martir
Helas et nest ce pas assez

From MS Brit. Mus. Royal 16 F ii, foll. 25 b-26.
Also in Paris, Bibl. Nat. fonds fr. 25458,
pp. 60-61.

ffor whi to iape not lustith me trewly   15
Wherfore y the right humbly requere
To take fro me that thus me sett afyre
The greef and smert / a welaway syn
     thou
Vnto the deth as hast ybrought me nere
Allas allas and is this not ynough   20

I may wel bere eche payne or displesere
Saue only on which on me causith dy
That y so longe dwelle fro my lady dere
Whom y haue chose to loue no wondir
     why
ffor tyme agoon as in hir company   25
Lefft y myn hert / my ioy and my desere
That neuyr sith list come / to do me
     chere
ffor werry there in no thing lo they mowe
Thus lyve y sovl without ioy or plesere
Allas allas and is this not ynough   30

To balade now y haue a fayre leysere
All othir sport is me biraught as now
Martir am y for loue and prisonere
Allas allas and is this not ynow

From MS Brit. Mus. Harley 682, foll. 27 b-28a.

XIV

Trop long temps vous voy sommeillier
Mon cueur en dueil & desplaisir
Vueilliez vous ce jour esueillier
Alons au bois le may cueillir
Pour la coustume maintenir   5
Nous orrons des oyseaulx leglay
Dont ils font les bois retentir
Ce premier jour du mois de may

Le dieu damours est coustumier
A ce jour de feste tenir   10
Pour amoureux cueurs festier
Qui desirent de le seruir
Pour ce fait les arbres couurir
De fleurs & les champs de vert gay
Pour la feste plus embellir   15
Ce premier jour du mois de may

To longe for shame and all to longe
     trewly
Myn hert y se thee slepe in displesere
Awake this day awake o verry fy
Lete vs at wode go geder may in fere
To holde of oure oold custome the
     manere   5
Ther shall we here the birdis synge and
     pley
Right as the wood therwt shuld forshy-
     uere
This ioly tyme this fresshe first day of
     may

The god of loue this worldis god myghti
Holdith this day his feste to fede and
     chere   10
The hertis of vs poore louers heuy
Which only him to serue sett oure desere
Wherfore he doth affoyle the trees sere
With grene / and hath the soyle yflowrid
     gay
Only to shewe his fest to more plesere 15
This ioly tyme this fresshe first day of
     may

Bien scay mon cueur que faulx dangier
Vous fait mainte paine souffrir
Car il vous fait trop eslonguier
Celle qui est vostre desir   *20*
Pour tant vous fault esbat guerir
Mieulx conseillier je ne vous scay
Pour vostre douleur amendrir
Ce premier jour du mois de may

Myn hert thou wost how daungere hath
  on whi
Doon thee endure full greuous paynes
  here
Which doth the longe thus absent thi
  lady
That willist most to ben vnto hir nere   *20*
Wherfore the best avise y kan thee lere
Is that thou drawe thee to disportis ay
Thi trowbely sorow therwt to aclere
This ioly tyme this fresshe first day of
  may

Lenuoy

Madame mon seul souuenir   *25*
En cent jours nauroye loisir
De vous raconter tout au vray
Le mal qui tient mon cueur martir
Ce premier jour du mois de may

My first in thought / and last my lady
  dere   *25*
Hit axith more then this oon day leysere
To telle yow loo my greef and gret affray
That this wolde make myn hert a poore
  martere
This ioly tyme this fresshe first day of
  may

From MS Bibl. Nat. fonds fr. 25458, p. 71. Text
  not in Brit. Mus. Royal 16 F ii.

From MS Brit. Mus. Harley 682, fol. 33.

XV

Balade

Las mort qui ta fait si hardye
De prendre la noble Princesse
Qui estoit mon confort ma vie
Mon bien mon plaisir ma richesse
Puis que tu as prins ma maistresse   *5*
Prens moy aussi son seruiteur
Car iayme mieulx prouchainement
Mourir que languir en tourment
En paine soussy et douleur

Allas deth who made thee so hardy
To take awey the most nobill princesse
Which comfort was of my lyf and body
Mi wele my ioy my plesere and ricchesse
But syn thou hast biraft me my mays-
  tres   *5*
Take me poore wrecche hir cely servi·
  ture
ffor leuyr had y hastily forto dy
Than langwysshe in þis karfull tragedy
In payne sorowe and woofull aventure

Las de tous biens estoit garnie   *10*
Et en droitte fleur de ieunesse
Je pry a dieu quil te mauldie
Faulse Mort plaine de rudesse
Se prinse leussiez en viellesse
Ce ne fust pas si grant rigueur   *15*
Mais prinse las hastiuement
Et mas laissie piteusement
En paine soussi et douleur

Allas nad she of eche good thing plente *10*
fflowryng in youthe and in hir lustynes
I biseche god a cursid mote thou be
O false deth so full of gret rudenes
Had thou hir taken in vnweldynes
As had thou not ydoon so gret rigure   *15*
But thou alak hast take hir hastily
And welaway this left me pitously
In payne sorow and wooful aventure

Las ie suy seul sans compaignie
Adieu ma dame ma leesse   *20*
Or est nostre amour departie
Non pourtant ie vous fais promesse
Que de prieres a largesse

Allas alone am y without compane
ffare well my lady fare well my gladnes
Now is the loue partid twix you and me
Yet what for then y make yow here
  promes
That wt prayers y shall of gret larges

Morte vous seruiray de cuer
Sans oublier aucunement   25
Et vous regretteray souuent
En paine soussy et douleur

Here serue yow ded while my lyf may
  endure
Without forgetyng in slouthe or slog-
  ardy   25
Biwaylyng oft yowre deth wt wepyng ey
In payne sorow and wofull aventure

Dieu sur tout souuerain seigneur
Ordonnez par grace et doulceur
De lame delle tellement   30
Quelle ne soit pas longuement
En paine soussy et douleur

O god that lordist euery creature
Graunt of thi grace thi right forto mesure
On alle the offensis she hath doon wil-
  fully   30
So that the good sowle of hir now not ly
In payne sorow and wofull aventure

From MS Brit. Mus. Royal 16 F ii, foll 93b-94a.
Also in Paris, Bibl. Nat. fonds fr. 25458,
pp. 82-83.

From MS Brit. Mus. Harley 682, foll. 38b-39a.
  There are some erasures and alterations in
  this text, for which see Notes.

XVI

Balade

Quant souuent me ramentoit
La grant beaute dont estoit plaine
Celle que mon cuer appelloit
Sa seule dame souueraine
De touz biens la vraye fontaine   5
Qui est morte nouuellement
Ię dy en plourant tendrement
Ce monde nest que chose vaine

When y revolue in my remembraunce
The bewte shappe and þe swete eyen
  t(w)ayne
Of hir y callid myn hert hool plesaunce
Mi lyvis ioy my sovl lady souerayne
Of eche good thewe that was þe fressh
  fountayne   5
Which newly deth hath tane O welaway
ffor which y say wt wepyng eyen t(w)ay
That this world nys but even a thyng in
  vayne

Ou viel temps grant renom couroit
De crisayde yseud helayne   10
Et maintes autres quon nommoit
Parfaictes en beaulte haultaine
Mais au derrain en son demaine
La mort les prist piteusement
Parquoy puis veoir clerement   15
Ce monde nest que chose vaine

In tyme apast ther ran gret renomaunce
Of dido cresseid Alcest and Eleyne   10
And many moo as fynde we in romaunce
That were of bewte huge and welbesayne
But in the ende allas to thynke agayne
How deth hem slew and sleth moo day
  bi day
Hit doth me wel aduert this may y say 15
That this world nys but even a thyng in
  vayne

La mort a voulu et vouldroit
Bien le congnois mettre sa paine
De destruire selle pouoit
Leesse et plaisance mondaine   20
Quant tant de belles dames maine
Hors du monde car vrayement
Sans elles a mon iugement
Ce monde nest que chose vaine.

Me thenkith that deth cast bi his gouernaunce
fforto distroy all worldly plesere playn
fforwhi he doth therto his gret puyssh-
  aunce
That hath allas so moche fayre folkis
  slayn   20
And dayly slethe / what ioy doth he
  refrayne
Out of this world and bryngith in such
  dismay
ffor without them y iuge this mafay
That this world nys but even a thyng
  in vayn

Lenuoy

Amours pour verite certainte   *25*
Mort vous guerrie fellement
Se ny trouuez amendement
Ce monde nest que chose vaine

From MS Brit. Mus. Royal 16 F ii, foll. 95b-96.
Also in Paris, Bibl. Nat. fonds fr. 25458,
p. 86.

O god of loue thou may perseyue cer-
   tayne   *25*
To myn entent that deth thee warrith ay
So se y wel but though hit menden may
That this world nys but even a thyng
   in vayne

From MS Brit. Mus. Harley 682, foll. 42b-43a.

XVII

Balade

Le lendemain du premier io*ur* de may
Dede*n*s mon lit ainsi que ie dormoye
Au poi*n*t du io*ur* maui*n*t q*ue* ie songay
Qur deuant moy vne fleur ie veoye
Qui me disoit Amy ie me souloye   *5*
En toy fyer / car pieca mon party
Tu tenoyes / mais mis las en oubly
En soustenant la fueille contre moy
Jay merueille que tu veulx faire ainsy
Riens nay meffait se pense ie vers toy   *10*

The secund day of fayre fresshe lusty
   May
As half in slepe in slombir half wakyng
Me mette this sweuene in spryngyng of
   þe day
How to me came a flowre this resonyng
Me and seide / my frend y had trustyng *5*
Whilom that thou had holde on my parte
But now me thynke thou hast forgoten
   me
And strengthist lo the leef ageyn me sore
I merveyle wherin y haue greuyd thee
Me thynke y haue deservid not wher-
   fore   *10*

Tout esbahy alors ie me trouuay
Si respondy au mieulx q*ue* ie sauoye
Tresbelle fleur onques ie ne pensay
Faire chose que desplaire te doye
Se pour esbat auenture menuoye   *15*
Que ie serue la fueille cest an cy
Doy ie pourtant estre de toy bany
Nennyl certes ie fais comme ie doy
Et se ie tiens le party quay choisy
Riens nay meffait se pense ie vers toy   *20*

Sore basshid y when y this herde hir say
Aftir my rewde havoure this answeryng
Moost goodly flowre god helpe me so al-
   way
As y thought neuyr doon ayenst yow
   thyng
Yow to displese but happe of such ches-
   yng   *15*
The leef to serue this heyre hath made
   me he
Ought ye therfore me blame then nay
   parde
Syn so to doon is vsid evirmore
And ye me blame as for my poore dewte
Me thynke y haue deservid not wher-
   fore   *20*

Car no*n* pourtant honneur te porteray
De bon vouloir quelq*ue* part q*ue* ie soye
Tout pour lamour dune fleur q*ue* iamay
Ou temps passe / dieu doi*n*t que ie la
   voye
En paradis apres ma mort en ioye   *25*
Et pource fleur chierement ie te pry
Ne te plains plus car cause nas pourquoy
Puis que ie fais ainsi que tenu suy
Riens nay meffait se pense ie vers toy

Als yow in cheef that do y honoure ay
What part y am as is me well sittyng
All for oon flowre that me was tane
   away
In tyme a past god graunt vs sone metyng
In paradice the howre of my deiyng   *25*
O flowre wherfore ye not displesid be
ffor cause therto well wote y noon nave ye
Though that y levys were a thousand
   skore
Whi blame ye me whi shewe ye crewelte

Lenuoy

La verite est telle que ie dy   *30*
Jen ·fais iuge Amo*ur*s le puissant roy
Tresdoulce fleur point ne te cry mercy
Riens nay meffait se pense ie vers toy

From MS Royal 16 F ii, foll. 97b-98a. Text also
   in Paris, Bibl. Nat. fonds fr. 25458, pp.
   88-89.

Me thynke y haue deservid not wher-
   fore   *30*

The trouthe is this hit light is forto se
God be my Juge y kan no ferthirmore
ffor where ye seine y axen shulde merce
M*e* thynke y haue deservid not wherfore

From MS Brit. Mus. Harley 682, fol. 44.

XVIII

Chancon

En la forest damoureuse t*ri*stesse
Ung io*ur* mau*in*t qua p*ar* moy cheminoye
Ie re*n*contray lamoureuse deesse
Qui mappella demandant ou ialoye
Ie respondy que par fortune estoye   *5*
Mis en exil en ce bois long temps a
Et qua bon droit appeller me pouoye
Lomme esgare qui ne scet ou il va

En sourriant par (sa) tresgra*n*t hum-
   blesse
Me respondy amy se ie sauoye   *10*
Pourquoy tu es mys en ceste destresse
A mon pouoir voulentiers tayderoye
Car ia pieca ie mis ton cuer en voye
De tout plaisir ne scay qui len osta
Or me desplaist qua present ie te voye *15*
Lomme esgare qui ne scet ou il va

Helas dis ie souueraine princesse
Mon fait sauez po*ur*quoy le vo*us* diroye
Cest par la mort qui fait a tous rudesse
Qui ma tollu celle que tant amoye   *20*
Qui estoit tout lespoir que iauoye
Qui me gardoit sy bien maco*m*paigna
En son viuant que poi*n*t ne me trouuoye
Lomme esgare qui ne scet ou il va

Lenuoy

Aueugle suy ne scay ou aler doye   *25*
De mo*n* basto*n* affin q*ue* ne fouruoye

In the forest of noyous hevynes
As y went wandryng in the moneth of
   may
I mette of loue the myghti gret goddes
Which axid me whithir y was away
I hir answerid as fortune doth convey   *5*
As oon exylid from ioy al be me loth
That passyng well all folke me clepyn
   may
The man forlost that wot not where he
   goth

Half in a smyle ayen of hir humblesse
She seide my frend if so y wist ma fay *10*
Wherfore that thou art brought in such
   distresse
To shape thyn ese y wolde my silf assay
ffor here to fore y sett thyn hert in way
Of gret plesere y not whoo made thee
   wroth
Hit grevith me / thee see in suche
   aray   *15*
The man forlost that wot not where he
   goth

Allas y seide most souereyne good p*ri*n-
   cesse
Ye knowe my case what nedith to yow
   say
Hit is thorugh deth that shewith to all
   rudesse
Hath fro me tane that y most louyd ay *20*
In whom that all myn hope and comfort
   lay
So passyng frendship was bitwene vs
   both
That y was not / to fals deth did hir
   day
The man forlost that wot not where he
   goth

Thus am y blynd allas and welaway   *25*
Al fer myswent with my staf grapsyng

Ie. voy tastant mon chemin ca et la
Cest grant pitie quil conuient que ie soye
Lomme esgare qui ne scet ou il va

From MS Brit. Mus. Royal 16 F ii, foll. 131b-132.
    Text also in Paris MS Bibl. Nat. fonds fr.
    25458, pp, 89-90.
    1. Paris reads *dennuyeuse tristesse*.
    9. *sa* is inserted from Paris.
    18. *diroye* is from Paris.   Royal reads
    coniroye.
    The French was printed in the 1501 *Jardin
    de Plaisance*, fol. 201b; see facsimile is-
    sued by the Soc. d. anc. textes fr.

wey
That no thyng axe but me a graue to
    cloth
ffor pite is that y lyue thus a day
The man forlost that wot not where he
    goth

From MS Brit. Mus. Harley 682, fol. 46 b-47 a.

XIX

Balade

Le beau soleil le iour saint Valentin
Qui aportoit sa chandelle alumee
Na pas long temps entra par vng matin
Priueement en ma chambre fermee
Celle clarte quil auoit aportee   5
Sy mesueilla du somme de soussy
Ou iauoye toute la nuyt dormy
Sur le dur lit damoureuse pensee

Ce iour aussi pour partir leur butin
Des biens damours faisoyent assemblee 10
Tous les oyseaulx qui parlans leur latin
Cryoyent fort demandans leur liuree
Que nature leur auoit ordonnee
Cestoit dun per comme chascun choisy
Sy ne me peuz rendormir pour leur cry 15
Sur le dur lit damoureuse pensee

Lors en mouillant de lermes mon coissin
Je regretay ma dure destinee
Disant oyseaulx ie vous voy en chemin
De tout plaisir et joye desiree   20
Chascun de vous a per qui luy agree
Et point nen ay. car Mort qui ma trahy
A pris mon per dont en dueil ie languy
Sur le dur lit damoureuse pensee

Lenuoy

Saint Valentin choisissent cest annee 25
Ceulx et celles de lamoureux party
Seul me tendray de confort desgarny
Sur le dur lit damoureuse pensee

From MS Brit. Mus. Royal 16 F ii, fol. 134. Text
    also in Paris, Bibl. Nat. fonds fr. 25458,
    p. 93.
    Paris reads in line 3—*entra vn bien matin*.
    In 8, 16, 24, 28 it reads *dennuieuse pensee*.
    Line 20, omitted by Royal, is here given
    from Paris.

Whan fresshe Phebus day of seynt val-
    entyn
Had whirlid vp his golden chare aloft
The burned bemys of it gan to shyne
In at my chambre where y slepid soft
Of which the light that he had wt him
    brought   5
He wook me of the slepe of heuynes
Wherin forslepid y all the nyght dowtles
Vpon my bed so hard of newous thought

Of which this day to parten there bottyne
An oost of fowlis semblid in a croft   10
Myn eye biside and pletid ther latyn
To haue wt them as nature had them
    wrou3t
Ther makis forto wrappe in wyngis soft
ffor which they gan so loude ther cries
    dresse
That y ne koude not slepe in my distres 15
Vpon my bed so hard of newous thought

Tho gan y reyne wt teeris of myn eyne
Mi pilowe and to wayle and cursen oft
My destyny and gan my look enclyne
These birdis to and seide ye birdis
    ought   20
To thanke nature where as it sittith me
    nou3t
That han yowre makis to yowre gret
    gladnes
Where y sorow the deth of my maystres
Vpon my bed so hard of noyous thought

Als wele is him this day that hath him
    kaught   25
A valentyne that louyth him as y gesse
Where as this comfort sole y here me
    dresse
Vpon my bed so hard of noyous thought

From MS Brit. Mus. Harley 682, foll. 47b-48a.

XX

Chancon

Prenez tost ce baiser mon cuer
Que ma maistresse vous *present*e
La belle bonne ieune et gente
Par sa tresgrant grace et doulceur   5
Bon guet feray sur mon honneur
Affin que danger riens nen sente
    Prenez etc.
Dangier toute nuyt en labeur
A fait guet or gist en sa tente
Acomplissez brief vostre entente   *10*
Tandis quil dort cest le meilleur
    Prenez &c.

English from MS Brit. Mus. Harley 682, fol. 77b.
French from MS Brit. Mus. Royal 16 F ii,
fol. 124b; copy also in Paris, Bibl. Nat.
fonds fr. 25458, p. 271.

Take take this cosse atonys atonys my
    herte
That thee presentid is of thi maystres
The goodly fayre so full of lustynes
Only of grace to lessen wt thi smert
But to myn honoure loke thou well
    avert   5
That daunger not parseyue my sotilnes
    Take take this
    That thee
Daunger wacchith al nyght in his shert
To spye me in a gery currisshenes   10
So to haue doon attones let se thee
    dresse
While in a slepe his eyen ben covert
    Take take this
    That thee

XXI

Chancon

Ie ne vueil plus rie*n*s q*ue* la mort
Pource que voy que reconfort
Ne puet mon cuer esleesser
Au moins me pourray ie vanter
Que ie seuffre douleur a tort   5
Car puis que nay despoir le port
Damours ne puys souffrir leffort
Ne doy ie donc ioye lasser
    Ie ne &c.
Au dieu damour ie men rapport   *10*
Quen pains suys boute sy fort
Que pouoir nay plus dendurer
Sen ce point me fault demourer
Quant de moy ie my accort
    Ie ne &c.

English from MS Brit. Mus. Harley 682, fol. 68a.
French from MS Brit. Mus. Royal 16 F ii,
fol. 117b; copy also in Paris, Bibl. Nat.
fonds fr. 25458, p. 251.

More then the deth nys thyng vnto me
    leef
Syn recomfort vnto my karfull greef
May noon be found to ioy my woofull
    hert
But as a wrecche avaunt y may of smert
That wrongfully my payne is to geef   5
ffare well hope for noon may me releef
Thorugh loue fortune hath cast me to
    myschef
Which shapen had my deth to fore my
    shert
    More then the
    Syn recomfort   10
    May noon·ben
O god of loue thou wost y am no theef
Nor fallyng of my trouthe thou kan not
    preef
Whi shall y dey then wolde y fayn aduert
Although from deth y kepe not now
    astert   *15*
Though that he stood right even here at
    my sleve
    More then the
    Syn recomfort
    May noon ben

XXII

Chancon

De la regarder vous gardez
La belle que sers ligement
Car vous perdrez soudainement
Vostre cuer se la regardez
Se donner ne le luy voulez   5
Clignez les yeux hastiuement
   De la. &c.
Les biens que dieu lui a donnez
Amblent vng cuer soubtilement
Por ce prenez auisement   10
Quant deuant elle vous vendrez
   De la regarder. &c.

English from MS Brit. Mus. Harley 682, fol. 72a.
 French from MS Brit. Mus. Royal 16 F ii,
 fol. 119a; text also in Paris, Bibl. Nat.
 fonds fr. 25458, p. 254.

Bewar y rede yow loke here not vpon
The goodly fayre that y loue feithfully
ffor ye shall lese yowre hert even sodayn-
 ly
If so be that ye cast her lokyng on
Wherfore but ye lust gefe yowre hert
 anoon   5
Shette vp yowre eyen and close hem we
 surely
   Bewar y
   The goodly
ffor the bewte she hath bi god alon
Hit stelith lo an hert so pratily   10
That but ye bet abowt yowre silf aspy
Or ye be war yowre hert shall be goon
   Bewar y
   The goodly

XXIII

Chancon

Ie me mets en vostre mercy
Tresbelle bonne ieune et gente
On ma dit questes mal *con*tente
De moy ne scay sil est ainsy
De toute nuyt ie nay dormy   5
Ne pensez pas que ie vous mente
   Ie me metz &c.
Pource treshumblement vous pry
Que vous me dictes vostre entente
Car dune chose ie me vante   10
Quen loyaulte nay point failly
   Ie me metz &c.

The English text is from MS Brit. Mus. Harley
 682, fol. 83a; the French from Brit. Mus.
 Royal 16 F ii, fol. 129a, compared with the
 text in Paris, Bibl. Nat. fonds fr. 25458,
 p. 278.

I put my silf vnto youre mercy lo
Moost goodly fayre most replete of
 bounte
Hit seid me is that ye are wroth wt me
Not wot y whi nor where hit be or no
But all the nyght ne slepen y for woo 5
Saue thenke and muse wherfore that hit
 shuld be
   I put my
   Most goodly
Allas beth not so moche to me my foo
But youre entent wherfore as let me se 10
ffor this y vaunt my silf that y am he
That kepe his trouthe and shall wherso y
 go
   I putt my
   Most goodly

FROM HARDYNG'S CHRONICLE
Henry V and the Battle of Agincourt

John Hardyng was born in 1378, of a Northern family, and at twelve years of age entered the service of the Earl of Northumberland. He was at the battle of Shrewsbury in 1403, and witnessed the death of his master "Hotspur". He then went into the service of Sir Robert Umfraville, in which he remained for the rest of his life. With Sir Robert he took part in the battle of Agincourt, and saw other foreign service. According to a rubric in MS Lansdowne 204, he was at Rome in 1424. Sir Robert later made Hardyng constable of his castle of Kyme, Lincolnshire, where Hardyng lived for many years; he was working on his Metrical Chronicle as late as 1464, when he was eighty-six years old, and it does not seem probable that he long survived that date.

Hardyng was commissioned by the English Crown to seek in Scotland for evidence of the feudal relation between that country and England, and much time was spent in this search. The documents which he brought forward to attest the homage due from Scotland to the English sovereign were, however, too probably forged by himself; and this and his constant demand to be rewarded for "discovering" them have seriously damaged his reputation with modern students. Nor is that reputation raised by his Chronicle, which, extending from mythical. times to his own day, rarely contains anything independent of previous chronicles.

He several times rewrote his work for different royal patrons. The earlier recension, of which the unique copy is Lansdowne 204 of the British Museum, and which was apparently the presentation text offered to Henry VI, concludes with the death of Hardyng's master, Sir Robert Umfraville, in 1436; it is of about 2700 stanzas in rime royal. Kingsford considers that it was partly composed between 1440 and 1450. A different and briefer version was subsequently prepared for Edward IV; the MS Harley 661, which Lee in the DictNatBiog terms "the best of the later versions", has less than 1800 stanzas. There are two MSS in the Bodleian Library, one (Arch. Selden B 10) bearing the arms of Percy Earl of Northumberland (ob. 1527). In 1543 Richard Grafton the printer issued two editions of Hardyng's work, following one of the later recensions, but in a form differing from any surviving copy; and in 1812 Sir Henry Ellis edited one of these.

Two brief bits from MS Harley 661 are printed by Wülker, Altengl. Lesebuch, ii: 73-75. Two stanzas were printed by Mrs. Cooper in her (1737) Muses' Library.

There is no literary merit whatever in Hardyng's work; its doggerel stupidity shows the uselessness of battle, foreign travel, and scholarly pursuits to summon any real response from a "spirit dried up and closely furled".

For discussion of Hardyng and his Chronicle, see C. L. Kingsford on The First Version of Hardyng's Chronicle, in Engl. Hist. Review 27:462-482 (1912).

See Kingsford, English Historical Literature in the Fifteenth Century, Oxford, 1913, chapter vi. Kingsford considers that a comparative edition of the various recensions of the Chronicle would be of no value. The differences between them, he says, are so great that no "critical" edition is possible.

On Hardyng's language see W. Hagedorn, Ueber die Sprache einiger nördlicher Chaucerschüler, Göttingen 1892, p. 15.

On Agincourt see Sir N. H. Nicolas' History of the Battle of Agincourt, 1832. He prints

1) on pp. 301-329 a poem from MS Harley 565, which is attributed to Lydgate; this is in 3 passus, and covers not only Agincourt but the preceding siege of Harfleur and the subsequent triumphal entry of Henry into London.

2) along with the above, on pp. 303-325, a similar but shorter poem, from Hearne's edition of Elmham's life of Henry V, the text offered by a Cottonian MS now lost, Vitellius D xii.

3) in his Appendix, pp. 69-77, a poem on the same subject, from a black letter copy. This is also to be found in Hazlitt's EEPopPoetry ii :92-108, and in Arber's Engl. Garner, Westm., 1897, viii :13-24, its text there modernized and ascribed to Lydgate.

Thomas Wright, in his PolitPoems ii :123-27, prints eight stanzas of verse on the battle, which appear in MS Cott. Cleopatra C iv with a prose account.

The Latin prose of the Gesta Henrici Quinti, see ed. by Williams, London, 1850, was used by Hardyng for this poem, according to Kingsford as above p. 49. It is translated into English and printed by Nicolas as above, pp. 183-300.

Other verses on the battle or on Henry's return are printed by Nicolas, pp. 67-8, 78-86.

Capgrave's allusion to the battle, in his Chronicle of England, ed. Rolls Series, 1858, is very slight.

On Oldcastle see the poem of Hoccleve in the EETS ed. of his work, iii :8 ff.

[MS Brit. Mus. Lansdowne 204, chapter 211]

Henry his sonne / that prynce of wales was than
On seynt Cuthbert / day than next folowynge
In marce was crounde / as I remembre can
And als ennoynte / at Westmynster for kynge
Of whom the reme / was glad with oute lesynge   5
Obeyand hym / in alkyns ordynaunce
As subgytz owe / to ryall gouernaunce

2

In his friste yer / the Cobham Errytyke
Confedred with / lollers incipient
Agayne the Chirche / arose and was full lyke   10
It haue distroyed / by thar intendement
Had noght the kynge / than made suppowelment
And toke thaym vp / by gode inspeccioun
That friste bygan / that insurreccioun

3

Than fled the lorde / Cobham erronyouse   15
To Wales so / with lollers many one
Musyng in his / oppynyoun venymouse

How that he myght / the chirche distroy anone
Bot god that sytte / in heuen aboue allone
Knowyng his herte / naked of gode sentement   20
Lete hym be take / to haue his Jugyment

4

That prisonde was / at london in the Toure
Of whiche he dyd / eschape away by nyght
And taken was agayn with in an houre
And after sone / dampned by law and right   25
ffor errisy / by all the Clergy sight
And brent he was / tyll askes dede and pale
Thurgh cursed lyfe / thus came he in grete bale

5

The kynge than sette / vpon all rightwysnesse
Of morall wytte / and all benygnyte   30
All openly / he ordeynde in expresse
That all men myght with oute diffyculte
The Archebisshop / of yorke vysyte and se

That Rychard Scrope / so hight full
graciouse
ffor whom god shewed / myracles plentyuouse   35

6

Kynge Rycharde als / at langley leyde in
erthe
Agayne his wyll / and all his ordynaunce
By comaundement / of kynge Henry the
ferthe
ffor folke of hym / shulde haue no remembraunce
The kynge toke vp / with riall ordynaunce   40
And toumbed fayre / byside his wyfe
quene Anne
With all honoure / that myght be done
by manne

7

The kynge so than / right in his seconde
yer
In his parlement / by gode benyvolence
At laycestr / foure dukes made in fer 45
His brother Thomas / duke of Clarence
His brother John / for grete expedience
Duke off Bedford / he made by hole de-
cre
That next was than / sette in all dignyte

8

His brother Vmfray / next hym he dyd
create   50
The duke so than / of Gloucestre by
style
Thomas Bewford / his Eme Erle of
Dorsette
He made than duke / of Excester that
while
And thar he graunte / than as I can
compyle
Henry Percy his londes / that wer in
tayle   55
To sewe thaym oute / by lawe and gouer-
nayle

9

On Mawdelayne day the thirde yer of his
rygne
Syr Robert than / Vmframvyle dyd so
ryde
In Scotlande so / and to none wolde re-
sygne
His power right / bot on hym toke that
tyde   60
That laboure hole / and toke hym to his
gyde

And tolde hym whare / he shulde hym
brynge and lede
Whar that he toke grete gode with outen
drede

10

And faught with thaym / at Greterigge
in batayle
Whare eghtene score / of Scottes were
dede and slayne   65
Nyne hundre fled / he folowed at thair
tayle
On whom he made / grete chace the
sothe to sayne
Twelfe myle on lenghe / with thaym he
rode agayn
Whare in the chase / bot with ffyve
hundre men
He toke thaym vp / and slew thaym
fleand then   70

11

At lammesse after / the kynge to Normandy
At hampton was / with all his hoste to
sayle
Whare than the Erle of Cambrige certanly
The lorde Scrope als / Sir Thomas gray
no fayle
The kynges deth / had caste for thair
avayle   75
Of whiche the kynge was ware and toke
all thre
And heded hem at hampton by decre

12

And helde hys way / to harflete than
anone
And wanne it so / and made ther of
Captayne
His Eme the duke / of Excester allone 80
Ande homwarde went / by Calays so
agayne
At Agyncourte / the ffrensshe hym mette
sertayne
And with hym faught / with hoste in-
nomerable
Whare thay were take / and wonne with
outen fable

13

The duke was take / that day of Orlience   85
The duke also / of Burboyne certaynly
The Erle wendome / that was of grete
credence

And *sir* Arthur / of Bretayn verryly

*   *   *   *   *   *   *   *

With many mo / of other prisoners *90*
That taken wer / as sayne Cronyclers

14

The dukes thre / of Bare and Alaunson
And of loreyne / were in that batayle
   slayn
And for thair lyfes / they payed no more
   raunson
Who to thayr wyfes / no more cam
   nought agayne
Bot on that grounde / thar dyde thay
   certayn
ffourty thousonde thar layde thair lyfes
   to wedde
ffor thair raunson / me thought thay had
   wele spedde
15
On oure syde / was of yorke Duke Edward slayne
A myghty lorde / and ffull of sapience   *100*
And few elles mo / of Englisshe men
   certayne
As I consayue / that were of reuerence
That was bot grace / of goddes omni-
   potence
ffor Englisshe men / nyne thousond
   noght excede
That faught agayne / an hundre thousonde in dede   *105*
16
On seynt Crispyne / and Crispynian day
This batayle sore / certanly was smyten
At Agyncourte / as thay with sette his
   way

ffor whiche the kynge / gan fight as wele
   was wyten
With thaym anone / whare wer slayne
   vnsmyten   *110*
Thousondes smored / thurgh thayr multitude
That wolde haue fledde / fro his excelsitude

17

The yere of Criste / a thousonde and
   foure hundre
And seuentene eke / whan that this same
   batayle
Was smyten so / and of the regne no
   wonder   *115*
The thirde yere was / that tyme with
   outen fayle
And home thay came / than to thair
   moste avayle
Thurgh Pykardy / by Guynes and Calays
   than
And thare thay shipte / and into Englond
   wan

18

In Englonde than / in the somer seson   *120*
The Emperour / of Rome *sir* Sygismounde
Was with the kynge / and made by grete
   encheson
Of the Garter / a knyght so in that
   stounde
And to the reule / and ordreur sworne
   and bounde
And had his stall / vpon the kynges lifte
   honde   *125*
In the Colage / of seynt George I vndyr-
   stonde

LONDON LICKPENNY

This poem narrates in stumbling metre, but with freedom and vivacity, the experiences of a poor Kentishman in Westminster and London. The author, speaking in his own person, represents himself as going the round of the lawyers in Westminster Hall to get a hearing for his case; but as he has no money, no one will take it up. He leaves Westminster and goes through the city of London, among the hawkers and vendors, to Billingsgate, where he would fain ferry over to the Surrey and Kent side of the Thames. Here again his lack of money is against him, but ultimately he gets back to his plow, resolved to meddle no more with the law.

A similar descriptive effort is seen in the seventeenth-century poem The Puisnes Walks about London, printed in Reliquiae Antiquae, ii :70, from MS Harley 3910. And cf. the Latin parody in Carmina Burana, pp. 22-23; also the complaint against the ecclesiastical law-courts printed from Harley 2253 by Wright in his Political Songs. . . John to Edward II, 1839, p. 155, and by Böddeker, Altengl. Dichtungen, p. 107.

Of the poem two recensions are known, in MSS Brit.Mus.Harley 367 and Harley 542. Both volumes are miscellaneous collections, the latter written for the most part in the tiny needle-script of John Stow (died 1605) and the other composed of papers of Stow's age or later. Stow's own copy, here printed, names no author; but in his Survey of London he gives a synopsis of part of it and attributes it to Lydgate; see the ed. of the Survey by Kingsford, Oxford, 1908, i :217. And the recension of Harley 367, in a loose scrawl not that of Stow, is headed "London Lyckpeny A Ballade compyled by Dan Iohn Lydgate monke of Bery about . . . yeres agoe, and now newly ouersene and amended." A blank is left by the scribe before the word yeres. Both recensions were printed parallel by me in Anglia 20 :404-420 (1898), with the suggestion that part at least of the "amended" condition of the Harley 367 text was its change of the eight-line stanza as copied by Stow to the seven-line stanza. I also seconded the rejection of the poem from the Lydgate canon, made by ten Brink in a note to vol. ii of his History of English Literature.

But the Harley 367 version, which is in its own heading stated to be an alteration from Lydgate, has been many times printed as his :—by Strutt in Horda Angelcynnan, London, 1775-6; by Hughson in his 'London,' 1805, ii :124-7; by Sir Harris Nicolas in his Chronicle of London, 1827, appendix; by Halliwell in his ed. of Lydgate's Minor Poems, 1840; by Gilfillan in his Specimens of the Less-Known British Poets, Edinburgh, 1860, i :49; by Henry Morley in his Shorter English Poems, 1876-82, p. 53; by Skeat in his Specimens of Engl. Lit. 1394-1579, fifth ed. Oxford, 1890; by H. M. Fitzgibbon in Early Engl. Poetry, London, 1887; by Bronson in his Old and Middle Engl. Poems, 1910, pp. 166-69. The Harley 542 recension, that for which we have Stow's assertion of Lydgate's authorship, was printed by Nicolas as above, by me as stated, and by Sir Frederick Bridge in his Old Cryes of London, London, 1921, pp. 16-20.

Since the appearance of the two texts in Anglia, there has been some tendency to reject the poem from the Lydgate canon, notably in Dr. MacCracken's introd. to his volume of Lydgate's Minor Poems, EETS 1911; but the earlier formula is followed by Saintsbury in his Engl. Prosody, i :225, by the Cambridge

Hist. of Eng. Lit. ii :228, by Courthope in his Hist. Eng. Poetry, i :326, and by
the New Eng. Dict. s. v. *common pleas.*
Halliwell meddled with the title, changing it to *London Lackpenny.* Skeat
corrected this "popular etymology", but it reappears in Courthope and in Compton-
Ricketts' London Life of Yesterday, p. 88. Skeat compared James Howell's *Lon-
dinopolis,* 1657, where it is said that London is called Lickpenny, just as Paris is
called Pickpurse, because of its expensiveness.
The text is discussed by J. H. Kern in Neophilologus iii :286-300.

london licpenye /

In london there I was bent
I saw my selfe, where trouthe shuld be a
 teynte
fast to westminstar ward I went
to a man of lawe, to make my complaynt
I sayd for maris love, that holy seynt 5
have pity on the powre, that would procede
I would gyve sylvar, but my purs is faynt
for lacke of money, I may not spede /

2

As I thrast thrughe out the thronge
amonge them all, my hode was gonn 10
netheles I let not longe,
to kyngs benche tyll I come
by fore a juge I kneled anon
I prayd hym for gods sake he would take
 hede
full rewfully to hym I gan make my
 mone 15
for lacke of money I may not spede /

3

benethe hym sat clerks, a great rowt
fast they writen by one assent
there stode vp one, and cryed round
 about
Richard Robert and one of Kent 20
I wist not wele what he ment
He cried so thike there in dede
there were stronge theves shamed & shent
but they that lacked money mowght not
 spede /

4

vnto the comon place y yowde thoo 25
where sat one with a sylken houde
I dyd hym reverence as me ought to do
I tolde hym my case, as well as I coude
and seyd all my goods by nowrd and by
 sowde
I am defrawdyd with great falshed 30

he would not geve me a momme of his
 mouthe
for lake of money, I may not spede /

5

Then I went me vnto the Rollis
before the clerks of the chauncerie
there were many qui tollis 35
but I herd no man speke of me
before them I knelyd vpon my kne
shewyd them myne evidence & they began to reade
they seyde trewer things might there
 nevar be
but for lacke of money I may not
 spede / 40

6

In westminster hall I found one
went in a longe gowne of ray
I crowched I kneled before them anon
for marys love of helpe I gan them pray
as he had be wrothe, he voyded away 45
bakward, his hand he gan me byd
I wot not what thou menest gan he say
ley down sylvar, or here thow may not
 spede /

7

In all westminstar hall I could find nevar
 a one
that for me would do, thowghe I shulde
 dye 50
wtout þe dores, were flemings grete woon
vpon me fast they gan to cry
and sayd mastar what will ye copen or by
fine felt hatts, spectacles for to rede
of this gay gere, a great cause why 55
for lake of money I might not spede /

8

Then to westminster gate y went
when the sone was at highe prime
Cokes to me, they toke good entent
called me nere, for to dyne 60
and proferyd me good brede ale & wyne

a fayre clothe they began to sprede
rybbes of befe, bothe fat and fine
but for lacke of money I might not
    spede /

9

In to london I gan me hy
of all the lond it bearethe the prise
hot pescods,one gan cry
strabery rype,and chery in the ryse
one bad me come nere and by some spice
pepar and saffron they gan me bede   70
clove, grayns, and flowre of rise
for lacke of money I might not spede /

10

Then into Chepe I gan me drawne
where I sawe stond moche people
one bad me come ner, and by fine cloth of
    lawne
paris thred, Coton, and vmple
I seyde there vpon I could no skyle
I am not wont there to in dede
one bad me by an hewre, my hed to hele
for lake of money I might not spede / 80

11

Then went I forth by london stone
Thrwghe out all canywike strete
drapers to me they called anon
grete chepe of clothe, they gan me hete
then come there one, and cried hot shepes
    fete
Risshes faire & grene, an othar began to
    grete
both melwell and makarell I gan mete
but for lacke of money I myght not
    spede /

12

Then I hied me into estchepe
one cried ribes of befe, and many a pie 90
pewtar potts they clatteryd on a heape
ther was harpe pipe and sawtry
ye by cokke, nay by cokke some began to
    cry
some sange of Jenken and Julian, to get
    them selvs mede
full fayne I wold hadd of that mynstralsie
but for lacke of money I cowld not
    spede /

13

Into Cornhill anon I yode
where is moche stolne gere amonge
I saw wher henge myne owne hode
that I had lost in westminstar amonge þe
    throng   100
then I beheld it with lokes full longe
I kenned it as well as I dyd my crede
to by myne owne hode agayne, me thought
    it wrong
but for lacke of money I might not
    spede /

14

Then came the taverner,and toke (me)
    by þe sleve   105
and seyd ser a pint of wyn would yow
    assay
syr quod I it may not greve
for a peny may do no more then it may
I dranke a pint, and therefore gan pay
sore a hungred away I yede   110
for well london lykke peny for ones &
    eye
for lake of money I may not spede /

15

Then I hyed me to byllingesgate
and cried wagge wagge gow hens
I praye a barge man for gods sake   115
that they would spare me myn expens
he sayde ryse vp man,and get the hens
what wenist thow I will do on þe my
    almes dede
here skapethe no man, by nethe ij pens
for lacke of money I myght not spede /

16

Then I conveyed me into Kent   121
for of the law would I medle no more
by caws no man to me would take entent
I dight me to the plowe, even as I ded be-
    fore
Ihesus save london, that in bethelem
    was bore   125
and every trew man of law god graunt
    hym souls med
and they that be other, god theyr state
    restore
for he that lackethe money, wt them he
    shall not spede /
    Explicet london lykke peny /

THE LIBEL OF ENGLISH POLICY

Lines 1-563

This "libel", or "little book", of English policy, was written by an unknown hand soon after 1436. The copies of it thus far listed are orthographically poor, full of errors and variants; they differ also somewhat in length, the text of Bodl. Laud 704 having 1156 lines, but others less. A marked difference among the thirteen (or fourteen) known MSS[1] is in the stanzas of epilogue. One type of this epilogue is addressed to Lord Hungerford, i.e., Walter baron Hungerford, who was prominent in the royal council from 1426 to 1449; it is found in three MSS and in the print by Hakluyt, 1599, from a text not now known but apparently better than the surviving copies. This recension was printed, from Laud 704, by Wright in his Political Songs and Poems, 1859-61, ii:157-205. Wright's text was revised and annotated by W. Hertzberg, with an introduction by R. Pauli, Leipzig, 1878; but this edition standardizes the spelling and emends freely. The other epilogue, also of two stanzas, is addressed to three persons, "bishop and yerle and baron plentivous", no names being given; a copy is printed in the Notes below. Another difference between the two recensions is found in line 9; the Laud MS there says of the emperor Sigismund "whyche yet regneth", while the later recension reads "which late regned" or "of high renowne". As Sigismund died in December 1437, and as the text of both recensions alludes to the attack on Calais by the duke of Burgundy in 1436 and to the taking of Harfleur in the same year, we can date the Laud type of text very closely; but there is as yet no means of dating the other recension. Sir George Warner, in his critical edition of the poem, considers that it cannot be separated from the earlier form of text by any such interval as Hertzberg conjectured, but probably followed soon.

The poem, written in five-beat couplets, is arranged in twelve chapters of unequal length, with a stanzaic prologue and epilogue. Certain of the chapters list the "commoditees" of Spain, Portugal, Brittany, Scotland, Hainault, Genoa, Ireland, etc., each description leading to an urgent demand on Government to control all this sea-borne trade bound for the marts of Flanders past English shores. Illustrative anecdotes are interspersed,—Edward III's dealings with the duke of Brittany, the sharp practices of Venetian woolbuyers, Hankyn Lyons the pirate, the wisdom of King Edgar, the prowess of Henry the Fifth. The writer's recurrent and constantly emphasized themes are the need for English sovereignty of the Channel or "narrow sea", and the need for stringent laws controlling foreign woolbuyers in England.

Great difficulties attend the attempt to generalize about English commerce and industry in the fifteenth century. Besides the lack of available information on many points, there is the contradiction between records existing for one part of the country and those remaining for others. It would seem, to steer a middle course, that the English agricultural districts were in this period depressed, often impoverished, while many of the towns, especially those engaged in the cloth trade, were

---

[1] Bodl. Laud 704, Pepys 1461 at Magdalene College Cambridge; two copies in Brit. Mus. Harley 78 (the second imperfect at close); Harley 271, Harley 4011 impf. at close; Brit. Mus. Adds. 40673 and Cotton Vitellius E x, the latter damaged by fire; Bodl. Rawlinson poetry 32 and All Souls College, Oxford, ciii; codices of the Cowper and of the Gurney collections; the former Phillipps MS 8299, now no. 140 of the Huntington Library, California. Add the MS back of the Hakluyt print.

rapidly rising into wealth and power. The way in which the busy East and South coast towns, with their foreign commerce and their active manufacturing gilds, adopted the system of money payments and of credit, organized for overseas trade, and made themselves heard in Parliament, is a world removed from the situation of the stagnant country manor, its owner unable to collect his dues, harassed by the difficulty of procuring labor, and often semi-isolated by the badness of the roads. It is with the prosperous trading towns that the Libel of English Policy deals; the voice of the rimester is that of the ambitious thriving exporter, the eager partisan of "protection" and of the sovereignty of the narrow sea.

England had long been aware of her advantage of position, lying just off the French and Flemish coasts, at the throat of the water route from Mediterranean countries to Flanders and to the Baltic. She had, however, made no effort to assert this advantage beyond the theoretical assumption to herself of "the sovereignty of the sea". This "sovereignty" seems to have consisted in requiring salute from all foreign shipping in the Channel to any English craft there encountered, and was not carried to exaction of tribute such as Venice imposed upon all shipping in the Adriatic, as Genoa sought to demand from craft entering the Ligurian Sea, or as Denmark and Sweden practiced in the Baltic. England did not even prohibit the Dutch from fishing freely in the Channel waters, until Stuart times; and although in 1420 such restraining legislation was petitioned for, Henry V refused.

One reason for this abstinence may have been England's lack of power to enforce the claim, and another may have been her unwillingness to antagonize nations who were not only her customers, but in large measure the carriers of her foreign trade. At the opening of the fifteenth century England was still far behind Flanders, Genoa, Venice, and other countries in her shipping. The bulk of what reached her shores and of what was carried away,—wine, silks, cloth, oil, spices as imports, and raw wool, tin, lead, etc., as exports—came and went in foreign bottoms. English merchants visited the great foreign fairs, but the volume of trade thus obtained did not induce them to build and man their own ships for transportation. Until the Hundred Years' War broke out, England as a market was relatively unimportant, and her traders betook themselves for custom to the fairs or "marts" of Burgundy and Champagne.

These fairs are, with the "staple" system of English exports and other restrictions on international commerce, the marked peculiarities of medieval trade. Until late in the Middle Ages the volume of trade in any one place was not constant enough to warrant the permanent domicile of merchants there. Hence the institution of fairs or marts, sometimes under the shadow of a renowned saint or relic, sometimes determined by a convenient road or river, but usually coinciding with Church festivals so as to catch the stream of pilgrims, and always "sublet" by some seigneur to a town or a monastic brotherhood, for value received. These latter in their turn leased the booths, arranged hostel for the travellers, and collected dues on the sales. The fairs lasted from eight days to eight weeks, and filled the year in pretty regular sequence. Thus, Troyes had a summer fair and a winter fair; and in the intervening time, from Sept. 14 to Nov. 2, was held the fair of St. Ayoul; from the date of the Troyes winter fair's closing, Jan. 1, to the Wednesday before mid-Lent, extended the fair of Lagny; and that of Bâr followed on the six weeks assigned to Lagny, etc. The most important French fairs lay along a topographical line from Provence to Flanders through the valleys of the Rhone,

Saône, Somme, Oise, Seine; here were the towns of Montpellier, Nimes, Lyon, Besançon, Troyes, Paris, Beauvais, Arras, and Calais. To these centers streamed at the appointed time the trade of Europe, moving on to the next fair northward or southward as the merchant's advantage might dictate. At the greater fairs were to be seen not only Northerners with their furs, Englishmen with their wool, and Provençals with their wines and cheeses, but Lombards with their silks, Spaniards with their leather, Genoese with armor and swords, Venetians with jewels and laces, Germans with linens, Orientals with dyestuffs, spices, coffee, drugs, and slaves. Both geographical and political position favored the county of Champagne, where lay several of these towns, down to the fourteenth century. Such an influx of Mediterranean and Flemish merchants was made possible not only by the great rivers, but by the political neutrality of the counts of Champagne; and when, by the marriage of its heiress Jeanne to Philip IV of France in the early fourteenth century, the county was drawn into the quarrels of the Domain Royal, its commercial prestige declined with the departure of its peace. No part of France, not even Normandy, suffered more than Champagne and Burgundy during the Hundred Years' War; and long before that war was at its height the fairs of eastern France had yielded priority to those of the Low Countries. Bruges, and later Antwerp, became the principal marts of Western Europe, and to them, as to other Flemish towns now rising into prominence, went the stream of Mediterranean commerce.

That stream was no longer overland; the war-conditions of the French valleys forbade. The trade route north and south became a sea-route, which, of course, traversed the English Channel; but off the coasts of France and of the Low Countries there raged all through the later Middle Ages violent and continual sea-warfare. It was not so much by bands of pirates fighting for their own hand, as in the North Sea, that the Channel and the adjacent waters were infested, but by the plague of privateering, of warfare licensed by royal letters of reprisal for injury already received. Overtly the rulers of France, of England, of the Low Countries, framed treaties covering commercial matters and entered formal legal protest against any breach of maritime law by their neighbors; but covertly they issued to their belligerent subjects these documentary permissions to obtain a revenge which the law's delay denied. As Malo expresses it in his Les Corsaires Dunkerquois, "in spite of the agreements almost yearly between English and Flemings, Flemings and Dutch, in spite of the alliances between France and Burgundy, the sea remained the theatre of incessant warfare, of a legalized brigandage." Merchant ships sailed with convoys, heavily armed, from La Rochelle, from Hull, or from Bruges; but the corsair fleet swooped out of St. Malo or from behind the dunes of the Zwyn and fell upon the laden keels. The records of the time are full of petitions for indemnification, of narratives of cruelty such as the wholesale killing of crews or the abandoning of them in small boats, foodless and waterless, far from land. The coast towns of France and of Southern England were exposed to the descent of pirates, licensed or unlicensed; some communes maintained guards in their harbors; and the sea-robbers were so well-informed and so bold that when Henry IV crossed the outer Thames in 1405, he narrowly escaped capture, although he was convoyed by ships of war. Part of his retinue and of his baggage was indeed taken.

The author of the Libel speaks of this piracy or privateering in his third and fourth chapters and in a few lines devoted to Hankyn Lyons, the French sea-marauder. But his main interest is elsewhere. He insists upon the need for English dominance of the Channel, for acquiring a naval supremacy so evident that every nation shall be obliged to cultivate English friendship lest it be forbidden passage through English waters, and also upon the need for retaliating against foreign exactions by placing restraints on foreign merchants similar to the restraints imposed abroad on English merchants.

The whole medieval trade between England and the Continent was conducted under restrictions. In the first place, the English sovereign, in order to collect the export duty on the wool which was England's main article of commerce, named certain ports as licensed for the shipment, and stationed his collectors there. Edward III, by his Ordinance of the Staple, 1353, specified Newcastle, York, Lincoln, Norwich, Westminster, Canterbury, Chichester, Winchester, Exeter, Bristol, as "staple towns"; each inland town of this list had its port appointed, Hull for York, Yarmouth for Norwich, Sandwich for Canterbury, etc. To these towns came the foreign buyers of wool, bringing their money or their goods for exchange, in a tide which grew steadily greater after the decay of the fairs of Champagne, and which continued to flow alongside the prosperity of the fairs of Flanders. What vexes our author is that the visiting merchant is not held to residence in one place, obliged to "go to host"; and also that such a merchant is not compelled to keep his stay in England within narrow limits such as were imposed upon the English merchant abroad. There had been from Edward I to Henry VI a series of enactments directed to control of the visiting alien; but these had fallen into desuetude or had been evaded; the Libel indignantly demands their enforcement, and in a marginal note beside lines 474 ff. of our manuscript some scribe or reviser comments with disgust on the "wyles and giles" by which the laws were subverted.

Our "poet" must have had a strong personal interest in the wool trade, his country's greatest commercial activity. His indignation has often the ring of individual as much as of national feeling; compare for instance his description of the double-profit system practiced by the Venetians on the commodity and on the exchange. Indeed, despite its limping doggerel expression, the work is a human document throughout. There is a French prose Débat des Hérauts, written perhaps a score of years later than the Libel, 1453-1461, in which the heralds of France and of England argue before Dame Prudence the claims of their respective countries to honor; but that essay is much more general in its terms than is the Libel, lacks its vivacity, and yields the student no such amount of information. The Libel is a poor enough thing as literature, the average product of the fifteenth-century tendency to put into verse any kind of information, were it on husbandry, on table manners, on cookery, on alchemy; but as a revelation of national and personal egoism it has the passion of an Agincourt ballad.

It was printed, from an unknown MS, by Hakluyt as below, and from Laud 704 by Wright as mentioned ante; Wright was revised by Hertzberg, and Hakluyt's text is reprinted by Benham, Univ. of Washington Press, Seattle, 1922. There is a bit of Wright's text repr. in A. S. Cook's Literary Mid. Eng. Reader, Boston, 1915. A critical edition by Sir George Warner, Oxford Univ. Press, is dated 1926. In Brit. Mus. Lansdowne 796 is a condensed rewriting of the Libel into quatrains; this was printed by Wright in his Polit.Poems, ii:282-7. The work has been freely used by historians of English commerce.

SELECT REFERENCE LIST X

Débat des hérauts . . . etc., SATF 1871 (see p. 219 here).

Fortescue, Sir John (d. 1476), is reputed author of a brief prose work on the Comodytes of Englond, printed with his life and works, London, 1869, i:549-554. "Commodities" to Fortescue and his age meant "advantages"; and he enumerates England's rivers, havens, and minerals, besides mentioning her soil as good for sheep and emphasizing that her people are better fed and better clothed than any other nation's. When listing the exports of various countries, he remarks that the goods of all nations are "uttered" in Flanders.

Forrest's Pleasant Poesye of Princelie Practise, 1548, deals among other things with the wool trade; see extracts from it as appendix to Herrtage's ed. of Starkey's Dialogue, EETS 1878, under title England in the Reign of Henry VIII.

Hakluyt, The Principal Navigations, Voyages, Traffiques, and Discoveries of the English Nation, 1598-1600. Text of our poem, repr. as above.

Lydgate's Horse, Goose, and Sheep, ed. Degenhart, Leipzig, 1900, discourses, 288 ff., on the importance of the sheep to England.

Schanz, Englische Handelspolitik gegen Ende des Mittelalters, etc., Leipzig, 1881.

Cunningham, W., Growth of English Industry and Commerce, 3d ed., Cambridge, 1896.

Huvelin, Essai historique sur le droit des marchés et des foires, Paris, 1897.

Fulton, T. W., The Sovereignty of the Sea, Edinburgh, 1911.

Malo, Les corsairs dunkerquois, Paris, 1913.

Kingsford, English Historical Literature in the Fifteenth Century, Oxford, 1913.

Warner, ed. The Libelle of Englyshe Polycye, Oxford, 1926; see introd.

[MS Brit. Mus. Harley 4011, fol. 120a]

HERE BEGYNNETHE THE PROLOGE OF THE LIBELLE OF ENGLISSH POLICIE EXHORTYNG
ALL ENGLONDE TO KEPE THE SEE ENVYROUN AND NAMLY THE NAROW SEE.
SHEWYNG WHAT PROFITE COMETH THEREOF AND ALSO WHAT
WORSHIP AND SALUACION TO ENGLOND

The trew processe . of Englissh policye
Off outward to kepe this lond in rest
Off oure Englond that no man may denye
Men say of sothe this is the best
Who sailethe Southe Northe Est or
   West   5
Cherissh marchauntes kepe the admyralte
That we be maisters of the narow See

2

ffor Sygismond the grete Emperoure
Whiche reigned whan he was in this lond
With kyng Henry the fifte prince of
   honour   10
Here moche glorye as hym thought he
   fond
A myghty lond whiche had take on hond
To werre in ffraunce and make mortalite
And were ever wele kept rounde aboute
   the See

On the MS see the Notes, p. 478.

3

And to the kyng thus he seid my brother
Whan he parseived Caleys and Dover 16
Of all your townes to chese of one and
   other
Kepe the see and sone to come over
And werre outward and your ream to re-
   cover
Kepe this tow townes sir to your maieste
As your twayn eyen kepe wele the narowe
   see   21

4

ffor if this see be kept in tyme of werre
Who can here passe without Daunger or
   wo
Who may ascape who may myschief deferre
Whan marchaundise may not foreby
   go   25
ffor nedis must than take trusse every fo
fflaundres Spayn and all other trust to me

Or els hyndred are the(i) for this narow
See

5

Therfore I cast me by a litelle writyng
To shew at eye this conclusion   *30*
ffor conscience and for myn Acquytyng
Ayenst god and ayenst Abusion
And cowardise and to our enemyes con-
fusion
ffor ·iiij· thynges oure noble sheweth to
me
Kyng · shipp · Swerd · and power of the
See   *35*

6

Where ben our shippes wher ben thei be
come
Our enmyes bid vs for the shipp set a
shepe
Allas our rule halteth it is be nome
Who dare wele sey that lordship shold
take kepe
I wille assay though myn hert begynne to
wepe   *40*
To do this werke yf we wille ever thee
ffor verray shame to kepe the narow see

7

Shall ony prynce what so be his name
Whiche hathe nobles moche like to oures
Be lordes of the See as fflemynges to our
blame   *45*
Stoppe vs · take vs · and so make fade the
floures
Of Englissh astate and disteyn oure
honoures
ffor cowardise allas it shold so be
Therfore I begynne to write of this narow
See

OFF THE COMMEDITEES OF SPAYN AND OF
FFLAUNDRES

Here begynneth the profites in certayn *50*
With commoditees that comethe out of
Spayn
And marchaundise who so wille wete
what it is
Ben ffyges raysyns wyne Bastard and
datis
Likorise Sivile oyle and Grayn
White castell Sope and wexe certayn *55*
Iren wolle wadmole Gotefelle and kid-
felle also
ffor poynt makers full nedfull ben thei
two

Saffron Quyksiluer whiche Spaynyssh
marchaundye
Is in to fflaundres shipped full craftely
Vnto Bruges as to her staple fayre   *60*
To haue at Scluse her haven to repaire
Whiche is cleped the Swyn theire shippes
gidyng
Where many a vesselle are bydyng
But thise marchauntees wt thaire shippes
grete
And such chaffare as thei bye and gete *65*
By the waies must nedes take on hond
By the costes to passe of our Englond
Betwixe Dover and Caleis this is no
doute
Who can wele els suche matirs bryng
aboute
And thise seid marchauntes (dis)charged
be   *70*
Of marchaundise in fflaundres nere the
See
Than thei ben charged agayn with mar-
chaundie
That to fflaundres longeth full richely
ffyne cloth of Ipre that named is better
than oures
Clothe of Curryk fyne clothe of all col-
oures   *75*
Moche ffustian and also lynnen clothe
But ye fflemynges though ye be wroth
The grete substaunce of your cloth atte
fulle
The clothe ye make of our Englissh
wolle
Than may it not synke in mannes
brayn   *80*
But that it must thise marchaundise of
Spayn
Bothe out and in by oure costes passe
He that seith nay in witte is like an asse
Thus yf the see were kept I dare wele
sayn
We shold haue pease wt the growndes
twayn   *85*
ffor Spayn and fflaundres is as eche other
brother
And neither may live welle with outen
other
They may not live to maynteyn theire
degrees
Wtouten our Englissh commoditees
Wolle and tynne of our Englond   *90*
Susteyneth comons fflemynges I vndir-
stond
Than yf Englond wold his wolle restrayn

ffro fflaundres this foloweth in certayn
fflaundres of nede must with vs haue
  pease
Or els it is distroied with outen lease 95
Also yf fflaundres thus Distroied be
Some marchaundise of Spayn wolle never
  thee
ffor distroied it is and as in chief
The wolle of Spayn it cometh not to preef
But yf it be tosed and menged wele 100
Amonge Englissh wolle the gretter dele
ffor Spaynyssh wolle in fflaundres Draped
  is
And ever hathe be that men hathe mynd
  Iwis
And yit wolle is one of the chief mar-
  chaundie
That longeth to Spayn who so list
  aspie   105
It is of litell valew trust vnto me
Wt Englissh wolle but yf it menged be
Thus yf the see be kept than harken hedir
Yf thise two londes come not to gedir
So that the fflete of fflaundres passe
  nought   110
That in the narow see it be not brought
Into the Rochell to seke the fumouse
  wyne
Ne into Bretons baye for salt so fyne
What is than Spayn what is fflaundres
  also
As who seith naught the thrifte is all
  ago   115
ffor the litell lond of fflaundres is
But a staple to other londes Iwis
And all that groweth in fflaundres grayn
  or sede
May not a monthe fynde hem mete and
  brede
What hathe than fflaundres be fflemynges
  leef or lothe   120
But a litell madder and fflemyssh clothe
By drapyng of our wolle in substaunce
Liven her comons this is her governaunce
With out whiche thei may not live at ease
Thus must thei sterve or with vs haue
  pease   125

OFF THE COMMODITEES OF PORTYNGALE

The marchaundise also of portyngale
Into Dyvers londes come to sale
Portyngalers wt vs haue truse in honde
Whos marchaundise commeth moche in
  to Englond

Thei ben our ffrendes wt thaire commoditees   130
And we Englisshe passen into her coun-
  trees
Her lond hathe Oyle · Wyne · osay · wexe
  · and grayn
ffigges · Raisyns · hony · and Cordewayn
Datis · salt hides · and suche marchaundye
And yef thei wold to fflaundres passe fore
  bye   13.
Thei shold not be suffred ones ne twyes
ffor supportyng of oure cruell enemyes
That is to sey fflemynges wt her gile
ffor chaungeable the(i) are in litell while
Than I conclude by resons many moo 140
Yeff we suffred neither frende ne foo
What for enemye and supportyng
Passe ffore by vs in tyme of werryng
Sithe oure frendis wold (not) ben in
  cause
Off our hyndryng yef reson lede this
  clause   14.
Than nedes ffro fflaundres pease shole
  be to vs sought
And other landes shold seche pease doute
  it nought
ffor fflaundres is staple as men telle me
Of all nacions of cristente

OFF THE COMMODITEES OF LITELL
              BRETAIGNE

Furthermore to write I am fayn   150
Somewhat spekyng of litell Bretaigne
The commoditees therof is and was
Salte · wynes · creste clothe · and Canvas
And the lond of fflaundres sikerly
Is the staple of theire marchaundie 15.
Whiche marchaundise may not passe
  away
But by the costes of Englond this is no
  nay
And of this Bretaigne who so the trouthe
  beleves
Are the grettest robbers and theves
That haue ben in the see many a yere 160
That oure marchauntes haue bought all
  to dere
ffor thei haue take notable good of oures
On this seid see thise seid pillours
Called (of) Seint malouse and els where
Whiche to their Duke none obeisaunce
  wold bere   16.
With such coloures we haue ben hyndred
  sore

And fayned pease is called no werre here-
fore
Thus thei haue ben in dyuerse costes
many
Of our Englond mo than reherse can I
In Norfolke costes and in other places
aboute   *170*
Robbed brent and slayn by many a route
And thei haue also (raunsomed) towne
to towne
That into regions of bost haue ronne the
sowne
Whiche haue ben ruthe to this ream and
shame
Thei that the see shold kepe are moche
to blame   *175*
ffor Bretaigne is of easy reputacion
And Seint Malouse turneth hem to repro-
bacion

A STORY OF KYNG EDWARDES ORDENAUNCE
FOR BRETAIGNE

Here bryng I in a story to me lent
That a good Squyer in tyme of parlia-
ment
Toke vnto me wele written in a
scrowe
That I comoned with both wt hye and
lowe
Of whiche all men Accorded vnto one
That it was done not many yeres Agone
But whan that noble Kyng Edward the
thirde
Reigned in grace right thus it be tid *185*
For he had A man*er* Iolesye
To his marchauntes and loved hem hertlye
He felt wele the waies the rules of the
see
Wherby marchauntes myght haue pros-
perite
Ther(for) Harflete and Houndflete did
he make   *190*
And grete werres that tyme were vndir
take
Bytwene the kyng and the Duke of
Bretaigne
Atte last to falle to pease bothe were
fayn
Vpon whiche made by convencion
Our marchauntes made hem redy
bown   *195*
Toward Bretaigne wt their*e* marchaundie
Wenyng hem frendes and thedir yode
boldly
But sone Anon our*e* marchauntes were
Itake

And we sped neuer the better*e* for truses
sake
They lost her goodes her money and her*e*
spendyng   *200*
Than thei complayned hem vnto the kyng
Than woxe the kyng wrothe and to the
Duke sent
And complayned how suche harme was
hent
Vndir convencion and pease made so re-
fused
The Duke sent Ayene and hym ex-
cused   *205*
Rehersyng that the mounte of seint
Michell
Nor seint Malous wold never A dele
Be subiecte vndir his governaunce
Ne be vndir his obeisaunce
And so with out hym thei did that
dede   *210*
Amendes he wold none make he seide
Wherfor the kynge in hast sette a Iuge-
ment
Wtout callyng of any parliament
Or grete tary to take longe Avise
To fortefye anon he did devise   *215*
Our Englissh townes that is to sey
Dertmouth Plymouthe and Fowey
And yaf hem help and notable pusaunce
Wt Insistence to sette hem in govern-
aunce
Vpon litell Bretaigne for to werre   *220*
Than good see men wold not deferre
But bete hem home that thei myght not
route
Toke prisoners And lerned hem to loute
Than the Duke in like wise
Wrote to the Kynge for the truse   *225*
The Kyng Aunswered how his mayne
wode
Wt grete power were passed over the
flode
To distroie the Dukes londe
Ayenst his wille I vndirstonde
And whan the Duke say how that townes
thre   *230*
Shold haue distroied his countre
He than made suerte trew and not fals
ffor mount Michell and seint Malous als
And for all the parties of litell Bretaigne
Whiche to obeye as seid was were not
fayne   *235*
So that all the lyf (tyme) of the kynge
Marchauntes had pease wt out warryng

He made a statute for lombardes in this
  lond
That thei shold in no wise take on hond
Here to enhabite to charge and dis-
  charge   240
But · xl · daies no more had thei large
This good kynge of suche Apreef
Kept his marchauntes in the see fro
  myschief

OF THE COMODITEES OF SCOTLOND AND
     DRAPYNG OF HER WOLLE IN
             FFLAUNDRES

Also over all Scotland the commoditees
'Are felles hides and of wolle the flees 245
All this must passe by vs away
In to fflaundres by Englond this is no
  nay
And all her wolle is draped for to selle
In the townes of poperyng and of Belle
Which the Duke of Gloucestre in grete
  Ire   250
ffor her falshede sete vpon a fire
And yit thei of Belle and Poperyng
Coude never drape her wolle for any
  thyng
But yef thei had englissh wolle wt all
Our goodly wolle it is so generalle   255
Nedfull to hem of Spayn and Scotland
  als
And other costes this (sentence) is not
  fals
Ye worthi marchauntes I do it vpon yow
That this is trew ye wote wele how
ffor the staple of that marchaundie   260
Of Scotland is fflaundres truly
Than the Scottes ben charged at eye
Out of fflaundres wt litell mercerye
And grete plente of haberdasshe ware
And (half ther shippes) wt cart wheles
  bare   265
And (with) Barowes are laden in sub-
  staunce
Thus must rude ware ben her cheve-
  saunce
So may thei not forbere this fflemyssh
  lond
Therfore yef we wold manly take on hond
To kepe the see fro fflaundres and fro
  Spayn   270
And fro Scotland and fro litell Bretaigne
We shold right sone haue pease for all
  her bostes
ffor thei must nedes passe by oure Eng-
  lisshe costes

OF THE COMMODITEES OF PRUCE AND HIGH
    DUCHE MEN AND ESTERLYNGES
[48 lines of Harl. 4011 are now omitted
in this print. The passage in other MSS
has 54 lines.]
OF þE COMMODITEES OF þE JANUAYSE &
       HER GRETE CARRIKES
The Januays comen in sondry wise
Into this lond wt dyuerse marchaundise
In grete Carrikes arraied wt outen lak
With clothes of gold and Siluer & pepir
  blak   325
Thei brynge with hem waad grete plente
Wolle oyle waad asshen by vessels in the
  see
Coton Roche Alom and good gold of
  Jean
And thei ben charged with wolle ayen
And wollen clothe of oures of coloures
  all   330
And thei aventure as ofte it dothe befalle
Into fflaundres wt suche thynges as thei
  bye
That is theire chief staple sikerly
And yef thei wold be our (fulle) enmyes
Thei shold not passe our stremys Iwise

OFF THE COMMODITEES OF THE VENYSIANS
  AND FFLORENTYNES WT THEIRE GALIES
The grete Galeys of venyse and fflorence
Be wele laden with thynges of compla-
  cience
All Spicery and Grocers ware
Wt swete wynes all maner of chaffare
Apes / Japes / and Marmesettes /
  tayled   340
Nifles / trifles / that litell haue availed
And other thynges whiche thei blere wt
  our eye
Whiche thynges be not Duryng that we
  bye
ffor moche of this chaffare that is vnstable
Might be for born for thei ben disceiv-
  able   345
And yitt I wene as for infirmitees
In Englond are suche commoditees
Wt out help of any other londe
Whiche by witte and practik bethe I
  founde
That all humours myght be voided
  sure   350
Of that we gadir in our englissh cure
That we shold haue no nede to Scamonye
Turbit / Euforbe / Correcte / Dagardye
Rubarbe / Sene / and yit thei bene towo
  nedfull
But ther ben thynges also spedfull   355

That growen here as thise thynges fayned
Lette of this matir no man be dismaied
But that a man myght void in firmyte
With out thise drugges fro be yonde the
    see
And yf ther shold be except ony thyng *360*
It were but Sugre trust to my senynge
He that trusteth not to my sentence
Lette hym better seche experience
In this matir I wille no ferther plese
Who so not beleveth let hym leve and
    cease   *365*
Thus thise Galeys fore theire likyng ware
And etyng ware beren hens our best
    chaffare
Clothe wolle and Tynne whiche as is
    seid beforn
Out of this lond myght worse be for-
    born
ffor eche other lond of necessite   *370*
Haue grete nede to bye one of thise thre
And we resceive for hem in to this cost
Ware and chaffare that lightly wille be
    lost
And wold Ihesu that our lordes wolde
Considre this welle bothe yonge and
    olde   *375*
Namly elder that haue experience
That myght the yonger exhorte to pru-
    dence
What harme what hurt what hyndraunce
Is Done to vs vnto our grete grevaunce
Of such londes and of thise nacions *380*
As experte men shew by probacions
By writyng Are discovered our counseils
By fals colours alway the countertails
Of oure enemyes that dothe vs hyndryng
Vnto oure goodes our Ream and to the
    kyng   *385*
As wise men haue shewed welle at eye
And all this is coloured by marchaundie

AN ENSAMPLE OF A GRETE DISCEITE

Also thei bere the gold out of this lond
And sowketh the thrifte out of our hond
As the waspe sowketh hony of the be *390*
So mynnyssheth our commodite
Now wolle ye here how thei in Cottes-
    wold
Were wonte to borow as it shold be sold
Here wolles good as fro yere to yere
Of clothe and tynne thei did in like
    maner   *395*
And in theire Galeys shipp theire mar-
    chaundie
Than some at venyse of hem wille it bye

Thei vtter ther the chaffare by the peyse
And lightly also ther thei make her reise
And whan the goodes ben at venyse
    solde   *400*
Than to cary her chaunge thei ben full
    bolde
Into fflaundres whan thei this money haue
Thei wille it profir their sotelte to save
To englissh Marchauntes to yeve it out
    by eschaunge
To be paid agayn thei make not straunge
Here in Englond semyng for the better
At the resceivyng and sight of lettir
By ·iiij· pens losse in the noble rounde
That is·xii·d·losse in the goldyn
    pounde
And yef we wille haue of payment   *410*
A ffull monthe than must we assent
To·viij·d·losse that is shillynges twayn
In the englisshe pounde and ofte sone
    agayn
ffor two monthes·xij·d·must hym pay
In the englisshe pounde what it is to
    say   *415*
But·iij·shillynges so that in poundes
    fele
For hurte and harme hard it is wt hem to
    dele
And whan englisshe marchauntes haue
    content
This eschaunge in Englond by assent
Than thise venysians haue in wone   *420*
And ffiorentynes to bere her gold sone
Over the see into fflaundres agayn
And thus thei live in fflaundres sothe to
    sayn
And in london with suche chevesaunce
That men calle vsure to oure losse and
    hyndraunce   *425*

ANOTHER ENSAMPLE OF A GRETE DISCEITE

Now listen wele how thei made vs a
    baleys
Whan thei borowed atte towne of Caleys
As thei were wonte their wolle to hem
    lent
ffro yere to yere thei shold make pay-
    ment
And somtyme·ij·yere and·ij·yere *430*
This was faire lone but yit wolle ye here
How thei to Brigges wold her wolle carry
And for hem take payment without tary
And selle it fast for redy money in hond
ffor·L·pounde losse thei wold not wond
In a thousand pounde and live therby
Tille the day of payment easely

Come agayn in eschaunge makyng
ffull like vsure as men make vndirtakyng
Than whan this payment of a thousand
   pounde   440
Was welle content thei shold haue chaf-
   fare sounde
Yf thei wold fro the staple fulle
Resceive   agayn · iiij · thousand   pounde
   of wolle
In Cotteswold also thei ride aboute
All Englond and byen wt out dowte 445
What thei list wt fredom and fraunchise
More than we englisshe may gete in any
   wise
But wold god that without lenger delayes
Here galeys were vnfraught in · xl ·
   dayes
And in · xl · dayes charged agayn   450
And that they myght be put in certayn
To go to host as we with hem do
It were expediente that thei did right
   so
As we do ther yf the kyng wold it
A what worship wold falle to englissh
   witte   455
What profite also to our marchaundie
Wiche wold of nede be cherisshed hert-
   lye
I wold wete whi our navie failethe
Whan many a foo vs atte dore assailethe
Now thise days that yef ther come a
   nede   460
What navie shold we haue it is to drede
   [12 lines omitted in this print]

NOW TO THE PRYNCIPALL MATIR

What reason is it that we shall go to host
In her countrees and in this englissh
   cost   475
They shall not so but haue more liberte
Than we our self now also mote I the
I wolde men shold to yiftes take none
   hede
That letteth our thing publius for to
   spede
ffor this we see wele every day at eye 480
Giftes and festes stoppen our policye
Now se that foles ben either thei or we
But ever we haue the worse in this coun-
   tre
Therfore lette hem vnto host go here
Or be we fre wt hem in like manere 485
In theire countrees and yf it wold not be
Compelle hem vnto host and ye shall se

Moche avauntage and moche profite arise
Moche more than I can write in any wise

OFF OURE DISCHARGE AND CHARGE AT HER
MARTES

Conseive wele here that englisshe men at
   martes   490
Ben discharged for all her craftes and
   artes
In the Braban of her marchaundye
In · xiiij · daies (and) agayn hastly
In the same · xiiij · daies are charged efte
And yf thei abide lenger all is be refte 495
Anon thei shold forfaite theire goodes
   alle
Of marchaundise it shold not better falle
And we to martes of Braban charged ben
With englisshe clothe full goode (and
   fayre) to sen
We ben ayene charged with mercery 500
Haberdassh ware and wt Grocery
To whiche Martes that englissh men calle
   faires
Eche nacion maketh ofte her repaires
Englissh . ffrenssh . Duche . lombardes
   and Januayes
Cathalons thedir make her waies   505
Scottes . Spaynardes . Irissh men ther
   abides
Whiche grete plente bryngen of Irissh
   hides
And I here sey that we in Braban bye
More plente of theire marchaundye
In comon vse than dothe all other na-
   cions   510
This I haue herd of marchauntes rela-
   cions
And yf the englissh be not in the martes
Thei ben feble and as naught ben her
   partes
ffor thei bye more and fro purse put out
ffor marchaundise than all the other rout
And þe see were kept þt shippes shold
   not bryng ne fecche   516
Than the carrys wold not thedir strecche
Than shold tho martes full evell thee
Yif we manly kept about the see

OFF THE COMMODITEES AND MARCHAUN-
DISE OF BRABAN SELANDE AND HENAUDE

The marchaundise of Braban and Seland
Bethe madir and wad that dyers take on
   hond   521
To dyne wt Garlik and Oynons

And Salt fyssh als for husbondes and
    comons
But thei of Selond at Caleis bye our
    felles
And our wolle that english men hem
    selles   525
And the chaffare that englissh men byen
In the martes no man may denyen
It is nat made in Braban that countre
It cometh out of henavde and not by the
    see
But all by land Icaried and fro ffraunce
ffro Burgayn Camerite Colayn in sub-
    staunce
Therfore at martes yef ther by ony re-
    straynt
Men seyn playnly that list no fables paynt
Yef englissh men be with draw away
Is grete rebuke losse and affray   535
As though we sent in to the land of
    ffraunce
xx · thousand men of (good) pussaunce
To werre vnto her hyndryng multiplye
So ben our englissh marchauntes neces-
    sarye
Whether it be thus assay and ye schull
    weten   540
Of men expert by whom I haue this
    writen
ffor seid is whan this caried marchaundie

Draweth as moche to valew sikerly
As all the good that cometh in schippes
    thedir
Whiche englissh men bye most and bryng
    hedir   545
ffor her martes ben feble shame to say
But englissh men thedir dresse her way

A CONCLUSION OF THIS DEPENDYNG OF
          KEPYNG OF þE SEE

Than I conclude yf men so moche be of
    lond
Were by carres brought vnto her hond
Were þe see welle kept in govern-
    aunce   550
Thei shold by see haue no delyueraunce
We shold hem stoppe and hem distroye
As prisoners we shold hem noye
And so we shold of our cruell enemyes
Make our frendes for fere of marchaun-
    dise   555
Yf thei were not suffred forto passe
Into fflaundres but we (be) fre as glasse
And as Brasile not tough ne abidyng
But whan grace shyneth than sone we are
    slidyng
We wille it not resceive in any wise 560
That maketh lust envye and Covetise
Expounde me this and the sothe Ifynde
Bere it away and kepe it in your mynde

[The text continues for about 500 lines more]

GEORGE RIPLEY: THE COMPEND OF ALCHEMY

Preface and Prohibicio

Of George Ripley, canon of Bridlington in Yorkshire and an alchemical writer, little is known but his work. His Compend of Alchemy was dedicated to Edward the Fourth in 1471, and in 1476 Ripley presented to Nevill archbishop of York a similar work in Latin, the Medulla Alchimiae, with a request for a home in some religious house. Manuscripts of both works are fairly numerous, and in many of those of the English poem there appears a preface of sixteen lines assigning it to Ripley, mentioning his study in Italy, and saying that he dwelt "aforetime" at Exning or Yxning. We have as yet no more information about him.

Manuscripts of the Compend are not yet listed, and probably not all recognized. That at Aberystwyth, South Wales, from which I print the Prohibicio, came to light in 1912; codices are known at Corpus Christi College Oxford, Univ. Libr. Cambridge Ff ii:23, Trinity College Cambridge O 2,16 and O 5,31, and Harley 367 of the British Museum, in the hand of John Stow. The preface to the poem is in Brit. Mus. Sloane 299, and there is a fragment in Univ. Libr. Cambridge Kk vi:30.

The Compend was printed in 1591, and in Elias Ashmole's Theatrum Chemicum Britannicum, 1652. In 1658 appeared Ripley Reviv'd: or an Exposition upon Sir George Ripley's Hermetico-Poetical Works; see Corser's Collectanea, ix:197.

The work consists of a dedicatory letter to Edward the Fourth, in thirty eight-line stanzas; Ripley therein says that he was earlier called upon to impart his knowledge to the king, while he was at the University of Louvain; that he wrote Edward thence secretly, and is now prepared to reveal much more valuable information to his sovereign, and to him alone. A general prologue of thirteen seven-line stanzas follows this letter, and the preface follows upon the prologue. This preface, of twenty-nine stanzas rime royal, closes with a list of the twelve chapters of the ensuing work; and to these twelve chapters, which constitute the body of the Compend, there is added a final "Prohibicio" of fifteen stanzas. Despite the attempt at lofty and "aureate" language in the preface, the work has no claim whatever to be considered literature; but it has an antiquarian value, and a value as parallel or footnote to Chaucer's Canon's Yeoman's Tale. Indeed, Ashmole includes in his Theatrum both Chaucer's tale and Lydgate's Churl and Bird, which he entitles Hermes Bird, and to which he gives an alchemical interpretation.

Royal interest in alchemy, as shown by both Henry the Sixth and Edward the Fourth, was doubtless responsible for the reappearance of the pseudo-science after its suppression during the early fifteenth century. Several of the numerous writers contemporary with Ripley are represented in Ashmole's volume, where may be read Norton's Ordinall of Alchemy, Charnock's Breviary of Natural Philosophy, and various briefer anonymous pieces, all with introductions and notes by Ashmole, an ardent believer in the science. The student may consult also Gower's Confessio Amantis, iv: 2450-2630, the EETS edition of the Boke of Quynt Essence, Lydgate's Secreta Secretorum, Ben Jonson's Alchemist as ed. by Hathaway, 1903, Waite's translation of Paracelsus, London, 1894, Thorndike's History of Magic, N. Y., 1923, Skeat's notes to the Canon's Yeoman's Tale, etc.

But from the summary of alchemical principles, given in my notes below, no clear and definite explanation must be expected; the subject is too cloudy and fantastic to admit of such statement.

I use the form of title as in the MSS, passing over the modern "Compound of Alchemy". The word *compendium* or *compend* meant a succinct statement, which was apparently Ripley's intention. Of other works by him, as listed by Bale and repeated by Ashmole, I take no account here; the question of a Ripley canon is not yet investigated.

Most of the copies of the Compend which I have examined are poorly written, often contained in sixteenth-century compilations of alchemical works. The Aberystwyth codex is a notable exception. It is a paper volume of 27 leaves, 17 by 11 inches, sewed into a vellum cover, and is of the Compend only. The hand is large and somewhat coarse, the ink still very dark and the paper clean and white. Mutilations of some lower leaf-corners injure the text occasionally. The last two folios, not needed for the Compend, are filled by a later hand with writing and pen-drawings. There is no letter to Edward the Fourth; the work begins with the prologue and goes through the Prohibicio. Other MSS lack sometimes the Prohibicio, sometimes the prologue; the Cambridge Ff volume is often rubbed to illegibility. I use the Aberystwyth codex for the Prohibicio here, and print some stanzas of the preface (not the prologue) from the Ff and the Corpus texts.

Oh hyghe incomperable and moste glori-
　ose trinyte
Whose lumynouse beames obtundythe *our*
　speculation
Oh onehede in sothe oh trynhede in deite
Of Iierarchycall Iubilesses the gratulat
　gloryfycation
O pietouse pueryfyer of Soules & pure
　perpetuation
Of deviant into daunger oh drawer moste
　debonayr
In thys envyouse valey of vanyte Oh our
　exalter

*　*　*　*　*　*

5

And among other whych ben pro*ffessed
　to thee
I me present as one wyth humble sub-
　myssyon　　　　　　　　　　　30
Thy servant besechyng that I may be
And trev in lyvyng accordyng to my pro-
　fessyon
In order . channon reguler of Brydellyng-
　ton

Besechyng thee lord . thou wylt me spare
And to thy trew *s*ervant thy secret de-
　clare

6

In þe begy*n*nyng when thou madest all
　off noght
A globous matter & dark vnder confu-
　syon
By thee the begy*n*ner mervelusly was
　wrought
Conteynyng materyally all thyngs wyth
　out dyvysyon
Of whych thou madst in vj days clere
　dystynccion　　　　　　　　　　40
As in the genysses of the same doth
　recorde
Then heuen and erth were *p*erfected wyth
　þi worde

7

So thorow thy wyll and power out of
　one mas
Consumed . was made all thyngs that
　beyng is
But in thy glory . afore . as maker thou
　was
Now is and shall . wyth out end be Iwys
As a most reverent god . florysshyng in
　all *p*erfeccyon
Of whose innvmerable gyfftes . hath re-
　ceyved many one

Stanza 1 is from the MS Ff ii, 23 of Univ. Libr. Cambridge, but the remaining stanzas of the Preface are from the Corpus copy, as the Ff is badly rubbed. I number the lines of Preface and Prohibicio separately, and without recognition of other parts of the work.

And to sum the secret of the phylosophers
      stone

8

For of one mas was made all thyng   *50*
And ryght so must it in our practyse be
All our secrets of one ymage must spryng
In phylosophers books therfore who lyst
      for to see
Our stone is called the les world one of
      three
Magnesia also of sulphur and mercury
Proporcyonat by nature most perfectly

9

But many one marvayle and marvayle
      maye
And muse on such a marvylous thyng
What is our stone syth phylosophers doo
      say
To such as ever be itt sekyng   *60*
It foules and fysshes to vs doo bryng
Ech man hath it . and it is in ech place
In thee and me . in ech thyng tyme and
      space

10

To this I answere that mercury it is Iwis
But not the commen called quyksylver by
      name
But mercury wythout whych nothyng
      beyng is
All phylosophors truly say the same
But symple sekers put them in blame
Sayeng they hyde it . but they be blame
      worthy
Whych be no clarks and wyll medle wyth
      phylosophy   *70*

11

But thogh it mercury be . yet wysely
      vnde(r)stande
Wherin it is and where thou shalt it seche
Els I thee counsayle take not thys work
      in hande
For phylosophors flatters fooles wyth a
      fayer spech
(But lyste to me for trulye I will þe
      teche)
Whych is the mercury most profytable
Beyng to thee not deceyveable

12

It is more nygh in sum thyng then in
      sum
Therfore take tent . what I to thee wryte

For yf thou never to the knowledge
      com   *80*
Therof yet shalt thou me not wytt
For I wyll truly thee exyte
To vnderstand now mercurys three
The keyse whych of our scyence be

13

Raymond*us* his menstrues he doth them
      calle
Wythout whych truly no truth is done
But two of them be superfycyall
The thyrd essencyall of sonn and mone
Her propertyse I wyll declare ryght sone
And Mercury of other mettall essen-
      cyall   *90*
Is the pryncyple of our stone materiall

14

*Non est mercurius de sole & luna sed de
      alio metallo*

In sonn and mone our menstru is not
      sene
It not aperyth but by effect to syght
That is the stone of whych I mene
Who so our wrytyng conceyveth ryght
It is a soule a substance bryght
Of sonn and mone a subtyle influence
By whych þe erth receyveth resplendence

16

Factum calcem

Bodys wyth the fyrst we calcyne natur-
      ally
Perfect . but none whych be vnclene
Except one whych is vsyally
Named by phylosophors the lyon grene
He is the meane . the sonn & þe mone
      betwene   *110*
Of ioynyng tyncture wyth perfectnes
As Gebar therto bereth wytnes

17

*Distillat calcem in furnace reverbera-
      cionis*

Wyth the second whych is an humydyty
Vegetable revyvyng that before was ded
Both pryncyples materyall must losyd be
And formals els standeth they lytle in sted
Thes menstrues therfore (know) I thee
      rede
Wythout whych neyther treu calcynacyon
Don may be . neyther naturall dis-
      solucyon

18

Recepit flegma per se distillando

Wyth the thyrd humydyty most perma-
  nent   120
Incombustyble and vnctuus in his nature
Hermes tree to asshis is brent
It is our naturall fyer most sure
It is our Mercurius our sulphur wyth
  tincture pure
Our soule our stone borne vp wyth wynde
In the erth engendred bere thys in thy
  mynde

19

Thys stone also tell thee I dare
Is the vapour of metalls potencyall
How thou shalt gett it thou must beware
For invysyble truly is thys menstruall 130
How be it wyth the second water phylo-
  sophycall
By seperacyon of elements it may appere
To syght in forme of water clere

20

Off that menstru by labor exuberate
And with it may be made sulphur of
  nature
If yt be kyndly acuate
And sirculate into a spryt pure
Then to dyssolve thou mayst be sure
The bace wyth yt in dyvers wyse
As thou shalt know by thy practyse   140

21

Circulare lyqidum in siccum est acuare

That poynt þerfore in hys dew place
I wyll declare wyth other mo
Yf god wyll graunte me space and grace
And me preserve in lyff from wo
As I thee tech looke thou doo so
And for thy fyrst ground pryncypall
Vnderstand thy waters menstruall

22

And when thou hast made cyrculacyon
Encresyng not wastyng moysture rady-
  call
To thy bace by offten subtylacyon   150
Wyll lyghtly flow as wax apon metall
Then lose it wyth thy vegytable men-
  struall
Tyll thou hast oyle therof in coloure
  bryght
Then is that menstru vysyble in syght

23

An oyle it is draune out in colour of
  golde
Or lyke therto . out of our fyne red lede
Whych Raymonde sayd when he was olde
Much more then gold wyll stand in stede
For when he was for age nygh dede
He made ther of aurum potabile   160
Whych (hym) revyved as men may see

24

ffor so together may they be cyrculate
That is to say that oyle and that vegytable
  menstruall
Eyther so by laboure exvberat
And made by crafft a stone celestyall
Of nature so fyery that we doo call
Our basylysk eyther our cockatryce
Our grete Elyxer moste of pryce

25

Whych as the syght of a basylyske
  abiecte
Kylleth   so slayeth the crude Mer-
  curye   170
When ther upon it is proiecte
In twynklyng of an eye most sodaynly
That Mercury then tayneth permanently
All bodys to sonn and mone perfect
Thus gyde thy bace both red and whytt

27

But into chapters thys (treatis) I shall
  devyde
In number . xij . wyth dew recapytulacyon
Superfluus rehersall I laye asyde
Intendyng onely to gyve trew informa-
  cyon
Both of the theoryk and practycall opera-
  cyon
That by my wrytyng who so wyll gvyded
  be
Of hys intent perfectly spede shall he

28

The fyrst chapter shalbe of naturall cal-
  cynacyon   190
The second of dyssolucyon secret and
  phylosophycall
The thyrd of our ellementes seperacyon
The fowerth of coniunccyon matrymony-
  all
The .5. of putrefaccyon then folow shall

Of congelacyon albyfycatyve shalbe the
    syxt
Then of cybacyon the seventh shall folow
    next

29

The secretes of our sublymacyon the .8te.
    shal shew
The .9th. shalbe of fermentacyon

The tenth of our exaltacyon trew
The eleventh of our mervylous multy-
    plycacyon   *200*
The 12th of proieccyon then recapytula-
    cyon
And so thys tretys shall take an ende
By the helpe of god as I intende . /
    Thus endyth the preface . /

PROHIBICIO

Affter all thys I wyll thow vnderstonde
ffor thy sauegard what I haue done
Meny experymenttes haue I hade in honde
As I fownd wretyn for sune and mone
Whych I wyll tell the rehersyng soone
Begynnyng at vermylon whyche provyd
    nowght
And mercury sublymyd whych I dere
    bowght

2

I made solucions meny on
Off spyryttes fermenttes salttes Iren and
    stele
Wenyng so for to make ower stone   *10*
But faythfully I lost yche dele
After my bokys yet wrowght I well
Whych euer ontrewe I provyd
And that made me full sore agrevyd

3

Water corosyves and water ardente
In whych I wrowght in diuers wysse
Many on I made but all was schent
Egge schelles I calcynyd twysse or
    thrysse
Oyles from calcys I made aryse
And every element from other twyne *20*
But profyte fond I ryght none therin

4

Also I wrowght in sulphure and in vi-
    triall
Wych folys do call the grene Lyon
In arsnyke in orpement fowle mut them
    befall
In debily principio was myne Incepcion
Therfore was ffrawde in fine my conclu-
    cion
And thus I blewe my thryft at the colle
My clothys were bawdy my stomake was
    neaver holle

5

Sall armonyake and sandyvere
Sall alkeley sall alembroke sall alter   *30*
Sall peter sall tartour sall comen sall
    geme moste clere

Sall vytre sall sode of thes be ware
ffro the odovre of quyke syluer kepe the
    fare
Medyll not wt mercury precypytate
Nother with Inperfyte bodys rubyfycate

6

I provyd vrynes egges here and blode
Es vste and crokfere wych dyd me no
    goode
The scalys of Irene whych smethys of
    smytys
Letarge and antymony not worth too
    myttes
Bothe rede and whyght whych wer
    vntrewe   *40*
The sowle of saturne and also markesyte
Off wych gay tynctures I made to schewe

7

Oyle of lune and water wt labowre grete
I made yt calcynyng wt salt preperate
And be yt selfe wt vyolent heate
Gryndyng wt venyger tyll I was fatygate
And also wt aqua vite wt spycys accu-
    ate
Vppon a marbyll stone whych stode me
    ofte to coste
And oyles wt corrosyves but all was lost

8

Meny a malgam dyd I make
Wenyng to fyx hem to gret avayle
And therto sulphure dyd I take
Tartour egges whyghtes and oyle of the
    snayle
But euer of my purpose dyd I fayle
What for the more and what for the lesse
Euermore sumthyng wantyng ther was

9

Wyne and mylke oyles and renett
The slyme of sterrys that fall vppon
    grownd

Stanza 6. The line arrangement is wrong. The
    order in Ashmole's print is 36, 38, 37, 41,
    39, 42, 40.

Celydony with secundynes and meny mo
   yet
In thes I practysyd as was in bokys
   fownd   60
I wan ryght nowght but lost meny a
   pound
Off mercury and metalles I made crystall stonys
Wenyng it had bene a worke for the
   nonys

10

Thus I rostyd and broylyd as on of gevers
   cokys
And oftentyme my wynnyng in the asches
   I sowght
ffor I was dysseyuyd wt meny falce bokys
Wherby vntrewly meny tymes I wrovght
But all such experymenttes avaylyth
   ryght nowght
But browght me in daynger and comber-
   aunce
By los of my gooddys and meny other
   grevaunce

11

Now for the love of ouer lady suche lewdnes eschewe
Nor medyll wt no falshod whych proved
   never well
Assaye when thow wylte and thow schalt
   fynd me trewe
Wyn schalt thow ryght nowght but lose
   euery dele
Penys in thy pawkener few schalt thow
   fele
In smokes and in smelles thow schalt
   haue mykell woo
That vnneth for syknes on the grownd
   schalt thow goo

12

I saw neaver trew werke trewly but one
Off the wych in thys treatys before I
   haue tolde
Stond onely therby for to make ower
   stone   80
ffor therby may thow wyne both syluer
   and golde
Vppon my wretyng therfore to grownd
   the beholde
ffor so schalt thow lese nowght yff god
   be thy guyde
Trust to my doctryne and therto Abyde

13

Remembre how man ys most noble creature
In composycyon ertly that euer god
   wrovght
In whom ys of .4. elementtes propor-
   cyonnyd by nature
A newtriall mercurialyte whych costyth
   ryght nowght
Owte of hys mynerue by marte yt ys
   browght
ffor ower metalles be nowght els but ower
   myners too   90
Off ower sune and mone wysse Raymonde
   saythe soo

14

The clernes of the mone and of the sune
   so bryght
Into thes too myners descendyd secretly
How be yt the clernes ys hyd from thy
   syght
By crafte thow schalt make yt appere
   opynly
Thys hyde stone thys on thyng therfore
   putryfye
Washe hym wt hys owne broth tyll
   whyght he become
Then ferment hym wyttely . loo here ys
   all and somme

15

Nowe vnto god almyghtye I the commende
Whych gravnte the grace to knowe thys
   on thyng   100
ffor now ys thys treatysse browght to
   an ende
And god for hys mercy vnto hys blys
   vs bryng
Sanctus sanctus sanctus where angellys
   doth syng
Praysyng wt owte sesyng hys gloryows
   mageste
Whych he in hys kyngdome vs graunte
   for to see
     Amen

[Below is a rubric by the scribe in doggerel]

Hec auctor parse qui scripsit ritmica parte
Tu miserere sibi qui dedit ista tibi
Diuicias dat corporeas tu spirituales
Dans Impende sibi que prece visque tibi
    Explicit Rypla

THE COURT OF SAPIENCE

The fifteenth-century poem bearing this title, and long, though mistakenly, attributed to John Lydgate, is composed of two books quite different from each other in character, the material of the first being theological, that of the second largely encyclopedic. In Book i the subject is the strife between Mercy and Peace, Righteousness and Truth, as to the fate of Adam or Mankind, the disobedient servant. This strife, when at the height, when Mercy has swooned and Peace has fled into the wilderness, is appeased by Sapience's advice to Christ that the solution lies with him, in his submission to human life and human death for Mankind's redemption. He carries this out; Man is forgiven; and the Four Daughters of God are reunited in happiness. The whole story is narrated by Sapience herself to a learner, the author, who has sought her for advice on his own affairs; and at its close, with Book i, she invites the listener to accompany her to her dwelling. The wonders of the journey and of that dwelling, often presented merely by lists, fill the second book, with theological material again at its close. This second book is the longer, of 201 stanzas in rime royal; Book i has with the prologue 129 stanzas.

Three written copies are known to exist. The first, in the library of Trinity College Cambridge, there marked R 3,21, lacks the ten stanzas of opening prologue, and stops some 30 stanzas short of the close of Book ii, although with a colophon by the scribe asserting conclusion. It has also three cases of omitted or amalgamated stanzas, gaps noted on the margin by John Stow the antiquary, who at one time owned the volume, and has himself a copy of the poem in his MS Brit. Mus. Adds, 29729; Stow's copy was made from the Caxton print, and was executed in 1558. The third MS-text is in Brit. Mus. Harley 2251, and is of 63 stanzas only, breaking off with the mutilation of the volume at close. Four (non-consecutive) stanzas from Peace's appeal to God the Father in Book i, beginning "O Mercifull and O merciable", are found combined with other stanzas in the MS Trin. Coll. Cambr. R 3,19, and have been thence printed as noted in my Chaucer Manual, p. 442. Bits are in Dibdin's Typographical Antiquities, i:325-30, from Caxton, and in Miss Spurgeon's Chaucer-Allusion, i:16-17.

The Caxton print of ?1481, which may not long postdate the composition of the poem, remains in four copies, one in the British Museum, one at St. John's College, Oxford, another (Earl Spencer's) at the John Rylands Library, Manchester, and another privately owned. Wynkyn de Worde issued an edition in 1510, of which there is a copy in the British Museum; and my text here cited is partly from a copy of de Worde checked by Caxton-collations made for me, and partly from a rotograph of the Trinity MS belonging to the Modern Language Association of America.

There are two modern editions. That by Dr. Robert Spindler, Munich diss. and printed Leipzig, 1927, has appeared; that for the EETS by Miss Katherine Salter Block is under way.

Stephen Hawes, in stanza 186 (chap. xiv) of his Pastime of Pleasure, included the Court of Sapience, or *a* Court of Sapience, among the works of Lydgate. The Caxton print bears no author's name, but Hawes was supported by Stow, who not only put "compyled by John Lydgate" to his own copy, but wrote it after heading and colophon of the Trinity MS, whose scribe made no statement as to author. Warton and Dibdin accepted this, and Schick, page cx of his edition of Lydgate's Temple of Glass, had no doubt as to the genuineness of the ascription. But MacCracken, page xxxv of his introduction to Lydgate's Minor Poems, vol. i, EETS, refused to believe the poem by Lydgate, and it is hard to see how any close examination could leave Lydgate's authorship unquestioned. Spindler, *op. cit.*, presents the case fully. There is nothing in Lydgate's style or in the movement of his mind which resembles this direct and often very vigorous workman; Lydgate's hesitant repetitions, his jarring verse-structure, are not here; the mode in which knowledge is displayed, although pedantic, is not Lydgatian.

The text of the poem is not in very good condition in any one copy; but when the blunders and omissions of the Trinity scribe are rectified by comparison with Caxton, Trinity's consistent orthography, fairly sound rhythm, and careful marginalia give an interesting result.

The Trinity College MS is on paper, an amalgamation of many separate booklets; this, the third, is of 33 written and one blank leaf, in one neat compact professional hand, with a full equipment of marginalia for the reader's guidance and with many interspersed Latin passages, some lengthy, all carefully "engrossed". The preceding booklet of the volume, carrying Pety Job, is in the hand of the scribe of MSS Harley 2251 and Adds. 34360 of the British Museum; this is important in view of the existence of our poem also in the Harley volume. The Trinity scribe's spelling and language are late; he regularly writes *theym,* and uses the rune, even for *the* or *that,* in only one case so far as I have noted.

As above remarked, Hawes mentions this poem, or a poem by this title, in his list of Lydgate's works; see line 1301 of the Pastime of Pleasure, here. The frequent use by Hawes of terms found in the Court of Sapience, such as *depured, gilt, gay and glorious, redolent, reflair,* makes it probable that he read and admired this text. Burkart, pp. 51-54 of his Hawes dissertation mentioned p. 271 here, argued the influence of the Court of Sapience on Hawes, not only as regards vocabulary but on conception and management of the Pastime. Natter, as mentioned *ibid.,* opposes the latter argument. Full discussion of Hawes' relation to this poem will doubtless come with an edition of either work as a whole; it may then also appear that the similarity in subject between chapters xi-xiv of Lydgate's Life of Our Lady and the Court of Sapience book i misled Hawes as to authorship of our poem. For this similarity see Schick, page cii of the introduction to his edition of the Temple of Glass; the Lydgatian heading there quoted, the "Dispute between Mercy and Peace, Righteousness and Truth, for the Redemption of Mankind", could easily be used of the first half of the Court of Sapience. Note also that those chapters of the Life of Our Lady, with that heading, occur separately in at least one manuscript, now Huntington 144, from the Huth Library, and once in the possession of John Stow.

Dr. Hope Traver, in her monograph on The Four Daughters of God (Bryn Mawr, 1907), devotes pp. 152-58 to a rapid summary of the contents of book i of this poem, and mentions at least three sources for its material,—Grosseteste, Bonaventura, and Deguileville's Pèlerinage de Jésu-Crist. Of the second book no detailed study has yet (1927) appeared, but the author's familiarity with the Seven Liberal Arts indicates a man well-educated and alertly curious. There are dry theological passages in book i, and some barren lists in book ii; but there are also striking lyrical passages in the former book, striking descriptive bits in the latter. Whoever made the compilation, although unoriginal enough, was observant, energetic, free of formula, often vigorous of speech; his control of rhythm and language is good, his rime living, his syntax clear. There is none of Lydgate's floundering, either in verbiage or in sentence-structure. To make this evident, I cite a passage or two from the first (or theological) book, before a set of extracts from the second is presented.

[From Caxton's print, no date]

The labero*us* & ye most merueylo*us* werkes
Of sapience syn firste regned nature
My purpos is to tell as writen clerkes
And specyally her moost notable cure
In my fyrst book I wyl preche & depure 5
It is so plesaunt vnto eche persone
That it a book shal occupye alone

2

Sone after this I shal wysedom descryue
Her blessyd howshold / and her wonnyng place
And than retourne vnto her actes blyue 10
As she them wrought by tyme, processe & space
Al this mater she taught me of her grace
I spak with her / as ye may here and rede
For in my dreme I mette her in a mede

3

O clyo lady moost facundyous   15
O rauysshyng delyte of Eloquence
O gylted goddes gay and gloryous
Enspyred with the percyng Influence
Of delycate heuenly complacence
Within my mouth late dystylle of thy showres   20
And forge my tonge to glad myn audytours

4

Myn ignoraunce whome clowded hath eclippes
With thy pure bemes illumyne al aboute
Thy blessyd breth lete refleyr in my lyppes
And with the dewe of heuen thou them degoute   25
So that my mouthe maye blowe & encense oute

The redolent dulcour Aromatyke
Of thy depured lusty Rethoryck

5

I knowe my self moost naked in al artes
My comune vulgare eke moost interupte   30
And I conuersaunte & borne in the partes
Wher my natyf langage is moost corrupt
And wyth most sondry tonges myxt & rupte
O lady myn wherfor I the byseche
My muse amende, dresse / forge / mynysse & eche   35

6

For to al makers here I me excuse
That I ne can delycately endyte
Rude is the speche of force / whiche I must vse
Such infortune my natyf byrth may wyte
But O ye lordes whiche haue your delyte
In termes gay / and ben moost eloquent
This book to yow no plesaunce may present

7

But netheles as tasted bytternesse
Al swete thyng maketh be more precious
So shal my book extende the godelynesse   45
Of other auctours whiche ben gloryous
And make theyr wrytyng delycyous
I symple shal extolle theyr soueraynte
And my rudenes shall shewe theyr subtylyte

8

Gower chaucers erthely goddes two   50
Of thyrste of eloquent delycacye
With al your successoures fewe or moo
Fragraunt in speche / experte in poetrye
You ne yet theym in no poynt I enuye
Exyled as fer I am from youre glorye 55
As nyght from day / or deth from vyctorye

1. Three-line capital T.
Stow's copy places the bar as does Caxton, and differs textually by omitting *of* from 12, inserting *thee* after *O* in 15, and changing *thy* to *the* in 28.

9

I you honoure / blysse / loue and glory-
   fye
And to whos presence my book shal
   atteyne
His hastyf dome I praye hym modefye
and not detraye / ne haue it in dysdayne
For I purpoos no makyng for to dystayne
Meke herte / good tonge / and spyryte
   pacyent   62
Who hath these thre / my book I hym
   present

10

And as hym lyst lete hym detray or adde
For syth I am constreyned for to wryte
By my souerayne / and haue a mater
   glad
And can not please paynte enourne ne
   endyte
Late ignorance & chyldhode haue the
   wyte
I aske no more / but god of his mercy
My book conferme from sklaunder and
   enuy   70

Explicit Prohemium

[The author of the poem, mated by Dame
Fortune in the chess-play of life, is bidden
by Reason to seek Sapience; he falls asleep,
and in that sleep his spirit passes through a
desert place inhabited by wild beasts "in
deuouryng expert". Beyond, in a heavenly
mead by the River of Quiet, he finds Dame
Sapience, to whom he swears fealty. She is
resting from the performance of a task which
she narrates to him,—a story we have just
briefly summarized. The definitely religious
or theological material of this first book
puts it outside our consideration in this
volume; but one passage may be cited, not
merely for its quality but for its possible
influence upon Stephen Hawes. It is from
Peace's farewell to the courts of light and
love, and fills stanzas 64-69. Line-numbers
as in Spindler's ed. of the poem.]

64

O seraphin yeue vp thyne Armony
O Cherubin thy glory do away
O ye thronys late be all melody
Youre Ierarchy discryuyd ys for ay   445
Youre maystresse see in what aray
She lyth in sowne ylorne wt debate
ffarewell farewell pure housbold desolate.

Stow spells *poyn*, *spryte*, in 54, 62; otherwise
he is almost the duplicate of Caxton.
445. Read *disteynd*. 454. Read *ouer set*.

65

O souuerayn myghty dominacions
O ye vertues and potestates   450
O principates wt all yowre heuynly sowns
Archaungelles Aungelles O thryes thre
   estates
Youre spouse dame pease euer set ys wt
   debates
Now may ye wepe and Ierarchies thre
Youre ordres now may nat restoryd
   be   455

66

Farewell ye all . Dame Mercy lyth in
   sowne
ffor sothfastnes accusyd hath made man-
   kynde
And ryghtwysnes that sheld (to) all
   reasowne
Hath dampnyd hym as crewell and vnkynde
Mercy ne pease for theym may no grace
   fynde   460
Natwtstandyng iugement may haue no
   sawte
Because of pease but hit be execute

67

Wo worth debate that neuer may haue
   pease
Wo worth penaunce that asketh no pite
Wo worth vengeaunce whyche mercy
   may not cease   465
Wo worth iugement that hath noon equyte
Wo worth that trewthe that hath no
   charyte
Wo worth that Iuge that may none gylty
   saue
And wo worth that ryght that may no
   fauour haue

68

Farewell Saturne Ioue / Mars and Phe-
   bus bryght   470
ffarewell Venus and farewell Mercury
ffarewell the shynyng lady of the nyght
I was your guyde but now awey go I
O cruell Mars thy tempestious fury
Now mayst thow shew and Jubiter thyne
   Ire
Now mayst thow rynge wt dartys full of
   fyre

69

I was the ryng that helde yow all togedyr
I brydelyd yow and set yow in acorde

458. The MS has *do*.

But now · I · go ywys and I wote not
  whydyr
Wherfore of force ye must fall to dis-
  corde   480
O ye souerayn of all batayle the lord
Now mayst thow sende aftyr (Comet)
  thy messingere
To signify that batayle nygheth nere

[The second book makes a complete
change of subject. Its proheme is:]

130

(Forth) to procede in (mater) of my
  booke
To preche and discryue the solempne
  mansioun
Of sapience most heuynly on to looke
Whos feete byn set in all perfeccioun
And to auoyde the oblocucioun
Of false tonges and thanke for to deserue
Thow graunt me grace (o good goddesse)
  Mynerue   910

131

My (style) thow dresse my langage thow
  depure
My wyt thow force thow mynyster of
  matyer
ffor syth I am most symple creature
I nyl vsurpe in thy place to apyer
But thow me guyde and shew on what
  manyer
I shall pronounse thynges whyche thow
  dost me se
Thy refrendary oonly wyll I be

132

The pure knowlage and verrey (sente-
  ment)
Of thy wysdom was neuer my dowere
But as the (sonne in) lyght most ex-
  cellent   920
Wt hys beames the mone illumyneth clere
So done allwey wysemen thorow foolys
  lere
Therfore thy wysdom as thow lyst me
  teche
O lady myne in my booke woll I preche

482. MS *Cornet;* Caxton as above. 904. MS has
First, maner. 910. MS has *thow good.* 911.
MS *styll.*
918. MS *sentment.* 920. MS *sonny.* 934. MS
of. 937, 941, 942, 943, MS *On, that, another,
hys.*

[Sapience now invites the author to accompany her to her home.]

Forth went we tho vnto a ryueres syde
Whos name ys Quyete full of all swetenes
Oute (ouer) whyche wt Archys hygh
  and wyde
A brege was set full of all lustynes 935
The marbyll stoone the solempne worthy-
  nes
(Of) Geometry shewyd on suche wyse
So good a werk that no wyght cowde
  deuyse

135

The pylours strong enarchyd wt effect
Wt pynnacles and towres full of blysse
And allured clene (gaue) suche a dygne
  prospect
That suche (a) brege was neuer seen
  ywysse
And on a towre (this) scrypture wretyn
  ysse
Who dredeth god com yn and ryght well
  come
ffor drede of god ys wey of all wysdome   945

[They cross the bridge, and note that the
gravel of its bed and banks is all of precious stones; in nineteen following stanzas
these stones are alphabetically enumerated
and their virtues given, from alabaster to
zyngynt. As his authority the poet refers
to the Lapidary, to Isidor, or Dioscorides,
or Bartholomaeus. The reader may change
the names of the stones at pleasure, says the
writer; he himself has used Latin "for the
more surete". There now follows a description of the river, with a praise of water the
element, a list of the rivers of the world,
and reference to the Hexameron of Basilius
and to the fifteenth book of Bartholomaeus
for more information. Stanzas 172 to 181
contain a "descripcio piscium", with a list
of nine authorities for the reader desirous
of more knowledge. From these two sections I give two stanzas each:]

166

Basilius in hys Exameron
Discryueth watyr and hys propurte
Whoso hath lust may loke hym opon
But · I · myself wyll fle prolyxite
And of my ryuer speke as lyketh me 1160
What shuld I say to her and to beholde
All erthely thyng passeth a thowsand
  folde

167

Hys heuynly sowne his grones delicate
Hys swete (murmour) hys subtyle course
and (stylle)
Hys fresshe colour whyche no storme
may abate   1165
His vapour swete hauyng (reflyer) at
wyll
Myght (saye) askaunce / on thys wyse
be I wyll
ffor to excyte owte from the heuens place
Nature to come to se of my solace

172

Thys lusty fyssh (within) thys ryuer
swete
Theyre swymmyng course (whiche we)
fynnys clepe
They put in vse to bere and swymme and
fleete   1200
Now at the ground and now aboue they
(lepe)
Now dysseueryd and now apon an hepe
Now heere now theere now endelong now
ouerthwert
The syght of theym myght (hele eche
wounded) hert

173

Som had a lust to (sewe) the sonnys
(lyght)
Som to the pryuate vmbre gon to attende
And gadreth in (theyr) bodyes to the
syght
Shot oute on (lengthe) theyre corage to
extende
Theyr parfyte blys nature myght nat
amende
Of net and hooke ne deceyte were they
aferde   1210
What shuld I say they had an heuen in
erde

[A description of the mead and its flowers
now follows, extending through the 189th
stanza, when the "descripcio arborum" is
reached. I give two of its nine stanzas.]

190

An heuenly woode / was on that other
syde   1325
And (closed) in wt a ryuer aboute
Plantyd at lust wt trees full of pryde
The (blossmy) bowys vnto the erthe gan
loute
The Cedyr tre presumptuous and stoute
Hauyng dysdeyne (in erthe) oonly to
abyde
Among the sterres hys hede began to
hyde   1330

191

He and the palme and (eke) the gret
Cypres
Gan ryse borioune and refleyre wt al
delyte
The bowes brought forth frute of all
gentylnes
And yaue vmbre vnto the solempne syght
Wt double (blysse) eche tree was in-
signyte   1335
Wt frute (to) man wt vmbre to the
ground
Thus hongor there ne heete myght ha-
bound

[The list of birds, which next follows, is
subjoined entire.]

199

The best byrdes in theyre melody
Theyre heuynly voyce gan to entewne
anon
Theyre aungelyk rauysshyng Armony
Oute thorough the heuen in to the hygh-
est trone   1390
Gan perse and passe the ix · ordres ech-
one
O cherubyn they sayd com hyder to vs ·
Lerne wt that tewne thow shalt syng
Sanctus ·

200

The (throstell coke) opon the Cedre
grene
The nytyngale vppon the blossom thorn
The noble swan wt whyte federes shene
The Ientyll lark fleyng among the corn
Ne seaseth nat to syng from euen to
morn

Bracketed readings are from Caxton. The MS
has: 1164 myrrour, fall; 1166 reflex; 1167 I say;
1198 wtoutyn; 1199 wt; 1201 fleete; 1204
wonder an; 1205 sowe grace; 1207 theym; 1208
leyngth.

Bracketed words are from Caxton's print. The
MS reads: 1326, clothyd; 1328, blossom; 1329,
omission; 1331 also; 1335 bysse, which is crossed
out; 1336, omission; 1394, trustylcok.

Wt all other fowles of pure plesaunce
Theyr voyce gan daunt vnto the concord-
aunce   *1400*

201

Iche other foule in kynde there had hys
blysse
Hys lust hys comfort and hys sustenaunce
They had no nede Roueyn to vse ywysse
Iche thyng obeyed to theyr hert*es* ples-
aunce
Debate ne stryfe discorde ne yet dis-
taunce   *1405*
Among theym myght nat engendryd be
Ichone other supportyd in degre ·

202

The prowde Pecok hys tayle began to
whele
On whyche the sparkyng son so purely
brent
That to the syght he semyd eu*er*ydele
An Archaungell downe from the heuyn
sent   *1411*
All heuynly colours in hym was content
Hys tayle the flowres the byrdys eke
ywys
The ey the nose the eare fed wt all blys

203

The Egle fresshe sou*er*ayn of fowles all
The goode Goshawke the gentyll faucon
of pryce   *1416*
Wt all other that (to) disport royall
Dysposyd byn ther regnyth at deuyse
The gentyll Doufe innocent of all vyce
The Turtyll trew the ffenix singuler *1420*
In lust and blysse togedyrs all they were

204

The holsom P*er*trege and the Pellicane
The sparow (eke) the plouers and the py
The Popingeay the Cok the hen the Crane
Theyre names all here for to specyfy *1425*
Hit nedeth nat for eu*er*yche (foule)
shortly
That ys in kynde and hath in v*er*tew
myght
In all comfort reioysyd there hys (flyght)

205

They flee at lust there ys nought theym
to let

Bracketed readings are from Caxton's print. In
lines 1417, 1423, 1426, 1469, the MS omits *to,
eke, foule, the.* In 1428 it reads *myght;* in
1431 *let;* in 1467 *flowres.*

They bylde in blys they haue all liberte
They nede not (drede) for gyldyr ne for
net   *1431*
fflee where they wyll they byn in all
sewrtee
The wynde the rayne nor noon adu*er*site
May theym distorbe all ioy ys they*m*
among
The heuyn aboue delyteth in theyr song
Explicit descripcio Auium
Incipit descripcio Animalium

[Four stanzas are now given to a list of
animals, after which follows a stanza of
"Recapitulacio", and the arrival of the
travelers at the home of Sapience:]

210

The watyrs sowne the lusty fysshe and
fayre
The good seasoun ye yongly son and
bryght   *1465*
The meede the herbys the flowres and
theyre reflayre
The blossom bowes the (fowles) fresshe
of flyght
The tenore wynde wt hys brethe and hys
myght
Enspyryng thorough (the) blossoms at
deuyse
Depeyntyd new on heuynly paradyse *1470*

Explicit descripcio Animalium
*Incipit descripcio Castri & Mansionis
Sapiencie*

211

Whan I had seene that souu*er*ayn sol-
*em*pne syght
Dame Sapience led me a lytell besyde
Vnto a comly Castell shynyng bryght
fful of all solace delyte lust and pryde
In whos circuite wt vawtes large and
wyde   *1475*
Of parfyte blys y set were towrys seuene
The heyghte of whyche styeth vp to
heuene

212

The Dyke of hit formyd wt delyte
ffulfyllyd was wt the watyr of Quiete
The marble stoone the Alabaustre whyte
By geometry so frendly goon meete *1481*
That suche a wall in hede body and feete
Wt p*re*cyous stones illumyneth at deuyse
Was neuer seen hit passeth paradyse

213

Vppon a rooche hit was groundyd and
set   *1485*
And euery Botras full of ymagery
Yche pynnacle (coner) towre and toret
Wt golde and perle and stonys curyosly
Depeyntyd was and powdryd lustyly
And on the yate illumynyd wt all blys
Wt goldyn lettres thys wrytyn was ywys

214

Thys ys the wey to *vertew* and to grace
To konnyng knowlache wyt and all wys-
dom
Thys ys the wey vnto that heuynly place
There storme / ne stryfe / syn / vyce
ne euyll may com   *1495*
Thys ys the wey vnto that solempne
kyngdom
Where rest pease (blysse) and com*f*ort
(seceth) neuer
Com in who wyll and ryght welcom for
euer

215

Seuyn ladyes bryght downe fro the towres seuen
Came to the yate wt many ladyes moo
Seruaun*tes* to theym whos names I woll
neuen   *1501*
ffeyth hope / (tofore) wt Charyte dyd
go
Prudence wt wysdom dame ffortitude also
Wt Temp*er*aunce and Ryghtwysnes ywys
Met Sapience / and hertyly gon hyr
kys   *1505*

[The allegorical ladies who make up the
trains of each of the Virtues are listed in
the four following stanzas; Theology then
appears, escorted by "ladyes seuen", whose
names are given in the next stanza, viz.:]

221

There was Gramor grounde of Scienc*es*
all
And Dialatyk full of pure knowyng
And Rethoryk Science Imp*er*iall
Dame Arsmetryke was in p*r*oporcionyng
Geometry that mesureth eu*er*y thyng
The lady Musyk and Astronomy
These ladyes seuen seweth Theology

Bracketed readings are from Caxton's print. The
MS omits those of lines 1487, 1497 (*blysse*), and
1502. It reads *cesyd* in 1497.

[Dame Philosophy now comes down from
the "dongeon grete within the place" and
greets Sapience. Her nature is defined in
four stanzas, and the functions of her three
sisters, Phisica, Ethica, and Logica, in stanzas 227-231. On these three, says stanza
232, Divinity is grounded. An alternative
classification is then given, filling four stanzas, and in stanza 237 the observer enters
the first court, administered by Dame
Science. Here he finds "the phylosopher
with his companye" sitting in a goodly parlor. Stanza 240 enumerates the company:]

240

Arystotyll Aueroys and Avycen
Good Algazell Galien Apolonius
Pictagoras and Plato wt hys pen
Macrobius / Cato . Boecius
Raasis . Isaak . Calyxt . Orbacius
Salustius . Theophile . Ipocras
Wt many mo whos names I lete pas

[The second court is now entered, ruled by
Dame Intelligence; it is "full of all lust
and heuenly complacence", depainted with
the heaven, the hierarchies, and the "vnhappy chaunce" of Lucifer. A few of the
indwelling scholars of that "parlor pure"
are mentioned in stanza 245, but the multitude of them is too great for full enumeration, says the poet.
Next is the third court, Sapience's own,
"so rauysshynge and eleg aunte" that the
author, unable to describe it, cries out, "O
Priamus and thyn hall Ilion", how insufficient are you in comparison! It is hung
with tapestries of the parables, of Ecclesiasticus, Wisdom, Ecclesiastes; and on the
dais is portrayed "Mynerue that hyght Pallas", with spear, shield, serpent locks, clothing "Of colours thre delycious and stoute",
and an olive tree on which sits a "night
crow". Dame Sapience explains the attributes and powers of Minerva, stanzas 253-
255, referring to "Fulgencius in his Metho-
logye" as authority.
After mentioning Theology and some of
her listeners,—Holcot, Nottingham, Comes-
tor, St. Thomas, etc.,—the poet comes to
Grammar.]

259

Wyth Gramer was foure ladyes well be-
seene
Of the whyche the furst hyght Dame
Ortography
Wythin a parl*our* lusty fresshe and cleene

Ther was (eke) gentyll Ethymology *1810*
Diasintastica and prosody
These systres foure dyfferent in offyce
Seruyd Gramer as lady full of pryce

260

The furst taught lettres and how men
  shulde wryte
The second taught the partyes of rea-
  soun   *1815*
To telle yche worde trewly ys her delyte
Whyche ys nowne whyche v*e*rbe (and)
  whyche pronown
The thryd dyd teche parfyte construc-
  ciown
The last eche worde yaue hys tyme and
  hys accent
And in these fowre all Gramer ys content   *1820*

261

These foure s*e*ruyd that Science liberall
In wrytyng pronow(n)syng and con-
  struyng
Of letter sillable worde reason wt all
She hath her p*r*incipall consideryng
She ys the ground the yate the entryng
To all the noble artes liberall   *1826*
By her frendshyp they be made speciall

262

There was Moyses Cadm*us* and Card-
  menta
Eborard fferru*m* Iohn Garlond and
  Donate
Precyan Petyr Thomas de Hennoya *1830*
Lambard Papy they wryte erly and late
The Ianuense was there in gret estate
And Arystotyll for theyre bookes wyse
Catholicon and pariarmonise

263

Hugucion wt many auctors mo   *1835*
Wrytyng there was and lokyng on Gram-
  ere
Whos names all shortly I lete ouergo
They may nat do / but prolong my
  (matere)
Many a babe of sou*e*rayn heuynly chere
Desyrous all in konnyng to habound *1840*
Abowte Dame Gramer sate to haue theyr
  ground

Bracketed readings are from Caxton's print. In
lines 1810, 1817, the MS omits *eke, and*. In line
1838 it reads *tyme*.

[Dame Dialectic occupies the next "parlour full of blys", surrounded by eager pupils, to whom she reads Latin, and who ask
no other wage but that they may "dyscerne
and eke depure Trewthe from falshede".
Her clothing is "prowde and stoute, Of
differt Scire and of Incipit With Sophysms
depeynted full aboute." She teaches her
students the "comone treatyse", "Whiche
whatkyns what is a proposycyon What
thynge he is and his dyuysyon." The learn-
ers dispute briskly; "with sophysms
straunge maters they discusse And fast they
crye oft tu es Asinus." She reads them
"the vniuersals the predicamentes the
Topykes the principals the Elynkes." The
group of her listeners is described in nine
lines of famous names, including Alfred,
Juvenal, Mercurius, Demosthenes, Euclid,
Democritus, Physiologus, Ptolemy, and William de Conches.

Next, in her "parlour fresshe and precious", is "Dame Rethoryke modyr of Eloquence Most elegaunt most pure and gloryous." Her delicious speech ravishes all
her auditors:]

272

And many a Clerke had lust hyr for to
  here
Hyr speche to theym was parfyte sus-
  tynaunce
Yche worde of hyr depuryd was so
  clere   *1900*
And enlumynyd wt so parfyte plesaunce
That heuyn hit was to here her beau
  parlaunce
Her termes gay of facound sou*e*rayne
Cacephaton in noo poynt myght dysteyne

[In stanza 273 the author enumerates the
subjects of Rhetoric's teaching, and bids any
one who considers his writing dull and blunt
to go to "Tria sunt And to Galfryde the
poete lawreate To Ianuense a clerke of
gret astate", or to Tullius "the chosyn
spowse vnto thys lady fre", with his
"gyltyd craft".

After the usual catalogue of the principal
students clustered about Rhetoric, the author
proceeds to Arithmetic, stanzas 277-282, then
to Geometry, stanzas 283-288; under this
head is recounted the dispute between Aristotle, Albert, and Ptolemy as to the extent
of the earth's circuit. To Music are given
stanzas 289-299, the manuscript breaking
off with stanza 297 complete, and a colophon
as if finished. Astronomy has the following
sixteen stanzas, which include a censure of

the "Gentiles" for identifying the planets
with gods, and for raising "fysshe and bestiall" to the heavens. The author also denounces the "old error" of astrology.]

311

O mysbeleue merueylous for to neuene
O cursed blyndenes of these gentyles all
Whiche demyn fysshe / and bestyall be
   in heuen
For gloryfyed regnaunt perpetuall
As Rame / bore / crabbe / and bere in
   specyall   *2175*
Hounde / lyon / swan / the egle eke in
   fere
Whome they worshyp for Ioues chyfe
   squyre

312

She tolde also of batayll destyne
And how in sterres some men haue suche
   byleue
That in theyr byrthe ryght by neces-
   syte   *2180*
Ordeyned is all that hym shall please or
   greue

This olde errour our doctours done re-
   preue
Socrates the same with Arystotyll sayth
Notwithstondynge they were not of our
   fayth

313

(For) yf a man were in his natyuyte *2185*
Constreyned to his sondry artes all
Them for to do ryght by necessyte
Why sholde good men haue laude in
   specyall
Or myslyuers to punysshement be thrall
Good Isodre maketh this reson   *2190*
In dampnynge of this false oppynyon

[Astronomy is left behind, and Faith leads
the learner to her tower, where, in a "parlour full solacious", sit the apostles writing
the articles of our faith. Fourteen stanzas
are filled by a digest of these truths, and
the work then closes with a list of the things
all Christian men and women are bound to
learn. This last part is in prose.]

Stanzas 311 ff. are from the Caxton text. Line
2185, Caxton reads *Or.*

STEPHEN HAWES: THE PASTIME OF PLEASURE

(Extracts)

We know very little of Stephen Hawes. He was allowed mourning-cloth after the death of Henry VII's queen in 1502; he dedicated his Pastime of Pleasure to Henry VII in 1506, styling himself one of the grooms of the king's chamber; he may be the "Mr. Hawse" who received payment for a play in 1521 from the king; and in 1530 he is mentioned in the past tense by Feylde, in his Controversy between a Lover and a Jay. The notices of him by Bale in his 1557 Catalogus Scriptorum and by Antony à Wood in his 1691 Athenae Oxonienses are too conventionally flowery to deserve much consideration; they assign to Hawes an University education, a great store of learning, and extensive travels, to which à Wood adds the more lifelike detail that Hawes was highly esteemed by the king for "his facetious discourse and prodigious memory, which last did evidently appear in this, that he could repeat by heart most of our English poets, especially Jo. Lydgate, a monk of Bury, whom he made equal in some respects with Geff. Chaucer."

Hawes has left five poems, the two longer of which are allegorical-didactic fictions, the three shorter didactic or "occasional" with no element of fiction. The largest of his poems, the Pastime of Pleasure, is of 5770 lines, mainly in rime royal; it is to be dated 1506, as said. The other allegorical fiction, the Example of Virtue, was presented to Henry VII in 1504; it is of 2100 lines in rime royal.

Both these poems are narrated in the first person; each hero, Youth or Virtue in the earlier work, Graunde Amour in the Pastime, is aided by a gracious woman-counsellor to win a bride; both youths must fight monsters to prove their worth; both are triumphantly wedded to the beloved; and each poem extends to the old age and death of the hero. This last is an awkward device for a first-person narrative, but is carried by Hawes in the Pastime even to his own epitaph and to Fame's adding of his name to those of the Nine Worthies. There are many resemblances in episode and in diction between the two poems; Hawes repeated in the Pastime every device, narrative or rhetorical, which he had used in the Example; but the Pastime is much enlarged, as compared with the Example, by its addition of the education of the hero and of his visit to the Seven Liberal Arts in their Tower of Doctrine.

This allegorizing of University education, and the parallel of Hawes' narrative here to the Vision Delectable earlier composed by Alfonso de la Torre for a young Spanish prince, tempt the student to see in the Pastime a treatise possibly planned for the young prince Henry, son of Henry VII to whom the work is dedicated. If such be the case, the close similarity between poems written only two years apart may be treated as deliberate on Hawes' part, the educational "cantos" being the raison d'être of the Pastime, and the chivalric cantos expanded in treatment to support the importance of the perhaps suggested work.

The Pastime, as remarked, falls into two parts, the cleric or scholastic and the chivalric. In the former of these the hero receives his book-education, and is accepted by La Bell Pucell, the heroine; in the second he makes himself worthy of her by slaying a series of monsters. Through these encounters he is accompanied by a comic servitor, Godfrey Gobelive, and the parts of the poem in which Godfrey comes to the front are written in couplets instead of the usual rime royal. The kinship of this portion of the poem with the Morality plays is obvious, while the romances, and Lydgate's translation of Deguileville's Pilgrimage of the Life of Man, have influenced the whole work in plan and in choice of episode. For the earlier, educational, chapters the sources are quite different. Burkart considered that the Court of Sapience was here Hawes' model, while Natter emphasizes the influence of the Margarita Philosophica of the Carthusian prior Reisch, printed in 1503. It is not clear to me that Hawes owed much to the plan of either work, although the vocabulary of the Court of Sapience, which Hawes believed to be Lydgate's, took a marked effect on him. Other works used by Hawes for these chapters are Caxton's Recuyell of the Histories of Troy, which is cited by name, Caxton's Mirror of the World, Donatus' Ars Grammatica Minor, and the pseudo-Ciceronian treatise on rhetoric, Ad Herennium, etc. The treatment of some of this material, notably that from Donatus' Grammar, is of the most scholastic and jejune sort, and as it is, e.g., accompanied by the hero's request to know what a noun substantive is, we may underline our suggestion that the *Pastime* is a very young prince's manual of education. See the note on lines 465-526 below. The influence of Chaucer and of Lydgate upon Hawes appears not in plan or vocabulary, but in certain details and rhetorical tricks, especially from the Temple of Glass and from the Troilus. For example, the dazzling palace upon which the eye cannot rest for brightness, the intervention of Venus to aid the lover, are devices of the former poem, while not only do the meeting and parting of the lovers show reminiscence of Troilus, but Hawes' use of "anaphora" is perhaps modelled on the passage near the close of Chaucer's poem. We have, however, to remark that his use is an abuse; see note on line 232 of Cavendish's Metrical Visions here. There are other traces of Hawes' reading in his English predecessors Gower, Chaucer, and Lydgate, although he has not caught up their lines or their turns of speech with half the fidelity of Lydgate's memory for Chaucer. He is a smaller man mentally than Lydgate; he is not so much hag-rid by the half-line formula, but he is much more a slave to rime and a hunter of the "aureate" word; his perceptions are duller, his temperament more pedantic. And there is a misuse or strain of words in him which is not found in Lydgate. When Hawes says of Priam, in cap. 20 of the Pastime (ed. 1845) that "His propre death him selfe he nutrifyed", this may be explained as a printer's or editor's error, but there are more than a few similar twists of language for rime's sake in the poem. True, there are also some fortunate touches. The trembling servitor's cry to the young knight, as the giant approaches,—"Take heed, quod he, here is a feend of hell!"; the Lydgatian sentiment—"Was never payne but it had joye at last"; the first view of Fame—"I sawe come ryding in a valey farre A goodly ladye" etc.;—most fortunate of all the (possibly proverbial) couplet

> For though the day be never so long
> At last the bells ringeth to evensong,—

these are high lights, but they are isolated spots in a very dull and long surface; and inasmuch as no writer is invariably inadequate, they prove nothing for Hawes. The approach of Fame, just mentioned, may have caught Spenser's eye; but the criticism which traces Spenser's "descent" from Hawes, even though it be Mrs. Browning's criticism, needs scrutiny. In the Cambridge History of English Literature, ii:266-7, are listed the agreements in theme and treatment between Hawes and Spenser; but although the aim of both writers is "to fashion a gentleman", as Spenser said of himself, that purpose of the Elizabethan age had already begun to stir at the court of Henry the Seventh, and had under both sovereigns much the same book-material with which to work. As regards detail, Spenser's Braggadochio, for example, may owe something to Godfrey Gobelive, but the idea of a comedy relief could well occur independently to a man of Spenser's ability, if the character be not accounted for by the Miles Gloriosus of the classics or a figure like the boastful servant of Herod in the Mysteries. Spenser, like Hawes, is a courtly allegorist; but he is not therefore borrower from the lesser man. As Saintsbury says, if he owes Hawes anything, it is a very small royalty. The Pastime is a mere rifacimento of stock medieval motifs, whether, as Warton suggested, it has a possible French "Passetemps" behind it, or not; in the Faerie Queene there has been a selection of such motifs as well as a transformation. Hawes' clumsy piecing-together of "properties" into a court-poem is without anything of Spenser's eye for the great or Chaucer's eye for the little.

But more than one historian of literature has praised Hawes. Warton, in the latter eighteenth century, called the Pastime of Pleasure an "unjustly neglected poem" which "contains no common touches of romantic and allegoric fiction", and in which also "the improved harmony of numbers and facility of diction" attained by Lydgate receive "new graces" from his disciple Hawes. And in our own time Churton Collins praised Hawes almost as warmly as he praised Lydgate, commending this poem for "its pathos, its picturesqueness, and its sweet and plaintive music". The fitness of these terms is, however, as questionable as is Churton Collins' laudation of the frequent "exquisite beauty" of Lydgate's verse. Spenser we may indeed call "picturesque", a picture-maker. His material is medieval, and he is not a great narrator; he has no development of character to present, and his episodes and transitions are conventional. But his highly sensitized soul, delighting in color, in glitter, in richness of sound, in delicacy of touch, lavished upon his limited gallery of subjects a wealth of sensuous description previously unmatched in English. His verse, moreover, was worthy of his pictures. With him there reappears a power lost since Chaucer's death, the poet's power to tread his measure with a sure and supple command of word, line, and paragraph, to bend language to his will.

This power is not in Hawes. He is a professional verse-maker, honest, dull, didactic, possessed of the dangerously little learning which breeds complacency, quite rhythm-deaf, insensitive to sight and sound, carrying out his puerile plan with stumbling clumsiness. We do mark some small gain over Lydgate in the comparative steadiness of Hawes' advance to his purpose; but we mark no real growth in narrative command. His conventional material is used with the vagueness, the awkwardness, of an earlier age, an age overschooled and undersensitized. He saw a tower and a tapestry, and had an impulse to depict the pursuit of the Ideal; there results the Pastime of Pleasure. Centuries later, a poet saw a tower and a tapestry, and dreamed the pursuit of an idea for Truth's sake; there results 'Childe Roland to the Dark Tower Came'.

SELECT REFERENCE LIST XI

No manuscript is known of any of Hawes' works, which in the prints are extremely rare. They are, in order of consequence:—

The Pastime of Pleasure, ca. 5770 lines, mainly in rime royal. Printed by de Worde in 1509 and 1517; copies in private possession. Printed by Wayland 1554, by Tottel 1555 (with woodcuts), and by Waley in 1555. The Wayland text is reprinted by Southey in his Select Works of the British Poets, 1831, the text of Tottel by Wright for the Percy Society, London, 1845. Both these modern editions omit some coarse lines from the Godfrey Gobelive portions of the poem. Selections are in Ellis' Specimens, 1811, in Skeat's Specimens of Eng. Lit. 1394-1579, in Ward's Eng. Poets i:175, in Arnold's Manual, in Flügel's Neuengl. Lesebuch, in Neilson and Webster's Chief Brit. Poets, 249-255. A bit is in Manly's Eng. Poetry, 59-60.

See discussion of the poem in Warton's HistEngPoetry, ed. Hazlitt, iii:169-188, in Morley's Engl. Writers vii, and in Berdan's Early Tudor Poetry, chap. ii: also as below.

The Example of Virtue, presented to Henry VII in 1504, is of 2100 lines in rime royal; it was printed ?de Worde ?1510, again 1530, and may be read in Arber's Dunbar Anthology, 1901, pp. 217-296, with modernized text.

The Conversyon of Swerers is of 307 lines, and the Joyfull Medytacyon, on the coronation of Henry VIII, is of 204 lines, both in stanza, and both printed de Worde 1509. They were reprinted for the Abbotsford Club in 1865 by David Laing. The former poem was also printed by Copland in 1551, by Butler in 1551.

The Comfort of Louers, of about 350 lines, was printed de Worde no date. The unique copy is in private possession. See Berdan op. cit., pp. 86-88.

Of these works the Pastime of Pleasure, because of its more elaborate structure and its supposed influence on Spenser, has received more attention. See:—

Fuhr, Lautuntersuchungen zu Stephen Hawes' Gedicht The Pastime of Pleasure Marburg diss., 1891.

Burkart, Stephen Hawes' The Pastime of Pleasure, A critical introduction to a proposed new edition of the text, Zürich diss., ?1900, pp. 60.

Zander, Hawes' "Passetyme of Pleasure" verglichen mit Spenser's "Faerie Queene" unter Berücksichtigung der allegorischen Dichtung in England, Rostock diss., 1906, pp. 114.

Natter, Untersuchung der Quellen von Hawes' allegorischem Gedicht "Pastime of Pleasure." Munich diss., pubd. Passau, 1911.

Rhodenizer, V. B., Studies in Stephen Hawes' Pastime of Pleasure, Harvard diss., 1918. In typescript in the Harv. Univ. Library. A careful study of Hawes' motifs and stage properties, especially as derived from the romances; valuable for late medieval authors other than Hawes.

On Hawes see also the Cambr. Hist. Eng. Lit. vol. ii, chap. ix, by William Murison; see Saintsbury's Hist. Eng. Prosody i:235-39; see Courthope's Hist. Eng. Poetry i:380.

[Dedication to Henry VII (part)]

4

Your noble grace, and excellent hyenes
For to accepte I beseche ryght humbly,
Thys little boke, opprest wyth rudenes
Without rethoryke, or colour crafty: 25
Nothynge I am experte in poetry,
As the monke of Bury, floure of eloquence
Which was in the time of great excellence,

5

Of your predecessour, the·v·kyng Henry,
Unto whose grace, he dyd present 30
Ryght famous bokes, of parfit memory:
Of hys faynyng wyth termes eloquent.
Whose fatall ficcions, are yet permanent.
Grounded on reason, wyth cloudy fygures
He cloked the trouth of al his scriptures.
                                35

6

The light of trouth, I lacke cunnyng to
  cloke
To drawe a curtayne, I dare not to pre-
  sume
Nor hyde my matter, with a misty smoke
My rudenes cunnyng, dothe so sore con-
  sume
Yet as I may, I shall blowe out a fume *40*
To hyde my mynde, vnderneth a fable
By couert coloure, well and probable.

7

Besechyng your grace, to pardon mine
  ignoraunce
Whiche this fayned fable, to eschue idle-
  nes
Haue so compiled, nowe without doubt-
  aunce   *45*
For to present, to your hye worthines
To folowe the trace, and all the perfitenes
Of my master Lydgate, with due exer-
  cise
Suche fayned tales, I do fynde and deuise.

8

For vnder a coloure, a truthe may arise *50*
As was the guise, in olde antiquitye
Of the Poetes olde, a tale to surmise
To cloke the trouthe, of their infirmitye
Or yet on ioye, to haue moralitye
I me excuse, if by necligence   *55*
That I do offende, for lacke of science.

*Youre graces most bounden seruaunt Stephen
Hawes, one of the gromes of your maiesties
Chambre, the .xxi. yeare of your prosperous
raygne.*

HOWE GRAUND AMOUR WALKED IN A MEDOWE,
AND MET WITH FAME, ENUIRONNED WITH
TONGUES OF FIRE. CHAP. I.

When Phebus entred was, in Geminy
Shinyng aboue, in hys fayre golden spere
And horned Dyane, then but one degre
In the crabbe had entred, fayre & cleare
When that aurora, did well appeare   *5*
In the depured ayre, and cruddy firma-
  ment

Text from: *The Historie of graunde Amoure and
la bell Pucel, called the Pastime of plesure,
conteining the Knowledge of the Seuen sciences
& the course of mans life in this world. Jnuented
by Stephen Hawes, grome of Kyng Henry the
seuenth his chamber.*
*Newely perused and imprynted by John Wayland
. . .* [etc.   Place and date in the colophon,
London, June 1, 1554.   Copy in the British
Museum, pressmark C.39.d.58.]

Forthe then I walked, without impediment

2

In to a medowe bothe gaye and glorious
Whiche Flora depainted with many a
  colour
Like a place of pleasure most solacious *10*
Encensyng out, the aromatike odoure
Of zepherus breathe, whiche that euery
  floure
Throughe his fume dothe alwaie en-
  gender
So as I went among the floures tender

3

By sodaine chaunce, a faire pathe I
  founde   *15*
On which I loked, and right oft I mused
And then all about, I behelde the grounde
With the faire pathe, whiche I sawe so
  vsed
My chaunce or fortune, I nothing re-
  fused
But in the pathe, forth I went a pace *20*
To knowe whither, and vnto what place

4

It woulde me bryng, by any similitude
So forth I went, were it ryght or wrong
Tyll that I sawe, of royall pulcritude
Before my face, an ymage fayre and
  strong   *25*
With two fayre handes, stretched out
  along
Unto two hye wayes, there in particion
And in the right hande, was this descrip-
  tion

5

This is the strayght waye of contempla-
  cion
Unto the ioyfull tower perdurable   *30*
Who that wyll walke, vnto that mancion
He must forsake, all thynges variable
With the vayne glory, so muche deceyu-
  able
And though the way, be hard and daun-
  gerous
The last ende therof, shalbe ryght pre-
  cious.   *35*

6

And in the other hande, ryght fayre
  wrytten was
This is the waye, of worldly dignitye
Of the actiue lyfe, who wyll in it passe
Unto the tower, of fayre dame beautye

Fame shal tell hym, of the way in cer-
taintye 40
Unto la bell pucell, the fayre lady excellent
Aboue all other, in cleare beauty splendent

7

I behelde ryght well, bothe the wayes
twayne
And mused oft, whyche was best to take
The one was sharpe, the other was more
plaine 45
And vnto myselfe, I began to make
A sodayne argument, for I myght not
slake
Of my great musyng, of this royall ym-
age
And of these two wayes, so muche in
vsage

8

For thys goodly picture was in altitude,
Nyne fote and more, of fayre marble
stone 51
Ryght well fauoured, and of great alti-
tude
Thoughe it were made, full many yeres
agone
Thus stode I musynge, my selfe all alone
By right long tyme, but at the last I
went 55
The actyue way, with all my whole en-
tent

9

Thus all alone, I began to trauayle
Forthe on my waye, by long continu-
aunce
But often times, I had great maruayle
Of the by pathes, so fulle of pleasaunce 60
Whiche for to take, I had great doubt-
aunce
But euermore, as nere as I myght
I toke the waye, whiche went before me
right

10

And at the laste, when Phebus in the west
Gan to auayle, with all his beames merye
When cleare Dyana, in the fayre south-
est 66
Gan for to ryse, lightyng our emispery
With clowdes cleare, wythout the stormy
pery
Me thought a farre, I had a vysyon
Of a picture, of marueylous facyon. 70

11

To whiche I went, without lenger delaye
Beholdyng well, the right faire portay-
ture
Made of fine copper, shynyng faire and
gaye
Full well truely, accordyng to measure
And as I thought, nine fote of stature 75
Yet in the breast, with letters fayre and
blewe
Was written, a sentence olde and true

12

This is the waye, and the sytuacion
Unto the toure, of famous doctrine
Who that will learne, must be ruled by
reason 80
And with all his diligence, he must en-
cline
Slouthe to eschue, and for to determine
And set his hert, to be intelligible
To a willyng herte, is nought impossible

13

Beside the ymage, I adowne me sette 85
After my laboure, my selfe to repose
Till at the last, with a gaspyng nette
Slouth my head caught, with his whole
purpose
It vayled not, the bodye for to dispose
Againste the heade, when it is applied 90
The heade must rule, it can not be denied

14

Thus as I satte, in a deadly slomber
Of a great horne, I hearde a royall blast
With which I awoke, and had a great
wonder
From whence it came, it made me sore
agast 95
I loked about, the night was well nere
past
And fayre golden Phebus, in the morow
graye
With clowdes redde, began to breake the
daye

15

I sawe come ridyng, in a valey farre
A goodly Ladye, enuironned about 100
With tongues of fire, as bright as any
starre
That fiery flambes, ensensed al way out
Whiche I behelde, and was in great doubt
Her Palfrey swift, rennyng as the winde
With two white greyhounds, that were
not behind 105

16

When that these greyhoundes, had me so
    espied
With faunyng chere, of great humilitie
In goodly haste, they fast vnto me hied
I mused why, and wherfore it shoulde be
But I welcomed them, in euery degree 110
They leaped oft, and were of me right
    faine
I suffred them, and cherished them againe

17

Their collers were of golde, and of tys-
    sue fine
Wherin their names, appeared by scrip-
    ture
Of Dyamondes that clerely do shine 115
The letters were grauen fayre and pure
To reade their names, I did my busye
    cure
The one was gouernaunce, the other
    named grace
Then was I gladde, of all this sodayne
    cace

18

And then the Ladye, with fiery flambe 120
Of brennyng tongues, was in my pres-
    ence
Upon her palfrey, whiche had vnto name
Pegase the swifte, so faire in excellence
Whiche sometime longed, with his premi-
    nence
To kyng Percius, the sonne of Jubiter 125
On whom he rode, by the worlde so
    farre

19

To me she saied, she marueyled muche
    why
That her greyhoundes, shewed me that
    fauoure
What was my name, she asked me truely
To whom I saied, it was la graunde
    Amoure   130
Besechyng you to be to me succoure
To the tower of doctrine, and also me
    tell
Your proper name, and where you do
    dwell.

20

My name quod she, in all the world is
    knowen
Iclipped Fame, in euery region   135
For I my horne in sundrye wise haue
    blowen

After the deathe, of many a champion
And with my tongues, haue made aye
    mencion
Of their great actes, agayne to reuiue
In flamyng tongues, for to abide on
    liue.   140

21

It was the custome of olde antiquitye
When the golden world, had domination
And nature highe, in her aucthoritie
More stronger had, her operation
Then she hath nowe, in her digres-
    sion   145
The people then did, all their busye payne
After their death, in Fame to liue agayne

22

Recorde of Saturne, the first kyng of
    Crete
Whiche in his youth, throughe his dili-
    gence
Founde first plowing, of the landes swete
And after this, by his great sapience 151
For the commen profite, and beneuolence
Of all metalles, he made diuision
One from another, by good prouision.

23

And then also, as some Poetes fayne 155
He founde shotyng, and drawyng of the
    bowe
Yet as of that, I am nothynge certaine
But for his cunnynge, of hye degre and
    lowe
He was well beloued, as I do well knowe
Throughe whose laboure, and aye busy
    cure   160
His fame shall liue, and shall right long
    endure

24

In whose time raigned, also in Thessayle
A parte of Grece, the kyng Meliȝyus
That was right strong, and fierce in
    battaile
By whose laboure, as the storye sheweth
    vs   165
He brake first horses, wilde and rigorious
Teachyng his men, on them right wel to
    ryde
And he him selfe, did first the horse be-
    stryde.

25

Also Mynerue, the right hardy Goddesse
In the same time, of so hyghe re-
    nowne   170

Uainquished Pallas, by her great worthines
And first made harneys, to laye his pride
adowne
Whose great defence, in euery realme
and towne
Was spredde about, for her hye chyualrye
Whiche by her harneys, wanne the victorye   *175*

26

Dothe not remayne, yet in remembraunce
The famous actes, of the noble Hercules
That so many monsters put to vtteraunce
By his great wisdome, and hye prowes
As the recule of Troye, beareth good
witnes   *180*
That in his time, he would no battayle
take
But for the wealthe, of the commens sake

27

Thus the whole mindes, were euer fixt
and set
Of noble men, in olde time to deuise
Suche thinges as were, to the commen
profite   *185*
For in that time, suche was their goodly
guise
That after death, their fame shoulde arise
For to endure, and abide in mynde
As yet in bokes, we maye them written
fynde

28

O ye estates, surmountyng in noblenes *190*
Remembre well, the noble paynyms all
Howe by their labour, they wanne the
highnes
Of worthy fame, to raygne memoriall
And them applyed, euer in speciall
Thinges to practise, whiche should pro-
fite be   *195*
To the comen wealth, and their heires
in fee.

OF THE SWETE REPORT OF FAME, OF THE
FAIRE LADY LA BEL PUCEL, IN THE TOWER
OF MUSIKE. CHAP. II.

29

And after this, Fame gan to expresse
Of ieopardous waye to the tower peril-
lous
And of the beautye, and the semelinesse
Of la bel Pucell, so gaye and glorious *200*
That dwelled in the tower so marueylous

Unto which might come, no maner of
creature
But by great laboure, and hard aduenture

30

For by the waye, there lye in waite
Gyantes great, disfigured of nature *205*
That all deuoureth, by their euil conceite
Against whose strength, there may no
man endure
They are so huge, and strong out of
measure
With many serpentes, foule and odious
In sundry likenesse, blacke and tedi-
ous   *210*

31

But beyonde them, a great sea there is
Beyonde whiche sea, there is a goodly
land
Most full of fruite, replete with ioye and
blisse
Of right fine golde, appeareth all the
sande
In this faire realme, where the tower
doth stand   *215*
Made all of gold, enameled aboute
With noble stories, whiche do appeare
without

32

In whiche dwelleth by great aucthoritye
Of la bel Pucell, whiche is so fayre and
bryght
To whom in beautye, no peare I can
see   *220*
For lyke as Phebus, aboue all starres in
lyght
When that he is, in his spere aryght
Dothe excede, with his beames cleare
So dothe her beauty, aboue other ap-
peare

33

She is bothe good, aye wise, and vertu-
ous   *225*
And also discended of a noble lyne
Ryche, comely, ryght meke, and bounte-
ous
All maner vertues, in her clearely shine
No uyce of her, maye ryght longe domyne
And I dame Fame, in euery Nacion *230*
Of her do make the same relation.

34

Her swete report, so my hart set on fyre
With brennyng loue, most hote and feruent

That her to see, I had great desyre
Saiynge to Fame, O Ladye excellent 235
I haue determined in my iudgement
For la bel Pucell, the most fayre ladye
To passe the waye, of so great ieopardye.

35

You shall quod Fame, attayne the victory
If you wyll do, as I shal to you say   240
And all my lesson, retayne in memory
To the tower of doctrine, ye shall take
    your waye
You are now wythin a dayes iourney
Both these greyhoundes, shal kepe you
    company
Loke that you cherishe them full gentely

36

And countenaunce the goodly portres,
Shall let you in, full well and nobly
And also shewe you, of the perfectnes
Of all the seuen sciences, ryght notably
There in your mynde, you may entent-
    ifely   250
Unto dame doctrine, geue perfite audi-
    ence
Whiche shall enfourme you, in euery
    science

37

Fare well she sayed, I may not nowe
    abide
Walke on your way, with all your whole
    delite
To the tower of doctrine, at this morowe
    tide   255
Ye shall to morowe, of it haue a syght
Kepe on your waye, nowe before you
    ryght
For I must hence, to specifye the dedes
Of their worthines, accordyng to their
    medes.

38

And with that she did, from me de-
    parte   260
Upon her stede, swifter then the wynde
When she was gone, full wofull was my
    hart
With inward trouble, oppressed was my
    mynde
Yet were the greyhoundes, left with me
    behind
Whiche did me comforte, in my great
    vyage   265
To the tower of doctrine, with their
    fawning courage.

39

So forthe I went, tossynge on my brayne
Greatly musynge, ouer hyll and vale
The way was troublous, & ey nothing
    playne
Tyll at the laste, I came to a dale   270
Beholdyng Phebus, declinyng lowe and
    pale
With my greyhoundes, in the fayre twy
    light
I sate me downe, for to rest me all
    nyght

40

Slouthe vpon me, so fast began to crepe
That of fyne force, I downe me layed 275
Upon an hyll, with my greyhoundes to
    slepe
When I was downe, I thought me well
    apayed
And to my selfe, these wordes then I
    sayed
Who will attaine, sone to his iourneys
    ende
To nourishe slouthe, he may not condis-
    cende.   280

HOWE FAME DEPARTED FROM GRAUNDE
AMOURE, AND LEFT WYTH HYM GOUERN-
AUNCE AND GRACE, AND HOWE HE WENT
TO THE TOWER OF DOCTRINE. CA.III.

41

Thus then I slept, til that Auroras bemes
Gan for to spreade, about the firmament
And the clere sunne, wt his golden
    stremes
Began for to rise, faire in the orient
Without Saturnus, blacke encombrement
And the little birdes, makyng melodye 286
Did me awake, with their swete armony.

42

I loked about, and sawe a craggy roche
Farre in the west, neare to the element
And as I did then, vnto it approche   290
Upon the toppe, I sawe refulgent
The royall tower, of morall document
Made of fine copper, wt turrettes faire
    and hye
Which against Phebus, shone so marueyl-
    ously

43

That for the verye perfect brightnes, 295
What of the tower, and of the cleare
    sunne

I coulde nothing beholde the goodlines
Of that palaice, where as doctrine did
  wonne
Tyll at the last, with misty windes donne
The radiant bryghtnes, of golden Phe-
  bus   *300*
Auster gan couer, wyth clowdes tene-
  brus.

44

Then to the tower I drewe nere and nere
And often mused, of the great hyghnes
Of the craggy rocke, which quadrant
  did appeare
But the fayre tower, so muche of riches
Was all about, sexangled doubtles   *305*
Gargeyld with greyhoundes, & with many
  lyons
Made of fyne golde, with diuers sundry
  dragons

45

The little turrets, wyth ymages of golde
About was set, which with the wynde aye
  moued   *310*
Wyth propre vyces, that I did well be-
  holde
About the towers, in sundry wise they
  houed
Wyth goodly pypes, in their mouthes
  ituned
That wyth the wynde, they pyped a
  daunce
Iclipped, amour de la hault pleasaunce. *315*

HOWE HE WAS LET IN BY COUNTENAUNCE
THE PORTERES, AND OF THE MARUEL-
OUS BUILDYNGE OF THE SAME TOWER.
CAPITULO · III ·

46

The tower was greate, and of maruelous
  wydenesse,
To whiche there was, no way to passe
  but one
Into the tower, for to haue an intresse
A grece there was, ychesyled all of stone
Out of the rocke, on whyche men did
  gone   *320*
Up to the tower, and in likewise did I
Wyth bothe the greyhoundes, in my com-
  pany

47

Tyll that I came, to a royall gate
Where I sawe standyng, the goodly portres

Whiche axed me, from whence I came
  alate   *325*
To whom I gan, in euery thing expresse
All myne aduenture, chaunce and busines
And eke my name, I tolde her euery dell
When she hearde thys, she liked me ryght
  well

48

Her name she sayed, was called countenaunce   *330*
In to the busy court, she did me then
  leade
Where was a fountayne, depured of
  pleasaunce
A noble spring, a royal conduit heade
Made of fyne golde, enameled with
  redde
And on the toppe, foure dragons blew
  and stoute   *335*
This dulcet water, in foure partes did
  spoute

49

Of whiche there flowed, foure riuers
  right cleare.
Sweter then Nysus, or Ganges was their
  odour
Tygrys, or Eufrates, vnto them no pere
I dyd then taste, the aromatike licoure *340*
Fragrant of fume, swete as any flower
And in my mouthe, it had a marueylous
  cent
Of diuers spices, I knew not what it
  mente

50

And after this, furder forthe me brought
Dame countenaunce, into a goodly hall
Of Jasper stones, it was wonderlye
  wrought   *346*
The windowes cleare, depured all of
  christal
And in the roufe, on hye ouer all
Of golde was made, a right crafty vyne
In stede of grapes, the Rubies there did
  shyne.   *350*

51

The flore was paued, with berall clarified
With pillers made, of stones precious
Like a place of pleasure, so gayely glori-
  fied
It might be called, a palaice glorious
So muche delectable, and solacious *355*
The hall was hanged, hye and circuler
With clothe of arras, in the richest maner

52

That treated well, of a full noble story
Of the doubty waye, to the tower perillous
Howe a noble knight, shoulde winne the
victory　　　360

[The rest of this stanza, and 7 more, describe the tapestry, which depicts the events
to be narrated in the poem, ending with the
wedding of the hero and La belle Pucell.]

60

And eke the clothe, made demonstration
How he wedded, the great ladye beaute-
ous　　　415
La bell Pucell, in her owne dominacion
After his labour, and passage daungerous
With solemne ioye, and mirthe melodious
This famous storye, well pyctured was
In the fayre hall, vpon the arras.　　420

61

The marshall, yclipped was dame Reason
And the yewres, also obseruaunce
The panter Pleasaunce, at euery season
The good butler, curteys continuaunce
And the chiefe coke, was called temper-
aunce,　　　425
The lady chamberlayne, named fidelitye
And the hye stewarde, Liberalitye.

62

There sate dame Doctrine, that lady gent
Whyche called me, vnto her presence
For to knowe all the whole entent
Of my commyng, vnto her excellence
Madame I sayed, to learne your scyence
I am comen, now me to applye
Wyth all my cure, in perfect studye.

63

And yet also, I vnto her then shewed 435
My name and purpose, without doublenes
For very great ioye, than were endued
Her cristall eyes, full of lowlines
When that she knewe, for very sikernes
That I was he, that should so attayne 440
La bell Pucell, with my busy payne.

64

And after this, I had right good chere
Of meate and drinke, there was great
plentye
Nothing I wanted, were it chepe or dere
Thus was I serued, wt delicate dishes
dainty　　　445

And after this, with all humilitie
I went to doctrine, praiyng her goo
grace
For to assigne me, my first learnyng
place

65

Seuen daughters, most expert in cun-
nyng
Without foly, she had well engendred 45
As the seuen Sciences, in vertue so shin-
yng
At whose encrease, there is great thanke
rendred
Unto the mother, as nothing surrendred
Her good name, and her dulcet sounde
Whiche did engender, their originall
ground.　　　45

66

And first to gramer she first me sent
To whose request, I did well obey
With diligence, forth on my way I went
Up to a chambre, depaynted fayre and
gaye
And at the chambre, in right riche araye
We were let in, by highe aucthoritye 46
Of the ryght noble, dame congruitie.

[Chapter v is Grammar, chap. vi Logic,
chap. vii Rhetoric, chap. viii Invention, a part
of Rhetoric. In chap. v Graunde Amour begs
to knowe what a noun substantive is:—]

To whom she answered, right gently
agayne　　　53
Saiyng alwaye, that a nowne substantyue
Might stande without helpe of an ad-
iectyue

77

The latyne worde, whiche that is referred
Unto a thing, whiche is substantiall
For a nowne substantiue, is well auerred
And with a gender, is declinall　　53
So, all the eyght partes in generall
Are latyn wordes, annexed proprelye
To euery speache, for to speake formally

[Chapters vi and vii are omitted. Stanza
3, etc., of viii follow:]

95

It was the guyse, in olde antiquitye
Of famous poetes, ryght ymaginatife 66
Fables to fayne, by good aucthoritye
They were so wyse, and so inuentyfe
Theyr obscure reason, fayre and sugra-
tyfe

Pronounced trouthe, vnder clowdy fygures
By the inuention, of theyr fatall scriptures 665

96

And thirdly, they had suche a fansy
In thys hye art, to be intelligible
Their fame encreasyng, euermore truely
To slouthe euer, they were inuyncible
To their wofull hartes, was nought im-
possible 670
Wyth brennyng loue, of insaciate fyre
Newe thynges to fynde, they set their
desyre

97

For thoughe a man, of hys propre mynde
Be inuentyfe, and he do not applye
His fantasye, vnto the busye kynde 675
Of hys cunnynge, it may not ratifye
For fantasye, must nedes exemplifye
His new inuention, & cause hym to en-
tende
Wyth whole desyre, to bryng it to an
ende

98

And fourthly, by good estimation 680
He must number, all the whole circum-
staunce
Of this matter, with breuiacion
That he walke not, by long continuaunce
The perambulat way, full of all variaunce
By estimacion, is made annunciate 685
Whether the matter, be long or breuiate

99

For to Inuention, it is equipolent
The matter founde, right well to com-
prehende
In suche a space, as is conuenient
For properlye, it dothe euer pretende 690
Of all the purpose, the length to extende
So estimation, may ryght well conclude
The perfite number, of euery similitude

100

And yet then, the retentife memory
Whiche is the fift, must euer agre-
gate 695
All matters thought, to retayne inwardlye
Tyll reason therof, hath made a probate
And by scripture, will make demonstrate
Outwardly, accordyng to the thought
To proue a reason, vpon a thyng of
nought 700

101

Thus when the fourth, hath wrought ful
wonderly
Then must the mynde, worke vpon them
all
By cours ingenious, to runne directly
After their thoughtes, then in generall
The mynde must cause them, to be mem-
orial 705
As after this, shall appeare more openlye
All whole exprest, by dame Philosophye.

102

O trust of vertue, and of royall pleasure
Of famous Poetes, many yeres ago
O insaciate couetise, of the special treas-
ure 710
Of newe inuencion, of idlenes the fo
We may you laude, and often praise also
And specially, for worthy causes thre
Whiche to this daye, we may bothe here
and see

103

As to the first, your whole desire was
set 715
Fable to fayne, to eschue idlenes
With ampliation, more cunnyng to get
By the laboure, of inuentife busines
Touchyng the trouthe, by couert likenes
To disnull vice, and the vycious to blame
Your dedes therto, exemplified the same.

104

And secondly, right well you did endite
Of the worthy actes, of many a conquer-
oure
Throughe which labour, that you did so
write
Unto this daye, rayneth the honoure 725
Of euery noble, and myghty warriour
And for your labour, and your busy paine
Your fame yet liueth, & shal endure cer-
taine

105

And eke to praise you, we are greatly
bounde
Because our cunnyng, from you so pre-
cedeth 730
For you therof, were first originall
grounde
And vpon your scripture, our science en-
sueth
Your splendent verses, our lightnes renueth
And so we ought, to laude and magnifie

Your excellent springes, of famous
poetry   *735*

106

But rude people, opprest with blindnes
Against your fables, will often solisgise
Suche is their minde, such is their folish-
nes
For they beleue, in no maner of wyse
That vnder a coloure, a trouth may
aryse   ,   *740*
For folyshe people, blynded in a matter
Will often erre, when they of it do clatter

107

O all ye cursed, and suche euil foles
Whose sightes be blynded, ouer all with
foly
Open your eyes, in the pleasaunt
scholes   *745*
Of parfect cunnyng, or that you replye
Against fables, for to be contrarye
For lacke of cunnyng, no maruell though
you erre
In suche scyence, whiche is from you so
farre

108

For now the people, whiche is dull and
rude   *750*
If that they do reade, a fatall scripture
And can not moralise, the similitude
Whiche to their wittes, is so harde and
obscure
Then will they saye, that it is sene in vre
That nought do poetes, but depaynt and
lye   *755*
Deceiuyng them, by tongues of flattery.

109

But what for that, they can not defame
The Poetes actes, whiche are in effect
Unto them selues, remayneth the shame
To dysprayse that, which they can not
correct   *760*
And if that they, had in it inspect
Than they would it praise, and often
eleuate
For it shoulde be to them, so delicate.

[Chap. x, on Disposition, 12 stanzas, and
most of chap. xi, on Elocution, 40 stanzas,
are omitted.]

158

Cunnyng is lyght, and also pleasaunt *1100*
A gentle burden, wythout greuousnes
Unto hym, that is ryght well appliaunt

For to beare it, with all his busines
He shall attaste, the welle of fruitefulnes
Whiche Uirgil clarified, and also Tul-
lius   *1105*
With latyn pure, swete, and delicious.

159

From whence my master lidgate derified,
The depured rethorike, in Englyshe lan-
guage
To make our tongue, so clearely purified
That the vyle termes, shoulde nothing
arage   *1110*
As like a pye, to chatter in a cage
But for to speake, with rethorike form-
ally
In the good order, withouten vylany.

160

And who his bokes, list to heare or see
In them he shall finde, elocution   *1115*
With as good order, as any maye be
Kepyng full close, the moralization
Of the trouthe, of his great intencion
Whose name is regestred, in remem-
braunce
For to endure, by long continuaunce

[One more stanza completes xi. Chap xii,
8 stanzas, treats of Pronunciation; chap.
xiii, 8 stanzas, of Memory. Two stanzas
of chap. xiv are omitted; then:]

180

O pensyfe harte, in the stormy pery
Mercury northwest, thou maist se ap-
peare   *1255*
After tempest, to gladde, thine emispery
Hoyse vp thy sayle, for thou must drawe
neare
Towarde the ende, of thy purpose so
cleare
Remembre the, of the trace and daunce
Of poetes olde, wyth all thy puruey-
aunce.   *1260*

181

As moral Gower, whose sentencious dewe
Adowne reflareth, with fayre golden
beames
And after Chaucers, all abroade dothe
shewe
Our vyces to clense, his depured streames
Kindlyng our hartes, wyth the fiery
leames
Of morall vertue, as is probable   *1266*
In all his bokes, so swete and profitable

182

The boke of fame, whiche is sentencious
He drewe him selfe, on his owne inuen-
tion
And then the tragidies, so piteous   *1270*
Of the nintene ladyes, was his translation
And vpon his ymagination
He made also, the tales of Caunterbury
Some vertuous, and some glad and merye

183

And of Troylus, the piteous doloure   *1275*
For his ladye Cresyde, full of doublenes
He did bewayle, full well the langoure
Of all his loue, and great vnhappines
And many other bokes doubtles
He did compyle, whose goodly name   *1280*
In prynted bookes, dothe remayne in
fame.

184

And after him, my master Lydgate
The monke of bury, did him well apply
Bothe to contryue, and eke to translate
And of vertue, euer in especially   *1285*
For he did compyle, then full ryally
Of our blessed ladye, the conuersation
Saynt Edmundes life, martred with
treason

185

Of the fall of Princes, ryght wofully
He did endite, in all piteous wise   *1290*
Folowyng his auctoure, Bocas rufully
A ryght great boke, he did truely com-
pryse
A good ensample, for vs to despyse
This worlde so full, of mutabilitie
In whiche no man, can haue a certainte.

186

And thre reasons, ryght greatly profit-
able
Under coloure, he cloked craftely
And of the chorle, he made the fable
That shitte the byrde, in a cage so closely
The pamflete, sheweth it expreslye   *1300*
He fayned also, the court of sapience
And translated, with all his diligence.

187

The great boke, of the last destruction
Of the citye of Troye, whylome so fam-
ous
Howe for a woman, was the confusion
And betwene vertue, and the life vicious
Of Gods and Goddesses, a boke solacious

He did compyle, and the tyme to passe
Of loue he made, the bryght temple of
glasse

188

Were not these thre, greatly to com-
mende   *1310*
Which them applied, such bokes to con-
triue
Whose famous draughtes, no man can
amend
The tyme of slouthe, they did from them
driue
After their deathe, for to abide on lyue
In worthy fame, by many a nacion   *1315*
Their bokes, their actes, do make rela-
tion

189

O master Lydgate, the most dulcet
spryng
Of famous rethoryke, wyth ballade royall
The chefe originall, of my learnyng
What vayleth it, on you for to call   *1320*
Me for to ayde, nowe in especiall
Sythen your bodye, is now wrapte in
chest
I pray God to geue, your soule good rest

190

O what losse is it, of suche a one
It is to great truely, for me to tell   *1325*
Sythen the tyme, that his life was gone
In all this realme his pere did not dwell
Aboue all other, he did so excell
None sythe his tyme, in arte woulde suc-
cede
After their death, to haue for their
mede   *1330*

191

But many a one, is ryght well expert
In this cunnyng, but vpon aucthoritie
They fayne no fables, pleasaunt and
couerte
But spende their time, in vaynefull vanitie
Makyng ballades, of feruent amitie   *1335*
As gestes and trifles, without fruitefulnes
Thus all in vayne, they spende their busi-
nes

192

I little or nought, expert in poetrye
Of my master Lidgate, will folowe the
trace

1330. Insert *fame* after *have*, as in reprint of
the 1555 text.

As euermore, so his name to magni-
fye   *1340*
With suche little bokes, by Gods grace
If in this worlde, I may haue the space
The little cunnyng, that his grace me sent
In tyme among, in suche wise shalbe
    spent.

193

And yet nothing, vpon presumption *1345*
My master Lydgate, I will not enuy
But all onely, is myne intencion
With suche laboure, my selfe to occupy
As white by blacke, dothe shyne more
    clearely
So shal their matters, appeare more pleas-
    aunt   *1350*
Bisyde my draughtes, rude, and ignoraunt

[The next chapter, xv, of 7 stanzas, deals
with Arsmetrik. Chap. xvi, of music,
opens :]

201

When splende*n*t Phebus, in his middaye
    speare
Was highe in Gemine, in the freshe sea-
    son
Of lustye Maye, with golden beames
    cleare
And darke Dyane, made declination
When Flora florished, in this nacion *1405*
I called vnto minde, right inwardly
The report of Fame, so muche ententiflye

202

Of la bell Pucell, in the tower musicall
And ryght anone, vnto the tower I went
Where I sawe, a temple made of Crys-
    tal   *1410*
In whiche musyke, the lady excellent
Played on base organes, expedient
Accordyng well, vnto dyopason
Dyapenthe, and eke dyetesseron

[Seventy more stanzas complete the chapter, in which Graunde Amour sees and dances
with La Bell Pucell, goes from her to a
temple to bewail his passion and there is met
by Counsel, who reminds him of the miser-
ies of lovers of olden time, but advises him
to pluck up heart. Chap. xviii, 40 stanzas,
is a disputation between Graunde Amour
and La bell Pucell. In chap. xix, 24 stanzas,
she accepts his love, but at once departs
in a ship. Graunde Amour is consoled by
Counsel in chap. xx, 20 stanzas. In chap.
xxi he betakes himself to Geometry, in xxii
to Astronomy; chap xxiii is "Of the direct

operation of Nature", xxiv on the five wits,
xxv on the supernal bodies. In chap. xxvi
Graunde Amour comes to the tower of Chivalry, and then visits the temple of Mars,
where he hears discourse on knighthood, is
made knight, and sets out on horseback for
adventures. In xxix he encounters a foolish
dwarf, who accompanies him as his varlet.
The portions of the work dealing with this
dwarf, Godfrey Gobelive, are in couplets, and
attempt a realistic use of Kentish dialect as
well as a comic effect. Godfrey counsels
Graunde Amour against women and marriage, and tells a clumsy story of Virgil
the enchanter. They enter the temple of
Venus, and Graunde Amour presents his bill
of complaint. Venus writes a letter for him
to La Bell Pucell, and the knight and his
varlet continue their travels. Chap. xxxiii
follows.]

HOWE GRAUNDE AMOURE DISCOMFITED THE
GYAUNT WITH THREE HEADES, AND WAS
RECEIUED OF THREE FAYRE LADYES.
CAPI. XXXIII

538

When golden Phebus, in the Capricorne
Gan to ascende, fast vnto Aquary *4215*
And Janus bifrus, the croune had worn
With his frosty bearde in January,
When cleare Dyana, ioyned with Mercury
The cristall ayre, and assured firmament
Were all depured, without encumbre-
    ment.   *4220*

539

Forthe then I rode, at mine owne aduen-
    ture
Ouer the mountaines, and the craggy
    rockes
To beholde the countres, I had great
    pleasure
Where corall growed, by ryght hye
    stockes
And the Popingayes, in the tree toppes
Then as I rode, I sawe me beforne *4226*
Beside a well hang, bothe a shelde and a
    horne

540

When I came there, adowne my stede I
    light
And the faire bugle, I right well behelde
Blasyng the armes, as well as I myght
That was so grauen, vpon the goodly
    shelde
First all of siluer, did appeare the felde
With a rampyng Lyon, of fine golde so
    pure   *4233*

And vnder the shelde, there was this
    scripture.

541

If any knight, that is aduenturous
Of his great pride, dare the bugle blowe
There is a gyaunt, bothe fierce and rigor-
    ious
That with his might, shall him sone ouer-
    throw
This is the waye, as ye shall nowe knowe
To la bell Pucell, but withouten faile *4240*
The sturdy gyaunt, will geue you battaile.

542

When I the scripture, once or twise had
    reade
And knewe therof, all the whole effect
I blewe the horne, without any dreade
And toke good hart, all feare to abiect
Makyng me ready, for I did suspect
That the great gyaunt, vnto me woulde
    haste
When he had hearde me, blowe so loude
    a blast.

543

I alite anone, vpon my gentle stede
About the well, then I rode to and fro
And thought right well, vpon the ioyfull
    mede   *4251*
That I shoulde haue, after my payne and
    wo
And of my lady, I did thinke also
Tyll at the last, my verlet did me tell
Take hede quod he, here is a fende of hell

544

My greyhoundes leaped, and my stede did
    start
My spere I toke, and did loke about
With hardy courage, I did arme my hart
At last I sawe, a sturdy gyaunt stoute
Twelue fote of length, to feare a great
    route   *4260*
Thre heades he had, and he armed was
Bothe heades and bodye, all aboute with
    brasse

545

Upon his first heade, in his helmet crest
There stode a fane, of the silke so fine
Where was written, with letters of the
    best
My name is falshode, I shall cause encline
My neighbours goodes, for to make them
    myne
Alway I get, their lande or substaunce
With subtile fraude, deceypt, or variaunce

546

And when a knight, with noble chyualry
Of la bell Pucell, shoulde attayne the
    grace   *4271*
With my great falshode, I worke so sub-
    tilly
That in her hart, he hath no dwellyng
    place
Thus of his purpose, I do let the case
This is my power, and my condicion
Loue to remoue, by a great illusion

547

And of the seconde heade, in a silken tas-
    sell
There I sawe written, ymagination
My crafty witte, is withouten fayle
Loue for to bring, in perturbacion *4280*
Where la bell Pucell, woulde haue affec-
    tion
To graunde amoure, I shall a tale deuise
To make her hate him, and him to despise.

548

By my false witte, so muche ymaginatife
The trouthe ful oft, I bryng in disease
Where as was peace, I cause to be strife
I will suffer no man, for to liue in ease
For if by fortune, he will be displease
I shall of hym, ymagen suche a tale
That out of ioye, it shall turne into bale.

549

And on the thirde heade, in a stremer
    grene   *4291*
There was written, my name is pariury
In many a towne, I am knowen as I
    wene
Where as I list, I do great iniury
And do forswere my selfe full wrong-
    fully
Of all thinges, I do hate conscience
But I loue lucre, with all diligence

550

Betwene two louers, I do make debate
I will so swere, that they thinke I am
    true   *4299*
For euer falshode, with his owne estate
To a lady cometh, and sayeth to eschue
An inconuenience, that ye do not rue
Your loue is nought, ymagination know-
    eth
I sweare in likewise, and anone she
    troweth

551

That we haue saied, is of very trouthe
Her loue she casteth, right cleane out of
minde
That with her loue, she is wondersly
wrough
With fayned kindenes, we do her so
blinde
Then to her louer, she is full vnkinde
Thus our thre powers, were ioyned in
one   *4310*
In this mighty gyaunt, many dayes agone

552

And when that I, had sene euery thing
My spere I charged, that was very great
And to this gyaunt, so fiercely commyng
I toke my course, that I with him mette
Breakyng my spere, vpon his first helmet
And right anone, adowne my stede I light
Drawyng my swerde, that was faire and
bright.

553

Iclipped Clara prudence, that was faire
and sure
At the gyaunt I stroke, with all my vale-
aunce   *4320*
But be my strokes, might right well en-
dure
He was so great, and huge of puysaunce
His glaue he did, against me aduaunce
Whiche was ·iiii· fote, and more of
cuttyng
And as he was, his stroke dischargyng

554

Because his stroke, was heauy to beare
I lept aside, from him full quickely
And to him I ranne, without any feare
When he had discharged, agayne full
lightly
He rored loude, and sware I shoulde
abye   *4330*
But what for that, I strake at him fast
And he at me, but I was not agast.

555

But as he fought, he had a vauntage
He was right hye, and I vnder him lowe
Till at the last, with lusty courage
Upon the side, I gaue him suche a blowe
That I right neare, did him ouerthrowe
But right anone, he did his mighte en-
large
That vpon me, he did suche strokes dis-
charge

556

That I vnneth, might make resistence *4340*
Against his power, for he was so strong
I did defend me, agaynst his vyolence
And thus the battayle, dured full right
long
Yet euermore, I did thinke among
Of la bell Pucell, whom I shoulde at-
tayne
After my battailles, to release my payne

557

And as I loked, I sawe then auale
Fayre golden Phebus, with his beames
redde
Then vp my courage, I began to hale
Whiche nighe before, was agone and
deade   *4350*
My swerde so entred, that the gyant
bledde
And with my strokes, I cutte of anone
One of his legges, amiddes the thyghe
bone.

558

Then to the grounde, he adowne did fall
And vpon me, he gan to loure and glumme
Enforsyng him, so for to ryse withall
But that I shortly, vnto him did come
With his thre heades, he spitte all his
venyme
And I with my sworde, as fast as coulde
be   *4359*
With all my force, cut of his heades
three.

559

When I had so, obtayned the victory
Unto me then, my varlet well sayed
You haue demeaned you, well and
worthely
My greyhoundes lept, and my stede then
brayed
And then from farre, I sawe well arayed
To me come ridyng, thre ladyes right
swete
Forthe then I rode, and did with them
mete

560

The first of them, was called Ueritie
And the seconde, good Operation
The thirde also, yclipped Fidelitie *4370*
All they at once, with good opinion
Did geue to me, great laudation
And me beseched, with their hart entire
With them to rest, and to make good
chere.

561

I graunted them, & then backewarde we
   rode
The mighty gyaunt, to se and beholde
Whose huge bodye, was more then fiue
   cart lode
Whiche lay there bledyng, that was al-
   most colde
They for his deathe, did thanke me many
   a folde
For he to them, was enemy mortall *4380*
Wherefore his thre heades, they toke in
   speciall

562

And then Ueritie, on the first fane
Did set aloft, of falshode the heade
And good Operacion, in likewise had tane
Of ymagination, that full sore then
   bledde
Upon his heade aloft, vpon his banner
   redde
And in likewise, Fidelitie had serued
Periuries heade, as he had well deserued

563

And with swete songes, and swete armony
Before me they rode, to their fayre
   castell   *4390*
So forthe I rode, with great ioye and
   glory
Unto the place, where these ladyes did
   dwell
Set on a rocke, beside a spryng or a
   well
And fayre Obseruaunce, the goodly por-
   tresse
Did vs receiue, with solemne gladnes

564

Then to a chamber, that was very bryght
They did me leade, for to take mine ease
After my trouble, and my great sturdy
   fight
But thre woundes I had, causyng my dis-
   ease   *4399*
My payne and wo, they did sone appease
And healed my woundes, with salue aro-
   matike
Tellyng me of a great gyaunt lunatike.

565

Whose name truely, was called Uariaunce
Whom I shoulde mete, after my depart-
   yng
These ladies, vnto me did great pleasaunce
And in the meane while, as we were
   talkyng

For me my supper, was in ordeynyng
Thus when by temperaunce, it was prepared
And then to it we went, and ryght well
   fared

566

Tell me quod Ueritie, if you be con-
   tent   *4410*
What is your name, so hye aduenturous
And who that you, into this coast hath
   sent
Madame I saide, I was so amorous
Of la bell Pucell, so fayre and beauteous
La graunde amoure, truely is my name
Whiche seke aduentures, to attayne the
   fame

567

A ha quod she, I thought asmuche before
That you were he, for your great hardi-
   nes
La bell Pucell, must loue you euermore
Whiche for her sake, in your hye nobles
Dothe suche actes, by chyualrous excesse
Her gentle hart, may nothing denye *4422*
To rewarde your mede, wyth loue full
   feruently.

568

Thus did we passe time, in all maner of
   ioye
I lacked nothing, that might make me
   solace
But euermore, as noble Troylus of Troye
Full oft I thought, on my faire ladyes
   face
And her to se, a muche lenger space
When time was come, to rest I was
   brought
All to me longyng, there lacked right
   nought   *4430*

569

What shoulde I wade, by perambulucion
My time is shorte, and I haue farre to
   sayle
Unto the lande, of my conclusion
The winde is east, right slowe without
   fayle
To blowe my shippe, of diligent trauayle
To the last ende, of my matter troublous
With waues enclosed, so tempestuous.

570

Right in the morowe, when aurora clere
Her radiaunt beames, began for to
   spreade
And splendent Phebus, in his golden spere

The crystall ayre, did make fayre and
　redde　　　　　　　　　　　　　*4441*
Darke Dyane, declinyng pale as anye
　ledde
When the little byrdes, sweetly did syng
Laudes to their maker, early in the morn-
　yng.

CAPIT. XXXIIII

571

Vp I arose, and did make me readye
For I thought long, vnto my iourneys
　ende
My greyhoundes lept, on me right merely
To cheare me forwarde, they did conde-
　scende
And the thre ladies, my cheare to amende
A good breakefast, did for me ordayne
They were right gladde, the gyaunt was
　slayne.　　　　　　　　　　　　*4451*

[The work extends through 45 chapters
and a brief author's "Excusation" at close;
in all 759 stanzas, and, with the two passages in couplets, of about 5765 lines. The
story, beyond chap. xxxiii, takes Graunde
Amour to the palace of Comfort under
guidance of Dame Perseveraunce; he then
vanquishes a giant with seven heads, continues to the palace of Patience, and slays
a dragon. As the smoke from the death-
throes of the "blacke and tedyous" monster
passes away, the mansion of La Bell Pucell
becomes visible. The hero is welcomed, and
the marriage ceremony performed. Many
years of happiness ensue; then, says the
author, Old Age warned me, soon Death
arrested me, and all my life was spent. In
chap. xlii Remembrance makes his epitaph,
modeling it on *Earth upon earth.* Fame
then praises him, comparing him to each of
the Nine Worthies. Time combats Fame's
pretensions to confer immortality, and Eternity utters a closing moralization.]

WILLIAM NEVILL

THE CASTELL OF PLEASURE

(Extracts)
and
DIALOGUE BETWEEN NEVILL AND COPLAND

Nothing is known of William Nevill except that he was the second son of Richard Nevill, Baron Latimer. His elder brother John, third baron Latimer, who died in 1543, was the husband of that Katharine Parr who later became the sixth wife of Henry the Eighth. We infer from the words of Copland to Nevill, in the introductory stanzas, that this poem was written in Nevill's youth; it was printed by Pepwell in 1518 (whence this text) and Dibdin describes a print, undated but ?earlier, by de Worde. From this dialogue it might be inferred that Copland was the responsible printer; but as he was for some time employed by de Worde in an "editorial" capacity, it is possible that he could arrogate to himself the rôle of publisher in this discussion.

The figure of Robert Copland, fl. 1508-1547, is of interest to the student of the later Transition. His own typographical work is not very good, and the dozen or so books from his press are nearly all slight. But he differs from his employer de Worde and resembles Caxton in his literary attempts and his translations; he goes further than Caxton, however, in his adoption of a "popular" tone when writing his two independent works. These compositions, Jyl of Brentford's Testament and The Hye Way to the Spyttel Hous, although unoriginal in plan and clumsy in execution, are frankly human in their material; and it is the double strain in Copland, the address to the two publics as in Skelton, which marks him so plainly with the stamp of the Transition. When he translates, and often in his prologues and epilogues to other men's work, he uses affectations and Latinisms; he talks of "odiferaunt flowers", of "misorned language", of "the divine savitude of God", etc. These are concessions to "high style", which Chaucer's Host might have scorned; but at the next moment Copland can speak as directly, as practically, and with as broadly coarse an appeal as Skelton himself or Harry Bailly himself.

Copland translated, from the French, the Kalender of Shepeherdes, the romances of King Apollonius of Tyre, of Helyas, and of Ipomydon, the Secret of Secrets, three marriage poems, etc. He added a long verse-invocation to Chertsey's Passion of Our Lord, appended stanzas on French dances to Barclay's book on French pronunciation, and stanzas on Newfangleness to the 1530 print of Chaucer's Parlement of Foules; to William Walter's translation of Boccaccio's Guiscard and Sigismonda he wrote a prologue, epilogue, and various interspersed comments, and to this poem the introductory and final stanzas as here printed. Most of these productions are wooden, aimed at a public of aristocratic or didactic tastes; but in his Hye Way, especially, there is some real feeling for nature as well as for human nature. And the same thing might be said of Nevill's picture of the fall of evening, although he even more than Copland is deeply branded with the iron of Hawes' formulae and Hawes' vocabulary.

Pepwell, the printer of this text of Nevill, followed the "editorial" procedure of Caxton and of Copland by prefixing to Anslay's translation of the Cité des

Dames a verse-prologue of four stanzas in rime royal; this is reprinted by Flügel in Anglia 12:13-14.

SELECT REFERENCE LIST XII

Dibdin, Typographical Antiquities: or the History of Printing in England, Scotland, and Ireland, etc. London, 1810-19, 4 vols.

> The unique copy of the de Worde print of this poem is discussed ii:371-2; it was then in the Roxburghe collection, dispersed 1812. Copland is discussed *ibid.*, iii:111-126, and his stanzas appended to the Parlement of Foules are reprinted *ibid.*, ii:268-70.

Handlists of English Printers 1501-1556, London, 1895-1913, 4 vols., compiled by Gordon Duff, H. R. Plomer, etc.

Plomer, Wynkyn de Worde and his Contemporaries, London, 1925.

Copland's Hye Way is reprinted in Utterson's Select Pieces of Early Popular Poetry, ii:1-50, and in Hazlitt's Early Popular Poetry iv:17-72. For a discussion of the poem see Herford's Literary Relations of England and Germany, 357-62. There is an extract from the poem in Flügel's Neuengl. Lesebuch, pp. 203-6.

On Copland's appendix to Barclay see Flügel *ibid.* 423; and for one of his marriage poems translated from the French see Hazlitt, *op. cit.*, iv: 73-80, and also Wright's Poems of Walter Mapes, Camden Society, 1841, p. 295, from the text in MS Bodl. Digby 181. This latter was long ascribed to Lydgate.

Flügel's Lesebuch gives one stanza of Nevill's poem, at p. 17, and in the Notes, pp. 374-5, prints Copland's prologue-stanzas.

Coplande the prynter to the auctour

Your mynde consydered / & your good entent
Theffecte regarded / in euery maner case
Your cyrcunstaunce / and labour dylygent
Who wyll construe / is of grete effycace
(Y)our sentences morally tenbrace
Concerneth reason of lauryate grauyte
Yonge tender hertes / talecte with amyte

Your aege also flourynge in vyrent youthe
So to bestowe is gretely to commende
Bookes to endyte of maters ryght vncouthe   *10*
Ensample gyuynge to all suche as pretende
In tharte of loue theyr myndes to condescende
In termes fresshe / theyr courage to endewe

Not with rude toyes / but elegant and newe

Yet ben there many that lytell regarde
Your pleasures castell / inhabyte with Beaute
And I am sure wold gyue but small rewarde
For this your labour / and studyous dyte
But had ye compyled some maner subtylte
Lucre to gete / theyr neyghbour to begyle   *20*
They wolde alowe it a perfyt dyscrete style

Thauctour

My boke of loue / belonges to no suche arte
But to the pleasure / is his hoole affeccyon
Of gentyll people / whiche lyketh to take parte
In pleasaunt youth / with amorous dyleccyon
Honour regarded / in clene cyrcunspeccyon
Layenge aparte / all wylfull vayne desyre
To conforte them that brenne in louynge fyre

Text from: *The Castell of pleasure. The conueyaunce of a dreme how Desyre went to ye castell of pleasure / Wherin was the gardyn of affecyon inhabyted by Beaute to whome he amerously expressed his loue / vpon the whiche supplycacion rose grete stryfe dysputacion / & argument between Pyte & Dysdayne.*—(Colophon) Printed by Harry Pepwell, London, 1518. (Brit. Mus. black letter, 18 leaves, no pagin., in sixes.)

Copland

Bokes of loue innumerable prynted be
I mene of ladyes / and many a hardy
   knyght   30
Withoute regarde of sensuall nycete
In loue exployntynge / truly with all
   theyr myght
But loue of golde / these dayes blyndeth
   the syght
Of men and women / hauynge theyr
   chefe delyte
Onely for mede to do theyr appetyte.

Thauctour

Emprynt this boke / Coplande at my
   request
And put it forth to euery maner state
It doost no good lyenge styll in my chest
To passe the tyme some wyll bye it algate
Cause it is newe / compyled now of late
At leest way yonge folke / wyll gladly
   seke recure   41
Beauty to gete in the toure of pleasure.

[Copland]

At your instaunce / I shall it glad(l)y
   impresse
But the vtteraunce I thynke wyll be but
   smale
Bokes be not set by / theyr tymes is past
   I gesse
The dyce and cardes / in drynknge wyne
   and ale
Tables / cayles / and balles / they be
   now set a sale
Men lete theyr chyldren vse all suche
   harlotry   48
That byenge of bokes they vtterly deny

Finit prologus

En passant le temps sans mal penser
Tornyng & trauersyng hystoryes vn-
   ste(d)faste
In Ouydes bokes of transformacyon
It was my fortune and chaunce at the
   laste
In ouertornyng of þe leues to se in what
   facyon
Phebus was inflamyd by inspyracyon
Of cruell cupyd to hym immercyable
Whiche of hym was worthy no commen-
   dacyon
Shewyng hymselfe alwayes deceyuable
Therfore I wolde gladly yf I were able
The maner playnly and in few wordes
   dysclose   10

How phebus and cupyd togyder were
   compenable
Fyrst it to shewe I wyll me dyspose

Phebus set on pryde and hault in corage
Spake these wordes of grete audacyte
Cupyde thou boy of yonge and tender
   aege
How mayst thou be so bolde to compare
   with me
These arowes becomes me as thou mayst
   clerely se
Wherwith I may wounde bothe man and
   beste
And for that at all creatures be subgect
   to the
So moche is thy power lesse than myn at
   eche feste   20
Well well sayd cupyde it lyketh you to
   geste
This sayd / he assended to the mount
   pernassus
On the hyght his armis shortly abrode
   he keste
And sayd I trust I shall this in haste
   dyscusse.

For a profe he toke forth of his arowy
   quyuer
A golden darte with loue ryght peny-
   trable
Made sharp at the poynt that it myght
   enter
With it he stroke phebus with a stroke
   ryght lamentable
It to resyste he was weyke and vnable
The stroke of his power who can or may
   resyste   30
But he must obey / and to loue be agre-
   able
Constreygned by cupyde which may
   stryke whom he lyst
An other darte he toke soone in his fyste
Contrary to thoder ledyn blont and heuy
With this he stroke Phebus loue or she
   wyste
So that the more he desyred the more
   she dyd deny

Her name was daphnys which was deuoyed of loue
By dame saunce mercy which made hym
   to complayne
Cupyde in sondry wyse his power dyde
   proue
On thone with loue on thoder with dysdayne   40

Thone dyde fle thoder wolde optayne
Thone was glad thoder was in wo
Thone was pencyfe and oppressyd with
　　payne
Thoder in Joy cared not though it were
　　so
By fere and dysdayne she dyd hym ouergo
Lyke to an hare she ranne in haste
He folowed lyke a grehounde desyre
　　wrought hym wo
But all was in vayne his labour was but
　　waste.

The nyght drew nye the day was at a
　　syde
My herte was heuy I moche desyred rest
Whan without comfort alone I dyd abyde
Seynge the shadowes fall from the hylles
　　in the west　　　　　　　　　　　　52
Eche byrde vnder boughe drewe nye to
　　theyr nest
The chymneys from ferre began to smoke
Eche housholder went about to lodge his
　　gest
The storke feringe stormes toke the
　　chymney for a cloke
Eche chambre & chest were sonne put
　　vnder locke
Curfew was ronge lyghtes were set vp in
　　haste
They þt were without for lodgynge soone
　　dyde knocke
Which were playne precedentes þt day
　　was clerely paste.　　　　　　　　60

Thus a slepe I fell by a sodayne chaunce
Whan I lacked lyght alone without com-
　　forte
My sore study with slouthe dyde me
　　enhaunce
Myn eyes were heuy my tonge without
　　dysporte
Caused many fantasyes to me to resorte
My hert was moche musynge my mynde
　　was varyaunt
So I was troubled with this vngracyous
　　sorte
That my herte & mynde to slouthe short-
　　ly dyde graunt　　　　　　　　　68
About the whiche whyles I was atend-
　　aunt
Sodaynly came Morpheus & at a brayde
Not affrayd but lyke a man ryght valy-
　　aunt
Couragyously to me th(e)se wordes he
　　sayde.

Morpheus

Well knowen it is and noysed for a trothe
Though perchaunce it hath not attayned
　　yet to your audyence
How Desyre in mynde hath made a
　　solempne othe　　　　　　　　　　75
Beaute to serue without resistence
So to contynue he dothe ryght well pre-
　　pence
Durynge his lyfe with loue stedfast and
　　sure
In parfyte loue to kepe one contynuaunce
It is his mynde to do her suche pleasure.

On faruent loue he sette holy his mynde
Loue is his pleasure yet loue putteth hym
　　to payne　　　　　　　　　　　　82
Moche rule I ensure you hath nature and
　　kynde
In hym as is possyble in one to remayne
He wold fayne haue release and dare
　　not yet complayne
Howbe it to suche a poynte he is now
　　brought
That eyther to shewe his minde he must
　　shortly be fayne
Or elles his Joye is clerely solde and
　　bought.

For the whiche it is done me to vnder-
　　stande
That he wyll shortly now expresse his
　　entent　　　　　　　　　　　　　90
And this they say he wyll take on hande
To go to her presence wherfore be dyly-
　　gent
And walke with me and be obedyent
And I shall soone knowe how he shall
　　spede
I must of duety holde me content
So ye supporte me alwaye whan I haue
　　nede.

The montayne of courage

This sayd sodaynly by a chaunce repent-
　　ine
I was ascendynge a god(e)ly montayne
About the whiche þe sonne ouer eche syde
　　dyd shyne
Wherof the colour made my herte ryght
　　fayne　　　　　　　　　　　　100
To se the golden valeys bothe fayre and
　　playne
But whan I to the toppe was nye auaunced

None of my Joyntes coude to gyder con-
tayne
For Joy my herte lepyd and my body
daunced.

What call ye this hyll I pray you tell
This is the mountayne of lusty courage
This hath ben inhabyted of many a rebell
As vnkyndnes / enmyte / dysdayne /
and dotage   108
But now they be dystroyed by marcyall
apparage
So that now adayes here dwelleth none
Yet dysdayne hath goten a more stately
aduauntage
For in the castell of plesure she troubles
many one.

Now goodly Justes here on they excercyse
By thactyfnes of many a champyon
And these well gargeled galeryes they
dyde deuyse
To thentent that ladyes myght haue prospeccyon
And to suche as were worthy graunte loue
& affeccyon
And also whan theyr lust were theyr
courage to vse
To daunce amonges theym they toke a
dyreccyon
As they myght well and not theym selfe
abuse   120

Whan I aduerted of these galeryes þe
quadrant facyon
The meruelous mountayne so well made
playne
Me thought that syth the incarnacyon
Was neuer seen a more goodly mountayne
For Joy my herte leped I was so fayne
Of it I was so ioyous and so well appade
I coude in no wyse my mynde refrayne
To suche tyme this as prayse of it I
made

O Puyssaunt courage chefe cause of comforte
Thou mayst well be nye the castell of
pleasure   130
O hyll thupholder of all doughty dysporte
Of marcyall manhode thou art the treasure
Out of thy bankes is goten the vre

That causeth the pastymes of parfyte
prowes
O mountayne god graunt the long to
endure
Syth thou art the lanterne of lastynge
lustynes

So forth we walked on that goodly hyll
To that we came to the bankes syde
To se the fayre castell than we stode styll
And to se the rennynge ryuer there we
dyd abyde   140
To haue a lowe water we taryed the
tyde
The name of this water then thus he dyde
expresse
To dystroye chaungeable & people op-
pressyd with pryde
They call this water the lauer of lowly-
nes

On the stones of stedfastnes rennes this
water clere
To ouercome folkes chaungeable & proud
of hert & minde
Suche men shall be put in ryght grete
daunger
For than swellyth the water contrary to
his kynde
So that they can not the steppynge stones
fynde
By the meane wherof they be troubled
so sore   150
With the wylde wawes waueryng with
the wynde
That for lake of helpe they are ryght
soone forlore.

But blessyd be god we came in good
season
Well passe this same I trust we shall in
haste
Be not to slowyshe but arme you with
reason
How ye shall gete ouer in mynde afore
well caste
To be to forwarde ye may soone make
waste
So forth we went in pacyent humylyte
And whan I this water was well past
I loked backe and sayd this in breuyte. 160

O lowly lauer slydyng ou(e)r the stones
of stedfastnes
O ryall ryuer whiche proueth perfytely

All proude people that delytes in double-
nes
Thou drownest them in thy stremys ryght
   shortly   *164*
Thou hast a more praysable proprety
Then euer hadde the well of helycon
The moder of mekenes conserve the per-
petually
Syth thou arte the moder water of ver-
tues many one

So whan I towarde the castell dyrected
   my loke
Whiche then was not from me a full
   stones caste   *170*
I remembred that I had redde in many
   a boke
That in this place of plesure were many
   a stormy blast
Notwithstandynge I thought all perylles
   had be past
Whan I sawe of this castell the royall
   gates
Yet afore I knewe that pleasour coude not
   last
There as dysdayne is in fauour with
   estates.

This royall castell was on eche syde
   quadraunt
Gargaled with goodly grehoundes &
   beastes many one
The tyrannous tygre the stronge &
   myghty elephaunt
With a castell on his backe whiche he
   bare alone   *180*
The lyons fyry eyes with rubyes there
   shone
        [No gap in text]
The golden grephyn with a rufull mone
Stode there as desolate of lyuely creature.

The walles were allectyng of adumantes
The wyndowes of crystall were well for-
   tyfyed
And as I was lokynge on these ele-
   phauntes
On the gates two scryptures I aspyed
Theym for to rede my mynd than I
   applyed
Wryten in gold and indye blew for folkes
   fortheraunce   *190*
They betoken two wayes as after well I
   tryed

These scryptures as I remembre thus
   sowned in substaunce

Who as in to this place wyll take his
   entrynge
Myst of these wayes haue fre eleccyon
Yf he lyst be lusty lepe daunce and senge
Or yf in worldly welthe he set his affec-
cyon
In honour ryches or prosperous inuen-
cyon
He shall be conueyed yf he wyll so ensewe
Elles to the scrypture vnderneth let hym
   gyue intencyon
Whiche is set out in letters of indye
   blewe.   *200*

Whose doth sette his pleasure and delyte
His faruent herte to conioyne stedfastly
On the loue of Beaute a blossom ryght
   whyte
Or on ony of her ladyes lete hym enten-
   tyfely
Be content his mynde and courage to
   apply   *205*
To suche as to conduyt all folkes lyeth in
   wate
For none can without theyr leue passe
   theym by
Nor yet attayne to beautes hygh estate

This sayd my mynde musyd gretely
Whiche of these wayes I was best to take
Wherby I called to remembraunce shortly
How Hercules of aege but tendre and
   wake
Newe at yeres of dyscresyon his mynde
   sore brake
Whan he sawe two wayes þe one of ver-
   tute þe oder of plesure
And of the nyght it caused hym ryght oft
   to wake   *215*
By cause he knewe not the waye of per-
   fyte mesure.

Yet suche was his fortune ryght happy
   was his chaunce
Whiche toke the way so moche praysable
This to plesure and welth dothe men
   auaunce
This other dooth enduce one to be amy-
   able   *220*
I am hereby moche troubled my mynde
   is vnstable
What remedy shall I fynde to make my
   mynd stedfast

I wyll endeuer me to reason to be con-
formable
All my wyttes serched I trust it so to
caste

This golden scripture is ryght moche
pleasaunte
And hath dampned the eyes of men many
one
I am sore troubled to whiche waye
sholde I graunte
Syth I am now here in maner as man
alone
This loue lasteth whan all ryches is gone
Therfore I thynke it best with it to be
content   230
Consyderynge that fewe theyr mysfor-
fortune wyll mone
That haue mo faces than hertes as dayly
is euydent.

[He chooses the "surest" way and enters
the castle, where he is welcomed by Comfort,—"Wheder wyll ye to the hall or to
Beaute now expresse." He wishes to go
into Beauty's presence; Kindness must then
lead him, and Comfort returns to the gate.
They enter the garden of Affection, "enuy-
roned with emyraudes." He misses Morpheus, sees him talking with Fantasy, and Kindness turns him over to Fantasy. They proceed, and he sees the tree of Pyramus and
Thisbe, which fills him with sadness. Fantasy discourses to him, with mythological
examples, on the necessity of attaining pleasure through pain. He is then turned over
to Eloquence, and through the boughs of
an arbor they hear Fantasy ask Beauty if
Desire may approach. The transition is very
clumsily managed, viz.]

Than she talked to me of Vlysses
Thellynge me that he was a man ryght
eloquent
Than to lene at the herbar where Beaute
sat at ese
It pleased Eloquence / yet the bowes
were so bent
That we coude not se through / yet
fantasy was present
As we well herde by her communyca-
cyon   430
And shewynge the maner of desyres en-
tent

She ordered her wordes moche after this
facyon.

[Desire approaches Beauty and begs her
favor. Before she can reply, Disdain censures his boldness. Pity intervenes on his
behalf, and she and Disdain quote mythological examples against each other. They
are interrupted by the arrival of Credence,
who has been summoned by Fantasy. Beauty
thanks her, and accepts Desire. Desire re-
joices in three stanzas beginning "O precyous
pryncesse of preelecte pulcrytude." Disdain
goes away disgusted; all the lovers rejoice,
and the noise causes Morpheus to vanish.
The author awakes, and resolves to write
his dream, that all may know this world is
but fleeting. The third stanza after his
awakening is:]

Where is Sampson for all his grete
strength   830
Or where is the sage Salomon for all
his prudence
Deth hath and wyll deuoure all at length
for where is Vlysses for all his eloquence
Where become Crassus for his ryches and
opulence
Where is Lucres for all her chastyte
Where is Alexander whiche subdued to
his obedyence
Moche of the worlde by his marcyalte
Where is Tully whiche had pryncypalyte
Ouer all oratours in parfyte rethoryke
Where be all the foure doctours of dy-
uynyte   840
Where is Arystotyll for all his phyloso-
phy & logyke

[Having considered the matter, the author
sees:]

That this amerous study of Cupyde and
Phebus
Was cause therof which coude not be
denyed
Therfore in mynde I dyde playnly dyscus
That I wolde study nomore and specyally
thus
I wold muse nomore in the euenynge so
late   875
But conclude this shortly in wordes com-
pendyous
Lest I shold be as I was erste in myser-
able estate
     *Volunte ie ay mais ie ne
     veulx mon cuer chaunger.*

¶ *Thenuoye.*

¶ Go humble style submytte the to correccyon
  Be not so bolde to presume to the
  presence
Of ony but suche as be enuyronde with
effeccyon
  Let theym arrect theyr eeres to rebuke
  thy neglygence
To theym thou perteynest of due congruence   5
  Let theym more curyously thy rurall
  termes affyle
How thou sholdest be amended they
haue best intellygence
  Therfore submytte the to theym my
  poore & humble style

¶ yf ony that be more sad delytynge
in grauyte
  And yf forther age wold agayne the
  gyue euydence   10
Sayng they were wel ocupyed þt were
troubled with þe
  Wrote not Ouyde in as low style which
  yf they prepence
They may thynke þt I to auoyde of
slouthe þe vyolence
  Made thys without cloke or rethorycall
  language
Thynkynge that I ought not of due
conuenyence   15
  Wryte the in so hyghe style as wyse
  storyes and sage.

Finis.

Lenuoy de Robert Copland lymprimeur.
A ton aucteur / vaten petit liuret
Et luy prier / dexcuser ton empraint
Ce fault ya / de par moy incorrect
Par sa copie souuent iestois constraint
De diuigner / ou lencre cestoit destaint
Ce nonobstant / ien ay fait mon debuoir
Pour son plesir / dassembler blanc et
  noir.

Treshonoure filz / du seigneur latimer
Surnomme Neuyl / de noble parentaige
O maistre guillaume / en sens at vertu
  cler
Aucteur de ce / comme bon clerc et
  saige
A vous / ie recommande cest ouuraige
De moy indigne / si non par vostre suf-
  fraunce
En ce monstrant / ma folle ignoraunce.

R. Coplande to thauctour.

Take ye in gre / o worthy mayster myne
This rubryke frensshe / in verses incorrect
No meruayle is / though theyr speche be
not fyne
For in scole nor countre / I neuer toke
effect   20
And from your boke / let them be vndeiect
Without your lycence / yf I dyde them
impresse
Pardon I praye you / of this my homely-
nesse

En passant le temps sans mal pencer
Quod Coplande.

ALEXANDER BARCLAY

Alexander Barclay has been claimed as both Scotsman and Englishman; it seems probable that he was born, as his contemporary Bullein asserts, to the north of the Tweed, but he spent much of his long life (?1475-1552) in England, in the service of the Church. His first known literary work was an (anonymous) paraphrase of Gringoire's Chasteau de Labeur, printed in England about 1505 and twice later. This poem, nearly all in eight-line stanzas, is a dull didactic dream in which the troubled author is browbeaten by various personified Virtues and Vices; neither in subject nor in execution has it interest for the modern student, although it apparently commanded some public in its own time. A far greater success was Barclay's next undertaking, the paraphrase of Sebastian Brant's Ship of Fools, dedicated by the translator to his patron Bishop Cornish, who had presented him to a chaplaincy in Devonshire; the work was published in 1509.

Barclay seems to have spent some years in Devonshire at St. Mary Ottery, a town known to modern readers as the original of "Clavering St. Mary's" in Thackeray's Pendennis. Perhaps at the death of his patron Cornish in 1513, perhaps earlier, Barclay left Devonshire and joined the Benedictine monastery of Ely. There he translated, for Sir Giles Alington, Mancini's Latin treatise entitled The Mirror of Good Manners. It is noteworthy that he refused the first task offered him by his new patron, the "abridging to amende and from corrupte Englishe in bettar to translate" Gower's Confessio Amantis. The reasons assigned for his refusal were the wanton character of some of Gower's stories, and the "importable labour" of the task for Barclay's "weake wittes" and "hoare heres". The Eclogues were not at this time published or completed; but the Ship of Fools had made for Barclay a great reputation in England, so great that in 1520 Sir Nicholas Vaux, writing from the Field of the Cloth of Gold, begged Wolsey to send over Master Barclay the Black Monk and Poet, "to devise histories and convenient raisons to flourisshe the buildings and banquet house withal." We recall the pageant speeches, the tapestry verses, and the stanzas for towering cakes or "soteltees" at royal dinners, written by an elder monk, and see that Barclay had inherited the functions of Lydgate.

While at Ely Barclay probably translated the Life of St. George, which is dedicated to Bishop West of Ely; and it is possible that the Eclogues, which contain references to West's predecessor Bishop Alcock, were translated during Barclay's residence there. How long that residence lasted we do not know, but Barclay eventually left Ely for Canterbury and the Franciscan order. Six years before his death, when a man of seventy, he received from different patrons two vicarages in the Established Church; and in the year of his death he was given a Church appointment in London. The Life of St. Thomas which bears Barclay's name may have been done while he was a monk at Canterbury; but how he spent his later years, or what was the reason for his transfer of monastic allegiance, we do not know. The only detail of his character that emerges from the flat dulness of generality is his lively antipathy to Skelton. This breaks out at the close of the Ship of Fools and in the Eclogues; had the *Contra Skeltonum* been preserved, which Bale includes among Barclay's works, we might have known more of the relation between the two professional poets.

Barclay's list of patrons is a solid one; to the various Bishops who employed his pen and to Sir Giles Alington we must add the duke of Norfolk, for whom Barclay executed a prose translation of Sallust and compiled a French handbook. Norfolk's second son, Lord Edward Howard, is commemorated in the fourth Eclogue.

The Eclogues were not so popular with Barclay's own time as was the Ship of Fools; but his reputation now rests pretty equally on the two works. In both cases, although a translator, Barclay introduced a new literary form among his countrymen as definitely as did Wyatt or Surrey; in both cases, although a translator, Barclay sets forth his own views and makes his own excursus at will, like all medieval paraphrasers. He was restricted in the tone of these additions by his obedience to clerical tradition; yet his descriptions of contemporary manners in the satire and his landscape-glimpses in the Eclogues have some independent value. As is true of Nevill, and still more of Gawain Douglas, we catch hints of an on-ward-pressing reality through the heavy veil of the conventional.

Barclay was no "laureate" praised of Erasmus, but he very possibly commanded as much Latin and French as did Skelton. He makes no restless parade of authorities, and does no juggling with words in Skelton's manner; he is too much the decorous Churchman for Skelton's horseplay, far more like Lydgate than like his unruly raffish contemporary. Barclay seems indeed to have known and used the work of Lydgate. Some influence of the Fall of Princes may be traced in the Ship of Fools, and in Jamieson's edition, i:189, we find a reference to "Bochas". The moralizing envoys which Barclay adds after the separate chapters of the Ship of Fools are perhaps modeled on Locher's less frequent summaries; but the attempt to differentiate the envoy metrically by using an eight-line stanza instead of a seven-line reminds us of Lydgate's occasional procedure in the Fall of Princes. It is, however, infrequently that Barclay writes more than the single stanza as an envoy, and he has very little of Lydgate's refrain or attempted *tour de force* in rime; see as exceptions Jamieson's edition, i:266-68, ii:164, 284-85. Rare also is the echo of Lydgate's words; but compare Jamieson i:219—

> There is concorde, here is no thynge but stryfe,
> There is all rest, and here is care and payne

with the Fall of Princes i: 666 ff.—

> There is delit and heer is sorwe & care
> There is ioie and heer is heuynesse.

The phraseology as to universal Death and his dance, Jamieson, ii:119, etc., may owe something to the Dance of Paul's and the verses of Lydgate.

But Barclay's vocabulary and verse-management differ from those of Lydgate. Although Barclay works some words hard,—*enormity, inconvenient, laudable,*—he does not strain them as Lydgate strains *cast, caught, recure*. He is as free from cumbrous Latinisms as was Lydgate; words like *caduke* and *fatigate* are rare; but also rare are padding phrases, which cannot be said of Lydgate. And Barclay's syntax is clear, which is not one of Lydgate's merits. In the verse-management of the Ship of Fools or of the Eclogues there is little skill or variety; Barclay's most interesting departure from equivalent line-work is in the song of Lust (see Jamieson ii: 290-92), which should be compared with the Palladius prologue and links here printed p. 202, with the Kyrie of the Lover's Mass, and with two passages in Chaucer's Anelida, 272-80, 333-41. There is also in the Ship of Fools (Jamieson ii:317-21) a passage in four-beat lines. Generally speaking, Barclay's rhythm, although without technical beauty or conscious management, runs free from the Lydgatian gasping half-line movement and the Lydgatian harshness of repeated variant.

To this stylistic mixture of a small positive improvement with a large negative inertia, Barclay's substance corresponds in its mingled quality. With plenty of interest in the living beings around him, in the homely actualities of street life or rural life, Barclay has no wider Renaissance feeling, no wonder, no curiosity, no eagerness. He is as much against study of the world as he is against astrology and alchemy; he is so against excess in all things that he represses enthusiasm. He has no sense of humor and no sense for values; he presents his material humanly to a certain extent, but not humanely. We are indeed in a larger and more normally furnished room than Hawes would open to us; but its windows do not admit the air of the world.

BIBLIOGRAPHY

There is no known manuscript of any of Barclay's works. The printed eds. are:—
The Castell of Labour. By Vérard, Paris ?1503. Only fragments known.
> By Pynson ?1505. By de Worde 1506. (Brit. Mus., ULC.) By de Worde ?1510. (Brit. Mus.).
> Facsimile of the 1506 text for the Roxburghe Club, 1905, with introd. by A. W. Pollard and with the 1501 French text of Gringoire.
The Shyp of Foles of the Worlde. Printed by Pynson 1509. (Brit. Mus., Bodl.).
> Reprinted by Jamieson as below p. 299. Used in Flügel's Neuengl. Lesebuch, and here.
> Printed as "Stultifera Nauis—The Ship of Fools" by Cawood, London, 1570. To this Cawood appended the Eclogues and the Mirror of Good Manners, with no separate title-page. His text of the Ship is used by Zarncke as below for citations; for the other poems see as below.
The Egloges (i-iii only). No date nor printer. Unique? see Jamieson, p. ciii.
The Fourthe Eglogge——. Pynson, no date. Unique? see Jamieson, p. ciii.
The Fyfte Eglog——. de Worde, no date. ?1509. (Brit. Mus.) This last reprinted for the Percy Society, ed. Fairholt, 1847.
The Egloges—— (i-iii only), John Herforde, no date.
The Egloges—— (i-iii only), Humfrey Powell ?1548. (Brit. Mus.) Prologue is here reprinted from this text.
Certayne Egloges—— (i-v) in Cawood as above, 1570. Cawood's text reprinted by the Spenser Society, 1885. Cawood is used here for Eclogue iv.
The Introductory to Wryte and to Pronounce Frenche. W. Copland, 1521. (Bodl. unique.) Parts are reprinted in Ellis' Early Engl. Pronunciation, iii:803-13.
The Myrrour of Good Manners. Pynson, no date, ?1523. (Brit. Mus.) Printed by Cawood 1570 as above. His text reprod. Spenser Society as above.
Cronycle compyled—— by ——Sallust. Twice by Pynson, n.d. Both in Brit. Mus. and in ULC; one in Bodl. Brit. Mus. dates ?1520.
Cronicle of Warre. The same work, corrected by T. Paynell. Printed by Waley 1557. (Brit. Mus.)
The Lyfe ——of——Saynt George. Pynson, ca. 1530. A bit reprinted in G. Mackenzie's Lives and Characters of the Most Eminent Writers of the Scots Nation, Edinburgh, 1708-22, 3 vols., ii:291.

The Lyfe of Saynte Thomas. Pynson ?1520. (Brit. Mus.)

Ascribed to Barclay are a treatise on Holy Church oppressed by the French King, and a transl. of Friar Haython's Travels; see Jamieson as p. 299 below.

Extracts from Barclay are in J. Sibbald's Chronicle of Scottish Poetry, Edinburgh, 1802, ii:391-438 (part of Eclogue v, and from the Ship of Fools). Flügel's Neuengl. Lesebuch has, pp. 90-94, extracts from prol. to eclogues, prol. to ecl. v, a bit from ecl. v; on pp. 104-110 are extracts from the Ship. Mrs. Elizabeth Cooper, in her very interesting Muses' Library, London, 1737, included, pp. 33-44, some thirty stanzas of the Ship of Fools, with introd. note.

SELECT REFERENCE LIST XIII

For Barclay's life see:—
> Jamieson in the introd. to his ed. of the Ship of Fools, as on p. 299 here.
> A. W. Ward in the Dict. Nat. Biog.
> W. E. A. Axon on Alexander Barclay and Manchester, in the Proceed. Man-chester Literary Club, 1895.
> J. R. Schultz in JEGcPhil 18:360-68, reprinting Bale's life of Barclay and valuable bits from Brewer's Letters and Papers of—Henry VIII.

On his work in general see:—
> Warton-Hazlitt, Hist. Eng. Poetry iii:189 ff.; Morley's Eng. Writers, vii. chap. 4; Koelbing in Cambr. Eng. Lit., iii, chap. 4; Berdan in ModLangReview 8:289-300 and in chap. 4 of his Early Tudor Poetry. See R. 'M. Alden's Rise of Formal Satire, Univ. Penna., 1899, and S. M. Tucker's Verse Satire in England before the Reformation, Columbia Univ., 1908.

On the Ship of Fools and the Eclogues see under those heads below.

THE SHIP OF FOOLS

When the Narrenschiff of the German Sebastian Brant appeared, in 1494, printing was still a new art, and had until then been used to preserve the monuments of an ecclesiastical and an aristocratic past. The Narrenschiff, as Max Müller remarks, was "the first printed book to treat of contemporaneous events and living persons"; and although to us today its satire seems very general and its imaginative powers very limited, it came to fifteenth-century Germany and France as a new and interesting departure from the conventional methods so long in vogue. It was immediately translated into Latin by Locher, with the consent and supervision of Brant; this Latin was used by Rivière for his French verse-translation of the same year, 1497; and Dutch and English, as well as other French and Latin paraphrases, attest the widespread appeal of the new form. Of these paraphrases the English was the latest, in 1509; in July of that year de Worde issued a prose translation by Henry Watson, done from Drouyn's French prose rendering of Rivière at the bidding of Margaret countess of Richmond; and in December Richard Pynson issued the much more elaborate work of Barclay.

Fraustadt (as below) and Berdan (as ante) opined that Barclay used his sources exactly in the order in which he himself names them,—"Latin, Frenche, and Doche". He had before him Locher, Rivière, and Brant; and according to these students, the Latin is constantly his original, the French is often used, and the German rarely. This statement has been amended by the Dutch Franciscan scholar Fr. A. Pompen, who presents detailed proof that Barclay at no time made use of Brant, but depended almost entirely on the Latin, with some traces of

Rivière. It is Locher whom Barclay calls his "Actour"; and it is Locher's Latin which he prefixes, chapter by chapter, to his work. The admirable edition of Barclay's Ship of Fools by Jamieson, which reproduces the woodcuts of 1497, does not reprint these Latin passages, thus depriving the modern student of the possibility of watching Barclay's method of work; and the same economy has of necessity ruled here.

Barclay's poem is even less a "translation" of Locher than Lydgate's Fall of Princes was a translation of Laurent and Boccaccio. Like Lydgate, like all medieval and many modern translators, Barclay followed the general plan of his original, brought forward the same figures, and narrated substantially the same things of them; but the verbal relation of his text to its antecedent is extremely free, and the translator added detail or comment at his pleasure to the text before him. These additions by Barclay swell his poem to over 14,000 lines,—four times the size of Locher.

· The conception of the work is that of the exhorter in his pulpit denouncing sin and folly in a long catalogue-sermon, with the variation that the pulpit is the poop of a ship, and that the generalities of the Seven Deadly Sins are concretized into attacks on the vices and stupidities of the day,—backbiting, dancing, extravagant dressing, the disturbing of Church sanctity, etc. The ship never departs, and there is no description of life on board, no such scenic movement as Chaucer would have created. Had Chaucer used the ship-framework, we should have had developments in the stage-management; a man would have fallen overboard, others would have quarreled, boats putting off from shore would have raced and collided, and the characteristic follies of the passengers would have been displayed less by the captain than by their reproaches to one another or by their own braggadocio. Barclay is, however, more vivacious than Gower; and among his didactic exhortations his contemporaries found a gallery of portraits to recognize,—the besotted student, the bushy-haired gallant, the shrewish wife, the ignorant physician, the greedy usurer, and many others. On these recognitions doubtless rested much of the appeal of the Ship of Fools to the sixteenth century; but it is noticeable that although literary historians insist on the popularity of the poem, there was no reprint of Barclay in England for sixty years after its first appearance. During that period, 1509-1570, there was indeed one reprint at least of Watson's translation, in 1517; but Chaucer was printed four times, and Lydgate's Fall of Princes three times.

SELECT REFERENCE LIST XIV

Zarncke's ed. of the Narrenschiff, Leipzig, 1854, has, in its appendix ii, extracts from the French transls. by Rivière and by Drouyn, from Barclay (the Cawood print), and from Henry Watson. There are also, pp. 210-17, extracts from Locher's Latin, and, pp. 217-20, from that of Badius.

Jamieson, Edinburgh, 1874, edited The Ship of Fools translated by Alexander Barclay, 2 vols. The prefatory note states that the text, even to the punctuation, is exactly as in the 1509 edition. The woodcuts are facsimiles from those in the Basel ed. of the Latin, 1497. Locher's Latin is not reprinted.

Herford, Literary Relations of England and Germany in the Sixteenth Century, Cambridge, 1886. See chap. vi.

Fraustadt, Ueber das Verhältnis von Barclay's "Ship of Fooles" zur lateinischen, französischen, und deutschen Quelle, Breslau diss., 1894.

Dalheimer, Die Sprache Alexander Barclays in "The Shyp of Folys", Zürich diss., 1897.

Pompen, Fr. A., The English Versions of The Ship of Fools, London, 1925.

Extracts are in Flügel's Neuengl. Lesebuch i: 104-110.

For discussion of Barclay see refs. p. 298 *ante*.

THE SHYP OF FOLES OF THE WORLDE
[Pynson, 1509]

¶ *Here begynneth the prologe.*

Amonge the people of euery regyon
And ouer the worlde / south north eest
   and west
Soundeth godly doctryne in plenty and
   foyson
Wherin the grounde of vertue & wysdome doth rest
Rede gode and bad / and kepe the to the
   best   5
Was neuer more plenty of holsome doctryne
Nor fewer people that doth thereto enclyne

2

We haue the Bybyll whiche godly doth.
   expresse
Of the olde testament the lawes mysticall
And also of the newe our erour to re-
   dresse   10
Of phylosophy and other artes liberall
With other bokes of vertues morall
But thoughe suche bokes vs godly wayes
   shewe
We all ar blynde no man wyll them ensue

3

Banysshed is doctryne / we wander in
   derknes   15
Throughe all the worlde : our selfe we
   wyll not knowe
Wysdome is exyled / alas blynde fol-
   ysshenes
Mysgydeth the myndes of people hye and
   lowe
Grace is decayed / yll gouernaunce doth
   growe
Both prudent Pallas and Minerua are
   slayne   20
Or els to heuyn retourned are they agayne

4

Knowledge of trouth / Prudence / and
   iust Symplicite
Hath vs clene left: For we set of them
   no store.
Our Fayth is defyled loue / goodnes /
   and Pyte:
Honest maners nowe ar reputed of: no
   more.   25
Lawyers ar lordes: but Justice is rent
   and tore.
Or closed lyke a Monster within dores
   thre.
For without mede : or money no man can
   hyr se.

5

Al is disordred: vertue hathe no rewarde.
Alas / Compassion: and Mercy bothe ar
   slayne.   30
Alas / the stony hartys of pepyl ar so
   harde
That nought can constrayne theyr folyes
   to refrayne
But styl they procede: and eche other
   meyntayne.
So wander these foles: incresinge with-
   out nomber.
That al the worlde they vtterly encomber.

6

Blasphemers of Chryst: Hostlers: and
   Tauerners:
Crakars and bosters with Courters auen-
   terous /
Bawdes and Pollers with comon extor-
   cioners
Ar taken nowe adayes in the worlde
   moste glorious.
But the gyftes of grace and al wayes
   gracious   40
We haue excluded. Thus lyue we carnal-
   ly:
Utterly subdued to al lewdnes and Foly.

7

Thus is of Foles a sorte almost innumerable.

The Pynson print of 1509 is described by Jamieson in his ed. of the Ship of Fools i:xcviii; see *ibid.* for the various Latin and English prefatory bits preceding this Prologue, which is on fol. ix ff. of the 1509 volume.

Defilynge the worlde with syn and Vylany.
Some thynkynge them self moche wyse
& commendable   45
Thoughe al theyr dayes they lyue vn-
thryftely.
No goodnes they perceyue nor to no
goode aplye.
But if he haue a great wombe ⸫/ & and
his Cofers ful
Than is none holde wyser bytwene London and Hul.

8

But to assemble these Foles in one
bonde   50
And theyr demerites worthely to note.
Fayne shal I shyppes of euery maner
londe.
None shalbe left: Barke / Galay / Shyp
/ nor Bote.
One vessel can nat brynge them al aflote.
For yf al these Foles were brought into
one Barge   55
The bote shulde synke so sore shulde be
the charge.

9

The sayles are hawsed / a plesant cole
dothe blowe.
The Foles assembleth as fast as they may
dryue.
Some swymmeth after: other as thycke
doth rowe
In theyr small botes / as Bees about a
hyue   60
The nomber is great / and eche one
doth stryue
For to be chefe as Purser and Capytayne
Quarter mayster / Lodesman or els Bote-
swayne.

10

They ron to our shyp / eche one doth
greatly fere
Lyst his slacke paas / sholde cause hym
byde behynde   65
The wynde ryseth / and is lyke the sayle
to tere
Eche one enforseth the anker vp to wynde
The se swellyth by planettes well I fynde
These obscure clowdes threteneth vs
tempest
All are nat in bed whiche shall haue yll
rest   70

11

We are full lade and yet forsoth I
thynke

A thousand are behynde / whom we may
not receyue
For if we do / our nauy clene shall synke
He oft all lesys that coueytes all to haue
From London Rockes almyghty god vs
saue   75
For if we there anker / outher bote or
barge
There be so many that they vs wyll ouer-
charge

12

Ye London Galantes / arere / ye shall
nat enter
We kepe the streme / and touche nat
the shore
In Cyte nor in Court we dare nat well
auenter   80
Lyst perchaunce we sholde displeasure
haue therfore
But if ye wyll nedes some shall haue an
ore
And all the remenaunt shall stande afar
at large
And rede theyr fautes paynted aboute our
barge

13

Lyke as a myrrour doth represent agayne
The fourme and fygure of mannes coun-
tenaunce   86
So in our shyp shall he se wrytyn playne
The fourme and fygure of his mysgouern-
aunce
What man is fautles / but outher igno-
raunce
Or els wylfulnes causeth hym offende: 90
Than let hym nat disdayne this shyp /
tyll he amende

14

And certaynly I thynke that no creature
Lyuynge in this lyfe mortall (and) tran-
sytory
Can hym selfe kepe and stedfastly endure
Without all spot / as worthy eternall
glory   95
But if he call to his mynde and memory
Fully the dedys both of his youthe and
age
He wyll graunt in this shyp to kepe some
stage

15

But who so euer wyll knowlege his owne
foly
And it repent / lyuynge after in sympyl-
nesse   100

Shall haue no place nor rowme more in
   our nauy
But become felawe to pallas the goddesse
But he that fyxed is in suche a blynd-
   nesse
That thoughe he be nought he thynketh
   al is well
Suche shall in this Barge bere a babyll
   and a bell   105

16

These with other lyke may eche man se
   and rede
Eche by themselfe in this small boke
   ouerall
The fautes shall he fynde if he take good
   hede
Of all estatis as degres temporall
With gyders of dignytees spirituall   110
Both pore and riche / Chorles and Cyte-
   zyns
For hast to lepe a borde many bruse
   theyr shynnys

17

Here is berdles youth / and here is
   crokyd age
Children with theyr faders that yll do
   them insygne
And doth nat intende theyr wantones to
   swage   115
Nouther by worde nor yet by discyplyne
Here be men of euery science and doctryne
Lerned and vnlerned man mayde chylde
   and wyfe
May here se and rede the lewdenes of
   theyr lyfe

18

Here ar vyle wymen: whom loue Immod-
   erate   120
And lust Uenereall bryngeth to hurt and
   shame
Here ar prodigal Galantes: wyth mouers
   of debate.
And thousandes mo: whome I nat wel
   dare name.
Here ar Bacbyters whiche goode lyuers
   dyffame.
Brakers of wedlocke / men proude: and
   couetous: 125
Pollers / and pykers with folke deli-
   cious.

19

It is but foly to rehers the names here
Of al suche Foles: as in one Shelde or
   targe.

Syns that theyr ·foly dystynctly shal
   apere
On euery lefe: in Pyctures fayre and
   large.   130
To Barclays stody: and Pynsones cost
   and charge
Wherfore ye redars pray that they both
   may be saued
Before God / syns they your folyes
   haue thus graued.

20

But to thentent that euery man· may
   knowe
The cause of my wrytynge: certes I in-
   tende   135
To profyte and to please both hye and
   lowe
And blame theyr fautes wherby they may
   amende
But if that any his quarell wyll defende
Excusynge his fautes to my derysyon
Knowe he that noble poetes thus haue
   done   140

21

Afore my dayes a thousande yere ago
Blamynge and reuylynge the inconuen-
   yence
Of people / wyllynge them to withdrawe
   therfro
Them I ensue: nat lyke of intellygence
And though I am nat to them lyke in
   science   145
Yet this is my wyll mynde and intencion
To blame all vyce lykewyse as they haue
   done /

22

To tender youth my mynde is to auayle
That they eschewe may all lewdenes
   and offence
Whiche doth theyr myndes often sore as-
   sayle   150
Closynge the iyen of theyr intellygence
But if I halt in meter or erre in elo-
   quence
Or be to large in langage I pray you
   blame nat me
For my mater is so bad it wyll none other
   be

¶*Here begynneth the foles and first in-
   profytable bokes.*

[Woodcut of a spectacled figure in cap and
   bells at a desk piled with books.]

23

I am the firste fole of all the hole nauy
To kepe the pompe / the helme and eke
   the sayle   156

For this is my mynde / this one pleas-
oure haue I
Of bokes to haue grete plenty and aparayle
I take no wysdome by them: nor yet
auayle
Nor them perceyue nat: And then I
them despyse   160
Thus am I a foole and all that sewe that
guyse

24

That in this shyp the chefe place I
gouerne
By this wyde see with folys wanderynge
The cause is playne / and easy to dys-
cerne
Styll am I besy bokes assemblynge   165
For to haue plenty it is a plesaunt thynge
In my conceyt and to haue them ay in
honde
But what they mene do I nat vnderstonde

25

But yet I haue them in great reuerence
And honoure sauynge them from fylth
and ordure   170
By often brusshynge / and moche dyly-
gence
Full goodly bounde in pleasaunt couer-
ture
Of domas / satyn / or els of veluet pure
I kepe them sure ferynge lyst they sholde
be lost
For in them is the connynge wherin I
me bost   175

26

But if it fortune that any lernyd men
Within my house fall to disputacion
I drawe the curtyns to shewe my bokes
then
That they of my cunnynge sholde make
probacion
I kepe nat to fall in altercacion   180
And whyle they comon my bokes I turne
and wynde
For all is in them / and no thynge in my
mynde.

27

Tholomeus the riche causyd longe agone
Ouer all the worlde good bokes to be
sought
Done was his commaundement anone 185
These bokes he had and in his study
brought

Whiche passyd all erthly treasoure as he
thought
But neuertheles he dyd hym nat aply
Unto theyr doctryne / but lyued unhap-
pely

28

Lo in lyke wyse of bokys I haue store 190
But fewe I rede / and fewer under-
stande
I folowe nat theyr doctryne nor theyr
lore
It is ynoughe to bere a boke in hande
It were to moche to be (in) suche a
bande
For to be bounde to loke within the
boke   195
I am content on the fayre couerynge to
loke

29

Why sholde I stody to hurt my wyt
therby
Or trouble my mynde with stody ex-
cessyue
Sythe many ar whiche stody right besely
And yet therby shall they neuer thryue
The fruyt of wysdom can they nat con-
tryue   201
And many to stody so moche are in-
clynde
That vtterly they fall out of theyr mynde

30

Eche is nat lettred that nowe is made a
lorde
Nor eche a clerke that hath a bene-
fyce   205
They are nat all lawyers that plees doth
recorde
All that are promotyd are nat fully wyse
On suche chaunce nowe fortune throwys
hir dyce
That thoughe one knowe but the yresshe
game
Yet wolde he haue a gentyll mannys
name   210

31

So in lyke wyse I am in suche case
Thoughe I nought can I wolde be callyd
wyse
Also I may set another in my place
Whiche may for me my bokes excercyse
Or else I shall ensue the comon gyse 215
And say concedo to euery argument
Lyst by moche speche my latyn sholde
be spent

32

I am lyke other Clerkes whiche frowardly
　　them gyde
That after they ar onys come vnto pro-
　　mocion
They gyue them to plesour theyr stody
　　set asyde.　　　　　　　　　　220
Theyr Auaryce couerynge with fayned
　　deuocion.
Yet dayly they preche: and haue great
　　derysyon
Against the rude Laymen: and al for
　　Couetyse.
Though theyr owne Conscience be blynd-
　　ed wt that vyce

33

But if I durst trouth playnely vtter and
　　expresse.　　　　　　　　　　225
This is the special cause of this Incon-
　　uenyence.
That greatest foles / and fullest of
　　lewdnes
Hauynge least wyt: and symplest Science
Ar fyrst promoted: and haue greatest
　　reuerence
For if one can flater / and bere a hawke
　　on his Fyst　　　　　　　　　230
He shalbe made Person of Honyngton
　　or of Clyst.

34

But he that is in Stody ay ferme and
　　diligent.
And without al fauour prechyth Chrystys
　　lore
Of al the Comontye nowe adayes is sore
　　shent.
And by Estates thretened to Pryson oft
　　therfore.　　　　　　　　　　235
Thus what auayle is it / to vs to Stody
　　more:
To knowe outher scripture / trouth /
　　wysedom / or vertue
Syns fewe / or none without fauour dare
　　them shewe.

35

But O noble Doctours / that worthy ar
　　of name:
Consyder our olde faders : note wel theyr
　　diligence:　　　　　　　　　240
Ensue ye theyr steppes : obtayne ye such
　　fame,
As they dyd lyuynge : and that by true
　　Prudence.

Within theyr hartys they planted theyr
　　scyence
And nat in plesaunt bokes. But nowe
　　to fewe suche be.
Therefore in this Shyp let them come
　　rowe with me.

¶*The Enuoy of Alexander Barclay Translatour exortynge the Foles accloyed with
　　this vice to amende theyr foly.*

36

Say worthy doctours and Clerkes curious:
What moueth you of Bokes to haue such
　　nomber.
Syns dyuers doctrines throughe way con-
　　trarious.
Doth mannys mynde distract and sore
　　encomber.
Alas blynde men awake / out of your
　　slomber　　　　　　　　　　250
And if ye wyl nedys your bokes multy-
　　plye
With diligence endeuer you some to oc-
　　cupye.

*　　*　　*　　*　　*　　*

¶*Of newe fassions and disgised Gar-
　　mentes.*

66

Who that newe garmentes loues or deuys-
　　es.
Or weryth by his symple wyt / and
　　vanyte
Gyuyth by his foly and vnthryfty gyses
Moche yl example to yonge Comontye.
Suche one is a Fole and skant shal euer
　　thee　　　　　　　　　　　460
And comonly it is sene that nowe a dayes
One Fole gladly folowes another wayes.

67

Drawe nere ye Courters and Galants dis-
　　gised
Ye counterfayt Caytifs / that ar nat con-
　　tent
As god hath you made : his warke is
　　despysed
Ye thynke you more crafty (than) God
　　o(m)nipotent
Unstable is your mynde : that shewes by
　　your garment.
A fole is knowen by his toyes and his
　　Cote.
But by theyr clothinge nowe may we
　　many note.

68

Aparayle is apayred. Al sadness is de-
cayde 470
The garmentes ar gone that longed to
honestye.
And in newe sortes newe Foles ar
arayede
Despisynge the costom of good antiquyte.
Mannys fourme is disfigured with euery
degre
As Knyght Squyer yeman Jentilman and
knaue / 475
For al in theyr goynge vngoodely them
behaue

69

The tyme hath ben / nat longe before
our dayes
Whan men with honest ray coude holde
them self content.
Without these disgised: and counterfayted wayes.
Wherby theyr goodes ar wasted / loste /
and spent. 480
Socrates with many mo in wysdom excellent.
Bycause they wolde nought change that
cam of nature
Let growe theyre here without cuttinge
or scissure.

70

At that time was it reputed to lawde and
great honour.
To haue longe here: the Beerde downe to
the brest 485
For so they vsed that were of moste
valour.
Stryuynge together who myht be godly-
est
Saddest / moste clenely / discretest /
and moste honest.
But nowe adayes together we contende
and stryue.
Who may be gayest: and newest wayes
contryue. 490

71

Fewe kepeth mesure / but excesse and
great outrage
In theyr aparayle. And so therin they
procede
That theyr goode is spent: theyr Londe
layde to morgage.
Or solde out right: of Thryft they take
no hede.

Hauinge no Peny them to socour at
theyr nede. 495
So whan theyr goode by suche wasteful-
nes is loste.
They sel agayne theyr Clothes for half
that they coste.

72

A fox furred Jentelman: of the fyrst
yere or hede.
If he be made a Bailyf a Clerke or a
Constable.
And can kepe a Parke or Court and
rede a Dede 500
Than is Ueluet to his state mete and
agreable.
Howbeit he were more mete to bere a
Babyl.
For his Foles Hode his iyen so sore doth
blynde
That Pryde expelleth his lynage from
his mynde.

73

Yet fynde I another sorte almoste as bad
as thay 505
As yonge Jentylmen descended of worthy
Auncetry.
Whiche go ful wantonly in dissolute
aray.
Counterfayt / disgised / and moche vn-
manerly
Blasinge and garded: to lowe or else to
hye.
And wyde without mesure: theyr stuffe
to wast thus gothe 510
But other some they suffer to dye for
lacke of clothe

74

Some theyr neckes charged with colers /
and chaynes
As golden withthes: theyr fyngers ful of
rynges:
Theyr neckes naked: almoste vnto the
raynes
Theyr sleues blasinge lyke to a Cranys
wynges 515
Thus by this deuysinge suche counterfayted thinges
They dysfourme that figure that god hymselfe hath made
On pryde and abusion thus ar theyr
myndes layde

75

Than the Courters careles that on theyr
mayster wayte

Seinge hym his Uesture in suche fourme
abuse   *520*
Assayeth suche Fassion for them to
counterfayte.
And so to sue Pryde contynually they
muse.
Than stele they: or Rubbe they. Forsoth
they can nat chuse.
For without Londe or Labour harde it is
to mentayne.
But to thynke on the Galows that is a
careful payne.   *525*

76

But be it payne or nat: there many suche
ende.
At Newgate theyr garmentis ar offred
to be solde.
Theyr bodyes to the Jebet solemly ascende.
Wauynge with the wether whyle theyr
necke wyl holde.
But if I shulde wryte al the ylles manyfolde,   *530*
That procedeth of this counterfayt abusion
And mysshapen Fassions: I neuer shulde
haue done.

77

For both States / comons / man / woman / and chylde
Ar vtterly incly(n)ed to this inconuenyence.
But namely therwith these Courters are
defyled.   *535*
Bytwen mayster and man I fynde no
dyfference.
Therfore ye Courters knowledge your
offence.
Do nat your errour mentayne / support
nor excuse.
For Fowles ye ar your Rayment thus to
abuse.

78

To Shyp Galauntes come nere I say
agayne.   *540*
Wyth your set Busshes Curlynge as men
of Inde.
Ye counterfayted Courters come with
your fleinge brayne
Expresed by these variable Garmentes
that ye fynde.
To tempt chast Damsels and turne them
to your mynde
Your breste ye discouer and necke. Thus
your abusion   *545*
Is the Fendes bate. And your soules confusion.

79

Come nere disgysed foles: receyue your
Foles Hode.
And ye that in sondry colours ar arayde.
Ye garded galantes wastinge thus your
goode
Come nere with your Shertes brodered
and displayed.   *550*
In fourme of Surplys. Forsoth it may be
sayde.
That of your Sort right fewe shal thryue
this yere.
Or that your faders werith suche Habyte
in the Quere.

80

And ye Jentyl wymen whome this lewde
vice doth blynde
Lased on the backe: your peakes set a
loft.   *555*
Come to my Shyp. forget ye nat behynde.
Your Sadel on the tayle: yf ye lyst to sit
soft.
Do on your Decke Slut: if ye purpos
to come oft.
I mean your Copyntanke: And if it wyl
do no goode.
To kepe you from the rayne ye shall haue
a foles hode.   *560*

81

By the ale stake knowe we the ale hous
And euery Jnne is knowen by the sygne
So a lewde woman and a lecherous
Is knowen by hir clothes / be they cours
or fyne
Folowyng newe fassyons / not graunted
by doctryne   *565*
The bocher sheweth his flesshe it to sell
So doth these women dampnyng theyr
soule to hell

82

What shall I more wryte of our enormyte
Both man and woman as I before haue
sayde
Ar rayde and clothyd nat after theyr
degre   *570*
As nat content with the shape that god
hath made
The clenlynes of Clergye is nere also
decayed.
Our olde apparale (alas) is nowe layde
downe
And many prestes asshamed of theyr
Crowne.

---

573. The bracketed word (alas) is so bracketed
in the text. Similarly in lines 8460, 13809,
13878.

83

Unto laymen we vs refourme agayne 575
As of chryste our mayster in maner halfe
asshamed
My hert doth wepe: my tunge doth sore
complayne
Seing howe our State is worthy to be
blamed.
But if all the Foly of our Hole Royalme
were named
Of mys apparayle of Olde / young /
lowe / and hye /   580
The tyme shulde fayle: and space to me
denye.

84

Alas thus al states of Chrysten men de-
clynes.
And of wymen also disfourmynge theyr
fygure.
Wors than the Turkes / Jewes / or
Sarazyns.
A Englonde Englonde amende or be
thou sure   585
Thy noble name and fame can nat en-
dure
Amende lyst god do greuously chastyce.
Bothe the begynners and folowe(r)s of
this vyce.

¶ *The enuoy of Alexander barclay þe*
translatour.

85

Reduce courters clerly vnto your re-
m(em)brance
From whens this disgysyng was brought
wherein ye go   590
As I remember it was brought out of
France.
This is to your plesour. But payne ye had
also.
As French Pockes hote ylles with other
paynes mo.
Take ye in good worth the swetnes with
the Sour.
For often plesour endeth with sorowe
and dolour.   595

86

But ye proude Galaundes that thus your-
selfe disgise
Be ye asshamed. beholde vnto your
Prynce.
Consyder his sadnes: His honestye de-
uyse
His clothynge expresseth his inwarde
prudence

Ye se no Example of suche Inconuen-
yence   600
In his hyghnes: but godly wyt and grauyte.
Ensue hym : and sorowe for your
enormyte.

87

Away with this pryde / this statelynes
let be
Rede of the Prophetis clothynge or vesture
And of Adam firste of your ancestrye 605
Of Johnn the Prophete / theyr clothynge was obscure
Uyle and homly / but nowe what creature
Wyll them ensue / sothly fewe by theyr
wyll
Therfore suche folys my nauy shall fulfyll

* * * * * *

Of the folysshe descripion and inquisi-
cion of dyuers contrees and regyons

Who that is besy to mesure and com-
pace   6930
The heuyn and erth and all the worlde
large
Describynge the clymatis and folke of
euery place
He is a fole and hath a greuous charge
Without auauntage / wherfore let hym
discharge
Hym selfe / of that fole whiche in his
necke doth syt   6935
About suche folyes dullynge his mynde
and wyt.

That fole / of wysdome and reason doth
fayle
And also discression labowrynge for
nought.
And in this shyp shall helpe to drawe the
sayle
Which day and nyght infixeth all his
thought   6940
To haue the hole worlde within his body
brought
Mesurynge the costes of euery royalme
and lande
And clymatis / with his compace / in
his hande

He coueytyth to knowe / and compryse
in his mynde

Euery regyon and euery sundry place
Whiche ar not knowen to any of man-
kynde   *6946*
And neuer shall be without a specyall
grace
Yet suche folys take pleasour and solace
The length and brede of the worlde to
mesure
In vay(n)e besynes / takynge great
charge and cure   *6950*

They set great stody labour and besynes
To knowe the people that in the east
abyde
And by and by theyr measures after
dres
To knowe what folke the west and north
part gyde
And who the sowth / thus all the worlde
wyde   *6955*
By thes folys is meated by ieometry
Yet knowe they scant theyr owne vnwyse
body

Another labours to knowe the nacions
wylde
Inhabytynge the worlde in the North
plage and syde
Metynge by mesure / countrees both
fyers and mylde   *6960*
Under euery planete / where men sayle
go or ryde
And so this fole castyth his wyt so wyde
To knowe eche londe vnder the fyrma-
ment
That therabout in vayne his tyme is
spent

Than wyth his compace drawyth he
about   *6965*
Europe / and Asye / to knowe howe
they stande
And of theyr regyons nat to be in dout
Another with Grece and Cesyll is in
honde
With Apuly / Afryke and the newe
fonde londe
With Numydy and / where the Moryans
do dwell   *6970*
And other londes whose namys none can
tell

He mesureth Athlant / calpe / and cappadoce
The see of Hercules garnado and Spayne

The yles there aboute shewynge all in
groce
Throwynge his mesure to Fraunce and
to Brytayne   *6975*
The more and lesse / to Flaundres and
almayne
There is no yle so lytell that hath name
But that these Folys in hande ar with the
same

And regyons that ar compasyd with the
se
They besely labour to knowe and vnderstande   *6980*
And by what cause / nature or prop-
ertye
The se doth flowe / nat ouercouerynge
the londe
So he descrybyth his cercle in his honde
The hole worlde: leuynge no thynge behynde
As in the Doctrynes of Strabo he doth
fynde   *6985*

Whiche wrote in bokes makynge declara-
cion
Somtyme hym groundynge vpon auctoryte
Howe eche Royalme and londe had sytuacion
Some in brode feldes some closyd with
the see
But ye geometryans that of this purpose
be   *6990*
Ye ar but folys to take suche cure and
payne
Aboute a thynge whiche is fruteles and
vayne

It passyth your reason the hole worlde
to discus
And knowe euery londe and countrey of
the grounde
For though that the noble a(u)ctour
plinius   *6995*
The same purposyd / yet fawty is he
founde
And in Tholomeus great errours doth ha-
bounde
Thoughe he by auctoryte makyth mencyon
Of the descripcion of euery regyon

Syns these a(u)ctours so excellent of
name   *7000*
Hath bokes composyd of this facultye

And neuer coude parfytely perfourme
   the same
Forsoth it is great foly vnto the
To labour about suche folysshe vanyte
It is a furour also one to take payne 7005
In suche thynges as prouyd ar vncer-
   tayne

For nowe of late hath large londe and
   grounde
Ben founde by maryners and crafty
   gouernours
The whiche londes were neuer knowen
   nor founde
Byfore our tyme by our predecessours
And here after shall by our successours
Parchaunce mo be founde / wherin men
   dwell   7012
Of whome we neuer before this same
   harde tell

Ferdynandus that late was kynge of
   spayne
Of londe and people hath founde plenty
   and store   7015
Of whome the bydynge to vs was vncer-
   tayne
No christen man of them harde tell be-
   fore
Thus is it foly to tende vnto the lore
And vnsure science of vayne geometry
Syns none can knowe all the worlde per-
   fytely   7020

¶ *Thenuoy of Barklay.*
Ye people that labour the worlde to
   mesure
Therby to knowe the regyons of the same
Knowe firste your self / that knowledge
   is moste sure
For certaynly it is rebuke and shame
For man to labour. onely for a name 7025
To knowe the compasse of all the worlde
   wyde
Nat knowynge hym selfe / nor howe he
   sholde hym gyde
   *   *   *   *   *

Of the arrogance & pryde of rude men
       of the countrey.
The rustycall pryde of carles of the
   londe   8437
Remaynyth nowe / whiche I intende to
   note
Whiche theyr owne pryde nat se nor
   vnderstonde

Wherfore they coueyte with me to haue a
   bote   8440
And so they shall / but whan they ar a
   flote
Let them me pardon / for I wyll take no
   charge
Of them: but them touche and let them
   ren at large

Of husbonde men the lyfe and the nature
Was wont be rude and of symplycyte 8445
And of condicion humble and demure
But if a man wolde nowe demande of me
Howe longe agone is syns they thus haue
   be
I myght well answere it is nat longe
   agone
Syns they were symple and innocent
   echone   8450

And so moche were they gyuen to
   symplenes
And other vertues chefe and pryncipall
That the godly trone of fayth and
   righ(t)wysnes
Had left great townes lordes and men
   royall
And taken place amonge these men rur-
   all   8455
All vertues: stedfastnes iustyce and lawe
Disdayned nat these pore cotis thekt with
   strawe

There was no disceyt nor gyle of tymes
   longe
Amonge these men: they were out chasyd
   and gone
For iustyce (as I haue sayd) was then
   amonge   8460
And of long tyme there kept hir chayre
   and trone
Of brynnynge Auaryce amonge these met
   was none
No wrongfull lucre nor disceytful auauntage
Infect the myndes of men of the vyllage

That is to say they knewe none vsury
No hunger of golde dyd theyr myndes
   confounde   8466
They knewe no malyce: nor pryde of
   theyr body
Nor other vyces that trowbleth nowe the
   grounde
They coueyted nat to greatly to abounde

In proude aparayle / lyke Cytezeyns
excellent   *8470*
But theyr hole lyfe was symple and innocent

But nowe the lyfe of eche carle and
vyllayne
Is in all maners chaungyd euen as clene
As if the trone moste noble and souerayne
Of rightwysenes: amonge them had neuer
bene   *8475*
Of theyr olde vertues nowe is none in
them sene
Wherby they longe were wont themself
to gyde
Theyr lyfe is loste and they set hole on
pryde

Theyr clothes stately after the courters
gyse
Theyr here out busshynge as a foxis
tayle   *8480*
And all the fassions whiche they can
deuyse
In counterfaytynge they vse in aparayll
Party and gardyd or short to none auayle
So that if god sholde theyr bodyes
chaunge
After theyr vesture theyr shape sholde
be full strange   *8485*

Thus is theyr mekenes and olde symply-
cyte
Tournyd by theyr foly to arrogance and
pryde
Theyr rightwysenes / loue and fydelyte
By enuy and falshode nowe ar set asyde
Disceyt and gyle with them so sure doth
byde   *8490*
That folke of the towne of them oft
lerne the same
And other newe yllis causynge reprofe
and shame

Theyr scarsnes nowe is tournyd to couetyse
They onely haue golde and that / in abun-
daunce
Theyr vertue is gone / and they rotyd in
vyce   *8495*
Onely on riches fixed is theyr pleasaunce
Fye Chorles amende this mad mysgouern-
aunce

What mouyth you vnto this thyrst feruent
Of golde: that were wont to be so innocent

What causeth you thus your lyfe to
change   *8500*
To cursyd malyce from godly innocence
Nowe Carles ar nat content with one
grange
Nore one ferme place / suche is theyr
insolence
They must haue many / to support theyr
expence
And so a riche / vyllayne proude and
arrogant   *8505*
Anone becomyth a couetous marchant

Than labours he for to be made a state
And to haue the pryuelege of hye nobles
Thus churlys becomyth statis nowe of
late
Hye of renowne without all sympyl-
nes   *8510*
But it is great foly and also shame doutles
For Carles to coueyt this wyse to clym
so hye
And nat be pleasyd with theyr state and
degre

T(h)enuoy of Barclay the Translatour
Fye rurall carles awake I say and ryse
Out of your vyce and lyfe abhomynable
Namely of pryde / wrath / enuy and
couetyse   *8516*
Whiche ye insue / as they were nat
damnable
Recouer your olde mekenes / whiche is
most profytable
Of all vertues / and be content with your
degre
For make a carle a lorde / and without
any fable   *8520*
In his inwarde maners one man styll
shall he be.

   *   *   *   *   *   *

Here purpose I no farther to procede
Let euery man chose for hym selfe a
place   *13796*
As he shall in this boke ouer se or rede
For hym moste mete: man knoweth best
his case
And here shall I by goddes helpe and
grace

Drawe all my Nauy / to hauyns for to
  rest   13800
For fere of wynter stormes and tempest

Wysdom hath gyuen me this commaunde-
  ment
My wyt is wery: my hande and hede also
Wherfore I gladly with all my herte as-
  sent
And lepe a borde / amonge the other
  mo   13805
But in my iournay: if that I haue mysgo
By bytynge wordes or scarsnes of scyence
I yelde me vnto men of more prudence

It is no meruayle (the trouth playnly to
  say)
Syth I a mayster without experyence
Of worldly thynges haue erred from the
  way   13811
By ignoraunce / or slouthfull neglygence
Let none be wroth for blamynge his offence
For if his lyfe fro synne be pure and
  clere
No maner hurt is sayde agaynst hym
  here   13815

Within a myrrour / if thou beholde thy
  chere
Or shap of face: if thy colour be pure
Within the myrrour to the it shall apere
But if that thou be foule of thy fygure
The glas shall shewe the same I the in-
  sure   13820
Yet blame thou nat the myrrour for the
  same
But thy owne shap thou ought rebuke
  and blame

The myrrour showys eche man lyke as
  they be
So doth my boke / for who that is in
  syn
Shall of his lyfe / the fygure in it
  se   13825
If he with good aduertence loke therin
But certaynly his reason is but thyn
For his yll lyfe if he my boke despyse
For them I laude that vertue exercyse

Let nat the redar be discontent with this
Nor any blame agayne me to obiect

Thoughe that some wordes be in my boke
  amys
For though that I my selfe dyd it correct
Yet with some fautis I knowe it is infect
Part by my owne ouersyght and neglygence   13835
And part by the prynters nat perfyte in
  science

And other some escaped ar and past
For that the Prynters in theyr besynes
Do all theyr werkes hedelynge / and in
  hast
Wherfore if that the redar be wytles
He shall it scorne anone by froward-
  nes   13841
But if the reder wyse / sad and discrete
  be
He shall it mende: laynge no faut to me

It is ynoughe if my labour may be sene
Of lernyd men / and theyr mynde to
  content   13845
For nought is pleasaunt before a Folys
  iyen
And to be playne it was nat myne intent
At my begynnynge to Folys to assent
Ne pleas theyr myndes by sparynge of
  theyr vyce
But it to shewe: and that in playnest
  wyse   13850

Therfore let Folys haue theyr wordes
  vayne
Whiche nought can do / but without
  reason chat
All others dedes / by lewde tunge to dis-
  tayne
And if theyr belyes be full / and chekis
  fat
Let Clerkes speke / and they haue scorne
  therat   13855
They knowe no thinge: yet wolde / they
  fayne haue prayse
And theyr owne dedes onely doth them
  please

With suche Folys I ende my besynes
Whiche all thynge blame / and vtterly
  dispyse
Yet all theyr lyfe they passe in ydyl-
  nes   13860
Or in theyr bely fedynge in bestely wyse

But this I fynde / that no man can
  deuyse
A thynge so crafty / so good and excellent
Or yet so sure: that may eche man con-
  content

What warke is that: that may eche man
  content   *13865*
No worldly thynge: forsoth I trowe the
  same
Thoughe Virgyll were a poet excellent
Afore all other / shynynge in lawde and
  fame
Yet some there were whiche dyd his
  warkes blame

Jerome with other Doctours certaynly
Cowde nat theyr warkes defende well
  from enuy   *13871*

Holde me excusyd: for why my wyll is
  gode
Men to induce vnto vertue and goodnes
I wryte no Iest ne tale of Robyn hode
Nor sawe no sparcles ne sede of vycious-
  nes   *13875*
Wyse men loue vertue / wylde people
  wantones
It longeth nat to my scyence nor cun-
  *n*ynge
For Phylyp the Sparowe the (Dirige)
  to synge.

BARCLAY'S ECLOGUES: THE PROLOGUE AND ECLOGUE IV

There are five of Barclay's eclogues, of which the first three were amplified
from the Miseriae Curialium of Pope Pius II (Aeneas Sylvius Piccolomini), who
died in 1454. The fourth and fifth are similarly expanded from the fifth and
sixth eclogues of Baptista Mantuanus, 1448-1516. Barclay's prologue to the group
is also based upon Mantuanus, and utilizes Mantuan's statements about the partial
execution of his work in youth in such a way that we are in doubt whether Barclay
asserts this of himself or not. Berdan remarks that the last two eclogues must
have been done at much the same time as the first three, since the prologue to all
is based on Mantuan.

The work of Mantuan, a Christian monk and General of the Carmelite Order
during the last three years of his life, is abundant and varied. His ten eclogues,
imitated from Virgil, were first printed on the Continent in 1498, and frequently
until the first English edition of 1519. For two hundred years after their appearance they were a school-text in England; Colet, drawing up his statutes for the new
St. Paul's School, included Mantuan in a list of Latin authors otherwise solidly
Christian in substance; and two generations later the boy Shakespeare must have
learned some of his "small Latin" from Mantuan, whom he quotes in act IV,
scene 2, of Love's Labour's Lost. And although Spenser took an earlier and
greater Mantuan for his model, there are more than a few traces of the Carmelite
monk in the Shepherd's Calendar.

The fourth eclogue of Barclay, here reprinted from the text of 1548, is based
on the fifth eclogue of Mantuan; but while the Latin is of 190 hexameter verses,
the English runs to 1158 pentameter lines. Part of this difference is due to the
two inserted recitations by the poor shepherd-poet, amounting with their connective to about 380 lines; and the introductory setting of Barclay adds another 36
lines. But the difference between the remaining 740 verses of Barclay and the
190 of Mantuan is one of method rather than of additions; it is caused by Barclay's
discursiveness. Every speech is lengthened and every motive repeated; and although a good deal of interesting descriptive detail is also added, the most of
the increase in bulk is due, as in the Ship of Fools, to moralizing comment or
exhortation.

In spite of this long-winded treatment, Barclay's management of his material in this eclogue has interest. He uses the Latin for his main structure, the attempt of a poor poet-shepherd to obtain the patronage of a richer but illiterate and niggardly neighbor. Into this frame Barclay works a double attempt at pleasing the imaginary patron, something on the Chaucerian pattern of a first essay interrupted and a second carried through; the second inserted poem is an elegy modelled on a French original, mourning with Barclay's actual patron the duke of Norfolk on the death of his son. Barclay then returns to Mantuan, and closes as does the Latin, with the listener's refusal to pay for his entertainment.

This second inserted poem, an elegy on Admiral Lord Howard, who was killed in a naval engagement in 1513, is said by Professor Mustard (ModLangNotes 24:8-10) to owe something to Le Temple d'Honneur et de Vertus, a poem written in 1503 by Jean Lemaire de Belges to bewail the death of the duke of Bourbon. This suggestion, accepted by Lee in his French Renaissance in England, is rejected by Berdan, Romanic Review 2:422. It does not indeed appear that the English poem owes the French much more than the title. The French has a high mountain crowned by a noble temple of Honor, to which press the valiant and worthy; but this is frequent in medieval allegory, and appears quite as plainly in another poem by Lemaire de Belges, his Concorde des deux Langages, of 1511, with the addition also of a detail present in Barclay and not in the French Temple d'Honneur, the extreme difficulty of ascending the mountain. Barclay's fierce guardian of the entrance, by him named Labor, is not in Lemaire de Belges' Temple-poem; but in the Concorde-poem, where the temples of Venus and of Minerva are described, there is a loud-voiced porter of the Venus-temple, named Danger, who brandishes a staff and demands fees of the suppliants. This porter, a comic figure, hurls the poet's proffered manuscript behind the altar in contempt.

In Gringoire's Chasteau de Labeur, translated earlier by Barclay, the narrator enters on "the waye of grete payne called dylygence", accompanied by Lust to Do Good, Good Will, and Good Heart. They come to a fair castle, resplendent and joyous; the traveler would enter, but the porter Besynesse resists, saying that no one enters except by meekness. The porter's wife Cure, however, intercedes, and the wayfarer is admitted. He learns that Travail and Pain are captain and mistress of the castle, and he addresses himself to the assigned task. There is no description of Labour's figure such as Barclay here gives, and which has aroused the interest of students.

SELECT REFERENCE LIST XV

Kluge, Spenser's Shepheards' Calendar und Mantuan's Eclogen, in Anglia 3:266-74.
Mustard, W. P., ed. of Mantuan's Eclogues, Baltimore, 1911. See paper by Mustard in Trans. Amer. Philol. Assn., 40:151-183.
Reissert, Die Eklogen des Alexander Barclay, Hannover, 1886.
J. R. Schultz, Alexander Barclay and the Later Eclogue-Writers, in ModLangNotes 35:52-4. (Googe and Spenser show no influence of Barclay whatever; Francis Sabie very little. Reason,—the overshadowing fame of Mantuan.)
Berdan, Early Tudor Poetry, N. Y., 1920.

[THE PROLOGUE TO THE ECLOGUES]

The famous Poetes, with the Muses nyne,
With wyt inspired, fresh, pregnant &
  diuyne.
Say boldly, indite, in style substanciall:
Some in poemes, hye and heroicall.
Some them deliteth, in heuy Tragedies: 5
And some, in wanton or mery Comedies.
Some, in Satiers, agayne vices dare carpe:
Some, in sweete songes, accordant with
  the harpe,
And eche of these all, had laude and ex-
  cellence:
After their reason, and style of elo-
  quence.   10
Who, in fayre speache, coulde brefely
  comprehende:
Most fruitful matter, men dyd him most
  commende
And who were fruitlesse, and in speache
  superflue:
Men by their writyng, scantly set a que.
Therfore, wyse Poetes, to sharpe & proue
  their wyt: 15
In homely ieastes, wrote many a mery
  fyt.
Before they durst be, of audacitie:
Tauenture thynges, of weyght and graui-
  tie.
In this same maner, the famous Teocrite:
First, in Siracuse, attempted for to
  wryte.   20
Certayne Eglogues, or speaches Pastor-
  all:
Inducyng Shepherdes, men, homely and
  rurall.
Which in playne language, accordyng to
  their name:
Had sondry talkyng, some in myrth and
  game.
Sometyme, of thynges, more lyke to
  grauitie: 25
And not excedyng, their small capacitie.
Most noble Uirgill, after him, long
  whyle,
Wrote also Egloges, after lyke maner
  style.
His wyttes prouyng, in matters Pastorall:
Or he durst ventre, to style Heroicall. 30
And in lyke maner now, lately in our
  dayes:
Hathe other Poetes, atempted the same
  wayes.
As the most famous, Baptist Mantuan:

The best of that sorte, synce Poetes first
  began.
And Frances Petrarke, also in Italy, 35
In lyke maner style, wrote playne and
  merily.
What shall I speake, of the father aun-
  cient:
Which in breife language, both playne
  & eloquent:
Betwene Alathea, Seustis, stout and
  bolde:
Hath made rehersall, of all the stories
  olde.   40
By true histories, vs teachyng to abiect:
Agaynst vayne fables, of olde Gentyles
  sect.
Besyde all these, yet fynde I many mo:
Which hath employed, their diligence
  also.
Betwene Shepheardes, as it were but a
  fable:
To write of matters, bothe true and prof-
  itable.
But all their names, I purpose not to
  write,
Which in this maner, made bookes in-
  finite.
Now to my purpose, their workes worthy
  fame:
Dyd my yong age, my herte greatly in-
  flame.   50
Dull slouth to eschew, my selfe to exer-
  cise:
In suche small matters, or I durst enter-
  prise.
To hyer matter, lyke as these chyldren do:
Whiche first vse to crepe, and after-
  warde to go.
The byrde vnused, first fliyng from her
  nest: 55
Dare not aduenture, and is not bolde
  nor prest:
With wynges abrode, to flye as dothe the
  olde:
For vse and custome, causeth all thynges
  be bolde.
And lytell connyng, by crafte and exer-
  cyse:
To perfecte science, causeth a man to
  ryse.   60
But ear the Paynter, can sure his crafte
  attayne,
Much frowarde facion, transformeth he
  in vayne.

But rasyng superflue, and addyng, that
    dothe want:
Rude pictures is made, both perfect and
    pleasant.
So, where I in youth, a certain warke
    began: *65*
And not concluded, as ofte doth many a
    man.
Yet thought I after, to make the same
    parfyte:
But long I myssed, that which I first dyd
    wryte.
But heare a wonder, I .xl. yere saue
    twayne,
Procedyng in age, founde my first youth
    agayne.   *70*
To fynde youth in age, is a probleme
    diffuse:
But now heare the truthe, & then no
    longer muse.
As I late tourned, olde bookes to and fro:
One lytle treatyse, I founde among the
    mo.
Bicause that in youth, I dyd compile the
    same: *75*
Egloges of youth, I called it by name.
And seyng some men, haue in the same
    delyte:
At their great instance, I made the same
    parfyte.
Addyng and batyng, where I perceyued
    neade:
All them desyring, which shall this trea-
    tyse reade.   *80*
Not to be greued, with my playne sent-
    ence,
Rudely conueyed, for lacke of eloquence.
It were not sittyng, a hearde or man
    rurall,
To speake in tearmes, gay and rethoricall.
So teacheth Orace, in arte of Poetry, *85*
That writers namely, their reason should
    apply.
Meete speache appropryng, to euery per-
    sonage:
After his estate, behauour, wyt, and age.
But if that any woulde, now to me abiect,
That this my labor, shalbe of small effect.
And to the reader, not greatly proffit-
    able,   *91*
And by that manner, as vayne and re-
    proueable.
Bicause it maketh, onely relacion,
Of Shepheardes manner, and disputacion.

If any suche reade, my treatyse to the
    ende,   *95*
He shall well perceyue, if he therto en-
    tende.
That it conteyneth, bothe laudes and ver-
    tue,
And man enformeth, misliuyng to eschue.
With diuers bourdes, and sentences
    morall:
Closed in shadow, of speaches Pastor-
    all.   *100*
As many Poetes, as I haue sayde beforne:
Haue vsed long tyme, before that I was
    borne.
But of their writyng, though I ensue the
    rate,
No name I chalenge, of Poete Laureate.
That name, vnto them, is meete, and dothe
    agree: *105*
Which writeth matters, with curiositee.
Myne habite blacke, accordeth not with
    greene:
Blacke, betokeneth death, as it is daily
    seene,
The greene, is pleasaunt, fresh, lust and
    iolitie:
These two, in nature, hath great diuer-
    sitie,   *110*
Then, who woulde ascribe, excepte he
    were a foole,
The pleasaunt Lauret, vnto the mourn-
    yng coole.
Another rewarde, abydeth my labor:
The glorious syght, of God my Sauior.
Which is cheife Shepherde, and head
    of other all: *115*
To him, for succour, in this my warke,
    I call.
And not on Clio, nor olde Melpomene:
My hope is fixed, of him ayded to be.
That he, me direct, my mynde for to ex-
    presse:
That he, to good ende, my wyt and pen
    addresse.   *120*
For to accomplyssh, my purpose and en-
    tent:
To the laude and pleasure, of God omni-
    potent.
And to the profyte, the pleasure and the
    meede.
Of al them which shal, this treatise heare
    & reede.
But to the **reader**, **now** to retourne
    agayne: *125*

Fyrst, of this thyng, I wyll thou be cer-
tayne.
That . x . Egloges, this hole treatyse dothe
holde:
To imitate, of other Poetes olde.
In which Egloges, Shepherdes thou mayst
see,
In homely language, not passyng their
degree.   *130*
Some, disputyng, of Courtly Misery:
Sometyme, of Uenus deceatfull tiranny.
Sometyme, commendyng loue, honest, and
laudable

Sometyme, dispisyng loue, false, deceau-
able.
Somtyme, dispisyng, and blamyng au-
arise: *135*
Sometyme excityng, vertue to exercyse.
Sometyme, of warre, abhoryng the out-
rage:
And of the same tyme, the manifolde
damage.
And other matters, as after shall appeare:
To their great pleasure, whiche shal them
reade or heare.   *140*

THE FOURTH EGLOGE OF ALEXANDER BARCLAY,
entituled Codrus and Minalcus, treating of the behauour of Riche men agaynst Poetes

¶ *The Argument.*

Codrus a shepheard lusty, gay and stoute,
Sat with his wethers at pasture round
about,
And poore Minalcas with ewes scarse
fourtene
Sat sadly musing in shadowe on the
grene.
This lustie Codrus was cloked for the
rayne,   5
And doble decked with huddes one or
twayne,
He had a pautner with purses manyfolde,
And surely lined with siluer and with
golde,
Within his wallet were meates good and
fine,
Both store and plentie had he of ale and
wine,   *10*
Suche fulsome pasture made him a double
chin,
His furred mittins were of a curres skin,
Nothing he wanted longing to clothe or
foode,
But by no meane would he depart with
good.
Sometime this Codrus did vnder shadowe
lye   *15*
Wide open piping and gaping on the skye,
Sometime he daunced and hobled as a
beare,
Sometime he pried howe he became his
geare,
He lept, he songe, and ran to proue his
might,

When purse is heauy oftetime the heart is
light.   *20*
But though this Codrus had store inough
of good,
He wanted wisedome, for nought he vn-
derstood
Saue worldly practise his treasour for to
store,
Howe euer it came small forse had he
therfore.
On the other side the poore Minalcas
lay,   *25*
With empty belly and simple poore aray,
Yet coulde he pipe and finger well a
drone,
But soure is musike when men for hun-
ger grone,
Codrus had riches, Minalcas had cunning,
For God not geueth to one man euery
thing.   *30*
At last this Codrus espied Minalcas,
And soone he knewe what maner man he
was,
For olde acquayntaunce betwene them
earst had bene,
Long time before they met vpon the
grene,
And therfor Codrus downe boldly by
him sat,   *35*
And in this maner began with him to
chat.

Codrus first speaketh

Al hayle Minalcas, nowe by my fayth well
met,
Lorde Jesu mercy what troubles did thee
let,

That this long season none could thee
  here espy?
With vs was thou wont to sing full
  merily,   40
And to lye piping oftetime among the
  floures,
What time thy beastes were feding among
  ours.
In these olde valleys we two were wont
  to bourde,
And in these shadowes talke many a
  mery worde,
And oft were we wont to wrastle for a
  fall,   45
But nowe thou droupest and hast for-
  gotten all.
Here wast thou wont swete balades to
  sing,
Of song and ditte as it were for a king,
And of gay matters to sing and to endite,
But nowe thy courage is gone and thy
  delite,   50
Trust me Minalcas nowe playnly I espy
That thou art wery of shepheardes com-
  pany,
And that all pleasour thou semest to de-
  spise,
Lothing our pasture and fieldes in like-
  wise,
Thou fleest solace and euery mery fitte, 55
Leasing thy time and sore hurting thy
  witte,
In sloth thou slombrest as buried were
  thy song,
Thy pipe is broken or som what els is
  wrong.

Minalcas

What time the Cuckowes fethers mout
  and fall,
From sight she lurketh, hir song is gone
  withall,   60
When backe is bare and purse of coyne
  is light,
The wit is dulled and reason hath no
  might:
Adewe enditing when gone is libertie,
Enemie to Muses is wretched pouertie,
What time a knight is subiect to a
  knaue   65
To iust or tourney small pleasour shall
  he haue.

Codrus

What no man thee kepeth here in captiuitie,

And busy labour subdueth pouertie,
And oft it is better and much surer also
As subiect to obey then at freewill to
  go,   70
As for example beholde a wanton colte
In raging youth leapeth ouer hill and
  holte,
But while he skippeth at pleasure and at
  will
Ofte time doth he fall in daunger for to
  spill,
Sometime on stubbes his hofes sore he
  teares,   75
Or fals in the mud both ouer head and
  eares,
Sometime all the night abrode in hayle
  or rayne,
And oft among breres tangled by the
  mayne,
And other perils he suffreth infinite,
So mingled with sorowe is pleasour and
  delite: 80
But if this same colte be broken at the
  last,
His sitter ruleth and him refrayneth fast,
The spurre him pricketh, the bridle doth
  him holde,
That he can not praunce at pleasour
  where he wolde,
The rider him ruleth and saueth from
  daunger.   85
By which example Minalcas it is clere
That free will is subiect to inconuenience,
Where by subiection man voydeth great
  offence,
For man of him selfe is very frayle cer-
  tayne,
But ofte a ruler his folly dothe re-
  frayne,   90
But as for thy selfe thou hast no cause
  pardie,
To walke at pleasour is no captiuitie.

Minalcas

Seest thou not Codrus the fieldes rounde
  about
Compassed with floudes that none may in
  nor out,
The muddy waters nere choke me with
  the stinke,   95
At euery tempest they be as blacke as
  inke:
Pouertie to me should be no discomforte
If other shepheardes were all of the same
  sorte.

But Codrus I clawe oft where it doth
not itche,
To see ten beggers and halfe a dosen
riche, *100*
Truely me thinketh this wrong pertition,
And namely sith all ought be after one.
When I first behelde these fieldes from a
farre,
Me thought them pleasant and voyde of
strife or warre,
But with my poore flocke approching
nere and nere *105*
Alway my pleasour did lesse and lesse
appeare,
And truely Codrus since I came on this
grounde
Oft vnder floures vile snakes haue I
founde,
Adders and todes and many fell serpent,
Infecte olde shepe with venim violent, *110*
And ofte be the yonge infected of the
olde,
That vnto these fewe nowe brought is all
my folde.

Codrus

In some place is neyther venim nor serpent
And as for my selfe I fele no greuous
sent.

Minalcas

It were great maruell where so great
grounde is sene, *115*
If no small medowe were pleasaunt, swete
and clene,
As for thee Codrus I may beleue right
weele,
That thou no sauour nor stinke of mud
dost feele,
For if a shephearde hath still remayned
longe
In a foule prison or in a stinking gonge,
His pores with ill ayre be stopped so
echone *121*
That of the ayre he feleth small sent or
none,
And yet the dwellers be badder then the
place,
The riche and sturdie doth threaten and
manace
The poore and simple and suche as came
but late, *125*
And who moste knoweth him moste of
all they hate,
And all the burthen is on the Asses backe,

But the stronge Caball standeth at the
racke.
And suche be assigned sometime the flocke
to kepe
Which scant haue so muche of reason as
the shepe, *130*
And euery shepheard at other hath enuy,
Scant be a couple which loueth perfitely,
Ill will so reygneth that brauling be thou
sure,
Constrayned me nere to seke a newe
pasture,
Saue onely after I hope of better rest, *135*
For small occasion a birde not chaungeth
nest.

Codrus

Welere thou graunted that in a large
grounde
Some plot of pleasour and quiet may be
founde,
So where of heardes assembled is great
sorte,
There some must be good, then to the best
resorte. *140*
But leaue we all this, turne to our poynt
agayne,
Of thy olde balades some would I heare
full fayne,
For often haue I had great pleasour and
delite
To heare recounted suche as thou did
endite.

Minalcas

Yea, other shepheardes which haue
inough at home, *145*
When ye be mery and stuffed is your
wombe,
Which haue great store of butter, chese
and woll,
Your cowes others of milke replete and
full,
Payles of swete milke as full as they be
able,
When your fat dishes smoke hote vpon
your table, *150*
Then laude ye songes and balades magnifie,
If they be mery or written craftily,
Ye clappe your handes and to the making
harke,
And one say to other, lo here a proper
warke.
But when ye haue saide nought geue ye
for our payne, *155*

Saue onely laudes and pleasaunt wordes
vayne,
All if these laudes may well be counted
good,
Yet the poore shepheard must haue some
other food.

Codrus.

Mayst thou not sometime thy folde and
shepe apply,
And after at leasour to liue more quietly,
Dispose thy wittes to make or to endite,
Renouncing cures for time while thou
dost write.

Minalcas

Nedes must a Shepheard bestowe his
whole labour
In tending his flockes, scant may he spare
one houre:
In going, comming, and often them to
tende,   165
Full lightly the day is brought vnto an
ende.
Sometime the wolues with dogges must
he chace,
Sometime his foldes must he newe compace:
And oft time them chaunge, and if he
stormes doubt,
Of his shepecote dawbe the walles round
about: 170
When they be broken, oft times them
renue,
And hurtfull pastures note well, and them
eschue.
Bye strawe and litter, and hay for winter
colde,
Oft grease the scabbes aswell of yonge
as olde.
For dreade of thieues oft watche vp all
the night,   175
Beside this labour with all his minde and
might,
For his poore housholde for to prouide
vitayle,
If by aduenture his wooll or lambes
fayle,
In doing all these no respite doth re-
mayne,
But well to indite requireth all the
brayne.   180
I tell thee Codrus, a stile of excellence
Must haue all laboure and all the dili-
gence.

Both these two workes be great, nere im-
portable
To my small power, my strength is muche
vnable.
The one to intende scant may I bide the
payne,   185
Then is it harder for me to do both
twayne,
What time my wittes be clere for to
indite,
My dayly charges will graunt me no respite:
But if I folowe, inditing at my will,
Eche one disdayneth my charges to ful-
fill.   190
Though in these fieldes eche other ought
sustayne,
Cleane lost is that lawe, one may require
in vayne:
If coyne commaunde, then men count
them as bounde,
Els flee they labour, then is my charge
on grounde.

Codrus

Cornix oft counted that man should flee
no payne,   195
His frendes burthen to supporte and sustayne:
Feede they thy flocke, while thou doest
write and sing,
Eche horse agreeth not well for euery
thing.
Some for the charet, some for the cart or
plough,
And some for hakneyes, if they be light
and tough.   200
Eche field agreeth not well for euery
seede,
Who hath moste labour is worthy of best
mede.

Minalcas

After inditing then gladly would I drinke,
To reache me the cup no man doth care
ne thinke:
And oft some fooles voyde of discre-
tion   205
Me and my matters haue in derision.
And meruayle is none, for who would
sowe that fielde
With costly seedes, which shall no fruites
yelde.
Some wanton body oft laugheth me to
scorne,

And saith: Minalcas, see howe thy pilche
   is torne,   *210*
Thy hose and cokers be broken at the
   knee,
Thou canst not stumble, for both thy
   shone may see.
Thy beard like bristels, or like a porpos
   skin,
Thy cloathing sheweth, thy winning is
   but thin:
Such mocking tauntes renueth oft my
   care,   *215*
And nowe be woods of fruit and leaues
   bare.
And frostie winter hath made the fieldes
   white,
For wrath and anger my lip and tonge
   I bite:
For dolour I droupe, sore vexed with dis-
   dayne,
My wombe all wasteth, wherfore I bide
   this payne: *220*
My wooll and wethers may scarsly feede
   my wombe,
And other housholde which I retayne at
   home.
Leane be my lambes, that no man will
   them bye,
And yet their dammes they dayly sucke
   so dry,
That from the vthers no licoure can we
   wring,   *225*
Then without repast who can indite or
   sing.
It me repenteth, if I haue any wit,
As for my science, I wery am of it.
And of my poore life I weary am, Co-
   drus,
Sith my harde fortune for me disposeth
   thus,   *230*
That of the starres and planettes eche
   one
To poore Minalcas well fortunate is none.
Knowen is the truth if it were clerely
   sought,
That nowe to this time I still haue songe
   for nought:
For youth is lusty, and of small thing
   hath nede,   *235*
That time to age men geue no force nor
   heede.
Ages condition is greatly contrary,
Which nowe approcheth right still and
   craftyly,

But what time age doth any man op-
   presse,
If he in youth haue gathred no riches:
Then passeth age in care and pouertie,
For nede is grieuous with olde infirmitie:
And age is fetred oft time with care and
   neede,
When strength is faded and man hath
   nought to feede,
When strength is faded, then hope of
   gayne is gone,   *245*
In youthes season to make prouision,
The litle Emmet is wise and prouident,
In summer working with labour diligent,
In her small caues conueying corne and
   grayne
Her life in Winter to nourish and sus-
   tayne:
And with her small mouth is busy it
   cutting,
Least in her caues the same might growe
   or spring.
So man of reason himselfe reputing sage,
In youth should puruey, to liue theron in
   age.

Codrus

Men say that clerkes which knowe As-
   tronomy,   *255*
Knowe certayne starres which longe to
   desteny:
But all their saying is nothing veritable,
Yet heare the matter, though it be but a
   fable.
They say that Mercury doth Poetes
   fauoure,
Under Jupiter be princes of honour: *260*
And men of riches, of wealth or dignitie,
And all such other as haue aucthoritie:
Mercury geueth to Poetes laureate
Goodly conueyaunce, speeche pleasaunt
   and ornate,
Inuentife reason to sing or play on
   harpe,   *265*
In goodly ditie or balade for to carpe.
This is thy lot, what seekest thou riches?
No man hath all, this thing is true doubt-
   lesse.
God all disposeth as he perceyueth best.
Take thou thy fortune, and holde thee still
   in rest: *270*
Take thou thy fortune, and holde thy
   selfe content,
Let vs haue riches and rowmes excellent,

Minalcas

Thou haste of riches and goodes haboun-
daunce,
And I haue dities and songes of pleasaunce:
To aske my cunning to couetous thou
art,
Why is not thy selfe contented with thy
part,
Why doest thou inuade my part and portion,
Thou wantest (Codrus) wit and discretion.

Codrus

Not so Minalcas, forsooth thou art to
blame,
Of wronge inuasion to geue to me the
name.   *280*
I would no ditie nor ballade take thee fro,
No harpe nor armes which long to
Apollo:
But onely, Minalcas, I sore desire and
longe
To geue mine eares to thy sweete sound-
ing song.
It feedeth hearing, and is to one pleas-
aunt,   *285*
To heare good reason and ballade con-
sonant.

Minalcas.

If thou haue pleasure to heare my melody,
I graunt thee Codrus to ioy my armony,
So haue I pleasure and ioy of thy riches,
So giftes doubled increaseth loue doubt-
lesse.   *290*

Codrus

He of my riches hath ioy which loueth
me,
And who me hateth, nothing content is
he.
Enuious wretches by malice commonly
Take others fortune and pleasure heauyly.

Minalcas

In like wise mayst thou inioy of our
science,   *295*
And of our Muses though thou be fro
presence:
And of our cunning thou ioyest semblably,
If nought prouoke thee by malice and
enuy.

---

278. The bracketed word is so bracketed in the
text. Similarly in lines 411, 467, 587, 607,
629, 663, 811, 847, 911.

If I feede thy eares, feede thou my mouth
agayne,
I loth were to spende my giftes all in
vayne.   *300*
Meate vnto the mouth is foode and suste-
naunce,
And songes feede the eares with pleas-
aunce,
I haue the Muses, if thou wilt haue of
mine,
Then right requireth that I haue part of
thine.
This longeth to loue, to nourish charitee
This feedeth pitie, this doth to right
agree
This is the pleasure and will of God
aboue,
Of him disposed for to ingender loue.
All pleasaunt giftes one man hath not
pardie,
That one of other should haue neces-
sitie.   *310*
No man of him selfe is sure sufficistent,
This is prouision of God omnipotent.
That one man should neede anothers as-
sistence,
Thereby is ioyned loue and beneuolence.
Englande hath cloth, Burdeus hath store
of wine,   *315*
Cornewall hath tinne, and lymster wools
fine.
London hath scarlet, and Bristowe pleas-
aunt red,
Fen lande hath fishes, in other place is
lead.
This is of our Lorde disposed so my
brother
Because all costes should one haue neede
of other.   *320*
So euery tree hath fruit after his kinde,
And diuers natures in beastes may we
finde.
Alway when nature of thing is moste
laudable,
That thing men counteth most good and
profitable.
And euery person in his owne gift hath
ioy   *325*
The foole in his bable hath pleasure for
to toy.
The clerke in his bookes, the merchaunt
in riches,
The knight in his horse, harnes and
hardynes.

But euery person of his giftes and art,
When nede requireth should gladly geue
    some part. *330*
Such meane conioyneth in bonde of loue
    certayne,
Englande and Fraunce, Scotlande, Grece
    and Spain.
So hast thou Codrus of golde ynough in
    store,
And I some cunning, though fewe men
    care therfore.
Thou art beholden to Jupiter truely, *335*
And I beholden to pleasaunt Mercury,
Joyne we our starres, let me haue part
    of thine,
Concorde to cherishe, thou shalt haue part
    of mine.
Make thou Jupiter be frendly vnto me,
And our Mercury shalbe as good to
    thee *340*
If thy Jupiter geue me but onely golde,
Mercury shall geue thee giftes many-
    folde.
His pillion, scepter, his winges and his
    harpe,
If thou haue all these thou mayst grathly
    carpe.
And ouer all these geue thee shall Mer-
    cury *345*
The knot of Hercules inlaced craftyly.

Codrus

Lorde God, Minalcas, why haste thou
    all this payne
Thus wise to forge so many wordes in
    vayne.

Minalcas

That vayne thou countest which may
    hurt or inlesse *350*
Thy loued treasure, or minishe thy
    riches:
If thou wilt harken or heare my Muses
    sing,
Refreshe my mindes with confort and
    liking,
Rid me fro troubles and care of busynes,
Confort my courage which nowe is com-
    fortlesse. *355*
A clerke or poete combined with a boye,
To haunt the Muses or write hath litle
    ioy
The wit and reason is dull or of valour
Like as the body is called to honour.
When busy charges causeth a man to
    grone,

The wit then slumbreth, and Muses all
    be gone. *360*
A ditie will haue minde quiet and respite,
And ease of stomake, els can none well
    indite,
I sighe, I slumber, care troubleth oft my
    thought,
When some by malice mine art setteth at
    nought.
I hewle as a kite for hunger and for
    golde, *365*
For thought and study my youth appereth
    olde:
My skin hath wrinkles and pimples round
    about,
For colde and study I dreade me of the
    gowte.
When sickenes commeth then life hath
    breuitie
By false vnkindnes and wretched pouer-
    tie. *370*
If men were louing, benigne and chari-
    table,
Then were pouertie both good and toller-
    able:
But since charitie and pitie both be gone,
What should pouertie remayne behinde
    alone.
No man hath pitie, eche dayneth me to
    feede, *375*
I lost haue confort, but still remayneth
    neede:
I haue no wethers nor ewes in my folde,
No siluer in purse, I knowe not what is
    golde:
No corne on the grounde haue I whereon
    to fare,
Then would thou haue me to liue auoyde
    of care. *380*
Nay nay frende Codrus, trust me, I thee
    assure
Such maner salues can not my dolour
    cure.
Make thou me iocunde, helpe me with
    cloth and foode,
Clothe me for winter with pilche, felt
    and hoode.
Auoyde all charges, let me sit in my
    cell, *385*
Let worldly wretches with worldly mat-
    ters mell.
Succoure my age, regarde my heares
    gray,
Then shalt thou proue and see what thing
    I may:

Then shalt thou finde me both apt to write and sing,
Good will shall fulfill my scarcenes of cunning,   *390*
A plentifull house out chaseth thought and care,
Soiourne doth sorowe there where all thing is bare,
The seller couched with bere, with ale or wine,
And meates ready when man hath lust to dine.
Great barnes full, fat wethers in the folde,   *395*
The purse well stuffed with siluer and with golde.
Fauour of frendes, and suche as loueth right
All these and other do make thee full light,
Then is it pleasure the yonge maydens amonge
To watche by the fire the winters nightes longe   *400*
At their fonde tales to laugh, or when they brall,
Great fire and candell spending for laboure small,
And in the ashes some playes for to marke,
To couer wardens for fault of other warke.
To toste white sheuers, and to make prophitroles,   *405*
And after talking oft time to fill the bowles.
Where wealth aboundeth without rebuke or crime,
Thus do some heardes for pleasure and pastime:
As fame reporteth, such a Shepherde there was,
Which that time liued vnder Mecenas. *410*
And Titerus (I trowe) was this shepherdes name,
I well remember aliue yet is his fame.
He songe of fieldes and tilling of the grounde,
Of shepe, of oxen, and battayle did he sounde.   *414*
So shrill he sounded in termes eloquent,
I trowe his tunes went to the firmament.
The same Mecenas to him was free and kinde,

Whose large giftes gaue confort to his minde:
Also this Shepherde by heauenly influence
I trowe obtayned his perelesse eloquence.
We other Shepherdes be greatly different,   *421*
Of common sortes, leane, ragged and rent.
Fed with rude frowise, with quacham, or with crudd,
Or slimy kempes ill smelling of the mud.
Such rusty meates inblindeth so our brayne,   *425*
That of our fauour the muses haue disdayne:
And great Apollo despiseth that we write
For why rude wittes but rudely do indite.

Codrus.

I trust on fortune, if it be fauourable,
My trust fulfilling, then shall I well be able   *430*
Thy neede to succoure, I hope after a thing,
And if fortune fall well after my liking,
Trust me Minalcas, I shall deliuer thee
Out of this trouble, care and calamitie.

Minalcas

A Codrus Codrus, I would to God thy will   *435*
Were this time ready thy promise to fulfill
After the power and might that thou haste nowe.
Thou haste ynough for both, man God auowe.
If thy good minde according with thy might,
At this time present thou should my heart well light.   *440*
I aske not the store of Cosmus or Capell,
With silken robes I couete not to mell.
No kinges dishes I couete nor desire,
Nor riche mantels, or palles wrought in Tire:
No cloth of golde, of Tissue nor veluet,   *445*
Damaske nor Sattin, nor orient Scarlet.
I aske no value of Peters costly cope,
Shield of Minerua, nor patin of Esope.
I aske no palace, nor lodging curious,
No bed of state, of rayment sumptuous.

For this I learned of the Dean of Powles,
I tell thee Codrus, this man hath won
   some soules.
I aske no treasure nor store of worldly
   good,
But a quiet life, and onely cloth and
   foode,
With homely lodging to keepe me warme
   and drye   455
Induring my life, forsooth no more aske
   I.
If I were certaine this liuing still to haue,
Auoyde of trouble, no more of God I
   craue.

Codrus

This liuing haste thou, what needest thou
   complayne,
Nothing thou wantest which may thy life
   sustayne: 460
What feele man, pardie thy chekes be
   not thin,
No lacke of vitayle causeth a double chin.

Minalcas.

Some beast is lustie and fat of his nature,
Though he sore laboure, and go in bad
   pasture.
And some beast agayne still leane and
   poore is seene,   465
Thogh it fatly fare within a medowe
   greene.
Though thou would (Codrus) stil argue
   til to morow,
I licke no dishes which sauced be with
   sorowe.
Better one small dish with ioy and heart
   liking
Then diuers daynties with murmure and
   grutching.   470
And men vnlearned can neuer be con-
   tent,
When scolers common, and clerkes be
   present.
Assoone as clerkes begin to talke and
   chat,
Some other glowmes, and hath enuy
   thereat.
It is a torment a clerke to sit at borde, 475
And of his learning not for to talke one
   worde.
Better were to be with clerkes with a
   crust,
Then at such tables to fare at will and
   lust.

Let me haue the borde of olde Pithag-
   oras,
Which of temperaunce a very father
   was.   480
Of Philosophers the moderate riches
In youth or age I loued neuer excesse.
Some boast and promise, and put men
   in confort
Of large giftes, moste men be of this
   sort,
With mouth and promise for to be liber-
   all,   485
When nede requireth, then geue they
   nought at all.
All onely in thee is fixed all my trust,
If thou fayle promise then rowle I in
   the dust,
My hope is faded, then shall my songe
   be dom
Like a Nightingale at the solstitium. 490
If thou fayle promise, my comfort cleane
   is lost,
Then may I hange my pipe vpon the
   poste:
Shet the shop windowes for lacke of
   marchaundise,
Or els for because that easy is the price.

Codrus

Minalcas, if thou the court of Rome
   haste seene,   495
With forked cappes or els if thou haste
   beene,
Or noble Prelates by riches excellent,
Thou well perceyuest they be magnifi-
   cent.
With them be clerkes and pleasaunt Ora-
   tours,
And many Poetes promoted to honours,
There is aboundaunce of all that men
   desire,   501
There men hath honour before they it re-
   quire:
In such fayre fieldes without labour or
   payne
Both wealth and riches thou lightly mayst
   obtayne.

Minalcas

Thou art abused, and thinkest wrong
   doubtlesse   505
To thinke that I am desirous of riches.
To feede on rawe fleshe it is a wolues
   gise,
Wherfore he weneth all beastes do likewise.

Because the blinde man halteth and is
lame,
In minde he thinketh that all men do the
same.   *510*
So for that thy selfe desirest good in
store,
All men thou iudgest infected with like
sore.
Codrus, I couet not to haue aboundaunce,
Small thing me pleaseth, I aske but suffi-
saunce.
Graunt me a liuing sufficient and small,
And voyde of troubles, I aske no more
at all.   *516*
But with that litle I holde my selfe con-
tent,
If sauce of sorowe my mindes not tor-
ment.
Of the court of Rome forsooth I haue
heard tell,
With forked cappes it folly is to mell. *520*
Micene and Morton be dead and gone
certayne,
They, nor their like shall neuer returne
agayne.
O Codrus Codrus, Augustus and Ed-
warde
Be gone for euer, our fortune is more
harde.
The scarlet robes in songe haue small
delite,   *525*
What should I trauayle, in Rome is no
profite,
It geueth mockes and scornes manyfolde,
Still catching coyne, and gaping after
golde,
Fraude and disceyte doth all the world
fill,
And money reygneth and doth all thing
at will.   *530*
And for that people would more intende
to gile,
Uertue and truth be driuen into exile.
We are commaunded to trust for time to
come
Till care and sorowe hath wasted our
wisedome.
Hope of rewarde hath Poetes them to
feede,   *535*
Nowe in the worlde fayre wordes be
their mede.

Codrus

Then write of battayles, or actes of men
bolde,

Or mightie princes, they may thee well
vpholde,
These worthy rulers of fame and name
royall
Of very reason ought to be liberall. *540*
Some shalt thou finde betwene this place
and Kent,
Which for thy labour shall thee right
well content.

Minalcas

Yea, some shall I finde which be so prod-
igall,
That in vayne thinges spende and cleane
wasteth all:
But howe should that man my pouertie
sustayne,   *545*
Which nought reserueth his honoure to
mayntayne.
For auncient bloud nor auncient honoure
In these our dayes be nought without
treasure.
The coyne auaunceth, neede doth the
name deiect,
And where is treasure olde honour hath
effect.   *550*
But such as be riche and in promotion
Shall haue my writing but in derision.
For in this season great men of excel-
lence
Haue to poemes no greater reuerence,
Then to a brothell or els a brothelhouse,
Mad ignoraunce is so contagious. *556*

Codrus

It is not seeming a Poet thus to iest
In wrathful speeche, nor wordes dishonest.

Minalcas

It is no iesting, be thou neuer so wroth,
In open language to say nothing but
troth: *560*
If peraduenture thou would haue troth
kept still,
Prouoke thou not me to anger at thy
will.
When wrath is moued, then reason hath
no might,
The tonge forgetteth discretion and right.

Codrus

To moue thy minde I truely were full
lothe,   *565*
To geue good councell is farre from being
wrothe.

Minalcas

As touching councell, my minde is plen-
tifull,
But neede and troubles make all my rea-
son dull,
If I had councell and golde in like plentie,
I tell thee Codrus, I had no neede of
thee.   570
Howe should a Poet, poore, bare and
indigent,
Indite the actes of princes excellent,
While scant is he worth a knife his pipe
to mende,
To rounde the holes, to clense or picke
the ende.
Beholde, my whittle almoste hath lost the
blade,   575
So long time past is sith the same was
made:
The haft is bruised, the blade not worth
a strawe,
Rusty and toothed, not much vnlike a
sawe.
But touching this hurt, it is but light and
small,
But care and trouble is grieuous payne
withall.   580
Good counsell helpeth, making the wittes
stable,
Ill councell maketh the mindes variable,
And breaketh the brayne, diminishing the
strength,
And all the reason confoundeth at the
length.
Great men are shamed to geue thing
poore or small,   585
And great they denye, thus geue they
nought at all.
Beside this (Codrus) princes and men
royall
In our inditinges haue pleasure faint and
small.
So much power haue they with men of
might,
As simple doues when Egles take their
flight: 590
Or as great windes careth for leaues
drye.
They liue in pleasure and wealth continually,
In lust their liking is, and in ydlenes,
Fewe haue their mindes clean from all
viciousnes:

Pleasure is thing whereto they moste
intende,   595
That they moste cherishe, they would
haue men concend
If Poetes should their maners magnify,
They were supporters of blame and
lechery:
Then should their writing be nothing
commendable,
Conteyning iestes and deedes detesta-
ble,   600
Of stinking Uenus or loue inordinate,
Of ribaude wordes which fall not for a
state,
Of right oppressed, and beastly gluttony,
Of vice aduaunced, of slouth and iniury,
And other deedes infame and worthy
blame,   605
Which were ouerlonge here to recount
or name.
These to commend (Codrus) do not
agree
To any Poete which loueth chastitie.

Codrus

What yes Minalcas, some haue bene
stronge and bolde,
Which haue in battayle done actes manyfolde,   610
With mighty courage hauing them in
fight,
And boldly biding for to maynteyne the
right.
To thee could I nowe rehearse well nere
a score
Of lust nor riches setting no force ne
store.
Despising oft golde, sweete fare and
beddes soft,   615
Which in colde harnes lye on the grounde
full oft,
Closed in yron, which when their woundes
blede,
Want bread and drinke them to restore
and feede.
While some haue pleasure in softe golde
orient,
With colde harde yron their minde is well
content.   620
Such were the sonnes of noble lord
Hawarde,
Whose famous actes may shame a faint
cowarde.
What could they more but their swete
liues spende,

Their princes quarell and right for to
    defende:
Alas that battayle should be of that ri-
    gour,   625
When fame and honour riseth and is in
    floure,
With sodayne furour then all to quenche
    agayne,
But boldest heartes be nerest death cer-
    tayne.

Minalcas

For certayne (Codrus) I can not that
    denye,
But some in battayle behaue them man-
    fully,   630
Such as in battayle do actes marciall,
Laude worthy Poetes and stile heroicall:
The pleasaunt Muses which soundeth
    grauitie
Had helpe and fauour while these were
    in degree.
But sith stronge knightes hath left their
    exercise,
And manly vertue corrupted is with vice,
The famous Poetes which ornately indite
Haue founde no matter whereof to singe
    or write.
The wit thus dyeth of poetes auncient,
So doth their writing and ditie eloquent.
For lacke of custome, thought, care and
    penury,   641
These be confounders of pleasaunt poecy.
But if some prince, some king or con-
    querour
Hath won in armes or battayle great
    honour:
Full litle they force for to delate their
    fame,
That other realmes may laude or prayse
    their name.
Of time for to come they force nothing
    at all,
By fame and honour to liue as immortall:
It them suffiseth, they count ynough true-
    ly
That their owne realmes their names
    magnify.   650
And that for their life they may haue
    laude and fame,
After their death then seeke they for no
    name.
And some be vntaught and learned no
    science,
Or els they disdayne hye stile of elo-
    quence:

Then standeth the Poet and his poeme
    arere,
When princes disdayne them for to reade
    or here.
Or els some other is drowned all in golde,
By couetise kept in cares manyfolde.
By flagrant ardour inflamed in suche case,
As in time past the olde king Midas was.
Then of poemes full small pleasure hath
    he,   661
Couetise and clergy full lewdly do agree.
Beside this (Codrus) with princes com-
    monly
Be vntaught courtiers fulfilled with enuy.
Jugglers and Pipers, bourders and flat-
    terers,
Baudes and Janglers, and cursed aduout-
    rers:
And mo such other of liuing vicious
To whom is vertue aduerse and odious.
These do good Poetes forth of all courtes
    chase,
By thousande maners of threatning and
    manace,   670
Sometime by fraudes, sometime by ill
    reporte,
And them assisteth all other of their sort:
Like as when curres light on a carion,
Or stinking rauens fed with corruption:
These two all other away do beate and
    chace,
Because they alone would occupy the
    place.
For vnto curres is carion moste meete,
And also rauens fele stinking thinges
    sweete.
Another thing yet is greatly more damna-
    ble,
Of rascolde poetes yet is a shamfull
    rable,   680
Which voyde of wisedome presumeth to
    indite,
Though they haue scantly the cunning
    of a snite:
And to what vices that princes moste
    intende,
Those dare these fooles solemnize and
    commende.
Then is he decked as Poete laureate,
When stinking Thais made him her grad-
    uate.
When Muses rested, she did her season
    note,
And she with Bacchus her camous did
    promote:

Such rascold drames promoted by Thais,
Bacchus, Licoris, or yet by Testalis,   *690*
Or by suche other newe forged Muses
   nine
Thinke in their mindes for to haue wit
   diuine.
They laude their verses, they boast, they
   vaunt and iet,
Though all their cunning be scantly
   worth a pet.
If they haue smelled the artes triuiall,
They count them Poetes hye and heroic-
   all.
Such is their foly, so foolishly they dote,
Thinking that none can their playne er-
   rour note:
Yet be they foolishe, auoyde of honestie,
Nothing seasoned with spice of grauitie,
Auoyde of pleasure, auoyde of eloquence,
With many wordes, and fruitlesse of sen-
   tence.   *702*
Unapt to learne, disdayning to be taught,
Their priuate pleasure in snare hath
   them so caught:
And worst yet of all, they count them ex-
   cellent,
Though they be fruitlesse, rashe and im-
   prouident.
To suche Ambages who doth their minde
   incline,
They count all other as priuate of doc-
   trine,
And that the faultes which be in them
   alone,
Also be common in other men eche one.
Thus bide good Poetes oft time rebuke
   and blame,   *711*
Because of other which haue despised
   name.
And thus for the bad the good be cleane
   abiect,
Their art and poeme counted of none
   effect.
Who wanteth reason good to discerne
   from ill
Doth worthy writers interprete at his
   will:
So both the laudes of good and not
   laudable
For lacke of knowledge become vituper-
   able.

Codrus

In fayth Minalcas, I well allowe thy wit,
Yet would I gladly heare nowe some
   mery fit   *720*

Of mayde Marion, or els of Robin hood,
Or Bentleys ale which chaseth well the
   bloud:
Of perte of Norwiche, or sauce of Wil-
   berton,
Or buckishe Joly well stuffed as a ton:
Talke of the bottell, let go the booke for
   nowe,
Combrous is cunning I make to God a
   vowe.
Speake of some matter which may re-
   fresh my brayne,
Trust me Minalcas, I shall rewarde thy
   payne.
Els talke of stoutenes, where is more
   brayne then wit,
Place moste abused that we haue spoke
   of yet.   *730*

Minalcas

Of all these thinges language to multi-
   ply,
Except I lyed, should be but vilany.
It is not seeming a Poete one to blame,
All if his hauour hath won diffamed
   name.
And though such beastes pursue me with
   enuy,   *735*
Malgre for malice, that payment I de-
   fye.
My master teacheth, so doth reason and
   skill,
That man should restore, and render good
   for ill.

Codrus

Then talke of somewhat, lo it is longe
   to night,
Yet hath the sonne more then an houre
   of light,   *740*

Minalcas

If I ought common sounding to grauitie,
I feare to obtayne but small rewarde of
   thee:
But if I common of vice or wantonnes,
Then of our Lorde shall my rewarde be
   lesse,
Wherefore my ballade shall haue con-
   clusion   *745*
On fruitfull clauses of noble Salomon.

Codrus

Sing on Minalcas, he may do litle thing,
Which to a ballade disdayneth the hear-
   ing:
But if thy ditie accorde not to my minde,

Then my rewarde and promise is behinde,   *750*
By mans manners it lightly doth appere,
What men desire, that loue they for to
  here.

Minalcas

Though in thy promise I finde no cer-
  tentie,
Yet of my cunning shalt thou haue part
  of me,
I call no muses to geue to me doctrine,
But ayde and confort of strength and
  might diuine,
To clere my reason with wisedom and
  prudence
To sing one ballade extract of sapience.

———

As medoes paynted with floures redolent
The sight reioyce of suche as them be-
  holde :   *760*
So man indued with vertue excellent
Fragrantly shineth with beames many-
  folde.
Uertue with wisedome exceedeth store of
  gold,
If riches abound, set not on them thy
  trust.
When strength is sturdy, then man is pert
  and bolde,   *765*
But wit and wisedome soone lay him in
  the dust.

That man is beastly which sueth carnall
  lust,
Spende not on women thy riches or sub-
  staunce,
For lacke of vsing as stele or yron rust,
So rusteth reason by wilfull ignoraunce,
In fraudfull beautie set but small pleas-
  aunce,   *771*
A pleasaunt apple is oft corrupt within,
Grounde thee in youth on goodly gouern-
  aunce,
It is good token when man doth well
  begin.

Ioy not in malice, that is a mortall sinne,
Man is perceyued by language and doc-
  trine,   *776*
Better is to lose then wrongfully to winne,
He loueth wisedome, which loueth disci-
  pline :
Rashe enterprises oft bringeth to ruine,
A man may contende, God geueth victory,
Set neuer thy minde on thing which is not
  thine,   *781*

Trust not in honour, all wealth is transitory,

Combine thou thy tonge with reason and
  memory,
Speake not to hasty without aduisement,
So liue in this life that thou mayst trust
  on glory,   *785*
Which is not caduke, but lasting perma-
  nent.
There is no secrete with people vinolent,
By beastly surfeit the life is breuiate,
Though some haue pleasure in sumptu-
  ous garment,
Yet goodly manners him maketh more
  ornate.   *790*

Codrus

Ho there Minalcas, of this haue we
  ynough,
What should a Ploughman go farther
  then his plough,
What should a shepherde in wisedome
  wade so farre,
Talke he of tankarde, or of his boxe of
  tarre.
Tell somewhat els, wherein is more conforte,   *795*
So shall the season and time seeme light
  and short.

Minalcas

For thou of Hawarde nowe lately did
  recite,
I haue a ditie which Cornix did indite :
His death complayning, but it is lamentable
To heare a Captayne so good and honorable,   *800*
So soone withdrawen by deathes crueltie,
Before his vertue was at moste hye degree.
If death for a season had· shewed him
  fauour,
To all his nation he should haue bene
  honour,
Alas, bolde heartes be nerest death in
  warre,   *805*
When out of daunger cowardes stande
  a farre.

Codrus

All if that ditie be neuer so lamentable,
Refrayne my teares I shall as I am able.
Begin Minalcas, tell of the bolde hawarde,
If fortune fauour hope after some re-
  warde.   *810*

Minalcas

I pray thee Codrus (my whey is weake
  and thin)
Lende me thy bottell to drinke or I begin.

Codrus

If ought be tasted, the remnant shall pall,
I may not aforde nowe for to spende out
  all.
We sit in shadowe, the sunne is not fer-
  uent,   *815*
Call for it after, then shall I be content.

Minalcas

Still thou desirest the pleasure of my art,
But of thy bottell nought wilt thou yet
  depart,
Though thou be nigard, and nought wilt
  geue of thine,
Yet this one time thou shalt haue part of
  mine.   *820*
Nowe harken Codrus, I tell mine elegy,
But small is the pleasure of dolefull
  armony.

*The description of the Towre of vertue
and honour, into the which the noble
Hawarde contended to enter by
worthy actes of Chiualry.*

Minalcas speaketh

High on a mountayne of highnes maruelous,
With pendant cliffes of stones harde as
  flent,
Is made a castell or toure moste curious,
Dreadfull vnto sight, but inwarde excellent.
Such as would enter finde paynes and
  torment,
So harde is the way vnto the same mountayne,
Streyght, hye and thorny, turning and
  different,
That many labour for to ascende in
  vayne.   *830*

Who doth perseuer, and to this toure
  attayne
Shall haue great pleasure to see the build-
  ing olde,
Joyned and graued, surmounting mans
  brayne,
And all the walles within of fynest golde,
With olde historyes, and pictures many-
  folde,
Glistering as bright as Phebus orient,

With marble pillers the building to vpholde,
About be turrets of shape most excellent.

This towre is gotten by labour diligent,
In it remayne such as haue won honoure
By holy liuing, by strength or tourna-
  ment,   *841*
And moste by wisedome attayne vnto this
  towre:
Briefely, all people of godly behauour,
By rightwise battayle, Justice and equitie,
Or that in mercy hath had a chiefe plea-
  sour:
In it haue rowmes eche after his degree.

This goodly Castell (thus shining in
  beautie)
Is named Castell of vertue and honour,
In it eyght Henry is in his maiestie
Moste hye enhaunsed as ought a con-
  querour: *850*
In it remayneth the worthy gouernour,
A stocke and fountayne of noble pro-
  geny,
Moste noble Hawarde the duke and pro-
  tectour,
Named of Northfolke the floure of chiu-
  alry.

Here is the Talbot manfull and hardy,
With other princes and men of dignitie,
Which to win honour do all their might
  apply,
Supporting Justice, concorde and equitie:
The manly Corson within this towre I
  see,
These haue we seene eche one in his
  estate,   *860*
With many other of hye and meane de-
  gree,
For marciall actes with crownes laureate.

Of this stronge castell is porter at the
  gate
Strong sturdy labour, much like a cham-
  pion,
But goodly vertue a lady moste ornate
Within gouerneth with great prouision:
But of this castell in the moste hyest
  trone
Is honour shining in rowme imperiall,
Which vnrewarded of them leaueth not
  one
That come by labour and vertue princi-
  pall.   *870*

Fearefull is labour without fauour at all,
Dreadfull of visage, a monster intreat-
    able,
Like Cerberus lying at gates infernall,
To some men his looke is halfe intoller-
    able,
His shoulders large, for burthen strong
    and able,
His body bristled, his necke mightie and
    stiffe,
By sturdy senewes his ioyntes stronge
    and stable,
Like marble stones his handes be as stiffe.

Here must man vanquishe the dragon of
    Cadmus,
Against the Chimer here stoutly must he
    fight,   880
Here must he vanquish the fearefull Peg-
    asus,
For the golden flece here must he shewe
    his might:
If labour gaynsay, he can nothing be
    right,
This monster labour oft chaungeth his
    figure,
Some time an oxe, a bore, or lion wight,
Playnely he seemeth, thus chaungeth his
    nature.

Like as Protheus oft chaunged his stat-
    ure,
Mutable of figure oft times in one houre,
When Aristeus in bondes had him sure:
To diuers figures likewise chaungeth
    labour,   890
Under his browes he dreadfully doth
    loure,
With glistering eyen, and side depend-
    aunt beard,
For thirst and hunger alway his chere is
    soure,
His horned forehead doth make faynt
    heartes feard.

Alway he drinketh, and yet alway is
    drye,   895
The sweat distilling with droppes aboun-
    daunt,
His breast and forehead doth humours
    multiply
By sweating showres, yet is this payne
    pleasaunt:
Of day and night his resting time is
    scant,
No day ouerpasseth exempt of busynes,

His sight infourmeth the rude and ignor-
    ant,
Who dare perseuer, he geueth them
    riches.

None he auaunceth but after stedfastnes,
Of litle burthen his bely is, and small,
His mighty thyes his vigour doth ex-
    pres,   905
His shankes sturdy, and large feete with-
    all:
By wrath he rageth, and still doth chide
    and brall,
Such as would enter repelling with his
    crye,
As well estates as homely men rurall
At the first entry he threatneth yrefully.

I trowe olde fathers (whom men nowe
    magnify)
Called this monster Minerua stoute and
    soure,
For strength and senewes of man moste
    commonly   913
Are tame and febled by cures and laboure.
Great Hercules the mighty conquerour
Was by this monster ouerccome and
    superate,
All if he before vnto his great honour
The sonne of Uenus had strongly subiu-
    gate.

Who would with honour be purely laure-
    ate,
Must with this monster longe time before
    contende,   920
But lightly is man ouercome and fati-
    gate,
To lady vertue if he not well intende:
When strength is febled she helpeth at
    the ende,
Opening the gates and passage to honour,
By whose assistaunce soone may a man
    ascende   925
The hye degrees of the triumphant Tour.

Mankinde inflamed by goodly behauour
Of lady vertue come to this towre with
    payne,
But for the entree pretendeth them rigour
Many one abasheth, rebuking backe
    agayne: 930
To purchase honour they would be glad
    and fayne,
But fearefull labour, the porter is so fell,
To them proclaming, their enterprise is
    vayne,

Except they before with him contende
and mell.

Here moste of all muste mans might ex-
cell   *935*
With stedfast courage and sure per-
seueraunce,
Els shall this monster him backe agayne
repell,
But man preuayleth by long continuaunce.
No costly treasour nor Jewell of pleas-
aunce
Without price or payne can man in earth
come by: *940*
So without labour doth vertue none
aduaunce
To parfite honour and noble seignory.

Faynt cowarde mindes soone at the first
escry
Of sturdie labour, fall to the grounde as
lame,
Els runne they back warde fast fleing
cowardly,   *945*
As hartles wretches caring nothing for
shame:
But noble heartes to win immortall name,
Fight at these gates till they ouercome
labour,
Then lady vertue with good report and
fame
Suche knightes gideth to laude and hye
honour.   *950*

But cruell fortune to some is harde and
soure,
That after trauell and many deadly
wounde,
When lady vertue should graunt to them
this toure
Then frowarde fortune them beateth to
the ground: *954*
Of this examples ouer many do abounde,
But chiefly this one, the noble lorde
Hawarde,
When he chiefe honour was worthy to
haue founde,
False death and fortune bereft him his
rewarde.

Longe he contended in battayle strong
and harde,
With payne and labour, with might repelling wrong,   *960*
No backe he turned as doth some faint
cowarde,

But with this monster boldly contended
long,
When he had broken the locke and doores
stronge,
Ouercome the porter, and should ascende
the toure,
To liue in honour hye conquerours
amonge,   *965*
Then cruell fortune and death did him
deuoure.

Though he were borne to glory and
honour,
Of auncient stocke and noble progenie,
Yet thought his courage to be of more
valour,
By his owne actes and noble chiualry.
Like as becommeth a knight to fortifye
His princes quarell with right and equitie,
So did this hawarde with courage val-
iauntly,   *973*
Till death abated his bolde audacitie.

O happy Samson more fortunate then he
Onely in strength, but not in hye courage,
O cruell fortune why durst thy crueltie
This floure of knighthood to slea in lusty
age,
Thou hast debated the floure of his lin-
age,
If thou had mercy bewayle his death thou
might,   *980*
For cruell lions and mo beastes sauage
Long time not ceased for to bewayle this
knight.

O death thou haste done agaynst both
lawe and right,
To spare a cowarde without daunger or
wounde,
And thus soone to quench of chiualry the
light,   *985*
O death enuious moste enemie to our
grounde,
What moste auayleth thou soonest doest
confounde:
Why did not vertue assist hir champion?
Thou might haue ayded, for soothly thou
was bounde,
For during his life he loued thee
alone,   *990*

O God almightie in thy eternall trone,
To whom all vertue is deare and accept-
able,
If reason suffred to thee our crye and
mone,

This dede might impute and fortune la-
    mentable,
Thou might haue left vs this knight moste
    honorable,   995
Our wealth and honour to haue kept in
    degree:
Alas why hath death so false and dis-
    ceyuable,
Mankinde to torment this will and liber-
    tie?

It quencheth vertue, sparing iniquitie,
The best it striketh, of bad hauing dis-
    dayne,   1000
No helpe nor comfort hath our aduersi-
    tie,
Death dayly striketh though dayly we
    complayne:
To treate a tiran it is but thing in vayne,
Mekenes prouoketh his wrath and tiran-
    ny,
So at our prayer death hath the more
    disdayne,   1005
We do by mekenes his furour multiply.

If some fell tiran replete with villany
Should thus haue ending the dede were
    commendable,
But a stoute captayne disposed to mercy
So soone thus faded, the case is lament-
    able,   1010
Was he not humble, iocunde and compan-
    able,
No man despising, and first in all labour,
Right wise with mercy debonair and tret-
    able,
Mate and companion with euery souldier.

Uice he subdued by goodly behauour, 1015
Like as a rider doth a wilde stede subdue,
His body subiect, his soule was gouern-
    our,
From vice withdrawen to goodnes and
    vertue,
When pride rebelled mekenes did it es-
    chue,
Free minde and almes subdued auarice:
Alway he noted this saying iuste and
    true,   1021
That noble mindes despised couetise.

His death declareth that slouth he did
    despise,
By hardie courage as fyrst in ieopardie,
Alway he vsed some noble exercise, 1025
Suche as belongeth to worthy chiualrie,

In him was there founde no sparkle of
    enuy,
Alway he lauded and praysed worthynes,
Suche as were doughtie rewarding large-
    ly,
Wrath saue in season he wisely coulde
    repres.   1030

Of wine or Bacchus despised he excesse,
For mindes kindled to actes marciall,
Seking for honour and name of doughti-
    nesse,
Despiseth surfet and liuing bestiall,
In him no power had luste venereall, 1035
For busy labour and pleasaunt abstinence
All corporall lust soone causeth for to
    fall,
No lust subdueth where reigneth dili-
    gence.

He was a piller of sober countenaunce,
His onely treasour and iewell was good
    name,   1040
But O cursed death thy wrathfull vio-
    lence,
By stroke vnwarned halfe blinded of his
    fame,
Whom may I accuse, whom may I put in
    blame,
God for death, or fortune, or impotent
    nature,
God doth his pleasour, and death will
    haue the same   1045
Nature was mightie longe able to endure,

In fortune is the fault nowe am I sure,
I would if I durst his tiranny accuse:
O cursed fortune if thou be creature,
Who gaue thee power thus people to
    abuse,   1050
Thy mutable might me causeth oft to
    muse,
When man is plunged in dolour and dis-
    tresse,
Thy face thou chaungest, which did earst
    refuse,
By sodayne chaunces him lifting to rich-
    esse.

And suche as longe time haue liued in
    noblenes   1055
Anone suche plungest in payne and pouer-
    tie,
Wealth, honour, strength, right, iustice
    and goodnes,
Misery, dolour, lowe rowme, iniquitie,

These thou rewardest like as it pleaseth
thee,
To mans merite without respect at all,
One this day being in great aucthori-
tie,   *1061*
Agayne to morowe thou causest for to
fall.

When man is worthy a rowme imperiall,
On him thou glowmest with frowarde
countenaunce,
Weake is thy promis reuoluing as a
ball,   *1065*
Thou hast no fauour to godly gouern-
aunce,
No man by merite thou vsest to aduaunce,
O blinded fortune ofte time infortunate,
When man thee trusteth then falleth some
mischaunce,
Unwarely chaunging his fortune and es-
tate.   *1070*

Tell me frayle fortune, why did thou
breuiate
The liuing season of suche a captayne,
That when his actes ought to be laureate
Thy fauour turned him suffring to be
slayne
I blame thee fortune, and thee excuse
agayne,   *1075*
For though thy fauour to him was rigor-
ous,
Suche is thy custome for to be vncer-
tayne,
And namely when man is hye and glori-
ous.

But moste worthy duke hye and victori-
ous,
Respire to comfort, see the vncertentie
Of other princes, whose fortune pros-
perous   *1081*
Oftetime haue ended in harde aduersitie:
Read of Pompeius whose pereles dignitie
Agaynst great Cesar did wealth of Rome
defende,
Whom after fortune brought in captiui-
tie,   *1085*
And he in Egipt was headed at the ende.

In likewise Cesar which did with him
contende,
When all the worlde to him was subiu-
gate,
From his hye honour did sodenly descende,

Murdred in Rome by chaunce infortu-
nate.   *1090*
Cato and Seneke, with Tully laureate,
These and mo like for all their sapience
Hath proued fortune, sore blinding their
estate,
By wrongfull slaunders and deadly vio-
lence.

To poore and riche it hath no difference,
Olde Policrates supposing perill past, *1096*
With death dishonest ended his excel-
lence,
Great Alexander by fortune was downe
cast,
One draught of poyson him filled at the
last,
Whom all the worlde earst could not
saciate: *1100*
What is all honour and power but a
blast,
When fortune threatneth the life to
breuiate.

Beholde on Pirrus the king infortunate
With a small stone dead prostrate vpon
the grounde,
See Ualerian brought downe from his es-
tate,   *1105*
From his empire in Percy thrall and
bounde.
Of olde Priamus it is in writing founde,
Howe he by Pyrrus was in his palace
slayne,
Paris and Hector receyued mortall
wounde,
To trust in fortune it is a thing in
vayne,   *1110*

The mightie Cyrus a king of Realmes
twayne
Was slayne and his hoste of Thomiris
the quene.
Thus is no matter of fortune to complayne,
All that nowe falleth of olde time hath
bene sene,
This shall be, this is, and this hath euer
bene,   *1115*
That boldest heartes be nearest ieopardie,
To dye in battayle is honour as men
wene
To suche as haue ioy in haunting chiualry.

Suche famous ending the name doth
magnifie,

Note worthy duke, no cause is to com-
    playne,   *1120*
His life not ended foule nor dishonestly,
In bed nor tauerne his lustes to mayn-
    teyne,
But like as besemed a noble captayne,
In sturdie harnes he died for the right,
From deathes daunger no man may flee
    certayne,   *1125*
But suche death is metest vnto so noble a
    knight.

But death it to call me thinke it vnright,
Sith his worthy name shall laste per-
    petuall,
To all his nation example and clere light,
But to his progeny moste specially of
    all,   *1130*
His soule is in pleasour of glory eternall,
So duke most doughty ioy may that noble
    tree,
Whose braunches honour shall neuer fade
    ne fall,
While beast is on earth or fishes in the
    sea.

Lo Codrus I here haue tolde thee by and
    by   *1135*
Of shepheard Cornix the wofull elegy,
Wherin he mourned the greeuous payne
    and harde,
And laste departing of the noble lord
    Hawarde,
More he indited of this good Admirall,
But truely Codrus I can not tell thee
    all.   *1140*

Codrus

Minalcas I sweare by holy Peters cope,
If all thing fortune as I haue trust and
    hope,
If happy winde blowe I shall or it be
    longe
Comfort thy sorowe and well rewarde thy
    songe,
What tary man a while till better fortune
    come,   *1145*
If my part be any then shall thy part
    be some.

Minalcas

If thou in purpose so to rewarde my hire,
God graunt thee Codrus thy wishing and
    desire.

Codrus

Forsooth Minalcas I wishe thee so in
    dede,
And that shalt thou knowe if fortune
    with me spede,   *1150*
Farewell Minalcas, for this time, dieu te
    garde,
Neare is winter the worlde is to harde.

Minalcas

Go wretched nigarde, God sende thee
    care and payne,
Our Lorde let thee neuer come hither
    more agayne,
And as Midas, God turne it all to golde
That euer thou touchest or shalt in
    handes holde,   *1156*
For so muche on golde is fixed thy liking,
That thou despiseth both vertue and cun-
    ninge.

Thus endeth the fourth Egloge.

JOHN SKELTON

Our conclusions as to Skelton's work are based on scarcely a fourth of what he wrote, if we take his own list in the Garland of Laurell as trustworthy. We have but one of his three or more dramatic pieces, no one of his larger didactic compositions, doubtful bits of his religious verse, none of his translations except an incomplete copy of the Diodorus Siculus. Much of the lighter verse which he describes with such gusto is unknown to us, and time has preserved only his "satire" in any amount.

Nevertheless, we are on fairly safe ground in making our generalizations. The way in which Skelton distributes his emphasis in cataloguing his works shows us that he took satisfaction in his smartly colloquial and ribald writing; and of that type of his production we have numerous specimens. His lighter lyric, inserted into the Garland of Laurell, he can hardly have bettered under any of the titles he there mentions; and his success in addressing a superior to whom he wishes to show respect, in that poem, causes us no regret at the loss of his verse written for royalty. We may, with Dyce, deplore the loss of the Ballad of the Mustard Tart and of the Mourning of the Mapely Root; but we can afford to lose the didactic, the monitory, the pompous Skelton, and we have material to recognize the roistering, abusive, voluble Skelton as clearly as if we possessed another volume filled with his How to Die, his advice to the Prince of Wales, and his attacks on Mistress Anne.

John Skelton, born about 1460, was a Cambridge graduate, and early made a reputation for classical learning. In 1490 Caxton, writing a preface to his translation of the Aeneid, begs Skelton's criticism, praising his scholarship and mentioning versions of Diodorus Siculus and of Cicero's letters Ad Familiares as by him. Caxton also says that Skelton had lately been created poet laureate at Oxford; in 1493 Skelton received the same honor at Cambridge, and Robert Whitinton, maker of various grammars printed by de Worde, calls Skelton "Louaniensis" in a Latin eulogy printed by Dyce, i:xvi-xix. As the Cambridge record terms Skelton "poeta in partibus transmarinis atque Oxon. laurea ornatus", we are tempted to believe that Skelton had indeed received the crown at Louvain; but the records of that University do not—or did not—chronicle the award. The laureate-rank, it may be observed, was much the same as our Litt. D. or LL. D.; it was held by other men of literary activity in Skelton's time, e.g., by Whitinton and by Bernard André, the blind historiographer of Henry the Seventh.

In 1498 Skelton took holy orders, passing rapidly through the three degrees in about as many months; this may have been that he might qualify for his duties as tutor to the young prince Henry. He was holding that post when Erasmus, in his ode De Laudibus Britanniae, of 1500, praised Skelton's scholarship; and he had written, or soon wrote, various works for his royal patrons, which are not now known. He celebrated Prince Arthur's creation as the Prince of Wales and Prince Henry's elevation to the dukedom of York; he composed a Speculum Principis for his pupil (see the Garland, line 1202); and the translation mentioned in line 1194 of that poem was perhaps done for the mother of Henry the Seventh.

Skelton's tutorial duties seem to have been over by 1503, when we find him holding the rectory of Diss, in Norfolk, a post doubtless conferred on him as reward for his services at Court. This change of locale marks a definite change in his utterance. He had been academic, didactic, conventional; he had lamented the death of Northumberland, he had paid homage to royalty, he had translated the classics, using the accepted literary vocabulary and moulds. But there now appears a difference in his thought and expression. Whether he resided for long periods at his new position or not, his withdrawal from Court seems to coincide with the appearance of the characteristic "Skeltonicall" metre and with the dominance of censure or satire in his verse.

Between his earlier conventional work and the rapid, short-breathed verse into which Skelton now breaks, rimed in groups of three to six lines of usually three beats and carrying voluble, often coarse, description and abuse, there intervenes a poem still in the orthodox seven-line stanza, but free in spirit,—the Bowge of Court. This poem should be compared with the Ship of Fools; it is the outcome of a general impulse of the time, an expression of that newly powerful bourgeois spirit which found its voice most easily in attack. The contrast between the adolescent awkwardness of method in the poem and the mature inherited form is more striking than that between the intent of Hawes or Barclay and their expression. Barclay's stiffness and Hawes' senility sink below the level of the stanza and are unable to fill it; Skelton seems to twist and struggle in the form, like a powerful unmannerly dog in harness. But with Philip Sparrow, written early in his tenure of Diss, and in the free couplet, Skelton passes over into his own province.

He never again appears to such advantage, for more than a few lines, as in this light occasional poem, written to please a young girl, and lamenting for her, now in earnest, now with banter, now with teasing magniloquence, the death of her pet sparrow under the claws of the family cat. His later coarseness and virulence are not here; his classical knowledge is lightly handled; and his extravagance of vocabulary, his fondness for jargon and word-puzzles, for heaped alliteration, for a medley of pothouse vulgarisms, proverbs, and Latinisms, has not yet obsessed him. We can see the indications of these traits; but they are under control.

So far as we can judge from his extant work, Skelton must have settled conclusively into the smartly-crackling, quick-fire verse-movement used in Philip Sparrow. He took pride in it, notwithstanding the objections of formal versifiers like Barclay; he says, speaking as Colin Clout, that "though my ryme be ragged, tattered and jagged,—If ye take well therwith, It hath in it some pyth." Certainly this loosely metred, indeterminate line-sequence gave Skelton greater freedom of movement than rime royal. But it also removed all bonds from a spirit reckless and restless; it permitted the noisy vehemence of Ware the Hauke, the Replycacion, the poem against the Scots; it permitted the wallowing coarseness of Elynour Rummyng; it permitted the snarling of the Wolsey-poems. When objurgation was made so easy, the impulse was speedily gratified.

The verse-form found its imitators later; but Elizabethan and Stuart critics regarded it with disfavor. Puttenham called Skelton "a rude ragling rimer"; Browne and Wither said his reed jarred; Drayton censured him. A period in which drama and criticism were considering form would not, indeed, value a man for whom the word was of so much more moment than was structure, for whom recurrence meant more than pattern.

What the course of life was which threw off these poems, we do not know with certainty. Tradition says that Skelton as a rector "was more fit for the stage than for the pulpit"; anecdotes were long current of the irregularity of his life,

and vulgar jests were readily attributed to him. Some connection he had for a
time with Wolsey, and this connection turned into enmity, which forced Skelton
to take sanctuary at Westminster, where he died in 1529. How long he was there
we do not know. He made visits in other counties than that of his benefice, as we
learn from his own words; he was more than once the guest of the College of
Bonshommes at Ashridge, Buckinghamshire, and he was entertained by the Countess of Surrey at Sheriff Hutton Castle in Norfolk, writing there his Garland of
Laurell.

This poem, which of course postdates all the long list of Skelton's writings
enumerated in it, was printed in 1523, and is conjecturally assigned to 1520, when
Skelton was about sixty years old. It is a composite in tone and in form, and is
in some ways the most interesting of Skelton's surviving works. Speaking in his
own person, the poet narrates a dispute between Fame and Pallas, in the grand
council of poets, as to Skelton's right to the laurel; he describes the making of a
garland for him by the Countess of Surrey and her ladies, and the joy of the
assembled poets on beholding his coronal. Skelton obviously endeavored to express himself here with a dignity and sobriety befitting the occasion; and he therefore resorted to the seven-line stanza for most of his poem. But he breaks into
lyric as he turns from the Countess to her waiting-women, and at the mention of
Philip Sparrow, in his catalogue of his own work, he whirls off again into the
rattling short line. More than once, in the course of the poem, he is tempted down
a bypath of personal rancor or of vulgar jocularity; he drags himself back each
time with an effort, but the difficulty with which he avoids the indecorous, the
voluble, and the violent is quite plain. It is also plain how much more clearly
he sees himself than he does his hostess; he lauds her in careful stanzas, but the
full paean of praise he reserves for himself. As Dyce remarks, there is no second
example in literature of a poet's deliberately writing sixteen hundred lines in his
own honor.

Commenting on the Garland in this same passage (i:xlix), Dyce opines that
the poem cannot be reckoned among Skelton's best; but, he adds, "it contains several
passages of no mean beauty, which show that [Skelton] possessed powers for the
higher kind of poetry, if he had chosen to exercise them; and [it] is interspersed
with some lyrical addresses to the ladies who weave his chaplet, which are very
happily versified." Our emphasis would fall somewhat differently. These inserted
lyrics appeal to us more than they did to Dyce; we hear in them a slender but true
prelude to the full orchestration of the Elizabethan lyric, and we may feel all the
more interest because of the machine-made setting in which they appear. "Prior
himself," says Saintsbury, "has nothing more graceful and delicate."

We do not however feel justified, because of these few notes of lyric, in regarding Skelton as a metrical genius. The racing short line which is most characteristic of him is not a thing of beauty. Its source is uncertain. Schipper considered that it arose from the dissolution of the Early English alliterative line, and
Saintsbury seems to suggest that the frequent internal rime of long-line poems led
to the use of short lines. Brie, in Englische Studien 37:80, takes the view that
Low Latin hymns, independently imitated in secular verse by French and by English writers, popularized short lines such as those of Skelton; and the development
of complex stanza and of lyrical line in West Europe strongly favors this suggestion. Such a hymn as that printed by Koenigsfeld, Lateinische Hymnen aus dem
Mittelalter, 1847, pp. 238 ff., is illuminating :—

Tandem audite me,
Sionis filiae!
Aegram respicite
Dilecto dicite .   .   .

Lines like these appear in the modern languages as well as in Latin. Lee, in his French Renaissance, pp. 194-5, cites from Skelton's contemporary, Martial d'Auvergne; and they had been employed by Trevisa, following Higden's Latin as in the Polycronicon, i:394-7 of the Rolls Series edition. They can be found also in the Italian, e.g., of Guittone d'Arezzo. But in all these cases it is more a matter of line than of line-grouping in which the resemblance to Skelton consists. Rarely do the Latin, the French, the Italian, the earlier English, run other than in pairs; only in Martial d'Auvergne do we find the variation from two to four rimes in a sequence, or from two to three as in a hymn to St. Remigius printed by Mone in his Hymni Latini, iii:490-91. Skelton not only chooses the short line, he abandons the structural balance of lines. Whether he misunderstood the grouping of Latin lines or not is immaterial here; the point is that even if we discover an example of such irregular line-grouping of earlier date, we shall expect to discover behind it a man of the same rebellious temperament as Skelton. For such a movement fits exactly what Skelton wished to say, and fits the style in which he said it. He was a man of coarse, vigorous, and restless fibre, of huge vanity, bad temper, and no self-control. With more command of himself, more learning, and a critical theory, he might have done work resembling that of Ben Jonson; as it was, he swung from enforced conventionality and pedantry to a series of outbursts personal and local. He has no outlook on life or on letters in the true sense.

His style shows in the same way the lack of balance in his nature. He resorts to mystifications and to jargon as did the decadent grammarians of late Roman time, or as did a Gallic spirit restless as his, but finer than his,—François Villon. He pours out lists longer than those of Lydgate, whole catalogues of Greek myths and Latin authors; and these he intermingles with homely proverbs and with colloquialisms. Everything is in excess; he cannot call Wolsey or Garnesche names without emptying the dictionary of thieves' lingo; and he hurls opprobrious epithets without pause or choice of weapon. Never is there in his work what Elton terms the "precision of insult" attained by the Roman or by the eighteenth-century English satirist. Skelton aims not at clarity but at speed, not at form but at fluency; and the race of his metre, the rattle of his epithets and allusions, suit the narrowly personal and occasional character of his work. But that a temperament has run away with an intellect we may judge from his University honors, from the praise of Caxton and of Erasmus, and from a very few words of his own. It was no incompetent literary critic who said of Chaucer that "no word he wrote in vain", and of Lydgate that "it is diffuse to find The sentence of his mind".

Like most occasional literature, Skelton's production has been classed as satire. If satire be a criticism of life, an observer's comment on the mistakes and the follies of mankind, it is obvious that the mood and the method of such comment will vary widely. Should the observing spirit be tolerant and even amused, cognizant always of its own kinship with humanity, we have the "satire" of Horace, of Chaucer, of Jane Austen. But if that spirit denounce, if by its angry derision it assert its superiority to humanity, the result is also called "satire", but we have Juvenal or Skelton. Moreover, beside this difference in mood, which our terminology does not recognize, there may be divergence of method. Indirect satire uses the minimum of comment, and often appears best in narrative; while 'direct satire prefers that comment which passes so easily into the didactic or the vituperative. If direct didactic satire be written in a society which, like the medieval, is strictly grouped, criticism will be of types rather than of persons, and will pass easily into general invective, as in the Ship of Fools. If by force of personal circumstances direct "satire" be aimed at an individual instead of a class, the result may become mere snarling, as in Skelton. Few are the men who can, like Chaucer, invest a class with individuality, and then hold the balance steady between censure and tolerance. Skelton was no such man, nor was Barclay.

It was Skelton's vain and violent temperament which led him to the intense personality of his criticisms. No happy man speaks with this voice, but a man dissatisfied with life's verdict on him, turbulent under restraining circumstances, looking with unfriendly eye at his fellow-creatures. Twice, in all his existing work, does he depart from that tone,—when addressing a young girl in Philip Sparrow, and when paying his devoirs, a soothed and flattered guest, to a group of noble ladies. He is not there the Skelton of literary history, the author of the raucous violence of the Wolsey poems and of the deliberate squalor of Elynour Rummyng; but he is a Skelton whom the after-world values more.

BIBLIOGRAPHY AND SELECT REFERENCE LIST XVI

Existing MS-copies of Skelton's work are:—

Against Garnesche. Brit. Mus. Harley 367.

Colin Clout, and Speke, Parrot. Brit. Mus. Harley 2252. A fragm. of Colin is in Brit. Mus. Lansdowne 762.

The Garland of Laurell. Brit.Mus.Cotton Vitellius E x (imperfect).

The Lament for the Earl of Northumberland. Brit.Mus.Royal 18 D ii, a Percy MS.

Manerly Margery. Brit.Mus.Adds. 5465, the "Fairfax MS".

To Mistress Anne. On the guard-leaf of Trin.Coll.Cambr. R. 3,17 (says Brie).

Recule against Gaguyn. A few lines are perhaps preserved in Trin.Coll.Cambr. 2,53. See Brie, EnglStud 37:31-2.

Rose both White and Rede. Exchequer Rolls B 2,8. Printed by Dyce as below, i after Preface. Printed by C. C. Stopes, Athenaeum 1914 i:625 as previously unpublished. Identified by Brie, EnglStud 37:49-50, with the "Boke of the Rosiar" in Skelton's list; already queried by Dyce.

The short poem entitled I, liber, et propera, see Corpus Christi Coll. Cambr. 432.

The Latin hymn Salve plus decies; see Brit.Mus.Adds. 4787.

Why Come Ye Nat to Court? frag. in Bodl. Rawlinson C 813; see Archiv 85:429-36.

Wofully Araid. Brit.Mus.Adds. 5465, and on the flyleaf of a 1496 print of Boethius; see Dyce i, page ci. In the Athenaeum 1873 ii:697 is publ. a text differing from Dyce's. See Brie, loc.cit.

The prose transl. of Diodorus Siculus, incomplete, is in Corpus Christi Coll. Cambr. 357. It is to appear EETS.

The Lament for Edward IV is in Brit. Mus. Harley 4011 and in Stow's MS Brit. Mus. Adds. 29729. Authenticity questioned.

Printed Editions.

The first collected edition of Skelton's works was issued by Thomas Marshe in 1568. Previously there had been printed:—

Ballad of the Scottish King. Faukes, 1513. Discovered 1878, facsimile ed. by Ashton, London, 1882.

The Bowge of Court. de Worde, no date, twice.
Colin Clout. By Kele, Wyght, Kitson, Veale, ?Godfray, no dates.
Comely Coystroun. ?Pynson, no date.
Garland of Laurell. Faukes, 1523. (Brit.Mus.)
Magnifycence. ?Rastell, no date. (Univ.Libr.Cambr. Impf. in Brit. Mus.)
   Reprinted by the Roxburghe Club, 1821; a facsimile issued in Tudor Fac-
   similes, 1910. Ed. by Ramsay, diss., 1905, for EETS 1908.
Philip Sparrow. By Kele, Toye, Wight, Kitson, Veale, Waley, no dates.
Replycacyon. By Pynson, no date.
Why Come Ye Nat to Court? By Kele, Wyght, Kitson, Veale, no dates.
Pynson printed, no date, a four-leaf pamphlet of "ballads and ditties solacious";
   a larger collection was pubd. by Kynge and Marshe, no date, and reprinted
   by Day, by Lant. See Dyce.
Later separate prints were:—

Tunnyng of Elynour Rummyng. 1624. (Bodleian, Huth) Repr. Harleian Miscellany, vol. i.
Thomas Marshe's Pithy Pleasaunt and Profitable Workes of Maister Skelton, London, 1568, was reprinted London, 1736.
Skelton's Works were printed in vol. ii of Chalmers' British Poets; they were edited by
   the Rev. Alexander Dyce, London, 1843, 2 vols., still the standard edition. Dyce's
   text and his introd. and notes, whole or part, were reprinted Cambridge, 1855,
   Boston, 1856, 1866, 1887. The fairly comprehensive selection ed. by Richard
   Hughes, London, 1924, uses Dyce's text, but has no notes other than glosses to
   text.
Selections, with a life by Sanford, Phila., 1819-23.
In Southey's Select Works of the British Poets, 1831, are Colin Clout, Philip Sparrow.
In Skeat's Specimens, vol. iii, Oxford, 1871 ff., are passages from Why Come Ye,
   Philip Sparrow.
In Flügel's Neuengl. Lesebuch, Halle, 1895, are the Garland, lines 323 ff., Ware the
   Hauke, Why Come Ye, Philip Sparrow, etc.
In Manly's English Poetry 1170-1892 are bits of Philip Sparrow, Why Come Ye,
   Colin Clout.
In Headlam's Selections from British Satirists, London, 1897, are extracts from the
   Bowge of Court, Colin Clout, Speke Parrot.
Selections from Skelton were ed. W. H. Williams, London, 1902. i.e. The Bowge of
   Court, Philip Sparrow, Why Come Ye, Colin Clout. Notes and glossary.
Neilson and Webster, Chief British Poets, 1916, contains Philip Sparrow, Elynour
   Rummyng, Colin Clout, Garland of Laurel, Lullaby. (Spelling modernized.)

   On Skelton see:—
Schöneberg, Die Sprache John Skeltons in seinen kleineren Werken. Marburg diss.,
   1888, pp. 62.
Rey, Skelton's Satirical Poems in Relation to Lydgate's Order of Fools, Cocke
   Lorell's Bote, and Barclay's Ship of Fools, Berne, 1899.
Koelbing, Zur Charakteristik John Skelton's, Stuttgart, 1904.
Thümmel, Studien über John Skelton, Leipzig, 1905.
Brie, Skelton-Studien, in Englische Studien 37:1-81 (1906).
——Zwei verlorene Dichtungen von John Skelton, in Archiv 138:226-8 (1919).
Bischoffsberger, Einfluss John Skelton's auf die englische Literatur, Freiburg diss.,
   1914, pp. 80.
A. S. Cook, Skelton's Garland of Laurel and Chaucer's Hous of Fame, in MLReview
   11:9 (1916).

R. L. Dunbabin, Notes on Skelton, in MLReview 12:129 and 257 (1917).
Berdan, The Poetry of Skelton, in Romanic Review 6:364.
——On the Dating of Skelton's Satires, PMLA 29:499-516.
——"Speke Parrot." An interpretation, in MLNotes 30:140-44.
Se Boyar, Skelton's Replycacion, in PMLA 28:244-45.
Warton, History of English Poetry, ed. Hazlitt, 1871, iii:268-90.
Berdan, Early Tudor Poetry, N. Y., 1920.
Koelbing, in Cambr. History of English Literature, iii chap. 4.
Herford, Literary Relations of England and Germany in the Sixteenth Century,
       Cambridge, 1886.
Saintsbury, English Prosody, i:235,240-45.
Tucker, Verse Satire in England before the Renaissance, N. Y., 1908.
On the play of Magnificence see The Library, series 3, vol. 4:393-408.

[MS Brit. Mus. Cotton Vitellius E x]

Arrectynge my Syght toward the Zodiak
The signnys twelue for to beholde afar
When Mars Retrogradant reuersid his
    bak
Lorde of the yere in his Orbicular
Put vp his sworde for he kowde make
    no war: 5
And when Lucyna plenarly did shyne
Scorpioune ascenddinge degrees twiys
    nyne

2

In place alone then musinge in my
    thowght
How all thynge passithe as dothe the
    sommer floure
On euery half my resons forthe I
    sowght   10
How ofte fortune variythe in an howre
Now clere wedder forthwithe a stormmy
    showre
Al thynge compassid no perpetuyte
Bot now in welthe now in aduersite

3

So depely drownnyd I was in this dumpe
Encrampisshed so sore was my conceyte
That me to rest I lent me to a stumpe 17
Of (an oke) that sumtyme grew ful
    streite
A myghty tre and of a nobille heyghte

Whos bewte blastid was withe the boys-
    ters wynde
His levis lost the sap was frome th
    rynde

4

Thus stode I in the fryththy forest (
    Galtres
Ensowkid with sylt of the myry moes
Where harttis belluynge embosid wt di
    tres
Ran on the raunge / so longe: that
    suppose
ffew men can telle now where the hync
    calf gose
ffaire fall that foster that so kan bate h
    hownde
Bot of my proces now turne we to th
    grownde:

5

While I stode musinge in this medita
    cioune
In slumbrynge I fille and halfe in
    slepe:
And wheither it were of Imagynacioun
Or of humors superfiu that often wil
    krepe
Into the brayne by drynkkynge ou(
    depe /
Or it procedid of fatall persuasioune
I kan not wele telle yow what was th
    occasioun

6

Bot sodenly at onys as I me auysid
As one in a traunce or in an extasy
I saw a pauylioune wonderly disgisyd
Garnnysshid freshe after my fantasy
Enhachid with perle and stonys preciou
    ly

The grounde engrosid and bet with burne
   gold
That passinge goodely it was to behold

7

Withe in it a prynces excellente of porte
Bot to recounte her riche habilymente
And what astatis to her did resorte   *45*
There to am I fulle insufficiente
A goddes Immortall she did represent
As I hard say Dame Pallas was her
   name
To whome suppleyd the roiall quene of
   ffame:

8

The quene of ffame to Dame Pallas
Prynces mooste pusaunt of higth pre-
   hemynence   *50*
Renowmmyd lady above the starry heven
All other transcendinge of verey congru-
   ence
Madame regent of the Scyence sevene
To whose astate all nobilnes most lene
My supplicacioune to yow I arrecte   *55*
Where of I beseke yow to tender the ef-
   fect

9

Not vnremembred it is vnto *your* grace
How ye yave me in roiall commaund-
   ment
That in my cowrte Skelton shuld have a
   place
By cause that his tyme he studiowsly
   hath spent   *60*
In *your* seruyce: And to the accomplish-
   ment
Of *your* request / regesterd is his name
Withe Laureate Tryumphe in the courte
   of ffame

10

Bot goode madame the acustome and vsage
Of auncyent Poetis ye wote ful wele
   hathe bene   *65*
Them self to enbissy withe all ther hole
   corage
So that ther workkis myght famowsly be
   sene
In figure where of they were the laurelle
   grene
Bot how it is Skelton is wonder slak
And as we dare we fynde in hym grete
   lak: *70*

11

ffor ne were only he hathe *your* promo-
   cioune
Owte of my bokis fulle sone I shulde hym
   race
Bot sithe he hathe tastid of thensugerd
   pocioune
Of Elyconys wel / reffreshid withe *your*
   grace
And wille not endeuoure hym self to pur-
   chace   *75*
The fauor of ladys wt wordis electe
It is fyttynge that ye most hym correcte:

12

Dame Pallas to the quene of ffame
The sum of *your* purpose as we ar auysid
Is for that *our* seruaunte is sumwhat to
   dulle:
Where in this aunswere for hym we have
   comprisid   *80*
How ryuers ryn not tille the sprynge be
   fulle
Better a dum mowthe than a braynles
   skulle
ffor if he gloriowsly pullishe his matter
Then men wille say how he dothe bot
   flatter

13

And if hym fortune to wright trew &
   playne   *85*
As sumtyme he mooste vicis remorde
Then sum wille say he hathe bot litille
   brayne
And how his worddis wt reson wille not
   corde
Beware for writynge remaynnythe of
   recorde
Displese not an hunderd for on mannys
   plesure   *90*
Who writithe wisely hathe a grete tresure

14

Also to furnnyshe better his excuse
Ouyde was bannysshid for soche a skille
And many mo whome I kowde enduse
Juvenall was tiret parde for to kylle *95*
ffor þt he enveiyd: yit wrate he none
   Ille
Savynge he rubbid sum on the gall
It was not for hym to byde the tryall

15

In generall wordis I say not gretely nay
A Poete sumtyme may for his plesure
   taunt   *100*

Spekynge in Parabols: how the fox the
gray
The gander the goose: and the huge
Oliphaunt
Went wt the pokok agayne the fesaunt
The lesarde kam lepynge and said that
he must
Withe helpe of the ram ley all in the
dust: *105*

16

Yit dyuerse that be Industriows of reson
Sumwhat wold gadder in ther coniecture
Of soche an enderkkid chapiter sum
seson
How be it it were hard to constru this
lecture
Sophisticatid craftily is many a confec-
ture   *110*
Another mannys mynde diffuse is to ex-
pound
Yit harde is to make bot sum fawte be
fownd

17

The Quene of ffame to Dame Pallas
Madame wt fauour of your benygne suf-
feraunce
Vnto your grace then make I this motyve
Whereto made ye me hym to avaunce *115*
Vnto the rowme of laureat promotyve
Or where to shuld he have that preroga-
tyve
Bot if he had made sum memoriall
Where by he myght have a name Im-
mortall

18

To passe the tyme in slawthfulle Idyl-
nes   *120*
Of youre roiall palace it is not the gise
Bot to do sumwhat eche man dothe hym
dres
ffor how shuld Cato els be callid wise
Bot that his bokis whiche he did devise
Recorde the same: or why is had in
mynde   *125*
Plato: bot for he laft wrytinge behynde

19

ffor men to loke on: Aristotille also
Of Philosophers callid the pryncipall
Olde Dyogenes wt other many mo
Dymostenes that Oratour roiall   *130*
Whiche yave Eschynes soche a cordiall
That bannysshid was he by his proposi-
cion
Ageyne whome he kowde make no con-
tradiccion

20

Dame Pallas to the quene of fame
Softe goode my sister and make there a
pause
And was Eschynes rebukyd as ye say *13.*
Remember yow wele: Poynte wele that
clause
Wherefore then rasid ye not away
His name: Or why is it I yow pray
That he to your courte is goynge and
commynge
Sithe he is sclaunderde for defaute of
konynge   *140*

21

The quene of ffame to Dame Pallas
Madame your opposelle is wele inferrid
And at your auauntage quykly it is
Towchid: And hard for to be debarrid
Yit shall I awnswere your grace as in
this
Withe youre reformacioun if I say amys
ffor bot if youre bownte did me assure
Myne argument els kowd not longe en-
dure   *147*

22

As towchinge that Eschynes is rememberd
That he so shuld be me semythe it is
syttynge
All be it grete parte he hathe surren-
dered   *150*
Of his honour: whos dissuasyve in writ-
ynge
To korage Demostenes was moche ex-
citynge
In settinge owght freshely his crafty
persuasioun
ffrome whiche Eschynes had noone Euasioun

23

The cause why Demostenes so famowsly
is brutyd   *155*
Only procedid for that he did owtray
Eschynes: whiche was not shamefully
confutid
Bot of that famows Orator I say
Whiche passid all other: wherfor I may
Amonge my recordis suffir hym namyd
Sithe thowthe he were venquisshid yit
was he not (shamyd)   *161*

24

As Jerome in his preambille ffrater Ambrosius

---

161. MS mutilated. Word supplied from 1523 ed.

ffrome that I have saide in no poynte
   dothe vary
Where he reporttithe of the coragiows
Wordis: that were moche consolatory *165*
By Eschynes rehersid. to the grete glory
Of Dymostenes that was his vtter fo
ffew shall ye fynde or noone þt wille do
   so

25

Dame Pallas to the quene of ffame
A thonke to have ye have wele deservyd
Your mynde that kan mayntene so ap-
   parently   *170*
Bot yit a grete parte ye have reservid
Of that most folow then consequently
Or els ye demene yow inordynatly
ffor if ye laude hym whome honour hathe
   opprest
Then he that dothe worst is as goode as
   the best   *175*

26

But whome that ye fauour I se wele
   hathe a name
Be he neuer so litille of substance
And whome ye love not ye wold put to
   shame
Ye counterway not euynly youre bal-
   aunce
As wele foly as wisdome ofte tyme ye
   auaunce   *180*
Reporte risithe many dyuerse waiys
Sum be moche spoken of for makinge of
   fraiys

27

Sum have a name for thefte and brybery
Sum be callid crafty that kan kit a purse
Sum men be made of for ther mokery *185*
Sum karefulle kokolddis sum have ther
   wyvis kurse
Sum famows wetewolddis and they be
   moche wurse
Sum liddurns sum losellis sum nowghtty
   pakkis
Sum facers sum bracers and sum make
   grete krakkis

28

Sum drunken dastarddis wt ther dry
   sowllis   *190*
Sume sluggishe slouens that slepe day &
   nyght
Ryote and reuelle be in your courte rollis
Mayntenans and myscheif theis be men
   of myght
Extorcioun is kounttid withe yow for a
   knyght

Theis pepille by me have noone assigne-
   ment   *195*
Yit ryde they and ryn they from karlyle
   to kente

29

Bot litille or no thynge shall ye here telle
Of them that have vertu by reson of
   konyng
Whiche souereynly in honor shuld excelle
Men of soche maters make bot a mummyng   *200*
ffor wisdom and sadnes be set owte a
   sunnyng
And soche of my seruaunttis as I have
   promotid
One fawte or other in them shall be notid

30

Eyther they shall say he is to wise
Or els he kan nowght bot when he is at
   skole   *205*
Prove his wit saithe he at karddis or dise
And ye shall fynde wele he is a verrey
   fole
Twishe / set hym a chayre or reche hym
   a stole
To syt vpon / and rede Jak Athrvmmys
   bibille
ffor truly it were pyte that he sat
   ydyll   *210*

31

The quene of ffame to Dame Pallas
To make repugnaunce ageyne þt ye have
   said
Of verey dewte it may not wele acorde
Bot your benynge sufferaunce for my discharge I laid
ffor that I wold not withe yow fall at
   discorde
Bot yit I beseke your grace that recorde
May be browght forthe soche as kan be
   fownde   *216*
Withe laureate tryvmphe why Skelton
   shuld be krownd

32

ffor els were to grete a derogacioun
Vnto your palace oure nobille courte of
   ffame
That any man vnder supportacioun   *220*
Withe owght deservynge shuld have the
   best game:
If he to the ampille encrese of his name

Can ley any workkis that he hathe com-
   pilyd
I am contente that he be not exilid

33

ffrom the laureate Senate : by force of
   proscripcioun   *225*
Or els ye know wele I kan do no les
Bot I most bannyshe hym frome my
   Iurisdiccioun
As he that aquayntithe hym wt Idelnes
Bot yf that he purpose to make a redres
What he hathe done let it be browght
   to sight   *230*
Graunte my peticioun I aske yow bot
   right

34

Dame Pallas to the quene of ffame
To your request we be wele condiscendid
Calle forthe let se where is your claryon-
   ar
To blow a blast withe his longe brethe
   extendid
Eolus your trumpet whiche knowen is so
   far   *235*
That Bararag blowithe in euery marciall
   war
Let hym blow now that we may take the
   vew
What Poet*is* we have at oure retenew

35

To se if Skelton dare put him self in
   prees
Amonge the thikkest of all the hole
   rowghte   *240*
Make noyce Inowthe for claterars love no
   pece
Let se my sister now spede go abowght
Anon I say this trumpet were fownd oute
And for no man hardly let hym spare
To blow bararag brag til bothe his yen
   stare   *245*

[Vitellius MS mutilated. Text below from
the Faukes print of 1523.]

36

Forth with there rose amonge the thronge
A wonderfull noyse / and on euery syde
They presid in faste / some thought they
   were to longe
Su*m*e were to hasty & wold no man byde
Some whispred some rownyd / some
   spake / & some cryde   *250*
With heuynge and shouynge haue in and
   haue oute

Some ranne the nexte way sume ranne
   abowte

37

There was suyng to the quene of fame
He plucked hym backe / and he went a
   fore
Nay hold thy tunge quod a nother let me
   haue the name   *255*
Make rowme sayd a nother ye prese all
   to sore
Sume sayd holde thy peas thou getest here
   no more
A thowsande thowsande I sawe on a
   plumpe
With that I harde the noyse of a trumpe

38

That longe tyme blewe a full timorous
   blaste   *260*
Lyke to the boryall wyndes whan they
   blowe
That towres / and townes / and trees
   downe caste
Droue clowdes together lyke dryftis of
   snowe
The dredefull dinne droue all the rowte
   on a rowe
Some tremblid / some girnid / some
   gaspid / some gasid   *265*
As people halfe peuysshe or men that
   were masyd

39

Anone all was whyste as it were for the
   nonys
And iche man stode gasyng & staryng
   vpon other
With that there come in wonderly at ones
A murmur of mynstrels / that suche a
   nother   *270*
Had I neuer sene some softer some
   lowder
Orpheus the traciane herped meledyously
Weth Amphion and other musis of ar-
   chady

40

Whos heuenly armony was so passynge
   sure
So truely proporsionyd and so well did
   gree   *275*
So duly entunyd with euery mesure
That in the forest was none so great a
   tre
But that he daunced for ioye of that gle
The huge myghty okes them selfe dyd
   auaunce

And lepe frome the hylles to lerne for to
   daunce   *280*

41

In so moche the stumpe where to I me
   lente
Sterte all at ones an hundrethe fote backe
With that I sprange vp towarde the tent
Of noble dame Pallas wherof I spake
Where I sawe come after I wote full
   lytyll lake   *285*
Of a thousande poetes assembled to
   geder
But phebus was formest of all that cam
   theder

42

Of laurell leuis a cronell on his hede
With heres enscrisped yalowe as the
   golde
Lamentyng daphnes whome with the darte
   of lede   *290*
Cupyde hath stryken so that she ne wolde
Concente to phebus to haue his herte in
   holde
But for to preserue her maiden hode
   clene
Transformyd was she in to the laurell
   grene

43

Meddelyd with murnynge the moost parte
   of his muse   *295*
O thoughtfull herte was euermore his
   songe
Daphnes my derlynge why do you me
   refuse
Yet loke on me that louyd you haue so
   longe
Yet haue compassyon vpon my paynes
   stronge
He sange also how the tre as he did
   take   *300*
Betwene his armes he felt her body quake

44

Then he assurded into his exclamacyon
Unto Diana the goddes inmortall
O mercyles madame hard is your con-
   stellacyon
So close to kepe your cloyster virgynall
Enhardid adyment the sement of your
   wall   *306*
Alas what ayle you to be so ouerthwhart
To bannysshe pyte out of a maydens harte

302. this exclamacyon Marshe.

45

Why haue the goddes shewyd me this
   cruelte
Sith I contryuyd first princyples medy-
   cynable   *310*
I helpe all other of there infirmite
But now to helpe my selfe I am not able
That profyteth all other is no thynge
   profytable
Unto me / alas that herbe nor gras
The feruent axes of loue can not re-
   presse   *315*

46

O fatall fortune what haue I offendid
Odious disdayne why raist þu me on this
   facyon
But sith I haue lost now that I entended
And may not atteyne it by no medyacyon
Yet in remembraunce of daph(n)es
   transformacyon   *320*
All famous poetis ensuynge after me
Shall were a garlande of the laurell tre

47

This sayd a great nowmber folowyd by
   and by
Of poetis laureat of many dyuerse na-
   cyons
Parte of there names I thynke to spece-
   fye   *325*
Fyrste olde Quintiliane wt his declyna-
   cyons
Theocritus with his bucolycall relacyons
Esiodus the Icononucar
And homerus the ffresshe historiar

48

Prynce of eloquence tullius cicero   *330*
With salusty ageinst lucius catelyne
That wrote the history of iugurta also
Ouyde enshryned with the musis nyne
But blesses Bacchus the pleasant god of
   wyne
Of clusters engrosyd with his ruddy
   droppes   *335*
These orators and poetes refresshed there
   throtis

49

Lucan with stacius in Achilliedos
Percius presed forth with problemes
   diffuse
Uirgill the mantuan with his eneidos
Juuenall satirray that men makythe to
   muse   *340*

Stanza 49 is from Marshe; not in Faukes.

But blessed Bacchus the pleasant god of
    wyne
Of clusters engrosed with his ruddy
    flotes
These orators & Poetes refreshed their
    throtes

50

There titus lyuius hym selfe dyd auaunce
With decadis historious whiche that he
    mengith   *345*
With maters that amount the romayns in
    substaunce
Enyus that wrate of mercyall war at
    lengthe
But blessed bachus potenciall god of
    strengthe
Of clusters engrosid wt his ruddy droppes
Theis orators and poetis refreshed there
    throtis   *350*

51

Aulus Gelius that noble historiar
Orace also with his new poetry
Mayster Terence the famous comicar
With plautus that wrote full many a
    comedy
But blessed bachus was in there company
Of clusters engrosyd with his ruddy
    dropis
Theis orators and poetis refresshed there
    throtis

52

Senek full soberly wt his tragedijs
Boyce recounfortyd with his philosophy
And maxymyane with his madde di-
    tijs   *360*
How dotynge age wold iape with yonge
    foly
But blessyd bachus most reuerent and
    holy
Of clusters engrosid with his ruddy dropis
Theis orators and poetis refresshed there
    throtis

53

There came John bochas wt his vol-
    umys grete   *365*
Quintus cursus full craftely that wrate
Of alexander / and macrobius that did
    trete
Of scipions dreme what was the treu
    probate
But blessyd bachus that neuer man for-
    gate

---

353. Faukes *conucar.*

Of clusters engrosed with his ruddy
    dropis   *370*
These orators and poetis refresshid ther
    throtis

54

Poggeus also that famous florentine
Mustred ther amonge them with many a
    mad tale
With a frere of fraunce men call sir
    gagwyne   *375*
That frownyd on me full angerly and
    pale
But blessyd bachus that bote is of all
    bale
Of clusters engrosyd with his ruddy
    dropis
Theis orators and poetis refresshid there
    throtis

55

Plutarke and Petrarke two famous clark-
    is   *380*
Lucilius and valerius maximus by name
With vincencius in speculo þt wrote noble
    warkis
Propercius and Pisandros poetis of noble
    fame
But blissed bachus that mastris oft doth
    frame
Of clusters engrosed with his ruddy
    dropis
Theis notable poetis refresshed there
    throtis   *385*

56

And as I thus sadly amonge them auysid
I saw Gower that first garnisshed our
    englysshe rude
And maister Chaucer that nobly enter-
    prysyd
How that our englysshe myght fresshely
    be (ennewed)
The monke of Bury then after them en-
    suyd   *390*
Dane John Lydgate theis englysshe poetis
    thre
As I ymagenyd repayrid vnto me

57

To geder in armes as brethern enbrasid
There apparell farre passynge beyonde
    that I can tell
Wt diamauntis and rubis there taber-
    (de)s were trasid   *395*

---

389. Faukes reads *amende.* Word from Marshe.
395. Reading amended from Marshe.

None so ryche stones in turkey to sell
Thei wantid nothynge but the laurell
And of there bounte they made me godely
   chere
In maner and forme as ye shall after
   here

58
Mayster Gower. To Skelton.
Brother Skelton your endeuorment   *400*
So haue ye done that meretoryously
Ye haue deseruyd to haue an enplement
In our collage aboue the sterry sky
By cause that (ye) encrese and amplyfy
The brutid britons of brutus albion   *405*
That welny was loste when that we were
   gone

59
Poeta Skelton to Maister Gower.
Maister Gower I haue nothyng deserued
To haue So laudabyle A commendacion
To yow thre this honor shalbe reserued
Arrectinge vnto your wyse examina-
   cion   *410*
How all that I do is vnder Refformation
For only the Substance of that I entend
Is glad to please and loth to offend

60
Mayster Gower. To Skelton.
Counterwayng your besy delygence
Of that we beganne in the supplement *415*
Enforcid ar we you to recompence
Of all our hooll collage by the agrea-
   ment
That we shall brynge you personally
   present
Of noble fame before the quenes grace
In whose court poynted is your place *420*

61
Poeta Ske(l)ton answeryth.
O noble Chaucer whos pullisshyd elo-
   quence
Oure englysshe rude so fresshely hath set
   out
That bounde ar we with all deu reuerence
Wt all our strength that we can brynge
   about
To owe to you our seruyce / & more if
   we mowte   *425*
But what sholde I say ye wote what I
   entende
Whiche glad am to please and loth to
   offende

404. Word supplied from Marshe. Stanza 59 is
from Marshe: not in Faukes.

62
Mayster Lydgate. To Skelton.
So am I preuentid of my brethern tweyne
In rendrynge to you thankkes meritory
That welny no thynge there doth re-
   mayne   *430*
Wherwt to geue you my regraciatory
But that I poynt you to be prothonotary
Of fames court by all our holl assent
Auaunced by pallas to laurell prefer-
   ment

63
Poeta Skelton answeryth
So haue ye me far passynge my meretis
   extollyd   *435*
Mayster lidgate of your accustomable
Bownte / and so gloryously ye haue en-
   rollyd
My name / I know well beyonde that I
   am able
That but if my warkes therto be agreable
I am elles rebukyd of that I intende *440*
Which glad am to please and lothe to
   offende

64
So finally when they had shewed there
   deuyse
Under the forme as I sayd to fore
I made it straunge & drew bak ones or
   twyse
And euer they presed on me more and
   more   *445*
Tyll at the last they forcyd me sore
That wt them I went where they wolde
   me brynge
Unto the pauylyon where pallas was syt-
   tyng

65
Dame Pallas commaundid þt they shold
   me conuay
Into the ryche palace of þe quene of
   fame   *450*
There shal he here what she wyl to hym
   say
When he is callid to answere to his
   name
A cry anone forthwt she made proclame
All orators and poetis shulde thider go
   before
With all the prese that there was lesse
   and more   *455*

66
Forth wt I say thus wa(n)drynge in my
   thought

How it was or elles wt in what howris
I can not tell you / but that I was
    brought
In to a palace wt turrettis and towris
Engalared goodly with hallis and bow-
    ris   460
So curiously / so craftely / so connyng-
    ly wrowght
That all the wor(l)de I trowe and it
    were sought

67

Suche a nother there coude no man fynde
Wher of partely I purpose to expounde
Whyles it remanyth fresshe in my
    mynde   465
Wt turkis and grossolitis enpauyd was
    the grounde
Of birrall enbosid wer the pyllers rownde
Of Elephantis tethe were the palace gatis
Enlosenged with many goodly platis

68

Of golde entachid with many a precyous
    stone   470
An hundred steppis mountyng to the
    halle
One of iasper a nother of whalis bone
Of dyamauntis pointed was the wall
The carpettis within and tappettis of
    pall
The chambres hangid with clothis of
    arace   475
Enuawtyd wt rubis the vawte was of this
    place

69

Thus passid we forth walkynge vnto the
    pretory
Where þe postis were enbulyoned wt
    saphiris indy blew
Englasid glittering wt many a clere story
Jacinctis and smaragdis out of the florthe
    they grew   480
Unto this place all poetis there did sue
Wherin was set of fame the noble quene
All other transcendynge most rychely be-
    sene

70

Under a gloryous cloth of astate
Fret all with orient perlys of garnate 485
Encrownyd as empresse of all this
    wor(l)dly fate
So ryally / so rychely / so passyngly
    ornate

---

460. *Engolerid* Faukes: reading from Marshe.

It was excedyng by yonde the com-
    mowne rate
This hous enuyrowne was a myle a bout
If . xij . were let in . xij . hundrethe stode
    without   490

71

Then to this lady & souerayne of this
    palace
Of purseuantis ther presid in wt many a
    dyuerse tale
Some were of poyle & sum were of trace
Of lymerik / of loreine / of spayne of
    portyngale
Frome napuls / from nauern & from
    rounceuall   495
Some from flaunders / sum fro the se
    coste
Some from the mayne lande / some fro
    the frensche hoste

72

With how doth þe north what tydingis
    is in þe sowth
The west is wyndy / the est is metely
    wele
It is harde to tell of euery mannes
    mouthe   500
A slipper holde the taile is of an ele
And he haltith often that hath a kyby
    hele
Some shewed his salfe cundight some
    shewid his charter
Some lokyd ful smothely and had a fals
    quarter

73

With sir I pray you a lytyll tyne stande
    backe   505
And lette me come in to delyuer my lettre
A nother tolde how shyppes wente to
    wrak
There were many wordes smaller and
    gretter
With I as good as thou / I fayth and no
    better
Some came to tell treuth / some came to
    lye   510
Some come to flater / some came to spye

74

There were I say / of all maner of sortis
Of dertmouth / of plummouth / of por-
    tismouth also
The burgeis / and the ballyuis of the . v .
    portis

With now let me come / and now let me
   go   *515*
And all tyme wandred I thus to and fro
Tyll at the last theis noble poetis thre
Unto me sayd / lo syr now ye may se

75

Of this high courte the dayly besines
From you most we but not longe to
   tary   *520*
Lo hither commyth a goodly maystres
Occupacyon famys regestary
Whiche shall be to you a sufferayne ac-
   cessary
With syngular pleasurs to dryue away
   the tyme
And we shall se you ageyne or it be
   pryme   *525*

76

When they were past & wente forth on
   there way
This gentilwoman that callyd was by
   name
Occupacyon in ryght goodly aray
Came towarde me and smylid halfe in
   game
I sawe hir smyle and I then did the
   same   *530*
With that on me she kest her goodly loke
Under her arme me thought she hade a
   boke

77
Occupacyoun to Skelton.

Lyke as the larke vpon the somers day
Whan titan radiant burnisshith his bemis
   bryght
Mountith on hy wt her melodious lay *535*
Of the sone shyne engladid with the
   lyght
So am I supprysd wt pleasure and de-
   lyght
To se this howre now that I may say
How ye are welcome to this court of
   aray

78

Of your aqueintaunce I was in tymes
   past   *540*
Of studyous doctryne when at the port
   salu
(Ye) fyrste aryuyd whan broken was
   your mast
Of worldly trust then did I you rescu

542. Faukes *The.*

Your storme dryuen shyppe I repared
   new
So well entakeled what wynde that euer
   blowe   *545*
No stormy tempeste your barge shall ouer
   throw

79

Welcome to me as hertely as herte can
   thynke
Welcome to me with all my hole desyre
And for my sake spare neyther pen nor
   ynke
Be well assurid I shall a quyte your
   hyre   *550*
Your name recountynge be yonde the
   lands of tyre
From sydony to the mount olympyan
Frome babill towre to the hillis Gaspian

80
Skelton poeta answeryth

I thanked her moche of her most noble
   offer   *554*
Affyaunsynge her myne hole assuraunce
For her pleasure to make a large profer
Enpryntyng her wordes in my remem-
   braunce
To owe her my seruyce wt true perseuer-
   aunce
Come on with me she sayd let vs not
   stonde
And with that worde she toke me by the
   honde   *560*

81

So passyd we forthe in to the forsayd
   place
With suche communycacyon as came to
   our mynde
And then she sayd whylis we haue tyme
   and space
To walke where we lyst / let vs somwhat fynde
To pas þe tyme with / but let vs wast no
   wynde   *565*
For ydle iangelers haue but lytill braine
Wordes be swordes and hard to call
   ageine

82

In to a felde she brought me wyde and
   large
Enwallyd aboute with the stony flint
Strongly enbateld moche costious of
   charge   *570*
To walke on this walle she bed I sholde
   not stint

Go softly she sayd the stones be full
glint
She went before and bad me take good
holde
I sawe a thowsande yatis new and olde

83

Then questionyd I her what thos yatis
ment　　　575
Wherto she answeryd and breuely me
tolde
How from the est vnto the occident
And from þe sowth vnto the north so
colde
Theis yatis she sayd which that ye beholde
Be issuis and portis from all maner of
nacyons　　　580
And seryously she shewyd me ther de-
nominacyons

84

They had wrytyng sum greke / sum
ebrew
Some romaine letters as I vnderstode
Some were olde wryten / sum were
writen new
Some carectis of caldy / sum frensshe
was full good　　　585
But one gate specyally where as I stode
Had grauin in it of calcydony a capytall
. A .
What yate call ye this / and she sayd
Anglea

85

The beldyng therof was passynge commendable
Wheron stode a lybbard crownyd wt
golde and stones　　　590
Terrible of countenaunce and passynge
formydable
As quikly towchyd as it were flesshe and
bones
As gastly that glaris as grimly that
gronis
As fersly frownynge as he had ben
fyghtyng
And with his forme foote he shoke
forthe this wrytyng　　　595

Cacosinthicon ex industria
Formidanda nimis Iouis vltima fulmina
tollis
Vnguibus ire parat loca singula liuida
curuis

Quam modo per phebes Nummos raptura
celeno
Arma / lues / luctus / fel / vis / fraus
barbara tellus
Mille modis erras odium tibi querere
martis
Spreto spineto cedat saliunca roseto

86

Then I me lent and loked ouer the wall
Innumerable people presed to euery gate
Shet were þe gatis thei might wel knock
& cal
And turne home ageyne for they cam al to
late
I her demaunded of them and ther as-
tate　　　600
Forsothe quod she theys be hastardis and
rebawdis
Dysers / carders / tumblars with gam-
bawdis

87

Furdrers of loue with bawdry aqueinted
Brainles blenkardis that blow at the cole
Fals forgers of mony for (coynnage)
atteintid　　　605
Pope holy ypocrytis as they were golde &
hole
Powle hatchettis þt prate wyll at euery
ale pole
Ryot / reueler / railer / brybery theft
Wt other condycyons that well myght
be left

88

Sume fayne them selfe folys & wolde
be callyd wyse　　　610
Sum medelynge spyes by craft to grope
thy mynde
Sume dysdanous dawcokkis þt all men
dispyse
Fals flaterers that fawne the & kurris of
kynde
That speke fayre before the & shrewdly
behynde
Hither they come crowdyng to get them
a name
But hailid they be homwarde wt sorow
and shame

89

With that I herd gunnis russhe out at
ones
Bowns / bowns / bowns / that all they
out cryde

---

605. Bracketed word from Marshe: Faukes *kown-
nage.*

It made sum lympe legged & broisid
there bones
Sum were made peuysshe porisshly pynk
iyde   *620*
That euer more after by it they were
aspyid
And one ther was there I wondred of his
hap
For a gun stone I say had all to iaggid
his cap

90

Raggid and daggid and cunnyngly cut
The blaste of þe byrnston blew away his
brayne   *625*
Masid as a marche hare he ran lyke a
scut
And sir amonge all me thought I saw
twaine
The one was a tumblar þt afterwarde
againe
Of a dysour a deuyl way grew a Jentilman
Pers prater the secund tha(t) quarillis
beganne   *630*

91

Wt a pellit of peuisshenes they had such
a stroke
That all þe dayes of ther lyfe shall styck
by ther rybbis
Foo / foisty bawdias sum smellid of the
smoke
I saw dyuers þt were carijd away thens
in cribbis
Dasyng after dotrellis lyke drunkardis þt
dribbis   *635*
Theis titiuyllis wt taumpinnis wer
towchid & tappid
Moche mischefe I hyght you / amonge
theme ther happid

92

Sometyme as it semyth when þe mone
light
By meanys of a grosely endarkyd clowde
Sodenly is eclipsid in the wynter night
In lyke maner of wyse a myst did vs
shrowde   *641*
But wele may ye thynk I was no thyng
prowde
Of that auenturis whiche made me sore
agast
In derkenes thus dwelt we tyll at the last

93

The clowdis gan to clere / þe myst was
rarifijd   *645*

In an herber I saw brought where I was
There birdis on the brere sange on euery
syde
With alys ensandid about in compas
The bankis enturfid with singular solas
Enrailid with rosers and vinis engrapid
It was a new comfort of sorowis escapid

94

In the middis a coundight that coryously
was cast
With pypes of golde engusshing out
stremes
Of cristall the clerenes theis waters far
past
Enswymmyng wt rochis / barbellis / and
bremis   *655*
Whose skales ensiluered again the son
beames
Englistered: þt ioyous it was to be holde
Then furthermore aboute me my syght
I reuolde

95

Where I saw growyng a goodly laurell tre
Enuerdurid with leuis contynually grene
Aboue in the top a byrde of araby   *661*
Men call a phenix: her wynges bytwene
She bet vp a fyre with the sparkis full
kene
With braunches and bowghis of þe swete
olyue
Whos flagraunt flower was chefe pre-
seruatyue   *665*

96

Ageynst all infeccyons with (r)ancour
enflamyd
Ageynst all baratows broisiours of olde
It passid all bawmys that euer were
namyd
Or gummis of saby so derely that be solde
There blew in that gardynge a soft pip-
lyng colde   *670*
Enbrethyng of zepherus wt his pleasant
wynde
All frutis (&) flowris grew there in there
kynde

97

Dryades there daunsid vpon that goodly
soile
Wit(h) the nyne muses pierides by name
Phillis and testalus ther tressis with
oyle   *675*
Were newly enbybid: and rownd about
the same

---

656. This line from Marshe; omitted by Faukes.

Grene tre of laurell moche solacyous game
They made / with chapellettes and gar-
    landes grene
And formest of all dame flora the quene

98

Of somer: so formally she fotid the
    daunce   *680*
There cintheus sat twynklyng vpon his
    harpe stringis
And iopas his instrument did auaunce
The poemis and storis auncient in bryngis
Of athlas astrology and many noble
    thyngis
Of wandryng of the mone / the course
    of the sun   *685*
Of men and of bestis and where of they
    begone

99

What thynge occasionyd the showris of
    rayne
Of fyre elementar in his supreme spere
And of that pole artike whiche doth
    remayne
Behynde the taile of vrsa so clere *690*
Of pliades he prechid wt ther drowsy
    chere
Immoysturid wt mistyng and ay droppyng
    dry
And where the two tr(i)ons a man shold
    aspy

100

And of þe winter days that hy them so
    fast
And of the wynter nyghtes that tary so
    longe   *695*
And of the somer days so longe that doth
    last
And of their shorte nyghtes / he browght
    in his songe
How wronge was no ryght / and ryght
    was no wronge
There was counteryng of carollis in meter
    and verse
So many : that longe it were to re-
    herse   *700*

101
Occupacyon. To Skelton.
How say ye: is this after your appetite
May this contente you & your mirry
    mynde
Here dwellith pleasure wt lust & delyte
Contynuall comfort here ye may fynde
Of welth & solace no thynge left be
    hynde   *705*

All thynge conuenable here is contryuyd
Where with your spiritis may be reuyuid

102
Poeta Skelton answeryth
Questionles no dowte of that ye say
Jupiter hym selfe this lyfe myght endure
This ioy excedith all wor(l)dly sport &
    play   *710*
Paradyce / this place is of syngular
    pleasure
O wele were hym that herof myght be
    sure
And here to inhabite / and ay for to
    dwell
But goodly maystres one thynge ye me
    tell

[Text following is from MS Cotton Vitellius E x]

103
[Occupacyon. To Skelton.]
Of your demaunde shew me the content
What it is and where vpon it standdis
And if there be in it any thynge ment
Where of the awnswere restithe in myne
    handdis
It shall be losond fulle sone owte of the
    banddis
Of skrupulows dought: wherefor your
    mynde discharge   *720*
And of your wille the playnnes shew at
    large

104
Poeta Skelton to Occupacioun
I thanke yow goodely mastres to me moost
    benygne
That of your bownte so wele have me
    assuryd
Bot my request is not so grete a thynge
That I ne force what thowthe it be dis-
    curyd   *725*
I am not woundid but that I may be
    kuryd
I am not ladyn of liddernes withe lumpis
As dasid dotarddis that dreme in ther
    dumppis

105
Occupacioun to Skelton
Now what ye mene I trow I coniecte
God geve yow goode yere ye make me
    to smyle   *730*
Now by yowre faythe is not this the
    effecte

Heading to Stanza 103 from Faukes.

Of yowre questioun ye make all this
    whyle
To vnderstande who dwellythe in yonder
    pyle
And what blunderar is yonder that plaiyth
    diddil diddil
He fyndithe owght fals mesuris of his
    fond fyddille   735

Interpolata / que industriosum Postulat
interpretem / satira in vatis adversarium

Tressis Agasonis Species *prior* altera
    Daui
Aucupium culicis limis dum torquet
    ocellum
Concipit: Aligeras rapit [a]ppetit aspice
    muskas:
Maia que*que* fouet fouet aut que Juppiter
    aut que
ffrigida / Saturnus . Sol . Mars. Venus .
    algida Luna
Si tibi contingat verbo aut committere
    scripto
Quam sibi mox tacita sudant precordia
    culpa
Hinc ruit in flammas / stimulans hu*nc*
    urget et iſlum
Inuocat ad rixas . vanos tamen excitat
    ignes
Labra mouens tacitus rumpantur vt ilia
    Codro
            .14.4.7.2.17.18.14.14.
            .18.19.1.8.17.12.14.14.

106
Hys name for to know if that ye lyst
Enuyows Ranco*ur* truly he hyght
Beware of hym I warne yow for and ye
    wist
How daungerows it is to stop vp his sight
Ye wolde not dele wt hym thowthe that
    ye myght   740
ffor by his devillishe dryfte and graceles
    prouysioun
An hole reme he is habille to set at dyvy-
    sioun
107
ffor when he spekithe fayrest then thynk-
    kithe he moost Il
fful gloriowsly kan he glose thy mynde
    for to fele
He wille stir men to brawlyng and syt
    hym self stil   745

Figures are in the prints:
        17.   4. 7.   2. 17. 5. 18.
        18. 19. 1. 19.   8. 5. 12.

And smyrke lyke a smytthy kur at
    sparkkis of stele
He kan neuer leve warke while it is
    wele
To telle all his towchis it were to grete
    wunder
The deuelle of helle and he be seldome
    asunder

108
Thus talkynge we went in at a posterne
    gate   750
Turnnyd on the right hand by a wyndyng
    stayre
She browght me in to a goodely chaum-
    ber of astate
Where the nobille Countes of Surrey /
    in a chayre
Sat honorably / : to whome did repayre
Of ladis a beuy / wt all du reuerence   755
Syt downe fayre ladis and do yo*ur* dili-
    gence

109
Com forthe Jantilwomen I pray yow she
    sayde
I have contryvyd for yow a goodely
    warke
And who kan worke best now shall be
    asaiyd
A coronelle of laurel withe verduris light
    and darke   760
I have devisid for Skelton my clarke
ffor to his seruyce I have soche regarde
That of oure bownte we will hym re-
    warde

110
ffor of all ladis he hathe the library
Ther namys recountynge in the courte
    of ffame   765
Of all Jantylwomen he hathe the scruteny
In famys courte reporttynge the same
ffor yit of women he neuer sayd shame
Bot if they wer Counterfett*es* that wom-
    en them call
That liste of ther lewdenes withe hym for
    to brall :   770

111
Wythe that the tappettis and Carpettis
    were layd
Where on theis ladis softly myght rest
The saumplar to sow on the lasis to
    enbrayd
To weue in the stole sum were fulle prest
Withe slaiys withe tauellis with heddell*es*
    wele drest   775

The frame was browght forthe withe his
wouynge
God yeve them goode spede ther worke
to begyn

112

Sum to enbrawder put them in prece
Wel gydyng the glutton to kepe streyght
ther sylk
Sum pyrlynge of golde ther worke to
encrese   *780*
Withe ffynggers smale and handdis
whyght as mylke
Withe reche me that skene of tuly silke
And wynde me that botum of soche a hu
Grene rede tawny whyht blak purpulle
and blu

113

Of broken workis wrowght many a
goodely thynge   *785*
In castinge in turnnynge in florisshinge
of flow*res*
Withe burris rowthe and buttunis surfullinge
In nedel warke reisinge bothe birddis and
bow*res*
Withe vertu enbesid all tymes and howrys
And truly of ther bownte thus were they
bente   *790*
To worke me this chapelet by goode
auysemente:

114
Occupacioun to Skelton

Beholde and se in youre aduertisement
How theis ladis and Jantilwomen all
ffor yowre plesure do ther endeuorment
And for youre sake how fast to worke
they fall   *795*
To youre remembraunce wherefor ye
most call
In goodely worddis pleasantly comprisid
That for them sum goodely conceyte be
deuysid

115

Wythe proper captaciouns of benyuo-
lence
Ornatly pullisshid after y*our* faculte *800*
Sithe ye most nedis afforce it by pretence
Of youre professioun vnto humanyte
Commensynge y*our* proces after ther de-
gre
To eche of them rendrynge thonkkis com-
mendabill
Wythe sentence fructuows and termmys
couenabill   *805*

---

784. *blak* is not in Faukes or Marshe.

116
Poeta Skelton

Auaunsynge my self sum thonk to de-
serue
I me determynd for to sharpe my pen
Deuowtly arrectynge my prayer to Myn-
erue
She to vowche saue me to enforme and
ken:
To Marcury also hartly praiyd I then *810*
Me to supporte to helpe and to assist
To gyde & to gouerne my dredefulle
tremlyng fyst

117

As a maryner that masid is in a stormmy
rage
Hardly bestad driven is to hope
Of that the tempestuows wynde wille
aswage   *815*
In troste where of counforte his harte
dothe grope
ffrome the Ankker he kyttithe the gabille
rope
Commyttithe all to god and lettithe his
ship ride
So I beseke J*he*su now to be my gyde

118
To the Right nobille Countes of Surrey

After all duly orderd obeisaunce   *820*
In humbille wise as lawly as I may
Vnto yow madame. I make reconusaunce
My lif enduringe . I . shall bothe wright
and say
Recounte . reporte . reherce withe owte
delay
The passinge bownte of y*our* nobille es-
tate   *825*
Of hono*ur* and worship whiche hathe the
formar date

119

Lyke to Argyua by Juste resemblaunce
The nobille wif of Polymytes kynge
Prudent Rebecca of whome remem-
braunce
The bibille makithe: withe whos chast
lyvynge   *830*
Y*our* nobille demenor is counterweiynge
Whos passinge bownte and right nobil
astate
Of hono*ur* and worship it hathe the for-
mar date

120

The nobille Pamphila quene of the grekis
land

Habilymenttis roiall fownd owte endus-
   triowsly   835
Thamar also wrowght withe her goodely
   hand
Many dyvisis passinge kuriowsly
Whome ye represent and exemplify
Whos passinge bownte and right nobille
   astate
Of honour and worship it hathe the for-
   mar date   840

121

As dame Thamaris whiche toke the kinge
   of Perse
Cyrus by name / as writithe the story
Dame Agrippina also I may reherce
Of Jantylle corage the perfight memory
So shall your name endure perpetually
Whos passinge bownte and right nobille
   astate
Of honor and worship it hathe the former
   date

122

To my lady Elisabethe [Howarde]
To be your remembrancer Madam I am
   bownd
Lyke to Aryna maydenly of porte
Of vertew konyng the wel and parfight
   grownd   850
Whome dame Nature as wele I may re-
   porte
Hathe freshely enbewtid withe many a
   goodely sorte
Of womanly feturis / : whos florisshinge
   tender age
Is lusty to loke on plesant demure and
   sage:

123

Goodely Creisseyda fairar than Poly-
   cene   855
ffor to envyve Pandarus appetite
Troylus I trow if that he had yow sene
In yow he wold have set his hole delight
Of all your bewte I suffice not to wright
Bot as I sayde your florisshynge tender
   age   860
Is lusty to loke on plesant demur & sage

124

To my lady Myrryel [Howarde]
My lytille lady I may not leue behynde
Bot do her seruyce nedis now I must
Benygne kurteise of Jantille harte and
   mynde

Bracketed words from Faukes of 1523.

Whome fortune and fate playnly have
   discust   865
Longe to enioy plesure delight and luste
Enbuddid blossome withe rosis rede of
   hu
The lylly whight your bewte dothe renew:

125

Compare yow I may to Cydippes the
   mayd
That of Aconycus when she fownd the
   bille   870
In her bosum: lorde she was afraiyd
The ruddy shamefastnes in her visage
   fylle
Whiche manner of abashemente becam
   her not Il
Right so madame the rosis rede of hu
Withe lyllis whight your bewte dothe
   renew   875

126

To my lady Dakers
Zeuxes that enpycturid fayre Elene the
   quene
Yow to deuyse his craft were to seke:
And if Apelles your countenaunce had
   sene
Of porturature whiche was the famows
   greke
He kowde not deuyse the lest poynte of
   your cheke   880
Prynces of yowthe and floure of goodely
   porte
Vertew konynge solace plesure counfort

127

Paregall in honour vnto Penolope
That for her trowthe is in remembraunce
   had
ffayre Dyanyra surmountynge in bewte
Demure Dyana womanly and sad   886
Whos lusty lokis make heuy harttis glad
Prynces of yowthe and flowre of goodely
   porte
Vertew konyng solace plesure conforte:

To mastres Margery Wentworthe
Wythe Mageran Jantel   890
The flowre of goodlihode
Enbrawderd the mantel
Is of your maydenhode

Playnly I kan not glose
Ye be as I dyvyne   895
The praty prymerose
The goodely columbyne

Withe Mageran Jantel
The floure of goodlihode
Enbrawderd the mantel   900
Is of your maydenhode

Benygne curteise & meke
Withe wordis wele deuysid
In yow who list to seke
Be vertewys wele comprisid   905

Wythe Mageran Jantyl
The floure of goodlyhode
Enbrawderd the mantyl
Is of your maydenhode:

To mastres Margarete Tylnney
I yow assure   910
ffulle wele I know
My besy cure
To yow I ow
Humbly and low
Commendinge me   915
To your bounte

As Machareus
ffayre Canace
So . I . Iwus
Endeuour me   920
Your name to se
It be enrold
Wryttyn wt gold

Phedra ye may
Wele represente   925
Intentyve ay
And diligente
No tyme mysspent
Wherefor delight
I have to wright   930

Of Margaryte
Perle oryente
Lodestar of lyght
Moche relucent:
Madame regent   935
I may yow call
Of Vertuys all

To mastres Jane Hasset
What thowthe my pen wax faynte
And hathe small lust to paynte
Yet shall there no restraynte   940
Cause me to cese
Amonge this prese
ffor to encrese
    Your goodely name

I wille my self apply   945
Trost me intentyvely
Yow for to stellify
And so observe
That ye ne swerve
ffor to deserve   950
    The courte of fame

Sythe mastres Jane Hasset
Smale flowris helpt to set
In my goodely chapelet
Therefor I render of her the memory 955
Vnto the legend of fayre Laodomy:

To mastres Isbill Pennel:
By seynte mary my lady
Youre mammy and your dady
Browght forthe a goodely baby
My maydyn Isabel   960
Reflayringe Rosabel
The flagrant Camamel
The ruddy Rosary
The souereyne Rosemary
The praty strawbery   965
The Columbyne the nept
The Jeloffer wele set
The proper vyolet
Ennewyd (your) colour
Is like the daisy flour   970
After the Apryle shour
Star of the morow gray
The blossom on the spray
The fresshest flour of may
Maydenly demure   975
Of womanhode the lure
Wherefor I yow assure
It wer an hevenly helthe
It wer an endles welthe
A lif for god hym (selfe)   980
To here this nytyngale
Amonge the byrddis smale
Warbolynge in the vale
Dug Dug
Jug Jug   985
Goode yere and goode luk
Wyth chuk chuk . chuk chuk:

To mastres Margarete Hussey:
Myrry Margarete as mydsomer floure
Jantylle as fawkon or hauke of the towr
Withe solace and gladnes   990
Moche myrthe and no madnes
All goode and no badnes
So Joyously

So maydenly
So womanly   995
Her demenynge
In euery thynge
ffar far passinge
That I kan endight
Or suffice to wright   1000
Of myrry margaret as mydsomer flowre
Jantille as faukon or hawke of the towre
As pacient and as stille
And as fulle of goode wille
As the fayre Isyphill   1005
Colyaundar
Swete pomaunder
Goode Cassander
Stedfast of thowght
Wele made wele wrowght   1010
ffar may be sowght
Erst than ye kan fynde
So kurteise so kynde
As myrry Marget the mydsomer flowre
Jantille as fawkon or hawke of the towre

To mastres Geretrude Statham

Thowthe ye were harde harttid
And I withe yow thwartyd
With worddis that smarttid
Yit now dowtles ye geve me cause
To wright of yow this goodely clause   1020
Mastres Geretrude
Wt womanhode endude
Wt vertew wele renewde
I wille that ye shall be
In all benygnyte   1025
Lyke to dame Pasiphe
ffor now dowtles ye geve me cause
To wright of yow this goodely clause
Mastres Geretrude
Wt womanhode endude   1030
Withe vertew wele renewde
Partly by your counselle
Garnnysshid withe laurelle
Was my freshe coronelle
Wherfor dowtless ye geve me cause   1035
To wright of yow this goodely clause
Mastres Geretrude
Withe womanhode endude
Withe vertu wele renewde

To mastres Isbell Knyght

Bot if I shulde aquyte your kyndnes   1040
Els say ye myght:
That in me were grete blyndnes
I for to be so myndles

And kowde not wright:
Of Isbel Knyght: 1045

It is not my kustome nor my gyse
To leve behynde:
Her that is both maydenly & wise
And specially whiche glad was to deuyse
The mene to fynde: 1050
To plese my mynde:

In helpynge to warke my laureel grene
Withe silke and golde:
Galathea the maide wele besene
Was neuer half so fayre as I wene 1055
Which was extolde:
A thowsand folde:

By Maro the mantuane prudent
Who list to rede
Bot and I had leysor competente   1060
I kowde shew soche a presedente
In verey dede
How ye excede:

128
Occupacioun to Skelton

Wythdraw your hand the tyme passithe
    fast
Set on your hede this laurelle whiche is
    wrowght   1065
Here ye not Eolus for yow blowithe a
    blast
I dare wele say that ye and I be sowght
Make no delay for now ye most be
    browght
Before my ladis grace the quene of fame
Where ye most brevely aunswere to your
    name   1070

129
Poeta Skelton

Castinge my sight the chaumber aboute
To se how duly eche thinge in Order was
Toward the durre as we were komynge
    owte
I saw Master Newton sit withe his com-
    pas
His plummet his penselle his specktakils
    of glas   1075
Deuysinge in picture by his industryows
    wit
Of my Laureell the proces euery whit

130

fforthwt vpon this as it were in a
    thowght
Gower Chawser Lydgate theis iij   1079

Before rememberd: kurteisly me browght
In to that place where as they left me
Where all the saide poetis sat in ther
degre
But when they saw my lawrelle rychely
wro(wght)
All thos þt they ware were counterfettis
they (thowght)

131

In comparison of that whiche I ware *1085*
Sum praisid the perle sum the stonys
bright
Wele was hym that there vpon myght
stare
Of this worke they had so grete delight
The silke the golde the flour*es* freshe to
sight
They saide my laureel was the goodely-
est   *1090*
That euer they saw: and wrowght it was
the best

132

In her astate there sat the nobille quene
Of fame / : *p*erceyvynge how that I was
kum
She wonderde me thowght at my laurelle
grene
She lokid hawtely and yave on me a
glum   *1095*
There was not a worde amonge them then
bot mvm
ffor eche man harkend what she to me
wold say
Where of in substance I browght this
away

133
The quene of ffame to Skelton

My frynde sithe ye are before vs here
*p*resent
To aunswere vnto this nobille audyence
Of þt shall be resond yow ye most be
content: /
And for asmoche as by the higthe pre-
tense
That ye haue now thorow preemynence
Of laureat promocioun / : *yo*ur place is
here reservyd
We wille vnderstand how ye have it
deservid   *1105*

134
Poeta Skelton to the quene of ffame

Right higthe and myghtty prynces of
(astate)
In famows glory all other transcenddinge
Of *yo*ur bownte the acustomabille rate
Hathe bene fulle oftene and yit is en-
tendinge   *1109*
To all that to reson is condiscendynge
Bot if hastyve credence by mayntenaunce
of myght
ffortune to stande bytwene yow and the
light

135

Bot soche evydence I thynke for me to
enduce
And so largely to ley for myn Indemnyte
That I troste to make myne excus *1115*
Of what charge so euer ye ley ageyne me
ffor of my bokis parte ye shall se
Whiche in *yo*ur recorddis I know wele
be (enrolde)
And so Occupacioun *yo*ur regester me
told

[Vitellius MS defective.   Text below
        from Faukes.]

136

Forth with she commaundid I shulde take
my place   *1120*
Caliope poynted me where I shulde sit
With that occupacioun presid in a pace
Be mirry she sayd be not aferde a whit
Your discharge here vnder myne arme
is it
So then commaundid she was vpon this
To shew her boke: and she sayd here it is

137
The quene of fame to occupacioun.

Yowre bokes of rememb*ra*uns we will
now þt ye rede
If ony recordis i*n* noumbyr ca*n* be founde
What Skelto*n* hath compilid & wryton in
dede
Rehersyng by ordre & what is the
grownde   *1130*
Let se now for hym how ye can expounde
For in owr courte ye wote wele his name
can not ryse
But if he wryte oftenner than ones or
twyse

1083, 1084. Mutilations of MS supplied from
    Faukes.

1107, 1118. MS defective.   Text from Faukes
    print.

138
Skelton Poeta.

With that of the boke losende were the
  claspis
The margent was illumynid all with gold-
  en railles   *1135*
And byse: enpicturid wt gressoppes and
  waspis
Wt butterflyis and fresshe pecoke taylis
Enflorid wt flowris and slymy snaylis
Enuyuid picturis well towchid & quikly
It wolde haue made a man hole þt had
  be ryght sekely   *1140*

139
To be holde how it was garnysshyd &
  bounde
Encouerde ouer wt golde of tissew fyne
The claspis and bullyons were worth a
  thousande pounde
Wt balassis & charbuncles the borders did
  shyne   *1144*
With aurum musicum euery other lyne
Was wrytin: and so she did her spede
Occupacyoun immediatly to rede

140
Occupacyoun redith and expoundyth sum
parte of Skeltons bokes and balades wt
ditis of plesure in asmoche as it were to
longe a proces to reherse all by name þt
he hath compylyd &c.

Of your oratour and poete laureate
Of Englande his workis here they be-
  gynne   *1149*
In primis the boke of honorous astate
Item the boke how men shuld fle synne
Item royall demenaunce worshyp to wyne
Item the boke to speke well or be styll
Item to lerne you (t)o dye when ye wyll

141
Of vertu also the souerayne enterlude
The boke of þe rosiar: prince arturis
  creacyoun   *1156*
The false fayth þt now goth which dayly
  is renude
Item his diologgis of ymagynacyoun
Item antomedon of loues meditacyoun
Item new gramer in englysshe compylyd
Item bowche of courte where drede was
  be gyled

142
His commedy achademios callyd by name
Of tullis familiars the translacyoun

Item good aduysement that brainles doth
  blame
The recule ageinst gaguyne of the frenshe
  nacyoun   *1165*
Item the popingay þt hath in commenda-
  cyoun
Ladyes and gentylwomen suche as deseruyd
And suche as be counterfettis they be
  reseruyd

143
And of soueraynte a noble pamphelet
And of magnyfycence a notable mater
How cownterfet cowntenaunce of the
  new get   *1171*
Wt crafty conueyaunce dothe smater and
  flater
And cloked collucyoun is brought in to
  clater
Wt courtely abusyoun: who pryntith it
  wele in mynde
Moche dowblenes of the worlde therin he
  may fynde   *1175*

144
Of manerly margery maystres mylke
  and ale
To her he wrote many maters of myrthe
Yet thoughe ye say it ther by lyith a
  tale
For margery wynshed and breke her
  hinder girth
Lor(de) how she made moche of her
  gentyll birth   *1180*
With gingirly go gingerly her tayle was
  made of hay
Go she neuer so gingirly her honesty is
  gone a way

145
Harde to make ought of that is nakid
  nought
This fustiane maistres and this giggisse
  gase
Wonder is to wryte what wrenchis she
  wrowght   *1185*
To face out her foly wt a midsomer mase
Wt pitche she patchid her pitcher shuld
  not crase
It may wele ryme but shroudly it doth
  accorde
To pyke out honesty of suche a potshorde

Patet per versus.

Hinc puer hic nat*us*: vir *con*iugis hinc
  spolia*tus*

Iure thori: est: fetus deli de sanguine
   cretus
Hinc magis extollo quod erit puer alter
   apollo
Si queris qualis: meretrix castissima
   talis
   Et relis et ralis: et reliqualis
   A good herynge of thes olde talis *1190*
Fynde no mor suche fro wanflete to
   walis
   Et relequa omelia de diuersis tractati-
   bus

146

Of my ladys grace at the contemplacyoun
Owt of frenshe in to englysshe prose
Of mannes lyfe the peregrynacioun
He did translate / enterprete and dis-
   close   *1195*
The tratyse of triumphis of the rede rose
Where in many storis ar breuely con-
   tayned
That vn remembred longe tyme remayn-
   ed

147

The duke of yorkis creauncer whan Skel-
   ton was
Now Henry the . viij . kyng of Englonde
A tratyse he deuysid and browght it to
   pas
Callid speculum principis to bere in his
   honde
Therin to rede and to vnderstande
All the demenour of princely astate
To be our kyng of god preordinate *1205*

148

Also the tunnynge of elinour rummyng
Wt colyn clowt / iohn iue / with ioforth
   iack
To make suche trifels it asketh sum kon-
   nyng
In honest myrth parde requyreth no lack
The whyte apperyth the better for the
   black   *1210*
And after conueyauns as the world goos
It is no foly to vse the walshemannys
   hoos

149

The vmblis of venyson / the botell of
   wyne
To fayre maistres anne þt shuld haue be
   sent
He wrate therof many a praty lyne *1215*
Where it became and whether it went

And how that it was wantonly spent
The balade also of the mustarde tarte,
Suche problemis to paynt it longyth to
   his arte

150

Of one adame all a knaue late dede and
   gone   *1220*
Dormiat in pace / lyke a dormows
He wrate an epitaph for his graue stone
Wt wordes deuoute and sentence ager-
   dows
For he was euer ageynst goddis hows
All his delight was to braule and to
   barke   *1225*
Ageynst holy chyrche the preste and the
   clarke

151

Of phillip sparow the lamentable fate
The dolefull desteny and the carefull
   chaunce
Dyuysed by Skelton after the funerall
   rate
Yet sum there be there wt that take greuaunce   *1230*
And grudge ther at wt frownyng countenaunce
But what of that: hard it is to please
   all men
Who list amende it let hym set to his
   penne

For the gyse now a days
Of sum iangelyng iays   *1235*
Is to discommende
Þt they can not amende
Though they wolde spende
All the wittis they haue
What ayle them to depraue   *1240*
Phillippe sparows graue
His dirige: her commendacioun
Can be no derogacyoun
But myrth & consolacyoun
Made by protestacyon   *1245*
No man to myscontent
With phillippis enteremente

Alas that goodly mayd
Why shulde she be afrayd
Why shulde she take shame   *1250*
That her goodly name
Honorably reportid
Shulde be set and sortyd
To be matriculate
With ladyes of astate   *1255*
I coniure þe Phillip sparow

By hercules þt hell did harow
And wt a venomows arow
Slew of the epidawris
One of the centauris   *1260*
Or onocentauris
Or hippocentaurus
By whos myght and maine
An hart was slayne
Wt hornnis twayne   *1265*
Of glitteryng golde
And the apples of golde
Of hesperides with holde
And with a dragon kepte
That neuer more slepte   *1270*
By merciall strength
He wan at length
And slew gerione
With thre bodys in one
With myghty corrage   *1275*
A dauntid the rage
Of a lyon sauage.
Of diomedis stabyll
He brought out a rabyll
Of coursers and rounsis   *1280*
Wit(h) lepes and bounsis
And wt myghty luggyng
Wrastelynge and tuggyng
He pluckid the bull
By the hornid scull   *1285*
And offred to cornucopia
And so forthe per cetera

Also by hecates powre
In plutos gastly towre
By the vgly Eumenides.   *1290*
Þt neuer haue rest nor ease
By þe venemows serpent
That in hell is neuer brente
In lerna the grekis fen
That was engendred then   *1295*
By chemeras flamys
And all the dedely namys
Of infernall posty
Where soulis fry and rosty
By the stigiall flode   *1300*
And the stremes wode
Of cochitos bottumles well
By the feryman of hell
Caron wt his berde hore
That rowyth wt a rude ore   *1305*
And wt his frownsid fortop
Gydith his bote wt a prop
I coniure phillippe & call
In þe name of kyng Saull
Primo regum expres   *1310*

He bad the phitones
To witche craft her to dres
And by her abusiouns
And damnable illusiouns
Of meruelous conclusiouns   *1315*
And by her supersticiouns
Of wonderfull condiciouns
She raysed vp in þe stede
Samuell that was dede
But whether it were so   *1320*
He were idem in numero
The selfe same Samuell
How be it to Saull he did tell
The phillistinis shulde hym askry
And the next day he shulde dye   *1325*
I wyll me selfe discharge
To letterd men at large
But phillip I coniure the
Now by theys names thre
Diana in the woddis grene   *1330*
Luna that so bryght doth shene
Proserpina in hell
That thou shortely tell
And shew now vnto me
What the cause may be   *1335*
Of this proplexyte

Phillyppe answeryth

Inferias phillippe tuas Scroupe pulcra
    Iohanna
Instanter peciit: cur nostri carminis
    illam
Nunc pudet: est sero: minor est: infamia
    vero

Then such that haue disdaynyd
And of this worke complaynyd
I pray god they be paynyd
No wors (than) is contaynyd   *1340*
In verses two or thre
That folowe as ye may se

Luride cur liuor volucrum pia funera
    damnas
Talia te rapiant rapiunt que fata volu-
    crem.
Est tamen inuidia mors tibi continua

152

The gruntyng (& the) groynninge (of
    the) gronnyng swyne
Also the murmyng of the mapely rote
How the grene couerlet sufferd grete
    pine   *1345*

1340. Faukes *and;* Marshe *than.*
1343. Bracketed words from Marshe's ed.

Whan the flye net was set for to catche
  a cote
Strake one with a birdbolt to the hart
  rote
Also a deuoute prayer to moyses hornis
Metrifyde merely / medelyd with stormis

153

Of paiauntis þt were played in ioyows
  garde   *1350*
He wrate of a muse throw a mud wall
How a do cam trippyng in at the rere
  warde
But lorde how the parker was wroth with
  all
And of castell aungell the fenestrall
Glittryng and glistryng and gloryously
  glasid   *1355*
It made sum mens eyn: dasild and dasid

154

The repete of the recule of rosamundis
  bowre
Of his pleasaunt paine there and his glad
  distres
In plantynge and pluckynge a propre
  ieloffer flowre
But how it was sum were to recheles
Not withstandynge it is remedeles
What myght she say: what myght he do
  therto
Though iak sayd nay: yet mok there
  loste her sho

155

How than lyke a man he wan the barbi-
  can   *1364*
With a sawte of solace at the longe last
The colour dedely swarte blo and wan
Of exione her lambis dede and past
The cheke and the nek but a shorte cast
In fortunis fauour euer to endure
No man lyuyng he sayth can be sure *1370*

156

How dame minuerua first found þe olyue
  tre: she red
And plantid it there where neuer before
  was none: vnshred
An hynde vnhurt hit by casuelte: not
  bled
Recouerd whan the forster was gone:
  and sped
The hertis of the herd began for to
  grone: and fled   *1375*
The howndis began to yerne & to quest:
  and dred

Wt litell besynes standith moche rest:
  in bed

157

His epitomis of the myller & his ioly
  make
How her ble was bryght as blossom on
  the spray
A wanton wenche and wele coude bake a
  cake   *1380*
The myllar was loth to be out of the way
But yet for all that be as be may
Whether he rode to swassham or to some
The millar durst not leue his wyfe at
  home

158

Wt wofully arayd and shamefully be-
  trayd   *1385*
Of his makyng deuoute medytacyons
Uexilla regis he deuysid to be displayd
Wt sacris solempniis and other contem-
  placyouns
That in them comprisid consyderacyons
Thus passyth he the tyme both nyght
  and day   *1390*
Sumtyme wt sadnes sumtyme with play

159

Though galiene and diascorides
With ipocras and mayster auycen
By there phesik doth many a man ease
And though albumasar can þe enforme
  and ken   *1395*
What constellacions ar good or bad for
  men
Yet whan the rayne rayneth and þe gose
  wynkith
Lytill wotith þe goslyng what þe gose
  thynkith

160

He is not wyse ageyne þe streme þt
  stryuith
Dun is in þe myre dame reche me my
  spur   *1400*
Nededes must he rin that the deuyll dryu-
  it
When the stede is stolyn spar the stable
  dur
A ientyll hownde shulde neuer play the
  kur
It is sone aspyd where the thorne prik-
  kith
And wele wotith the cat whos berde she
  likkith   *1405*

161

With marione clarione sol lucerne
Graund iuir: of this frenshe prouerbe
   olde
How men were wonte for to discerne
By candelmas day what wedder shuld
   holde
But marione clarione was caught wt a
   colde colde   *1410*
      [anglice a cokwolde]
& all ouercast wt cloudis vnky*n*de
This goodly flowre wt stormis was vntwynde

162

This ieloffer ientyll / this rose this lylly
   flowre
This prime rose pereles / this propre
   vyolet
This delycate dasy / this strawberry
   pretely set   *1415*
This columbyne clere and fresshest of
   coloure
Wt frowarde frostis alas was all to fret
But who may haue a more vngracyous
   lyfe
Than a chyldis birde and a knauis wyfe
      Thynke what ye wyll   *1420*
      Of this wanton byll
      By mary gipcy
      Quod scripsi scripsi
      Uxor tua sicut vitis
      Habetis in custodiam   *1425*
      Custodite sicut scitis
      Secundum lucam .&c.

163

Of the bone homs of a shrige besyde
   barkamstede
That goodly place to Skelton moost kynde
Where the sank royall is crystes blode so
   rede   *1430*
Where vpon he metrefyde after his
   mynde
A plesaunter place than a shrige is harde
   where to fynde
As Skelton rehersith with wordes few
   and playne
In his distincyon made on verses twaine

Fraxinus in cliuo : fro*n*detqu*e* viret sine
   riuo
Non est sub diuo : similis sine flumine
   viuo.

1411. Bracketed words from Faukes; not in Marshe.

164

The nacyoun of folys he left not be-
   hynde   *1435*
Item apollo that whirllid vp his chare
That made sum to s(n)urt and snuf in
   the wynde
It made them to skip to stampe and to
   stare
Whiche if they be happy haue cause to
   beware
In rymyng and raylyng with hym for to
   mell   *1440*
For drede that he lerne them there A.
   B. C. to spell

165

Poeta Skelton

With that I stode vp halfe sodenly a
   frayd
Suppleyng to fame I besought her grace
And þt it wolde please her full tenderly
   I prayd
Owt of her bokis apollo to rase   *1445*
Nay sir she sayd : what so in this place
Of our noble courte is ones spoken owte
It must nedes after rin all the worlde
   a boute

166

God wote theis wordes made me full sad
And when that I sawe it wolde no better
   be   *1450*
But that my peticyon wolde not be had
What shulde I do but take it in gre
For by iuppiter and his high mageste
I did what I cowde to scrape out the
   scrollis
Apollo to rase out of her ragman rol-
   lis   *1455*

167

Now here of it erkith me lenger to
   wryte
To occupacyon I wyll agayne resorte
Whiche rede on still as it cam to her
   syght
Rendrynge my deuisis I made in des-
   porte
Of the mayden of Kent callid coun-
   forte   *1460*
Of louers testamentis and of there wan-
   ton wyllis
And how iollas louyd goodly phillis

168

Diodorus Siculus of my translacyon
Out of fresshe latine in to oure englisshe
   playne

Recountyng commoditis of many a
   straunge nacyon   *1465*
Who redyth it ones wolde rede it agayne
Sex volumis engrosid to gether it doth
   containe
But when of the laurell she made rehersall
All orators and poetis wt other grete
   and smale

169

A thowsande thowsande I trow to my
   dome   *1470*
Triumpha triumpha they cryid all aboute
Of trumpettis and clariouns the noyse
   went to rome
The starry heuyn me thought shoke wt
   the showte
The grownde gronid & tremblid þe noyse
   was so stowte
The quene of fame commaundid shett
   fast þe boke   *1475*
And ther with sodenly out of my dreme
   I woke

170

My mynde of the grete din was somdele
   amasid
I wypid myne eyne for to make them
   clere
Then to the heuyn sperycall vpwarde I
   gasid
Where I saw Janus wt his double
   chere   *1480*
Makynge his almanak for the new yere
He turnyd his tirikkis his voluell ran fast
Good luck this new yere the olde yere is
   past
   Mens tibi sit consulta petis: sic con-
   sule menti
   Emula sis iani retro speculetur et ante
Skeltonis alloquium Librum suum.
Ite britannorum lux : O radiosa britan-
num
Carmina nostra pium vestrum celebrate
   catullum.
      Dicite Skeltonis
      Vester adonis erat.
      Dicite Skeltonis
      Vester Homerus erat.
Barbara cum lacio pariter iam currite
   versu.
Et licet est verbo pars maxima texta
   britanno.
      Non magis incompta:
      Nostra thalya patet.
      Est magis inculta:
      Nec mea caliope.

Nec vos peniteat liuoris tela subire.
Nec vobis peniteat rabiem tolerare cani-
nam.
      Nam Maro dissimiles
      Non tulit ille minas.
      Immunis nec enim
      Musa nasonis erat.

Lenuoy

Go litil quaire
Demene you faire   *1485*
Take no dispare
Though I you wrate
After this rate.
In englysshe letter
So moche the better   *1490*
Welcome shall ye
To sum men be
For latin warkis
Be good for clerkis
Yet now and then   *1495*
Sum Latin men
May happely loke
Upon your boke
And so procede
In you to rede   *1500*
That so in dede
Your fame may sprede
In length and brede
But then I drede
Ye shall haue nede   *1505*
You for to spede
To harnnes bryght
By force of myght
Ageyne enuy
And obloquy   *1510*
And wote ye why
Not for to fyght
Ageyne dispyght
Nor to derayne
Batayle agayne   *1515*
Scornfull disdayne
Not for to chyde
Not for to hyde
You cowardly
But curteisly   *1520*
That I haue pende
For to deffend
Under the banner
Of all good maner
Under proteccyon   *1525*
Of sad correccyon
With toleracyon
And supportacyon
Of reformacyon

If they can spy   *1530*
Circumspectly
Any worde defacid
That myght be rasid
Els ye shall pray
Them that ye may   *1535*
Contynew still
With there good wyll
Admonet Skeltonis: omnes / arbores
Dare locum viridi lauro / Iuxta genus
    suum
           Fraxinus in siluis: altis
           In montibus Orni.
           Populus in fluuiis Abies
           Patulissima Fagus.
Lenta Salix platanus pinguis ficulnea
    ficus
Glandifera et Quercus / pirus / esculus
    ardua pinus.

Balsamus exudans; oleaster / oliua min-
    erue
Iunipirus Buxus: lentiscus cuspide lenta.
Botrigera & domino vitis gratissima
    Baccho
Ilex & sterilis / labrusta per rosa colonis
Mollibus exudans fragrancia thura Sa-
    beis
Thus: redolens arabis pariter notissima
    mirrha
Et vos o corili fragiles: Humilesque
    mirice.
Et vos o Cedri redolentes vos quoque
    mirti.
Arboris omne genus viridi concedite
    Lauro.

Prenness En gre

GEORGE CAVENDISH: METRICAL VISIONS

The author of a prose narrative of Cardinal Wolsey's closing years, written evidently by one closely connected with Wolsey, was long supposed to be Sir William Cavendish. Early biographical and genealogical compilations such, e.g., as the Biographia Britannica of 1741-66, mentioned the fact that the work had sometimes been attributed to Sir William's elder brother George, but rejected the possibility. In 1814, however, an essay by Joseph Hunter established the author as George Cavendish, gentleman-usher to the Cardinal. This essay is reprinted by Singer, as below, in his edition of the biography.

George Cavendish, born about 1500, died 1561 or 1562, became connected with the Cardinal's household in 1526 or 1527, and remained with his lord until Wolsey's death in 1530. He lived thereafter a quiet country life, although his younger brother William rose to title and fortune; the memoir of Wolsey was the work of these years, and is almost our first piece of separate biography in English, preceded only by More's (unfinished) life of Richard the Third. The work had an extensive circulation in manuscript among the generation just following the Cardinal's death, but was not published until 1641, doubtless because of the author's frank comments on Tudor royalty. Some fifteen or more manuscripts of it exist; one of these, believed to be in Cavendish's own hand, contains also a set of poems, death-laments by Wolsey, by Anne Boleyn and her fellow-sufferers, by King Henry, by Surrey, and many others. These poems are in the same script as is the prose Life of the same volume, and the comments which follow each lament are headed "Lauctour G. C." Their first (and only) editor, Singer, had no hesitation in ascribing these "Metrical Visions" to George Cavendish also.

Not only in plan but in execution the poems show the influence of Lydgate's Fall of Princes; and we may remark that an edition of that work had appeared in 1554, the next earlier print being in 1527. There is the same defile of the mourning figures past the author, the same comment of the author upon each figure; there is the same emphasis on the fickleness of Fortune, who is called "gery fortune furious and wood", as by Lydgate in book iii, line 2405; there are occasional attempts at the use of refrain in the author's comment or envoy, as Lydgate had used it; there is obvious borrowing in Cavendish's lines 167-8 (see note here); and Cavendish's lines 246-252 are lifted bodily from Fall of Princes iii :3760 ff.

It is very improbable that Cavendish's verse exerted any influence on the Mirror for Magistrates, which was coming into existence just as Cavendish finished his Visions. The tragedy of Wolsey, by Thomas Churchyard, which is included in the Mirror, owes nothing to the living, if awkward, stanzas by Cavendish put into Wolsey's mouth. Nor does the later poem of Storer show any trace of Cavendish's verse. Thomas Storer published in 1599 The Life and Death of Thomas Wolsey Cardinall—etc.; and this was reprinted Oxford, 1826, and included in Part ii of Park's Heliconia, 1815. Storer's poem is of 241 stanzas rime royal, and is divided into three parts, Wolsey Aspirans, Wolsey Triumphans, Wolsey Moriens. It has a few passages of interest, especially in the regret of Wolsey at losing Henry's friendship; "I am the tombe where that affection lies", and its following lines, have an Elizabethan ring.

But neither Storer, nor Churchyard, nor Cavendish in his verse has any touch to bear comparison with the closing sentences of Cavendish's own prose. His "Visions" are clumsy and stilted, loaded with rhetoric and fettered by formulae; they have indeed their verities, but it is only when we turn to the prose life of Wolsey that a human voice speaks simply and freely. There every page has its interest, every page is candid; but the close is worthy of Bunyan. Cavendish has been summoned, after the Cardinal's death, to report to King Henry; and the Duke of Norfolk, acting as the king's intermediary, concludes the business with Cavendish. "He showed me," says Cavendish, "how the king was my good and gracious lord, and had given me six of the best horses that I could choose amongst all my lord's cart horses, with a cart to carry my stuff, and five marks for my cost homewards, and hath commanded me ten pounds for my wages being behind unpaid and twenty pounds for a reward.——And he willed me to meet with him the next day at London; and there to receive both my money, my stuff, and horses that the king gave me; and so I did; of whom I received all things according, and then I returned into my country."

The manuscript from which I print, Egerton 2402 of the British Museum, contains only Cavendish's life of Wolsey and the appended poems, here unique. The "Metrical Visions", as their first editor Singer entitled them, are separately paged, 1 to 58, and their leaves are confused in binding, as has been noted on the lower margins already by a ?Stuart hand. The page-order should be:—1-20, 35, 36, 41-54, 37-40, 21-34, 55-58. That is, the manuscript being in sixes and in fours, the bunch 21-34, composed of one six and two fours, was exchanged for the similarly-composed bunch 41-54, the latter being thrust in between the first and second leaves of the gathering 35-40. The Life and the Visions are in the same hand, a somewhat crabbed script said by Singer to be that of Cavendish himself; facsimiles of it are included in Singer's 1825 edition, to face page xvii of vol. i. The scribe of the poems made frequent alterations as he wrote, inserting words with a caret, deleting, rewriting. It would seem that Cavendish closed off and then continued his work from time to time; for twice at least in the long series of lamenting personages a "Finis" has been put, and then more material, of later date, added. After mourning, in his own person, the death of Edward VI, Cavendish welcomes the accession of Mary, whom he describes as a maiden queen; but the final poem of the series bewails Mary's death, and mentions her successor Elizabeth. Yet the colophon which follows upon this and upon the author's farewell address to his book runs:—"Finie et compile le xxiiij jour de Junij anno regnorum Philippi Rex et Reg. Mariae iiijti & vti. Per le auctor G. C." Below which, and apparently later, appears "Novus Rex Nova Lex Nova sola Regina proborum pene ruina",— such a comment as a devout Catholic might permit himself to his private journal on the Protestant Elizabeth's accession. Considering the disorder of leaves, we may query if Cavendish himself separated them in order to force in the Epitaph of Queen Mary, after he had written his Philip and Mary colophon. For although the date of that colophon is 1558, the fourth year of Philip and fifth of Mary, yet Mary died in November 1558, five months after the June date which Cavendish there gives.

The first edition of the life of Wolsey and the poems, from the authoritative "autograph" manuscript, was by Samuel Weller Singer, London, 1825, two vols. Singer's text is in the main correct, although he "slightly" modernized the orthography. He omits occasionally in our parts of the poem, as noted lines 38, 1119, and line 1368 entire; he inserts in 272, 1193, epilogue 39; in 1182, 1400 by error, and epilogue 8, he alters. He appended much valuable illustrative material. In his second edition, London, 1827, one vol., the poems were cut to little more than Wolsey's own lament. Other editors of the Life have passed the poems unmentioned.

Singer's 1827 text of the Life was reprinted by Henry Morley in his Universal Library, London, 1885, again 1887, accompanied by Churchyard's Wolsey-stanzas from A Mirror for Magistrates, but not by the Visions or by any allusion to them. Morley's error of "1815" instead of "1825" in describing Singer's first edition has been copied by later editors and even by the Dict. Nat. Biog.

The Life of Wolsey was edited by F. S. Ellis for the Kelmscott Press in 1893, from the "autograph" MS but with no mention of the Visions. Ellis' text, the spelling modernized, was printed in the Temple Classics, 1893, with Churchyard's poem, but with no mention of the Visions. Singer's text was reprinted Boston, 1905, with Ellis' corrections; no mention of the Visions.

In the Letters of Royal and Illustrious Ladies of Great Britain, ed. Mary A. E. Wood, 3 vols., London, 1846, Cavendish's stanzas on the Countess of Salisbury and on Lady Jane Grey are printed in the Notes, iii:94-5 and 273-4, from Singer.

Previous to Singer the memoir had been published in 1641, in a garbled form, as "The Negotiations of Thomas Wolsey the Great Cardinal" etc. This was reprinted 1667, 1706, and in the Harleian Miscellany, 1744-46 and later. It was also included in Joseph Grove's history of the life and times of Cardinal Wolsey, London, 1742-44, four vols. Grove, who reproduced the 1641 text, is said by Singer to have later discovered its unsoundness, and to have issued privately, in 1761, a few copies from manuscript.

The Life was printed in vol. 1 of Christopher Wordsworth's Ecclesiastical Biography, 1818 and later, from four MSS, not including the "autograph" text; Wordsworth therefore knows nothing of the poems. The text of his fourth edition was reprinted by J. Holmes, London, 1852, and a "slightly altered" text by "E. H.", London, 1855.

In 1901 the Life was reprinted in London by Grace H. M. Simpson, from the 1667 text. She asserts that this is the earliest, and that the author was William Cavendish; she refers to the Biographia Britannica.

[MS Brit. Mus. Egerton 2402]

Prolougus de lauctor G. C.
In the monyth of June / I lyeng sole alon
Vnder the vmber of an Oke / wt bowes
  pendaunt
Whan Phebus in Gemynys / had his
  course ouergoon

Corrections are made by the scribe, viz.:—1, *of* is inserted with a caret; similarly *mean* in 5, *in* in 6, *all* in 22. Singer in 13 reads *gystes,* which he explains as "gests, actions"; he reads *devysing* in 18; he alters *lion* to *Leo* in 6; and he omits the third *of* in 7 and *this* in 20. In 25 he reads *spent.*

And entred Cancer / a sygne retrogradaunt
In a mean measure / his beames rady-
  aunt   5
Approchyng lion / than mused I in
  mynd
Of ffikkellnes of ffortune / and of the
  course of kynd

2

Howe some are by fortune / exalted to
  riches

And often suche / as most vnworthy be
And some opp*ressed* / in langor and
   syknes /   *10*
Some waylyng lakkyng welthe / by
   wretched po*ue*rtie
Some in bayle & bondage / and some at
   libertie
Wt other moo gyftes / of ffortune
   varyable
Some pleas*au*nt / some mean / and some
   onp*ro*fitable

3

But after dewe serche / and better ad-
   viseme*nt*   *15*
I knewe by reason / that oonly god
   above
Rewlithe thos thyng*es* / as is most convenyent
The same devydyng / to man for his behove
Wherfore dame reason / did me p*er*-
   swade & move /
To be content / wt this *m*y small estat   *20*
And in this matter no more to vestigate /

4

Whan I had debated / all thyng in my
   mynd
I well considered / myn obscure blynd-
   nes
So that non excuse could I se or fynd
But that my tyme / I spend in Idelnes *25*
ffor this me thought / and trew it is
   doughtles
That sence I ame a reasonable creature
I owght my reason & wyt to put in vre /

5

Than of what matter / myght I devise
   & wright
To vse my tyme / and wytte to exercyse   *30*
Sythe most men haue / no pleas*u*re or
   delight
In any history / wtout it sownd to
   vice /
Alas shold I than / that ame not yong
   attise
Wt lewed ballat*es* faynt hart*es* to synne
Or flatter estat*es* / some fauo*ur* of them
   to wynne /   *35*

6

What than shall I wright / the noble
   doughtynes

Of estat*es* / that vsed is nowe a dayes
I shall than lake just matter / for gredy
   couetousnes
Of vayn ryches / w*hi*ch hathe stopt all
   the wayes
Of worthy Chyvallry / that now dayly
   sore dekayes   *40*
And yet thoughe some behaue them nobly
Yet many ther be / that dayly dothe the
   contrarye

7

ffor some lovyth meate fynne & delicious
And some baudye brothes / as ther edu-
   casion hathe be
So some lovethe v*er*tue / and some tales
   vicious   *45*
Sewerly suche tales / gett ye non of me
But to eschewe all Oci*o*site
Of ffortunes fykellnes / here after shall
   I wright
Howe greatest estat*es* / she ou*er*throwyth
   by myght

8

Thoughe I onworthe this tragedy do begyne   *50*
Of pardon I pray / the reders in meke
   wyse
And to correct / where they se fault
   therin
Reputyng it for lake / of connyng excercyse
The cause that moved me / to this enter-
   price
Specyally was / that all estat*es* myght
   se   *55*
What it is to trust to ffortunes mutabyl-
   ite

9

Wt pen & ynke I toke this worke in
   hand
Redy to wright the deadly dole / & whofull playnt
Of them whos fall the world dothe vnderstand
W*hi*ch for feare made my hart to
   faynt /   *60*
I must wright playn / colo*ur*s haue I
   none to paynt
But termes rude / ther dolo*ur*s to compile
An wofull playnt must haue an wofull
   style

---

41. *Some* inserted by scribe with a caret, as is
   dothe in 42.

10

To whome therfore / for helpe shall I
  nowe call
Alas Caliope my callyng wyll vtterly refuse /   65
ffor mornyng dities / and woo of for-
  tunes falle
Caliope dyd neue*r* / in hir dyties vse
Wherfore to hir I myght my selfe abuse
Also the musis that on Parnasus syng
Suche warblyng dole / did neue*r* tempor
  stryng   70

11

Nowe to that lord / whos power is
  celestiall
And gwydyth all thyng of sadnes and
  of blysse
Wt humble voyce / to the I crie & call
That thou woldest direct / my sely pen
  in this
ffor wantyng of thy helpe / no ma*r*vell
  thoughe I mysse   75
And by thy grace / thoughe my style be
  rude
In sentence playn / I may full well conclude

12

Nowe by thy helpe / this history I wyll
  begyn
And ffrome theffect varie nothyng at all
ffor if I shold / it ware to me great
  synne   80
To take vppon me a matter so substan-
  cyall
So waytie so necessarie of ffame pe*r*-
  petuall
And thus to be short / oon began to
  speke /
Wt deadly voyce / as thoughe his hart
  wold breke /

ffinis Quod G. C.
Le Historye Cardinalis Eboracensis

13

O ffortune / q*u*od he / shold I on the
  complayn   85
Or of my necligence that I susteyn this
  smart
Thy doble visage hathe led me to this
  trayn
ffor at my begynnyng / thow dydest ay
  take my part
Vntill ambysion had puffed vppe my hart

Wt vaynglory . honor . and vsurped dignyte   90
fforgettyng cleane my naturall mendycitie

14

ffrom poue*r*tie to plentie w*hi*che nowe I
  se is vayn
A cardynall I was and legate de latere
A bysshope & archebysshope / the more
  to crease my gayn
Chauncelor of Englond / fortune by hir
  false flatere   95
Dyd me ava*u*nce / and gave me suche
  auctorytie
That of hyghe & lowe I toke on me the
  charge
All Englond to rewle / my power extendyd large

15

Whan ffortune wt fauo*u*r had sett me
  thus alofte
I gathered me riches / suffisa*u*nce cowld
  not content   100
My fare was supe*r*fluo*u*s / my bed was
  fynne & softe
To haue my desiers / I past not what I
  spent
In yerthe suche abounda*u*nce / ffortune
  had me lent
Yt was not in the world / that I cowld
  well requyer
But fortune strayt wayes / dyd graunt
  me my desier   105

16

My byldyng*es* somptio*u*s / the roffes w.
  gold & byse
Shone lyke the sone / in the myd day
  spere
Craftely entayled / as connyng cowld
  devyse
Wt imag*es* embossed / most lyvely did
  appere
Expertest artificers / that ware bothe
  farre & nere   110
To beatyfie my howssys / I had them at
  my wyll
Thus I wanted nought / my pleas*u*rs to
  fullfyll /

17

My Galleryes ware fayer / bothe large &
  long
To walke in theme / whan that it lyked
  me best
My gardens swett / enclosed wt walles
  strong   115

Enbanked wt benches / to sytt & take my
rest
The knott*es* so enknotted / it cannot be
expr*est*
Wt arbors and alyes / so pleas*a*unt &
so dulce
The pestylent ayers / wt flauours to repulse

18

My chambers garnysht / wt aras fynne
Importyng p*er*sonag*es* / of the lyvelyest
kynd   *121*
And whan I was disposed / in them to
dynne
My clothe of estate / there redy did I
fynd
ffurnysshed complett accordyng to my
mynd
The subtill p*er*fumes / of muske and
swett amber   *125*
There wanted non / to p*er*fume all my
chamber

19

Plate of all sort*es* / most curiously
wrought
Of facions newe / I past not of the old
No vessell but sylu*er* byfore me was
brought
ffull of dayntes vyaund*es* / the some cannot be told   *130*
I dranke my wynne alwayes in sylu*er* &
in gold
And dayly to s*er*ue me / attendyng on
my table
Seru*au*ntes I had / bothe worsh(i)pfull
& honorable

20

My crossis twayn / of silu*er* long &
greate
That dayly byfore me / ware caried
hyghe   *135*
Vppon great horses / opynly in the strett
And massie pillers / gloryouse to the eye
Wt pollaxes gylt / that no man durst
come nyghe
My presence / I was so pryncely to be-
hold
Ridyng on my mule / trapped in silu*er*
& in gold   *140*

21

My legantyn pr*er*ogatyve / was myche to
myn avayle

---

136. The scribe inserts *the* with a caret; so the
second *in* of 140.

By v*er*tue wherof / I had thys highe pr*e*-
emynence
All vacant benefic*es* / I dyd them strayt
retaylle
Presentyng than my clarke / asson as I
had intellygence
I pr*e*ventid the patron / ther vaylled no
resistence   *145*
All bysshoppes and pr*e*latt*es* / durst not
oons denay
They doughtyd so my power / they
myght not dysobey

22

Thus may yow se / howe I to riches
did attayne
And wt suffisaunce / my mynde was
not content
Whan I had most / I rathest wold com-
playn   *150*
ffor lake of good / alas howe I was
blent
Where shall my gatheryng / and good be
spent
Som*m*e oon p*er*chaunce / shall me therof
discharge /
Whome I most hate / and spend it owt at
large

23

Syttyng in Jugement / p*ar*cyall ware my
domes   *155*
I spared non estate / of hyghe or lowe
degree
I preferred whome me lyst / exaltyng
symple gromes
Above the nobles / I spared myche the
sp*iritu*altie
Not passyng myche / on the temperaltie
Promotyng suche / to so hyghe es-
tate   *160*
As vnto prync*es* / wold boldly say chek
mate /

24

Oon to subdewe / that did me allwayes
fauour
And in that place an other to au*au*nce
Ayenst all trewthe / I did my besy labor
And whilest I was workyng / witty
whiles in fraunce   *165*
I was at home supplanted / where I
thought most assur*au*nce
Thus who by fraud / ffraudelent is found
ffraude to the defrauder / wyll aye re-
bound

25

Who workyth fraude / often is disceyved
As in a myrror / ye may beholde in
me　　　　　　　　　　　　　　*170*
ffor by disceyt / or I had it perceyved
I was dissayved / a guerdon met parde
ffor hyme that wold / ayenst all equyte
Dysseyve the innocent / that innocent
was in deade
Therfore justice of justice / ayenst me
must procede　　　　　　　　*175*

26

ffor bye my subtill dealyng / thus it came
to passe
Cheafely disdayned / ffor whome I toke
the payn
And than to repent / it was to late alas
My purpose I wold than haue chaynged
fayn
But it wold not be / I was perceyved
playn　　　　　　　　　　　*180*
Thus venus the goddesse / that called is
of love
Spared not wt spight / to bryng me
frome above /

27

Alas my souerayn lord / thou didest me
avaunce
And settest me vppe in thys great pompe
& pryde
And gayest to me thy realme in gouern-
aunce　　　　　　　　　　*185*
Thy pryncely will / why did I sett a
side
And folowed myn owen / consideryng
not the tyde
Howe after a floode / (an) ebbe com-
mythe on a pace
That to consider / in my tryhumphe /
I lakked grace /

28

Nowe fykkell fortune / torned hathe hir
whele　　　　　　　　　　*190*
Or I it wyst all sodenly / and down she
dyd me cast
Down was my hed / and vpward went
my heele
My hold faylled me / that I thought suer
& fast
I se by experyence / hir fauour dothe
not last
ffor she full lowe nowe hathe brought
me vnder　　　　　　　　　*195*

188. MS reads *and ebbe.*

Thoughe I on hir complayn alas it is no
wonder

29

I lost myn honour my treasure was me
berafte
ffayn to avoyd / and quykly to geve
place
Symply to depart for me no thyng was
lafte
Wtout penny or pound / I lyved a certyn
space /　　　　　　　　　*200*
Vntill my souerayn lord / extendyd to
me hys grace
Who restored me sufficient / if I had
byn content
To maynteyn myn estate / bothe of lond
& rent

30

Yet notwtstandyng / my corage was so
hault
Dispight of myn ennemyes / rubbed me
on the gall　　　　　　　　*205*
Who conspired together / to take me wt
asault
They travelled wtout triall to geve me
a fall
I therfore entendyd / to trie my frendes
all
To forrayn potentates wrott my letters
playn
Desireng ther ayd / to restore me to
fauour agayn　　　　　　　*210*

31

Myn ennemyes perceyvyng / caught therof dysdayn
Doughtyng the daynger / dreamed on the
dought
In councell consultyng / my sewte to
restrayn
Accused me of treason / and brought it
so abought
That travellyng to my triall / or I could
trie it owte　　　　　　　　*215*
Deathe wt his dart / strake me for the
nons
In Leycester full lowe / where nowe
lyethe my boons

32

Loo nowe may you se / what it is to
trust
In wordly vanytes / that voydyth wt the
wynd

The scribe has inserted, with a caret, *it* in 214,
nowe in 217.

ffor deathe in a moment / consumyth all
  to dust   *220*
No honor . no glory / that euer man
  cowld fynd
But tyme wt hys tyme / puttythe all owt
  of mynd
ffor tyme in breafe tyme / duskyth the
  hystory
Of them that long tyme / lyved in glory

33

Where is my Tombe / that I made for
  the nons   *225*
Wrought of ffynne Cooper / that cost
  many a pound
To couche in my Carion / and my rotten
  boons
All is but vaynglory / nowe haue I
  found
And small to the purpose / whan I ame
  in the ground
What dothe it avaylle me / all that I
  haue   *230*
Seyng I ame deade / & layed in my
  grave /

34

ffare well Hampton Court / whos ffound-
  er I was
ffarewell Westmynster place / nowe a
  palace royall
ffarewell the Moore / lett Tynnynainger
  passe
ffarewell in Oxford / my Colege Cardynall   *235*
ffarewell in Jpsewich / my Scole gramat-
  icall
Yit oons ffarewell I say / I shall you
  neuer se
Your somptious byldyng / what nowe
  avayllethe me

35

What avayllyth / my great aboundaunce
What is nowe laft / to helpe me in thys
  case   *240*
Nothyng at all / but dompe in the
  daunce /
Among deade men / to tryppe on the
  trace /
And for my gay housis / nowe haue I
  this place
To lay in my karcas / wrapt in a shette
Knytt wt a knott / att my hed and my
  feete   *245*

36

What avaylleth / nowe my ffetherbeddes
  soft
Shettes of raynes / long large & wyde
And dyuers devysis / of clothes. chaynged
  oft
Or vicious chapleyns / walkyng by my
  syd
Voyde of all vertue / fulfilled wt pryde
Whiche hathe caused me / by report of
  suche fame /   *251*
ffor ther myslyvyng / to haue an yll
  name /

37

This is my last complaynt / I can say you
  no moore
But farewell my seruaunt / that faythe-
  full hathe be
Note well thes wordes / quod he / I
  pray the therfore   *255*
And wright them thus playn / as I haue
  told them the
All which is trewe / thou knowest it
  well parde
Thou faylledest me not / vntill that I
  dyed
And nowe I must depart / I may no
  lenger byde /

ffinis
Thauctor G. C.

38

Whan he his tale had told / thus in
  sentence   *260*
His dolorous playnt / strake me to the
  hart
Pytie also moved me / to bewayll his
  offence
And wt hyme to wepe / whan I did
  aduert
In his aduersyte / howe I did not departe
Tyll mortall deathe / had gevyn hyme
  his wou(n)d   *265*
Wt whome I was present / and layed
  hyme in the ground

39

Whan I had wept / and lamentyd my
  ffyll
Wt reason perswaded / to hold me content
I aspied certyn persons / commyng me
  tyll
Strayngely disguysed / that grettly did
  lament   *270*

And as me semed / this was ther entent
On ffortune to complayn / ther cause not
　　slender
And me to requyer ther ffall to re-
　　member

*　　*　　*　　*　　*　　*

The Erle of Surrey

158

What avauntage had I to be a dukes
　　heyr　　　　　　　　　　　　*1105*
Endowed wt suche qualities / as fewe in
　　my tyme
Lakkyng no thyng / that nature myght
　　repayr
In dewe proporcyon / she wrought hathe
　　euery lyne
Assendyng ffortunes whele / made lyke
　　to clyme
Syttyng in myn abode / supposyng to
　　sitt fast　　　　　　　　　　*1110*
Wt a sodeyn tourne she made me dissend
　　as fast

159

Whoo trustith in honor / and settythe
　　all hys lust
In wordly riches / hauyng of theme
　　aboundaunce
Lett hyme beware / and take good hede
　　he must
Of subtill ffortune / wt dissemblyng
　　countenaunce　　　　　　　　*1115*
ffor whan she smylyth / than hathe she
　　least assuraunce
ffor the fflatteryng world / dothe often
　　them begyle
With suche vayn vanyties / alas / alas /
　　the whyle /

160

I haue not only / my self nowe ouer-
　　throwen
But also my ffather / wt heares old &
　　hoore　　　　　　　　　　　*1120*
Allthoughe his actes marsheall be right
　　welle knowen
Yet was myn offence / taken so passyng
　　sore
That I nedes must dye / and he in prison
　　for euermore
Shall still remayn / ffor it wyll not
　　avaylle

1111. MS crosses out *she.*
1116. *She* is inserted with caret before *least.*

All his great conquestes / wherin he did
　　prevayle /　　　　　　　　　*1125*
161
O Julyus Cesar / O thou myghty con-
　　queror
What myght thy conquestes & all thy
　　victorye
The prevayle / that of Rome was Em-
　　peroure
Whos prowes yet remaynyth / in mem-
　　orye
Whan Brewtus Casseus / wt ffalce con-
　　spyracye　　　　　　　　　　*1130*
Ayenst the in the Capitoll / did contend
Than all thy worthynes / could the not
　　defend
162
Also Scipio of Affrican / that for the
　　co(m)en wele
Of Rome the Empier / the Citie beyng
　　in distresse
Lykly to be subdewd / than euery dele
By Anyballes / valyaunt hardynes *1136*
And dyuers noble victoryes as the his-
　　tory dothe expresse
That he atchyved / to the honor of the
　　town
Cowld not hyme prevaylle / whan ffor-
　　tune lyst to frown

163
Thes myghty Champions / thes valyaunt
　　men　　　　　　　　　　　　*1140*
Who for the publyke whele / travelled
　　all theyr lyfe
Regarded not ther ease / nowther where
　　or when
But most valyauntly / wt corage inten-
　　tyfe
Defendyd the wele publyke / ffrome all
　　myschyfe
Yet was ther nobles / put in oblyvion
And by matters conspired / brought to
　　confusion　　　　　　　　　*1146*
164
Loo the reward alas that men shall haue
ffor all ther travelles in ther dayes old
Wt small spot / ther honor to deprave
Alas it causithe full often / mens hartes
　　to be cold　　　　　　　　　*1150*
Whan suche chaunces / they do behold
How for oon offence / a thousaund con-
　　questes valyaunte
Can haue no place ther lyves make war-
　　raunt

165

Therfore noble ffather / hold your self
  content
And wt your Captyfe lyve / be ye no
  thyng dysmayd   1155
ffor you may se / in historys playn &
  evydent
That many noble persons / as ye are
  hathe byn dekayed
The chaunce therfore of ffortune / nedes
  must be obeyed /
And perpetuall prisonment / here shalbe
  your Gwerdon
And dethe for my desertes / wtout remyse & pardon   1160

166

ffor all my knowlege / wysdome & science
That god hathe me endowed / all other
  to precell
Gave me here / but small preemynence /
All thoughe some ware aduaunced in the
  comen wele /
ffrome basse estate / as experience
  dothe tell   1165
ffor suche vertues / as vices in me ac-
  compted were
Caused me to be doughted / and in great
  feare /

167

That thyng which in some / deseruyth
  commendacion
And hyghly to be praysed / as verteus
  commendable
Beyng estemed therfore / worthy exalta-
  cion   1170
And to be auaunced / to dygnyties honorable
I assure yow ware to me / nothyng prof-
  etable
ffor suche some tyme / as are but vayn
  and idell
Disdaynythe all them / that owght to
  rewle the bridell

168

Therfor ffarewell / my peers / of the
  noble sect   1175
Desiryng you all / my fall for to be hold
Lett it a myrror be / that ye be not
  enfecte
Wt ffolyshe wytte / wherof be not to
  bold
My warnyng to yow / is more worthe
  than gold

An old prouerbe there is / which trewe
  is at thys day   1180
The warned is halfe armed / thus I
  hard men saye /

169

I thought of no suche chaunce / as nowe
  to me is chaunced
I trusted so my wytt / my power & myn
  estate
Thynkyng more rather / highly to be
  auaunced
Than to be deposed / as I haue byn but
  late /   1185
Be it right or wrong / loo I haue lost my
  pate
Ye se thend / of many noble estates
Take a vowe of me / & of some your
  late mattes

170
Thauctor G. C.

Wt that he vanysshed / I wyst not
  whether
But a way he went / and I was left
  alone   1190
Whos wordes and talke I gathered them
  together
And in this sentence rewde / wrott them
  euerychone
Yet was my hart with sorowe full woo-
  begon
So noble a yong man / of wyt & excellence /
To be condempned / for so small offence   1195

[Three stanzas of Lenvoy de le auctor
follow, then:—]

174
Lauctor G. C.

Intendyng here to end / this my symple
  worke
And no further to wade / in this on-
  savery lake
My penne was fordulled / my wyttes began to lurke /
I sodenly trembled / as oon ware in a
  brake   1220
The cause I knewe not / that I shold
  tremble & shake
Vntill dame fame I hard / blowe hir
  trembleng trompe
Which woofull blaste brought me / in
  a soden dompe

175

Dame ffame I asked / why blowe ye your
   trom(p)e so shryll
In so deadly a sownd / ye make my hart
   full sorry   *1225*
She answered me agayn / and sayd /
   Sir so I wyll
Deade is that royall prynce / the late
   viijth Harry
Wherfor adewe / I may no lenger tarry
ffor thorowghe the world I must / to
   blowe this deadly blast
Alas thes woofull newes / made my hart
   agaste /   *1230*

176

I went my wayes / and drewe my self
   aside
Alon to lament the deathe of this royall
   kyng
Parceyvyng right well / deth wyll stope
   no tyde
Wt kyng or kaysier / therfore a wonder-
   ouse thyng
To se howe will in them dothe raygn
   makyng ther reconyng   *1235*
Euer to lyve / as thoughe deathe ware
   of them a feard
To byd them chekmate / & pluke them
   by the berd /

177

To ffynysshe thys worke / I did my self
   dispose
And to conclude the same / as ye byfore
   haue red
I leaned to my chayer / entendyng to repose   *1240*
In a slepie slomber I fille / so hevy was
   my hed
Morpheus to me appered / and sayd he
   wold me lede
My spyrittes to revyve / and my labor
   to degest
Wt whome ffantzy was redy / and stayed
   in my brest /

178

ffantzy by & bye / led me as I thought
To a palice royall / of pryncely Edy-
   fice   *1246*
Plentyfully furnysshed / of riches it
   lacked nought
Astonyed not a littill / of the wofull
   cries

1224. MS writes *shyrll.*
1240. Singer reads *on my chayer.*

Which I hard there / wt many wepyng
   eyes
Euer as we passed / frome place to
   place /   *1250*
I beheld many a pityfull bedropped face

179

So that at the last / to tell you playn &
   right
We entred a chamber / wt out light of
   the day
To whome wax candelles gave myche
   light
Wherin I parceyved a bed of royall ar-
   ray   *1255*
To the which I approced / makyng no de-
   lay /
Wherin a prynce lay syke / wt a deadly
   face
And cruell Attrophos standyng in that
   place /

180

Clotho / I aspied also / that in hyr hand
   did support
A distaffe wherof the stuffe / was well
   nyghe spent   *1260*
Which lacheses dothe spynne / as poetes
   dothe report
Drawyng the lyvely thred / tyll Attropos
   had hent
Hir sharped sheres / wt a full consent /
To shere the thred / supporter of hys
   lyfe
Ayenst whome ther botyth / no preroga-
   tyfe   *1265*

181

Attendyng on his person / was many a
   worthy grome
Where he lay syke / to whome syknes
   sayd chekmate /
All thoughe he ware a prynce / of highe
   renome
Yet syknes regardyd not hys Emperyall
   estate
Tyme approched / of his lyfe the fynall
   date /   *1270*
And Attrophos was prest / his lyves
   thred to devyde
Hold thy hand / quod he / and lett thy
   stroke abyde /

182

Henricus Rex loquetus ad mortem
Geve me leve Attrophos / my self for to
   lament

Spare me a lityll / for nature mak*es* me
    sewe
The ffleshe is frayle / and lothe for to
    relent   *1275*
ffor deathe wt lyfe cannot be shett in
    mewe
They be contrari*au*nt / there is no thyng
    more trewe
ffor lyfe ayenst dethe / allwayes dothe
    rebell
Eche man by experience / naturally this
    can tell /

183

ffrome Clothos distafe / my lyvely stuffe
    is spent   *1280*
W*h*iche Lachesis the slender thred hathe
    sponne
Of my lyfe Emperyall / and thou At-
    trophos hast hent
The sharped sheres / to shere my feble
    throme
That the warbeled spendell / no more
    abought shold ronne /
And of my regall lyfe / thus hast thou
    great disdayn   *1285*
So slender a thred / so long shold it
    susteyn

184

But leave of Attrophos / thou ned*es* not
    make suche hast
My symple lyfe / wt vigor to confound
Thy sheryng sheres / thou shalt but
    spend in wast
ffor the spyndell*es* end / alredy is at the
    ground   *1290*
The thred ontwynned cannot more be
    twound
Great folly in the / that tak*es* suche idell
    paynne
To slee that thyng / that is all redy
    slayn /

185

Wherfore leave of Attrophos / for end
    of lyfe is deathe
And deathe I se / is end of world*es*
    payn   *1295*
What shalt thou wyn than / to stope my
    faynted brethe
Sythe well thou knowest / whan that
    thou hast me slayn
To welle or woo I shall oons rise agayn
Thoughe in thy fury / my lyfe nowe thou
    devoure
To sle me agayn / it shall not lie in thy
    power   *1300*

186

Slee me not Attrophos but lete spyndell
    ronne
W*h*ich long hathe hanged / by a feoble
    lynne /
ffor whan Lachesis / hir fyned fflees
    hathe sponne
The spyndell woll fall / thou seest well
    wt thyn eyen
No stuffe is laft / agayn the thred*es* to
    twn   *1305*
So slender it is / that wt oon blast of
    wynd
The thred will breke / it is so slakley
    twynd

187

But nowe alas / that eu*er* it shold befall
So fam*ou*s a prynce / of ffame so notable
That ffame wt defame / shold the same
    appall   *1310*
Or cause my concyence / to be so on-
    stable
W*h*ich for to here / is wonderous lament-
    able
Howe for the love / and fond affeccion
Of a symple woman / to worke all by
    collusion

188

I brake the bond of mariage / and did
    my self inclyne   *1315*
To the love of oon in whome was all my
    felicitie
By means whereof / this realme is
    brought in rewyn
Yet notwtstandyng / I ned*es* wold ser*ue*
    my ffantzye
So that all my lust / in hir was ffyxt as-
    suredly
W*h*ich for to colo*ur* / I colored than my
    case   *1320*
Makyng newe lawes / the old I did de-
    face /

189

Wt coloure of concience / I colored my
    pretence
Entendyng therby / to sett my bond at
    lybertie
My lust*es* to frequent / and haue of them
    experience
Sekyng but my lust / of onlefull lech-
    erye   *1325*
Wherof the slaunder / remaynythe still
    in me
So that my wilfullnes / and my shamfull
    trespace

Dothe all my magestie / and noblenes deface

190

Whan Venus veneryall / of me had
domynacion
And blynd Cupydo / my purpose did
auaunce　　　　　　　　　　　　　*1330*
Than willfull lust / thoroughe Indiscres-
sion
Was chosyn Juge to hold my ballaunce
Of onlefull choyse / by whos onhappie
chaunce
Yt hathe darked my honour / spotted
fame & glory
Which causithe my concience / oft to be
full sory　　　　　　　　　　　　　*1335*

191

Alake therfore / greatly I ame ashamed
That thus the world / shold knowe my
pretence
Wherwt my magestie / is slaundred &
defamed
Thoroughe this poysoned / lecherous
offence
Which hathe constrayned / by mortall
violence　　　　　　　　　　　　　*1340*
So many to dye / my purpose to attayn
That nowe more grevous / suerly is my
payn /

192

Thoughe I ware myghty / and royall in
pieusaunce
Havyng all thyng / in myn owen demayn
Yet was my reason / vnder the obey-
saunce　　　　　　　　　　　　　*1345*
Of fflesshely lustes / fetered in Venus
chayn
ffor of my lust / will was my souerayn
My reason was bridelled / so by sen-
sualite
That wyll rewled all / wtout lawe &
equytie

193

After I forsoke / my first most lawfull
wyfe　　　　　　　　　　　　　　*1350*
And toke an other / my pleasure to full-
fill
I chaynged often / so inconstant was
my lyfe
Deathe was the meade / of some that
did non ill
Which oonly was / to satisfie my wyll
I was so desirous / of newe to haue my
lust　　　　　　　　　　　　　　*1355*

Yet could I fynd / non lyke vnto the
furst /

194

In excellent vertues and wyfely trouthe /
In pryncely prudence / and whomanly
port
Which ffloryshed in hir / evyn frome
hyr youthe
So well disposed / and of so sad a sort
To all men it was / no small comfort
And synce the tyme / that I did hir de-
vorse /
All Englond lamentithe / and hathe ther-
of remorse

195

Hir to commende & prayse / evyn at
the ffull
As she was worthy / it lyethe not in my
myght　　　　　　　　　　　　　*1365*
My wytt and connyng / is to grosse &
dull
Hir worthynes / in so rude a stile to
wright
ffor she may be compared / evyn of
very right
Vnto pacient Greseld / if euer there ware
any
ffor lyke hyr paciente / there hathe not
regned many :　　　　　　　　　*1370*

196

What inconvenyence / haue I nowe
brought to passe /
Thoroughe my wilfullnes / of willfull
necligence
Wtin thys realme / fare frome the welthe
it was
Yt nedes not therfore / to geve you intelligence
ffor you haue fillt the smart / and the
indygence /　　　　　　　　　　　*1375*
Wherfore to make / any ferther declara-
cion
Yt ware to me / but an idell occupacion /

197

ffor all my conquestes / and my royall
powers
My plesunt tryhumphes / and my bankettyng chere
My pryncely port / and my youthfull
powers　　　　　　　　　　　　　*1380*
My great liberalites / vnto my darlynges
dere
My Emperyall magestie / what ame I the
nere

ffor all my great aboundaunce / no
thyng can me defend
ffrome mortall dethe / all fleshe must
haue an end

198

Who had more Joyes / who had more
pleas*ure*   *1385*
Who had more riches / who had more
abondaunce
Who had more joyell*es* / who had more
treas*ure*
Who had more pastyme / who had more
dal*y*aunce
Who had more ayed / who had more
all*y*aunce
Who had more howsis / of pleas*ure* &
disport   *1390*
Who had suche plac*es* as I for my comfort

199

All thyng to reherce / wherin I toke
delight
A long tyme I assure you / wold not
suffice /
What avayllythe nowe / my power &
my myght
Synce I must dye / & shall no more
aryse   *1395*
To raygn in this world / nor seen wt
bodely eyes
But as a clott of claye / consume I must
to dust
Whome you haue seen / to raygn in
welthe & lust /

200

ffarewell my nobles / ffarewell my *pre-*
latt*es* pasturall
ffarwell my noble dames / ffarewell you
pieusell*es* fayer   *1400*
ffarewell my Citezens / ffarewell my
Com*ens* all /
ffarewell my howsses / where I was wont
repayer
ffarewell my gardens / ffarewell the
pleas*a*unt ayer
ffarewell the world / ffarewell eche creature
ffarewell my ffrend*es* / my lyfe may no
more endure /   *1405*

201

Adewe myn Impe / adewe my relyke
here
Adewe my sonne Edward / sprong of the
royall race /

Of the wight roose and the rede / as it
may well appere
Lord god I beseche the / to send hyme
of thy grace
Pr*o*sperously to raygne / and long to
enioy my place /   *1410*
To thy will & pleas*ure* and the co*m*en
welthe /
Justly here to gou*er*ne / in great Joy
& helthe /

202
Lauctor G. C.

Wt that I sawe his brethe / fast consume away
And lyfe also / allthoughe he ware a
kyng /
Whan deathe was come / ned*es* he must
obeye   *1415*
ffor dethe is indyfferent / to eche creature lyvyng
He sparithe none / all is to hyme oon
rykconyng /
All estates by deathe must end / there
is none other bootte
Loo here nowe I lie / q*uo*d he / vnder
nethe y*our* foote /

203

Makyng thus an end / of his most dolorous talke /   *1420*
I strayt awoke / owt of my sobbyng
slomber
Morpheus than forsoke me / and forthe
began to walke
But ffantzy wt me abode / who did me
myche encomber
Puttyng me in remembra*u*nce / of the
lamentable nomber
W*hi*ch in my slepe I sawe / wt eu*er*y
circu*m*stance /   *1425*
Yt was no small greave / to my dull
remembra*u*nce /

204

And whan I degested / eche thyng as it
was
I cowld but lament / in my faythfull
hart
To se the want / of *our* wonted solas
Wt whome I ned*es* must take suche
equall part   *1430*
And than to my remembra*u*nce / I dyd
agayn reu*er*t
Recountyng his noblenes / shortly to conclude

Wrott than thus his Epitaphe / in sentence brefe & rude /

Epytaphe
Victoryously didest rayn /
The viiijth Herrye
Worthy most souerayn
Tenthe worthy worthy /

A Jupiter of providence /
A strengthe of Herculus
A Mars of excellence /
A paynfull Pirrus

A Ceser of clemancye
A Corage of Hector   *10*
A Salomon in sapience
An Armez of Arthore

A Cicero in eloquence /
A hardy Anyball /
A Davyd in prudence /
A Allexander liberall

A Plato in peace
Of beawtie an Absolon

An Achilles in presse
In gouernaunce Agamemnon   *20*

A force of Sampson
A Charlmayn in myght
A Godfray of Bulloyn
A Rowlond in fyght /

An holy Phocion
A contynent ffabricyus
An intier Caton
A pieusaunt Pompeyus

A Marcus Marcellus
A Sipio Affrican   *30*
A Ceaser Julius
An other Octauyan

This beawtie of Britayne
Reyned prosperously
Of progeny Grecean
Dissendyd lynyally

Whos honour to magnefie
The myghty power dyvyn
Hathe chosen hyme for (thye)
Above the sterres to shyn   *40*
ffinis G. C.

---

8. *Pirrus.* Singer prints *Janus.*
25-6. Praise of Henry VIII for the austerity
of Phocion or the frugality of Fabricius is
nearly as much out of place as for the
clemency of Caesar, line 9.
35. *Grecean.* Englishmen claimed descent from a
mythical Brutus or Brut, a Trojan hero who
found his way to Britain after the fall of

Troy. This however constitutes no Grecian
inheritance. See note Garland 405.
39. The MS reads *thyn,* which is at the extreme
edge of the leaf. Singer printed *thyn eie,*
probably thinking that *eie,* "aye," had been
trimmed away. I prefer to consider that
Cavendish meant "forthye," i.e., *therefore,*
and wrote *thyn* by attraction of the rime
above and that approaching.

MORLEY'S TRANSLATION OF PETRARCH'S TRIUMPH OF LOVE, BOOK I

Henry Parker, eighth (or tenth?) baron Morley by right of his mother, born 1476 and died 1556, was for years gentleman usher to Henry the Eighth, and resident at the royal court. His connection with both Wyatt and Surrey is noteworthy in view of his similar literary interests. His daughter Jane married George viscount Rochford, cousin to Surrey and brother to Anne Boleyn, with whom Rochford suffered death; another daughter married Sir John Shelton, whose child Mary not only owned and annotated one of the few existing manuscripts of Wyatt's poems, but has written her name at the foot of a page carrying the unique copy of his acrostic-poem on the name *Sheltun*.

The similarity in literary interest among Wyatt, Surrey, and Morley has, however, not the smallest parallel in literary command. Morley read Italian, an accomplishment of which he was proud; and he executed numerous translations from Italian or from Latin, often presenting them to the princess Mary, King Henry's eldest daughter. In the dedication to his prose translation of the Dream of Scipio, offered later to the "Lady Mary suster" of Edward VI, Morley says that it had been his habit to send the princess each year either a Latin work by some Christian doctor or something translated by himself. Other translations by him, still existing in the gift-copies, are dedicated to Henry VIII or to a lord of the court; these never have any literary value, but the prefixed addresses are of antiquarian interest. That accompanying the prose translation of Boccaccio's De Claris Mulieribus, offered to Henry VIII, was printed by Waldron in his Literary Museum, London, 1792, and reprinted thence by Paget Toynbee in his Dante in English Literature, i:33-35. That prefixed to the translation of Turrecremata's commentary on Psalm 36, with an accompanying "sonnet", was printed by Flügel in Anglia 13:73-75, and is addressed to "the Lady Mary doughter" of Henry the Eighth. The prose translation of Plutarch's life of Agesilaus was dedicated to Lord Cromwell; in it Morley tells Cromwell that the work "was translated from Greke into Latyn by Antony Tudartyn and drawen out of Latyn into Englishe by me Henry Lord Morley". Other translations by Morley, still in manuscript, are preserved in the British Museum collection of Royal MSS, as below.

Morley's Italian work has more interest for us than have his translations from the Latin;—the prose rendering of Masuccio's forty-ninth novel offered to Henry VIII, and the ambitious attempt in verse at Petrarch's Trionfi, dedicated to the young Lord Maltravers, from which selection is here made. Maltravers, son of the earl of Arundel, is the same youth who is lamented in a poem printed in Tottel's Miscellany, p. 118 of the Arber edition, and there said to be from Dr. Haddon's Latin. The date of Maltravers' death is in the text given as July 31 in the fourth year of Queen Mary, i.e., 1556, and he is stated to have been nineteen years old at the time. Since Morley himself died in 1556, aged eighty, and would hardly have offered the Petrarch-translation to a very young boy, he was probably over seventy when this work was undertaken.

The Trionfi of Petrarch show, more than any other part of his writing, the influence of Dante's Commedia. Like the Commedia, their dominant figure is that of the beloved lady; and there are constantly situations, choices of material, and turns of phrase, which show study of Dante's masterpiece. The Trionfi were very widely circulated, often with the Sonette and Rime. Hundreds of MSS exist, and after the first printing in 1470 the editions follow almost annually for years. The work was translated into French prose by La Forge and printed as early as 1514, with several reprintings. Whether one of those editions, or the verse-translation into French by Jean Maynier baron d'Oppède, printed 1538, was seen by Morley, whether he used a manuscript or a print of the Italian, we do not know. He professes great admiration for Petrarch and for the Trionfi, which he places above all work done in any vulgar tongue,—without recognition of Dante. True, Dante is mentioned, and is given formal precedence over Petrarch, in Morley's earlier dedication of the De Claris Mulieribus to King Henry; but Morley there says what we can well believe true, that there was at that time in Italy scarcely a prince or noble gentleman who had not Petrarch's poems in his hands. It was Petrarch, in less degree Serafino, who caught the English ear of Wyatt, and who attracted that of many another Tudor poet. The Court of Love stencil, and the "conceits" of Petrarch, had more validity for the mid-sixteenth century than had Dante; only Sackville, in his Induction, printed 1563, turns to the stronger spirit.

  There is indeed in the Trionfi's blending of allegory, pageant, classic legend, and worship of the Lady, as in its interlinking plan, just the sort of material and of structure which would please adolescent Tudor literature. The six Trionfi form a series. In the first of them, that of Cupid or Love, the onlooker sees humanity vanquished by the winged god, who is in turn compelled to yield to Chastity in the second of the poems, as Chastity falls before Death in the third, the Triumph of Death. Death is then triumphed over by Fame, who is later obliged to surrender to Time, and Time to Eternity or Divinity. Compare the appearance of Death, Fame, Time, and Eternity, one following another, at the close of Hawes' Pastime of Pleasure.

  The whole was never completed; among the mass of existing MSS there are variants which show the poet retouching his work to the end of his life; but of a final version, or of any one recension as nearer definitive than the others, it is impossible to speak. Our uncertainty as to which recension Morley used is increased by the freedoms and the inaccuracies of his handling, through which his original can often not be discerned; cf., e.g., lines 10, 131-2. If one compares his translation with the two main types of Petrarchan text as edited by Appel, it will appear that Morley leans sometimes to one type, sometimes to the other. See for instance his lines 93, 229 with the Laurentian-Parma recension, and then his lines 8, 30, 36, 200 with the Casanatensis type.

  A mere glance over Morley's work will show the inadequacy of his imagination and the poverty of his ear. His rhythmic peculiarities are not the conscious licences of the competent poet nor the struggles of a strong and gifted spirit with language; they are the deaf stupidities of the complacently ignorant versifier. His value for the modern reader resides in the likenesses and differences between him and his contemporary and fellow-courtier Wyatt. On the one hand, both read Italian, both translated Petrarch, both found it difficult to adjust language to the pentameter line; one the other hand, Wyatt ventured into terza rima and the sonnet, while Morley stayed by the couplet or prose. It is worth noticing not only that Wyatt moved better in his couplet than in his sonnets, and that he chose or modelled a sonnet-form clinched by a couplet, but that later translations of this same Trionfo, in 1644 and in 1807, preferred the couplet. English has always leaned to the couplet-structure.

In the Italian there are 160 lines of terza rima; the translation by Anna Hume in 1644 kept to the same number of verses, but that of Henry Boyd in 1807 runs to 196, that of Morley to 250 lines. Morley's expansion is due in many cases to lines and half-lines of padding for rime's sake; see note on line 16. But he also expands to display his knowledge, as in lines 21-24 with their picture of a Roman triumph, or in the biographical details added to Petrarch's list of lovers, lines 200 ff. Mistranslations occur; see notes on 103, 210, 229.

I subjoin brief passages from the opening of the Hume and the Boyd translations, to illustrate the difference in rhythmical flow.

> It was the time when I do sadly pay
> My sighs, in tribute to that sweet-sour day
> Which first gave being to my tedious woes;
> The sun now o'er the Bull's horns proudly goes,
> And Phaeton had renew'd his wonted race;   (1644)

> The fatal morning dawn'd, that brought again
> The sad memorial of my ancient pain;
> That day, the source of long-protracted woe,
> When I began the plagues of Love to know.
> Hyperion's throne, along the azure field,
> Between the splendid horns of Taurus wheel'd;
> And from her spouse the Queen of Morn withdrew
> Her sandals, gemm'd with frost-bespangled dew.   (1807)

The whole of each version may be read in a volume of Petrarch's sonnets, Triumphs, and other poems, translated by various hands, with a life of the poet by Thomas Campbell prefixed, London, 1859, again 1901. And it may be added that the Triumph of Death was translated into terza rima by Mary Sidney countess of Pembroke two generations later than Morley; her work is printed in PMLA 27 :47-75 by Frances Young.

The present text is reprinted from Cawood's edition pubd. during the reign of Mary, ca.1555; it was reprinted for the Roxburghe Club in 1887, and this canto, the first part of the "Triumphus Amoris", was printed (with modernized orthography) by G. F. Nott in his edition of Wyatt and Surrey, 1815, i: appendix 36. Much of the dedication to Lord Maltravers is printed by Flügel in Anglia 13: 72-3 footnote; and in his Neuengl. Lesebuch i :111 Flügel reprinted the twenty opening lines of this "canto", from Cawood. Morley's "sonnet" on the Psalms, printed by Flügel, *ibid.*, p. 110, and in Anglia as cited, p. 75, is given here from MS. Brit. Mus. Royal 18 A xv, the presentation copy to the Princess Mary.

SELECT REFERENCE LIST XVII

Wyatt's poems are ed. by Miss Foxwell in two vols., London, 1913.
Morley's translations still in MS are listed in the Dict. Nat. Biog. article on him; see earlier, Walpole's Catalogue of Royal and Noble Authors, London, 1759, i :92-96.
The Masuccio novel and its dedication are printed by Brie in Archiv 124 :46-57.
Petrarch's Trionfi are ed. by Appel, Halle, 1901.

The Catalogue of Western MSS in the Old Royal and King's Collections, 4 vols.,
  is of 1921. See, e.g., for Morley the Seneca in 17 A xxx, the Dream of Scipio
  in 18 A lx, the Athanasius in 17 C xii.
Two brief bits by Morley, the lines beginning "Neuer was I lesse alone", and those
  beginning "All men do wisshe", are printed by Flügel in his Lesebuch, pp. 37-8,
  and also in Arber's Surrey and Wyatt anthology, 1900, pp. 128-9. The latter
  was also printed in Bliss' Athenae Oxon. i :118, the former in the British Bibliog-
  rapher, iv :107, and in Foxwell's Wyatt, ii :162-3. The source of this stanza is
  discussed MLNotes 24 :54,123,226 and 34 :122,441. Its theme is cited by Petrarch
  in his De vita solitaria as from Scipio and Cicero; Morley may have taken it
  from him.

[The Dedicatory Letter]

Unto the mooste | towarde yonge gentle Lord Matrauers | sonne and heyre apparaunt
to the worthy and noble | Earle of Arundel, your poore frende Henry Par | ker
knyght, Lorde Morley, prayeth to God that | the vertue whiche doth floryshe in you
in | this youre tender age, maye more and | more increase in you, to the comfort | of
all that loue you, vnto the | laste age.

The fables of Isope (mooste towarde younge Lorde) are not only had in commendation amonge the Philosophers, as with Plato, Aristotle, & diuerse other of ye
moste excellent of them, but also the deuines, when in theyr preachynges there cometh
to theyr purpose any matter, to rehearse to the rude people, they alledge the allegorye
sence of them, to the muche edification of the hearers. I saye therfore, that amonge
other his wyttye fables (not to you noble gentleman vnknowen) he telleth, how that
the cocke scrapynge on a doungehill, found a precious stone, and when he sawe it,
disdayninge, he spurned it from hym, sayinge, what haue I to do with the, thou
canste not serue me to no kynde of vse, and so dispysynge it, left it where as it laye
on the dongehyll styll. Euen so there be a number of that sorte, that percase when
they shall eyther heare redde, or them selfe reade this excellent tryumphes, of this
famous clercke Petrarca, shall lytle set by them, and peraduenture caste it from them,
desyrynge rather to haue a tale prynted of Robyn Hoode, or some other dongehyll
matter then of this, whiche I dare affirme, yea, and the Italians do the same, that the
diuine workes set aparte, there was neuer in any vulgar speech or language, so notable
a worke, so clerckely done as this his worke. And albeit that he setteth forth these
syxte wonderfull made triumphes all to the laude of hys Ladye Laura, by whome he
made so many a swete sonnet, that neuer yet no poete nor gentleman could amend,
nor make the lyke, yet who that doth vnderstande them shall se in them comprehended
al morall vertue, all Phylosophye, all story all matters, and briefely manye devyne
sentences theologicall secretes declared. But alas who is he that will so reade them,
that he wyl marke them, or what prynter wyll not saye, that he may winne more gayne
in pryntynge of a merye ieste, then suche lyke excellente workes, suerlye (my good
Lorde) very fewe or none, whyche I do lamente at my harte, consyderynge that aswel
in French, as in the Italyan (in the whyche both tongues I haue some lytle knowledge)
there is no excellente worke in the latyn, but that strayght wayes they set it forth in
the vulgar, moost commonly to their kynges and noble prynces of theyr region and
countreys : As one of late dayes that was grome of the chaumber with that renowmed
and valyaunte Prynce of hyghe memorye, Fraunces the Frenche kynge, whose name
I haue forgotten, that dydde translate these tryumphes to that sayde kynge, whyche
he toke so thankefullye, that he gaue to hym for hys paynes an hundred crounes, to
hym and to his heyres of inheritaunce to enioye to that value in lande for euer, and
toke suche pleasure in it, that wheresoeuer he wente amonges hys precyous Iewelles, that
booke was always caryed with hym for his pastyme to loke vpon, and as much estemed
by hym, as the rychest Diamonde he hadde : whiche sayde booke, when I sawe the

    From :—The tryumphes of Fraunces Petrarcke, translated out of Italian into English by Henrye Parker
knyght, Lord Morley. [Colophon] Printed at London in Powles Churchyarde at the sygne of the Holy
Ghost, by John Cawood, Prynter to the Quenes hyghnes. [After 1553].

coppye of it, I thoughte in my mynde, howe I beynge an Englishe man, myght do as well as the Frenche man, dyd translate this sayde worke into our maternall tounge, and after much debatyng with my selfe, dyd as your Lordshyppe doth se, translate the sayde booke to that moost worthy kynge our late soueraygne Lorde of perpetuall memorye kynge Henrye theyghte, who as he was a Prynce aboue all other mooste excellente, so toke the worke verye thankefullye, merueylynge muche howe I coulde do it, and thynkynge verelye I hadde not doone it, wythoute helpe of some other, better knowynge the Italyan tounge then I: but when he knewe the verye treweth, that I hadde traunslated the worke my selfe, he was more pleased therewith then he was before, and so what his highnes dyd with it, is to me vnknowen, one thynge is, that I dyd it in suche hast, that doubtles in many places (yf it were agayne in my handes) I thynke I coulde well amende it, albeit that I professe, I haue not erred moche from the letter, but in the ryme, whiche is not possible for me to folow in the translation, nor touche the least poynt of the elegancy that this elegant Poete hath set forth in his owne maternall tongue. But as it is, if in the translation there be any thynge to be amended, or any wyll depraue it, I shall praye you (mooste noble younge Lorde) the very myrroure of al the yonge noble gentlemen of this realme in vertue, in learnynge, and in all other feates appertaynyng to such a Lorde as you be, to defende it a-agaynst those that will more by enuy then by knowledge depraue it, and then I do not feare but those that knowe and can speake the Italian, will beare with the simple translation, and commende the worke, as it is so muche commendable, that it can not be to dere bought, I desyre god noble yonge gentleman, to make the lorde Matrauers an olde gentleman, and | then thy worthy father the Earle of Arundell | my most speciall good | Lorde and frend, shall make | an olde Earle and lyue | *vsque in senium et senectum.* | *Dixi* |

Henry Morelye.

The first Chapter of the Tryumphe of Loue.

In the tyme of the Renewinge of my sus-
   pyres
By the swete remembraunce of my
   louely desyres
That was the begynnynge of soo longe a
   payne
The fayre *Phebus* the bull dyd attayne
And warmyd had the tone and tother
   horne   5
Wherby the colde wynter stormes were
   worne
And *Tytans* chylde with her frostye face
Ran from the heate to her aunciente
   place
Loue, grefe, and complaynt, oute of rea-
   son
Had brought me in such a case that sea-
   son   10
That myne eyes closed, and I fell to
   reste
The very Remedye to such as be oppreste
And ther on the grene, as I reposed fast
Sodenly me thought, as I myne eyes vp
   cast
I sawe afore me a maruelous great
   lighte   15
Wherin as well comprehend then, I
   myghte

Was doloure ynough wyth smale sporte
   & play
And thus in my dreame musyng, as I
   laye
I sawe a great Duke victorious to beholde
Tryumphyng on a chayre, shynyng as
   golde   20
Muche after the olde auncient sage wyse
That the bolde Romayns vsed in there
   guyse
When to the Capytoll the vyctors were
   brought
With right riche Robes curiously were
   wrought
I that such sightes was not wont to se 25
In this noyous worlde wherein I fynde
   me
Uoyde from the olde valure & yet more
   in pryde
Sawe comming towardes me ther on
   euery side
Dyuerse men wyth straunge and queynte
   arraye
Not vsyd amonge vs at this present daye
Which made me wonder what persons
   thei shuld be   31
As one glad to learne, and some new
   thinges to se

There sawe I a boye on a firye chayre on
  hyghte
Drawen with foure coursers all mylke
  whight
Wyth bowe in hande and arrowes sharpe
  & keene   35
Against whome no shylde nor helme so
  sheene
Myght in no wyse the mortale stroke
  wythstand
When he shote wyth his most dreadfull
  hande
To this also a straunge sight to se
Two wynges vpon his shoulders had he 40
Wyth coloures more then I can wryte or
  tell
A thousande dyuers this I noted well
And all the rest were nakyd to the skynne
Aboute the chayre where that this boye
  was in
Some laye there deade gapynge on the
  grounde   45
Some with his dartes had taken meny a
  wound
Some were prysoners and could not scape
  away
But folowed styll the chayre nyght and
  day
I that sawe this wonderfull straunge
  sight
To know what it mente, dyde that I
  myght   50
Tyll at the last I dyd perceaue and se
My selfe to be amonge that company
So had loue led me on that dawnce
That as it lyked her, so must I take the
  chawnce
I then among that great number in that
  place   55
Lokyng here and there in eche mannes
  face
Yf any of myne Acquayntaunce I coulde
  se
But none was there except perchaunce
  that he
By age or death or payne was chaunged
  quyte
As that I neuer had hym knowen by
  syght   60
Wyth folowing that great kyng in that
  houre
That is the grounde and cause of all
  dolowre

Thus all astonied as I loked here and
  there
All sodenly afore me then dyd there ap-
  peare
A shadowe much more sadde for to re-
  garde   65
Than all the reste that I had sene or
  harde
This sayd shadowe called me by name
And sayd by loue is gotten all this fame
Whereat I marueyled and sayde to hym
  agayne
How knowest thou me, to learne I wold
  be faine   70
For who thou arte I doo not knowe at all
So wonderous derke is here thys ayre
  and all
That I can nether perceaue nor yet well
  se
What man thou art nor whence þt thou
  should be
To that anone this shadowe to me sayde
I am thy frende thou nedest not be dis-
  mayde   76
And borne in Toscane where þu was
  borne perdye
Thyne auncient frende if that thou lyst
  to se
His wordes whiche that I knewe by
  dayes paste
By his speche, I knewe hym at the last 8c
All though his face, I coulde not then
  well se
And thus in talkyng together went we
And he beganne and thus to me dyd
  saye
It is right longe and thereto many a day
That I haue loked the my frynde to se 85
Amonge vs here in this our companye
For thy face was to me a token playne
That ones thou shouldest know loues
  payne
To whome I made aunswere and sayde
These wordes by me they cannot be de-
  nayde   90
But the sorowe the daunger and the
  dreade
That louers haue at the ende for theyr
  meade
So put me in feare, that I left all asyde
Leste that my seruyce should be cleane
  denyde
Thus sayd I and when he well percey-
  ued   95
Myne entention and my wordes conceyued

Smylynge he sayde what flame of fyre
Hath loue kyndled in thy hartys de-
    syre
I vnderstode then lytle what he ment
For his wordes vnto my heade then went
As fyrme and fast sure set anone   *101*
As they had bene prynted in a marbell
    stone
And thus for the newe game that I be-
    gane
I prayde hym tell me of verie gentlenes
    than
What people these were that afore me
    went   *105*
He aunswered bryfely to myne intente
That I should knowe what they should be
And be shortly one of theyr companye
And that it was my destany and lotte
That loue shoulde tye for me such a
    knotte   *110*
That I shoulde fyrst chaunge my heade
    to graye
Or that I coulde vnclose that knot away
But to fulfyll thy yonge desyre sayth he
I shall declare what kynde of men they
    be
And fyrst of the capteynes of them all *115*
His maner playne declare the I shall
This is he that loue the worlde doth
    name
Bytter as thou shalt well conceyue the
    same
And much the more when the tyme shall
    be
That thou shalt be amonge this companie
A meke chylde in his lustye yonge
    age   *121*
And in elde one all full of rage
Well knoweth he that thys hath prouyd
When thou by hym art heaued and
    shoued
Thy selfe shall well see and vnder-
    stand   *125*
What a maister thou hast then in hande
This god hath his fyrst byrth of ydelnes
Noryshed with mankyndes foly and wan-
    tones
And of vayne thoughtes plesaunt and
    swete
To a sage wyse man nothynge mete *130*
Callyd a god of the people most vayne
All be it he geueth for theyr rewarde
    and payne
Some the death forthwyth out of hande
Some alonge tyme in miserye to stand
To loue I say them that loues not hym *135*

Fast tyed and fetred both cheke and
    chynne
Nowe haue I declared to the this goddes
    feste
Nowe wyl I tell the in order of the reste
Hym that thou seest that so lordely doth
    go
And leadeth wyth hym his loue also *140*
It is the valeaunte Cesar, Julius
Wyth hym is quene Cleopatra the beuti-
    ouse
She tryumphes of hym and that is good
    ryghte
That he that ouercame the worlde by
    myght
Should hymselfe ouer commen be   *145*
By his loue euen as thou mayest se
The next vnto hym is his sonne deare
The great Augustus that neuer had peare
That louyde more iustly then Cesar
    playne
By request hys Lyuya he dyd obtayne *150*
The thyrde is the dyspytefull tyraunte
    Nero
That furyously as thou seest doth go
And yet a woman hym ouercame
Wyth her regardes Lo she made hym
    tame
Beholde the same, is the good Marcus
Worthy to haue prayse for his lyfe ver-
    tuouse   *156*
Full of phylosophy both the tounge and
    breste
Yet for Fausteyn he standeth (at) ar-
    reste
The tother two that stand hym by
That loke both twayne so fearefullye *160*
The tone is Denyse the tother Alexander
That well was rewarded for his sclaunder
The tother was he that soore complayned
Under Antander wyth teares vnfayned
The death of Creusa and toke awaye *165*
The loue from hym as the poete doth
    saye
That toke from Euander his sone deare
Among the rest thou mayest se hym
    here
Hast thou harde euer reason heretofore
Of one that neuer would consent more
To hys stepmothers foull and shamefull
    desires   *171*
But flye from her syght and her attyres
But wo alas that same chast honest mynde
Was his death as thou mayst playnely
    fynde

158. The printed text reads *as* instead of *at.*

Because she chaunged hyr loue vnto hate
Phedra she hyght that caused the de-
  bate   176
And yet was it hyr owne Death also
A sore punyshment vnto both them two
To (Theseus) that deceyued Adryan
Wherefore it is full often founde than
That one that blameth another parde 181
He hym selfe is more to blame then he
And who so he be wythouten any doubte
That by fraude or crafte doth go aboute
Another that trusteth hym for to be-
  guyle
Yt is good reason that wyth that selfe
  wyle   186
He be seruyd wyth that same sawse
Lo what it is a louer to be false,
This is he the famouse worthy knyght
That betwyxt two systers standeth vp-
  ryghte   190
The tone by hym was cruelly slayne
The tother his loue in ioye dyd remayne:
He that goeth with hym in the route
It is Hercules, the stronge, fierce, and
  stoute
That loue caused to folowe hyr daunce:
To other whiche in louynge had harde
  chaunce
It is Achylles the Greke so bolde
That for Polexemes loue dyed, as it is
  tolde.
There mayst thou see also Demophone
And Phylys hys loue, that sore dyd
  mone   200
Hys absence, wherby that she dyed.
Lo those that stande vpon the tother syde
Is Iason, and Medea that for his loue
Deceaued hyr father his trueth to proue
The more vngentle is Jason in dede   205
That gaue hyr suche rewarde for hyr
  mede.
Hysyphyle foloweth and she doth wayle
  also
For the barbarouse loue was taken hyr
  fro
Next in ordre there commeth by and by
He that hath the name moost excel-
  lently   210
Of bewtye, and with hym commeth she
That ouersone behelde his beutye
Wherby ensued innumerable of harmes
Thoroughe out the world by Mars
  charmes
Beholde I praye the among the com-
  panye   215
Enone complaynynge full heauely

For Parys that dyd hyr falsly betraye
And toke in hyr stede fayre Helen awaye
Se also Menelaus the Grekysse kynge
For his wyfe Helene in great mourn-
  ynge   220
And Hermon the fayre Horestes for to
  call
And Laodome that standeth all apall
Crye for hyr love the good Protheosso-
  laus
And argia the faythfull for Pollynisus
Here I pray the, the greuous lament-
  ynges   225
The syghes, the sorowes, and the bewayl-
  ynges
Of the myserable louers in this place
That are brought into so dolorous case
That there spyrytes they are about to
  rendre
Unto the fals God that is so sclendre 230
I can not nowe tell the all the names
That the false God of loue thus tames
Not onely men that borne be mortall
But also the hyghe great Goddes super-
  nall   234
Are here in this greate and darke presse
What shulde I any more nowe rehearse
Se where Uenus doth stande with Mars
Whose heade and legges the yron doth
  enbrase
And Pluto and Preserpyne on the other
  syde
And Iuno the ielyous for all hyr pryde
And Apollo with his gaye golden lockes
That gaue vnto Uenus scornes and
  mockes   242
Yet in Thessalia with this boyes fyrye
  darte
This great God was pearsed to the harte
And for conclusion, the Goddes and God-
  desses al   245
Of whome Uarro doth make rehearsall
Beholde how afore loues chayre they goo
Fast fettred and chayned from toppe to
  too
And Jupiter, hym selfe, the great myghty
  kynge
Amonge the other, whiche is a maruelous
  thing.   250

[There follow Chapter ii, 274 lines, Chapter iii, 278 lines, Chapter iv, 222 lines.
Next comes the *Triumph of Chastity*, 278
lines; then the *Triumph of Death*, in two
parts, of 222 and 224 lines. The Triumphs
of Fame, Time, and Divinity (or Eternity)
complete the work.]

A "SONNET" ON THE PSALMS

The manuscript now marked Royal 18 A xv, of the British Museum, is the gift-copy to the princess Mary Tudor of Morley's prose translation of Turre-cremata's commentary on the thirty-sixth Psalm. It is of nine leaves only; and on the last page, following the translation, we find:—

*Carmina Maphei Vegii Laudensis de vtilitate psalmor*um

> Orpheu sileto abijcite Mercurii lyram
> Et tu Tripus obliterate Delphice.
> Nam Dauid ad nos spiritus pulsans lyram
> Mysterior*um* operta patefecit dei.
> Miraculor*um* signat veterum copiam.
> Creata sit creantis in laudem sui.
> Preseruat omnes initians misteriis.
> Inter futura aperit iudici*um* iudiciis.

The Englyshe of thies verses. In an Italion Ryme called . Soneto .

> Orpheus with thy musyke and all thy pryde.
> And thou Mercurius do thy harpe away
> And thow three fotede Apollo . I . do say
> Sett your Armony quyte and clene asyde.
> ffor dauid that the spryte of trueth tryde.
> Playnge on hys harpe the swete holy lay
> The mysterys of god dothe manifestly play
> In shewynge vs christe that on the crosse dyede
> And all creatures exhorteth to commende
> The hyghe god and celestiall kynge.
> And made with hys worde eury thynge.
> As the Iudge of vs all at the latter ende.
>   Then let vs pretende
> Hys name to gloryfy hys mercy to reherse.
> Whiche Dauid harppes on in many a swete verse.
>   Finis.

The Latin which Morley translates was written by Mapheus Vegius of Lodi, who died in 1457. The Maxima Biblioteca Veterum Patrum, Leyden, 1677. contains in its vol. 26, pp. 632-787, a collection of Vegius' work in prose and verse,—religious, didactic, allegorical, and pseudo-classical. The best-known of these compositions is a supplementary or ·thirteenth book to the Aeneid, which is to be found in many early editions of Virgil, and was included in Douglas' translation of the Aeneid. In the Carmina Illustrium Poetarum Italorum, 11 vols, Florence, 1719-26, are printed (vol. 10) many epistles and epitaphs by Vegius, some "rustic-alia", and (vols. 6 and 7) various poems addressed to Vegius by his contemporaries.

This poem on the Psalms is not in either of the above-mentioned collections.

With Morley's application of the term "soneto" to his 15-line rendering of the Latin cp. Gascoigne's (1563) definition in his *Certayne Notes*. Gascoigne there says,—"some think that all Poems (being short) may be called Sonets", but that he can best allow the word to be used of poems having fourteen lines, each line with ten syllables. In 1869 the editor of Hearne's Reliquiae (see p. 218 here) applied the term "sonnets" to roundels translated from Charles d'Orléans; one of these may be read on p. 231 above.

WALTON'S TRANSLATION OF BOETHIUS

1 ff. Apologies for "rude langage" and for "wittes dulle" are formula with late medieval writers. Courtly versifiers often protested that the noble lady their subject was far beyond her servant's powers of description, or indeed beyond that of any human tongue; writings of a more intellectual cast bewailed the poet's inferiority to his model or his non-acquaintance with the Muses. Such apologies are often accompanied by the stereotyped request for the reader's indulgence or for his corrective hand; and all this material was properly found in the prologue, with echo sometimes in the envoy or epilogue. Its appearance elsewhere in the work marks a growth towards individual expression.

Another line of that growth was in the conception of the prologue itself. One type of the medieval prologue was the scholastic, organized according to Aristotle; it is discussed by Hope Allen in Romanic Review 8:454 ff. In its stricter early medieval construction it persists in such later works as Brunetto Latini's Trésor, in Dante's Convito, in Bokenam's Legends. Its function was the preliminary stating of the "four causes" of the work which followed, causes "material, formal, final, and efficient". The efficient cause, Bokenam says, is the author, the final cause his purpose; the matter of the work and its arrangement are included under the two other heads. But another type of prologue, which we may call the "rhetorical", gained ground as the scholastic method relaxed; it is discussed in the pseudo-Ciceronian treatise Ad Herennium, the source of so much of the rhetorical theory of the latter Middle Ages.

An "exordium", says the Ad Herennium i, 4, may precede the argument for a cause which is either honest, vicious, doubtful, or humble; each of these is defined and the management of the audience for each is counselled. There are two sorts of exordia, that which the Greeks call the prohemium and that which is termed the epodos or "insinuatio". The proheme endeavors to attune the minds of the listeners, to render them sympathetic toward a doubtful or a vicious case, attentive to a humble case. If the case be an honorable one, the proheme may or may not be used.

Study of English prologues or prohemes written in the Transition age shows very plainly the attempt to win the sympathy and attention of the reader. In a literary period so controlled by aristocratic patronage this would naturally be the case; the author's self-depreciation, his entreaty for indulgence, are aimed at the patron's sympathy, just as the frequent praise of literature aims at holding his attention. And eulogy of the noble patron is of course to be expected in work done to order. It was the freer relation of author to the larger public, if only in the author's thought, which brought about the great contrast between most medieval prologues and the prologues of Chaucer, even of Gower; and it is the relapse to protected literature which stamps most of the prologues of the fifteenth century. A comparative study of prologues in this period would have value for this reason alone, for there can be traced in each writer of the Transition, in Hoccleve's evasion of the prologue, in Walton's quiet business-like treatment, in Lydgate's effusive obedience to code, in all the later combinations of tone, the varying relations between the stereotype and the increasingly plastic state of a literature which was responding to social change.

It is clarity which Walton seeks; and after complying briefly with conventional requirement in his preface, he devotes a prologue to the historical setting of the Consolatio.

4. *yowre hest,* the command of Elizabeth Berkeley, according to the 1525 print as mentioned in the introd. above. The absence of emphasis from Walton's allusion to his supposed patroness should be compared with the tone e.g. of Hoccleve, of Lydgate, and of the Palladius-translator towards Gloucester; see pp. 90, 203, here.

13-17 may be paraphrased: "I pray to God so to help me with his inspiration that it (the text of Boethius) be not defouled nor corrupted by my translation,—to God, who is both lock and key to wisdom, that I vary not from the text—"etc.

14, 16. Schümmer in his critical edition puts a semicolon after each of these lines, thus destroying the syntactical connection. With 16 cp. Bokenam as cited note on 44 below.

17. *As for,* etc. This use of *as* to introduce a precatory clause is characteristic of MidEng; cp. KnTale 1458, "As sende love and pees bitwixe hem two", or Hoccleve's LettCupid 30, "As doth me grace" etc.

18. *his.* The neuter pronoun *its* is a late coinage, rare in Shakespeare and not in the 1611 version of the Bible.

19. *And wordes eke.* This is an unusual statement for a medieval translator; the general attitude is that of Lydgate in the Dance Macabre 666,—"Not worde by worde but folwynge the substaunce". Bokenam, finishing his life of St. Agnes, says, line 680 ff., that he has followed St. Ambrose

> Not wurde for wurde for þat ne may be
> In no translacyoun aftyr Ieromys decre
> But fro sentence to sentence.

St. Jerome, in his epistle Ad Pammachium, no. 57 of his Epistles, declares that he has endeavored "non verbum e verbo, sed sensum exprimere de sensu" in translating from the Greek. He supports himself by reference to Cicero and to Horace's Ars Poetica; and further on in the same letter he says, of interpreting the Apostles and Evangelists to elucidate the Old Testament,—"sensum quaesisse, non verba; nec magnopere de ordine sermonibus curasse, dum intellectui res pareret." Also, in writing to Theophilus, epistle 114, Jerome says that his disciple should endeavor, when translating, "ut nihil desit ex sensibus, cum aliquid desit ex verbis." Jerome's words became law to the medieval mind; John of Salisbury dresses the principle more gracefully, but nevertheless conforms to it, when he writes (Polycraticus v:2) that he works "ita tamen ut sententiarum vestigia potius imitarer, quam passus verborum."

25. This and the following stanza are printed by Todd in his Illustrations of Gower and Chaucer, page xxxii; also by Skeat, Oxford Chaucer ii:xvi-xvii.

26-27. So far as we know, Walton was preceded in English only by King Alfred's prose, by the anon. Old Eng. alliterative version of the Metra, and by Chaucer. We do not however know the date of that revamping of Chaucer's first book which is preserved in the fifteenth-century MS Bodl. Auct. F. 3, 5. And it must be noted that *sum,* as here used by Walton, may be either plural or singular.

29. *word for word.* Chaucer's translation is closer to the Latin than is Walton's; his principal divergences from Boethius are the doubling of terms to translate a single Latin word, and the frequent insertion of explanatory glosses. The adoption of some of these glosses into Walton's text is, as Cossack points out, one of the clearest proofs of Walton's study of Chaucer.

37. *doþ trete.* On the auxiliary *do* in MidEng, especially in Walton, see p. 89 of Hittmair's monograph in Ref.List below. Cp. *dede* line 56 below.

38. *book of moralite.* Gower's Confessio Amantis.

44. *Witnes vppon Ierome,* etc. The passage referred to is probably that in Jerome's letter to Eustachius, no. 22 of his Epistles as ed. in Migne's Patrologia Latina. Jerome there asks what Horace has to do with the Psalter, or Virgil with the Gospels; "we ought not", he says, "to drink at the same time from the cup of Christ and from the cup of demons." He narrates a dream in which he was castigated before the Throne for his love of heathen authors; to his assertion that he was a Christian the Divine Voice replied, "Thou liest, thou art a Ciceronian." And punishment followed, until he repented.

With Walton's disclaimer here we may compare Lydgate in the Life of Our Lady:—

> Nether to clyo ne to calyope
> Me list not calle for to helpe me
> Ne to no muse my poyntel for to gye
> But leve al this and say vnto marie. . . .

Cp. also St. Edmund i. 90-92. Bokenam in his prolocutory to the life of St. Mary Magdalen says, line 234 ff.

> Wher fore lord to þe alone I crye
> Wych welle art of mercy & of pyte
> And neyther to Clyo ner to Melpomene

> Ner to noon oþir of þe musys nyne
> Ner to Pallas Mynerue ner Lucyne
> Ner to Apollo wych as old poetys seye
> Of wysdam beryth both lok & keye
> Of gay speche eek & of eloquencye
> But alle þem wyttyrly I denye. . . .

Similarly Hardyng, in cap. vi of his Chronicle as printed by Grafton in 1543, enumerates a list of "old false gods" and says: "All these I wyll refuse nowe and defye And to ye God in heauen I praye in magestie My wytte to enforce—" etc. See Barclay's eclogue iv:755-6, p. 329 here, and his prologue 116-17.

58. *welles of Calliope*. With this mode of protesting incapacity cp. Chaucer, prol. to the FranklTale,—

> I slep never on the mount of Parnaso
> Ne lerned Marcus Tullius Cithero,—

the hint for which probably came from Persius' prologue to his satires,—

> Nec fonte labra prolui caballino
> Neque in bicipiti somniasse Parnasso
> Memini, ut repente sic poeta prodirem.

Chaucer is imitated by Lydgate, by Bokenam, Burgh, and others. See Lydgate's Troy Book iii:554-56, where Lydgate says of Chaucer:

> For in makyng he drank of þe welle
> Vndir Pernaso þat þe Musis kepe
> On whiche hil I myght neuer slepe. . . .

See also the envoy to Lydgate's Miracles of St. Edmund, the Fall of Princes iii:8-17 as printed p. 174 here, and FaPrin ix:3436-38, p. 187 here; see Burgh as printed p. 189 here. Bokenam in the prol. to his St. Anna says:

> For Tullius wolde me neuer non teche
> Ne in Parnase wher Apollo doth dwelle
> I neuer slepte—

The Pilgrimage to Parnassus act i, Sidney's "I never drank of Aganippe well", etc. return to the classics for their inspiration.

60-61. Walton here names the three Furies, and rejects them as sources of inspiration. Chaucer, in Troilus iv:22-24, had set England the fashion of invoking the Furies for a tragic composition. Lydgate appeals to the Furies in Troy Book iii:5443 ff., Duobus Mercatoribus stanza 73. Does Walton's language here indicate knowledge of Chaucer's Troilus?

81-88. This stanza, the second of the prologue, is by some of the MSS, as here, marked "Nota per exemplum"; this may have led to its separate copying into commonplace-books. The (later) MS Selden B 24, for instance, has this isolated stanza, marking it "Qd Chaucere", and the lines were therefore included by Morris in the Aldine Chaucer, (see my Manual, pp. 448-9). It is in Ellesmere 26 A, 13 of the Huntington Library, in Petworth 8, in Advocates Libr. Edinburgh 1, 1, 6, is at the end of Brit. Mus. Adds. 29729 (John Stow's MS), and on the endleaf of the Gower-MS formerly Phillipps 8192, with other bits. It appears in Harley 2251, fol. 152 b, as if it were the last stanza of Lydgate's Wicked Tongue. It is also in Brit. Mus. Royal 20 B xv, see Brusendorff, p. 436.

With the phrase "parelouse pestilence" in line 87 cp. the closing sentence of Boethius' book iii prose 5, and its rendering by Chaucer, MerchTale 549 f. The ascription of this (detached) stanza to Chaucer in Scottish MSS may be responsible for the phrase in Henryson's Fables, 598. See Lydgate's Troy Book iv:4517-18.

89. *oon þe principall*. This usage, instead of our modern *one of the principal*, is regular in MidEng, also *oon* with the superlative, e.g. "she was oon the faireste under sonne", FrankTale 6. On Nero see below, line 94 note.

92. *hym selfe*. The use of *himself* etc. as nominative can be exemplified from all periods of English; cp. Robert of Gloucester, Chaucer's CanYeoTale 431, Macbeth iv, 3:150, Tennyson, Aylmer's Field 596,—"The dagger which himself Gave Edith." This fact is used as argument in note on FaPrinces A 303.

94. *his maistir*. The philosopher and rhetorician L. Annaeus Seneca, tutor of the youthful Nero, was condemned to death by the emperor, A.D. 65, on suspicion of complicity in a conspiracy. Boethius, who perhaps was attracted to that example by his own situation, discusses Nero in book ii metre 6, book iii metre 4 and prose 5. The persecution of Christians by Nero was however the principal reason for the horror in which the Middle Ages held his name.

101. *Paule writeth þus*, etc. The persecutions of Christians by Nero and by Domitian were regarded by the Middle Ages as the activity of Antichrist, and Nero was often identified with the evil force described by St. Paul in 2d Thessal. ii, 3-4,—"et revelatus fuerit homo peccati, filius perditionis" etc.

105. *techeth*. For note on verbal plural in—*th* see Cavendish 1261 here. See line 367 below.

125. *a conquerour*. Theodoric the Ostrogoth, a Christian, was encouraged by the Eastern Roman emperor Zeno to march against the heathen Odoacer, the Germanic invader of Italy, whom Theodoric overthrew, making himself the master of Italy and Western Roman Emperor in 493. He ruled ably and peacefully for thirty-three years, during which time the Eastern emperors were Zeno, Anastasius, and Justin.

136. *perelus with to dele*. For word-order see note on Thebes 35.

139 ff. Walton, like many medieval chroniclers, connects the fall and death of Boethius with Theodoric's alleged persecution of Trinitarian Christians, thereby making Boethius a religious martyr. But most of the long reign of Theodoric was conspicuously tolerant; himself an Arian, he made no move against the orthodox. It was in 523 that the Eastern emperor Justin (see line 163) made a proclamation against Manichaean and other heretics, an action which roused Theodoric to protest. At nearly the same time a conspiracy against Theodoric was discovered, fomented from the East, and Boethius was imprisoned on suspicion of complicity in this. Boethius' own account of the circumstances, as given in book i prose 4 of the Consolatio, describes his repeated opposition to "graft" by highly-placed officials, his defence of unpopular men, and one case of his withstanding the emperor's will; of doctrinal differences we hear nothing.,

143. *hym presente*. An ablative absolute.

154-5. *colors . . . of rethoryk*. See note on FaPrinces G 46.

168. *arrians,* Arians, adherents to the doctrines of Arius, presbyter of Alexandria in the fourth century, who denied that Christ was consubstantial, i.e. of the same essence, with God. Arian opinions were embraced by a large part of the Church, and the fourth century was torn with dissension.

169 ff. Paulus Diaconus, a Lombard historian of the 8th century and reputed continuer of Eutropius in a Historia Romana, has in book xvi of that work a narrative of these events. He says that in the sixth year of his reign the orthodox Eastern emperor Justin moved against heretics; that Theodoric, "Ariana lue pollutus", sent Pope John and several dignitaries to Constantinople to protest, threatening to put "universos Italiae populos" to the sword unless Justin abandoned his purpose; that the embassy implored Justin, with tears, to save Italy, and that Justin yielded to their entreaties. But as the embassy "in itinere demorantur", Theodoric, "rabie suae iniquitatis stimulatus", executed both the "catholicos viros" Boethius and Symmachus. (See ed. in Monumenta Germaniae Historiae, 1878.) There is nothing in Paulus Diaconus to match Walton's lines 195-198.

188. *for þaire avne beste,* for their own good, to save their own necks.

200. *þaire olde gouernaunce*. Paulus Diaconus has *suo iuri.*

207-8. Boethius is said to be buried in Pavia, twenty miles from Milan, where he was slain.

209 ff. Somewhat different accounts of Pope John are given by Paulus, and by Gregory of Tours in his De Gloria Martyrum cap. 40. Paulus says that when Pope John on his return went to Theodoric at Ravenna, Theodoric, "ductus malitia quod eum Justinus catholicae pietatis defensor honorifice suscepisset", threw him and his fellow-ambassadors into prison, where

the pope soon died. There is nothing as specific in Paulus as is line 214 here. Gregory does not mention any embassy to Constantinople, but says that the pope endeavored to dissuade Theodoric from his intended persecution of Trinitarians, the emperor imprisoned him, etc.

217. For the slaying of Symmachus, ex-consul and Boethius' father-in-law, see 169; see FaPrinces H.

219. *heroicus.* The 1525 print of Walton has here, as often, a prose note in elucidation. According to Cossack, *op. cit.,* p. 14, it reads: "Vir heroicus ys man geuen al to contemplation and to vertu in whom al flesly passyons ben quenched and repressed." Cossack remarks that a Latin source for this part of Walton's text is obvious, or the Latin word would not have been dragged in.

224. The *he* refers to Theodoric, whose death in 526 closely followed those of Boethius and of Pope John.

223. Walton now cites Gregory as his authority. The passage may be found in Migne's Patrologia latina ed. of Gregory's works, Dialogue iv cap. 30, p. 368,—"De morte Theoderici regis Ariani". Travellers to the island of Lipari, visiting a holy hermit who dwelt there, were told by him of the emperor's death. To their denial and disbelief the hermit replied that the day preceding he had seen Theodoric led between Pope John and Symmachus, his hands bound, shoeless and ungirt (discinctus), and cast into the crater (ollam) of Vulcan. (The substance of 234 ff. is not in Gregory.) And on their return to Italy the travellers found that Theodoric had died on the day specified by the hermit. (Most of this is also in Paulus Diaconus *op. cit.*)

231. By *vlcane,* or the pot of Vulcan, the still smoking crater of Vulcano is meant,—one of the Lipari Islands, a volcanic group north of Sicily.

244. According to Schümmer, all MSS present this short line; the print reads—*haue ofte seyde,* etc.

249 ff. The text of Boethius now begins. Wülker prints lines 249-344, and book i metre 5 entire, from this MS, with no mention of Walton's name. Note the alliteration in the two opening stanzas. Note that in the Trésor Amoureux conjecturally ascribed to Froissart it is said of Boethius that by Envy he was brought—

> Où il disoit: Las! qu'il m'ennoie,
> Je vi le temps que je faisoie
> En paix, en recreacion
> Chançonnettes où je prenoie
> Parfaite consolacion! . . . (ed. Scheler iii :216-17)

253. *redyng.* So most MSS; Phillipps 1099 and Harley 43 read *rendyng,* and Balliol 316 B is corrected by an inserted *n.* The Latin *lacerae Camenae* and Chaucer's *rendinge Muses* show the true form of the word, but *reding* probably appealed to the scribes as connecting the Muses with letters; and the horizontal line, for the omitted nasal, over the vowel, was either unnoticed or ignored. Skeat ii :xxiv puts this use of the participle in the list of Chaucer's "inaccurate, unhappy, or insufficient" renderings. See Troilus iv :358, "And with his chere and loking al totorn"; and note that Coluccio Salutati (died 1406) says in one of his letters that the Muses are *integrae* when wisdom is joined to eloquence and sound reason does not oppose, but are *lacerae* if wisdom and reason be lacking to eloquence. See Emerton, Humanism and Tyranny, Cambridge, 1925, p. 329. Wülker, accepting *redyng,* explained as "die mir ratenden, die zu mir sprechenden Musen". The 1525 print of Walton changed to "Lamentable Muses".

255-56. Added by Walton, as are 257-8, 272.

273-80. See Lydgate's DuorMercat 743-46, and the note on FaPrinces, p. 185 here. See also Orléans xv, and Chaucer's Troilus iv :503-4.

283. The *he* refers to Death, in line 284. Note Walton's use here of Chaucer's gloss, as frequently. Chaucer has "the sorowful houre that is to seyn the deeth". For *sodainly* Walton has no authority.

285. *sche,* i.e. Fortune.

289-96. This stanza is expanded from two lines of the Latin.

298. *fyngres folde.* Walton departs from the Latin for the sake of rime; Chaucer and other workers in prose are literal.

299-300 are added by Walton, also 303-4.

307. *brend semyng.* The Latin is "ardentibus et . . . perspicacibus". Chaucer has "iyen brenninge and cleer seinge". The Walton MSS vary, writing *brennyng, brenned, brennes.* Two MSS write "—as fire clere".

309. *As þogh.* So the MSS, according to Schümmer. The print has *Al,* not *As.*

310. *corage.* This very frequent Middle English word meant "temperament, mind, spirit". By the end of the 17th century it had become limited to its present meaning.

313 ff. This stanza is full of borrowings from Chaucer.

315. *extent.* This reading is found, says Schümmer, in four MSS and the print; it is much more plausible than the *existent* of Royal and of nine other MSS.

318-19. Mainly padding by Walton.

322. Chaucer has "subtile craft of perdurable matere". The Latin is "subtili artificio indissolubili materia perfectae". Putting *perdurable* under rime, Walton was obliged to pad the lines riming with it.

328 is added by Walton because his adoption of the word *elde* from Chaucer, in 326, compelled him to pad.

330, 332. Walton does not use the explanatory glosses incorporated by Chaucer into his text. Boethius, in the dialogue with Porphyrius, says "Est enim philosophia genus, species vero eius duo, una quae θεωρητική dicitur, altera quae πρακτική, id est speculativa et activa." In Chaucer the two species are termed "the lyf actif and the lyf contemplatyf".

333. Chaucer, following the Latin, says "there were".

338. The translation of *abstulerant* as *born away* (so in Chaucer), and its use in rime, forced Walton to pad the riming lines.

346. *approchen.* The Latin is *adsistentes,* "standing by". It is Chaucer who says *aprochen,* as also *endytinge wordes* in line 347.

349. *þis companye.* Walton softens here, using the same word by which, in 373, he renders the Latin *chorus.* Boethius' *scenicae meretriculae* is translated by Chaucer "comune strompetes of the stage", by Queen Elizabeth "stagis harlotz", by Colvile "crafty harlots", by Cooper "seducing mummers".

354. Walton moves *swete venim* from a preceding sentence in Boethius to this.

356. *full affeccioun.* Three MSS, says Schümmer, scattered in various parts of the genealogical tree, write *foule* instead of *full.* To this they could be led by the pressure of the context. Walton errs in *full;* the Latin sentence contains *uberem,* but not in syntactical connection with *affectuum.*

358 ff. Walton here renders the Latin better than did Chaucer. Boethius wrote: "mentes assuefaciunt morbo non liberant". This the 1609 translator gives as "accustom men's minds to sickness instead of curing them". When Chaucer wrote "they holden the hertes of men in usage but they ne delivere not folke fro maladye", he connected *morbo* with *liberant.*

360. *aswage.* This transitive use of *assuage* is not cited by the NED until the Lover's Mass, a text which the Dictionary ascribes to Lydgate. See Mass 162.

362. By rendering *profanum* as *foole vnprofitable* (from Chaucer), Walton found himself obliged to pad the lines agreeing in rime.

366. Instead of *&,* several MSS have *in;* the Latin is *in eo.* Chaucer here translates: "for why, in swiche an unprofitable man, myn ententes ne weren nothing endamaged." Queen Elizabeth renders correctly, ending "For by suche our worke had got no harme." Walton's aim is blind, but he seems to be using the Latin rather than Chaucer, and to have gone wrong. Boethius wrote: "nihil in eo nostrae operae laederentur." Walton treated the verb as if singular, with *nihil* as subject and *nostrae operae* a genitive singular dependent on *nihil.* His *not* means nought.

367. Royal, says Schümmer, is the only MS reading *þeie;* others have *þis, þese,* Walton does not transfer to his text the *Eleaticis atque Academicis* which Boethius specifies with *studiis,* and which Chaucer retains, adding the explanatory phrase *in Grece.*

369. *ye filthes.* The Latin is *Sirenes;* Chaucer and Colvile use *mermaidenes,* Queen Elizabeth *Sirenes swite.* Possibly Walton here transfers some of the force unused in his line 349 above.

372 is inserted by Walton; note the rime.

375. Walton omits the *blush* of the original.

381 is inserted.

386. *on þe corner.* Chaucer, *the uttereste corner;* Boethius *in extrema parte,* i.e. at the foot.

388. This line is short in the Royal and Balliol MSS, as in most others; Harley 43, a text usually careless and unreliable, reads "That so with teris wepynge was be wett", and Trinity also has the word *wepynge.*

391-2 are padded.

B. BOOK II METRE 5: THE FORMER AGE

In this metre are found a number of Chaucerian phrases, from the prose, not from the verse; e.g., helden hem apayed, outrage, trewe feldes, hoolsom slepes, cruel clariouns ful hust, egre hate, a precious peril. It is printed by Skeat, Oxford Chaucer ii:xvii-xviii.

6. *sese their talent,* quench or satisfy their desire. This meaning for *talent* is usual in OFr and MidEng; *sese* is to be taken transitively, as *cesse,* "make to cease".

8. Walton incorporates in his text the Chaucerian gloss, "that is to seyn, they coude make no piment nor clarrie." See Roman de la Rose 8418-19, "Et de l'iaue simple bevoient Sans querre piment ne clare".

10. *venim.* Most of the early translators thus render *veneno,* which is rather "dye".

13-14. Here Walton renders, not unhappily, "Vmbras (dabat) altissima pinus."

21. *armour,* Chaucer *armures.* A number of Boethius-MSS have instead of *arma* the word *arua,* "fields". Cp. footnote p. 96 here.

24. *reward,* i.e. regard, consideration of the fact that he must lose his blood.

28. *more fersere.* The double comparative and double superlative are not uncommon in Middle English. See, e.g., *most fresshest* La Belle Dame 105, *most surest* Troy Book iii:47, *more lyker* Hawes' Pastime 607, etc. Cavendish in his prose life of Wolsey is addicted to their use.

29-31. Here the syntax seems broken. "Alas, who was the man who would concern himself (with) the gold and gems thus hidden? who first began to mine I cannot say, but (I know) that"—etc.

Queen Elizabeth's transl. of this metre is appended, from the EETS print.

Happy to muche the formar Age
With faithful fild content
Not Lost by sluggy Lust
that wontz the Long fastz
To Louse by son-got Acorne
that knew not Baccus giftz
With molton hony mixed
Nor Serike shining flise
With tirius venom die
Sound slips Gave the grasse
ther drink the running streme
Shades gaue the hiest pine
The depth of sea they fadomd not
Nor wares chosen from fur
Made Stranger find new shores

Than wer Navies Stil
Nor bloudshed by Cruel hate
Had fearful weapons staned
What first fury to foes shuld
any armes rayse
Whan Cruel woundz he saw
And no reward for bloude?
Wold God agane Our formar time
to wonted maners fel
But Gridy getting Loue burnes
Sorar than Etna with her flames
O who the first man was
of hiden Gold the waight
Or Gemmes that willing lurkt
The deare danger digd?

It will be observed that the Elizabethan feeling for language and rhythm is not shared by Elizabeth.

C. BOOK II, METRE 7

From Chaucer's prose are: liften up hir nekkes, maketh egal and evene, stinting of fame (this last from Chaucer's added gloss).

2. The sense-order of the words is—"Sovereign joys for to be in renown", i.e., whoever ignorantly thinks that joy is there.

3. Read *As* instead of *And;* see note on line 17 of A above. The Latin is *cernat,* i.e. "Let him behold".

3-5. See Chaucer's Parlement of Foules 57, where Chaucer is using the Somnium Scipionis, of which see lines 135 ff.

5-8 are expanded.

9. *what aylen,* etc. So MS Balliol A. The subject is apparently *men,* but this personal use of the verb is rare. *proute* is a normal OEng form beside *proude,* which died out by the end of the fifteenth century.

13. *resoun.* So MS Balliol. We expect *renoun;* the Latin has *fama;* and see 37 below.

13 ff. Stewart says of the Latin here that it is an "anticipation of Villon". Rather say that the stanzas are dominated by the "Ubi Sunt" motive so frequent in the latter Middle Ages; see introd. to extract C from Lydgate's Fall of Princes, p. 169 here.

21. *we trowe.* Other MSS, *I trowe.* The phrase is inserted for rime, as is *overblowe,* 24.

22. *Brutus.* When King Alfred renders this passage of Boethius, he adds here the explanation—"oððe naman Cassius". See note on *Brutus Cassius.* Brutus is probably however L. Junius Brutus, the inflexible consul who condemned his two sons to death for conspiracy against the Republic, and for whom Rome wore twelve months' mourning; Fabricius, consul and military commander, was famous for his frugality and his uprightness; stern Cato, the Censor, was the model of austerity to his time.

24. Chaucer has "marked with a few lettres". MSS Balliol 316 A and Harley 43 read as does Royal.

27, 28 are inserted, as are 31, 32.

29. *fforwiþ.* Balliol 316 A, *ffor why.* Should we adopt this latter reading, we could paraphrase: "wherefore, when ye pass from this life, ye ben unable to be known".

33. Chaucer and Gower are named together, conventionally. See pp. 96-97 here.

35. *yow selven.* Balliol, *your seluen.*

D. BOOK III, METRE 12

With the serious simplicity of the story of Orpheus, as told here, by Chaucer, and by Boethius, compare the attempted waggishness of the version in Lydgate's FaPrinces i:5776 ff., there filling eleven stanzas, of which I quote the third, fourth, and fifth from the text as ed. Bergen, Carnegie Instit. and EETS 1923-27.

> An harpe he hadde off Mercurius
> With the which Erudice he wan
> And to Bachus as writ Ouidius
> Sacrifises ful solempne he began
> And onto helle for his wiff he ran
> Hir to recure with soote touchis sharpe
> Which that he made vpon his heuenli harpe

> But whan that he this labour on hym took
> A lawe was maade which that bond hym sore
> That yiff that he bakward caste his look
> He sholde hire lese & seen his wiff no more
> But it is seide sithen gon ful yore
> Ther may no lawe louers weel constreyne
> So inportable is ther dedli peyne

> Yiff summe husbondis hadde stonden in the cas
> Ta lost her wyues for a look sodeyne
> Thei wolde ha suffred and nat seid allas
> But pacientli endured al ther peyne
> And thanked god that broken was the cheyne
> Which hath so longe hem in prisoun bounde
> That thei be grace han such a fredam founde

The tone of this latter stanza continues through the rest of the story. It is not derived from the French prose of Laurent, which Lydgate is in general following, and as I have suggested p. 95 here, may be an attempt to divert the Duke of Gloucester, the patron of Lydgate's translation.

10. The *houndes fell* are added by Walton to the lions of the Latin.

12. Punctuate with a pause after *hound;* lines 13 and 14 are closely connected.

15, 16, 23, 24, are added by Walton.

28. *welles thre.* The numeral is added by Walton. It was a frequent medieval error to speak of Helicon as a fountain. On the slopes of Mt. Helicon, the haunt of the Muses, were the spring Hippocrene and the fount Aganippe; Walton may have thought of Helicon as a third fount.

29. *modres.* So all MSS which I have consulted; we expect the nominative? But the text here is unclear; there is no predicate for *dere Calliope,* and emendation is necessary. The Latin is *deae matris fontibus hauserat.*

34. *nelle.* Hades or Pluto, god of the lower world.

35. *lawnesse.* For the spelling cp. *avne,* "owne", line 188 of A ante.

36. *at.* To *ask at* is MidEng idiom; see Troilus ii:894, but cp. *ibid.* 896.

40. Walton renders *stupet* as "falle on slepe". The Latin is: "Stupet tergeminus nouo Captus carmine ianitor"; Chaucer translates the verbs "caught and all abayst".

52. *surfetoures.* Walton's translation of *sontes,* "the guilty", is more definite than Chaucer's "the sowles". The 1609 version has "the guilty souls".

45. *swift.* Chaucer renders "Velox praecipitat rota" as "the overthrowing wheel".

47-48. "And Tantalus, although he had long been tortured by thirst, desired no water."

49. *gryp.* Chaucer, "the fowl that hight voltor".

53 is inserted for rime.

61-2. This well-known passage of Boethius,—"Quis legem dat amantibus? Maior lex amor est sibi",—is used by Chaucer in Troilus iv:618, KnTale 306.

63. *neygh out of þe bondes blake.* Boethius, "noctis prope terminos"; Chaucer, "almost at the termes of the night, that is to seyn, at the laste boundes of helle".

64-5. The Latin is simply:—"Vidit, perdidit, occidit". Chaucer renders,—"lokede abakward on Eurydice his wyf, and loste hir, and was deed". Walton was doubtless influenced by the coming *mentem,* "mind", which he uses as rime-word, to the weakening of *occidit;* but Chaucer gives an erroneous translation, as do many others. The 1609 rendering, uncorrected by Stewart in the Loeb Library ed., is "doth lose and kill her and himself". But Boethius, who was a sound and able metrist, uses not the transitive verb *occīdit* but the intransive *occĭdit;* he says that Orpheus looked on Eurydice, and lost her, and was undone. For his climax-verb Boethius may have had in mind the phrase of Virgil, Georg. iv:491-2, "ibi omnis Effusus labor"; he certainly did not intend to assert Orpheus' immediate death, as Skeat's note on the Chaucerian passage suggests. (I am here indebted to Prof. G. L. Hendrickson of Yale University.)

E. PREFACE TO BOOKS IV AND V: BOOK IV, PROSE I AND METRE I

Walton is about to attempt the most abstruse part of Boethius' discussion, that dealing with predestination and free will. As he begins, he makes, in his own person, a renewed protestation of his insufficiency "to the height of this great argument"; and either because of the increased difficulty of his task or because of some external cause unknown to us, he changes at this point from the eight to the seven-line stanza. His proheme is lyrical, deprecatory, suppliant; its dignity and its command of verse are notable.

3. *Conteyned.* This word may be *Conceyued.* See lines 14, 44 below.

8-11. See Job chap. 38.

20. *Ye ben.* Walton may be addressing his patroness, although the absence of any word of respect or gratitude is in that case peculiar. He may mean Boethius.

21-22. These lines are apparently bound together syntactically. Walton is compelled, he says, to show himself overbold (in discussing the questions) "of hap", etc.

22. *Of hap of fortune and of destine.* Cp. Chaucer's phrase, CTprol 846, "Were it by aventure or sort or cas"; see KnTale 607 etc., Lydgate's Troy Book iii:2815 etc., Dante's Inferno 32:76, "Se voler fu, o destino, o fortuna".

24. *Supposyng* may be parsed as agreeing with *mynde.* These questions of predestination, says Walton, have bewildered many a mind which thinks that our free will, etc.

23-25, 26. Note the rime.

39. *wel & wo.* Cp. Chaucer's "Wo was his cook", CTprol. 351.

47. *failleth of his ende,* fails to accomplish its purpose.

49. *So may we,* i.e., "So little may we", etc.

50. Schümmer inserts *the* before *movynge,* from one MS and the print of 1525. The meaning is that fire, by the impelling power of its nature, rises.

66. *wonder lustilye.* Boethius, "leniter suauiterque", Chaucer "softly and delitably".

67. This line is inserted by Walton.

70. *interrupcion.* This word, and *interrupt,* are mainly used by Lydgate and by Hoccleve to mean infringement of law, breach of the peace, etc. In a minority of cases they are applied to speech, e.g. Troy Book iv:4808. Not in Chaucer. Cp. Alanus' De Planctu Naturae, prose iv, "praefata narrationi meorum verborum parenthesi syncopatae tenorem hujus quaestionis inserui, dicens:—"

71. Chaucer writes "gyderesse of verrey light", which Walton may be following, although the Latin "ueri praeuia luminis", gives most of the clue. It frequently happens that when Walton is literal in his translation, he necessarily comes close to Chaucer's consistently literal version.

73. *anon to þis.* Latin, *usque ad huc;* Chaucer, "hider to". Cp. Richard the Redeless ii:126. "anon to the skynnes". See 151 below.

77. *byknowen.* So the Balliol MS. Harley 43 reads *vnknowen,* which gives better sense than either Balliol, or Royal's *we knowen.*

89. *Bot,* etc. We expect *Swiche* rather than *But;* see the Latin, and Chaucer's "that swiche thinges ben doon", etc. Note *Bot* in line 86.

93. *Abhomynable.* This spelling, which has been attributed to the Latinizing tendencies of a later period of English, and explained as a false etymology from *ab hominibus,* is fairly frequent in the Transition. It and other *h*-forms are regular in the Bodley 263 MS of FaPrinces, as ed. by Bergen; and the spelling occurs in Latin. See Ship of Fools 8515.

100. "For if those things stand formally, to which we have already assented, then thou shalt hereafter acknowledge", etc.

103. The MSS which I have used read *he speketh.* Read *we speketh?* For such a verb-form cp. line 100, A 105 *ante,* etc. The Latin is *loquimur;* Chaucer, "I speke".

117-119 are inserted.

123-5. The rime-arrangement here is inaccurate. Walton may have been thinking of the sequence in eight-line stanzas such as he had been writing.

125. *cariage.* Boethius *vehiculis,* Chaucer *sledes.*

128-133. This passage of Boethius is used in Chaucer's HoFame 973-78.

131. *he.* Walton's change of pronoun, from *it* in line 130, is also in Chaucer. The word *deviseth,* and that line, are inserted for rime; so line 137.

133. The Latin is "nubesque postergum videt".

139-40. Chaucer says "the olde colde Saturnus". See Thebes prol. line 3, "Satourn olde with his frosty face".

145-47 are padded by Walton.

146. *be holden.* Shall we read *he beholdeth,* or insert *al* to remedy this short line, taking *be holden* as *are held?*

148 is not in Boethius nor in Chaucer, and the rest of the stanza is padded.

152. The pronouns are confusing. *He* here and in 155 refers to God; the other cases of *he,* and the *his* of 152, refer to the mind.

158, 159 are closely bound; read with comma after *place.* The word *reduce* here, as frequently in the Transition, means to lead back; see Lydgate's Troy Book ii:183.

HOCCLEVE

LA MÂLE RÈGLE

1. Hoccleve opens with a paean in praise of Hygeia or Health; but his lyrical note is not supported by "aureate language", as often in medieval prologues; see Ripley's Compend of Alchemy or the Court of Sapience.

5. *aduersitee,* adverse action. So line 47 and in Regement of Princes 390.

22. *feeste fro penaunce.* "Now I can tell the difference between a feast-day and a fast-day; but when I was in health I made none."

31. *lym . . . gore.* The term "gore" for "gown" is frequent in the romances; the word "lym" was interpreted by Mason as "active instrument". Cp. our "limb of the law".—"His hand should not have clutched my sleeve."

36. *put . . . assay,* "tried it".

38. *But what!* Cp. *Quid enim!* e.g. in Philippians i:18 or in WBTale 58. Very frequent in medieval rhetorical writers.

39. With the alliteration cp. 220 below.

50. *holde . . . in chief.* Tenure *in capite,* or direct holding from the lord of the soil, implied under the feudal system homage or "reverence". The tenant, as a vassal, swore allegiance and obedience.

62. *inprudence.* Mason writes *imprudence,* the EETS *inpudence.*

63. *curse . . . & warie.* Doublets are frequent in Hoccleve; see Regement 2304, 2422, 2490, 2546-7, 2663, 2803, etc.

67. *Regnynge which* is an ablative absolute.

70. Instead of *resoun,* as in the MS and in Mason, the EETS reads *reform.*

78. *brydillees,* without bridle. See note on Epithalamium 88, Cavendish 1348.

79. *hony and gall.* This is a very frequent antithesis in late Middle English literature. The "two tuns" of Fortune or of Jupiter contained the sweet and the bitter; see Lydgate's ResonandSens 50 ff., Troy Book ii:65, DuobMercat 697 ff., Gower's Confessio vi:330 ff., also Lydgate's many references to sugar as hiding gall, e.g. FaPrinces A 243 and note.

85. *Salomon wroot.* See Prov. xi:14, xv:22, xx:18, xxiv:6. See Hoccleve's Dialogue 451-2.

95. *rype . . . pit.* See Hoccleve's Complaint 266; see Chaucer's MerchTale 157.

106. *in tyme,* at regular hours. Cp. 110 below.

113. *The custume,* the custom-house, or receipt of custom, i.e., the gluttonous mouth.

121. *Bachus and his lure.* The bush of Bacchus, the accepted sign of a wine-shop, is compared to the "lure" or bit of leather garnished with feathers which was used by fowlers to induce the soaring hawk to return. This line I would punctuate otherwise than in the EETS ed., with no comma after *lure,* but a comma after *Bachus.*

126-8. *With outen daunger,* without any compulsion. "Unless I was so heavily in debt or so pressed with business" etc. Note the rime of *hye me :tyme,* with an apparently silent *-e* in the verb.

130. Cp. London Lickpenny, p. 238 here.

138. Cp. SqTale 264, "—lusty Venus children dere". The phrase "fressh repeir" means "lively visiting".

143. *Poules heed,* the sign of a tavern, the Paul's Head.

146. *wafres thikke,* cakes substantial or abundant.

149. *for the maistrie.* See Prol. to CantTales 165. Tyrwhitt noted that old medical books applied the phrase *pour la maistrie* to remedies which were super-excellent. See Hoccleve's Dialogue 565.

150. *warme with.* The word-order here is modern, not as in Thebes 35 and refs. there.

173 ff. "And yet my will (to blame others) was good, if I could have managed to suppress my cowardice." Cp. Pope, Epistle to Arbuthnot, line 203, "Willing to wound, and yet afraid to strike".

188. *priueseel,* the Privy Seal office, where Hoccleve was employed. Apparently the clerks dwelt there. See line 300.

193. "Because the roads were rutted and muddy", Hoccleve would pay a boatman and go by the river.

197. The EETS word-order is wrong.

202. *in myn audience,* in my hearing. Hoccleve is shrewd, although vain.

211. *faueles tonge.* The tongue of Favel or Flattery is again alluded to in lines 223, 244, 247, 284, 287. All medieval treatises on the governance of princes are strenuous against flattery; see for example Hoccleve's own Regement lines 3039 ff., 4446 ff. Dante put flatterers deep down in hell, see Inferno xviii. On *favel* see Skeat's note to Piers Plowman, C-text iii :6.

233. *book of nature of beestes.* This is not Albertus Magnus' De naturis animalium, where the chapter on Sirens, book xxv chap. 53, is very brief and bald. It seems to be rather from Theobaldus' Physiologus de naturis duodecim animalium; there the, chapter De Syrene contains all the descriptive matter which Hoccleve gives, and this is followed by an "allegorizing" of the siren's "natura biformis" to mean human duplicity of character, smooth speech and injurious action. When here speaking of flattery, Hoccleve might well recall this interpretation of the siren's wiles. See note on 249 below.

236, 240. *spekth, swich.* So the MS and Mason; the EETS reads *spekith, which.*

249. *Holcote.* The story of Ulysses and the Sirens is told by Robert of Holkot (died 1349) in his commentary Super Sapientiam Salomonis, lectio 64. Holkot is discussing "dangers of the sea"; he describes the Sirens, who he says were three in number, and gives an allegorical interpretation, saying that "moraliter Vlixes sapiens interpretatur et designat mentem in qua prudentia inhabitare debet." Another "danger of the sea" described is Circe, for whom Holkot refers to Boethius bk. iv, metre 3. Hoccleve has possibly another use of Holkot in lines 300-04, see Note.

258. *prudence.* Mason reads *providence,* wrongly.

265. *A nay.* Mason *Ah nay;* EETS *As nay,* for which emphatic negative cp. Roberte the Deuyll, in Hazlitt's EEPopPo i :860. The MS has a peculiar punctuation mark after *A*; see p. 60 ante.

269. *a myte . . . deere,* "too expensive, if valued at a mite".

270. *priuee and appert,* privately and openly. The lord favors the adroit courtier both when alone and in public.

280. "And he bids him begone quickly, with bad luck to him."

294. The comma inserted by the EETS editor disturbs the sense.

301. *malencolie.* Melancholy, or black bile, was one of the four "humors" of the body, the others being blood, phlegm, and choler. The preponderance of any one humor determined the "complexion" of the individual, whether sanguine, choleric, phlegmatic, or melancholic. If this preponderance of black bile were not excessive, the "melancholic" man was distinguished by steadiness of purpose and soundness of judgment, e.g., Hector. But in excess the melancholic temperament meant sullenness, jealousy, obstinacy.

300-04. The rhetorical device here employed, the linking of stages up to a climax, is termed *gradatio*: see the pseudo-Ciceronian treatise Ad Herennium, the source of so much medieval rhetorical principle, pp. 326-27. It may be noted that this particular passage is cited, as from Tullius, in the same commentary of Holkot which Hoccleve used for lines 249 ff. above. See lectio 84 of Holkot.

305. "Let us go on to the next point, late hours."

312. *cam.* So the MS and Mason. The EETS reads *can.*

319-20. Note the lively management.

321. *Prentys and Arondel,* companions of Hoccleve. These two names appear in a petition of 1431; see Proceedings of the Privy Council iv :77, cited EETS ed. of Hoccleve, i :page xxxv note. Other fellow-clerks are named in the supplication To Somer, see p. 66 here.

349. *My thank is qweynt,* "gratitude due me is all wiped out."

354. *old Clerkes,* etc. See Chaucer's Melibeus, B 2405; cp. Dance Macabre 344 and the French, line 272.

380. The MS omits *an,* which is supplied in brackets. See Hoccleve's poem for Chichele, EETS i :67, line 20; see the WBprol. 659, Lydgate's Troy Book ii :4043.

391. *so do.* MS and Mason thus; EETS reads *do so.*

417. *the Fourneval.* Thomas Nevil, lord Fournival, was in 1405 appointed subtreasurer, with Sir John Pelham.

421. *theschequeer,* the Exchequer, from which office Hoccleve's yearly ten pounds was paid in instalments; he is asking for that due at Michaelmas, "Michel," September 29.

423. The Latin side note is: Annus ille fuit ann*us* restrictionis annuitat*um.* The "ferne yeer", or previous year, is evidently overdue also.

430. *estaat real,* royal power.

432. *Wherfore.* So the MS and Mason; the EETS reads *Therfore.*

442. *Shameth.* Mason reads *Shunneth,* incorrectly.

446. Cp. Lydgate's Letter to Gloucester, stanzas 1 and 6, p. 149 here.

TO SOMER

This half-jesting, half-earnest, and wholly punning supplication to Sir Henry Somer, the subtreasurer, must have been sent later than 1408, when Somer was appointed a baron of the Exchequer. Its exact date is uncertain, although it was obviously sent at Christmas-time.

It was printed by Mason, by Morley, in EETS ed. i:59, and in Neilson and Webster p. 204. Its first three stanzas are on three rimes, and are linked by rime.

12-14. Read with a stop after *lust,* and then paraphrase "According to the maturity of our fruits, last Michaelmas was the time of year for the harvest of our seed." Evidently the previous quarter's salary was unpaid, for all four men.

20-22. "Whether our accounting shall soon make us sail with our ship to a safe harbor." For the pun on *ships* cp. Letter to Gloucester line 17 and note; the English gold noble and half-noble bore the stamp of a ship. "If you list" begins a new sentence.

25-6. *Offorde.* See note on this man by Kern in Anglia 40:374.

33 ff. This roundel is in almost the briefest form possible to that metrical type; see note on lines 57-73 of the Lover's Mass here, where other late MidEng. roundels are listed. Three more by Hoccleve are printed in this volume.

TO CARPENTER

The person to whom this poem is addressed was probably John Carpenter, town clerk of London 1417-1438, a man of large means and a public benefactor. It was he, for instance, who according to Stow paid for the painting-up of Lydgate's Dance Macabre text in the cloisters of old St. Paul's.

The poem was printed by Mason, and in EETS ed. i:63.

8. This "expression" refers to the line of initials in the margin, representing the creditors of Hoccleve, who would fain be "even" with him, that is, clear up their accounts.

22-4. Hoccleve begs Carpenter to stand surety for him, and prevent his arrest for debt.

23. The MS has not *hem.*

27-8. The meaning seems to be: "However completely you may settle the business, and however speedily, I can permit that for the ending of my anxiety."

THREE ROUNDELS

From among the many begging-letters and laments for money-scantness in this period, cp. here Froissart's Dit dou Florin, a dialogue with the last coin in his purse. The French poem is however of 490 lines; see Scheler's ed. of Froissart, ii:220-34.

In these roundels, note that the scribe has not filled out the repetition of the first member, which is characteristic of the form; he writes only a word or two of it.

The poems are printed EETS ed., vol. ii, and earlier in Academy for 1892, i:542. For (3) see EETS ed. i, foot of xxxviii.

(1)

6. *streite.* Read with a following question-mark. Hoccleve tells Lady Money that when she was shut up in his purse he never kept her close pent,—far from it, he let her out.

11. *saillen.* Perhaps again an allusion to the ship stamped on the English gold coins. See note on line 21 of the poem To Somer.

13. *right a feynt,* a right feigned, i.e. a mere show of good spirits.

(2)

5. *cheertee.* This word is much used by Hoccleve. It means "affection, value"; the phrase here is "thou settest no store by me".

7-8. "At the urge of your excessive expenditure I became extravagant (or dissolute)." The word *delauee* is also used by Hoccleve in Jereslaus' Wife line 901, in the Regement 4624; and it occurs in line 40 of the Ballad of Good Counsel printed by Skeat vii :286. It was used by Chaucer in the Parson's Tale; and it is in Laurent's French transl. of the De Casibus ii chap. 14, a passage which Lydgate materially changes. Chatterton took up the word, writing it as *deslavate,* and using the substantive *deslavatie.*

10,12. After each of these lines read a question-mark.

(3)

With this burlesque of a lover's "praise of my lady" cp. the *Balade Plesaunte* and the poem beginning *O Mossie Quince,* both in MS Trin.Coll.Cambr. R 3, 19 and both printed thence as noted in my Chaucer Manual, pp. 428,442. On a very reduced scale, this is a feature-by-feature description, recognized as code in medieval court-poems lauding a beloved lady. Such may be seen in Matthew of Vendôme's Ars Versificatoria (ed. Faral, pp. 129-30), or in Geoffrey de Vinsauf's Nova Poetria, *ibid.,* lines 563 ff. of the text, or in the Architrenius of Johannes de Altavilla bk. ii, or in Alanus' Anticlaudianus i chap. 7, or in the Historia Troiana of Guido delle Colonne where Helen is described. On the last-named it may be noted that when Lydgate in his Troy Book reaches that point (ii :3643 ff.) he says lines 3676-77, that Guido depicts Helen "by ordre ceryously From hed to foot", but that he has no sufficient English, wherefore (3689-90) he refers his readers to Guido. A clumsy imitation of the method is made by the fifteenth-century author of the poem "How A Lover Praiseth his Lady", printed ModPhil 21 :379-95, which see for notes on medieval modes of description.

7-8. *pentice,* etc. Her nose is a penthouse, which keeps the rain out of her mouth even were she lying *vprightes,* i.e. on her back.

DIALOGUE WITH A FRIEND

(EETS edition i :p. 128)

The MS here used, Bodl. Selden supra 53, is described with its copy of Lydgate's Dance Macabre, p. 124 here. In this poem it shows a number of minor differences from the Durham MS-text printed by the EETS. The word-order differs in lines 502, 525, 540, 548, 559, etc. The particles *that, it,* give the scribe especial trouble; see their omission or insertion in lines 507, 513, 529, 531, 686, 710, 733, 746, 779; also *ther,* 757, and *thei* 776.

533. *now is lieutenant.* Gloucester was appointed Lord Lieutenant of the kingdom Dec. 30, 1419. In early February, 1421, the king returned to England with his newly-wedded queen; in early June Gloucester went with Henry to France, and came back the next spring, replacing Bedford as regent or lieutenant some time before May, 1422, when Bedford accompanied Queen Katherine and the infant prince to France. He held this post until Henry's death, when the king's will provided for the establishment of a Council during the prince's minority.

542-3. The Durham MS printed by the EETS has in the margin : scilicet de secundo redditu suo de ffrancia.

548. *with to glade.* The usual medieval word-order; see note on Mâle Règle 150.

550. The EETS text reads *god* instead of *him.* The phrase is an ejaculation.

561. This MS omits the rime-word *Vegece,* i.e., Vegetius' Art of Chivalry, a work highly valued in the Middle Ages, and among those recommended by Hoccleve for Oldcastle's reading in place of his dangerous incursions into Holy Writ; see the poem to Oldcastle, line 196

The work had been translated into French by Jean de Meun and also by Jean de Vignay(?); into English for Sir Thomas Berkeley in 1408. See the SATF edition of 1897, the Brit.Mus. catalogue of Royal MSS under 18 A xii, 20 B xi. The omission of the word is probably due to the scribe's intention of rubricking it later, as was often done with special words.

563. A headless line.

565. *for the maistrie.* See note on Mâle Règle 149.

566. *Bygonde,* etc. "Beyond (the sea) he hath wel proved", etc.

567. *Chirburgh.* See note on line 576 below.

573. *Duke Herry.* As no prince of the blood royal, fighting in France, bore the name Henry, I would interpret this allusion as to Henry the Fourth, whom Hoccleve may call "duke" to distinguish him from the reigning king. The words *this prince,* in line 574, are then in the nominative case.

576. *Costantin.* The district of the Côtentin, or outer peninsula of Normandy, was overrun by Gloucester after Easter 1418; he encountered serious resistance only at Cherbourg, which stood a fairly long siege, surrendering October first.

577. *bi preising.* EETS ed. reads *hy preysynge.*

579. *a worthi stile,* a dignified title or reputation.

581. The EETS has no *and that is.*

583. Note the metaphor.

587-8. "Lest I might perchance reduce his credit, if through my ignorance (ignorantly) I should enumerate (i.e. understate) them." The word *allege* has in late Mid.Eng. a meaning of "lighten, reduce", although it is thus applied usually to pain or misery, as in Lover's Mass 160. Cp. Chaucer's Troilus iv:802-5.

586-7. *Humfrey,* interpreted as "homme ferai". This mode of elucidation is characteristically medieval. Hoccleve exaggerates it into a "conceit" in his Complaint of the Virgin Mary, EETS ed. i, p. 6; but a very marked example of the method is Giovanni del Virgilio's explanation of the name *Prometheus* as from *"pro* id est provisio, *me* id est mentis, *theus* id est divine, unde prometheus id est provisio divine mentis." (See Dante and Giov. del Virgilio, by Wicksteed and Gardner, 1902, p. 318.) Compare Holkot's fantasy on *Ave,* the first word of the Salutation to Mary, as a reversal of *Eva,* the source of human unhappiness; the passage is in lectio 195 of the Commentary on Sapience, a book cited by Hoccleve in Mâle Règle 249,— see note. Chaucer "interprets" the name *Melibeus,* see line 2600 of that Tale.

592 ff. "Warlike Mars, at his birth, gave him that name" etc. Mars presided over Humphrey's birth, says Hoccleve.

610 ff. Apparently the words *O lorde* are an ejaculation, with no reference to an earthly nobleman. Read them with a question-mark after *dide,* line 613, and interpret "whether fere or cowardyse" as "Was it fear or cowardice?"—an ironical question. Gloucester's daring at the siege of Rouen is described in John Page's (contemporary) poem, written by an eyewitness; it is pubd. by the Camden Society, where, on p. 11, we find:—

> Glouceter that gracyus home
> From the sege of Chirborough he come
> At the Port Synt Hyllarye
> Fulle manfully loggyd he
> In caste of stone in schot of quarelle
> He dradde hym for noo perelle
> But wanne worschyppe with his werre
> And lay hys enmys fulle nerre
> Thanne any man that there was
> Be xl rode and more in spas.

Later in the same poem we read that the besieged's shots wrought much damage to the English,—"And namely Gloucester that lord so dere, For he was loggyd them so nere."

613. *dide.* Read with question-mark after *dide.* Cp. Lydgate's FaPrinces ix:3423, "As Petrark did, and also Iohn Bochas". Or the confession of the Earl of Cambridge after discovery of the conspiracy against Henry the Fifth, that certain men knew not of the extent of the plan, "but Grey dyd". See Rymer's Foedera, ix:300-01.

616. *what* is an exclamation.

620. *ascance.* Shakespeare, Lucrece 637, uses *askance* as a verb,—"turn away". Can it here have the meaning "Begone!"? In the Court of Sapience ii:1167 we find: "Myght saye askaunce on thys wyse be I wyll"; which I would interpret as "Go to! I shall be as I am moved to be!" The student will distinguish between this word and *ascaunces,* meaning *as if,* for which cp. Chaucer's Troilus i:292, translating Boccaccio's *Quasi.*

623. *ministrith.* An imperative;—"give me some!" Read with pause after *Can I* in 622, comma after *you* here.

626. Read with a question-mark after *of.*

631. In the EETS ed. this line has no *to,* and Furnivall interprets *that* as meaning *what,* i.e., "what book".

638-42. Cp. Chaucer's Troilus i:1065 ff., a passage which Kittredge has shown to be from Geoffroi de Vinsauf's Nova Poetria 43-45.

640. *mental ye.* This phrase, and *inward sight,* are frequent in Lydgate. See FaPrinces i:17, v:453, Troy Book ii:2138, 3180, iv:177, 5045, v:51, 815, 1709, 3059, 3447. Cp. Chaucer's MLTale 454-5; and cp. Isidor's Etymologiae xi:1,20, where the power of sight is divided as "externa aetherea luce aut interno spiritu lucido". See St. Augustine, Confess. vii:ch. 17; see Boethius, Consol. Philos. iii, metr. 11.

643, 657, 662. The EETS ed. reads *for the deffaute, I now byseeche, Syn now,* etc.

669. *quarter sak,* a sack holding a quarter of a hundredweight, double the usual size.

675. The EETS ed. reads *mis-berynge.*

691. *make partie,* "put up a fight".

694. *The wyf of Bathe.* See WBTale 81, 88.

721. *evere.* EETS *ay.*

724. See Genesis iii:15.

727-8. Hoccleve's hand with a jest against women is lighter than Lydgate's.

733-34. See Genesis iii:16.

736. See the conclusion of the Wife of Bath's prologue.

751. "for the sake of him that died," i.e. "In God's name, how am *i* at fault?"

752. The EETS ed. reads *dar I me auante,* i.e., "I dare assert".

755, 756. The EETS reads *largeliche, swart wrooth.*

759. *for youre fader kyn,* a common asseveration; see its use by the Host, headlink to the MoTale, 43.

764 ff. Cp. Chaucer ProlCantTales 731 ff.

772. *conpleiningly,* under protest. Cp. Lydgate's expressions of reluctant disgust as he translates attacks on women in the Troy Book, e.g., i:2100, ii:3560.

778. EETS ed. reads *woot I neuere,* etc.

780-2. Note the quick crisp dialogue here. The only bit comparable in Lydgate is the dispute between Boccaccio and Brunhilda, FaPrinces ix:190 ff.; but that moves in much larger courses, and is a translation. Cp. Chaucer's dialogue in the BoDuchesse, especially 749-57, 1045 ff., 1308-10.

789. *kut to kepe.* The NED says that this phrase is "of obscure origin", and suggests that it means "keep your distance, be reserved". The earliest cited case is from the Coventry Play of the Woman Taken in Adultery; the culprit is told by her captors that she shall be taught "bettyr to kepe thi kutte". The next case is this passage, then Skelton's Philip Sparrow 118. It seems to me that in all these cases a better interpretation is "be on guard, mind yourself".

791. EETS has no *nowe.*

806. *as wisly god me blesse.* An asseveration.

810. *bite me the crowe.* Perhaps "May I die!" i.e., may crows or carrion birds peck me!

818-19. Note the like rime. Provided the two words were different parts of speech, the usage was allowable in Middle English. It was very common, and unrestricted, in French; note the greater frequency of such rimes in e.g. Chaucer's Book of the Duchesse as compared with his later work.

820. *Romayn dedis,* the Gesta Romanorum, a Latin collection of anecdotes and tales, of the late thirteenth or early fourteenth century; author uncertain. It is discussed by Warton in a special section of his HistEngPoetry, see ed. by Hazlitt i :238 ff., and was used by Gower, Hoccleve, and Shakespeare. The Latin is ed. by W. Dick, Leipzig 1890, earlier by Oesterley. An Eng. prose translation is in MS Harley 7333, etc., ed. by Sir F. Madden for the Roxburghe Club, ed. EETS 1879. Modern Engl. transl. by Charles Swan, N. Y., 1924.

826. *sope.* Manufactured in England in the fourteenth century. The word is used in the transl. of Jeremiah ii :22 and of Malachi iii :2, and means there a lye, or water alkalised by vegetable ashes. The Vulgate word in both cases is *herba.*

IN PRAISE OF CHAUCER
(from the Regement of Princes)

1956. *ffadir,* i.e., the old beggar with whom Hoccleve has been talking, who has advised him to write.

1968. *synguleer.* This word, in Chaucer and in Middle English, meant "separate, single, private, especial". Cp. FaPrinces A 447 here,—"to censure in especial"; cp. the phrase "synguleer bataile" as "single combat", *ibid.* ii :4305, and that of "syngular profites" as "individual advantages", *ibid.* iii :1249. In St. Albon ii :92 we read "Not singuler founde nor yet parciall". And note the tautology in FaPrin. iii :2258,—"a special syngulerte".

1971. *He name.* Read *His name;* the scribe errs.

1978. *I ment* is one word, the past participle *meant.* See 2090, 2100.

2083. Death is treated as feminine in this line and in 2099, 2101, 2103, 2105.

2090. *I now* is one word, i.e., *enough.* Cp. *I leche,* i.e., *yliche,* "alike", in 2100.

2091-92. "I would that that cumberworld were slain."

2096-97. The syntax is muddled, but the meaning is: "No more, as experience shows, (to) an excellent faithful servant than to a vicious lord."

2105. *nedes do moot sche.* Compare Guillaume de Machaut, in the Jugement de Roy de Behaingne 730, of Fortune's variance,—"Car elle fist dou faire son devoir", etc. See Chaucer's handling, BoDuchesse 675-82. See Boethius ii prose 1.

4978 ff. Hoccleve says that Chaucer has discussed the keeping of the Sabbath holy, and that a prince who would be obeyed by his subjects must obey God's command on this point and on others. See the Parson's Tale 667.

4987. *ful many a lyne.* Of poems by Chaucer to the Virgin we have the A. B. C., the Invocation at the opening of the Second Nun's Tale, and the Prioress' prayer at the beginning of her Tale.

4995-8. *here his likinesse.* The portrait of Chaucer which appears on the margin of a few MSS of the Regement at this point is our most authentic representation of him. That of the codex Harley 4866 is closely duplicated in the volume formerly Phillipps 1099, now in the hands of Dr. Rosenbach of New York City; and although a half-length, it is apparently the same picture as the Sloane portrait in the National Portrait Gallery and the "Clarendon" portrait, which are full-length. An identical full-length is on the single sheet of vellum marked MS Adds. 5141 in the British Museum; and the only difference of type between them and the half-length as here is that the MS-artist has turned the right hand of Chaucer from the penner which hangs upon his breast to point at the stanza mentioning his likeness. In MS Royal 17 D vi's copy of the Regement the portrait on the margin is quite other than these, a full-length in another pose; see its reproduction in Spielmann's Portraits of Chaucer to face p. 120, and see reprods. *ibid.,* of other Chaucer portraits. Most MSS of the Regement are without the picture; it has been cut out of Harley 4826, but was never in Brit.Mus. Adds. 18632, Arundel 59, Harley 116, Harley 372, Royal 17 C xiv, Royal 17 D xviii, Royal 17 D xix, Sloane 1212, Sloane 1825, Ashmole 40, Dugdale 45. Regarding the Regement-MSS of the University Library, Cambridge, and of Cambridge colleges, I cannot speak; but neither the official catalogues nor Spielmann's monograph mention the existence of a Chaucer-portrait in any of them, as is also the case with the two McClean MSS in the Fitzwilliam Museum, Cambridge.

Brit.Mus.Arundel 38, the gift-copy to Prince Henry of Hoccleve's poem has on fol. 37 a miniature of Hoccleve presenting the book; but leaf 91, which probably carried a portrait of Chaucer, has been cut out, and with it lines 4990-5042. The leaf was lacking in Urry's time; see preface to the 1721 Chaucer.

THE CHURL AND THE BIRD

1. *Problemes,* etc. The MSS Harley, Caligula, and Trinity read as here; Lansdowne and Hh read *Problemys liknessis and figures,* Hh altering the last word to *signes.* The subject has no verb; should we omit *And* from line 3 we get a predicate.

6-9. *Like as the Bibyll.* See Judges ix:8-15.

13. *tarage.* See note on line 350 below.

15. *Poetes Laureat.* Lydgate is alluding to Aesop, whom he terms "this poyet laureat" in the prologue to his version of some of the Fables. The name was given in the late Middle Ages to a man honored by an University degree, e.g., Bernard André the blind historiographer of Henry VII, Whitinton the grammarian, Skelton; or it was applied to eminent poets generally. Higden so terms Homer; Burgh, in his letter to Lydgate, applies the word to Boccaccio; in his Kingis Quair, stanza 197, King James applies it to Gower and to Chaucer; Dunbar in his Golden Targe uses ·it of Lydgate. See introd. to Skelton here.

29. Lydgate here comments on the use of the "fable" to convey a lesson; this was the accepted medieval and Christian view of literature, especially of poetry. See e.g. FaPrinces iii:3830-31, where the French original says that poetry, like Holy Scripture, reveals "soubz couerture de figures . . . . les choses advenir". Boccaccio at this point has:—"ignari plerique existiment . . . . poetas mendaces et fabulosos homines esse . . . Sola quantum humane imbecillitati possibile est sancte pagine vestigia sequi conata. Nam prout illa divine mentis arcana prophetis futura que sub figurarum tegmine reserauit, sic et hoc celsos suorum conceptus sub figmentorum velamine tradere orsa est."

Hawes in his Pastime 659-665 recognizes this as the correct procedure, but he laments *ibid.* 737 ff. that the dull rude people fail to understand the method. Nevill in his envoy line 14 states that his "humble style" is due to his having worked "without cloke".

35. *paunflete,* pamphlet. The uses of this word by Hoccleve, RegPrinces 2060, and by Lydgate here, are two of the earliest in English. See Skelton, Garland 491.

43-44. Cp. Henryson, Fables 1944-45,—"Quhilum thair wynnit in a wildernes. As myne authour expresli can declair."

50 ff. See Skelton in his Garland, stanzas 93, 94, 95.

51. *couerd.* This reading, *coueryd,* is also in MSS Hh and Kk; Harley, Trinity, and Lansdowne have *turued,* and Caligula *clowryd.* See the turfed seats pictured in the Roman de la Rose, reproduced from MS in Amherst-Cecil's history of gardening in England, ed. of 1910, to face pp. 50, 56. Cp. Chaucer's Troilus ii:820-22 for Cressida's garden; cp. the "benched herber grene" in Black Knight 125-6. In Wordsworth's Descriptive Sketches 19 sod seats are mentioned.

52. There is no verb for *condites.*

53-4. *ayenst the sonne shene.* The same phrase is in Troy Book i:1268; cp. *ibid.* ii:2460, and cp. the rivers of FaPrinces i:577-78. Running water was a necessary furnishing of a medieval garden.

55. *burbly.* This is the only case given in NED.

56. *shewing.* We expect a finite verb.

59. *gold were,* golden wire. The likening of hair to gold wire is a very frequent simile in Lydgate and in later poets; Schick, note on Temple of Glass 271, cannot trace the comparison earlier. See Troy Book i:1977, 2042, ii:4741-2, iii:4125, iv:6424, etc.

60, 61. If these lines were transposed the order of thought would be clearer.

68. *Alceste.* With this mention of the wife of Admetus as if she were a star, the daystar, cp. Chaucer's Legend, prol. (A) 513-15,—

> No wonder is thogh Iove hir stellifye
> As tellith Agaton, for hir goodnesse
> Hir whyte coroun berth of hit witnesse.

The writer Agaton has been no further identified than by Sandras, who suggested (Etude sur Chaucer 115-16), that an Agaton might be meant whose comedy "The Flower", now unknown, is mentioned in Aristotle's Poetics. With the Chaucerian passage cp. Lydgate's allusions to the daisy as Alceste's flower, Secrees 1305-6, and Looke in thy Mirour, printed Halliwell, p. 161. In TemGlass 70-74 he mentions the transformation of Alceste into a daisy. Cp. Court of Love 103-5. Gower's treatment of Alceste, Confessio vii:1917-43, is very brief and bald, as is that of Fulgentius in his Mythologiae.

It may be noted that Shirley, in his compendium of the Legend, the "Cronycle made by Chaucier", copied in MS Ashmole 59, confuses Alcestis and Alcyone in his last stanza. Printed Chaucer Soc., Odd Texts, pp. vi ff.

73. *sugred.* See notes on Thebes 52 and FaPrinces A 243.

74. *draw along,* drawn along, prolonged. See Walton A 288, C 33, FaPrinces ii:900, v:659.

75. *that all the wood rong.* Cp. PoFoules 491-4, FlLeaf 100, BlKnight 45, Troy Book i:3933, Cuckoo 99-100, Kingis Quair stanza 33. Marie de France in her fable "De volucribus et rege eorum", line 12, says "Kar tut le bois fist retentir".

76. This line read in Longleat "On the morowe", etc. The corrector struck out *On* and wrote *Tyl.* Cp. Troy Book iv:4024, "Til on a morwe whan Phebus shoon ful bri3t", and a nearly identical line FaPrinces v:1524. Also St.Albon i:349 and cp. Chaucer's Legend 773. Cp. also Thebes 4014, FaPrinces iii:2383.

87-8. See Barclay, Eclogue iv:63, p. 317 here.

96 ff. Here and 120 ff., cp. the Manciple's Tale 59-70; cp. Boethius' Consolatio, iii metre 2:19 ff.

115. MSS Linc. and Lansd. read *morwenyng,* Caligula *in the gray mornynge.*

122. *wastel breed.* This was the food of the Prioress' little dogs, CTprol. 147.

124-6. See Lydgate's Aesop, fable i:174-5 (Zupitza) :—

> Set more store I haue hit of nature
> Among rude chaffe to shrape for my pasture.

132. *bere at the stake.* Bear-baiting was a popular pastime in England earlier than Elizabeth's time.

143. *maugre thyn hede,* "in spite of you". See KnTale 311, NPTale 592, WBTale 31, and often.

145. Cp. Parlament of Byrdes 69-70, ed. Hazlitt in EEPopPoetry iii:167 :—

> For the byrde that can not speake nor syng
> Shall to the kytchyn to serue the kynge.

162. Cp. Lydgate's St.Margaret 216, "Trust me welle this no feyned tale".

175. *lyme twiggis* (see line 192). Limed twigs were smeared with birdlime, a viscous preparation made from the bark of holly (NED) to hold the feet of birds fast. See Piers of Fulham as below, line 185 note.

177. *fetters.* The Longleat MS reads *feders,* feathers. Cp. PoFoules 346, where the Oxford MSS change *eles,* "eels", to *egles,* "eagles"; and *ibid.* 521, 588, where some MSS change *faconde,* "eloquent", to *faucon,* "falcon", under pressure of the many bird-allusions of the poem. Note also the Trin.Coll. text of Lydgate's fable of the Wolf and the Lamb, where, in line 85, the scribe has altered the correct *wole,* "wool", to *wolf.*

182. *treacle,* triacle, a remedy, "theriacum"; originally an antidote against poison. A dignified word in this period, often applied by Lydgate to Christ or to the Virgin; now transferred to a substance resembling in appearance the liquid in which the medieval remedy was given.

185-6. Cp. Kingis Quair stanza 135,—"For as the foulere quhistlith in his throte Diuersely to counterfete the brid And feynis mony a suete and strange note That in the busk for his desate is hid Til sche be fast lokin his net amyd." Cp. Piers of Fulham, in Hazlitt's EEPopPo ii :94-96.

206-7. See Lydgate's Thebes 3447-49.

209-10. *clymbe to high,* etc. One of Lydgate's most frequent metaphors, especially in his Fall of Princes; it depends on Fortune's wheel. Other MSS read—*torne felyth oft his fall vnsoft.*

213-14. Hawes' Example of Virtue, stanza 59, has "For a thing lost without recover Look that thou never be too pensive."

220. Cp. Chaucer's Legend, B-prol. 134 ff.,—"hem thoughte hit did hem good To singe of him, and in hir song despyse The foule cherl that for his covetyse Had hem betrayed with his sophistrye."

227. MSS Linc., Lansd., Hh, read "riht to pleyne & maken dool"; Trinity has—"compleyn & make", etc.; Harley has "to compleyn and make", etc. See Troy Book i :1918, "þou mygtest wel compleyne and make dool."

232. *Iagounce.* The French poem has "Qui apelee est Iacintus Vne once peise bien ou plus." See descr. of the stone Hyacinthus in Evax, De Gemmis. This work (transl. by Moller, Wittenberg, 1574) is cited by Lydgate in his fable of the Cock and Precious Stone, so closely related to this poem. Evax, "rex Arabum", is there mentioned by name, as in the Italian L'Intelligenza, a fourteenth-century poem. See lines 152 ff. of Lydgate's fable, Archiv, vol 85.

239 ff. Cp. the virtues of "jasp" as listed by Henryson in his Fables 120 ff.

259. *perry . . . garnade.* Old French *pierrerie,* precious stones. *Garnade,* i.e. Granada, was under the Moorish dynasty of the Nasrides, 1238-1492, the seat of a brilliant civilization, the wealthiest of Spanish cities, and the centre of the European jewel-trade. See Garl. 485.

260 ff. A favorite theme with Lydgate. Cp. his fable of the Cock and Precious Stone lines 187 ff.—

> Thus euery þyng foloweþ hys nature
> Pryncys to reygne knyghtys for batayll
> Plowmen for tylþe shypmen forto sayll.

See also his poem with refrain "Thus euery thyng draweth to his semblable", in Harley 2251 and Ashmole 59, of which a stanza is cited in note on line 351 below; see a similar poem with the refrain "Utter thy Langage", in Halliwell MinPo, p. 173; see FaPrinces iii :3786-3822, and the original in Laurent's French, iii chap. 14. See Barclay, Ecl. iv :325 ff., as here.

266. *lapidary.* Chaucer, HoFame 1352, refers to the "Lapidaire". Various catalogues of precious stones and their virtues were current in the Middle Ages. That of "Evax rex Arabum" is cited in note on line 232 above; that of Marbodus, bishop of Rennes in the 11-12th centuries, was widely known; the material of Isidor, Etymol. xvi cap. 9, and of Vincent de Beauvais in his Speculum Naturale, was also much used. See Pannier, Les lapidaires français des xii, xiii, et xiv siècles, Paris, 1882.

275. This comparison was proverbial for dullness of perception. See Chaucer's Troilus i :731; see his Boethius v prose 4 and Skeat's note.

276. For the expression see Chaucer's Troilus v :1433, KnTale 980; see 340 below.

280. This was a proverb;—"Whoever is serf to a boor is wretched". See 371, 374 below.

290. The Longleat scribe ignores the peculiarly Lydgatian form of *continue,* which is necessary for rime.

306. *All is not gold,* etc. This very old proverb is often cited by Lydgate; see FaPrinces iv :2707, 2944, viii :3160; see Midsummer Rose, stanza 2, in Halliwell MinPo, p. 22. Chaucer uses the saying in CanYeoTale 409-10. It is found in Alanus' Parabolae iii :1 as "Non teneas aurum totum quod splendet ut aurum".

345. Cp. CantTales prol. 9.

350. *tarage.* This word, apparently meaning "character, savor, quality", is of uncertain origin, and is almost exclusively used by Lydgate. Henryson has it once at least, but it took no root in the language.

351 ff. This theme is closely allied to that touched on in line 260 above. Lydgate was perhaps influenced by the passage on dreams which Chaucer, PoFoules 99-105, drew from Claudian; but he is hardly likely to have known Propertius, Eleg. II, i:43-44, "navita de ventis, de tauris narrat arator, Enumerat miles vulnera, pastor oves." See the theme again in the poem mentioned in note on 260 above; I cite from MS Harley 2251, fol. 19b:—

> With philosophres . trete of philosophie
> With the marchant . trete of riches
> With the poete . trete of poetrye
> With gentilmen . trete of gentilnes
> And serve a cherle . aftir his rudenes
> Who currieth hors . resortith to the stable
> Plowman in tilth . sette al theyr besynes
> Thus euery thyng . drawith to his semblable

356-7. MSS Trinity and Calig. agree with Longleat here; others have line 357 as 356, and as 357 have "The hunter to speke of venerye".

359. *popyngay,* parrot. The parrot was in this period valued as an accessory to luxurious life. Elizabeth of York, queen of Henry VII, paid in July 1502 the sum of 13 shillings and fourpence for a parrot, the same sum which she paid the musician Cornish for setting a carol in December, 1502, and the same sum which she paid weekly for the diet and clothing of her three young kinsfolk, the Courtenay children, with their three servants, in the country. See Nicolas' Privy Purse Expenses of Elizabeth of York, London, 1830, pp. 62-3, 30, 83.

363. *hensforth my lyvyng.* An accusative of duration of time.

374-5. This proverb is in Skelton's Garland lines 1418-19, also in Barclay's transl. of Mancini,—"Amonge olde parables this often haue I read, A vilayns subiect, a ielous boyes wife And a childes birde are wo and harde bested."

379. *Goo litil quayeer.* On this very old form of envoy see Tatlock in ModPhil. 18:115-118.

380. *my maistir.* See introduction above.

385. See note on Cavendish line 52.

HORNS AWAY

10. *Charbonclis.* The carbuncle or ruby, very highly valued by the Middle Ages, was believed to emit light in darkness. In the De Planctu Naturae of Alanus, which Lydgate quotes just below, we find:—"Carbunculus, qui solis gerens imaginem, suo radiationis cereo noctis proscribens umbracula" etc. The same is recorded in Bartholomaeus Anglicus' De Proprietatibus Rerum, xvi:26; and references to the stone in early French and English are very numerous. See Chaucer's Legend 1119, Lydgate's Troy Book ii:1027-30, iii:4787-9. In Renaud's Li Biaus Desconus 1897-1900 a carbuncle lights the castle at night.

17-22. *Aleyn,* Alanus de Insulis, died 1202. His De Planctu Naturae is here referred to, but not correctly. Lydgate confuses the description of Nature there found with the description of Venus in the PoFoules, where Chaucer says that Nature, presiding over the birds, is attired as Aleyn describes her; later in the poem, lines 269-73, Chaucer says of Venus that she lies covered below the breast with "a subtle kerchef of Valence". Alanus' description of Nature gave the goddess an elaborate diadem, carefully listing the stones, and a robe, mantle, and tunic on which were depicted all living and growing things. Lydgate has fused recollections, and given Nature as headgear the coverlet of Venus. But in his ResonandSens, 407 ff., he follows Alanus.

23. *Texemplyfye,* etc. This line is wrongly printed NED, s.v. *exemplify,* as "I exemplefye", etc. It is "To exemplify".

27. *Heleyne,* etc. This is a very brief use of the common medieval list. See the Epithalamium for Gloucester 71 and note.

32. *Ther bewte couthe.* Apparently an ablative absolute; "their beauty being so evident". In such case, *hornys wer* means simply "horns were", and not "the defence of horns".

37. *arche wyves.* This phrase is used by Chaucer in the envoy to the Clerk's Tale, where Skeat explains it as "ruling wives". For *arch* in this sense the earliest NED citation is of 1547; for the sense of "clever, crafty", the earliest is of 1662.

45. *Peysed.* We might conjecture *Peysyth* here, on the analogy of *Yeuyth,* line 48, but the ablative absolute is very common in Lydgate.

49. *Grettest of vertues,* etc. Lydgate says the same thing in his St. Albon i:480-1,— "the chefe founderesse Of all vertues / that called is mekenes." And in the same poem i:487-8, he says that humility "bereth vp all / and hath the souereynte." Cp. *ibid.* 493-4. In the Wisdom of Solomon x:12 it is godliness, not humility that is "stronger than all". No exact parallel to Lydgate's phrase is found in Proverbs; but see xv:33, xvi:19, xviii:12. Tennyson, in the Holy Grail 145, refers to "True humility, the highest virtue, mother of all"; and his commentator Lester cites Philippians ii:3-8. See James iv:6, 1st Peter v:5.

52. Cp. St. Albon iii:569, "Take hede hereto and yeueth good audience."

59-64. There are no predicate verbs for the subjects.

60. *iust convenience,* i.e., "by perfect agreement (are) all virtues conjoined."

62. *roose of Jerycho,* etc. See the poem beginning "Queen of heuene" etc., printed by MacCracken i:284, line 27:—"Rose of Iherico groweth noon so fressh in May."

BYCORNE AND CHICHEVACHE

It was suggested, p. 114 *ante,* that the text of this poem in MS Trin.Coll.Cambridge R 3, 20 was the source of the text as in MS Harley 2251. A possible point against this is the appearance of *not,* line 28, in the later MSS, but lacking in Shirley's copy; another point is the reading of line 98. It should also be noted that Shirley transposed stanzas 2 and 3, marking them in the margin as *a* and *b* for correction; but the Harley scribe paid no attention to this, and the false sequence of stanzas as in his text remains in Dodsley, in Montaiglon, in Halliwell, in Morley, and in Neilson and Webster. Some of Shirley's orthographic tricks are evident; his *eo* for long *e,* as in lines 71, 74, 75, 82, 86, 93, 104, 105, 108, 124, 127; his *nuwe* for *newe,* 112; his *filowing* for *following* as in the margin beside stanza 4; and note his frequent inorganic final *e,* as in *cane, frome,* etc.

13. *in sentence.* This word signified "meaning, import". So in CTprol 800, "Tales of best sentence and most solas". So in NPTale 345, "Ma dame, the sentence of this Latin is". It could also mean "opinion", see Troy Book ii:2697, 3006, etc. But the phrase is often with Lydgate a mere padding-formula, as here; and see Troy Book i:428. Cp. also Churl 302, Horns 15, ResonandSens 6448, FaPrin. i:3316.

16. *foode.* The MS wrongly reads *foote.*

17. *men.* The Harley MS omitted this word, and a later hand has inserted, with caret, *husbondis,* the *h* written badly. Halliwell read this *husks never* and his error is preserved by Montaiglon and by Neilson, but not by Dodsley or by Morley.

21. The MS reads *Lyke luk,* etc.

22. Cp. the French "Bigorne suis en Bigornois". See Archiv 114:80.

31. *at þe countretayle,* in retort. The tally and countertally, two halves of a hazel or ash rod, were used in the days before written accounts were common. They were scored across, split lengthwise, and given to the two parties in a bargain. When payment was due, the tally and countertally were produced. Hence the figurative sense as here and in ClTale envoy.

32. *hewe.* The NED interprets this as "to strike". Its only other citation is from Addison. See Doctor Doubble Ale, line 32, in Hazlitt's EEPopPo iii:316. The usage in FlCourtesy 158, Troy Book i:1230-32, is another idiom.

35. The NED cites this passage under *forbear* 7 as "to refrain from using, uttering". The sense seems to be "cannot restrain (overbear) their husbands in speech". The Harley MS reads *oon woord,* as if "one word".

38. *per living;* an accusative of duration of time; "all their life long". See 48.

41. *chaumpartye.* Latin *campi-partem,* a divided field; French *chaumpart.* Chaucer, KnTale 1091, used the word in the sense of "partnership in power". Lydgate, says the NED,

seems to have misunderstood "holde chaumpartye" as "to hold rivalry or contest with, to resist". He was followed by some of the 16th century archaists, says NED.

71. *O noble wyves.* Cp. the Clerk's envoy, passim, for this and various other phrases here borrowed by Lydgate.

85. *In existence,* in reality. Used definitely in this sense HoFame 266, but here merely padding for rime. Cp. 13 above, on the same rime-sound.

88. *bountee,* etc. "Or more patient than Griselda, to augment their excellence." Bounty and beauty were two main categories of perfection; see Flower of Courtesy 216-217, where the poet says that "bountee and beautie both in her demeyne, She maketh bountee alwey souereyne". That is, graciousness has with her precedence over physical perfection. See also Gower's ballade 31, in ed. by Macaulay i:363. From its first usage in English, ca. 1300, the word *bounty* has also a narrower sense of "kindness, liberality"; see ResonandSens 6160 ff., but see *ibid.* 6450. Cp. Shakespeare's song "Who Is Sylvia," in Two Gentlemen of Verona,— "Is she kind as she is fair? For beauty lives with kindness". And cp. BoDuch 1195-8, also its direct sources, Machaut's Roi de Behaingne 461-2, Remède de Fortune 1671-83. See the variant-stanza in one MS of Chaucer's Troilus, printed in Root's ed., p. 140.

91. *to breke with my faaste,* to break my fast with. For the word-order, see Thebes 35 and note.

96. *more þane thritty Mayes.* The French text (Montaiglon xi:284) says "Des ans y a plus de deux cens"; that in Archiv 114:83 reads "Il y a des ans bien deux cens". Whether Lydgate, by altering into this phrase, means that thirty years have elapsed since Chaucer wrote his Griselda, is uncertain.

98. This line gave the scribes some trouble. Harley writes "But yit oon Gresield", etc.; R 3, 19 has "But oone lyke Gresild", etc. If we keep this reading, we must render *fonde* in 98 as "discover", in 99 as "found".

105 ff. In the Bigorne text printed Archiv 114:80 there is at this point a stanza uttered by a wife who sees Bigorne about to lay hold on her husband. Lydgate has a stanza of lament by a husband.

110. *an impossible.* In English of this period, *impossible* was frequently a substantive. See WB prol. 688 etc., and many cases in Lydgate, e. g., FaPrin. i:6857.

115. *made þeyre avowe,* sworn. On many formal occasions, when a lord and his courtiers pledged themselves to some undertaking, their oaths were made upon the body of a bird. The Vows of the Swan were taken by Edward I in 1306, when, according to the chronicler Matthew of Westminster, two swans appeared before the king as he was knighting his son previous to the invasion of Scotland. Cp. especially here the Vows of the Peacock. The peacock was in Greek and Roman times regarded as one of the greatest of table delicacies; Cicero, writing to Paetus, bids his correspondent marvel at his temerity in entertaining Hirtius (a well-known gourmand) when he has no peacock to set before him. In the Middle Ages the peacock was "la viande des preux"; at state banquets it was formally set upon the table by the lady of greatest rank or beauty, to the accompaniment of music; and it was placed before the most honored guest that he might carve it. It became customary for the carver, and in turn the knights present, to pledge themselves to further achievement in the names of "God, Our Lady, the ladies, and the peacock". Les Voeux du Paon, written about 1310 by Jacques de Longuyon, describes such a feast, such vows, and their fulfilment; see Ward, Cat. of Romances, i:146. That Lydgate knew the custom, and perhaps knew of Longuyon's epic, appears from his allusions to the "vowes of pecok"; a stanza in his Midsummer Rose, pr. Halliwell, p. 22, contains the lines:—

> Where ben of Fraunce all the dozepiere
> Which in Gaule had the governaunce?
> Vowes of pecok with all ther proude chere?
> The worthy nyne with all ther high bobbaunce?

See Gaston Paris, La littérature française au moyen-âge, p. 76; see Koeppel in Archiv 108:29.

There is also in French a poem entitled Les Voeux du Héron, prescribing vows taken by Edward III and many of his court in 1338, pledging Englishmen to perform marvels in their invasion of France; these vows were sworn at the instigation of Robert d'Artois, an exiled Frenchman, who served at the King's banquet a roasted heron with the taunt that as it was the most timid of birds it should be an example to the most cowardly of men. This poem is printed in La Curne de Ste. Palaye's Mémoires sur l'ancienne chevalerie, iii.

In the prologue to the tale of Beryn we find "I make a vowe to the pecock"; and when Chaucer's Sir Thopas, line 151, swears "by ale and breed", it is probably intended as a burlesque of the solemn oaths taken upon the dish of honor, the peacock.

116. Harley 2251 reads *exile for euer pacience*. The words *for evir* have been written on the margin of our text, in darker ink, with a caret after *exyle*.

117. *cryed wolffes hede obedyence*. An outlaw, in the fifteenth century, was said to carry a wolf's head on his shoulders, because he was hunted down like a wolf, the terror of the English medieval countryside. See Gamelyn 700, 710, 722. Lydgate uses the expression in FaPrinces vii:1261, "Cried woluis hed was vertuous sobirnesse", i. e. "It was cried,—Away with virtuous soberness!"

120. The MS R 3, 19 reads *fast full longe*.

PROLOGUE TO THE SIEGE OF THEBES

1 ff. A temporal clause describing the season of the year is a favorite mode of opening with medieval writers. Nigel Wireker's Contra Curiales begins:—

> Postquam tristis hiems Zephyro spirante recessit
> Grando, nives, pluviae, consuluere fugae,
> Terra, parens florum, vires rediviva resumpsit.   (Wright, Satir. Po. i)

The Metamorphosis Goliae of Walter Map begins:—

> Sole post arietem taurum subintrante
> Novo terrae faciem flore picturante.

The fourth book of Guido delle Colonne's Historia Trojana, cited by Skeat in his note on the opening of Chaucer's Prologue, begins:—Tempus erat quo sol maturans sub obliquo Zodiaci circulo cursum sub signo iam intrauerat Arietis; see my Chaucer Manual, p. 267.

The combination of mythology with nature-description in a temporal clause opening with *When* became still more common after Chaucer. In Lydgate's Troy Book it frequently serves as an introduction to a new phase of the story, cp. i:3094, 3907, ii:3319, 5070, etc.; he uses it also Secrees 1296, Pedigree of Henry VI line 287 ff., etc. The printer Copland's rejection of the method, and some modern acceptances of it, are noted with Cavendish's Metrical Visions, line 1 here. In this poem Lydgate has the date of the Canterbury Pilgrimage in mind, and says that the sun has entered the Bull, the next constellation to the Ram which Chaucer mentioned in his line 8.

Observe the sentence-structure of this opening in comparison with that of Chaucer. Chaucer's first eighteen lines assure us of his full command of complex phrasing, his clear view of his goal. In line 12, *Than longen folk* is the prompt and expected conclusion of the *Whan* of lines 1 and 5. But Lydgate's endeavor to imitate this poise expresses itself only in beginnings and rebeginnings, in an accumulation of clauses to their final exhaustion in line 78—or 91?—without reaching a principal verb. His habitual use of the ablative absolute and of the participles as a finite verb, as here, is one of his most baffling ineptitudes; see lines 17, 35, 49, 53, 55, 56. But even were finite verbs substituted, the construction of the paragraph as a whole would not be established; this idiosyncrasy of Lydgate's is an additional complication, not a fundamental cause of his incoherence.

3. *Satourn old*. Saturn was decribed by Albricus, De Deorum Imaginibus, as "homo senex, canus, prolixa barba, curvus, tristis et pallidus, tecto capite, colore glauco." He is so described in Lydgate's ResonandSens 1347, 3091, 3103; Sackville in his Induction line 3 borrows this verse from Lydgate.

8. *Shour . . . made avale*. If Saturn were in Virgo and the moon were in opposition to him, she must be in Pisces, a "watery" sign.

19. Koeppel suggested here "Complet are told", to obtain a finite verb. See his monograph as *ante* p. 120, note on his p. 12. The change would however stabilize only one clause.

22. *Some of desport,* etc. These same phrases appear in the description of Chaucer's work FaPrinces i :344; see p. 162 here.

32. *And eek also.* This accumulation of emphasis, used by Chaucer, e.g. HoFame 178, is frequent in Lydgate. I have noted four other cases in Thebes, four in ResonandSens, fifteen in the Troy book. It occurs in the Serpent of Division, p. 55.

33. Lydgates here credits the Pardoner with the Summoner's appearance and conduct.

35. *to angre with,* to anger. This locution, instead of "to anger the Friar with", is regular in Middle English. .Chaucer, Prol. 791, has "To shorte with our weye"; Gower, Confessio i :2172, has "To tendre with the kinges herte"; Piers Plowman (B) vi :297, has "And profred Perse this present to plese with hunger"; Lydgate, Bycorne 91, has "to breke with my fast", Dance Macabre 86, "to wrappen in my body", Troy Book ii :6238, "to glade with the eyr". See also Orléans xx :4, p. 231 here. Hoccleve, Mâle Règle 150, has the modern word-order.

51. *many prouerbe.* The Middle Ages set high value upon proverbs, maxims and "sentences". The extracts from classical writers which appear and reappear in medieval authors are by preference "auctoritees", scraps of moral or practical wisdom. This lasted long. When the second edition of Speght's Chaucer was issued in 1602, it announced on its titlepage, among other improvements, "Sentences and proverbs noted". This noting is done by tiny pointing hands along the margins of the text, sometimes only one on a page, sometimes, as in the Melibeus, ten or twelve. The difference between this and the modern view of literature is clearly illustrated by this choice of notes. In Chaucer's Prologue, where we would mark the opening spring symphony, which, as Lowell said, still at the thousandth reading lifts the hair upon our foreheads with a breath of uncontaminated springtide; where we quote lines of character-description, of the Prioress' smiling, of the Shipman's tempest-shaken beard,—the medieval reader made a very different selection. The first line of the Prologue which is marked in the 1602 edition is 443, "For gold in phisik is a cordial"; three lines in the description of the Parson are noted, 500, 503, and 505; and other lines are 563, 652, 731, 741, and 830. This annotation is not retained in the 1687 Chaucer.

52. *his sugred mouth.* The term *sugred* is extremely common in Lydgate. He talks of sugared sounds, sugared eloquence, sweet sugared harmony, the sugared aureat liquor of the Muses, the god who sugars the tongues of rhetoricians, etc. Chaucer, translating the phrase of Boethius, "melliflui canit oris Homerus", rendered it "Homer with the honey mouth, that is to say, Homer with the swete ditees." Possibly it was this phrase which suggested Lydgate's "sugred ditees of Omere", (FaPrinces ix :3402); but the term *sugred* is rare in Chaucer (cp. Troilus ii :384) and Gower does not use the word freely.

We should note that the Latin *mellea,* "honeyed", would naturally give in Middle English the term *sugared,* since the sugar of the Middle Ages, a very expensive luxury obtained principally from Venice, was a viscous liquid or thick syrup, not unlike prepared honey. It was not until late in the fifteenth century that a Venetian discovered the art of refining and hardening the product. Such phrases as those of Ausonius in his Epistles, "quam mellea res sit oratio", or "melleum eloquium", could lead direct to "sugared eloquence".

The word was used by other than Lydgate; cp. Test. of Love i :4, Court of Love 22, Bokenam's St. Anne 57-59, Skelton's Garland of Laurell 73-4, etc.

55-56. These phrases, and a line from Chaucer's Prologue, are echoed in Caxton's proheme to his second edition of the Canterbury Tales; see Flügel's Neuengl. Lesebuch, p. 6. Caxton there says of Chaucer that "he comprehended hys matere in short / quyck / and hye sentences / eschewynge / prolyxyte / castyng away the chaf of superfluyte / and shewyng the pyked grayn of sentence / utteryd by crafty and sugred eloquence".

58. *ded mete.* This use of the verb *do* as an auxiliary, rare in earlier English, and appearing in Chaucer only in interrogative construction (Monk's Tale 442, 444), is very common in Lydgate. In fact, the weakening of *do* into such usage is a feature of fifteenth-century grammar. See Hittmair, Das Zeitwort 'do' in Chaucer's Prosa, 1923, pp. 85 ff. The Kentish form *ded* may be noted.

65. See line 136; and cp. St. Albon i:130, "None so hardy to be therto contrarye".

68-9. *Hap or fortune.* Cp. Chaucer's Prologue 846, "Were it by aventure, or sort, or cas"; and from the many similar cases in Lydgate's Troy Book take iii:2815, "Were it be hap auenture or caas". Note also Dante, Inferno xxxii:76, "Se voler fu, o destino, o fortuna".

72. *vowes to aquyte.* The sick who called upon a saint to heal them were bound when recovered to pay their thanks at his shrine; cp. Chaucer's Prol. 17-18. Cp. also Bokenam's prol. to St. Magdalen 112-13, "My pylgrymage . . . wych promysyd I to saynt Jamys wyth hert entere Had to performe þe same yere."

73. *of black and not of grene.* Black was the color of the ascetic, of mourning, of the Benedictine monk; green that of youth, vigor, joyousness. See Barclay, Ecl. prol. 107; see Deschamps' balade, Oeuvres iii:224, "Ainçoix pour vert me vueil de noir vestir".

75. The adornment of a horse's trappings, especially the bridle, with bosses and bells of silver, was a frequent medieval mode of display; cp. Skeat's note on CantTales prol. 170. Lydgates's bridle, as described here and 85 below, indicated poverty.

76. *My man toforn,* etc. Cp. Chaucer, CanYeo headlink 13-14.

90. *a wonder thred bar hood.* See Shirley's allusions to Lydgate's poverty, in the poem printed p. 196 here, lines 37-44.

93. *ny3 fyfty 3ere of age.* Koeppel, in his diss. on this poem above mentioned, pp. 11 ff., argues the date of the Siege of Thebes from this passage.

95. *As I haue hight.* It is not clear whether this means "According to my promise", or "As for my name".

96. *wel broke ye youre name,* "well profit you your name!" Cp. Chaucer's Legend, prol. (B) 194; cp. Beryn 66, "broke wel thy name", King Horn 206, "wel bruke þu þi nevening".

100. *hagys.* A sort of meat-loaf, cooked like a large sausage in the maw of the animal; see a verse-recipe printed Anglia 36:372, and one printed in the EETS volume of cookery-books, p. 39. The dish is still made in Scotland; see Burns, To a Haggis. Wülker, in his text as above, was led by his use of Stow's poor copy to render this word as *bagys*, bags. See also note on 162 below.

101. *A ffranchmole a tansey or a froyse.* Verse-recipes for these dishes are printed Anglia 36:373 and in the EETS vol. above mentioned, pp. 39, 45, 86. A franche mole was not unlike a haggis; a tansey and a froyse were pancakes. Gower, Confessio iv:2732, says of Somnolence that he "brustleth as a monkes froise Whanne it is throwe into the panne." The froise or pancake made with fish was an especially common dish with monks because of their many fast-days.

102. *sclender is youre koyse.* The word *koyse, coise* is very rare in Mid. Engl. and Old French. Gower, Confessio i:1734, calls the hideous old wife whom Florent is forced to wed "this foule grete coise"; Godefroy, in his dictionary of Old French, cites the fifteenth play of St. Nicholas for the word, and queries its meaning. There also occurs, see Hartshorne's Ancient Metrical Tales, p. 118, the phrase "coisy fish", meaning apparently coarse or worthless fish.

110. The bracketed word is not in the MS.

117-18. These herbs are remedies for flatulence or colic, the *collis passioun* of line 114.

124. *parcel afore pryme,* a little before dawn. Prime, the first period of the day, was originally reckoned from six A. M., then from sunrise. The use of *parcel* with a phrase, as here, is exemplified by NED from Lydgate only.

126. *by kokkis blood,* by God's blood. For this corrupted form cp. Chaucer, Mancprol. line 9, Parson's prol. 29; London Lickpenny 93.

142. *platly.* This word, like *pleinly, sothly* is much used by Lydgate for mid-line padding. Cp. in the Troy Book iv lines 79, 93, 139, 425, 447, 615, 618, 665, 681, etc.

155. *Ospryng.* This town was about ten miles on the London side of Canterbury.

160. *be 3our Cristene name.* This tag not only served to fill out a line, but gave the identification which the medieval mind so desired. Cp. Nun's Priest's prol. 42, "or dan Piers by your name"; DoctTale 213, "Virginia by thy name"; Gower's Confessio i:1541, "And

seide Florent be thi name". Cp. Bokenam, St. Magd. prol. 75; cp. Barclay, Eclogue i, prol. 19, "Himselfe he called Cornix by his name". Skelton's usage of the phrase in Garl. 381 is not a tag; see note *ibid*.

162. *portoos,* a breviary, Old French *portehors*. See Chaucer, Shipman's Tale 131, "For on my porthors here I make an ooth". The porthors was often of great beauty and value; Henry the Fourth bequeathed his to his son Henry the Fifth, who left it to Bishop Beaufort, cp. Wylie's Henry the Fourth iii:233. John of Gaunt also bequeathed to Beaufort, then Bishop of Lincoln, "mon messale et mon portheus", see Armitage-Smith's life of Gaunt, p. 428. In catalogues of medieval libraries we frequently find the "porthors" very richly executed. Wülker, following Stow's text, printed *portes* here, and interpreted it as "gates" or "lips". See note on line 100 above.—*a twenty deuelway,* i.e., in the name of twenty devils. See Chaucer, MillTale 527, Reves Tale 337; Chester Play of Noah's Flood 219, etc.

165. *a Iape, no Iape.* The MSS vary in the word appearing before *Iape;* Arundel omits. The word *jape,* "jest", is used by the Host when ordering the Pardoner to narrate, Pard. headlink 33, "Tel us som mirth or japes right anon".

166. *rouncy.* This may be an error by Lydgate, as Chaucer assigns a rouncy, or common cart-horse, to the Shipman.

167. Cp. the Clerk's headlink, "But precheth nat, as freres doon in Lente".

169. *bekke,* beak, nose. The earliest example of this word given NED is of 1598. Cp. Troy Book ii:5781, "And noddeth ofte with his Iowsy hed". See MancTale 346.

170. *draweth to effekke,* "amounts to something, has weight". The word *effecte* has in this MS been altered to *effekke;* both forms appear in the MSS of the poem.

THE DANCE MACABRE

The poem is headed in Brit. Mus. Harley 116 "The Daunce of Macabre". Bodl. Laud 735 and this MS have only "Verba translatoris"; Bodley 221 has no heading.

Of the B-recension MSS, Bodley 686 heads the poem "Here begynneþ a tretys of the daunce of Poulys other weyes called Makabre;" Corpus writes "The Daunce of Powlys"; Lansdowne and Lincoln Cathedral have as heading "Incipit macrobius".

The five opening stanzas here are not in the B-recension.

6. *þat be* refers to *folkes* in line 1.

20. *depict . . . in a wal.* Cp. Horse Goose and Sheep 18, Utter Thy Language (Min Po 173) 97.

24. *Machabres daunce.* The earliest known use of this phrase is in the Respit de Mort of Jehan le Fèvre, ca. 1376. He there says:—

> Je fis de macabre la dance,
> Qui toutes gens maisne a sa tresche
> Et a la fosse les adresche
> Qui est leur derraine maison.

The passage is printed by Gaston Paris, Romania 24:130. Apparently the next recorded use of the phrase is in the Journal d'un Bourgeois de Paris sous Charles VII, printed by Labarre in his Mémoires pour servir à l'histoire de France, 1729, and by Tuetey in 1881 for the Soc. de l'histoire de Paris, etc. The diarist says that a preacher speaking in the cloisters of SS. Innocents was "à l'endroit de la danse macabre"; and some pages earlier he states that the Dance was begun about August 1424 and finished by the following Lent. In a description of Paris compiled by Guil. de Metz about 1434, the fresco is mentioned as the Dance Macabre; in a poem written by Jehan Regnier after his imprisonment in 1432, he says "Si fault-il aller a la dance De macabre la très-diverse"; the French MSS use that heading, as do the many prints. Lydgate adopted the phrase, and incorporated it in his text; a few usages of it in later English are mentioned in the Introduction *ante,* but the B-recension, which is without Lydgate's prologue of explanation, does not preserve the French name.

The word *macabre* is still a difficulty to philologists. It has been explained as from the Arabic maq-abir, a place of sepulture; see Seelmann, p. 24 and his reference to Van Praet, author of the suggestion. This etymology is refused by Mâle, who in his work on French medieval religious art, p. 390 note, says that the only possible derivation is by popular modification of the name of the Maccabees, the Jewish warrior-heroes. He points to the Latin heading "Macchabaeorum chorea", the Dutch term "Makkabeus danz", (see Romania 24:588). The NED adopts this explanation; but no connection has yet been shown with any church or festivity sacred to the Maccabees. Another etymology is from Macarius, the name of a hermit-saint who may then be the hermit appearing in the Campo Santo fresco at Pisa and in some of the poems. Yet another, advocated by Gaston Paris as above, treats Macabre as the surname of the earliest painter of the Death-picture; and that the word was indeed a surname in medieval France is easily proved; see my paper MLNotes 24:63 for example. For a résumé of the discussion see Huet, Notes d'historie littéraire, iii, Paris, 1918. See Mâle as cited for treatment of the Dance as a dramatic performance.

The word *dance* has here its frequent medieval sense of a procession, a chain or file formed in dancing; such a dance had generally a leader, as in the Flower and Leaf. The phrase *olde daunce* meant "experience".

25. *atte þe leste.* The medieval scribe frequently contracted *at þe* into *atte;* he has here written both the contracted and the full form.

26. *her sterying,* their suggestion and urging. See MaReg 192, Thebes 235.

27. Lydgate here says that he executed his translation at the suggestion of French clerks. Warton-Hazlitt iii:55 has corrected Warton's earlier assertion that the monk worked at the request of the Chapter of St. Paul's,—a statement retained by the DNB. The DNB also says that this poem is of 24 quatrains, and mentions MS Lansdowne 699.

31. *mirrour.* See note FaPrinces G 179 for another usage of this metaphor; here the meaning is "example".

41 ff. This first stanza from the French illustrates Lydgate's adherence to the rime-sounds of his original.

46. The B-recension alters to "daunce which that ye see". Note the excision of the word *makabre.*

60. The B-recension alters to "chirche most in especiall".

64. *to god is the honour.* It might seem that Lydgate here mistranslated the French "Aux grans maistres est deu honneur"; but at least one French MS, Bibl. nat. fonds latin 14904, writes "est dieu lonneur".

68. The B-recension has *seynt* before *Petris.*

71. *ffor such honour,* etc. is the reading of the Lincoln Cathedral MS.

75. *appil round.* The orb or sphere was, with the sceptre and sword, an imperial attribute. This is not the *appil round* of line 288.

83. *gein.* Harley 116 reads *bote,* Ellesmere *geyne,* the B-recension *gyn.*

86. *To wrappe in my body.* See note on Thebes 35 here.

87. Harley 116 reads "And þervppon I may me sore complayne"; Bodley and Corpus "full sore I may compleyne"; Ellesmere agrees with Selden.

101. *grys ne ermyn.* These valuable furs might be worn by high ecclesiastics. See line 250.

103. *lyved wel.* Ellesmere reads as Selden; Harley 116, *conceyued well;* B-type MSS, *lerned wel.*

107. This phrase, *Com forth,* is addressed to the Lady of Great Estate 185, to the Squire line 217, to the Abbot line 233, to the Bailiff line 265, to the Astronomer line 281, to the Sergeant line 361, and to the Gentlewoman line 449. See note on 153.

109. Ellesmere and Selden both omit *for.* Harley 116 reads "for all your highnesse".

117. See line 308.

120. *he shal al,* etc. So Ellesmere. Harley 116 and the B-type MSS have *we shul all,* etc.

136. Note the use of *do* as an auxiliary, and cp. lines 287, 507, 619. See notes on Dial. 613, Thebes 58.

137 ff. The address of Death to the Constable is rewritten in the B-recension, the character summoned being termed the Prince. It runs, in Bodley 686:—

Right myghti prince beth ryght wel certeyn
This daunce to you is not eschewable
ffor more mighty þan euer was Charlemayn
Or worthi Artour of prowes ful notable
With al his knyghtes of þe rounde table
What myght þer platis ther Armes or maile
Ther stronge curage ther scheldes defensable
To deth avayle when he doth hem assaile

Note the retention of A-type rime-sounds.

141-2. There is no verb for these subjects. See line 433.

153. *whi...withdrawe.* Cp. *what do ye ...tarie* in line 297, or *Com forth* as in 107 etc., for the dramatic quality of the text.

174. This line reads in the B-version "Was in estate and worldely worschip to glade".

179. *my thanke also deuised,* "acknowledgment also rendered to me".

185-200. These Princess-stanzas are not in the French or in the B-recension.

195. Selden omits pronoun; Ellesmere reads *moste y nedes fote;* Harley and Trin. have *I*.

198. *trace sewe,* follow the steps. To follow or "sewe" the traces of Homer or of old authors, to dance the trace of lovers, etc., are phrases frequent in the fifteenth century and earlier. See prol. to Chaucer's Legend 285, his Gentilesse 3; see the play of Mankind, where the minstrels are bid to play "the common trace", and where Titivillus says of the leading character, "I shall make him to dance another trace".

199-200. *oure.* Selden, Bodley 221, Laud, read *3oure.*

205. *dredly.* Most MSS *dredeful.*

207. *broughte to lure.* A metaphor from hawking. The falcon which had flown at its prey was reclaimed or recalled to the wrist of the master by calls and by the display of a lure, i. e. a bit of leather furnished with feathers to resemble a small bird. The metaphor is so common in MidEng as to be proverbial; see the WBprol 415 and cp. RevesTale 214, also two occurrences at least of the same proverb in Lydgate, in the fable of the Wolf and the Lamb and in Utter thy Language. In a still older form it is used by John of Salisbury, Polycraticus v, cap. 10, "uacuae manus temeraria petitio est". The metaphor occurs in Lydgate's Letter to Gloucester 37 (see p. 150 here) and it continues to modern times, as in Swinburne's "Time stoops to no man's lure".

210. Harley 116 has...*ye me bringe.*

211. *a symple ferye,* an ordinary holiday or *feria,* a weekday on which work was suspended, but not a feast-day.

212. *me list no þing syng,* I am not at all disposed to sing.

213. The omission of the principal verb, here *is,* is common in Lydgate.

215. *þat* is not in Trin. or Corpus.

220. *at youre vnkouþe deuise,* to your special desire. See prol. to Thebes 99.

225-232. The rimes in this stanza have a monotony not seen in the French.

230. *euery day is prime,* every day is a beginning. See note on Thebes 124. For this more general use of *prime* cp. Lydgate's FaPrinces i:738, "Off chaung it was to hem a newe pryme".

235. *heed* in Harley, Trinity; Ellesmere *hede; hood* in Selden, Laud, Bodl. 221.

241. *envie.* From the context there seems a confusion in Lydgate's mind between the Old French *envie,* "wish, desire", and *enuie* "disgust, repulsion, annoyance". The original "De cecy neusse point enuie", means "For this (summons) I have no desire"; but Lydgate seems to institute a contrast between the loss of power and the death as a cloisterer.

249-64. The Abbess-stanzas are not in the French. The B-recension alters them.

250. *mantels furred.* The use of fur was very general in medieval England. Poor men wore sheepskin for warmth; the rich and those of high rank used ermine, vair and gris. Chaucer's Monk, the Cardinal of this poem (line 101), Mercury as Doctor of Physic in Henryson's Testament of Cresseid 251, all wear rich fur. Such display by Churchmen, as also the secular cut of their robes, was censured by the Archbishop of Canterbury in 1342.

251. *passing of greet,* of passing great.

257 ff. The reply of the Abbess is rewritten in the B-recension, and deprived of force or color.

> Alas that deth hath so for me ordeyned
> That in no wise I kan him not eschewe
> Vnto this daunce of ryght I am constreyned
> That here with other y moste his trace sewe
> This pilgrimage to euery man is dewe
> A ernest matere a matere of no Iape
> Who that is redy schal neuer rewe
> The hour abydyng god hath for him schape
>
> (MS Bodley 686)

261. *chekes . . . vernysshed.* The Abbess painted her face. See in FaPrinces i:6525 ff., with mention of "farcing and popping" 6563, the long catalogue of women's arts in disguising figure, hair, and complexion; this list is much expanded from Boccaccio by Laurent, Lydgate's French original. See also the Troy Book ii:2685-99. As at this time all worldly license was imitated by the Church, regardless of archiepiscopal censure, we may suppose that Lydgate is here speaking by the book. The nuns who entertained Rozmital and his Bohemians at Neuss in 1465 were "acquainted with the most excellent dances." See Mrs. Cust's *Gentlemen Errant,* p. 16, and her references.

262. *Vngirt . . . at the large.* "At large" means at liberty; cp. HoFame 745, WBprol 322, etc. To walk ungirt is probably a reflection on the nun's chastity. In Nigel Wireker's 12th century Speculum Stultorum (ed. Wright, Anglo-Latin Satirical Poets, i:94) one of the censures of nuns is "Cingula nulla ferunt". And on p. 96, *ibid.,* the speaker Brunellus announces that in his new and easygoing Abbey, where there are to be the prancing horses of the Templars, the rich food of the Cluniacs, etc., he will adopt from nuns their custom "zonam semper abesse meam". The girdle as a symbol of chastity plays an important part in canto v of the Faerie Queene.

265 ff: After the Abbess the B-recension has instead of the Bailly the Justice. A citation will show the difference of this addition from the movement of Lydgate.

> Thik honde of your my lorde Justice
> That hath rewled so longe in lawe
> Wel may men holde you ware and wise
> So that this drawght be wel ydrawe
> Escape schal not ye wolde ye neuer so fawe
> Suche dome to haue / as ye haue yeue in soth
> Therfor men seyn of an old sawe
> Wel is him alwey that wel doth
>
> (MS Bodley 686)

The conception of the Bailly here is that of the officer of justice under a county sheriff, who made arrests, as in Piers Plowman B ii:59, and not as in Chaucer's Prologue, the agent of a manorial lord. In either capacity he was a well-hated personage, his position affording him every opportunity for extortion. —*knowen,* cp. *loken* in line 281.

270-72. Observe the like rime, verb and substantive.

275. *chaunge.* Read *chaunce,* i.e., fortune.

276. *what me list to spede,* to promote whatever pleased me.

282. *Instrumentis of Astronomy.* By this is not meant the telescope, which was unknown before 1600 except to a few individuals who did not realize its practical importance, and who used it mainly in "natural magic" (Encyl. Brit.). Lydgate is probably alluding to armillary spheres, which were known already to Hipparchus and Ptolemy; or he may have in mind the astrolabe and cross-staff, which were used in taking altitudes; cp. line 283. Columbus and Vasco da Gama had these and the compass; the sextant was unknown until the 18th century.

292. *domefiyng.* The location of the planets in their respective "houses" of the Zodiac, preparatory to casting a horoscope. There is no corresponding word in the French, and this is the first citation of the word by the NED. See FaPrinces i:299, p. 161 here.

297. *what.* The line should perhaps be punctuated with an exclamation-point after this word, which would then be an introductory ejaculation, as in Chaucer's Prologue 854. The meaning *why* would suit well with the context, but I find no cases of such use.

298. *aver,* possessions; in the French, line 226, *avoir.* Harley, Trinity, and the B-recension change to *honeur, onneur.*

306. *and may it not assure.* Here *may* is the infinitive, as in Caxton, Foure Sonnes of Aymon, "As longe that I shalle may bere armes". The meaning is "To leave all this and be unable to assure it, be certain of it". Cp. the use of *mowe* in Troy Book i:4016, "schal nat mowe sustene"; see also *ibid.* i:1134, ii:4210, iv:1063, 6497; see Hoccleve's Mâle Règle 148, and *mow* in Chaucer's Boethius v prose 4:163, Gower's Confessio ii:1670.

308. See line 117.

311. *recure,* recover, take back. This variant form of the verb *recover* is exceedingly common, even characteristic, in Lydgate. It occurs about a hundred times in the FaPrinces and nearly as often in the Troy Book, largely as a rime-word. The parallel form *discure* is not so common, and both are only occasional in Lydgate's contemporaries; they are not in Gower's Confessio, and Chaucer has apparently but one case, *discure,* BoDuchesse 549. The use of *recure* by Spenser should be noted.

When translating here, Lydgate retained the French rime-words *nature* and *creature,* rejecting *norriture* and *droiture;* the -ure words which he substituted, *assure* and *recure,* led him into difficulties. He seems to have read the French (stanza 30) with a full stop after *demeurent,* taking it to mean "do not endure", and to have treated *monde* as a nominative.

313. *prebende.* An ecclesiastical living; the portion of the revenues of a cathedral or collegiate church granted to a canon or member of the chapter as his stipend. (NED) See line 596.

313 ff. The Canon-stanzas are somewhat altered in the B-recension, but the A-rimes are kept.

339. *do carie,* etc. "I have caused many a bale to be carried". This old active use of *do,* so regular in Chaucer, is rare in Lydgate. See note on line 136.

344. Cp. the line "Who al embraceth litel shall restraine", in the Proverbs attributed to Chaucer. See Hoccleve's Mâle Règle 353-55; see the French *Dance,* line 272.

350. *memoire.* The OFr *avoir memoire en* meant *penser à,* acc. to Godefroy. There is no *en* in the French here, stanza 35, but the meaning seems to be "have no mind to longer life." Lydgate's use of *memorie* to translate the word is peculiar.

356. *by kindly mocioun,* by natural impulse.

368. MSS Bodley 221, Laud 735, Trinity, and Ellesmere agree with Selden. Harley has *deth is a strong;* Corpus 237, and the B-group, read "Thowghe he be myghty dethe is yit mor stronge".

374. *þou3 I hadde it sworn,* though I had vowed against it. Common in Chaucer, see Troilus iv:976, KnTale 1666, etc.

377 ff. In this stanza Lydgate departs from the French (st. 39) in all but the last two lines.

392. This proverbial expression is differently twisted in PoFoules 592.

393 ff. The Usurer is not in the B-recension, and the removal of this very typical figure is an interesting point of difference between the two texts. The term "usury" was in the Middle Ages applied to all lending of money upon interest. The practice had been severely condemned by the ancient Jews (Exod. 22:25, etc), and by the Greek and Roman law-codes. For a man did not borrow, as frequently today, to push his undertaking or meet a temporary need, but when in a state of extreme distress. Unable to repay, he was often obliged to surrender his personal liberty; see Nehemiah 5:5. In both Greece and Rome a large part of the population, originally small proprietors, had become practically enslaved; and the failure of national feeling because of this must have contributed to the fall of the Empire. The Christian Fathers condemned "usury" in the strongest terms; even before the Council of Nicæa (325) we find legislation against it as practised by clerics, and the Church's penalties for it were by later councils extended to laymen also. The Council of Vienne, in 1311,

declared it heresy to defend the legality of usury. In the fifteenth century, however, the whole character of borrowing changed with the development of the trading class, and in spite of the bull of Sixtus V (Detestabilis Avaritiae) in 1586, the Church was obliged to modify her position. See Cunningham's Christian Opinion on Usury, 1884; see art. in Dict. of Religion and Ethics.

The effect of this Church doctrine was to throw most medieval moneylending into the hands of the Jews, which increased the popular abhorrence of them. See Confessio Amantis vii:3239 ff., Piers' Plowman B xviii:104, Chaucer's Prioress' Tale 39 ff.; see such English statutes as that of 5th Henry IV against the "horrible & dampnable peeche de Usure" which is practised "tres sotilment" by "gentz estraunges". See the many examples in the Elizabethan drama.

401. In the French, stanza 42, one line begins "Je vais mourir"; cp. the Vado Mori discussed in introd. above, and such French poems as the Mirouer du Monde, in which each stanza begins with that phrase.

407. *by kinde or fatal chaunce,* "by nature or by accident of fate".

409 ff. Stanza 52 is not in the French, in the B-type, or in Harley 116.

417. *on 3oure vryne.* The ancient medical theory of the four bodily "humors", and of the "complexions" which resulted from the dominance of any one of them, regarded disease as the excess of one of the humors. Traces of this excess would be found in the bodily excretions; the testing of the urine in particular was raised into an elaborate pseudo-science. Each of the senses of the examining physician was called into play in the tests; see the picture of a doctor in his robes holding a glass vessel to the light, reprod. from a 1490 copy of the works of Galen, in Studien zur Geschichte der Medizin, Leipzig, 1907, plate i of vol. i. In Hoccleve's tale of Jonathas the physician comes to the sick woman, "sy hire vryne & eeke felte hir pous". In Hawes' Pastime lines 1645-7 we have "'A physycien truely can lyttel descerne Ony maner sekenes wythout syght of vryne." The notion persisted long; see second Henry IV, act I sc. 2, or Twelfth Night III sc. 4, etc.

427. *speculatyf and . . . practyk.* Medicine in its medieval state was linked with both astrology and alchemy or pseudo-chemistry. It determined theoretically the proper times for preparing and administering its practical remedies, and a long struggle was required to substitute for this "magic natural" the knowledge gained by direct experiments. Chaucer's Physician, Prol. 411 ff., was grounded in astronomy; he knew how and when to make the "image" of his patient and how to treat that image so as to help the sufferer.

Barclay, Ship of Fools, ed. Jamieson i:261, speaks of foolish physicians who neglect the speculation which is the chief thing in medicine. Jonson in Volpone, II, sc. 1, alludes to "the theorick and practick in the Aesculapian art". See note on Walton A 332 here.

429. *A3ens pestilence.* The French, stanza 45, speaks only of "maladie" in general. The outbreak of the plague in London in 1426, the date suggested for this translation, may be noted.

433. There is no verb for *3e.* Cp. lines 141-2.

433-48. These stanzas are not in the B-recension.

434. *grene age.* The color green connoted youth and vigor, as in the leaf; in a bad sense, as of the transitoriness of the leaf, it connoted inconstancy. See the poem Against Women Unconstant, printed by Skeat with Chaucer's works, i:409.

446. *wel besein,* well beseen, i.e. arrayed or equipped. Used by Chaucer and Gower, very frequent in Lydgate,—see TemGlass 1167 and Schick's note there. In the Assembly of Gods 275-6 Juno appears "ful rychely beseene" in a surcoat as bright as glass; the Flower and the Leaf, the Garland of Laurell, the Palice of Honour, Orléans as translated here xvi:12, Spenser, etc., all use the word.

448. A proverb in more than one language. Caxton's Recuyell, ed. Sommer ii:461, has "lyke as a small rayne abayteth or lyth doun a grete wynde". In Monaci's chrestomathy of Italian, p. 219, Guido delle Colonne is cited—"E pogo piagio grande vento attera."

449-464. These stanzas are not in the French; they are retained in the B-recension.

451. The beloved of Achilles, the faithful wife of Ulysses, the faithless but lovely wife of Menelaus stolen by Paris, constantly appear in Lydgate's lists of noble dames; see his Epithalamium 71, and note there for other refs.

455. *daunger . . . lad ʒoure reine,* "though disdain has hitherto guided you". The word *danger* meant in Mid. Eng. "power" (Chaucer's Prol. 663), "difficulty'" (WBprol 521), "haughtiness" (Anelida 186). For the metaphor, derived from the leading of the horses of dignitaries on state occasions, see Epithalamium 88.

456. *arestid . . . doubilnesse,* i.e. "Your fickle shiftings are forced to cease". *Doubleness* was the most frequent of medieval flings at women. See the poem so entitled in Skeat vii:291; see Anelida 159; see Troy Book i:1850, 2094, etc.

459. *yseide chekmate,* "said checkmate". The French phrase *eschec mat,* "the king is dead", from the Arabic *shak mat,* signifies to chess-players that the game is over. To "say checkmate" to any one was accordingly to defeat, to undo him. The metaphor is exceedingly common in Middle English; see note on FaPrinces D 52.

468. *to do folke refuge,* "For money you have undertaken to give people protection."

481 ff. The Juror is not in the French; the character is retained by the B-recension. The medieval juror's functions were wider than in our day. Under Richard I the assessment of taxes was entrusted to juries acting under knights of the shire; and as this duty implied the valuation of land and property, the opportunity for unscrupulousness was great. The juror was hated equally with the summoner, and second only to the usurer. It is however not always clear whether the word is employed in its legal sense or in the general sense of one who swears, i.e. swears falsely. In Lydgate's fable of the Hound and Sheep the "jurors" inveighed against are the false witnesses who take oath to a lie; but in his description of the golden world, FaPrinces vii:1183, the line "Fraude, fals meede put bakward fro iorours", the reference is probably to the legal juror, as is clearly the case here. See note below.

482. *questes doste embrace.* "Shire questes" were judicial inquiries; to *embrace,* in law-language, was to give bribes, especially to a jury or inquest; see NED. Cp. the Towneley Mysteries 22:24, where Pilate declares that "all fals endytars, quest-gangars, and Iurors" are welcome to him; cp. the acts of Henry VII against "unlawful mayntenours, ymbrasours, and Iurrours".

490. *The belle wedir,* the bellwether. In Troilus iii:198 we have "which of yow shall bere the bell To speke of love aright", which is first citation in NED, sense 7, for "take first rank, be the best". This word is contemptuous; this is the earliest citation NED.

495. *write.* Note the use of *write* in this supposedly spoken text. Cp. Chaucer's SecNun's Tale 78.

497 ff. The two stanzas of the Minstrel are rewritten in the B-recension. The text of Lansdowne 699 (Bodley 686 has not this character) runs:—

> Gentil menstral / shewe now thi witt
> How thou canst pleye / or foote ariht this daunce
> I dar weel sei / that an harder fitt
> Than this / fil neuyr to thi chaunce
> Look ther fore / what may best avaunce
> Thi sowle as now / & vse that I reede
> Refuse nyce play / & veyn plesaunce
> Bettir late / than neuyr to do good deede
>
> Ey benedicite / this world is freele
> Now glad / now sorry / what shal men vse
> Harpe lute phidil / pipe farewell
> Sautry Sithol / & Shalmuse
> Al wordly myrthe / I here refuse
> God graunte me grace / of sich penaunce
> As may myn old / synnes excuse
> For alle be nat mery / that othir whyle daunce

509-10. The syntax here is awkward, as often in Lydgate.
512. Cp. line 392 above, and note.

513 ff. The Tregetour, or Juggler, is not in the French, nor in the B-recension, nor in the Trinity MS of the A-recension. It appears from Lydgate's words that John Rikil or Rickhill, the juggler of Henry the Fifth, outlived his royal master, but had just died at the time this translation was made. I have not found his name among those of Henry's minstrels and fools, see Rymer's Foedera ix:255, 260, 336, x:287; but there is a John Michel in the list of 1415, who is not mentioned with the royal minstrels to whom money is granted by Henry VI in 1423 as having been in his father's service.

For the arts of tregetours see Chaucer's Franklin's Tale and the notes of Tyrwhitt and of Skeat on its line 413; see also HoFame 1260, 1277, and Skeat's note; see Squire's Tale 210-11. It will be observed that in this list the Tregetour precedes the Parson; but this is possibly because a definite individual formerly of the royal household, is named; for the German law-code of the 13-14 centuries placed the bastard children of monks below the peasant, "superior only to the juggler". See Lea, Sacerdotal Celibacy, p. 336.

For the introduction of a known and named contemporary into this list of types cp. the Fuckardus or member of the wealthy mercantile family of the Fuggers, who appears, after the Mercator, in the Latin death-dance printed at Antwerp in 1533; see the reprint by Douce in his Dance of Death, ed. 1902, p. 19. Cp. also a poem by Cornelius Arnold, 1775, entitled The Mirror, in which a number of personages are seized by Death, among them David Garrick. There is in this poem no dialogue-method or class-arrangement; the personages are a Knight, the Lord Mayor "Sir Thrifty Gripe", one "Sir Epicure", a beauteous dame, a beau, a fawning reverend, "Sir Politick", an actor, a physician, Robustus, a roaring blade, Prudella, a lawyer, a lustful old man, a group of fiddlers, dancers, jockeys, poetasters, etc. The beggar who sues to Death is refused. The actor is Garrick, who although not named is fully described and his most famous triumphs enumerated; the poem is dedicated to him. It is of 44 Spenserian stanzas.

523. *cours of sterres*. It appears from the FranklTale 545 ff. that the tregetour, like the physician, calculated the position and motion of the heavenly bodies as a preliminary to the exercise of his art, which must select the auspicious moment. See note on line 427 above.

529 ff. The character of the Parson or Curate is not in the B-recension. He bears no resemblance to Chaucer's Parson; cp. lines 530-32 with Prologue 486.

532. Again in 541 Lydgate distinguishes between tithes, or assessed tenths of the parish property, due the Church, and the offerings or oblations voluntarily made. Cp. Chaucer's Wife of Bath and her insistence on going up first to the altar to make offering, Prol. 450; also his Parson, *ibid.*, 486, 489.

561. *Cordeler*. This name was given in France to the Franciscan Observantists, a reform-movement of the Franciscans which began at Foligno about 1390 and spread northward. In 1415 the Council of Constance allowed them a vicar of their own, and by the end of the Middle Ages they had some 1400 houses. They carried on the vow of poverty so characteristic of the Order, but they attached more value to study than did the earlier Franciscans, and were noted for the denunciatory vigor of their sermons, as Lydgate here says,—amplifying the French.

589. With this line and speech cp. Spenser's ShepCal, January, 29-30; cp. also the poem said to have been written by Chidiock Titchbourne in 1586, the night before his execution for complicity in the Babington plot. I cite from MS Harley 36.

> My prime of youth is but a frost of cares
> My feast of ioye is but a dishe of paine
> My croppe of corne is but (a) field of tares
> And all my goodes is but vaine hope of gaine
> The daye is fled, and yet I sawe no sonne
> And nowe I live, and nowe my life is donne
>
> My springe is past, and yet it hath not sprunge
> The fruite is deade, and yet the leaves are green
> My youth is paste, and yet I ame but yonge

I sawe the worlde, and yet I was not seene
My thrid is cutt, and yet it is not sponn
And now I live, and nowe my life is donne

I sought for death, and found it in the wombe
I lookt for life, and yet it was a shade
I trade the grounde, and knewe it was my tombe
And nowe I dye, and nowe I am but made
The glasse is full, and yet my glasse is ronne
And now I live, and nowe my life is donne

593 ff. The character of the Clerk is not in the B-recension.

602. *ffro my seruice.* So the Ellesmere MS, etc. Read *for my seruice?*

606. *To late ware,* i.e., "It is too late to beware."

621-3. Lydgate uses participles instead of finite verbs.

623-4. The second halves of these lines are altered in the B-recension to read respectively "such as I have assayed" and "but he that halt him payed". Possibly the notion of "great habondance" offended the reviser when connected with hermit-life.

625 ff. Death's reply to the Hermit is not in the B-recension.

633. Note the allusion to the picture for which the text was written. The B-recension changes lines 634, 638 so as to remove the pictorial quality.

641 ff. This stanza is marked "Machabre doctour" in the French MS Bibl.nat.fonds français 14989. The B-recension rewrites the stanza.

642. With the French cp. the Italian Lauda, pubd. by Vigo, Danze Macabre, p. 101; the second stanza there reads:—"Questa vita e come vento Che 'n un punto passar via."

643. *Wake or winke.* This formula, like *flete or synke,* is common for rime's sake in Middle English. See Chaucer's Pity 109, 110, PoFoules 482, Anelida 182, KnTale 1539; see the Confessio iii:1628, vi:334-5, Court of Love 311, Lydgate's Troy Book i:439, iv:3825, etc. For the variant *slepe or wake* see SecNunTale 153, FlCourtesy 95, Troy Book iv:4123, v:271, etc.

657 ff. This envoy is not in the B-recension.

660. See note on Cavendish's Visions 52, p. 527 here.

665 ff. This stanza was printed by Mrs. Elizabeth Cooper in her Muses' Library, 1737.

666. *Not worde by worde,* etc. See note on translation, Walton's Boethius A 19.

670. Lydgate sometimes gives his name in his compositions; see prol. to Thebes 92, Troy Book v:3468. He mentions his birthplace in the prol. to his Fables of Aesop 32, in FaPrinces viii:194, cp. ix:3431.

672. See Chaucer's Venus line 81.

LA DANCE MACABRE : FRENCH TEXT

The manuscript from which the French Dance Macabre is here printed is no. 139 of the Bibliothèque Communale at Lille. It is bound with a printed copy, by Colard Mansion, of Gerson's Dictes moraux des philosophes, marked Inc.D ii. The MS is of twenty leaves, containing a prose note on a sermon by Aubert Archbishop of Cologne and a note on the Mass, the Dance Macabre, the Trois Mors et Trois Vifs, and a copy of the Visio Philiberti, in French verse. There are no headings or titles; the only ornament is coarsely-executed red capitals. The poem is written in long lines, in a commonplace but fairly early hand. Whether this volume still exists or not I cannot say. The Lille city-buildings were badly damaged by fire during the German occupation, and many books were destroyed; but the fate of this particular volume I have been unable to learn.

Other texts of the French Dance Macabre which I have examined are:—

Bibl.nat.fonds lat. 14904, formerly St. Victor 516. A paper MS of nearly 200 leaves; has, prefixed, 72 leaves of vellum carrying tractates by Gerson and by Nicolas de Clemangis, especially the former, with the Dance among them. No ornament or color in the 72 leaves. Observe the association of the Dance Macabre again with the work of Gerson.

Bibl. nat. fonds français 25434. A small volume, formerly a Celestins MS. Neatly written in small square hands, and containing various Dances and Débats, also Alain Chartier's Breuiaire des nobles.

Bibl. nat. fonds français 25550. Vellum and paper, in various hands, some bad. A composite MS. The Dance is in two hands, the second a loose scrawl.

Bibl. nat. fonds français 1186. Paper, of 108 leaves, containing the Epistle of Othea to Hector, the Dance aux Aveugles, Dance Cupido, Dance de Fortune, etc.

Bibl. nat. fonds français 14989. A tiny book of fifteen leaves, containing the Dance only, in a hand ? later than the fifteenth century.

Bibl. nat. fonds français 995, formerly du roi 7310. A gorgeous halfhundred of vellum leaves, the upper half of each page a beautifully executed picture; very elaborate borders. The Trois Mors et Trois Vifs, and the Dance des Femmes, follow the Dance Macabre.

Bibl.nat.fonds français 1181 I have not seen. Langfors, *Les Incipit*, p. 237, mentions a MS in the Musée Condé at Chantilly, one at Tours, and one in the Bibl. nat. fonds français 1055.

[Lille MS]

Discite vos Coram cunctis qui cernitis istam
Quantum prosit honor gaudia diuicie
Tales estis enim natura morte futuro
Qualis in effigie mortua turba vocat

O creature raisonnable / qui desire vie eternelle
Tu as cy doctrine notable / pour bien finer vie mortelle
La danse macabre sappelle / qui chascun a danser aprent
A homme et femme est naturelle / mort nespargne petit ne grant

2

En ce miroir chascun peult lire Qui le conuient ainsy danser   10
Cilz est heureux qui bien sy mire Le mort le vif fait auancer
Tu vois les plus grans commencher Car il nest nulz qui mort ne fiere
Cest piteuse chose y penser Tout est forgie dune matiere

3

[DEATH]   Vous qui viuez certainement Quoy quil tarde ainsy danserez
Mais quant dieu le scet soullement Aduisez comment vous ferez   20
Damp pappe vous commencerez Comme le plus digne seigneur
En ce point honnourez serez Aux grans maistres est deu honneur

4

[POPE]   He fault il que la danse maine Le premier qui sui dieu en terre
Jay eu dignite souueraine / En leglise comme saint pierre
Et comme aultres mort me vient querre / Encor point morir ne cuidasse   30
Mais la mort a tous maine guerre / Peu vault honneur qui si tost passe

5

[DEATH]   Et vous le non pareil du monde Prince et seigneur grant emperere
Laissier fault la pomme dor ronde / Armes ceptre tymbre baniere
Je ne vous lairay pas derriere / Vous ne pouez plus seignourir
Je maine tout cest ma maniere . Les filz dadam fault tous morir   40

6

[EMPEROR]   Je ne say deuant qui Jappelle / De la mort quainsy me demaine
Armer me fault de pic de pelle / Et dun lincheul ce mest grant paine
Sur tous ay eu grandeur mondaine / Et morir me fault pour tout gage
Et quest ce de mortel demaine Les grans ne lont pas dauantage

Latin, Line 1. *coram*] *choream* B. N. 14904.   24. *est dieu* etc., B. N. 14904.
3. *natura*] *matura* B. N. 14904.

7

[DEATH]   Vous faittes lesbahy ce samble Cardinal sus legierement   *50*
                   Sieuez les aultres hastiuement / Riens ny vault esbahissement
                   Vous auez vescu haultement / Et en honneur a grant deuis
                   Prenez en gre lesbatement / En grans honneurs se pert laduis

8

[CARDINAL]   Jay bien cause de mesbahir /Quant Je me voy de sy pres pris
                   La mort mest venu enuayr / Plus ne vestiray vaire ne gris   *60*
                   Chappeau rouge & chappe de pris / Me fault laissier a grant destresse
                   Je ne lauoye pas apruis Toute Joye fine en tristesse

9

[DEATH]   Venez noble Roy couronnez Renomme de force & proesse
                   Jadis fustes aduironnez / De grans pompes de grant noblesse
                   Mais maintenant toute hautesse / Laisserez vous nestes pas seul   *70*
                   Peu aurez de vostre ricesse / Le plu rice na que vng linceul

10

[KING]   Je nay point aprins a danser / A notte na danse si sauuaige
                   Helas on peult voir et penser / Que vault orgueil force lignage
                   Mort destruit tout cest son vsage / Aussi tost le grant que le mendre
                   Qui moins se prise plus est sage / A la fin fault deuenir cendre   *80*

11

[DEATH]   Patriarce pour basse chiere / Vous ne pouez estre quitte
                   Vostre double croix quauez chiere / Vng aultre aura cest equite
                   Ne pensez plus a dignite / Ja ne serez pappe de Romme
                   Pour rendre compte estes cite / folle esperance dechoit lomme

12

[PATRIARCH]   Bien perchoy que mondains honneurs / mont decu pour dire le voir   *90*
                   Mes Joyes tournent en doleurs Et que vault tant dhonneur auoir
                   Trop hault monter nest pas sauoir / Haulx estas gettent gens sans nombre
                   Mais peu le veullent parceuoir A hault monter le fais encombre

13

[DEATH]   Cest de mon droit que je vous maine / A la danse gent Connestable
                   Le plus fort comme Charlemaine / Mort prent cest chose veritable   *100*
                   Riens ny vault chiere espouentable / Ne forte armur a cest assault
                   Dun cop Jabas le plus estable / Riens nest darmes quant mort assaut

14

[CONSTABLE]   Jauoye encore intencion / Dassaillir chasteaux forteresses
                   Et mener a subiection / En acquerrant honneur ricesses
                   Mais Je voy que toute prouesse / Mort met au bas cest grant despit   *110*
                   Tout luy est vng douceur rudesse / Contre la mort nul na respit

15

[DEATH]   Que vous tirez la teste arriere / Arceuesque tirez vous pres
                   Auez paour que on ne vous fiere / Ne doubtez vous venrez apres
                   Nest pas tousiours la mort empres / Tout homme elle sieut coste a coste
                   Rendre conuient debtes et prestz / Vne fois fault compter a loste   *120*

64. Lille, by error, reads—*tritresse.*

16

[ARCHBISHOP] Las Je ne say ou regarder Tant suit par mort a grant destroit
Ou fuieray Je pour moy garder / Certes qui bien la congnoistroit
Hors de raison Jamais nystroit Plus ne giray en chambre painte
Morir me conuient cest le droit / Quant faire fault cest grant [contrainte]

17

[DEATH] Vous qui entre les grans barons / Auez eu renon cheuallier   130
Oublies trompettes clarons / Et me sieuez sans sommeillier
Les dames solies resueillier / En faisant danser longue piece
A aultre dansse fault veillier Ce que lun fait lautre despiece

18

[CHEVALIER] Or aige este auctorisie en pluiseurs fais et bien fame
Des grans et des petis prisie / Auec ce de dames ayme   140
Ne oncques ne fui diffame / A la court de seigneur notable
Mais a ce cop suis tout pasme / Desoubz le ciel na riens estable

19

[DEATH] Tantost naurez vaillant ce pic / Des biens du monde & de nature
Euesques de vous est il pic / Non obstant vostre prelature
Vostre fait gist en aduenture / De vos subgets fault rendre compte   150
A chascun dieu fera droitture / Nest pas asseur qui trop hault monte

20

[BISHOP] Le cuer ne me peult resiouir / des nouuelles que mort maporte
Dieu vouldra de tous compte oyr / Cest ce que plus me descomforte
Le monde aussy peu me conforte / Qui tous a la fin desherite
Il retient tout nul riens nemporte / Tout se passe fors la merite   160

21

[DEATH] Auancies vous gent escuier Qui sauez de danser les tours
Lance porties et escu hier / Et huy vous finerez voz Jours
Il nest riens qui ne prengne cours / Dansez et pensez de suir
Vous ne pouez auoir secours / Il nest nul qui puist mort fuir

22

[SQUIRE] Puis que mort me tient en ses las Aumoins que Je puisse vng mot dire   170
Adieu deduit adieu soulas / Adieu dames plus ne puis rire
Pensez de lame qui desire repos ne vous chaille plus tant
Du corps qui tous les Jours empire / Tout faut pourrir on ne scet quant

23

[DEATH] Abbe venez tost vous fuyez Nayes Ja la chiere esbahie
Il conuient que la mort sieuez Combien que moult lauez haye   180
Commandez adieu labbeye Qui gros et gras vous a nourry
Tost pourriras a peu daye / Le plus grant est premier pourry

24

[ABBÉ] De cecy neusse point enuye Mais Il conuient le pas passer
Las or nay Je pas en ma vie garde mon ordre sans casser
Gardez vous de trop embracher / vous qui viuez au demourant   190
Se vous voulez bien trespasser On sauise tart en morant

126. Lille, by error, reads—pointe.   128. Lille reads *grant contraire*; B.N. 14904, 25434,—*contrainte*.

25

[DEATH]   Bailly vous sauez quest Justice Et hault et bas en mainte guise
Pour gouuerner toute polisce Venez tantost a ceste assise
Je vous adiourne de main mise Pour rendre compte de voz fais
Au grant Juge qui tout vng prise Vng chascun portera son fais   *200*

26

[BAILLY]   Heu dieu vecy dure journee De ce cop pas ne me gardoye
Or est la chance bien tournee Entre Juges honneur auoye
Et mort fait raualler ma joye Qui ma adiourne sans rappel
Je ny voy plus ne tour ne voye / Contre la mort na point dappel

27

[DEATH]   Maistre pour vostre regarder En hault ne pour vostre clergie   *210*
Ne pouez la mort retarder / Cy ne vault riens astrologie
Toute la genealogie / Dadam qui fut le premier homme
Mort prent ce dist theologie / tout fault morir pour vne pomme

28

[ASTRONOMER]   Pour science ne pour degrez Ne puis auoir prouision
Car maintenant tous mes regrez / Font morir a confusion   *220*
Pour finale conclusion / Je ne say riens que plus descripue
Je pers cy toute aduision Qui vouldra bien morir bien viure

29

[DEATH]   Bourgois hastez vous sans tarder / Vous nauez auoir ne ricesse
Qui vous puist de mort retarder / Se des biens dont eustes largesse
Auez bien vse cest sagesse / Daultrui vient tout Aultrui passe   *230*
ffolz est qui damasser se bless / On ne scet pour qui on amasse

30

[BOURGEOIS]   Grant mal me fait si tost laissier / Rentes maisons cens nourreture
Mais poures riches abaissier / Tu fais mort telle est ta nature
Sage nest pas la creature / Damer trop les biens qui demeurent
Au monde / et sont siens de droiture / Ceux qui plus ont plus enuis meurent

31

[DEATH]   Sire chanonne prebendez / Plus naurez distribucion
Ne gros ne vous y atendez Prenez cy consolacion
Pour toute retribucion / Morir vous conuient sans demeure
Ja ny aurez dilacion / La mort vient quand on ne garde leure

32

[CANON]   Cecy gaires ne me conforte / Prebendez fuis en mainte eglise   *250*
Or est la mort plus que moy forte / Qui tout emmaine cest la guise
Blanc supplis et aumuce grise / Me fault laissier & a mort rendre
Que vault gloire sy tost bas mise / A bien morir doit chascun tendre

33

[DEATH]   Marchant regardez par decha Pluiseurs pays auez cherchiez
A pie a cheual de piecha / Vous nen serez plus empeschies   *260*
Jl conuient que par cy passez / De tous soings serez despeschies
Tel couuoite qui a assez / Vecy voz daranis jours marchies

227. *retarder*] *garder*, B. N. 14904.
230. *A aultruy passe.* B. N. 14904.
252. *La guise*] *sa guise*, B. N. 25434; B. N. 14904 as here.

255. Lille MS.—*pas mise;* B. N. 14904 *bas misse.*
264. B. N. 14904, 25434—*vostre desrain marchie.* Both these MSS have line-order 260, 264, 261, 262, 263.

34

[MERCHANT]   Jay este amont et aual Pour marchander ou Je pouoye
              Pour long tamps a pie a cheual / Mais maintenant pers toute Joye
              De tout mon pouoir acquerroie Et ay assez mort me constraint   270
              Bon fait auoir moyenne voye Qui trop embraisse mal estraint

35

[DEATH]   Alez marchant sans plus rester Ne faites ja cy residence
              Vous ny pouez riens conquester / Vous aussy homme dabstinence
              Chartreux prenez en pacience / De plus viure nayes memoire
              ffaites vous valoir a la dansce / Sur tout homme mort a victoire   280

36

[CHARTREUX]   Je suis au monde piecha mort Pourquoy de viure ay moins enuye
              Ja soit que tout homme craint mort Puis que la char est assouuye
              Plaise a dieu que lame rauye Soit es cieulx apres mon trespas
              Cest tout neant de ceste vye / Tel est huy qui demain nest pas

37

[DEATH]   Sergent qui portez celle mache / Il samble que vous rebellez   290
              Pour neant faittes la grimace / Se on vous grieue sy appellez
              Vous estes de mort appellez Qui sy rebelle Jl se dechoit
              Les plus fors sont tost rauallez / Nest sy fort qui aussi fort ne soit

38

[SERGEANT]   Moy qui suy Royal officier / Comment mose la mort frapper
              Je faisoie mon office hier Et elle me vient huy happer   300
              Je ne say quel part eschapper / Je suis pris decha et dela
              Malgre moy me laisse attraper / Enuis meurt qui apris ne la

39

[DEATH]   Ha maistre par la passerez / Nayes Ja soing de vous deffendre
              Plus homme ne espouenterez / Apres moine sans plus attendre
              Ou pensez vous cy fault entendre Tantost aurez la bouce close   310
              Homme nest fors que vent et cendre / Vie dhomme est moult peu de chose

40

[MONK]   Jamaisse mieulx encore estre En cloistre et faire mon office
              Cest vng lieu deuot et bel estre Or ay Je comme fol et nice
              Ou tamps passe commis maint vice / Dequoy nay pas fait penitance
              Souffisant dieu me soit propice / Chascun nest pas Joyeux qui dansce   320

41

[DEATH]   Vsurier de sens desriglez / Venez tost et me regardez
              Dusure estes tant auueuglez / Que dargent gaignier tout ardez
              Mais vous en serez bien lardez Car se dieu qui est merueilleux
              Na de vous pitie tout perdez A tout perdre est cop perilleux

42

[USURER]   Me conuient Jl sy tost morir / Ce mest grant paine & grant greuaunce   330
              Et ne me pourroit secourir Mon or mon argent ma cheuance
              Je vois morir la mort mauance Mais Jl men desplait somme toute
              Quesse de malle acoustumance / Tel a beaux yeulx qui ny voit goutte

296. B. N. 14904 reads *Il nest fort quaussi fort ne soit.*

43

Vsure est tant mauuais pechie Comme chascun dit & racompte
Et cest homme qui approuchie Se sent de la mort nen tient compte   *340*
Meismes largent que ma main compte Encore a vsure me preste
Jl denra de retour au compte Nest pas quitte qui doit de reste

44

[DEATH]
Medecin a tout vostre orine Veez vous Jcy que amender
Jadis seustes de medecine Assez pour pourueoir commander
Et vous vient la mort demander Comme aultres vous conuient morir   *350*
Vous ny pouez contremander Bon mire est qui se scet garir

45

[PHYSICIAN]
Longtamps a quen lart de phisique Je ay mis toute mestudie
Jauoye science et practique pour guarir mainte maladie
Je ne say que Je contredie / Plus ny vault herbe ne rachine
Nautre remede quoy qon die / Contre la mort na medecine   *360*

46

[DEATH]
Gentil amoureux Josne et frisque Qui vous cuidies de grant valoir
Vous estes pris la mort vous picque Le monde lairez a doleur
Trop lauez ayme cest folour Et a morir peu regarde
Tantost vous changerez coulour Beaute nest que ymage farde

47

[GALLANT]
Helas or ny a il secours / Contre mort / adieu amourettes   *370*
Moult tost va Jonnesse a decours / Adieu chappeaux boucages flourettes
Adieu amans et pucellettes / Souuiengne vous de moy souuent
Et vous mirez se saiges estes Petite pluye abat grant vent

48

[DEATH]
Aduocas sans long proces faire / Venez vostre cause plaidier
Bien auez sceu les gens attraire De pieca non pas dhuy ne dier   *380*
Conseil ne vous peult cy aydier Au grant Juge vous fault venir
Sauoir le direz sans cuidier Bon fait Justice preuenir

49

[ADVOCATE]
Cest bien droit que raison se face Ne Je ny say mettre deffence
Contre mort na respit ne grace Nul nappelle de sa sentence
Jay eu de lautruy quant Je y pense Dequoy Je doubte estre repris   *390*
A craindre fait Jour de vengence / Dieu rendra tout a Juste pris

50

[DEATH]
Menestrez qui danses et nottes Sauez et auez bel maintien
Pour faire esiouir sos et sottes /Quen dittes vous alons nous bien
Monstrer vous fault puis que vous tien Aux autres cy vng tour de danse
Le contredire ny vault rien Maistre doit monstrer sa sciance   *400*

51

[MINSTREL]
De dansser ainsy neusse cure Certes tres enuis Je men mesle
Car de mort nest paine plus dure / Jay mis soubz le banc ma vielle
Plus ne corneray sauterelle Ne aultre danse mort me retient
Jl me fault obeir a elle Tel danse a qui au cuer nen tient

383. B. N. 14904 reads *Sauoir se deues*, etc.   391. B. N. 14904 reads *A craindre est le jour*, etc.

52

[DEATH]   Passez Cure sans plus songier Je sens questes abandonnez   *410*
Le mort le vif souliez mengier Mais vous serez aux vers donnez
Vous fustes Jadis ordonnez Miroir daultrui estre exemplaire
De voz fais serez guerdonnez A toute paine est deu sallaire

53

[PARSON]   Vueille ou non Jl fault que me rende Jl nest homme qui mort nasaille
Hee de mes parociens offrande Narray Jamais ne funeraille   *420*
Deuant le Juge fault que Jaille Rendre compte las dolloureux
Or ay grant paour que ne faille Qui dieu quitte bien est eureux

54

[DEATH]   Laboureux qui en soing et paine Auez vescu tout vostre tamps
Morir fault cest chose certaine Reculler ny vault ne contens
De mort deuez estre contens Car de grant soussy vous deliure   *430*
Approchies vous Je vous attens / Fol est qui cuide tousiours viure

55

[LABORER]   La mort ay souhaidie souuent Mais voulentier Je la fuysse
Jamaisse mieulx feist pluye ou vent / Estre es vingnes ou Je fouysse
Aultre plus grant plaisir y prinse Car de paour pers tout propos
Or nest Jl qui de ce pas ysse Au monde na point de repos   *440*

56

[DEATH]   Faittes voye vous auez tort / Laboureux apres cordeliers
Souuent auez preschie de mort / Se vous devez moins marueillier
Ja ne sen fault esmay baillier Jl nest sy fort qui mort nareste
Sy fait bon a morir veillier A toute heure la mort est preste

57

[CORDELIER]   Quest ce de viure en ce monde Nul homme a sceurete ny demeure   *450*
Toute vanite y abonde Puis vient la mort qui tout court sceure
Mendicite point ne masseure Des malfais fault payer lamende
En petite heure dieu labeure / Sage est le pecheur qui samende

58

[DEATH]   Petit enfant nagaires ne Au monde auras peu de plaisance
Vieng a la danse sans mener Comme aultres Car mort a puissance   *460*
Sur tous du Jour de la naissance Conuient chascun a mort offrir
ffol est qui nen a congnoissance Qui plus vit plus a a souffrir

59

[INFANT]   A A A Je ne say parler Enffant suy Jay la langue mue
Hier nasqui huy men fault aller Je ne say quentree & yssue
Riens nay meffait mais de peur sue / Prendre en gre me fault cest le mieux
Lordonnance dieu ne se mue / Aussy tost muert Jonne que vieux

60

[DEATH]   Cuidez vous de mort eschapper Clerc esperdu pour reculler
Il ne sen fault Ja defripper Tel cuide souuent hault aller
Quon voit a cop tost raualler Prenez en gre alons ensamble
Car riens ny vault le rebeller / Dieu pugnist tout quant bon lui samble   *480*

414. B. N. 14904 reads—*daltrui & examplaire.*   452. B. N. 14904 has—*qua tous cour seure.*
441. Lille miswrites *tost* for *tort.*   468. B. N. 14904 has *Je ne fais quentrer,* etc.

61

[CLERK] ffault Jl que Jonne clerc seruant Qui en seruice prent plaisir
Pour cuider venir en auant Meure si tost cest desplaisir
Je sui quitte de plus choisir Aultre estat Jl fault quainsy dansce
La mort ma prins a son loysir Moult remaint de ce que fol pensce

62

[DEATH] Clerc point ne fault faire reffus De danser faites vous valoir   *490*
Vous nestes pas seul leuez sus Pourtant moins vous en doit challoir
Venez apres cest mon vouloir Homme nourry en hermitage
Ja ne vous en conuient doloir / Vie nest pas seur heritage

63

[HERMIT] Pour vie dure ou solitaire Mort ne donne de vie espace
Chascun le voit sy sen fault taire Or requier dieu que vng don me face   *500*
Cest que tous mes pechies efface Bien sui contens de tous ses biens
Desquelz Jay vse de sa grace / Qui na souffissance Jl na riens

64

[DEATH] Cest bien dit / ainsy doit on dire Jl nest qui soit de mort deliure
Qui mal vit Jl aura du pire Sy pense chascun de bien viure
Dieu pesera tout a la liure / Bon y fait penser soir & main   *510*
Meilleur science na en liure / Jl nest qui ait point de demain

65

Vng roy mort tout nu couchie en uers
Vous qui estes en pourtraiture / Veez danser estas diuers
Pensez quest humaine nature Ce nest fors que viande aux vers
Je le monstre qui gis enuers Sy ay Je este Roy couronnez
Tels serez vous bons et paruers Tous estas sont aux ver donnez   *520*

66

Vng maistre qui est au bout de la dance
Riens est dhomme qui bien y pensce Cest tout vent chose transitore
Chascun le voit par ceste dansce Pour ce vous qui veez listore
Retenez le bien en memoire / Car homme et femme elle ammoneste
Dauoir de paradis la gloire / Eureux est qui es cieulx fait feste

67

Mais aucun sont a qui nen chault / Comme sil ne fust paradis
Ne enfer helas Jlz auront chault / Les liures que firent Jadis
Les sains le monstrent en beaux dis Acquittez vous qui cy passez
Et faittes bien plus que nen dis / Bien fais vault moult aux trespassez *536*

Mortales dominus cunctos In luce creauit
Vt capiant meritis gaudia summa polj
Felix ille quidem mentem iugiter illuc
Dirigit atque vigil noxia queque cauet
Nec tamen Infelix [sceleris] quen penitet actj   5
Quique suum facinus plangere s(e)pe solet
Sed viuunt homines tamquam mors nulla sequatur

487. B. N. 14904,—a son plaisir.
513. B. N. 14904 Vous qui en ceste pourtraiture.
Latin, line 5. Sceleris is from B. N. 14904; Lille

reads sterilis. Lille in 6 has spe, in 7
vimunt(ur).

Et velud infernis fabula vana foret
Cum doceat sensus viuentes more resoluj
Atque herebj penas pagina sacra probet   10
Quas qui non metuit Jnfelix prorsus & amens
Viuit et exinitus sentiet ille rogam
Sit igitur cuncti sapientes viuere certent
Vt nichil inferni sit metuenda palus

EPITHALAMIUM FOR GLOUCESTER

1. *gladde aspectis,* favoring regard. See FaPrin.E 88 here, and see FaPrin. iii :2763, of Fortune's face; see Thebes 218, 275, 383-4, and Root's notes on Chaucer's Troilus ii :682, iii :716.

14. *Jubiter's cheyne.* Jupiter maintained the sanctity of laws, oaths, and treaties; his consort Juno presided over marriage. In the next two stanzas Lydgate is not clear. Alliance excludes strife, he says; then, that wars are predetermined in the stars; then that God, by instituting marriage, has made it possible to contravene the stars. His misuse or omission of verbs, as e.g. line 21, confuses still more.

21. "(Of which) the first cause (is) portrayed in the stars."

24. *to voide.* If we read *do voide,* the sense will be "Nor force destiny to yield, except God, who rules all", etc.

29-31. "There is more than one example in books, (whoso will consider the deeper meaning) carried out in olden time", etc.

31. *Calydoyne and Arge,* Calydon and Argos. See note on 138 below, and Troy Book v :1207 ff.

42. *werre stynt.* The marriage of Henry V to the French princess /Katherine, in 1420, was supposed to end the war and to secure the French crown to their descendants.

55. *duchy of Holand.* See introduction above.

56. *Brutus Albyoun,* the Albion of Brut, a mythical warrior who wandered thither after the fall of Troy, and founded a settlement. See Garland 405.

69-70. "whose birth to describe, (she) is by descent" etc.

71 ff. This list of personages with whom comparison is made is a convention often used by Lydgate. He has two such catalogues in this poem, one of women and one of men; there is a long list of women in the Flower of Courtesy, a still longer in the Valentine to the Virgin, printed by MacCracken, p. 304 ff.; there is one of men in the Coronation of Henry VI, and shorter lists in TemGlass 405 ff., Horns Away 27 ff., and the Troy Book envoy. See the list in Black Knight 365 ff., or the prose Epistle of the Lover's Mass, p. 213 here, or Cavendish, p. 382 here. See Feylde's Controversy between a Lover and a Jay; see p. 69 of the Percy Society ed. of Hawes' Pastime.

72. *Polixseene.* Polyxena, the daughter of Priam, beloved by Achilles. See note Garl. 855.

77. *be.* The scribe inserted this word above, with a caret.

83-4. The word *beo,* 83, is omitted by the scribe. With the rime-words here, *comprehendid: amendid,* cp. the same two-line formula in FlCourtesy 188-9, DuorMercat 391-2, Albon i :386-7, St. Edmund i :408-9; and in Chaucer's Anelida 83-4. It might be suggested that the 1532 print of the Flower of Courtesy, our only text, be read *comprehende* in line 188 instead of *commende,* with Skeat's added *her.* But see ResonandSens 327-8 beside *ibid.* 1101-2.

87. *avysee.* This word, meaning "well-advised", is fairly common in Lydgate; there are a dozen cases in the Troy Book alone. It is used by Chaucer in the Legend 1521; and I may suggest that the rime-word in FlCourtesy 142 is *avisee,* as in 215, rather than the emendation offered by Skeat.

88. *brydil leede,* a very common metaphor in Lydgate. See "And thus fals lust doth your bridil leede", FaPrinces i :838; see *ibid.,* 1394, 1999, 2520, 6729, etc.

96. *Nowe,* omitted from the text, is supplied in the margin by Shirley, with a caret.

99. *A heven it is.* A Chaucerian locution. Cp. "It was an heven upon him for to see," Troilus ii :637; similarly *ibid.,* ii :826, iii :1742, SqTale 271, 558. Lydgate uses the phrase Troy Book i :2048-9, etc. The word *paradys* instead of *heven* appears in Troy Book i :1590, St. Albon i :261, etc; see Reproof 5-6 here.

104-5. *Hir.eyeghen saygne,* etc. Cp. Chaucer's BoDuch 876-7, "... hir eyen seyde ... my wrath is al foryive". Cp. p. 286 of the transl. of Orléans ed. for the Roxburghe Club,—"Me thynkith yowre eyen mercy seith."

112. *Ce bien raysoun.* This was presumably the motto of Jacqueline. The use of such mottoes was extremely common in this period; a long list may be read in the Assembly of Ladies.

114. "One of those the greatest-born alive."

123. *oon þe beste.* This Middle English idiom is recurrent in both Chaucer and Lydgate; cp: "among kynges he was oon the beste", FaPrinces i :5979, or "oon the best knyht", *ibid.,* viii :3227, etc.

129. *daring doo.* This is termed by NED a "pseudo-archaism", and explained as a verbal phrase, "daring to do", which was in later English treated as a substantive combination. See Chaucer's Troilus v :837, "dorring don"; the passage is imitated by Lydgate, Troy Book ii :4861 ff., see 4869. Spenser, ShephCal. October 65 and December 43, Faerie Queene ii :4, 42 and vi :5,37, uses the word substantively, as does Scott in Ivanhoe. But Lydgate's treatment here has all the appearance of a substantive.

133. *hous of ffaame.* Cp. "Set and registred in the Hous of Fame", FaPrinces iv :122,— "May be registrid in the Hous off Fame", *ibid.* vi :514, etc. See note on FaPrin. B 95 here, and see Troy Book iii :4254.

134. *worþy nyen,* the Nine Worthies, i.e., Hector, Alexander, Caesar, Joshua, David, Judas Maccabaeus, Arthur, Charlemagne, Godfrey of Bouillon. In the presentation of the Nine Worthies in Shakespeare's Love's Labor's Lost, Pompey and Hercules are included.

138. *Tedeus,* Tydeus, son of Oeneus king of Calydon, who, being obliged to flee from his native country, took shelter with the king of Argos, wedded his daughter, and became the father of a son Diomedes who subsequently rescued the Calydonian royal house from usurpers. Tydeus' figure is greatly magnified in the form of the Theban story used by Lydgate for his Siege of Thebes, and the mention of Tydeus as a superman, both here and in St. Edmund i :1036, suggests comment as to the relative dates of these works.

143. *with þe Allegorye.* The text of Scripture was held to require several interpretations, the "literal, tropological, allegorical, and anagogical". Until the work of Erasmus and Colet, in the late fifteenth and early sixteenth centuries, the Bible was treated predominantly by the allegorical method of exposition. Gloucester's MSS presented to Oxford·include many works of this sort.

148. With this list see note on line 71 above.

161. *Sanz plus vous belle.* Gloucester's heraldic motto was "Loyalle et belle"; he may have used a special motto for Jacqueline. Cp. the two mottoes of the Black Prince, "Homout" for war, "Ich dene" for peace.

176. *ymeneus,* Hymen, god of marriage; usually said to be a son of one of the Muses. With this line cp. Thebes 826.

178. *Juvo.* Shirley's spelling of Juno. She presided over marriage.

179-80. *Phylogenye.* A false rendering by Shirley of *Philology,* whose marriage to Mercury god of eloquence was described by Martianus Capella in a work of the fifth century, one of the influential books of the Middle Ages. Lydgate refers to it in Thebes 833-44, in St. Edmund i :95-104; see also FaPrinces iii :66, and Chaucer's MerchTale 488-90.

182. *thryes thre.* This convenient rime-formula is often used by Lydgate when he mentions the Muses. See Thebes 832, FaPrinces i :459, iii :12. Or the formula is "in noumbre nyne", as in St. Edmund i :91, FaPrinces iv :76.

189. *neodful.* Shirley's spelling of *needful.*

LETTER TO GLOUCESTER

4. *hand . . . quake.* The quaking hand or pen is a very frequent device with Lydgate; see TemGlass 947, BlKnight 181, St. Margaret 57, St. Edmund iii :89, St. Albon i :928, Troy Book i :4427 etc., FaPrinces i :5517 etc. Chaucer has the locution Troilus iv :13-14.

9 ff. The first group of metaphors is medical. Gloucester, a man of self-indulgence, was constantly under medical care, and took great interest in medicine; his library contained many books on the subject. Cp. Hoccleve's Mâle Règle 446-8.

12. *Dragge nor dya.* Cp. *dyas and dragges,* Piers Plowman B xx :173. The word *dragge,* an early form of *drug,* was accord. to NED used only in plural; but see the sing. here and in line 55. *Dia* means any medical preparation; it is the Greek prefix "through" used as a separate word. —*Bury town.* Was Lydgate writing at the monastery?

17. *Ship was ther noon,* etc. The metaphor changes to monetary, and means that there was no gold coin in Lydgate's purse. In this period the noble, half-noble, and quarter-noble bore on the obverse the design of a crowned king in a ship; cp. Hoccleve's poem to Somer line 21, and the "vj shippis grete", i.e., six gold nobles, of EETS ed., i, p. 64. Similar metaphors are used by Aristophanes, who in The Birds calls Athenian coins "owlets", from the stamp they bore; and by Dante, who in Paradiso xviii :133 censures the Papacy for preferring John the Baptist to Peter or Paul,—this meaning the figure of John on the gold florin. Also, in A Mirror for Magistrates ii p. 134 (Haslewood's ed.) the poem on Humphrey of Gloucester says of Beaufort (stanza 24) that "Not God's angels, but angels of old gold Lift him aloft."

seilis reed, etc. In this period sails were stained red or particolored. See Nicolas' Hist. of the Royal Navy i :469, 471, and the directions for dyeing the sails of Edward III's ship; see Chaucer's Legend 654 for Cleopatra's "purpre sail," i.e., crimson.

20. *ebbe.* See FaPrinces iii :69 for note.

25. *from the Tour.* The Mint was in the Tower of London after 1329, but for how long is uncertain. See Ruding, Annals of the Coinage of Britain, 5 vols., 1817-19.

27. *ffretyng Etik,* a devouring fever. This phrase, "gredy etik", and the word *etik* are common in Lydgate. See line 45 below; see FaPrinces ii :3739-43, 3889-92, iii :138, 695, 3724, 4286, 4029, iv :1103, vi :1323, etc.

28. *cotidian.* A fever persisting daily, instead of recurring as tertian or quartan.

29. *Sol and Luna,* the sun and moon, i.e., alchemical terms for gold and silver. Neither planet was shining upon the poet.

30. *no cros,* etc. The English silver coins of the fifteenth century bore on the obverse a crowned male head ("visage"), and on the reverse a large slender cross.

35-6. *an ernest grote.* The agreement between buyer and seller was clinched by payment of a groat as "earnest-money" or guarantee. When the bargain was completed in an ale-house, as was frequently the case, the groat was spent in liquor.—*stant in aventure,* stands in peril, is shaky.

37. *callyd to the lure,* summoned to Indigence by her lure. See note on Dance Macabre 207 for *lure.*

39. *recure.* This form of *recover,* used transitively, is exceedingly common in Lydgate, and common in him alone. See note on Dance Macabre 311 here.

43. *boklersbury,* the London street occupied by grocers and apothecaries; see Stow's Survey, ed. Kingsford, i :260.

46. *aurum potabile,* drinkable gold, the alchemical specific against age and its ills; see Ripley's Compend, line 160 here.

47. *quynt essence,* the "fifth essence", the element above the four earthly elements of earth, air, fire, and water; i.e., ether. Later, the concentration of pure quality in anything. —*In,* read *Is?*

51. *tonne attamyd,* pierced (and drained) your cask. The verb *attame* rarely has in Lydgate the simple original meaning "to pierce, to broach", as literally in Piers Plowman B xvii :68, metaphorically in Chaucer's prologue to the NPTale 52. It usually means in Lydgate "to lay hands on, meddle with, undertake".

52. *nichil habet.* A nihil or nichil was the return made by a sheriff to the executor when the party named in the writ had no goods on which levy could be made. The first case NED is of 1585.

53. *tisyk,* phthisis, i.e., consumption with its attendant dry cough or asthma.

59. *cros nor pyl.* The cross was the mark stamped on the obverse of English silver coins; see note on line 30 above. The "pile" was the depression made by the stamping instrument on the reverse of such a coin.

FALL OF PRINCES : A

1 ff. Lydgate's opening prologue restates a part of Laurent's, declaring the right of translators to remake, describing the magnitude of this particular task, and commenting on the folly of princes in supposing Fortune to be stable. The immediate problem is then taken up, and in his own person Lydgate laments his incapacity and his loss of his lodestar Chaucer. The well-known list of Chaucer's works follows, after which, remarking that poets were of old held in high esteem by princes, Lydgate proceeds to the praise of his patron Humphrey of Gloucester. With another regret as to his own inadequacy, Lydgate closes the prologue.

The portion of this which is derived from Laurent is relatively small, and is much padded by Lydgate, who also occasionally misunderstands his original;—see below 4-5 and 36-37. Laurent's first desire, in his own proheme, was to explain why he was executing another version of the De Casibus, which he had so recently translated. He says that a man diligent in the pursuit of knowledge may change his "conseil de bien en mieulx", just as à potter may break his vessel to give it a better form. And such license to improve holds good not merely for a man's own work but for that of another, if the task be undertaken without "enuye ne arrogance". Then Laurent says that he has already translated this work, following closely the subtle artificial language of Boccaccio; but that even those who call themselves clerks and men of letters suffer from great ignorance, and he has come to realize the necessity of rendering Latin books in such terms as can be understood without much labor. He then commends the De Casibus as of "tres singulier prix", and its lesson as greatly needed; he states his intention of giving at length those histories which Boccaccio had merely touched, by which he evidently means the group-chapters with their brief mention of many notables. He considers that in so passing them over Boccaccio was brief not from lack of knowledge but because he thought others as well-informed as himself. He, Laurent, will enlarge on these points to give the work completeness.

This prologue is modified by some of the French printers, and the form of its text which Lydgate used is uncertain. It may be read, as printed by du Pré, Paris 1483, in Bergen's ed. of FaPrinces, i, pp. lii-liv. A text from MS is printed by Hortis, Opere latine del Boccaccio, Trieste, 1879, pp. 740-742.

4-5. Laurent, describing the scope of the De Casibus, says that it includes the histories of all the great from the beginning of the world "iusques a Iehan roy de France mort prisonicr en angleterre." The assumption that this last event marks the date of Laurent's work is Lydgate's error.—*Theere,* i.e., *The yeere.*

13-14. For the simile of the potter cp. Jeremiah 18 :4.

20. *Fro good to better.* In Laurent, "de bien en mieulx". The French phrase, as also "de mieulx en mieulx", seems to have been frequent in courtly poetry. Granson uses the latter in one of his ballade-refrains, and it appears in Lydgate's Temple of Glass 310. The phrase "De bien en mieulx" was apparently one of Charles V's mottoes, see Delisle's Librairie de Charles V, i:128. We find "Fro good to better" in Lydgate's St. Edmund i:361 and in his Pilgrimage 23696; the phrase "Fro wele to better" is in the Flower and Leaf 550. Similarly, "Fro bet to wers" appears in FaPrinces v:2339.

21-22. Note the stanza-liaison, frequent in this poem, and not uncommon in Lydgate.

24. *chaff . . . corn.* See Chaucer, Legend 312, 529, and MLTale 603.

27. *colours,* i.e., of rhetoric. See note on G 46 below, on Cavendish's Visions 61.

29-35. This follows Laurent:—"que on le face par bonte de couraige & par mouvement de pure charite qui en soy ne contient enuye ne arrogance."

36-37. Lydgate thinks that the previous translation of the De Casibus was not by Laurent. But the French is explicit.

45-46. *requerid Off estatis,* urged by men of rank. Laurent says "a lenhortement & requeste daulcuns."

50-77. An excursus by Lydgate.

78-84. This is an expansion of Laurent's words as to the ignorance of even the clerks in his time; see above.

85-91. Here Lydgate restates Laurent's announced intention of filling out the parts of the De Casibus which Boccaccio had treated summarily. As pointed out in the introduction to the poem here, such an expansion destroyed Boccaccio's effect of varied focus. See note on 141-154 below.

92-98. Although this expansion of Laurent's words apparently is endorsed by Lydgate, it can be paralleled by many passages rejecting "prolixite" or refusing to describe in detail. Each is a formula.

99-126 expand two sentences of moderate length in the French.

127-140 expand phrases of a long sentence in Laurent.—140. *prince edward,* the Black Prince, victor at Poitiers.

141-154. Lydgate follows Laurent in his alteration of Boccaccio. The Latin is: "Absit tamen vt omnes dixerim [i.e., that I should discuss *all* illustrious men and women]. Quis enim mortalium tanti foret vt infinito posset labori sufficere? Set ex claris quos clarissimos excerpsisse sat erit." The text of Boccaccio used by Laurent we do not yet know, but Laurent gives no part of this reason, saying that Boccaccio did not make his omissions because of ignorance, but because "les reputa communes et cogneues aux autres comme a soy."

162-175. Here Lydgate uses a bit not of Laurent's own preface, but of his translation of Boccaccio's preface, which was retained in the second French version. In some MSS the text is more complete than in others; see Bergen's ed. i, p. li. There we find "comme se ilz eussent endormie fortune par herbes ou par enchantemens ou ainsi comme se ilz eussent fermees leurs seignouries a croz de fer a roche daymant."

182. *seith . . . chekmat.* See note FaPrinces D 52 here.

183-224 are an excursus by Lydgate.

205 is parenthetical.

211-12. For this proverb see Chaucer's SqTale 483. Skeat there cites from Othello ii,3:276, from Cotgrave, from George Herbert. Holthausen, Anglia 14:320, gives 14th century examples, mainly Latin and German; and Lowes, Archiv 124:132, prints a passage from Jacobus de Voragine. It was evidently a commonplace of the Middle Ages; it occurs in a French collection of proverbs cited by Naetebus, p. 137, in the Geneva text of Proverbes des Philosophes as ed. by Ritter, 1880, and is used by Surrey in his poem opening "Suche way-warde wais hath Love".

239. Cp. Lydgate's DuorMercat. 498-99, Black Knight 176-77, and line 456 below.

241-45. This refusal of Calliope and the Muses to aid in "compleynyng" is a formula, a convention of formal poetry. See below 456-58, Temple of Glass 952-4, Troy Book iii:5428 ff. Chaucer in his Troilus had twice called upon the Furies to assist in narrating his tragedy.

243. *sugre . . . galle.* The Muses, Lydgate says, refuse to mingle the sugar of their "rethorik swete" with the bitterness of woe. In Lydgate and the Transition poets, elo-quence is "thensugerd pocioun of Elyconys welle", as Skelton says. See GarlLaurell 73-4, Court of Love 22, Bokenam's St. Anne 57, etc. Also, when Fate or Fortune overthrows the proud, the sugar of life is "meynt with bittir gall" (FaPrinces i:4536) and the tragedy is consummated. Here and in 456-58 below the Muses take no part in woful narrative; in Thebes 828 ff. they are not present at the inauspicious wedding of Oedipus. See also Duor-Mercat. 505 ff.

246 ff. This long passage on Chaucer, by no means the only allusion in this poem, could hardly have been included without Gloucester's approval. In this connection we may

query if Humphrey's naming of his illegitimate daughter "Antigone" was so much classical as in remembrance of "Antigone the whyte", her of the sweet song, in Chaucer's Troilus.

248-9. The Monk's Tale is meant; see FaPrinces ix:3421-27.

253-73. The mention of comedies and tragedies in conjunction sends Lydgate on a digression to Seneca's tragedies, Cicero's "fressh ditees", Petrarch's De Remediis utriusque Fortunae, and Boccaccio. The "ditees" ascribed to Cicero mean not so much his surviving bits of verse as his "dictes" or utterances.

257. *petrak.* The spelling of Petrarch's name as *Patrak* or *Petrak* is frequent if not predominant in English MSS; it occurs in a number of CantTales MSS in the Clerk's headlink, and in MSS of this poem. See Bergen's ed. iii:3859, viii:61, 66, 87, 183, etc. And Delisle's Librairie de Charles V mentions, p. 371, "un livre appellé Patrac." See line 37 of extract K, below.

259. The work here alluded to is Petrarch's De remediis utriusque fortunae, which as Lydgate says is divided into two books of dialogues, the first set between Gaudium (or Spes) and Ratio, the second between Dolor and Ratio. There was a copy of "Franciscus de remediis fortuitorum" among the manuscripts which Gloucester in 1439 presented to the University of Oxford. The work is again alluded to in this poem iv:109.

281 ff. After a transitional stanza, Lydgate returns to the matter of Chaucer's works. Skeat comments on this list in Oxford Chaucer i:22-25. The stanzas containing it are printed in my Chaucer Manual, pp. 58-60 from the 1554 print of the FaPrinces, and by Miss Spurgeon in Chaucer Allusions i:37-43 from MSS Harley 1766 and 4203.

284. *trophe.* There are but two known occurrences of this word in Middle English, one in Chaucer's Monk's Tale 127, the other here. Discussion of Chaucer's "Trophee" has thus far most substantially resulted in Kittredge's suggestion of a confusion, by Chaucer or in Chaucer's source, between the "trophees" or columns set up by Hercules and Bacchus at the two ends of the world, and a book or author narrating the life of Hercules, of whom the Monk is speaking. This confusion, as Kittredge points out, might be caused by such a phrase as "ad Herculis Liberique trophaea", which occurs in the so-called Letter of Alexander to Aristotle; the word *Liber* (Bacchus) might be understood as *liber* (book). See Kittredge's paper in the Putnam Anniversary Volume, 1909.

An earlier explanation of the MoTale allusion was Skeat's identification of "Trophee" or "Pillar" with Guido delle Colonne or Guido de Columpnis, in whose Historia Trojana Hercules is a figure, and who might be cited, by his translated surname, as authority for statements about Hercules.

But although the passage of the MoTale was doubtless known to Lydgate, it was not certainly in his mind here; and part of what he says is based on a quite different, and definite, piece of knowledge. He is aware that the original of Chaucer's Troilus was written in Italian, "in lumbard tunge", and he says that this original was called *Trophe*. He does not say, any more than Chaucer said, that the principal source of *Troilus* was the same "Bochas" whom he is here following for the Fall of Princes; and it may be that he does not know it. But while Chaucer acknowledged none but a Latin source for his romantic tragedy, Lydgate is possessed of the fact that the original was in Italian. Two questions therefore follow:—Where did Lydgate obtain that fact?—and,—Why does he call Boccaccio's Filostrato "Trophe"?

On the former point, Prof. Kittredge, in his study of Chaucer's Lollius, HarvStudClass-Philol 28, asserts that Chaucer's setting-up of "Lollius" to represent his various sources for the Troilus was a transparent literary artifice well understood by contemporary men of letters, and that Chaucer himself gave his "hearty consent" to the "common knowledge" that the work was really from the Italian. This passage of Lydgate Prof. Kittredge regards as proof. But considering Lydgate's dependence upon Gloucester's library in this translation, I think it as probable that his information regarding a "Lombard" original of the Troilus derived from an Italian scholar in Gloucester's entourage, or from Gloucester himself, the owner of so many Petrarch and Boccaccio volumes. The monk's scrap of knowledge about Dante, his access to Coluccio Salutati's declamation on Lucretia, came in all likelihood from his patron; and if Humphrey recognized the debt of Chaucer to the Italian for his Troilus-story, he was critic of letters as well as patron and collector. This is conjecture, and not fact; but there seems more probability of it than of the situation which Prof. Kittredge's clairvoyance has depicted.

On the second point there is little to be said. Although Chaucer made occasional use of Guido delle Colonne's Historia Trojana in his Troilus, it is unlikely that Lydgate's "Trophe" refers to Guido, as Skeat has suggested for Chaucer's Trophee in the MoTale. Lydgate knew Guido, and had translated his Trojan chronicle in the Troy Book, there speaking constantly of the author as "Guido". Moreover, he is here definitely talking of a book not in Latin. Prof. Kittredge opines that Lydgate has carelessly shifted the Monk's Tale allusion, and that as "a constitutional blunderer" his statement "need trouble us no further". Upon which I may comment that even a Homer-epigone nods not all the time. The connection of "Trophee" with the Troilus is at present unclear to us; but more knowledge of manuscript-conditions may yet show us that the transfer of names has an explanation.

For an interesting suggestion on the gloss "Ille vates Chaldaeorum Trophaeus" in two of the best of the CantTales MSS, see Tupper in MLNotes, vol. 31.

291. Chaucer's translation of Boethius' De Consolatione Philosophiae.

292. The bracketed word is from MS Bodley 263; our MS reads &.

294. *thastlabre,* the Astrolabe. Tottel's 1554 print reads "that labour".

299-300. *domefieng,* etc. Late medieval Latin *domificare,* "to build houses", was used astrologically to mean "to divide the heavens into twelve equal houses or mansions, to locate the planets therein". This is the first case cited NED, and Hawes, Pastime of Pleasure, is the second. See Dance Macabre 292.

root . . . ascendent. The root or radix, in astrology, was the basis of any calculation, perhaps a nativity, perhaps the position of a planet. See Chaucer's Astrolabe ii § 44, MLTale 314. The ascendent was that part of the ecliptic which was at any time rising above the horizon. See the Astrolabe ii § 3, lines 23-24, and especially § 4. With this line cp. Lydgate's Thebes 370, "The root ytaken at the ascendent".

south is miswritten for *souht.*

303. *Dante in inglissh / hym silff so doth expresse.* This line has occasioned much discussion, which it may be convenient to restate in two sections,—opinion as to the first half of the line and opinion as to the latter half. Prof. Skeat, Oxford Chaucer i:22-25, comments only on the first half, which he considers as referring to the Hous of Fame. His reasons are that Lydgate would certainly mention that work, and would naturally mention it in connection with the Death of Blanche the Duchess, as Chaucer had in the Legend, line 418 of the prologue. Still stronger, indeed conclusive to Skeat's mind, is the influence of Dante upon the Hous of Fame, of which he considers that Lydgate is thinking when he applies this name to the poem. Of the second half of the line Skeat says only that it is "rather dubious"; he paraphrases—"Chaucer expresses himself (therein) like Dante."

MacCracken, in the N.Y.Nation for 1909, ii:276-77, offers a solution which like Skeat's emphasizes mainly the first half of the line. But he argues, and justly, that Lydgate is not capable of any such critical dictum, such implied comparison of poems so different in form and tone as are the Divina Commedia and the Hous of Fame; the more incapable because Lydgate's knowledge of Dante was very slight. MacCracken's suggestion is that as the next two poems in this list, Ceys and Alcyone and the Death of Blanche, are "piteous", Lydgate introduces them by saying that Chaucer therein writes as Dante, author of the "piteous" story of Ugolino, would express himself in English. On this theory, the Hous of Fame is not mentioned by Lydgate; which need not surprise us in so careless a workman.

Both Skeat and MacCracken, in their paraphrases and comments, treat the second half of the line as meaning "expresses himself", as reflexive. I have however pointed out, Anglia 36:375-6, that the NED has no case of *express* in reflexive usage before Shakespeare, and that, as *himself* has in all periods of the language served as a nominative, this half-line must be paraphrased "he himself says so". (Compare in this connection Thebes 2442, "—hym-silf in ordre did expresse".) This being so, then *he* must mean Chaucer; and any interpretation of the first half of the line must be shaped by this fact. Should we take *Dante in inglissh* as referring to the story of Ugolino, in the Monk's Tale, and point both to the separate mentions of Melibeus, of Griselda, of the Monk's Tale, in lines 249, 346-350, and to Chaucer's own naming of Dante as he ends the Ugolino-story, we should still have to recognize that Lydgate's telling of the Pisan tragedy, FaPrinces ix:2051-55, makes no mention of Chaucer, and is dismissed with five lines. The tale which in this Prologue the monk singled out and described in accordance with Chaucer's own reference to Dante as its author, he would, on this explanation, have totally forgotten when he arrived at the ninth book of his translation. This is perhaps not impossible for Lydgate; it is not impossible that he noticed Chaucer's mention of Dante more than he did the heading of that particular tragedy in the Monk's tale. But the first half of the line remains "dubious", rather than the second, which is linguistically clear. On the line see Brusendorff, p. 151.

It may be added that in the many scores of usages of *expresse* by Lydgate, with whom the word is a favorite, I have noted no case of the reflexive; nor in any writer of this period. The phrasing "as he seith hymselue", FaPrinces vi:3170, may be compared here. In these extracts it is G 223.

304. *ciex and alcione.* This story forms part of the Boke of the Duchesse, and is separately mentioned ML headlink 57. It may once have been an independent poem.

314. See Parl. of Foules 540.

318. This translation is not now known to exist.

319. *of the leoun.* Mentioned in the Retractation to the Canterbury Tales, but not now known. Perhaps, as Tyrwhitt suggested, a translation of Machaut's Dit du Lion.

321-3. "The Broche of Thebes" is the title of the Complaint of Mars in MS Harley 7333; see my Manual, p. 384.—Note the stanza-liaison.

324. *Ouyde.* Lydgate is in error. It is Statius who mentions the fatal brooch, or rather bracelet, so desired of Theban women, in his Thebais ii:265. Chaucer, in his Mars 245-260, extends the maleficent effect to men, and Lydgate follows him.

330. *at requeste of the quene.* Lydgate may be recalling incorrectly the close of the prologue to Chaucer's Legend of Good Women, where Love bids the poet give the queen his book, when finished, "at Eltham or at Shene". This passage is not in the Cambridge Gg text of the prologue.

330-36. This passage is used in the Schole-House of Women, ed. Hazlitt, EEPopPoetry iv:141-2.

331. The Legend of Good Women.

332. *bounte & fairnesse.* See note on Bycorne 88.

334-36. This is what Skeat would call "a waggish comment" by Lydgate. The words *And for* in 334 oblige us to read a comma at end of 336, and make Lydgate say that Chaucer turned to the Canterbury Tales because he could not complete the Legend as commanded. This is doubtful.

345. *sentence,* sense, substance. See 448 below, Chaucer's Prologue 306, 800, NPTale 345, Troilus iii:1327, etc.

342-5. See Lydgate's prologue to Thebes, 22-23.

346. The story of Melibeus, from the Cant.Tales.—348. The Clerk's Tale.

350. The Monk's Tale.

353. *virrelaies,* virelays. A virelay was a poem in strophes, on two rimes, the last rime of each strophe becoming the first rime of the next strophe; e.g., *aab aab aab bcc,* etc.

365-8. In Higden's Polychronicon iii cap. 42 (Rolls Series ed.) we find:—"Auditorium Tullii Caesar intravit. Cui cum assurgeret Tullius, Caesar prohibuit, dicens 'Non assurgas mihi, maior est enim sapientia quam potentia.' Cui Tullius: 'Orbis victori non assurgam?' Et Caesar, 'Et tu maiorem lauream adeptus es quam propagare terminos Romani imperii.' Cuius verbi occasione lex a Caesare emanavit ut nemo codicem tenens aut legens cuiquam assurgat."

375-6. As pointed out Anglia 38:135-6, this allusion, with line 406, enables us to date the prologue of the Fall of Princes. Koeppel, interpreting the phrase "which is now in fraunce" to mean Gloucester, connected it with the duke's 1424-5 campaign in Flanders.

But from the next line we learn that Gloucester at time of writing was "lieftenant" of Britain; to fill this office he must be in England. And as the phrase "which is now in fraunce" could in Lydgate's syntax equally well apply to Henry VI, whose absence in France would compel the appointment of a lieutenant, it is clear that Henry was out of England and Gloucester acting as lieutenant, when Lydgate wrote these lines. This was noted by Schick, Temple of Glass, introd. p. cv. The date would then be between April 1430 and January 1432; Schick fixes on 1430,—but see note on 406 below.—Observe stanza-liaison 378-9, 385-6.

387. *commune*, converse. This word was used in the late MidEng period alongside the more frequent *common*, which it ultimately displaced.

389. *contune*. This variant on *continue*, of obscure formation, occurs three times in the Romaunt of the Rose, is frequent in Lydgate and in Bokenam, and goes no further. Its presence in "fragment B" of the Romaunt is with some scholars an argument for Lydgate's authorship of that part of the translation. The word occurs in Lover's Mass 13.

391-2. *And wher he loueth*, etc. These lines may be conventional praise of Gloucester for a virtue highly commended by medieval poets, although quite foreign to the duke's temperament; they may be an allusion to Gloucester's motto, "Loyalle et belle"; and they may hint at the circumstances of the moment. Gloucester, after a passionate and ill-advised marriage with Jacqueline of Holland in 1424, had forsaken her, and had caused public scandal by his connection with Eleanor Cobham. When the earlier union was annulled, he made Eleanor his duchess, some time between 1428 and 1431. Lydgate, who is now probably writing in 1431, had written not only an Epithalamium for the marriage with Jacqueline (see p. 144 above), but ? a lament over Gloucester's desertion of her and infatuation with Eleanor, an infatuation piously attributed to witchcraft. (See text of the poem in Anglia 27:393 ff.) We may query if the second marriage was recent when Lydgate wrote this passage, if he is here justifying Gloucester, by his phrase "without cause", for the rejection of Jacqueline.

398. *hym silff to ocupie*. This reflexive use of *occupy* is earlier than the NED citations of 1555, 1604. Cp. note on 303 *ante*.

406 ff. *To punysshe alle tho*, etc. A yet closer approximation to the date of this Prologue may be obtained from these lines. In the spring of 1431 there were various outbreaks of Lollardy in the south of England, all of which were rigorously put down by Gloucester's government, acting in the king's absence, and he himself was present at the beheading, at Oxford, of a small band of recalcitrants led by the bailiff of Abingdon. This was in May, 1431. As a matter of politics, Gloucester made much of his loyalty to the Church, and Lydgate is very probably referring to this occasion. The date of the Prologue would then be between May 1431 and the New Year of 1432, when Henry VI returned from France and Gloucester's lieutenancy ended. See other allusions to these outbreaks in the Palladius-prologue line 51, and cp. note on that passage.

409. *synglar*, singular. This word has usually in Lydgate the force of "especial, particular"; but the phrase "synguler bataile", as in FaPrinces i:5455, etc., means "single combat"; and in a number of cases the word means "personal, individual", e.g., FaPrinces iii:1249, etc.

431. Cp. the management of line 454.

456. *Ditees of murnyng*, etc. Cp. lines 24-5 above.

459. *in noumbre thries thre*. A formula for rime; see note on line 182 of the Epithamium above. See also FaPrinces i:3758, ii:3237, Kingis Quair, stanza 19.

464-5. The verb-forms are confused and confusing. *To hynder* is equivalent to "hindering".

465. *Hauyng* is to be parsed with the *me* of line 463.

466. *To the tragedies*, i.e., "for the tragedies".

FALL OF PRINCES : B

1. *abrayde*, start up. The Old Eng. transitive vb. *abregdan* was in Mid. Eng. intransitive, one of its senses being "to break into motion or speech". It is frequent in Lydgate, more so than in Chaucer; see G 174 here, and Churl 83.

6. The text of the Carnegie ed. reads "be will were so disposid". The meaning apparently is "were so shaped by our inclinations". Cp. the various readings *wel, wil*, in

Chaucer's PoFoules 214, and the possible confusion between Voluptas the daughter of Cupid and Voluntas, "will", as Chaucer or his scribe may have misread Boccaccio.

4-18. As remarked in the introd. above, Lydgate here dilutes Gower's balanced "opposites".

22-25. A characteristic Lydgatian repetition.

33-35. See Ovid's Heroides xi:124, Gower iii:293-4. This is a stock idea; see Shakespeare's Winter's Tale iii:2, 236. With line 34 cp. Lydgate's Troy Book i:892.

45 ff. Lydgate's tenderness for an innocent helpless child is also expressed i:3219-20, 3236, 4022, ii:3135—"with lippis tendre & softe",—ii:3143,—"In childli wise on hir gan to smyle",—iv:3929, viii:1187.

49. *the goodly ffayre.* With the substantival use of the singular adjective cp. *lusty* in Troilus iii:354, *fre* in FlCourtesy 222, Compl. to his Lady 104.

50. *A mouth he hath,* etc. This expression, here highly pathetic, occurs several times in Lydgate. In the Troy Book iii:4178 it is said, of Troilus grieving over Cressida, that "He had a mouþe but wordis had he noon". In TemGlas Compl. 49 the lover says "A tunge I haue but wordys none". In ResonandSens 6268, FaPrin i:4742, similar phrases are used sardonically of women in general, and in St. Albon ii:401-2, 1398 ff., the eyes, ears, and arms of idols are so described. Cp. "Anon he lost þe offys of spekyng", Troy Book iii:5530. Donne, in his Progress of the Soul, writes "A mouth, but dumb, he hath".

For the different color taken by a line in its different contexts cp. Chaucer's use of "Allone withouten any companye" in KnTale 1921 and in MillTale 18; see note on Charles of Orléans xvi:20 here.

60. A favorite line with Lydgate. See ii:2918, vi:807 of the FaPrinces, also Troy Book ii:4248, iv:4383, v:1563.

59-63. An example of Lydgate's real feeling and muddled expression. The arbitrary omission of the auxiliary or of the subject of the verb, the use of the ablative absolute, the forcing of participles to function as finite verbs, are constant weaknesses with him. One might suggest emending *considred* to *considre* in line 62; but the construction as it stands is common enough in Lydgate.

With line 62, "lyppes soffte as sylk," cp. FaPrin ii:3135. For the simile cp. St. Margaret 416, ResonandSens 1643, TemGlas 540, PilgrMan 24446,—each case riming with *milk*.

64-65. Cp. Jeremiah, Lament. i:12, "O vos omnes qui transitis per viam, attendite et videte an sit dolor sicut dolor meus." In Aeschylus' Promethus, Io cries "Who of the company of the unfortunate endure sufferings such as mine?" (Smyth's trans.) Cp .Ovid, Metam. iii:442,—"ecquis, io silvae, crudelius, inquit, amavit?" And Dante, Inferno 28:132, "vedi se alcuna (pena) è grande come questa." The same thing is said by Brunhilde in FaPrinces ix:473-4.

65. *comparable.* This word and *incomparable,* neither cited NED anterior to Lydgate, are used by him, especially the latter, in rime a number of times.

70. *corage.* For note on this word, see B 62 of Walton's Boethius here.

81. *be lady,* etc. Bergen's text reads *be lord & souereyne.*

82. *at me so dysdeyne.* This locution is more frequent in Mid. Eng. than that of line 139 below, now the standard.

95. To Virgil, Aeneid vi:173-197, Fame is a messenger oftener of evil than of good, "tam ficti pravique tenax quam nuntia veri". To Ovid she is "Fama loquax", a disseminator of falsehood; but the description of her palace in Metam. xii:39-63 stirred the imagination of later poets. Both Petrarch in the Trionfo della Fama and the Amorosa Visione, and Chaucer in the third book of his Hous of Fame, dwell upon her powers and her abode, treating her less as messenger than as divinity. Lydgate, FaPrinces i:5111, vi:109-119, speaks of Fame's two trumpets, a detail he could get from Chaucer. The golden, or favorable, trumpet, is mentioned FaPrinces i:3013, vi:3093, ix:3468, the other trumpet i:5117 and vii:418. The swiftness of evil Fame Lydgate mentions here and in FaPrinces iv:2373; the palace or house of Fame is named *ibid.* iii:2352, iv:122, v:420, vi:514, viii:26, 2735, Troy Book iii:4254, Epithal. 133. The table of Fame is alluded to in FaPrinces iv:999. See Hawes 136, Cavendish 1222.

99. Cp. Barclay's Eclogue iv:1043.

101-2. "There is no way to mitigate these slanderous reports for our exculpation, unless Cupid be blamed."

106 ff. This digression is at first sight tasteless and no more. But inept as it is, it endeavors at a reasoning-out of circumstance such as Chaucer seeks in Troilus' long musing on predestination, iv:960-1078, or such as he puts into Cressida's mouth, iii:813-40. And "Cupid", to us so insipid, represents the force of Love, over which clerks and chevaliers argued scholastically. Lydgate's expression is weak enough, but he is following code.

108. *mesour,* moderation, "mensura", the golden mean of rhetorical as well as of moral code. See note on "reason", line 110 below, and see MLReview 21:380-4 on "The Conception of *Mesure* in some Medieval Poets". Cp. *moderatio* in the de Vinsauf passage cited in note on G 193 below.

110. *reson.* This word meant not only "a comment, a word, an argument", as in Fa-Princes G 117 or Garl. 10, but also a systematic arrangement, the principle of such order, a scheme of "mesure". The latter, a technical term of rhetoric, is thus used by Chaucer, CTprol 37, Troilus iii:1408-9, HoFame 707-8, etc.; and when so used, it is similar to the phrase *by ordre,* cp. notes on Shirley I:26 and on Roundel 3 here. For *reson* in this sense see MLReview 21:13-18.

112. Supply *he* before *yiveth.*

115. *arke,* the part of a circle which a heavenly body appears to pass through, either above the horizon (diurnal) or below it (nocturnal). See MerchTale 551.

117. *lures.* See note Dance Macabre 207.

127-8. See Chaucer's Troilus iv:798.

130. *Vnto . . . ward.* See FaPrinces ix:1806, Hoccleve EETS ed. i:50 line 44, Dial. 469, Jonathas 65; see Lydgate's DuorMercat. 791, St. Margaret 90, etc., for this idiom.

143-4. Ovid, Petrarch, Gower, are all particular about this picture of Canace, who has her pen in her right hand, the sword in her left. According to Ovid, Heroides xi:89-90, the child has already been taken away; according to Gower and to Lydgate, it is in its mother's "barm". I cannot cite the word *barm* from Lydgate elsewhere, and the NED does not cite it between A. D. 950 and Douglas (1513). It is in Chaucer's MoTale 76, 450, SqTale 631, ClTale 495.

154. *save: bathe.* Lydgate has a number of cases of assonance. The TemGlass has three, 125-6, 858-9, 1017-18; the Black Knight has three, 274-6, 284-5, 460-1; Thebes has one, 1247-8; the DuorMercat has two, 202-3 and 293-4. I have noted at least fifteen in the Troy Book, mainly on *p* and *k,* but have not observed others in that poem. Chaucer has but one clear case of assonance, Troilus ii:884-6; that in BoDuch 79-80 is susceptible of explanation. *—the silff, itself,* i.e., Canace's very blood.

FALL OF PRINCES : C

2. Compare Dante, Inferno 26:118, "Considerate la vostra semenza",—though said in a very different spirit.

3. *discencioun.* The quarrel between Romulus and Remus. See FaPrinces ii:4072 ff.

16. *triumphe usurpyng.* Caesar's demand for a triumphal entry and honors, on his return from Britain and Gaul, was refused by Pompey and the Senate from fear of Caesar's waxing power; civil war followed. The matter of the Roman triumph was very interesting to Lydgate; he goes into particulars in book iv, lines 519 ff., and still more fully in ?his prose Serpent of Division, which narrates the Caesar-Pompey quarrel. He also discusses "crowns" in FaPrinces iv:239 ff. The word *usurp* is occasionally employed by Lydgate in the sense of "claim," as here. See FaPrinces i:5669-70, ii:2719-20, iv:1228-29.

18. *serious.* This word, frequent here and in the Troy Book, is explained by Skeat, note on MLTale 87, as "minutely, with full details". It can have the force of "in sequence, serially". See Thebes 333, "Cereously be lyneal discent".

19. *Octavyan.* Octavianus Augustus, Caesar's nephew and successor.

20. *Wher is become,* i. e., "What is become of?" See Libel 36, Garland of Laurell 1216.

21. After this line there is inserted in Dr. Bergen's edition of the poem a stanza found only in the 1554 print and in one MS. I have not included it, and the numbering of this text is not correspondent with Bergen's beyond this point.

22. *cheef lanterne.* This term, or "light", is used by medieval writers to imply super-excellence in the person described, or to assert that he guides lesser men as does one bearing a lantern. Laurent's French prose, Lydgate's principal source, speaks elsewhere of Hector as "lumière de prouesse et de chevalerie"; Athens is "lumière de philosophie", and "lumi-ère de Grèce", in the same way that Cicero calls Rome "lux orbis terrarum". When Dante addresses Virgil, Inferno 1:82, as "degli altri poeti onore e lume", he is probably thinking in the second of these senses, as was the Psalmist in 119:105, which Wyclif translates "Lan-terne to my feet thy word and light to myn pathe". Cp. Dante in Purgat. 1:43, 22:67, fol-lowing Seneca or Ennius; and Chaucer, Legend 926, following Dante.

27. *declyne.* Trajan would not "decline on",—lean toward, favor,—any party.

29-35. The Middle Ages regarded Virgil not only as a poet and philosopher, but as a beneficient magician; see Comparetti's *Vergil in the Middle Ages.* The story here told was long current without Virgil's name as the worker of the wonder, e. g. in Jacobus de Voragine's Legenda Aurea cap. clvii, earlier in the Mirabilia Urbis Romae of ca. 1150, and earlier yet in a MS of the 8th century cited by Keller, Li Roman de Sept Sages, 1836, p. ccvii. In the twelfth and thirteenth centuries this marvel, with others, was ascribed to Virgil; in chap. clxxiv of Alexander Neckam's De Naturis Rerum, late 12th century, we are told that Virgil constructed at Rome a palace in which were statues representing the subject provinces of the Empire, each statue bearing a bell which rang if that province meditated revolt. Vincent de Beauvais has the same story in his Speculum Historiale (before 1264) at the opening of his discussion of Virgil, book vi, chap. 61; and in the Polychronicon of Higden, trans-lated by Trevisa, this building is more than once mentioned. In the Rolls Series ed. of Trevisa, i:217-19, the building is described, but attributed to witchcraft; in iv:243-45 Virgil is named as its builder, and Neckam as source of the fact. Laurent repeats the legend, see FaPrinces ix:20 ff. He does not mention Virgil as the builder, but says that the emperor Phocas gave to Boniface, "le quart pape depuis sainct Gregoire", this "pantheum", which he describes, and recounts how Boniface dismantled it and consecrated it to Our Lady and all the saints. Lydgate, at that point in his translation, says nothing about Virgil, as Laurent had not; he muddles the names of Gregory and Boniface, and refers to "poetis and Fulgence" for the story of the statues. I do not find anything about the "pantheon" in Fulgentius; Lau-rent in his rendering fuses, as do some earlier writers, the image-filled "Salvatio Romae" and the pagan temple hallowed by Boniface.

44. This MS and Royal 18 D v omit the word *enrichyng* at the end of the line; I sup-ply it from Harley 1245. In Bergen's edition there is a typographical error in the order of words.

69. *thordris nyne.* The nine grades of angels, viz., Seraphim, Cherubim, Thrones, Domin-ions, Virtues, Powers, Principalities, Archangels, Angels. So Dante, Paradiso 28:98 ff., fol-lowing Dionysius' De Caeleste Hierarchia. See FaPrinces ix:2399 ff.

74. *wordli.* An exceedingly frequent MS-spelling for *worldly.*

76. *bowe . . . chyne,* bow thy shin, kneel. One might consider that in FaPrinces iii:2594, viii:497, this word meant *chin.* In iv:3637, "Tascende the mounteyn feeble wer ther chynes", the meaning is clear. Cp. iii:3132, iv:2536, vii:442, viii:995, 2091; Troy Book i:3066.

85. *Cast vp,* i.e., Consider. See Thebes 1687, Troy Book iv:4959. With this passage cp. Lydgate's St. Albon ii:1745-61.

88. *Now briht,* etc. The balance of "opposites" by the word *Now* is a device Chaucer and Lydgate could find, e.g., in the Romaunt of the Rose, 6327 ff. Chaucer uses it briefly and colloquially in KnTale 674-7; Lydgate has it, in this poem, ii:4554, iii:1321, 4337, iv:623, 1987, v:439, and especially in the description of Fortune vi:55-69, 169-71, 192-4.

93. *Cirenes.* Lydgate's allusions to sirens are frequent. See this poem i:5157, ii:658, 4245-9, iii:1637, 3708, 4610, vi:69-70, etc.; cp. his ResonandSens 1772-5, 4098, 5257, 6732; cp. Troy Book v:2054 ff., Letter to My Lady of Gloucester stanza 10. He could get his

material from Isidor's Etymologies xi :3, 30, or from Hugh of St. Victor, De Bestiis et Aliis Rebus, ii cap. 32; or he could find a brief account in another part of Laurent's French, book i chap. 18.

96. *Synderesis*, or Synteresis, Aquinas' term for conscience as applied to human conduct. In his translation of Deguilleville's Pilgrimage, 4963 ff., Lydgate gives a definition of synderesis as "the hiher party of Resoun". Hoccleve uses the same source, see EETS ed. iii p. xxv, line 76. In the Assembly of Gods, 937 ff., Synderesis aids Conscience, the judge of the combat between Virtues and Vices. Milton in his Commonplace Book copies a definition of Synderesis as a "natural power of the soul, set in the highest part thereof, moving and striving it to good, and abhorring evil. And therefore Sindrisis never sinns nor erres. And this Sindirisis the Lord put in man to the intent that the order of things should be observed."

Vincent de Beauvais, Speculum Historiale i cap 40, has "Sinderesis est scintilla conscientie in speculamentis constituta, cuius est peccato remurmurare & errata corrigere. & hec est que movet liberum arbitrium in bonum commune, et retrahit a malo communi" etc. He says it is extinct in the devil and in the damned, but not in Jews, nor quite so in heresiarchs.

FALL OF PRINCES : D

8. *I meene as thus.* Such an explanation by a writer of his own words, scholastic in its origin, is very frequent in Chaucer, for example; and the usage is continued by his followers. See for instance the Kingis Quair, stanzas 72, 78, 79, 123, 129, 184. It was much used by Chaucer in his Boethius-translation, when he was incorporating glosses to make the text clearer to his readers. And Dante's use of *dico*, although generally a mode of emphasis or of filliping the attention, is sometimes directly parallel to Chaucer's "This is to meene"; cp. Inferno 4 :66, "la selva, dico, di spiriti spessi". And note *ibid.*, 14 :7-8.

A similar turn of words is employed by Chaucer in a way which to a modern ear sounds mischievous. In Troilus ii :904-5 he says :—

> The dayes honour and the hevenes ye
> The nightes fo (al this clepe I the sonne)—

and, with a fuller formula, FranklTale 289-90,

> For th' orisonte hath reft the sonne his light
> This is as much to seye as it was night.

But if this latter is in intent a burlesque, what of the parallel passage in Fulgentius' Mitologiarum, bk. i? After protracted and somewhat turgid description of night, in verse, Fulgentius says: "ut, in verba paucissima conferam, nox erat." This particular Chaucerian passage took effect on his followers; cp. the Kingis Quair stanza 72, "This is to say, approche gan the nyght",—and Lydgate's Troy Book iv :3582-3 :—

> And Espirus gan his ligte to shede
> þis to seyn, for it drowe to nygt,—

also, *ibid.,* iv :629, "þis to seyne þe sonne went doun". See also *ibid.,* iii :15, 2749.

It is doubtful if either King James or Lydgate read humorous intent into the Chaucerian phrase which was serving as their model. But Lowell, in his essay on Chaucer, says of the FranklTale passage that the poet "turns round upon himself and smiles at a trip he has made into fine writing"; and Mackail, in his Springs of Helicon, p. 59, remarks of it: "It may be suspected that Chaucer is making fun of Dante". On this point note Matthew of Vendôme's "ut sit sensus 'jam diescebat' ",—after a citation of Aeneid iv :584. See Faral, p. 185.

Other passages in which Chaucer's "I seye" is parallel to Dante's scholastic *dico* are MLTale 162-3, ClerkTale 410 ff., FranklTale 337-40; in the two latter he repeats himself emphatically. The locution is very common in Lydgate, usually in the form as here; it is more frequent as explanation than as emphasis, and often seems merely padding.

8-21. For this apology see note on Walton A 58. Calliope, the muse of epic poetry and eloquence, and Clio the muse of history, are frequently mentioned together by Lydgate; see

Thebes 831, Epithal. 181, Troy Book prol. 40, 46, iii :5445, Life of Our Lady as cited by Schick TemGlas note on 958.

10. *rethorik . . . floure.* The term *flowers* was often used by medieval writers for the adornments of rhetoric, beside the term *colours.* Both are found in Cicero, cp. De Oratore iii :25, where he says that *oratio* is adorned *quasi colore quodam* and *quasi verborum senten-tiarumque floribus.*

12. *in noumbre thries thre.* For note on this rime-tag see FaPrinces A 459, Epithal. 182.

16. *Pegase.* In Greek mythology, the spring Hippocrene, upon Helicon, was opened by the thrust of Pegasus' hoof. Fulgentius says merely "Musarum fontem ungula sua rupisse fertur",—without connecting the kick of Pegasus, as fuller myth does, with the song-contest of the Pierides and the Muses, the rising of Helicon in rapture while the Muses sang and Jupiter's command to Pegasus to thrust the mountain back. An almost identical line is in Troy Book i prol. 45.

19. *tame ther tunnys.* The word *tame* is a shortened form of *attame,* frequently used by Lydgate in its sense of "to broach, to open as a cask is opened". It seems to have here the force of "to sample". Cp. "Who that wil entren to tamen of the sweete", DuobMercat. 701.

20-21. *poliphemus . . . Argus.* Argus had many eyes, Polyphemus but one. In this poem ix :3335 Lydgate says of himself "Myn eyen mystyd and dirked my spectacle". Possibly he, like Hoccleve and Bokenam, had weak or overworked eyes; see Bokenam p. 23, line 657-8, Hoccleve to Oldcastle 417-20, and to the duke of York 57-59.

22-23. *Our life here short,* etc. Cp. the line-movement of the opening of Chaucer's PoFoules. Cp. for the wording the prologue of John of Salisbury to his Polycraticus, bk. i :—"Siquidem vita brevis, sensus herbes, negligentia torpor, inutilis occupatio, nos paucula scire permittunt : et eadem iugiter excutit, et avellit ab animo fraudatrix scientiae, inimica et infida semper memoriae noverca, oblivio." The use of the last phrase in line 30 below makes it probable that Lydgate has the Polycraticus in mind rather than a more general observation like that of Vincent of Beauvais in his Speculum Naturale :—"Quoniam multitudo librorum et temporis brevitas memorie quoque labilitas non patiuntur cuncta que scripta sunt pariter animo comprehendi—"etc.

30. *stepmodir.* John of Salisbury's phrase, as above. The metaphorical use of *noverca* is very common in the latter Middle Ages. Fulgentius and Matthew of Vendôme, especially the latter, employ it frequently. Vendôme in his Tobias, 2123-4, says : "Vocum congeries prolixa noverca favoris Displicet, excurrit, labitur, auris abest"; and Bokenam in his St. Margaret 941-3 speaks of prolixity as "Stepdame of fauour aftyr the sentence. In a vers of Mathu Vindocinence"—referring obviously to the passage just cited. Lydgate, FaPrinces iv :150-51, calls idleness the stepmother of science and cunning; *ibid.,* i :4811 hasty credence is the stepmother of good counsel; *ibid.,* ii :643 flattery is stepmother to virtue; and so in iii :3980 of Will and Wit, in v :3045-7 of Covetousness and Worthiness. Cp. also PilgLifeMan 15985-7, Secrees 665. The metaphor in Matthew of Vendôme occurs, e. g., Tobias 193-4, 811-12, Ars Versificatoria end of part i and passim there; see Faral, pp. 118, 163, etc.

36. *were,* i.e., doubt, perplexity.

38. The punctuation in the Carnegie edition is erroneous. The phrase "who euer list to lere" is one of Lydgate's lumps of padding, is parenthetical, and should be set off by commas.

41. *with a maas,* i. e., with mace, or the staff carried by a sheriff's officer, by one who makes an arrest.

46. *felt quake.* The quaking hand or pen is a favorite mode with Lydgate of asserting his inadequacy for his task. Chaucer had used the locution, Troilus iv :13-14, and it is found, e.g., in Lydgate's BlKnight 181, TemGlas 947, St. Marg. 57, St. Edmund iii :89, AlbonandAmph. i :928, LettGlouc 4, Troy Book i :4427, ii :145, iii :5425, v :1044, Secrees 334, 1555, FaPrinces i :5517, 7023, ii :1022, iii :3684, iv :3495, v :2133, vi :2989, ix :3307. See Hawes, Example of Vertu stanza 112, Skelton's GarlLaurell 812.

52. *stood chek maate,* was nonplussed, helpless. This also is a favorite locution with Lydgate. It appears in Chaucer's Troilus ii :754 as "say chekmate", i.e., force to a halt, to

submission; see BoDuch 659-60. See Hoccleve's Lerne to Dye 181; see Dance 459, Cavendish 161.

63. *Pierides & Meduse.* Lydgate has said that the Muses show him no favor; he now says that only to the unworthy rivals of the Muses, those daughters of Pierus who attempted to assert their own supremacy in song, and to stony Medusa, can he look for aid.

66. *Mercurie . . . and Philologie.* Mercury and Philology are referred to together in TemGlas 129, where the allusion is to their marriage as described by Martianus Capella in one of the widely read books of the Middle Ages. The names also appear together Epithal-Glouc. 179-80 with reference to their marriage, which is described by Lydgate Thebes 833-44. Here the two are rather thought of as presiding over eloquence, the special province of Mercury, as Lydgate says ResonandSens 1657 ff., Troy Book ii:2499-2501, 5605-8, FaPrinces ii:4544-5. See St. Edmund i:99-101.

69. *ebb.* A frequent metaphor with Lydgate; see this poem i:4422-24, 6079, iii:355-58, ix:3348-51, Troy Book ii:456, LettGlouc 20.

67-9. With these lines cp. LettGlouc 20-24.

78. *ertheli.* Harley 1245 reads *hertely.*

82. The bracketed phrase is from MS Harley 1245; our MS by error repeats from 79 as "list nat to aduertise".

83. *to greue.* Harley 1245, or *greve.*

92. Translation of Laurent now begins. In the French there is no distinct prologue to this Book; the introductory simile (in the printed ed. here used) runs without break into the dispute of Fortune and Poverty which follows. In Boccaccio's Latin, however, the eleven-line prologue is set off separately, and its first half is, as printed in Paris n. d. by Jehan Petit:—"Consverere longum ac laboriosvm iter agentes / non solum aliquando consistere /sudores abstergere / corpus leuare / auram captare lenem / & sitim poculis pellere: Set etiam in tergum facie versa / iam acta metiri spatia / opida recolere / flumina / montes / vallesque / & aequora / recensere. Et dum toti itineri quod preteritum est / eximunt: Non modicum sibi / ad laboris residuum / virium superaddere." Laurent renders this:— "Pelerins & autres voyageurs qui font aucun long & labourieux chemin ont de coustume soy arrester / & aucunesfois torcher la sueur de leur visage / et la lautre fois mettre ius leurs fardeaulx pour aleger le corps & autrefois prendre le vent fres et souef / et boire ou vin ou eaue pour oster la soif & si ont de coustume de veoir & abater combien ils ont fait apres ce quilz ont tourne le dos a aucun notable lieu dont ils se sont partis / ils recordent entre eulx le nombre et les noms des chasteaulx / des riuieres / des valles / des montaignes / et des mers que ils ont passees / & quant ils rabatent de tout leur chemin ce qui en est fait ils prennent en leurs cueurs forces et allegences plus quilz nen auoient pour acomplir le remanant du labour & du chemin." (From the Petit print, Paris 1538).—With this pilgrim-simile cp. the Lover's Mass, Epistle in prose, p. 212 here; and see p. 209 here.

FALL OF PRINCES : E

In this extract Lydgate is very prone to the absolute treatment of participles and to the omission of the verb-subject; cp. lines 13, 15, 16, 17, 19, 27, 31, 50, 53, 70, 76, 90, 103.

11. *Germanye.* The Bergen ed. reads *Lumbardie.*

13. *peisid . . . seyn.* An ablative absolute. "This matter having been examined and weighed",—nevertheless Caesar had no guerdon, no triumph.

16. *appesid,* were appeased. Laurent says: "appaisa les discentions civiles".

17. Vincent of Beauvais, Speculum Historiale, vi., cap. 37, "De initio imperii Cesaris", gives Sichardus as his authority for the statement: "Denique Cesar Romam reuersus rerum summam ac potentiam quam Greci monarchiam vocant solus sibi presumpsit." Lydgate makes no use of Laurent's repeated emphasis on the graciousness and leniency of Caesar as compared with other despots.

18. *xiiiine regiouns.* Rome was divided into fourteen regions, Italy into eleven. This may be a miswriting for xiiiine.

19-21. The refusal of the triumph to Caesar is again mentioned.

20. *recure.* See note Dance Macabre 311. Our MS erroneously reads *replye,* under influence probably of the rime-word.

21. Other MSS *request* instead of *conquest.*

25. *doomys . . . dresse,* administer judgments.

37. Cp. similar line Knight's Tale 152.

42. *parody.* This word, probably a reshaping of French *période,* "duration", was used by Chaucer, Troilus v:1548, to mean "term of life". Lydgate employs it four times in this poem, twice in the Troy Book, and elsewhere; but it was not longer preserved in English. The 1554 print of the Fall of Princes renders the word here as *periody;* and the scribe of Harley 2251, copying a poem which is printed Halliwell MinPo, p. 126, changes it to *paradice.*

43. *Tongilyus.* Lydgate's source for this bit of information is perhaps the same as that of the De Nugis Curialium, or rather of the Dissuasio Valerii ad Rufinum which is incorporated in the fourth Distinction of the De Nugis, and which had a large circulation as a separate work, being sometimes attributed to St. Jerome. Walter Map mentions the story merely to urge on his correspondent that however humble the source of advice, it should be heeded lest worse follow. See p. 146 of the ed. by Wright, p. 149 of the ed. by M. R. James. The same name is given to the warner of Caesar in the Serpent of Division, see *ibid.,* p. 64; and the phrase of introduction is there identical, "a pore man called Tongilius". Map says "Tongillo humili quidem sed divino", making Tongillus a soothsayer; Laurent says that "vne sedulle" was offered Caesar, mentioning no name for its bearer.

48. *ambicious necligence.* The "necligence", Caesar's delay to read the warning scroll, is deplored by both Laurent and the author of the Serpent of Division. Laurent says that Caesar was "trop tardif", and that the tragic outcome should teach all to be prompt in opening and reading their letters.

50. *consistory.* This word was used in the Middle Ages for any dignified assemblage, but is now restricted to an ecclesiastical sense.

54. *bodkyns.* Laurent says "dagues assez longues et estroictes, presque a facon de greffes." Chaucer says "boydekins".

63, 70, etc. *Brutus Cassius.* This fusion of the two names was made by Chaucer in the Monk's Tale 707; and he was followed by Lydgate on at least four separate occasions, viz., this, the Serpent of Division, the Coronation Address to Henry VI, and the poem printed Halliwell MinPo, p. 125. Bradshaw, in his life of St. Werburgh, line 1714, has *Cassius Brutus;* and Cavendish in his Metrical Visions, line 1130 (Surrey), has *Brewtus Cassius.* Both these men derive from Lydgate, who derives from Chaucer; where Chaucer obtained the error is not yet clear, and it is singular that in the same tale in which he uses material from Dante's Inferno, canto 33, and sends his readers to Dante, he should ignore a fact extremely clear from a reading of canto 34, where Brutus and Cassius hang separately from the jaws of Lucifer. The only case of the error earlier than Chaucer which I have as yet noted is in King Alfred's translation of Boethius chap. 19,—"Brutus oþre naman Cassius",—an addition by Alfred to the text. Any brief colorless narrative, such as perhaps an epitome of Orosius, which used the sign for *et* between the two proper names, could start the error. Thus, as Prof. John L. Lowes points out to me, we find in Philargyrius' fifth-century commentary on Virgil:—"Tiberius Caesar Iulius et Antonius contra Cassium Brutum civile bellum gesserunt." Note that Lydgate's usual source for this poem, Laurent's French, is quite definite on Brutus and Cassius, speaking of "les deux coniurateurs"; see note on F 15 below. And Coluccio Salutati, in his De Tyranno, discusses at length the propriety of Dante's handling of the two tyrannicides. Lydgate very probably knew no more of Coluccio than the "Lucretia" which Gloucester ordered him to work into the Fall of Princes book ii; but his ignoring of Laurent is a different matter. For the reverse sort of error, with other names, see note on Barclay's Ship of Fools prol. line 20.

69. *to lustris,* two lustres, i. e., ten years. It was just about ten years from Caesar's second invasion of Britain to his assassination in 44 B. C.

82. "Add the unhappy fate of Caesar."

95. *malencolik vengeaunce.* The chronicler Sichardus, from whom Vincent of Beauvais often draws, and Laurent, both emphasize the leniency of Caesar after his assumption of

power. Apparently Lydgate's rime-scheme drives him to a different statement. Of the four humors, sanguine, phlegmatic, choleric, and melancholic, the last-named, determined by a preponderance of the black bile, was said by medieval medicine to cause gloom, sulleness, and irascibility. The phrase here fits Achilles sulking in his tent or raging against the slayers of Patroclus,—but not Caesar.

FALL OF PRINCES : F

8. *Brutus Cassius.* See note on E 63 ante.

10-12. Decius Brutus, according to MacCallum, in his *Shakespeare's Roman Plays,* "the least erected spirit of the group". He was killed in Gaul while trying to escape to join Brutus and Cassius in Macedonia, B. C. 43.

13. *what costis,* etc., "wherever one may go".

15 ff. Lydgate here disregards all of Laurent's narrative. The French says that "Anthoine filz de seur" was by Caesar's will named second of the heirs and executors; "et octouien nepueu aussi de cesar fut premier heritier"; etc. Octavian fought five battles against the rebels, and afterwards "vng cheualier appelle Decius Brutus confessa a octouien la maniere de la coniuration faicte contre Cesar / et pource que Decius Brutus auoit este vng des coniurateurs / il luy requist pardon en luy monstrant signe de repentance." Then, says Laurent, Dolabella killed Trebonius, another conspirator; "et Decius Brutus vng autre des meurtriers fut prins et occis en France ou il sen estoit fuy." Then Basilius is disposed of; then Brutus and Cassius ("les deux coniurateurs") gather head at Athens and at Rhodes; Octavian and Antony, "iustes vengeurs", pursue them into Macedonia, where there is a great battle. Brutus and Cassius kill each other in despair. Other nobles are drawn into the miserable conflict, among them Tullius.

15. *thre yere.* There is nothing of this time limit in Laurent; Lydgate, in line 19, refers to "auctours". He could read in Vincent of Beauvais' Speculum Historiale, book vi, cap. xlii,—"percussorum cesaris fere neque triennio quisque amplius superuixit",—etc.

Observe, in this stanza, Lydgate's weak repetition; the last two lines restate the two opening lines of the stanza.

22 ff. Laurent has at this point in his work nothing about tyrannicide; but he elsewhere touches on the question, one which aroused much discussion in the century, and had since John of Salisbury's inadequate argument. See Emerton, Humanism and Tyranny, Boston, 1926; see Lydgate's Fall of Princes ix:1443 ff. and note the solemn popular vote there, justifying the deposition and killing of Andronicus.

FALL OF PRINCES : G

3. *laumpe and lanterne.* See note, FaPrinces C 22.

5. *barein style.* See note on Nevill envoy 12.

10. *flours,* i. e., of rhetoric. See note, FaPrinces D 10.

17. *termes and resouns,* i. e., set phrases and words. For this meaning of "terms" cp. CantTales prol. 325, 641, Pard. headlink 25, CanYeoTale 845; for the use of "reason" to mean "word, motto, speech", cp. Libiaus Desconus 3218, 3221, 3430, 4280, 4931, 4948, Squire of Lowe Degre 214, Chaucer's Troilus i:796, Henryson's Testament of Cressida 606, FaPrinces ii:2327, and the Orléans transl. here printed, xviii:4.

Another and very important medieval use of the word *reason* is in the larger sense of "decorum", closely corresponding to the *ordo, ordine,* of late Latin rhetoricians and of Italian philosophic poets before Dante. See Goffin in MLReview 21:13-18 for Chaucer's use of *reason* in such sense; and cp. Jacopone da Todi's *laude,* e.g. as cited by Gardner, Dante and the Mystics, 1913, for praise of Order. Cp. also the use of Reason in contrast with Sensuality, the bridled with the unbridled; not only in Lydgate's poem of that name, but in his St. Edmund i:398, his St. Albon ii:16, his Troy Book ii:1821-3, FaPrinces i:6200, 6257, ii:579-80, 2535-6, etc. Note Hamlet's "blood and judgment". For the limited simple usage of the word as here see note on Shirley I:78.

19. The syntax is here broken and bewildered; the movement would be clearer were this line omitted. In 21 *to* is repeated, though already in line 19; see a similar confusion in FaPrinces i:3246-48 and ii:2325-27; also iv:26-28.

22. *kauht a fantasie.* To catch envy, catch an indignation, catch a melancholy, especially to catch a fantasy, are stereotyped phrases in Lydgate. Chaucer in the MLTale 628 uses "caught a gret motyf", and in FrklTale 12, 792 we find—catch a pity, catch routh. The word *supprisid* means, as in Chaucer, "overcome by feeling".

24. *skie.* In Chaucer's HoFame 1600 this word means *cloud,* as it usually does to Gower. For Lydgate it usually means *cloud;* and this phrase,—see also FaPrinces i:3539, ix:2020, Pilgrimage 9626,—seems to be "a cloudy mass of cloud".

32. The subject of *spak* is not in the text.

33-35. *Too colours sein;* i. e., "to see two colors". Laurent writes:—"quant deux choses contraires sont mises lune pres de lautre / elles se monstrent plus legierement." Chaucer made a similar remark, Troilus i:642-3; and Lydgate uses it again Temple of Glass 1250. See Hawes' Pastime, line 1349; see Skelton's Garland 1210, Spenser's Faerie Queene iii:9,2.

Observe the like rime 35-36. The rime on *other* was often awkwardly managed by early poets; Lydgate is sometimes reduced to use of the padding phrase "I meene non othir", when he has *brothir* in rime,—see FaPrinces v:3025-6, and see Troy Book ii:5439-40, 5965-6, etc. Chaucer manages better; see HoFame 2101-2, PoFoules 566-7, BoDuchesse 891-2, Troilus iv:608-9, KnTale 273-4, etc.; but he has some difficulty HoFame 795-6, 815-6.

36. *In phebus presence,* etc. The comparison of the "sun passing the stars", whether to exalt some person praised or to describe the inferiority of the lover-disciple, is very frequent in medieval literature. We find in the Carmina Burana no. 143: "Sol solis in stellifero Stellas excedit radio"; Chrétien de Troyes, in his Yvain 3245 ff., writes "Si con cierges antre chandoiles Et la lune antre les estoiles Et li solaus desor la lune." Machaut in his Fontaine Amoureuse says "Aussi com li solaus la lune Vient de clarte Avait elle les autres sormonte De pris." See Chaucer's PoFoules 299-300, Lydgate's Flower of Courtesy 113-14, his Temple of Glass 251-2, his St. Albon i:288-90, his Secrees 344, 348, FaPrinces ii:995-6, ix:1878, 2350-51, 3415-16, Troy Book ii:8471-2; see Metham's Amoryus and Cleopes 148 ff., Hawes' Pastime 221-4 as here and p. 185 of the Percy Soc. edition. See Bradshaw's St. Werburge i:733-5; and further in note on K 29-30 below.

42. *quaking hond.* See note FaPrinces D 46.

43-49. There is no principal verb or clause here.

46. *colours . . . of eloquens.* "Colours" were embellishments of style, ornaments of diction. The phrase "colours of rhetoric" is extremely common in English and French medieval writers. Its use to mean definite categories of ornamentation goes back to the pseudo-Ciceronian treatise Ad Herennium, which contains a list, with definitions, of the various "exornationes" of formal speech; this is retained by the Latin grammarians and by Italian and French writers of the later Middle Ages. The eight "colors of rhetoric" listed by Dante's teacher Brunetto Latini in his Livre dou Trésor were Ornament, Circumlocution, Comparison, Exclamation, Fable, Transition, Demonstration, and Repetition. Under Demonstration Brunetto cites a description of Iseult, feature by feature; for this mode of praising the lady see note here on Hoccleve's third Roundel. Under Ornament Brunetto says that a simple statement, such as "Jules Cesar fu empereres de tout le monde", should be expanded by longer and more becoming words; the writer should say "The prudence and valor of Julius Caesar brought all the world into subjection to him, and he was lord and emperor of the whole earth."

The earlier categories of "colors" were much expanded by later medieval rhetoricians; they are enumerated in the "Arts of Poetry" collected by Langlois, Paris, 1902, and by Mari, Milan, 1899; see also in especial the Latin treatises edited by Faral, Paris, 1924, comprising Matthew of Vendôme and Geoffrey de Vinsauf. It is in Ornament and Repetition that the greatest amount of development takes place; the French treatises of Deschamps and of Alain Chartier discuss elaborate stanza-forms, acrostic-stanzas, groups of lines beginning with the same word or phrase, repetitions of the same word-base in different forms, etc. Among the sub-forms of Repetition we find lines ending with the word on which they opened, as in

Cavendish 212 here; or a sequence of lines each catching up the last word of the preceding verse,—i.e., enchained lines; or stanzas similarly enchained. See for example the elegy inserted into Barclay's fourth eclogue, where the last rime of one stanza is the opening rime-sound of the next; or see the prologue to Palladius here. For still more elaborate echoes see Naetebus' book on the non-lyric strophe-forms of early French poetry, and see Butler's Forerunners of Dante. In our own time J. C. Squire's Wind at Evening is a very studied and graceful chain-line poem.

From Dante down, such rhetorical effects have been recognized. Dante was austerely sparing in his use of lines with identical beginning, somewhat freer in his admission of words built on an identical base; the passage with recurrent *onor—*, Inferno 4:72-80, is the longest in his work. It was more or less imitated by Tennyson at the opening of The Marriage of Geraint, with the word *love;* and Tennyson has used groups of lines beginning alike with far more freedom than Dante. A more delicate form of this "color of rhetoric" is the grouping by Shelley or by Keats of adjectives with similar prefixes or suffixes; for example,—"With feet unwet, unwearied, undelaying," (Prometheus Unbound iii, 3:157); or in the opening of Hyperion,—"His old right hand lay nerveless, listless, dead, Unsceptred; and his realmless eyes were closed." But the sensitized modern ear has sought a variety and attained a delicacy not in the medieval code.

With the approach and arrival of humanism in England, many other modes of ornament became prevalent. The list of classical (and Biblical) examples was developed, naturally, far beyond what the classical or post-classical mind had deemed appropriate; Latin tags, borrowed or manufactured polysyllables, plays upon words, were everywhere. Lydgate does not employ the play upon words, as Ovid had employed it; but his admiration for "aureate language" is very great. Indeed, we cannot always interpret a digression, or even a tedious repetition of material, by him, as a proof of his incompetence and dulness. He, or Cavendish, or many a late medieval writer, may be following a principle, that of rhetorical ornamentation and expansion. The result is undoubtedly similar, for the average reader, to what pure dulness would produce; but the student perceives an attempt, however clumsy, to follow a code. See note on Cavendish line 232.

52. *afforcid his corage.* See same phrase Churl 64.

55. *ditees.* This word may mean in Mid. Eng. either "compositions" or "compositions in verse, songs". For the former sense see the Romaunt of the Rose 5285-6, "And whilom of this (amitee) Spak Tullius in a ditee", i. e., De Amicitia; see FaPrinces A 256, G 225. For the latter sense see FaPrinces A 352, 456 above.

63. As Koeppel points out in his De Casibus monograph, p. 65, Lydgate took Laurent's *translata*, "transplanted", to mean "translated". The French is: "Tulle non pas seulement translata lart de rhetorique de Grec en langage latin / mais augmenta accreut & aorna la science tellement que par luy elle creust & croist"—etc. Isidor, in his Etymologies ii:2, says that "haec autem disciplina [i. e., rhetoric] a Graecis inventa est, . . . translata in latinum a Tullio . . ." This statement is correctly rendered by Lydgate in FaPrinces vi:3300-01.

67. The vices of Rome, mentioned by Laurent, are omitted by Lydgate.

69. *tyme.* Accusative of duration.

71, 75. There is no auxiliary for the verb.

80. There is no principal verb for *Catalina.* Lydgate omits mention of Catiline's noble origin and picture of his financial difficulties, except for a slight allusion to the latter in line 93.

96. "Found out means, did devise ways to his purpose", etc. The omission of the subject and the connective makes the syntax unclear.

102. Lydgate omits the go-between Fulvia mentioned by Laurent.

109. Lydgate reduces to generalities Laurent's vigorous description of Cicero shattering "par tres aigres & mordantes parolles. . . la paresseuse souffrance des senateurs."

116. Laurent here dwells on Catiline's courage, and has no moralizing such as Lydgate's in 118-19.

122. *Ceregus.* Read *Cetegus.*

125-6. *Tulliane . . . the prisoun.* Laurent gives this detail. There was on the Capitoline a prison built by Servius Tullius, but from the twelfth century the name "Tullian" was incorrectly applied to the locality on which stood a prison erected by Appius Claudius. Cicero had no connection with either. See Gregorovius, Gesch. der Stadt Rom in Mittelalter, iv:350, note 2.

127. Between the material of this and of the preceding stanza there intervenes in Laurent and in Boccaccio an interesting simile omitted by Lydgate. It runs in the Latin: "Sic armatos duces togatus excessit Cicero si is medicus praeferendus est qui secretam adque laetiferam intestinorum vomicam argumentis exclusit et repulit; ei qui vulnus adparens et si maximum sit vnguentis et arte traxit in cicatricem." We may note here Boccaccio's reminder of Cicero's own line of verse,—"Cedant arma togae . . ." etc.

133. *clergy,* learning. Bergen's text reads *polycie.*

140. Here Boccaccio said: "vt Plotinum Gallum / qui primus vrbi rhetoricam Latine monstrauit / & Miltacilium Plotum & alterum ex Graccis / atque Hortensium / aliosque elegantissimos oratores / Graecosque veteres anteiret." Laurent wrote: "que il surmonta aussi en rethoricque Milius catilius / et Gracius / et Hortense & autres plusieurs orateurs latins treselegans et autres anciens orateurs de Grece." The word *Policius* here reads in other MSS *Plocius*; the reference is to Plotius Gallus, of whom it is recorded: "Plotius Gallus primus Romae latinam rhetoricam docuit." See Jerome's comment. on Eusebius, ed. Migne, viii:528; and note that the name is not in Laurent. "Gracce" is probably the younger Gracchus, a most brilliant orator.

145. The subject of the verb is again omitted.

146-7. *The golden trumpe.* This allusion is drawn from Chaucer's HoFame iii, where Aeolus, at Fame's command, blows good report through his golden trumpet, ill report through one of brass. See Cavendish, line 1222 here.

154. *lanterne . . . & liht.* See line 3 above, and note on FaPrinces C 22.

156-68. This is from Laurent, with praise of Cicero's "doulce et amesuree prononciation de voix".

159. Laurent gives the names of the defendants.

160-1. The text printed by Dr. Bergen reads *repreeff* at close of 161,—an error by contamination in our text.

172. Note the elision of *that he was.*

173-5. *platon . . . bees . . . hony.* The story of the bees moistening the lips of the infant Plato with honey is in both Laurent and Boccaccio, in John of Salisbury's Polycraticus i, chap. 13, and in Valerius Maximus i, chap. 6.

178. *sours and welle.* This phrase, also *gynnyng and grounde,* are frequent in Lydgate. In this poem i:3887 Atreus is "of tresoun sours and welle"; in viii:2976-7 Arthur's court is "sours and welle" of martial deeds, etc. Cp. Skelton, Garland 850.

179. *merour.* Insistence that a knight or a lady is "the glass" not merely of fashion but of all virtues, is exceedingly frequent in medieval literature. In Chaucer's MLTale 68, Constance is "mirrour of alle curteisye"; the lady of Lydgate's Temple of Glass 754 is "mirour of wit"; in this poem vii:784 Nero is "cheef merour of diffame". For use of the term Speculum or Mirror in titles of books see note on Ship of Fools 85.

183. Lydgate omits to mention Cicero's return to Rome, which Laurent describes.

186. Lydgate omits the names given by Laurent.

193. *pronunciacioun,* "oratorical delivery". This is the NED's earliest case of the word in this sense; Laurent speaks at this point of Cicero's "doulce et amesuree prononciation de voix". But Lydgate is using, I think, Vinsauf's De arte versificandi. In Faral's edition of that work, p. 318, we find Pronunciation termed "quasi totius orationis condimentum, ut sine qua totum est insipidum et inconditum. Pronuntiatio sic describitur a Tullio in Rhetoricis: 'Pronuntiatio est vocis, vultus, gestus moderatio cum venustate'". By *Rhetoricis,* Vinsauf means the pseudo-Ciceronian treatise Ad Herennium, see Marx's ed., p. 188, bk. i, 2. For Vinsauf's further discussion, see note on 197 below.

The next chapter of the Fall of Princes, against "Ianglers and Diffamers of Rethorique", gives, following Laurent, five "banners of eloquence", viz., Invention, Disposition, Elocution,

Pronunciation, Remembrance. In Ad Herennium and in Isidor's Etymologies ii :3, Memory precedes Pronunciation in the list; in the Margarita Philosophica perhaps known to Hawes and in Hawes' Pastime 659 ff., the order is as in Lydgate. See note on Hawes *loc. cit.*

196. *His thank receivith.* "He earns his reward." (?)

197-203. *glad mateere . . . glad cheere.* Lydgate omits Laurent's comment that in a mere reading of Cicero one must lose his "bonne prononciation et bel maintien"; in the English we find instead this passage, which appears again 3347 ff. as "An heuy mateer requereth an heuy cheer To a glad mateer longeth weel gladnesse". Here, line 203, Lydgate ascribes the dictum to Cicero. The passage of de Vinsauf above cited continues: "Si materia fuerit de dolore, vox et vultus et gestus debent conformari materiae et testes esse doloris. Si fuerit de gaudio, similiter vox et vultus et gestus debent attestari laetitiae" etc. If Lydgate read this passage, he might not perceive the change from the Rhetoricis citation to Vinsauf's own words, and might thus credit all to Cicero. Something similar, indeed, may be read near the close of the De Oratore; and the precept was general, from Horace's "Tristia maestum Vultum verba decent," (Ars Poetica 105) to Chaucer's Troilus i :12-14. But Chaucer says nothing of Cicero in connection with the dictum. See the Troy Book iii :5455-56; see note on Cavendish line 63.

208-10. Laurent introduces these homely details more artistically. After saying, as above, that no reading of Cicero can produce the effect of his delivery, and that he himself is powerless to describe such eloquence, he adds that he will pass over mention of Cicero's wealth, his wife, his friends, because such details are not wisely mingled with account of the honor paid Cicero for his especial virtues. He then goes on to recount Cicero's banishments and death; Lydgate inserts, from Vincent de Beauvais, a list of his works.

211 ff. For this list of Cicero's works Lydgate refers, line 215, to Vincent of Beauvais; see the Speculum Historiale, ed. 1494, book v, chap 6. He uses, however, not all of the books mentioned by Vincent, whose list is: De Officiis, De Amicitia, De Senectute, De Oratore, De Paradoxis, the Philippics, two books of "Rethoricorum", the Tuscular disputations, twelve books of orations, six books of invectives, De Legibus, De Fine Boni et Mali, De Natura Deorum, De Divinatione, De Fato, De Creatione Mundi, Ad Hortensium, De Partitione Orationis, the Academics. To Vincent's list Lydgate adds the Dream of Scipio, De Lege Agraria, De Gloria, De Re Publica.

218. *the dreme of Scipioun.* This narrative was by Cicero included in book vi of his De Re Publica, of which portions only have come down to us; but the "Somnium Scipionis" was preserved in a commentary by Macrobius, and attained great popularity in the Middle Ages. See, for example, Chaucer's PoFoules.

221. *of cithe lond.* Read "of tilth of lond"; so other MSS and the 1554 print. By this is probably meant the three orations De Lege Agraria, in which Cicero combated the proposal of a tribune to purchase and distribute lands in Italy. Vincent does not separately mention the work.

223. *as he sayth himselue.* Cp. "himself so doth express", A 303 here. Does Cicero say this?

228. Lydgate returns to Laurent as his source.

233. *In campania at Ative.* Laurent gives no name to the city; Lydgate could obtain his *Atine* (the MS wrongly writes *Ative*) either from Boccaccio or from Valerius Maximus; in the latter the dream of Cicero, not in Laurent, is fully given.

239-41. Cp. the opening of Dante's Inferno.

250-52. The pronouns are confused. The "seriaunt" is to convey Cicero to the sepulture of Marius.

277-78. Again, as often, the ablative absolute.

279. *beyng of assent* probably refers to Cicero.

281. *ffaryman.* Laurent has "vne ville appelle Fornian". Cicero's country seat near Formiae is meant.

285. *Inuentiff.* Bergen's text reads "invectiff scripture", which must be correct.

287. *Cleopatraas.* This form is regular in Lydgate, and occurs in Chaucer, see Legend 582, 601, 604. Laurent does not mention the name here.

291. At this point Laurent tells the story of Popilius Lena's debt of gratitude to Cicero; Lydgate defers it until after narrating the murder. It is given at length in Valerius Maximus v, chap. 3. Both in the MS and in the French and English early prints the ingrate's name is written with nasal mark above the *o*. The free use of Pompey's name in this part of the poem may have led by contamination to the writing *Pompilius*.

292. *who* is omitted before *gat*.

295 ff. Clumsily expressed. The sense is: "By virtue of the commission given to Popilius, who took licence and liberty from Antony, it followed that the chief rhetorician who ever was in the city, he who among Romans added dignity to Rome, was slain."

301. This renders Valerius Maximus' statement that Popilius "rogavit" to be sent on the errand of execution.

306-8. Laurent's comment on Antony's vengeance for Cicero's "invective" is that it is unwise in this world to tell the whole truth, because of the hate thereby incurred. The Frenchman drops a bit of practical wisdom; the English monk repeats a proverb.

309-15 are added by Lydgate. Lines 311-12 mean that whoever is in heart treasonable determines to do ill in return for good will. Between 314 and 315 supply "that it is".

317. This MS did not complete the line; bracketed words from Harley 1245.

320. *to heere abhominable* is parenthetical. On the orthography see Walton E 93 note.

321-2 means that he, Cicero, while living, took upon him to write, etc.

321-6. Laurent laments "le sage et venerable test de Tulle en qui estoit enclose toute eloquence latine", and the right hand with which so many notable books were written. He narrates how head and hand were set up on two lances, but has nothing of 327-30 as here; the rest of his chapter demands of God why his fire, his thunderstroke, his earthquake, did not overwhelm the "mauldit varlet" Popilius.

With this lament for head and hand cp. that for the lips of Orpheus, Ovid's Metam. xi:41-43, and the mention of Ceyx's hand *ibid.,* xi:560-61.

FALL OF PRINCES : H

1. *Symak.* Symmachus, Boethius' father-in-law, an ex-consul, historian, and patriot, one of the most cultivated men of his time, was involved in Boethius' fate. See Walton A 217 ff. *ante*.

11. *a geyn to,* against two.

11 ff. Boethius has told his own story of his resistance to the "graft" practised by unscrupulous Imperial officials; see the Consolatio bk. i, prose 4. Of the full account Lydgate uses very little.

12. *wiht.* Our MS writes *whiht*.

15. *Theodorik,* Theodoric the Ostrogothic Emperor, treated by Lydgate solely as usurper and tyrant; this view he could get from Laurent, see introd. *ante*.

19. *Dide,* i.e., *he did,* with the omission of subject as so frequently in Lydgate and occasionally in Chaucer. See 33 and 35 below.

23. *his comon.* Bergen's text reads *the comon,* i.e., the common people.

28. *Pauye,* Pavia in Lombardy, about 20 miles from Milan, and one of the leading cities in Italy under the Lombard emperors. Until 1584, a tower in Pavia was pointed out as Boethius' place of detention. Laurent says nothing of Pavia, only of Ravenna, whither the prisoner was first sent. Boccaccio speaks of Ravenna as Boethius' earlier prison, "Ticinum", i.e. Pavia, as the place of his death. See Walton A 207-222.

32-55. This meager treatment of Boethius as philosopher and as (supposed) Christian is surprising in a Churchman and a disciple of Chaucer. With the anticlimax of the last line, forced by the rime, cp. Chaucer's Troilus iv:25, 762, MoTale 3948; see an egregious case in the lines printed in my Chaucer Manual, p. 398-9. The finale of Lydgate's St. Giles— "Thi goost to God conveied vp by grace With hooly angelis moneth of Septembre",—is less absurd than at the first glance, because the poem was probably for use on the saint's day, and the emphasis thus understandable.

Laurent says nothing of a work on the Trinity by Boethius, and the library of Bury St. Edmunds, Lydgate's Abbey, contained only the Consolatio and the treatises on Music and on Arithmetic; see Dr. James on the Abbey, p. 30.

FALL OF PRINCES : K

4. *colours of cadence,* ornament by ?rhythm or measure. For *cadence* the NED cites first Chaucer's HoFame 112, "In ryme or elles in cadence". Gower, Confessio iv:2413-15, says that "Heredot" was earliest in the science "Of meter of rime and of cadence". The Coventry Mysteries speak of "gramer cadens and of prosodye". In Wyntoun's Orygynall Cronykill the word obviously means rhythm, as it does to Douglas; and in several fifteenth-century cases the term is applied to rhythmic prose. Thus, a piece of Latin copied by Shirley into MS Ashmole 59, fol. 77, is headed as "prosed in feyre cadence"; and in Brit.Mus.Royal 12 B xvii a tract on prose rhythm is headed "Iam de cadenciis". Skeat in his note on the line HoFame 112 opined that *cadence* may possibly have meant couplet-lines, while *rime* meant their grouping into stanzas. But see above.

Lydgate uses this same phrase in the envoy to his St. Edmund; in the Troy Book prol. 362 he speaks of "craft and cadence", and in Guy of Warwick 588 he says he "hadde of cadence no colour". A poem attributed to Lydgate by Shirley in Ashmole 59 fol. 18 speaks of "metres and cadence". For the term *colour,* "rhetorical ornament", see note on FaPrinces G 46.

5. *moral Senec,* Seneca the moralist, "most grave in his discourse". In A 253 *ante* Lydgate spoke of Seneca as a tragic writer, but "of great moralite". Koeppel, p. 62-3 says that although Boccaccio made two Senecas out of the tragedian and the philosopher, Lydgate knows that they are one.

11. *do correccion.* The usual request of the poet endeavoring to please a patron. See note on Cavendish 52 here. The MS erroneously reads *ffauoutre.*

13. *colours.* Lydgate plays on the double meaning of the word, as actual hue and as rhetorical ornament.

15 ff. The monk now disclaims knowledge of Virgil, of Homer, of Dares Phrygius, of Ovid and of Chaucer's "balladis". So far as the Fall of Princes is concerned, no direct acquaintance with Virgil appears, although his works are enumerated iv:67-91 and his name mentioned with praise. In the same passage various works by Ovid are listed, and of the Metamorphoses at least Lydgate had direct knowledge, see p. 92 here. Homer, it is needless to say, Lydgate did not know; Dares Phrygius, whose meagre Latin account of the Trojan War was used by Guido delle Colonne, is mentioned by Lydgate Troy Book i:310 as one of the predecessors of his own author, Guido. The list of these predecessors, there given, is Ovid, Virgil who followed Homer, Lollius, and above all "Dares Frigius" and "Dytes eke"—i.e. Dictys Cretensis, and then Guido. What Lygate means by declaring his ignorance of Chaucer's sovereign ballads we do not know, nor exactly what he means by that term.

23. *in fantasy.* Bergen's text, *mi fantasy.*

24-28. The mention of Gower and of Strode, together, is evidently a following of Troilus v:1856-57; the same descriptive epithets are used. The monk adds to this brief list of English writers the hermit of Hampole, reputed translator of the Stimulus Conscientiae.

29-30. *As the . . . sonne,* etc. A favorite simile with Lydgate. See note on G 36 *ante,* to which add Seneca's "Quemadmodum minuta lumina claritas solis obscurat", epist. lxvi to Lucilius; cp. also Ovid, Metam.ii:722-24, and Petrarch, In Vita, canzone 12, lines 69-70, 218.

31. *cacheth.* Other MSS *chaceth.*

37. *Petrake.* On this spelling see note A 257 *ante.* The Liber Augustalis may be meant.

41. *did.* Note the "modern" usage, as in 37. See note Dance 136, and *do* in Glossary.

42-3. Partial liaison of stanzas. See note Mass 74-97.

45. Lydgate here gives the name of the Suffolk village in which he was born, and whence he probably took his name. See this poem viii:194, and note to Dance 670.

48. On the life of St. Edmund, king of the East Angles at the time of the Danish incursions, and of his martyrdom and miracles, Lydgate composed a poem in three books, at the bidding of his abbot, for King Henry VI. The royal presentation copy still exists, Harley 2278 of the British Museum.

49. *Oxne.* Hoxne, twenty miles from Thetford; the site of the battle in which Edmund was slain. He was ultimately interred at Bury St. Edmunds, later the site of the monastery to which Lydgate belonged.

51-3. For this mode of disclaiming inspiration see note on Walton A 58 here. Chaucer, in the Franklin's headlink, joined Parnassus and Cicero as sources of eloquence; and he was followed by Bokenam as cited. But Lydgate here uses *Citheron* instead of Cicero, in which he is justified by classic myth, for the range of mountains between Boeotia and Attica, called Cithaeron, was sacred to Dionysus and to the Muses. See also Burgh's letter to Lydgate, line 7 and note. The Roman de la Rose, 15865, 15867, made Cithaeron the special abode of Venus, and also gave the word a short penult, kept by Chaucer, KnTale 1078, 1365, and by Lydgate as cited in the note on Burgh 7. Lydgate uses the word again in FaPrinces ix:3592; but in this latter passage it is not certain whether Cithaeron or Cicero is meant, and the scribes add to the uncertainty. In the FranklTale many MSS write *Cithero, Scithero,* just as some write Marcus Tullius *and* Cicero; and in the Court of Sapience we find *Cythero* among philosophers.

BURGH'S LETTER TO LYDGATE

1-2. *Nat dremyd I,* etc. See note on Walton A 58.

3. *the pale pirus.* A miswriting by Stow or his original is here probable. Stow wrote *priu,* struck it through, and proceeded with *pirus.* Possibly Pieria, one of the earliest places where the Muses were worshipped; but why *pale*?

5. *Tagus.* Allusions to the river Tagus and its golden sands are several times made by Ovid and by Claudian. Boethius in the Consolatio iii metr. 10 speaks of "Tagus aureis harenis", but Chaucer does not transfer the bit elsewhere. Isidor twice mentions Tagus, Etymol. xiii:21,33 and xiv:4,29; and in the fifteenth century the river again becomes literary material, still more so in the Renaissance. See FaPrinces iii:3734, Douglas' Palice of Honour, prol. 42, the Epist. Obscurorum Virorum, p. 23 of the 1909 edition, Wyatt, Browne's Britannia's Pastorals, etc.

7. *Citero or elicon.* Stow's script may be read either *Cicero* or *Citero,* i.e., Mt. Cithaeron in the latter case. Steele and Foerster print *Cicero;* but the confusion is so frequent in MSS, the use of *Tullius* as Cicero's name so regular in this period, and the coupling with Mt. Helicon so plain that Burgh, at least must have meant *Cithero.* The word was regularly scanned with short penult in Middle English. See its use by Lydgate in Troy Book ii:3456, 3635, iv:4602, 5708. See note on Mass line 5 and on FaPrinces K 51-3.

The mountain Helicon and its spring were often confused by medieval writers, because of ambiguity already in the Aeneid vii:641, Dante's Purgatorio 29:40. Boccaccio is clear, Teseide i:1 and xi stanza 63; but Chaucer is not, HoFame 521-2, Anelida 15-18, Troilus iii:1809-10; nor is Lydgate, Troy Book prol. 42, i:1612, iii:5432, TemGlass 706, St. Edmund envoy. Cp. Court of Love 22, Skelton's GarlLaurell 73-4 and Philip Sparrow 609-10; especially Spenser, ShepCal April 41-2. See Pilgrimage to Parnassus act i.

8. *founde.* Steele prints *formde.*

9. *moste.* The MS writes *noste.*

10. *Aristotell,* etc. Burgh may mean Aristotle, Gorgias, and Hermogenes, as Stow writes, or Aristotle, Gorgias, and Hermagoras as in Isidor, Etymol, ii, 2. Aristotle's Art of Rhetoric is meant. Gorgias is not the sophist contemporary with Socrates, but a later author of a treatise on the figures of speech, partly preserved in a Latin paraphrase,—see Halm's Rhetori Latini Minores, Leipzig, 1863. Hermogenes was a Greek rhetorician of the second century, author of a treatise on oratory still in existence,—see Halm as above. Hermagoras, also a Greek rhetorician, was contemporary with Cicero. Hermogenes is mentioned in Lydgate's Secrees 964, 1023, etc.

13. *tullius* etc. Marcus Tullius Cicero, Francis Petrarch, Quintilian. The linking of Petrarch's name with those of the elder writers is noteworthy.

16. *torqwat souereyne. Boethius,* i.e., Anicius Manlius Torquatus Severinus Boethius. See p. 39 here.

17. *Naso,* i.e. Ovidius Naso. His Metamorphoses are meant by line 18, which is muddled in transcription.

20. *porcyus,* i.e. Persius.—*marcyan,* printed *marycan* by Steele, is Martianus Capella, author of the De Nuptiis Mercurii et Philologiae.

21. *lauriate bocase.* Boccaccio was not "laureate" in the sense in which Petrarch was; he never received the laurel crown. But the term was applied in this period to many great writers, see note on Churl 15.

22. *seyne.* Steele prints *peyne.*—*Innat sapience.* See Hoccleve's Regement 2130.

23. See note on FaPrinces D 10.

30. *booke wt . . . clasppes seven.* The allusion is to the seven liberal arts, which enclose the volume of literature and of science.

34. *a benedicite.* The two lines are an admiring exclamation—"Ah, Heaven bless you, Master Lydgate, what a man you are!" Steele prints *di benedicite.* Cp. Chaucer's BoDuchesse 859, 895, 919.

40. *garland of Ive.* The ivy garland had in ancient times no special meaning, as had the wreaths of laurel, grass, bay, oak, and olive. The garland of bay was at Athens worn by orators while speaking, and that of olive was given to victors in the games or to specially-deserving citizens. Either bay or olive would single Lydgate out more than does the garland of ivy which, mingled with wool or with flowers, was worn by any Greek or Roman on festival occasions.

43. *chebri place,* etc. Burgh here gives the place of his letter; see introduction *ante.* Foerster would interpret *chebri place* as "shivery place", alluding to the winter weather; but this appears to me very doubtful. The word *shiver* has indeed the modern sense in Black Knight 230, but the transference of meaning Foerster suggests has no example in the NED before 1850, and is strongly modern in feeling. I would sooner expect "Chebri Place" to be the name of the building in which Burgh is writing; for a number of localities and manorhouses in Essex were known as "Places", and one of the Abbey-tenements may have borne that title from its former owner. There was, for instance, a family Chevere (or Cheever?) in that part of Essex. I have, however, not found the name in the list of the Abbey's possessions. See Morant, Hist. and Antiq. of Essex, London, 1768, i:327-338, especially 335 note.

45. *mount Canace.* Boccaccio's De Montibus says of Mt. Canatus, in Spain, that it is "excelsus", has a deep black lake atop, and is so often the source of tempest that it is believed to be the abode of demons; which, Boccaccio adds, "meo iudicio fabulosa".

50 ff. Burgh gives his date of writing as December the eleventh, but gives no year. If the letter were actually sent, omission of the year would be natural.

51. *chare,* chariot. Steele prints *share.*

SHIRLEY'S TABLES OF CONTENTS : I

26. *ordre.* The medieval rhetorical code required an "orderly" exhaustive tabulation of qualities or points. On its feature-by-feature description see note on Hoccleve's third Roundel, *ante;* on the sections of an argument or list cp. Chaucer's Second Nun's Tale 358, "It were ful hard by ordre for to seyn How many wondres Jesus for hem wroghte."

Compare also such phrases as "the ordre of compleynt", Chaucer's Mars 155, or "the ordre of endityng", Hoccleve's poem to the Duke of York 50, for *order* as "rhetorical code." Cp. Lydgate's very frequent use of *ceriousli,* "serially".

35. Chaucer's translation of Boethius' Consolatio is followed in the MS by a prose tractate on the martyrdom of Nicodemus, which fills the next twenty pages. Shirley says that this translation from the Latin was made by John Trevisa for his patron Thomas lord Berkeley. Berkeley was father of that Elizabeth Countess of Warwick who accepted the

dedication of John Walton's Boethius-translation; see p. 39 here. He commissioned from John Trevisa (1326-1412) translations of Higden's Polychronicon and of Bartholomaeus' De Proprietatibus Rerum; various other works are less certainly ascribed to Trevisa, e.g., Englishings of Vegetius' De Re Militari and of Aegidius de Colonna's De Regimine Principum.

49. *maystre of þe game*, Master of Game, a treatise on hunting by Edward second duke of York. This has been edited by W. A. and F. Baillie-Grohman, with an introd. by Theodore Roosevelt, London, 1904, again 1909.

Edward York, killed at Agincourt in 1415, is the Aumerle of Shakespeare's Richard II. He dedicated his work to Henry prince of Wales, afterward Henry the Fifth, whose Master of Game, i.e. of the Hunt, he was.

57. *To alle.* Read *So alle?*

66. *Regula sacerdotalis.* This article does not come next in the MS, but after the Complaint of the Black Knight, which now follows. The *Regula* fills four and one-half leaves, prose, and in its colophon is the phrase "tam dominis quam communibus" which Shirley uses in line 18 of this poem. Shirley professes ignorance of the tractate's authorship.

70-71. On these lines I can throw no light. They seem more useful as rime-connectives than as sense-connectives.

72-86. This passage is cited, and the whole verse-table discussed, by Schick, pp. lxxxii-iii of his introd. to the EETS edition of the Temple of Glass.

73. *of a knyght.* Lydgate's Complaint of the Black Knight; see my Chaucer Manual, p. 413.

78. Cp. Hall's Chronicle (1548), "Gounes embrodred with reasons of golde that sayd *adieu Iunesse.*"

81. *cloþed in black.* Lydgate belonged to the Benedictines or Black Friars. Shirley's tone of familiarity toward Lydgate should be noted; cp. the following piece of verse.

87. *oþer balades.* The remainder of MS Adds. 16165 is filled with Chaucer's Anelida, Lydgate's St. Anne and his Departing of Chaucer, Richard Beauchamp Earl of Warwick's poem to Lady Despenser, and by a number of short amatory verse-bits. Warwick's poem has been edited by MacCracken in PMLA 22:597; the Departing of Chaucer was printed by me in ModPhil 1:333-36, repr. by Ruud in *Thomas Chaucer*, pp. 119-121. See my Manual, p. 327.

92. *ebounden.* Note the peculiar Shirleyan spelling, and cp. *ellas* in II:43, *filowiþe* in 45 here.

SHIRLEY'S TABLES OF CONTENTS : II

In this text, of 1558, observe the constant writing *ye* for older *þe.* The use of *y*, in print and in script, to replace the obsolete rune so similar in shape, has led to our pseudo-archaism of "Ye olde".

12. *coth.* The MS so reads; but it may be that *ooth* was intended; in either case, a padding phrase.

16. "What were (once) widely scattered are afterwards here brought together." The pause is in front of *eft.*

21. *humayne pilgrymage.* This prose translation, ? of Deguileville's *Pèlerinage de la vie humaine* may or may not be ascribed by Shirley to Lydgate, according as one treats line 24. Lydgate executed a verse-translation of Deguileville's second recension, which is ed. EETS 1899-1904, and a prose Englishing of the earlier French recension is printed by the Roxburghe Club, 1869. The relations of the Englishings of Deguileville are not clear.

It is to be noted that although Stow in this part of his volume, foll. 132a-179a, is transcribing from Shirley, and from the existing MS Trinity College R 3, 20 (see pp. 79, 194 ante), the Trinity volume does not now contain the Pilgrimage-translation. But as that volume's first existing quire is marked xiiij, and as there is an isolated copy of the prose translation, filling 93 leaves though imperfect, in the Sion College Shirley MS, I have queried if the Sion MS be the missing Shirley gatherings, once part of the Trinity codex.

23. *many a roundell and balade.* The Trinity MS contains a number of French roundels by the duke of Suffolk; and many of its poems, especially the French, are headed "Balade gaye et gracieux", etc. Shirley cannot apply "many a roundell" to Lydgate.

25. *sugred mouthe.* See note on Thebes 52.

29-30. *pleyinges . . . of kynges.* Probably the royal mummings are meant.

31. Supply *is* before *so.*

32. "He ought to receive a formal expression of gratitude from all our nation."

40 ff. "I believe his nobles (i.e., gold coins) are spent, and nearly all his shillings." Note Lydgate's pleas for money, as in the Letter to Gloucester, here printed, p. 149. With 42 cp. Thebes 90.

45. *sainte margarete.* This poem is printed by MacCracken i:173 ff., from the Durham MS. All that intervenes between the Pilgrimage-translation and this poem on fol. 178 is summarily mentioned by Shirley. He now pauses over a translation commissioned by the countess of March, and as a Londoner he mentions the countess' burial place in London.

57. *by lordes and by clerkes.* This statement represents the whole MS better than it does the leaves after the Life of St. Margaret.

61. *persayue,* etc. The MS writes without the *er*-flourish.

71. *correcte.* Shirley asks his readers to correct metrical and scribal errors. It may be that the modesty, or assumed modesty, of an author in making this conventional plea received emphasis from his realization of scribal carelessness.

76. *grac.* So in the MS.

84. *weddinge.* Is *reading* meant? See Shirley I:100.

88. *when you list send.* Shirley's function as a book-lender is plainly stated.

90. *as . . . owne man,* "as much as if I were actually of your household."

94. The last word is partly deleted, and doubtless should be so entirely.

99. *in ernest nor in game.* A convenient padding phrase; see Troilus iv:1465, Troy Book iv:4559, v:2687, etc.

REPROOF TO LYDGATE

The MS Fairfax 16 of the Bodleian Library at Oxford, the source of our text, is a thick but not large vellum volume of 336 leaves, written almost entirely in one clear neat firm book-hand; one of its copied poems postdates the death of Henry the Fifth in 1422. It bears on leaf 14 verso an elaborate illumination to illustrate Chaucer's *Mars,* which faces the picture; in the border of this are the arms of Stanley-Storeton-Hooton. Its contents are listed pp. 334-35 of my Chaucer Manual, where, on p. 338, will be found a parallel-table proving the close relationship between this volume and two others of the Bodleian Library. The Fairfax scribe, although insensitive to the value of *-e* final (see ModPhil 23:129-52), is steadily consistent in orthography and above the average in accuracy.

Since the publication of my Chaucer Manual, the then unpubd. texts of Fairfax have appeared in print; the series of short poems on foll. 318a-329a was ed. by MacCracken in PMLA 26:142 ff.; the poem "How a Lover Praiseth his Lady" was pubd. by me in Mod Phil 21:379-95; the Lover's Mass is again printed here p. 207; and one of the short poems ed. by MacCracken, the Reproof to Lydgate, is included in this volume, as here.

4. *slouthe,* sloth or remissness. As Sloth was one of the Seven Deadly Sins for a Christian, so was it most blameworthy in a lover. Gower in his Confessio bk. iv illustrates the failing by several narratives, among them that of Demophoon and Phyllis, in which latter he twice speaks of Demophoon's "sloth" in not returning to the deceived and despairing Phyllis. Lydgate, BlKnight 380, also mentions the "sloth" of Demophoon, which he would not get from Chaucer's Legend 2394 ff., since Chaucer denounces the traitor Demophoon, taking his key from Ovid's Heroides ii. The "sloth" mentioned by Orléans, extract vi here, seems to be merely neglect on the lady's part; and see TemGlas 379, FlandLeaf 549. A more serious and philosophical conception of "sloth" in love is that of Dante in the Purgatorio, where the seven capital sins are treated as arising from disordered love. Sloth is there deficient love, the loving too little what should be the goal of the mind's desire. See Gardner, Dante and the

Mystics, 1913, pp. 55-57 and mark the notion of *ordo* or *reason* as the essence of *virtus*. See note on FaPrinces G 17 here.

5. *wytt the.* Probably miswritten for *wytt ye,* the *y* treated as the rune *th.*

6. See prol. to the Legend of Good Women (B) 202.

14. The MS omits *to.*

29. MacCracken, *loc. cit.,* above, says "This is certainly a burlesque of Lydgate's style."

31. *colours,* i.e., of rhetoric; see note FaPrinces G 46 above.

36 ff. Lydgate is now censured for saying that love is dotage, that great clerks have yielded to it, that women are false and fickle, and that they can pretend love without feeling it.

40. MacCracken, *loc. cit.,* above, says "This is certainly a parody on the moral poem by Lydgate with the refrain 'Who sueth vertu vertu he shal lere'." It may be, however, that both pieces of verse used a current proverb.

58. The MS has *myned* instead of *meuyd.*

65. *Thynk whens,* etc. Cp. Hoccleve's Letter of Cupid 178, "Take hede of whom / thou took thy bygynnyng". Another and different use is Ovid's in Metam. iii:543, "Este, precor, memores qua sitis stirpe creati",—and Dante's Inferno xxvi:118. The MS writes *thom* instead of *thou.*

66. The MS writes *Hastow thou not,* etc.

67. *not fair.* I do not find this apparently modern locution in Chaucer, but it occurs a number of times in Lydgate; see ResonandSens 1448, FaPrinces i:2624, 4171, iv:2148, etc.

79, 80, 81. These are in the MS arranged as 80, 81, 79, with scribal marks for transposition.

TRANSLATION OF PALLADIUS

PROLOGUE

In this original prologue prefixed to the Palladius-translation, the author's business is almost entirely praise of his patron Gloucester. With it compare Hoccleve's praise of the duke, Dialogue lines 532-616, Lydgate's prologue to FaPrinces 373-420 and his Epithalamium, also his Letter to the duke; cp. the Libel of English Policy 250-51, the extract from Hardyng's Chronicle 49-50.

The prologue is heavy with "rhetorical color". Observe not only the internal rime in single verses, but the linking of stanza by phrase-echo. Such technique is much more elaborate, but less pleasing, than that of the Lover's Mass (see p. 211 here), or of parts of Chaucer's Anelida. Necessarily the poet has difficulty in fitting speech to such a form, and is driven to twist syntax or force the senses of words. Thus, in line 8 he says "To rade error from my balade and do Pallade [so as] to glade his excellence",—i.e., Gloucester. And at the opening the sense apparently is:—"The All-Creator of creatures chose to establish agriculture (and set it) to endure in nature and in art; and (that Creator chose) to assign duke Humphrey his part in each respect, adding honor so great that we see the duke as flower of princes." In the second stanza the opening phrase "His excellence" is the object of *extende* in line 14; and I take "Thy Providence" as its subject:—"Thy Providence so chooses to extend his excellence."

16. *an ace.* For this and for the *ace apoynt* of line 17 I can offer little. The author himself considers it necessary to explain the second phrase. The ace, especially the ambes-as or double ace, was the lowest cast at dice, consequently, a failure. Regarding *apoynt* I can suggest only the rare Old French use of *apointer* to mean "deceive, ensnare".

18. Read with period after *honde;* the two and a half lines following are a question.

22. *lame* is used by Transition writers to mean "inadequate, imperfect". Cp. Chaucer's Troilus ii:17. There is a full stop at the end of the line.

23. By *myghtiest* the poet probably means the great nobles and Churchmen of the time. We may note that at this moment, ca. 1440, Gloucester's power and influence were on the wane, whether this translator knew it or not.

28. I read with stop at end of the line.

29. *the Sapient secounde.* Apparently the translator says that the lieutenant or "second" to all-sapient God is found in Gloucester. This is no more extreme than his declaration in book i:1194, also of Gloucester,

> But God me semeth best thou mayst resemble
> ffor verite Iustice and mansuetude.

The use of *secounde* is not infrequent in Middle English; e.g., Troilus is termed "Hector the secounde" in Lydgate's Troy Book ii:288, iv:2344, following Chaucer's Troilus ii:158, v:834-40; and Chaucer is following Guido delle Colonne. In FaPrinces iv:3961, Arsinoe is called "Venus the seconde".

31. *founde* means to test, try, learn by experience.

35-37. "To see whose virtue and to do pleasure to it", etc., many "have resorted with great honor and gifts".

37, 38. "And some under this flower (i.e. Gloucester) are here." The translator is apparently working at one of Gloucester's castles; in 102-3 the men alluded to are members of Gloucester's household. See introduction *ante.*

42. Full stop at end of the line. Lines 43-47 are all interrogative.

43. *The duc periure,* the perjured duke, i.e., Philip of Burgundy, who after supporting for some years the English claim to the French crown, at length abandoned that position and threw his influence for the French king. A Flemish force under Burgundy invested Calais and its English garrison in 1436. Gloucester, who had been made Lieutenant of Calais in the preceding year, crossed the Channel with an English force; but the Burgundian army was already in retreat, and after ravaging some Burgundian territory Gloucester returned to England to meet an enthusiastic popular welcome. Cp. a poem jeering at the craven Flemings, included in one version of the Brut, or English Chronicle,—see ed. of the Brut for EETS 1906-08, ii:582. MacCracken has ascribed this poem to Lydgate. Cp. the undoubted Lydgate poem, Horse Goose and Sheep, 413-420.

50. *kouthe pike him fro,* could get any advantage over him. In Chaucer's Legend 2467, "And piked of her al the good he mighte", the word means literally "robbed", but this use seems more like the modern colloquial "get any change out of him".

51. *Sharp or Wawe,*—if they had a happy time with the law!—In 1431 John Scharpe of Wigmoreland created a commotion by distributing bills in London, Coventry, Oxford, and other towns, against the great possessions of the clergy and suggesting their appropriation to help the poor. Gloucester, who was at the time Protector during the king's absence in France, arrested Scharpe and several others, who were all hanged or beheaded. See the Annales Monast. S. Albani, ed. 1870, i:63; see Proceed. Privy Council iv:89,99,107. In 1427 one William Wawe, who had attacked and robbed a nunnery near St. Albans, was tried before Gloucester in London as a heretic and outrager of the Church, and was hanged. The insistence upon these facts by this translator and by Lydgate (see p. 163 here) may show Gloucester's wish to keep alive the popular idea of him as champion of the Church; cp. introduction above.

52-53. These lines present difficulty. Liddell states that against 52 is in the margin a cross; as this was the usual scribe's note of a correction to be made, and as at present the rime here is over-rich, Liddell substitutes for the *unto* of 52 the word *undo* and puts a following comma. His paraphrase of 52 would then probably be: "(Say) if right was found undone in all this land"; but 53 remains difficult. Did we retain the *unto* of 52 we might paraphrase the two lines: "(Say) if right was found in all this land until he put his hand to the rudder to govern it." But either there or with the rime-change it is necessary to explain the apparent plural-form *doon* with a singular subject.

57. Read question or exclamation after *sothe.*

60. *and Orliaunce ennoye.* In 1439 the Beaufort party, always antagonistic to Gloucester, pressed strongly for a peace with France and for liberation of the duke of Orléans, a prisoner since Agincourt. Gloucester opposed both moves, but the liberation of Orléans was decided on, despite a formal and weighty protest from Gloucester, for which see Rymer's Foedera x:764-767 or Vickers' life of the duke, pp. 264-65. His arguments, which

of course stressed the dying commands of Henry the Fifth, aroused so much popular feeling that they were answered by the other Lords of Council in the name of the boy-king; see Stevenson, Letters and Papers ii:451-60, Vickers, op. cit., p. 267. Orléans was set free in Nov. 1440; and when, on the preceding Aug. 28, he took solemn public oath never to move against the English king, Gloucester left Westminster Abbey and the ceremony and went direct to his post in South Wales. It thus seems probable not only that "Orliaunce ennoye" refers to Humphrey's efforts to prevent the French duke's liberation, but that this translation if supervised by Gloucester, must antedate August 1440 as well as postdate November 1439 and the first gift of books to Oxford.

68. *hem connect.* Liddell punctuates with a semicolon after *connect* and period after *enclude*, line 67 running over into 68. The translator seems to have been led by his closing phrase in 64, "al vertu is", to start his next stanza with a definition of virtus. He may be using for it a Latin source, which I have not identified; and his adoption of the word *intellect* drives him to a somewhat unusual group of rime-words, *connect, confect, provect.* I might paraphrase: "If mercy (piety?) be adorned with knowledge, (and if) fear of the Lord hold them connected together."

72. Pause after *werkis;* the rest of the line is an interrogation.

73. *felyng.* Here and in line 91 this word apparently means "to grasp mentally". See Libel 188. See also Walton's Boethius, v prose 4:145, "As be exsaumple myght þou feelen yit". In 91 the word is glossed *sentiunt* by the scribe, while the *fele* of 89 is glossed *plures.* We may paraphrase the awkward stanza: "Another testing so the philosopher in books of natural philosophy, as is physics; so prompt also to proffer metaphysic, or each art quadrivial; and who hath the practical with the theoretical" etc. A description of Gloucester is intended.

76. *quadriuial.* The quadrivium joined with the trivium to make the seven liberal arts; it included Arithmetic, Geometry, Music, and Astronomy, while the trivium (see 79, 80) included Grammar, Logic, and Rhetoric. See the Court of Sapience, or Hawes' Pastime of Pleasure, from among countless medieval works on the Seven Liberal Arts.—*practic With theoric.* See notes on Dance Macabre 427, on Walton A 332; see Confessio Amantis vii: 1499 ff., 1649 ff.

78. *Politic,* etc. In an explanatory Latin comment near the opening of the Court of Sapience, we read that "Policia" is, according to Aristotle, Arnulphus, Kilwardby, and Isidor, to be divided into monastic, economic, and civil or politic. Monastic deals with the administration of the individual, economic with that of the household, politic with that of the subjects in a state. See Gower as cited above, and Macaulay's note, vol. iii, p. 522.

82. *al thorgh se,*—"to see (understand) philosophy thoroughly".

86-88. This stanza apparently says that acquired knowledge is a high possession, that natural gifts are no small endowment, and that it is a proper procedure to depend upon "tresor" if a wise use of the science of physiognomy judge each organ and feature. The pseudo-Aristotelian Secreta Secretorum devotes a long section to physiognomy; but the exact force of *tresor* I cannot interpret, unless it refers to the Secreta itself,—see Lydgate's translation, line 592.

89. *At Oxenford* etc. Gloucester made two princely gifts of books to the University of Oxford, one in November 1439, the second in February 1443. His first donation, of 129 volumes, was sent in answer to an appeal from the scantily-equipped University; the delivery was made by Master Gilbert Kymer and by Ralph Drew. The second gift, of 135 volumes, was delivered by Master William Say and Ralph Drew. The University acknowledged the donations with warm gratitude, drew up lists of the books, and provided for their storage in a "cista trium philosophiarum et septem scientiarum liberalium", whence they might be borrowed by Masters under special indenture. Annual masses were to be said for Gloucester and for his consort forever, etc.

These lists are printed by Anstey in his Munimenta Academica, 1868, ii:758-772; but there is nothing either there or in the Epistolae Academicae Oxon., 1898, to indicate that the duke equipped an University reading-room with desks. A letter from the University to Humphrey, after the first gift, speaks of the need for a larger reading-room because of the increased number of readers; but Humphrey, says Vickers, p. 406-7, seems to have ignored the hint.

The recurrent *They, these other, They,* mark out different classes of readers. There are pauses after *methaphisic,* line 91, and *natural,* line 92. With 89 the stanza-linking ceases, also the internal rime-echo; there are reappearances of the latter in 107, 117, 123, 124.

93. "Here (close) by is theology to be met with."

102-104. These men must have presented their works to Gloucester before this translation was executed in 1440. Whethamstede, Abbot of St. Albans and counsellor of Gloucester in literary matters, is praised by Lydgate in St. Albon and Amphabell (done to Whethamstede's order) for his "gaye librarye" and for his scholarly industry. He compiled a Granarium, or De Viris Illustribus, which Lydgate mentions, and which appears in the 1443 list of Gloucester's gifts to Oxford. The work still exists, part 1 in Brit. Mus. Cotton Nero C vi; part 2 in Cotton Tiberius D v, very badly damaged by fire; part 4 in Brit. Mus. Adds. 26764. *Pers de Mounte,* Peter de Monte of Venice, dedicated to Gloucester his treatise De virtutum et vitiorum inter se differentia, which is probably meant by the next to the last entry of the 1443 list, "De vitiorum inter se". *Titus* is Titus Livius of Friuli, an Italian and Gloucester's resident poet, who wrote a Latin life of Henry the Fifth at the duke's command. *Anthony* is Antonio da Beccaria of Verona, Gloucester's secretary, who translated at his master's order several theological treatises by Athanasius. Capgrave the prior of Lynn in Norfolk is not here mentioned; he dedicated to Gloucester his commentary on Genesis, which is in the 1443 list. Upton is not mentioned, nor Lydgate, but they both translated into English, which may have seemed negligible to our author except in his own case.

104. There is a pause after *least.*

109. *taught me metur make.* How to estimate this curious and important statement we are not certain. The management of rhythm in the body of the translation is so good, and the text so careful of *e*-final, that a strict supervision over it is obvious. Such a supervision, by Gloucester himself, is asserted in the January and February epilogue-stanzas, here printed; but how far the duke was responsible for the sound and competent rhythm we do not and cannot know. Certainly no amount of correction could have put the management of Lydgate's Fall of Princes on a par with this. The flourished trickery of the prologue gives no real idea of this translator's ability to cope with his main problem, which he handles easily and well.

111-112. Compare the Lover's Mass 115 ff.

113-16. The translator's personal grievance breaks into expression, but is quickly curbed. Nothing is known of the circumstances, nor can be until the translator is identified. The late E. W. B. Nicholson, Bodley's Librarian, suggested John Walton; but the ability of the two men in handling difficult Latin is the only point of similarity to be noted.

PALLADIUS: EPILOGUE-STANZAS

A

1. *A now,* Ah now! Liddell suggests "And now".

2. *crossis make,* to make crosses, the recognized method of indicating, in the margin, the need for correction in the text. These crosses are sometimes lightly scratched, sometimes in faint crayon or ink easy of erasure.

3. *plummet.* Whether the implement used by Gloucester was the egg-shaped pointed plummet of lead, such as a surveyor carries today, or a sort of crayon pencil, cannot be determined. See Garland 1075 and note 1074 *ibid.*

4. *straunge eschaunge,* strangely altered.

5. *no leue I take,* i.e., I slip away quietly.

6. *do forth,* continue? This line is puzzling. Does the author first withdraw quaking and then submit himself?

B

6. *by what,* etc. Liddell reads this "Ey what" etc., that is, "Ah, what have I to do?" This gives better sense and a more dramatic meaning. A question mark is then to be understood after *correcte,* and after *done.*

7. In this line, in A 4 above, and previously, note how the scribe indicates a new sentence, in mid-line, by a capital. In C 6, however, the capital means the Deity.

C

1. "And here I find an end sooner than I thought."

2. "(What) art taught before is finished this month."

4. "That chose to be born of one for every one."

6-8. The last sentence of this stanza begins either with *Ay* or with line 7; there is a comma-pause after *make.* "So bear up thy prince's deeds from darkness, while I set to work at May."

D

3-4. "I see my guide far ahead, and I follow him, although I do not attempt to be as swift as he."

5. *o god allone.* Liddell suggests *of God allone,* the reading of the Oxford MS.

6. "O hope, free of drop of sin or fraud."

THE LOVER'S MASS

5. *Cytheron.* This may be the mountain, or may be Venus,—Cytherea. See note FaPrinces K 51; see Burgh 7 and note.

15-40. Compare the "confession" of Troilus, in Chaucer's poem ii:523 ff., and see Root's (522) note in his edition of the poem.

53. *The* is miswritten by the scribe, for *Ther?*

56. *Genius.* This name is given to the mystagogue of Nature, or "prélat Venérien", in. Alanus' De Planctu Naturae, prose ix, in the Roman de la Rose, in the Confessio Amantis, in Lydgate's Reson and Sensuality 6623, 6677, in his Troy Book iv:6975-6, in Lemaire de Belges' Concorde des deux Langages, in Marot's Temple de Cupido. See Spenser, Faerie Queene ii:12, 47, iii:6, 31.

57-72. The Officium is a roundel, i.e., a poem of unequally tripartite structure on two rimes, repeating its opening lines in two other positions in the poem. Scribes often write only the first word or two of the repeated lines, as here.

The roundel was originally a French "rondet de carole", or lyric sung in dance. Roundels appear inserted into thirteenth-century romances, e.g., the Cléomades 5497-5504, 5513-20; and thereafter they developed as an independent literary form, in various lengths according to the number of thematic lines. Roundels occur in earlier English at the close of Chaucer's Parlement of Foules, in Lydgate's Entry of Henry VI into London and in his Pedigree of Henry VI, at close. Four by Hoccleve are printed here pp. 67, 68; a roundel to Fortune, with Lydgate's Pedigree-roundel, is printed by Ritson, Ancient Songs i:128-9; and Lydgate's first roundel above mentioned is discussed by Schleich, Archiv 96:193. All these, except perhaps the Fortune-roundel, were intended for singing; and the employment of the roundel-form in this part of the Mass should be noted. Three roundels, entitled Merciles Beaute, are printed by Skeat i:387-8 with the work of Chaucer; they are preserved in one MS only, without mark of authorship.

The earl of Suffolk has left several roundels written in French; see print by MacCracken in PMLA 26:142 ff. English translations of several roundels by the duke of Orléans are printed in this volume, pp. 221-3, 231-2.

74-97. In these Kyrie stanzas two "rhetorical colors" are employed, internal rime and stanza-linking. Internal rime was twice used by Chaucer in his Anelida, in groups of nine verses, 272-8, 332-41; and we find similar nine-line stanzas at the close of Douglas' Palice of Honour. Here the stanza is of eight verses, the internal rime changing with each verse; but in the three eight-line stanzas at the close of Henryson's Prayer for the Pest, in a stanza closing part ii of the Palladius-translation, and in one strophe of the Song of Lust in Barclay's Ship of Fools (ii :290), the rime-management differs each time. Palladius and Henryson both construct the stanza *ababbcbc,* but while Henryson shifts his (often three-fold) internal rime with every line, Palladius uses a twofold *b*-rime within his *a*-lines and an *a*-rime within his *b*-lines. Barclay, changing his internal rime with each verse, builds his stanza *aabbaabb.* None of these is therefore exactly parallel to the stanza as constructed here or to the Anelida-stanza ; but their common refusal of the Anelida-stanza of nine lines, which is reproduced by Douglas, is noteworthy. The use of internal rime by Dunbar in part of each stanza of his Ballat to Our Lady, when taken with this general divergence from the Chaucerian model, indicates that not so much Chaucer as a known rhetorical device was in the minds of these post-Chaucerian versifiers, who each varied to suit himself.

A brief treatment of medial or "leonine" rime is in the *Laborintus,* see Faral, p. 362.

The enchaining of stanzas, by phrase, word, or rime, has a longer history. It is found, in English, in Laurence Minot, in the Pearl, in Sir Perceval of Galles, in the archetype of the Awnters of Arthur, in various poems of MS Harl 2253 as ed. in Böddeker's Altenglische Dichtungen, etc. Italian, Provençal, and early French poets use the device ; see, e.g. the 19th canzone of Guittone d'Arezzo ; see Butler's Forerunners of Dante nos. i, xiii, xxii, xlv ; see Naetebus, pp. 143-4, 164, 174, 181-2. Lydgate makes an attempt at it in Black Knight 217-45. A reduced form of stanza-linking, by rime only, is employed by Barclay in the Tower of Virtue poem inserted into his fourth eclogue ; see p. 330 here. For a modern example see Alfred Perceval Graves' "When Adam's eyes childwise."

123. For this thought see Troilus i :950-52, iii :1060-62 ; see Lydgate's Guy of Warwick 81-85 ; see Dunbar's Of the Changes of Life ; see Orléans' poem "Aftir wynter the veer with foilys grene". Cp. the Palladius-prologue, line 112 here. And see Matthew of Vendôme's lines from the Tobias 457-8 :—

> Flores post hiemem, post absinthim risum
> Praestas post lacrimas, post tenebrosa iubar.

146. With the Epistle cp. such addresses to the "fedeli d'Amor", or initiates of love, as in Dante's Vita Nuova. For a contact between the pilgrim-simile here and in Boccaccio's De Casibus bk. iii see the introduction to this poem ; and for the text of Laurent's transla-tion of Boccacio at this point see the note to FaPrinces C 92.

151. Read with comma after *Joye.*

155. *vse a maner to reste on ther wey.* Laurent has "ont de coustume de soy arrester".

157. *alleggen ther wery lemys.* Laurent has "aleger le corps".

160-1. *somme . . . vsen to gadren wyne.* Can this be a misunderstanding of Laurent's "prendre le vent fres et souef"? Is *vent* taken as *vin*? The next clause, in both Laurent and Lydgate, treats of water and wine-drinking.

159. *asswage.* This is the earliest NED case of this word in this sense, Lydgate being treated as the author. He uses it frequently in the Troy Book and the FaPrinces.

160. *how myche they hd passyd.* Laurent has "combien ils ont fait"; the FaPrinces iii :112 has "whiche thei ha passyd". The French continues "apres ce quilz ont tourne le dos a aucun notable seteys dont ils se sont partis". The passage is loosely and verbosely rendered in the FaPrinces, but Lydgate seems to understand the French, which this writer does not follow.

165. *entytlen hem,* make notes on, keep a journal. This seems a reflexive use, but is not so recognized by the NED. See a non-reflexive use in FaPrinces ix :1885, and a half-score of cases in Lydgate's Secrees, also non-reflexive.

167. Lydgate in the FaPrinces omits rivers and sea from his list.

184-5. *The holy legende of Martyrs of Cupydo.* The Legend of Good Women, so called in the Man of Law's prologue, includes women only. The author says that after noting the fidelity of Troilus, the truth of Penelope, the purity of Polyxena, the generous trust of Dido, he often read this holy legend, also the story of Tristram and Isolde, and the meagre rewards of Palamides. In Lydgate's Black Knight 330, Palamides the unsuccessful lover of Isolde is mentioned, and two stanzas given to him. Tristram is one name of a list, *ibid.*, 366. Tristram and Isolde are mentioned in Lydgate's Temple of Glass 77-79, in the PoFoules 290, in the Confessio vi:471, viii: 2500.

The notion of "martyrs of Cupid" was general. Charles of Orléans, ed. d'Héricault i:24, says that he ought to be called martyr, "Se Dieu d'Amours fait nulz amoureux saints"; and Villon in his Petit Testament 47-8 said "ie suis amant martir, Du nombre des amoureux sains."

CHARLES D'ORLÉANS

A. POEMS WRITTEN IN ENGLISH

Of these eleven poems, ten are rondeaux and one (IX) is written in stanza. The rondel or rondeau, a favorite French courtly verse-form, is a short poem of unequally tripartite structure, which repeats its opening line or lines in two other positions in the poem, one being at close. See note on Mass 57.

The first two of these poems appear together on one page of the "autograph" MS, a page which according to Champion is in the hand of Charles himself. Hence the use of the Northern rune þ in I:9, II:1, 4, 9, is noteworthy when compared with the Grenoble MS' *your* instead of *þy* in II:1, 4 (I cite from Champollion-Figeac's edition, not from the MS, unseen by me.) The Grenoble scribe, or his editor, also expanded final *e*-flourishes to *er* in some cases, but in yet more cases rendered it as *-ing*. Those English texts are otherwise defaced by a great number of misunderstandings and miswritings, some of which are emended by MacCracken, who however leaves standing the *cryst* of I:5, the *tho fy* of II:11.

I

Printed by Champollion-Figeac, p. 269, from the Grenoble MS; reprinted by Sauerstein, pp. 65-6, by MacCracken, PMLA 26:177. It was printed from a Bibl.Nat.MS by Mlle. de Keralio, and reprinted from her by Walpole, as cited p. 216 here. Keralio's principal differences from the present text are: *thys message* (1), *plesant* (2), *in leed* (3), *all yat* (9), and in line 4 *clenching* instead of *lettyng*. She reads *this viage* in line 11.

MacCracken emends *of tymys* (11) to *ofttym y;* but the line as here has both sense and syntax, agreeing with the construction of line 10. MacCracken retains the (Grenoble) *folywing* of 12, though removing an excrescent *-ing* from earlier lines.

For the theme of the poem cp. d'Héricault's ed. of Charles, i:37, 39, 59; all of these exist in English translation, see the Roxburghe Club print of Brit. Mus. Harley 682, pp. 38, 44, 66. The French of the last-mentioned opens "Mon cueur est devenu hermite En l'ermitage de Pensée." Cp. lines 9, 10 here.

II

Printed by Champollion-Figeac, pp. 269-70; repr. by Bullrich, by MacCracken, *loc. cit.*, 177-8. It was printed by Mlle. de Keralio and repr. from her by Walpole, as above p. 216 Keralio's variants are *thows* (1, 2, 9 etc.), *hope y viage* (1), *of my message* (4); she omits *is* (12), writes *yat y* in 9, and renders 5 as "Us hat that had letting of thy passage". This is obviously a misreading of *W* to *Us*. Neither the Grenoble nor this MS writes the *W;* MacCracken emends to *Wher that hyt be* etc.

The Grenoble MS otherwise abounds in errors. The word *taryd* is each time written *carydge; blake* (12) is written *clake; nay* (10) is written *way;* and line 11, soundly preserved in de Keralio's text, is given as "And tho fy syngling et dauns or lagh and play". MacCracken leaves *tho fy* unrectified; *thof* is however a by-form of *though*, see no. xix below. In line 9 Grenoble omits the initial *T* of *Thow;* MacCracken emends to *Who*.

For the theme of the poem cp. d'Héricault's ed. of Charles, ii:22, 54. Neither of these poems is translated in MS Harley 682.

III

Printed in Champollion-Figeac's ed. of Charles, p. 265; repr. by MacCracken, *loc. cit.*, pp. 174-5.

The use of the rune in line 1, and in the next poem lines 4, 10, 11, should be noted with Champion's statement, *op. cit.,* p. 47, that pp. 299-314 of the "autograph" MS are the work of an English scribe. If this be so, the writing of *guippe* for *keep* in IV A 6 is peculiar.

IV A

Printed by Champollion-Figeac, p. 266; repr. by MacCracken, *loc. cit.,* p. 175.

The reading *guippe* for *keep* in line 6 is apparently an ear-error, as is *do wel* for *dwel* in line 10. Both appear also in the Grenoble MS printed by Champollion.

IV B

Printed by Ellis, Specimens of Early Engl. Poets, i:253; in the London Magazine for 1823, pp. 301-6; printed by Costello, Specimens of the Early Poetry of France, 1835, p. 138; printed by Sauerstein, p. 64.

In this Royal text the roundel-form is muddled, lines 4 and 5 run together. The word *kepe* (5) appears in its proper form; line 7 has undergone miswritings which are eye-errors, *I must* being rendered *Iniust,* and *hertles* as *helis.* If the archetype indicated the *er* of *hertles* by the usual flourish, this latter error would be easy.

V

Printed by Champollion-Figeac, pp. 266-7; repr. MacCracken, *loc. cit.,* pp. 175-6.

The French editor has *tvewe* in line 2, *serve* instead of *sume* in line 6, and *Thousches* at opening of line 8.

The poem is clumsily expressed, but apparently says that after a half-year of waiting and a time of endured disdain, an embrace is a jewel full dear: but that the lover must be on the alert against a ?jealous guardian. The phrase *fore against,* line 11, is first cited by NED from the year 1494, with the meaning "directly opposite, facing".

The rune again appears, line 11.

VI

Printed by Champollion-Figeac, pp. 266-7; repr. MacCracken *loc. cit.,* pp. 175-6.

This roundel contains in its line-initials the name *Anne Molins,* a fact pointed out by me in ModPhil 22:215. In Romania 49:580 ff., M. Pierre Champion published an interesting passage from King Réné's Cuer d'Amours Espris (cited above p. 220), which says that Charles learned English while a prisoner, from a lady to whom he paid court and addressed poems. As the duke undoubtedly had social intercourse with his various English gaolers, he may well have met a daughter of the house of Molyneux; she may have been in the train of a greater lady, just as the damsels to whom Skelton addresses the lyrics of his Garland of Laurell were associated with the countess of Surrey. The family of Molyneux or Moleyns was an ancient and dignified house; its most conspicuous figure was Adam de Moleyns, bishop of Chichester and keeper of the Privy Seal, who died in 1450. His connections with French affairs were many, and he was more than once associated in diplomatic business with the earl of Suffolk, who was for four years Charles' guardian. De Moleyns was of the Lancashire branch of the family; his sister Katharine was duchess of Norfolk; of another sister, Anne, nothing is recorded; his brother's daughter Anne became the wife of Sir Richard Nevil.

Champollion-Figeac prints *let have have* in line 6, *a vende* in line 8; MacCracken emends to *let hym have,—an ende.* The latter phrase may however mean "a turning". The French editor has line 10 as here; MacCracken omits *not.* In line 11, the word *hys* is perhaps the verb *hies,* "hastens"?

VII

Printed by Champollion-Figeac, p. 267-8, repr. by MacCracken, *loc. cit.,* p. 176.

The French editor writes *puyd* for *payd* in line 1, *nuans* for *auans* in line 3, *fraichyedness* in line 4, *Ye go* for *Ys go* in line 10.

VIII

Printed by Champollion-Figeac, pp. 267-8, repr. by MacCracken, *loc. cit.,* pp. 176-7.

IX

Printed by Champollion-Figeac, pp. 268-9; printed by MacCracken, *loc. cit.,* pp. 160-61, from the MS Bodl. Fairfax 16 fol. 321, where the stanzas form one of a group of English amatory poems, for which MacCracken suggests the earl of Suffolk as author. On this hypothesis, the poem would have been preserved in Charles' "album" as so many other poems by his fellow-versifiers were preserved. And it is to be noted that its form and flow differ sharply from those of Charles' rondeaux here printed.

The "autograph" and the Grenoble MSS agree in some textual differences from the Fairfax copy. They read *to se fro* in line 2, where Fairfax reads *to and fro;* they read *Me thyng* in line 8, where Fairfax reads *Me thynk;* they read *wehout* in line 10, where Fairfax reads *wythout;* they read *makyth alwey* in line 18, where Fairfax reads *makyth now;* they write *sykyrvenes, sykyrnenes* in line 20, where Fairfax writes *sykernes.*

In line 16 Fairfax has no *the;* in line 19 it writes *wost.* The French editor's text shows *worst* in line 19, omits *I* from line 5, and has other divergences.

X

Printed by Ellis i:253; in the London Magazine and in Costello as under IV B above. Printed by Champollion-Figeac, p. 455, repr. by Bullrich, *op. cit.* Printed by MacCracken, *loc. cit.,* p. 178; printed by Sauerstein, p. 65.

XI

Printed as is no. X, omitting Costello.

Ellis suggested *Be ware* in line 1 instead of *Ne were,* an emendation incorporated into the London Magazine text. The *com smert* of line 5 is possibly *con* (can) *smert;* for *And* in line 8, read *An,* i.e., *If.*

B. TRANSLATIONS FROM CHARLES' FRENCH

XII

Printed in the Roxburghe Club ed. of these translations, pp. 36-7.

1. *As mot,* etc. The use of *as* with the imperative to express a wish is very frequent in Middle English. Cp. KnTale 1444, MillTale 591, MLTale 761, Troilus ii:1025, etc.

11. *wrappid & wounde.* See ClTale 527, PoFoules 670-71.

18. *hir hit mevyng,* urging on her the fact that, etc.

24. *To,* i. e., Till.

26. *Of which,* i. e., "From whom".

29-30. *lennuy* is omitted in transl. Supply *al?*

With the poem cp. Pope's Epistle of Eloisa to Abelard, lines 51 ff.

XIII

Printed in the Roxburghe Club edition, pp. 62-3.

5. *Whi dost thou straunge,* "Why art thou distant, aloof"? See Chaucer, PoFoules 584, Troilus ii:1660, Skelton's Garland 444, etc.

8. The scribe has marked *ben* for erasure and put *leve* in the margin.

10. *ynough* is pronounced to rime with *how,* i.e., as *enow.* This *w*-form is the old plural of the word, an archaism in Modern English.

15. *to iape not lustith me,* "it is not my intention to jest".

19. *as hast,* i.e., thus hast. See xv:15 below.

22. The second *on* is written over an erasure.

28. *ffor werry* may be understood as a single word, the verb *forweary,* to become exhausted. "They may (*mowe*) grow weary in the lady's company in no respect." Or, *for* may be the conjunction. The use of *lo* as a line-filler is very frequent in this translator;

note Chaucer's Troilus i:397, 845, ii:255, 1433, 1633, 1743, iii:1341, iv:284, 1231, 1319, v:54, 127, 461, 704, 1828.

XIV

Printed in the Roxburghe Club edition, pp. 74-5. Printed in Park's 1806 ed. of Walpole (see p. 217 here) i:184-85.

The -ir and -ay rimes of the French are retained as -er and -ay, -ey.

4. *at wode,* to the wood. *geder may,* gather the appropriate Mayday green branches or flowers. See Knight's Tale 654.

7. *Right as the wood,* etc. See Chaucer's PoFoules 493, Lydgate's Black Knight 46.

8. *first day of may.* See note on xvii below.

13. *affoyle.* Neither the NED, Godefroy, nor Cotgrave gives this word. The sense of "beleave", i e. to adorn with leaves, lies very near, cp. *foille, fueille,* leaf. Cotgrave has the substantive *foyle* as the setting of precious stones, the mounting of a mirror, etc.:—our word *foil.* In such latter case, this word might be a coinage for metre, such as *apast* in xvi:9, a word used also in the romances.—*trees.* Scanned disyllabic? Cp. PoFoules 173, Prol. CT 607.

15. Note the French, and the position of *to* after its case; see xix:20 below.

17. *on whi.* Read *and whi?*

19. Here *absent* is probably a transitive verb; "doth remove, keep away, thy lady from thee".

20. *That,* i. e., *who,* refers to *thee,* to the lover.

XV

Printed in the Roxburghe Club edition pp. 87-88.

With this outcry against Death cp. Chaucer's BoDuchesse 475-83; see Floris and Blanchefleur 281 ff.; see Machaut's motet printed by Chichmaref ii:487; see Villon's rondeau "Mort, iappelle de ta rigueur", in von Wurzbach's edition, p. 100; see Pugliese's "Morte, perche m'ai fatte si gran guerra", in Butler's Forerunners of Dante or in Monaci, p. 92. The ring of the Floris and Blanchefleur bit is much nearer Boethius (see lines A 277-80 of Walton) than is this purely court-poem. Note the treatment of the French rime-sounds.

11. *fflowryng in youthe.* A stock phrase. See Lydgate's St. Margaret 439; and for similar phrase "Flouryng in vertu" see *ibid.,* 96, FaPrinces iii:3165, etc.; the phrase "flouryng age" occurs often in this period.

14. *Had* is altered from *hadest,* and after *taken* a word is erased, apparently *yet. vnweldynes* is the inactivity of age. Gower in the Confessio vii:1855 uses *unwelde* as the opposite of *deliver;* Lydgate, FaPrinces i:2259, uses *weeldi* as equivalent to *deliver,* "active". For the phrase "vnweldy croked age" see Scogan's Moral Balade line 145, in Skeat vii:242; see Lydgate's FaPrinces i:1686, 2127, iii:5117, etc.; and cp. Romaunt of the Rose 4886, etc.

15. *As had,* i.e. "So had". See above, xiii:19.

16. *take* shows an erased *n.*

17. *this* is written over an erasure.

19. *Alone . . . wtout compane.* The phrase "seul sans compaignie" occurs also in Orléans' twelfth ballade, see ed. by d'Héricault i:26. Machaut, in his Dit dou Lyon 182, speaks of walking "Par le vergier sans compaignie"; Christine de Pisan in her poem Seulete, ed. SATF i:12, has as line 3, "Seulete suy, sanz compaignon ne maistre". The phrase "seus sans compaignie" appears in Venus la Déesse, quatrain 229, (see ed. Foerster, Bonn, 1880). Cp. Bartsch's Chrestomathy of Old French, 11th ed., pp. 146, 151, 231, 262. Dante, Inferno 23:1, says that he and Virgil were "soli e senza compagnia"; cp. his Vita Nuova, section 12, line 6 of its ballata. Petrarch, In Vita 135, line 6 (canzone 18), describes "un augel . . . sol, senza consorte"; cp. *ibid.* 106, line 4. Chaucer uses the phrase three times, KnTale 1921, MillTale 18, Melibeus 2749-50. In Gower's Confessio iii:1220 we find "Solein withoute compaignie" applied to Diogenes. The Old Eng. Dream of the Rood 123-4 has "þaer ic ana waes Maete werode". Hawes employs the phrase in his Pastime 1938, (p. 78 of the Percy Soc. edition).

Here and in line 25 the *wi* of *without* has been erased.
25. *in* is inserted above the line.
30. The *is* of *offensis* has been erased.

XVI

Printed in the Roxburghe Club edition, pp. 94-5.
With the opening cp. Shakespeare's sonnet xxx.
1. The Paris MS of the French reads *souuenir* instead of *souuent*.
2. This MS very frequently writes *tayne* for *twayne*, as here. See the repetition in line 7, and cp. "hir goodely eyen twoo" of Lydgate's New Year poem, pr. Anglia 32:190 ff., line 46.
3. *myn hert.* Read *hertis*, but note the French.
8. Note the padding *but even* for rhythm, and cp. *O welaway* of line 6 for rime.
11. The English omits Yseult and adds Dido and Alceste, probably with reminiscence of Chaucer.
17. Death is feminine in the French, where line 19 ends "s'elle pouoit". Notice the skilful amplification of the English in this stanza, but the twist of "Hors du monde" to another purpose.
27. "unless it should improve"? "even though it should improve"?

XVII

Printed in the Roxburghe Club edition, pp. 99-100.
1. *The secund day*, etc. The three opening days of May were those of the festival. It is on "Mayes day the thridde" that Pandarus feels love's pain, Troilus ii:56. The Cuckoo and Nightingale is timed on "the thridde night of may", line 55. In Octovien de St. Gelais' Séjour d'Honneur the hero embarks with Sensuality on his voyage on May 2. Orléans has a French ballade beginning "Le premier jour du mois de May"; transl. also into English, see Roxburghe Club edition, p. 97.
2. *half . . . half.* The French does not say this, but that the lover was asleep. In the rondeau by Orléans, printed d'Héricault ii:98, is the phrase "moitié veillant". This was a medieval formula; see the opening line of La Belle Dame; see Lydgate's PilgrLifeMan 222. Perhaps cp. the phrase "neither living nor dead" from Alanus down to Shelley, e. g. De Planctu Naturae prose 3, Dante's Inferno 34:25, Chaucer's Troilus iii:79, Gower's Confessio i:289, Shelley's Epipsychidion 309.
4-8. Here is mentioned the strife of Flower and Leaf; see p. 259 here.—*lo* is again used to fill out the line.
12. "In my clumsy fashion", etc. Note the French.
15-16. "But the fortune of such choice hath made me this year *he* who is to serve the Leaf." Note the case of *he*; and read *yere* instead of *heyre*,—French "cest an". Is it likely that the author of this translation himself would have written *heyre*?
22. *what part y am*, wherever I am.

XVIII

Printed in the Roxburghe Club edition, pp. 105-6. Translated in the London Magazine for Sept. 1823, pp. 301-6.
1. *noyous.* The translation is closer to the Paris than to the Royal text of the French. Cp. xvi:1, and the refrain line of xix.
3. *I mette.* Mark the difference from *Me mette* in xvii:3.
6. *al be me loth*, "although it displeases me". Changed from the French for the sake of rime. Cp. BoDuchesse 8, Legend 1639, etc.
15. *thee see*, "to see thee".
23. *to*, i.e. *till.—did hir day*, caused her to die.
27 is added to the French. With the picture cp. PardTale 400 ff.

XIX

Printed in the Roxburghe Club edition, pp. 107-9.

Observe in this poem the rime of *thought* with *aloft*, etc. See the romance of **Eger** and Grine 261-2, Sir Isumbras 222-3, 445-6, Perceval de Galles 161-3. In the prol. to Shakespeare's Winter's Tale, act. iv, *daughter* and *after* are rimed; in Chamberlayne's Pharonnida, of 1659, such rimes as *thought: soft* occur. See the writing *thof* for *though* in ii:11 here; other cases in the Roxburghe ed. are on pp. 30, 55, 64, 75, 180, 198, 207, 221.

1, 2. Cp. the Squire's Tale 663, followed by Lydgate's Troy Book i:626 and by the Flower and Leaf at opening; see Skelton's Garland 1436, and the Serpent of Division, ed. MacCracken, p. 55,—"When þe same golden wayne of Titan . . . is whirlid vp", etc.—*day of seynt valentyn* is accusative of specification,—"on the day".

6. *He wook* is confusing. Read *Awook?* See BoDuchesse 1324.

8, 16, 24, 28. The text is nearer the Paris than the Royal version. See xvi:1, xviii:1.

11. *pletid ther latyn*, pleaded in their speech. See PoFoules 495, SqTale 427,—both bird-passages. The word *latyn* or *leden* had come to mean "speech".

13. *wrappe . . . soft*. See the PoFoules 670.

14. This does not render line 12 of the French, which is very close to Chaucer's PoFoules 491, "The noyse of foules forto ben delivred".

20. *These birdis to,* to these birds. See xiv:15.

27. *this comfort sole,* "without this comfort". French *desgarny,* etc.

XX

Printed in the Roxburghe Club edition, p. 159. This is an especially successfuf translation.

4. *to lessen wt.* Cp. Thebes 35, Bycorne 91, and notes, for this word-order.

XXI

Printed in the Roxburghe Club edition, p. 146. This poem is one of the four printed from Hearne's Diaries (1712) in Anglia 17:445-7, and by Bliss as on p. 218 here.

5. *to geef,* Old Eng. *to giefe,* "dirt cheap". The sense is "is underrated, held cheap". Note the retention of this early native idiom, and also a coinage like *affoyle,* xiv:13 *ante.*

8. *my deth . . . shert.* See the Knight's Tale, Troilus iii:733, Lydgate's BlKnight 489, Partonope of Blois 109, etc.; also Wyatt in the poem beginning "Alas the greiff".

15. *y kepe,* etc. "I have no desire to escape from death."

XXII

Printed in the Roxburghe Club edition, p. 151. Translated by Costello as p. 219 here.

4. Inversion for rime's sake.

5. *but ye lust,* etc. "unless you desire to give".

XXIII

Printed in the Roxburghe Club edition, p. 167.

5. *ne slepen y.* This seems an early case of the incorrect use of *-n* in the verb-singular, as it was later abused by, e.g., Urry in his 1721 ed. of Chaucer. See *I ben* in xiii:8 *ante*; and see "the greef y han" on p. 61 of the Roxburghe print, in rime; and see the 1840 ed. of **Guy** of Warwick, p. 297,—"He seemed as it weren a fend þat comen weren out of helle".

HARDYNG'S CHRONICLE

THE BATTLE OF AGINCOURT

The MS, Brit. Mus, Lansdowne 204, has many marginal summaries to chapters and stanzas. Beside stanza 1 is: "The vij Book *primum* Ca*pitulum.* Henry the fyfte kynge of Englonde & ffraunce and lorde of Irelonde duke of Normandy Guyen & of Aungevy." In the right hand margin is: "No*ta* q*uo*d Cronica istius Regis Henrici patet in quadam cronica

Magistri Norham doctoris Theolo*giae* & *secundum* quod compilator hui*us* libri vidit & audiuit."
There are English summaries beside stanzas 2, 5, 6, 7, 8, etc.

2. *seynt Cuthbert day*, March 20. Hardyng is inaccurate. Henry IV died on March 20,
1413, and Henry V was crowned on Passion Sunday, April 9, in a heavy snowstorm. This
error was amended by Hardyng in later versions of the Chronicle; cp. the text of this
stanza in the Grafton-Ellis ed. of 1812:—

> Henry his sonne that prynce of Wales was than
> On Saynt Cuthbertes day in March folowynge
> Kyng was, so as I remembre canne:
> On Passyon Sonday after was this kyng
> Anoynted and crowned without taryeng,
> The ninth daye it was of April so
> With stormes fell and haylestones greate also.

6. *obeyand*. The participle here shows the Northern ending, as does *fleand* in 70.

8. *Cobham Errytyke,* Cobham the heretic. Sir John Oldcastle, Lord Cobham, was an
earnest disciple of Wyclif. His activity in supporting and disseminating Lollard doctrines
brought down on him the wrath of the Church, and after the passing of Henry V's statutes
against heresy not all Oldcastle's distinguished military record nor his personal friendship
with Henry could save him. He was cited before the Bishops, examined, and adjudged a
heretic. He was committed to the Tower, but escaped, and was at large for four years,
when he was captured, brought to London, and hanged and burned in 1417. The orthodox
Hoccleve has a poem of pious denunciations against Cobham, printed EETS ed. i:8; and the
Liber Metricus of Elmham, printed in the Memorials of Henry V, Rolls Series 1858, is
equally fierce. Later Oldcastle became a sort of half-mythical figure; from Shakespeare's
(first) Henry Fourth i, scene 2:48 it may be inferred that there was an early play in which
he figured. His "Examination" may be read in Arber's Engl.Garner, vol. vi. See Tennyson's poem on Oldcastle.

9. *lollers*, Lollards. See Skeat's note on CantTales B 1173.—*incipient*. The Grafton-
Ellis text reads *insapient*, "foolish".

11. *it haue*, "it to have".

12. *suppowelment*, aid, support. The word *suppowaile, sowponaile*, is frequent in this
sense in Lydgate. See, e.g.,Thebes 267, "As his Pyler & his sowpowayle", or FaPrinces iv:39,
"And registreer to suppowaile trouthe". See Dance 663.

13. *toke them vp*. The sense of "capture, arrest" for this phrase is more modern. It
may mean "overtook", i.e., after pursuit. Grafton-Ellis has a different line.

24. What ground Hardyng had for the statement that Oldcastle was recaptured within
an hour of his escape from the Tower is not clear. There was some mystery about the
means of his escape. Redman,—see the Memorials of Henry V above cited—says that he was
either helped by his friends or bribed his guards, and fled into Wales, where "ad breve et
perexiguum tempus permansit". This remark as to the length of Oldcastle's stay in Wales
Hardyng may have misinterpreted to refer to the period of his freedom, which was, however, as said, four years.

26. *by all the Clergy sight*, i.e. in all the clergy's sight, or opinion?

34. *Rychard Scrope*. Richard le Scrope, Archbishop of York, was executed for treason in
1405 by Henry the Fourth. He was buried in York Minster, and the men of his county
elevated their fallen leader to the rank of martyr. Miracles were said to be wrought at his
tomb, and although the Church never canonized him, he was known in the North of England
as St. Richard Scrope. His nephew Henry le Scrope was implicated in the Earl of Cambridge's conspiracy against Henry V, and was summarily executed in 1415, on the eve of
Henry's departure for France.

36. *Kynge Rycharde,* etc. Richard II of England, deposed by Henry of Lancaster,
afterward Henry the Fourth, was probably murdered while a prisoner in Pontefract Castle,
Yorkshire, a few months after his deposition. The popular pity and interest for him were
so great that Henry IV surrounded his death and burial with secrecy, and interred him in a

church at Kings Langley, near Windsor, instead of in the tomb Richard had built for himself and his first wife Anne of Bohemia in Westminster Abbey. But Henry V removed Richard's body to its proper place in the Abbey tomb.

45. *laycestr,* Leicester, where the Parliament of 1414 was held.

46. Thomas duke of Clarence, third son of Henry the Fourth, fell in the French war in 1421, a year before the king's death.

47. John duke of Bedford, Henry V's next brother, was the most able and highminded of the brothers; he carried on the French war after Henry's death.

50. *Vmfray.* Humphrey duke of Gloucester, Henry the Fourth's youngest son. See the notes on him as listed in the Glossary.

52. *Bewford.* This is Thomas Beaufort, one of the children of John of Gaunt, duke of Lancaster, by his mistress Katherine Swynford, whom Gaunt ultimately married as his third wife. Her children, all born previously, were legitimised by Richard II, but barred from succession to the crown. This uncle of Henry V was made duke of Exeter by the king; another uncle, the Cardinal Bishop of Winchester, was a man of great wealth, who after Henry's death struggled with Humphrey of Gloucester for control of the infant king and the national affairs.

55-56. Henry Percy, "Hotspur", eldest son of the earl of Northumberland, fell at Shrewsbury fighting against Henry IV, and according to Shakespeare died by the hand of "Prince Hal" himself. As the father also had conspired against the House of Lancaster, the Percy name was attainted and the estates reverted to the crown; but in 1414 Henry V restored the family honors to Hotspur's son, another Henry Percy. It is this restoration which Hardyng mentions.

Whenever an English noble holding fief direct from the Crown succeeded to title and estates, it was necessary for him to "sue out" or present his claim, do formal homage, and receive his inheritance from his feudal lord. It was the traversing of such established right by Richard II, who seized the Lancastrian estates on John of Gaunt's death, which brought Henry of Lancaster (afterwards Henry IV) back from temporary banishment to insist upon his claim; and the dispute led directly to Richard's fall.

57. *Mawdelayne day,* St. Mary Magdalen's day, July 22.

58-63. This muddled statement seems to be that Sir Robert Umfraville (Hardyng's patron), entrusted with an expedition against the Scots, took full control of it, and directed the nominal guide whither he should lead the party,—from which expedition he, Umfraville, derived great credit. In line 61 *toke hym to* has the force of "betook him to", i.e., addressed himself to.

64. *thaym,* i.e., the Scots. "Greterigge" is rendered "Geteryng" in the Grafton-Ellis text.

70. *toke thaym vp,* overtook them. See note on line 13 above.—*fleand,* see line 6.

71. *lammesse.* "Lammas" is celebrated on August 1. The word is derived from O. E. *hlaf,* a loaf, and *maesse,* mass, and denotes the harvest festival, at which bread was made from the first ripe corn.

72. *hampton.* Southampton, whence the French expedition sailed under Henry V to the conquest of Normandy. Here was settled the fate of the Earl of Cambridge, Henry Lord Scrope, etc., whose conspiracy against the king was discovered on the eve of departure. See note on line 34 above.

78. *harflete,* Harfleur in Normandy. Henry laid siege to this town the middle of August 1415, and it surrendered on Sept 22. See the first poem on Agincourt mentioned at close of introd. *ante.*

85. *Orlience.* The duke of Orléans whose capture at Agincourt is here mentioned is the poet-prince Charles of Orléans, translations of whose verse are included in the present volume.

86. *Burboyne.* This is Jean de Bourbon, born 1381, who remained in captivity in England for 18 years, and died there in 1434, after paying a ransom of 300,000 crowns three times over to no avail. It is asserted by French writers that Henry V on his deathbed charged his brother to keep Bourbon and Orléans prisoners at all costs until the establishment of Henry VI upon the throne of France.

87. *wendome,* Louis de Bourbon, count of Vendôme.

88. *sir Arthur of Bretayne.* Arthur duke de Richemont, afterward duke of Brittany, prisoner in England until 1420.—Line 89 is missing from this MS, but has been recognized in the numbering. The Grafton-Ellis text is at this point quite different; it condenses the material of stanzas 13 and 14 into one strophe, and does not use the second half of stanza 14 as here. A mention of Boucicault marshal of France as an eminent prisoner is perhaps the content of the line here missing.

92-93. The French dukes of Bâr, Alençon, and Lorraine, slain at Agincourt, are now named.

97. *layde . . . to wedde,* pledged. O. E. *wedde,* a pledge or forfeit.

99. Edward second duke of York, who commanded the van at Agincourt, was the eldest son of Edmund the first duke, son of Edward III.

104-5. Hardyng's figures here and in line 97 are not in accord with scholarly investigation and estimate. The English army may have numbered 15,000 men; the French was, according to Ramsay's Lancaster and York, "certainly three times as numerous", perhaps of 50,000 men. Monstrelet, the French chronicler, gives the French loss at 10,000, and English writers state theirs to have been from 14 men to 1,600 men.

106. *Crispin and Crispinian day,* October 25.

111. *smored,* smothered. Rendered "smouldered to death" in Leland's Itinerary i:4-5.

118. *Thurgh Pykardy* etc. From inland Normandy a force marching to English-held Calais would cross Picardy, and pass Guines.

121. *Sygismounde.* The emperor Sigismund, also king of Hungary and of Bohemia and brother to Anne of Bohemia wife of Richard II, is degraded in modern estimation by his betrayal of the reformer John Huss, who came to the Council of Constance (1414) trusting in the imperial safe-conduct. Sigismund later visited France and England; he was in France in March 1416, and arrived in England May first. His visit, which lasted until latter August, was elaborately celebrated, and left many echoes in fifteenth-century writings; see for instance the Libel of English Policy, printed here, lines 8 ff. Henry V made Sigismund a knight of the Garter, as Hardyng says; on that occasion the emperor presented the head of St. George to the Order, and Ramsay, in his Lancaster and York i:234 note, cites to show that the relic was preserved until Henry VIII's time.

123. *the Garter.* The Order of the Garter was established by Edward III in 1349, five years after Philip of Burgundy's establishment of the Order of the Golden Fleece. It was founded on St. George's day, April 23, and its patrons were the Holy Trinity, the Virgin, St. Edward the Confessor, and St. George. As the last-named was patron saint of England, he was often considered especial patron of the Order, which was thus sometimes called the "Order of St. George". As originally constituted, it was made up of twenty-five Knights Companions and the Sovereign; each had a stall in St. George's Chapel, Windsor, where the annual assembly was held. The Order was reorganized and enlarged in 1831.

LONDON LICKPENNY

1, 2. In the latter "amended" version of Harley 367, these lines read:—"To london once my stepps I bent Where trouth in no wyse should be feynt".

12, 25, 33. Upon these three Courts of Law see Stow's Survey of London, ed. Kingsford, ii:118. They were all in Westminster Hall. "At the entry on the right hand the common place [i. e. Common Pleas], where ciuill matters are to be pleaded, especially such as touch lands or contracts; at the vpper end of the Hall, on the right hand or Southest corner, the king's bench, where pleas of the Crowne haue their hearing; and on the left hand or Southwest corner sitteth the Lord Chancellor, accompanied with the master of the Rowles and other men . . . called maisters of the Chauncerie." This last-named court handled all cases relating to revenue, and the King's Bench and Common Pleas, as Stow says, took cognizance respectively of trespasses against the King's peace and of disputes between private persons.

20. The clerk apparently calls the names of the parties concerned in the next action. See lines 155-59 of the Satire on the Consistory Courts, printed by Böddeker in his Altengl. Dichtung, p. 107; see the 14th Coventry Play.

26. The silken hood was worn by sergeants; only a sergeant could plead in the Court of Common Pleas. See note on 31.

31. *momme of his mouthe.* Here cp. Piers Plowman (B) prol. 210-15:—"ʒit houed there an hondreth in houues of selke Seriauntz it semed that serueden atte barre Plededen for penyes and poundes the lawe. And nouʒt for loue of owre lorde vnlese here lippes onis. Thow myʒtest better mete the myste on Maluerne hulles Than gete a momme of here mouthe but money were shewed".

35. *qui tollis.* This line and its companion are rewritten in the later version of the poem. The Latin phrase, evidently a legal formula, may be the summons to complainants to stand forth, i.e. "Thou who hast a grievance, present it".

42. *gowne of ray.* Ray, a striped cloth, was much worn by lawyers; see Assembly of Gods 550 for Minos in his "roob of ray".

51. *flemings grete woon,* a great crowd of Flemings. Both felt hats and spectacles, offered for sale by the Flemish traders so numerous in London at this time, are appropriate merchandise for a country which specialized in cloth-making and was the first in Europe to develop the art of lens-grinding.

54. *spectacles.* Spectacles had not long been in use in England. Hoccleve in his poem to Oldcastle, line 417, describes them, and in his poem to the Duke of York he says that his own vanity prevents his use of them. Bokenam, in his St. Margaret, lines 657-8, says that his eyes "bleynte shuld be, ner helpe of a spectacle". And Lydgate, FaPrinces ix:3335, describes his "eyen mystyd and dirked my spectacle". Flemish fifteenth century tapestries and paintings show spectacles in use, e. g. by St. Peter in a large tapestry hanging in the Museum of Fine Arts, Boston.

58. *at high prime.* Nine o'clock in the morning; see Skeat's note on Piers Plowman (C) ix:119. Laborers and artisans then took the first hearty meal of the working day, which began very early. See Chaucer's Troilus ii:1557.

59. *Cokes,* etc. The vendor-calls of cooks and taverners are mentioned in Piers Plowman prol. 225-9. See Hoccleve's Mâle Règle 57 for cooks at Westminster Gate, and 89 below for others near Billingsgate, on the river.

65. *In to London.* In the fifteenth century Westminster and the City of London were separated by the "Liberties", a district partly open and partly occupied by the walled residences of nobles, the buildings of the Temple, etc. Our countryman crossed Long Ditch after leaving Westminster Hall by the Gate, walked by White Hall along the Strand, entered the City through Ludgate, and passed along Fleet Street to St. Paul's and the west end of Cheapside.

67 ff. This poem contains some of the earliest records of London street cries. Later they attracted the attention of musicians, and in the seventeenth century combinations of them, known as "fancies", were arranged. On them see Bridge, Old Cryes of London, 1921; *ibid.,* pp. 36-39, is such a compilation, repr. from the Roxburghe Ballads vii:57.—*in the ryse,* on the twig or branch.

76. *vmple.* Fine gauze or lawn; see the Assembly of Ladies 471, in Skeat's Chaucer, vol. vii. This word is removed in the Harley 367 remodeling of our poem.

77. *could no skyle,* had no knowledge.

81. *London Stone.* Stow in his Survey, i:224-5, gives various theories as to the purpose served by this stone. The antiquary Camden first suggested, says Kingsford, that it was a Roman "milliarium", or central stone from which distances were measured along the great roads to the north and west. In Stow's day the stone was very large, was near the middle of Candlewick (now Cannon) Street, and was supported by iron bands. What remained of it was in 1798 built into the wall of St. Swithin's Church near by.

The streets traversed by the author are West Cheap (Cheapside today) and its eastward continuation Cornhill; Candlewick or Canwick Street and its continuation Eastcheap run east and west nearer the river. He seems to have wandered back to Cornhill after being in Eastcheap, and then to have turned south down to the Thames at Billingsgate, just beyond London Bridge. Lacking his two pence for the ferry, he may have crossed the bridge into Southwark, and so got back to Kent and his plow.

93. *ye by cokke,* etc. "Yea, by God". See the Manciple's prologue, the Parson's prol. 29, in the CantTales; see the Plowman's Tale 1271 in Skeat vii.

94. *Jenken and Julyan.* Evidently a song or songs by itinerant beggars. St. Julian was the patron saint of hospitality, but the poem does not read *St.* Julian.

100. *in westminstar.* These words are perhaps an explanatory gloss which has been worked into the text.

105. *the Taverner.* A wine-dealer. The MS writes *my* instead of *me.*

114. *wagge . . . gow hens.* The word *wagge* may be either verb or substantive. The verb means "begone" in Elizabethan writers; the subst. means "fellow". For *gow,* "go we", "let us go", cp. Troilus ii:615, 1163, v:402; see the first Digby Mystery, line 276.

118. "Do you think I will choose you as a subject for almsgiving?" The MS has made a correction of *my* to *no,* in which case we must put our question after *thow,* and treat the rest of the line as an assertion.

THE LIBEL OF ENGLISH POLICY

The MS here used, Brit. Mus. Harley 4011, is a paper volume containing various entries in both verse and prose, written partly by W. Grauell, who has executed the copy of our poem, and partly by W. Woodeward. It contains three short poems by Lydgate, the second and third being extracts from the Fall of Princes; Lydgate's Life of our Lady, etc.; a copy of the Mappula Anglie attributed to Bokenam, see EnglStud 10:1-40; etc.

2. *Off outward.* i. e., from outside.

4. The Cotton MS reads: "Ner say of sooth but it is one of the best". Laud is very similar; this MS is inferior in sense.

5. *Who sailethe.* A better reading is "as who seith", in the Laud MS. See line 115.

7. *narow See,* the English Channel.

8. Beside stanza 2 is the marginal rubric:—"Videns Imperator Sigismonde duas villas inter ceteras Anglis .d. Calisiam (et) Doveriam ponens suos duos digitos super suos duos oculos ait regi ffrater custodite istas suas villas sicut vestros oculos &c". For Sigismund's visit to England in 1416 see note on line 121 of Hardyng's Chronicle here.

9. *Whiche reigned.* The Laud MS reads "Whyche yet regneth"; Harley 271 and Harley 78 (fol. 35) read "Wiche late reyned"; the Cotton MS, "Of high Renowne". The difference in tense marks the earlier and the later recension, Laud's composition dating before the death of Sigismund in December 1437.

20. *sir.* Other MSS *sure,*—a better reading.

25. The Laud MS reads: "What marchaundy may forby be agoo". Our text gives the sense of "When commerce cannot go past, who can escape (business) misfortune?

34-35. In the margin the scribe has written:—"Quatuor considerantur in moneta aurea anglicana quod dicitur nobile S. Rex Navis Gladius et potestatem super mare. In quorum obprobrium hijs diebus britones minores & fflandrenses &c. dicunt Anglicis tollite de nobile vestro Navem & imponite ovem. Intendentes quare sicut quondam A tempore Edwardi tercij Anglici erant domini maris modo hijs diebus sunt vecordes victi & ad bellandi & mari conservandi velud oves & sicut sepissime patet eorum derisio &c."—*oure noble.* The gold coin called the noble bore a crowned male figure holding a sword and seated in a ship on the waves. See line 17 and note, of LettGlouc., here.

37. *set a shepe.* The increase of England's sheepfarming in this period was associated by her enemies with her decline in naval power. See Capgrave's De Illustribus Henricis, line 135:—"Cachinnant de nobis inimici et dicunt 'Tollite navem de pretiosa moneta et imprimite ovem'."

38. *our rule halteth,* our sovereignty is lame, loses strength.

39. "Who is bold enough to bid our government be on the alert"?

44. Warner notes that nobles similar to those of England were struck in Flanders, and were forbidden currency in England because of their lighter weight.

45. *as.* MS Laud reads *and.*

57. The "points" of a medieval gentleman's dress were a set of leather thongs upon the lower part of the doublet and the upper part of the hose or breeches; these had to be tied or "trussed" to support the hose. Point-making was a separate occupation, and required delicate leather.

60. *staple fayre.* See introd. to this text for note on the fairs of the Low Countries.

61. *To haue.* A better reading is *They have,* as in MS Laud.—*Scluse,* Sluys, the port of Bruges.

62. *the Swyn,* the small arm of the North Sea, called the Zwyn, where the modern canal of Bruges terminates. When this silted up, in the late fifteenth century, the commercial prosperity of Bruges waned.

74. *cloth of Ipre.* The clothmaking of Ypres and of Ghent is mentioned ProlCT 447.

75. *Curryk.* Laud 704 reads *Curtryke,* i. e., Cortoriacum, the Courtrai of modern Belgium, busy then as now in the weaving of linen and cotton.

79. Other MSS read "Ye wote ye make (it) of—"etc.

80-82 is a question. "Do you not get it through your head (that)" etc.

85. *the growndes twayn,* the two lands of Spain and Flanders.

91. *comons fflemynges,* the Flemish common people.

95. *with outen lease,* verily. A tag for rime.

112. *the Rochell,* La Rochelle, on the French coast north of the mouth of the Garonne; a centre of the wine-trade.

113. *Bretons baye.* Warner cites Nicolas as identifying this bay with that of Bourgneuf, south of the Loire. It was granted by Edward III to Walter de Bentley in 1349, and was a centre for the salt trade.

120. *leef or lothe,* i. e., willy-nilly. A padding phrase frequent for rime.

122. *in substaunce,* a padding phrase; "for the most part".

132. *osay.* In Piers Plowman prol. 228-9 are mentioned "white wyn of Osey and red wyn of Gascoigne Of the Ryne and of the Rochel". Hakluyt in his Voyages i:188 assigns Osey to Portugal; Skeat considers the word as a corruption of Alsace, which fits the Rhine district named in Piers Plowman. But see Warner's note.

142. The passage is confused in our MS and in Laud; the sense is clearer in Harley 271 with which Harley 78 fol. 38 closely agrees:—

> Vn to oure sayd enmyes by se to resorte
> In tyme of warre & them to soporte
> Seth our frendis owe not for to be the cavse
> Of our hyndryng þan reson schewith þis cawse . . .

The author is really discussing the impossibility of neutrality.

144. Our MS omits the negative present in other MSS.

161. "This fact our merchants have realized all too dearly."

163. *thise seid pillours.* Laud reads "these fals coloured piloures".

164. *Seint malouse.* The town of St. Malo was until the 19th century a centre of corsair activity.

172. Our MS reads *recunsomed.* Laud reads "towne by towne".

173. This probably corrupt line gave the scribes trouble. Texts vary between *regnes* and *regions, best* and *bost.* The sense apparently is that the story of these misdeeds has gone far and wide. Cp. the Inferno 27:78, "ch'al fine della terra il suono uscie", from Romans x:18.

176. *Easy reputacion,* ill repute.

179. *a good Squyer.* Warner identifies this man, mentioned as "Hampton squyere" in the later version of the Libel, with John Hampton, squire of the body to the king, Master of the Ordnance, etc.

181. The Laud MS has only one *with*. The sense is—"that I have discussed with men of rank and with commoners".

184. *third*. Read *thrid* for rime.

188. Laud and the Hakluyt print read:—"He feld the wayes to rule well the see." For this use of *felt* see Pallad. prol. 73 and note.

190. *Harflete and Houndflete,* i. e. Harfleur and Honfleur, important trading towns at the mouth of the Seine, taken and retaken during the Hundred Years' War.

194. Laud reads "Upon the whyche" etc.; that is, this peace having been made by agreement, the merchants ventured out.

200. *money*. Laud reads *navy*.

202. *the Duke,* i. e., of Brittany, as in 192.

203-4. "How such injury was estopped by convention, and the peace just made was nullified by this conduct."

206, 208. Mont St. Michel and St. Malo, strongholds of Breton piracy, which their Duke at first declares are beyond his control.

211. Laud reads "But whan the kyng anone had takene hede."

216. Laud has *iij* after *townes.*

217 ff. King Edward issues to the energetic seaport towns of Dartmouth, Plymouth, and Fowey, authority to avenge England on the Breton robbers.—*fortefye,* i.e., to strengthen, assist.

221. *see men,* seamen.

222. *thei myght not route,* could not assemble, unite to resist.

225. *for the truse.* Laud reads "as he fyrst dyd dewysse".

235. *as seid was* is parenthetical.

236. The bracketed word is from other MSS. After this line other texts have a couplet not in Harley 4011.

238-41. *He* is King Edward, who by an act of 1343 ordered that Lombards and other alien merchants should be taxed if they outstayed their forty days on English soil.

249. In the margin is:—"Hic patet de incendio villarum de Poperyng & de Belle per ducem Gloucestrie & suos." The Flemish towns of Poperinghes and of Bailleul were sacked by Gloucester's forces in a punitive expedition, 1436, after Philip of Burgundy's attempted seizure of Calais. See the Ballad against the Flemings, Ref. List vi, p. 145.

253. *for any thyng,* at all costs. See Prol CT 276.

257, 265, 266, 334. The bracketed words are in other MSS.

258. *I do it vpon yow,* I call upon you, put it up to you.

262. This line gave the scribes trouble. Laud has *knowen* after *charged;* Cotton reads *charged knowen that ye;* Harley 78 has *charged ayen wt outtyn ly,* and Harley 271 is similar. The phrase *at eye* usually means "clearly, obviously"; it is here so used lines 30, 386, 480, and in the Palladius prol. 32, 33. One might surmise that *charged at eye* meant "loaded to the hawseholes", which were called *eyes;* but this is surmise.

263-4. A distinction is made between mercery and "haberdasshe ware". The former was textile fabrics; although the earliest English use of the word haberdassher is connected with cap-making, the 16th cent. users of the term defined it to mean French or Milan caps, daggers, swords, glasses, etc., or birdcages, lanterns, etc. Our writer seems to distinguish between fabrics and hardware.

325. *Siluer.* MSS Laud and Harley 271 read *sylke.*

326. *waad* is probably *woad,* a plant yielding a blue dye.

327. *Wolle oyle,* wood-oil, used in the draping of cloth.

329. Laud and Cotton fill out the line at close with *I wene,* Harley 78 and 271 with *bedene.*

338. The Company of Grocers, incorporated in London about 1344, was composed of wholesale dealers in spices and foreign foodstuffs. Spices were extensively used on the medieval table and in cooking because the lack of refrigeration made it necessary to disguise the taste of meats and fish past the prime. They were of course high-priced, and "things of complacience", i.e., luxuries.

340. *Apes / Japes / and Marmesettes.* This line is cited NED for *jape,* which is explained as "trifle, toy, trinket". In Skelton's Magnificence 1132-34 these three words are also linked. Marmosets, or small monkeys, were favored pets in the houses of the rich, as contemporary paintings show us.

341. *nifles,* things of naught. See Chaucer's SummTale 52, Skelton's Magnif. 1143. With this passage cp. Browne, Britannia's Pastorals ii, song 4 near close.

342. *blere with our eye,* "with which they blear our eye", i.e., deceive us. For the idiom see Reve's Tale 129; for the use of *with* see note Thebes 35 here.

344. Other MSS have *wastable* instead of *unstable.*

351. *cure* seems to mean pharmacopoeia.

352. In the margin is: "Of dragges materiall for resceites of medecyne."—*scamonye,* a gum from the roots of Convolvulus Scammonia, native in Syria and in Asia Minor, was a strong purgative.

353. *Turbit.* Turbith, or turpeth, was a cathartic drug prepared from the root of East Indian jalap.—*euforbe,* euphorbia or milkweed, growing in warm climates, secretes a milky juice used to purge phlegm.—*correcte* is noted by NED only as "some medicinal herb".—*dagardye* or diagrydium was a preparation of scammony, see 352.

354. *Rubarbe Sene,* rhubarb and senna.—*towo* may be *two*; Laud has *to,* the Harleys *full.*

356. *fayned* is an error; read *forsayd,* with the two Harley MSS; Laud has *said.*

361. *senynge* is probably written for *seyinge,* as in Laud.

364. Read *prese,* as in MS Laud, instead of *plese.*

366-67. *likyng ware and etyng ware,* luxuries and food-stuffs, already named, for which England exchanges her necessities.

369 means "which can ill be spared".

382-3. That is, these travelling alien merchants spy out our economic conditions and plans, and write them in report; then by disguised schemes are pushed their countertails, i.e. opposed plans.—The countertally and tally were originally the two halves of the scored account-rod, split and given respectively to seller and purchaser, in the days before written accounts were general. Here the word is metaphorical.

388. This illustration is of great value to economic historians, although the badness of the MSS and the confusion of the pronouns make it difficult to follow. The first complaint is the usual one, of the drain of gold from England; see Cunningham pp. 395 etc. Then it would seem that the Cotswold men sold their wool on credit to Italian merchants, who retailed it in Italy at higher prices, took their Italian gold to Flanders and loaned it, making a further profit there while their English creditors waited.

405. *make not straunge,* do not shrink from.

407. *lettir* seems to be the Venetians' bill of exchange, which when cashed in England meant a loss of fourpence in the noble, twelvepence in the pound.

410 says apparently that if Englishmen desired payment a month ahead of maturity they must accept a discount of two shillings in the pound, three shillings if two months ahead. The writer reckons eightpence per noble, and three nobles equal a pound. On the English gold retailed in Flanders another usurious profit follows; see note Dance Macabre 393 on usury.

426 ff. is another case of "deceit". The foreign dealer sold at Bruges for cash the wool he had purchased in England on time-note of one or two years; then taking a five per cent. loss on the cash transaction, he lent the money out at interest until maturity, making profit enough to purchase more wool at the Staple.

438. Read with a comma after *agayne*; *day* is the subject of *come.*

443. Harley 78 and 271 read *iij* instead of *iiij,* and Laud reads *her.*

444. The free travel of the foreign merchant about England is indignantly contrasted by the author with the restrictions imposed upon English merchants abroad.

449 ff. A time-limit of forty days for the discharge and re-loading of alien merchant's ships is demanded.

452, 474. *go to hoste.* In continuance of an earlier policy, it had been ordained by a statute of 5th Henry IV that in every town and port to which aliens resorted there should be a sufficient "host" or guardian assigned to them by the mayor or bailiff, and that such aliens should dwell only under his control. This however was not strictly enforced, and the Rolls of Parliament all through the reigns of Henry V and Henry VI are dotted with petitions from English traders praying for more restraints on visiting foreign merchants. A marginal note against this passage is: "Here is to be noted þat sithen this seid ordenaunce of writyng thei haue be ordeyned to go to host in london.—But how þis pollecy is subuerted it is mervayle to know þe wyles and giles."

461. The 12 lines of Harley 4011 now omitted are paralleled by 22 in other texts.

478. A complaint of "graft".

479. *publius* is an error for *public; thing publius* is *res publica.*

481. "Bribes and entertainments are used to thwart the normal growth of our commerce."

481, 506, 510, 525. Observe the various plural endings.

490. Only 14 days are allowed us in Brabant for unloading and loading, says our writer.

493, 499. Bracketed words are from other texts.

502. *faires.* See introduction to this text.

516. *And* is written for *an,* "if".

517. The means of land transportation would not suffice to handle the sea traffic, were that checked.

522. *dyne.* Read *dyen,* as in the Cotton MS. A comma, in sense, follows *wt.*

531. *Burgayn,* etc. Burgundy, Cambrai, Cologne.

537. The bracketed word is from other texts.

538. *multiplye.* Read *multifarye,* as in Laud.

542. *whan this caried.* Other MSS *that this cartyd.*

548. *men.* Other MSS *neuer.* See line 4 above. The *of* is superfluous.

552. MSS Laud and Harley 271 read "and we shuld hem distroye".

553. Other MSS have before *noye* either *bring to* or *take and.*

554. A marginal note reads: "Note of defautes lettyng of our good spede in policie."

557-8. The Laud MS reads: "but we be frail as glasse"; Harley 78, "but we by for a glasse"; Cotton has "but we be freely I gesse". Our MS omits *be,* and should read *fraile* for *fre. Brasil* is miswritten for *brotyll* as in other MSS. Punctuate with a full pause after *fflandres.*

[No more of the *Libel* is here printed.]

As mentioned in the introduction to this text, the epilogue differs in the two recensions of the poem. The first copy of Harley 78 has no epilogue, and a condensed conclusion. The epilogue of Harley 78 (second copy) runs with that of Laud and Pepys. Harley 271, Gurney, Brit.Mus.Adds. 40673, Bodl.Rawlinson poetry 32, and (probably) the mutilated Cotton Vitellius E x, alter one stanza of the epilogue to address three unnamed lords instead of Baron Hungerford as in the earlier recension. Phillipps 8299 (now Huntington 140) I have not seen, nor the Cowper MS. All Souls College, Oxford, ciii, is impf. at close, as is Harley 4011. I print below the text of Harley 271.

> Go forthe lytle bylle & mekly schew þis face
> Apperyng euer wt humbell contenance
> & pray my lordes to take In grace
> In apposell & cherisch þe & a Avaunce
> To hardyness yf þt no variaunce
> þou hast sore thowt trowthe be full experience
> Auutors & resons if owȝt falle in substaunce
> Remytt to hym þt geff þe pis science
>
> To the gret prelate þe heyghest so confessor
> The gret mayster of þe gretest housse
> Cheff tresorere of the gret socoure

Ꝋesschop Cherle and barouη plentivous
Of high wytt*es* lordes thre famous
To examene thy doubled rendytee
I offer þe tham to be *gra*cious
To myn excuse farwell my own trete

(In line 12 *cherle* should be *erle*.)

Warner suggests as the first of these three nobles either John Stafford, bishop of Bath and Wells, or Henry Cardinal Beaufort, bishop of Winchester; as the second, William de la Pole earl of Suffolk, steward of the king's household; as the third, Ralph Cromwell. See Warner's notes.

RIPLEY'S COMPEND OF ALCHEMY

A Note on Alchemy

Alchemy in its widest sense has a philosophical basis. It pretends, and has pretended, to no miracle, but asserts its entire dependence upon the laws of nature. It maintained, as Plato maintained in the Timaeus, that all matter is in essence one; behind all visible phenomena there is an Essential, and from this one "prima materia" or "remote matter", differentiated into four elements of earth, air, water, and fire, God created the whole world of things. The substances known to us are complexes, full of admixtures and impurities, but nevertheless each containing some portion of that "remote matter", which well-directed effort can disengage and refine. This separation of the "prima materia", or "elixir", or "philosopher's stone", or "powder of projection", from the gross burden of ordinary matter was the central problem of the alchemists. An important point, of course, was to begin this process of separation as near as possible to purity; and alchemists very early agreed in identifying the "prima materia" with mercury,—not crude mercury, but that sublimed "mercury of the philosophers" which was most immediately resident in mercury, and could be obtained from it by removing the fluidity, the volatility, and other disturbing attributes of ordinary mercury.

The ancient or medieval student of chemistry (alchemy) guided his procedure as much by theory as by practice; philosophy and analogy were as important to him as experiment or observation. Stephanus of Alexandria, a seventh century writer, said, for example, that a metal was, like man, composed of a body and a soul. The soul of anything in nature was its most subtle essence, its natural tinctorial spirit. And if matter was to become perfect, it must be stripped of its physical qualities, its grosser body, so that its soul might be set free. The second cardinal dogma of alchemy, that substances were within limits capable of transformation into one another, was also based on analogy and theory. Since an oxide-bearing rock could be forced by heat into the semblance of iron, and this iron by more heat or by exposure to the air could pass back into the state of oxide; since all matter decayed, changed, and was born again, it followed that the whole creation was in a ceaseless flux, that the "prima materia" or soul of things was continually receiving and discarding qualities. And the adept by study could reproduce and develop those processes. None but a charlatan would pretend that anything non-metallic, as eggshells or ashes, could be transmuted into the highest of metals, gold; but the baser metals, such as iron or lead, could, on alchemical theory, be deprived of their own superficial qualities, could be reduced to their ultimate metallic base, and then, by addition of the qualities peculiar to gold, could be transmuted into the nobler metal. A chief agent in this transmutation was the "prima materia" or "remote matter". The management of the stages by which "remote matter" was first found, then intermingled with an inferior substance so as to give the common metal-base, and then refined so as to become gold, was the most desired and most difficult art of the alchemist. In Jonson's Alchemist, act ii, scene 3, we find the arch-swindler Subtle saying that "remote matter" is a "humid exhalation" called "materia liquida or the unctuous water", and that when intermingled with a certain "crasse and viscous portion of earth", the result would be the elementary matter of gold. The theory underlying all this process was at first solely "chemical", but was applied with increasing frequency to medicine, especially by Paracelsus in the sixteenth century.

The science of alchemy reaches back much further than the sixteenth century. Many of its practitioners claimed the god Hermes as father of the art; treatises in Greek exist, and Arabic sources are claimed for many Latin treatises of the Middle Ages. The Arabian Jaber or Geber, of the eighth-ninth century, and the Spanish mystic Raimon Lull or Lully, who died in 1315, had probably little or no share in the alchemical treatises which passed as theirs; but Albertus Magnus, Roger Bacon, and Arnoldus Villanovanus,—Chaucer's "Arnold of the Newe Toun" in the CanYeoTale,—were great thirteenth-century names. Among the crowd of teachers there were differences of detail, but some general tenets were common to all. There were four spirits, or substances by means of which bodies could be changed,—mercury, sulphur, arsenic, and sal ammoniac. There were three "menstrues" or liquors, which were respectively animal, vegetable, and mineral, and were presided over by Sol, Luna, and Mercury. Every metal had in the cycle of existence previously been "water mineral", and had in itself the potentiality of a liquid state. In seeking a solution, any substance must be "loosed in its own menstrue", (Jonson's Alchemist ii,3 :281) that is, a vegetable menstrue must not be employed to dissolve animal or mineral. The metals were seven: mercury (which was thus both body and spirit), gold, silver, iron, tin, copper, and lead. In alchemical jargon, the names of the planets were applied to the metals; gold and silver were Sol and Luna, iron Mars, tin Jupiter, copper Venus, lead Saturn. Gold was to be formed from purified mercury and a small portion of pure sulphur. To arrive at this union, the spirits and bodies must be subjected to a long and complicated series of processes, chief among which was the action of heat. According to Geber, these processes were sublimation, or the rendering a body vaporous; then volatilisation or condensation; distillation; calcination; coagulation or crystallisation; incineration, etc.

Great stress was laid upon the purity of the substance used, and upon right composition. God had made all things in "number, ponder, and measure"; and an alchemical procedure must heed these subtle laws. When the four elements are wisely joined in a body, the color will rise toward perfection; inward natural heat will begin to work, excited by outward artificial heat; and the process of change. is comparable, said the analogy-hunting alchemists, to human digestion. The index to a right progress of this digestion is the color of the composition at various stages Color was highly important in alchemy. It was believed, e.g., that any metal potentially all metals, and that the predominance of the quality which individualized each was expressed in its color. To change silver to gold was to remove whiteness and substitute yellowness, or, as the alchemist would say, to dealbificate and then citrinate. The function of the "philosopher's stone" was colorative or "tinctorial". The comparison with the art of the dyer was constantly in the minds of the alchemists, and one reason for the superiority of gold to other metals was its refusal to be decolorized, its resistance to fire. To obtain a superficial coloration was mere dyeing; real coloration implied a transformation of the metal.

In maintaining the proper heat for the proper length of time, in carrying each operation to its right pitch, lay unlimited possibilities of error and of excuses for fraud. There were no means of test such as we use today in experiment; and when failure arrived, as it regularly did, the alchemist and his assistant accused one another (see Canon's Yeoman's Tale) of wrong temperature, wrong ingredients, wrong material burned for the fire:—and everything was begun again. We may marvel that the belief persisted; but there has always been and always will be a type of mind which receives Moses' striking the rock as proof of the doctrine that mineral is potentially liquid, or which is impressed by the treatment of two substances as father and mother, by the theory that months of slow incubation in a closed vessel are necessary to produce the offspring. Kings have on occasion been as credulous as commoners; the interested belief of Henry VI and Edward IV is probably responsible for the mass of treatises on the subject in the late fifteenth century. But the failure of the alchemists continued, and the art at length retired from its attempts at transmutation and emphasized its philosophical tenets, finding then, as Hathaway remarks, the audience which spiritualism and theosophy have today with us.

6, 7. Ashmole reads "O deviaunt fro danger"—and "Fro thys envyos valey".

36 ff. Here is stated the basic alchemical position,—that the one Primal Substance, containing all things potentially, was separated by the Deity at creation.

38. *begynner* is in apposition with *thee.*

44. *Consumed.* Ashmole reads *Confused,* with better sense. See line 37.

47-49. Here the rime-scheme is broken; the fifth should rime with the fourth and does not. The lines are quite different in Ashmole, where the rime-arrangement is preserved.

49. *sum* is contrasted with *many one* of line 48. Norton's Ordinal (see p. 15 in Ashmole) says that as there be but seven planets among the host of heaven, "Soe among millions of millions of Mankinde Scarslie seaven men maie this Science finde."

54. *the les worlde,* the microcosm. Norton's Ordinal, p. 62 of Ashmole, says that among creatures these two alone "Be called Microcosmus, Man and our Stone". See *ibid.,* p. 85-6 for the stone as the microcosm, and, e.g., Lydgate's ReasonandSens 540 ff. for man as the microcosm; cp. Sieper's note on line 552 *ibid.—one of three.* Ashmole reads *one and three.*

59 ff. The movement of idea here seems to be,—"What is this stone, when philosophers say to those seeking it that each man has it" etc.

69. The first *they* means the philosophers, the second "the symple sekers".

75. This line, omitted by Corpus, is here supplied from the MS Ff.ii, 23; Stow, in Harley 367, has it as line 74, and 74 as 75.

85. *Raymondus,* Raymund Lully, the thirteenth-century Spanish mystic and philosopher, to whom unfounded tradition attributed a number of alchemical works.

88. *sonn and mone,* gold and silver; see Note on Alchemy *ante.*

106. *the fyrst,* the first or animal menstruum, sal.

109. *the lyon grene.* The glossary of alchemical terms appended by Waite to his ed. of Paracelsus says that the Green Lion is mineral, and the base of all menstrua or solvents, the fixed part of matter, capable of resisting the action of fire. His strength is "vernant and greene evermore enduring", according to Bloomfield's Blossoms, in Ashmole p. 312; *ibid.* p. 278, in the "Hunting of the Greene Lyon", this menstruum is said to be metallic vitriol, the priest who weds Sun and Moon, etc.

111. *tyncture,* see Note on Alchemy *ante,* par. 4.

112. *Gebar,* Geber, an Arabian chemist of the 8th century, the supposed author of numerous alchemical treatises the origin of which is now dated about the thirteenth century. See line 64 of the Prohibicio and note.

113. *the second,* the second or vegetable menstruum, sulphur, more humid than the first.

116. *formals.* Read *formall?* Both the material and the formal principle must be dissolved, says Ripley.

117. Ashmole supplies the word.

120. *the thyrd humydyte,* mercury, the essence underlying metals.

122. *Hermes tree.* In the various processes of alchemical experiment aiming at the pure white elixir or stone, a black deposit was encountered. Waite's transl. of Paracelsus i:68 says that "when the philosophers have put their matter into the more secret fire, and when with a moderate philosophical heat it is cherished on every side, beginning to pass into corruption, it grows black. This operation they call putrefaction, and they call the blackness by the name of the crow's head". Other names, says Ripley in his first book, on Calcination, are the ashes of Hermes tree, or the toad of the earth. Comparison of the "prima materia" to a golden tree may be found in Paracelsus as cited, i :54.

133-34. These lines are closely bound syntactically.—*by labor exuberate,* rendered fruitful by labor. This case cited NED.

136. *kyndly acuate,* etc., properly refined ("sharpened") and passed into a pure spirit. Ashmole reads "well and kyndly".

149. *cyrculacyon.* Ashmole reads *Calcination.*

151. The "circulation", if properly made, will cause the compound to flow over the base as smoothly as wax flows over metal. Then "loose" i.e. dissolve it, etc.

160. *aurum potabile*, drinkable gold, the elixir of life. Use of this is ascribed to Lully. See Lydgate's Letter to Gloucester, line 46.

161. *hym* is inserted from Ashmole's text.

166. Ashmole reads "we yt call".

169. *Our basylyske*, etc. The basilisk or cockatrice, the "little king" of serpents, was a mythical creature having legs, wings, a serpentine tail, and a puffed crest. Its look was possessed of death-dealing power, even from a distance; as Sir Thomas Browne says in his Vulgar Errors, "this venenation shouteth from the eye". Bloomfield the alchemist, in his Blossoms,—see Ashmole, pp. 318, 322,—says that Raymond called the Stone "Basiliske and Cocatrice"; and he himself uses the same terms, by metaphor, to indicate the marvellous and unique qualities of the stone.—*abiecte*, prone? The basilisk could slay without moving from its usual position. But Ashmole here reads "hys object", evidently interpreting *sight* as "glance".

173. *tayneth*, kindles.

174. *perfect*. Read *perfyt*, for rime.

183. The bracketed word is supplied from Ashmole's text.

187. *theoryk and practycall*. See notes on Walton A 332, Dance Macabre 427.

190 ff., Ripley now enumerates the twelve processes or "gates" of the art of alchemy, to each of which he devotes a chapter of his work. The first is of natural calcination, i. e., the reduction to powder by means of heat. The second is of solution, the third of separation, the fourth of conjunction; by the fifth, "putrefaction", the alchemists understood a breaking-down process: the sixth step was congelation accompanied by whitening, and the seventh cibation, by which alchemists meant the adding of fresh substances to compensate for the evaporation which had taken place. The eighth process was sublimation, and the ninth fermentation; after these followed exaltation, or the raising of qualities to a higher degree, multiplication, and finally projection, the end and crown of all. To these twelve chapters Ripley devotes, respectively, 22, 15, 18, 15, 51, 30, 6, 8, 19, 11, 9, and 8 stanzas. A recapitulation of 11 stanzas then follows and a Prohibicio is appended to all.

The Prohibicio

4.. *fon sune and mone*, for Sun and Moon, i. e., for gold and silver. See CanYeoTale 887.

6. *vermylon*, vermilion, the red mercuric sulphide used by alchemists. Later, any red pigment.

15. *water corosyves and water ardente*, acids and spirits.

20. *calcys*. A calx, in alchemy, was a powder produced by thoroughly burning a mineral or metal.

23. Vitriol, says Ripley, is called the Green Lion by fools. See note on 109 *ante*.

24. *arsnyke*. Arsenic, in its alchemical sense, might be the Mercury of the philosophers when in the stage of putrefaction. *Orpement* is yellow arsenic. See CanYeoTale 269-70.

25. *In debily principio*, etc. The contrast is between *principio* and *fine*. A poor beginning makes a bad ending.

29 ff. give a list of salts:—sal ammoniac, sandiver (the liquid saline floating on glass after vitrification), sal alkali, alembroth or the double chloride of mercury and ammonium, sal altincar or borax, saltpetre, sal of tartar, sal comen or meconic acid, sal-gem or rock-salt, vitriol, and sal soda. See CanYeoTale 231 ff. for some of these terms.

36 ff. Ripley now enumerates the false methods which he unsuccessfully tried; cp. also Norton's list, p. 39 in Ashmole. In chapter 8 of Paracelsus' Aurora of the philosophers (see Waite's transl. i:55), Paracelsus says that some have sought the stone in hairs, urine, hen's eggs, milk, in calx of eggshells, in galls of oxen, and in dragon's blood. Others, he says, take a score of lizard-like animals, shut them in a vessel, and make them mad with hunger, so that they devour one another until but one survives. This one is then fed with filings

of copper and it is supposed that by his digestion of the copper he will bring about the desired transmutation into gold. Such experimenters then burn the lizard into a red powder, which they think must be gold; but they are deceived, says Paracelsus.

37. *Es uste,* aes ustum, the crocus of copper or crocus of Venus. The method of making this is described by Paracelsus, see Waite's translation i:141-2. The copper, in thin plates, is smeared with salt and vinegar, burnt in a blast furnace, and dipped in vinegar and sal ammoniac. This process is repeated, the scales being scraped off each time, until the plates are nearly consumed. Then the vinegar is extracted by distillation, and is allowed to coagulate into a very hard stone, which is the crocus of copper used in alchemy.—*crokfere,* crocus ferri, the crocus or yellow powder of iron; peroxide of iron.

39. *letarge,* litharge, protoxide of lead. The rime should be *worth a myte.—antymony,* antimony, sometimes classed as a metal, sometimes as a non-metal; one of the elementary bodies. Etymology unknown; popularly explained as "anti-moine", hence called monksbane.

41. *The sowle of Saturn,*—the sal of Saturn? sugar of lead.—*markesyte,* marcasite, iron pyrites, which often had the lustre of gold. Waite says that all stones which contained any proportion of metal were called marcasite by the alchemists.—For the wrong line-arrangement in this stanza see footnote to text.

43. *Oyle of lune,* oil of silver. Paracelsus, in Waite's transl. ii:140, gives a recipe for making "the oil and quintessence of Luna".

47. *aqua vite.* Ashmole reads "a quantity".

48. In one of the minor alchemical tracts printed by Ashmole, p. 205, the worker is bidden to take "the red substance" and break it on a marble stone.

53. *oyle of the snayle.* The NED notes the use of snail-oil, as late as 1887, as remedy for backache.

57. *rennet.* A mass of curdled milk found in the stomach of an unweaned calf, and used to curdle milk for cheese. Mentioned among natural liquors by Norton, see p. 79 of Ashmole.

58. *slyme of sterrys.* According to the NED, the alga Nostoc, which appears as a jelly-like mass on dry soil after rain, was popularly supposed to be the remains, or "slime", of fallen stars or meteors. This assertion is found in Paracelsus.

59. *celydony.* This probably means not the fabled stone found in the entrails of a swallow, but the plant celandine, from which, says Paracelsus, some alchemists have pressed a juice, boiled it, put it in the sun, and after coagulation pounded it to a fine black powder, which should by projection turn Mercury into Sol, but does not.—*secundynes,* afterbirths. It may be noted that in a Herbal of 1526 amber is said to be the secondine cast by a whale.

63. *for the nonys,* suited for the occasion. See note Garl. 267.

64. *on of gevers cokys,* one of Geber's cooks. To the Arabian Geber, as above noted, line 112, were attributed many alchemical works. See for this locution Norton's Ordinal as printed by Ashmole, p. 103, "manie of Gebars Cookes"; and see the poem by Sir Edward Kelle, printed *ibid.* p. 324, beginning "All you that faine Philosophers would be And night and day in kitchin broyle, Wasting the chipps of ancient Hermes tree," etc.

88. *newtriall mercurialyte.* Ashmole reads *A naturall Mercuryalyte.* This is the first NED citation of *mercuriality* as "the mercurial part of something".

89. *Owte of hys mynerue by marte,* etc. Ashmole reads "Out of his myner by Arte", etc., and the Corpus MS reads *arte.* The NED defines *minera* as the matrix in which a precious stone or metal was supposed by the alchemists to grow, and cites Ripley.

THE COURT OF SAPIENCE

is neither annotated nor glossed.

HAWES: THE PASTIME OF PLEASURE

In his dedication to King Henry the Seventh, Hawes makes the conventional protestations of his rudeness and dulness, and lauds the "fatal fictions" of his master Lydgate. In the tone of his excuses he closely follows Lydgate, whom he treats with the same respect which Lydgate showed for Chaucer, and Chaucer for Dante or Virgil. The theory of poetry stated in 34-42 is that current in medieval formal poetry, that, as Spingarn phrases it, "the reality of poetry is dependent on its allegorical foundations; its moral teachings are to be sought in the hidden meanings discoverable beneath the literal expression". Thus, John of Salisbury praises Virgil, "qui sub imagine fabularum totius philosophiae exprimit veritatem" (Polycraticus vi, cap. 22; see *ibid.*, ii, cap. 15). Dante in Inferno ix:63 calls upon his readers to observe the "dottrina che s'asconde Sotto il velame degli versi strani." See note on Churl and Bird 29 here, and the paragraphs on allegory in Gen. Introd.

25. *colour crafty.* See note on FaPrinces G 46.

28, 29. Observe stanza-liaison; also between stanzas 1 and 2, 3 and 4, 42 and 43, 186 and 187, 550 and 551, 555 and 556, 564 and 565, 570 and 571 of the poem.

33. *fatall.* See note on line 665 below.

44. *to eschue idlenes.* See note on line 1313 below, and on Cavendish, lines 24-30.

1 ff. *When . . . etc.* The usual temporal-astronomical opening; see note on Thebes 1.

6. *depured . . . cruddy.* The adjective *depured* is a favorite with Hawes, and is probably taken from the Court of Sapience, where its use is frequent. It is occasional in Lydgate and in Bokenam, but it is not in Chaucer. The use of *cruddy,* "curdled", to describe the sky, is very interesting to the modern student, who thinks of Shelley's "crudded rack" or "curdling winds". The likeness between the torn white clouds of morning and the integument of curdling milk is sufficiently marked to rouse curiosity as to Hawes' intention here. The passage is the earliest of the few NED citations. Had Hawes for an instant his "eye on the object", instead of blindly repeating conventional phrases as usual?

8. *gaye and glorious.* Used again 200, 1400, 2504, 3181, 4880, 5264, 5616; see note on line 353. The phrase is in Bradshaw's St. Werburge i:1786.

11-13. Possibly a recollection of Chaucer's opening to the CantTales.

15-18. In the Example of Virtue, stanza 26 begins "A path we found, right greatly used".

19. *chaunce or fortune.* This and similar couplings are very frequent in Lydgate, not uncommon in Chaucer. Note the "aventure or sort or cas" of the CTprologue 846, the "aventure or cas" of Knight's Tale 216, the many cases in Lydgate's Troy Book, e. g., "of caas or aventure" i:34, "hap or sort" iii:5315, etc. Note Dante's "Se voler fu, o destino, o fortuna", Inferno 32:76. But Hawes' phrase, as often Lydgate's, is a synonym instead of a distinction.

27. The two ways are those of the Active and the Contemplative Life. A choice of paths is a frequent motif in medieval literature, but the contrast is oftener between Voluptas and Virtus (as in the choice of Hercules) or Idleness and Occupation (cp. Pilgrimage of the Life of Man 11232 ff.) or Reason and Sensuality, as in Lydgate's poem 637 ff., than as here.

29 ff. The most famous example of the inscription at entrance, that over the gate of the Inferno in Dante's third canto, is imitated by Chaucer PoFoules 127 ff. There is a brief inscription on the entrance tower of the Court of Sapience, see ii:40-42 *ibid.* See below 78 ff.

73. *shynyng.* The print has *shydyng;* and in 72 it reads *portayture.* For copper as material for statues cp. note here on Cavendish line 225. For the use of *picture* as "image" the NED gives first the Coventry Plays, then this passage, etc.

78. *situacion..* Hawes frequently, under coercion of rime, uses a sounding Latin abstract term in a forced sense, e. g.:—

. . . it shall to him *exemplify*	Pastime 1214
. . . she can *exhort* Of La Bell Pucell . . .	Pastime 4588
. . . they did then *conject* To make . . .	Pastime 4896
. . . the high *promotion* Of la Bell Pucell's domination	Pastime 5113
. . . I cannot *extend* the goodlyness Of this palace . . .	Pastime 5198

87. *gaspyng nette.* This may be a printer's error for *galpyng,* i.e. "gaping, yawning", in which case the rhetorical figure is parallel to Chaucer's "slepy yerd", KnTale 529, or to the

"trembling trompe" of Cavendish's Metrical Visions 1222. The NED treats the word here as *gasping*.

92. *deadly slomber*, profound slumber. Cp. Lydgate's *mortal slepe*, Troy Book v:2072. Note the assonance.

93. The wakening of the sleeper by a loud or musical sound is a favorite device in medieval dream-poetry. The voice of birds is used in Chaucer's PoFoules, followed by Lydgate's Black Knight, by the Cuckoo and Nightingale, and by Dunbar's Thrissill and Rois. In the BoDuchesse Chaucer uses the castle-bell; in the Parlement of Thre Ages it is the blast of a bugle, in Dunbar's Goldin Targe the noise of guns, which wakes the sleeper. Differing modes are the dreamer's fall from the bridge in Douglas' Palice of Honour, the water springing in his face at the close of the Assembly of Ladies. In the Kingis Quair, Fortune takes the poet by the ear. See Cavendish's Visions 1222.

97. *morow gray*. This phrase, used by Chaucer at the opening of his Mars, reappears in the Flower of Courtesy 9, the Troy Book i:3078, 3098, iii:3760, v:2958, and often elsewhere in Lydgate. See also the introduction to Orléans, p. 215 here, other cases in Hawes, and later English writers such as William Browne the student of Lydgate.

99. This description of the approach of Fame is one of the few really good bits in the poem.

106 ff. With the arms of Henry VII and of Henry VIII two greyhounds were often used as supporters; Fame's bestowing of them, under the names of Governance and Grace, on the youthful prince, is a workmanlike blend of allegory and compliment.

121. *was in my presence*. Hawes has of course no notion of following the procedure of Dante, who often obtains his "dream-effects" by saying that some one "was there", without mentioning the approach or using such words as "came", "crossed", "rowed", etc.

125. *kyng Percius*. Perseus, son of Zeus and slayer of Medusa, has no connection in myth with the winged steed Pegasus except that in the moment of Medusa's death her son by Neptune, the flying horse, was born. It was Bellerophon, slayer of the Chimaera, who rode Pegasus. Rhodenizer suggests that Caxton's comparison of Perseus' spreading fame to the flying steed led Hawes to this statement; see Recuyell, ed. Sommer i:196.

129. The request for the name is as usual in medieval work. When names are not given, the writer thinks it necessary to apologize; cp. PoFoules 287, BlKnight 124, FlandLeaf 150, 273, Thebes 3195, AssGods 406, 1542, 1598, etc.

130-1. The confusion of direct and indirect discourse, and the use of the participle as a finite verb, are very Lydgatian. See for the latter Thebes prol. *passim*.

136. *my horne haue blowen*, etc. See Cavendish's Visions 1222; see this poem 5498, or p. 210 of the Percy Soc. edition. See note on FaPrinces B 95 here.

145. *in her digression*, i. e., in the decline of the world.

146, 148. The phrases *busy payne, Record of,* are Lydgatian. The former occurs again 441, 727, the phrase *busy cure* 117, 160.

148 ff. Fame now discourses on the "first finders" of arts in the golden age. The chapter in Lydgate's FaPrinces, ii:2409 ff., is not used; Hawes takes his material, as Rhodenizer points out, from Caxton's Recuyell, to which he refers in line 180. He also uses the book, calling it "the Trojan story", in ExamVirtue stanzas 87-89. The "finding" of agriculture by Saturn is described at the very opening of the Recuyell, the mining and working of the metals a little later, see p. 117 of Sommer's edition.

163 ff. *Melizyus*. The importance of King Melizyus in this poem should be noted. At his court the youthful hero receives his training in the arts of chivalry, and from the king personally the order of knighthood. If this poem has a connection with the young prince Henry (see note on 106 above) a compliment to the reigning sovereign would be entirely in place. In the Recuyell (ed. Sommer i:14), "Mellyseus" is lord of the city of Oson; on p. 70 he is king of Epirus; on p. 144 "the kyng of Mollose", who has "founden the craft to tame and breke horses" leads a hundred Centaurs to the aid of Jupiter. Rhodenizer suggests a confusion between the two names in Hawes' mind. The fact that "Millesius", i.e. Thales of Miletus, is one of the seven sages in the Court of Sapience has no connection here.

169 ff. Minerva's gift of arms to man, and her conquest of the giant Pallas, whose name she took, are in the Recuyell (Sommer i:38). See also the ExamVirtue, stanza 37. Lydgate's list makes Pallas the inventor of weaving, see note on 148 above.

180. Hercules' life and deeds are fully narrated in the Recuyell.

196. *heyres in fee,* the heirs of feudal privileges and obligations.

205. *Gyauntes.* A frequent feature of the romances, see e. g. Sir Tristrem, Sir Perceval, Sir Beves of Hamtoun.

210. *serpentes . . . blacke and tedious.* The latter epithet is used by Lydgate of abstractions; cp. "on this mater is tedious for to abyde", FaPrinces vii:460, "tedius to here", Troy Book iii:5565. He also uses *tediouste* to mean "prolixity", cp. DuorMerc 900. But Hawes regularly, and Barclay occasionally, use this word of concrete things; Barclay writes of a "tedious shout", of "infernal floodes tedious and horrible"; and Hawes, always coupling the word with black, applies it to devils, to serpents, and to the evil spirit expelled from a dragon. See this poem 953, 2229, 5090, and ExamVirtue stanza 270.

211. For *beyonde* the Percy Society text reads *behynde.*

216-17. The outer walls of the tower are "enamelled" as were those of the garden in the Roman de la Rose, with paintings. In the Assembly of Gods the outside of the walls of Dame Doctrine's foursquare arbor were painted with figures. See further on in this poem, 5122-3 and 5177-8, pp. 195, 197 of Percy Soc. edition.

219. Delete *Of?*

221. *lyke as Phebus.* See note on FaPrinces G 36 here for this locution in formal verse.

246. The porter of Venus, in the PoFoules, is Richesse; the portress of the Roman de la Rose is Idleness; in the Assembly of Ladies the portress is called Countenance, as• here. For a full household staff of such allegorical figures see this last, and also the French poem printed by Meyer in Romania 15:241-6. See 421 below.

249. *the seuen scyences.* Graund Amoure is to receive something parallel to an University education. Of the seven liberal Arts, the trivium was made up of grammar, logic, and rhetoric; the quadrivium of arithmetic, music, geometry, and astronomy. See Abelson, The Seven Liberal Arts: a study in Medieval Culture, N. Y., 1906. See also the essay on these Arts in the Vision Delectable of Alfonso de la Torre, by J. P. W. Crawford in Romanic Review 4:58-75, and the earlier paper by d'Ancona in vol. 5 of L'Arte, on the influence of Martianus Capella as seen in frescoes, tapestry, etc. of the pre-Renaissance. See the Court of Sapience, book ii.

266. *fawning courage,* i. e., ingratiating ways, obedient spirit. On the word *courage* see note above on Walton A 310.

269. Perhaps read *ek* for *ey?*

272. *twylight.* The first NED citation is from Lydgate's Troy Book i:2733. Of his several uses of the word, that *ibid.,* iii:2677 ff. is accompanied by a definition.

275. *fyne force,* stern necessity, perforce. See Chaucer's Troilus v:421.

281. This chapter-heading is out of place; it should precede stanza 38.

286. For the awakening by birds cp. note on line 93.

289. *the element,* the upper air. See Comus 299.

292. *Document,* instruction. In the ExamVirtue prol. 3, Hawes cites St. Paul as saying "All that is written is to our document". He is probably quoting 2d Tim. iii:16.

293. *copper.* The use of metal or of precious stones in architecture (also amber, coral, and jet) is a constant feature of the romances and of medieval tales of marvel such as Mandeville's Travels. Chaucer's house of Fame is of beryl, and the palace of Venus, in the PoFoules, is of brass set on jasper pillars; in Caxton' Recuyell the tower in which Danaë is imprisoned is "alle of copper", and Douglas' palace of Honour is of beryl upon a marble rock.

We may also remember that when Henry VIII later erected his palace of Nonesuch he covered the timbers with lead and gilded them. The taste of the time, as well as the romance-formula, is expressed in this detail of Hawes' poem; and much later, when Keats in his Endymion or Tennyson in his Palace of Art, was creating a mythical building, he sought glitter to enhance its beauty.

297. In Lydgate's Temple of Glass 20 ff. the brilliancy of the building blinds the gazer until "certain skyes donne" cover "the stremes of Titan". In Douglas' Palice of Honour, "For brichtnes scarslie blenk thairon I mocht", says the author.

301. Auster, the south wind, was supposed to bring mist and fog.

305. The definiteness of this description suggests that Hawes had at least a picture in mind. In the Margarita Philosophica the tower of Philosophy is hexagonal, but the full-page cut shows it standing apparently in the street of a city; see reproduction in The Legacy of the Middle Ages, Oxford, 1926, to face p. 272. The foursquare base may have been added from some woodcut or pageant-setting seen by Hawes; neither Chaucer's HoFame nor Lydgate's TemGlas nor the Court of Sapience gives any statement as to the shape of the rock-base.

309. The castles of the romances, the palaces of Chaucer, of the Court of Sapience, and of Douglas, are all equipped with pinnacles. In Hawes' ExamVirtue stanza 27 the castle of Fortune has high diamond towers "with fanis wavering in the wind"; and Douglas' Palice of Honour has "goldin fanis waifand with the wind", also "pinaclis quhilk like to Phebus schone". See also this poem, p. 196 of the Percy Soc. ed. In this last extract, and here, the special feature is the musical quality of the wind-moved turrets. Chaucer, HoFame 1193 ff., fills his pinnacles with enshrined figures of singers; Tennyson, in the Palace of Art, tips his turrets with figures which seem to toss incense from golden cups.

311. *propre vyces.* The word *vyces* may mean a screw, a turning shaft; cp. the pseudo-Chaucerian Isle of Ladies 1312, in which the writer, ascending "a winding stayer keeps hold on "the vice" as he climbs. The adjective means that each pinnacle had its own.

315. *dance Iclipped,* etc. The more popular "caroles" and group-dances bore the names of their thematic lines or their place of origin, etc. Some mentioned in the Tournois de Chauvenci (ed. Delmotte, Valenciennes, 1835) are *Béguignaige, Ermite, Pélérinaige, Provencel, le Chapelet.* And in line 1528 below the musicians are bidden to play "Mamours the swete and the gentill daunce".

331. *besy court.* Probably a misprint for *base court,* "lower or main court", the French "basse cour". See lines 2942, 5140, where the correct form appears.

337. The four rivers of medieval allegorized gardens and palaces were ultimately modelled on the four rivers of Paradise, which are named lines 338-9. In the Palace of Art Tennyson modifies the convention into four courts, each with "the golden gorge" of a dragon spouting forth "a flood of fountain-foam".

338. *Nysus* is an error for *Nilus,* the Nile. Cp. note on line 87 above.

347. The crystal windows, usually "depured" as here, are always noted by Hawes. See this poem 1360, 1468, 2502, 5176, 5197; see the ExamVirtue stanzas 28, 46, 70, 174. So in the romances, e.g., Sir Degrevaunt 1441-54; so in Mandeville's Travels.

349-50. Hawes invariably shows great interest in the roofs of his buildings, which are either "knotted" curiously or equipped with precious stones, especially the radiant carbuncle. See also his ExamVirtue stanzas 32, 238. With this grapevine of gold and rubies Rhodenizer compares the similar vine in the hall of the Great Khan, described by Mandeville chap. 23 of his Travels as of gold with clusters of fine grapes made of white crystal, yellow topaz, red rubies, green emeralds, and black onyx. Other descriptions of the roof in this poem are 1359, 1467, 2504-6, 3180, 3240, 3701, 4112, 5181-6, 5192. See note on Cavendish's Visions line 106; see Shelley's Revolt of Islam, i, stanzas 51, 52.

353. *gayely glorified.* This phrase also occurs 597, 3194, and ExamVirtue stanza 77. It is a variant of the phrase *gaye and glorious* as in line 8, etc. Cp. *gaye and gorgeous,* 2833.

356-7. The same two lines recur 1469-70.

358-420. The coming story of Graund Amoure, up to his wedding, is given by anticipation in this tapestry. There is a curious parallel in the novel *This Freedom,* temporarily popular in the third decade of the twentieth century; its author says of his heroine, "We'll fix her stage from first to last, then see her walk upon it." Events to come are then outlined, after which the narrative begins. Hawes may have been influenced by the Knight's Tale 1175-80.

421-7. With the careful apportioning of household duties among allegorical female figures cp. the Assembly of Ladies, where Discretion is purveyor, Countenance porter, Belchere marshal, Largesse steward, Remembrance chamberlain, Aviseness secretary, Temperance chancellor, etc. See also Douglas' Palice of Honour, ed. Small i:68; and see the French poem cited in note on 246 ante.

453-5. The meaning seems to be that Doctrine has given birth to these seven daughters without lessening her own authority.

462. *Congruitie.* In the fullpage illustration of the Margarita Philosophica entitled "Typus Gramatice", the learner is presented by Grammar, or Nicostrata, with a key inscribed "Congruitas", which opens the tower of Philosophy.

463-526 are omitted from this selection of passages. In them Grammar receives and addresses the learner, and instructs him in "Donat", i.e. the Ars Grammatica Minor of Donatus, the usual medieval text-book. Four stanzas epitomize the hero's study, and six, chapter 6 entire, dispose of Logic. Rhetoric, the next sister, is given much more space, and discourses through a number of chapters.

The approach to the Seven Arts is quite different in Hawes from the approach in the Court of Sapience. In the earlier work the seven sisters are found in the third court of Sapience's palace, and are by no means the principal figures of the narrative. Much is made of their pupils, whose names are carefully given; and the account of their teachings is often very technically phrased, and far from puerile as is the instruction here. It might almost be suspected from the full treatment of Rhetoric here that the young prince for whom the poem was intended was at the time engaged with that particular branch of study. There is no such proportion in the Court of Sapience, where Rhetoric has six stanzas and Dialectic or Logic seven; and in the Margarita Philosophica the section of Rhetoric fills 23 pages as compared with Dialectic's 64 and the seventy-two devoted to Grammar.

527-536 are retained from the chapters on Grammar, Logic, and Rhetoric now omitted, in order to illustrate the extreme definiteness of Hawes' pedagogic intention.

659 ff. Hawes now formulates his theory of sound composition, insisting upon the necessity of a fable of "clowdy fygure", and censuring the dull rude people who think themselves deceived by a poet if they have to interpret his meaning; see note on Churl and Bird 29 ante. He then proceeds to give the five parts of Rhetoric. These are, as in the usual medieval text-books, ultimately from the pseudo-Ciceronian treatise Ad Herennium, see *ibid.*, i chap. 2; but instead of following the order of that treatise, "inventio, dispositio, elocutio, memoria, pronuntiatio", Hawes puts Pronuntiatio before Memoria. In this he agrees with Lydgate's FaPrinces vi:3319-3360, and with the Margarita Philosophica. See note FaPrinces G 193 here.

663. *obscure reason,* "veiled discourse". The word *reason* often means "utterance" in Middle English; and see the French Li Biaus Desconus, Lydgate's Troy Book ii:5392, etc. etc. Cp. for the theory Dante in the Inferno ix:62-3,—"la dottrina che s'asconde Sotto il velame degli versi strani." See note *ante* on Churl and Bird 29.—*obscure* means "hard to understand". First case NED for this sense is of 1495; but see FaPrinces vi:2339, "to whom she gaff an ansuere ful obscure."

665. *fatall scriptures.* In Chaucer's MLTale 163 *fatal* means "fraught with destiny"; and so in Lydgate, where Minos' hair is fatal, FaPrinces i:2528. But Hawes gives the word the meaning "prophetic"; in ExamVirtue he writes of "poetes that were fatall"; and cp. dedication here, line 33, also 751, 813; cp. Skelton's Garland 34.

670. *wofull hartes.* Why woeful?

674. *and,* i.e., *an,* "if".

675-79. Hawes' meaning seems to be that Invention must be supported by Industry. The *exemplify* of 677 may be one of his grandiloquent polysyllables inexactly employed,—see introd. *ante*—or Hawes may mean that the working-out in narrative "exemplum" of something found by Invention is necessary to successful literary work.

692-3. After praising brevity, Hawes says that it is necessary to estimate what length of treatment is fitted for the matter in hand.

730-32-33. Note the rime on accented *-eth,* and cp. the procedure of Sir Thomas Wyatt.

737. *solisgyse,* "syllogize", i.e., argue, dispute. First used, according to NED, in the Assembly of Gods.

752. *moralyse the similitude,* "interpret the fable". The same phrase is used at the opening of The Craft of Lovers, see my Chaucer Manual, p. 420. Skeat in his Chaucer Canon, p. 121, thinks the phrase was there a marginal note which has crept into the text.

757. *what for that* is an ejaculation.

763. Chapters X and XI are now omitted.

1107. *derified,* "derived". In the Percy Soc. edition, *veryfyde.*

1110. *arage.* The two examples of this word in NED are both transitive. Hawes apparently uses it intransitively, "to be enraged"; such twisting is not uncommon in his work.

1121. Chapters XII and XIII are omitted.

1255. *Mercury northwest.* Compare the much-debated passage in PoFoules 117, "As wisly as I saw thee north-northwest", i.e. the planet Venus. Cp. Hamlet's "mad north-northwest".

1257. *Hoyse vp thy sayle,* etc. Cp. opening of the second book of Troilus.

1259. *trace and daunce,* manner and procedure.

1260. *thy.* The later print, of 1555, reads *the.*

1261 ff. Hawes' allusions to Gower, Chaucer, and Lydgate are interesting. I reprint the three closing stanzas of the Example of Virtue, from the unique copy of de Worde's 1510 print in the Pepysian collection, Magdalene College, Cambridge.

> O gower fountayne moost aromatyke
> I the now lake for to depure
> My rudnes with thy lusty retoryke
> And also I mys as I am sure
> My mayster Chaucers to take the cure
> Of my penne for he was expert
> In eloquent termes subtyll and couert
>
> Where is now lydgate flourynge in sentence
> That shold my mynde forge to endyte
> After the termes of famous eloquence
> And strength my penne well for to wryte
> With maters fresshe of pure delyte
> They can not helpe me there is no remedy
> But for to praye to God almyghty
>
> for to dystyll the dewe of influence
> Upon my brayn so dull and rude
> And to enlumyn me with his sapyence
> That I my rudnes may exclude
> And in my mater well to conclude
> Unto thy pleasure and to the reders all
> To whome I excuse me now in generall
>   Explicit exemplum virtutis

1268 ff. In discussing Chaucer's work, Hawes distinguishes between invention, translation, and imagination; this may be a mere coercion by rime, but the description of the Legend of Good Women as a translation is noteworthy, also the term "sentencious" as applied to the Hous of Fame. Hawes names, of Chaucer's work, the Hous of Fame, the Legend, the Canterbury Tales, Troilus, and "many other bokes" remaining in print. At the time Hawes wrote, there was no collected edition of Chaucer; there were in existence four editions of the Canterbury Tales, two of which were by Caxton; from the same press had been issued Troilus, Boethius, the Hous of Fame, and eight of the minor poems, including the Parlement of Foules. There was no text of the Legend in print when Hawes wrote.

1286 ff. A selected list of Lydgate's work follows. It runs: the Life of Our Lady, St. Edmund, the Fall of Princes, the Churl and Bird, the Court of Sapience, the Troy Book, a "boke solacious" of gods and goddesses, and the Temple of Glass. Of these eight, the first, fourth, fifth, and eighth had been printed by Caxton, and the Assembly of Gods (the "boke solacious"?) and Fall of Princes by de Worde, anterior to the date at which Hawes is writing. This attribution of the Temple of Glass to Lydgate is accepted by scholars, but neither the Assembly of Gods nor the Court of Sapience is viewed as his. See p. 100 here.

1286. *ryally.* The text reads *nyally.*

1297. See note on Churl 29.

1313. *the tyme of slouthe.* This is corrected by the 1555 editor to *The synne,* etc. Sloth was one of the Seven Deadly Sins, and writers of this period freqently state that their purpose in writing is "to eschewe idilnesse, modir of vycis". See, e.g., Lydgate's FaPrinces i:4685-6, vi:234, vii:696-7, etc. Cp. the Franciscan phrase "ad repellendam otiositatem"; and see Caxton's insistence on writing as safeguard against sloth, in the Recuyell and elsewhere. See note on lines 24-30 of Cavendish's Visions.

1318. *ballade royall.* The application of "rime royal" to the seven-line stanza rimed *ababbcc* is by the NED *et al.* ascribed to its use in the post-Chaucerian "Kingis Quair" of King James of Scotland. MacCracken however points out the term in Quixley's ?1402 translation of Gower's French ballads; see MLNotes 24:31.

1330. The 1555 text reads "to haue fame for their mede", supplying the omission.

1334-37. According to Hawes, the making of love-songs was as favored an occupation at the court of Henry VII as we know it to have been at the court of his son.

1349. See Chaucer's Troilus i:642-3 for this more or less proverbial parallel between the heightening of white by black and the aggrandizement of a great writer by a humble follower. It is especially developed by Lydgate, FaPrinces vi:2969-82; see also his Temple of Glass 1250, and cp. Skelton, Garland of Laurell 1210, Spenser's Faerie Queene, iii:9, 2, 4. See note FaPrinces G 33-35 here.

1351. Chapter XV is omitted from these extracts.

1401 ff. Another temporal-astronomical beginning, as in Lydgate's Thebes 1 ff., or at the opening of this poem. It is now May; the sun is in Gemini.

1404. *darke Dyane,* the unillumined moon.

1412-14. *base organes,* etc. In the Margarita Philosophica the woodcut of "Typus Musica" represents Music as a female figure holding a placard of musical notation and surrounded by performers on various instruments, harp, viol, organ, etc. With the chapter is a diagram of the groupings of musical tones. Under the all-inclusive Bis Diapason are the subdivisions Diapason and Diapason-cum-Diapenthe; under the Diapason or octave appears Diapenthe the interval of a fifth, and under Diapenthe the Diatessaron or Tetrachord, the interval of a fourth.

4213. Another temporal-astronomical opening, as in 1401 above. Lydgate, in his Troy Book, frequently marks thus a new phase of his story.

4215. Aquarius is next Capricorn in the Zodiac.

4216. *Janus bifrus.* This should be "bifrons", or two-browed; the print failed to recognize the horizontal mark over the vowel indicating an omitted nasal. Janus, in Roman mythology, presided over the beginnings of all things, was porter of Heaven, and guardian of gates on earth. He was represented with two heads because every door looks two ways.

4224-5. *corall . . . . rockes . . . toppes.* Hawes probably uses coral to make the landscape magical. According to Bartholomaeus' De Proprietatibus Rerum, coral was a tree as long as it remained under water, but on being drawn out turned to stone. Note the assonance of *rockes: toppes.* This un-Chaucerian license is fairly frequent in Lydgate.

4225. *popingayes,* parrots, favorite birds with medieval courts because of their decorative plumage and peculiar ways.

4230. *blasyng,* i.e., *blazoning,* or interpreting the devices upon a shield.

4255 ff. *Take hede,* etc. In the romance of Sir Degore 321-2 (see Utterson's Select Pieces of Early Popular Poetry, 1817, i:113-155) the giant is described "to loke on as I you tell As it had bene a fiende of hell." So in Guy of Warwick, when the hero encounters the giant Colbrond:—"Swiche armour as he hadde opon Ywis no herd ye neuer non Bot as it ware a fende of helle" (see ed. of 1840, p. 393). On p. 297 of the same text it is said of the Saracen giant that "He semed as it weren a fend þat comen weren out of helle."

4261. In Caxton's Recuyell, Hercules encounters the giant Cerberus with three heads, then the Hydra with seven heads.

4266. *cause encline,* cause to encline. Hawes' twisting of word-use again.

4288. *be displease.* There is apparently text-corruption here.

4291. *stremer grene.* Green was the color of fickleness.

4301-3. Clumsy change from indirect to direct discourse.

4307. *wondersly wrough.* The reprint of 1555 reads *wonderly wroth,* which restores the rime. Note reading of line 346.

4319. Hawes gives a name to his hero's sword, a trait frequent in the romances. Cp. Arthur's Excalibur, Sir Beves' Morgelai, Grine's Erkyn, Horn Childe's Bittofer, Torrent's Adolake. And in the Pilgrimage of the Life of Man, Moses gives Manhode the sword Versatile, Grace Dieu giving him the sword Righteousness.

4332. *what for that.* An ejaculation, as in line 757 above.

4344-45. In Caxton's Recuyell, ed. Sommer i:26, Hercules remembers Megaera as he fights.

4358. *venyme* should be *venum,* "venom", as in the 1555 text.

4363. The 1555 text garbles *demeaned you* to *demaunded.*

4364. *brayed.* This term was formerly applied to the voices of various animals. Caxton uses it of the elephant, and in book ii of the Recuyell the lions attacking Hercules "brayed in her throtes". The Italian poet Pugliese, of the 13th century, wrote "Gli auscelletti odo bradire", applying the word of same etymology to birds.

4386. *Upon,* at opening of the line, has apparently been intruded into the text from the second half-line. It is not in the 1555 edition.

4406. The verb *talk* is rarely used by Chaucer, somewhat more freely by Lydgate.

4411. The hero's name is asked; see note on 129 above.

4416. The 1555 text reads: "to attayne the same".

4426. The allusion is to Chaucer's Troilus i:358 ff. The movement of thought in 4427 is "and desired to see her still longer".

4431. Chaucer uses *wade* of conversation in Troilus ii:150; so does Capgrave in his St. Katherine iv:1624, and Cavendish as here, line 1218. For the ship-metaphor see note on 1257 *ante.*

444-45. The chapter-heading is out of place; it should precede line 4438.

NEVILL AND COPLAND: THE CASTELL OF PLEASURE

DIALOGUE

1 ff. Copland uses his participles very clumsily. Putting a semicolon or full stop at the end of line 4, we may paraphrase: "Your mind being considered (etc.), the effect being regarded (etc.), your circumstance and labor is of great efficacy (for him) who will examine it." Although the word "concern", line 6, is used by Lydgate to mean, "discern, perceive",— see FaPrinces i:6719, iii:1346, 4766, etc.,—it seems here to have more the later sense of "relate to, bear on". The last three lines of the stanza might then be paraphrased: "To adopt your moral teachings has a bearing on reason, (and tends) to draw young hearts with affection."

Beside this loose management of the participle, which reminds us of Lydgate, and the inversions, we observe in Copland's opening compliment to Nevill a further beclouding of the intention by the arbitrary use of Latin abstract words wrenched from their normal meaning.

This wrenching, we may remark, is not characteristic of Lydgate, but is frequent in Hawes; see for instance the note on line 78 of the Pastime of Pleasure. But such flourishing of terms does not go through Copland's introduction; although it reappears in his envoy, the most of these stanzas express the opinion of a practical business man, or a comment on the degeneracy of the times.

With this dialogue as introduction compare the method of Hoccleve in opening both his De Regimine Principum and his series of poems intended for Gloucester.

16. *inhabyte with Beaute.* See line 107; see Lydgate's Troy Book i :854.

32. *exployntyng.* Read "exploytyng", i.e., "succeeding". See Lydgate's FaPrinces v :713, vi :517, 542, etc. He uses it to mean "make to succeed", and the noun *expleit* as synonymous with "good speed".

38. *doost* should be *dooth.*

43. *At your instaunce.* Copland perhaps means an arrangement such as was frequent between Caxton and his noble patrons, who engaged to take "a reasonable number of copies" and to give him some material help otherwise. See p. 14 here.

47. *Tables / cayles / and balles,* i.e., backgammon, ninepins, and ball-playing.

THE CASTELL OF PLEASURE

1 ff. As Chaucer had done in the Book of the Duchesse and Parlement of Foules, Nevill starts his work with the reading of an old book, in this case the Metamorphoses of Ovid. He chances on the story of Phoebus' wounding by the arrow of Cupid, and his consequent passion for Daphne. His lines 13-48 should be compared with Metam. i :454-549.

11. *were compenable,* "were associated", i.e., what the conversation was.

17. *becomes me.* Ovid, "decent umeros nostros".

19-20. Nevill here muddles the Latin. It is Cupid, not Phoebus, who says (Metam. i :464-5), "quantoque animalia cedunt cuncta deo, tanto minor est tua gloria nostra." That is, "by as much as all living things are less than deity, by so much less ,is thy glory than mine." To this add the typographical error of the inserted *at* in line 19.

38. *dame saunce mercy.* As Daphne was vowed to virginity and the service of Diana, it may be that *dame* here is miswritten for *Diane.*

49. *at a syde.* Perhaps "at the moment of departure". Early Eng. *sithe* meant "a going, a journey". The last NED citation in this meaning is from the ,Towneley Mysteries, 1460.

49 ff. The ice of convention falls from Nevill's eyes and tongue in this stanza; but the conventional dream nevertheless follows. The lines, 49-60, are included in Flügel's Neuengl. Lesebuch, 1895, p. 17.

63. *enhaunce.* The NED gives one example, from 1632, of the "misuse" of this word to mean "surpass". This appears to be its force here, "overmaster".

79. The twelve-line stanza is now exchanged for the eight-line.

84. *in one,* i.e., in one man?

88. *solde and bought.* A proverbial expression, "all over with, done for". Cp. Richard III, act V, sc. 3 :306.

89. *it is done me,* etc. "I am given to understand." Cp. "I do you to wit."

95-6 are apparently the author's reply to Morpheus.

105 is spoken by the author, the rest of the stanza by Morpheus.

109. *apparage* is explained by NED as "rank", and illustrated from Hawes' ExamVirtue. Both there and here the sense "prowess" would better fit.

115. *gargeled galeryes.* See note on 178, and cp. Surrey's Complaint at Windsor, where the ladies watch the contestants from above.

119. *toke a dyreccyon.* Cp. Hawes' wresting of word-meaning for rime; see note on the Pastime line 78.

133. Nevill's meaning is that from courage comes the delight of the tourney. He may be using *ure* in a double sense, the *ore* from the Hill of Courage and the *practice* that upholds "doughty disport"; (*ure* can derive from *augurium,* "destiny", *opera,* "custom, practice", or *hora,* "hour". Lydgate-MSS usually spell it *ewre*).

151. Nevill, like Hawes, uses alliteration as a verse-ornament.

178. *Gargaled,* etc. The tower is "gargoyled" with various animals, among which the greyhound is first mentioned. See note on Hawes 106; and in 307 of the Pastime the Tower of Doctrine is "Gargeyld with grayhoundes and with many lyons". In chap. 26 of the Pastime the Tower of Chivalry, on a rock, is quadrant and is "gargeylde wyth beastes".

183. *grephyn,* "griffin". These mythological creatures, called by Aeschylus the "sharp-beaked unbarking dogs of Zeus", were mentioned by Pliny as "ferarum volucre genus". They were winged lions with the beaks of birds and with blazing eyes; they were supposed to guard the treasures of the Ind from those who would seize gold. They symbolized strength and guardianship, and their duty placed them in watchful antagonism to men. Hence, probably, Nevill speaks of their being "desolate of lyuely creature", and terms them "golden". But the "ruful mone" is perhaps for rime.

185-6. Nevill follows the procedure of Hawes in describing the "bejewelled" architecture and the windows. See notes on 347, 349-50 of the Pastime.

191-3. The two ways and their two "scryptures" are as in the Pastime 27-42; see note on 27 *ibid.* for Hercules' choice between Pleasure and Virtue, a choice referred to by Nevill in line 212 below.

209. Nevill muses as did Hawes line 44 of the Pastime.

214. In the fable of Prodicus, fifth century B.C., Hercules does not see two ways, but two female figures who discourse of their different ways, that of Pleasure and that of Virtue. Barclay (see ed. Ship of Fools by Jamieson ii:287) says however that he saw in a dream the two ways. The more obvious story-form must therefore have displaced the earlier.

425. *She* is Eloquence, who is escorting the dreamer.

427. *to lene at the herbar,* to listen outside the flower-walls of the arbor, as in La Belle Dame sans Merci 195.

830 ff. The Ubi Sunt motif; see FaPrinces, extract C here, introduction.

840. *the foure doctours,* i.e., Ambrose, Jerome, Augustine, Gregory.

872. *thereof, i*.e. of his dream.

NEVILL: ENVOY

1. *Go humble style,* etc. See note on Churl 379.

4. *arrect,* etc. The first NED case of to *arrect* or prick up (the ears) is of 1646.

12. *Ouyde . . . low style.* Nevill compares his work with that of Ovid in its lack of "rethoriques". See Lydgate's definition of "humble style" in FaPrinces vi:102-4:

> Nat maad corious be non auauntage
> Of rethoriques with musis for to stryue
> But in pleyn foorme ther deedis to descryue.

Ovid's style appears to us decidedly rhetorical; but Nevill continues by pointing out that his simple matter is not worthy the "high style" befitting wise and serious stories. The term "high style" was used by Chaucer in the Clerk's prol. and Tale 41,1092; see my Chaucer Manual, p. 252. On the "colors of rhetoric" see note FaPrinces G 46 here.

13. *to auoyde . . . slouthe.* See note on Hawes' Pastime, line 1313.

14. *with cloke,* i.e., under a fable or allegory. See note on Churl line 29, and cp. Hawes' Pastime, lines 659 ff.

COPLAND: ENVOY

16. *This rubryke,* i.e., this part or section of the work, with its heading. Titles or summaries were usually written in red, "rubricked"; and the term was extended to mean parts of the work thus marked.

18. *toke effect.* Again a wrenching of word-meaning; see notes on Nevill 119 and on the Pastime, line 78.

BARCLAY: THE SHIP OF FOOLS

7. *doth.* The plural in *-th* is frequent in Barclay; cp. lines 23, 206, 249, 6997, 7001, 8490, 8509. See also Walton's Boethius A 105 and Note, Cavendish 1261 and Note.

20. *Pallas and Minerva.* For this division of the goddess see Dunbar's Goldin Targe 78. Hawes' Pastime, chap. 36, lines 4914 etc., makes "dame Pallas" a goddess, while in chap. 27, lines 3271 etc., Minerva is at the court of king Meligius as instructress in arms. A similar splitting of Tullius and Cicero is made in the Confessio Amantis iv:2647-8, and earlier by Alars de Cambrai as cited Hist. Litt. de la France xvi:218. Alars also made Virgilius and Maro two people, as John of Salisbury does with Suetonius Tranquillus, see his Polycraticus viii:18 *ad finem.* For the reverse error see note on Brutus Cassius, FaPrinces E 63 here.

27. *lyke a Monster.* In the time of Shakespeare and Jonson, London abounded in exhibitors of "monsters", creatures which either were abnormal in physical structure or had been taught tricks; see The Tempest II, scene 2, and III, scene 2, also Jonson's Bartholomew Fair V, scene 3. This passage shows that earlier in the century the "monster" was exhibited, behind closed doors for better security of the owner's income.

36-7. The marginal note is "Horatius in sermonibus". The second satire of Horace's first book begins:—"Ambubiarum conlegia, pharmacopolae, Mendici, mimi, balatrones, hoc genus omne." Locher's Latin uses the word *pharmacopolas* in line 21; hence probably the reference.

43-49. The marginal note is: "Eccles. primo. Peruersi difficile corriguntur Et stultorum infinitus est numerus. Prouer. xxvi." The citation is from Ecclesiastes i:15; Proverbs xxvi deals with fools.

68. *by planettes.* The navigator finds in the stars adverse conditions.

74 is a proverb; cp. Lydgate's Dance Macabre 344, "Who al enbraceth litel shal restreine", and its French original, "Qui trop embraisse mal estraint", line 271 on p. 431 here. The same French sentence is at the head of a poem by Deschamps (see ed. by Tarbé i:32). Chaucer quotes it as a proverb in the tale of Melibeus, and it appears in the "Proverbs" ascribed to him.

75. *London Rockes.* This phrase I cannot satisfactorily explain. I find no evidence as to actual rocks in the Thames, nor any jesting use of the phrase to describe the low marshy banks of the river. It is possible that there is here a misprint of *Rocks* for *Docks,* a term used as early as Douglas' Aeneid and Leland's Itinerary to denote the bed in which a ship is anchored.

78. *arere.* Apparently an exclamation:—"Get back!" In Jamieson's ed. of the whole poem i: p. 297 we find the foolish night-serenaders made to "stande arere" by missiles flung from the windows. See also Eclogue iv:655. Cp. *Avaunt!*

85. *myrrour.* An exceedingly common metaphor in medieval literature. The number of volumes entitled Speculum or Mirror,—Ecclesiae, Laicorum, Peccatoris, Historiale, Myrrour of Life, Mirouer du Monde, Miroir aux Dames, Mirror for Magistrates, etc., is beyond count. The metaphor was as common in discourse as in title, cp. e.g., Lydgate's Dance Macabre 31, 637; cp. line 13186 here, etc., etc.

86-7. Beside these lines the print has "Speculum stultorum" in the margin.

92-3. In the margin the print has "Seneca Prouer.", transferred from Locher's Latin. Locher's text at that point is: "Nemo caret vitiis, nemo est sine crimine vite." Just below, against 95-98, is: "Quis potest dicere mundum est cor meum purus sum a peccato." This is from Proverbs xx:9. In 93 the bracketed word is from the 1570 ed.; our text reads *in.*

105. *babyll,* i.e., bauble, the imitation sceptre carried by the professional fool, resembling the modern "rattle" of a small child. See 502. Cromwell termed the Parliamentary mace "that bauble".

114. *insygne.* French *enseigner,* "educate". Note Barclay's use of a French term in rime. In the margin by this stanza is "Pedes enim eorum ad malum currunt et festinant ad effundendum sanguinem. Prouer. i. Ps. xlviii." The citation is from Proverbs i:16, but ends "ut effundant sanguinem". There is a similar text in Isaiah lix:7, but not in Psalms.

126. *delicious*, i.e., sensual, voluptuous. Caxton in the Golden Legend speaks of monks as "ouer delicious"; and Palsgrave in his 1530 dictionary defines it as "daynty mouthed or delycate".

131. The 1570 text changes *Pynsones* to *the Printers.*

134. In the margin is "Scribendi causa". The poet's conception of his duty and function, from Plato to George Meredith, is one of great interest. Browning, in The Glove, writes, "For I,—so I spoke—am a poet; Human nature,—behooves that I know it!" Meredith (Melampus) says that vitality resides in song solely "where earth and her uses to men, their needs, their forceful cravings, the theme are: there is it strong." Bunyan says that the Pilgrim's Progress was written "mine own self to gratify". Dante in the Vita Nuova says that he cannot do his lady justice with his praises, but speaks "to discharge his mind". None of these was the average medieval position. Barclay, translating and expanding the prologue of Locher to the Ship, declares that no poets write unless it be for the reader's pleasure or profit, or both; that poets teach what is good and what is evil, and that their intention has ever been to reprove vice and to commend virtue. He is undertaking the work to promote wisdom and to cleanse the vanity and madness of foolish people. Again, in the brief prose "Argument" just before the first book, Barclay says that he writes both to "auoyde the execrable inconuenyence of ydilnes, whyche (as saint Bernard sayth) is moder of all vices", and to deride fools. Henryson commends the sweet rhetoric of fables, but says they were first written to reprove misliving. The disappearance of the plea of "virtuous besynesse" as a literary motive and the frank recognition of pleasure to individual or group in its place is a mark of the Renaissance, and runs parallel with the crowding out of allegory by pure story. See notes on Hawes' Pastime 1313, Cavendish 24-30; see FaPrinces iii: 3823-36.

142. *inconuenyence*, "impropriety, unseemly wrong-doing", as in lines 534, 600 below, and often in this period. Cp. Cavendish 1371. In line 226 it means "injury", as in Hawes' Pastime, chap. 10, line 818, a passage not reproduced here.

148. In the margin is "Excusatio scribentis".

154. A passage of prose follows, introducing the "Boke". It is headed by Jamieson i:17 "The Argument", and may be read either there or in Flügel's Neuengl. Lesebuch, p. 104.

156. *pompe.* Is this misprinted for "poupe", the poop or high afterpart of the ship where the master stands, as in 162? The writing *pompe* is retained in the 1570 text; and cp. Cocke Lorels Bote, "some roped ye hoke, some ye pompe and some ye launce." The corresponding Latin line is: "rego docili vastaque vela manu".

162. In the margin appears "Diodorus Siculus li.i.", and just below it "Ecclesi. xij". The opening chapter of Diodorus the Sicilian's (Greek) Biblioteca Historica lauds the endeavor of historians to teach mankind "praeteritorum exemplis quid nobis appetendum sit quidve fugiendum". This Latin citation is from the transl. of the first five books of Diodorus by Poggio Bracciolini, printed 1472, 1476, 1496, ?1515, etc. We do not know whether Poggio, or Skelton's transl. of Diodorus, or a mere transfer of the marginal reference from Locher, is behind Barclay's use of the name here. The Ecclesiastes reference is to verse 129:— "Faciendi plures libros nullus est finis; frequensque meditatio carnis afflictio est".

166-68. In the margin is:—"Dabi*tur* liber nescienti*bus* lit*er*as. Esaie. xxix". See xxix:12 *ibid.*

181. *comon*, commune, talk. A frequent word with Barclay; see, e.g., Eclogue iv:472, 541. The Cawood print of 1570 changes to *comment.*

183. *Tholomeus.* In the margin is:—"Ptolome*us* philadetemus meminit Jo Sephus li.xij". In Josephus' Antiquitates Judaeorum xii cap. 2 it is said of Ptolemy Philadelphus' library that the king endeavored to gather all the books of the known world. Locher's text has "philadelphus", accurately.

190. In the margin is:—"Qui par*um* studet par*um* proficit glo. Li. vnicui*que* C. de prox. sacr. scri." I have not worked out this reference.

194. The 1570 edition reads *in*, our text *it.*

209. *the yresshe game.* "Irish" was a game resembling backgammon, but more complicated. Nares in his Glossary refers to the "Compleat Gamester" of 1680.

216. *Concedo.* "I assent." The Latin is:—"At si cum doctis versor concedere malo Omnia: ne cogar fors verba latina profari", etc. Watson translates:—"I shall condyscende vnto all theyr preposycyons for fere that I sholde not be reproched of that that I haue so euylly lerned."

231. *Honyngton or of Clyst.* These small Devonshire parishes,—Honiton and six places named Clyst,—were in the vicinity of St. Mary Ottery, where was Barclay's chaplaincy at this time. What personal animus may lie behind the allusion we do not know; but Pompen, p. 207, notes that the incumbent of Honiton, from 1505 till 1517, was Henry Ferman or Feyrman. See Pompen as cited; see Jamieson i:221; and cp. Skelton's Ware the Hauke.

235. The 1570 text omits *to Pryson.*

245. The last line of Locher's Latin at this point is:—"Auriculis asini tegitur sed magna caterua"; in the margin beside which is "Persius".

250. In the margin is:—"Translatio a somniantibus".

252. *occupye.* This word frequently means "to use" in late Middle English. In Cavendish's life of Wolsey we hear of "broken plate and old, not worthy to be occupied". See Exodus xxxviii:24, Judges xvi:11. In Lydgate, however, this sense is infrequent, and his usage is more commonly like ours. It is reflexive in FaPrinces A 398.

Two chapters are now omitted, on Evil Counsellors and on Avarice.

456 ff. Extravagantly cut and ornamented dress and headgear, curled, frizzed, and padded hair, as worn by upper-class men and women, were constant topics of satire in this period. See the dramas, from the 25th Coventry Play and the Woodstock Play to Medwall's Nature and its figure of Pride. See the introduction to Horns Away, p. 110 here, with refs. to contemporary verse and pictures. See lines 514, 533, 541, 8479-85 below; and with it cp. the sobriety of Henry VII, as described by John Blacman in his memoir of Henry, Cambridge, 1919.

466. The 1570 edition reads:—"you wiser then God omnipotent".

470. "The mode of dress has deteriorated. All sobriety is gone".

498. *of the first yere,* etc. That is, newly raised in rank; a metaphor from hunting. The antlers of a buck are said to be of the "first head" until he is at least five years old. "Of the first year" would be a still greener dignity.—*foxfurred.* Furs were most carefully prescribed and proscribed by the various English Acts of Apparel. By that of 1363 no yeoman or his family was to wear any rich fur, "mes soulment d'aignel, conil, chat, et goupil", i.e., lamb, cony, cat, and fox. In the petition of 1402 no "vadlet" is permitted any fur but lamb, fox, cony, and otter. By the law of 1465 sable and ermine were restricted to lords, and by that of 1509-10 sable could be worn only by earls and yet higher ranks. A foxfurred gentleman is therefore so new in gentlemanhood that he still wears the fur of his native yeoman class.

509, 514. *to lowe* probably alludes to the cut of clothing at the neck. While in Henry VI's time both sexes covered the neck and throat completely, in the reign of Henry VII men as well as women were bare-necked. The English fop at this period cut his doublet in a V as deep as that of a modern woman of fashion. A similar change from one extreme to the other may be seen in the styles of hair and shoes; cp. notes on 541, 8480 below, and the difference between the headdress of Richard II's time and the low flat cap of latter Edward IV, as described in the introd. to Horns Away *ante.*

512-13. *chaynes as withthes,* chains like (plaited?) golden rushes.

515. The wearing of "grosses Maunches pendants ouertez ne closez", i.e., big hanging sleeves open or closed, was petitioned against by the Commons in 1402. In 1406 they repeated the request to the King that such sleeves, and long gowns touching the ground, be forbidden; they also asked that sleeves "tranchez des peces", i.e., slashed, jagged in patterns at the edges, be prohibited. At this time sleeves were often made separate from the rest of the garment, of very rich stuffs, and either cut into roses, birds, etc., along the border, or trailing nearly to the ground, or padded to great dimensions,—"blasinge". By the 1465 Act of Apparel, early in Edward IV's reign, no yeoman or man of lower degree was to stuff his doublet with any bolster, wool, or cotton. See the prologue to the 25th Coventry Play, where Lucifer describes a dandy's costume.

In France especially the sleeve was further adorned by devices and mottoes, a custom followed by the higher classes in England. Charles of Orléans wore on his sleeve the words of a song and its notes, embroidered in seed pearls and precious stones. In the Epithalamium for Gloucester, 112, 161, are mentioned "mottoes" which may have been used in this manner. And it may be remarked that in the MS of the Fall of Princes, formerly Phillipps 4254, two of the miniatures show gallants who have devices embroidered on the left leg of the hose.

523. *Rubbe.* This orthography appears several times in the 1509 print of the Ship; see Jamieson i:80, ii:101. On ii:202 it is spelled *rebbing.*

527-9. The garments of a condemned criminal were sold after he had been hanged at Newgate. His body remained hanging, at least on a country gallows, until the neck broke away.

533-6. The manuscript-illuminations and the monuments of the time bear Barclay out in this statement; and the Acts of Apparel not only bewail the "inordinate Aray", but endeavor to force men and women to dress "according to their degrees". Impoverishment of the less wealthy, and class-confusion, were the arguments of the Commons in their various petitions to the sovereign. From that of 1363, which presents both these reasons, to that of 1465, there were three abortive attempts at controlling dress, the petitions of 1379, 1402, and 1406; only the second of these drew an assent, a very general one, from the king. See Rotuli Parliam. ii:278-82, iii:66, 506, 593, v:504. The law of 1465 was re-enacted in 1477 (Rot. Parl. vi:188-9), when the Commons declare that it had not been enforced, and that matters are worse than ever. There is then provided a system of collecting fines; but it was of no avail, and in 1482 (Rot. Parl. vi:220), the law was again enacted. Nothing more appears until the opening of Henry VIII's reign, 1509-10, when an Act of Apparel was passed (Statutes of the Realm iii:8-9), and is re-enacted 1514-15 and 1532-33. There was another such statute under Mary; see Statutes iv:239. That all the statutes on the matter were virtually a dead letter may be inferred from the satires of the two centuries.

541. *set Busshes.* See 8480 below. A gallant's hair, from the reign of Richard II to that of Edward IV, was curled and bushed like that of a Polynesian savage. In Medwall's play of Nature, printed 1516-20, the character of Pride says that he knits up his long hair at night and combs it out crisp and shining for the daytime. Other allusions by Barclay are in Jamieson ii:97, 268.

Fraustadt points out, p. 41 of his monograph as *ante,* that Barclay changes Locher's Ethiopians, as the source of this fashion, to "men of Inde". The same change is made in another passage of Barclay; see Jamieson ii:264. It is possibly because Vasco da Gama's opening of the sea-route to India in 1498, between the Latin and the English versions of the Ship, had created a general European interest in India; but it is also true that "the gretter Inde" had represented fabulous wealth and incredible marvel to the Western imagination long before da Gama. Some part in this change made by Barclay was perhaps due to the convenience of *Inde* as a rime-word.

This fashion, like that of neckwear, headdresses, and shoes, changed to the extreme when it changed. In 1521 Francis the First of France introduced the mode of close-cut hair, and a little earlier the long peaked men's shoes were replaced by the clumsy broadtoed footwear seen in the portraits of Henry VIII.

542-3 etc. *fleinge brayne.* The "inconstant mind" of the gallant is expressed by his extravagant parti-colored often-changed clothing.

553. *in the Quere,* in the choir. Their fathers were mass-priests?

555. Barclay censures dresses laced in the back, and high pointed headgear.

556. Delete the period at the end of the line as in the print.

557. *sadel.* I can throw no light here except to query if Barclay can mean the long train, often worn gathered up and fastened at the back of the waistband.

558-9. *decke slut. Copyntanke.* The word *copyntanke* (*copatain* in Shakespeare's Tam. Shrew V, 1:69), is first used here, according to the NED, and is found only in XVIth-century texts. It means a high sugarloaf hat, and its etymology, although probably French, is not clear.

The only meaning for the word *slut* which seems applicable here is that of "an oven-mop", recorded from Shropshire in the Engl. Dialect Dictionary. It is possible that Barclay first disrespectfully terms the high hat with its mass of ribands and veils a "deck mop", and then makes amends by giving it its foreign name. Cp. Lydgate's "humorous" procedure in FaPrinces ii :3360 ff.

575. By letting the tonsure grow the cleric "re-forms" himself to the appearance of a layman.

597. *your Prynce*. The Ship of Fools was published in December 1509, and Henry VII died in April of that year. The phrases here used seem more applicable to him than to Henry VIII, and this early part of the translation may have been executed before his death.

6930 ff. In Jamieson's edition of Barclay, this chapter is at p. 23 of vol. ii.

6953. "And then they take measures to know", etc.

6968. These place-names are largely adopted from the Latin. *Moryans,* or Barbary Moors, are also mentioned in Eclogue v; Athlant and Calpe are Atlas and Gibraltar, the latter being one of the two jaws of the Straits of Hercules; *Garnado* is Granada. Barclay does not mention the Northern lands "hynder Norvegen und Thyle", Iceland and "Pylappenland", which Locher had already dropped, except Thule, in translating the German of Brant. He adds to Locher's strong Mediterranean interest an allusion to the "newe fonde londe", line 6969. The coast of Labrador had been visited by the Portuguese in 1501, and in that year and in 1502 Henry VII had granted some Bristol and Portuguese merchants the right to make a voyage of discovery. In 1502 he paid twenty pounds to "the merchants of Bristoll that haue bene in the Newefounde Launde", and in 1503, 1505, he rewarded men who brought him hawks, wildcats, and popinjays from "the Newfounded Island". Hakluyt also speaks of three wild men who were captured "in the Newfound Island" and brought to court. *Hickscorner* mentions the "newfound island" in its list of places visited; and in Letters and Papers of Henry VIII, ed. Brewer iii :366, there are mentioned in the inventory of Lord Darcy's goods, 1520, nine pieces of hangings "having the story of the new funnd island". See Pollard's Reign of Henry VII, ii :345-47.

6973. *the see of Hercules*. Probably that part of the Mediterranean adjacent to the Straits of Hercules?

6985, 6995, 6997. *Strabo, plinius, Tholomeus*. The Geographia of Strabo, written under Augustus, the Historia Naturalis of Pliny the Elder, born just as Strabo died, and the "Instructions for the Drawing of Maps" written by Ptolemy in the second century, are the three great geographical reference-books of the Middle Ages. The churchman Barclay is by no means anticipating the anti-Ptolemaic theory of the solar system; but his criticism of these mighty authorities is noteworthy. Compare, in the second book of the Court of Sapience, the "processus" of Geometry, where the various theories of the earth's measurement, by Aristotle, Albertus, and a follower of Ptolemy, are given, and it is said "thus one clerk doth another confound".

7005. "It is a mad thing for any one to take trouble", etc.

7007-15. Allusion is here made to recent discoveries:—that of Newfoundland in 1501, the return of Vasco da Gama in 1503 from around the Cape of Good Hope to India, the earlier success of Columbus. *Ferdinandus* is Ferdinand V of Castile and II of Aragon, "the Catholic", husband of Isabella (who died 1504), and patron of Columbus.

8444 ff. Cp. the description of the Golden Age and the simplicity of manners then, in Virgil's Georgics i :125 ff., Ovid's Metamorphoses i :89 ff. and xv :96 ff., Hesiod as cited by Diodorus Siculus v, chap. 4, Boethius' De Consolatione ii metre 5, Chaucer's translation The Former Age, Lydgate's FaPrinces vii :1153 ff., Spenser's Faerie Queene ii, 7 :16, Browne's Britannia's Pastorals ii, song 3, Thomson's Spring 235 ff., Beattie's Minstrel ii, stanza 38.

8465. On usury see note Dance Macabre 393.

8480. *here out busshynge*. See 541 and note. In Barclay's Eclogue ii it is said that women most love those "well decked with large busshes set".

8503. *one grange,* etc. Neither to Barclay's mind nor to that of most Englishmen did it appear unfitting that an English cleric should hold more than one benefice; and "plurality" was not removed from the Church for centuries. But that a churl should own more than one homestead or farm was scandalously greedy.

8509. *churlys becomyth statis.* This may be a general conclusion from the preceding, and it may perhaps hint at Wolsey, to whom Barclay is supposed to have been antagonistic. Wolsey, the son of a well-to-do butcher or grazier, had received an University education, had been introduced to the notice of Henry VII, and had "of late" been made the King's chaplain, in 1507, the year before Barclay began his translation. Henry made him dean of Lincoln in early 1509, and Henry VIII on his accession in April of that year made Wolsey his almoner. In that capacity Wolsey was particularly distasteful to the old nobility. In the first of Barclay's eclogues is an allusion to "butchers dogges wood" (i.e. mad), which has been interpreted as meaning Wolsey; and documents printed by Brewer, Letters and Papers of Henry VIII, indicate that Barclay had incurred the suspicion of the Cardinal. See Schultz as *ante*, p. 298.

8515. *abhomynable.* For the spelling see note on Walton E 93 here.

13796-8. "A place . . . most meet for him."

3827. *reason . . . thyn.* Cp. Merch Tale 438, "my wit is thinne". ProlCantTales 748 has "my wit is short".

13836-9. Note Barclay's comment on printers.

13869. For a censure of Virgil see Macrobius' Saturnalia as cited by Skelton in the Garland of Laurell 380-84 note.

13874-8. Barclay ends with blame of vicious literature; cp. the remarks of Nevill and Copland at the opening of the Castell of Pleasure, p. 289 here. The names here singled out are Robin Hood and Philip Sparrow; and also in Eclogue iv:721 Barclay casts slur on Robin Hood. Ward, Catal. of Romances i:507, opined that Skelton, to whom Barclay had a strong antipathy, was probably author of a Robin Hood interlude or pageant; Brie, Engl Stud. 37:32-7, supports this.

In Roy's Rede Me and Be Not Wroth, ed. Arber, p. 64, it is said that the "frantyke foly" of the bishops forbids the use of the New Testament in English, "but as for tales of Robyn hode / With wother iestes nether honest or goode / They have none impediment". See Morley's language in his prose dedication, p. 386 here.

sparcles, scattered particles, whether of fire or not. The word, as verb or as substantive, is frequent in this period, from Caxton on. In Barclay's fifth eclogue we find "sprinkled and sparkled abrode"; Surrey in his Aeneis is fond of the term, which Wyatt also uses; in Sackville's Induction 464 he speaks of "spercled tresse", meaning scattered or dishevelled locks.

BARCLAY'S ECLOGUES: THE PROLOGUE AND THE FOURTH ECLOGUE

The text of this prologue shows the peculiar and apparently unreasonable notions of a sixteenth-century printer as to punctuation. The old cesural bar of the scribes, which had itself become a carelessly-handled convention before it passed away, is quite regularly replaced by a mid-line comma; and in a large number of cases the second line of a couplet closes with a full stop, the first with a colon, regardless of the flow of the sense. It is these frequent arbitrarinesses of method, alongside the better-judged handling of a few texts, e.g., in the Chaucer of 1561, which make the early history of English punctuation a psychological problem. The meddling of John Stow with Chaucerian rhythm, although it proves that he failed to hear -*e* final, proves also that he actually read the text; the more reasonable punctuation in his 1561 Chaucer may be due to the same cause, although the question has not yet been investigated. But the pointing here is quite mechanical and stupid; the reader should cancel it mentally in order to get the flow of Barclay's meaning.

Barclay's prologue bears but small relation to the dedicatory prose preface of Mantuan. It begins with Barclay's own survey of previous eclogue-writing. He names Theocritus, Virgil, and Mantuan, giving the palm to Mantuan in "that sorte". Petrarch follows, and then, unnamed, Theodulus, author of an "Ecloga" written in the seventh or eighth century, a dialogue between the shepherd Pseustis and the shepherdess Alithia, representing Falsehood and Truth, and discussing heathendom and Christianity with many examples from history or myth in support of the argument. Barclay then says that a youthful work is here revised and completed by him; he generalizes for a number of lines on this point, where Mantuan says briefly that he found a work of his youth which he had supposed destroyed, that he has polished it, and has added two more eclogues done later. The close agreement of line 73 with Mantuan's "intellexi apud quendam litterarium virum esse quendam libellum meum" causes us to doubt whether the experience here described is actually Barclay's or is imitated from Mantuan. The remainder of the prologue seems to be Barclay's own.

THE PROLOGUE

3. "They say boldly, they indite", etc.

14. *a que*, a half-farthing or quadrans, often abbreviated to *q* in accounts. The same phrase occurs in Barclay's Mirror of Good Manners; and see Skelton's Magnificence 36.

21. *Eglogues*. This word, first cited NED as of 1514, is used by Lydgate in Fall of Princes iii :110.

30. *style Heroicall*. See note on *style*, Nevill envoy 12.

31. *in our dayes*. Mantuan died in 1516.

32. *Hathe*. See note on Cavendish 1261.

37-42. *the father*, etc. See above.

51. *slouthe to eschewe*. See note on Hawes 1313, Cavendish 24-30.

78. *great instance*, urgent request.

85 ff. Horace in the Ars Poetica 114 ff. says, in Conington's translation:—"Gods should not talk like heroes, nor again Impetuous youth like grave and reverend men; Lady and nurse a different language crave, Sons of the soil and rovers o'er the wave."

98. *by that manner*, because of this mode of presenting my material.

100. *Closed in shadow*. Barclay means the same thing that Lydgate or Hawes means by "the veil of the fable". See notes Churl and Bird 29-30, Hawes' dedic. 34-42, etc.

104. *Poëte Laureate*. See note on Churl and Bird 15, Burgh 21.

107. *blacke . . . greene*. See note on Thebes prol. 73.

116-17. See note on Walton A 44.

127. There are not ten eclogues by Barclay preserved, but five. Mantuan had ten, Virgil ten, Petrarch twelve.

131. *Courtly Misery*. The title of the poems by Aeneas Sylvius Piccolomini, which Barclay follows in the first three eclogues, is Miseriae Curialium.

THE FOURTH ECLOGUE

Compare Spenser, Shepherd's Calendar, October. The names of the interlocutors here are, according to Mantuan, eclogue 5, Silvanus and Candidus, Silvanus being the rich and stingy sheepowner. Barclay substitutes Codrus and Minalcas. The latter is Virgilian, from the fifth eclogue; and in that same poem line 11 are mentioned the *iurgia Codri* or quarrels of Codrus, while in viii:26 Codrus is represented as envious. See the Carmina Burana II close,—"quia Codro codrior omnibus abundas"; is this a Virgilian allusion?

1-36. Barclay's stage-setting has no parallel in Mantuan.

16. *wide open*, i.e., on the back, relaxed. See Sir Degrevaunt 3352, Morte Arthure 2147, Beryn prol. 1293.

18. "Peered to see how his garments became him."

63. See Churl and Bird 87-8.

71 ff. This "example" is not in Mantuan.

137. Perhaps read "wel ere", i.e., "just now you conceded".

145. Read "Ye other shepherds"; Mantuan has "Vos quibus est res ampla domi", etc. 145-151 is quite closely from Mantuan.

162. *Renouncing cures*. Mantuan has:—"positis vitam traducere curis".

167-178. The description of a shepherd's duties fills two lines of Latin.

170. *daube*, lay on as whitewash. In Eclogue v one of the shepherd's labors, repairing the holes in his sheepcote, is to "stop them with stubble, eft daube them with some clay".

180. Mantuan 18-19 has:—"laudabile carmen. Omnem operam totumque caput . . . requirit."

185. "I can hardly support the burden of attending to one."

190. "Every one disdains to perform my tasks."

194. "—then my work is ruined".

195-200 are inserted by Barclay to break the long speech; see 459-62. Note the rime 199-200. Cornix is the principal speaker in Mantuan's sixth eclogue, used by Barclay for his fifth; he says nothing of this sort, however, and the sentiment is not in keeping with Codrus' later stinginess. If Barclay had any plan of making the niggard expansive until he had obtained his end, the management is interesting.

212. For this light and colloquial touch, and for lines 210-15, the Latin has only:—"tibi paenula, dicunt, . . . trita, genu nudum, riget hispida barba".

216. of leaues bare. Mantuan has "iam silvae implumes".

228-9. With the repetition of weary cp. Mantuan's repetition of paenitet thrice in two lines.

233 represents ut nosti in the Latin.

236. "At that time men give no thought to age."

247. Mantuan line 36 reads:—"formica, brevis sed provida bestia."

257. Barclay cannot pass unchallenged the acceptance of stellar influence on human fate in the Latin. Cp. his chapter against "astronomy" in the Ship of Fools, Jamieson ii :18. In the preface to his translation of Mancini we find:—"Helped by milde Planet and constellation. If Planets haue power or may helpe any thing." The Latin there is:—"Sydera coniuncta, sydera si qua valent." Mantuan himself, ecl. vii :181-2, makes Cornix say that "qui numerant stellas et se comprendere fata posse putant, stulti".

273-294. These four speeches are in Mantuan of two lines each.

286. reason and ballade consonant, sense and sound agreeing. Cp. such a title as Browning's Bells and Pomegranates.

295-346. This speech is of eleven lines in Mantuan.

296. fro presence, i.e., although thou art far from the Muses' presence, through us may come enjoyment of them.

301-2. Mantuan says, "Carmina sunt auris convivia, caseus oris". Note his word-play auris: oris, and cp. John of Salisbury's scitu: situ, urbis: orbis, militia: malitia; Fulgentius' famae: fami; Alanus' nomen: numen, etc.

315-18 are added by Barclay; see the FaPrinces viii :2685 ff. and note on Churl 260.

317. lymster, Leominster, in the west of England, near the Welsh border.

327. See Chaucer's adaptation from Claudian in PoFoules 99-105, and see note on Churl 351.

346. knot of Hercules, one of the attributes of Mercury; the twist of the serpents on his staff or caduceus. The allusion is to Hercules' strangling of two serpents while he was yet an infant; the phrase is explained by Macrobius in his Saturnalia i chap. 19 thus:—"Hi dracones parte media voluminis sui invicem nodo, quem vocant Herculis, obligantur" (Mustard).

347-8. Mantuan's shepherd says: "Vana supervacuis inculcas plurima verbis." The reply begins: "Vana inquis—" etc.

355. boye, a serving-knave; Prompt. Parv. scurrus. The meaning is that the attempt to labor hard, like a servant, is impossible if one is to "haunt the Muses".

385. Auoyde all charges, remove all responsibilities.

388. "Then shalt thou see and test what I am able to do".

399. Barclay expands somewhat Mantuan's sketch of a winter evening's amusements around the hearth; his eight lines represent five Latin. The prophitroles of 405 I cannot explain; the look of the word tempts one to suggest a game such as Ragman Roll, in which various written "fortunes", rolled together, were drawn out in turn by the players and read aloud. But such an amusement seems too "literary" for the group here described. See note on GarlLaurell 1455. With the description cp. Thomson's Winter 617-29, Milton's L'Allegro 100-15.

411. *Titerus,* Tityrus, i.e., Virgil.

414, 415. Cp. use of *sound* with that in 633, and see note *ibid.*

416. Mantuan 88 says: "et magno pulsabat cantu".

419-28. The parallel lines in Mantuan are:—

> eloquium fortuna dabat. Nos, debile vulgus,
> pannosos, macie affectos, farragine pastos,
> Aoniae fugiunt Musae, contemnit Apollo.

423. *frowise, froyse?* See note on Thebes 101.—*quacham* is not in NED or Eng. Dialect Dict.

425. *rusty meates,* foul food.—*inblindeth.* See use of *blind* in lines 1042, 1093, as "to make decrepit, dull".

431. Render with strong pause after *succoure.*

438. *man God auowe,* man may declare to God. See 726 below. The modern locution is "I'll tell the world". Cp. *and God toforn,* Troilus iii:1639, etc.

441. *Cosmus or Capell.* The wealth of Cosmo de' Medici of Florence was proverbial. Capell was the name of a great Austrian family, owners of vast landed estates in the fourteenth century. Their male line became extinct in 1408, and their possessions passed by marriage to the house of Lichtenstein.

444-6. Mantuan has only:—"Serica pallia, Tyrias chlamydes." The Acts of Apparel of Henry VIII and his predecessors specify these same costly stuffs named by Barclay as to be worn only by nobles.

447-8. Mantuan 98 has:—"non patinam Aesopi fames clipeumve Minervae." Mustard notes that this is Clodius Aesop, a Roman tragic actor of Cicero's time, of great wealth, who according to Pliny, Nat. Hist. x:141, served at a banquet a patina or pie of rare singing birds. This extravagance became proverbial. It was the son of this Aesop who is said to have dissolved and drunk a pearl. The shield of Minerva was also a large and costly pie, made of peacocks' brains, flamingoes' tongues, etc., and so called from its size.

To these classical examples Barclay adds "Peter's costly cope". Both here and in line 1141, where the miserly Codrus swears by "holy Peter's cope", the phrase may mean "a treasure". The NED under *cope* cites from Barclay's contemporary Whitinton, who in his Vulgaria quaedam cum suis vernaculis, printed in 1527, has "wolde spend Goddes cope (Tantaleas opes)". The NED suggests connection of the gold-idea with the stars, and the cope as heaven. See Beryn 453, where "siker as of goddis cope" apparently means "not sure at all".

451. Mantuan 101 has: "haec me iam pridem memini didicisse sub Umbro." The teacher from whom Mantuan makes his poet-shepherd derive his learning is Umber, Mantuan's name in his eclogues for his own master Gregorio Tifernate. Barclay makes a similar allusion to the Dean of St. Paul's, Colet.

459-62. This interruption by Codrus, not in Mantuan, is probably introduced by Barclay to make the dialogue brisk. Cp. 195-200, 609-28. Barclay adds 463-78.

479-80. *olde Pithagoras.* The Greek teacher Pythagoras, of the sixth century B.C., was a proverb for his doctrines of moral abstinence, extended by later popular belief to physical abstinence. The *Pythagorae mensae* of Mantuan 104 are dinners of herbs, with no meat.

490. Mantuan in ecl. ii:46-7 says, "finem philomena canendi fecerat" in the heat of summer. See also his ecl. v:108-9, the source of this passage.

496. *forⁱed cappes* were worn by bishops. Mantuan 112 says "pontifices". Read the line: "Or else if thou hast been with the forked caps."

507-8. Mantuan 115 has: "vesci Et lupus omni animal crudis existimat escis."

519. *I haue heard tell.* Mantuan says:—"Romana palatia vidi."

521. *Micene and Morton.* John Morton, Archbishop of Canterbury and Chancellor of the realm 1486, Cardinal 1493, previously Bishop of Ely, had died in 1500. *Micene* is perhaps Richard Mesyn or Misyn, Bishop of Dromore, who had died about 1462. He was the translator of Hampole into English, and as a Carmelite may have been conspicuous in Barclay's memory.

523-4. Mantuan 121 reads:—"Occidit Augustus numquam rediturus ab Orco."

525 ff. With Mantuan's censure of Rome's greed and Barclay's adoption of it unexpanded cp. Wyatt's expansion and emphasis on Alamanni's censure in his first satire, to Poyntz.

543-556. Three lines in Mantuan.

557-8. The couplet of the English is a single line in the Latin.

567-8. Mantuan has: "Consilii locuples ego, sed pauperrimus auri."

578. *a sawe,* etc.   Mantuan 141 has: "ut dentata acies veterique simillima serrae."

584. *at the length,* at length, finally. Cp. *at the large,* 81.

590-91. Mantuan 147 has: "ut frondes Aquilo, mare Libs, vineta pruinae."

596. *concend.* This is the only citation NED, which interprets "kindle, inflame". Why not "concede, agree to"? This spelling for *consent* is not impossible.

602. "Which do not become a man of position."

605. *deedes infame.* Mantuan has "infamibus actis".

606. *ouerlonge here.* This is a very frequent device of narrators. See, e.g., the tales of Knight and Squire, Lydgate's Thebes.

609-28 is inserted by Barclay to break the longest speech of the Latin. Cp. 459-62.

633. Mantuan 155 has "graves Musae." Barclay's use of *sound* as a transitive verb governing an abstract noun is not common in Mid Eng; but cp. Prol CT 275, "Souning always the encres of his winning".

634. "While these were in power."

639. Mantuan 159 has: "occidit ingenium vatum, ruit alta poesis."

643-652. Four lines in Mantuan.

654. *hye stile.* See notes here on Nevill's envoy line 12, and FaPrinces G 46.

659. Mantuan 165 has: "curis flagrantibus ardet."

686 ff. Thais, an Athenian courtesan, accompanied Alexander the Great to the East. Virgil in eclogue x mentions Lycoris as a Roman courtesan, and Barclay ecl. ii alludes to her. Testalis, "Thestylis", is referred to by Barclay in ecl. ii and by Skelton in his Garland 675; the name is taken either from Virgil's second eclogue or from Mantuan iv :176. The passage from Barclay's ecl. ii is: "Yet is it pleasour to handle and to toye With Galatea, Licoris, or Phillis, Neera, Malkin or lustie Testalis." Compare, without comparison, Milton's Lycidas 68-9.

688. *camous did promote.* Here I can only conjecture. The meaning of *camous* is a flat nose; see Chaucer's Reeve's Tale 14, 54, and Lydgate's Secrees 2623. If it be used here to mean "a flat-nosed (i.e., sensual and boorish) person", then Barclay says that Thais and Bacchus take their opportunity to push such a disciple (Skelton?) when true poetry is no longer practised. One might interpret that Thais tipped up her nose while drinking, as Milton's Death "upturned his nostril wide" (Par. Lost x :279-80), but there would be no apparent connection with what Barclay is saying in the rest of the passage. See Skelton's Elynour Rummyng 28.

689. *drames.* This is the earliest NED citation for the use of *drama* in its modern sense. But does it not mean "writers of plays"?

695. *artes triuiall.* The three arts of the Trivium, or fundamental University course in Grammar, Logic, and Rhetoric.

702. *fruitlesse of sentence,* empty of wisdom. This passage, 699 ff., is parallel to Mantuan's line 179,—"insulsi, illepidi, indociles, improvidi, inepti".

707. Mantuan has: "qui solet his vacuas praebere ambagibus aures."

708. "They count all others as devoid of judgment."

719-1140 are inserted by Barclay into the plan of the Latin eclogue.

721. The illiterate Codrus praises songs of Robin Hood; see note on line 13874 of the Ship of Fools here.

722. *Bentleys ale.* In ecl. ii one of the shepherds says "This ale brewed Bentley, it maketh me to winke."—*chaseth.* See Barclay's transl. of Mancini,—"though labour hath sore chased thy bloud". We might expect *chafeth*?

723-4. These are apparently women of the town, vulgar versions of Lycoris and Thestylis.

726. "Knowledge is a bore, I declare to God." See 438 and note. In Roy's Rede Me and Be Nott Wroth, ed. Arber, p. 62, one speaker says that he has explained a point and the other replies, "that thou hast, I make god a vowe". Cp. the use of "God to recorde", etc. in Skelton's Why Come Ye 483, in Godly Queen Hester 599, etc.

729-30. This couplet apparently refers to a rival of the poet. Minalcas, who has refused to sing of the vulgar subjects suggested by Codrus, refuses also to attack the envious of "diffamed name". Can this mean Skelton? does "Place most abused" refer to Skelton's rank of laureate?

736. *Malgre for malice.* In his fifth eclogue Barclay uses *malgre* (or, *maugre*) as a substantive:—"I thought no mauger, I tolde it for a bourd." The NED exemplifies the word as a substantive, meaning "ill, will", from 1320 to 1542. This passage means "To render ill will for malice, I refuse such payment".

755-56. The poet will call on no Muses to aid him; see note on Walton A 44.

759-60. In 746 Barclay announces that his ballad is to be based on "noble Salomon", in 758 that it is extract of Sapience,—perhaps the apocryphal book of Wisdom, which bears Solomon's name. No line of the four stanzas is exactly copied from a verse of Wisdom, but many of its principles are restated. Thus with 763-4 cp. Wisdom viii:10, 11, 19, xi:4, 28, xvi:16, xxiii:5; with 766 cp. Wisdom xxviii:11; with 775 cp. Wisdom i:4; with 783 cp. Wisdom xxi:23; with 784 cp. Wisdom xiv:29 and xxix:20; with 788 cp. Wisdom xxiii:5. There is but a general parallel between these stanzas and the De Quatuor Virtutibus translated from Mancini by Barclay.

791. Compare, so far as narrative management is concerned, the Host's interruption to the Rime of Sir Thopas. Most of Codrus' objection, however, is of the "Shoemaker, stick to your last!" type.

794. *boxe of tarre.* The constant companion of the shpeherd, used to heal scabs or wounds on the sheep. In the Assembly of Gods Pan has "a gret tar box hangyng by his side"; in As You Like It, act iii, the shepherd's hands smell of tar. Drayton in his fourth eclogue says of his shepherd that "His tarbox on his broad belt hung". See note on Piers Plowman (C) x:262-3.

798. Cornix is the name which Barclay often gives himself in these poems. See 1136.

811-20. As in 459-62, Barclay breaks up a long speech by a short one.

823 ff. The relation of this inserted elegy to Jean Lemaire de Belges' Temple dHonneur et de Vertus is briefly discussed in the introd. above. We may note that except between lines 878 and 879, 894 and 895, each stanza of Barclay picks up the rime of that preceding. For the subject of the elegy, Sir Edward Howard, see note on 853 below.

850. *enhaunsed,* etc., "elevated as is due a conqueror". The Scots had just been defeated, and their king slain, at Flodden Field. The English army was commanded by Thomas Howard, earl of Surrey, made Duke of Norfolk immediately after. See Cavendish 1121.

853. *Moste noble Hawarde,* etc. This is Thomas Howard, second duke of Norfolk, died 1524. Although attainted and imprisoned for his support of Richard III, Howard was subsequently restored to his honors by Henry VII, and under Henry VIII was an influential member of Council and an able military commander. He won the battle of Flodden Field in 1513, when seventy years old; and so highly did Henry value his judgment that he was made guardian of the realm during the king's absence at the Field of the Cloth of Gold. The duke had by his two wives eleven sons and seven daughters; see Barclay's line 852.

His second son, Sir Edward Howard, was a gallant sea-fighter. After two daring raids on the French coast in 1512, he was made Lord High Admiral; and the next year he was killed in a third expedition. His death was felt as a national disaster. His wife was by an earlier marriage to Sir William Parker the mother of Henry Lord Morley, whose verse-work is discussed in this volume.

It was the wife of Sir Edward's elder brother, the third duke, who patronized Skelton, and for whom he wrote, at Sheriff Hutton, the Garland of Laurell. See the appendix to vol. i of Nott's Wyatt and Surrey, *passim.*

855. *Talbot.* George Talbot, earl of Shrewsbury, died 1541, bore the sword at the coronation of both Henry VII and Henry VIII, was an executor of Henry VII's will, a joint

ambassador to the Pope in 1511, Lieutenant-General of the King's army in Picardy in 1513, etc. One of the most powerful of English nobles, of whom Wolsey wrote to the king:—"as active a capitaine as can be chosen within your realm".

859. *Corson.* This is probably Sir Robert Curzon or Corson, also termed Baron Curson, who in 1513 was Henry VIII's master of ordnance; see various mentions of him in Brewer's Letters and Papers of Henry VIII, vol. i. He is called "master of the rearward" in entry no. 4354 *ibid.,* and in entry no. 1757 is said to be "of Ipswich".

867. For note on the double superlative see Walton's Boethius B 28 here.

871 ff. Critics have praised this portrait of Labor, which I have not traced to any earlier source. The word of course means Effort. The opposing guardian of an entrance, in medieval romance and allegory, is usually a monster, from Cerberus to Milton's Sin and Death. Barclay's business here was to depict a figure definitely human, at once terrible and admirable; and he staggers somewhat under difficulties. He begins a list of "labors" with the dragon slain by Cadmus, the Chimaera overcome by Bellerophon, and the conquest of the Golden Fleece by Jason. His imagination is then apparently attracted to the labors of Hercules, and in 885 he mentions the oxen (of Geryon), the boar (of Erymanthus), the lion (of Nemaea). This variety of animal form sends his mind to Proteus and the changes assumed when Proteus attempted escape from the grasp of Aristeus,—see the fourth Georgic of Virgil; and for other accounts of the forms taken by the sea-god see the fourth book of the Odyssey or Ovid's Metamorphoses viii :732-4.

876-8 repeats the rime-word; in 878-9 the stanza-liaison by rime is broken, as in 894-5.

879-80. The management of these two lines, with the different placing of the word *Here,* recalls Inferno iii :14-15. This is not, however, saying that Barclay knew Dante's poem.

883. "He cannot of himself get anything."

895. *Alway he drinketh,* etc. It is the characteristic of "idropesie" in medieval thought that his thirst "crescit indulgens", as in Horace, Odes ii, 2:13, Gower's Confessio v:253-4, Lydgate's FaPrinces vii:998. This last reads: "The mor he drank the mor he was athrust". Barclay uses the touch here to make the giant's laborious sweat a realistic portrait.

901. "The sight of him instructs the rude."

905. *doth expres.* On the *-th* plural see notes Walton A 105 and Cavendish 1261. On *express* see note FaPrinces A 303 here.

912. *monster Minerua,* etc. Here I can only conjecture. Hercules was ultimately overcome by his labors, says Barclay, although at the opening of life he had chosen the path of Virtus rather than that of Pleasure. This story of the "Choice of Hercules" Barclay had translated when doing the Ship of Fools; see Jamieson ii :287, 302. On such a suggestion, the "sonne of Venus", line 918, would be a covering phrase for Pleasure; we may recollect that the daughter of Cupid was named Voluptas. But why Minerva or Pallas should be identified with this monster Labor is unclear, unless the similarity of their high inflexible purpose be dwelt on to the exclusion of all else.

916. *ouerccome and superate.* The spelling is as in the text. Such word-pairs, English and Latin often, are not uncommon in Barclay, and are frequent in Lydgate and in Early English generally. See line 921 here; see "more ewrouse or happy" in Eclogue v and in the preface to the translation of Mancini, also, e.g., in Lydgate's FaPrinces iv :3831.

929. "But because the entrance offers difficulty to them." In Chaucer's Troilus iv :922 *pretend* means *tend;* in Douglas' Aeneis and in Barclay's fifth eclogue it means *portend.*

969. "Yet his spirit (courage) thought itself of more worth" than inherited glory.

983 ff. With this reproach to Death compare the FaPrinces iii :3655 ff., Troy Book iii :5475 ff., Skelton's elegy on the earl of Northumberland, on the duke of Bedford (?), etc. Barclay is free from Lydgate's allusions to the Parcae, but "cries out on Fortune" quite according to medieval code. Love-laments of the period are more the direct address to Death, like Barclay's here; see Orléans' poem xv here and notes *ibid.*

994. "This act (of injustice) we might impute" etc. Read the passage with a comma after *suffred* and none after *mone,* in line 993. The first case NED of *impute* in the sense of *accuse* is of 1596.

998. "This will and liberty to torment mankind"?

1022. This line is aimed at the niggard Codrus.

1042. See 1093 for similar use of *blind* as "deprived of".

1043. See line 99 of FaPrinces extract B here.

1044. The meaning is,—shall I blame God for his death, or Fortune? Cp. FaPrinces i:2195, ii:3717, 3748, 4284, etc. for mention of God and Fortune as co-deities; denied however, *ibid.* i:4977-78.

1074. Read with a comma after *turned*.

1075-78. With this "exculpation" of Fortune cp. Boethius' De Consolatione ii prose 1, Machaut's Roy de Behaingne 725-34, Chaucer's Troilus i:848-49.

1083 ff. A list of unfortunate great now follows:—Pompey, Caesar, Cato, Seneca, Cicero, Polycrates, Alexander, Pyrrhus, Valerian, Priam, Paris, Hector, Cyrus.

1093. "Fortune hath tried, sorely dimming their dignity".

1097. *death dishonest.* Polycrates, tyrant of Samos, was hanged as "to alle folk odious", see FaPrinces iv:1094.

1103. *Pirrus.* Pyrrhus king of Epirus, while invading Argos B. C. 273, was killed by a tile flung from a housetop by a woman. Lydgate, FaPrinces iv:3880, has a different story.

1112. *Thomyris.* This savage queen of the Massagetae, who defeated Cyrus and plunged his head in a bath of blood, exercised a strong fascination on the early Renaissance. Lydgate deals with her FaPrinces ii:3844 ff., giving her no praise; but see note on Skelton's Garland 827 ff. here.

1115 ff. The close of the elegy, with its dignified exhortation to the bereaved father to recall the "dulce et decorum" of his son's death, is like the close of Lemaire de Belges' Temple d'Honneur. Note lines 1124, 1127-8.

1142. Here Mantuan begins again. The nine lines of the Latin ending are closely followed by Barclay. In 1141 the "holy Peters cope" of the English represents "per Superos, per Olympica numina". See note on 447-8 above; see TemGlass 117.

SKELTON: THE GARLAND OF LAURELL

1 ff. The astronomical opening; see note on Thebes 1 here. Mars is retrograde, going down the sky; Scorpio is 18 degrees high; the moon is full.

16. *encrampisshed,* etc. "My imagination was so straitly bound." See Chaucer's Anelida 171, Lydgate's FaPrinces i:3623, Flower of Courtesy 49, for this word.

17. With this leaning of the poet against a stump cp. Drayton's picture of his shepherd Rowland "leaning on a rampike tree", (i.e. one dead at the top), eclogue i, stanza four. Drayton's preface compares Barclay and ?Skelton, whom he calls Scoggin.

22. *forest of Galtres.* This great forest extended all around Sheriff Hutton, the seat of the Duke of Norfolk in Yorkshire, where Skelton was at this time the guest of the duke's daughter-in-law, the countess of Surrey. The forest was in part swampy, says Dyce, citing Camden's Britannia; see line 23 below.

27. *faire fall,* etc., "Success to that forester that can so bate his hound". The exact force of *bate* here is uncertain; it usually means to check, restrain.

34. *fatall persuasioun,* "prophetic assurance". See note on Hawes 665. Skelton foresees what is to happen to him.

36. *as I me auisid,* as I took note. At the opening of the Inferno Dante says *mi ritrovai,* "I came to myself". He too has slept, as Skelton has.

53. *Scyence seven.* See note on Hawes line 249.

71. "If it were not that he has your support."

73-4. *thensugerd pocioune,* etc., the sugared draught of Helicon's spring. See note on *sugared,* Thebes 52, on Helicon, Burgh's Letter 7. Cp. Bokenam's prol. to St. Agnes, "sugird welle in Elicona"; cp. "sugar dropis swete of Helicon", Court of Love 22; see Skelton against Garnesche, 98-99. The Roman poet Claudian, in his Laus Serenae, has "mella Heliconis".

77. *fyttynge*. In line 149 *syttynge* is similarly used. Either is appropriate, and either may be a misprint.

93-7. In defence of Skelton's "trew and playne" writing, Pallas adduces the cases of Ovid and of Juvenal, banished and threatened with death for similar free censure of the powerful. The reason for Ovid's banishment by Augustus has never been known; and the belief that Juvenal's visit to Egypt was a sort of exile because of his satiric attack on the imperial favorite has no certain basis.

97. *rubbid sum on the gall,* touched a sore spot for somebody. The NED cites Chaucer's WifeBath's Tale 84, and then this passage. See Cavendish 205.

101 ff. Skelton here sketches an animal-fable, and makes Pallas say that faultfinders might try to put an injurious interpretation on what the poet had written for his own pleasure. This passage seems to be a defense of something written by Skelton, using animals as poetic material, which had brought him under suspicion.

112. *fawte,* fault. This word was pronounced without the *l*-sound down to the nineteenth century; note Pope's rimes *sought: fault,* Iliad v :15-16, *thought: fault,* Odyss. xvii: 16-17. See Nevill 187-8 here.

114. *make I this motyve,* "propound this argument". The NED cites this passage to illustrate the meaning "a motion, proposition". The word has, I would suggest, much the meaning of *opposaile* below, i.e., of a propounded difficulty or question requiring answer. See Hoccleve's Lerne to Die 564, and see one of the many cases in Capgrave's St. Katherine, iv :1884,—"This is my motyf, an answere I desyre." Cp. *ibid.,* ii :1236, iv :1572, 1856, etc.

125-6. With this line-flow, run over and pausing sharply after the first foot of the following line, cp. lines 137-8, 143-4, 156-7, 164-5; and note 436-8, 656-7. It is more effective in Chaucer's BoDuchesse 22-23, 78-79, 111-12, 227-8, 1275-76; and in modern work such as Shelley's Hellas, Swinburne's Tristram of Lyonesse, the device is very conscious and emphatic.

130 ff. So full is the discussion of the relations between Demosthenes and Aeschines which Skelton now makes, that we may conjecture an allusion to himself and some rival poet under this disguise. Aeschines, for years the rival of Demosthenes, was at last defeated by him in public argument, and left Athens. It perhaps adds a special force to this comparison that the question argued was the legality of the golden crown which the State proposed to confer upon Demosthenes for his services.

141-3. "Your query in opposition is well put, and vigorously developed to your advantage; it is hard to combat." The word *opposaile* is first cited NED from Lydgate, see FaPrinces iii :431, v :2268. It occurs both times in rime, and with no such word in the antecedent French. It is also used in the earlier form of the envoy to the Libel of English Policy, not in rime.

151-3. "Whose attack in writing was very effective in urging Demosthenes to set out brilliantly his well-wrought argument, from which Aeschines had no escape."

162-7. A letter of St. Jerome to Paulinus, prefixed to the translation of the Vulgate by Jerome, begins :—"Frater Ambrosius tua mihi munuscula perferens, detulit simul—" etc. In the letter Jerome illustrates the greater force of the spoken as compared with the written word by an anecdote of Aeschines. "Unde et Aeschines cum Rhodi exularet, et legeretur illa Demosthenis oratio, quam adversus eum habuerat, mirantibus cunctis atque laudantibus, suspirans ait :—'Quid si ipsam audissetis bestiam sua verba resonantem!'"

188-9. *liddurns* or *lidderons* (cp. Ital. *ladrone*) means in sixteenth century English "rascals, scoundrels". Used by Skelton in Magnificence line 1919.—*losellis,* losels or worthless fellows, used from Langland down, and revived by Browning and other modern writers.—*facers* are swaggerers, bullies.—*bracers* is not in the NED, but cp. *bracery,* corruption, cited NED from a 1540 text. However, the word is in the rules of the charter of the Company of Musicians, incorporated 1640, forbidding "facing, bracing, evil reproaching, or affraying". This seems to connote violent deeds or talk.—*nowghtty pakkis* is used in a de Worde text of 1531, cited NED, as synonymous with "wretched livers". In Cotgrave's Dictionary *putaigne,* "harlot", is rendered "naughty pack".

192. "Riot and Revel are in the list of your household."

193. *Mayntenans,* maintenance, the keeping of an army of retainers paid or protected by the lord, was an evil legislated against in England by Richard II, and overcome through Henry VII's militia-system and the transfer of civil cases to the Star Chamber. Its abuse—the Earl of Warwick was escorted to Parliament by six hundred men wearing his badge and pledged to him—was according to historians a prime cause for the long-drawn out Wars of the Roses. See Hoccleve's RegPrinces 2791 ff.

196. *karlyle to kent,* Carlisle to Kent, from North to South of England.

201. *set oute a sunnyng,* idle in the sun, like useless or unnecessary things.

209. *Jak Athrommys bibille,* Jack o' Thrums' Bible. The same phrase occurs in Skelton's Magnificence, line 1427, and Jack a Thrums is mentioned in the third Garnesche poem, line 204, and in Colin Clout 284. Dyce refers to a burlesque printed in Reliquiae Antiquae i :84, in which are mentioned two noted preachers, "Jacke a Throme and Jone Brest Bale; these men seyd in the bibull that an ill drynker is unpossibul hevon for to wynne; for God luffus nodur hors nor mare, but mere men that in the cuppe con stare." Note also that Jack Drum's Entertainment, referred to in the Three Ladies of London, written about 1584, is a thrashing. Is "Jack a Thrums" the type of an illiterate tosspot, and his "Bible" the bottom of a tankard?

215. The printed eds, read *good record.* MS omits.

217. Note the inversion, and cp. lines 230, 232, 415, 417, 419, 879.

235. In the third book of Chaucer's Hous of Fame, Eolus is Fame's trumpeter.

236. *Bararag.* We would say "Tarantara". See line 245.

238. *at our retenew,* at our cost and charge. The phrase today would be "in our retinue", meaning the organization of household dependents.

239. *put hymself in prees.* This phrase, meaning to put one's self forward, compete for, take a risk, is used by Chaucer PoFoules 603, Scogan 49, Former Age 33. It is very frequent in Lydgate, and appears in Hoccleve, Bokenam, etc. Wyatt has it; but Spenser, ShepCal October 70, does not treat it as a reflexive.

242. The prints have *spede you.* MS omits.

243. "Let this trumpeter be produced at once!"

251. "Have in! Have out!" i.e., "Let me in! Get out!" are the cries of the rivals for Fame's favor.

260. *timorous blaste. Timorous* may mean terrible; see the NED citations, which do not include this passage. Cp. such phrases as Chaucer's "slepy yerde", KnTale 529, Cavendish's "trembling trompe", Visions 1222, Spenser's "slombring dew", Faerie Queene i, 1:36, Sandys' "drowsie rod", (translating Ovid's *virga movente soporem*), Milton's "oblivious pool", Par.Lost i :266, and his "forgetful lake", ii :74; cp. Thomson's "panting height", Summer 1670.

267. *for the nonys,* for the occasion. This phrase early became stereotyped, and part of its uses in late Middle English are such, part real. In Chaucer's Troilus iv :185, 428, it is living, probably also in ProlCT 379, but not so in Prologue 545, KnTale 21, 565, etc. With Lydgate it is oftener stereotyped than real; see Thebes 311, but Troy Book i :1315. This latter line has "as it wer for the nonys", like the Skelton line here, and as in Beryn 544. Hawes, Wyatt, etc., use the phrase; in our day it has been revived by Browning at its full original value; see Ring and Book x :41, Two Poets 1108-9, and cp. Childe Roland 179. In the epil. to Pacchiarotto, Browning uses it to contrast with "for the future".

270. *a murmur of minstrels.* Dyce compares "a noise of musicians" etc., in early plays by Lyly, Jonson, etc. This group includes Orpheus the Thracian and Amphion of Arcadia.

290. Daphne, pursued by Phoebus Apollo, fled him because Eros had stricken her with the leaden dart which expels love. See Ovid, Metam. i :471.

296. *O thoughtful herte,* etc. As Dyce notes, Lydgate opens his Life of Our Lady with this phrase. Skelton also used Lydgate's entire line in a poem to a lady named Katherine,—see Dyce i :25, where it will be seen that the stanza-initials give "Kateryn". Another phrase in the Kateryn-poem also occurs line 315 here. And there is a similarity in the opening line of a poem copied by MS Bodl. Fairfax 16,—"O wofull hert prisound in gret duresse." Mac-Cracken, printing this last-named poem in PLMA 26 :160, reads the line "—profound in gret duresse".

300. "As he did take the tree", etc.

301. This line is from Ovid, Metam. i:554,—"sentit adhuc trepidare novo sub cortice pectus."

302. *his.* Marshe's edition reads *this.*

304. *hard is,* etc. "Your star is unrelenting, unfavorable."

305. *cloyster virginall,* physical chastity.

306. "Hardened adamant is the cement of your wall."

310-14. These lines from Ovid, Metam. i:521-4. Marshe reads *gresse* in 314.

315. "The fervent accesses, burning fever-attacks, of love." A similar phrase, "feverous axys", occurs in Skelton's Kateryn-poem mentioned in note on 296 above; it is in the line preceding that modeled on Lydgate. The term *access* for recurrent ague-fits is used in Chaucer's Troilus ii:1316, in Lydgate's Temple of Glas 358 (see Schick's note), in the Cuckoo and Nightingale, etc.

320. What Ovid makes Apollo say is that if Daphne cannot be his love she shall be his tree, that he will always wear the laurel, and that it shall be worn by victorious generals.

324. See notes on ChurlandBird 15, Burgh 21. Dyce points out that "poetis laureat" means those holding degrees in the Trivium of Grammar, Logic, and Rhetoric, and that *poet* was used to signify a writer of either verse or prose, a maker.

326. *declynacyons.* Marshe's edition reads "Declamations".

326 ff. Skelton proceeds to display his learning by a list of writers and works from Quintilian to Lydgate. Quintilian's "Declamations" are now considered spurious. Theo-critus' "bucolycall relacyons" are his idyls, in which pastoral setting and story are mingled. Hesiod the "economist" or writer on husbandry is named in line 328, misprinted "Eliodus" by Faukes; *Icononucar,* as Dyce notes, is miswritten for Oeconomicus or Economicar (see line 353). Homer is in line 329 termed "the ffresshe historiar", i.e. vigorous narrator. Stanza 48 presents Cicero, Sallust's Catiline and his Jugurthine War, and Ovid. Skelton does not say that the Jugurtha has been translated by Barclay; the work appeared in 1520.

334-6. Read *blessed* in 334, as in 341, 348, etc.; MS *blesses.* The stanza-refrain uses assonance, *droppes: throtis,* as printed by Faukes; note Marshe's different reading, line 342.

337 ff. This stanza mentions Lucan, Statius and his Achilleis (only a fragment of which exists), Persius, Virgil, and Juvenal. Persius' *problems diffuse* may mean the veiled allusions of his satires, and it may mean only Skelton's desire for *pr*-alliteration. Virgil's Aeneid, and Juvenal who makes men thoughtful, follow. The word *satirray* is not in the NED, but obviously means satirist. 339 has no rime for 341.

342. The reading *flotes* instead of *droppes* is peculiar to the Marshe print, from which this stanza is taken to supply a gap in Faukes' text. The word perhaps means "flowings"; cp. *flotesse,* scum, skimmings.

344 ff. This stanza mentions Livy and Ennius. To Livy are ascribed "decades". His history of Rome was not so arranged by himself, but the scribes of it, already at the close of antiquity, imposed such a grouping on his material. Ennius' Annales are probably meant by line 347, but the work does not exist.

351 ff. Here are named Aulus Gellius the historian, Horace, Terence, and Plautus. Horace is credited with a "new poetry", a possible confusion, as Warton suggests, of the title of his Ars Poetica with that of Vinsauf's Nova Poetria.

358 ff. Skelton proceeds to Seneca's tragedies, Boethius' Consolatio, and Maximian's elegies, which latter are termed "mad ditties". Of Maximian's six elegies, the fifth, as Dyce remarks, may be described in line 361; in that poem Maximian narrates a love-adventure between himself in his later years and a "puella".

365 ff. This stanza mentions "John Bochas", i.e. Boccaccio, Quintus Curtius, and Macro-bius. By the "volumys grete" of Boccaccio are meant his Latin works, the De Casibus Virorum Illustrium, De Claris Mulieribus, De Genealogia Deorum. Quintus Curtius was the author of De Rebus Gestis Alexandri Magni. Macrobius' principal works are the Saturnalia, which Skelton does not mention, and a commentary, or "treu probate", on the Somnium Scipionis; this dream was contained in one of the lost books of Cicero's De Re Publica, and is preserved only by Macrobius.

372-6. Poggio of Florence and the French friar Gaguin are now named. Skelton does not allude to Poggio's Latin translation of (part of) Diodorus Siculus, used by himself for his version (see 1463 ff. below); what he mentions is the Facetiae, a collection of anecdotes and jests very popular in the sixteenth century, but now classed among the incredibly indecent productions of the Italian Renaissance. It gave Poggio a great reputation; Gawain Douglas names him with Plautus and Persius. Line 376 alludes to the quarrel between Skelton and Robert Gaguin, the leader of humanism in Paris, head of the Order of the Maturins, and royal ambassador to England in 1490, when he and Skelton may have met. We have no knowledge of this "flyting" other than Skelton's mention, line 1165 below, of his "recule against gaguyne", a work preserved only in fragments (see Brie in Englische Studien 37 :32).

380-4. Plutarch and Petrarch, Lucilius, Valerius Maximus, Vincentius, Propertius, and Pisander are next mentioned. Plutarch's Lives were translated from Greek into Latin, complete, by Campano, a pupil of Valla, and printed at Rome in 1470. Petrarch's Latin works, to which alone Skelton is probably alluding, include a Ciceronian treatise De remediis utriusque fortunae, many letters on the model of Cicero's, verse-eclogues, an epic entitled Africa, etc. Lucilius, a Roman satirist, is known to us only by fragments of his works. Valerius Maximus is the author of Factorum et Dictorum Memorabilium Libri, a compilation of anecdotes of "human interest" into groups according to the moral they point; the book was very popular in the late Middle Ages because of these two qualities. The phrase "by name", applied to Valerius, is not padding here, but a discrimination between him and Valerius Flaccus. See note on Thebes line 160. *Vincencius in speculo* alludes to Vincent of Beauvais, the thirteenth-century compiler of a huge four-part encyclopedia entitled the Speculum Majus, and divided into Naturale, Morale, Doctrinale, and Historiale. Propertius is the Roman writer of elegies. Pisander was the name of two Greek poets; the work of neither survives, but in Macrobius' Saturnalia (see note on 365 above) a carping guest at the banquet accuses Virgil, whose work is under discussion, of having stolen nearly all of the second book of the Aeneid from Pisander.

386. "And as I thus soberly looked about among them."

387-91. Skelton here links in apparent equality Gower, Chaucer, and Lydgate; but in Philip Sparrow 783 ff. he is amply shrewd in his judgment of the three elder poets. Other writers were less critical; see introd. to Lydgate, page 96, and see Walton's Boethius A 33-40 here, King James in the last stanza of the Kingis Quair, the Court of Sapience as printed p. 260 here, Hawes line 1261 ff. here and note, Feylde's prologue to Controversy between a Lover and a Jay.

397. Skelton's vanity is painfully obvious here, as in 1470.

402. *enplement*. The medieval French word *emplement* means approximately "arrival at goal, consummation".

405. *Brutus Albion*. Britain was supposedly founded by Brutus the Trojan, descendant of Aeneas, who came from Italy thither, and settled London as "New Troy". So says Geoffrey of Monmouth, the Welsh historiographer of the twelfth century. See note on Cavendish epitaph 35 here.

413. This line is used as refrain 427, 441. Note the repetition of 334-6.

415, 417, 419, are all inverted sentences; the latter half of each line is to be read first. See line 217.

436-7, 437-8. Cp. the run-over of 125-6 and note there.

442. *shewyd ther deuyse*, played their part. See FaPrinces v :2404.

455. A comma is to be understood after *was*.

460 ff. Observe the number of formations with the prefix *en*, a favorite device with Skelton. See 648 ff.

479. *clere story*. The upper part of a building, especially a church, which is free to light and air, and has a series of windows. Skelton's is the earliest non-ecclesiastical use, says NED. See Twelfth Night iv, 2:41.

485. *perlys of garnate*. The allusion here may be to Granada, at this time the center of the European jewel-trade. See note Churl and Bird 259. Caxton renders "von dosoye et de garnate" as "wyn of oseye and of Garnade".

492. *purseuantis,* etc. Pursuivants, i.e., heralds or newsbringers, with reports from Apulia (Poyle), Thrace, Limerick (Ireland), Lorraine (eastern France), etc.

495. *nauern,* etc. Navarre, a territory part French part Spanish, lying on both sides of the Pyrenees, is often mentioned in literature of this period. See FaPrinces viii :2884, ix :2459, 2471, Court of Love 1229, Skelton's poem Against the Scots 153, Lyndesay's Dreme 729-30, the poem Doctor Doubble Ale (89) in Hazlitt's EarlyPopPoetry iii, etc. Earlier uses cp. Laurence Minot, poem iv :70, the romance of Octavian 962, the poem King Berdok, etc. On this last the Cambr. Hist. Eng. Lit. ii :315 says "Strathnaver". One of the main roads from Spanish Navarre north led through Roncesvalles, "rounceuall", where part of Charlemagne's army suffered defeat in 778, and where a later church was famous.

497. *the mayne lande.* Probably the Almayne land, Germany.

500-502 are proverbs.

504. *fals quarter.* Dyce explains this from a seventeenth-century handbook on Armory as meaning a soreness on the inside of the hoof.

512-14. All sorts of men were there, from Dartmouth, Plymouth, Portsmouth; the bailiffs and burgesses of the Cinque Ports, i.e., of Dover, Sandwich, Romney, Hastings, Hythe. Skelton enumerates the most important commercial coast towns of England, his imagination passing from west through south to southeast.

522. *Occupacyon.* In the following passage Skelton states, in his own way, that the "eschewing of idleness", his industry in study and in writing, is the source of his fame. See notes here on Hawes 1313, Cavendish 24-30.

533-36. Skelton here suddenly gives a glimpse of lyrical power; the picture of the rising lark, springing from this pretentious and feeble allegory, gives us a shock of pleasure, all the greater because the line-movement reminds us of a true poet's: "Like to the lark at break of day arising From sullen earth". Most poets are touched to finer speech by the lark; Dante, Chaucer, Lydgate's lark "with notis newe hegh vp in the ayr", Milton's herald lark, come to the memory. William Browne and Beattie hear the song as "shrill", and pay less attention to the morning freshness of it. The nineteenth century is impressed by the invisibility of the music, as indeed was Charles Cotton in the seventeenth century. Hood · speaks of "vanished larks", Keats of the "skysearching lark", and the lark "lost" in the sky. Mrs. Browning's lark is "sucked up out of sight In vortices of glory and blue air", Tennyson's is "a sightless song", Browning's is "emballed by its own crystal song". Tennyson in The Princess harks back to the epithet "shrill"; Meredith calls the bird "dewdelighted",—and see his poem The Lark Ascending; to Christina Rossetti the lark is "hopeful". Galsworthy says that the lark "dripped his beads of song"'; Amy Lowell sees him "shooting up like a popgun-ball"; Joseph Auslander hears him "arguing with the sun", or "talking madness in some corner of the sky".

541 ff. There seems here an allusion to a turning-point in Skelton's life, when his "mast of worldly trust" was broken, perhaps by the death or alienation of a powerful patron, and when his assiduity in study repaired his fortunes.

550 ff. *a quyte your hyre,* reimburse you for your trouble. Skelton's name is to be sounded beyond Tyre, from Sidon to Olympus, from Babel to the Caspian hills.

561-2. There is here, as in Barclay's eclogue iv :879-80, a momentary reminder of the method of Dante; see Inferno iv :104, vi :113.

563 *whylis . . . space.* See ProlCantTales 35.

564-5. Cp. Dante's request to Virgil, Inferno xi :13-14,—"alcun compenso . . . trova, che il tempo non passi perduto".

567. *Wordes be swordes,* etc. A proverb.

590, 595. The leopard has an upraised paw resting on a scroll bearing the inscription. Line 595 is followed by a "cacosyntheton", or, in Greek, something ill put together. The subject is Industry; Skelton's six Latin lines show borrowings from classical authors, which Dyce points out. The second and third lines of the group are modeled on Juvenal's Satire viii :129,—

> Nec per conventus et cuncta per oppida *curvis*
> *Unguibus ire parat nummos raptura Celaeno,*

and the last line echoes Virgil's eclogue v:16. Dyce says that these lines are beyond his comprehension. Skelton seems to say that Industry (?) bears weapons more to be feared than are the bolts of Jove; that she is as ready to use her curved talons as is a harpy to snatch money. Then, enumerating the disputes of a fierce world, he adds: "Thou wanderest a thousand ways to seek for thyself the strife of Mars, that the wild nard may give place to the scorned and thorny rose-tree." Is he alluding to his own industrious use of letters as a weapon of attack?—These six lines are not included in our line-numbering, nor are subsequent Latin passages; the numbering of Dyce's edition therefore ceases now to agree with this.

604. Dyce cites but dismisses the suggestion that alchemists are here meant. See note on 607 below.

606. *pope-holy.* In the Romaunt of the Rose 415 Chaucer thus translates the French *papelardie,* "hypocrisy". The word is there possibly an adjective; it is such in Piers Plowman B 13:284, in the Ship of Fools, ed. Jamieson i:154, in Skelton's Magnificence 467 and in his ?Replycacion, ed. Dyce i:209. In the poem printed as by Lydgate, Halliwell, MinPo 27-46, it is a substantive.—*golde and hole,* "precious and perfect".

607. *powle hatchettis.* The NED, citing Skelton only, says "an opprobrious appellation". Skelton uses it also in a poem printed Dyce i:22-3. As he there employs the phrase "blynkerd blowboll", may it be that the expression "blow at the cole", above cited 604, is to be read "at the bole"? See Colyn Blowbole's Testament for the use of the word *blowbole* to mean "drunkard"; in Barclay's first eclogue Godfrey Gormand "blows in a bole", and in Lydgate's Mumming at Hertford the wife of Hob the Reeve sits "bolling at the nale" all day, and "hathe for the collyk pouped in the bolle".

613. "That fawn on thee and curs by nature. That—".

618. *Bowns,* etc. In modern parlance, "Bang, bang, bang".

623. *gunstones.* Dyce notes that this term was retained after iron shot had supplanted round stones for artillery.

626. *Masid as a marche hare,* wild as a hare in March,—the breeding time for hares. Earliest case of the locution in NED is 1529.

628. Skelton here fetches a slap at one of his opponents, whom he describes as a "tumbler" or mountebank, who later became a "dysour" or sneering jester, and then a gentleman. He is, adds Skelton, a second Piers the prater, who begins quarrels. The "Piers the prater" carries a modern student's thought to Piers Plowman and its attack on social abuses, but there is no certainty as to Skelton's meaning here.

629. *a deuyl way.* Cp. Chaucer's MillProl. 26 etc., and the phrase "a twenty devil way" in MillTale 527 etc. The exclamation is equivalent to "the devil take him!"

633. *foisty bawdias.* This exclamation occurs also in the fourth poem against Garnesche, line 76. It is used, with "Stryke pantnere", as formulae before drinking in The Kyng and the Hermyt, printed by Hazlitt, EEPopPo i, see lines 346, 349, etc.

635. *Dasyng,* or staring stupidly, *after dotrellis,* in the manner of dotterels or foolish birds easily caught, "like drunkards that drivel".

636. *Theis titiuyllis,* etc. Titivillus is the name given to the devil-figure of the Towneley Mysteries and other late medieval plays. The term became synonymous with any evil-meaning evil-doing person. Skelton says that these men were hit and "plugged" with tampions, the wooden stoppers of cannon-mouths.

646 ff. With the description of this garden cp. that depicted by Lydgate in the Churl and the Bird. Observe again the lavish coinage of words with prefix *en,* as in 460 ff.

646. "I saw where I was brought in an arbor." Note the inversion, and cp. 654. For the arbor see note on Cavendish 115-18; and cp. also the arbor of Doctrine, in the Assembly of Gods, with its painted walls. In the Augsburger Geschlechtertanz, of 1522, is depicted an arbor in a tree, reached by stairs; see Jahrb. d. kgl. preuss. Kunstsammlungen 32:230.

656-7. Again the run-over through one foot of the succeeding line, as in 125-6. With this line cp. Churl 53.

664. In the margin is "Oliua speciosa in campis".

665. The olive branches, symbols of peace, beat or blew up a fire against all rancor. We may perhaps note that a crest of the Howards of Norfolk was a pair of expanded wings. Note the linking to next strophe.

666. In the margin is "Nota excellentiam virtutis in oliva".

670. *soft pipling colde*. This phrase is used in George Macdonald's David Elginbrod.

675. *Thestylis*. See note on Barclay's eclogue iv:690.

681. *Cintheus*. Apollo; so called, as his sister Diana is called Cynthia, from their birth-place, Mt. Cynthus.

682-97. Dyce cites the passage, Aeneid i:740 ff., which Skelton here uses:—

> Cithara crinitus Iopas
> Personat aurata, docuit quae maxumus Atlas.
> Hic canit errantem lunam, solisque labores;
> Unde hominum genus, et pecudes; unde imber, et ignes;
> Arcturum, pluviasque Hyadas, geminosque Triones;
> Quid tantum Oceano properent se tinguere soles
> Hiberni, vel quae tardis mora noctibus obstet.

683. *The poemis*, etc. Either read *That* for *The*, or *he* for *in*.

691. *drowsy chere*. This term as applied to the Pleiades I cannot explain. The Hyades, sisters to the Pleiades, are termed by Virgil (see note above) *pluvias*, and by Horace *tristes*; see Carmina i, 3:14.

693. *trions*, or triones, ploughing-oxen; a name for the seven principal stars of Ursa Major, i.e. Charles' Wain. The Latin, as cited above, has "geminosque Triones", probably referring to both Ursa Major and Ursa Minor. The first citation of *trions* in NED is of 1594.

699. *counteryng*, singing counter, or by way of "embroidery" upon the simple air.

713. The opening *And* seems superfluous.

725. "That I care very much if it be disclosed", care to disclose it.

727-8. "I am not weighed down with lumps of sluggishness [note the inversion] as are bewildered dotards who dream in their stupidity."

730. *goode yere*. A formula-imprecation,—"Good luck to you!" See 986 below.

736. The Latin heading after this line means:—"A satire against a poet is interpolated, which it requires industry to understand." The set of numbers appended to the Latin, although reproduced here as in the Cotton MS, must be emended to the form given by the prints if the name of the person attacked by Skelton is to be deciphered. The puzzle was solved by the late Henry Bradley, in the Athenaeum 1896 ii:83; he explained that if the five vowels be represented by the numbers 1 to 5, and the consonants by their numbers in the alphabet, there will result from these figures the name *Rogerus Stathum*. Of this personage nothing is yet known; but as one of the ladies-in-waiting addressed by Skelton later in this poem is Gertrude Statham, and as Skelton hints that he had spoken sharp words to her on a previous occasion, it may be that the man Statham, her kinsman, was also a member of the Countess' household and an object of Skelton's uneasy jealousy.

The Latin verses have various classical echoes, pointed out by Dyce. The phrase *non tressis agaso,* "a hireling not worth three groats", is from Persius, Sat. v:76. Davus is in Plautus and Terence the name of a slave. The phrase *tacita sudant praecordia culpa,* "sweat with the silent consciousness of sin", is from Juvenal, Sat. i:167, and the words *labra . . . tacitus* are from Persius, Sat. v:184. From Virgil, eclogue vii:26, is the half-line *rumpantur ut ilia Codro,* "that Codrus' sides may burst". Skelton's portrait is of a clownish slave who rolls his eyes asquint as he catches parasites. If it happen, says Skelton, that you mention the things pleasing to Maia or to Jupiter, then suddenly he sweats in silent consciousness of wrongdoing; he flames up, urges this man and that man to strife; but none the less he fans useless fires, murmuring silent wishes that Codrus may burst his sides.

The list of deities here agrees with the seven fundamental metals of alchemy, as a marginal note in the prints states. It may be that Statham was interested in that science.

753. *Countes of Surrey*. This is Elizabeth Stafford, daughter of Edward duke of Buckingham, and second wife of Thomas Howard earl of Surrey, elder brother of the Admiral Howard who is lamented in Barclay's fourth eclogue. Surrey later, in 1524, became duke of

Norfolk; he was twenty years older than his wife, and the marriage was unhappy. See the duchess' later letters to Thomas Cromwell, lord of the Privy Seal, complaining bitterly of her husband's cruelty, niggardliness, and infidelity; these are printed in vol. i of Nott's ed. of Wyatt and Surrey, appendix nos. xxvii-xxxi, and a letter from the duke as no. xxxii. In these letters the duchess several times states that she has borne her husband five children. The eldest of these was Henry Howard earl of Surrey, the poet, who was at this time not more than three years old, while his mother was twenty-six. She was residing with her father-in-law at his estate of Sheriff Hutton. Her mother-in-law, Norfolk's second duchess, Agnes Tilney, is not of the little family circle which Skelton addresses.

769. "That call themselves women."

771. Skelton now draws a graceful picture of the "group of noble dames" at their needle-work. Sewing, lacemaking, weaving, embroidering, are the various occupations; some work on "samplers" (773) or braid lace (773), and some set themselves to weave in the *stool,* a stretcher or tambour-frame mounted on legs for the worker's convenience. In line 775 are enumerated some of the necessary appliances, the *slaiys,* sleys or weavers' reeds, the heddles or cords sustaining the warp on the loom. Tuly or tewly silk, mentioned in 782, is dark red; the *botum* or bottom of 783 is a skein of thread or the clew on which to wind a skein. The *tavels* of 775 are bobbins on which silk for the shuttle is wound; see Skelton's poem Comely Coystroun 34.

776-7. Observe the rime of *ng:n,* also in 779-82 the identical rime.

779. *glutton.* This term is clear from the context; but the NED recognizes no meaning which would would apply here.

785. *broken workis,* not defined in NED, may perhaps, like *broken ground,* be a raised surface, say of heavy embroidery.

786-7. *Castinge* is the making of knots on the ends of cords; *turnnynge* is twisting; *florisshinge of flowers* is the adding of curved lines waving from the blossoms over the groundwork. *burris rowthe* are raised rings; *buttunis surfullinge* means the embroidery of button-like knots.

801 ff. The sense is that you, Skelton, have to devise this "goodly conceit" (798) because you lay claim to the profession of humanity, i.e., the humanities, polite literature. Acknowl-edgments are to be made "after ther degre", that is, in order of the ladies' rank.

812. *tremlyng fyst.* Lydgate's phrase is "quaking pen".

823. *my lif enduring,* during my life.

826. "Which hath the highest quality (?) of honor and worship." This line is used as refrain, as was 336 *ante.—former date* is used by Skelton in his Northumberland 18.

827 ff. Skelton here makes some use of Boccaccio's De Claris Mulieribus. In that work Argia wife of Polynices is discussed in chap. 27, Pamphila in chap. 42, "Thamar" queen of Scythia in chap. 47, "Thamaris pictrix" in chap. 54, and Agrippina in chap. 88. Between Argia and Pamphila Skelton inserts the Biblical Rebecca. The selection of Pamphila and of "Thamar pictrix" (stanza 120) is obviously to draw the parallel between their occupations and that of the Countess at the time of Skelton's writing. Pamphila's discovery of silkworm culture and of the mode of weaving silk is described by Boccaccio more fully than here; Skelton brushes it all into one generalized line. He could get such a condensed version from Pliny's Natural History xi:26; but neither there nor in Boccaccio is Pamphila more than "mulier" or "femina". Thamyris daughter of Mycon the painter was herself an artist; pos-sibly the similarity of names takes Skelton from her to "dame Thamaris" the victor over Cyrus. But Queen Tomyris and Agrippina seem extraordinary selections from classical story to compare with English noblewomen. It is however true that Tomyris exercised a strong attraction on the Early Renaissance. In the set of tapestry verses sent to Queen Elizabeth by order of Catherine de Medicis, the gift copy of which is now MS Brit. Mus. Royal 20 A xx, Tomyris opens the list of 18 famous queens, and is followed by Artemisia, Esther, Plotina wife of Trajan, Eudoxia wife of Theodosius, Zenobia, Helena mother of Constantine, Clo-tilde,—then by French, Spanish, and English princesses. In Feylde's Controversy we hear (sarcastically?) of Tomyris "so hynde"; in Douglas' Palice of Honour a group of queens is "Semiramis, Thamar, Hippolita, Penthessilea, Medea, Zenobia"; Deschamps mentions

"Tamaris l'onouree" next after Hippolyta; Lydgate in the FaPrinces ii:3844 ff. narrates at length her slaying of Cyrus, Sackville in his Buckingham tragedy (Mirror for Magistrates) more briefly; Barclay ecl. iv:1112 merely mentions her. It might be remarked that just as the Transition or Early Renaissance included Thamaris among great queens, so it included Pasiphae and Sextus Tarquinius among great lovers. The Spaniard Ruiz, in his Libro del buen amor, did the latter, and Feylde the former, along with Scylla and Canace; Feylde's tone may be questioned.

848-61. The Lady Elizabeth Howard who is here addressed is probably the third daughter of the then duke of Norfolk by his second wife Agnes Tilney. As the duke married in 1508-9, and as their son was born 1509-10, the third daughter cannot in 1520 have been more than a child of five or six. Cp. 853 below.

849. Skelton compares Lady Elizabeth to "Aryna". Dyce suggests that this may mean Irene daughter of Cratinus, described by Boccaccio as above (chap. 57) as an artist and the daughter of an artist.

850. "The well and the perfect basis of virtue and knowledge." Cp. Lydgate's frequent complimentary phrases "sours and welle", "gynnyng and grounde".

855. *Polycene.* Polyxena daughter of Priam, beloved of Achilles, was in the Middle Ages proverbial for beauty and for fidelity in love. See, e.g., the balade of Chaucer's Legend; see Lydgate's Epithalamium 72 here.

862. The Lady Muriel Howard may be, as Dyce queries, a daughter of the earl and countess of Surrey. According to the countess' own statement, cited note on 753, *ante,* she bore her husband five children; the eldest of these, afterwards the poet, was in 1520 only about three years old, and his sister Mary a year or so younger. Between them and the youngest son, born about 1529, intervened two children of whom nothing is recorded, and who died early. Perhaps the "lytille lady" Muriel is one.

869. *Cydippes,* Cydippe, whose lover Acontius obtained her avowal by flinging at her feet an apple wrapped with a letter or "bille", which she unthinkingly read aloud.

876. *my lady Dakers.* Dyce identifies this lady as the wife of Thomas lord Dacre, and granddaughter of the then duke of Norfolk by his first wife Elizabeth Tilney. The married granddaughter of the first duchess and the girl daughter of the second duchess are thus associated here with the wife of the heir-apparent, the countess of Surrey. Skelton is classical and complimentary in his address of Lady Dacre. He praises her beauty, which he declares neither Zeuxis nor Apelles could paint, and compares her to Penelope, Deianira, and Diana. He does not specifically mention Diana's supremacy in weaving (see Ovid's Metamorphoses vi), nor Penelope's industry at the loom.

879. With the inversion cp. line 217 above.

890-1063. In these seven short-line lyrics, addressed apparently to damsels of the countess' household, Skelton's tone and touch change. There are still cumbrous classical allusions, but the line-movement is fresh and lilting, and the scent of flowers is about the reader. The first of the poems, to Margery Wentworth, is unsubstantial, for three of its five stanzas are identical; but its singing quality is marked. Observe the keeping of reference to the occupation of the group, in the embroidery-simile.

Margery Wentworth is probably the daughter of Sir Henry Wentworth, eldest son of an ancient Yorkshire house, who by his marriage with the daughter of Sir Philip Despenser had acquired the manor of Nettlestead, Suffolk. This daughter, who died 1550, married Sir John Seymour, by whom she became mother of Henry VIII's wife Jane Seymour, and grandmother to Edward VI. Note that she here outranks all the other ladies-in-waiting.

890. *mageran Jentil.* Dyce quotes Gerard's Herbal to show that this term was applied to the best sort of marjoram.

910. Mistress Margaret Tilney, here addressed, must be a kinswoman of either the first or the second duchess of Norfolk, both of whom bore that surname. The student may find food for conjecture in Skelton's language to her; he compares himself to Macareus the brother-lover of Canace, and likens her to Canace and to Phaedra, thus using two of the more impossible stories of antiquity, of the type rejected by Chaucer in the prologue to his Man of Law's Tale. Dyce quotes a passage from Feylde's Controversy between a Lover and

a Jay to show that the sixteenth century could see in Phaedra, Progne, Pasiphae, and Canace, examples of "true love". But, as said note 827 *ante,* Feylde's tone is not certain; nor is Skelton's here.

919. *Iwus,* "iwis"; cp. German *gewiss,* "certainly". The *i-* of this word is a survival of the OldEng past-participial *ge-* prefix, in this case of the verb *witan,* to know. Modern English constantly confuses the word with an imaginary *I wis,* treating *I* as a personal pronoun. So frequently in Browning.

932. *perle oryent,* i.e., margaret, a pearl. See 485 *ante.*

938 ff. The Jane Hassett here addressed, called Jane *Blenner haiset* in the printed eds., is surmised by Dyce to be perhaps a daughter of Sir Thomas Blennerhassett, who was one of the executors to the second duke of Norfolk a few years later.

947. *stellify.* This word in its first sense meant "to place among the constellations", as Jupiter raised Castor and Pollux, etc.; see HoFame 1002-08. Hence "to make a member of the Olympian group", as Philology by her marriage to Mercury. See Temple of Glass 136. Hence, "to exalt, extol".

956. *Laodomy,* Laodamia, one of the classical types of womanly constancy. After the death of her husband Protesilaus at Troy, she had an image of him made, upon which she centered all her grief. When her father destroyed this, she killed herself.

957. To Isabel Pennell, now addressed, Skelton uses a much livelier and more familiar tone.

969, 980. The MS reads *her, sefhe.*

976. *lure.* See note Dance Macabre 207. As the lure used in recalling hawks was the model of a bird, the sense here may be that of "type, model". But the NED gives no authority for such interpretation.

988. Margaret Hussey, another of the countess' gentlewomen, is now addressed. The rimes of the lyric again run in threes, except for the opening and closing lines; but the verselength is varied. My numbering hereafter departs further from that of Dyce, who breaks some of the lines written long by the manuscript.

989. *hauke of the towr.* A highflying or "towering" hawk; see Magnificence 926.

1005. *Isyphill.* Hypsipyle, the beloved of Jason, was another favorite classical heroine of the Middle Ages. Chaucer includes her in his Legend of Good Women, and part of her story is told by Lydgate, Thebes 3028 ff., with a reference there to Boccaccio's De Claris Mulieribus.

1007. *pomaunder.* French pomme d'ambre, a ball, or box containing a ball, of perfumes and spices, carried in the latter Middle Ages as a specific against the plague or as a luxury. Cardinal Wolsey used often an orange so stuffed; see line 125 of Cavendish here for note.

1008. *Goode Cassander.* Does Skelton mean Cassandra, or the herb cassawder, cassava?

1011-12. "Far may be sought before you can find" etc.

1016. See note on 736 for similarity of name between this lady-in-waiting and the Roger Statham there described.

1026. *dame Pasiphe.* Pasiphae, wife of King Minos of Crete, was mother of the monster Minotaur by a bull. See notes on 827, 910 *ante.*

1054, 1059. Delete the colon at end of 1057 and place period at end of 1059. Skelton says that Galatea was extolled by Virgil; she is briefly mentioned in the third eclogue, but her story is more fully told in Theocritus.

1074. *Master Newton.* Dyce makes no note at this point. Apparently the duke's household included a man whose occupation was draughting, illuminating, and scrivener-work. He is using compasses, a plummet or ?leadpencil, a penselle or brush of fine hair; he wears spectacles. For these last see note on line 54 of London Lickpenny here. The word *pencil* is used to mean "brush" as late as Tennyson, Gardener's Daughter 26; the term *plummet* for a leadpencil is not cited NED earlier than 1634, but see note here on Palladius, line 3 of extract A.

1108 ff. "The usual amount of your grace has been and yet is in proportion to all which suits with reason, unless hasty credence, by the urge of force, should happen to stand" etc.— *fortune,* 1112, is a verb, as in 85 above.

1134-40 are used, with appropriate border, as title page to Madden's Illuminated Ornament, London 1833.

1135. *golden railles.* The NED gives no clue here. What is meant may be something like "strap-work", which the NED defines as "an ornament consisting of a narrow fillet or band arranged in loops, sometimes of two such bands interlaced". This was much used in the 15th and 16th cents., especially in Flanders and Germany. Gollancz speaks of the Shirley MS now owned by the Prince of Wales (see p. 193) as having "borders of gold strap-work and flowers".

1145. *aurum musicum.* Read *aurum mosaicum,* a bronze powder used by painters.

1148. In the margin by stanza 140 is, in small type:—"Honor est benefactiue operacionis signum: Aristotiles: Diuerte a malo & fac bonum: Pso. Nobilis est ille quem nobilitat sua virtus: Cassianus. Proximus ille deo qui scit racione tacere. Cato. Mors vltima linea rerum. Horat."

1150 ff. A list of Skelton's works now follows. Many of them are lost; and in giving the catalogue, Occupation makes no distinction as to length or importance, nor as to date of composition. Manerly Margery is discussed through two stanzas, while the translation of Cicero's Ad Familiares is given one line. The early-executed rendering of Diodorus Siculus is mentioned far down the list, line 1463.

Skelton opens, stanza 140, with books on Honorous Estate, on How Men Should Flee Sin, on Royal Demeanor, on How to Speak Well, on How to Die. None of these has yet been identified with existing work; the last-mentioned is perhaps, as Dyce suggested, a version of the same original as Caxton used for his 1490 "Crafte to Know Well to Dye". There follow in stanza 141 the Interlude of Virtue, the Book of the Rosiar, Prince Arthur's Creation (i.e., assumption of the dignity of Prince of Wales, in 1489), a book on False Faith, dialogues of Imagination, "Antomedon of love's meditation", a new grammar, and the Bowge of Court. The last exists; and Brie identifies the Book of the Rosiar with the poem printed by Dyce i to follow page viii. See EnglStud 37:49. Upon Antomedon, or better "Automedon", line 1159, Brie has an important note in Archiv 138:228. Among the poets of the Anthologia Graeca, he tells us, was an epigrammatist named Automedon, to whom there are assigned eleven epigrams. The tenth is, in the Latin version of Duebner's ed. ii:294,—

> Felix *est* primum quidem qui nulli quidquam debet;
> dein qui non duxit uxorem, tertio qui est sine liberis.
> si vero insanus uxorem duxerit quispiam, habet gratiam,
> si defodiat statim uxorem, dotem nactus magnam.
> Haec edoctus sapiens esto; incassum vero Epicurum sine
> ubi *sit* vacuum quaerere, et quae sint monades.

Brie remarks that however trivial this seems to us, it had interest for the Renaissance; it was for instance translated by Ronsard in 1560.

1155. In the margin by stanza 141 is:—"Virtuti omnia parent: Salust. Nusquam tuta fides: Virgilius. Res est solliciti plena timoris amor. Ouid. Si vacet vsus quem penes &c. Horace."

1162 ff. In stanza 142 are listed a comedy Academios and the translation of Tully's (i.e., Cicero's) Ad Familiares, neither now known; a book Good Advisement (not known, but see Skelton's Replycacion 360-61), the Recule against Gaguin, a few lines of which have been discovered by Brie (see EnglStud 37:32), and The Popinjay, which is perhaps the existing Speke Parrot.

In the margin by this stanza is: "Non est timor dei ante oculos eorum. Spalmo. Concedat laurea lingue. Tullius. Fac cum consilio & in eternum non peccabis. Salamon."

1169 ff. This stanza mentions a pamphlet on Sovereignty (not known), and Magnificence. In the margin by this and the next stanza is:—"Non mihi sit modulo rustica papilio. Vates. Dominare in virtute tua. Pso. Magnificauit eum in conspectu regum. Sapiencia. Fugere pudor verumque fidesque. In quorum subiere locum fraudesque dolique. Insidieque et vis et amor scileratus habendi. Ouid. Filia Babilonis misera. Psalmo."

1176 ff. Two stanzas are now devoted to the various poems addressed to "Manerly Margery", only one of which is known today. Skelton breaks into rollicking doggerel coarseness as easily as he had earlier broken into song; he either likes his subject here or believes it interesting to the countess, for he disports himself at length with allusion incomprehensible to us. We perceive only that "Margery" is a woman of loose life but pretended honesty. Something further about her may be contained in the Latin verses, as yet unsolved. These Latin lines are omitted from the numbering here, while the two English lines are included. The last Latin line is unconnected with what precedes, and serves to summarize work by Skelton.

1183. In the margin by stanza 145 is:—"De nihilo nihil fit. Aristotiles. Le plus displeysant pleiser puent."

1188. Cp. the proverbial "It may well ryme but it acordeth nought", used as refrain in the poem printed as Lydgate's by Halliwell, Min Poems, p. 55.

1191 ff. As Dyce notes, "my ladys grace" perhaps refers to the countess of Derby, mother of Henry VII; see also Brie in EnglStud 37:9. By the Peregrination of Man's Life Skelton may mean a translation of Guillaume de Deguilleville's Pèlerinage, a very popular three-part poem of the fourteenth century, the first of the three pilgrimages being of man's life, the second of the soul, the third of Christ. Lydgate's verse-translation of the first part exists, but Skelton's prose is today unknown. Of the Red Rose treatise nothing is now known.

Beside stanzas 146 and 147 runs the marginal note:—"Notat bellum cornubiense quod in campistribus & in patencioribus vastique solitudinibus prope Grenewich gestum est." Beside 146 is the note:—"Apostolus. Non habemus hic ciuitatem manentem sed futuram perquerimus".

1199. In the margin by stanza 147 is:—"Erudemini qui iudicatis terram. Pso."

1202. This treatise, written for Henry VIII's boyhood, is not now known. Skelton was at the time "creancer" or tutor to the boy-prince. Dyce remarks that a manuscript of Precepta Moralia compiled by Skelton for Henry was once in the library of Lincoln Cathedral, but is now missing. Such handbooks were very numerous in the late Middle Ages; cp. Hoccleve's Regement of Princes, Ashby's Active Policy of a Prince, Barclay's transl. of Mancini, Hawes' effort to combine precept and entertainment in his Pastime of Pleasure, Spenser himself,—etc. For the Speculum-title see note on Ship of Fools 85.

1206-07. The Tunnyng of Elynour Rummyng and Colin Clout still exist. John Ive is possibly, as Dyce suggests, a lost work using the heretical teacher John Ive's name in its title. Ioforth Iack means "Get up, Jack!" and Dyce thinks that the phrase was used as a sort of refrain in the poem John Ive. But it must be noted that as "with Colyn Clout" introduces a separate work, a separate poem may here also be meant.

In the margin by stanza 148 is:—"Quis stabit mecum aduersus operantes in iniquitatem. Pso. Arrident melius seria picta iocis. In fabulis isopi."

1210. whyte . . . blacke. See note on Hawes' Pastime 1349.

1211. conueyauns, conveyance, is cunning, underhand dealing. See the play Magnificence.

1212. vse the walshemannys hoos. Dyce explains this as parallel to the proverbial use of "shipman's hose" to mean something which can be indefinitely adapted and stretched. See Colin Clout 780.

1213. These poems do not exist. A poem addressed to "Mistress Anne" is printed by Dyce i:20, and a fragmentary copy of another is printed by Brie in Engl Stud 37:29-30, from a text discovered by him on a guardleaf of MS Trin. Coll. Cambr. R 3, 17.

In the margin by stanza 149:—"Implent veteris Bacchi pinguisque ferine. Virgilius. Aut prodesse volunt aut delectare poete. Horace."

1216. Where it became, "what became of it". See FaPrinces C 20 here.

1218. The Ballad of the Mustard Tart is now unknown.

1220. Adame all. This epitaph may be read in Dyce i:171-3. Line 1221 means "let him sleep in peace like a dormouse".

In the margin by stanza 150 is:—"Adam adam vbi es. genesis. Resp. Vbi nulla requies vbi nullus ordo sed sempiternus horror inhabitat. Job".

1227 ff. Philip Sparrow was contemptuously treated by Barclay; see the close of the Ship of Fools. Although the Ship was printed in 1508, twelve years earlier than the Garland was written, it must be that Barclay's scorn still rankled, or that there had been more recent criticism, by Barclay or another. For the allusion to Philip Sparrow sends Skelton off on a detour of a hundred lines in the short couplet of that poem, an excursus which indeed appears in the early prints as "an adicyon made by Maister Skelton". See Dyce i :90-92.

In the margin by stanza 151 is :—"Etenim passer inuenit sibi domum. spalmo".

1242. *His dirige,* etc. Skelton says : "What ails (such jangling jays) to carp at Philip Sparrow's grave, at his dirige?" Her commendation, i.e., the praise of Philip's owner in the poem, cannot be matter of fault finding; it was joyous material, put in so that no one be displeased at the burial-song for Philip.

1250-55. In praising Jane or Joanna Scrope, the young girl-owner of Philip Sparrow, Skelton compares her to Lucretia, Polyxena, Calliope, Penelope, etc. She was thus "set and sorted", that is, placed and classed, with women of dignity.

1257. Hercules took out of hell Cerberus, his own friends Theseus and Pirithous, and Alcestis. The term "harrow hell" is applied in Middle English to Christ's descent into hell and removal from it of Adam, Eve, and the patriarchs, as related in the apocryphal gospel of Nicodemus. Warner, describing Hercules' exploits in his Albion's England, book i, says that he "harrowed Hell".

1259. Is Skelton thinking of Georgics iii :44,—"domitrix Epidaurus equorum"? Is he arbitrarily connecting that place with the horse-men, and constructing a form for rime?

1264. Hercules wounded and captured, but did not slay, the Maenalian hind, which had horns of gold and hoofs of brass. This was his fourth labor.

1267 ff. Hercules' eleventh labor was the obtaining of the apples of the Hesperides, which were guarded by a serpent. His tenth labor was the slaying of the three-bodied Geryon.

1277. *lyon sauage,* the Nemaean lion, slain as the first labor.

1278-81. The mares of Diomed were captured as Hercules' ninth labor.

1280. The rouncy was a common hackney or nag, more a farmhorse than a "steed".

1282-7. The bull here mentioned is a shape taken by the river-god Achelous, who fought in that form with Hercules for the possession of Deianira, but was defeated and deprived of one of his horns. Ovid, Metam. ix :86-7, says that the Naiads changed this horn into the horn of plenty; he makes Achelous say :—

> Naides hoc, pomis et odoro flore repletum,
> Sacrarunt; divesque meo Bona Copia cornu est.

1288. Skelton has conjured Philip Sparrow by Hercules, who harrowed Hell; now he calls on him by Hecate's power in the underworld, by the Eumenides or Fates, by the Lernaean hydra, by the Chimaera (1296), by the river Styx (1300), by Cocytus, by Charon, by Saul and the incantations of the witch who raised Samuel, by Diana, Luna, and Proserpine,— by all those who have power in Hades; then he asks (1336) what is the cause of this perplexity?

1310. *Primo regum expres,* "in the first book of Kings expressly set forth".

1311. *Phitones.* A Pythoness or witch is a woman possessed of an evil spirit which speaks. The name is ultimately from the Vulgate; in First Chronicles x :13 the modern rendering "one that hath a familiar spirit" appears as "pythonissa"; and in First Samuel xxviii :7 the witch of Endor is "mulier pythonem habens". The NED opines that a connection with Pythia was felt in the coinage of the word. In the form *Phitonesse* it is frequent in Middle English; see Chaucer's HoFame 1261, Friar's Tale 212, Gower's Confessio iv :1937, etc. The NED cites *Pythoness* as late as Byron.

1321. *idem numero,* the same (as) in the Book of Numbers.

1326-7. Skelton says: "I will leave it to lettered men generally to say (whether that spirit were the same Samuel as appears in the Book of Numbers)". See Lydgate's FaPrinces ii :451 ff.

1330-32. Diana is invoked in her three forms, earthly, heavenly, infernal.

1337. The words "Phillyppe answeryth" are found in the margin by the Latin line beginning "Nunc pudet"; it is probable that they refer only to the latter part of that line. The sense is: "O Philip, fair Joanna Scrope urgently implores thy deeps of hell; why does she now shrink in modesty from our song?—It is [too?] late; infamy is less than truth."

1342. The sense is: "Why, O sallow Envy, dost thou condemn the pious funeral rites of a bird? May such Fates snatch thee as snatch the bird! But envy is to thee an unending death." (Does this point at Barclay?)

1343. In the margin by stanza 152 is:—"Porcus se ingurgitat ceno & luto se immergit: Guarinus Veronensis. Et sicut oportorium mutabis eos & mutabuntur. Pso. C. Exultabuntur cornua iusti: spalmo." The same collocation of gr-words appears in the second poem against Garnesche; see Dyce i:118 line 2.

1344. "The mourning of the maple-root". Dyce points out that this lost poem is probably alluded to in one line of a song of 1609,—"Why weepst thou, maple root?"

1345-7. On this poem I can give no information; the lines may or may not sketch the plot of the Maple Root.

1348. *Moyses hornis.* The Vulgate translation of Exod. xxxiv:29 says that Moses, descending from Sinai, knew not "quod cornuta esset facies sua ex consortio sermonis Domini". St. Jerome, making the translation, was here misled by the Hebrew word meaning "to emit rays", which also meant "to put forth horns". Hence the horned Moses of Michelangelo; hence, e.g., Lydgate's allusions PilgLifeMan 1398, 1580, and Proc. Corpus Christi 50.

1349. *stormis.* Marshe reads *scornes.*

1350. *paiauntis,* etc. Dyce in a long note argues that this stanza does not refer to "theatrales ludos" such as Bale includes in his list of Skelton's writings, but to "things that were done" in Joyous Gard. As this was the name of Lancelot's castle, Skelton may be alluding to some aristocratic escapade or pageant of which the countess knew, and perhaps of which he had written disguisedly.

1351. *muse.* Marshe reads *mows.* In the margin here is:—"Tanquam parieti inclinato & macerie depulse. spalmo. Militat omnis amans et habet sua castra Cupido. Ouid."

1354. Dyce cites Cavendish's use of this phrase to mean Castle St. Angelo in Rome. But a student who reads, in Brewer and Gairdner's Letters and Papers of Henry VIII, ii:1510-11 etc., the long list of names of halls, tents, and pavilions, may query if this name were not applied to some English building, or even some pageant such as the "Gardyn de Esperance" described *ibid.,* p. 1509.

1357 ff. Again Skelton pours out a stream of disguised allusions, which his older hearers may have understood, but which are blind to us. Line 1357 means "the recital of the group of poems dealing with Rosamond's Bower". As the phrase "mok loste her sho" in 1363 seems to be part of a narrative of a love-affair, it may be used as was the phrase "tread her shoe amiss", which meant sexual misdoing, for a woman. But in Why Come Ye 83 the locution is less probably of this sort.

In the margin by the stanza is:—"Introduxit me in cubuculum suum. Cant. Os fatue ebullit stultitiam. Cant."

1358. *pleasaunt paine,* etc. This rhetorical device of "opposites" goes back, like so much else of late medieval poetic mannerism, to Ovid. Schroetter in his Ovid und die Troubadours points out that "pleasant pain" was a commonplace of Roman elegies, later a commonplace of Provençal lyric. He cites Ovid's *dulce malum,* the Troubadours' *doussa dolors.* Medieval Latin rhetoricians worked the device freely; St. Augustine uses it, and it is very frequent in Alanus. Chaucer is sparing of it; see Troilus ii:1099; and Lydgate has not many cases. It is often employed by Petrarch.

1367. *Exione.* Possibly Hesione, sister of Priam, taken captive by King Telamon and the Greeks in an expedition which slew Priam's father Laomedon and ravaged Troy, see Lydgate's Troy Book ii. It was in revenge for this that Paris made his incursion into Greece and carried off Helen, a deed followed by the Ten Years' War. Hesione herself plays no part in the Troy Book, but her name appears in some late medieval lists; e.g., Feylde in his Controversy says "Where is Semele and Iocasta, Cleoparte and Ixionya?" etc. And Douglas in his Palice of Honour, ed. Small i:23, writes "Jole, Hercules, Alcest, Ixion". Christine de Pisan in the Epistle of Othea mentions "Esyona". The Troy Book story of Hesione is quite other than the usual classical narrative as in e.g., Diodorus Siculus iv, chap. 42, or as in Hyginus' Fabulae no. 89.

Lines 1367 and 1368 are quite inexplicable to me. Marsh reads "her lambe is".

In the margin by stanza 155 is:—"Audaces fortuna iuuat. Uirgilius. Nescia mens hominum sortis fatique futuri. Uirgilius" (Aeneid x:501).

1371-7. The structure of this stanza is freakish. The usual rime-scheme is kept, but there is appended to each line a foot monorimed throughout, while the five-stress movement is quite lost.

In the margin by the stanza is:—"Oleeque minerua inuentrix. Georgicorum (see i:18-19). Atque agmina cerui puluerulenta glomerant. Eneid. 4" (see 154-5).

1377. A proverb:—With little occupation much rest is possible.

1378 ff. In the margin by this stanza is:—"Due molentes in pistrino vna assumetur altera relinquetur. Isaias. Foris vastabit eum timor et intus pravor. Pso."

1383. *Swassham and Some,* i.e., Swaffham(?) and Soham. Swaffham is in Norfolk, about 25 miles from Norwich, and Soham is six miles from Ely. Both places have fine early churches.

1385 ff. In the margin by this stanza is:—"Opera que ego facio ipsa perhibent testimonium de me. In euang. &c."—*wofully arayd.* A poem opening thus has been preserved, and is printed with Skelton's work by Dyce i:141. Brie in EnglStud 37:22-25 discusses this text and an earlier using the same phrase; he concludes that the poem printed by Dyce is probably not Skelton's.

1386. Another inverted line; see 217 *ante* and note. This line is appositive with that preceding.

1387. *Uexilla regis.* Dyce identifies this with a poem which he prints i:144. Brie, EnglStud 37:25-6, questions.

1388. *sacris solempniis.* Dyce doubts if this be a transl. of the Latin hymn beginning "Sacris solemniis juncta sunt gaudia".

1392 ff. In the margin by stanza 159 is:—"Honora medicum propter necessitatem creauit eum altissimus &c. Superiores lationes influunt in corpora subiecta et disposita &c. Nota."

1392-3. Here are mentioned a group of ancient physicians, Galen, Dioscorides, Hippocrates, Avicenna.

1395. Albumazar, an Arabian astrologer of the ninth century.

1397 ff. Skelton now runs into a whirl of proverbs and madcap nonsense. Stanza 160 is a compound of proverbs. Line 1400, "Dun is in the myre", is a Christmas game the title of which coincided with or passed into a proverb; the meaning is, "We are in a tight place". See Skeat's note CantTales H 5.

1399. In the margin beside this stanza is:—"Spectatum admisse risus teneatur amor. Horace."

1401-02 are transposed in the Faukes print.

1406 ff. In the margin is:—"Lumen ad reuelacionem gentium. Pso. clxxv." If "sol lucerne" means "sunlight" and "grand iuir" means "long winter", the French proverb here referred to is parallel to the Anglo-Saxon saying that if the ground hog sees his shadow on February second (Candlemas Day) there will be six weeks more of winter. The "Marion clarion" part of the stanza alludes probably to some story of Skelton's own making, and says that cold and clouds descended upon this goodly flower and untwined her (i.e., tore her to pieces). The bracketed addition to line 1410 appears only in the Faukes print, and may be a gloss.

1413 ff. In the margin is:—"Uelut rosa vel lilium O pulcherrima mulierum. &c. Cant. ecclesia."

1418-19. See the proverb in Churl and Bird 374. Barclay in his Mancini-translation also uses it.

1420 ff. In the margin is:—"Notate verba signata misteria. Gregori."

1422. *mary gipcy.* St. Mary Egyptiaca, the "Egipcien Marie" of Chaucer's Man of Law's Tale 402, is often confused with St. Mary Magdalen by the similarity of their stories.

1423. *Quod scripsi, scripsi.* So said Pilate, John xix:22.

1424-27. Dyce thinks that Skelton alludes to Luke i:13. If we credit Bale's report that Skelton was disciplined for maintaining an illegal wife, we might refer to Luke xx:35.

1428, 1432. Marshe reads *Asshrige*. Dyce has a full note here. There was a College of the Bonhommes at Ashridge in Buckinghamshire, which cherished as relic a portion of the blood of Jesus, brought over in the reign of Henry III by Edmund of Cornwall, the king's nephew and founder of the College. Another portion of the sacred blood, "sang royall", was deposited at Hailes Abbey; see PardTale 324 and Skeat's note. Both societies were in consequence sought by many pilgrims, and must have kept open house, see line 1432. On the Ashridge fraternity see Todd, History of the College of the Bonhommes at Ashridge, London, 1823. It may be remarked that the noble "Ellesmere" manuscript of the Canterbury Tales is possibly of Ashridge provenance.

1434. Skelton says that he has made a "distinction", or definition of the College, which follows in the two Latin lines. In these, the "fraxinus in clivo" is an ash-tree on a cliff or ridge,—Ashridge; and it flourishes without a supply of living water.

1435 ff. In the margin is:—"Nota. Penuriam aque nam canes ibi hauriunt ex puteo altissimo. Stultorum infinitus est numerus, &c. Ecclesiasticus. Factum est cum apollo esset corinthi: Actus apostolorum. Stimulos sub pectore vertit Apollo. Uirgilius.—*The nacyoun of folys.*" This was connected by Dyce with The Boke of Three Folys, which he reprinted i:199 from the 1568 Skelton. But Brie, EnglStud 37:18-21, points out that these three prose chapters are from the translation of the Ship of Fools made by Henry Watson and pubd. slightly earlier than that of Barclay. We have accordingly to say that Skelton's work here mentioned is unknown to us.

1436. *Apollo . . . whirllid vp his chare.* This line is the first of two which are all that remain of a third part of Chaucer's Squire's Tale. It seems to have caught the fancy of later versifiers. The author of the Flower and the Leaf begins his poem with it; the translator of Charles d'Orléans uses the line, see p. 230 here; and apparently Skelton opened one of his tirades with it. This poem he now wishes to efface from Fame's record, but she refuses,—stanza 165.

1442 ff. In the margin is:—"Fama repleta malis per virilis euolat alis, &c."

1449 ff. In the margin is:—"Ego quidem sum Pauli, ego Apollo: Cor."

1455. *ragman rollis.* This phrase is variously applied in Middle English to an important legal document and to a game, the point of contact being that in the game a roll of verses, individual "characters", was used, having separate pendent strings like the pendent seals of the document. The word "ragman" is still in dispute etymologically; Skeat (Piers Plowman A prol. 73 and C xix:122) suggests a Scandinavian connection with the word *ragmenni*, "coward". Such a term might have been applied to the Scottish nobles who signed allegiance to Edward I, and thereafter, on this theory, any document with seals might be so called. But Nares and others think that the game may have antedated the use of the word for lawdocuments; with this opinion I may compare the French poem in Montaiglon and Raynaud's Recueil général des Fabliaux, 1878, iii:247-8. Here an aristocratic company plays at "roy-qui-ne-ment", a sort of forfeits-game. Froissart twice mentions the game, and Langlois in Roman. Forsch. 23:163-73 discusses it, citing an allusion as early as 1285. With the *roi* of this game cp. the Greek game Basilinda and its elected king, also the late Mid Eng (tautological?) use of *King Ragman*. The word *ragment* came to mean any sort of discourse; see its use by Douglas, Dunbar, and Lyndesay. Gower, Confessio viii:2378-9, mentions the game; Udall in his transl. of Erasmus' Apophthegms, 1542, renders "Fescennina carmina" by "ragmans rewe", and then explains the word as "a long iest that raileth on any person by name" etc. Here the phrase means "list".

1456 ff. In the margin is:—"Malo me galathea petit lasciua puella. Virgilius. Nec si muneribus certes concedet Iollas. 2. Bucol."

1460-62. Three lost works by Skelton are now mentioned:—Of the Maiden of Kent called Comfort, Of Lovers' Testaments, and How Iollas Loved Phillis. Iollas is mentioned in Virgil's second eclogue, line 57, as a wealthy rival to Corydon. In the collection of Bucolica brought together by the printer Oporinus in 1546 are eclogues entitled *Iolas*, by an unknown author and by Stigelius.

1463 ff. In the margin is:—"Mille hominum species & rerum discolor vsus. Horace.— *Diodorus Siculus.* This translation of part of Diodorus, done from the Latin of Poggio, was mentioned by Caxton in the preface to his 1490 translation of the Aeneid, along with the translation of Cicero's Letters; both must therefore have been executed in Skelton's young manhood. An imperfect copy of the Diodorus exists in MS 357 of Corpus Christi College, Cambridge.

1470 ff. In the margin is:—"Millia milium & decies millies centena millia &c. Apocalipsis. Uite senatum laureati possident. Ecclesiastica. Cauit."

1480. *Janus* refers to an approaching January. The Latin following stanza 170 says:— "Dost thou desire to know what meaning may be in this for thee? Then advise thy mind; like Janus, look forward and back." Note the feminine *aemula*; Skelton is addressing a woman. Marshe's edition reads *Mens*, Faukes' *Meus*; Marshe reads *sis* in the second line, Faukes *sit*. In the margin by the Latin couplet is:—"Uates".—Skelton now addresses his book, using Latin and English in turn. He says: Go forth, O radiant light of the Britons! Our songs, do ye celebrate your worthy British Catullus! Say that Skelton is your Adonis, your Homer!

CAVENDISH'S METRICAL VISIONS

1 ff. Cavendish fixes the date of his poem astronomically, as Chaucer did the prologue to the Canterbury Tales, as Lydgate did his Siege of Thebes, Black Knight, etc., and as did many earlier writers; see note on Thebes lines 1 here. Cavendish's contemporary Robert Copland, in his Hye Wey to the Spyttel Hous, expressly declined such mode of dating a work; but modern poets have not ignored the effect of allusion to the great stars or constellaions. Thus Chatterton in his February, Thomson at the opening of his Autumn and of his Winter; thus Tennyson in the third part of Maud; thus Hardy in the second chapter of Far from the Madding Crowd,—"The Dog Star and Aldebaran, pointing to the restless Pleiades, were halfway up the southern sky". Still more archaic is the method of Housman,—"The sun at noon to higher air. Unharnessing the silver Pair That late before his chariot swam, Rides on the gold wool of the Ram". We may recollect Housman's strong interest in astrology.

4. *sygne retrogradaunt*. This means that the constellation or "sign" was on the western or descending side of the meridian line.

24-30. *Idelnes*. Sloth was one of the Seven Deadly Sins, and medieval writers frequently state that their work is undertaken to avoid the "mater vitiorum omnium". Peckham, Archbishop of Canterbury 1279-1292, in his treatise De Paupertate chap. 9, says "Labor principaliter inventus est pro otio excludendo". De Vignay in the prol. to his transl. of the Legenda Aurea speaks of the dangers of "oysiuete", and Chaucer at the opening of the Second Nun's Tale says that he intends to eschew idleness; see Brown in ModPhil 9:1-16 on the source. The lover in Chaucer's Book of the Duchesse wrote songs to keep himself from idleness; the compiler of the Scottish Legendary, ca. 1400, worked "for til eschew idilnes". Copland in the prol. to his Kalender of Shepeherdes gives the same reason for his undertaking; and the list could be indefinitely extended. See note on Hawes 1313 here, and for sloth in a lover see note on Reproof line 4. See also line 47 below, Barclay's prol. ecl. 51, Ship 134, etc.

31-2. Compare Copland's introd. to Nevill as *ante*, p. 289.

38. Cavendish says that should he choose as his theme the high courage of men of rank, he would lack examples of it in England because covetousness has so sorely impaired chivalry. Cp. Copland as just noted.

52. The request to correct is very common in the medieval period. Chaucer at the close of his Venus apologized for his inadequacy; and the phrases of excuse which he put into the mouth of his Franklin were taken as model by Lydgate, by Bokenam, and by others, who added to the apology an entreaty that the patron correct shortcomings. Chaucer makes such a request only at the close of his Troilus, and addresses it to fellow-writers, to Gower and to Strode; but Lydgate is profuse of it. See for instance Dance Macabre 660, Churl and Bird 385, ResonandSens 32-40, Troy Book i:30 ff., the close of St. Edmund, etc. When translating Laurent's version of the De Casibus, Lydgate could also find it in the French,— "ie le laisse et remetzı en la correction et amendment des sages hommes". Cp. also the last

stanza of La Belle Dame, Skelton's Garland 1525 ff., very often in Caxton, etc. In the Temple of Glass 1400 Lydgate says that he himself will correct if his patroness so desires. It is possibly the dependence of formal literature on patronage which gives this request to correct so wide a currency. See note on Shirley II: 71 here.

61. *colours.* This word has in late Middle or early Modern English three senses:—(1) pretext, as in FaPrinces i:5223, "Under a colour off liberalitie"; (2) rhetorical ornament, see note on FaPrinces G 46 here; (3) the fable under which a moral truth is conveyed; see Hawes' Pastime 740, 1297.

63. *wofull style.* Chaucer, Troilus i:12-14, said that a "sory chere'" suits well a sorrowful tale; and in SqTale 102-4 he said "Acordaunt to his wordes was his chere, As techeth art of speche hem that it lere". Lydgate, making similar statements in Black Knight 183-4, Troy Book iii:5453-57, especially FaPrinces vi:3144-50 (G 197-203 here), says in the last-named passage that men may read this doctrine in Tullius. In De Oratore ii:148, §35, we read "—ut eius . . . vultus denique perspiciamus omnis, qui sensus animi plerumque indicant". See also *ibid.,* iii:221, §59, and cp. Ovid, Fasti ii:755, "—facies animo dignaque parque fuit". Alanus says in his Anticlaudianus iii, cap. 4:7, 8 that the countenance is "nuntius, interpres verax animique figura". See Lydgate's description of the actors, Troy Book ii: 905 ff.; see Hawes' Pastime 1172 ff. Allied are FaPrinces ix:3447 and Henryson's Testament of Cresseid 1-2. See note on FaPrinces G 197 here.

65 ff. *Caliope wyll refuse,* etc. This line is imitated from FaPrinces prol. 241, see p. 160 here. In it and in 456-58 Lydgate says that ditties of complaining do not fit Calliope and the Muses. He had already said this in the Temple of Glass 952-4; and the rhetorical question of that passage,—"Allas to whom shal I for help call?" is repeated FaPrinces prol. 240 and by Cavendish 64 here. Chaucer had said, Troilus i:6, 7 and iv:22-24, that the Furies alone are fit patronesses of a woeful tale; and Lydgate adopts this convention, e.g., in DuorMerc 505, Troy Book iii:5428 ff. Cavendish calls on God for aid, though not rejecting the Muses for religious reasons, as Walton had done, see his Boethius A 60-64 and note.

79. *frome.* The writing of an inorganic final e is frequent in Cavendish's orthography; cp., in these extracts, *frome* 182, 1359, 1373, *bye* 176, *hyme* 173, 263, 266, 1139 and epitaph 39, *ame* 229, 231, 1382, *theme* 114, 1113, *whome* 154, 157, 266, 1316, etc. This inorganic e is also frequent in the copies of Chaucer and of Lydgate executed by John Shirley.

85. Cavendish opens his pageant of the fallen great with Wolsey, his late master, Cardinal and Archbishop of York,—*Eboracensis.* The career of Wolsey, born a grazier's son, educated at Oxford, favored by Henry because of his conspicuous ability, and deprived of his enormous wealth and power when his arrogance and excess, more especially his failure to obtain Henry's divorce from Katharine, had aroused the despot's anger,—is one of the perennially interesting stories of the world.

93. *legate de latere.* There are three classes of Papal legates,—legati nati, legati missi, and legati a latere. The first-named hold this ambassadorial power by virtue of their office; the second are deputed by the Pope for some special occasion, and the third, chosen by the Pope from among the Cardinals, exercise his power in some foreign country, where they reside. See note on 141.

101. *fynne* instead of *fyne.* Note the similar orthography in 43, 226; note *fynne: dynne* in 120-122; note *wynne* 131, *lynne* 1302, also *basse* 1165, *mattes* for *mates* in 1188. That a soft bed was a luxury in the Middle Ages we may infer from 246 and from Dance Macabre 252. The inventory of Wolsey's possessions written out in MS Brit. Mus. Harley 599 lists, in the expenditures for 1527, "A bedde for my Lordes owne lying, 8 mattresses, every one of them stuffed with 13 pounds of carded wulle". See Hoccleve's Lerne to Dye 778, and the original in Suso's Horologium,—"Tolle, tolle a me lectisterniorum molliciem", etc.

104-5. This means that there was nothing in the world Wolsey could desire which Fortune would not at once give him.

106. Very little remains of the interior decoration of Hampton Court, to which Cavendish is probably alluding here; but Law, in his History of Hampton Court Palace (1885) i:53, describes the beautiful ceiling of one small room still existing, ribbed with moulded wood, gilt, and with a light blue ground. The interest of the late Middle Ages in the roofs

of halls and reception rooms was very great; cp. Hawes' Pastime 349-50 and refs. given in note. Cp. also the romances, e.g. Syr Degrevaunt, for roofs "craftely entaylled".

111. *Expertest artificers*. A large number of the painters, carvers, and workers in plaster or terra-cotta who were employed on Hampton Court Palace by Wolsey were Italians. Many Italian artists were settled in or near Winchester, and the South-England great houses dating from Tudor times still show traces of their handiwork. Eminent men such as Rovezzano, Torrigiano, Maiano, executed commissions for Wolsey and for other English patrons; cp. note regarding Wolsey's tomb, line 225 below. The ten terra-cotta medallions done by Maiano for Wolsey are still at Hampton Court.

113. *Galleryes*. This especial feature of Wolsey's architecture is described in a contemporary Italian letter cited by Law, *op. cit.* above i:127, as consisting of long porticoes with windows on each side, looking on garden or river, the ceilings marvellously wrought, etc. It was Wolsey's habit in inclement weather to walk meditating in his galleries instead of in his gardens.

114. Here is still the Middle English construction *it lyked me,* where the modern is *I liked*. See Walton A 41, etc.

115-18. *Garden . . . arbors*. Wolsey's gardens, at Hampton Court and at York Place, were the objects of his most interested attention, and were laid out with great care. A walled garden was the fashion of the time, and had long been so; see the Roman de la Rose, Froissart's Paradys d'Amour, Lydgate's Black Knight, Reson and Sensuality, Churl and Bird, etc. No garden was complete without its arbor, set either high upon the mound, in a nook in the wall, or behind a thick hedge. In the last case, the hedge was made of trees so thickly intertwined with climbing plants that the occupant of the arbor was completely screened from observation. See the Pearl 38, Chaucer's prol. to the Legend 97, the Kingis Quair 213, La Belle Dame 191, the Flower and Leaf 49, 64, Hawes' Pastime 1939, 1962, Skelton's Garland 646, etc. At Hampton Court there were at least two arbors; and Wolsey loved to sit in one of these at evening to say his devotions.

117. *knottes*, i.e. flowerbeds laid out in fanciful intricate designs. In Cecil's Hist. of Gardening in England, ed. 1910, p. 76, are cuts of some of these knots. Inside the rectangular flowerbed an elaborate design in curves was laid out, the lines of which were either formed of box, thrift, savory, marjoram, on the general level of the bed, or the pattern was of raised earth, held in place by brick, tile, or lead, and artificially colored. This latter practice is condemned by Bacon in his essay Of Gardens; and the green knots were far more favored. Within the divisions of the pattern thus made the bed was filled with flowers, and green was used as border to the whole. Care had to be exercised to keep the knots from growing into the filling of the bed; cp. Shakespeare's Richard II act ii scene 4:46. Knots in a garden are mentioned by Hawes, Pastime chap. 18 line 1955, and also in roofs, see note on line 106 above.

119. *pestylent ayers*. It was the general medieval belief that disease and pestilence were caused and spread by bad air. Many authorities opined that the ultimate cause of the Black Death which ravaged Europe in the latter fourteenth century was the inauspicious conjunction of Saturn, Jupiter, and Mars in the sign of Aquarius in 1345. There was in consequence, said the medical faculty of Paris, a struggle between the sun and the sea in the Orient which produced a thick stinking mist; and this mist spread gradually to Europe. Terrific earthquakes in Greece, Cyprus, and Italy in 1348 were accompaniments of this pestilential fog. Whoever breathed such an atmosphere suffered a putrid corrupton of the blood in the lungs and heart; consequently all who wished to escape infection must purify the air about them, and must bleed and purge. The south wind, the bringer of evil from the world's centre of contagion, must be carefully avoided. Fires were to be kept blazing in the house; the leaves of the baytree, the juniper, and wormwood, were to be strewn about; the floors were to be sprinkled with vinegar, and the hands and face frequently washed with vinegar and water. Sanitary measures were also advised for towns; refuse was not to lie in the streets. Lydgate in his Troy Book ii:749 ff. enlarges on the sewerage system of New Troy, and describes how the gutters were so constantly flushed that no filth could be seen anywhere,—"Whereby þe town was outterly assured From engendryng of al corrupcioun, From wikked eyr and from infeccioun, þat causen ofte by her violence Mortalite and gret pestilence."

A garden was thus not merely an aesthetic delight, but an hygienic precaution, to the medieval mind. Hawes, in his Pastime 1924-5, speaks of walking "among the floures of aromatic fume The mysty ayre to exyle and consume". And whenever writers of this period allude to morning mists or to the danger of the south wind, it is these theories which are at the back of their minds. See note on 125 below.

120-1. Tapestry was a passion with Wolsey. He purchased scores of sets at a time, and Sir Richard Gresham was especially commissioned to obtain in Flanders the many hangings for Hampton Court. See the comment of Skelton, evidently an eyewitness, in Colin Clout 942 ff.; and see Law's Hist. of Hampton Court Palace i chap. 5. A condensed list of the Cardinal's tapestries, made when his goods were handed over to Henry VIII, is in Brewer's Letters and Papers of Henry VIII, iv:2763 ff. Many of these were of Scriptural subjects, but many also of the story of Priam, the Romaunt of the Rose, the Triumphs of Petrarch, the Wheel of Fortune, etc. Others were hunting scenes, studies of flowers, trees, etc. The fourteenth and fifteenth centuries made a distinction between ordinary tapestry and tapestry à personnages; the latter presented heroes and scenes of history or romance, and the weave was full of human figures, often with verses in the bordure and scrolls of identification or of speeches on the shoulders or pennons of the principal actors. "Tapestry ystoriée" was the term applied to such hangings; see EnglStud 43:10-26 for note on two sets of verses composed by Lydgate for this purpose; see also Bycorne and Chichevache, p. 114 here.

123. *clothe of estate,* the canopy over the seat of honor. See Cavendish's Life of Wolsey. ed. 1827, p. 113, with its mention of "my lord Cardinal sitting under the cloth of estate"; and see also *ibid.,* 117, 195, 211, etc., Skelton's Garland 484, Paradise Lost x:445-6.

125. The use of perfumes was not only a luxury but an hygienic precaution in an age of the pestilence and "the sweating sickness". Cavendish says in his Life, ed. 1827, p. 106, that whenever the Cardinal was receiving a throng of suitors he moved among them "holding in his hand a very fair orange, where the meat or substance within was taken out, and filled up again with the part of a sponge, wherein was vinegar, and other confections against the pestilent airs". Perfumes were frequently used in such a "pomaunder", see note on Skelton's Garland 1007. The musk and ambergris here mentioned as used in the chamber were too costly for any but the wealthy; poorer people used bay leaves, etc.; see note on 119 *ante.*

127. *Plate.* There is an "Account of Plate, Gold and Silver, made for Cardinal Wolsey from the 9th Year of Henry VIII unto the 19th",—printed from MS in John Gutch's Collectanea Curiosa, Oxford, 1781, ii:334-344. Cavendish in his Life mentions Wolsey's plate on p. 195.

133. *seruauntes.* Fiddes in his Life of Wolsey ed. 1726, p. 100, says that the Cardinal's household numbered 800; Law in his Hampton Court i chap. 7 says 500. Cavendish's Life, ed. 1827, p. 96 ff., enumerates the principal officers.

134. *Crossis twayn.* These, and the pillars and pole-axes mentioned in 137-8 below were borne before Wolsey on all formal occasions. Cavendish, *op. cit.,* p. 94, says that the crosses were carried "whithersoever he went or rode, by two of the most tallest and comeliest priests that he could get within all his realm"; and p. 108 he describes Wolsey as riding "upon his mule with his crosses, his pillars, his hat, and the great seal, to his barge". Also, *ibid.,* p. 150, Wolsey starts on his embassy to France having "before him his two great crosses of silver, two pillars of silver, the great seal of England, his cardinal's hat, and a gentleman that carried his valaunce, otherwise called a cloakbag". It is perhaps on this last passage that a drawing is based which is incorporated in Stephen Batman's copy of Cavendish's Life, in MS Douce 363 of the Bodleian Library at Oxford, and which is reproduced in both editions of Cavendish, at i:87 and 149 respectively. But neither this sixteenth-century picture nor Roy's "Rede Me and Be Nott Wrothe", a contemporary attack on Wolsey, agrees exactly with Cavendish. Roy (see ed. Arber, 1871, p. 56) says that the two crosses are borne first by two priests, and that two laymen bearing the pillars follow, just preceding "my lord on his mule". He continues, "On each syde a pollaxe is borne / Which in none wother use are worne. Pretendyng some hid mistery." Cavendish, *op. cit.,* 105-7, says that Wolsey in going to Westminster Hall was preceded by two crosses, by two great silver pillars, and by a mace

of silver gilt, "having about him four footmen with gilt pollaxes in their hand". The drawing shows no pole-axe bearers; Wolsey, rides quite alone, preceded by two crosses, these by the two pillar-bearers, and these by the bearers of the Great Seal and of the Cardinal's hat, all mounted. It must however be noted that in this drawing Wolsey is inaccurately represented as bearded. Of the two crosses, one is simple, the archiepiscopal or legantine; the other is that of a Primate or Patriarch, with two transoms, indicating the double supremacy as a Metropolitan and as in authority over other Metropolitans. This double cross, according to Rock, Church of Our Fathers (1905) ii:180 ff., "was used in very few places and for a very short period". It existed, says, Rock, more in the imagination of painters, as did the Papal three-transomed cross entirely. Wolsey's insistent use of it alongside his archiepiscopal cross, and still more his parade of pillars and pole-axes, aroused the irritation of his contemporaries. The former were taken to symbolize his function as a pillar of the Church; but the pole-axes were not understood. Skelton in Speke Parrot 510 sneers at both; Roy as cited says the pole-axes pretend some hid mystery; Robert Barnes, in his Supplication to Henry VIII, recounts his dispute with Wolsey over the extravagance of these costly emblems. See Works of Tyndale, Frith, Barnes, Lond., 1573, pp. 214-15, and Cavendish (1827), note to pp. 109-111.

141. *legantyn prerogative*. Wolsey was in 1516 made the Pope's legate a latere; see note on line 93 above. By virtue of this special power he might convoke all British ecclesiastical courts, and exercise visitatorial powers over all monasteries and colleges. His assumption of this office and use of it to raise his authority above that of the king was the leading article of the 43 accusations brought against him in Oct. 1529 by the Lords. See Letters and Papers of Henry VIII, iv:2712-13, and Fiddes' Life of Wolsey, ed. 1726, pp. 172-79. Wolsey's attorneys pleaded for him that he did not know he was "in contempt" in so doing, and he threw himself on the king's mercy. The bill was dropped, but Wolsey accepted the king's commands as if he had been found guilty. See note on 198.

143-5. Cavendish makes Wolsey say that when a benefice fell vacant he at once appointed his clerk to it to keep it in his jurisdiction, thus preventing, i.e. anticipating, the patron or owner of the living in disposing of it.

148. Note the use of *yow* as nominative, and cp. 218.

161. *say chek mate*. Cp. 1237, 1267. For note see Dance Macabre 459, FaPrinces D 52.

165. *whiles*, wiles, schemes. For the orthography cp. *whofull* 58, *whele* 1141, *whomanly* 1358.—In 1408 *wight* is written for *white*. The meaning of 165-182 is that while Wolsey was in France in 1527 the infatuation of Henry for Anne Boleyn nullified all his plans. Thus Venus, as he says 181, overthrew him, "brought me from above".

167-8. These two lines agree closely with Lydgate's FaPrinces ii:4437-38 :—

> For who with fraude fraudulent is founde
> To a diffraudere fraude will ay rebounde.

See also Lydgate's Frog and Mouse fable, last stanza, and the stanza beginning "Deceit deceiveth and shal be deceived", copied separately in Fairfax 16, Harley 7578, Hatton 73 (flyleaf), Douce 45, Trin. Coll. Camb. R 3, 20, and the Bannatyne MS. Shirley in the Trinity MS writes "A Proverb" in the margin; and Lydgate evidently worked up proverbial material, with a play upon words which contributed to the popularity of the saying. For this latter see the ringing of changes on a wordbase in Dante's Inferno iv:72-80.

170. *mirror*. See notes FaPrinces G 179, Ship of Fools 85.

177. *disdayned* (by him) *for whom I toke the payn;* that is, Henry, for whom Wolsey's efforts were made, disdained and spurned him.

188. A proverb, and a frequent metaphor with Lydgate, see note on FaPrinces D 69 here.

190-92. *fykkell fortune*. A frequent pictorial representation of Fortune, in the latter Middle Ages, showed her presiding over a wheel, on the rim of which were human figures in different positions. When these figures numbered four, that atop was a crowned and exultant king, marked "Regno"; on one side was a figure climbing, marked "Regnabo"; the opposite side showed him falling headlong, and was inscribed "Regnavi"; and a prostrate body underneath the wheel was lettered "Sum sine regno". Such a drawing is reproduced in

Schmeller's Carmina Burana, Breslau, 1883, p. 1, a different design as frontispiece to vol. i of Bergen's ed. of the FaPrinces, Carnegie Instit., 1923. Early eds. of the FaPrinces, e.g., that of 1554, have at the opening of book vi a cut of hundred-handed Fortune ruling a wheel crowded with figures; and K. Weinhold, in his monograph Glücksrad und Lebensrad (Abhandl. d. kgl. Akad. d. Wissenschaften, Berlin, 1892), describes pictures in MSS of Boethius and of Brunetto Latini. Modifications may be seen in drawings by ?Hans Burgkmaier for Petrarch's De remediis utriusque fortunae, Augsburg 1532, reproduced in Hirth's Les grands illustrateurs i:221-2, also in the earliest German editions of the Ship of Fools, etc. The idea of the Wheel of Life, more than that of the Wheel of Fortune, is present in the seventeen sculptured figures which border the upper half of the great rose-window of the south portal at Amiens, and in the twelve figures of St. Etienne de Beauvais' north transept.

Whenever the late Middle Ages turned to the theme of fickle Fortune,—and that was constantly—some such picture of her and her wheel, whether with four figures or with many, was in their minds. That Cavendish so imagined her we can see from this passage, from a phrase in his prose Life of Wolsey,—"climbing thus hastily on Fortune's wheel",—or from lines in his Surrey tragedy, 1109-11 here. We may remember that a tapestry of the Wheel of Fortune was in Wolsey's possession; see note on 120-1 above. It may be added that this typically medieval treatment of Fortune and her wheel roots in both Boethius and Dante; see the De Consolatione ii prose 2, the Inferno vii:67 ff. On the whole subject see H. R. Patch, The Tradition of the Goddess Fortuna in Mediaeval Philosophy and Literature, Northampton, Mass., 1922. See also description in the Morte Arthure, EETS, 3260-67.

198. ffayn to avoid, "I was fain to depart". In 1529 Wolsey was ordered by Henry to yield up all his benefices and possessions and retire to Esher, a manor not far from Winchester. Later the Cardinal was directed to remove to his Archbishopric of York, which Henry restored him in February 1530; but a few months subsequently he was suddenly accused of high treason and ordered to London. On the journey he fell ill, and died at the Abbey of Leicester; see line 217.

200-203. When Henry restored Wolsey to the Archbishopric of York, he returned his fallen favorite about three thousand pounds in money, and goods, furniture, etc., of the value of £3600 more. See the 1827 Cavendish, appendix, p. 507. Wolsey had been for some time quite without funds.

205. rubbed me on the gall. See Skelton's Garland 97; but see also "rubbyth me on the splene", Visions, p. 34 of the 1827 edition, for the possible meaning "rouse my spleen, stir up my gall".

207. letters playn. Wolsey appealed privately to the French ambassador to beg King Francis' intercession on his behalf, as in 209-10 below. This appeal was betrayed by the Cardinal's Italian physician to the English Lords in Council, with addition of false details likely to arouse Henry's anger. Wolsey's enemies saw their opportunity to degrade him yet more completely. The arrest was made on November 7, and he died November 29.

209. caught . . . dysdayn. See note on FaPrinces G 22 here.

215. travellyng to my triall. See note on line 198 above. The phrase here means "traveling to my trial"; but in line 207 travelled means "travailed".

222-24. Of this sort of word-manipulation Cavendish is fond. Elsewhere in the Visions we read "When lust was lusty, wyll did hyme advaunce To tangle me with lust where my lust did requier", etc. See 1310, 1320 below, 167-8 above.

225. my Tombe. Wolsey had planned an elaborate mausoleum for himself, the work of the Florentine artist Rovezzano, who came to England about 1520. It was not complete at the time of Wolsey's fall, and the king seized it for himself. Rovezzano was called upon for an inventory of the material in his hands; and this list is printed by Blomfield in his Hist. of Renaissance Architecture in England, i:13. It includes:—4 graven copper pillars; 4 angels to kneel at the head and foot of the tomb, ready gilt and burnished; 4 angels with candlesticks to stand on the said pillars; 4 naked children to stand at the head and foot of the tomb with the arms; 2 pieces of copper with epitaphs; a tomb of black touchstone 7 feet by 4 feet, and 2 1/2 feet high; 4 copper leaves for the corners of the tomb; 12 pieces of black touchstone, and 8 of white marble, for the base of the tomb; a step of black touchstone (etc., etc.). The

work was continued by Rovezzano, who used, for Henry's enlarged plan, more than 2000 additional pounds of copper; Henry was to have had a recumbent figure of himself, many figures of the apostles, etc. The work however was never finished, and although Charles the First intended the tomb for himself, Parliament after his execution sold all the bronze and copper. In 1806-10 the sarcophagus was used for the burial of Nelson in St. Paul's. See A. Higgins' paper on the work of Florentine sculptors in England, Archaeol. Journal, Sept. 1894.

Henry VIII had previously contracted with Torregiano, in 1519, to make for him and Katharine of Arragon a tomb of white marble and black touchstone, one-fourth larger than that which the artist had made for Henry VII; it was to be completed in four years under Wolsey's direction. See Brewer's Letters and Papers iii:2. We may note that the tomb ordered by Richard II for Anne was to be made by London masons, and that London copper-smiths were to furnish the images for it. See Rymer's Foedera vii:795-7.

227. *to couche in.* See note on Thebes 35. Cp. 244 below.

232. *Hampton Court,* etc. This stanza contains a list of Wolsey's principal residences and foundations,—Hampton Court, Westminster Place or York Place (now Whitehall), The Moor, "Tynnynainger" or Tittenhanger, Cardinal College (now Christ Church College Oxford), and the Ipswich Grammar School. The last of these was not yet erected at Wolsey's fall, and was re-founded by Elizabeth; it was intended to serve as preparatory school for Wolsey's "Cardinal College", of which hardly more than the great kitchen was completed when Wolsey's career ended. Henry VIII subsequently re-founded and renamed it. Hampton Court and York Place are the best-known of Wolsey's palaces; Tittenhanger was in Hertfordshire, a manor belonging to the Abbey of St. Albans, which was one of Wolsey's holdings. The Moor was also in Hertfordshire, near Rickmansworth; it was built by an earlier Archbishop of York, and came into Wolsey's hands about 1525; he rebuilt the palace. See Robert Bayne's Moor Park, London, 1871. It is Hampton Court with which Wolsey's name is most intimately connected, though little remains of his buildings there, Henry VIII and later sovereigns having made extensive changes. Wolsey leased in 1514 about 2000 acres on the Thames, and erected a huge brick palace with a frontage of 400 feet, containing nearly a thousand rooms. He not only equipped his buildings with an excellent water supply, and drained them in the most approved manner, but laid out elaborate gardens (see stanza 17), and lavished immense sums on interior decorations and furnishings. There were for instance 280 guest rooms, with beds of velvet or satin and counterpanes of satin or damask richly embroidered; two hundred feather-beds are inventoried in the list of the Cardinal's possessions in MS. Brit. Mus. Harley 599, and the expenditure on gold and silver plate represents more than seven millions of American money. See note on 127 above; and see Law's Hampton Court as cited, note on 106 above.

This device of a series of lines beginning alike, "anaphora" or "epanophora", is frequently used in medieval formal poetry. Like all the "colores rhetorici" lightly handled by Ovid, still more lightly by Dante, it is overworked by the average medieval writer. Matthew of Vendôme or Alanus parades all these "exornationes"; anaphora is a feature of the Provençal "enueg"; it appears in the Roman de la Rose (see ed. Méon ii:pp. 13-15, 334-5, 366 etc.), in Christine de Pisan, Marie de France, Granson, etc.; Chaucer has three notable examples of it near the close of his Troilus; Gower employs it, cp. Confessio prol. 935 ff., iii:279 ff., v:2469-81; Lydgate, Hawes, Dunbar, Henryson, Douglas, all avail themselves of this "color", as do the romancers. In the Squyr of Lowe Degre 941-954 is a sequence of lines beginning "Farewell", as here; see also stanzas 14 and 15 of the Lament for the Duchess of Gloucester (Eleanor Cobham), printed in Wright's PolitPoems ii:205-8, in Anglia 26:177-80 by Flügel, in the EETS Songs and Carols etc. by R. Dyboski.

The difference between the tiresome over-emphasis of Hawes in chaps. 21, 31, of the Pastime and the sparing use of the device by Keats in Endymion iii:543-6, in Isabella 417-20, or by Tennyson in the Holy Grail 473-6, Guinevere 467-72, Enoch Arden 590-92, or in Meredith's Love in the Valley 113-116, Sage Enamoured 292-94, is the same difference as exists between Dante's restraint (Inferno v:100-106) in the three successive terzine beginning *Amor,* and the 31 lines beginning *Amors,* inserted into the Roman de la Rose by a fifteenth-century scribe; see Méon's ed. ii:pp. 19-22. To this latter workman and to Hawes, as to Lydgate, quantity produced effect.

242. The allusion probably is to the Dance Macabre or Dance of Death. In Cavendish's time Lydgate's verses and the accompanying paintings were still in the churchyard of St. Paul's Cathedral. See the text here, p. 124.

246-54. With the change of *meyne* to *chapleyns* in 249, this stanza is taken complete from Lydgate's FaPrinces iii:3760 ff. Cp. line 101 above with 246 here.

247. *shettes of raynes,* "sheets of Rennes". A fine linen was made at Rennes in Brittany; see Chaucer's BoDuchesse 255, see the Squyr of Lowe Degre, 842, see Skelton's Colyn Clout 316 and Magnyfycence 2042.

249. *vicious chapleyns.* Wolsey's chaplain Dr. John Allen, according to Fiddes' life of the Cardinal, p. 372, rode in a kind of perpetual progress from one religious house to another, drawing from them large sums for his master's use. This was at last so bitterly complained of that the king compelled Wolsey to promise to offend no more in such manner. On p. 205 Fiddes says "That whereby the Cardinal seemeth to have given the greatest and most general disgust was his erecting the Legate's court and employing a person as judge in it, charged with much rapine and extortion,"—this person being the chaplain Allen. See note on 141.

254-58, 264. Cavendish was proud of his fidelity to Wolsey.

269. This is the method of the Fall of Princes, even more of Boccaccio's De Casibus its ultimate original, where inserted and generalized groups break the succession of individual laments. Of the personages intervening between Wolsey and Surrey in this poem, the viscount Rochford, brother to Anne Boleyn, and the grooms of Henry's chamber Norris, Weston, Brereton, and Smeaton, were all accused with Anne of adultery, and all executed. Cavendish gives from three to seven stanzas to each of the lesser men, and sixteen to Anne Boleyn, who follows in the list. Next comes a group of minor figures accused of rebellion and murder in Henry's reign and executed by him; then Cromwell earl of Essex, who had been one of Cavendish's fellow-servants in Wolsey's household, who rose to the chancellorship after Wolsey's death and More's resignation, and went to the scaffold a bare two months after he was made earl. Next come the lords Exeter and Montagu, beheaded for treason; Queen Katharine Howard and the king's page Culpepper; the viscountess Rochford; the countess of Salisbury; the earl of Surrey.

1105 ff. Henry Howard earl of Surrey, lyric poet and blank-verse translator of the Aeneid, was beheaded by Henry VIII a very short time before the king's own death in 1547. Henry was then mortally ill, and filled with anxiety for the future of his son; and the enemies of the Howards persuaded the king that Surrey and his aged father the duke of Norfolk aspired to make themselves guardians of the boy Edward and to rule through him and the princess Mary. Of the frivolous pretexts upon which Surrey was sentenced, Cavendish seems to have known only the flimsiest, the charge that Surrey, by quartering upon his shield the arms of Edward the Confessor, had committed an act of high treason. To this line 1195 doubtless alludes. Surrey went to the block, but the death of Henry saved his father after the warrant had actually been made out. The old duke remained a prisoner in the Tower for seven years, and died immediately after liberation and restoration to his honors, aged 83. See note on 1121 below.

1109. *whele* (I) *made lyke to clyme.* See note on 190-92 above.

1121. *actes marsheall,* martial deeds. Norfolk was captain of the English vanguard when his father, Thomas Howard second duke, won the battle of Flodden Field in 1513 over the Scots. He was at various times lieutenant-general of forces sent abroad, lord lieutenant of Ireland, and warden of the Scottish marches. See Barclay, ecl. iv:850, 853, notes.

1130. *Brewtus Cassius.* See note on FaPrinces E 63 here.

1133 ff. This stanza is very Lydgatian in its confused verb-management.

1137. *dothe expresse.* The convenience of this verb for rime with abstract terms in *-nesse* made its use exceedingly common in Lydgate and in later formal writers of the period,— Bokenam, Capgrave, Bradshaw, Barclay. It does not appear in the reflexive construction, but *dothe expresse, did expresse,* are freely used, especially by Lydgate. See note on FaPrinces A 303 here.

1149. *deprave.* This transitive use of the verb occurs in Lydgate, cp. FaPrinces A 447 here; it is more frequent in Hawes.

1151 is a short line.

1155. Singer puts a semicolon after *lyve,* thus wrecking the sense. See 1314, 1356.

1157. *hath byn dekayed,* have been overthrown, have fallen from high estate. This use of the verb *decay* appears in the sixteenth century, and is frequent in Spenser.

1164-1174. This passage says that the qualities which had raised low-born men to high rank were accounted dangerous in men already high-born like Surrey, who met only disdain from "suche" (men) as were vain and idle.

1177. *myrror.* See note on Barclay's Ship of Fools 85.

1182. Singer substitutes *shame* for *chaunce* in the middle of the line.

1184. *more rather.* The double comparative and double superlative are frequent in Cavendish.

1186. *lost my pate.* Until after the seventeenth century, says the NED, the word *pate* had not its present ridiculous connotation. See Beryn, prol. 139.

1188. *Take a vowe.* This seems to mean "Take my assurance". It is thus not the same locution as "make avowe", e.g., in Barclay's fourth eclogue 438, 726.

1193. The scribe inserts *wt sorowe,* with a caret.

1217. Cavendish more than once made an end of his Visions, and again took them up. At the close of the Wolsey tragedy he wrote *Finis;* here he says that after finishing the lines on Surrey he intended to stop; after the epitaph of Henry VIII he writes *Finis G. C.,* and just before the stanzas on the death of Edward VI another *Finis* stands in the manuscript. At the end of Queen Mary's epitaph is "Fiat. Fiat. Finis". This is followed by the author's address to his book and by the colophon, which, as remarked in the introduction here, sets a date for completion five months anterior to the death of Mary. The piecemeal composition of the Visions is obvious.

1220. "As if one were in a brake, like one who is in a brake." The word *brake* in late Middle English meant a cage, snare, dilemma; the first case NED is from Skelton's Elynour Rummyng 325.

1222. *trembling trompe,* i.e, trumpet which causes trembling. See *timorous blast* in Skelton's Garland 260, and note *ibid.* For the use of a loud sound to waken a sleeper or turn a narrative cp. Hawes 93 note. For Fame's trump blown at the death of a champion see Hawes 136 and note.

1237. *chekmate.* See note on 161 above.—*pluk them by the berd.* A mark of contempt. See, e.g., the romance of Sir Degrevaunt 835-6,—"I shal schak hym by the berd þe nexte tyme we mete". To meet an opponent "in the beard" was to face him, e.g., in combat; see Troilus iv:41, Lydgate's Troy Book ii:6283, iii:1203, and often. To "make a man's beard" was to deceive him. See WBprol. 361, Beryn 436, 485, 622.

1241. The device of a sleep for changing scene in narrative is more than common in medieval formal verse.

1245. *by & bye,* immediately. The phrase also means "in sequence", see Morley 209 and note.

1246. Henry VIII died at Whitehall, the palace he took from Wolsey; Whitehall is in Westminster.

1251. *bedropped face,* face dripping with tears. Cp. "so dropping was her wede", Flower and Leaf 371. The NED has no case of *bedropped* between Gower's Confessio vii:4832 and Paradise Lost x:527.

1259 ff. The three Fates, Clotho, Lachesis, and Atropos, are present at Henry's death-bed, drawing and cutting the thread of his life.

1261. *as poettes dothe.* The use of the verb in *-th* with a plural subject may be dialectal, a survival of the old Southwestern plural; or it may be an extension of that use of a singular verb with plural subject which has always been sporadic in English,—influenced sometimes in this latter case by the feeling that a collective subject has singular force. See line 1366 below, also lines 1174, 1327-8, 1394; see the Lover's Mass 127, Libel of Eng. Policy 389, 510, Hawes' Pastime 206. There are several cases in Walton's Boethius; see A 105 and note.

1283. *throme,* thrum, the part of the warp unwoven, at the sides of the finished web.

1288. *vigor.* Perhaps read *rigor?*

1293. Compare Antigone 1030, τίς ἀλκὴ τὸν θανόντ᾽ ἐπικτανεῖν, "what valor to slay the slain?"

1302-4. Note the rime.

1309-10. For the word-play see 222 and note; cp. 1320-22.

1314. Singer puts a period at the end of this line, as in 1356, although in both cases there is syntactical connection with the next stanza. See note on 1155.

1315 ff. This extremely outspoken language regarding Henry VIII made the publication of the Visions even more impossible than that of the Life of Wolsey. Cavendish was a strong Roman Catholic, and rejoiced at the accession of Mary; but his opinions about her father were none the less too dangerous for publication.

1348. *bridelled.* This metaphor is very common in Lydgate; see Epithal. for Gloucester 88 and note; see his Thebes 2704-5, Troy Book prol. 6, ii :6628, v :1369, etc. For the conjunction of Reason and Sensuality ("blood and judgment") see e.g. FaPrinces i :6200, 6257, ii :579-80, 2535-6, etc.

1355-56. Note the rime.

1368. Singer omitted this line.

1369. *Greseld.* At the very time of Cavendish's completion of this set of poems, June 1558, there appeared a poem on Katharine of Arragon by William Forrest, chaplain to Queen Mary, entitled Grisild the Second. See the edition for the Roxburghe Club, 1875, by Macray. From the Privy Purse Expenses of the Princess Mary, ed. Madden, 1831, we see that in 1523, when the scholar Ludovico Vives drew up a scheme of education for Katharine's use in training her daughter, he included, as one of the few fictions permitted, "Gresilda vulgata jam fabula".

1371. *inconvenyence.* This word had for Lydgate or for Cavendish much more force than for us. In this stronger sense it is frequent in Barclay; see note Ship of Fools 142.

1378-80. Observe the identical rime.

1379. *bankettyng chere.* The same phrase is used by Holinshed in his Scottish Chronicle, according to the NED.

1385 ff. See latter part of note on 232 *ante.*

1400. *pieuselles,* pucelles, maidens. Singer prints *prensells.*

1406. *Impe,* scion, especially of a noble house. The first case given by NED in this sense is from Hoccleve's De Regimine Principum 5442; the word is used by Hall in his 1548 Chronicle, also of Prince Edward.

Epytaphe. Singer, in a note on this epitaph, refers to the *Coplas* of Jorge Manrique on his father's death, written in Spain in the mid-fifteenth century. He reprints the part in question, which is here given:—

En ventura Octaviano
Julio Cesar en vencer
Y batallar
En la virtud Africano
Hanibal en el saber
Y trabajar

En la bondad un Trajano
Tito en liberalidad
Con alegria
En sus brazos un Troyano
Marco Tulio en la verdad
Que prometia

Antonio Pio en clemencia
Marco Fabio en igualdad
Del semblante
Adriano en eloquencia
Theodosio en humildad
Y buen talante

Aurelio Alessandro fue
En diciplina y rigor
De la guerra
Un Constantino en la fe
Y Camilo en el amor
De su tierra

The use of a list of great ancient names, when praising a contemporary, is so frequent with medieval rhetoricians that I point out no kinship here other than that of descent from a common ancestor or stock. Compare Lydgate's procedure in his poem on the Coronation of Henry VI (printed by Wright, PolitPoems ii :141), where Solomon, David, Samson, Joshua, Judas Maccabaeus, Alexander, Julius Caesar, "Brutus Cassius", Hector, Fabricius,

Zenocrates, Scipio, Titus, Trajan, Tiberius, Gratian, Justinian, Octavian, Constantine, and the pious emperor Sigismund, the betrayer of Huss, are marshalled as examples of the virtues. The list includes most of the Nine Worthies (see note on Epithal. 134 here), but the additions are in several cases interesting; "Brutus Cassius" is praised for foresight, Tiberius for "fredam and gentilesse".

The change of metrical form, when narrative gives way to lyric, is to be expected even in the Transition; and Cavendish does not imitate the Spanish stanza. But the possibility that he knew of the poem is not excluded; see introduction to the Lover's Mass, p. 209 here, and consider his possible meeting with servants of Katharine of Arragon.

The Historia Trojana of Guido delle Colonne, ed. of 1486, has after the close of its text the epitaphs of Hector and of Achilles.

The Epitaph is followed, in Cavendish's work, by two stanzas of author's comment, which rebegin the series after the "Finis" below the Epitaph. There follow:—Seymour, Somerset, Arundel, Stanhope, Vane, and Partridge, then another "Finis"; the re-opening is "Lauctor in Mortem Edwardi VI"; and after this ensues a praise of Queen Mary. The tragedies of Northumberland, of Suffolk, and of Lady Jane Grey follow, and next is an "Epitaphe on the Late Quene Marie", beneath which is "Fiat. Fiat. Finis". Six stanzas of author's address to his book follow, and the colophon.

LORD MORLEY'S TRANSLATION OF PETRARCH'S TRIUMPH OF LOVE

DEDICATORY LETTER

Robyn Hoode. Cp. Barclay's scorn, Ship of Fools 13874-8.—*swete sonnet.* Petrarch's sonnets were often included in the MSS of his Trionfi.—*story all,* i.e., storiall, "historical".—*ryme.* Morley undoubtedly means that he cannot manage the terza rima scheme.

THE TRIUMPH OF LOVE, BOOK I

1. *In the tyme,* etc. Petrarch begins "Al tempo che rinova i miei sospiri", etc. He is dating his poem on April 6, the anniversary of his first meeting with Madonna Laura; and in verse 8 of the Italian he imagines himself "al chiuso loco", i.e., Vaucluse, his country home, and the scene of that meeting. This latter allusion escapes Morley, unless his "myne eyen closed" in line 11 is an erroneous attempt at it. Petrarch's choice of dawn as the time of his vision was to the medieval reader assurance of its truth. See Albertus Magnus De Somno; see Ovid's Heroides 19:195-6,—

> Namque sub Aurora, jam dormitante lucerna,
> Somnia quo cerni tempore vera solent.

See Dante's Inferno 26:7,—"Ma se presso al mattin del ver si sogna".

7. *Tytans chylde,* etc. Petrarch's "fanciulla di Titone" refers to Aurora, either as bride of Tithonus or as daughter of the Titan Hyperion. According to Skeat, Chaucer has confused Titan and Tithonus in Troilus iii:1464; one of the Troilus MSS, Harley 2392, has there a side-note, "Aurora: amica solis". Lydgate at the opening of Troy Book iii makes Phoebus the husband of Aurora. In the attempt to secure a rime to *place,* the "soggiorno" of the Italian, Morley has translated *gelata* by the phrase applied to Saturn in Lydgate's Thebes prologue line 3.

16. This line is padding for rime; cp. also 18, 38, 39, half-lines 41 and 42, 44, 48, 49, 54, 63, 78, 89, 116, 124, 126, 130, 132, 135, 137-8, 140, 154, 156, 168, 174, 198, 202, 217-18, 232, 236, 245.

28-32 have no parallel in the Italian. 32 is apparently twisted from Petrarch's 21, but line 20 of the Italian, "levando gli occhi gravi e stanchi", is omitted. Mrs. Hume renders,—"And having raised mine eyes, which wearied were, To understand this sight was all my care".

43. Read this line with period at close.—*all the rest* means all the rest of Cupid's body.

45. Petrarch does not say that any were lying on the ground.

50-54. Mrs. Hume's fairly accurate version is:—"Glad to learn news I rose, and forward pressed So far, that I was one amongst the rest; As if I had been kill'd with loving pain Before my time", etc.

62. Petrarch describes the king as he who is thirsty of tears, "sempre di lagrime digiuno"; Morley blurs this into a medieval formula.

65. *more sadde.* Petrarch says "less sad".

68. *fame* is dragged in for rime. What Petrarch says is:—"This is what comes of loving."

72-4 are taken from the newcomer's speech by Morley, and given to the dreamer.

100. *then.* Petrarch says that *now,* i.e., later, those words are recorded in his memory.

103 is a mistranslation. What Petrarch says is:—"And because of my forward youth, which makes mind and tongue bold and hardy, I asked him" etc.

115. Read *capteyn.*

116 is weakened. It is in the Italian:—"who thus deprives (men) of life and liberty".

135-8 are added by Morley.

150. *By request.* Augustus compelled the husband of Livia to divorce her, B.C. 38, in order that he himself might marry her. She was at the time pregnant, and one at least of the early prints, that of Venice 1519, reads *pregnante* here instead of *pregando.* Morley had *pregando* before him, and his *By request* is a softening, though less so than his rendition of Petrarch's *tolse,* "seized", as *obtayne.*

161. *Denyse,* etc. The elder Dionysius, tyrant of Syracuse, was intensely suspicious, and similar but less extravagant tales are related of Alexander. Morley follows Petrarch in mentioning only the "paura e sospetto" of the two sovereigns; but like Petrarch he includes them among those conquered by love. Lydgate in his FaPrinces iv:799 ff. treats at length of Dionysius' unbridled cruel lust, saying nothing of his suspicion.

162. *sclaunder.* Petrarch says "temer", i.e., fear.

163-7. These lines allude to Aeneas, whose wife Creusa was separated from him during the flight from Troy. He mourned for her at the foot of Mt. Ida, near the Greek colony of Antander; and later, in Italy, he wedded Lavinia the betrothed of Turnus. Turnus also is not directly named, but identified as the slayer of Evander's son. Petrarch was driven to this circumlocution by his use of *Alexandro* in rime; and Morley follows him.

170. *one.* Hippolytus son of Theseus. Not named by Petrarch for several lines.

178-9. Petrarch here says, in one of the two main recensions of his text, that Phaedra's death was "vendetta" for Hippolytus, Theseus, and Ariadne whom Theseus had earlier deceived. When Morley uses the phrase *them two,* he seems to follow the other main recension, however. In 179 the printed edition reads *the sens* instead of *Theseus.*

180-87 expand two lines of Petrarch.

187-8. Note the rime indicating a silent *l* in *false.* See note on Garland 112.

189 ff. Theseus is meant, between the sisters Ariadne and Phaedra. He carried off both from Crete after the slaying of the Minotaur, and on the voyage deserted Ariadne for Phaedra. He did not slay either, as Morley asserts in 191. Petrarch says that Theseus stands "fra due sorelle morte", and then makes the rhetorical antithesis, in the next line, that "the one rested her joy in him, he rested his joy in the other". Morley runs the word *morte,* a plural, into connection with the following "L'una di lui", and says that the one was slain by Theseus. The antithesis he spoils.

194 ff. A list of lovers follows:—Hercules, Achilles and Polyxena, Demophoon and Phyllis, Jason, Medea, and Hypsipyle; then unnamed at first, are Paris and Helen, then Oénone. Next are Menelaus, Hermione and Orestes, Laodomia and Prothesilaus, Argia and Polynices. This is the standard list. Chaucer in the (unfinished) Legend of Good Women included Hypsipyle, Ariadne, and Phyllis; and in the introduction to the Man of Law's Tale he mentions all these women but Polyxena, Helen, Oenone, and Argia. Lydgate in his Thebes has the story of Argia and Polynices, in his Troy Book those of Polyxena and of Helen. These latter two are often named in his lists of fair ladies; see the Dance Macabre 451-2, the Flower of Courtesy 190-1, and the entire list in the latter poem.

205-6 do not follow the Italian. Petrarch says at this point, of Medea, that "even as she was cruel to her old father and to her youthful brother, so much had she reason to curse her own lot".

209. *in ordre by and by,* arranged one after the other. For "by and by" cp. AssGods 302, "Next to Cupido in ordre by and by", and very many cases in Lydgate. For the phrase "by ordre" see note on Hoccleve's third Roundel, p 405 here.

210-12. The pronouns are all of the wrong gender. It is Helen who "hath the name of bewtye"; Morley's omission of "pastor" to identify Paris increases the vagueness.

213. *innumerable of harmes,* the Trojan War. Petrarch says "gran tempeste".

214 is a clumsy makeshift for rime.

229-30. Here Morley's error drives him to absurdity. What Petrarch says is "Hear the cries which the spirits address to him who thus leads them". In one of the main types of Italian text the verb for "address" is *diero,* in the other *rendero.* Apparently Morley had the latter before him; and having translated it *render,* he drags in the word *slender* for rime.

235. Morley omits the "shadowy myrtles" which Petrarch borrows from Aeneid vi :443-4; he has instead "a greate and darke presse".

241-2. *Apollo,* etc. The reference is probably to Apollo's love for the two Thessalian sisters Daphne and Cyrene, daughters of the river-god Peneus.

246. *Uarro.* M. Terentius Varro, a voluminous author of the first century B. C., wrote forty-one books "Antiquitatum rerum humanarum et divinarum", of which fragments are preserved by citation in the writings of the Church Fathers Augustine, Tertullian, and Lactantius. In that work Varro made an elaborate classification of the Greek and Roman deities. According to Sandys ii :13, Boccaccio was the first humanist to quote Varro, and may have been the discoverer of the archetypal manuscript.

LIST OF ABBREVIATIONS AND SELECT REFERENCE LIST

(See also separate Reference Lists *s.v.* in Glossary.)

Adds., applied to a manuscript, indicates one of the "Additionals" sub-collection of the British Museum.

Ad Herennium. A rhetorical treatise long ascribed to Cicero; ed. by Marx, Leipzig, 1894.

Alanus. Alanus de Insulis or Alain de Lille, a twelfth century rhetorical writer, in Latin. Works ed. in Migne's Patrologia Latina, vol. 210; his Anticlaudianus is ed. by Thomas Wright in Anglo-Latin Satirical Poets of the Twelfth Century, ii : 268 ff.; his De Planctu Naturae, *ibid.*, 429 ff. The latter work is translated into English by D. M. Moffatt, N. Y., 1908. On Alanus see H. O. Taylor, The Medieval Mind, London, 1911, vol. ii.

Albon *or* St. Albon. Lydgate's metrical life of Saints Albon and Amphabell, ed. Horstmann, Berlin, 1882.

Allegory. See under Virgil.

Anglia. Zeitschrift für englische Philologie, Halle, 1878 ff. quarterly. Anglia Beiblatt, containing reviews, 1890 ff.

Anticlaudianus. See under Alanus.

Archiv. Archiv für das Studium der neueren Sprachen und Litteraturen, 1846 ff.

Arundel. A sub-collection of MSS in the British Museum.

Ashmole. A sub-collection of MSS in the Bodleian Library, Oxford.—Elias Ashmole's Theatrum Chemicum Britannicum, a collection of treatises on alchemy, London, 1652.

AssGods. The Assembly of Gods, a poem formerly ascribed to Lydgate, and ed. as his for the EETS in 1895 by O. L. Triggs. See my Chaucer Manual, p. 407.

AssLadies. The Assembly of Ladies, a poem of unknown authorship, printed by Skeat in Chaucerian and Other Pieces, pp. 380 ff. See my Chaucer Manual, p. 408.

Barclay. See pp. 295 ff. here. Barclay's Ship of Fools is ed. Jamieson, 2 vols., Edinburgh, 1874.

Bartholomaeus Anglicus. Of the thirteenth century; was author of the encyclopedia De Proprietatibus Rerum, Englished by Trevisa in 1398; no modern edition. "Gleanings" from it, translated, constitute R. Steele's *Mediaeval Lore,* London, 1893. See Voigt in Engl. Stud. 41 : 337-9.

Bedford. Hoccleve's poem to the duke of Bedford, p. 76 here.

Berdan. Early Tudor Poetry, 1485-1547, by John M. Berdan, N. Y., 1920.

Bergen, Henry. Editor of Lydgate's Troy Book for the EETS, 1906, 1908, and of Lydgate's Fall of Princes for the Carnegie Institution of America, 1923, 1927.

Beryn. A supplementary Canterbury tale, of unknown authorship. Unique copy in the Northumberland MS of the Canterbury Tales, ed. for the Chaucer Society 1876.

Bibl.nat. The Bibliothèque nationale at Paris.

Bibl.nat.fonds français. The "fonds français" MSS, or French section of the MS collection in the Bibliothèque nationale.

BlKnight. Lydgate's poem The Complaint of the Black Knight. Edited by Krausser in Anglia 19: 211 ff., and by Skeat in Chaucerian and Other Pieces. See my Chaucer Manual, p. 413.

Boccaccio. The Opere Volgari were edited by Moutier, Florence, 1827-34, 17 vols. Several poems are separately ed. in the Biblioteca Romanica, notably Il Filostrato; and of this poem there is a stanzaic translation by H. M. Cummings, Princeton, 1924. Editions of the Decameron are very numerous. None of the three Latin works is accessible in a modern edition; they are: De Casibus Virorum Illustrium, De Claris Mulieribus, and De Genealogia Deorum. The first-named is the ultimate source of Lydgate's Fall of Princes, see p. 151 here; of the second Skelton makes some use in his Garland of Laurel, see p. 518 here; and the third is often mentioned in these Notes. On Boccaccio's Latin works see Hortis, Opere latine del Boccaccio, Trieste, 1879; on the relation of the De Casibus to Lydgate see vol. iv of Bergen's ed. of the Fall of Princes, introd., and also Koeppel as p. 151 foot, here.

Bodl. The Bodleian Library at Oxford.—One of the "Bodley" sub-collection of MSS there.

BoDuch. Chaucer's Boke of the Duchesse.

Boethius. See pp. 39 ff., p. 185.

Bokenam. Osbern Bokenam, author of a fifteenth-century collection of saints' lives, ed. Horstmann, Heilbronn, 1883.

Brown's Register. A Register of Middle English Religious and Didactic Verse, ed. Carleton Brown, Oxford, 1916, 2 vols.

Bradshaw, Henry, (died 1513). Author of a verse-life of St. Werburge, ed. by Horstmann for the EETS, 1887.

Bradshaw, Henry. Librarian of the University Library, Cambridge, England, 1867-86. See my Chaucer Manual, p. 520.

Brit.Mus. The British Museum, London.

Brusendorff. Author of The Chaucer Tradition, Copenhagen and Oxford, 1926.

Burgh. Burgh's Letter to Lydgate, see pp. 188 ff. here.

Bycorne. Lydgate's Bycorne and Chichevache, see pp. 113 ff. here.

Calig. The mark of a MS in the Cottonian collection of the British Museum, and from the case of that collection bearing the bust of Caligula. See my Chaucer Manual, p. 511.

CambrHEL. The Cambridge History of English Literature, Cambridge, 1907 ff.

CantTales. The Canterbury Tales of Chaucer.

CanYeoTale. Chaucer's Canon's Yeoman's Tale, from the Canterbury Tales.

Capgrave. John Capgrave, eminent Churchman of the fifteenth century, author among other of a life of St. Katherine. See under Gloucester.

Carmina Burana. A collection of vigorous Latin verse of the Middle Ages, ed. by Schmeller, 1883.

To Carpenter. Poem by Hoccleve, printed p. 67 here.

Cavend. The Metrical Visions of George Cavendish, see pp. 368 ff. here.

Caxton. See Gen. Introd. pp. 9, 35; see p. 88.

Chaucer Manual. Chaucer, a Bibliographical Manual, by E. P. Hammond, N. Y., 1908. Supplement to appear.

Chaucer, Praise of. Extracts from Hoccleve's Regement of Princes, see p. 74 here.

Chaucer Society. For publications see my Manual, pp. 523 ff.

Chrétien de Troyes, of the twelfth century. Author among other of the romance of Yvain, cited Gen. Introd. p. 31, 32. The Works are ed. by Foerster, 4 vols., Halle 1884-99.

Christine de Pisan, died ca. 1430. Oeuvres poétiques are ed. by Roy for SATF., 3 vols., 1886-96. Her Chemin de Long Estude is ed. R. Püschel, Berlin, 1881. Her Epistle of Othea to Hector was transl. by Stephen Scrope and ed. by Warner for the Roxburghe Club, 1904. Many other works, some inedited.

Churl. Lydgate's Churl and Bird; see p. 102 here.

ClTale. The Clerk's Tale, from the Canterbury Tales.

Compl. to his Lady. A Complaint to his Lady, a poem printed with the work of Chaucer by Skeat, i: 360. See my Chaucer Manual, p. 411.

Confessio. Gower's Confessio Amantis, ed. with the other works of Gower by G. C. Macaulay, Oxford 1899, 4 vols.; also EETS.

Copland. .Robert Copland, printer and editor, also writer; see p. 287 here.

CourtLove. The Court of Love, an anonymous poem ed. Skeat vii: 409. See my Chaucer Manual, p. 418.

CourtSap. The Court of Sapience, a poem ascribed to Lydgate by Hawes. Ed. by Spindler, Leipzig, 1927. Extracts pp. 258 ff. here.

CT. Chaucer's Canterbury Tales. CT prol., the General Prologue to the Tales.

Cuckoo. The Cuckoo and the Nightingale, a poem ed. Skeat vii:347. See my Chaucer Manual, p. 420.

Dance. Lydgate's Dance Macabre, printed pp. 124 ff. here. French text of the poem, pp. 427 ff.

Deguilleville, Guillaume de, of the fourteenth century. Author of a three-part Pilgrimage:—the Pèlerinage de la Vie Humaine, the Pèlerinage de l'Ame, the Pèlerinage de Jésu Christ. The first of these was Englished, verse, by Lydgate; see my Chaucer Manual, p. 76.

De Planctu Naturae. See under Alanus ante.

Deschamps, Eustace. French contemporary of Chaucer, died ca. 1406. His works are ed., in 11 vols., for the SATF., 1878-1903. See my Chaucer Manual, p. 77.

Dial. Hoccleve's Dialogue with a Friend: extract printed here p. 69 ff.

Dibdin. Typographical Antiquities, London, 1810-19, 4 vols. Antiquated but still useful. For works supplementing it see Handlists, and see Blades on Caxton.

diss., dissertation.

DNB or Dict Nat Biog. The British Dictionary of National Biography, with its supplements. Living personages not included. See pp. 98, 419 here.

DoctTale. The Doctor's Tale, from the Canterbury Tales.

Donatus. See under Grammarians.

Douglas, Gavin. Scottish poet, died 1522. Bishop of Dunkeld, translator of the Aeneid. Works edited for the STS by Small, 4 vols., Edinburgh, 1874.

Du Cange. Glossarium mediae et infimae latinitatis, 1678. Edited by Henschel, 10 vols., 1882-88. Antiquated but still useful.

Dunbar, William. Scottish poet, died ca. 1520. Poems edited for the STS by Small, Mackay, and Gregor, 1888-93; ed. in one volume by H. B. Baildon, Cambr. Univ. Press, 1907.

DuorMerc or DuobMercat. Lydgate's Fabula Duorum Mercatorum, ed. Zupitza-Schleich, Strassburg, 1897.
Dyce. The Poetical Works of John Skelton, with notes, by the Rev. Alexander Dyce, 2 vols., London, 1843.

Ecl.,Ecl.prol. Barclay's Fourth Eclogue, pp. 312 ff. here and his prologue, *ibid*.
Education. In the Universities, see Rashdall's Universities of Europe in the Middle Ages, 2 vols., Oxford, 1895; see H. Parker in English Historical Review, vol. 5 (1890); see Abelson's Seven Liberal Arts, Columbia Univ., 1906. In the schools, see Leach's Schools of Medieval England, London, 1915; see Foster Watson's English Grammar Schools to 1660, Cambridge, 1908. In the Inns of Court, see the bit in Fortescue's De Laudibus Legum Angliae, and see the chapter on Chaucer's Education in Manly's New Light on Chaucer, N. Y., 1926. See the chapter on Education in vol. ii of the Cambridge Hist. Eng. Literature; and Seebohm's Oxford Reformers for a study of Colet and his school at St. Paul's.
EEPopPo. Remains of the Early Popular Poetry of England, ed. W. C. Hazlitt, 4 vols., London, 1864-66.
EETS. The Early English Text Society, founded 1864 and still active.
Egerton. The mark of a MS-subcollection in the British Museum.
Ellesmere. The mark of a MS owned by the Earl of Ellesmere. The noble copy of the Canterbury Tales once owned by Lord Ellesmere has passed to the Huntington collection in California; and the copy of poems by Lydgate, etc., formerly marked Ellesmere 26 A 13, is also now of that library, but retaining the early mark.—See refs., p. 58 here.
EncyclBrit. The Encyclopedia Britannica.
EnglStud. Englische Studien, Heidelberg, 1877 ff., quarterly.
Epithal. Lydgate's Epithalamium for Gloucester, printed pp. 142 ff. here.

Fairfax. The mark of a small sub-collection of MSS in the Bodleian Library at Oxford. For the most important, no. 16, see my Chaucer Manual, p. 333 ff.
Fall, FaPrin. Lydgate's Fall of Princes, ed. Bergen 1923-27, 4 vols. Extracts pp. 150 ff. here.
Faral. Editor of Les arts poétiques du xii et du xiii siècle, Paris, 1924. Texts, with introductions, of the more important Latin rhetoricians in that period; includes Matthew of Vendôme's Ars Versificatoria, Gaufrid de Vinsauf's Poetria Nova and his De Arte Versificandi, Evrard l'Allemand's Laborintus. Supersedes Leyser as below, and supplements the collection of Mari, I Tratti Medievali di Ritmica Latina, Milan, 1899, also that of Langlois, Recueil d'arts de séconde Rhétorique, Paris, 1902. On the general subject see also Norden, Die antike Kunstprosa vom vi Jahrhundert vor Christo bis in die Zeit der Renaissance, Leipzig, 1898, 2 vols. See under Rhetoric below.
On Faral see Sedgwick in Speculum ii: 331-342.
Filigranes. See collection ed. by C. M. Briquet, 4 vols., Paris, 1907.
Fitzwilliam MS of Palladius. See p. 202 here.
FlandLeaf. The anonymous poem, The Flower and the Leaf, ed. Skeat in Chaucerian and Other Pieces, pp. 361 ff. See my Chaucer Manual, p. 423.
FlCourt. The Flower of Courtesy, a poem presumably by Lydgate. Text in Skeat as just cited, p. 266; see my Chaucer Manual, p. 424.

Flügel, Ewald, died 1914. Co-editor of Anglia, where are printed many articles
    by him. Editor of a Neuenglisches Lesebuch, Halle, 1895, vol. i only
    published.
FranklTale. The Franklin's Tale, from the Canterbury Tales.
Fulgentius, died 533 A.D. Works, ed. by Helm, Leipzig, 1898, include a Myth-
    ologicon much read in the Middle Ages, also an allegorical interpretation of
    Virgil.
Furnivall. Frederick James Furnivall, died 1910, founder and indefatigable edi-
    tor for the Ballad Society, the Chaucer Society, the Early English Text
    Society, etc. See my Chaucer Manual, p. 522.

Gamelyn. The Tale of Gamelyn, found in many MSS of the Canterbury Tales.
    Edited by Skeat, Oxford, 1884, 1893. See my Chaucer Manual, p. 425.
Garl. Skelton's Garland of Laurel, printed pp. 336 ff. here.
Gen. Introd. The General Introduction to this volume.
Gesta Romanorum. For note on this collection of anecdotes and stories see my
    Chaucer Manual, p. 90. The Latin is edited by Oesterley, Berlin, 1871 *et seq.*,
    and by Dick, Leipzig, 1890; transl. into English by Charles Swan, see ed. N.
    Y., 1924.
Gower. See under Confessio above; see pp. 21, 96, 164 ff.
Grammarians. See Grammatici Latini, ed. H. Keil, Leipzig, 1857-78, 7 vols. and
    suppl., for Donatus, Priscian, etc.
Guido. Guido delle Colonne, translator, from Benoit's French, of the Historia
    Trojana; cited by Lydgate as source of his Troy Book. No modern edition.
Guy of Warwick. By Lydgate; see pp. 96, 100 here.

Halliwell, MinPo. A Selection from the Minor Poems of Dan John Lydgate, ed.
    by J. O. Halliwell, London, for the Percy Society, 1840. Ill done, with much
    spurious matter.
Handlists. Handlists of English Printers, 1501-1556. London, 1895, 1896, for
    the Bibliographical Society. See my Chaucer Manual, p. 548.
Hardyng. The extract from Hardyng's Chronicle, printed pp. 233 ff. here.
Harl. As applied to a MS, one of the sub-collection formerly owned by Lord
    Harley, and now in the British Museum.
Harv.Stud. Studies and Notes in Philology and Literature, pubd. under the
    direction of the Modern Language Departments of Harvard University,
    1892 ff.
Hawes. Stephen Hawes' Pastime of Pleasure, from which extracts are printed pp.
    268 ff. here.
Hazlitt. W. C. Hazlitt, editor of the 1871 revision of Warton's History of Eng-
    lish Poetry, on which see my Chaucer Manual, p. 556-57. Editor of Remains
    of Early Popular Poetry, as above; etc. etc.
Henryson, Robert, "the schoolmaster of Dunfermline," died ca. 1506. The most
    Chaucerian of the "Scottish Chaucerians". Poems ed. G. Gregory Smith for
    the Scottish Text Society, 3 vols., 1906-14. An ed. in one volume, with texts
    selected and slightly modernized, is by W. M. Metcalfe, Paisley, 1917. See
    p. 25 here.
Hh. Class-mark of MSS in the University Library, Cambridge.

Higden. Compiler of the Polychronicon, ed., with Trevisa's English translation, for the Rolls Series, 1865. The Polychronicon was completed in 1387.

HistEEPO. Warton's History of English Poetry; see under Hazlitt above.

HM. The usual mark of a MS in the collection of the late Henry E. Huntington, San Gabriel, California.

HoFame. Chaucer's Hous of Fame.

Horns. Lydgate's poem Horns Away, printed pp. 110 ff. here.

HorGoSheep. Lydgate's poem The Horse, the Goose, and the Sheep, ed. Degenhart, Leipzig, 1900.

How A Lover. The anonymous poem "How a Lover Praiseth his Lady", printed by me in Modern Philology 21 : 379-395.

Hunterian. The mark of MSS in the University Library, Glasgow.

Huntington. See under HM above.

Hye Way to the Spyttelhous. See under Copland here.

Hyginus. A mythographer, died ca. A.D. 17. His Fabulae are in Scriptores Rerum Mythicarum Latini Tres, ed. Bode, Kiel, 1834.

Isidor. Isidor bishop of Seville, "Isidorus Hispalensis", died ca. 636 A.D. His Opera are in Migne's Patrologia latina, vols. 81-84; his principal work, the Etymologiarum sive Originum libri XX, is ed. by W. M. Lindsay, Oxford, 1911, 2 vols.

Isle of Ladies is ed. Sherzer, Berlin diss. 1905. See my Chaucer Manual, p. 429.

James I king of Scotland. See under Kingis Quair.

Jamieson. Editor of Barclay's Ship of Fools, q.v.

James, Dr. Montague Rhodes, Compiler of many catalogues of MSS in the libraries of Cambridge, especially of those in Trinity College, 4 vols., Cambridge 1900-04; author of a volume on the Abbey of St. Edmund at Bury, Cambridge, 1895.

Jardin de Plaisance. A fifteenth-century French compilation of amatory and didactic prose and verse, facsimiled for the Soc. des anciens textes français, 1910.

JEGcPhil. The Journal of English and Germanic Philology, Bloomington, Ills., U. S. A., 1897 ff. Quarterly.

John of Salisbury, English schoolman of the twelfth century, author of the Polycraticus, a work (Latin) on the vices and follies of courts; of the Metalogicus; etc. His Opera are pubd. in Migne's Patrologia latina, vol. 199; and the Polycraticus is edited by C. C. J. Webb, Oxford, 1910. See H. O. Taylor's Medieval Mind, vol. ii; see Schaarschmidt's Johannes Sarisberiensis, Leipzig, 1862.

Kingis Quair. The single poem by King James I of Scotland; accessible in ed. by Skeat, Scottish Text Society, 1884, or in ed. of Medieval Scottish Poetry by G. Eyre-Todd, Glasgow, 1892. See also Alex. Lawson, London, 1910. A monograph by J. T. T. Brown, Glasgow 1896, on the authorship of the poem, opened a discussion; see Jusserand in Révue historique, vol. 64, R. S. Rait, The Kingis Quair and the New Criticism, Aberdeen, 1898.

Kingsford, C. L., died 1927. Editor of Stow's Survey of London, 2 vols., Oxford, 1908; author of English Historical Literature in the Fifteenth Century, Oxford 1913, and of Prejudice and Promise in Fifteenth Century England, Oxford 1925, etc.

Kk. Class-mark of MSS in the University Library, Cambridge.

KnTale. Chaucer's Knight's Tale, from the Canterbury Tales.

Koeppel. Emil Koeppel, died 1917, author of monographs on Lydgate's Fall of Princes and on his Siege of Thebes; see pp. 151, 120 here.

La Belle Dame. La Belle Dame sans Mercy, ed. Skeat vii: 299.

Laborintus. See under Faral above.

Lansd., Lansdowne. Mark of a collection of MSS in the British Museum, so called from its former owner.

Laurent. Laurent de Premierfait, fifteenth-century French translator of Boccaccio, etc.; see p. 150 here, and passim under Fall of Princes; see Notes on that poem, A 3, 36, 79, etc.

Legend. Chaucer's Legend of Good Women.

LettGlouc. Lydgate's Letter to Gloucester, see p. 149 here.

Leyser. Historia Poetarum et Poematum Medii Aevi, 1721. Now largely superseded by Faral, q.v.

LGW. Chaucer's Legend of Good Women.

Libel. The Libel of English Policy, see pp. 240 ff. here.

Lickp. London Lickpenny, see p. 237 here.

Liddell. See under Palladius, p. 202 here.

Linc. The mark of a MS owned by Lincoln Cathedral.

Longleat. The mark of a MS in the library of the Marquess of Bath, at Longleat House.

MacCracken. Editor of The Minor Poems of John Lydgate, vol. i, EETS 1911. Contains essay on the Canon, and Religious Poems. Reference to the paper on the Canon is frequent here.—Editor of The Serpent of Division, see p. 101 here.—See under FaPrinces A 303 here (Notes) for suggestion as to "Dant in English".—See under Orléans, p. 218 here, for suggestion as to authorship; see pp. 79, 198, note on Garl. 296, on Orl. I-XI.

Machaut, Guillaume de, died ca. 1377. Oeuvres, ed. Hoepffner, Soc. des anciens textes français, 3 vols., 1908-1921. Poésies lyriques, ed. V. Chichmaref, Paris, 1909.

Macrobius. Of the fifth century. Author of the Saturnalia, a report of conversations at a banquet, really an encyclopedia thinly disguised. Author of Commentarii in Somnium Scipionis, a treatise which preserves for us part of Cicero's De Republica. Macrobius is ed. by Eyssenhardt, Leipzig, 1893; on him see Whittaker's study, Cambridge, 1923, and chap. viii of Glover's Life and Letters in the Fourth Century, 1901.

Magic. See under Thorndike.

Magnificence. Skelton's play of that name; ed. by Ramsay for EETS, 1908.

Mâle, E. L'art réligieux de la fin du moyen-âge en France. Paris, 1908.

Malory, Sir Thomas. See Gen. Introd. pp. 30, 34, 36. See the many eds. of his Morte dArthur; see Vida D. Scudder, Le Morte dArthur of Sir Thomas Malory and its Sources, London and N. Y., 1917.

MancTale. Chaucer's Manciple's Tale, in the Canterbury Tales.

Mandeville. His Travels were ed. 1889 for the Roxburghe Club by Sir George Warner, with the original French; by A. W. Pollard, London 1900; by Hamelins for the EETS, 1919.

Map, Walter. Of the twelfth century, a Welshman writing in Latin. Author of De Nugis Curialium, ed. Wright for the Camden Society in 1850, and ed. by M. R. James, Oxford, 1914; transl. into English, with notes, by Frederick Tupper and M. B. Ogle, N. Y., 1924. Map is also redactor of the Arthurian romances, and supposed author of a quantity of bitter "Goliardic" verse, ed. for the Camden Society, 1841, by Wright, as "Poems of Walter Mapes". See Hinton in PMLA 32:81-132, Bradley in Engl. Histor. Review 32:393-400. See note on FaPrinces E 43 here.

MaReg. Hoccleve's Mâle Règle, printed p. 60 here.

Margarita Philosophica. See p. 269 here.

Mars. Chaucer's Complaint of Mars.

Martianus Capella. Of the latter fifth century, author of De Nuptiis Mercurii et Philologiae, an encyclopedic work popular throughout the Middle Ages. It is ed. Eyssenhardt, Leipzig, 1866. See note on FaPrinces D 66 here.

Mass. The Lover's Mass, printed p. 207 here.

Matthew of Vendôme. See under Vendôme.

McClean. Mark of a MS of the McClean bequest, at the Fitzwilliam Museum, Cambridge.

Melibeus. Chaucer's tale of Melibeus, in the Canterbury Tales.

MerchTale. Chaucer's Merchant's Tale, in the Canterbury Tales.

Metam. Ovid's Metamorphoses. Convenient edition in the Loeb Library, 2 vols., 1916.

MidEng. Middle English.

Migne. Editor of the Patrologia Cursus Completus, of which the Patrologia Latina fills 225 vols., Paris, 1844-55, and includes the Latin works of all fathers, doctors, and authorities of the Church, from the apostolic age to the time of Pope Innocent III. Ill-printed, and with many errors, but offering much material not yet better edited.

MillTale. The Miller's Tale, in the Canterbury Tales.

MinPo. Minor Poems, i.e. of Lydgate. See Halliwell.

ML.Notes. Modern Language Notes, Baltimore, 1886 ff.

MLReview. The Modern Language Review, which in 1905 succeeded the Modern Language Quarterly. Cambridge, Eng.; quarterly.

MLTale. The Man of Law's Tale, in the Canterbury Tales.

ModPhil. Modern Philology. University of Chicago, 1903 ff.; quarterly.

Monaci. Editor of Crestomazia Italiana dei Primi Secoli, 1912.

MoTale. The Monk's Tale, in the Canterbury Tales.

Naetebus. Die nichtlyrischen Strophenformen des altfranzösischen, Leipzig, 1891.

NED. The New English Dictionary, Oxford 1888-1927. Additions and corrective suggestions, see p. 87; see, in Glossary, under *amount, degest, erronyouse, engrosid, frowise, lurke, mortalite, obscure, prouect, salarie, satirray, ?spare, sufficistent, trions, vauntwarde*. In the Notes see Walton A 360, Horns 23, 37, Thebes 169, LettGlouc. 12, 55, FaPrinces A 398, B 143, Mass 165, Orl. v, Hawes 87, 494, 663, Nevill 49, Nevill envoy 4, Garl. 785, 1074, Ecl. 596, 994, Ecl. prol. 21, Cavend. 1251. See under *affoyle, drames, glutton, lauer, plummet, quacham*. On the Dictionary's attribution of poems see Mass, p. 208, Lickp., p. 238.

Neilson. Neilson and Webster's ed. of The Chief British Poets of the Fourteenth and Fifteenth Centuries. Boston, n.d. (?1916).

Nevill, Nevill dial., Nevill envoy. The extracts from Nevill's Castell of Pleasure, p. 287 here.

NPTale. The Nonne Prestes Tale, in the Canterbury Tales.

OEng. Old English.

OFr. Old French.

Orl. The translations from Charles d'Orléans' verse, pp. 214 ff. here.

Pallad. The translation of Palladius De re rustica; prologue printed p. 202 here.

Pallad.A,B,C,D. The four "linking-stanzas" from the above work, p. 206 here.

PardTale. The Pardoner's Tale, from the Canterbury Tales.

ParsTale. The Parson's Tale, from the Canterbury Tales.

Phillipps. Many Chaucer and Lydgate MSS were formerly in the great collection of the late Sir Thomas Phillipps, at Cheltenham, but are now all in other libraries. No. 9053 (miscell.) is Brit. Mus. Adds. 34360; no. 4255 (Fa-Princes) is in the hands of Quaritch; nos. 8117 and 8118 (FaPrinces) are owned by Robert Garrett of Baltimore and John Gribbel of Philadelphia; no. 8151 (Hoccleve) is now HM 111 of the Huntington Library, California, and no. 8299 (miscell.) is no. 140 of the same library. Other Phillipps MSS are at present (1927) in the hands of Dr. A. S. W. Rosenbach of New York viz.:—nos. 1099 (Hoccleve and Walton), 4254 (FaPrinces), 6570 (fragments of the CantTales), 8136 and 8137 (CantTales), 8192 (Gower's Confessio) 8250 (Chaucer's Troilus).

Piers Plowman. Edited by Skeat, 2 vols., Oxford, 1886. Cited by either the A,B, or C-recension, and by Passus or section.

PilgLifeMan. Lydgate's verse-translation of Deguilleville's Pèlerinage de la Vie Humaine, ed. for EETS 1899-1904, as The Pilgrimage of the Life of Man.

Pity. Chaucer's poem so entitled.

PMLA. Publications of the Modern Language Association of America, 1884 ff.; quarterly.

PoFoules. Chaucer's Parlement of Foules.

Polit.Poems. Political Poems and Songs . . . from the Accession of Edward III to that of Richard III, ed. by Thomas Wright, 1859-61, for the Rolls Series, 2 vols.

PolReligLove Poems. Political, Religious, and Love Poems, ed. Furnivall for the EETS in 1866, and revised 1903.

Praise of Chaucer. Three extracts from Hoccleve's De Regimine Principum, in praise of his master; see p. 74-75 here.

PriorTale. The Prioress' Tale, from the Canterbury Tales.

Priscian. See under Grammarians.

Prohib. The final chapter or "Prohibitio" of Ripley's Compend of Alchemy. See p. 256 here.

ProlCT. The Prologue to the Canterbury Tales.

Prompt. Parv. Promptorium Parvulorum, the first English-Latin dictionary, ed. for the EETS by A. L. Mayhew, 1908.

Quaritch. The foremost bookdealing business of the English-speaking world takes its name from its founder, the late Bernard Quaritch.

Rashdall. See under Education *ante*.

RefList. This Reference List.

RegPrinc. Hoccleve's poem The Regement of Princes, or De Regimine Principum; extracts pp. 74-75 here. Edited entire for the EETS in vol. iii of
Hoccleve's works, 1897.

Reliq.Antiq. Reliquiae Antiquae, ed. J. O. Halliwell and Thomas Wright, 2 vols.,
London 1841-43. A collection of shorter poems and scraps from MSS, in
several languages.

Renaud. See Gen. Introd. pp. 32-33.

Reproof. A Reproof to Lydgate, printed p. 198 here.

ResonandSens. Lydgate's poem Reson and Sensuality, ed. for the EETS 1901-3.

Rhetoric. See under Faral *ante,* and under Vendôme below. The Poetria of
Johannes de Garlandia is ed. by Mari in Rom. Forsch. vol. 13. For earlier
treatises see collection ed. by Halm, Rhetores Latini Minores, Leipzig, 1863;
see under Ad Herennium *ante.*

Ripley. The extracts from George Ripley's Compend of Alchemy, here printed p.
252. See also under Prohibicio.

Rolls Series. The series of Chronicles and Memorials of Great Britain and Ireland during the Middle Ages, pubd. under the direction of the Master of the
Rolls, in London.

Romania. Paris, 1872 ff.; quarterly.

Rom.Forsch. Romanische Forschungen, Erlangen, 1833 ff.; quarterly.

Rom.Review. Romanic Review, New York (Columbia Univ.), 1910 ff.; quarterly.

RomRose. Le Roman de la Rose, a French poem of the 13th century, of enormous
influence in West Europe. Translated or partly translated by Chaucer; see
my Manual, p. 450. Edited by Méon in 1814, by Michel in 1864, by Marteau
in 1878-80, by Langlois, SATF, 5 vols., 1914-1924.

Rosenbach. Dr. A. S. W. Rosenbach, bibliophile and dealer, New York City.

Round. One of Hoccleve's three roundels here printed p. 68.

Royal. As applied to a MS, one of the Royal collection of the British Museum.
See Catalogue of the Western MSS in the Old Royal and Kings' Collections,
London, 1921, for full descriptions and much information.

Rylands. The John Rylands Library at Manchester, England.

Rymer's Foedera. Foedera, Conventiones, Litterae, et cujusque generis Acta
Publica (etc.) 1101-1654. 20 vols. London, 1704-35.

Salisbury, John of. See John of Salisbury.

Sandys. History of Classical Scholarship, by J. E. Sandys, Cambridge 1903-08,
3 vols.

SATF. Société des anciens textes français, Paris. Issues one or more medieval
French texts each year.

SatirPoets. The Anglo-Latin Satirical Poets and Epigrammatists of the Twelfth
Century, ed. Thomas Wright, 2 vols., London, 1872.

SecNunTale. The Second Nun's Tale, in the Canterbury Tales.

Secrees. The Secrees of Olde Philisoffres, by Lydgate and ?Burgh. EETS 1894.

Selden. Class-mark of a collection of MSS in the Bodleian Library.

Serpent of Division. Prose tractate probably by Lydgate; ed. MacCracken, Oxford, 1911.

Servius. See under Virgil.

ShephCal. The Shepherd's Calendar of Spenser.

Ship. Barclay's rendering, from Locher, of Brant's Ship of Fools. See extracts
    pp. 298 ff.

Shirley. John Shirley, fifteenth-century copyist of Chaucer and Lydgate; see p.
    191 here.

Sir Thopas. Chaucer's Rime of Sir Thopas, in the Canterbury Tales.

Skeat, Walter William, died 1912. Author of various works on English philology,
    and editor of many Early English texts. See his "Oxford" edition of
    Chaucer, 6 vols., 1894 and subsequently, and especially the supplementary
    volume "Chaucerian and Other Pieces," cited here as *vii.*—Skeat was also
    editor of a volume of Specimens of English Literature 1394-1579, Oxford,
    1871 and many reprints, cited here as *Specimens.* This volume followed on
    R. Morris' Specimens of Early English Literature (the Old Eng. Homilies to
    King Horn), and on Morris and Skeat's companion volume covering Robert
    of Gloucester to Gower.

Sloane. As applied to a MS, one of the collection in the Brit. Mus. bearing that
    name.

Somer. Hoccleve's poem to the sub-treasurer Somer; see p. 66 here.

Specimens. See Skeat.

Speculum. Publ. quarterly, 1926 ff., by the Medieval Academy of America,
    Boston, Mass.

Speght. Editor or part-editor of the Chaucer of 1598; see my Manual, pp.
    122-128.

SPT. Supplementary Parallel Texts of Chaucer's Minor Poems, Chaucer Society.

Spurgeon, Caroline F. E. Compiler of : Five Hundred Years of Chaucer-Criticism
    and Allusion, Chaucer Society, 1908-1926, five parts.

SqTale. The Squire's Tale, in the Canterbury Tales.

Stow, John. See p. 193 here; and see under Kingsford.

STS. The Scottish Text Society, founded 1884.

Summ.Catal. A Summary Catalogue of Western Manuscripts in the Bodleian
    Library at Oxford which have not hitherto been catalogued in the quarto
    series. Oxford 1895—in progress. Vols. III-VI have appeared; vols. I and
    II are to be a new edition of the Old Catalogue by Bernard etc., 1697, and of
    this vol. I part i has been pubd., 1922.

Tanner. The class-mark of a collection of MSS in the Bodleian Library, Oxford.

TemGlass. Lydgate's Temple of Glass, ed. for the EETS 1891 by Dr. Schick.

ten Brink. ten Brink's (unfinished) History of English Literature was pubd.
    1877-89, and transl. into English in 1883-93. See my Chaucer Manual, p.
    555, and for ten Brink's other volumes see p. 556; see *ibid.* p. 520.

Test. Lydgate's Testament; see p. 101 here, also pp. 79-80.

TestLove. The Testament of Love, a prose treatise of the fourteenth century;
    see ed. in Skeat vol. vii.

Thebes. Lydgate's Siege of Thebes; prologue printed pp. 118 ff. here.

Thorndike. History of Magic and Experimental Science during the First Thirteen
    Centuries of our Era, by Lynn Thorndike, 2 vols. New York, 1923.

Trevisa. John of Trevisa, died 1412, did most of his translation for Thomas lord
    Berkeley. His version of Higden's Polychronicon, finished in 1387, is ed. in
    the Rolls Series 1865; his transl. of Bartholomaeus' De Proprietatibus Rerum
    was finished in 1398.

Trin.Coll. The mark of a Trinity College MS, either at Cambridge or at Oxford. The Oxford college distinguishes by a following numeral; the great Cambridge college classes its MSS under various alphabetical divisions, having the more important English MSS in class R. Thus,—the often-mentioned Shirley MS R 3,20.

Tyrwhitt. Thomas Tyrwhitt, classical and English scholar, executed the first critical edition of the Canterbury Tales entire. See my Chaucer Manual, pp. 205 ff.

Ubi Sunt motif. See p. 169 here.

ULC. The University Library, Cambridge, England.

Utter thy Language. Poem by Lydgate, ed. Halliwell MinPo, p. 173.

Venus. Chaucer's poem The Complaint of Venus.

Vendôme, Matthew of, or Matthaeus Vindocinensis. A twelfth-century rhetorician, two of whose works are ed. by Faral as *ante*. Matthew's importance has not yet been estimated for Chaucer and the Chaucerians, although notes on the subject are beginning to appear, see e.g. Goffin in ModLangReview 21:13, and Prof. Manly's Warton lecture on Chaucer and the Rhetoricians, pubd. Oxford, 1926. Matthew's Tobias was ed. by Mueldener, Göttingen, 1855, from 6 MSS in German libraries. His Ars Versificatoria was ed.. Bourgain, Paris, 1879, and by Faral as *ante;* portions are in Reliq. Antiq. ii: 257 ff., reprinted in Migne, vol. 205, where is also the Tobias from the ed. by Hering of 1642. Matthew's collection of model letters is printed by Wattenbach in Sitzungsberichte der königl. bayerischen Akademie der Wissenschaften, Munich, 1872, iii: 561-631.

Vincent de Beauvais. Compiler of a four-volume encyclopedia in the thirteenth century,—the Speculum Historiale, Speculum Doctrinale, Speculum Naturale, and a Speculum Morale not certainly by Vincent.

Vinsauf, Gaufrid or Geoffroi de. Of the thirteenth century; author of a rhetorical treatise for which see Faral as *ante*.

Virgil. See in especial Comparetti's Vergil in the Middle Ages, Eng. transl., London, 1895. For the allegorical interpretation of Virgil see Servius' commentary, ed. Thilo and Hagen, Leipzig, 1878-87, 3 vols.; see under Fulgentius.

Walton. Extracts from John Walton's transl. of the Consolatio Philosophiae are here printed pp. 39 ff.

Ward, Catal. Catalogue of Romances in the Manuscript Department of the British Museum, ed. H. L. D. Ward, completed by J. A. Herbert. London, 1883 ff., 3 vols.

Warton, HistEEPoetry. See under Hazlitt *ante,* and see my Chaucer Manual, p. 556-57.

Watermarks of paper, see under Filigranes.

WBprol., WBTale. The Wife of Bath's prologue and tale, in the Canterbury Tales.

Wells. A Manual of the Writings in Middle English 1050-1400. By J. E. Wells. London and New Haven 1916; first supplement 1919.

Wright,Politpoems,—SatirPoems. See *ante* under those abbreviations, and under Map.

Wülker. Editor of an Altenglisches Lesebuch, 2 vols., Halle, 1874-80. Editor of Anglia for years, and late professor at the University of Leipzig.

SELECT GLOSSARY AND FINDING LIST

No attempt is made here to include all variants in spelling, for example as between -i- and -y-, or to cite words of which the meaning is recognizable despite slight archaism, such as list; nor is any attempt made to elucidate terms like Hector or Mercury, or to catalogue all mentions of names. The constant reference to Lydgate or to Chaucer, in the various Introductions here, would if recognized extend this Index beyond all bounds; and to collect all the echoes of the Bible or all the proverbial material or all the cases of alliteration would be a labor in itself. An asterisk, following a line-number, means that a note on the word is to be found there. The Court of Sapience extracts are neither annotated nor glossed.

A, Ah! Walton A 273, MaReg. 265*, FaPrin. D 78, Pallad. A 1, Burgh 34, Reproof 64, Orl. xiii: 12, 18, Libel 455, Ship 585, Ecl. 435;—on, Nevill dial. 47.

aart, art, MaReg. 32.

abasched, abaisshid, abashed, Walton A 382, Dance 89, 98, FaPrin. G 16.

abate, to bring down, Dance 12, 150.

abhomynable, abominable, Walton E 93*, FaPrin. G 320, Ship 8515.

abiect, to cast out, cast down, Hawes 4245, Ecl. 713;—to object, Ecl. prol. 41, 89;—*a.* prone, Ripley 169*.

abit, *v.* abides, Dance 405, FaPrin. E 104.

abood, *s.* delay, FaPrin. B 150;—*v.* remained, FaPrin. G 69, 116, 236.

abraid, abrayde, *v.* speak out, start up, Churl 83, FaPrin. B 1*;—*v.* to approach, FaPrin. A 451, G 174.

abrode, abroad, FaPrin. G 147, etc.

absent, *v.* Orl. xiv: 19*.

Absolon, Cavend. epit. 14.

abuse, to be mistaken, Ecl. 505; *see* Cavend. 68.

abusion, *s.* abuse, Libel 32, FaPrin. D 113.

abye, to pay dearly, Hawes 4330.

abyt, *s.* habit, Walton A 375.

acate, *s.* purchasing, MaReg. 181.

access, Garl. 315*.

accessary, *s.* aid, support, Garl. 523.

accloyed, hampered; Ship, heading on p.304.

accuate, acuate, *a.* sharpened, refined, Ripley 136*, Prohib. 47.

accusith, *v.* discloses, MaReg. 40. See Chaucer RomRose 1591.

ace, *s.* Pallad. 16, 17*.

Achilliedos, Garl. 337*.

aclere, *v.* to clear, Orl. xv: 23.

acquite, aquytte, acquitted, Thebes 29, see 72.

acustomabill, usual, Garl. 1108.

adauntid, *v.* beat down, Garl. 1276.

a dewe, adieu, Dance 166, 200.

admittible, admissible, MaReg. 299.

aduenture, risk, Hawes 4221;—chance. Ecl. 178.

aduersite, opposition, attack, MaReg. 5*, 47.

aduerte, aduertise, to attend, notice, Dance 615, FaPrin. A 202, D 79, Orl. xvi:15, Nevill 121;—to know, Orl. xxi:14;—to consider, FaPrin. A 164, Cavend. 263.

aduertence, attention, Dance 2, Ship 13826.

aduertisement, attention, Garl. 792.

aduisement, consideration, Ecl. 784, Cavend. 15.

adumantes, diamonds, Nevill 185.

aduoutrers, adulterers, Ecl. 666.

adyment, adamant, Garl. 305.

aege, age, Nevill dial. 8, Nevill 16, 212.

affeccioun, interested desire, FaPrin. A 368, C 64.

affore, afforn, before, Churl 118 etc., Dance 5, etc., Thebes 124, FaPrin. E 58 etc., Morley 15.

afforcid, *v.* strengthened, Dance 140, FaPrin. G 52. See Churl 64.

affoyle, Orl. xiv: 13*.

affray, terrifying, Churl 222; — discomfiture, Libel 535.

affter, according to, Churl 321, FaPrin. A 361, 432, G 199, Shirley I: 11, Reproof 32, 78, Orl. ix: 3, vii: 1, Prohib. 12, Ship 570, Ecl. prol. 10, 88, Ecl. 321, Garl. 39, 800, 1431;—afterward. FaPrin. A 103, 123, G 264, 274, Hawes 1263.

after one, on one pattern, Ecl. 102.

affyaunsynge, pledging, Garl. 555.

afor, aforn, before, Dance 376, Epithal. 3, Mass 9, etc.

afourme, read **aforne,** i.e., previously, Dance 274.

Agellius, Aulus Gellius, i.e., A. Gellius.

agerdows, sour-sweet, Garl. 1223. Fr. *aigre-doux.*

ageyn, back, Walton D 59, FaPrin. D 97, 99;—in return, Ship 85, Cavend. 1226.—for, To Somer 19.

ageyn, ayens, against, Churl 53 etc., Dance 349 etc., Epithal. 45, FaPrin. B 47, D 96, H 11, Hardyng 10, 37, 105 etc., Nevill envoy 10, Garl, 103, 211, 656, 1116:—for, FaPrin. G 76, Garl. 1359, 1509, 1513, 1515. þere ageyne, thereagainst, on the contrary, Walton E 106.

aght, aught, MaReg. 319, Roundel 2.

agilte, offended, Dial. 751.

Agincourt, Shirley I: 54. Hardyng as p. 233.

agone, ago, FaPrin. A 302, Ship 8448, etc.

agoo, gone, Walton C 28.

agreeth, suits, Ecl. 198, 201.

ai, aye, always, FaPrin. D 67.

I am aknowe, I confess, Mass 15.

at al, completely, Churl 272, Epithal. 100.

alak, alack! Orl. xv: 16.
alate, recently, Hawes 325.
Alathea, Ecl. prol. 39*.
Alaunson, Alençon, Hardyng 92.
albe, although, FaPrin. E 21.
Albumasar, Garl. 1395.
albyfycatyve, whitening, Ripley 195.
Albyoun, Albion, Shirley I: 60.
Alcest, Alcestis, Churl 68, Orl. xvii: 10.
Alchemy, *see* Ripley.
Alcione, Alcyone, FaPrin. A 304.
Alcreatour, Creator of all, Pallad. 2.
alegge, to state, Dial. 588*, Shirley I: 69.
aleven, eleven, Burgh 54.
Aleyn, Alanus de Insulis, Horns 17*. *See* Ref. List.
algate, anyway, MaReg. 183, FaPrin. B 26, Ripley 180, Nevill dial. 39.
Alisaunder, Alexander, FaPrin. E 92. *See* Nevill 836, Ecl. 1098, Garl. 367, Cavend. epit. 12.
alite, mounted, Hawes 4249.
alkyns, of every kind, Hardyng 6.
all, *s.* awl, FaPrin. E 54.
allay, *s.* alloy, Horns 6.
Allecto, one of the Furies, Walton A 61.
allectyng, alluring, Nevill 185. *See* **talecte.** First case NED 1528.
alleggen, to relieve, FaPrin. G 255, Mass 160. *See* Dial. 588*. *See* **alegge.**
Allegory *discussed,* Gen. Introd. p. 28. *See* Epithal. 143*.
allewei, always, FaPrin. C 25, G 229.
all if, although, Ecl. 157, 734, 917.
allonly, solely, Orl. ix: 22.
alloone, all one, united, Epithal. 18.
Almayne, Alemannia, Germany, Ship 6976.
allmeest, almost, Pallad. A 4.
almes, charity, Ecl. 1020. *See* FaPrin. A 206.
alom, alum, Libel. 328.
alon, ?alone, all one? Orl. xxii: 9.
Alone without company. See note, Orl. xv:19.
alowe, to praise, Dial. 717, Nevill dial. 21, Ecl. 719. Lat. *allaudare.*
als, as, Walton A 19, Libel 355, 363; —also. Hardyng 4, 36, 74, Libel 233, 256, 523, Orl. xix: 25; —so. Libel 477; —for? Orl. xvii: 21, xix: 25.
alsapyent, all-wise, Pallad. 10.
alys, alleys, Garl. 648, Cavend. 118.
ambages, *s.* obscurities, double meanings, Ecl. 707.
ambicious, haughty, FaPrin. E 48.
ameede, miswritten for **amende.** FaPrin. A 40.
amenusyng, diminishing, FaPrin. C 107.
amiddes, in the midst of, Hawes 4353.
amitie, amyte, fervent affection, Hawes 1335, Nevill 7.
among, therewith, Dial. 792, FaPrin. D 106, E 97, Mass 176, Lickp. 98, Hawes 1344, 4344; —sometimes, FaPrin. A 120, ?363, ?D 106.
amongys, among, Mass 28.
amount, to increase in estimation, Garl. 346. First case NED 1563.
Amphion, Garl. 273.

ampille, ample, Garl. 222.
ampty, empty, Walton, A 270.
an, on, Dance 190.
Anaphora, *See* note Cavend. 232.
and, an, if, Dial. 766, LettGlouc. 1, Burgh 41, Shirley I:72, Orl. xi:8, xvii:19, Libel 516, Hawes 674, Garl. 462, 738, 1060, Cavend. 188.
and eke also, Thebes 32*.
anende, constantly, Pallad. B 3.
an hondryd, a hundred, Mass 185.
annexed, Hawes 591.
annunciate, announced, Hawes 685.
annys, anise, Thebes 118.
anon riht, immediately, FaPrin. G 23. So **anon,** Hardyng 18.
anon to, as far as, Walton E 73, 151.
Antigone. *See* note FaPrin. A 246.
antimony, Prohib. 39*.
Anyball, Hannibal, Cavend. epit. 14, Cavend. 1136.
apall, *a.* pale, aghast, Morley 222.
aparayle, equipment, Ship 158; —apparel, Ship 470, 492, 580, 8470, 8482.
apast, past, Orl. xvi:9, xvii:24. NED gives cases from the romances.
apayed, pleased, Hawes 277.
apayred, impaired, made worse, Ship 470.
apese, to mitigate, FaPrin. B 16, D 109. *See* **appease.**
Apollo, a work by Skelton, Garl. 1436, 1445, 1455.
Apology, *See* Correcte, request to. *See* Walton A 1*, 58*.
apon, upon, Ripley 152.
apoynt, Pallad. 17*.
appade, appayed, pleased, Nevill 126.
appall, to fade, to lose color or vigor. MaReg. 310, Thebes 44, FaPrin. A 395; — to cause to lose strength, Cavend. 1310.
apparage, apparatus? Nevill 109.
Apparel, Acts of, *See* notes, Ship 498, 515, 533.
apparence, appearance, Horns 2, Dance 351, 522.
appease, to relieve, Hawes 4400. *See* **apese.**
appert, open, MaReg. 270, Orl. xi:8.
appliaunt, diligent, docile, Hawes 1102.
apply, to tend, Ecl. 159.
appoorte, *s.* bearing, Epithal. 86.
appreued, approved, Shirley I:6, 42.
appropryng, assigning, Ecl. prol. 87.
apreef, *s.* approved worth, Libel 242.
Apuly, Apulia, in southern Italy, Ship 6969.
ar, are, FaPrin. B 69 etc.
arace, aras, Arras tapestry, Garl. 475, Cavend. 120.
arage, to enrage? Hawes 1110.
aray, condition, Orl. xviii:15; — court of aray, a formally summoned court, Garl. 539.
arayed, prepared, Walton A 238.
arbitrye, judgment, Walton E 36.
arbor. *See* Nevill 427*, Cavendish 115-118* Garl. 646.
arche wyves, Horns 37*.
ardente, spirituous, Prohib. 8.

arere! Ship 78*; — behind, at disadvantage, Ecl. 655.

arestid, checked, Dance 456.

arett, to consider, repay. Orl, xiii:14.

arghnesse, timidity, MaReg. 435.

Argia, Morley 224.

Argus, FaPrin. A 383, D 21.

Aristeus, Ecl. 889*.

Aristotell, Aristotle, Praise of Chaucer 2088, Burgh 10, Nevill 841, Garl. 127.

arke, arc, FaPrin. B 115*.

Arnold, Cornelius, poem by, *see* note Dance 513.

arrayed, put forth, Walton C 4; —placed, Libel 324.

arrect, to raise (the eyes), to prick up (the ears) Garl. 1, 808, Nevill envoy 4*; —to submit? Garl. 55, 410*.

arrest, standeth at, "is held in durance", Morley 158.

Arrians, Arians, Walton A 168*, 177, 182, 192, 199.

arsnyke, arsenic, Prohib. 24.

artid, to cause, compel, MaReg. 396, 438.

artike, Arctic, Garl. 689.

Arts, the Seven Liberal, *see under* Seven etc., *below*.

as, so, thus, Walton A 16, Orl. xiii:19, xv:15; — as if, FaPrin. A 167, 169 etc.

as, introducing a clause, *see* note, Walton A 17; Orl. xii:1,*, xxiii:10.

asaiyd, assayed, tested, Garl. 759.

ascaunce, Dial. 620*, Orl. vii:6.

ascendent. *See* FaPrin. A 300*.

askes, ashes, Hardyng 27.

askry, to assail with a shout, Garl. 1324. *See* escry.

as nowe, just now, at once, Dance 192, Orl. xiii:32.

aspectis, Epithal. 1*, FaPrin. E 88.

assay, to try, test, use, Walton B 7, MaReg. 36, Horns 14, FaPrin. A 195, Shirley I:48, II:61, Orl. xviii:12, Lickp. 106, Prohib. 73, Libel 40, 540, Ship 521.

assencioun, ascension, the rising arc of a planet, FaPrin. C 71.

assent, agreement, Churl 18, 171.

assise, assize, session of justice, Dance 267.

asson, as soon, Cavend. 144.

Assonance, *see* FaPrin. B 154*, Hawes 92-4, 4224*, Garl. 335-6, etc., 980, Cavend. 162-4, 272-3, 1281-3.

assoyle, absolve, Shirley I:38.

assur, azure, FaPrin. K 12.

assuraunce, security, FaPrin. E 96.

assurded, broke out, (O. F. *assourdre*, to rise up), Garl. 392; only case in NED.

assure, to find safety, Pallad. 43; —assured, Mass 11.

assured, azured, Hawes 4219.

asswagin, to assuage, FaPrin. D 95, Mass 159.

astat, *see* estate.

asterte, to escape, avoid, MaReg. 96, Churl 111, Dance 510, FaPrin. B 29, 152, Orl. xi:11, xxi:15.

astonid, astonished, FaPrin. D 132, G 15.

aswage, to assuage, Walton A 360*. *See* **asswagin**.

at al, completely, Churl 272; —in every way. Epithal. 100.

atame, to lay hands on, Walton C 36.

atchyved, achieved, Cavend. 1138.

ateynt, attained, Lickp. 2.

Athlant, Atlantis, Ship 6972.

athlas, Atlas, Garl. 684.

Athrvmmys, Garl. 209*.

atonys, attonys, at once, Orl. xxi:1, 11.

attame, to broach, i.e., drain, LettGlouc. 51*.

attaste, to taste, experience, Hawes 1104.

atte, at the, Walton A 130, 132, Dance 25*, FaPrin. D 69, G 164, Libel 193, 427, etc.

atteinted, accused, Garl. 605; —stained, Mass 149.

atteyne, take a hand, FaPrin. A 107.

attise, to entice? Cavend. 33.

attyres, solicitations, Morley 172.

atwen, between, FaPrin. A 266, C 122.

atwyte, to blame, FaPrin. B 99.

auale, to fall, Thebes 8; —to set, sink, Hawes 65, 4347; —to bend, conform, Dance 347; —s. profit, Prohib. 51, etc.

auans, to advance, Orl. vii:3; —to put forward, Garl. 806.

auayle, be of profit, Ship 148; —s. profit, Ship 159.

auctor, autour, author.

auctoritee, authority.

auctorised, authorized, Dance 177; —recorded? FaPrin. A 154.

auctrice, *s.* (feminine) authority, Dial. 694.

audience, *s.* hearing, MaReg. 202, Horns 44, Hawes 251, Nevill 74.

auenter, to venture, Ship 80. **auenterous,** venturesome, Ship 37.

auenture, *s.* chance, lot, Dance 658, FaPrin. B 112, 114, G 284, Reproof 35, Mass 132, Orl. xv:9, 18, etc.; —*v.* to venture, Libel 331.

in auenture, in danger, Churl 208, LettGlouc. 36.

auertise, to consider, FaPrin. A 186. *See* **aduerte**.

aught, ought, Shirley II:32. **auhte,** ought, FaPrin. G 324.

Augustus, Morley 148, *see* Octavian.

auisines, judgment, Orl. ix:6.

me auysid, I took note, Garl. 36. *See* Garl. 78, 386.

Aulus Gellius, Garl. 351. *See* Agellius.

auncetry, ancestry, Ship 506.

on aunter, in case, Walton A 55.

auoyde, *a.* devoid, Ecl. 380, 458, 699, 701; — *v.* remove, Ecl. 385.

aureat, golden, FaPrin. A 461, C 13.

Aureate Language, *see* p. 25, 453, *see* MaReg. 1*.

aurum musicum, Garl. 1145*.

aurum potabile, LettGlouc. 46*, Ripley 160.

Auster, the south wind, Hawes 301*.

autentyk, authentic, Epithal. 36.

auter, altar, Mass 2.

"Autograph MS" of Orleans, p. 217.
auycen, Avicenna, Garl. 1393.
avaunt, awaunt, s. and v. boast, MaReg. 6,
  Walton A 289, Orl. xxi:4.
aver, possession, Dance 298*.
avert, to advert, attend, Orl. xx:5.
avis, auys, consideration, Walton A 111, 198,
  Dance 96, FaPrin. A 307, Pallad. 42, Libel 214.
avise, to give thought, Dance 248.
avise, avysee, prudent, FaPrin. A 71, Epithal.
  87*.
avisement, prudent consideration, FaPrin. E
  34.
avisioun, vision, FaPrin. G 256.
avne, own, Walton A 188.
avoyd, to banish, remove, FaPrin. A 439, B 78,
  Ecl. 385; —to depart, Cavend. 198.
awail, s. profit, FaPrin. G 258.
awaiteþe, lies in wait for, Bycorne 128.
awaityng, ambush, FaPrin. A 63.
awhappyd, stupefied with fear, FaPrin. B 141.
awne, own, Walton A 323.
axe, axyth, etc., to ask.
axes, s. access, Garl. 315*.
ayed, s. aid, Cavend. 1389.
ayein, ayen, again, Churl 69; —in return, Orl.
  xviii:9, Libel 329, 500; —thither, Pallad. 36; —
  against, Dance 79, 152, 280, 349, 380, 418, 422,
  447, 474, 613, 618, Reproof 70.
aȝens, against, Dance 429, 432, 442, 479, 598.
ayenst, toward, Libel 32; —against, Libel 32,
  Cavend. 164, 173, etc.
aylen, to ail, Walton C 9.

baar, v. bore, Roundel 1.
babill, Babel, Garl. 553.
babyll, bauble, Ship 105*, 502, Ecl. 236.
Bacchus, FaPrin. C 90, D 68, Ecl. 690, 1031,
  Garl. 334, 341, etc.
bace, (chemical) base, Ripley 139, 150, 175; —
  down, Walton A 256.
bad, Walton A 269.
badder, worse, Ecl. 123.
bagge, purse, MaReg. 163.
bake, back, Mass 157.
balade, stanza, Shirley I:79; —a poem in stanzas, a poem, Shirley I:87, (see II:23), Pallad. 6,
  Hawes 1335, Ecl. 142, 151, 286, 745, 747, 758,
  see Cavend. 134; —to make stanzaic verse, Orl.
  xiii:31.
balassis, grouped rubies used as ornaments,
  Garl. 1144.
bale, s. ill, Hardyng 28, Hawes 4290, Garl.
  377.
baleys, bundle of twigs for flogging, Libel 426.
ballade royal, Hawes 1318*.
ballyuis, bailiffs, Garl. 514*.
bankettyng, a. festal, Cavend. 1379.
bansshid, banished, FaPrin. F 18, G 231, H 27.
bararag, Garl. 235*, 245.
baratows, tricky, Garl. 667.
barbellis, fish of the carp-tribe, Garl. 655.
barbican, outer defence of a castle, Garl. 1364.
Bare, Bâr, Hardyng 92.

barm, bosom, FaPrin. B 146*.
base organes, Hawes 1412*.
basse, low, Cavend. 1165.
basshid, was abashed, Orl. xvii:11.
bastard, a sweet Spanish wine, Libel 53.
bastile, a small fortress, a barricade? FaPrin.
  D 31.
basylyske, basilisk, Ripley 169*.
batail, armed force, FaPrin. D 25.
batallous, warlike, Dial. 592.
bate, to check? Garl. 27*; —s. bait, Ship 546; —
  batyng, reducing, Ecl. prol. 79.
baudye, bawdy, coarse, dirty, Prohib. 28, Cavend. 44.
bawme, balm, Thebes 17, FaPrin. D 18, Garl. 668.
be, by, Walton A 8, C 34, E 6, 91, 102, Churl
  153, Thebes 113, 166, FaPrin. A 95, B 64, 119,
  136, D 58, E 3, G 165, 265, 279, Orl. ix:6,
  Prohib. 45.
beatyfie, to beautify, Cavend. 111.
bebled, covered with blood, Walton B 21.
it became, i.e; (what) became of it? Garl. 1216.
is become, i.e., (what) has become of it? Fa-
  Prin. C 20*, 43, Libel 36, Nevill 834.
bed, v. bade, Garl. 571.
bede, to offer, Lickp. 70.
bedleem, Bethlehem, Horns 54.
beeldyng, building, FaPrin. C 30.
beet, to beat, Walton A 316.
Begging letters, see MaReg. 417ff., To Somer,
  To Carpenter, Roundel 1, LettGlouc.
Beginnings of Lines alike, Cavend. 232*. Beginning, mode of, Thebes 1*, Cavendish 1.
begone, begun, Garl. 686.
behight, promised, Dance 239, Mass 92.
behove, s. need, Cavend. 18.
bekke, beak, nose, Thebes 169*.
bellewedir, bellwether, Dance 490*.
beldyng, building, FaPrin. C 3, Garl. 589.
belluynge, bellowing, Garl. 24.
ben, bene, v. are, Dance 635, Shirley II:40,
  Libel 36, etc.
benome, stupefied, rendered helpless. The
  past part. of O. E. beniman, in Mod. Eng.
  erroneously treated as "benumbed", Libel 38.
beo, beon, Shirley's spelling of v. "be".
ber, to bear, FaPrin. K 56.
berall, beryl, Hawes 351. See birall.
berd, beard, Cavend. 1237*.
bere, bier, Orl. xiii:7; —beer, Ecl. 393.
berefte, taken away, Libel 495.
berthen, burden, Dance 136, Mass 157.
besched, besought, Hawes 4373.
beseene, besein, Dance 446*, Garl. 483, 1054;
  see Orl. xvi:12.
beseke, to beseech, FaPrin. K 9, Garl. 56, 215,
  818. See byseeke.
besi, diligent, FaPrin. G 251.
bestad, pressed by circumstance, Garl. 814.
besynesse, earnest effort, Walton A 141, Fa-
  Prin. A 275, Garl. 1377.
bet, bete, beat, beaten, MaReg. 434, Libel 222,
  Garl. 41, 663.

bet, bette, better, Bedford 9, Churl 377, Thebes 145, 151, 172, Dance 645, FaPrin. A 467, Orl. xxii:11.

beth, are, Pallad. 83, Libel 349, 521;—*imperat. plu.*, be, Churl 368, Thebes 97, Orl. xxiii:9.

beþynke, to devise, contrive, Walton B 9.

betid, happened, Libel 185.

bett, beaten, FaPrin. K 47.

Bewford, Beaufort, Hardyng 52*.

bexample, by example, FaPrin. C 126.

bi, from? Orl. xxii:9. *See* by.

Bibliographies; *see* Reference Lists; *see* for Lydgate, p. 98, for Orleans, pp. 215 ff.

bide, i.e., bye, to endure, Ecl. 711.

bifru(n)s, two-faced, Hawes 4216*.

biheest, promise, Dial. 598.

bihoueth, it is necessary, Dance 168.

bileven, to remain, Dance 93.

bille, a written composition, LettGlouc. 49.

bilt, built, FaPrin. G 260.

biraft, biraught, bereft, Orl. xiii:32, xv:5.

birall, byral, beryl, Churl 56, 93, Garl. 467. *See* berall.

bit, biddeth, MaReg. 280, Dance 269.

bitake, to recommend, Dial. 789.

biwepen, to bewail with tears, FaPrin. A 235.

biwreie, to betray, reveal, Dial. 599.

Black Death, *see* p. 10; *see* note Cavend. 119.

blasinge, Ship 509, 515*.

blasyng, Hawes 4230*, *see* 3169.

ble, countenance, Garl. 1379.

blenkardis, men with blinking eyes, dullards, Garl. 604.

blent, deceived, FaPrin. A 166, Cavend. 151.

blere, *v.* Libel 342*.

blere-eyed, with eyes tear-dimmed, Churl 187.

bleuh, blew, FaPrin. G 147.

blew, blue, Hawes 335.

blis, to bless, Walton A 49.

blo, livid, Garl. 1366.

blont, blunt, Nevill 34.

blowe, to break wind, Thebes 112; *see* Garl. 604*.

blyue, soon, quickly, Dial. 542, MaReg. 280, Churl 10.

bocase, Boccaccio, Burgh 21, Hawes 1291.

Boccaccio, *see* Fall of Princes, pp. 150 ff.; *see* Garl. 827 ff*.

Bochas, Boccaccio, FaPrin. A 2, 64, 114, 120, 141, 150, 269, 423, 469, G 27, H 2, K 37, Garl. 365. *See* bocase.

bocher, butcher, Ship 566.

bodkyns, daggers, FaPrin. E 54*.

boece, Boethius, FaPrin. A 291, Shirley I:27.

Boethius, *see* Walton's translation, pp. 39 ff.; *see* FaPrin. H, p. 185; *see* Burgh 16. *See* Boys.

boked, equipped with books, Pallad. 96.

boklersbury, Bucklersbury, (a London street), LettGlouc. 43*.

bole, Boole, a bull, the constellation Taurus, Thebes 2.

bondes, boundaries, Walton D 58, 63.

bone, a request, Walton A 194.

bonechife, bonchief, good fortune; the contrary of mischief, Walton A 256.

bone homs, Bonshommes, Garl. 1428*.

boos, a boss, ornamental knob, Thebes 85.

boost, boastfulness, FaPrin. C 58, 59.

bootte, bote, a resource, remedy, Dance 193 FaPrin. D 3, Garl. 377, Cavend. 1418.

bordure, border, Walton A 331.

bore, born, Dance 586, Lickp. 125.

born, borne, Pallad. 30.

borowe, to redeem, Dance 358;—to sell on credit? Libel 393, 427, (*see* note 388).

borowis, boroughs, towns, FaPrin. D 117.

borwid, borwith, borrowed, borrows, MaReg. 369.

boryall, Boreal, northern, Garl. 261.

bost, outcry, Libel 173*.

bot, bot if, *see* but; —only, Hardyng 69, 103.

bothes, both, FaPrin. B 128.

bottyne, booty, (Fr. *butin*), Orl. xix:9.

botum, a bottom or clew of thread, Garl. 783.

botyth, booteth, avails, Cavend. 1265.

bounsis, bounces or bounds, Garl. 1281.

bountee, *see* Bycorne 88*, Dance 197, FaPrin. A 333.

bourde, to jest, Ecl. 43; —a jest, Ecl. prol. 99.

bourder, a jester, Ecl. 665.

bowes, boughs, Nevill 428.

bowgy, bulgy, Roundel 3.

bown, ready, "bound", Libel 195.

bowns, bang! Garl. 618.

boy, *s.* menial, Ecl. 355.*

Boys, Boethius, FaPrin. H 3, 6, etc., Garl. 309.

boysters, boisterous, Garl. 20.

boystously, boisterously, Thebes 30.

boyueer, boveer, rustic churl, Churl 266, 355.

Braban, Brabant, Libel 492, 498, 508, 528.

bracers, Garl. 189*.

brake, a snare, Cavend. 1220*;—was disturbed, Nevill 213.

brall, to brawl, wrangle, Ecl. 401, 907, Garl. 770.

Brasile, *written by error for* brotil, brittle, Libel 558*.

at a brayde, instantly, Nevill 70.

brayed, Hawes 4364*.

brede, breadth, Garl. 1503.

bremis, bream, (a kind of fish), Garl. 655.

brend, fiery? Walton A 307*.

brenne, etc., to burn, Walton A 210, 235, B 27, D 17, Mass 110, Hawes 121, 233, 671, Nevill dial. 28.

brent, burnt, Dial. 499, Churl 178, Hardyng 27, Libel 171, Garl. 1293.

brest, the breast, Dance 260.

breteyne, Britain, FaPrin. A 377.

brettaygne, Britain, Epithal. 53.

breuiacion, shortening, Hawes 682.

breuiate, *v.* and *a.*, abbreviate, Hawes 686, Ecl. 788, 1071, 1102.

brevely, briefly, Churl 20, Garl. 1070, etc.

bribour, a rascal, robber, FàPrin. G 308, 319.

bride, briddes, etc., bird, etc., Churl 39, 72, etc.

bridle lead, Epithal. 88*; *see* Cavend. 1174, 1348*, MaReg. 78*.

Brigges, Bruges, Libel 432.

Bristowe, Bristol, Ecl. 317.

briton, Britain, Burgh 46, Garl. 405.

broche of Thebes, FaPrin. A 322-3*.

brodered, embroidered, Ship 550.

broisid, bruised, Garl. 619.

broisours,? bruisers, ruffians, Garl. 667.

broke, Thebes 96*.

broken, *see* Garl. 785*.

Broken backed lines, *see* p. 21, p. 84-5.

bronte, brunt, FaPrin. G 119.

brotilnesse, brittleness, fragility, FaPrin. D 24.

Browne, William, his MSS, pp. 58-59.

Brutes, of Brut, Epithal. 56*, FaPrin. E 68, *see* Garl. 405.

Brutus, Walton C 22*.

Brutus Cassius, FaPrin. E 63*, Cavend. 1130; *see* Walton B 22.

brutyd, bruited, renowned, Garl. 155, 405.

brydilless, without bridle, MaReg. 78*.

brynnynge, burning, Ship 8462.

buckishe, lascivious, Ecl. 724.

bull, (*see* bole), Morley 4.

bullyons, metal knobs as ornaments, Garl. 1143.

burbly, Churl 55*.

Burboyne, Bourbon, Hardyng 86*.

Burdeus, Bordeaux, Ecl. 315.

burgeis, burgess, Dance 297, Garl. 514.

burne, burnt, Garl. 41.

burris, raised rings, Garl. 787.

business, effort, Hawes 1337.

busy, *error for* base, Hawes 331.

but, FaPrin. A 114, *read* bit, i.e., biddeth.

but, but if, unless, Walton A 177, 192, C 24, D 57, MaReg. 57, 127, 129, Dial. 637, 810, Churl 133, Dance 399, FaPrin. A 326, Orl. xxii:5, Hardyng 19, 60, 96, Libel 100, 107, 254, 547, Ship 96, Garl. 119, 146, 439, 769, 1111.

but though, unless, Orl. xvi:27.

buttunis, buttons, knots, Garl. 787.

buxom, obedient, Dial. 687; *see* Roundel 2.

by, according to, Libel 521; —about, Hawes 126; —be, Libel 532.

by and by, in sequence, Dance 542, FaPrin. A 137, Shirley II:6, Ecl. 1135, Garl. 323, Morley 209*.—immediately, Cavend. 1245.

by caws, because, Lickp. 123, Garl. 60.

by cock, parde, Lickp. 93.

Bycorne, *see* Bycorne and Chichevache, p.113.

byde, to await, Garl. 98.

bydynge, existence, dwelling-place, Ship 7016.

bye, to buy, Lickp. 53, 69, 75, 79, 103, Libel 65, 397, 445, 508, Nevill dial. 39, 49, Ecl. 173, 223.

byfil, befell, Thebes 70.

bygonde, beyond (the sea), Dial. 566.

byll, piece of writing, Reproof 32, Garl. 1421. *see* bille.

byholde, to behold, Walton B 139.

byknowen, recognized, Walton E 77.

byleuyd, believed, Reproof 61.

beneþen, beneath, Walton A 329, 336; *see* Lickp. 119.

byrnston, brimstone, Garl. 625.

byse, dull blue, Garl. 1136, Cavend. 106.

byseeke, to beseech, MaReg. 411. *See* beseeke.

byseye, (*see* beseene), MaReg. 142.

bysynes, business, matter, Dance 303.

bytwix, bytwyne, between, Walton A 151, 230, Epithal. 196, Libel 192.

bywette, bewet, Walton A 388.

by yonde, beyond, Garl. 488.

caas, cas, case, FaPrin. E 46, G 102, etc.

caball, horse, Ecl. 128.

cace, case, matter, Hawes 119.

cacheth, chaseth? FaPrin. K 31*.

cadence, FaPrin. K 4*.

Cadmus, Ecl. 879.

Caesar, Julius, Epithal. 149, FaPrin. A 365, C 15, Ecl. 1084, 1087 ff., Cavend. 1126-32, Cavend. epit. 5, 31, Morley 141 ff.; his tragedy, pp. 176 ff.

caduke, transitory, Ecl. 786.

calcydony, chalcedony, Garl. 587.

calcys, Prohib. 19*.

caldy, Chaldaean, Garl. 585.

Calise, Calais, Pallad. 44.

Calliope, Walton A 58*, Epithal. 181, FaPrin. A 457, D 9, Cavend. 65*, 67, Garl. 1121.

Calpe, Ship 6972*.

camamel, camomile, Garl. 962.

camous, Ecl. 688*.

can, knows, knows how, Dial. 565, Dance 218, 571, Mass 21, Ship 212; —accomplishes, Ecl. 883; —*written for* gan, did, FaPrin. A 46.

Canace, her letter to Macaire, FaPrin. B; —a mountain, Burgh 45*.

canvas, Libel 153.

Canywike, the name of a London street, Lickp. 82*.

Capell, Ecl. 441*.

cappadoce, Cappadocia, Ship 6972.

captacions, ornaments, pleasing artifices, Garl. 799.

carders, card players, Garl. 602.

carectis, characters, letters, Garl. 585.

carfull, full of care, Orl. xiii:13; —woeful, Garl. 1228; *see* carfull.

cariage, transportation, Walton E 125.

carl, rustic churl, Churl 278, Ship 8437, etc.

Caron, Charon, Garl. 1304.

carpe, to talk, Churl 278, 337, Ecl. 266, 344, Ecl. prol. 7.

Carpenter, Hoccleve to, p. 67.

carres, *see* carrys.

carrikes, large ships, Libel 324.

carrys, land routes, Libel 517, 549.

Cartage, Carthage, Mass 183.

cassander, Garl. 1008*.

cast, cast him, etc., to intend, Churl 33, 80, 174, 363, Bycorne 44, FaPrin. A 100, G 312, Orl. xvi:17, Hardyng 75, Libel 29; —to consider, Nevill 156, 224.

castell, Castile, Libel 55.

castinge, Garl. 786*.

casuelte, chance, Garl. 1373.

catch, caught, FaPrin. G 22*, 165, Cavend. 211.

Cathalons, Catalans, Libel 505.

Catoun, Cato, Walton C 23, FaPrin. C 24, G 269, Ecl. 1091, Garl. 123, Cavend. epit. 23.

causa, cause, because, LettGlouc. 6, FaPrin. G 125, Nevill dial. 40.

for causa, because, Walton A 139.

Caxton, pp. 14, 35, 96; see Thebes 55-6

cayles, ninepins, Nevill dial. 47*.

caytiff, captive, Orl. xiii:6; —see Ship 464.

ceesse, to cease, Epithal. 44

cely, (silly), "poor", Churl 83, Bycorne 124, Orl. xv:6.

celydony, Prohib. 59*.

cent, scent, Hawes 342.

cercle, circle, Walton E 143; —a nautical instrument, Ship 6983.

ceriousli, serially, FaPrin. A 135. See notes Shirley I:26, Morley 209.

Cerberus, Ecl. 873.

certys, certainly, Mass 96, etc.

cessen, to cease, Mass 82; —to cause to cease, Walton A 196, B 6. See sese.

Cesyll, Sicily, Ship 6968.

chaffare, merchandise, bargain, Libel 65, 441, 526, etc.

chaier, see chare.

chance, lot, Dance 53, FaPrin. E 82, Hawes 19*.

chapytles, chapters, Shirley II:7.

charbonclis, carbuncles, Horns 10*, Garl. 1144.

chare, chaier, chayre, chariot, FaPrin. E 75, Burgh 51, Orl. xix:2, Morley 20, 48. But see chayre.

charet, carriage, Ecl. 199.

charge, responsibility, Dance 206, 272, Ship 6950, 8442, Ecl. 188, 190, 194, 359, 385, Cavend. 97; —load, Ship 56, 6933; —expense, Garl. 570.

charge, to make responsible, Dance 270; —to consider, Epithal. 30*; —to load, Libel 240.

charged, loaded, Libel 72, 262, 494, Ship 512; —laid in rest, Hawes 4313.

chartereux, a monk of the Charterhouse, Dance 347.

chat, talk, Ship 13852, Ecl. 473.

Chaucer, see Gen. Introd. 5, 11-12, 14, 18, 19, 21, 24, 26, 29, 31, 32. See Walton introd., Hoccleve introd., Lydgate introd., Churl introd., Bycorne introd., Thebes introd., FaPrin. introd., —See Hoccleve's stanzas to him, p. 74; portrait, see note on Praise of Chaucer 4995; see FaPrin. A 246, ibid. 275* ff. for list of his works; see introd. to FaPrin. B and H, see K 19-21, 34-41; see Shirley I:29-34; see Reproof 19; see Hawes 1263 ff. and note on 1261; see Garl. 388, 414-427, 1079. See under Griselda, Troilus, Wife of Bath.

chaumpartye, Bycorne 41*.

chaunge, read chaunce, i.e., cast of dice, lot, Dance 275.

chayre, seat, Ship 8461, Garl. 753, Cavend. 1240; —car, Morley 33, 44, 48.

chebri place, Burgh 43*.

to say checkmate, to call a halt, defeat, Dance 459*, FaPrin. A 182, D 52*, Cavend. 161, 1237, 1267.

cheertee, Roundel 2*.

chemeras, chimeras, Garl. 1296.

chepe, a bargain, Lickp. 84; —a London street, Cheapside, Lickp. 72.

chere, countenance, bearing, Walton A 347, 387, E 65, Churl 79, 296, Bycorne 94, Dance 90, 121, 372, 391, 621, Thebes 175, FaPrin. B 137, D 45, G 81, 197*, 200, Burgh 49, Pallad. A 4, Mass 84, Hawes 107, Ship 13816, Ecl. 893, Garl. 691, 1430.

chere, entertainment, Hawes 442, 4374, ?4449, Garl. 398, Cavend. 1379.

cherice, to cherish, MaReg. 282.

chese, to choose, Walton A 135, Churl 143, Thebes 133, Reproof 35, Libel 17.

chesyng, choosing, Orl. xvii:15.

chevesaunce, bargain, goods, Dance 404, Libel 267, 424.

Chichevache, see pp. 113 ff.

as in chief, especially, Libel 98. See •MaReg. 50*.

Chimer, Chimera, Ecl. 880.

chippe, ship, Dance 264.

Chirborwe, Chirburgh, Cherbourg, Dial. 567, 611.

chorle, churl, Churl passim, Hawes 1298, Ship 111, 8497.

chose, chosen, FaPrin. A 408, G 75, 132, Mass 150.

chyldre, children, Mass 150.

chynchy, stingy, MaReg. 136. See introd. to Bycorne and Chichevache.

chyne, FaPrin. C 76*.

Cicero, see Tullius. See Cavend. epit. 9.

ciex, Ceyx, FaPrin. A 304*.

Cintheus, Apollo, Garl. 681*.

Circes, Circe, FaPrin. C 92.

circumstance, detail, Cavend. 1425.

Cirenes, see Sirens.

Citero, Citheron, Burgh 7*.

Citharon, FaPrin. K 51*.

cithe, read tilthe, FaPrin. G 221*.

Cithera, Venus, FaPrin. D 13.

citheryn, a. citron, Churl 235.

clappid, etc., to prate, MaReg. 394, Bycorne 32.

clarified, made famous, Hawes 1105.

clarry, wine mixed with honey, Walton B 8.

claryonar, trumpeter, Garl. 233.

clatter, to chatter, Hawes 742. See Garl. 241, 1173.

Cleopatras, FaPrin. G 287*. See Morley 142.

clepen, clepid, clept, to call by name, to cry out, Walton A 168, 278, MaReg. 225, Dance 489, Burgh 50, Shirley 1: 60, 66, Orl. xviii:7, Libel 62.

for clere, for clearness, Walton A 307. Or for-clere, very clear?

clere story, Garl. 479*.
clergi, clergye, learning, Walton E 32, FaPrin.
G 133*, 150, Pallad. 97, Ecl. 662; —the clergy,
Ship 572.
Clio, Walton A 58*, Epithal. 181, FaPrin. D 10,
Ecl. prol. 117.
clipsen, to eclipse, Dance 13.
cloke, veil of allegorical language, Nevill envoy
14. See Churl 29*.
cloked, hid, veiled, Hawes 1297*, Garl. 1173.
See Churl 29*, FaPrin. G 46*.
cloos, stronghold, territory? Dial. 576.
Clotho, etc., Cavend. 1259 ff.
clowdes, the heavens, Hawes 68.
clowdy, veiled, Hawes 34, 664. See cloked.
clypsyd, eclipsed, Epithal. 29.
coast, part of the world, Hawes 4412, Ecl. 320.
See coost.
cochitos, Cocytus, the river or pit of hell, Garl.
1302.
cockatryce, Ripley 167*.
Cobham, Eleanor, duchess of Gloucester, see
pp. 143, 145.
Codrus, a speaker in Barclay's Eclogue iv.
cokers, leggings, Ecl. 211.
colage, collage, a college, an assembly, Hardyng 126, Garl. 403, 417.
cole, coolness, Ship 57.
colers, collars, Ship 512.
colle, coal, Prohib. 27.
collis passioun, Thebes 114, i.e., colica pas-
sio, the pain of colic.
colour, a pretext, Libel 166, 383, Cavend. 1322;
—color, FaPrin. G 33-35*; —a fable, Hawes
740, 1297, see dedic. 41-2; —rhetorical ornament, Walton A 154, FaPrin. A 27, 278, 452,
G 46*, K 4, Reproof 31, Hawes dedic. 25, 42,
Cavend. 61*, 232*.
colour, v. to disguise, Cavend. 1320, 1322.
colour, the symbolism of, Epithal. 107-110, Ecl.
prol. 107 ff.
coloured, given a false appearance, Libel 387.
Coluccio Salutati, see p. 91; see note FaPrin.
E 63.
colyaunder, coriander, Garl. 1006; see Thebes
118.
com, can, Orl. xi:5*.
comberaunce, encumbrance, difficulty, Prohib. 69.
combreworldes, cumberers of earth, nuisances,
MaReg. 225.
comicar, writer of comedies, Garl. 353.
comen, common, Hawes 196.
commen, common, Ripley 65, Hawes 185.
commens, the common people, Hawes 182.
com(m)on, to talk, discuss, Libel 181, Ship
181*, Ecl. 472, 741, 743.
commynalte, the communalty, Walton A 80.
comons, the common people, FaPrin. H 14, 23,
Libel 123, 523.
comontye, the common people, FaPrin.
A 207, Ship 234, 459.
compace, to enclose, Ecl. 168.
Compaigne, Campania, FaPrin. G 294.

companable, compenable, in company, Nevil[1]
11; —social, Ecl. 1011.
Comparative, double, Walton B 28, Hawes 144,
Cavend. 1184.
compassid, included, considered, Garl. 13.
compendyous, etc., brief, briefly, FaPrin.
A 90, G 4, H 22, Shirley II:5, Nevill 876.
competente, sufficient, Garl. 1060.
complacience, luxury, Libel 337.
compline, the last prayer-service of the day,
after sunset, Churl 67.
compownen, to reconcile, Walton E 42.
comprehended, Epithal. 83*. See Walton
E 44.
comprise, etc., to compose, describe, Pallad.
40, 41, Hawes 1292, Garl. 80; —to include,
Ship 6944, Garl. 905.
compyle, to collect, write, Hardyng 54, etc.
comune, common, Walton A 314, Shirley I:18.
comyn, cummin, Thebes 118.
comynly, in common, Walton D 20.
concedo, see Ship 216*.
conceit, opinion, thought, MaReg. 381, Dial.
591, 601, 658, Hawes 206, Ship 167, Garl. 16;
—device, plan, Garl. 798.
concend, Ecl. 596*.
conclusions, riddles, experiments, Dance 518.
condescend, to agree, consent, Dance 537,
LettGlouc. 2, Hawes 280, 4448, Nevill dial.
12?, Garl. 232, 1110.
condicioun, nature, disposition, Walton A 359,
Garl. 609? or "classes of society"?.
conductis, conduits, FaPrin. D 9.
conduyt, conduct, Nevill 206.
confect, made up, Pallad. 69.
confecture, compound, Garl. 110.
confedred, confederate, Hardyng 9.
confortatyff, remedy, LettGlouc. 11.
conforth, comfort, Orl. vi:6.
confrary, brotherhood, Mass 147.
congruence, fitness, Garl. 52.
coniecte, to guess, Garl. 729.
connyng, ability, art, Reproof 15, 27, Garl.
1208, Cavend. 108; —knowledge, Ship 175,
Ecl. prol. 59, Garl. 140, 198, 850; —a. wise,
Cavend. 53. See cunnyng.
consayue, to think, FaPrin. A 449, Hardyng
102.
consel, s. counsel, Pallad. 66.
consentant, in agreement, Walton A 131.
conseyt, opinion, Walton E 44, FaPrin. C 125,
Reproof 63. See conceit.
consistorye, place of assembly, assembly, Fa-
Prin. E 50, G 278.
consonant, harmonious, Ecl. 286.
consuetude, custom, Mass 154.
consuleere, consular, consul, FaPrin. G 75.
contagious, injurious, Ecl. 556.
contekk, contest, debate, Epithal. 20.
content, fulfilled, paid up, Libel 418, 441.
contesse, countess, Shirley II:52.
continuaunce, countenance, FaPrin. G 196.
contraire, contrary, FaPrin. C 52, etc.
contrarie, to oppose, Dance 156, 502.

contune, to continue, Churl 290, Thebes 140, FaPrin. A 62, 389*, Mass 13.

conuersation, mode of life, life, Dance 533, Hawes 1287.

conuysance, cognizance, Pallad. 55.

convenable, suitable, Churl 262, Garl. 706. *See* **couenable.**

convenience, fitness, Horns 60*, Nevill envoy 15.

convenient, suitable, Dial. 590*, Churl 16, Hawes 689, Cavend. 17.

conveyance, Garl. 1172, 1211*; –style, Ecl. 264.

conveyed, brought thither? Nevill 198.

coole, cowl, Ecl. prol. 112.

cooper, copper, Cavend. 226; *see* note on 225, and *see* Hawes 293*.

coost, coste, place, country, Walton A 179. *See* **coast, costis.—euery coost,** on every hand, Dance 158.

cope, Ecl. 447*, 1141*.

copen, to buy, Lickp. 53.

Copland, Robert. *See under* Nevill, p. 287.

copper, *see* **cooper.**

copyntanke, Ship 559*.

corage, spirit, temper, strength, Walton A 310*, Churl 45, 64, 82, Dance 436, LettGlouc. 54, FaPrin. A 395, B 70, D 68, G 16, 52, Reproof 38, Mass 103, 151, Nevill 13, etc., Ecl. 969, Garl. 66, 844, 1275, Cavend. 204, 1143, epit. 6. *See* **courage.**

coral, Hawes 4224*.

corde, to accord, Garl. 88.

cordeler, a Cordelier, a Franciscan friar of the strict rule, girt with the knotted cord, Dance 561*.

cordewayn, Spanish goat-leather from Cordova, Libel 133. *See* Sir Thopas 21.

coriandre, Thebes 118; *see* Garl. 1006.

corious, elaborate, Dance 672, FaPrin. C 30, Garl. 652. *See* **curious.**

Cornix, Ecl. 195*, 798, 1136.

corosyves, acids, Prohib. 8, 49.

correcte? Libel 353*.

Correct, request to, Churl 385, Dance 660, FaPrin. K 11, Shirley II:71*, Cavend. 52*.

Corson, Ecl. 859*.

Cosmus, Cosmo de' Medici, Ecl. 441*.

cosse, a kiss, Orl. xx:1.

Costantin, the Cotentin, Dial. 576*.

costious, costly, Garl. 570.

costis, places, FaPrin. F 13. *See* **coost.**

cote, coot, (a waterfowl), Garl. 1346; –a coat, Ship 468.

coth, disease, pestilence? Shirley II:12*.

cotidian, daily, daily fever, MaReg. 25, LettGlouc. 28*.

cotis, cotes, cottages, Ship 8457.

Cotteswold, Cotswold, the sheep-raising district of England, Libel 392.

couched, packed in layers, Ecl. 393; –to lay, Cavend. 227.

couenable, couenabill, fitting, Dial. 635, Garl. 805. *See* **convenable.**

could no skyle, possessed no knowledge, Lickp. 77.

coule, cowl, Shirley II:42.

coulpable, culpable, Reproof 55. *See* **coupable.**

coundight, conduit, Garl. 652.

counten, to make up account, Dance 160,542.

countirpeys, balance, counterpoise, LettGlouc. 26, FaPrin. E 79, Reproof 18.

countertails, counterstrokes, Libel 383*.

countertayle, Bycorne 31*.

countervayle, opposed weight, Churl 315.

counterwayng, balancing, Garl. 414; *see* 179.

counterweiynge, comparable, Garl. 831.

counteryng, singing an accompaniment to the melody or plain song, Garl. 699.

coupable, culpable, Dial. 688, FaPrin. G 319.

Cour Amoureuse, *see* p. 199 here.

courage, Hawes 266, 4335, Nevill 118. *See* **corage.**

cours, coarse, Ship 564.

coursidhede, cursedness, Walton E 87.

Court of Sapience, *see* Hawes 1301. Extracts from the poem, pp. 258 ff. here.

couthe, kouth, could, Walton A 248, 303, 330, B 2, 6, 9, ?Horns 32*. Reproof 12.

couthe, known, FaPrin. G 204.

covert, couerte, covered, Orl. xx:12;—of hidden meaning, Hawes dedic. 42, Hawes 1389. *See* Churl 29*.

crafty, expert, Hawes dedic. 25, Ship 7008; — elaborate, Hawes 405, Ship 13683. *See* Ecl. 346, etc.

crakars, braggarts, Ship 37.

crase, to break, Garl. 1187.

Crassus, Nevill 834.

crease, to increase, Cavend. 94.

creauncer, tutor, Garl. 1199.

credence, credit, dignity, Hardyng 87*.

Cresseid, Cressida, Orl. xvi:10, Hawes 1276, Garl. 855.

creste cloth, a linen fabric, Libel 153.

Creusa, Morley 165.

cristente, Christendom, Libel 149.

croft, a small field, Orl. xix:10.

crokfere, Prohib. 37*.

crokyd, bent, FaPrin. D 65, Ship 113.

cronell, coronal, Garl. 288.

crowne, a tonsure, Ship 574.

crudd, curds, Churl 124, Ecl. 423.

cruddy, Hawes 62*.

cunnyng, knowledge, FaPrin. A 432, Hawes 449, 717, 730, 746, 748, 1100, 1332, 1343, Ship 179, Ecl. 29, 275, 297, 334, etc.

Cupide, Cupid, Dance 445, FaPrin. B 102, C 89, Nevill 11, 15, 21, 32, 39, 871, Garl. 291, Cavend. 1330;—martyrs of, Mass 191*.

cure, care, attention, pains, MaReg. 261, 309, Churl 124, 327, Dance 205, FaPrin. G 251, Pallad. 40, 122, Libel 351*, Hawes 117*, 160, 434, Ship 6950, 6991, Ecl. 162, Garl. 912.

curiositee, rhetorical ornamentation, Ecl. prol. 106.

curious, intricate, elaborate, Walton A 11, Ship 246, Ecl. 449, 825. *See* Morley 24.

currishenes, dishonorable act, Orl. xx:10.

curteys, courteous.

custom, trade? LettGlouc. 23.

custoumable, accustomed, Mass 153.
custumed, habitual, Bedford 8.
cybacyon, Ripley 196*.
Cypyoun, Scipio, Epithal. 154.
cyrcunspeccyon, circumspection, Nevill 26.
cyrcumstaunce, detail?, effort?, Nevill dial. 3. *See* NED meanings 6 and 7.
Cyrus, Ecl. 1111.
cytezyns, citizens, Ship 111, 8470.
Cytheron, Mass 5*.

.d., pence, Libel 409, 412, 413.
dagardye, Libel 353*.
daggid, slashed, cut in long points, Garl. 624.
daliaunce, intercourse, talk, Walton A 361, Dial. 706, Dance 189, Cavend. 1388.
dame, i.e., dan, dominus, as a title, Shirley II:39, 47; also **Dane.**
Dante in English, *see* note on FaPrin. A 303.
Dante as known to Lydgate, p. 93 here.
Danys, the Danes, FaPrin. K 47.
Daphnes, Daphne, Garl. 290, 297.
Dares frigius, Dares the Phrygian, FaPrin. K 17*.
daring doo, Epithal. 129*.
dasid, etc., to daze, Garl. 635, 728, 1356.
dasild, dazzled, Garl. 1356.
dastarddis, dullards, sots, Garl. 190.
daswed, dazed, Bedford 9.
daunce, dance, Dance 24*, Orl. xi:9, Hawes 1259, Cavend. 241, Morley 53, 195.
daunger, danger, FaPrin. F 17, ?G 161, Libel 23;—tyranny, MaReg. 126*, Dance 455, FaPrin. A 63, Mass 86, Orl. v:4, xx:6, 9, Ecl. 1125;—bond to another's power, Walton E 11, Churl 85, 114;—**daungerous,** Dial. 745.
dawe, to be day, Thebes 129.
dawbe, to mend, Ecl. 170.
dawcokkis, male jackdaws, i.e., simpletons, Garl. 612.
day, to die, Orl. xviii:23.
dayneth, disdains, Ecl. 375.
dayse, days, Reproof 19.
De bien en mieulx, FaPrin. A 20*.
in deade, indeed, Cavend. 174.
deadly, profound, Hawes 92; —like death, Cavend. 84, 1257; —ominous, Cavend. 1225, 1229.
Dean of Powles, Ecl. 451*.
Death. *See* Dance Macabre, Orl. xv*, Ecl. 983*.
debarrid, stopped, Garl. 143.
debated, abated, Ecl. 979.
debily, Prohib. 25*.
debonayr, gracious, Ripley 6.
decertys, deserts, deservings, Mass 96.
decked, covered, Ecl. 6.
decke slut, Ship 558*.
declinall, declinable, Hawes 533.
declination, downward course, Hawes 1404.
declyne, to evade, FaPrin. G 115; —to incline, show favor, FaPrin. C 27.
dede, did, Walton A 56, Thebes 58, FaPrin. A 1, 49, 209, 249, 273, 275, etc., Lickp. 124.
dedis, deeds, Dial. 820*.

deel, part, MaReg. 153, Epithal. 105; *see* **dele.**
deemyng, judging, FaPrin. C 26.
deen, to dye, Walton B 9.
defye, to digest, Bycorne 42.
degest, to get over the effects of, Cavend. 1243, (NED first case 1576); —ponder, Cavend. 1427.
degree, place, position, rank, Walton A 293, E 157, MaReg. 317, Dance 101, 491, FaPrin. A 67, 361, Mass 28, Libel 88, Ship 474, 570, 8519, Ecl. prol. 130, Ecl. 846, 861, Garl. 803, 1082;—way, manner, Hawes 110.—**in degree,** in supremacy, Ecl. 634, 996; *see* 602.
deide, died, FaPrin. C 70.
deiect, to sink, Ecl. 549.
deied, etc., died, etc., FaPrin. F 21, Orl. xvii:25.
dekayed, etc., to bring low, Ship 470, 572, Cavend. 1157*.
delate, to spread afar, publish, Ecl. 645.
delavee, Roundel 2*.
dele, part, bit, Walton A 158, E 147, Dance 294, 408, Libel 101, 207, Cavend. 1135. *See* **dell.**
delice, *s.* delight, Walton A 109.
delicious, sensual, Ship 126*. *See* Cavend. 43.
dell, vale, Walton E 70;—part, Walton D 12, Hawes 328. *See* **dele, deel.**
demayn, domain, power, Cavend. 1344.
demene, to manage, Orl. ix:3, Hawes 4363.
demenaunce, demenynge, behavior, FaPrin. G 194, Garl. 996, 1152.
demerites, Ship 51.
Demophon, Morley 199.
dempte, deemed, FaPrin. G 27.
denay, to deny, Cavend. 146, Morley 90.
Denyse, Dionysius, Morley 161*.
depaint, adorned, depicted, FaPrin. B 106, Hawes 9, 459, 755. *See* **dopeynt.**
depart, to part with, Ecl. 14, 818; —to divide, separate, MaReg. 133, Dance 483.
depayseth, deprives of value, Walton C 17.
depraue, to speak ill of, stain, MaReg. 171, FaPrin. A 447, Garl. 1240, Cavend. 1149.
depured, purified, clear, Hawes 6*, 332, 347, 1108, 1264, 4220, etc.
derayne, derrain, to decide, offer for decision, Bycorne 6, Garl. 1514. (Late Latin *derationare.*
dere, to injure, Dial. 711.
derified, derived, Hawes 1107.
Description by order, *see* Roundel 3*, Shirley I:26.
descryve, to express, Epithal. 116.
desere, to desire, Orl. xiv:12. *See* **desier.**
desese, discomfort, FaPrin. G 247.
desier, desire, Cavend. 102, 105.
desteyned, besmirched, MaReg. 340. *See* Libel 47.
determine, to fix, assert, FaPrin. B 6, G 152.
dette, dettour, debt, etc., Walton E 11, Dance 159, Shirley II:66.
deu, due, FaPrin. G 153, Garl. 423. **A deu,** Adieu, *see* Dial. 504; *see* note Dance 64.
deueere, devoir, duty, FaPrin. F 5.

deuelway, Thebes 162*, Garl. 629.

deuise, describe, Churl 334, Dance 340, 483, etc., Ship 598;—arrange, Libel 215, ?Garl. 1387;—manage, Mass 26;—s. device, fancy, Dance, 220, 436, 483, Garl. 442*, 1459;—fashion, Cavend. 248.

deuised, given, Dance 179.

deuoyed, deprived, Nevill 37*.

deviant, one who turns aside, Ripley 6*.

Devices, see Mottoes. For Shirley's device see pp. 192-3 here.

dewren, etc., to endure, Orl. xii:33, xiii:11.

dewte, duty, Orl. xvii:19, Garl. 212.

deye, to die, FaPrin. B 26, 33, 84, 128, Orl. vi:8, xxi:14.

deynous, disdainful, proud, Dance 299, 364.

deynte, dignity, value, FaPrin. A 359.

Diana, FaPrin. C 87, Garl. 303.

diascorides, Garl. 1392*.

dictes, FaPrin. G 225.　See dite.

dide, died, Dial. 751.

Dido, Orl. xvi:10.　See Dydo.

diffautis, wrongdoings, FaPrin. B 122, G 160, 287.

diffied, disintegrated, FaPrin. G 329.

diffieng, defying, refusing, FaPrin. C 60.

diffuse, difficult, obscure, Ecl. prol. 71, Garl. 111, 338.

dight, set to, prepare, Walton D 71, Lickp. 124.

digne, worthy, FaPrin. F 26, G 131.

digression, decadence of moral quality, Hawes 145. For the rhetorical "digressio" see Gen. Introd. p. 25.

dilacioun, delay, Dance 314.

Diodorus Siculus, see notes Ship 162, Garl. 1463.

Dirige, dirge, Ship 13878*.

dirke, dark, Mass 128.

dirkid, darkened, FaPrin. D 21, 57.

discharge, to unload, Libel 70, 240, 491, Ship 6934, Garl. 720;—to unburden, Cavend. 153; —to excuse, Garl. 1326; to make void, FaPrin. B 40.—s. vindication, Garl. 213, 1124.

discommend, to dispraise, Garl. 1236.

discrive, to describe, Walton A 303, Dance 294.

discure, to discover, FaPrin. G 90, 100, Garl. 725.　See note Dance 311.

discusse, dyscus, to decide, determine, allot, Nevill 24, 873, Ship 6993, Garl. 865.

disese, discomfort, evil case, Walton A 255, 352, MaReg. 414, Hawes 4285, 4399.　See desese.

disespeirid, in despair, FaPrin. D 47.

disgysyd, decked, adorned, Garl. 38.

dishonest, wretched, shameful, Ecl. 1097.

disioynt, ill-wrought, Pallad. 18;—s. evil case, misery, Mass 75.

disnull, v. destroy, Hawes 720.

dispence, excuse myself, Pallad. D 4.

dispense, s. expense, Horns 55.

disporte, to give pleasure, Dance 324; — s. pleasure, Pallad. 35.

dissert, desert, worth, MaReg. 272.

disseruid, deserved, FaPrin. G 304.

disseuere, to depart, pass away, Dance 310.

disteyn, to stain, Libel 47.　See desteyn.

distincyon, a division of a composition, Garl. 1434.

distresse, trouble, pains, Shirley I:95.

distryed, destroyed, Walton A 255.

dite, dyte, ditijs, etc., "dicta", literary compositions, FaPrin. A 256*, 352, 456, G 55*, K 16, Nevill dial. 18, Garl. 360*, Cavend. 66, 67.

ditie, ditte, ditty, Ecl. 48, 351, etc.

diynge, dying, Dance 248.

do, s. doe, Garl. 1352.

do, dede, doon, etc., 1) causative, as in Chaucer; see e.g., Dance 339, Shirley I:17. 2) auxiliary; see e.g., Walton A 225, Thebes 58*, Dance 136*, FaPrin. A 303, G 136, etc. 3) independent verb; see e.g., Walton A 56, Dial. 613*, FaPrin. K 37, 41.

do forth, Dial. 524, Pallad. A 6*.

do it upon you, Libel 258*.

do on, put on, don, Ship 558.

document, Hawes 292*.

doke, duck, Churl 360.

dolven, dug, buried, Dance 558, Shirley I:22.

dom, dumb, Ecl. 489.　See dum.

domas, damask, Ship 173.

dome, doomys, etc., doom, judgment, FaPrin. E 25, F 7, Garl. 1470, Cavend. 155.

domefying, Dance 292*, FaPrin. A 299*.

dominacion, domain? Hawes 416.

dompe, to be downcast, Cavend. 241.　See dumpe.　NED 1530 first.—s. a depressed or musing state, Cavend. 1223.

domyne, to have power, Hawes 229.

dongel, dunghill, Churl 360.

donne, dun, FaPrin. K 31, Hawes 299.

dool, dolor, FaPrin. B 67, Mass 120, 130.

doomys, see dome.

dopeynt, Thebes 16.　See depaint.

dorste, dared, Walton D 15, etc.

dotrellis, Garl. 635*.

Double Compar. and Superl., Walton B 28*, FaPrin. C 19, 50, Ecl. 867, Cavend. 1184.

doublenes, Hawes 436, 1277, Garl. 1175.

doubletys, imitations, Horns 13*.

doubt, doubtaunce, dread, Hawes dedic. 45, Hawes 5, 103, Ecl. 169.

doubty, dreadful, Hawes 359.

dought, fear, Cavend. 212.

doughtyd, feared, Cavend. 147, 212, 1167.

doutfull, uncertain, Walton A 313.

drad, dreaded, Dance 491.

draff, s. refuse, Churl 256, 258.

dragge, drug, LettGlouc. 12*, 55.

drames, ?drama-writers, Ecl. 689*.

drape, etc., to weave into cloth, Libel 102, etc.

draughtes, attempts, works, Hawes 1312, 1351.

drauh, draw, FaPrin. C 64.

draw, to tend, approach, Churl 260, Thebes 170, FaPrin. H 1, Lickp. 73;—to amount, Libel 543.

drawe along, to protract, draw out, Walton A 288, C 33, Churl 74.

drede me, have fear, Dance 98.

dreepyng, drooping, FaPrin. C 88.

drempt, dreamed, FaPrin. E 96.

Dress, extravagance in, *see* pp. 110-11.

dresse (one's self), to prepare, set about, undertake, direct, Walton D 26, Dance 300, 611, 626, FaPrin. A 449, D 72, E 25, G 3, 51, 65, Orl. xix:14, 27, xx:11, Libel 547, Ship 6953, Garl. 122, 1312.

dreye, dry, Thebes 164.

dribbis, to dribble, slaver, Garl. 635.

drone, lower tube of a bagpipe, Ecl. 27.

dropsy, *see* Ecl. 895*.

drouh, drew, i.e., translated, FaPrin. K 28.

drouh him to, adhered to, FaPrin. G 269.

dud, did, Churl 63.

dulce, sweet, Cavend. 118.

dum, dumb, Garl. 82. *See* **dom**.

dumpe, fit of abstraction or depression, Garl. 15, 728. *See* **dompe**.

dure, door, Garl. 1402; —*v.* to endure, Mass 12, Libel 343, Hawes 4343.

durre, door, Garl. 1073.

duskyth, *v.* dims, Cavend. 223.

dy, die, Orl. xiii:22.

dya, *s.* LettGlouc. 12*.

dyane, the moon, Diana, Hawes 1404, 4218. *See* Garl. 303.

dyapenthe, Hawes 1414*.

Dydo, Dido, Epithal. 73, Mass 182. *See* **Dido**.

dyetesseron, diatessaron, Hawes 1414*.

dyffautes, faults, defects, FaPrin. B 122.

dygne, worthy, Mass 164.

dyleccyon, delight, Nevill dial. 25.

dymeynet, demeaned, Orl. viii:2.

Dymostenes, Demosthenes, Garl. 130, 152, 155, 167.

dyne, to die, Libel 522.

dynne, to dine, Cavend. 122.

Dyogenes, Garl. 129.

dyopason, Hawes 1413.

dyscomfet, discomfited, Orl. iii:7.

dyscusse, to decide, Nevill 24, 873. *See* **discusse**.

dysese, discomfort, unhappiness, FaPrin. B 18. *See* **desese**.

dysour, dice-player, Garl. 629.

dyssauyd, deceived, Prohib. 66.

ear, ere, Ecl. prol. 61.

earst, erst, Ecl. 33, 1053, 1100.

Earth upon Earth, alluded to in closing summary of Hawes. *See* ed. for EETS, and Wells, p. 387.

ebb, *s.* FaPrin. D 69*, Cavend. 188.

ebounden, bound, Shirley I:92.

ebrew, Hebrew, Garl. 582.

ecchoun, echoon, each one, Churl 109, FaPrin. C 41.

Ector, *see* Hector.

Ecuba, Hecuba, Epithal. 74.

Edmund, St., FaPrin. K 48.

Education, *see* introd. to Hawes; *see* in Ref. List.

Edward III, Libel 184 ff., Ecl. 523.

Edward VI, Cavend. 1407.

eende, end, FaPrin. G 256.

effekke, effect, Thebes 170.

effycace, efficacy, Nevill dial. 4.

eft, again, afterwards, MaReg. 408, Libel 494, Shirley II:16*, 88.

efte sone, afterwards, then, Walton A 196, D 60, 69, etc.

egall, equal, Epithal. 145, FaPrin. G 182. *See* Epithal. 134.

eger, eager, Walton B 20.

egloges, eclogues, Ecl. prol. 21*, 28, 76, 127, 129.

eied, eyed, equipped with eyes, FaPrin. A 383.

eir, heir, Dance 238.

eld, age, Walton A 267, 326, Morley 122.

eldres, elders, Shirley I:7.

elephant, Garl. 468. *See* **oliphaunt**.

Eleyne, Helen of Troy, Horns 27*, Dance 452, Epithal. 78*, Orl. xvi:10, Garl. 876, Morley 218, 220.

eleuate, to extol, Hawes 762.

elich, alike, Churl 48.

elicon, Helicon, Burgh 7*. *See* **Helicon**.

ellas, alas! Shirley II:43.

ellis, ellys, else, Dance 636, 641, 661, Shirley I:8, Orl. vi:4, Nevill 199, etc.

Elizabeth, Queen, her transl. of Boethius, *see* Walton A 366*, B notes.

eloquencyale, eloquent, Shirley I:31.

elthe, health, Mass 151.

Elyconys, of Helicon, Garl. 74.

embosid, foaming at the mouth, Garl. 24.

embossed, adorned in raised patterns, Cavend. 109.

embrace, *v.* Dance 482*.

eme, uncle, Hardyng 52, 80.

emforth, according to, Pallad. 12.

emispery, hemisphere, Hawes 67, 1256.

emmet, ant, Ecl. 247.

empier, empire, Cavend. 1134.

emprice, emprise, *s.* undertaking, Dance 178, 221, 655; —renown, Pallad. 38.

enaured, gilded, adorned, Pallad. 67.

enbateled, fortified, Garl. 570.

enbesid, busied, Garl. 789.

enbewtid, beautified, Garl. 852.

enbissy, *v.* busy, Garl. 66.

enbosid, embossed, Garl. 467.

enbrawded, etc., embroider, Garl. 778, 892.

enbrayd, *v.* braid, Garl. 773.

enbulyoned, bejewelled? Garl. 478.

enbybid, moistened, Garl. 676.

enchace, drive away, FaPrin. D 91.

encheson, occasion, Hardyng 122.

encline, to decay, lose value, Hawes 4266.

enclude, to hold together, Pallad. 68*.

encouerde, covered, Garl. 1142.

encrampisshed, cramped, bound, Garl. 16*.

enderkkid, *a.* obscure, Garl. 108.

endeuorment, endeavor, Garl. 794.

endewe, *v.* discipline, Nevill dial. 13.

endite, to write, Walton A 59, 155, 253, MaReg. 298*, FaPrin. G 41, Orl. xii:8, 24, Hawes 722, 1290, Nevill dial. 10, Ecl. 681; —to dictate, Walton A 347; —to indict, Dance 492.

enduce, to induce, Nevill 220.
endued, dewed, wet with tears, Hawes 437;—clothed, Garl. 1022, etc.
enduringe, during, Garl. 823*.
enduse, to adduce, Garl. 94, 1113.
enflorid, decked with ornaments? Garl. 1138.
enforced, stimulated, Walton E 53, 60, Churl 64.
enforsyng him, attempting, Hawes 4411. See Ship 67.
engalared, having galleries, Garl. 460.
engladid, gladdened, Garl. 536.
englasid, glazed, Garl. 479.
englistered, glistened, Garl. 657.
engrapid, hung with grapes, Garl. 650.
engrosid, swollen, Garl. 335, 342, 349, etc. (So Dyce. First case NED, 1561);—written, Garl. 1467;—?? Garl. 41.
engyne, "ingenium", ingenuity, Pallad. 85.
enhabite, dwell, Libel 240. See Nevill dial. 16.
enhachid, adorned, Garl. 40.
enhardid, hardened, Garl. 306.
enhaunce, overcome? Nevill 63;—to elevate, Ecl. 850.
enlosenged, patterned in lozenges, Garl. 469.
enmy, enemy, FaPrin. G 283.
ennewed, renewed, Reproof 7, Garl. 389, 969.
ennoy, annoy, Pallad. 60*.
ennoynte, anointed, Hardyng 4, Pallad. 54.
enormyte, flagrant wrongdoing, Ship 568, 602.
enow, ynow, enough, Dance 336.
enpauyd, paved, Garl. 466.
enplement, Garl. 402*.
enpreented, imprinted, LettGlouc. 56.
enprise, charge?, bidding, Churl 333.
enrailid, surrounded by a rail, Garl. 650.
ensaumple, to give example to, Dial. 604;—s. example, Hawes 1294.
enscrisped, crisped, curled, Garl. 289.
ensensed, etc., to sprinkle with odor, Hawes 11, 102.
enserched, searched out, Walton E 4.
ensewe, to follow, ensue, Nevill 198, Garl. 321, 390. See Ship 14, 62, 144, 215, 241, 603, 608, 8517, Ecl. prol. 103.
ensowkid, soaked, Garl. 23.
enstore, provide, Bycorne 103.
ensue, see ensewe.
ensure, to assure, Orl. ix:11, Nevill 83.
entachid, linked? Garl. 470.
entakeled, furnished with (ship's) tackle, Garl. 545.
entayle, quality, Churl 235.
entaylled, adorned or carved, Cavend. 108.
enteer, perfect, FaPrin. G 74, K 18. See entere.
entencioun, desire, intent, FaPrin. D 108.
entend, to give attention to, Dance 328, Fa-Prin. A 13, Shirley I:1, Hawes 678, Ecl. prol. 96; —to intend, Garl. 412, 426; —to tend, Garl. 1109?
entent, intention, Dance 33, 461, 531, 665, Fa-Prin. A 309, 428, B 155, G 97, Mass 10, 37, 155, Reproof 32, Orl. ix:17, xvi:26, xxiii:10, Hawes 56, 430, Nevill 431, Cavend. 271; —attention, Lickp. 59.

ententifely, attentively, Walton E 103, Hawes 250, 1407, Nevill 204.
enterchaungyng, interchanging, FaPrin. A 125.
entere, entire, Dance 659, FaPrin. G 74, Epithal. 178, Mass 1. See enteer.
entered, interred, Shirley II:51.
enterement, interment, Garl. 1247.
enterprysyd, endeavored, Garl. 388, Ecl. prol. 52.
entremete, to take part in, meddle with, Walton A 36, MaReg. 439.
entyrmete, see entremete.
entytlen, to write down under headings, Mass 165*.
enuawtyd, arched over, vaulted, Garl. 476.
enuerdurid, made green, Garl. 660.
enuolupid, enwrapped, MaReg. 245.
enuy, envie, to try to rival, Hawes 1346. See Dance 241*.
enuyronde, environed, Nevill envoy 3.
enuyrowne, around, Garl. 489.
enuyuid, to enliven, kindle, Garl. 856, 1139.
enveiyd, inveighed, censured, Garl. 96. First case NED 1529.
enviroun, round about, Dance 107. See enuyrowne.
Enyus, Ennius, Garl. 347.
Eolus, Aeolus, Garl. 235, 1066.
epitomis, brief writings, Garl. 1378.
equypollent, of equal worth, Epithal. 151, Hawes 687.
er, ere, Pallad. C 1.
-er, rime on, Nevill 25-27. See -eth.
eresy, errisy, heresy, Reproof 63, Hardyng 26.
erkith me, "it irks me", Garl. 1456.
ernest, Shirley II:99*.
ernestful, exacting?, MaReg. 293.
erronyouse, misguided, Hardyng 15. First case NED 1512.
errytyke, heretic, Hardyng 8.
erst than, before, Garl. 1012.
erste, first, Mass 30, Pallad. 118.
ertly, earthly, Prohib. 86.
erudice, Eurydice, Walton D 18, 64.
es, Lat. aes, brass or copper, Prohib. 37*.
eschape, escape, Hardyng 23.
eschaunge, Pallad. A 4*.
Eschines, Aeschines, Garl. 131, 135, 154, 157, 166.
escry, outcry, battle cry, Ecl. 943. See askry.
escuse, excuse, Reproof 80.
Esiodus, Hesiod, Garl. 328.
Esope, Aesop, Ecl. 448*.
Espirus, Hesperus, FaPrin. K 32.
esploye, Fr. esploier, s'avancer, i.e., to put one's self forward, Pallad. 58.
estchepe, Eastcheap, a London street, Lickp. 89.
estate, class, rank. Thebes 20, Dance 573, Epithal. 146, FaPrin. A 128, 167, 177, 181, 447, Shirley II:93, Ecl. 860, 1093, Garl. 54, 600, 1204, 1255, Cavend. 48, 55, 156, 1187, 1269, 1418;—higher rank, men of eminence, Churl 17, FaPrin. A 46, 67, Hawes 190, Nevill 176,

Ship 235, Ecl. 909, Garl. 45, Cavend. 35, 37;—
condition, Hawes 4300, Nevill 877;—dignity,
FaPrin. E 51, Garl. 752, 1092. *See* **state.**
cloth of astate, Garl. 484*, Cavend. 123.
este, east, Walton A 133.
ete, ate, Walton D 49.
–eth, rime on, Hawes, stanza 105.
etik, etiques, flushed "hectic" dry fever, Dance
398*, LettGlouc. 27, 45.
euasioun, escape, Garl. 154.
Etymology, *see* Dial. 586*.
euforbe, Libel 353*.
Eumenides, Garl. 1290.
ewre, to prosper, Orl. xii:31. *See* **ure.**
exaumplaire, model, Dance 534.
excelsitude, majesty, Hardyng 112.
excesse, excess? access? Hawes 4421.
exemplifye, to adduce as example, Hawes 677.
Exione, Garl. 1367*.
existent, Walton A 315*.
expedient, Libel 453, Hawes 1412.
expert, able, well-contrived, FaPrin. A 298.
exployntynge, performing exploits, Nevill dial.
32.
expresse, to tell, utter, FaPrin. A 303*, Hawes
197, 326, Nevill 90, 142, Ecl. prol. 119, Cavend.
117, 1137.
in expresse, expressly, Walton A 143, E 113,
Dance 269, Reproof 41, Shirley II:28, Pallad.
32, Hardyng 31.
expreslye, Hawes 1300.
exskus, excuse, FaPrin. B 101.
exuberate, Ripley 134*, 164.
exyte, excite, Ripley 82.
ey, ever, Hawes 269.
eye, ever, Lickp. 111;—to examine with the eye,
Pallad. 88?
at eye, at a glance, obviously, Pallad. 30, 386,
480, Pallad. 32, 33. *See* Libel 262*.
eyeghen, eyes, Epithal. 164, 167.
eyne, eyes, Orl. xix:17. *See* **iyen.**
eyre, air, Churl 22.
eyther, either, or, Ripley 164, 167.

faatal, *see* **fatal.**
fable, *see* Churl 29*, Hawes dedic. 34-42, Pastime
663*, Nevill envoy 14, Ecl. prol. 100.
Fabricius, Walton C 22*, Cavend. epitaph 22.
facers, Garl. 189*.
facoun, falcon, Churl 358.
faculte, ability, Garl. 800;—art, branch of learning, Ship 7001.
falle, to befall, MaReg. 74, FaPrin. G 24, Shirley I:50.—**fall not,** fit not, Ecl. 602.
ffaire fall, success befall, Shirley I:50, Garl. 27.
falls, false, FaPrin. A 320.
fallyng, failure, Orl. xxi:13.
Fame. *See* note FaPrin. B 95; *see* Epithal. 133,
Hawes 135 ff., Cavend. 1223 ff.
fane, banner, Hawes 4264;—vane, Hawes 4382.
ffantasien, to imagine, FaPrin. A 17, 23.
fantasy, opinion, FaPrin. E 59, G 22, Garl. 39;
—imagination, Hawes 675, 677.
ffantzy, fancy, Cavend. 1244, 1245, 1318, 1423.

ffardel, burden, FaPrin. D 106, Mass 156, 177.
fare, far, Prohib. 33, Cavend. 1373.
farsid, filled, well provided, MaReg. 13.
faste by, close by, Epithal. 20.
fatal, fateful, FaPrin. B 114, Garl. 316;—fore-
ordained, Dance 407, Epithal. 10, Garl. 34;—
prophetic, Hawes dedic. 33*, Hawes 665*,
751, Garl. 34.
fatenesse, fatness, Churl 11.
fatigate, wearied, Prohib. 46, Ecl. 921.
fauel, MaReg. 211*, 223, 244, 247, 284, 287.
fauour, appearance, Ecl. 426.
fautes, fawtes, faults, Ship 84, 108, 137, 139,
13834, Garl. 112*, 203.
fautles, faultless, Ship 89.
fawty, faulty, Ship 6996.
fayn, fain, Hawes 111;—to feign, Hawes 155,
716, 1301, 1357, 1389, 4308, Ship 52.
faynt, exhausted, Lickp. 7;—weak, Cavend. 34.
feard, afraid, Ecl. 894.
feare, to terrify, Hawes 4260.
fearefull, dreadful, Ecl. 881.
febled, enfeebled, Ecl. 923.
feblesse, weakness, Shirley I:12, II:13.
fee, Hawes 196*.
feere, fear, Walton D 16, 42.
in feere, together, Walton E 145, Bycorne 11,
Dance 95, 657, Epithal. 5, Orl. xiv:4, Hardyng
45. *See* **fere.**
fel, to feel, Mass 16.
fele, many, Pallad. 89, 106, Libel 416;—to examine, comprehend, Pallad. 73*, 91, Libel 188,
Garl. 744; *see* FaPrin. A 126;—to notice, Ecl.
114, 118, 122, 678*.
fell, cruel, Walton A 237, D 10, E 166, Ecl. 932,
1007.
felles, skins, Libel 245, 524.
felly, cruelly, FaPrin. B 114.
felt, felt hat, Ecl. 384;—*v.,* *see* **fele,** Libel 188.
femel, female, MaReg. 138.
ffemynyte, femininity, Horns 35.
fendis, of fiends, Dance 359.
fenestrall, windows, Garl. 1354.
fer, ferre, far, Walton A 12, 308, E 48, 59, Epithal. 46, FaPrin. A 245, B 95, 108, 115, D 56,
68, Orl. xviii:26, Nevill 54;—*s.* fear, Mass 33.
ferd, *see* **fforferd.**
Ferdinand, Ship 7015*.
fere, mate, Dial. 739;—*s.* fire, Churl 178;—far,
Shirley II:16;—fear, Libel 555. *See* **feere.**
ferforth, far, Walton E 52.
ferme place, a farm, Ship 8503.
fern ago, long ago, MaReg. 196.
ferneyeer, last year, MaReg. 423.
fers, fierce, Walton A 237, FaPrin. A 212.
fersere, fiercer, Walton B 28*.
ferthe, fourth, Hardyng 38.
ferye, holiday, Dance 211*.
fesaunt, pheasant, Garl. 103.
festes, entertainments, Libel 481.
fette, fetch, Dance 414.
feynt, insufficient, Thebes 104.
feyntice, weakness, FaPrin. D 96, Mass 169.
ff–. For words so beginning *see* under **f–.**

ffeueryeer, February, Pallad. A 7, B 5.
fil, befell, Churl 42, FaPrin. A 102, 104.
fill, fell, FaPrin. A 53, 271, B 152, Garl. 30.
filoweþe, followeth, Shirley I:45.
fine, end, Dance 32, 39, 640, Prohib. 26*;—
to end, Dance 430. *See* fyne.
fitte, song, section of a poem, Ecl. 55, 720.
flagraunt, fragrant, Garl. 665, 962.
flambe, flame, Walton A 234, E 45, Hawes 102, 120.
flatereris, flatterers, FaPrin. C 86.
fleand, fleeing, Hardyng 70; *see* 6*.
fleen, to fly, Churl 137.
ı ees, fleece, Walton B 10, Libel 245.
fleinge, inconstant, variable, Ship 542.
flent, flint, Ecl. 824.
ffleth, *v.* flies, FaPrin. B 95, 120.
fletinge, flowing, Thebes 17.
fleyen, to fly, Walton C 32.
fligh, flew, Churl. 171.
Flora, Thebes 13, Garl. 679.
florifie, to adorn with flowers, Pallad. 80, 81.
florthe, floor, Garl. 480.
flouring, vigorous? ornate? FaPrin. G 163.
Flower and Leaf strife, *see* p. 199. *See* Orl. xvii.
foisoun, plenty, Churl 130, 241, FaPrin. C 106, K 12, Ship 3.
foisty bawdias, Garl. 633*.
folde, bend, Walton A 298.
foly, foolish, Dance 128.
folynesse, folly, Walton A 368.
fond, silly, Ecl. 401, Garl. 735.
fond, found, Walton B 32, Bycorne 98, 99, Dance 20, Epithal. 10, FaPrin. A 76, D 62, G 96, Pallad. 30, 65.
foo, Phoo! Garl. 633.
foone, foes, Churl 238, Epithal. 164.
for, as, Hardyng 4;—because (of), Walton A 129, 299, D 43, E 12, 168, etc., MaReg. 335, FaPrin. A 451, G 269, Ecl. 797, 929, Garl. 214;
—in order that, Hardyng 39;—for? Orl. vii:6; —against, Ecl. 5.
for any thyng, Libel 253*.
for thy, *see* forthy.
forbere, do without, Bycorne 35*, Libel 268.
force, *s.* matter, consequence, MaReg. 305, Ecl. 236, 614;—*v.* to care, attach importance to, Ecl. 645, 647, Garl. 725. *See* forse.
fordoþe, destroys, Dance 117, 308.
fordullid, much dulled, Churl 340, Cavend. 1219.
fforferd, much terrified, Pallad. A 5.
fore, Orl. v:11*.
fore by, by, Libel 25, 135, 143.
forgate, forgot, Garl. 369.
forlete, forletten, to abandon, Walton A 106, 319, 326.
forlore, lost, Shirley I:8, Nevill 152.
forlost, lost, Orl. xviii:8, 16, 24, 28.
formals, Ripley 116*.
forme, front, first, Pallad. B 4, Garl. 595.
formely, formally, Walton E 100.
Former Age, Walton B.
former date, Garl. 826*.

formest, foremost, Garl. 287, 679.
fforpyned, tortured, Walton D 48.
fforride, riding ahead, Pallad. D 3.
forsayd, aforesaid, Garl. 561.
forse, *s.* care, Ecl. 24. *See* force.
forshyuere, to break in pieces, Orl. xiv:7.
forslepid, slept heavily, Orl. xix:7.
forster, forester, Garl. 1374; *see* 27.
for that, because, Thebes 140, Ecl. 531.
forther, earlier?, elder, Nevill envoy 10. *See* former date.
not forthi, nevertheless, Walton E 19, 47.
forthinkiþ me, gives me regret, Dance 275.
forthir, forthre, to further, support, FaPrin. D 62, K 4, Reproof 32, 49.
forthwt, forthwith.
forthy, therefore, MaReg. 356. *See* not forthi, yit forthy. See Cavend. 39*.
fortop, forehead, Garl. 1306.
fortune, to happen, Ship 176, Garl. 85, 1112; — to manage, favor, Epithal. 176.
Fortune exculpated, Ecl. 1075*.
Fortune's wheel, Cavend. 190-92*.
fortyfye, to support, to equip?, Nevill 186, Ecl. 971.
for well, farewell, Lickp. 111.
forwhy, wherefore, Orl. xvi:19;—because, Orl. xiii:15.
foryete, to forget, Dance 171.
foryetilnesse, forgetfulness, FaPrin. D 31.
foryeue, forgive, MaReg. 408.
fforyoven, forgiven, Epithal. 105.
foster, forester, Garl. 27; *see* 1374.
founden, tested? tried? Walton A 368. Old Eng. *fandian* ?
a fourme, Dance 274. Read a forne.
fowerth, fourth, Ripley 193.
fowles, fools, Ship 539.
foysoun, *see* foison, Ship 3.
fraiys, frays, quarrels, Garl. 182.
Franceis, i.e., Petrarch, FaPrin. K 38.
franchemole, Thebes 101*.
fraunchise, *s.* and *v.*, license, Dance 366, 469, 604.
frauncis, i.e., Petrarch, Burgh 13.
frawhydnes, frowardness, Orl. vii:4.
fre, Libel 557*. *Read* frele?
frequent, to use, practise, Cavend. 1324.
frere, friar, Garl. 375.
freshe, gay, gorgeous, Garl. 39.
fret, torn, Dance 341, Garl. 1417;—ornamented, Garl. 485.
frete, to devour, Dance 398, Epithal. 27.
frigius, Phrygian, FaPrin. K 17.
friste, first, FaPrin. G 58, 266, Hardyng 8, 14.
fro, from.
frowise, Ecl. 423. Same as froyse? Not in NED.
frownsyd, wrinkled, Garl. 1306.
froyse, Thebes 101*.
fryththy, having low woods, Garl. 22.
fulfill, to eke out, Ecl. 390.
fulfilled, filled, Ecl. 664, Ship 609.
fulle, atte fulle, as a whole. Libel 78.

fume, odor, smoke, Hawes dedic. 40, Hawes 13, 341.

fumouse, heady, vaporous, Libel 112.

funerall, ominous, "funeste", FaPrin. E 31.

fur, Dance 250*, Ship 498*.

furder, further, Hawes 344.

Furies not invoked, Walton 60-61*.

furour, madness, rage, Ship 7005, Ecl. 1006.

fury, fiery, Walton A 233.

ffustian, a coarse weave of cotton or flax, Libel 76. *See* Garl. 1184 for metaphor.

fuyre, fire, Walton B 28, E 45, 50, 134.

fuyres, furies, Walton D 41.

fy, Fie! Orl. xiv:3.

fyers, fierce, Ship 6960.

fylle, *v.* fell, FaPrin. B 152, Garl. 872.

fyn, *a.* close, FaPrin. G 164. *See under* **fyne.**

fyne, to end, Walton A 161, Dance 263, 430, Epithal. 44, FaPrin. C 62, G 124;—*s.* end, Dance 32, 39, 640, Epithal. 175, FaPrin. A 228, E 97, G 164, Mass 179.

fyne force, Hawes 275*.

fyned, wrought to delicacy, Cavend. 1303*.

fyt, Ecl. prol. 16. *See* **fitte.**

fyx, to make permanent, Prohib. 51.

gabille, cable, Garl. 817.

gadder, to gather, Garl. 107.

gadrid, gathered, FaPrin. G 10.

gadryn, to gather, Mass 158.

gaff, gave, FaPrin. D 14, E 89, K 6.

gagwyne, Gaguin, Garl. 375*.

galauntes, galaundes, gallants, Ship 540, 596.

galeys, galleys, Libel 336, Ship 53.

galiene, Galen, Garl. 1392*.

gall, *see* **honey and gall,** MaReg. 79*; *see* **rub on the gall,** Garl. 97*.

Galtres, Garl. 22*.

galwes, gallows, FaPrin. G 303.

gambawdis, *s.* gambols, Garl. 602.

gan, began, Walton A 140, 348, D 44, E 68, Churl 65, FaPrin. A 7, C 3, D 89, Orl. xix:3, Lickp. 52, Hawes 65, 197, 4215, 4355. *See* Hawes 67, 282.

gan, did (*auxil.*), Walton A 301, 387, D 17, Churl 10, 297, FaPrin. D 39, 46, 52, 72, 128, E 5, 24, 73, G 3, 15, 31, 51, 65, 96, 98, H 1, K 36, Lickp. 44, 46, 47, 65, 70, 73, 84, 87, 109, Orl. xix:14, Hardyng 109, Hawes 301, 326.

garded, trimmed or faced, Ship 509, 549, 8483.

Garden, Churl 47 ff.*, Garl. 646 ff., Cavend. 115-18*.

gargeled, gargeyld, equipped with gargoyles, Hawes 307, Nevill 115, 178.

garnade, garnado, Granada, Churl 259, Ship 6973. *See* Garl. 485.

Garter, Order of, Hardyng 123*.

gase, *s.* that which is stared at, Garl. 1184. *See* NED.

gasid, gazed, stared, Garl. 265.

Gaspian, Caspian, Garl. 553. (Marshe ed. reads **Caspian**).

gaspyng, Hawes 87*.

gastful, dreadful, Dance 564.

gat, got, FaPrin. E 68, G 292.

gayne, Bycorne 46. *Read* **gyn,** device?

Gayus Marrius, Caius Marius, FaPrin. G 243.

geare, equipment, Ecl. 18.

Gebar, Ripley 112*; *see* Prohib. 64*.

geder, to gather, Orl. xiv:4.

geef, *s.* Orl. xxi:5*, *see* xxii:5.

geet, raised, tossed up, Walton A 317.

gefe, to give, Orl. xxii:5.

gein, against, FaPrin. G 159.

Gemine, Gemynys, the constellation Gemini, Hawes 1403, Cavend. 3.

Genius, Mass 56*.

gent, noble, Hawes 428.

gentrye, noble blood, FaPrin. E 94.

gentyl, gentle, Shirley I:57.

gentyles, gentlefolk, Shirley I:84.

genysses, Genesis, Ripley 41.

gerdouns, guerdons, rewards, Mass 185.

gere, stuff, Lickp. 98.

gery, fickle, Orl. xx:10.

ges, to guess, Orl. iii:7, xix:26.

Gesta Romanorum, Dial. 820.

gest, guest, Nevill 55.

geste, *s.* and *v.*, jest, Hawes 1336, Nevill 21.

gestes, deeds, Dial. 820*.

get, fashion, Garl. 1171.

geue, to give, Lickp. 31, Hawes 251, etc., Ecl 320, etc.

gevers, Geber's, Prohib. 64*.

geyn, against, FaPrin. C 98;—*s.* remedy, help, Bycorne 46, Dance 83, 157, 603;—to avail, Dance 143.

giggisshe, flighty, wanton, Garl. 1184. First case NED.

giltees, guilty acts, Dial. 717.

girdle, meaning of, Dance 262*.

girnid, snarled so as to show the teeth, Garl. 265.

gise, guise, mode, Dance 218, 265, Garl. 121.

glacing, slippery, FaPrin. D 24.

glade, to gladden, Pallad. 8;—to rejoice, Churl 258, Pallad. 111.

glaue, sword, Hawes 4323.

glee, music, Garl. 278.

gleede, hot coal, MaReg. 159.

glint, slippery, Garl. 572.

globous, globe-shaped, Ripley 37.

gloire, glory, FaPrin. C 13.

gloriowsly, brilliantly, Garl. 83.

glose, to flatter, talk smoothly, MaReg. 266, Garl. 744, 894.

Gloucester, Humphrey, duke of: etymology of his name, Dial. 596-7; made duke, Hardyng 50; lieutenant of England, Dial. 533; against Orleans' liberation, Pallad. 60; marriage to Jacqueline, introd. to Epithalamium; his books, pp. 143, 145, and note on Pallad. 89; as bibliophile and patron, introd. and prol. to FaPrinces, introds. to Epithal. and to Letter, introd. to Pallad.; military commander, Dial. 576, 610, Libel 249; pious son of the Church, prol. to FaPrin., introd. to Palladius; name of his daughter, FaPrin. A 246*.

glowmes, is gloomy, Ecl. 474, 1064.

glum, a black look, Garl. 1095.

glumme, to look sourly, scowl, Hawes 4355.

glutton, Garl. 779*. Not in NED.
Go, little book; *see* Churl 379 note; *see* Nevill envoy 1, Garl. 1484.
god, good, FaPrin. D 39.
God avow, Ecl. 438*.
Gold, proverb on, Churl 306*.
Golden Age, Walton B, Ship 8444* ff.
goldissh, golden, Churl 306*.
gone, go, Hawes 320.
gonge, the privy-closet, Ecl. 120.
gonne, begun, FaPrin. H 13.
good, property, Churl 367.
goode yere, Garl. 730*, 986.
goordis, gourds, Mass 159, 176.
gorge, Gorgias, Burgh 10*.
Gorgones, Gorgons, FaPrin. C 95.
gose, goes, Garl. 26.
gossomer, gossamer, Horns 5, LettGlouc. 26.
gotefelle, goatskin, Libel 56.
goten, gotten, obtained, Nevill 111, 133, Ecl. 839, Morley 68.
gouernaunce, mode of life, Libel 123; —enterprise, Libel 219.
gouernour, guide, pilot, Thebes 79, Ship 7008.
gow, Go we! Lickp. 114*.
Gower, FaPrin. K 24*, Hawes 1261*, Garl. 387 ff., 1079. *See* p. 21.
goynge, gait, Ship 476.
Gracce, Gracchus, FaPrin. G 140*.
Gradatio, MaReg. 300-04*.
grame, woe, Walton C 37.
grange, farm Ship 8502.
grapsyng wey, feeling my way, Orl. xviii:26.
grathly, well, Ecl. 344.
gratulat, rejoicing, Ripley 4.
graued, engraved, Ship 133.
graunt, yield, Nevill 68.
gray, the badger, Garl. 101.
grayn, dye, especially scarlet dye, Libel 54; —grain, Libel 118.
gre, a stair, degree, Walton A 335, Dance 283. Lat. *gradum*.
greable, agreeable, Dial. 690.
greave, grief, Cavend. 1426.
grece, staircase, Hawes 319.
gree, to agree, Garl. 275.
in gree, kindly, Dance 599, Nevill envoy 15, Garl. 1452. Lat. *gratum*.
green, Dance 434*.
grekysshe, Greek, Walton A 330, FaPrin. G 61.
grene, immature, Mass 19, 171.
grephyn, griffin, Nevill 183*.
gressoppes, grasshoppers, Garl. 1136.
grete, to cry out, Lickp. 86.
greuance, sorrow, FaPrin. G 245, 255.
greuen, to suffer, Thebes 115.
greyhounds, Hawes 106*.
greyn, grain, Thebes 56.
Griselda, Bycorne *passim*, FaPrin. A 348, Cavend. 1369*.
in groce, "en masse"; *or* "in full"?, Ship 6974.
grocery, goods by wholesale, Libel 501.
grope, to probe, search, Garl. 611, 816.

grosely, heavily, Garl. 639.
grossolitis, *error for* chrysolitis, Garl. 466.
ground, theme, Garl. 28; —country, Libel 85; —floor, Garl. 41? 466; —earth, Orl. xii:23, Ecl. 986; —occasion, Epithal. 39.
grucche, to grudge, be unwilling, Dance 363, 598, FaPrin. B 52.
gryp, vulture, Walton D 49.
grys, gray fur, Dance 325.
guie, to guide, FaPrin. D 64.
guippe, *error for* keep? Orl. iv A:6.
guy, gye, to guide, MaReg. 387, FaPrin. G 132.
gyffen, given, Walton A 88.
gynne, to begin, Thebes 129, 168, FaPrin. A 136, C 2, Pallad. A 2.
gynyng, a beginning, FaPrin. C 2.

h, excrescent in spelling, *see* Walton E 93*.
ha, han, to have, Churl 99, Thebes 95, 103, Dance 170, FaPrin. A 130, 218, 274, B 70, E 62, K 83, Pallad. 21, Mass 85, Orl. xix:22, etc.
habille, able, Garl. 742.
habound, to abound, Orl. xii:1.
hagys, haggis, Thebes 100*.
hailid, pulled, Garl. 616.
Hair, *see* Ship 456*, 541*.
hale, to pull, Hawes 4349.
half, hallfe, side, Shirley II:19, Garl. 10.
halteth, limps, FaPrin. K 2, Libel 38, Ship 152, Ecl. 509, Garl. 502.
Hanibal, Hannibal, Epithal. 152.
hampton, Southampton, Hardyng 72, 77.
at the hand, near, Dance 158.
harde, heard, Ship 7017, Cavend. 1181, Morley 66, 169.
hardly, sorely, Garl. 814.
harneys, armor, Hawes 172, 175, Ecl. 1124, Garl. 1507.
hastardis, base fellows, Garl. 601.
haste, hasty, Churl 197.
hastly, in haste, Libel 493.
hastow, hast thou.
hastyue, hasty, Garl. 1111.
hath, *imper. plu.*, have, Shirley II:76.
hattered, hatred, FaPrin. G 288.
haue in, haue out, i.e., Get in, Get out! Garl. 251.
hauing, behaving, Ecl. 611; *see* 734; —possession, Walton B 27.
hault, high, Nevill 13, Cavend. 204.
haunt, to frequent, practise, Ecl. 356, 1117.
hauoure, behavior, manner, Orl. xvii:12, Ecl. 734.
Hawarde, *see* Howard.
hawe, fruit of the hawthorn, i.e., something valueless, MaReg. 380.
hawsed, hoisted, Ship 57.
Headless lines, *see* p. 21.
hearde, herdsman, Ecl. prol. 83, Ecl. 139, 408.
heares, hairs, Cavend. 1120.
heauely, heavily, sadly, Morley 216.
heaven to hear, etc. *See* note Epithal. 99. *See* paradyce.
Hecate, Garl. 1288.

Hector, Epithal. 138, FaPrin. E 94, Ecl. 1199, Cavend. epitaph 6.
heddelles, Garl. 775*.
heded, beheaded, Hardyng 77, Ecl. 1086.
hedelynge, headlong, Dial. 647, Ship 13839.
hedir, hither, Libel 108, 545.
on heed, ahead, Dial. 630.
heeght, i.e., hight, is called, Epithal. 47.
heelde, kept, held, FaPrin. G 210, K 3.
heep, a number of people or things, MaReg. 340, Lickp. 91.
heere, to hear, FaPrin. G 320.
hegged, hedged, Churl 49.
heghe, high, Epithal. 128.
hele, welfare, advantage, Walton A 134;—*v.* to cover, conceal, Lickp. 79.
Helen, of Troy, *see* **Eleyne.**
Helicon (*see* **elicon**), Walton D 28*, Burgh 5*, *See* Garl. 74.
helis, *error for* **hertles,** Orl. iv B:6.
heim, hem, them, Dance 414, Libel 326, etc.
helthe, healing? Garl. 978.
Helycon, Helicon, Nevill 166. *See* **Elicon.**
henavde, Hainault, Libel 529. *See* introd. to Epithal.
heng, hung, Walton A 382, Lickp. 99.
hennes, hens, hence, Walton E 162, Dance 656, Lickp. 114.
Henry V, *see* Epithal. 49, Hardyng; *see* p. 90.
Henry VII, *see* dedic. to Hawes.
Henry VIII, Ecl. 849, Garl. 1200, Cavend. 1227 ff., Morley dedic. letter.
hent, taken, Libel 203, etc., Cavend. 1262, 1282.
her, their, Dial. 671, etc., Thebes 30, Dance 12, Pallad. 31, Libel 131, Ripley 89, etc. *See* **hir, here.**
her aftir, hereafter, Dance 120.
herber, arbor, Nevill 427, Garl. 646*.
Hercules, Hawes 177, Ecl. 915, Garl. 1257 ff., Cavend. epitaph 2, Morley 194;—choice of, Hawes 27*, Nevill 214*;—knot of, Ecl. 346*.
herdys, herdboys, Mass 126.
here, to hear, FaPrin. A368, Shirley I:2, Pallad. 34, 60, Mass 86, Libel 508, Garl. 197, 451, 981, 1066, 1190, Cavend, 1312;—*s.* hair, Burgh 42, Prohib. 36, Ship 483, 485, 8480, Garl. 289;— their, Libel 394; —her, FaPrin. A 237, 242; —*s.* heir, Cavend. 140 .
herefore, heretofore, Libel 167.
heremyte, hermit, Walton A 227.
Ad Herennium, *see* MaReg. 300-04*, *see* notes FaPrin. G 197, etc.
heris, heres, hairs, Walton A 268, Burgh 42.
Hermon, Hermione, Morley 221.
heroicus, Walton A 219*.
hertis, harts, Garl. 1375.
hest, command, Walton A 4, 132, Pallad. 128; —promise, Mass 105.
hete, to offer, Lickp. 84.
hewe, Bycorne 32*.
hewle, to howl, Ecl. 365.
hewre, a cap, Lickp. 79.
heyre, *error for* **yere,** Orl. xvii:16.

hie, high, Pallad. 83. *See* **hih.**
hiere, her, Walton A 305.
hight, to be named, Thebes 95, Hardyng 34, Morley 176.
higth, high, Garl. 50, 1102, 1106.
hih, to hie, FaPrin. G 272;—high, Walton A 317, FaPrin. E 61, F 28, G 275, 305.
himself, as nominative, Walton A 92*, FaPrin. A 303*.
hippocentaurus, centaur, horse-man, Garl. 1262.
hir, hire, their, Walton A 350, Churl 22.
historiar, historian, Garl. 351.
hit, it.
ho, who, Dance 67, 119.
hokir, scorn, Dial. 741.
Holcot, MaReg. 249*.
hold, held, Churl 203, FaPrin. A 47, E 90, G 171, 258, Orl. xvii:6.
holde an hond, hold in hand, manage, Dance 190.
hole, holl, whole, Reproof 1, Shirley I:27, Hardyng 48, 61, Prohib. 28, Ship 579, 6941, 6984, 6993, 8471, Ecl. prol. 127, Garl. 66, 240, 433, 548, 553, 742, 858, 1140.
hole, wholly, Shirley II:6, Ship 8478.
holie, holly, wholly, Churl 287, FaPrin. E 1, G 92, Nevill 130.
homerus, Homer, Garl. 329. *See* **Omer.**
an honde, on hand, in control, Dance 190.
honey and gall, *see* MaReg. 79*.
hoo, Halt! Shirley I:33.
hool, whole, Dance 124, 145, Epithal. 197, FaPrin. C 68, Mass 1, Orl. xvi:3. *See* **hole.**
hoolde, *s.* hold, FaPrin. G 248.
Horace, *see* **Orace.**
hore, hoar, Walton A 268.
Horestes, Orestes, Morley 221.
horns, women's, *see* Horns Away, p. 110;—of Moses, Garl. 1348*.
hoso, whoso, Dance 67.
hospytlerys, hospitallers, members or residents of religious orders which cared for the sick, Mass 148.
host, go to, Libel 452*, etc.
hostlers, innkeepers, Ship 36.
hoten, hidden, Walton A 267. **hot,** Ship 593.
houe, to hover, Walton E 133, Hawes 312. *See* **howyng.**
Howard, Lord, Ecl. 621, 797, 853;—the Earl of Surrey, Cavend. 1105 ff;—*see* Garl. 848*, 862*.
howssys, houses, Cavend. 111.
howyng, hovering, Churl 224.
hoyse, to hoist, Hawes 1257.
huddes, hoods, Ecl. 6.
huge, great, Orl. xvi:12.
humors, *see* note FaPrin. E 95. *See* Libel 350.
Humphrey, etymology of, Dial. 596-7. *See* **Gloucester.**
hundrethe, hundred, Garl. 490, etc.
hur, her, Shirley II:52, 53.
husbondes, husbandmen, Libel 523.
huscht, hushed, Walton B 19.
huys, hues, Pallad. 62.

hy, to hie, Lickp. 15.
hyde, hidden, secret, Prohib. 96.
hye stile, *see* style.
hyegh, hyhe, high, Walton A 11, 88, etc., Bycorne 114, Epithal. 153, 180.
hyenes, highness, Hawes dedic. 22.
hyghte, height, Morley 33;—*v.* to assure, Garl.
637. *See* hight.
Hymen, *see* Ymeneus, Epithal. 176.
hynde, hind, female of the hart, Garl. 26.
hynderen, to hinder, FaPrin. G 202.
hynes, haughtiness, Dance 109.
hynge, hung, Pallad. C 5.
hys, *v.* hies? Orl. vi:11.
Hysyphyle, Hypsipyle, Morley 207. *See* Isyphill.
hyvye, Churl 276.

jacinctes, jacinths, Garl. 480.
Jacqueline of Hainault, pp. 144-45.
to iaggid, cut to pieces, Garl. 623.
iagounce, jacinth, Churl 232, 318*.
iangelers, chatterers, Ecl. 666, Garl. 566. *See*
Garl. 1235.
jantel, jantylle, wellborn or wellbred, Garl.
844, 864, 989, etc.; *see* 890.
jantilwomen, gentlewomen, Garl. 793.
Januays, the Genoese, Libel 322, 504.
Janus, Garl. 1430.
Ianyueer, January, Pallad. B 4.
iape, *s.* and *v.*, trick, jest, Churl 192, Thebes 185,
Orl. xiii:15, Garl. 361.
Iaques, Jacqueline, Epithal. 69.
Iason, Morley 203.
Ibroght, brought, Walton A 296.
icaried, carried, Libel 530.
iche, each, Garl. 268.
iclipped, called by name, Hawes 135, 315, 4319.
See yclipped.
Icononucar, Garl. 328*.
Idleness or Sloth. *See* Hawes dedic. 44, Hawes
711, Garl. 120, Cavend. 24-30*.
idrede, dreaded, Walton E 167.
Jean, Genoa, Libel 328.
ieet, jet, Roundel 3.
ieloffer, gillyflower, Garl. 967, 1359, 1413.
ielyous, jealous, Morley 240.
Ierome, St. Jerome, Walton A 19, 44*, Ship
13870, Garl. 162ˢ.
iet, to swagger, Ecl. 693.
I fayth, i'faith, in faith, Garl. 509.
ifeere, together, FaPrin. G 79.
ifounde, found, Libel 9.
ifynde, to find, Libel 562.
ihesu, Jesus, Libel 374.
jhewe, hewed, FaPrin. A 96.
Iierarchycall, hierarchical, Ripley 4.
Jleid, laid, FaPrin. A 168.
ill, bad, Ecl. 121, 582;—*s.* harm, Thebes 108.
See yll.
ilyke, equal, Walton A 129.
immercyable, merciless, Nevill 6.
immoysturid, saturated, Garl. 692.

impressid, imagined, MaReg. 175.
immuyn, immune, Pallad. D 6.
jmowled, mouldy, FaPrin. A 220.
impe, Cavend. 1406*.
importable, unbearable, FaPrin. D 48.
importyng, including, bringing in, Cavend. 121.
impossible, *s.* Bycorne 110*.
impute, to blame, Ecl. 994.
inblindeth, *v.* blinds, Ecl. 425.
incipience, insapience, unwisdom, Bedford 17.
incipient, Hardyng 9*.
inconuenyence, Ship 142*, 226, 534, 600, Ecl.
87, Cavend. 1371.
Inde, India, Ship 541. *See* ynde.
indigne, unworthy, Pallad. 87.
indite, *see* endite.
induce, to bring in, lead, Ship 13873, Ecl. prol.
22.
induring, during, Ecl. 456.
indye blew, deep blue, Nevill 190, 200, Garl.
478.
infame, infamous, Ecl. 605.
inferrid, adduced, brought forward, Garl.141*.
influence, favor, Ecl. 419.
inlesse, to diminish, Ecl. 349.
inowthe, enough, Garl. 241.
inperfyte, imperfect, Prohib. 35.
inportable, unbearable, Mass 175, 177. *See*
importable.
inspeccioun, vigilance, Hardyng 13;—insight
FaPrin. G 45.
instance, suggestion, Roundel 2.
insue, *see* ensue.
insure, to assure, Ship 13820.
insygne, to educate, Ship 114. (Fr. *enseigner*)
intencyon, attention, Nevill 199.
intende, to pay heed to, Ship 115, Ecl. 185, 531,
595, 683, 922.
intendement, intention, Hardyng 11.
intentyfe, attentive, Garl. 926, 946, Cavend.
1143.
intier, entire, complete, Cavend. epit. 23.
intreatable, intractable, pitiless, Ecl. 872.
intresse, entrance, Hawes 318;—concern, share
FaPrin. A 268.
inuentyff, *error for* invectyff, FaPrin. G 285.
inuentyfe, inventive, Hawes 674, 718.
inuident, envious person? Pallad. 16.
inwarde siht, creative mind, FaPrin. A 17.
See note Dial. 640.
joenesse, jeunesse, youth, Shirley I:78.
iolesye, jealousy, Libel 186.
iolite, gayety, Walton A 261.
Iollas, Garl. 1462*.
Ioly, Ecl. 724*.
Joone, John, Walton A 211.
Iopas, Garl. 682*.
iornee, iourne, journey, Dance 273, FaPrin.
D 50, 98, 114, etc
iowes, jaws, Roundel 3.
ioy, to make joyful, Orl. xxi:3.
joyelles, jewels, Cavend. 1387.
ipight, penetrated, set, Walton E 129.
ipocras, Hippocrates, Garl. 1393.

Ipre, Ypres, Libel 74.
iren, iron, Libel 56, Prohib. 38.
ironne, run, Dance 421.
irous, wrathful, violent, FaPrin. G 80.
Isyphill, Hypsipyle, Garl. 1005*. See Hysy-
    phyle.
itake, taken, Libel 198.
Itauȝt, taught, Dance 563.
Iubilesses, celebrations? Ripley 4.
Jubiter, Jupiter, FaPrin. E 87, 89, etc.
Judicum, the book of Judges, Churl 9.
juel, jewel, Orl. v:8.
iugurta, Jugurtha, Garl. 332.
iurediccion, jurisdiction, FaPrin. A 161.
juror, see Dance 481*.
iust, joust, Ecl. 66.
Iuvenall, Juvenal, Burgh 21, Garl. 95, 340.
Juvo, Juno, Epithal. 177.
ive, ivy, Burgh 40*.
iwis, iwus, iwys, certainly, Walton A 247, Libel
    103, 117, 335, Ripley 46, 64, Garl. 919*.
iyen, eyes, Ship 151, 503, 13846.

kannest, canst, Walton A 24.
karfull, woeful, Orl. xv:8, xxi:2. See carfull.
Katherine of France, Epithal. 47*.
kauht. See catch.
kechyn, kitchen, Churl 145.
keep, kepe, s. heed, MaReg. 195, Libel 39.
kempes, eels, Ecl. 424.
ken, to instruct, guide, Garl. 809, 1395.
kenned, knew, Lickp. 102.
kepe, kepte, to care, heed, MaReg. 425, Orl.
    xxi:15, Ship 180.
kerue, to carve, plow, Walton B 15.
keste, cast, threw, Nevill 23, Garl. 531.
keuered, covered, Walton B 30.
keuerchef, keverche, kerchief, Horns 21, 56.
keyse, keys, Ripley 84.
kid, made known, FaPrin. A 237.
kidfelle, kidskin, Libel 56.
kinde, nature, Churl 256, 407, FaPrin. G 35,
    Ecl. 321. See kynde.
kindly, natural, Dance 356. See kyndely.
kit, cut, Garl. 184.
knet, knotted, FaPrin. G 306.
kneuh, knew, FaPrin. G 148.
knottes, Cavend. 117*.
knowleching, knowledge, FaPrin. C 5, D 123.
knowlege, acknowledge, Ship 99, 537.
kokkis, God's, Thebes 126*.
kokolddis, cuckolds, Garl. 186.
konne, to be master of, know how, Walton E 32,
    Dance 420, Thebes 138.
konnynge, ability, knowledge, Dance 294, Fa-
    Prin. G 18, Burgh 42, Shirley II:37, Mass 26,
    Garl. 198, 850, 882, 889, 1208.
korage, to encourage, Garl. 152.
koude, could.
kouthe, known, FaPrin. G 204.
koyse, Thebes 102*.
krakkis, boasts, Garl. 189.
kunnyng, see konnynge.
kurris of kynde, curs by nature, Garl. 613.

kus, a kiss, MaReg. 155.
kut, Dial. 789*.
kyby, chapped, Garl. 502.
kylle, to be killed, Garl. 95.
kynde, kyndely, nature, natural, Walton A 359,
    372, E 14, 24, 44, 151, Horns 1, 23, 31, FaPrin.
    A 109, Shirley I:57, Orl.ix:2, Ripley 136, Nevill
    83, 148;—a. gracious, Pallad. C 3, Cavend. 7.
kynrede, kindred, FaPrin. E 1.
kyt, cut, Walton A 338. See kit.
kythe, to make evident, show, MaReg. 406.
kyttithe, cuts, Garl. 817.

L., fifty, Libel 435.
Labor, figure of, Ecl. 864 ff.
lace, a net, Dance 225;—v. to bind, Epithal. 13.
lacheses, Lachesis, Cavend. 1261, 1281.
lad, led, Dance 494, 546, 580.
ladyn, loaded, Garl. 727.
laft, left, Cavend. 1305.
lake, s. lack, FaPrin. G 18, K 2, 56, Mass 46,
    Garl. 285, Cavend. 38, 151.
lame, Pallad. 22*.
lammesse, Lammas-tide, Hardyng 71*.
lanterne, FaPrin. C 22*, G 8, 154, Nevill 136.
Laodome, Laodomia, Garl. 956*, Morley 222.
Lapidary, see note Churl 266.
large, free, Ship 153.
at large, at liberty, Churl 137, Dance 262, Ship
    83, 8443, Cavend. 154. See Libel 241; —in
    general, Garl. 1327.
larges, largesse, abundance, Orl. xv:23.
lark, see note Garl. 533-36, and see p. 83.
lasis, laces, Garl. 773.
lasse, less, Churl 338.
lassith, lessens, FaPrin. G 26.
at the longe last, finally, Garl. 1365, Ecl. 81,
    cp. 584.
late, v. let, Walton C 3, 5, FaPrin. K 56, Re
    proof 47, 62.
latyn, Orl. ix:11*.
lauer, a stream? Nevill 144, 161. NED says
    "basin of a fountain".
Laurent de Premierfait, FaPrin. introd.
laurere, laurel, Churl 25, 57, 116, 172, FaPrin.
    G 14.
lauret, laurel, Ecl. prol. 112.
lauriate, honored by or worthy of the laurel,
    Churl 15*, FaPrin. C 12, K 38, Burgh 21*,
    Nevill dial. 6, Ecl. prol. 104, Ecl. 263, 685,
    862, 919, 1073, 1091, Garl. 63, 116, 324 and
    introd.
lawly, lowly, Garl. 821; see Walton D 35.
lawre, laurel, Burgh 40.
lay, law? Walton A 103. Fr. lei.
laycestr, Leicester, Hardyng 45.
leames, rays, Hawes 1265.
lease, a lie, Libel 95. See lesyng.
leasing, losing, Ecl. 56.
leasour, leisure, Ecl. 160.
least, lest, Ecl. 252.
at least way, leastways, anyhow, Nevill dial.
    41.
leche, alike, Praise of Chaucer 2100*.

leche, s. physician, Dance 424.
lectrure, learning, FaPrin. A 384.
lede, lead, Burgh 47.
ledyn, leaden, Nevill 34.
leechys, physicians, LettGlouc. 9.
leef, pleasant, pleased, Orl. xxi:1, Libel 120*.
leet, caused to be, MaReg. 254.
leeued, believed, MaReg. 220.
left, lived? Walton A 220.
leften, to lift, Walton C 10, FaPrin. C 61.
legeble, legible, Burgh 27.
legende, reading, Shirley I:2.
legerdemayn, Dance 526.
leicer, leisure, FaPrin. A 232, 364, C 123.
lemys, limbs, Mass 157, Nevill 427.
lene, to lean, bow, Garl. 54;—lent me, leaned on, Garl. 17, 281.
lenger, longer, FaPrin. E 41, Libel 448, etc.
lengest, longest.
lenghe, length, Hardyng 68.
lept, leaped, Hawes 4364, 4382.   See Garl. 104, Hawes 111.
lere, to inform, teach, Thebes 36, FaPrin. A 43, Orl. xiv:21;—to learn, Churl 299, Dance 92, FaPrin. D 38, Burgh 11, 14, Mass 24.
lerned, taught, Libel 223.
lesard, lizard, Garl. 104.
lese, to lose, Walton B 24, Churl 95, 265, 270, Dance 400, FaPrin. G 36, Orl. xxii:3, Prohib. 83, Ship 74.
leste, to choose, Walton A 186, MaReg. 107, Dance 144;—least, Walton A 130, Dance 25, 320, 646, Garl. 880.
lesynge, a lie, MaReg. 223, Churl 200, Hardyng 5.
letarge, Prohib. 39*.
lete, to leave, Dance 110;—to cause to, FaPrin. E 45, Shirley I:39, Libel 363, 484;—to delay, Dance 567, Lickp. 11.
lete, for lette, to hinder, Walton A 259, Hawes 4274, Ecl. 38.
lette, to hinder, FaPrin. G 303, Libel 479;—s. hindrance, Walton A 389, MaReg. 174, Thebes 171, FaPrin. D 91, Orl. i:4, ii:5.
letuary, electuary, a thick sirupy medicine, LettGlouc. 43, 63.
leue, to believe? Libel 365, Shirley II:10;—to leave, Walton A 179; —? Dial. 714.
leve up, to leave, Dance 237.
leuer, leuyr, rather, Dial. 817, Churl 124, Dance 385, Orl. xv:7.
leuyng, living, FaPrin. B 66, C 9, G 321.
lewde, ignorant, Churl 311.   See Roundel 2, Churl 326, Prohib. 71, Ship 13853, Garl. 227, Cavend. 34; —sensual, Ship 553, 563.
lewdeness, Ship 119, 227, Garl. 770.
lewdly, badly, Ecl. 662.
leysere, leisure, LettGlouc. 2, Orl. xiv:26, xiii:31, Garl. 1060.
li, i.e., librae, pounds, MaReg. 421.
librair, library, Pallad. 96.
library, catalogue, Garl. 764.
Libye, Libya, FaPrin. E 8.

liche as, like, as if, Dance 3, 389; —as, Epithal. 78.
Licklider, his theory of verse, pp. 83-84.
lidderness, i.e., lithernes, sloth, timid inertia, Garl. 727.
liddurnes, blackguards, Garl. 188*.
liff, life, FaPrin. H 24.
lifly, living, Dance 538.   See lyvely.
lifte, left, Hardyng 125.
ligging, lyin꞉, recumbent.
light, alighted, Hawes 4228, 4317.
likerous, greedy, sweet-toothed, MaReg. 147.
likyng, delight, luxury, Libel 366, see note 338; Orl. xii:25, Ecl. 352.
lion, the constellation Leo, Cavend. 6.
List, the, as a rhetorical "color", Epithal. 71*.   See Cavend. epitaph.
list, v. wish.
listith on, listens to, Churl 275.
litel, lyte, little, Walton A 57, MaReg. 92, Dial. 506, Dance 322, 490, Burgh 11.
lith, imposes as a burden, requires? Dial. 682; —lies, FaPrin. B 49, 52.
on liue, alive, Walton A 184, Hawes 140, 1314.
Livius, Garl. 344.
lo! Walton D 66, Orl. xiii:28*.
lodesman, pilot, Ship 63.
on loft, aloft, Churl 209.
logged, lodged, Thebes 67, 78, etc.
loken, to look, Walton D 72.
lollers, Lollards, FaPrin. A 403, Hardyng 9*, 16.
Lollius, see note FaPrin. A 284.
londe, to bring, set? Pallad. 47.
London Rockes, Ship 75*.
lone, loan, Libel 431.
on long, in length, Walton C 33.
long, to belong, FaPrin. G 197, Libel 73, 105, Hawes 124, 4430, Ship 471, 13877, Ecl. 13, 256, 282, 305, Garl. 1219.
loodsterre, lodestar, Epithal. 191.
looke, look at, Shirley II:4.
loos, reputation, MaReg. 345. Lat. laus.
loose, to lose, Walton D 72.
lordshipeþe, rules, lords over, Epithal. 25.
lore, lost, MaReg. 349.
loreyne, Lorraine, Hardyng 93, Garl. 494.
lorn, lost, FaPrin. E 32; —deprived? Pallad. 34.
lose, to dissolve, Ripley 115, 152.
losellis, Garl. 188*.
losengeour, false flatterer, MaReg. 220.
losond, loosened, Garl. 719, 1134.
loþest, most loath or unwilling, Dance 312.
louh, low, FaPrin. A 128, 223.
loute, to bend low, submit, Libel 223.
lowis, Lewis.
lowre, to lower, look black, Walton A 258, Hawes 4354.
Lucan, Burgh 20, FaPrin. C 17, Garl. 337.
Lucilius, Garl. 381.
Lucine, Lucina, the moon, Thebes 7, FaPrin. C 90, G 37, K 31, Garl. 6.
Lucrece, Lucretia, Horns 29, Epithal. 75, Nevill 835.

lumpes, dullards, Garl. 727.

lune, Luna, the moon, i.e., silver, Prohib. 43*.

lure, *s.* Dance 207*, LettGlouc. 37, FaPrin. B 117; *see* MaReg. 121;—standard? Garl. 976.

lurke, to shirk work, be idle, Cavend. 1219 (first case NED, 1551); —to hide, Ecl. 60.

not lustith me, it pleases me not, Orl. xiii:15; *see* Orl. xxii:5.

lustris, FaPrin. E 69*.

ly, to lie, Shirley II:42.

lybbard, leopard, Garl. 590.

lych, like, FaPrin. B 106.

Lydgate, essay on, pp. 77-98; partial list of his work, 100-101; his metre, 83 ff.; his padding phrases, 88 ff.; his reading, 92-94; his use of Chaucer, 90-92; list of better lines by him,81-82; his writing about women, 95; his attitude to Nature, 95. He gives his name, Thebes 92, FaPrin. K 56; names his birthplace, FaPrin. K 45. His relation to Gloucester, introds. to Epithal. and to Letter, also to FaPrin. Alluded to Reproof 26 ff., by Shirley I:80, II:24, by Hawes 1261 note, 1282 ff., 1317 ff., 1339, 1346, dedic. 27, 48; by Skelton, Garl. 391 428 ff., 1079.

in lyke, alike, Walton C 19.

lyketh me, it pleases me, Walton A 41 (*but see* B 17), Cavend. 114.

lymster, Leominster, Ecl. 316.

lyn, to lie, FaPrin. A 70.

lynage, lineage, Walton C 15, etc.

lynkeld, linked, Bycorne 133.

lyst, lest, Ship 65, 81, 217, 587;—to will, Reproof 11, etc., Orl. ix: 4, 5, Ripley 53, etc.

lyste, to listen, Ripley 75.

lyte, little, Mass 21.

lyttler, lesser, Shirley II:10.

lyvely, of life, Cavend. 1262, 1280. *See* Cavend. 121. *See* lifly.

maad, made, FaPrin. H 18.

maas, mace, FaPrin. D 41*.

macabre, pronunciation of, p. 124 note; etymology of, *see* note on Dance 24.

MacCracken. *See* notes FaPrin. A 303, Garl. 296; *see* pp. 79, 198, 218.

macrobius, Garl. 367.

mad, made, Mass 148.

made, made of, held, regarded, Walton E 98, Garl. 185.

madir, madder, Libel 521.

mafay, My faith! Orl. xvi:23, xviii:10.

mageran, marjoram, Garl. 890, etc.

magre, maugre, in spite of, Dance 15. *See* malgre, maugre.

maintenance, Garl. 193*.

to maistresse, as a mistress, Dance 165.

maistrie, maystry, mastery, FaPrin. A 169, 399, Orl. xiii:4.

for the maistrie, MaReg. 149*, Dial. 565, Shirley I:42.

maistris, crafts, schemes, Dance 528, *see* Garl. 383.

make, mate, Orl. xix:13, 22, Garl. 1378.

makyng, composition, Walton A 39, Thebes 43, FaPrin. A 356, D 17, 28, Reproof 21,Shirley I:82.

malapertly, ill-advisedly, Epithal. 50.

male, portmanteau, Thebes 76.

malencolie, melancholy, MaReg. 301*.

malencolik, melancholic, Thebes 5, FaPrin. E 95*.

malgam, amalgam, Prohib. 50.

malgre, *s.* illwill, Ecl. 736*. *See* mawgree, Dial. 795.

maligne, to speak evil, FaPrin. G 84.

Malory. *See* Gen. Introd. pp. 34, 36.

manace, to menace, FaPrin. B 93, C 46, D 77.

maner, sort of, FaPrin. C 5.

man is, mannes, man's, Churl 247.

mansion, Thebes 11, FaPrin. A 299*.

Mantuan, Ecl. prol. 33; *see* introd. to Ecl.

Manuscripts: a) in lists.—Of Walton, p. 41; of Hoccleve, p. 57; of the Churl and Bird, p. 103; of Horns Away, p. 111; of Bycorne, p. 114; of the Siege of Thebes, p. 119; of the Dance Macabre, p. 125; of the French Dance Macabre, pp. 426-7; of the Fall of Princes, pp. 155-6; of the Libel of English Policy, p. 240 footnote; of Orléans, p. 217; of the Compend of Alchemy, p. 252.

b) singly.—Aberystwyth of Ripley, p. 253; Adds. 29729 (Stow) of Burgh and of Shirley II, p. 194; Arundel 38 of Hoccleve, p. 74; Arundel 119 of Thebes, p. 120; Bibl. nat., Paris, of Orléans, p. 217; Cotton Vitellius E x of Skelton, p. 342; Egerton 2402 of Cavendish, p. 369; Fairfax 16 of the Reproof and of the Lover's Mass, p. 461; Harley 542 of London Lickpenny, p. 237; Harley 682 of the Orléans translations, p. 217; Harley 1766 of the Fall of Princes, p. 156; Harley 2255 of the Letter to Gloucester and of Horns Away p. 79; Harley 4011 of the Libel, p. 478; Huntington 111 and Huntington 744 of Hoccleve, pp. 60, 57; Lansdowne 204 of Hardyng, p. 233; the Lille MS of the Dance Macabre, p. 426; Lincoln Cathedral and Longleat 258 of the Churl and Bird, pp. 103-04; Royal 16 F ii of Orleans, p. 217; Royal 18 A xiii of Walton, p. 41; Royal 18 A xv of Morley, p..391; Royal 18 D iv and D v of the Fall of Princes, p. 156; Selden *supra* 53 of the Dance Macabre and of Hoccleve's Dialogue, p. 124; Trinity College Cambridge R 3, 20 (Shirley) of Bycorne, of the Epithalamium, and of Shirley I, p. 79; Trinity College Cambridge R 3, 21 of the Court of Sapience, p. 259; Wentworth Wodehouse of Palladius, p. 202.

mapely, maple, Garl. 1344.

Mapheus Vegius, *see* p. 391.

marce, March, Hardyng 3.

March Hare, Garl. 626*.

marchaundye, merchandise, Libel 396, 456, 492, 509.

Marcus, i.e., M. Antoninus Pius, Morley 155.

marcyalte, martial prowess, Nevill 837.

marcyan, Martianus Capella, Burgh 20*.

margarete, gem, Churl 253.
margent, margin, Garl. 1135.
maris, Mary's, Lickp. 5, 44.
markesyte, Prohib. 41*.
Maro, Virgil, Garl. 1058.
marrius, Caius Marius, FaPrin. G 260.
marte, *error for* arte? Prohib. 89*.
martes, marts, Libel 518.
martys, of Mars, Epithal. 155.
marvelist, marvellous? Burgh 17*.
mas, substance, Ripley 43, 50.
masid, bewildered, Garl. 266, 626, 813.
mastris, works of skill or power, Garl. 383. *See*
    maistris.
mateeris, matters, Dial. 497, etc., FaPrin. G
    166, K 22, 24.
matriculate, enrolled, associated, Garl. 1254.
mattes, mates, Cavend. 1188.
maugre, mawgree, illwill, Dial. 795; —on
    pain of (losing), Churl 143; —in spite of, Dance
    15, 537, FaPrin. E 74. *See* malgre.
maundement, command, Walton A 190.
Mawdelayne day, St. Mary Magdalen's day,
    July 22, Ha dyng 57.
Maximian, Garl. 360*.
may as infinitive, *see* Dance 306*.
may, am able, Ecl. 388.
May-days, *see* Orleans xvii.
mayne, *see* meyne.
mayne land, i.e., Alemannia, Germany, Garl.
    497.
mayntenans, *s.* support, Garl. 193*, 1111.
mayster, master, Shirley I:49*, Ship 13810.
    See MaReg. 177, 201.
meade, meed, Cavend. 1353, Morley 92.
mean, medium, Cavend. 5, 14.
I mean, *see* note FaPrin. D 8.
measure, *see* note FaPrin. B 108. *See* order.
meated, meted, measured, Ship 6956.
Mecenas, Maecenas, Ecl. 410, 417.
med, meed, reward, Lickp. 126.
meddelyd, mingled, Garl. 295, 1349. *See* med-
    lid.
mede, meed, Walton A 238, E 85, 107, Lickp.
    94, Hawes 4251, 4423, Nevill dial. 35.
medlid, mingled, FaPrin. E 94. *See* med-
    delyd.
medoes, meadows, Ecl. 759.
Medusa, FaPrin. C 94, D 63.
meenys, means, FaPrin. G 96.
meest, most, greatest, Pallad. 24.
meet, measurement, Walton A 314; —a. suit-
    able, Ecl. prol. 87, 105. *See* mete.
meeued, moved, MaReg. 333.
megare, Megaera, one of the Furies, Walton
    A 61.
meigne, meynee, group of attendants, Wal-
    ton A 381.
Mel yus, Hawes 163 ff.*.
mell, take part, encounter, Ecl. 386, 442, 520,
    934, Garl. 1440.
him melle, concern himself, Walton B 29*.
Melpomene, Ecl. prol. 117.

melwell, cod, Lickp. 87.
memorial, memory, Dance 18; —remembrance,
    FaPrin. A 64; —in memory? Hawes 193, 705.
memory, memorial? Garl. 955.
memoyre, memory, Thebes 45, FaPrin. A 149,
    D 24.
men, to mean, Burgh 45.
mende, meant, Walton A 334.
mendycitie, low origin? Cavend. 91. NED
    "beggary".
mene reule, rule of moderation, MaReg. 352.
    See measure.
menged, mingled Libel 100, 107.
mengith, mingles, Garl.345.
menstru, solvent, Ripley *passim*.
menstruous, monstrous, Walton E 93.
mentayne, to maintain, Ship 524, 538.
mental eye, *see* note Dial. 640. *See* inwarde
    siht.
in ther menynge, by their intention, Shirley
    II:102.
merce, mercy, Orl. xvii:33.
mercerye, merchandise, Libel 263, 500.
Mercury, FaPrin. C 78, D 66*, Ecl. 259, 263,
    342, etc., Garl. 810.
Mercy belongs with Beauty. *See* Bycorne 88
    and note.
mercyall, martial, Garl. 347, 1271.
merely, merrily, Churl 97, 144, Hawes 4447,
    Garl. 1349.
meritory, deserved, Garl. 429.
merour, mirror, FaPrin. A 159, G 179*, 216*,
    227. *See* Dance 49. *See* myrrour.
merueiled, marvelled, Walton A 378.
meschief, misfortune, Walton A 158, etc., Ma-
    Reg. 53, FaPrin. B 71, H 1. *See* myschief.
mesour, measure, moderation, FaPrin. B 108*,
    Nevill 216, Ship 491.
mest, must, Walton A 135.
met, *a.* meet, suitable, Cavend. 172.
mete, to meet, Walton A 257, ?Lickp. 87; —a.
    suitable, Ship 501, 502, Ecl. 1126.
metely, fairly, Garl. 499.
metrifyde, made in metre, Garl. 1349, 1431.
mette, met, FaPrin. G 242, Orl. xviii:3; —a.
    meet, fitting, FaPrin. A 454.
me mette, I dreamed, Orl. xvii:3.
was mette, met, Walton A 391.
meueth, moves, Walton E 155.
meuyd, disturbed, Dial. 807; —suggested, Re-
    proof 58.
meuyng, moving, FaPrin. C 82, Orl. ix:2.
mewe, place of confinement, Cavend. 1276.
meynee, group of attendants, subjects, Walton
    A 130, MaReg. 202, Libel 226. *See* meigne.
meynt, mixed, LettGlouc. 55.
miche, much, Epithal. 198.
mid, amid, FaPrin. G 229.
Midas, Ecl. 660, 1155.
Minalcas, speaker in Barclay's Eclogue iv.
Minerva, shield of, Ecl. 448*. *See* Ship 20,
    Ecl. 912, Garl. 808, 1371.
minishe, to diminish, Ecl. 350.

ministrith, administers, Dial. 623.

mirror, MaReg. 330, Dance 31, 534, 637, Fa-Prin. A 159, G 179*, Ship 85*, Cavend. 170, 1177.

mirry, merry, Garl. 702, 988, 1001.

mis, amiss, Bedford 18.

mo, moo, more, many.

moch, much.

mocioun, urging, impulse, Dance 26, 356, Fa-Prin. G 274.

Molins, Anne, Orl. vi*.

momme, a mumble, Lickp. 31. *See* Garl. 1096.

monastic, Pallad. 78*.

mone, moon, month, Pallad. B 8, C 2.

Monster, *see* note Ship 27.

moordre, etc., murder, FaPrin. C 4, E 49, F 1, etc.

moose, moss, Garl. 23.

moot, mot, must, may.

moralise, to interpret, Hawes 752, cp. 1117.

more, greater, Ship 6976.

mornyng, mourning, Walton A 252, 297, Lett-Glouc. 5, Cavend. 66.

morowe gray, *see* note Hawes 97.

Morpheus, Cavend. 1242, 1422.

mortalite, death, Libel 13. Earlier than first case NED?

mortail, mortall, death-dealing, Dance 460, FaPrin. A 5, E 7, G 247.

mortified, injured fatally, caused the death of, MaReg. 212.

Moryans, Moors, Ship 6970.

Moses' horns, Garl. 1348*.

moost, must, Walton A 5, etc., Garl. 172, 796, 1070, etc.

moste, *v.* might, Walton A 177; —*a.* greatest, FaPrin. G 11, Orl. ix:25.

mote, must.

motli, Burgh 23*.

Mottoes. *See* Epithal. 112, 161*, Ship 515*.

motyve, Garl. 114*.

mought, *v.* might, Shirley II:63.

mout, to moult, Ecl. 59.

mouth he hath, FaPrin. B 50*.

mowe, may, Walton E 4, 38, MaReg. 148, Orl. xiii:28.

mowght, might, Lickp. 24.

mowte, *v.* might, Garl. 425.

much, great, Shirley II:37.

multiplye, Libel 538*.

mummyng, a slight thing, Garl. 200.

murmur, Garl. 270*.

murmyng, *error for* **murnyng,** mourning, Garl. 344. *See* 295.

muse, to ponder, Orl. xxiii:6, Hardyng 17, Hawes 109, 268, 303, Nevill 875, Ship 522, Ecl. prol. 72, Garl. 8, Morley 18; —*s.* meditation? Garl. 295; —*s.* opening in a fence or thicket made by small animals, Garl. 1351.

Muses not invoked, Walton A 44*, Ecl. prol. 117, Ecl. 755.

mvm, *See* **momme.**

mvt, must, may, FaPrin. B 14, etc., Prohib. 24.

myche, much.

mykell, much, Prohib. 76.

hath mynd, remember, Libel 103.

myleyne, Milan, Walton A 207.

myne, to penetrate, Walton B 31, FaPrin. C 125.

myner, Prohib. 90, 93; *see* **mynerue.**

mynerue, Prohib. 89*.

mynnyssheth, diminishes, Libel 391.

myrrour, Ship 85*. *See* **mirror.**

myry, miry, Garl. 23; —**myreth,** gets into the mire, MaReg. 355.

mys, amiss, Pallad. 18.

mys apparayle, improper apparel, Ship 580.

myschief, misfortune, FaPrin. B 161, G 161, H 1, Orl. xxi:7, Libel 24, etc. *See* **meschief.**

myschief, misfortune, FaPrin. B 161, Orl. xxi:7, Libel 24, etc. *See* **meschief.**

at myscheef, wretchedly, FaPrin. F 21, G 124.

myschevous, wretched, FaPrin. E 82.

mysse, amiss, Shirley I:71.

myst, must, Nevill 194.

myswent, gone astray, Orl. xviii:26.

myttes, mites, Prohib. 39.

—n in singular of verb, Orl. xxiii:5.

na, no, Shirley I:34.

nad, ne had, had not, Orl. xv:10.

Name, request for, *see* note Thebes 160, Hawes 129.

namelych, namely, Shirley I:59.

napuls, Naples, Garl. 495.

Narrative method. *See* FaPrin. A 92 ff. *See* Gen. Introd. p. 27 ff.

narwe, narrow, Walton A 213, Roundel 3.

nas, ne was, was not, Dial. 761, etc.

Naso, Ovid, Burgh 17.

naue, ne have, have not, Orl. xii:5, xvii:27.

Nauern, Navarre, Garl. 495*.

ne, nor, not.

neaver, never, Prohib. 28, 78.

nededes, needs, Garl. 1401.

nedes, necessarily, Libel 146.

neigh, near, Walton A 19, 377; —to draw near, *ibid.*, 385.

nenpayr, ne enpair, do not impair, Shirley II:68.

neodful, needful, Epithal. 188.

nept, catnip, Garl. 966.

ner, nor, Churl 175, 198, 240, 245, 307, Epithal. 24.

nere, ne were, were not, Dance 156.

nere, near, Walton A 385; —nearer, Hawes 302, Ecl. 105, Cavend. 1382.

Nero, Walton A 89*, Morley 151.

netheles, nevertheless, Lickp. 11.

neven, to name, tell, Burgh 33.

nevewe, nephew, FaPrin. F 3.

newe fonde londe, Newfoundland, Ship 6969*.

of newe, anew, recently, Dance 591, FaPrin. H 13.

newous, annoying, *see* Orl. xix: 8, 16, and the French of the Paris MS.

newtriall, neutral, Prohib. 88*.

nexst, next, so spelt by Shirley.

ney, neygh, nigh, near, Walton A 29, 267, 346;
  —nearly, Walton D 63.
nichil habet, LettGlouc. 52*.
nifles, Libel 341*.
nightirtale, night-time, MaReg. 306.
nill, ne will, will not, Shirley II:43, Pallad. 56.
Nine Orders, FaPrin. C 69*.
Nine Worthies, Epithal. 134*.
nis, ne is, is not.
nobles, gold coins, Libel 34*, 44, 408, Shirley
  I:86, II:40;—members of the nobility, Cavend. 1399.   *See* LettGlouc. 17*.
nobles, nobleness, excellence, FaPrin. A 425,
  C 13, 55, 74, D 86, E 88, G 53, 243, Hawes
  4420, Ship 8508, Cavend. 1145.
nobleye, nobility, Bedford 26.
noght, not.
noght for thye, not forthi, nevertheless, Walton A 31, E 19, 47.
noie, to annoy, injure, FaPrin. D 83.
nold, ne wold, would not, Walton A 179, etc.
nolle, the noddle, top of the head, Thebes 32.
nomo, no more, Orl. viii:7.
nons, nonys, in phrase **for the nonys,** Garl.
  267*, Prohib. 63, Cavend. 216, 225.
noot, *see* **not.**
nore, nor, Ship 8503.
note, not, ne wot, know not, MaReg. 329, Dial.
  619, Thebes 68, Dance 81, Shirley I:67, Orl.
  xviii:14.
nother, nor, Prohib. 35.
notty, heady, foaming, Thebes 110. Only citation NED of this variant of **nappy, noppy.**
notyd, marked, Mass 149.
nouelrie, novelty, MaReg. 38.
nought, not, Shirley I:4, Libel 110.
noumbre, number, FaPrin. D 12.
nouthir, neither, Dance 209, etc., Epithal. 34,
  Mass 34, 149, Ship 116.
noverca, *see under* **stepmother,** FaPrin. D 30*.
"Now," etc., *see* note FaPrin. C 88.
as nowe, at once, Dial. 621.
nowghtty pakkis, Garl. 188*.
nowrd, north, Lickp. 29.
noye, to annoy, Libel 553.
noyous, annoying, wearisome, Orl. xviii:1, xix:
  24, 28*, Morley 26.
noyse, fame, publicity, FaPrin. B 93, 119; —
  to make public, Nevill 73.
Numydy, Numidia, on the north coast of Africa,
  Ship 6970.
nuwe, new, Epithal. 60.
of nuwe, recently, Bycorne 113.
nyce, foolish, stupid, MaReg. 204, Dance 389.
nycetee, stupidity, folly, MaReg. 45, 404, Nevill dial. 31.
nyen, nine, Epithal. 134.
ny3, nigh, near, Thebes 93.
a nyht, at night, FaPrin. G 237.
nys, ne is, is not, Dance 196, Orl. xvi:8, etc.,
  xxi:1.
Nysus, *for* **Nilus,** the Nile, Hawes 338.
nyw, new, Orl. vii:10.

o, a, Walton C 36, etc.
o, on, oo, oone, one, Walton E 157, Churl 204,
  217, 346, Dance 56, 160, 176, 226, 400, 585,
  Thebes 60, 67, FaPrin. A 409, 442, B 35, E 72,
  F 11, 20, 27, Reproof 14, Orl. viii:10, xiii:22,
  Prohib. 17, 64, 96, 100, Garl. 90.   *See* **oon.**
obeisaunce, obedience, FaPrin. E 65, 93, Orl.
  viii:6, Libel 165, Garl. 820, Cavend. 1345.
obeyand, obeying, Hardyng 6.
oblacion, voluntary offering, Dance 532.
obscure, difficult to understand, Hawes 663*,
  753;—dark, Ship 69, Cavend. 23;—mean?
  Ship 606. NED has this sense only for persons.
obtundythe, dulls, overpowers, Ripley 2.
occupy, to use, Ship 252*.
ociosite, idleness, Cavend. 47; *see* note *ibid.*,
  24-30.
Octavian, FaPrin. C 19, F, Cavend. epit. 32.
oder, other, Nevill 214.
odible, odious, FaPrin. G 316.
of, off, FaPrin. D 68, G 301, 320, Mass 157, Prohib. 38, Hawes 4352, Cavend. 1294.
off, of, Epithal. 38, FaPrin. A 44, 463, etc., H 11,
  13, 25, 26, 33, 34, Reproof 20, Ripley 36, Prohib. 42.
off newe, newly, recently, FaPrin. H 13.
ofte sone, eftsoons, afterward, Libel 413.
of tymes, ofttimes, Orl. i:11, iv A:5, cp. B 4.
Oldcastle, Hardyng 8*.
oliphaunt, elephant, Garl. 102.
Omer, Omerus, Homer, FaPrin. K3,16, Burgh
  16; *see* Garl. 329.
on, *see* **o.**
after one, on one pattern, Ecl. 102.
onely, only.
all onely, only, Hawes 1347.
ones, ons, onys, oonis, once, Dance 20, Lickp.
  111, FaPrin. A 327, B 42, D 14, Orl. vi:6, 8,
  xiii:2, Libel 136, 143, Garl. 269, 282, 1447,
  1466, Cavend. 146, 237, Morley 88.
onipotent, omnipotent, Ship 466.
onlefull, unlawful, Cavend. 1325, 1333.
on lyue, alive, Shirley II:85.
onocentauris, ass-men, Garl. 1261.
onto, unto, Pallad. 22.
ontwyne, ontwynned, to untwine, etc., i.e.,
  to terminate, FaPrin. C 55, Cavend. 1291.
onworthe, unworthy, Cavend. 50.
onys, *see* **ones.**
oo, Oh! FaPrin. E 40, 48.
oon, one, Walton A 174, 179, FaPrin. G 234,
  291.   *See* **o.**
euer in oone, forever, Dance 3.
oon the, one of the, Walton A 174*, Epithal.
  123*, FaPrin. E 90.
oonli, only.
oost, host, Dance 160;—a crowd, Orl. xix:10.
opon, upon, Pallad. 21.
opposelle, Garl. 114*.
Opposites. *See* note Garl. 1358.   *See* p. 164.
or, ere, Walton E 30, MaReg. 29, 226, 292, 293,
  376, 444, Dial. 575, 648, 652, 793, Dance 226,
  231, 440, FaPrin. A 286, 301, Mass 192, Shir-

ley II:3, 67, Orl. xxii:12, Hawes 746, Nevill 35, Ecl. prol. 30, 52, Ecl. 812, 1143, Garl. 525, Cavend. 171, 191, 215, Morley 112.

Orace, Horace, Burgh 20, Ecl. prol. 85, Garl. 352.

orbicular, *s.* circuit, orbit, Garl. 4.

order, in the phrase "by ordre", *see* Shirley I:26*, Roundel 3*; cp. Morley 209.

Orders Nine, *see* Nine.

ordeynyng, preparation, Hawes 4406.

ordreur, order, Hardyng 124.

ore, oar, Ship 82.

orient, Eastern, Garl. 485, 932.

orisouns, orations, FaPrin. G 184, 224.

Orleans and Anne Molins, Orl. vi.

Orlience, Orleans, Hardyng 85. *See* pp. 221 ff., for texts of Orleans; *see* Pallad. 60 and note.

orloger, timekeeper, Thebes 122.

ormogenes, Hermogenes, Burgh 10*.

orpement, Prohib. 24*.

Orpheus, *see* Walton D; *see* Garl. 272.

ortagrafyure, orthography, Shirley II:70.

osay, Libel 132*.

o syde, aside, Orl. viii:11.

other, or, Churl 151. For rime on "other" *see* FaPrin. G 34-35*.

others, udders, Ecl. 148.

othre, others, FaPrin. G 88.

oueral, everywhere, Pallad. 63, Ship 107.

ouerblowe, passed like a wind, Walton C 23.

ouercharge, to overload, Ship 77.

ouergo, to outstrip, Nevill 45.

ouersayne, guilty of an oversight, Churl 269.

ouerthwart, contrary, Garl. 307.

ought, is owing to, Ecl. 850.

ougly, ugly, Dance 32.

Ouid, Ouyd, Ovid, FaPrin. A 324, K 18, Nevill 2, Nevill envoy 12, Garl. 93, 333.

oure, hour, Walton A 284, Dance 619, Reproof 10.

Out! an ejaculation, Walton A 277.

oute, aught, Walton A 117.

outerage, outrage, Walton B 3.

with outhyn, without, Orl. vii:9.

outher, or, FaPrin. G 201, Mass 158; —either, Ship 76, 89, 237.

outraie, to surpass, defeat, Bycorne 123, FaPrin. G 128, Garl. 156.

outrarious, outrageous, FaPrin. C 4, 9.

ower, our, Prohib. 10, 90, 91.

owght, out, Garl. 153, 221, 735.

Oxenford, Oxford, Pallad. 89.

oynons, onions, Libel 522.

pace, to pass, Dance 72, 656, FaPrin. H 5.

a pace, briskly, Hawes 20, Cavend. 188.

Padding Phrases, *see* pp. 88-89.

paiauntis, pageants, Garl. 1350.

pakkis, Garl. 189*.

Palamydes, Mass 185*.

palen, to make pale, Mass 84.

pall, a rich cloth, a canopy, Ecl. 444, Garl. 474.

Pallas, Hawes 170, Ship 20*, 102, Garl. 284 and *passim.*

pamflete, pamphlet, Hawes 1300. *See* Churl 35, Garl. 1169.

Pandarus, Garl. 856.

pantere, a swoop-net, Churl 77, etc.;—a clerk of the pantry, Hawes 423.

papelay, popingay, a parrot, Roundel 3.

paradise to see, etc., *see* note Epithal. 99.

parage, rank, lineage, Dance 8.

par cas, perchance, for example, Dance 411, FaPrin. G 284 (note the tautology).

parcel, a little, partly, Thebes 124, FaPrin. D 97.

parde, par Dieu, MaReg. 363, Dial.509,Thebes 125, Reproof 67, Orl. xvii:17, Ecl. 91, 309, 461, Garl. 95, 1209, Cavend. 172, 257. *See* Morley 77, 181.

paregall, fully equal, Garl. 883.

parelouse, perilous, Walton A 87, B 32.

parfit, parfyte, perfect, complete, FaPrin. K 26, Burgh 9, Hawes dedic. 31, Ecl. prol. 67, 78, etc.

parfourm, to complete, Epithal. 120, FaPrin. D 49. *See* **performe.**

Paris, son of Priam, Epithal. 135, Ecl. 1109, Morley 217.

parker, park-keeper, Garl. 1353.

Parnassus, *see* note Walton A 58. *See* Cavend 69. *See* **pernaso.**

parody, term of life, FaPrin. E 42*, 83.

parseyve, to perceive, Orl. xx:6.

what part, wherever, Orl. xvii:22.

parten, to divide, Orl. xix:9.

partes, profits, Libel 513.

partie, a part, i.e., geographical division, FaPrin. G 91;—part, side, Churl 204, FaPrin. A 315, C 27, G 181, Burgh 12, Mass 168, 188, Orl. xii:29, xvii:6; —direction, Dance 161;— party, case, FaPrin. G 167, ?271; —particolored, Ship 8483;—resistance, head against, Dial. 691.

partyng, departure, Dance 215.

Pasiphae, *see* Garl. 827*, 910*, 1026*.

passyng well, more than well, Orl. xviii:7, etc. *See* Dance 251.

passyoun, martyrdom, Shirley I:35.

past, pastry, Churl 151.

past not, etc., cared not, Cavend. 102, 128, 159.

pasture, food, feeding-place, Bycorne 12, 17, 83, Churl 123*, Thebes 101, 104.

pate, top of the head, Cavend. 1186*.

patere, to patter, repeat the paternoster rapidly, murmur rapidly, Thebes 163.

patin, Ecl. 448*.

Patronage. *See* Gen. Introd. pp. 6, 15, 35; *see* under **Gloucester.** *See* p. 95.

paunflete, pamphlet, Churl 35. *See* Hawes 1300, Garl. 1169.

pautner, a wallet, scrip, Ecl. 7.

Pauye, Pavia, FaPrin. H 2.

pawkener, *or* **pautner,** Prohib. 75.

paye, pleasure, Walton A 201, 340, Horns 46, Shirley II:62;—*v.* to please, Walton B 2.

payne, effort, Hawes 146, 441. *See* **cure** in 117.

paynfull, Cavend. epitaph 4.
paynyms, pagans, Hawes 191.
payse, to weigh, Walton C 12.   *See* peyse.
peakes, lofty headgear, Ship 555.   *See* introd.
   to Horns Away.
peare, *s.* peer, Hawes 220.   *See* pere.
Pegase, Pegasus, FaPrin. D 16*, Hawes 123,
   See Ecl. 881.
pegases, of Pegasus, Burgh 2.
peise, to weigh, Bedford 23.
peisid, weighed, FaPrin. E 13, F 27.
peisith, *v. imper.*, weigh, FaPrin. C 122.
pele, appeal, Dance 365.
pen, *see* quaking pen.
pencyfe, pensive, Nevill 43.
Penelope, wife of Ulysses, Horns 27, Dance
   452*, Mass 182, Garl. 883.
pennes, feathers, Walton E 121.
penselle, Garl. 1075*.
pentice, penthouse, Roundel 3*.
perambulat, circuitous, Hawes 684.
perambulucion, circumlocution, Hawes 4431.
Percius, Perseus, Hawes 125; —Persius, Garl.
   338.   *See* Burgh 20.
Percy, Persia, Ecl. 1106.
perdurable, of enduring strength, Walton A 322,
   Hawes 30.
perdye, *see* parde.
pere, *s.* peer, Hawes 339, 1328, Shirley I:30.   *See*
   peare.
perelus, perilous, Walton A 136, perlious,
   Churl 181.
performe, to complete, Mass 170, Ship 7002.
   See parforme.
pernaso, Parnassus, FaPrin. A 242, 458, D 13,
   G 10, K 52, Burgh 1; *see* Nevill 22.
perre, perry, Churl 259*, Horns 9.
Pers de Mounte, Pallad. 102-104*.
persaunt, keen, piercing, Burgh 46 (adj. used as
   subst?).
personage, parsonage, Dance 321.
peruerse, adverse, FaPrin. A 259.
pery, blast of wind, Hawes 68, 1254.
pescods, peascods, Lickp. 67.
pese, to be in peace, Orl. xiii:2.
Pestilence, *see* note Cavend. 119; *see* Dance 429.
pet, a breaking of wind, Ecl. 694.   Only citation NED.
Peter's cope, Ecl. 447*, 1141.
Petrarch.   *See* FaPrin. A 257, Ecl. prol. 35,
   Garl. 380.   *See* Burgh 13.
Petrake, FaPrin. A 257*, K 37.
peuishe, peevish, silly, stupid, Garl. 266, 620,
   see 631.
peyce, weight, Churl 314.
peyse, weight? piece? Libel 398; —to weigh,
   Churl 312.
peysith, to weigh, Churl 234, 318.   *See* peisid.
peysyble, peaceable, Bycorne 107.
Phebus passing the stars, *see* Sun.
Phedra, Morley 176; *see* note Garl. 910.
Philip Sparrow, *see* note Garl. 1227.
Philologie, FaPrin. D 66*, *see* Epithal. 179*.
phisionomye, physiognomy, Pallad. 87*.

phitones, Pythoness, Garl. 1311*.
Phocion, Cavend, epitaph 21.
Phylogeny, *error for* Philology, Epithal. 179*.
picture, image, Hawes 50, 70.
Pierides, FaPrin. D 63*, Garl. 674.
pietous, merciful, Ripley 5.
pieusaunce, puissance, Cavend. 1343.
pieusaunt, puissant, Cavend. epitaph 28.
pieuselles, pucelles, maidens, Cavend. 1400.
   See pucell.
pike, Pallad. 50*.
piked, picked, Thebes 56.
pikoys, pickaxe, Dance 84, 557.
pilche, a leather or coarse wool outer garment,
   Ecl. 210, 384.
piler, pillar, MaReg. 8.
pillion, a hat or cap, Ecl. 343.   Lat. *pilleus*.
pillours, robbers, Libel 163.
pine, pain, Garl. 1345.   *See* pyne.
piplyng, gently moving, Garl. 670*,   First case
   NED.
Pirrus, Ecl. 1103*, Cavend. epitaph 4.
pirus, Burgh 3*.
Pisandros, Garl. 383.
Pistoye, Pistoja, FaPrin. G 114.
Pithagoras, Ecl. 479*.
pitous, piteous, FaPrin. F 22, etc
pithth, pith, essence, strength, spirit, Epithal.
   30.
plage, region, Ship 6959.
platly, plainly, Dance 641, Thebes 142*.   *See*
   pleynly.
Plato, FaPrin. G 173-182*, Garl. 126, Cavend.
   epitaph 13.
Plautus, Garl. 354.
playn, smooth, Churl 50, 137, Hawes 45, 269;
   —to complain, Churl 245, 283, FaPrin. G 159.
plees, pleas, Ship 206.
plenerly, fully, Walton E 114, Garl. 6.
plentyuouse, abundant, Hardyng 35.
plesere, pleasure, Orl. xiv:15.
plete, etc., to plead a cause, to talk, Dance 466,
   FaPrin. G 156, 162, Orl. xix:11.
pleye, to make sport, Mass 80.
pleyne, to complain, Roundel 1; —*a.* full, Pallad. 21, Orl. xvi:18.   *See* playn.
pleynly, plainly, Thebes 71, 138.   *See* platly.
pleyntiff, Mass 146.
pleyntis, complaints, Roundel 2, FaPrin. G 199.
pliades, the Pleiades, Garl. 691.
Plinius, Pliny, Ship 6995*.
plummet, a pencil? Pallad. A 3*.   First case
   NED 1634.
plummouth, Plymouth, Garl. 513.
plumpe, a group, Garl. 258.
Plutarch, Garl. 380.
Pluto, Garl. 1289, Morley 239.
pockes, pox, venereal disease, Ship 593.
poecy, poetry, Ecl. 642.
Poet, function of, *see* note Ship 134.
Poggeus, Poggio, Garl. 373*.
points, Libel 57*.
poise, poesy, Burgh 39.
poites, poets, Churl 29.

pokok, peacock, Garl. 103.
Polexemes, *see* **Polyceene,** Morley 198.
Policius, FaPrin. G 140*.
Policrates, Ecl. 1096*.
poliphemus, Polyphemus, FaPrin. D 20.
Politic, Pallad. 78*.
pollers, extortioners, Ship 30, 126.
Polyceene, Polyxena, Horns 28*, Dance 451, Epithal. 72, Mass 182, Garl. 855*. *See* Morley 198.
pomaunder, Garl. 1007*.
pompe, Ship 156*.
Pompeie, Pompey, Epithal. 153, FaPrin. G 189, 268, Ecl. 1083, Cavend. epitaph 28.
ponyschement, punishment, Walton E 88.
pope holy, Garl. 606*.
poperyng, Popering, Libel 249*, 252.
popingay, parrot, Churl 359*, Hawes 4225. *See* **papelay.**
por, poor, Mass 146.
poraill, poor people, FaPrin. H 12.
porcyus, Persius, Burgh 20. *See* **Percius.**
porisshly, peeringly, with half-shut eyes, Garl. 620.
porpos, porpoise, Ecl. 213.
port, bearing, Dance 167.
port salu, safe haven, To Somer 22, Garl. 541.
portismouth, Portsmouth, Garl. 513.
portoos, Thebes 162*.
portyngale, Portugal, Garl. 494.
possede, to possess, Dance 126, 132.
posty, pouste, power, Garl. 1298.
potshorde, fragment of a broken earthen pot, Garl. 1189.
pouer, power, Walton A 85.
pouert, poverty, Walton A 81*.
pourveyed of, equipped with, Epithal. 124.
Powle hatchettis, Garl. 607*.
Powles, Paul's, St. Paul's, Ecl. 451*.
Powles heed, Paul's Head, a tavern sign, MaReg. 143.
poyle, Apulia, Garl. 493*.
poynt, to appoint, Garl. 420, 432, 1121; —*s.* point. *See* Libel 57*.
poysy, poetry, FaPrin. K 26.
practik, Walton A 330, 332*, Dance 427, Pallad. 76.
pratily, praty, pretty, etc., Churl 81, Orl. xxii: 10, Garl. 896, 965, 1215.
praysable, laudable, Nevill 165, 218.
prebende, Dance 313*, 326, 596.
prece, *see* **press.**
precedentes, signs, Nevill 60.
precell, to excel, Cavend. 1162.
in preciouste, as of value, Walton E 98.
preeff, proof, test, FaPrin. G 310, Libel 99; —*v.* to prove, Orl. xvi:13.
preent, print, Epithal. 30, 60.
preferre, to advance to dignity, FaPrin. A 251, 361, G 207, Cavend. 157.
premynence, preëminence, Horns 53, Hawes 124, Garl. 50, 1103.
prepence, to plan, intend, Nevill 77; —to consider, Nevill envoy 12.

preperate, prepared, Prohib. 44.
presid in a pace, hastened up, Garl. 1122.
press, put (one's self) **in,** to press forward, endeavor, Garl. 239*, 778.
prest, ready, hasty, Dial. 553, Pallad. 47, Orl. v:10, Garl. 774, Ecl. prol. 56, Cavend. 1271; —*s.* a loan, Dance 159.
pretence, assertion, reason, Garl. 801, Cavend. 1337.
pretende, to offer, Ecl. 929.
pretory, a hall or palace, Garl. 477.
preuyd, proved, Dial. 566, Reproof 60, FaPrin. E 11. *See* **prouyd.**
prevayle, to avail, Cavend. 1128, 1139.
preventid, anticipated, Garl. 428, Cavend. 145*.
Priamus, Ecl. 1107.
price, *see* **pris.**
pried, peeped, looked, Ecl. 18.
prike, FaPrin. K 28*.
prime, Thebes 124*, Dance 230*. *See* **pryme.**
prime rose, primrose, Garl. 1414.
principio, Prohib. 25*.
pris, prys, highest esteem, Thebes 46, Burgh 24, Shirley I:33, Lickp. 66.
prise, prisse, value, quality, Walton A 108, Churl 252, FaPrin. A 294, 409.
priuate, deprived of, Ecl. 708.
priuee, privately, MaReg. 270.
probable, evident, Hawes 1266.
probacion, experience, proof, Dial. 735, Libel 381, Ship 179.
probate, test, proof, Hawes 697; —interpretation, Garl. 368.
procede, to begin legal process, Lickp. 6.
proces, ordered material, Garl. 28; —narrative or argumentative presentation, Dance 465, FaPrin. A 127, 453, B 160, G 1, K 13, Garl. 803, 1077.
bi processe, in the course of events, FaPrin. B 7, etc.
Procession as a motif, *see* p. 126, 151.
profe, proof, Nevill 25.
proferryng, i.e., preferring, FaPrin. C 25.
proiecte, projected, Ripley 171.
projection, Ripley 190*.
prolle, to prowl, seek advantage from, Dial. 744.
Prologue, *see* Walton 1*.
promocioune, advocacy, Garl. 71.
promotyve, promotion, Garl. 116.
pronostik, prognostic, FaPrin. G 176.
Pronunciation, FaPrin. G 193*.
prop, pole, Garl. 1307.
proper, propre, pretty, Garl. 968, 1359, 1414; —one's own, Hawes 311.
Propertius, Garl. 383.
prophitroles, ? Ecl. 405*.
proplexyte, perplexity, Garl. 1336.
Prose in this volume, *see* Epistle of Lover's Mass, *see* dedic. letter of Morley.
Proserpine, FaPrin. C 90.
prospeccyon, a view, Nevill 116.
Protheus, Proteus, Ecl. 887.

prothonotary, protonotary, a principal notary or chief clerk, Garl. 432.

prouect, to carry forward, send forward, Pallad. 71. NED first 1652.

proueth, tests, Nevill 162. *See* Prohib. 36.

prouyng, testing, Ecl. prol. 29.

prouision, foresight, Ecl. 866.

proute, proud, Walton C 9*.

Proverbs, *see* note Thebes 51.

prow, advantage, Bycorne 113, Dance 557.

pryce, value, Ripley 168. *See* pris.

pryme, prime, Garl. 525. *See* prime.

pryncypalyte, supremacy, Nevill 838.

pryuely, privately, Orl. iv A:5, B:4.

Ptolemy, *see* Tholomeus.

publius, Libel 479*.

pucell, damsel, Hawes *passim. See* pieusell.

pulcritude, beauty, Hawes 24.

pullisshe, to polish, Garl. 83, 421, 800.

Punctuation, *see* Preface; *see* Ecl. prol introd.

punsshe, to punish, FaPrin. A 198, F 6, G 127.

purpartye, proportion or share, FaPrin. E 80.

purpos, the point, Churl 372.

Purpose in writing. *See* Hawes 1313*, Ship 134-7*, Cavend. 24-30*.

purpure, purple, Walton B 9.

purseuantis, pursuivants, messengers, Garl. 492*.

pursue, to persecute, Walton A 107, 167; —to pursue, Walton E 16.

purueyaunce, management, foresight, Dance 405, FaPrin. E 86, G 110, Hawes 1260.

pusaunce, power, Libel 218, 537, Hawes 4322.

pusaunt, puissant, Garl. 50.

put back, thwart, Mass 35.

put case, to raise the question of, Reproof 57.

putrefaccyon, putrefaction, Ripley 194, *see* 190*.

putryfye, to putrefy, Prohib. 96, *see* 190*.

pycche, to set, Walton E 121.

pye, magpie, Hawes 1111.

pyke, to pick, Garl. 1189.

pykers, thieves, Ship 126.

pyl, pile, the obverse of a coin, LettGlouc. 59.

pylled, bald, Thebes 32.

pyment, sweet wine, Walton B 8.

pynacles, Hawes 309*.

pynchid nat, raised no question, MaReg. 181.

pyne, pain, Walton E 75. *See* pine.

pynk iyde, pinkeyed, smalleyed or squint-eyed, Garl. 620.

pynned, bolted, barred, Churl 120.

pyrlynge, pirling, twisting, Garl. 780.

Pyrrus, Ecl. 1108*.

quacham, Ecl. 423. Only citation NED; no definition.

quadrant, foursquare, Nevill 121, 177.

quadriuial, Pallad. 76*.

Quaking hand or pen, LettGlouc. 4, FaPrin. B 142, D 46*, G 42.

quarter, Garl. 504*.

quayeer, quair, song or poem, Churl 379, Garl. 1484. *See* "Go little book".

qd, quod, said.

que, i.e., quadrans, a half-farthing, Ecl. prol. 14.

queint, extinguished, FaPrin. D 60. *See* qweynt.

queinte, artful? FaPrin. D 27.

quemyd, appeased, pleased, FaPrin. B 125.

quere, choir, Ship 553.

querele, quarrel, cause, Dance 83.

queste, to give tongue together, Garl. 1376.

queveryng, uncertain, FaPrin. E 96.

quik, to enliven, FaPrin. D 34; —in lifelike manner, Garl. 142, 1139; *see* 592.

Quintilian, Burgh 13, Garl. 326.

Quintus Cursus, Q. Curtius, Garl. 366.

quit, free, Dance 416.

quite, to requite, repay, Dial. 578, Dance 488, 629, FaPrin. A 290, G 308; —to bear one's self, Dance 480; —to acquit, FaPrin. A 290.

quook, quaked, shook, FaPrin. B 148.

qweynt, extinguished, blotted out, MaReg. 349.

qwynt essence, quintessence, LettGlouc. 47*.

qwyte, quit, emptyhanded, Burgh 12.

rabyll, rabble, Garl. 1279. *See* Ecl. 680.

race, to erase, Churl 301, Garl. 72. *See* rasid.

rad, etc., to read, Walton A 331, Horas 44, FaPrin. A 73, E 57, G 108, K 20, Mass 183.

rade, to remove, Pallad. 7.

ragman rollis, Garl. 1455*.

railles, Garl. 1135*.

raist, arrayest, i.e., treatest, Garl. 317.

rakil, unstable, reckless, MaReg. 83, Dial. 655.

rampyng, rampant, Hawes 4233.

rascolde, rascally, Ecl. 680, 689.

rasid, etc., to erase, Ecl. prol. 63, Garl. 137, 1445, 1455, 1533. *See* race.

raskaille, vile rabble, FaPrin. C 98.

rate, manner, Ecl. prol. 103, Garl. 1108, 1229, 1488.

rathe, hasty, soon, Walton A 268, D 62, Cavend. 150, 1184.

rather, earlier, former, Walton B 1.

ratifye, to confirm truth of, consummate? Hawes 676.

raught, reached, caught, Thebes 158, Dance 561.

raunge, range, Garl. 25. on the range, at liberty?

ray, a striped cloth, Lickp. 42*, Ship 478.

rayde, arrayed, Ship 570.

raynes, kidneys or loins Ship 514; —Rennes, Cavend. 247*.

Raysoun, Reason, Epithal. 89.

real, royal, MaReg. 430.

ream, realm, Libel 19, 174, 385.

reason, *see* resoun.

rebawdis, ribald fellows; Garl. 601.

rebuke, to repel, repulse, Ecl. 930, —s. Libel 535.

receyt, receipt, Epithal. 40.

recheles, reckless, Garl. 1360.

reclyne, to lean on, Pallad. 86.

reclus, a prisoner, LettGlouc. 59.

reconcile, to restore, FaPrin. G 262, 276.

reconusaunce, acknowledgment, Garl. 822.

recorde, to take note, FaPrin. E 104.
recounfortyd, comforted, Garl. 359.
recours, course, Walton E 145.
recule, recueil, collection of writings, Hawes 180, Garl. 1165, 1357.
recure, to recover, heal, obtain, Churl 207, 326, Dance 311*, 424, LettGlouc. 39, FaPrin. B 91, E 20, Mass 137, Nevill dial. 41.
rede, redde, etc., to advise, MaReg. 35, 86, 91, 105, 382, Dial. 719, 801, Reproof 77, Orl. xxii: 1; —advice, Churl 155, Dial. 619.
reduce, to lead back, Walton E 158, Ship 589.
redyng, Walton A 253*.
reed, read, FaPrin. G 203, 228;—advice, Ma-Reg. 108, Dial. 722.
Reference Lists:—I, to Gen. Introd., p. 38; II, to Walton, p. 41; III, to Hoccleve, p. 57; IV, to Bycorne, p. 115; V, to the Dance Macabre, p. 130; VI, to the Epithalamium, p. 145; VII, to the Reproof, p. 199; VIII, to Palladius, p. 203; IX, to the Mass, p. 210; X, to the Libel, p. 244; XI, to Hawes, p. 270; XII, to Nevill, p. 288; XIII, to Barclay, p. 298; XIV, to the Ship of Fools, p. 299; XV, to the Eclogue, p. 313; XVI, to Skelton, p. 340; XVII, to Morley, p. 385. *See* Bibliographies.
reffuce, outcast, FaPrin. B 116.
reflareth, distils, Hawes 1262. *See* Garl. 961.
refluent, back-flowing, Pallad. 12.
reformacion, correction, Garl. 145.
refrayne, to draw back, hold back, bridle, Walton A 114, MaReg. 338, Orl. xvi:21, Nevill 127, Ship 32, Ecl. 82, 90, 808.
refute, refuge, Dance 163.
regestary, registrar, Garl. 522. *See* Garl. 1119.
regraciatory, thanks, Garl. 431. NED gives Skelton only.
rehersall, mention, Garl. 1468.
reise, journey? profit? Libel 399.
rekne, rekune, to reckon.
relacions, narratives, Libel 511; *see* Hawes 231.
release, to relieve, Hawes 4346.
releef, to relieve, Orl. xxi:6.
relent, to yield, melt, Cavend. 1275. *See* Troy Book ii:5077.
reles, *s.* release, relief, Mass 109.
relucent, gleaming, Garl. 934.
relyke here, remaining heir, Cavend. 1406.
reme, realm, Hardyng 5, Garl. 742.
remedeles, without remedy, Garl. 1361.
remevyng, unstable, moving, FaPrin. C 86.
remorde, to carp at, rebuke, Garl. 86.
remue, remuwe, to remove, swerve, Epithal. 24, FaPrin. A 231.
remyse, remission, Cavend. 1160.
renett, rennet, Prohib. 57*.
renne, etc., to run, Walton B 11, D 8, MaReg. 78, Dial. 746, Nevill 140, 145, Ship 8443.
renomaunce, renown, Orl. xvi:9.
renommed, renoumyd, renowned, Horns 26, Epithal. 79, 127, FaPrin. G 67.
renoueld, renewed, Shirley I:94.
renude, renewed.

repair, a coming, frequenting, return, MaReg. 137, FaPrin. E 15, G 245;—to supply, Cavend. 1107; —a visit, Libel 61, 503; —to return, Reproof 65, Mass 81, 82.
repentine, sudden, Nevill 97.
repete, recital, Garl. 1357.
repreef, reproof, discredit, injury, Dial. 671, FaPrin. G 312.
reprehende, to reprove? Pallad. 16.
repugnaunce, opposition, Garl. 211.
reputing it for, imputing it to, Cavend. 53.
requeere, to require, FaPrin. G 199.
rerage, arrears, LettGlouc. 6.
rere warde, back entrance, Garl. 1352.
rescws, rescue, Dance 278.
resemblance, mirror, pattern, Dance 639.
reseruyd, put aside, Garl. 1168.
residewe, residue, FaPrin. D 50, etc.
Reson and Sensuality, *see* Cavend. 1348*.
resorte, to return, Churl 178, Dance 325, Fa-Prin. A 191, C 68; —*s.* visitation, Pallad. 23. *See* FaPrin. C 101.
resoun, reason, a word or saying, ?Walton E 72, FaPrin. G 17*, Garl. 10; —subject-matter, Ecl. 286, Ecl. prol. 10; —order or decorum, FaPrin. B 110, G 194;—to talk, address, Orl. xvii:4, Garl. 1101, Morley 169, (where Petrarch has *ragionar*).
respire, to recover (hope or courage), Ecl.1080.
respite, to interrupt, Walton A 252; —to hold back, FaPrin. B 101.
reste, to arrest, Dance 137, 567.
is reste, remains? Pallad. B 1.
restrayn, to hold back, Walton D 57, Libel 92.
retaylle, Cavend. 143*.
retayne, to maintain, Ecl. 222.
retenew, retinue, maintenance, Garl. 238.
retorryke, rhetoric, Shirley I:31.
retrogradaunt, retrograde, Garl. 3*, Cavend. 4.
reuerent, dignified, Walton A 305.
reuers, reverse, Dial. 735.
reule, rule, Hardyng 124. *See* **mene reule.**
reuolde, rolled or revolved, Garl. 658.
reward, to regard or look, Dance 331, Orl. xii:19; —reward? Walton B 24, Shirley II:44; —*s.* regard, Dance 331.
rewdisshe, rewde, rude, Orl. xiii:14, xvii:12.
rewe, rue, to have pity, Mass 87.
rewlyd, ruled, Orl. ix:6.
rewme, realm, Walton E 89, FaPrin. E 67. *See* **reme, ream.**
rewyn, ruin, Cavend. 1317.
Rhetorical Theory. See Colors of Rhetor Description by Order, Lists, Prologue.
riall, royal, Hardyng 40.
rialte, royalty, Dance 108.
ribaudye, ribaldry, Thebes 25.
Richard II, Hardyng 36.
Richard Hermyte, *see* FaPrin. K 27*.
riff, rife, current, Churl 372, FaPrin. G 205.
right, to make right, Pallad. 124.
now right, just now, Epithal. 158.
right wise, righteous, Ecl. 1013. *See* Dance 629.

rigorious, fierce, cruel, Hawes 166, 4237, Ecl. 1076*.

rigure, rigor, Orl. xv:15.

riht, right; —very, FaPrin. H 14;—a. direct, FaPrin. G 66.

rihtis, rites, FaPrin. C 75.

Rime on -*th, see* -**th**; of -*ft*: -*ght, see* Orl. xix.

rin, to run, Garl. 1401, 1448.

rise, rice flour, Lickp. 71.

risshes, rushes for floor coverings, Roundel 2, Lickp. 86.

Robin Hood, Ship 13874-88*, Ecl. 721, Morley dedic.

roche alom, rock alum, Libel 328.

rochis, roaches, fish, Garl. 655.

roffes, roofs, Cavend. 106*.

Rolle, Richard, *see* Richard Hermyte.

romain, Roman, FaPrin. G 157.

Romayn dedis, the Gesta Romanorum, Dial. 820*.

ronne, run, Pallad. D 1, Libel 173, Cavend. 1301.

roof described, Hawes 348-50*, Cavend. 106*.

rooff, pierced, FaPrin. B 151.

root. *See* FaPrin. A 300*.

roppys, the intestines, Thebes 115.

rosary, rosebush, Garl. 963.

rosers, rosebushes or rose-gardens, Garl. 650.

rosty, to roast, Garl. 1299.

rote, root, Garl. 1347;—**hart rote,** heart's root. —to rot, Dance 232.

rotyd, rooted, rotted? Ship 8495.

roufe, roof, Hawes 348.

rounceuall, Roncesvalles, Garl. 495.

rouncy, Thebes 166*.

round, around, Orl. xii:13.

roundel, To Somer 31, FaPrin. A 353, Shirley II:23*.

Roundels in this volume, pp. 67, 68, 211, 221-23, 231-32. *See* Note p. 466.

rounsis, Garl. 1280*.

rout, a multitude, Libel 515.

route, to snore, Thebes 110;—to assemble, Libel 222.

routhe, pity, FaPrin. H 7.

rowghte, rout, Garl. 240.

rowle, roll, Ecl. 488.

rowmes, positions, ranks, Ecl. 272, 846, 868, 1058, 1063;—place, space, Ship 101, Garl. 116, 256.

rownyd, whispered, Garl. 250.

rownyngely, in a whisper, MaReg. 172, Garl. 250.

rowthe, rough, Garl. 787.

royalme, realm, Ship 579, 6942, 6988.

rub on the gall, Garl. 97*, Cavend. 205*.

rubarbe, rhubarb, Libel 354.

rubbe, to rob, Ship 523*.

rubryke, rubric, Nevill envoy 16*.

rubyfycate, heated to redness, Prohib. 35. Only case NED.

rudesse, violence, Orl. xviii:19.

rusty, foul, Thebes 75, Ecl. 425.

ruthe, a pity, Libel 174.

ryall, ryally, royal, etc., Hardyng 7, Hawes 1286, Nevill 162, Garl. 487.

ryconyng, a reckoning, Cavend. 1235, 1417.

rygne, to reign, Hardyng 57.

rympled, wrinkled, Dance 200.

ryn, to run, Garl. 81, 196.

ryse, Lickp. 68*.

ryve, to split, Churl 282.

s as a verbal ending, Libel 158, 507, 525, Ripley 74, Prohib. 38, Nevill dial. 22, Nevill 17, 112, 145, 163, Ship 74, 208, 456, 462, 467, 582, 6958, 8507, 13823, Ecl. 474, Garl. 593, 635, 683, 716, 1211, 1526, Cavend. 40, Morley 135, 143.

saby, Sheba, Garl. 669.

sad, sadness, etc., serious, sobriety, Walton A 387, E 67, MaReg. 274, Dial. 558, Epithal. 85, FaPrin. A 71, C 24, G 198, 244, K 5, Pallad. 42, Nevill envoy 9, Ship 470, 488, 598, 13842, Garl. 201, 386, 886, 1391, 1526, Cavend. 1360; —sad, sadness, Cavend. 72, Morley 65?

safe, save, except, Dance 293, Reproof 74. *See* **sauf.**

Sails, *see* note LettGlouc. 17.

salarie, Dance 536. First case NED 1484.

salfe cundight, safe conduct, Garl. 503.

sall, salt, Prohib. 29*. *See* Notes for all the terms of this stanza.

salmes, psalms, Shirley II:28.

Salomon, Nevill 831.

salu, *see* **port salu,** Garl. 541.

salusty, Sallust, Garl. 331.

Samson, Nevill 839, Ecl. 975.

sandyvere, Prohib. 29*.

sank royall, Garl. 1430*.

satirray, Garl. 340*. Not in NED.

Saturn, Walton E 140, Thebes 3, FaPrin. C 64, Hawes 285.

sauf, save, except, FaPrin. K 14. *See* **safe.**

sauh, saugh, saw, Thebes 172.

saunce mercy, Nevill 38*.

sawe, to sow, Ship 13875.

sawh, saw, Walton, etc.

sawte, assault, Garl. 1365.

sawtry, psaltery, a stringed instrument, Lickp. 92.

say, saw, Libel 230, Garl. 623.

scamonye, Libel 352*.

scape, *s.* escape, Dance 501.

scapid, escaped, FaPrin. G 314.

scarcete, scarcity, FaPrin. D 18, 69.

schenschipe, destruction, injury, Walton A 65.

schent, injured, Walton E 86, Prohib. 18.

schold, schuld, should, Walton *passim.*

schrewes, evildoers, Walton A 88.

science, knowledge, Hawes 56, Ship 145, 243, 13807, 13836, 13877, Ecl. prol. 60, Ecl. 228, 653, Cavend. 1133, epitaph 30.

Scipioun, Scipio, FaPrin. C 10, G 218*. *See* **Cipioun.**

scissure, cutting? scissor? Ship 483.

sclaundre, slander, FaPrin. B 91, 98.

Scluse, Sluys, Libel 61*.

scole, school.

Scottish Poets, *see* Gen. Introd. p. 24-25.

scrowe, scroll, Libel. 180.

scut, rabbit, Garl. 626.
se, seen, Pallad. 82*. By error in Orl. ix:2*.
seche, seek, Dial. 658, Ripley 72, Shirley II:104, Libel 147, 363; —such, Orl. iv A:3.
sect, Cavend. 1174.
secundynes, Prohib. 59*.
see, seat, throne, Dance 14, see 66; FaPrin. A 68, 118; —sea, Ship 6973.
seek, seekly, sick, etc., Walton A 350, MaReg. 15.
seely, silly, simple, LettGlouc. 49.
seeth, sees, Dance 635; v. imper. see FaPrin. ● C 121.
seie, saw, Walton A 302; —say, Walton A 383.
seignory, lordship, Ecl. 942.
sein, to see, seen, FaPrin. D 101, G 33; —to say, Orl. xvii:33.
seist, seest, Churl 326.
were to seke, were inadequate, Garl. 877.
seknesse, sickness, Walton A 360.
selde, seelde, seldom, Walton A 328, MaReg. 73.
selle, cell, Walton E 165.
seller, cellar, Ecl. 393.
Selond, Zeeland, Libel 524.
seluen, self, Walton A 133.
seluerene, silver, FaPrin. C 67.
sely, "poor", Cavend. 74.
semachus, Symmachus, Walton A 217; see FaPrin. K 1.
semblabli, similarly, FaPrin. D 127, Ecl. 297.
semblid, assembled, Orl. xix:10.
sement, cement, Garl. 306.
sempte, seemed, FaPrin. A 431, 454.
sene, senna, Libel 354.
sene, seen, Hawes 754; —to see, Libel 499, Ecl. 115.
Senek, Seneca, FaPrin. A 253, C 24, K 5*, Ecl. 1091, Garl. 358.
senge, to sing, Nevill 195.
sengle, single, Dance 112.
sengulerli, particularly, FaPrin. A 447. See Praise of Chaucer 1968*.
sent, scent, Ecl. 114, 122.
sentence, sense, purport, Walton A 18, 32, E 18, Churl 2, 302, Thebes 54, FaPrin. A 345, 448, Shirley I:91, Nevill dial. 5, Ecl. 702, Cavend. 77, ?260; —utterance, opinion, Churl 321, Horns 15, Dance 431, FaPrin. K 5, 27; —subject, MaReg. 160.
sentencious, full of meaning, Hawes 1261, 1268.
senyng, Libel 361*.
septir, sceptre, Walton A 343.
seriaunt, sergeant, FaPrin. G 249.
serious, FaPrin. C 18*.
Serpent of Division, see p. 177.
seryously, serially, in sequence, Garl. 581. See ceriousli.
sese, to cause to cease, quench, Walton B 6.
sesyng, ceasing, Prohib. 104.
seteys, cities, Mass 162.
seth, sethen, since, Dance 99, 285, 628. See sith.

seth, v. imper. see, Orl. viii:10; —sees, FaPrin. B 122.
setten by, value, MaReg. 28. See FaPrin. A 184.
setyn, sat, Mass 174.
Seueryne, Severinus, a name of Boethius, FaPrin. H 35.
Seustis, Pseustis, Ecl. prol. 39*.
Seven Liberal Arts. See Hawes 249*, 463-526*, Garl. 53.
sewe, to follow, Walton A 260, Dance 198, FaPrin. A 230, Reproof 40, Ship 161, 522, Ecl. 767, Cavend. 1274; —to petition, plead legally, Reproof 79, Hardyng 56*.
sewr, sure, MaReg. 320.
sewte, suit, Cavend. 213.
sexangled, hexagonal, six-cornered, Hawes 306.
sey, saw, Libel 230.
seyne, seen, Walton A 25, 318, FaPrin. A 60?, E 13, Burgh 22, Mass 180; —to say, FaPrin. B 105, Pallad. 28, Libel 533; —to see, Pallad. 35.
seyng, seeing, FaPrin. A 165, Ecl. prol. 77.
shadde, shed, FaPrin. C 77.
shadow, shadwe, shadow, FaPrin. D 32, Ecl. prol. 100*. See under cloked, cloudy.
shape, to make, Orl. xviii:12.
shappe, shape, FaPrin. A 11, Orl. xvi:2.
sharp, rough, rugged, Hawes 45.
shene, bright, shining, Churl 53, 98, Mass 116, Morley 36.
shent, misused, Ship 234.
sheo, she, Epithal. 80.
shet, shette, shut, Churl 107, Orl. xxii:6, Pallad. 100, Ecl. 493, Garl. 598, 1475.
sheuers, pieces, Ecl. 405.
Ship on coins, To Somer 17, LettGlouc. 17*.
shitt, shut, Churl 120, 161, Hawes 1299.
shope me, set myself, Dial. 802.
shone, shoes, Ecl. 212.
shours, rainfalls, onsets, Dance 13.
shrape, to scrape, Churl 125.
shrewdly, shroudly, evilly, ill, Garl. 614, 1188.
a shrige, Ashridge, Garl. 1428, 1432*.
shul, shall.
siker, sure, Dial. 723.
sikerly, surely, Walton A 208, E 99, Libel 154, 333, 543.
sikernesse, security, Roundel 2, Dance 628, Epithal. 162, Hawes 439.
silff, self, FaPrin. A 369, G 301, 317, Orl. xviii: 12, xxii:11, xxiii:1, 11.
similitude, fable, Hawes 693, 752.
simulacioun, imitation, falsity, Dance 172.
singulere, FaPrin. G 57, 193, Garl. 649. See synguleer.
Sirens, MaReg. 249*, FaPrin. C 93*.
sit, etc., to be appropriate, MaReg. 329, 407, Churl 166, FaPrin. A 431, Orl. xvii:22, xix:21, Ecl. prol. 83. See sytte.
sith, sithen, since, Dial. 727, Churl 141, Dance 225, 278, FaPrin. A 252, 356, B 27, 100, D 114, Epithal. 159, 196, Burgh 17, Shirley II:75, Reproof 24, Libel 144, Orl. xiii:27, Ecl. 230, etc. See seth.

sith go ful yore, many years ago, Bycorne 100.
ofte sithes, often times, Churl 184, 375, Dance 177, 508, Epithal. 3.
sivile, Seville, Libel 54.
skapethe, escapes, Lickp. 119.
skene, skein, Garl. 782.
skie, sky, cloud, FaPrin. G 24*, K 31.
skile, course of reasoning, MaReg. 299.
skille, skyll, cause, reason, knowledge, Walton E 91, Lickp. 77, Ecl. 737, Garl. 93.
sklender, slender, Thebes 102. *See* Morley 230*.
slacke, slow, Ship 65.
slaiys, Garl. 775*.
slake, to abate, cease, Walton A 276, Hawes 47.
slauth, *see* **sloth**.
slawthfulle, Garl. 120. *See* **sloth**.
sleeth, slen, etc., to slay, MaReg. 19, Dance 7, FaPrin. B 59.
sleues, sleeves, Ship 515*.
slidyng, inconstant, Libel 559.
slipir, slippery, Roundel 2.
slipper, slippery, Garl. 501.
Sloth, Epithal. 141, FaPrin. A 399, 417, Reproof 4*, Orl. vi:11, xv:25, Mass 47, 91, Hawes 669, 1313*, Nevill envoy 13, Ecl. prol. 51, Ecl. 1023, Garl. 120, see 522, Cavend. 24-30*, see 47.
slowe, slouh, slew, Walton A 94, 97, 222.
slowyshe, slow, Nevill 155.
slyme, Prohib. 58*.
smaragdis, emeralds, Garl. 480.
smertly, briskly, Walton A 381.
smet, smote, FaPrin. G 320, see 301.
smethys, smiths, Prohib. 38.
smook, smoke, Walton A 327.
smored, smothered, Hardyng 111.
smyten, struck, fought, Hardyng 107, 115.
smyten of, smite off, FaPrin. G 301.
of smytys, smite off, Prohib. 38.
snayle, snail, Prohib. 53*.
snite, snipe, a game-bird, Churl 360, Ecl. 682.
snurt, to snort, Garl. 1437.
soche, such.
Socrates, Ship 481.
soden, sudden, FaPrin. E 83, etc.
soiour, sojourn, stay, Dance 378.
solace, pleasure, Garl. 1365.
solacious, pleasurable, Hawes 10, 355, 1307, Garl. 677.
solas, delight, Garl. 649.
solein, an independent role, "lone hand", Dial. 742.
solempnysed, Shirley II:32*.
solisgise, Hawes 737*.
Somer, Hoccleve to, p. 66.
all and somme, general and particular, Prohib. 98.
sonde, message, visitation, Dial. 522.
sondri, sundry, FaPrin. G 95, etc.
sone, soon, Dance 592, etc.
songe, sung, FaPrin. G 62, K 20.
sonnest, soonest, Dance 240.
sonnyssh, sunny, sunlike, Churl 59, 250.
sool, alone, Dance 110.

soor, sore, Epithal. 39.
soore, sorely, Walton C 6.
soote, sweet, FaPrin. G 175, 184; —*s.* sweat, FaPrin. D 105, Mass 156, 175.
sope, soap. Dial. 826*, Libel 55.
sorous, sorrows, Orl. ix:18.
sort, manner, Cavend. 1360; —condition, Nevill 67; —class, kind, Ship 43, Garl. 512; —to be classed, Garl. 1253.
sorte, number, Ecl. 139.
soso, after a fashion, Pallad. 109.
sorw, sorweful, sorrow, etc., Dance 151, FaPrin. B 65, etc.
sotelte, subtlety, Reproof 44, Libel 403.
soth, true, FaPrin. E 40.
sotill, subtle, able, Walton E 141.
souffren, to suffer, permit, Roundel 1.
souhte, sought.
soul, alone, Thebes 97.
soundeth, sounds, Ship 3; —to make sounds, Ecl. 414, 415; —to promote, tend to, Ecl. 633, 741. *See* **sownd**.
soupe, to sup, Thebes 98.
sovl, alone, Orl. xiii:29, xvii:4.
south, i.e., **souht**, sought, FaPrin. A 300.
sow, sew, Garl. 773.
sowde, south, Lickp. 29.
sowketh, sucketh, FaPrin. B 63, Libel 389, 390.
sowle, Prohib. 41*.
sownde, sowne, to tend toward, Dial. 758, Cavend. 32; —to sound, Walton D 27; —to be of a certain tenor, Nevill 192; —*s.* report, noise Libel 173. *See* **soundeth**.
sowponaile, aid, Dance 663. *See* **suppowelment**, Hardyng 12*.
spar, to fasten, Garl. 1402.
sparcles, scattered particles, Ship 13875*, Ecl. 1027.
spare, to spar, prop up? FaPrin. A 88. Not in NED in such sense, nor in Bergen.
in special, in detail, Dial. 582.
spectacles, FaPrin. D 20*, Lickp. 54*, Garl. 1075.
speculatif, theory, Dance 427*.
spede, to prosper, Mass 96, Lickp. 8 and *passim*, Hardyng 98, Libel 199, 479, Ripley 189, Nevill 94.
spedfull, helpful, Libel 355.
speere, speare, sphere, Walton E 132, etc., FaPrin. C 82, Hawes 2, 222, 1401, 4440, etc., Garl. 688, Cavend. 107.
spendell, spindle, Cavend. 1284.
sperycall, spherical, Garl. 1479.
spill, to come to grief, Ecl. 74.
spryngyng, a rising, Orl. xvii:3.
spyne, thorn, FaPrin. C 83.
stace, Stacius, Statius, Burgh 21, Garl. 337.
stal, stole, FaPrin. D 65.
stall, seat of honor, Hardyng 125.
Stanza-liaison, Mass 74-97*. *See* Pallad. prol. For simple enjambement, *see* Hawes dedic. 28-29*.
staple, staple fayre, a market, exchange, Libel 60, etc. *See* introd. to Libel.

stars, *see* sun.

state, class, rank, Dance 634, Nevill dial. 37, Ship 533, 578, 8513; —man of rank, Ship 8507, 8509, Ecl. 602. *See* estate.

stede, place, Garl. 1318.

stellify, to raise to the stars, i.e., to extol, Garl. 947*.

stepmodir, stepmother, *see* FaPrin. D 30*.

sterismon, steersman, Pallad. 11.

sterne, star? Pallad. 11; —rudder? *ibid.*, 53.

sterre, etc., star, Walton E 136, etc.

sterue, to die, Reproof 13, Mass 93, Libel 125.

steryng, urging, Dance 26*.

stieng, ascending, Walton E 128.

stigiall, of Styx, Garl. 1300.

stiketh by, is close at hand, Dial. 775.

stile, a pen, Dance 40, FaPrin. A 449, D 61, G 5, K 17?; —title, appellation, Dial. 579; —style, Nevill envoy 12*, Ecl. 181, 632, 654, Cavend. 1367. *See* style.

stired, incited, MaReg. 192. *See* steryng.

stockes, trunks, Hawes 4224.

stole, stool, Garl. 774, *see* note 771.

stood at, i.e., were in, FaPrin. G 191.

stood a bak, lacked success, FaPrin. D 56.

stound, time, Walton A 384, Orl. xii:3, Hardyng 123.

stoupe, to stoop, FaPrin. K 2.

Stow, *see* p. 193.

stowte, stout, Garl. 1474.

Strabo, Ship 6985*.

strake, struck, Hawes 4331, Garl. 1347, Cavend. 216, 261.

straunge, etc., disdainful, Dance 187, 299, 454, *see* Dance 505.

made it straunge, was aloof, refused, Orl. xiii: 5*, Libel 405*, Garl. 444.

straunge, *s.* foreigners, Pallad. 31.

stfawed, strewn, Churl 180.

strayt, immediately, Cavend. 143.

strecche, to suffice, Libel 517.

streit, strict, Churl 108.

strenges, strings, Walton D 26.

strengthist, strengthenest, Orl. xvii:8.

strett, street, Cavend. 136.

stroke, struck, Nevill 35.

Stroode, FaPrin. K 25.

strook, *s.* stroke, Dance 183.

stye, to ascend, Walton E 53.

style, title of rank, Hardyng 50; —pen or literary style, FaPrin. G 5, Nevill dial. 21, envoy 12, Ecl. 654, Ecl. prol. 3, 10, 28, 30, 36, Cavend. 63*, 76; *see* stile.

stynt, ended, Epithal. 42;—to end, Pallad. 46.

subgytz, subjects, Hardyng 7.

sue, *see* sewe.

suerte, security, firm bond, Libel 232.

sufferayn, sovereign, Walton A 68, Garl. 523.

sufficistent, sufficient, Ecl. 311. Not in NED.

sugratyfe, sugared, Hawes 663. *See* sugre.

sugre, sugrid, etc., sugar, Churl 73, Thebes 52*, FaPrin. A 243*, 461, K 16, Shirley II:25, Garl. 73-4*.

sum, a person, somebody, Walton A 27, Garl. 97, etc.

Sun passing the stars. *See* FaPrin. G 36*, K 29-30*, Hawes 222-24.—Not affected by clouds, FaPrin. G 24-26.

superate, conquered, Ecl. 916*.

superflu, superfluous, Ecl. prol. 13, 63, Garl.32.

Superlative, the use of double, FaPrin. C 19, 50, Ecl. 867. *See* note Walton B 28.

suppleyd, supplicated, Garl. 49, 1443.

supportacion, support, Shirley II:73.

suppowelment, aid, Hardyng 12*. *See* sowponaile.

supprisid, overcome, FaPrin. G 22*, Garl. 537.

surfullinge, embroidering, Garl. 787.

surmountynge, excelling, Garl. 885.

surpluage, surplusage, remainder, rest, Dance 36, FaPrin. D 120, G 166.

surquedie, pride, FaPrin. A 176.

surquidous, haughty, Dance 372, FaPrin. C 54.

Surrey. *See* p. 376 and note; Countess of Surrey, Garl. 753*.

suspyres, sighs, Morley 1.

sustren, sustres, sisters, Epithal. 182, FaPrin. A 242, D 12, Burgh 7.

suwe, to follow, pursue, Shirley I:72. *See* sewe.

suyng, the pleading of a suit, Garl. 253.

swage, to assuage, reduce, Ship 115.

swarte, black, Garl. 1366.

sweuene, dream, Orl. xvii:3.

Sword, the named, Hawes 4319*.

swown, swoon, FaPrin. B 1.

Swyn, Libel 62*.

sy, saw, Dial. 821.

syche, such.

at a syde, at close? Nevill 49*.

sydony, Sidon, Garl. 552.

Sygismounde, Sigismund, Hardyng 121*, Libel 8*.

syhes, sighs, FaPrin. B 65.

sykernesse, sykyrnenes, security, FaPrin. B 8, Orl. ix:20.

sylff, self, FaPrin. B 151, *see* 154.

sylt, soil deposited by water, sand, Garl. 23.

Symak, Symmachus, FaPrin. H 1*. *See* Semachus.

symplesse, simplicity, Shirley I:11, Mass 18.

symulacon, simulation, Mass 149.

symulacres, images, FaPrin. C 100.

syn, since, MaReg. 383, Roundel 2, Orl.xiii:18, xv:5, xvii:18, xxi:2.

Synderesis, FaPrin. C 96*.

syngler, especial, FaPrin. A 409, Garl. 524, 711.

synguleer, single, Praise of Chaucer 1968*. *See* FaPrin. A 409, G 57, 193.

syth, sythen, since, Orl. ix:5, 12, 19, Mass 52, Nevill 123, 136, 168, 228, Ripley 59, Hawes 1322, etc. *See* sith, seth.

sythe, times, Mass 123, 177. *See* sithes.

sytte, to be fitting, Hardyng 19, Garl. 149, *see* note on 77. *See* sit.

ta, to have.

taberdes, sleeveless surcoats, Garl. 395.

tabide, to abide, FaPrin. H 28, Mass 152.

tables, backgammon, Nevill dial. 47;—tablets, Mass 165.

tacounte, to account, Pallad. 104.
Tagus, the river, Burgh 5*.
taill, payment, due, To Somer 20.
take, to put, Prohib. 52;—given, FaPrin. B 144; pleased, enthralled, Walton D 39.
take on hond, to undertake, LettGlouc. 21, Libel 12, 66, 239, 269, Nevill 91.
taken, considered, Ship 39.
Talbot, Ecl. 855.
talecte, to allure, Nevill 7.　See allectyng.
talent, desire, Walton B 6.
talis, tales, Churl 366.
talkyng, Churl 142, Hawes 4406*.
talle, tale, Shirley II:104.
tame, to open, set abroach, FaPrin. D 19*. See attame.
tane, taken, Orl. xvi:6, xvii:23, xviii;20, Hawes 4440.
tansey, Thebes 101*.
Tapestry.　See Cavend. 120-21*.
Tapestry Verses.　See p. 114.
tappettis, figured cloths used as hangings, Garl. 474, 771.
tapplien, to apply, FaPrin. A 297.
tarage, Churl 13, 350*.
taraye, to array, Churl 47.
targe, shield, coat of arms, Ship 128.
tartour, tartar, Prohib. 53.
tath, taketh, Orl. xii:22, 28.
tathenis, to Athens, FaPrin. G 149.
tatteyn, to attain, Pallad. 22.
tauellis, Garl. 775*.
tauenture, to venture, Ecl. prol. 18.
taumpinnis, Garl. 636*.
taunt, to answer back, retort, Garl. 100.
tawoiden, to avoid, to banish, FaPrin. A 277. See avoyd.
tayle, tail, rear, Hardyng 66.
in tayle, entailed, Hardyng 55.
tayneth, kindles, Ripley 173.
Tedeus, Tydeus, Epithal. 138*.
tedious, Hawes 210*.
teene, anguish, Bycorne 81.
teermes, terms, Thebes 30.
teint, tainted, Dance 472, 487.
Temp!e of Glass.　See Hawes 1309.
tenbrace, to embrace, Epithal. 14, Nevill dial. 5.
tencrese, to increase, FaPrin. C 47.
tende, to attend, Ship 7018.
tendure, to endure, Epithal. 7, 161, Pallad. 2.
tenebrus, dark, Hawes 301.
tenlumyne, to illumine, FaPrin. C 13, K 13.
tent, heed, Ripley 79.
Teocrite, Theocritus, Ecl. prol. 19.　See Garl. 327.
Terence, Burgh 19, Garl. 353.
termes, terms, FaPrin. G 17*.　See teermes.
termyne, to determine, describe, Epithal. 69.
tessiphone, Tisiphone, one of the Furies, Walton A 60*.
Testalis, Thestylis, Ecl. 690*.　See Garl. 675.
texcluden, to exclude, Epithal. 61.
texecut, to execute, Epithal. 188.

texemplyfye, to exemplify, Horns 23*.
texpresse, to express, Pallad. 117.
a teynte, attained, Lickp. 2.
—th, verbal plural, Walton A 105*, 253, 254, C 25, D 42, E 100, Epithal. 78, FaPrin. D 25, 28, Hawes 206, etc., Nevill 24, Libel 50, 51, 510, Ripley 2, 116, Prohib. 68, Ship 7*, 23, 58, 115, 206, 521, 553, 6997, 7001, 8468, 8490, 13857, Ecl. prol. 5, 44, 106, 110, Ecl. 290, 425, 502, 529, 544, 591, 626, 633, 635, 672, 707, 845, 897, 905 ,1034, Garl. 696, Cavend. 42, 43, 217, 219, 1174, 1261*, 1328.
—th, rime on verb-ending.　See Hawes, stanza 105.
thabbey, the abbey, Burgh 43.
thactyfnes, the activity, Nevill 163.
Thais, Ecl. 686, 689.
thallpies, the Alps, FaPrin. E 66.
thamaris, Tomyris, Garl. 841*.　See Ecl.1112.
than, then, FaPrin. G 283, Hardyng 1, etc., Cavend. 38, 144.
thanke, thanks, credit, MaReg. 349, Dial. 587, Shirley I:16, 20.
thar, their, Hardyng 11; —there, Hardyng 54, 96, 119.
tharte, the art, Nevill dial. 12.
thassaut, the assault, Epithal. 163, FaPrin. A 236.
thastlabre, the Astrolabe, FaPrin. A 295*.
thauctour, the author, Shirley I:93, etc.
thawaityng, the lying in wait, FaPrin. A 63. ·
thaym, them, Reproof 55, Orl. ix:3, Hardyng 13.
the, pron. thee, Dial. 684, 688, etc., Churl 300, etc., FaPrin. B 76, 113, C 42,118,Orl. ii:10,ix: 11, 15, 16, 22, 26, xiii:16, Lickp. 117, Prohib. 5, Nevill envoy 10, Ship 7003, 13820, Garl. 612, 613, Cavend. 85, 255, etc.
theatryne, dramatist, Burgh 19*.
theder, thither, Walton E 48, Libel 197, 517, 544, 547, Garl. 287.
thee, the, to prosper, Libel 41, 97, 477, 518, Ship 460.
theere, the year, FaPrin. A 5.
Þees, these.
theffecte, the effect, the purpose, Nevill 2, Cavend. 79.
theih, though, FaPrin. A 229.
thekt, thatched, Ship 8457.
thellynge, telling, Nevill 426.
Þempire, the empire, FaPrin. C 16.
then, than, Churl 59, 98, 259, Pallad. 20, C 1, Orl. xxi:1, Hawes 261, 338, 4377, Ecl. 70, 123, 555, 729, 740, 777, 976; —thence, Walton A 215.
thend, the end, Cavend. 1187.
thenk, think, Walton E 49, Orl. xxi:6.
thenlumynyd, the illumined, Burgh 26.
Þensaumple, the example, Dance 19.
thensugerd, the sugared, Garl. 73*.
thentent, the intent, purpose, Nevill 115, Ship 134.
Theocritus, Garl. 327.　See Teocrite.

theoric, the theoretical aspect of a science or art, Pallad. 77, Ripley 187; *see* notes Dance 427, Walton A 332.

Þeos, these, Shirley I:93.

ther, their, FaPrin. A 244, G 128, 129, 130, etc., Orl. xix:9. *See* Garl. 394, 442, 526, 672, 1441, 1537.

Þerfro, from there, Dance 582.

ÞerÞe, the earth, Walton C 5.

therwt, therewith.

Þeternal, the eternal, Epithal. 27.

thexperience, the experience, FaPrin. E 9.

thewes, habits, virtues, Walton A 86, Orl.xvi:5.

thider, thither.

thikke, numerous, thick, MaReg. 146; —*adv.* Lickp. 22.

thilke, those, Walton D 36, Churl 291.

thin, meagre, Ecl. 214. *See* **thyn.**

Þinward, the inward, Epithal. 30.

"This is to say". *See* note on FaPrin. D 8.

Þo, thoo, those, Walton A 46, 49, 174, C 25, E 100, MaReg. 225, FaPrin. A 153, F 6, K 8, Pallad. 108, Epithal. 33, Orl. ix:5, Libel 518; —then, Walton A 125, B 19, D 45, FaPrin. G 249, Lickp. 25, Orl. xix:17.

thobeisaunce, the obeisance, obedience, Fa Prin. E 12.

thoder, the other, Nevill 34, 40, 41, 42, 44.

thof, though, Orl. ii:11; *see* note Orl. xix.

Tholomeus, Ptolemy, Ship 183*, 6997*.

Thomyris, Ecl. 1112*. *See* **Thamaris.**

thone, the one, Nevill 40, 41, 42, 43.

Þordeynaunce, the ordinance, Epithal. 22.

Þordre, the order, Epithal. 28.

thordris nyne, the nine orders. *See* FaPrin. C 69 note.

thorug, through, Dial. 588.

thoruh, through, FaPrin. E 57, etc.

thoruhgirt, pierced, FaPrin. E 37.

thousch, though, Orl. v:8.

thowthe, though, Garl. 725, 740, 938, 1016.

in a thowght, in a trice, Garl. 1078.

thrast, thrust, Lickp. 9.

threde, third, Churl 211, 330.

thret, threatened, Garl. 95.

thridde, third, FaPrin. G 122.

thries, thrice, FaPrin. D 12.

thrift, prosperity, Libel 115, 389, Prohib. 27.

thrist, *s.* and *v.*, thirst, Walton D 47, MaReg. 360.

thristy, thirsty, MaReg. 135.

throme, thrum, Cavend. 1283*.

Jack a' Thrum's bible. *See* note Garl. 209.

throwe, time, Dial. 649; —through, Garl. 1351

thrust, thirst, Dance 396, FaPrin. D 4, Mass 159.

thrysse, thrice, Prohib. 18.

thrwghe, through, Lickp. 82.

Þt, that.

thu, thou, LettGlouc. 49.

thupholder, the upholder, Nevill 131.

thuntrust, the untrust, instability, FaPrin. A 429

thurgh, through.

thwartyd, disputed, Garl. 1017.

thycke, numerous, Ship 59.

thye, Walton A 31. *See* **noght for thye.**

thylke, FaPrin. B 69. *See* **thilke.**

thymage, the image, FaPrin. C 34.

thyn, Ship 13827. *See* **thin.**

thyng, thinketh, Orl. ix:8.

Þynke, *see* beÞynke.

til, to, Epithal. 48.

tilthe, cultivation, Churl 355.

unto time, until, Churl 305.

timorous, Garl. 260*.

tirikkis, tricks? Garl. 1482. First case NED 1548.

tisyk, phthisis, LettGlouc. 53*.

Titchbourne, poem by, *see* note Dance 589.

titiuyllis, Garl. 636*.

titled, listed by title, Shirley II:5.

Tityrus, i.e., Virgil, Ecl. 411.

to, till, Orl. xii:24, xviii:23, Nevill 128, 138, 139; —too, Walton A 268, MaReg. 362, Churl 209, 325, Dance 248, 606, FaPrin. B 57, E 40, G 17, Shirley II:11, Nevill 157, Ship 153,194, 244, 509, Ecl. 275, 784, 1152, Garl. 204, 248, 249, 748, 1360, Cavend. 178, 1366; —two, Fa-Prin. E 69, H 11. *See* **too.**

to for, before, Dance 31, 472, 488, FaPrin. E 30, G 259, Mass 2, Orl. xviii:13, xxi:9.

toforn, before, Churl 252, Thebes 76, Dance 51, etc.

togedir, together, Libel 109, Garl. 286, 393.

togidre, together, Walton E 15, FaPrin. E 81, Nevill 103.

toiaggid, torn to pieces, Garl. 623.

toke, gave, FaPrin. E 45, Libel 180; —obtained, Hardyng 63.

toke on him, undertook, FaPrin. G 321*.

toke him to, Hardyng 61*.

tolde, accounted, Walton A 300.

Tomyris, *see* **Thamaris, Thomyris.**

tone, the one, FaPrin. D 38, Morley 5, 161, 191.

Tongilius, FaPrin. E 43*.

tonne, tun, LettGlouc. 51*.

too, two, FaPrin. A 259, G 33, 133, 159, H 18, 31, Prohib. 90, 93.

tookeneÞe, betokens, Epithal. 107.

toome, empty, Walton A 269.

topasion, topaz, sapphire, or precious stone, Churl 250.

torqwat, i.e., Boethius, Burgh 16*.

Toscane, Tuscany, Morley 77.

tosed, carded or combed, Libel 100.

tossyng on my brayne, turning over in my mind, Hawes 267.

tothir, the other, FaPrin. H 21, Morley 5, 159, 161, 163, 192, 203.

touchyng, concerning, FaPrin. H 32, Mass 17.

toumbed, entombed, Hardyng 41.

tow, to? Orl. v:2; —two, Libel 20; —to.....ward, *see* **ward.**

towche of, mention, MaReg. 320.

towchis, devices, tricks, Garl. 748.

towchyd, portrayed, expressed, formed, Garl. 143, 592, 1139.

trace, footing, step, moving procession, Dance 198*, Hawes dedic. 47, Hawes 1259, 1339, Cavend. 242;—to follow, Dance 46, 70, Pallad. D 3.
trace, Thrace, Garl. 493.
tragedy, FaPrin. K 35, Orl. xv:8, Hawes 1270, Cavend. 50.
Traian, Trajan, FaPrin. C 26.
Translation, theory of, Walton A 19*.
trasid, ornamented with tracery, Garl. 395.
trauayle, travel, Hawes 57, Ecl. 526;—labor, Ecl. 952, Cavend. 1148.
travelled, travailed, worked, Cavend. 207,1141; —travelled, Cavend. 215.
trayne, deception, Cavend. 87.
treacle, Churl 182*.
treate, to entreat, Ecl. 1003.
tregetour, Dance 513*.
tresor, Pallad. 86*.
treste, trust, Pallad. 49, 116, B 2.
tretable, docile, Ecl. 1013.
tretour, traitor, FaPrin. F 18, G 127, 316.
Trevisa. See Gen. Introd. p. 15, Shirley I:40.
trie, to test, Pallad. 85.
trifles, Libel 341, Hawes 1336.
trine, threefold, Pallad. 9.
trions, Garl. 693*. First case NED of 1594.
tristesse, sorrow, Dance 131.
triuiall, Ecl. 695*.
Triumph, FaPrin. A 366, C 16*, E 19, 73.
Troilus, Epithal. 136, Mass 181, Hawes 1275, 4426. See FaPrin. A 287*, Garl. 857.
trone, throne, seat, Ship 8453, 8461, 8474.
Trophe, FaPrin. A 284*.
troth, truth, Nevill 73.
trow, believe, Walton C 21, Garl. 729, etc.
trowbely, troubled, Orl. xiv: 23
trowghte, troth, Burgh 41.
Troy Book. See Hawes 1304.
trumpet, trumpeter, Garl. 235, 243.
truse, trusse, truce, Libel 26, 128, 199, 225.
truwe, true, Shirley I:56, etc.
tryce, to drag away, MaReg. 287.
trwly, truly, Walton A 105.
trynhede, Trinity, Ripley 3.
tryst, trust, Reproof 52.
trysteth, *plu. imper.* trust, Reproof 62. See **treste.**
Trystram, Tristan, Mass 184.
Tullius, i.e., Cicero, Praise of Chaucer 2085, Epithal. 151, FaPrin. A 255, 367, C 22, G *passim,* Burgh 13, Hawes 1105, Nevill 838, Ecl. 1091, Garl. 330, see 1163. Tragedy of Tullius, FaPrin. G.
tuly, dull red, Garl. 782*.
tunnys, tuns, FaPrin. D 19*.
turbit, Libel 353*.
turkis, turquoises, Garl. 466.
turvys, turfs, Churl 51 (variant).
Tuskan, Tuscany, FaPrin. G 59, 65, 91.
twein, twain, FaPrin. B 56, G 156, etc.
twen, between, Horns 5, FaPrin. A 264, D 50, G 268.
Twishe, Tush! Garl. 208.
twiys, twice, Garl. 7.

Two Ways, Hawes 27*, Nevill 191*, 214*.
twound, twined, Cavend. 1291.
twyes, twice, Libel 136. See **twiys.**
twylight, Hawes 272*.
twynd, twined, Cavend. 1307.
twyne, to separate, MaReg. 17, 42, 318, Prohib. 20, Cavend. 1305; —to wind, turn (a song), Dance 260.
by twyne, between, Walton A 333.
twynklyng, tinkling, Garl. 681.
twysse, twice, Prohib. 18, Garl. 444.
tyde, time, Hardyng 60.
tyll, to, Epithal. 197, Hardyng 27, Cavend. 269.
tyne, interval, Garl. 505.
tyred, tore, Walton D 50, 52.
tyryen, Tyrian, Walton B 10.
tyssue, tissue, Hawes 113.
tything, tidings, Churl 198, 202, Orl. ii:4.

Vado Mori text, p. 128.
vailith, to avail, Dance 132, 280, Hawes 1320, Cavend. 145.
Valence, Valenciennes, Horns 21.
Valerian, Ecl. 1105.
Valerius Maximus, Garl. 381*.
valour, valure, worth, Ship 486, Ecl. 357, 969, Morley 27.
Varro, Morley 246.
vauntage, advantage, Hawes 4333.
vauntwarde, vanguard, Shirley I:52. First case NED 1476; but see FaPrin. ix:1904.
vawte, vaulting, inner roof, Garl. 476.
vaylled, availed, Cavend. 145.
vaynefull, trivial, Hawes 1334.
Ubi Sunt motif, Walton C 13*, FaPrin. C introd., Nevill 830 ff.
vche, each, Pallad. 39, 88, 100.
uende, Orl. vi:8*.
vengoures, avengers, Walton D 41.
venim, etc., venom, Walton A 354, C 10, Hardyng 17, Hawes 4358.
ventre, to venture, Ecl. prol. 30.
venyger, vinegar, Prohib. 46.
verlet, varlet, Hawes 4254.
vermylon, vermilion, Prohib. 6*.
verray, etc., very.
vertute, virtue, Nevill 214.
vestigate, to investigate, Cavend. 21.
vew, *s.* survey, Garl. 237.
viagis, journeys, FaPrin. D 92, 102.
Vincencius, Vincent of Beauvais, FaPrin. G 215, Garl. 382*.
vinolent, wine-bibbing, Ecl. 787.
Virgil, Praise of Chaucer 2089, FaPrin. C 29*, K 15, Burgh 15, Hawes 1105, Ship 13867,Ecl. prol. 27, Garl. 339, 380-4*. See **Maro.**
virrelaies, virelays, FaPrin. A 353*.
Vlcan, Vulcanus, a volcano, Walton A 233*.
Vlysses, Nevill 425, 833.
vmber, shadow, Cavend. 2.
vmblis, entrails, Garl. 1213.
vmple, Lickp. 76*.
unconnyngly, ignorantly, Bedford 12.

vncouth, strange, Churl 74, Thebes 51, Dance 220, FaPrin. D 117, Nevill dial. 10.

unctuus, unctuous, oily, Ripley 121.

vncul, uncle, Pallad. 70.

vndeiect, not cast out, Nevill envoy 21.

vndirfong, to undertake, FaPrin. A 48, D 93, Mass 153.

vnkonning, ignorance, FaPrin. D 25, Mass 19.

vnkouthe, unusual, Shirley II:26. See vncouth.

vnlust, distaste, lack of desire, Dial. 537.

vnlusti, unhappy, Burgh 49.

vnmete, insufficient, Walton A 39, E 17.

vnneth, scarcely, with difficulty, MaReg. 216, 365, 400, Roundel 3, Pallad. 101, Prohib. 77, Hawes 4340.

vnponysched, unpunished, Walton E 81.

vnrecuperable, not to be recovered from, FaPrin. B 68.

vnselþe, misery, Walton A 251.

vnshred? Garl. 1372.

vnsmyten, unsmitten, Hardyng 110.

vnto, until, Walton D 58.

unto, read undo? Pallad. 52*; or, until?

vntretable, intractable, FaPrin. B 24.

vntwynde, broken apart, Garl. 1412.

vnweldynes, Orl. xv:14*.

unwarly, unawares, Walton A 265.

vnwyttyly, ignorantly, Walton C 1.

voluell, a device of graduated circles, used to ascertain the rising and setting of the moon, etc., Garl. 1432.

vowche saue, vouchsafe, Garl. 809.

vowe, Cavend. 1188*, Ecl. 438, 726. See note Bycorne 115.

voyd, etc., to avoid, Ecl. 88;—to be gone, MaReg. 280, Cavend. 219;—to expel, get rid of, Thebes 55, Epithal. 24, Libel 358.

vp so don, upside down, FaPrin. B 89, Lett-Glouc. 13.

vpfynde, to find out, Pallad. 85.

vpholde, to maintain, Ecl. 538.

vplandisshe, rustic, countrified, Shirley II:14.

vprightes, Roundel 3*.

vre, s. practice, Hawes 754, Cavend. 28;—fortune, lot, Reproof 34;—ore? Nevill 133*.

vrsa, the Bear, Garl. 690.

vrynes, urines, Dance 417*, Prohib. 36.

vsage, habit, Walton A 363.

vse, to be accustomed, FaPrin. D 92.

vste, burnt, Prohib. 37*. Lat. ustum.

usurpyng, claiming, FaPrin. C 16*. See Cavend. 90.

Usury, Dance 393 ff.*, Libel 425, Ship 8465.

vthers, udders, Ecl. 225.

vtter, to pass current, to sell, Libel 398.

vtteraunce, sale, Nevill dial. 44;—"outrance", Hawes 178.

vtterly, at all, Walton D 21;—completely, Ship 35, 203, 534, 13859.

vulgar, vulgar tongue, FaPrin. A 286, 317.

vyage, journey, Mass 153, Hawes 265.

vyces, Hawes 367*.

vyrent, flourishing, blooming, Nevill dial. 8.

waad, wad, woad, Libel 326, 521.

waad aschen, wood ashes, Libel 327.

wacche, watch, wakefulness, Dance 346.

wach, wakefulness, i.e., late hours, MaReg. 322.

wade, to proceed heavily, Hawes 4431*, Ecl. 793, Cavend. 1219.

wadmole, a coarse woollen cloth, Libel 56.

wafres, cakes, MaReg 146.

wagge, Lickp. 114*.

waiys, ways, Garl. 181.

wake, weak, Nevill 212.

wake or winke, Dance 643*.

Waking, devices for, Hawes 93 note. See note Cavend. 1222.

wan, v. got, i.e., arrived, Hardyng 119;—won, FaPrin. A 366, Prohib. 61, Garl. 1272, 1364; a. wan, Garl. 1366.

wanhope, despair, FaPrin. B 11.

wanne, won, Hardyng 79, Hawes 175,192.

war, ware, wary, cautious, Thebes 143, Dance 606.

war, ware, were, Burgh 54, Reproof 16, Cavend. 80, 110, 135, 155, 1164, 1172, 1220, 1236, 1268, 1343, 1369, 1377;—wore, Garl. 1084, 1085.

warbeled, whirling? Cavend. 1284.

to....ward, FaPrin. B 130*, Lickp. 3.

wardens, a kind of pears, Ecl. 404.

warie, to curse, MaReg 63.

Warwick, see note Shirley I:87.

wastelbrede, bread of fine flour, Churl 122.

wate, s. wait, Nevill 206.

waue, flicker, MaReg. 399.

wawes, waves, Nevill 151.

waytie, weighty, Cavend. 82.

wax, v. became, Walton A 299.

waytie, weighty, Cavend. 82.

wealthe, weal, Hawes 182, 196, Ecl. 1084. See welthe.

wedde, pledge, Hardyng 97.

wedder, weather, Garl. 12, 1409.

wedir, wether, Dance 490, FaPrin. G 328, Mass 106.

weel willy, favorable, Epithal. 186.

weengis, wings, FaPrin. A 436.

wehout, without, Orl. ix:10 (scribal error).

weie, to weigh, Dial. 600.

weies, ways, FaPrin. G 96.

welaway, Well away! Orl. xiii:18, xv:17, xvi:6, xviii:25.

welbesayne. See besein.

wele, well, Orl. xix:25;—weal, Orl. ix:4, Cavend. 1144, 1164.

weleful, full of weal, MaReg. 402, FaPrin. A 259.

welere, Ecl. 137*.

welny, well nigh, Garl. 430.

welthe, weal, fortune, Walton A 156, 249, 291, E 109, MaReg. 6, Garl. 14, 705, 979, Cavend. 1411.

wende, to turn, go, Walton A 214, Dial. 790, FaPrin. F 13. See wene, pret.

wendome, Vendome, Hardyng 87*.

wene, wende, etc., to deem, think, Walton C 33, Dial. 521, 784, Dance 552, 595, FaPrin. E 62, Pallad. C 1, Lickp. 188, Libel 197, Prohib. 10, 51, 63, Hawes 4293.

were, to wear, FaPrin. B 137, Orl. xvii:28, Garl. 68, 322.

were, *s.* doubt, difficulty, FaPrin. D 36 (here Bergen's text reads **werre**). *See* Orl. xiii:3; —wire, Churl 59.

wern, were, FaPrin. A 153, E 3, F 16, G 107; — to refuse, Walton A 279, MaReg. 430, 442.

wern, were, FaPrin. E 3, F 16, G 107; —to refuse, Walton A 279, MaReg. 430, 442.

werrai, very, FaPrin. A 216.

werre, to make war, Libel 19; —*s.* war, Dial. 818, Epithal. 125; —worse, Dial. 819.

werreie, to attack, make war, MaReg. 117, FaPrin. G 270.

werry, Orl. xiii:28*.

werryng, war, Libel 143.

wete, to know, Libel 52, 458, 540.

wetewolddis, cuckolds by consent, Garl. 187.

weth, with, Orl. iii:6, Garl. 273.

wexe, grown, Bycorne 104; —*s.* wax, Libel 55, 132.

wey, to weigh, Bedford 23, FaPrin. E 81.

weyke, weak, Nevill 29.

weylleway, FaPrin. B 45. *See* **welaway.**

wham, whom, FaPrin. G 41.

whar, where, Hardyng 62, 69, 73, 110.

whas, whose, Epithal. 69, 101.

what, as interjection, MaReg. 38, Dial. 616, Orl. xii:31, Ecl. 67, 1145.

what, why, Dance 297, Hawes 4431, Ecl. 526, 792, 793.

what for that, what of that! Hawes 757.

what for then, what of that? Orl. xv:22.

whele, weal, Cavend. 1141, cp. 1144.

wher, whether, Walton E 27, FaPrin. A 94, G 327, Orl. xxiii:4.

Where? *see* Ubi Sunt.

wherwt, wherewith.

whether, whither, Cavend. 1189, 1216.

whiles, *s.* wiles, Cavend. 165*.

whill, while, Orl. x:2.

white by black, *see* notes on FaPrin. G 33, Hawes 1349. *See* Garl. 1210.

whittle, knife, Ecl. 575.

whomanly, womanly, Cavend. 1358, *see* 165*.

whofull, woeful, Cavend. 58.

whois, whose, Churl 32.

whose, whoso, Nevill 201.

whow, how, Pallad. A 3.

whyght, white, Prohib. 40, 98. **egges whyghtes,** whites of eggs, Prohib. 53.

whyl, while, Orl. vi:10.

whylfulnes, wilfulness, Orl. vii:1.

whylk, which, Mass 77.

whyste, whist, quiet, Garl. 267.

wiche, which, Dance 2, etc., Mass 154, Libel 457.

wide open, flat on his back, Ecl. 16.

Wife, the patient, *see* **Bycorne;**—Wife of Bath, Dial. 694.

wight, weight? word-mass? Pallad. 124; —white, Cavend. 1408.

wiȝt, wiht, MaReg. 175, Dance 208, 583, 625, FaPrin. E 12.

wilfully, of free will, Walton E 38.

willi, willing, FaPrin. A 462.

Windows, Hawes 347*.

winke, Dance 643*.

wirche, to work, Dial. 647.

wise, to guide, Pallad. 42; —to instruct, *ibid.,* 107.

thus wise, in such manner, Ecl. 349.

wist, knew, Burgh 4, Lickp. 21, Orl. xviii:10.

wit, to know, Shirley I:62.

wite, to blame, Dial. 667; —to know, MaReg. 285.

with, *see* note Thebes 35.

withall, therewith, Hawes 4356.

withhalt, withholds, Dance 215.

withholde, kept, Garl. 1268.

withthes, bands of twisted twigs, ropes, Ship 513.

wode, furious, cruel, Libel 226, Garl. 1301. *See* wood.

wofull? Hawes 670.

wol, woll, *v.* will, Cavend. 1304.

wolde, would.

wolffes hede, wolf's head, Bycorne 117*.

wolgare, vulgar (tongue?), Shirley I:30. *See* vulgar.

woll, will, Cavend. 1304.

wolle, wool, Libel 56, 79, 90, Ecl. 147.

Wolsey, ?Ship 8509*, Cavend. 85 ff.

wombe, belly, Ship 48, Ecl. 146, 220, 221.

wond, to turn from, shrink, Dial. 523, Libel 435.

wonder, woundir, wonderfully, very, Walton A 26, 76, 154, 165, 173, 305, B 1, E 66, Garl. 69; —*a.* wonderful, Walton A 279, FaPrin. G 238.

wonderly, wonderfully, Walton D 8, Hawes 701, Garl. 38, 269.

wondersly, wonderfully, very, Hawes 4307.

wone, wonne, to dwell, Hawes 298; —*s.* custom, MaReg. 294, Libel 420.

woned, wont, Walton D 37.

wont, accustomed, Lickp. 78.

wood, furious, Walton B 22, Pallad. 13. *See* wode.

wook, woke, Orl. xix:6.

woon, number, Lickp. 51.

woot, to know, MaReg. 42.

wordli, worldly, Churl 378, FaPrin. C 74, Cavend. 219, 1113. Frequent in MSS.

worne, outworn? Morley 6.

worship, *s.* worth, honor, Dance 63, FaPrin. A 273, G 229, Mass 98, Garl. 1152; —to gain honor for, FaPrin. G 229, 298.

wot, woot, to know.

wost, wotst, thou knowest, Orl. xxi:12, ix:19.

wouch saue, vouchsafe, Shirley II:71.

woundir, *see* wonder.

wouynge, *s.* weaving, Garl. 776.

wowed, wooed, tempted, MaReg. 188.

woxe, waxed, grew, Libel 202.

wrake, vengeance, Mass 36; —wreck, Garl. 507.

wrate, wrote, Garl. 96, 347, 367, 1215, 1222, 1351, 1487.

wreche, vengeance, FaPrin. B 57.

wreke, avenged, Walton A 115, Dance 587.

wrenchis, shrewd turns, MaReg. 378, Garl· 1185.

wrete, written, Dial. 671.

wretyn, written, Prohib. 4.

wretyng, writing, Prohib. 82.

wright, write, Garl. 85.

wrotte, wrote, FaPrin. H 33.

wrough, rough, Hawes 4307.

wt, with.

wtin, within.

wtout, without.

wtstonde, withstand.

wul, v. will, Pallad. 58.

wych, which, Prohib. 23, 42, 79.

wyle, s. while, time, Dial. 578.

wyly, wily, Orl. vii:4.

wyne, to win, Garl. 152.

wynshed, kicked up, Garl. 1179.

wyre, i.e., were, doubt, Orl. xiii:3.

wysse, a. wise, Prohib. 91;—s. wise, manner, Prohib. 16.

wyten, known, Hardyng 109.

wytt, to know, Reproof 5, 62;—to blame, Ripley 81.

wyttely, wisely, Prohib. 98.

xiiine, thirteen, FaPrin. E 18.

xxti, twenty, MaReg. 111.

y, I, Walton passim, MaReg. passim, Orleans passim, etc.

y fere, see yfere.

y now, see ynow.

yaf, gave, Walton B 11, Dance 484, FaPrin.H 31.

yalowe, yellow, Garl. 289.

yatis, gates, Walton D 38, Garl. 574, 575, 579.

yave, gave, Garl. 58, 131, 1095.

yborn, born, Dance 577.

yche, each, Prohib. 11.

ychesyled, chiselled, Hawes 319.

ychon, each one, Shirley II:40.

yclipped, called by name, Hawes 421, 4370. See iclipped.

yconomye, economy, Pallad. 78*.

ydoon, done, Orl. xv:15.

ye, the, Shirley II, in Stow's hand, passim.

ye, yea, Epithal. 134, Lickp. 93;—eye, MaReg. 97, 98, Garl. 245.

yearth, earth, Shirley II:95.

yede, went, Lickp. 110.

yef, if, Libel 135, 141, 145, 269, 334, 410, 460, 532, 534. See yiff.

but yef, unless, Libel 254.

yelde, to return, i.e., as reward, Dial. 558; —to render, Dance 270. See yolde.

yelde me, submit myself, Ship 13808.

yeman, yeoman, Ship 475.

yen, eyes, Bedford 8, Garl. 245.

yerne, to pursue eagerly, Garl. 1376.

yerne, quickly, Epithal. 188.

yerthe, earth, Cavend. 103.

yeuyth, give (imper.plu.), Horns 48, 52.

yeve, etc., to give, Churl 14, 158, 197, 304, 322, Horns 13, LettGlouc. 42, FaPrin. B 112, C 5, 73, E 53, G 43, 202, Burgh 24, Libel 404.

yewres, i.e., eweress, she who fetches water for the guests' handwashing, Hawes 422.

yfere, in fere, in company, Dance 95, Mass 84.

yiff, if, Thebes 39, 112, 134, FaPrin. A 187, B 19, 93, Libel 519. See yef.

yiftes, gifts, Dance 622, Pallad. 37, 83, Libel 478.

yit, yet, Orl. ix:17, Libel 346, 354.

yit for thy, nevertheless, Dance 91.

yive, give, FaPrin. A 279, Mass 69, 118, 122.

yles, isles, Ship 6974, 6977.

yliche, alike, Dance 47.

ylle, evil, bad, Mass 106, Ship 19, 70, 459, 13828; —s. harm, Ship 593, 8492. See ill.

ymagen, imagine, invent, Hawes 4289.

ymaginatife, imaginative, Hawes 660, 4284.

ymaginid, imagined, contrived, FaPrin. G 93.

ymeeued, moved, MaReg. 391.

ymeneus, Hymen, Epithal. 176*.

ymeynt, mingled, Thebes 15.

ympnes, hymns, Shirley II:28.

ynamyd, named, Reproof 20.

ynde, of India, Churl 254, 308.

ynne, in, Walton D 43.

ynnynge, harvest, To Somer 15.

ynough, ynow, enough, Dial. 602, Orl. v:3, xiii:10, etc.

yode, went, Lickp. 97, Libel 197.

yoie, joy, FaPrin. A 371.

yolde, yielded, submitted, FaPrin. E 65; — paid, Dance 159.

yongly, youthful, Walton A 310.

yore, before, MaReg. 29.

yore agone, long ago, Epithal. 31, FaPrin. G 215.

yove, given, MaReg. 99, Horns 34, Thebes 46, Dance 38, FaPrin. G 144, Mass 68.

yowde, went, Lickp. 26.

yperborye, the Hyperborean, Burgh 48.

ypocrysye, hypocrisy, Mass 150.

yresshe game, Ship 209*.

yseide, said, Dance 459.

ysoude, Isolde, Mass 184.

yt, it; —that, in Shirley's abbreviation, II. See under ye. See Cavend. 104.